D0111620

ROGET'S THESAURUS

OF SYNONYMS AND ANTONYMS

BY

PETER MARK ROGET, M.D., F.R.S.

ENLARGED BY

JOHN LEWIS ROGET, M.A.

NEW EDITION REVISED AND ENLARGED BY

SAMUEL ROMILLY ROGET, M.A.

MODERN PROMOTIONS
A Division of Unisystems Inc., New York, New York 10022

PLAN OF CLASSIFICATION

TABULAR SYNOPSIS OF CATEGORIES

Class I. ABSTRACT RELATIONS

I. EXISTENCE

1°. ABSTRACT...........	1. Existence.	2. Inexistence.
2°. CONCRETE..........	3. Substantiality.	4. Unsubstantiality.
3°. FORMAL........... {	*Internal.*	*External.*
	5. Intrinsicality.	6. Extrinsicality.
4°. MODAL............ {	*Absolute.*	*Relative.*
	7. State.	8. Circumstance.

II. RELATION

	9. Relation.	10. Irrelation.
	11. Consanguinity.	
1°. ABSOLUTE.......... {	12. Correlation.	
	13. Identity.	14. Contrariety.
	15. Difference.	
2°. CONTINUOUS........	16. Uniformity.	16a. Non-uniformity.
	17. Similarity.	18. Dissimilarity.
3°. PARTIAL........... {	19. Imitation.	20. Non-imitation.
	20a. Variation.	
	21. Copy.	22. Prototype.
4°. GENERAL...........	23. Agreement.	24. Disagreement.

III. QUANTITY

	Absolute.	*Relative.*
1°. SIMPLE............	25. Quantity.	26. Degree.
	27. Equality.	28. Inequality.
	29. Mean.	
	30. Compensation.	
	By Comparison with a Standard.	
2°. COMPARATIVE....... {	31. Greatness.	32. Smallness.
	By Comparison with a similar Object.	
	33. Superiority.	34. Inferiority.
	Changes in Quantity.	
	35. Increase.	36. Decrease.
	37. Addition.	38. { Non-addition. Subduction.
	39. Adjunct.	40. Remainder.
		40a. Decrement.
3°. CONJUNCTIVE....... {	41. Mixture.	42. Simpleness.
	43. Junction.	44. Disjunction.
	45. Vinculum.	
	46. Coherence.	47. Incoherence.
	48. Combination.	49. Decomposition.

SYNOPSIS OF CATEGORIES

VII. CHANGE

1°. SIMPLE	140. Change.	141. Permanence.	
	142. Cessation.	143. Continuance.	
	144. Conversion.		
		145. Reversion.	
2°. COMPLEX	146. Revolution.		
	147. Substitution.	148. Interchange.	
	149. Changeableness.	150. Stability.	
	Present.	*Future.*	
	151. Eventuality.	152. Destiny.	

VIII. CAUSATION

1°. CONSTANCY OF SEQUENCE	153. { *Constant Antecedent.* Cause.	154. { *Constant Sequent.* Effect.	
	155. { *Assignment of Cause.* Attribution.	156. { *Absence of Assignment.* Chance.	
2°. CONNECTION BETWEEN CAUSE AND EFFECT	157. Power.	158. Impotence.	
	Degrees of Power.		
	159. Strength.	160. Weakness.	
	161. Production.	162. Destruction.	
	163. Reproduction.		
3°. POWER IN OPERATION	164. Producer.	165. Destroyer.	
	166. Paternity.	167. Posterity.	
	168. Productiveness.	169. Unproductiveness.	
	170. Agency.		
	171. Energy.	172. Inertness.	
	173. Violence.	174. Moderation.	
	175. Influence.	175a. Absence of Influence.	
4°. INDIRECT POWER	176. Tendency.		
	177. Liability.		
5°. COMBINATIONS OF CAUSES	178. Concurrence.	179. Counteraction.	

CLASS II. SPACE

I. SPACE IN GENERAL

1°. ABSTRACT SPACE	180. { *Indefinite.* Space.	180a. Inextension. 181. { *Definite.* Region. 182. { *Limited.* Place.	
2°. RELATIVE SPACE	183. Situation. 184. Location.	185. Displacement.	
3°. EXISTENCE IN SPACE	186. Presence.	187. Absence.	
	188. Inhabitant.	189. Abode.	
	190. Contents.	191. Receptacle.	

II. DIMENSIONS

1°. GENERAL	192. Size.	193. Littleness.	
	194. Expansion.	195. Contraction.	
	196. Distance.	197. Nearness.	
	198. Interval.	199. Contiguity.	
2°. LINEAR	200. Length.	201. Shortness.	
	202. { Breadth. Thickness.	203. { Narrowness. Thinness.	
	204. Layer.	205. Filament.	
	206. Height.	207. Lowness.	
	208. Depth.	209. Shallowness.	

SYNOPSIS OF CATEGORIES

4°. WITH REFERENCE TO DIRECTION—*cont.*...

305. Ascent.	306. Descent.
307. Elevation.	308. Depression.
309. Leap.	310. Plunge.
311. Circuition.	
312. Rotation.	313. Evolution.
314. Oscillation.	
315. Agitation.	

CLASS III. MATTER

I. MATTER IN GENERAL.......

316. Materiality.	317. Immateriality.
318. World.	
319. Gravity.	320. Levity.

II. INORGANIC MATTER

1°. SOLIDS.............

321. Density.	322. Rarity.
323. Hardness.	324. Softness.
325. Elasticity.	326. Inelasticity.
327. Tenacity.	328. Brittleness.
329. Texture.	
330. Pulverulence.	
331. Friction.	332. Lubrication.

2°. FLUIDS

1. *In General*

333. Fluidity.	334. Gaseity.
335. Liquefaction.	336. Vaporization.
337. Water.	338. Air.
339. Moisture.	340. Dryness.

2. *Specific*...

341. Ocean.	342. Land.
343. { Gulf. Lake.	
	344. Plain.
345. Marsh.	346. Island.

3. *In motion*

347. Stream.	
348. River.	349. Wind.
350. Conduit.	351. Air-pipe.

3°. IMPERFECT FLUIDS...

352. Semiliquidity.	353. Bubble.
354. Pulpiness.	355. Unctuousness.
	356. Oil.
	356*a*. Resin.

III. ORGANIC MATTER

1°. VITALITY

1. *In General*....

357. Organization.	358. Inorganization.
359. Life.	360. Death.
	361. Killing.
	362. Corpse.
	363. Interment.

2. *Special*

364. Animality.	365. Vegetability.
366. Animal.	367. Vegetable.
368. Zoology.	369. Botany.
370. Cicuration.	371. Agriculture.
372. Mankind.	
373. Man.	374. Woman.

SYNOPSIS OF CATEGORIES

(1) General		375. Sensibility.	376. Insensibility.
		377. Pleasure.	378. Pain.
	1. Touch	379. Touch.	
		380. { Sensations of Touch.	381. Numbness.
	2. Heat	382. Heat.	383. Cold.
		384. Calefaction.	385. Refrigeration.
		386. Furnace.	387. Refrigeratory.
		388. Fuel.	
		389. Thermometer.	
	3. Taste	390. Taste.	391. Insipidity.
		392. Pungency.	
		393. Condiment.	
		394. Savouriness.	395. Unsavouriness.
		396. Sweetness.	397. Sourness.
	4. Odor	398. Odor.	399. Inodorousness.
		400. Fragrance.	401. Fœtor.

2°. SENSATION

(2) Special

5. Sound

(i.) *Sound in General.*
402. Sound.   403. Silence.
404. Loudness.   405. Faintness.

(ii.) *Specific Sounds.*
406. Snap.   407. Roll.
408. Resonance.   408a. Non-resonance.
          409. Sibilation.
410. Stridor.
411. Cry.   412. Ululation.

(iii.) *Musical Sounds.*
413. { Melody.   414. Discord.
      Concord.
415. Music.
416. Musician.
417. Musical Instruments.

(iv.) *Perception of Sound.*
418. Hearing.   419. Deafness.

6. Light

(i.) *Light in General.*
420. Light.   421. Darkness.
     422. Dimness.
423. Luminary.   424. Shade.
425. Transparency.   426. Opacity.
     427. Semitransparency.

(ii.) *Specific Light.*
428. Color.   429. Achromatism.
430. Whiteness.   431. Blackness.
432. Gray.   433. Brown.
434. Redness.   435. Greenness.
436. Yellowness.   437. Purple.
438. Blueness.   439. Orange.
440. Variegation.

(iii.) *Perceptions of Light.*
441. Vision.   442. Blindness.
     443. Dimsightedness.
444. Spectator.
445. Optical Instruments.
446. Visibility.   447. Invisibility.
448. Appearance.   449. Disappearance.

SYNOPSIS OF CATEGORIES

Class IV. INTELLECT

Division (I.). Formation of Ideas

I. Operations of Intellect in General.....

450. Intellect.	450a. Absence of Intellect.
451. Thought.	452. Incogitancy.
453. Idea.	454. Topic.
455. Curiosity.	456. Incuriosity.
457. Attention.	458. Inattention.
459. Care.	460. Neglect.

II. Precursory Conditions and Operations......

461. Inquiry.	462. Answer.
463. Experiment.	
464. Comparison.	
465. Discrimination.	465a. Indiscrimination.
466. Measurement.	
467. Evidence.	468. Counter-evidence.
469. Qualification.	

III. Materials for Reasoning..........

Degrees of Evidence.

470. Possibility.	471. Impossibility.
472. Probability.	473. Improbability.
474. Certainty.	475. Uncertainty.

IV. Reasoning Processes .

476. Reasoning.	477. { Intuition. Sophistry.
478. Demonstration.	479. Confutation.
480. Judgement.	481. Misjudgement.
480a. Discovery.	
482. Over-estimation.	483. Under-estimation.
484. Belief.	485. { Unbelief. Doubt.

V. Results of Reasoning .

486. Credulity.	487. Incredulity.
488. Assent.	489. Dissent.
490. Knowledge.	491. Ignorance.
492. Scholar.	493. Ignoramus.
494. Truth.	495. Error.
496. Maxim.	497. Absurdity.

Faculties.

498. { Intelligence. Wisdom.	499. { Imbecility. Folly.
500. Sage.	501. Fool.
502. Sanity.	503. Insanity.
	504. Madman.

VI. Extension of Thought

1°. *To the Past...*

505. Memory.	506. Oblivion.
507. Expectation.	508. Inexpectation.
	509. Disappointment.

2°. *To the Future.*

510. Foresight.	
511. Prediction.	
512. Omen.	
513. Oracle.	

VII. Creative Thought...

514. Supposition.
515. Imagination.

Class V. VOLITION

Division (I.). Individual Volition

I. Volition in General

1°. Acts....

600. Will.	601. Necessity.
602. Willingness.	603. Unwillingness.
604. Resolution.	605. Irresolution.
604a. Perseverance. }	607. Tergiversation.
606. Obstinacy. }	
	608. Caprice.
609. Choice.	609a. Absence of Choice.
	610. Rejection.
611. Predetermination.	612. Impulse.
613. Habit.	614. Desuetude.

2°. Causes..

615. Motive.	615a. Absence of Motive.
	616. Dissuasion.
617. Plea.	

3°. Objects..

618. Good.	619. Evil.
620. Intention.	621. Chance.
622. Pursuit.	623. Avoidance.
	624. Relinquishment.

II. Prospective Volition.......

1°. Conceptional..

625. Business.
626. Plan.
627. Method.
628. Mid-Course.   629. Circuit.
630. Requirement.

2°. Subservience to Ends...

1. Actual Subservience.

631. Instrumentality.
632. Means.
633. Instrument.
634. Substitute.
635. Materials.
636. Store.
637. Provision.   638. Waste.
639. Sufficiency.
641. Redundance.   640. Insufficiency.

2. Degree of Subservience.

642. Importance.	643. Unimportance.
644. Utility.	645. Inutility.
646. Expedience.	647. Inexpedience.
648. Goodness.	649. Badness.
650. Perfection.	651. Imperfection.
652. Cleanness.	653. Uncleanness.
654. Health.	655. Disease.
656. Salubrity.	657. Insalubrity.
658. Improvement.	659. Deterioration.
660. Restoration.	661. Relapse.
662. Remedy.	663. Bane.

3. Contingent Subservience.

664. Safety.	665. Danger.
666. Refuge.	667. Pitfall.
668. Warning.	
669. Alarm.	
670. Preservation.	
671. Escape.	
672. Deliverance.	

Division (II.). INTERSOCIAL VOLITION

SYNOPSIS OF CATEGORIES

Class VI. AFFECTIONS

II. PERSONAL

1°. PASSIVE

827. Pleasure.	828. Pain.
829. Pleasureableness.	830. Painfulness.
831. Content.	{832. Discontent.
	{833. Regret.
834. Relief.	835. Aggravation.
836. Cheerfulness.	837. Dejection.
838. Rejoicing.	839. Lamentation.
840. Amusement.	841. Weariness.
842. Wit.	843. Dulness.
844. Humorist.	

2°. DISCRIMINATIVE

845. Beauty.	846. Ugliness.
847. Ornament.	848. Blemish.
	849. Simplicity.
850. Taste.	851. Vulgarity.
852. Fashion.	
	853. Ridiculousness.
	854. Fop.
	855. Affection.
	856. Ridicule.
	857. Laughing-stock.

3°. PROSPECTIVE

858. Hope.	{859. Hopelessness.
	{860. Fear.
861. Courage.	862. Cowardice.
863. Rashness.	864. Caution.
865. Desire.	867. Dislike.
866. Indifference.	
	868. Fastidiousness.
	869. Satiety.

4°. CONTEMPLATIVE

870. Wonder.	871. Expectance.
872. Prodigy.	

5°. EXTRINSIC

873. Repute.	874. Disrepute.
875. Nobility.	876. Commonalty.
877. Title.	
878. Pride.	879. Humility.
880. Vanity.	881. Modesty.
882. Ostentation.	
883. Celebration.	
884. Boasting.	
885. Insolence.	886. Servility.
887. Blusterer.	

III. SYMPATHETIC

1°. SOCIAL

888. Friendship.	889. Enmity.
890. Friend.	891. Enemy.
892. Sociality.	893. Seclusion.
894. Courtesy.	895. Discourtesy.
896. Congratulation.	
897. Love.	898. Hate.
899. Favorite.	
	900. Resentment.
	901. Irascibility.
	901a. Sullenness.
902. Endearment.	
903. Marriage.	{904. Celibacy.
	{905. Divorce.

	906. Benevolence.	907. Malevolence.
		908. Malediction.
2°. DIFFUSIVE.........		909. Threat.
	910. Philanthropy.	911. Misanthropy.
	912. Benefactor.	913. Evil doer.
3°. SPECIAL..........	914. Pity.	914a. Pitilessness.
	915. Condolence.	
	916. Gratitude.	917. Ingratitude.
4°. RETROSPECTIVE....	918. Forgiveness.	919. Revenge.
		920. Jealousy.
		921. Envy.

IV. MORAL

	922. Right.	923. Wrong.
1°. OBLIGATIONS.......	924. Dueness.	925. Undueness.
		927. Dereliction.
	926. Duty.	927a. Exemption.
	928. Respect.	929. Disrespect.
		930. Contempt.
	931. Approbation.	932. Disapprobation.
2°. SENTIMENTS........	933. Flattery.	934. Detraction.
	935. Flatterer.	936. Detractor.
	937. Vindication.	938. Accusation.
	939. Probity.	940. Improbity.
		941. Knave.
	942. Disinterestedness.	943. Selfishness.
	944. Virtue.	945. Vice.
3°. CONDITIONS........	946. Innocence.	947. Guilt.
	948. Good Man.	949. Bad Man.
	950. Penitence.	951. Impenitence.
	952. Atonement.	
	953. Temperance.	954. Intemperance.
		954a. Sensualist.
	955. Asceticism.	
4°. PRACTICE..........	956. Fasting.	957. Gluttony.
	958. Sobriety.	959. Drunkenness.
	960. Purity.	961. Impurity.
		962. Libertine.
	963. Legality.	964. Illegality.
	965. Jurisprudence.	
	966. Tribunal.	
	967. Judge.	
5°. INSTITUTIONS......	968. Lawyer.	
	969. Lawsuit.	
	970. Acquittal.	971. Condemnation.
		972. Punishment.
	973. Reward.	974. Penalty.
		975. Scourge.

V. RELIGIOUS

	976. Deity.	
1°. SUPERHUMAN BE-	977. Angel.	978. Satan.
INGS AND REGIONS..	979. Jupiter.	980. Demon.
	981. Heaven.	982. Hell.
	983. Theology.	
2°. DOCTRINES........	983a. Orthodoxy.	984. Heterodoxy.
	985. Revelation.	986. Pseudo-revelation.
3°. SENTIMENTS........	987. Piety.	988. Impiety.
		989. Irreligion.

ABBREVIATIONS, &c.

Adj.	*adj.*	Adjectives, Participles, and Words having the power of Adjectives.
Adv.	*adv.*	Adverbs and Adverbial Expressions.
Int.	*int.*	Interjections.
Phr.	*phr.*	Phrases.
V.	*v.*	Verbs.

The numbers are those of the headings, or Categories.

Words in italics within parentheses are not intended to explain the meanings of the words which precede them, but to indicate the nature of allied group of words under the numbers which follow them.

THESAURUS

OF

ENGLISH WORDS AND PHRASES

1. Existence.—N. existence, being, entity, *ens, esse,* subsistence, quiddity.

reality, realness, actuality; positiveness etc. *adj.*; fact, matter of fact, sober reality; truth etc. 494; actual existence.

presence etc. (*existence in space*) 186; coexistence etc. 120.

stubborn fact; not a -dream etc. 515; no joke.

substance, essence, prime constituent, hypostatis. [Science of existence], ontology.

V. exist, be; have -being etc. *n.*; subsist, live, breathe, stand, obtain, be the case; occur etc. (*event*) 151; have place, rank, prevail; find oneself, pass the time, vegetate.

consist in, lie in, reside in, inhere in.

come into -existence etc. *n.*; arise etc. (*begin*) 66; come forth etc. (*appear*) 446.

become etc. (*be converted*) 144; bring into existence etc. 161; coexist, preexist, endure etc. 141.

Adj. existing etc. *v.*; existent, subsistent, under the sun; in -existence etc, *n.*; extant; afloat, on foot, current, prevalent, rife, in force, -vogue; undestroyed.

real, actual, positive, absolute; true etc. 494; substan-tial, -tive; self-existing, -ent.

well-founded, -grounded; un-ideal, -imagined; not -potential etc. 2.

Adv. actually etc. *adj.*; in -fact, − point of fact, − reality; indeed; *de −*, *ipso-facto.*

2. Nonexistence.—N. nonexistence; inexistence, -subsistence; nonentity, *nil*; negativeness etc. *adj.*; nullity; nihil-ity, -ism; *tabula rasa,* blank; abeyance; absence etc. 187; no such thing. 4; nothingness, oblivion, *non esse.*

annihilation; extinction etc. (*destruction*) 162.

V. not -exist etc. 1; have no -existence etc. 1; be null and void; cease to -exist etc. 1; pass away, perish; be −, become-extinct etc. *adj.*; die out; disappear etc. 449; melt away, dissolve, leave not a rack behind, leave no trace; go, be no more; die etc. 360.

annihilate, render null, nullify; abrogate etc. 756; destroy etc. 162; take away; remove etc. (*displace*) 185.

Adj. inexistent, non-existent etc. 1; negative, blank, null and void; missing, omitted; absent etc. 187; visionary etc. 515.

unreal, potential, virtual; baseless, *in nubibus*; unsubstantial etc. 4; vain.

un-born, -created, -begotten, -conceived, produced, -made.

perished, annihilated etc. *v.*; extinct, exhausted, gone, lost, departed; defunct etc. (*dead*) 360; fabulous, ideal etc. (*imaginary*) 515; supposititious etc. 514.

Adv. negatively, virtually, etc. *adj.*

3. Substantiality.—N. substantiality, *hypostasis*; person, thing, object, article; something, a being, an existence; creature, body, substance, flesh and blood, stuff, *substratum*; matter etc. 316; physical nature.

[Totality of existences], world etc. 318; *plenum.*

Adj. substan-tive, -tial, concrete; hypostatic; personal, bodily; tangible etc. (*material*) 316; real, corporeal, evident.

Adv. substantially etc. *adj.*; bodily, essentially.

4. Unsubstantiality.—N. un-, in-substantiality; nothingness, nihility.

nothing, naught, *nil,* nullity, zero, cipher, no one, nobody; never −, ne'er -a one; no such thing, none in the world; nothing -whatever, − at all, − on earth; not a -particle etc. (*smallness*) 32; all - talk, − moonshine, − stuff and nonsense, matter of no import.

thing of naught, man of straw, John Doe and Richard Roe; *nominis umbra,* nonentity, figurehead, lay figure; flash in the pan, *vox et praeterea nihil.*

shadow; phantasm, phantom etc. (*fallacy of vision*) 443; dream etc. (*imagination*) 515; *ignis fatuus* etc. (*luminary*) 423; 'such stuff as dreams are made of,' thin air; bubble etc. 353; 'baseless fabric of a vision,' mockery.

hollowness, blank; vacuity, void etc. (*absence*) 187.

inanity, fool's paradise, fatuity, stupidity, emptiness of mind.

V. vanish, evaporate, fade, sink, fly −, die −, melt- away, dissolve, disappear etc. 449; become extinct, become invisible.

Adj. unsubstantial; fleeting; base-, ground-less; ungrounded; without −, − having no- foundation.

visionary etc. (*imaginary*) 515; immaterial etc. 317; spectral etc. 980; dreamy; shadowy; ethereal, airy, imponderable, tenuous, vague.

vacant, vacuous; empty etc. 187; eviscerated; blank, hollow; nominal; null; inane.

Phr. there's nothing in it.

5. Intrinsicality.—N. intrinsicality, inbeing, inherence, inhesion, immanence; subjectiveness; *ego;* essence; essentialness etc. *adj.*; essential part, essential stuff, substance, quintessence, incarnation, quiddity, gist, pith, core, kernel, marrow, sap, lifeblood, backbone, heart, soul, life, flower; important part etc. (*importance*) 642.

principle, nature, constitution, character, ethos, type, quality, crasis, *diathesis.*

habit; temper, -ament; spirit, humor, grain, disposition, streak, tendency etc. 176.

endowment, capacity; capability etc. (*power*) 157; moods, declensions, features, aspects; peculiarities etc. (*specialty*) 79; idiosyncrasy; idiocrasy; diagnostics.

V. be —, run- in the blood; be born so; be - intrinsic etc. *adj.*

Adj. derived from within, subjective; idiocratic, idiosyncratic, intrin-sic, -sical; fundamental, cardinal, normal, inherent, essential, natural; in-nate, -born, -bred, -dwelling, -grained; -wrought; radical, incarnate, thoroughbred, hereditary, inherited, immanent; congen-ital, -ite; connate, running in the blood; coeval with birth, genetic, ingenerate, - genite; indigenous; in the -grain etc. *n.*; bred in the bone, instinctive; inward, internal etc. 221; to the manner born; virtual.

characteristic etc. (*special*) 79, (*indicative*) 550; invariable, incurable, ineradicable, fixed, settled, constant, unchanging.

Adv. intrinsically etc. *adj.*; at bottom, in the main, in effect, essentially, practically, virtually, substantially, *au fond*; fairly.

6. Extrinsicality.—N. extrinsicality, objectiveness, *non ego;* extraneousness etc. 57; accident; letter of the law.

Adj. derived from without; objective; extrinsic, -sical; extraneous etc. (*foreign*) 57; modal, adventitious, additional, supervenient, fortuitous; a-, ad-scititious; incidental, casual, accidental, unessential, non-essential, accessory.

implanted, ingrafted; instilled, inculcated.

outward etc. (*external*) 220.

Adv. extrinsically etc. *adj.*

7. State.—N. state, condition, category, estate, lot, case, trim, mood, pickle, plight etc. 704; temper; aspect etc. (*appearance*) 448.

constitution, habitude, *diathesis;* frame, fabric etc. 329; stamp, set, fit, mold.

mode, modality, schesis; fettle; form etc. (*shape*) 240.

tone, tenor, turn; trim, guise, fashion, light, complexion, style, character.

V. be in —, possess —, enjoy —, labor under- a -state etc. *n.*; be on a footing, do, fare; come to pass.

Adj. conditional, modal, formal; structural, organic.

Adv. conditionally etc. *adj.*; as -the matter stands, — things are; such being the case etc. 8.

8. Circumstance.—N. circumstance, situation, phase, position, posture, attitude, place, point; terms; *régime;* footing, standing, status.

occasion, juncture, conjuncture; contingency etc. (*event*) 151.

predicament; emergen-ce, -cy; exigency, crisis, pinch, pass, push; turning point; crossroads.

bearings, how the land lies.

Adj. circumstantial; given, conditional, provisional; critical; modal; contingent, incidental; adventitious etc. (*extrinsic*) 6.

Adv. in the circumstances etc. *n.*, under the conditions etc. 7; thus, in such wise.

accordingly; that —, such- being the case; that being so, since, seeing that.

as matters stand; as -things, — times- go.

conditionally, provided, if, in case; if -so, — so be, — it be so; if it so -happen, — turn out; in the event of; in such a -contingency, — case, — event; provisionally, unless, without.

according to -circumstances, — the occasion; as it may -happen, — turn out, — be; as the -case may be, — wind blows; *pro re natâ.*

9. Relation.—N. relation, bearing, reference, connection, apposition, interconnection, concern, cognation; applicability, appositeness; correlation etc. 12; analogy; similarity etc. 17; affinity, intimacy, friendship; homology, alliance, homogeneity, association, rapport; approximation etc. (*nearness*) 197; filiation etc. (*consanguinity*) 11; interest; relevancy etc. 23; relationship, relative position; relativity; interrelation etc. 12.

comparison etc. 464; ratio, proportion.

link, tie, bond, bond of union.

V. be-related etc. *adj.*; have a relation etc. *n.*; relate —, refer- to; bear upon, regard, concern, touch, affect, have to do with; pertain —, belong —, appertain- to; have respect to; answer to; interest.

bring -into relation with, — to bear upon; connect, associate, draw a parallel; link etc. 43.

Adj. relative; correlative etc. 12; cognate; relating to etc. *v.*; relative to, in relation with, referable *or* referrible to; belonging to etc. *v.*; appurtenant to, in common with.

related, connected; implicated, associated, affiliated, akin, allied to; collateral, cognate, congenial, kindred, affinitive, *en rapport*, in touch with.

approxima-tive, -ting; approaching; proportion-al, -ate, -able; allusive, comparable.

in the same -category etc. 75; like etc. 17; relevant etc. (*apt*) 23.

Adv. relatively etc. *adj.*; pertinently etc. 23.

thereof; as -to, — for, — respects, — re-gards; about; concerning etc. *v.*; anent; relating —, as relates- to; with -relation, — reference, — respect, — regard-to; in respect of; while speaking —, *à propos* -of; in connection with; by the - way, — by; whereas; for —, in -as much as; in point of, as far as; on the -part, — score- of; *quoad hoc; pro re natâ;* under the -head etc. (*class*) 75- of; in the matter of, *in re.*

Phr. 'thereby hangs a tale.'

10. Irrelation. [Want, or absence of relation.]—**N.** irrelation, dissociation; inapplicability; inconnection; multifariousness; disconnection etc. (*disjunction*) 44; inconsequence, independence; incommensurability; irreconcilableness etc. (*disagreement*) 24; heterogeneity;

unconformity etc. 83; irrelevancy, impertinence, *nihil ad rem;* intrusion etc. 24.

V. have no -relation etc. 9 to, − bearing upon, − concern etc. 9 with, − business with; not -concern etc. 9; have -nothing to do with, − no business there; intrude, etc. 24.

bring −, drag −, haul −, lug- in head and shoulders.

Adj. irrelative, irrespective, unrelated, irrelated; arbitrary; independent, unallied; un-, dis-connected; adrift, isolated, insular; extraneous, strange, alien, foreign, outlandish, exotic.

not comparable, incommensurable, heterogeneous; unconformable etc. 83.

irrelevant; rambling etc. 279; inapplicable; not -pertinent, − to the purpose; impertinent, inapposite, beside the mark, *à propos de bottes;* away from −, foreign to −, beside- the -purpose, − question, − transaction, − point; misplaced etc. (*intrusive*) 24.

remote, far fetched, out of the way, forced, neither here nor there, quite another thing; detached, segregated, segregate.

multifarious; discordant etc. 24.

incidental, parenthetical, *obiter dictum,* episodic.

Adv. parenthetically etc. *adj.;* by the -way, − by; *en passant,* incidentally; irrespecitively etc. *adj.;* without reference, − regard- to; in the abstract etc. 87; *a se.*

11. Consanguinity. [Relations of kindred.]—N. consanguinity, relationship, kindred, blood; parentage etc. (*paternity*) 166; filiation, affiliation; lineage, agnation, connection, cognation, alliance; family -connection, − tie; ties of blood; blood relationship; nepotism.

kins-man, -folk; people; kith and kin; relation, -tive; connection; sib; next of kin; uncle, aunt, nephew, niece; cousin, -german; first −, second- cousin; cousin -once, − twice etc.- removed; near −, distant-relation; brother, sister, one's own flesh and blood.

family, patriarch, matriarch; fraternity; brother-, sister-, cousin-hood.

race, stock, generation; sept etc. 166 ; stirps, side; strain; breed, clan, tribe.

V. be -related etc. *adj.* − to; claim -relationship etc. *n.*- with.

Adj. related, akin, consanguineous, matrilinear, patrilineal, of the blood, family, allied, collateral; cog-, ag-, con-nate; kindred; affiliated, affine; fraternal, avuncular.

intimately −, nearly −, closely −, remotely −, distantly- related, − allied; german.

12. Correlation. [Double or reciprocal relation.]—N. reciprocalness etc. *adj.;* recipro-city, -cality, -cation; mutuality, correlation, correspondence, interdependence; interchange etc. 148; exchange, barter; interrelation, interconnection; alternation, see-saw.

V. reciprocate, alternate; interchange etc. 148; exchange; counterchange; interact, correspond, mutualize, give and take.

Adj. reciprocal, mutual, commutual, correlative; alternate; interchangeable; international; correspondent, complementary, analogous.

Adv. *mutatis mutandis; vice versâ;* each other; by turns etc. 148; reciprocally etc. *adj.;* to and fro etc. 314.

13. Identity.—N. identity, sameness, oneness, ditto, homogeneity; unity, coincidence, coalescence; convertibility; equality etc. 27; selfness, self, oneself; identification.

monotony, tautology etc. (*repetition*) 104.

synonym.

fac-simile etc. (*copy*) 21; *alter ego* etc. (*similar*) 17; *ipsissima verba* etc. (*exactness*) 494; same; self −, very −, one and the same; very −, actual-thing, no other.

V. be -identical etc. *adj.;* match, coincide, coalesce.

treat as −, render--the same , −identical; identify; recognize the identity of.

Adj. identical; self, ilk; the -same etc. *n.;* self same; synonymous; one and the same.

coincid-, coalesc-ent, -ing; indistinguishable; one; equivalent etc. (*equal*) 27; much -the same, − of a muchness; unaltered.

Adv. identically etc. *adj.;* on all fours; ibid-, -em.

14. Contrariety. [Non-coincidence.]—N. contrariety, contrast, foil, antithesis, oppositeness; counterpole; contradiction; antagonism etc. (*opposition*) 708; counteraction etc. 179.

inversion etc. 218; the -opposite, − reverse, − inverse, − converse, − antipodes, − other extreme etc. 237.

antonym.

V. be -contrary etc. *adj.;* contrast with, oppose; differ *toto coelo.*

invert, reverse, turn the tables etc. 218.

contra-dict, -vene; antagonize etc. 708.

Adj. contrar-y, -ious, -iant; opposite, counter, dead against; ad-, con-, reverse; opposed, antithetical, contrasted, antipodean, antagonistic, opposing; conflicting, inconsistent, contradictory, at cross purposes; negative; hostile etc. 708.

differing *toto coelo;* diametrically opposite; as opposite as -black and white, − light and darkness, − fire and water, − the poles, as different as chalk from cheese; 'Hyperion to a satyr;' quite the -contrary, − reverse; no such thing, just the other way, *tout au contraire.*

Adv. contrarily etc. *adj.; contra,* contrariwise, *per contra,* on the contrary, nay rather; topsyturvy; *vice versâ;* on the other hand etc. (*in compensation*) 30.

15. Difference.—N. difference, unlikeness; heterogeneity; vari-ance, -ation, -ety; diversity, dissimilarity etc. 18; disagreement etc. 24; disparity etc. (*inequality*) 28; distinction, contra-distinction; distinctness; discrepancy, divergence, contrast etc. 18; nonconformity, incompatibility, antithesis.

discord etc. 713.

modification, moods and tenses.

nice −, fine −, delicate −, subtle- distinction; shade of difference, *nuance;* discrimination etc. 465; *differentia.*

different thing, something else, variant, apple

off another tree, horse of another color, another pair of shoes; this that or the other.
V. be -different etc. *adj.;* differ, vary, ablude, mismatch, contrast; diverge −, depart −, deviate- -from; divaricate; differ -*toto coelo, — longo intervallo.*
disagree etc. 713.
vary, modify etc. (*change*) 140.
discriminate etc. 465.
Adj. differing etc. *v.;* different, diverse, divided, heterogeneous; distinguishable; varied, modified; divergent, incongruous, diversified, various; discrepant, dissentient, differential; divers, all manner of; variform etc. 81; discordant etc. 713.
other, another, not the same; unequal etc. 28; unmatched; widely apart.
distinctive, characteristic; discriminative; distinghishing.
Adv. differently etc. *adj.*
Phr. *il y a fagots et fagots; tot nomines tot sententiae;* one man's meat is another man's poison.

16. Uniformity.—N. uniformity; homogeneity, -ousness; continuity, stability, consistency; connatural-ity, -ness; homology; accordance; conformity etc. 82; agreement etc. 23.
regularity, constancy, even tenor, routine; monotony, evenness, sameness, dead level; steadiness, equability, unity.
V. be -uniform etc. *adj.;* accord with etc. 23; run through.
become -uniform etc. *adj.;* conform to etc. 82.
render uniform etc. *adj.;* assimilate, level, smooth, dress.
Adj. uniform; homo-geneous, -logous; of a piece, consistent, steady; connatural; monotonous, changeless, dreary, even, invariable, equable, level, regular, stereotyped, unchanged, unvarying; methodical etc. 60; habitual etc. 613.
Adv. uniformly etc. *adj.;* uniformly with etc. (*conformably*) 82; in harmony with etc. (*agreeing*) 23; in a -rut, − groove.
always, ever etc. 112; invariably, without exception, never otherwise; by clock-work; endlessly etc. 112.
Phr. *ab uno disce omnes.*

16a. Non-uniformity. [Absence or want of uniformity.]−**N.** diversity, irregularity, unevenness; multiformity etc. 81; unconformity etc. 83; roughness etc. 256; heterogeneity, heteromorphism.
Adj. diversified, varied, irregular, uneven, rough etc. 256; multifarious; multiform etc. 81; of various kinds; all -manner, − sorts, − kinds- of.
Adv. in all manner of ways, here there and everywhere.

17. Similarity.—N. similarity, resemblance, likeness, similitude, semblance; affinity, approximation, parallelism; parity; agreement etc. 23; ana-logy, -logicalness; correspondence, equality etc.
connatural-ness, -ity; brotherhood, family likeness.

alliteration, rhyme, pun.
repetition etc. 104; sameness etc. (*identity*) 13; uniformity etc. 16.
analogue; the like; match, *pendant,* fellow, companion, pair, mate, twin, double, counterpart, brother, sister; one's second self, *alter ego,* chip of the old block, *par nobile fratrum, Arcades ambo,* birds of a feather, *et hoc genus omne.*
parallel; simile; type etc. (*metaphor*) 521; image etc. (*representation*) 554; photograph; close −, striking −, speaking −, faithful etc *adj.* − likeness, − resemblance.
V. be -similar etc. *adj.;* look like, resemble, bear resemblance, favor; savor −, smack- of; approximate; parallel, match, rhyme with; take after; imitate etc. 19; run in pairs.
Adj. similar; resembling etc. *v.;* like, alike; twin.
analog-ous, -ical; parallel, of a piece; such as, so.
connatural, congeneric, allied to; corresponding, cognate; akin to etc. (*consanguineous*) 11.
approximate, much the same, near, close, something like, such like; a show of; mock, *pseudo,* simulating, representing.
exact etc. (*true*) 494; lifelike, faithful, realistic; true to -nature, − the life; the -very image − pic:ure- of; for all the world like, *comme deux gouttes d'eau;* as like as -two peas, − it can stare; *instar omnium,* case in the same mold, ridiculously like.
Adv. as if, so to speak; as −, as if- it were; *quasi,* just as, *veluti in speculum.*

18. Dissimilarity.—N. dissimil-arity, -itude; unlikeness, diversity, disparity, dissemblance; divergence, inequality, difference etc. 15; novelty; variation, variety, originality, disguise.
V. be -unlike etc. *adj.;* vary etc. (*differ*) 15; bear no resemblance to, differ *toto coelo.*
render -unlike etc. *adj.;* vary etc. (*diversify*) 140.
Adj. dissimilar, unlike, disparate; of a different kind etc. (*class*) 75; unmatched, unique; new, novel; unprecedented etc. 83; original.
nothing of the kind; no such −, quite another-thing; far from it, other than, cast in a different mold, *tertium quid,* as like a dock as a daisy, 'very like a whale;' as different as -chalk from cheese, − Macedon and Monmouth; *lucus a non lucendo.*
diversified etc. 16a.
Adv. otherwise, *alias.*

19. Imitation.—N. imitation; copying etc. *v.;* transcription; repetition, mimeograph, mimeotype, duplication, reduplication; quotation; reproduction.
mockery, mimicry, mime, simulation, personation; representation etc. 554; semblance, pretence; copy etc. 21; assimilation.
paraphrase, parody etc. 21.
plagiarism; forgery etc. (*falsehood*) 544.
imitator; echo, cuckoo, parrot, ape, monkey, mocking-bird, mimic, impersonator, copyist.
V. imitate, copy, mirror, reflect, reproduce, repeat, borrow; do like, echo, re-echo, catch; transcribe; match, parallel.

mock, take off, mimic, ape, simulate, personate, impersonate; forge; act etc. (*drama*) 599; represent etc. 554; counterfeit, duplicate; portray, parody, travesty, caricature, burlesque.

follow —, tread- in the- -steps, — footsteps, — wake- of; pattern after, take pattern by; follow - suit, — the example of; walk in the shoes of, take a leaf out of another's book, strike in with; take —, model -after; emulate.

Adj. imitated etc. *v.*; mock, mimic; counterfeit, false, pseudo; modelled after, molded on, paraphrastic; literal; imitative, apish; second-hand; imitable; sham etc. 545.

Adv. literally, to the letter, strictly, precisely, *verbatim, literatim, sic, totidem verbis,* word for word, *mot à mot.*

Phr. like master like man.

20. Non-Imitation.—N. no imitation, genuineness, originality; creativeness.

Adj. unimitated, uncopied; unmatched, unparalleled; inimitable etc. 33; *unique,* original, primordial, primary, pristine, underived, first-hand, archetypal, prototypal.

20a. Variation.—N. variation; alteration etc. (*change*) 140. modification, moods and tenses; modulation.

divergency etc. 291; deviation etc. 279; aberration; innovation.

V. vary etc. (*change*) 140. deviate etc. 279, diverge etc. 291.

Adj. varied etc. *v.*; modified; dissimilar etc. 18; diversified etc. 16*a.*

21. Copy. [Result of imitation.]—**N.** copy, facsimile, counterpart, *effigies,* effigy, symbol, image, form, likeness, similitude, semblance, resemblance, cast, electrotype, stereotype, tracing, ectype; imitation etc. 19; model, representation, adumbration, study; counterfeit presentment, portrait etc. (*representment*) 554.

duplicate; transcript, -ion; reflex, -ion; shadow, echo; chip of the old block; reprint, reproduction, casting, engraving, replica; transfer; second edition etc. (*repetition*) 104; *réchauffé* apograph, fair copy; revise.

parody, caricature, cartoon, burlesque, travesty, paraphrase.

servile -copy, — imitation; counterfeit etc. (*deception*) 545; *pasticcio.*

Adj. faithful; lifelike etc. (*similar*) 17.

22. Prototype. [Thing copied.]—**N.** prototype, original, model, pattern, founding, precedent, standard, scantling, type, arche-, anti-type; protoplast, copy-book, module, exemplar, example, ensample, specimen; paradigm; guide; templet; lay-figure.

text, copy, manuscript, MS., design; fugleman, keynote.

die, mold; matrix, engraving, last, plasm; pro-, proto-plasm; mint; seal, punch, *intaglio,* negative, stamp.

V. be —, set- an example; set a copy; standardize.

23. Agreement.—N. agreement; ac-cord, -cordance; unison, harmony, concord etc. 714; concordance, concert, understanding, convention, *entente -cordiale, consortium,* consensus of opinion, pact, mutual understanding, unanimity.

conformity etc. 82; conformance; uniformity etc. 16; consonance, consentaneousness, consistency; congruity, -ence; keeping; congeniality; correspondence, concinnity, parallelism, apposition, union.

fitness, aptness etc. *adj.*; relevancy; pertinence, -cy; sortance; case in point; aptitude, propriety, applicability, admissibility, commensurability, compatibility, suitability; cognation etc (*relation*) 9.

adaptation, adjustment, arrangement, graduation, accommodation; reconcil-iation -ement; assimilation; attunement.

consent etc. (*assent*) 448; concurrence etc. 178; co-operation etc. 709.

right man in the right place, very thing; quite —, just- the thing.

V. be -accordant etc. *adj.*; agree, accord, harmonize; correspond, tally, respond; meet, suit, fit, befit, do, adapt itself to; fall in —, chime in —, square —, quadrate —, consort —, comport- with; dovetail, assimilate; fit like a glove; fit to a -tittle, — T; match etc. 17; become one. consent etc. (*assent*) 488.

render -accordant etc. *adj.*; fit, suit, adapt, accommodate; graduate; adjust etc. (*render equal*) 27; dress, regulate, readjust; accord, harmonize, reconcile; fadge, dovetail, square.

Adj. agreeing, suiting etc. *v.*; in accord, accordant, concordant, consonant, congruous, consentaneous, correspondent, corresponding, homologous, congenial; becoming; harmonious, reconcilable, conformable; in -accordance, — harmony; — keeping, — unison, etc. *n.*;-with; at one with, of one mind, of a piece; consistent, compatible, proportionate, answerable; commensurate; on all fours.

apt, apposite, pertinent, pat; to the -point, —-purpose; happy, felicitous, germane, *ad rem,* in point, bearing upon, applicable, relevant, admissible.

fit, adapted, *in loco, à propos,* appropriate, seasonable, sortable, suitable, idoneous, deft; meet etc. (*expedient*) 646.

at home, in one's proper element.

Adv. *à propos of;* pertinently etc. *adj.*; pro rata.

Phr. *rem acu tetigisti,* the cap fits.

24. Disagreement.—N. disagreement, discord, -cordance; disunion, dissonance, dissidence, discrepancy; unconformity etc. 83; incongru-ity, -ence; discongruity, *mésalliance, oxymoron;* jarring etc. *v.*; clash, collision, dissension etc. 713; conflict etc. (*opposition*) 708; controversy etc. 720; falling out, wrangle, argument.

disparity, mismatch, misfit, disproportion; disproportionateness etc. *adj.*; variance, divergence, repugnance.

unfitness etc. *adj.*; inaptitude, impropriety; inapplicability etc. *adj.*; inconsistency, inconcinnity; irrelevancy etc. (*irrelation*) 10.

misjoin-ing, -der; syncretism, intrusion, interference; *concordia discors.*
fish out of water.
V. disagree; clash, quarrel, jar etc. (*discord*) 713; interfere, intrude, come amiss; not concern etc. 10; mismatch; *hymano capiti cervicem jungere equinam.*
Adj. disagreeing etc. *v.;* discordant, discrepant; at -variance, − war; hostile, antagonistic, repugnant, factious, contradictory, dissentious, incompatible, irreconcilable, inconsistent with; unconformable, exceptional etc. 83; intrusive, in-congruous; disproportionate, -ed; unharmonious; unconsonant; divergent, repugnant to.

inapt, unapt, inappropriate, inept, infelicitous, improper; unsuit-ed, -able; inapplicable; un-fit, -fitting, -befitting; unbecoming; ill-timed, ill-adapted, unseasonable, *mal à propos,* inadmissible; inapposite etc. (*irrelevant*) 10.

uncongenial; ill-assorted, -sorted, -matched; mis-matched, -mated, -joined, -placed; unaccommodating, irreducible, uncommensurable, unsympathetic.

out of -character, − keeping, − proportion, − joint, − tune, − place, − season, − its element; at -odds, − variance with.
Adv. in -defiance, − contempt, − spite-of; discordantly etc. *adj.; à tort et à travers.*

25. Quantity. [Absolute quantity.]—N. quantity, magnitude; size etc. ((*dimensions*) 192; amplitude, mass, amount, *quantum,* measure, measurement, substance, strength.
[Science of quantity.] Mathematics, Mathesis.
[Definite or finite quantity] arm-, hand-, mouth-, spoon-, thimble-, capful; stock, batch, lot, dose, ration, quotum, quota, pittance, driblet, part, portion etc. 51.
Adj. quantitative, some, any, more or less.
Adv. to the tune of.

26. Degree. [Relative quantity.]—N. degree, grade, extent, measure, proportion, amount, ratio, stint, standard, height, pitch; reach, amplitude, range, scope, size, caliber; gradation, shade; tenor, compass; sphere, station, rank, standing; rate, way, sort.
point, mark, step, stage etc. (*term*) 71; intensity, strength etc. (*greatness*) 31.
V. compare, graduate, calibrate, measure.
Adj. comparative; gradual, shading off, gradational; within the bounds etc. (*limit*), 233.
Adv. by degrees, gradually, inasmuch, *pro tanto;* how-ever, -soever; step by step, bit by bit, little by little, inch by inch, drop by drop, gradatim; by -inches, − slow degrees, − little and little; in some -degree, − measure; to some extent; just a bit.

27. Equality. [Sameness of quantity or degree.]—N. equality, parity, co-extension, symmetry, balance, poise; evenness, monotony, level.
equivalence; equi-pollence, -poise, -librium, -ponderance; par, quits; not a pin to choose; distinction without a difference, six of one and half a dozen of the other; identity etc. 13; similarity etc. 17; isotropism; coequality.
equalization, equation, equilibration, co-ordination, adjustment, readjustment.

drawn -game, -battle, draw, stalemate; neck and neck race; tie, dead heat.
match, peer, compeer, equal, mate, fellow, brother; equivalent.
V. be -equal etc. *adj.;* equal, match, reach, keep pace with, run abreast; come −, amount −, come upto; be −, lie- on a level with; balance; cope with; come to the same thing; level off.
render -equal etc. *adj.;* equalize, level, dress, balance, equate, handicap, give points, trim, adjust, poise; fit, accommodate; adapt etc. (*render accordant*) 23; strike a balance; establish −, restore- equality, − equilibrium; readjust; stretch on the bed of Procrustes.
Adj. equal, even, level, monotonous, coequal, symmetrical, coordinate;- on a -par, − level, − footing- with; up to the mark; equiparent.
equivalent, tantamount; quits; homologous; synonymous etc. 522; resolvable into, convertible, much at one, as broad as long, neither more nor less; much the same −, the same thing −, as good- as; all -one, — the same; equi-pollent, -ponderant, -ponderous, -balanced; equalized etc. *v.;* drawn; half and half; isochronous; isoperimetrical.
Adv. equally etc. *adj.; pari passu, ad eundem, caeteris paribus; in equilibrio;* to all intents and purposes.
Phr. it -comes, -adds up, − amounts- to the same thing.

28. Inequality. [Difference of quantity or degree.]—N. inequality; dis-, im-parity; odds; difference etc. 15; ill-balanced; unevenness; inclination of the balance, partiality; shortcoming; casting −make- weight; superiority etc. 33; inferiority etc. 34.
V. be -unequal etc. *adj.;* countervail; have −, give- the advantage; turn the scale; kick the beam; topple, -over; over-match etc. 33; not come up to etc. 34.
Adj. unequal, uneven, disparate, partial; un-, over-balanced; top-heavy, lop-sided.
Adv. *haud passibus aequis.*

29. Mean.—N. mean, medium, intermedium, average, run of the mill, normal, balance; mediocrity, generality, rule, ordinary -run, -ruck; golden mean etc. (*mid-course*) 628; middle etc. 68; compromise etc. 774; neutrality; middle point, middle course.
V. split the difference; take the -average etc. *n.;* reduce to a -mean etc. *n.;* strike a balance, pair off.
Adj. mean, intermediate; medial; middle etc. 68; average, normal, standard, neutral; middling, moderate.
médiocre, middle-class; *bourgeois,* commonplace etc. (*unimportant*) 643.
Adv. on an average, in the long run; taking - one with another, − all things together, − it for all in all; *communibus annis,* in round numbers.

30. Compensation.—N. compensation, equation; commutation; indemnification; compromise etc. 774; neutralization, nullification; counteraction etc. 179; reaction; measure for measure; retaliation etc. 718; equalization etc. 27; redemption, recoupment, recompense.

set-off, offset; make- casting-weight; counterpoise, equipoise, ballast; indemnity, reparation etc. 790; equivalent, *quid pro quo;* bribe, hushmoney, tribute etc. 784; amends etc. (*atonement*) 952; counterclaim, counterbalance, equiponderance, countervail, cross demand.

V. make -amends, − compensation; compensate, -pense; indemnify; counter-act, -vail, - poise; equiponderate; balance; out-, over-, counterbalance; set off, offset, cancel; hedge, square, give and take; make up -for, − lee way; cover, fill up, neutralize, nullify; equalize etc. 27; make good; redeem etc. (*atone*) 952; recoup, pay etc. 973.

Adj. compensat-ing, -ory; amendatory, reparative, countervailing etc. *v.;* in the opposite scale; equivalent etc. (*equal*) 27.

Adv. in -return, − consideration; but, however, yet, still, notwithstanding; neverthe-, nathless; although, though; al-, how-beit; in spite of, despite; mauger; at -all events, − any rate; be that as it may, for all that, even so, on the other hand, at the same time, *quoad minus, quand même,* however that may be; after all, − is said and done; taking one thing with another etc. (*average*) 29.

31. Greatness.−**N.** greatness etc. *adj.;* magnitude; size etc. (*dimensions*) 192; multitude etc. (*number*) 102; immensity, enormity, infinity etc. 105; might, strength, intensity, fulness; importance etc. 642; fame etc. 873.

great quantity, quantity, deal, power, sight, pot, volume, world; mass, heap etc. (*assemblage*) 72; stock etc. (*store*) 636; peck, bushel, load, cargo; cart −, wagon −, car −, truck −, shipload; flood, spring tide; abundance etc. (*sufficiency*) 639.

principal −, chief −, main −, greater −, major −, best −, essential- part; bulk, mass etc. (*whole*) 50.

V. be -great etc. *adj.;* run high, soar, loom up, tower, bulk large, transcend; rise −, carry- to a great height; know no bounds; scale, overtop, ascend.

enlarge etc. (*increase*) 35, (*expand*) 194.

Adj. great; greater etc. 33; large, considerable, fair, above par; big, massive, huge etc. (*large in size*) 192; ample; abundant etc. (*enough*) 639; Herculean etc. 159; full, intense, strong, sound, passing, heavy, plenary, deep, high; signal, at its height, in the zenith.

world-wide, wide-spread, extensive; wholesale; many etc. 102.

goodly, noble, precious, mighty; sad, grave, serious; far gone, arrant, downright; utter, -most; crass, gross, arch, profound, intense, consummate; rank, unmitigated, red-hot, desperate; glaring, flagrant, stark staring; thorough-paced, - going; roaring, thumping, thundering, strapping, whacking; extraordinary; important etc. 642; unsurpassed etc. (*supreme*) 33; complete etc. 52.

vast, immense, enormous, extreme; inordinate, excessive, extravagant, exorbitant, outrageous, preposterous, unconscionable, swinging, monstrous, over-grown; towering, stupendous, prodigious, astonishing, incredible; terrific, frightful; marvelous etc. (*wonder*) 870; grand.

unlimited etc. (*infinite*) 105; unapproachable, unutterable, indescribable, ineffable, unspeakable, inexpressible, beyond expression, fabulous.

un-diminished, -abated, -reduced, -restricted.

absolute, positive, stark, decided, unequivocal, essential, perfect, finished.

remarkable, of mark, marked, pointed, veriest; noticeable, uncommon, noteworthy, eminent etc. 873.

Adv. [in a positive degree] truly etc. (*truth*) 494; decidedly, unequivocally, purely, absolutely, seriously, essentially, fundamentally, radically, downright, in all conscience; for the most part, in the main.

[in a complete degree] entirely etc. (*completely*) 52; abundantly, etc. (*sufficiently*) 639; widely, far and wide.

[in a great or high degree] greatly etc. *adj.;* much, muckle, well, indeed, very, very much, a deal, no end of, most not a little; pretty, − well; enough, in a great measure, passing richly; to a - large, − great, − gigantic- extent; on a large scale; so; never −, ever- so; ever so much; by wholesale; mightily, mighty, powerfully; with a witness, *ultra,* in the extreme, extremely, exceedingly, intensely, exquisitely, acutely, indefinitely, immeasurably; beyond -compare, − comparison, − measure, − all bounds; incalculably, -infinitely.

[in a supreme degree] pre-eminently, superlatively etc. (*superiority*) 33.

[in a too great degree] immoderately, unduly, monstrously, grossly, preposterously, inordinately, exorbitantly, excessively, enormously, out of all proportion, with a vengeance.

[in a marked degree] particularly, remarkably, singularly, curiously, uncommonly, unusually, peculiarly, notably, signally, strikingly, pointedly, mainly, chiefly; famously, egregiously, prominently, glaringly, emphatically, strangely, wonderfully, amazingly, surprisingly, astonishingly, incredibly, marvelously, awfully, stupendously.

[in an exceptional degree] peculiarly etc. (*unconformity*) 83.

[in a violent degree] furiously etc. (*violence*) 173; severely, desperately, tremendously, extravagantly, confoundedly, deucedly, devilishly, with a vengeance; *à −, à toute- outrance.*

[in a painful degree] painfully, sadly, grossly, sorely, bitterly, piteously, grievously, miserably, cruelly, woefully, lamentably, shockingly, frightfully, dreadfully, fearfully, terribly, horribly, distressingly, balefully.

32. Smallness.—**N.** smallness etc. *adj.;* littleness etc. (*small size*) 193; tenuity; paucity; fewness etc. (*small number*) 103; meanness, insignificance etc. (*unimportance*) 643; mediocrity, moderation.

small quantity, *modicum, minimum;* vanishing point; material point, electron, atom, particle, molecule, corpuscle, point, dab, fleck, speck, dot, mote, jot, iota, ace; *minutiae,* details; look, thought, idea, *soupçon,* whit, tittle, shade, shadow; spark, *scintilla,* gleam; touch, cast; grain, scruple, granule, globule, minim, sup, sip, sop, spice, drop, droplet, sprinkling, dash, smack, tinge, tincture; inch, patch, scantling, dole; scrap, shred, tag, splinter, rag, tatter, cantlet, flitter, gobbet, mite, bit, morsel, crumb, seed, fritter, shive; snip, -pet; snick, snack, snatch, slip, scrag; chip, -ping; shiver, sliver, driblet, clipping, paring, shaving, hair.

nutshell; thimble-, spoon-, hand-, cap-, mouthful; fragment; fraction etc. (*part*)51; drop in the ocean, drop in the bucket.

animalcule etc. 193.

trifle etc. (*unimportant thing*) 643; mere —, next to- nothing; hardly anything; just enough to swear by; the shadow of a shade.

finiteness, finite quantity.

V. be -shall etc. *adj.;* lie in a nutshell.

diminish etc. (*decrease*) 36, (*contract*) 195.

Adj. small, little, tiny, weeny; diminutive etc. (*small in size*) 193; minute; minikin, fine, inconsiderable, dribbling, paltry etc. (*unimportant*) 643; faint etc. (*weak*) 160; slender, light, slight, scanty, scant, limited; meager etc. (*insufficient*) 640; sparing; few etc. 103; low, so-so, middling, tolerable, no great shakes; below —, under-par, — the mark; at a low ebb; halfway; moderate, modest; tender, subtle; petty, shallow, skin-deep.

inappreciable, evanescent, infinite-simal, homeopathic, very small, atomic, molecular, ultra-, -microscopic.

petty, shallow etc. 499.

mere, simple, sheer, stark, bare; near run.

Adv. [in a small degree] to a small extent, on a small scale; a -little, — wee, — tiny bit; slightly etc. *adj.;* imperceptibly; miserably, wretchedly; insufficiently etc. 640; imperfectly; faintly etc. 160; passably, pretty well, well enough.

[in a certain or limited degree] partially, in part; in —, to a certain degree; to a certain extent; comparatively; some, rather; in some -degree, -measure; some-thing, -what; simply, only, purely, merely; at —, at the- -least, — most; ever so little, as little as may be, *tant soit peu,* in ever so small a degree; thus far, *pro tanto;* within bounds, in a manner, after a fashion.

almost, nearly, well nigh, short of, not quite, all but; near —, close- upon; *peu s'en faut,* near the mark; within an -ace, — inch- of; on the brink of; scarcely, hardly, barely, only just, no more than.

[in an uncertain degree] about, therabouts, somewhere about, nearly, say; be the same -more, — little more- or less.

[in no degree] no- ways, — wise; not -at all, — in the least, — a bit, — a bit of it, — a whit, — a jot, — a shadow; in no -wise, — respect; by no -means, — manner of means; on no account, at no hand.

33. Superiority.—N. superiority, supremacy, majority; greatness etc. 31; advantage, odds, pull; preponderance, -ation; predominance, vantage ground, coign of vantage, prevalence, partiality; personal superiority; sovereignty etc. 737; nobility etc. (*rank*) 875; Triton among the minnows, *primus inter pares, nulli secundus,* superman; captain etc. 475.

supremacy, pre-eminence; primacy, lead, *maximum;* record; climax, crest, top; culmination etc. (*summit*) 210; transcendence; *ne plus ultra;* lion's share, Benjamin's mess; excess; bisque, surplus etc. (*remainder*) 40, (*redundance*) 641.

V. be -superior etc. *adj.;* exceed, excel, transcend; out-do, -balance, -weigh, -rival, -Herod, outrank, pass, surpass, surmount, get ahead of; over-top, -ride, -pass, -balance, -weigh, -match; top, o'er-top, cap, beat, win out, cut out; beat hollow; outstrip etc. 303; eclipse, throw into the shade, take the shine out of, put one's nose out of joint; have the -upper hand, — whip hand of, — advantage; turn the scale, play first fiddle etc. (*importance*) 642; preponderate, predominate, prevail; precede, take .precedence, come first; come to a head, culminate; beat etc. all others, bear the palm; break the record, take the cake.

become —, render- -larger, etc. (*increase*) 35, (*expand*) 194.

Adj. superior, greater, major, higher; exceeding etc. *v.;* great etc. 31; distinguished, *ultra;* vaulting; more than a match for.

supreme, greatest, maximal, maximum, utmost, paramount, pre-eminent, foremost, crowning; first-rate etc. (important) 642, (*excellent*) 648; unrivalled; peer-, match-less; none such, second to none, *sans pareil;* un-paragoned, -paralleled, -equalled, -approached, -surpassed; superlative, inimitable, *facile princeps,* incomparable, sovereign, without parallel, *nulli secundus, ne plus ultra;* beyond -compare, — comparison; culminating etc. (*topmost*) 210; transcendent, -ental; *plus royaliste que le Roi.*

increased etc. (*added to*) 35; enlarged etc. (*expanded*) 194.

Adv. beyond, more, over; over —, above- the mark; above par; upwards —, in advance- of; over and above; at the top of the scale, on the crest, at it height.

[in a superior or supreme degree] eminently, egregiously, pre-eminently, surpassing, prominently, superlatively, supremely, above all, of all things, the most, to crown all, *par excellence,* principally, especially, particularly, peculiarly, *a fortiori,* even, yea, still more.

Phr. 'we shall not look upon his like again.'

34. Inferiority.—N. inferiority, minority, sub-ordinancy; shortcoming, deficiency; handicap; *minimum;* smallness etc. 32; imperfection, shabbiness.

[personal inferiority] commonalty etc. 876; subordinate, substitute, sub.

V. be -inferior etc. *adj.;* fall —, come- short of; not -pass, — come up to; want.

become —, render- smaller etc. (decrease) 36, (*contract*) 195; hide its diminished head, retire into the shade, yield the palm, play second fiddle, take a back seat; bow.

Adj. inferior, smaller; small etc. 32; minor, less, lesser, deficient, minus, lower, subordinate, secondary; second-rate etc. (*imperfect*) 651; sub, subaltern; thrown into the shade; weighed in the balance and found wanting; not fit to hold a candle to.

least, smallest etc. (*see little, small etc.* 193); lowest.

diminished etc. (*decreased*) 36; reduced etc. (*contracted*) 195; unimportant etc. 643.

Adv. less; under —, below- -the mark, — par; at -the bottom of the scale, — a low ebb, — a disadvantage; short of, under.

35. Increase.—**N.** increase; augmentation, addition, enlargement, extension; dilatation etc. (*expansion*) 194; multiplication; increment, accretion; accession etc. 37; production etc. 161; development, growth; aggrandizement, aggravation, intensification; rise; ascent etc. 305; anabasis; ex-aggeration, -acerbation; spread etc. (*dispersion*) 73; flood-, spring-, -tide; gain, produce, profit etc. 618; booty, plunder etc. 793.

V. increase, augment, add to, enlarge; dilate etc. (*expand*) 194; grow, wax, mount, swell, get ahead, gain strength; advance; run —, shoot- up; rise; ascend etc. 305; sprout etc. 194.

aggrandize; raise; exalt; deepen, heighten; lengthen; thicken; strengthen; intensify, enhance, inflate, magnify, double, redouble; multiply; aggravate, exaggerate; ex-asperate, -acerbate; add fuel to the flame, *oleum addere camino*, superadd etc. (*add*) 37; spread etc. (*disperse*) 73.

Adj. increased etc. *v.;* on the increase, undiminished, additional etc. (*added*) 37; increasing etc. *v.;* growing, crescent, intensive, cumulative.

Adv. crescendo, increasingly.

Phr. *vires acquirit eundo.*

36. Non-Increase. Decrease.—**N.** decrease, diminution, lessening etc. *v.;* subtraction etc. 38; reduction, abatement, declension; shrinkage etc. (*contraction*) 195; coarctation; abridgment etc. (*shortening*) 201; extenuation.

subsidence, catabasis, wane, ebb-, neap-tide, decline; descent etc. 306; decrement, reflux, depreciation; erosion, wear and tear, deterioration etc. 659; anticlimax; mitigation etc. (*moderation*) 174.

V. decrease, diminish, lessen; abridge etc. (*shorten*) 201; shrink etc. (*contract*) 195; drop —, fall —, tail- off; fall away, waste, wear, erode; wane, ebb, decline; descent etc. 306; subside; deliquesce, melt —, die -away; retire into the shade, hide its diminished head, fall to a low ebb, run low, languish, decay, crumble, consume away.

bate, abate, dequantitate; discount; depreciate; extenuate, lower, weaken, attenuate, fritter away; mitigate etc.(*moderate*) 174; belittle, minimize; dwarf, throw into the shade; keep down, reduce etc. 195; shorten etc. 201; subtract etc. 38.

Adj. unincreased etc. (*see* increase etc. 35); decreased etc. *v.;* decreasing etc. *v.;* on the -wane etc. *n.;* deliquescent.

Adv. diminuendo, decrescendo, decreasingly.

37. Addition.—**N.** addition, annexation, adjection; junction etc. 43; super-position, -addition, -junction, -fetation; accession, reinforcement; increase etc. 35; increment, supplement; accompaniment etc. 88; interposition etc. 228; insertion etc. 300; summation etc. 85; adjunct etc. 39.

V. add, annex, adject, affix, attach, superadd, subjoin, superpose; clap —, saddle- on; tack to, postfix, append, tag; ingraft; saddle with; sprinkle; introduce etc. (*interpose*) 228; insert etc. 300.

become added, accrue; ad-, supervene; add up etc. 85.

reinforce, strengthen, swell the ranks of; augment etc. 35.

Adj. added etc. *v.;* additional; supplement, -al, -ary; suppletory, subjunctive; adjec-, adsci-, ascititious; additive, extra, spare, further, fresh, more, new, ulterior, other, auxiliary, supernumerary, accessory.

Adv. in addition, more, plus, extra; and, also, likewise, too, furthermore, further, item; and - also, — eke; else, besides, to boot, *et cetera;* etc.; and so -on, — forth; into the bargain, *cum multis aliis,* over and above, moreover.

with, withal; including, inclusive, as well as, not to mention, let alone; together —, along —, coupled —, in conjunction- with; conjointly; jointly etc. 43.

38. Non-Addition. Subduction.—**N.** sub-traction, -duction; deduction, retrenchment; removal; ab-, sub-lation; abstraction etc. (*taking*) 789; garbling etc. *v.;* mutilation, detruncation; amputation, severance; abs-, ex-, re-cision; curtailment etc. 201; minuend, subtrahend; decrease etc. 36; abrasion.

V. sub-tract, -duct; rebate, de-duct, —duce; bate, retrench; remove, withdraw; take — from, — away; detract.

garble, mutilate, amputate, sever, detruncate; cut -off, — away, — out; expurgate; abscind, excise; pare, thin, prune, decimate; abrade, scrape, file; geld, castrate, emasculate, unman, spay, caponize; eliminate.

diminish etc. 36; curtail etc. (*shorten*) 201; deprive of etc. (*take*) 789; weaken.

Adj. subtracted etc. *v.;* subtractive.

tailless, acaudal.

Adv. in -deduction etc. *n.;* less; short of; minus, without, except, excepting, with the exception of, barring, bar, save, exclusive of, save and except, with a reservation.

39. Adjunct. [Thing added.]—**N.** adjunct, addit-ion, -ament; *additum,* affix, appendage, annex; augment, -ation; increment, reinforcement, supernumerary, accessory, item; garnish, sauce; accompaniment etc. 88; adjective, *addendum,* accession, complement, supplement; continu-ation; extension, subscript, tag, appendix, postscript, interlineation, interpolation, insertion.

rider, codicil, off-shoot, episode, side issue, corollary; piece; flap, lapel, label, tab, strip, fold, lappet, apron, skirt, embroidery, trappings, *cortège;* tail, suffix etc. (*sequel*) 65; wing.

Adj. additional etc. 37.

Adv. in addition etc. 37.

40. Remainder. [Thing remaining.]—**N.** remainder, residue; remains, *remanet,* remnant, rest, relic, relict; leavings, heel-tap, odds and ends, cheese-parings, candle ends, orts; *residuum;* dottle, dregs, etc. (*dirt*) 653; refuse etc. (*useless*) 645; stubble, result, educt; fag-end, stub; ruins, wreck, skeleton, stump; *alluvium.*

surplus, overplus, excess; balance, complement; superfluity etc. (*redundance*) 641; surviv-al, -ance; afterglow.

V. remain; be -left etc. *adj.;* exceed, survive; leave.

Adj. remaining, left; left -behind, - over;

residu-al, -ary; over, odd; unconsumed, sedimentary; surviving; net; exceeding, over and above; outlying, -standing; cast off etc. 782; superfluous etc. (*redundant*) 641.

V. remain; be -left; left -behind, − over; redidual, -ary; over, odd; unconsumed, sedimentary; surviving; net; exceeding, over and above; outlying, -standing; cast off etc. 782; superfluous etc. (*redundant*) 641.

40a. Decrement. [Thing deducted.]—**N.** decrement, discount, rebate, defect, loss, deduction, eduction, tare; drawback; waste, wastage; reprise.

41. Mixture. [Forming a whole without coherence.]—**N.** mix-, admix-, commix-ture, -tion, mingling; commixion, immixture, interfusion, intermixture, alloyage, matrimony; junction etc. 43; combination etc. 48; entanglement, interlacing; miscegenation, interbreeding.

impregnation; in-, dif-, suf-, transfusion; infiltration; seasoning, sprinkling, interlarding; interpolation etc. 228; adulteration, sophistication.

[Thing mixed] tinge, tincture, touch, dash, smack, sprinkling, spice, seasoning, infusion, *soupçon*.

[Compound resulting from mixture] alloy, brass, bronze, pewter etc.; amalgam, *magma*, blend, half-and-half, *mélange, tertium, quid*, miscellany, *ambigu*, medley, mess, hash, hotchpotch, hodgepodge, *pasticcio*, patchwork, odds and ends, all sorts; jumble etc. (*disorder*) 59; salad, sauce, mash, *omnium gatherum*, gallimaufry, ragout, *olla podrida, olio*, salmagundi, *potpourri*, Noah's ark; texture, mingled yarn; mosaic etc. (*variegation*) 440.

half-blood, -caste, -breed, Eurasian; mulatto; terc-, quart-, quinteron etc.; quad-, octo-roon; *griffo, zambo;* cross, hybrid, mongrel etc. 83.

V. mix; join etc. 43; combine etc. 48; com-, im-, inter-mix; mix up with, mingle; com-, inter-, bemingle; shuffle etc. (*derange*) 61; pound together; hash −, stir- up; knead, brew; impregnate with; interlard etc. (*interpolate*) 228; intertwine, -weave etc. 219; associate with, miscegenate, interbreed.

be mixed etc.; get among, be entangled with.

instil, imbue; in-, suf-, trans-fuse; infiltrate, dash, tinge, tincture, season, sprinkle, besprinkle, attemper, medicate, blend, cross; alloy, amalgamate, compound, adulterate, sophisticate, infect.

Adj. mixed etc. *v.;* implex, composite, half-and-half, linsey-wolsey, hybrid, mongrel, heterogeneous; motley etc. (*variegated*) 440; miscellaneous, promiscuous, indiscriminate; miscible.

Adv. among, amongst, amid, amidst, with; in the midst of, in the crowd.

42. Simpleness [Freedom from mixture.]—**N.** simpleness etc. *adj.;* purity, homogeneity.

elimination; sifting etc. *v.;* purification etc. (*cleanness*) 652.

V. render -simple etc. *adj.;* simplify.

sift, winnow, bolt, eliminate; narrow down; get rid of, exclude etc. 55; clear; purify etc. (*clean*) 652; disentangle etc. (*disjoin*) 44.

Adj. simple, uniform, of a piece, homogeneous, single, pure, clear, sheer, neat; Attic.

un-mixed, -mingled, -blended, -combined, -compounded; elementary, undecomposed; unadulterated, -sophisticated, -alloyed, -tinged, -fortified; pure and simple.

free −, exempt- from; exclusive.

Adv. simply etc. *adj.;* only.

43. Junction.—**N.** junction; joining etc. *v.;* joinder, union; con-nection, -junction, -jugation, compendency, annex-ion, -ation, -ment; coalition; astriction, attachment, compagination, vincture, ligation, alligation; accouplement; marriage etc. (*wedlock*) 903; infibulation, inosculation, symphysis, anastomosis, confluence, communication, concatenation; concurrence, meeting, reunion; assemblage etc. 72.

copulation, coition, intercourse.

joint, joining, juncture, chiasma, pivot, hinge, articulation, commissure, seam, suture, gusset, stitch, splice; link etc. 45; miter, mortise.

closeness, tightness etc. *adj.;* coherence etc. 46; combination etc. 48.

V. join, unite; con-join, -nect; associate; put −, lay −, clap −, hang −, lump −, hold −, piece −, tack −, fix −, bind up- together; embody, re-embody; roll into one.

attach, fix, affix, saddle on, fasten, bind, secure, clinch, twist, make -fast etc. *adj.;* tie, pinion, string, strap, sew, lace, stitch, tack, paste, knit, button, buckle, hitch, lash, truss, bandage, braid, splice, swathe, gird, tether, moor, picket, harness, chain; fetter etc. (*restrain*) 751; lock, latch, belay, brace, hook, grapple, leash, couple, accouple, link, yoke, bracket; marry etc. (*wed*) 903; bridge over, span.

pin, nail, bolt, hasp, clasp, clamp, screw, rivet; impact, solder, braze, cement, set; weld −, fuse-together; wedge, rabbet, mortise, miter, jam, dovetail, enchase; graft, ingraft, inosculate; en-, in-twine; inter-link, -lace, -twine, -twist, -weave; entangle; twine round, belay; tighten; trice −, screw-up.

be -joined etc.; hang −, hold- together; cohere etc. 46.

Adj. joined etc. *v.;* joint; con-joint, -junct; corporate, compact; hand in hand.

firm, fast, close, tight, taut, taught, tense, secure, set, intervolved; in-separable, -dissoluble, -secable, -severable.

Adv. jointly etc. *adj.;* in conjunction with etc. (*in addition to*) 37; fast, firmly etc. *adj.;* intimately.

44. Disjunction.—**N.** dis-junction, -connection, -unity, -union, -association, -engagement, -sociation; discontinuity etc. 70; inconnection; abstraction, -edness; isolation; insul-arity, -ation; oasis; separateness etc. *adj.;* severalty; *disjecta membra;* dispersion etc. 73; apportionment etc. 786.

separation; parting etc. *v.;* detachment, segregation; divorce, sejunction, seposition, diduction, diremption, discerption; elision; *caesura*, division, subdivision, break, fracture, rupture, compartition, dis-memberment, -integration, -location; luxation; sever-, dis-severance; scission; re-, ab-scission; circumcision;

lacer-, dilacer-ation; dis-, ab-ruption; avulsion, divulsion; section, resection, cleavage; fission; separability; separatism.

fissure, breach, rent, split, rift, crack, slit, slot, incision.

dissection, anatomy; decomposition etc. 49; cutting instrument etc. (*sharpness*) 253; saw.

V. be -disjoined etc.; come —, fall- -off, — to pieces; peel off; get loose.

dis-join, -connect, -engage, -unite, -sociate, - pair; divorce, part, dispart, detach, uncouple, separate, cut off, rescind, segregate; set —, keep-apart; insulate, isolate; throw out of gear; cut adrift; loose; un-loose, -do, -bind, -tie, -hitch, - chain, -lock etc. (*fix*) 43, -pack, -ravel; disen-tangle; set free etc. (*liberate*) 750.

sunder, divide, subdivide, sectionalize, sever, dissever, abscind; cut; segment; in-cide, -cise; circumcise; saw, snip, nib, nip, cleave, rive, rend, slit, split, splinter, chip, crack, snap, break, tear, burst; rend etc. -asunder, — in twain; wrench, rupture, shatter, shiver, cranch, crunch, craunch, chop; rip up; hack, hew, slash; whittle; haggle, hackle, discind, lacerate, scamble, mangle, gash, hash, slice.

cut up, carve, quarter, dissect, anatomize; take —, pull —, pick —, tear- to pieces; tear to tatters, — piecemeal; divellicate; skin etc. 226; dis-in-tegrate, -member, -branch, -band; disperse etc. 73; dis-locate, -joint; break up; mince; com-minute etc. (*pulverize*) 330; distribute, appor-tion etc. 786.

part, — company; separate, leave; alienate, estrange.

Adj. disjoined etc. *v.*; discontinuous etc. 70; bipartite, multipartite, abstract; digitate; dis-junctive; isolated etc. *v.*; insular, separate, dis-parate, discrete, apart, asunder, far between, loose, free; unattached, -annexed, -associated, - connected; distinct; adrift; straggling; rift, reft, cleft, split.

[capable of being divided] scissile, partible, divisible, separable, severable, detachable.

Adv. separately etc. *adj.*; one by one, sever-ally, apart; adrift, asunder, in twain; in the abstract, abstractedly.

45. Vinculum. [Connecting medium.]—N. vinculum, link, *nexus*; connec-tive, -tion; junction etc. 43; bond of union, copula, intermedium, hyphen; bracket; bridge, stepping-stone, isthmus.

bond, tendon, tendril; fiber; cord, -age; riband, ribbon, rope, guy, cable, line, halser, hawser, paint-er, moorings, wire, chain; string etc. (*filament*) 205.

fastening, tie; liga-ment, -ture; strap; bowline, halliard, tackle, lanyard, rigging, shrouds; stand-ing —, running- rigging; traces, harness; yoke; band, -age; brace, roller, fillet; inkle; with, withe, withy; thong, braid; girder, tie-beam; girt, cinch, girth, girdle, cestus, garter, braces, suspenders; halter, noose, lasso, lariat, surcingle, knot, hitch, running knot, frog.

pin, corking pin, nail, brad, tack, skewer, staple, cleat, clamp; cramp, screw, button, buckle, clasp, hasp, hinge; hank, catch, latch, bolt, ring, latchet, pawl, tag; tooth; stud; hook, — and eye; morse, lock, holdfast, padlock, rivet; anchor, grappling-iron, drawbar, coupler, draw-

head, coupling, treenail, trennel, stake, pale, pile, post, bollard.

cement, glue, gum, paste, size, wafer, solder, lute, putty, bird-lime, mortar, stucco, plaster, grout.

shackle, rein etc. (*means of restraint*) 752; suspender etc. 214; prop etc. (*support*) 215.

V. bridge over, span; connect etc. 43; hang etc. 214.

46. Coherence.—N. co-, ad-herence, -hesion; - hesiveness; concretion, accretion; con-, ag-glutination, -glomeration; aggregation; con-solidation, set, cementation; sticking, soldering etc. *v.*; connection.

tenacity, toughness; stickiness etc. 352; insepara-bility, -bleness; bur, remora.

conglomerate, concrete etc. (*density*) 321.

V. cohere, adhere, stick, cling, cleave, hold, take hold of, hold fast, close with, embrace, clasp, hug; grow —, hang-together; twine round etc. (*join*) 43.

stick like -a leech, — wax; stick close; cling like -ivy, — a bur; adhere like -a remora, — Dejan-ira's shirt.

glue; ag-, con-glutinate; cement, lute, paste, gum; solder, weld; cake, coagulate, consolidate etc. (*solidify*) 321; agglomerate.

Adj. co-, ad-hesive, -hering etc. *v.*; tenacious, tough; sticky etc. 352.

united, unseparated, sessile, inseparable, in-extricable, infrangible; compact etc. (*dense*) 321.

47. Incoherence. [Want of adhesion, non-ad-hesion, immiscibility.]—N. non-adhesion; im-miscibility; incoherence; looseness etc. *adj.*; lax-ity; relaxation; loosening etc. *v.*; freedom; dis-junction etc. 44; rope of sand.

V. make -loose etc. *adj.*, loosen, slacken, relax; un-glue etc. 46; detach etc. (*disjoin*) 44.

Adj. non-adhesive, immiscible; incoherent, detached, loose, slack, baggy, lax, relaxed, flap-ping, streaming; dishevelled; segregated, like grains of sand; un-consolidated etc. 321; -com-bined etc. 48; non-cohesive.

48. Combination.—N. combination; mixture etc. 41; alloy; junction etc. 43; union, unification, synthesis, incorporation, amalgamation, embodiment, coalescence, crasis, fusion, blend, blending, absorption, centralization, federation.

compound, amalgam, composition, *tertium quid*; resultant, impregnation.

V. combine, unite, incorporate, alloy, inter-twine etc. 41; amalgamate, embody, absorb, re-embody, blend, merge, fuse, melt into one, con-solidate, coalesce, centralize, impregnate; put —, lump- together; federate, associate; fraternize; cement a union, marry, wed, couple, pair, ally.

Adj. combined etc. *v.*; conjunctive, conjugate, conjoint, allied, confederate; impregnated with, ingrained, inoculated.

49. Decomposition.—N. decomposition, analysis, diaeresis, dissection, resolution, catalysis, electrolysis, hydrolysis, photolysis, dis-solution; dispersion etc. 73; disjunction etc. 44;

putrescence, caries, necrosis, corruption etc. (*uncleanness*) 653.

V. decom-pose, -pound; analyze, disembody, dissolve; resolve −, separate- into its elements; electrolyze; dissect, decentralize, break up; disintegrate; disperse etc. 73; unravel etc. (*unroll*) 313; crumble into dust; decay etc. *n.;* deteriorate etc. 659.

Adj. decomposed etc. *v.;* catalytic, analytical.

50. Whole. [Principal part.]—N.

whole, totality, integrity; totalness etc. *adj.;* entirety, *ensemble,* collectiveness; unity etc. 87; completeness etc. 52; indivisibility, indiscerptibility; integration, embodiment; integer, integral.

all, the whole, total, aggregate, one and all, gross amount, sum, sum-total, *tout ensemble,* length and breadth of, Alpha and Omega, 'be all and end all,' lock, stock and barrel.

bulk, mass, lump, tissue, staple, body, torso, *compages;* truck, bole, hull, hulk, skeleton; greater −, major −, best −, principal −, main-part; essential part etc. (*importance*) 642; lion's share, Benjamin's mess; the long and the short; nearly −, almost- all.

V. form −, constitute- a whole; integrate, embody, amass; aggregate etc. (*assemble*) 72; amount to, come to.

Adj. whole, total, integral, entire; complete etc. 52; one, individual.

un-broken, -cut, -divided, -severed, -clipped, -cropped, -shorn; seamless; undiminished; undemolished, -dissolved, -destroyed, -bruised.

in-divisible, -dissoluble, -dissolvable, -discerptible.

wholesale, sweeping, comprehensive.

Adv. wholly, altogether; totally etc. (*completely*) 52; entirely, all, all in all, considering all things, in a body, collectively, all put together; in the -aggregate, − lump; − mass, − gross, − main, − long run; *en masse,* on the whole, as a whole, bodily, *en bloc, in extenso,* throughout, every inch; substantially.

51. Part.—N.

part, portion; dose; item, particular; aught, any; division, ward; subdivision, section; chapter, verse; article, clause, count, paragraph, passage; phrase; number, volume, book, fascicule; sector, segment; fraction, fragment; cantle, -t; frustum; detachment, parcel, unit, class etc. 75.

piece, lump, bit; cut, -ting; chip, chunk, collop, slice, scale, shard; lamina etc. 204; moiety; small part; morsel, scrap, crumb; particle etc. (*smallness*) 32; instalment, dividend; share etc. (*allotment*) 786.

débris, odds and ends, oddments, *detritus; excerpta;* member, limb, lobe, lobule, arm, wing, scion, branch, bough, joint, link, offshoot, ramification, twig, stipule, tendril, bush, spray, sprig; runner; leaf, -let; stump; constituent, ingredient, component part etc. 56.

compartment; department etc. (*class*) 75; county etc. (*region*) 181.

V. part, divide, break etc. (*disjoin*) 44; partition etc. (*apportion*) 786.

Adj. fractional, fragmentary; sectional, aliquot; divided etc. *v.;* in compartments, multifid, incomplete, partial, divided etc. 44.

Adv. partly, in part, partially; piecemeal, part by part; by -instalments, − snatches, − inches, − driblets; bit by bit, inch by inch, foot by foot, drop by drop; in -detail, − lots.

52. Completeness.—N.

completeness etc. *adj.;* completion etc. 729; integration; integrality.

entirety; universality; totality; perfection etc. 650; solid-ity, -arity; unity; all; *ne plus ultra,* ideal, limit.

complement, supplement, make-weight; filling up etc. *v.*

impletion; satur-ation, -ity; high water; high −, flood −, spring- tide; fill, load, bumper, belly-ful; brimmer; sufficiency etc. 639.

V. be -complete etc. *adj.;* come to a head.

render -complete etc. *adj.;* complete etc. (*accomplish*) 729; fill, charge, load, replenish; make-up, − good; piece −, eke- out; supply deficiencies; fill -up, − in, − to the brim, − the measure of; saturate etc. 869.

go the whole -hog, − length, go all lengths.

Adj. complete, entire; whole etc. 50; perfect etc. 650; full, good, absolute, thorough, plenary; solid, undivided; with all its parts.

exhaustive, radical, sweeping, thorough-go-ing; dead.

regular, consummate, unmitigated, sheer, unqualified, unconditional, free; abundant etc. (*sufficient*) 639.

brimming; brim-, top-ful; chock −, choke-full; as full as- an egg is of meat, − a vetch, − a tick; saturated, crammed; replete etc. (*redundant*) 641; fraught, laden; full-laden, -fraught, -charged; heavy laden.

completing etc. *v.;* supplement-al, -ary; ascititious.

Adv. completely etc. *adj.;* altogether, outright, wholly, totally, *in toto,* quite; over head and ears; effectually, for good and all, nicely, fully, through thick and thin, head and shoulders; neck and -heel, − crop; all out; in -all respects, − every respect; at all points, out and out, to all intents and purposes; *toto coelo;* utterly, clean, − as a whistle; to the -full, − utmost, − backbone; hollow, stark; heart and soul, root and branch; down to the ground.

to the top of one's bent, as far as possible, *à outrance.*

throughout; from -first to last, − beginning to end, − end to end, − one end to the other, − Dan to Beersheba, − head to foot, − head to heels, − top to toe, − top to bottom; *de fond en comble; à fond, a capite ad calcem, ab ovo usque ad mala,* fore and aft; every -whit, − inch; *cap-à-pie,* to the end of the chapter; up to the -brim, − ears, − eyes; as ... as can be.

on all accounts; *sous tous les rapports;* with a -vengeance, − witness.

53. Incompleteness.—N.

incompleteness etc. *adj.;* deficiency, short -measure, − wieght; shortcoming etc. 304; insufficiency etc. 640; imperfection etc. 651; immaturity etc. (*non-preparation*) 674; half measures.

[part wanting] defect, deficit, shortage, ullage, defalcation, omission, *caret;* interval etc. 198; break etc. (*discontinuity*) 70; non-completion etc. 730; missing link.

V. be -incomplete etc. *adj.;* fall short of etc. 304; lack etc. *(be insufficient)* 640; neglect etc. 460.

Adj. incomplete; imperfect etc. 651; unfinished; uncompleted etc. *(see* complete etc.

729); defective, deficient, wanting; failing; in -default, − arrear; short, − of; hollow, meagre, lame, half-and-half, perfunctory, sketchy; crude etc. *(unprepared)* 674.

mutilated, garbled, mangled, docked, lopped, truncated; bobtailed, cropped, bobbed, shingled.

in -progress, − hand; going on, proceeding.

Adv. incompletely etc. *adj.;* by halves.

Phr. *caetera desunt; caret.*

54. Composition.—N. composition, constitution, crasis, synthesis; make-up; combination etc. 48; inclusion, admission, comprehension, reception; embodiment, formation, conformation, production.

compilation etc. 72. *(musical)* composition etc. 415; painting etc. 556; writing etc. 590; typography etc. 591.

V. be -composed, − made, − formed, − made up- of; consist of, be resolved into.

include etc. *(in a class)* 76; subsume; synthesize; contain, hold, comprehend, take in, admit, embrace, embody; involve; implicate, drag into.

compose, constitute, form, make; make −, fill −, build- up; weave, construct, fabricate; compile; write, draw; set up *(printing)*; enter into the composition of etc. *(be a component)* 56.

Adj. containing, constituting etc. *v.*

55. Exclusion.—N. exclusion, non-admission, omission, exception, rejection, repudiation; exile etc. *(seclusion)* 893; preclusion, lock out, ostracism, prohibition; disbarment, expulsion, ban.

separation, segregation, seposition, elimination, coffer-dam.

V. be excluded from etc.

exclude, bar, ban; leave −. shut −, thrust −, bar- out; reject, repudiate, spurn, blackball; ostracize, boycott; lay −, put −, set-apart, − aside; relegate, segregate; throw overboard; strike -off, − out; neglect etc. 460; banish etc. *(seclude)* 893; separate etc. *(disjoin)* 44.

pass over, omit; garble; eliminate, weed, winnow.

Adj. excluding etc. *v.;* exclusive.

excluded etc. *v.;* unrecounted, not included in; inadmissible; preventive, interdictive.

Adv. exclusive of, barring, except; with the exception of; save, bating.

56. Component.—N. component; component −, integral −, integrant-part; element, constituent, ingredient, leaven; part and parcel; contents; appurtenance; feature; member etc. *(part)* 51; personnel.

V. enter into, − the composition of; be a - component etc. *n.;* be −, form- part of; merge −, be merged- in; be implicated in; share in etc. *(participate)* 778; belong −, appertain- to.

form, make, constitute, compose.

Adj. forming etc. *v.;* inclusive; inherent etc. 5.

57. Extraneousness.—N. extraneousness etc. *adj.;* extrinsicality etc. 6; exteriority etc. 220; alienism.

foreign -body, − substance, − element; alien, stranger, intruder, interloper, foreigner, tramontane, *novus homo*, new comer, immi-, emi-grant; creole, Afrikander; outsider, outlander, tenderfoot.

Adj. extraneous, foreign, alien, ulterior; exterior, external, outside, outlandish; oversea; tra-, ultra-montane.

excluded etc. 55; inadmissible; exceptional.

Adv. in foreign -parts, − lands; abroad, beyond seas, overseas.

58. Order.—N. order, regularity etc. 80; uniformity, symmetry, *lucidus ordo;* harmony, music of the .spheres.

gradation, progression; series etc. *(continuity)* 69.

subordination; course, even tenor, routine; method, disposition, arrangement, array, system, economy, discipline; orderliness etc. *adj.* rank, place etc. *(term)* 71.

V. be −, become- in order etc. *adj.;* form, fall in, draw up; arrange −, range −, place- itself; adjust; fall into −, take- -one's place, − rank; rally round; arrange etc. 60.

Adj. orderly, regular; in -order, − trim, − apple-pie order, according to Cocker, − its proper place, neat, neat as a pin, tidy, *en règle*, well regulated, correct, methodical, uniform, symmetrical, ship-shape, business-like, systematic; habitual; unconfused etc. *(see* confuse etc. 61) arranged etc. 60.

Adv. in order; methodically etc. *adj.;* in -turn, − its turn; step by step; by regular -steps, − gradations, − stages, − intervals; *seriatim*, systematically, by clockwork, *gradatim;* at stated periods etc. *(periodically)*138.

59. Disorder. [Absence, or want of Order, etc.]—N. disorder; derangement etc. 61; irregularity; anomaly etc. *(unconformity)* 83; anar-chy, -chism; want of method; dishevelment, untidiness etc. *adj.;* disunion; discord etc. 24.

confusion; confusedness etc. *adj.;* disarray, jumble, mix-up, huddle, litter, lumber; *cahotage;* farrago; mess, muss, mash, muddle, hash; hotch-potch; *imbroglio*, chaos, *omnium gatherum*, medley; mere -mixture etc. 41; fortuitous concourse of atoms, *disjecta membra*, *rudis indigestaque moles*.

complexity; complexness etc. *adj.;* com-, implication; intri-cacy, -cation; perplexity; network, maze, labyrinth, wilderness, jungle; involution, ravelling, entanglement; coil etc. *(convolution)* 248; sleave, tangled skein, knot, Gordian know, kink, web; wheels within wheels.

turmoil; ferment, etc. *(agitation)* 315; to do, trouble, pudder, pother, row, disturbance, convulsion, tumult, pandemonium, uproar, riot, rumpus, stour, scramble, *fracas*, embroilment, *mêlée*, spill and pelt, rough and tumble; whirlwind etc. 349; bear garden, Babel, Saturnalia, Donnybrook Fair, confusion worse confounded, most admired disorder, *concordia discors;* Bedlam −, hell- broke loose; bull in a china shop;

all the fat in the fire, *diable à quatre,* Devil to pay; pretty kettle of fish; pretty piece of -work, — business.

slattern, slut, sloven; draggle-tail.

V. be -disorderly etc. *adj.;* ferment, play at cross purposes.

put out of order; derange etc. 61; ravel etc. 219; ruffle, rumple; bungle, botch.

Adj. disorderly, orderless; out of -order; — place, — gear, — whack; irregular, desultory; anomalous etc. (*unconformable*) 83; aceph- alous, disorganized, straggling; un-, im-me- thodical; unsymmetric; unsystematic; untidy, slovenly, bedraggled, messy; dislocated; out of sorts; promiscuous, indiscriminate; chaotic, anarchical, lawless; unarranged etc. 60; con- fused, tumultuous, turbulent, tempestuous; de- ranged etc. 61; topsy turvy etc. (*inverted*) 218; shapeless etc. 241; disjointed, out of joint.

com-plex, -plexed; intricate, complicated, per- plexed, involved, ravelled, entangled, knotted, tangled, inextricable; irreducible.

troublous; riotous etc. (*violent*) 173.

Adv. irregularly etc. *adj.;* by fits and -snatches, — starts; pell-mell; higgledy-piggledy; .helter- skelter, harum-scarum; in a ferment; at -sixes and sevens, — cross purposes; upside down etc. 218.

Phr. the cart before the horse, chaos is come again.

60. Arrangement. [Reduction to Order.]—N. arrangement; plan etc. 626; preparation etc. 673; dispos-al, -ition; col-, al-location; disbribution; sorting etc. *v.;* assortment, allotment; grouping; apportionment, *taxis,* taxonomy, *syn-taxis,* grad- uation, organization, grading; re-organization, rationalization.

analysis, classification, division, digestion; systematism.

[Result of arrangement] order, orderliness, form, array; digest, synopsis etc. (compendi -um) 596; *syntagma,* table, atlas; register etc. (*record*) 551; score etc. 415; cosmos, organism, architecture.

[Instrument for sorting] sieve etc. 260; file, card index.

V. reduce to — , bring into- order; introduce order into; rally.

arrange, dispose, place, form; put —, set —, place- in order; straighten up, tidy up; set out, collocate, allocate, pack, marshal, range, size, rank, array, group, parcel out, allot, space, dis- tribute, deal; cast —, assign- the parts; dispose of, assign places to; assort, sort; sift, riddle; put —, set- -to rights, — into shape, — in trim, — in array.

class, -ify; divide; file, string together, thread; register etc. (*record*) 551; list, catalogue, tabulate, index, alphabeticize, graduate, digest, grade, codify; orchestrate, score.

methodize, regulate, systematize, standard- ize, co-ordinate, organize, settle, fix.

unravel, disentangle, ravel, card; disembroil.

Adj. arranged etc. *v.;* embattled, in battle array; cut and dried; methodical, orderly, regular, systematic, tabular.

61. Derangement. [Subversion of Order; bring- ing into disorder.]—N. derangement etc. *v.;* dis-

order etc. 59; evection, discomposure, dis- turbance; dis-, de-organization; involvement; dis- location; perturbation, interruption; shuffling etc. *v.;* inversion etc. 218; corrugation etc. (*fold*) 258; insanity etc. 503.

V. derange; dis-, mis-arrange; dis-, mis-place; mislay, discompose, disorder, de-, dis-organize; embroil, unsettle, disturb, confuse, trouble, per- turb, jumble, tumble; huddle, shuffle, muddle, toss, hustle, fumble, riot; bring —, put —, throw- into -disorder etc. 59; break the ranks, dis- concert, convulse; break in upon.

unhinge, dislocate, put out of joint, throw out of gear.

turn topsy-turvy etc. (*invert*) 218; bedevil; complicate, involve, perplex, confound; im-, em- brangle; tangle, en-tangle, ravel, tousle, dis- hevel, ruffle, rumple etc. (*fold*) 258; dement.

litter, scatter; mix etc. 41.

Adj. deranged etc. *v.;* syncre-tic, -tistic.

62. Precedence.—N. precedence; coming before etc. *v.;* the lead, *le pas;* superiority etc. 33; importance etc. 642; anteced-ence, -ency; anteriority etc. (*front*) 234; precursor etc. 64; priority etc. 116; precession etc. 280; antthe- tion, preference.

V. precede; come -before, — first; forerun, head, lead, take the lead; lead the -way, — dance; introduce, usher in; have the *pas;* set the fashion etc. (*influence*) 175; lead off, kick off, open the ball; take —, have- precedence; outrank; have the start etc. (*get before*) 280.

· place before; prefix; premise, prelude, preface.

Adj. preceding etc. *v.;* pre-, antecedent; an- terior, prior etc. 116; before; former, foregoing; before-, above-mentioned; aforesaid, said; precurs-ory, -ive; prevenient, preliminary, prefa- tory, introductory; prelus-ive, -ory; proemial, preparatory.

Adv. before; in advance etc. (*precession*) 280.

Phr. *seniores priores.*

63. Sequence.—N. sequence, coming after; going after etc. (*following*) 281; consecution, succession; posteriority etc. 117.

continuation; prolongation, order of succus- sion; successiveness; Elijah's mantle.

secondariness; subordinancy etc. (*inferiority*) 34.

V. succeed; come -after, — on, — next; follow, ensue, step into the shoes of; alternate.

place after, suffix, append.

Adj. succeeding etc. *v.;* sequent; sub-, con- sequent; sequacious, proximate, next; con- secutive etc. (*continuity*) 69; alternate, amoebaean.

latter; posterior etc. 117.

Adv. after, subsequently; behind etc. (*rear*) 235.

64. Precursor.—N. precursor, antecedent, precedent, predecessor; forerunner, van-courier, *avant-coureur,* pioneer, prodrome, *prodromos,* outrider; leader, bell-wether; herald, harbinger; dawn.

prelude, preamble, preface, prologue, fore- word, *avant-propos, protasis,* prolusion, proem, *prolepsis, prolegomena,* prefix, introduction;

lead, heading, frontispiece, groundwork;
preparation etc. 673; overture, voluntary, *exord-ium,* symphony, *ritornello;* premises.
prefigurement etc. 511; omen etc. 512.

Adj. precursory; prelu-sive, -sory, -dious; pro-emial, introductory, prefatory, prodromous, in-augural, preliminary; precedent etc. (*prior*) 116.

65. Sequel.—N. sequel, suffix, successor; tail,
queue, train, wake, trail, rear; retinue, suite;
appendix, postscript, subscript; epilogue; con-clusion; peroration; codicil; continuation, *se-quela;* appendage etc. 39; tail −, heel-piece; tag,
more last words; *colophon.*

follower, after-glow, -growth, -crop, -taste, -math.

after-part, -piece, -course, -thought, -game;
arrière pensée, second thoughts.

66. Beginning.—N. beginning, com-mencement, opening, outset, incipience, incep-tion, inchoation; introduction etc. (*precursor*) 64;
alpha; initial; foundation; inauguration, *début, le
premier pas,* embarcation, rising of the curtain;
zero hour; exordium, curtain raiser; maiden
speech; prelude; outbreak, onset, brunt; in-itiative, move, first move; gambit, narrow −,
thin- end of the wedge; fresh start, new depar-ture; forefront.

origin etc. (*cause*) 153; source, rise; bud, germ
etc. 153; egg, rudiment; genesis, birth, nativity,
cradle, infancy, incunabula; start, starting-point
etc. 293, dawn etc. (*morning*) 125.

title-page; head, -ing, caption; van etc. (*front*)
234.

en-trance, -try; inlet, orifice, mouth, chops,
lips, porch, portal, portico, *propylon,* door; gate,
-way; postern, wicket, threshold, vestibule; skirts,
border etc. (*edge*) 231; tee.

first -stage, − blush, − glance, − impression,
− sight.

rudiments, elements, outlines, *principia,* gram-mar, *protasis;* alphabet, ABC.

V. begin, commence, inchoate, rise, arise,
originate, institute, conceive, initiate, open,
dawn, set in, take its rise, enter upon, start; enter;
set out etc. (*depart*) 293; embark in.

usher in; lead -off, − the way; take the -lead, −
initiative; inaugurate, head; stand -at the head, −
first, − for; lay the foundations etc. (*prepare*)
673; found etc. (*cause*) 153; set -up, − on foot, −
agoing, − abroach, − the ball in motion; apply
the match to a train; launch, broach; open -up, −
the door to; set -about, − to work; make a -be-ginning, − start; handsel; take the first step, lay
the first stone, cut the first turf; break -ground,
− the ice, − cover; pass −, cross- the Rubicon;
open -fire, − the ball; ventilate, air; undertake
etc. 676.

come into -existence, − the world; make one's
début, take birth; burst forth, break out; spring
−, crop- up.

begin -at the beginning, − *ab ovo,* − again, −
de novo; start afresh, make a fresh start, shuffle
the cards, resume, recommence.

Adj. beginning etc. *v.;* initi-al, -atory, -ative;
inceptive, introductory, incipient; proemial, in-augural; incho-ate, -ative; embryonic, rudi-mental; primogenial; primeval etc. (*old*) 124;
rudimentary, aboriginal; natal, nascent.

first, foremost, front, leading, head; maiden.
begun etc. *v.;* just -begun etc. *v.*

Adv. at −, in- the beginning etc. *n.;* first, in the
first place, *imprimis,* first and foremost; *in
limine;* in -the bud, − embryo, − its infancy;
from -the beginning, − its birth; *ab -initio,* −
ovo, − *incunabilis,* primarily, originally.

67. End.—N. end, close, termination;
desinence, conclusion, *finis, finale,* period, term,
terminus, last, *omega;* extreme, -tremity; gable
−, butt −, fagend; tip, nib, point; tail etc. (*rear*)
235; verge etc. (*edge*) 231; tag, epilogue, perora-tion; *bonne bouche,* bitter end, tail end; terminal;
apodosis; appendix.

consummation, *dénouement;* finish etc. (*com-pletion*) 729; fate; doom, -sday; crack of doom,
day of Judgment, fall of the curtain, wind-up;
goal, destination; limit, stoppage, end all, de-termination; expiration, expiry; death etc. 360;
end of all things; finality; eschatology.

break up, *commencement de la fin,* last stage,
turning point; *coup de grâce,* death-blow; knock-out.

V. end, close, finish, terminate, conclude, be
all over; expire; die etc. 360; come −, draw- to a -close etc. *n.;* have run its course; run out, pass
away.

bring to an -end etc. *n.;* put an end to, make an
end of; determine; get through; achieve etc.
(*complete*) 729; stop etc. (*make to cease*) 142;
shut up shop.

Adj. ending etc. *v.,* final, terminal, definitive,
conclusive; crowning etc. (*completing*) 729; last,
ultimate; hindermost; rear etc. 235; caudal.

contermin-ate, -ous, -able.

ended etc. *v.;* at an end; settled, decided, over,
played out, set at rest.

penultimate; last but -one, − two, etc.

unbegun, uncommenced; fresh.

Adv. finally etc. *adj.;* in fine; at the last; once
for all.

68. Middle.—N. middle, midst, mediety; mean
etc. 29; medium, middle term; center etc. 222;
mid-course etc. 628; *mezzo termine; juste milieu*
etc. 628; half-way house, nave, navel, omphalos;
nucle-us, -olus.

equidistance, bisection, half-distance; equator,
diaphragm, midriff; interjacence etc. 228.

Adj. middle, medial, mesial, mean, mid;
middle-, mid-most; middling; mediate; inter-mediate etc. (*interjacent*) 228; equidistant; cen-tral etc. 222; mediterranean, equatorial.

Adv. in the middle; in the thick; mid-, half-way; midships, *in medias res.*

69. Continuity. [Uninterrupted se-quence.]—N. continuity; consecu-tion,, -tive-ness etc. *adj.;* succession, round, suite,
progression, series, train, chain; cat-, concat-enation; catena; scale; gradation, course, con-stant flow, perpetuity.

procession, column; retinue, *cortège,* caval-cade, rank and file, line of battle, array.

pedigree, genealogy, lineage; race etc. 166.

rank, file, line, row, range, tier, string, thread,
team; suit; colonnade.

V. follow in −, form- a series etc. *n.;* fall in.

arrange in a -series etc. *n.;* string together, catenate, file, thread, graduate, tabulate.

Adj. continu-ous. -ed; consecutive; progressive, gradual; serial, successive; immediate, unbroken, entire; linear; in a -line, − row etc. *n.;* uninter-rupted, -mitting; unremitting; perennial, evergreen; constant.

Adv. continuously etc. *adj.; seriatim;* in a -line etc. *n.;* in -succession, − turn; running, gradually, step by step, *gradatim,* at a stretch; in -file, − column, − single file, − Indian file.

70. Discontinuity. [Interrupted sequence.]—**N.** discontinuity; disjunction etc. 44; anacoluthon; interruption, break, fracture, flaw, fault, split, crack, cut; gap etc. *(interval)* 198; solution of continuity, *caesura;* broken thread; parenthesis, episode; rhapsody, patchwork; intermission; alternation etc. *(periodicity)* 138; dropping fire.

V. be -discontinuous etc. *adj.;* alternate, intermit.

discontinue, pause, interrupt; intervene; break, − in upon; interpose etc. 228; break −, snap- the thread; disconnect etc. *(disjoin)* 44.

Adj. discontinuous, unsuccessive, broken, interrupted, *décousu;* dis-, un-connected, discrete, disjunctive; fitful etc. *(irregular)* 139; spasmodic, desultory, intermit-ting etc. *v.;* -tent; alternate; recurrent etc. *(periodic)* 138; few and far between.

Adv. at intervals; by -snatches, − jerks, − skips, − catches, − fits and starts; skippingly, *per saltum; longo intervallo.*

71. Term.—**N.** term, rank, station, stage, step; degree etc. 26; scale, remove, grade, link, peg, round −, rung- of the ladder, *status,* position, place, point, mark, *pas,* period, pitch; stand, - ing; footing, range.

V. hold −, occupy −, fall into- a place etc. *n.*

72. Assemblage.—**N.** assemblage; col-lection, location, -ligation; compilation, levy, gathering, ingathering, mobilization, meet, foregathering, muster, *attroupement;* con-course, -flux, - gregation, -tesseration, -vergence etc. 290; meeting, *levée, réunion,* drawing room, at home; conversazione etc. *(social gathering)* 892; assembly, congress, eisteddfod; conven-tion, -ticle; gemote; conclave, etc. *(council)* 696; posse, *posse comitatus;* Noah's ark.

miscellany, *collectanea,* symposium; museum, menagerie, etc. *(store)* 636.

crowd, throng, multitude; flood, rush, deluge; rout, rabble, mob, press, crush, *cohue,* jam, horde, body, tribe; crew, gang, knot, squad, band, party; swarm, shoal, school, covey, flock.

herd, drove, kennel; array, bevy, galaxy; *corps,* company, troop, *troupe;* army, force, regiment, etc. *(combatants)* 726; host etc. *(multitude)* 102; populousness.

clan, brotherhood, association etc. *(party)* 712. volley, shower, storm, cloud.

group, cluster, Pleiades, clump, pencil; set, batch, lot, pack; budget, *dossier,* assortment, bunch; parcel; pack-et, -age; bundle, *fasciculus,* fascine, bale; ser-on, oon; faggot, wisp, truss,

tuft; shock, rick, fardel, stack, sheaf, swath, gavel, haycock, stook.

accumulation etc. *(store)* 636; congeries, heap, lump, pile, *rouleau,* tissue, mass, pyramid; drift; snow-ball, -drift; acervation, cumulation; amassment, glom-, agglom-eration; conglobation; conglomeration, -ate; coacervation, coagmentation, aggregation, concentration, congestion, *omnium gatherum, spicilegium,* black hole of Calcutta; quantity etc. *(greatness)* 31.

collector, gatherer; whip, -per in.

V. [be or come together] assemble, collect, muster; meet, unite, join, rejoin; cluster, flock, swarm, surge, stream, herd, crowd, throng, associate; con-gregate, -glomerate, -centrate; center round, *rendezvous,* resort; come −, flock −, get −, pig- together; forgather; huddle; reassemble.

[get or bring together] assemble, muster, mobilize; bring −, get −, put −, draw −, scrape −, lump- together; col-lect, -locate. -ligate; get −, whip- in; gather; hold a meeting; con-vene, - voke, -vocate; rake up, dredge; heap, mass, pile; pack, put up, truss, cram; acervate; ag-glomerate, - gregate; compile; group, aggroup, concentrate, unite; collect −, bring- into a focus; amass, accumulate etc. *(store)* 636; collect in a drag-net; heap Ossa upon Pelion.

Adj. assembled etc. *v.;* closely packed, dense, serried, crowded to suffocation, teeming, swarming, populous; as thick as hops; all of a heap, fasciculated; cumulative.

Phr. the plot thickens.

73. Non-assemblage. Dispersion.—**N.** dispersion; disjunction etc. 44; divergence etc. 291; scattering etc. *v.;* dissemination, broadcasting, diffusion, dissipation, distribution; apportionment etc. 786; spread, respersion, circumfusion, interspersion, spargefaction.

waifs and estrays, flotsam and jetsam, *disjecta membra.*

V. disperse, scatter, sow, disseminate, radiate, diffuse, shed, spread, ted, bestrew, overspread, dispense, disband, disembody, demobilize, dismember, distribute; apportion etc. 786; blow off, let out, dispel, cast forth, draught off; strew, straw, strow; spirtle, cast, sprinkle, shatter; issue, deal out, retail, utter; re-, inter-sperse; set abroach, circumfuse.

turn −, cast- adrift; scatter to the winds; sow broadcast.

spread like wildfire, disperse themselves.

Adj. unassembled etc. (*see* assemble etc. 72); dispersed etc. *v.;* sparse, dispread, broadcast, sporadic, widespread; far-flung; epidemic etc. *(general)* 78; adrift, stray; dishevelled, streaming.

Adv. *sparsim,* here and there, *passim.*

74. Focus. [Place of meeting.]—**N.** focus; point of- convergence etc. 290; corradiation; center etc. 222; gathering-place, resort; haunt; retreat; *venue, rendezvous;* rallying point, head-quarters, home, club; *dépôt* etc. *(store)* 636; tryst, trysting-place; place of -meeting, − resort, − assignation; *point de −, lieu de- réunion;* issue.

V. bring to- a point, − a focus, − an issue; focus.

75. Class.—N. class, category, *categorema,* head, order, section; division, subdivision; department, province, domain, sphere.

kind, sort, genus, species, variety, branch, family, race, tribe, caste, sept, clan, breed; *clique, coterie;* type, kit, sect, set; assortment; feather, kidney; suit; range; gender, sex, kin.

manner, description, denomination, persuasion, connection, designation, character, stamp; predicament; conviction etc. 484.

similarity etc. 17.

76. Inclusion. [Comprehension under, or reference to a class.]—N. inclusion, admission, incorporation, comprehension, reception.

composition etc. (*inclusion in a compound*) 54.

V. be -included in etc.; come −, fall −, range-under; belong −, pertain- to; range with; merge in.

include, compromise, comprehend, contain, admit, embrace, receive; enclose etc. (*circumscribe*) 229; incorporate, cover, embody, encircle.

reckon −, enumerate −, number- among; refer to; place −, arrange-under, − with; take into account.

Adj. includ-ed; -ing etc. *v.;* inclusive; comprehensive, all-embracing; congen-er, -erous; of the same -class etc. 75.

Phr. *et hoc genus omne,* etc.; *et caetera.*

77. Exclusion.*—N. exclusion etc. 55.

* The same set of words is used to express *Exclusion from a class* and *Exclusion from a compound.* Reference is therefore made to the former at 55. This identity does not occur with regard to *Inclusion,* which therefore constitutes a separate category.

78. Generality.—N. general-ity, -ization; universality; catholic-ity, -ism; miscel-lany, -laneousness; drag-net.

every-one, -body; all hands, all the world and his wife; any body, N or M, all sorts; *tout le monde.*

prevalence, run.

V. be -general etc. *adj.;* prevail, obtain, be going about, stalk abroad.

render -general etc. *adj.;* generalize; spread, broadcast.

Adj. general, usual, current, generic, collective; broad, comprehensive; sweeping; encyclopedical, panoramic, widespread etc. (*dispersed*) 73.

universal; catho-lic, -lical; common, worldwide; e-cumenical; transcendental; prevalent, prevailing, rife, epidemic, besetting; all over, covered with.

every, all; indeterminate, indefinite, unspecified, impersonal.

customary etc. (*habitual*) 613.

Adv. what-ever, -soever; to a man, one and all, without exception.

generally etc. *adj.;* always, for better for worse; in general, generally speaking; speaking generally; for the most part; in the long run etc. (*on an average*) 29.

79. Speciality.—N. speciality, *spécialité;* individ-uality, -uity; particularity, peculairity;

idiocrasy etc. (*tendency*) 176; personality, characteristic, mannerism, idiosyncrasy, attribute specificness etc. *adj.;* singularity etc. (*unconformity*) 83; reading, version, lection; state; *trait;* distinctive feature; technicality; *differentia.*

particulars, details, minutiae, items, counts; I, self, I myself, *ego;* my-, him-, her-, it-self.

V. specify, particularize, individualize, realize, specialize, designate, differentiate, determine, define, denote, indicate, itemize, detail.

descend to particulars, enter into detail, come to the point.

Adj. special, particular, individual, specific, proper, personal, intimate, original, private, respective, definite, concrete, determinate, especial, certain, esoteric, endemic, partial, party, peculiar, marked, appropriate, several, characteristic, diagnistic, exact, exclusive; singular etc. (*exceptional*) 83; idiomatic; typical, representative, distinctive.

this, that; yon, -der.

Adv. specially etc. *adj.;* in particular, *in propriâ personâ; ad hominem;* for my part.

each, apiece, one by one; severally, respectively, each to each; *seriatim,* in detail, bit by bit; *pro hac vice, − re natâ.*

namely, that is to say, *videlicet,* viz.; to wit.

80. Rule.—N. regularity, uniformity etc. 16; clock-work precision; punctuality etc. (*exactness*) 494; routine etc. (*custom*) 613; formula; system; rut; canon, convention, maxim; rule etc. (*form, regulation*) 697; key-note, standard, model; precedent etc. (*prototype*) 22; conformity etc. 82.

nature, principle; law; order of things; normal −, natural −, ordinary −, model- -state, − condition; standing -dish, − order; normality; Procrustean law; law of the Medes and Persians; hard and fast rule.

Adj. regular, uniform, symmetrical, constant, steady; according to rule etc. (*conformable*) 82; customary etc. 613; orderly etc. 58.

81. Multiformity.—N. multi-, omniformity; variety, diversity; multifariousness etc. *adj.*

Adj. multi-form, -fold, -farious, -generous; multiplex, variform, manifold, many-sided, multiplicate; omni-form, -genous, -farious; polymorphic; protean; heterogeneous, motley, mosaic; epicene, indiscriminate, desultory, irregular, diversified, different, divers; all manner of; of -every description, − all sorts and kinds; *et hoc genus omne;* and what not? *de omnibus rebus et quibusdam aliis.*

82. Conformity.—N. conform-ity, -ance; observance.

naturalization; conventionality etc. (*custom*) 613; agreement etc. 23.

example, instance, specimen, sample, quotation; exemplification, illustration, case in point; object lesson.

conventionalist, formalist, Philistine.

pattern etc. (*prototype*) 22.

V. conform to, − rule; accommodate −, adapt- oneself to; rub off corners.

be -regular etc. *adj.;* move in a groove; follow —, observe —, go by —, bend to —, obey- -rules, — precedents; comply —, tally —, chime in —, fall in-with; be -guided, — regulated- by; fall into a -custom, — usage; follow the -fashion, — multitude; pass muster, do as others do, *hurler aves les loups;* do at Rome as the Romans do; go —, swim- with the -stream, — current, — tide; tread the beaten track etc. (*habit*) 613; rubber-stamp; keep one in countenance.

exemplify, illustrate, cite, quote, put a case; produce an- instance etc. *n.*

Adj. conformable to rule, adaptable, compliant, consistent, agreeable; regular etc. 80; according to -regulation, — rule, — Cocker; *en règle, selon les règles,* well regulated, orderly; symmetric etc. 242.

conventional commonplace etc. (*customary*) 613; of -daily, — every day- occurrence; in the natural order of things; ordinary, common, — or garden, prosaic, habitual, usual.

in the order of the day; naturalized.

typical, normal, formal; canonical, orthodox, sound, strict, rigid, positive, uncompromising, Procrustean; point device.

secundum artem, ship-shape, technical.

exemplary, illustrative, in point.

Adv. conformably etc. *adj.;* by rule; agreeably to; in -conformity, — accordance, — keeping-with; according to; consistently with; as usual, *ad instar, instar omnium; more -solito,* — *majorum.*

for the sake of conformity; of —, as a matter of- course; *pro formâ,* for form's sake, by the card; according to plan.

invariably etc. (*uniformly*) 16.

for -example, — instance; *exempli gratiâ; e.g.; inter alia.*

Phr. *cela va sans dire, ex pede Herculem, noscitur a sociis.*

83. Unconformity.—N. non-conformity etc. 82; un-, dis-conformity; unconventionality, informality, abnormity, anomaly; anomalousness etc. *adj.;* exception, peculiarity, etc. 79; infraction —, breach —, violation —, infringement- of -law, — custom, — usage; eccentricity, *bizarrerie,* oddity, *je ne sais quoi,* monstrosity, rarity; freak of Nature.

individuality, idiosyncrasy, singularity, oritinality, mannerism.

aberration; irregularity; variety; singularity; exemption; salvo etc. (*qualification*) 469.

nonconformist; nondescript, character, original, nonsuch, monster, prodigy, wonder, miracle, curiosity, missing link, flying fish, black swan, *lusus naturae, rara avis,* queer fish; mongrel; half-caste, -blood, -breed; *métis,* cross breed, hybrid, mule, mulatto, sacatra, marabou; *tertium quid,* hermaphrodite, gynander, androgyn.

phoenix, chimera, hydra, sphinx, minotaur; griff-in, -on; centaur; hippogriff, -centaur; sagittary; kraken; cockatrice, wyvern, roc, liver, dragon, sea-serpent; mermaid; unicorn; Cyclops, 'men whose heads do grown beneath their shoulders;. Teratolgy.

fish out of water; neither -one thing nor another, — fish flesh nor fowl nor good red her-ring; one in a -way, — thousand; out-cast, -law; Ishmael, pariah; oasis.

V. be -unconformable etc. *adj.;* leave the beaten -track, — path; infringe —, break —, violate- a -law, — habit, — usage, — custom; drive a coach and six through; stretch a point; have no business there; baffle —, beggar- all description.

Adj. unconformable, exceptional; abnorm-al, -ous; anomal-ous, -istic; out of -order, — place, — keeping, — tune, — one's element; irregular, arbitrary; lawless, informal, aberrant, stray, wandering, wanton; peculiar, exclusive, unnatural, eccentric, crotchety, egregious; out of the -beaten track, — common, — common run, — pale of; misplaced; funny.

un-usual, -accustomed, -customary, -wonted, -common; rare, singular, *unique,* curious, odd, extraordinary, strange, monstrous; wonderful etc. 870; unexpected, unaccountable; *outré,* out of the way, remarkable, noteworthy; queer, quaint, nondescript, none such, *sui generis;* original, unconventional, Bohemian, unfashionable; un-described, -precedented, -paralleled, -exampled, -heard of, -familiar; fantastic, newfangled, grotesque, *bizarre;* outlandish, exotic, *tombé de nues,* preternatural; denaturalized.

heterogeneious, heteroclite, amorphous, mongrel, amphibious, epicene, half-blood, hybrid; androgyn-ous, -al; unsymmetric etc. 243.

qualified etc. 469.

Adv. unconformably etc. *adj.;* except, unless, save, barring, beside, without, save and except, let alone.

however, yet, but.

Int. what -on earth! — in the world!

Phr. never was -seen, — heard, — known- the like.

84. Number.—N. number, symbol, numeral, figure, cipher, digit, integer; counter; round number; formula; function; series.

sum, total, aggregate, difference, complement, subtrahend; product; multipli-cand, -er, -cator; coefficient, multiple; dividend, divisor, factor, quotient, sub-multiple, fraction; mixed number; numerator, denominator; decimal, circulating decimal, repetend; common measure, aliquot part; reciprocal; prime number; totitive, totient.

permutation, combination, variation; election. ratio, proportion; progression; arithmetical —, geometrical —, harmonical- progression; percentage.

figurate —, pyramidal —, polygonal- numbers.

power, root, exponent, index, logarithm, anti-logarithm; modulus.

differential, integral, fluxion, fluent.

Adj. numeral, complementary, divisible, aliquot, reciprocal, prime, fractional, decimal, figurate, incommensurable.

proportional, exponential, logarithmic, logometric, differential, fluxional, integral.

positive, negative; rational, irrational; surd, radical, real, imaginary, impossible.

85. Numeration.—N. numeration, numbering etc. *v.;* pagination; tale, tally, recension, enumer-

ation, summation, reckoning, computation, sup-
putation; calcu-lation, -lus; algorithm, rhabdology,
dactylonomy; measurement etc. 466; statistics.

arithmetic, analysis, algebra, fluxions;
differential −, integral −, infinitesimal-calculus;
calculus of differences.

[Statistics] dead reckoning, muster, poll, census, capitation, roll-call, recapitulation; account
etc. (list) 86.

[Operations] notation, addition, subtraction,
multiplication, division, proportion, rule of
three, practice, equations, extraction of roots,
reduction, involution, evolution, approximation,
interpolation, differentiation, integration.

[Instruments] abacus, swan-pan, logometer,
sliding −, slide- rule, tallies, Napier's bones, calculating −, adding- machine, difference engine;
cash register.

arithmetician, calculator, abacist; math-
ematician, actuary, statistician, surveyor,
geodesist.

V. number, count, tell; call −, run- over, take
an account of, enumerate, call the roll, muster,
poll, recite, recapitulate; sum; sum −, cast- up;
tell off, score, cipher, compute, calculate, set a
price, reckon, − up, estimate; suppute, add, sub-
tract, multiply, divide, extract roots.

check, prove, demonstrate, balance, audit,
overhaul, take stock; affix numbers to, page,
foliate, paginate.

amount −, come- to.

Adj. numer-al, -ical; arithmetical, analytic,
algebraic, statistical, numerable, computable,
calculable; commensur-able, -ate; incommen-
sur-able, -ate.

86. List.—N. list, catalogue, enumeration,
inventory, schedule; register etc. (record) 551;
account; bill, − of costs, syllabus; terrier, tally,
file; almanac, calendar, index, table, atlas, contents, card index; rota, ticket; book, ledger;
synopsis, catalogue raisonné; tableau, scroll,
manifest, invoice, bill of lading; prospectus,
programme; bill of fare, menu, carte; score,
census, statistics, returns; Red −, Blue −,
Domesday- book; cadaster; directory, gazetteer,
dictionary, glossary, lexicon, thesaurus, gradus.

roll; check −, chequer −, bead- roll, − of
honor; muster -roll, − book; roster, panel; cartulary, diptych.

V. list, enrol, schedule, register etc. n.; indent,
post, docket; matriculate.

Adj. cadastral, listed etc. v.

87. Unity.—N. unity; oneness etc. adj.; individuality; solitude etc. (seclusion) 893; isolation
etc. (disjunction) 44; unification etc. 48.

one, unit, ace; item; individual; solo, none else,
no other, naught beside.

V. be -one, − alone etc. adj.; dine with Duke
Humphrey.

isolate etc. (disjoin) 44.

render one; unite etc. (join) 43, (combine) 48.

Adj. one, sole, single, solitary, only- begotten;
individual, apart, alone; kithless.

un-accompanied, -attended; solus, single-
handed; singular, odd, unique, unrepeated,
azygous, first and last; isolated etc. (disjoined)
44; insular; unitary.

lone; lone-ly, -some; desolate, dreary.

in-secable, -severable, -discerptible; compact,
irresolvable.

Adv. singly etc. adj.; alone, by itself, per se,
only, apart, in the singular number, in the
abstract; one -by one, − at a time; simply; one
and a half, sesqui-.

Phr. natura il fece, e poi roppe la stampa.

88. Accompaniment.—N. accompaniment; appurtenance, adjunct etc. 39; context.

coexistence, concomitance, company,
association, companionship; part-, copart-ner-
ship; coefficiency.

concomitant, accessory, coefficient; companion, attendant, fellow, associate, consort,
spouse, colleague, fidus Achates; part-, co-partner; satellite, hanger on, shadow; excort, entourage, suite, cortège; convoy, follower etc. 65;
attribute.

V. accompany, coexist, attend, convoy,
chaperon; hang −, wait- on; go hand in hand
with; synchronize etc. 120; bear −, keep- company; row in the same boat; bring in its train,
associate −, couple- with.

Adj. accompanying etc. v.; concomitant,
fellow, twin, joint; associated −, coupled- with;
accessory, attendant, obbligato.

Adv. with, withal; together −, along −, in
company- with; hand in hand, side by side; cheek
by -jowl, − jole; arm in arm; there-, here-with;
and etc. (addition) 37.

together, in a body, collectively.

89. Duality.—N. dual-ity, -ism; duplicity; biplicity, -formity; span, polarity.

two, deuce, couple, couplet, doublet, brace,
pair, cheeks, twins, Castor and Pollus, gemini,
Siamese twins; fellows; yoke, conjugation, dyad,
distich.

V. [unite in pairs] pair, couple, bracket, yoke;
conduplicate, mate.

Adj. two, twain; dual, -istic; binary, binomial;
twin, biparous; dyadic; conduplicate; duplex etc.
90; tête-à-tête; paired; dihedral.

coupled etc. v.; conjugate.

both, − the one and the other.

90. Duplication.—N. duplication, doubling
etc. v.; gemi-, ingemi-nation; reduplication;
iteration etc. (repetition) 104; renewal.

V. double; re-double, -duplicate; geminate;
repeat etc. 104; renew etc. 660; duplicate, copy
etc. 21.

Adj. double; doubled etc. v.; bicameral,
bicapital, bi-fold, -form, -lateral, -farious, -
facial; two-fold, -sided, -headed, -edged etc.;
duplex; double-faced; twin, duplicate, ingem-
inate; second; dual etc. 29.

Adv. twice, once more; over again etc.
(repeatedly) 104; as much again; twofold.

secondly, in the second place, again.

91. Bisection. [Division into two parts.]—N.
bi-section, -partition; di-, subdi-chotomy; halv-
ing etc. v.; dimidiation; hendiadis.

bifurcation, forking, branching, furcation,
ramification, divarication; fork, prong; fold.

half, moiety.
V. bisect, halve, divide, split, cut in two, cleave, dimidiate, dichotomize, divaricate.
go halves, divide with.
separate, fork, bifurcate; branch -off, − out; ramify.
Adj. bisected etc. v.; cloven, cleft; bipartite, biconjugate, bicuspid, bifid; bifur-cous, -cate, -cated; semi-, demi- hemi-.

92. Triality.—N. triality, trinity,* triplicity.
three, triad, triplet, trey, trio, ternion, tri-nomial, leash; tierce; triennium; trefoil, triangle, trident, tripod, triumvirate, troika.
third power, cube.
Adj. three; tri-form, -nal, -nomial; tertiary; triune.
*Trinity is hardly ever used except in a theological sense; see Deity 976.

93. Triplication.—N. tripli-cation, -city; trebleness, trine, trilogy.
V. treble, triple, triplicate, cube.
Adj. treble, triple; tern, -ary; triplex, triplicate, threefold, trilogistic; third; trinal; trihedral.
Adv. three -times, − fold; thrice, in the third place, thirdly; trebly etc. adj.

94. Trisection. [Division into three parts.]—N. tri-section, -partition, -chotomy; third, − part.
V. trisect, divide into three parts, trifurcate.
Adj. trifid; trisected etc. v.; tripartite, -chotomous, -sulcate.

95. Quaternity.—N. quaternity, four, tetrad, quartet, quaternion, square, quadrature, quarter, quadruplet; quadrilateral, quadrangle, quatre-foil; quadriga.
V. reduce to a square, square.
Adj. four; quat-ernary, -ernal; quadratic; quar-tile, quartic, tetractic, tetrad, tetrahedral; quad-rennial; quadrivalent.

96. Quadruplication.—N. quadruplication.
V. multiply by four, quadruplicate, bi-quadrate.
Adj. fourfold; quad-ruple, -ruplicate, -rible; quadruplex; fourth.
Adv. four times; in the fourth place, fourthly.

97. Quadrisection. [Division into four parts.]—N. quadri-section, -partition; quarter-ing etc. v.; fourth; quart, -er, -ern; farthing (i.e. fourthing); quarto.
V. quarter, divide into four parts, quadrisect.
Adj. quartered etc. v.; quadri-fid, -partite.

98. Five, etc.—N. five, cinque, quint, quin-cunx, quintuplet, quintet, pentagon, pentameter, Pentateuch; six, half-a-dozen; sextet, hexagon, hexameter; seven, Heptarchy; eight, octet, octa-gon, octave; nine, three times three; ten, decade; eleven; twelve, dozen; thirteen; long −, baker's-dozen.
twenty, score; twenty-four, four and twenty, two dozen; twenty-five, five and twenty, quarter

of a hundred; forty, two score; fifty, half a hundred; sixty, three score, sexagenarian; seven-ty, three score and ten, septuagenarian; eighty, four score, octogenarian; ninety, four score and ten, nonagenarian.
hundred, centenary, hecatomb, century; hundredweight, cwt.; one hundred and forty-four, gross; bicentenary, tercentenary etc.
thousand, chiliad; myriad, millennium, ten thousand; lac, lakh, one hundred thousand, plum; million; thousand million, milliard.
billion, trillion etc.
V. centuriate.
Adj. five, quinary, quintuple; fifth; senary, sextuple; sixth; seventh; octuple; eighth; nine-fold, ninth; tenfold, decimal, denary, decuple, tenth; eleventh; duo-denary, -denal; twelfth; in one's 'teens, thirteenth.
vices-, viges-imal; twentieth; twenty-fourth etc. n.
cent-uple, -uplicate, -ennial, -enary, -urial; secular, hundredth; thousandth; millenary etc.

99. Quinquesection, etc.—N. division by -five etc. 98; quinquesection etc.; fifth etc.; decima-tion.
V. decimate, quinquesect.
Adj. quinque-fid, -partite; quinquarticular; octifid; decimal, tenth, tithe, teind; duodecimal, twelfth; sexagesimal, -genary; hundredth, centesimal; millesimal etc.

100. Plurality. [More than one.]—N. plurality; a -number, − certain number; one or two, two or three etc.; a few, several; multitude etc. 102.
Adj. plural, more than one, upwards of, some, certain; not -alone etc. 87.
Adv. et cetera, etc., etc.
Phr. non deficit alter.

100a. Fraction [Less than one.]—N. fraction, fractional part, fragment; part etc. 51.
Adj. fractional, fragmentary, partial.

101. Zero.—N. zero, nothing, naught, nought, duck's egg, goose egg; cipher, none, nobody; not a soul; âme qui vive; absence etc. 187; unsubstantiality etc. 4.
Adj. not -one, − any.

102. Multitude.—N. multitude; numerousness etc. adj.; numer-osity, -ality; multiplicity; profu-sion etc. (plenty) 639; legion, host; great −, large −, round −, enormous- number; a quantity, numbers, array, sight, army, sea, galaxy; scores, peck, bushel, school, shoal, swarm, draft, bevy, cloud, flock, herd, drove, flight, covey, hive, brood, litter, farrow, fry, nest; mob, crowd etc. (assemblage) 72; lots, loads, heaps; all the world and his wife.
[Increase of number] greater number, ma-jority; multiplication, multiple.
V. be -numerous etc. adj.; swarm −, teem −, crawl −, creep -with; crowd, swarm, come thick upon; outnumber, multiply; people; swarm like -locusts, − bees.
Adj. many, several, sundry, divers, various,

not a few; a -hundred, − thousand, − myriad, − million, − thousand and one; some -ten or a dozen, − forty or fifty etc.; half a -dozen, − hundred etc.; very −, full −, ever so- many; numer-ous, -ose; profuse, in profusion; manifold, multiplied, multitudinous, multiferous, multiple, multinomial, teeming, crawling, populous, peopled, crowded, thick, studded; galore.

thick coming, many more, more than one can tell, a world of; no end -of, − to; *cum multis aliis*; thick as -hops, − hail; plenty as blackberries; numerous as the -stars in the firmament, − sands on the sea-shore, − hairs on the head; and -what not, − heaven knows what; endless etc. (*infinite*) 105.

Phr. their name is 'Legion.'

103. Fewness.—N. fewness etc. *adj.*; paucity, small number; small quantity etc. 32; scarcity, sparsity; rarity; infrequency etc. 137; handfull; maniple; minority, exiguity.

[Diminution of number] reduction; weeding etc. *v.*; elimination, sarculation, decimation.

V. be -few etc. *adj.*

render -few etc. *adj.*; reduce, diminish the number, weed; eliminate, thin, decimate.

Adj. few; scarce; scant, -y; thin, rare, thinly scattered, few and far between; exiguous; infrequent etc. 137; *rari nantes*; hardly −, scarcely-any; to be counted on one's fingers; reduced etc. *v.*; unrepeated.

Adv. here and there.

104. Repetition.—N. repetition, iteration, reiteration, duplication, ding-dong, alliteration; *epistrophe;* harping, recurrence, succession, run; batto-, tauto-logy; monotony, tautophony; rhythm etc. 138; pleonasm, redundancy, diffuseness.

chimes, repetend, echo, *ritornello,* burden of a song, *refrain;* rehearsal; encore; *réchauffé, rifacimento,* recapitulation.

cuckoo etc. (*imitation*) 19; reverberation etc. 408; drumming etc. (*roll*) 407; renewal etc. (*restoration*) 660.

twice-told tale; old -story, − song, chestnut; second −, new- edition; reprint, new impression; return game, return match, reappearance, reproduction; periodicity etc. 138.

V. repeat, iterate, reiterate, reproduce, parrot, echo, re-echo, drum, harp upon, battologize, hammer, redouble.

recur, revert, return, reappear; renew etc. (*restore*) 660.

rehearse; do −, say- over again; ring the changes on; harp on the same string; din −, drum- in the ear; conjugate in all its moods, tenses and inflexions, begin again, go over the same ground, go the same round, never hear the last of; resume, return to, recapitulate, reword.

Adj. repeated etc. *v.*; repetition-al, -ary; recurrent, -ring; ever recurring; thick coming; frequent, incessant, redundant, pleonastic, tautological.

monotonous, harping, iterative; mocking, chiming; retold; aforesaid, -named; abovementioned, said; habitual etc. 613; another.

Adv. repeatedly, often, again, afresh, anew,

over again, once more; ditto, *encore, de novo, bis, da capo.*

again and again; over and over, − again; many times over; time- and again, − after time; year after year; day by day etc.; many −, several −, a number of- times; many −, full many- a time; times out of number, year in and year out, morning, noon and night; frequently etc. 136.

Phr. *ecce iterum Crispinus, toujours perdrix,* cut and come again; 'tomorrow and tomorrow.'

105. Infinity.—N. infini-ty, -tude, -teness etc. *adj.;* perpetuity etc. 112.

V. be -infinite etc. *adj.;* know −, have- no - limits, − bounds; go on for ever.

Adj. infinite, immense; number-, count-, sum-, measure-less; innumer-, immeasur-, incalcul-, illimit-, intermin-, unfathom-, unapproach-able; exhaustless, inexhaustible, indefinite; without - number, − measure, − limit, − end; incomprehensible; limit-, end-, bound-, termless; un-told, -numbered, -measured, -bounded, -limited; il-limited; perpetual etc. 112.

Adv. infinitely etc. *adj.; ad infinitum.*

106. Time.—N. time, duration; period, term, stage, space, span, spell, season; the whole -time, − period; course etc. 109.

intermediate, time, while, *interim,* interval, bit, pendency; inter-vention, -mission, -mittence, -regnum, -lude; respite.

era, epoch, éon, cycle, time of life, age, year, date; decade etc. (*period*) 108; moment, etc. (*instant*) 113; reign etc. 737.

glass −, ravages −, whirligig −, noiseless foot- of time; scythe.

V. continue, last, endure, go on, hold out, remain, stay, persist, abide, run; intervene; elapse etc. 109.

take −, take up −, fill −, occupy- time.

pass −, pass away −, spend −, while away −, consume −, talk against −, kill- time; tide over; use −, employ- time; tarry etc. 110; seize an opportunity etc. 134; waste time etc. (*be inactive*) 683.

Adj. continuing etc. *v.;* on foot; permanent etc. (*durable*) 110.

Adv. while, whilst, during, pending; during the -time, − interval; in the course of; for the time being, day by day; in the time of, when; meantime, -while; in the -meantime, − *interim; ad interim, pendente lite; de die in diem;* from -day to day, − hour to hour etc.; hourly, always; for a -time, − season; till, until, up to, yet; the whole −, all the- time; all along; throughout etc. (*completely*) 52; for good etc. (*diuturnity*) 110.

here-, there-, where-upon; then; *anno, Domini;* A.D.; *ante Christum;* A.C.; before Christ; B.C.; *anno urbis conditae;* A.U.C.; *anno regni,* A.R.; once upon a time, one fine morning.

Phr. time -runs, − runs against; *tempus fugit.*

107. Neverness.—N. 'neverness;' absence of time, no time; *dies non;* Tib's eve; Greek Kalends.

Adv. never; at no -time, − period; on no occasion, never in all one's born days, nevermore, *sine die.*

108. Period. [Definite duration, or portion of time.]—N. period; second, minute, hour, day, week, sennight, octave, month, moon, quarter, semester, year, *lustrum, quinquennium,* decade, *decennium,* indiction, lifetime, generation, epoch, era, cycle.

century, age, *millennium; annus magnus.*

Adj. horary; hourly, annual etc. (*periodical*) 138.

108a. Contingent Duration.—Adv. during - pleasure, — good behavior; *quamdiu se bene gesserit.*

109. Course. [Indefinite duration.]—N. course —, progress —, process —, succession —, lapse —, flow —, flux —, effluxion, stream —, tract —, current —, sweep —, tide —, march —, step —, flight- of time; duration etc. 106.

[Indefinite time] aorist.

V. elapse, lapse, flow, run, proceed, advance, pass; roll —, wear —, press —, drag- on; flit, fly, slip, slide, glide, crawl; run -its course.

out; expire; go —, pass- by; be -past etc. 122.

Adj. elapsing etc. *v.;* aoristic; progressive; transient etc. 111.

Adv. in due -time, — season; in -course, — process, — the fulness- of time; in time.

Phr. *labitur et labetur; truditur dies die; fugaces labuntur anni;* 'tomorrow and tomorrow and tomorrow creeps in this petty pace from day to day.'

110. Diuturnity. [Long duration.]—N. diuturnity; a -long —, length of -time; an age, a century, an eternity, aeons; slowness etc. 275; perpetuity etc. 112; blue moon.

dura-bleness, -bility; persistence, lastingness etc. *adj.;* continuance, assiduity, endurance, standing; permanence etc. (*stability*) 150; survival, -vance; longevity etc. (*age*) 128; distance of time.

protraction —, prolongation —, extension- of time; delay etc. (*lateness*) 133.

V. last, endure, stand, remain, abide, continue, brave a thousand years.

tarry etc. (*be late*) 133; drag -on, — its slow length along, — a lengthening chain; protract, prolong; spin —, eke —, draw —, lengthen- out; temporize; gain —, make —, talk against- time.

out-last, -live; survive; live to fight again.

Adj. durable; perdurable; lasting etc. *v.;* of long -duration, — standing; permanent, chronic, long-standing; intransi-ent, -tive; intransmutable, persistent; life-, live-long; longeval, long-lived, macrobiotic, diuturnal, sempervirent, evergreen, perennial; unin-, ter-, unremitting; perpetual etc. 112.

lingering, protracted, prolonged, spun out etc. *v.;* long-pending, -winded; slow etc. 275.

Adv. long; for -a long time, — an age, — ages, — ever so long, — many a long day; long ago etc. (*in a past time*) 122; *longo intervallo.*

all the -day long, — year round; the livelong day, as the day is long, morning, noon and night; hour after hour, day after day, etc.; for good; permanently etc. *adj.*

111. Transientness. [Short duration.]—N. transientness etc. *adj.;* evanescence, impermanence, fugacity, transitoriness, volatility, caducity, mortality, span; flash in the pan, nine days' wonder, bubble, May-fly; spurt; temporary -arrangement, interregnum.

velocity etc. 274; suddenness etc. 113; changeableness etc. 149.

V. be -transient etc. *adj.;* flit, pass away, fly, gallop, vanish, fade, fleet, melt away, evaporate; pass away like a -cloud, — summer cloud, — shadow, — dream.

Adj. transi-ent, -tory, -tive; passing, evanescent, fleeting; flying etc. *v.;* fug-acious, -itive; shifting, slippery; spasmodic.

tempor-al, -ary; provis-ional, -ory; cursory, short-lived, ephemeral, deciduous; perishable, mortal, precarious; impermanent.

brief, quick, brisk; cometary, meteoric, extemporaneous, summary; pressed for time etc. (*haste*) 684; sudden, momentary etc. (*instantaneous*) 113.

Adv. temporarily etc. *adj.; pro tempore;* for - the moment, — a time; awhile, *en passant, in transitu;* in a short time; soon etc. (*early*) 132; briefly etc. *adj.;* at short notice; on the -point, — eve -of; *in articulo;* between cup and lip.

Phr. one's days are numbered; the time is up; her to-day and gone tomorrow; *non semper erit aestas; eheu! fugaces labuntur anni; sic transit gloria mundi.*

112. Perpetuity. [Endless duration.]—N. perpetuity, eternity, timelessness; everness, aye, sempiternity, immortality, athanasia; everlastingness etc. *adj.;* perpetuation; infinite duration.

V. last —, endure —, go on- for ever; have no end.

eternize, eternify, perpetuate, immortalize.

Adj. perpetual, eternal, eterne; everlasting, -living, -flowing; continual, constant, sempiternal; co-eternal; endless, unending; ceaseless, incessant, uninterrupted, indesinent, unceasing; interminable, having no end; unfading, evergreen, amaranthine; neverending, -dying, -fading; deathless, immortal, undying, imperishable.

Adv. perpetually etc. *adj.;* always, ever, evermore, aye; for -ever, — aye, — evermore, — ever and a day, —, ever and ever; in all ages, from age to age; without end; world —, time- without end; *in saecula saeculorum;* to the -end of time, — crack of doom, — 'last syllable of recorded time;' till doomsday; constantly etc. (*very frequently*) 136.

Phr. *esto perpetuum; labitur et labetur in omne volubilis aevum.*

113. Instantaneity. [Point of time.]—N. instantane-ity, -ousness; sudden-, abrupt-ness.

moment, instant, second, minute; twinkling, trice, flash, breath, crack, jiffy, *coup,* burst, flash of lightning, stroke of time.

epoch, time; time of -day, — night; hour, minute; very -minute etc., — time, — hours; present —, right —, true —, exact —, correct-time.

V. be -instantaneous etc. *adj.;* twinkle, flash.

Adj. instantaneous, momentary, extempore, sudden, instant, abrupt; subitaneous, hasty; quick as- thought,* — lightning, — a flash; rapid as electricity.

Adv. instantaneously etc. *adj.*; in — in less than-no time; *presto, subito, instanter,* suddenly, at a stroke, like- a shot, — greased lightning; in a trice, in a moment etc. *n.*; eftsoons, in the twinkling of - an eye, — a bed post; at one jump, in the same breath, *per saltum, uno saltu;* at — , all at- once; in one's tracks; plump, slap; 'at one fell swoop;' at the same -instant etc. *n.*; immediately etc. (*early*) 132; *ex tempore,* on the -spot, — spur of the moment, — .dot; just then; slap- dash etc. (*haste*) 684; before you could -turn round, — say -knife, — Jack Robinson.

Phr. touch and go; no sooner said than done.
*See note on 264.

114. Chronometry. [Estimation, measurement, and record of time.]—N. chrono-, horo-metry, -logy; date, epoch; style, era.

almanac, calendar, ephemeris; register, -try; chronicle, annals, journal, diary, chronogram.

[Instruments for the measurement of time] clock, watch; chrono-meter, -scope, -graph; repeater, alarum; time-keeper, -piece; dial, sun-dial, *gnomon, pendule,* horologe, pendulum, hourglass, water clock, clepsydra.

mean —, Greenwich —, solar —, sidereal —, local —, summer- time; daylight saving.

chrono-grapher, -loger, -logist; annalist.

V. fix —, mark- the time; date, register, chronicle; measure —, beat —, mark- time; bear date.

Adj. chrono-logical, -metrical, -grammatical; isochronal.

Adv. o'clock; *a.m., p.m.*

115. Anachronism. [False estimate of time.]—N. ana-, meta-, para-, prochronism; *prolepsis,* misdate; anticipation, antichronism.

disregard —, neglect —, oblivion- of time. intempestivity etc. 135.

V. mis-, ante-, post-, over-date; anticipate; take no note of time.

Adj. misdated etc. *v.*; undated; overdue; out of date; anachronous etc. *n.*

116. Priority.—N. priority, antecedence, anteriority, pre-existence, precedence etc. 62; precession etc. 280; precursor etc. 64; the past etc. 122; premises.

V. precede, come before; forerun; antecede, go before etc. (*lead*) 280; pre-exist; dawn; premise, presage etc. 511.

be -beforehand etc. (*be early*) 132; steal a march upon, anticipate, forestall; have —, gain- the start.

Adj. prior, previous; preced-ing, -ent; anterior, antecedent; pre-existing, -existent; foresighted; former, foregoing; afore —, before-, above-mentioned; aforesaid, said; introductory etc. (*precursory*) 64; pre-war.

Adv. before, prior to; earlier; previously etc. *adj.*; afore, ere, theretofore, erewhile, ere —, before- -then, — now; erewhile, already, yet, beforehand; aforetime; on the eve of, in anticipation.

117. Posteriority.—N. posteriority; succession, sequence; following etc. 281; subsequence,

supervention; futurity etc. 121; successor; sequel etc. 65; remainder, reversion.

V. follow etc. 281 —, come —, go- after; ensue, result; succeed, supervene; step into the shoes of.

Adj. subsequent, posterior, following, after, later, succeeding, postliminious, postnate; successive etc. 63; postdiluvial, -an; *puisné;* posthumous; post-war, future etc. 121.

Adv. subsequently, after, afterwards, since, later; at a -subsequent, — later- period; next, in the sequel, close upon, thereafter. thereupon, upon which, eftsoons; from that -time, — moment; after a -while, — time; in process of time.

postcenal, postcibal, postprandial, after-dinner.

118. The Present Time.—N. the present -time, — day, — moment, — juncture, — occasion; the times, existing time, time being; twentieth century; nonce, crisis, epoch, day, hour.

age, time of life.

Adj. present, actual, instant, current, latest, existing, that is.

Adv. at this -time, — moment etc. 113; at the -present time etc. *n.*; now, at present.

at this time of day, to-day, now-adays; already; even —, but —, just-now; on the present occasion; for the -time being, — nonce; *pro hâc vice;* on the -nail, — spot; on the spur of the -moment, — occasion.

until now; to -this, — the present day.

119. Different Time. [Time different from the present.]—N. different —, other- time.

[Indefinite time] aorist.

Adj. aoristic.

Adv. at that —, at which- -time, — moment, — instant; then, on that occasion, upon.

when; when-ever, -soever; upon which, on which occasion; at -another, — a different, — some other, — any - time; at various times; some —, one- -of these days, — fine morning, — day; sooner or later; some time or other; once upon a time, once.

120. Synchronism.—N. synchronism; coexistence, coincidence; simultaneousness etc. *adj.*; concurrence, concomitance, unity of time, interim.

[Having equal times] isochronism, syntony. contemporary, coetanian.

V. coexist, concur, accompany, go hand in hand, keep pace with; synchronize, isochronize.

Adj. synchron-ous, -al, -ical, -istical; simultaneous, coexisting, coincident, concomitant, concurrent; coev-al, -ous; contempora-ry, -neous; coetaneous; coterminous, coeternal; isochronous.

Adv. at the same time; simultaneously etc. *adj.*; together, in concert, during the same time; in the same breath; *pari passu;* in the interim.

at the -very moment etc. 113; just as, as soon as; meanwhile etc. (*while*) 106.

121. Futurity. [Prospective time.]—N. futurity, -ition; future, hereafter, time to come; approaching —, coming —, after- -time, — age, — days, — hours, — years, — ages, — life;

morrow, to-morrow, by and by; millennium, doomsday, day of judgment, crack of doom, remote future.

approach of time, advent, time drawing on, womb of time; destiny etc. 152; eventuality.

heritage, heirs, posterity, descendants.

prospect etc. (*expectation*) 507; foresight etc. 510.

V. look forwards; anticipate etc. (*expect*) 507, (*foresee*) 510; forestall etc. (*be early*) 132.

come −, draw- on; draw near; approach, await, threaten; impend etc. (*be destined*) 152.

Adj. future, to come; coming etc. (*impending*) 152; next, near; near −, close- at hand; eventual, ulterior; expectant, prospective, in prospect etc. (*expectation*) 507.

Adv. prospectively, hereafter, on the knees of the gods, in future; to-morrow, the day after to-morrow; in -course, − process, − the fulness- of time; eventually, ultimately, sooner or later; *proximo; paulo post futurum;* in after time; one of these days; after a -time, − while.

from this time; hence-forth, -forwards; thence; thence-forth, -forward; whereupon, upon which.

soon etc. (*early*) 132; on the -eve, − point, − brink- of; about to; close upon.

122. Preterition. [Retrospective time.]—N. preterition, priority etc. 116; the past, past time; days −, times- -of yore, − of old, − past, − gone by; bygone days, good old days; old −, ancient −, former -times; fore time; yesterdays; the olden −, good old- time; auld lang syne; eld.

antiquity, antiqueness, *status quo;* time immemorial; distance of time; remote -age, − time; ancient history; remote past; rust of antiquity; ancientness.

pale-ontology, -ography, -ology; palaetiology, archaeology; archaism, antiquarianism, mediaevalism, pre- Raphaelitism; retrospection, looking back, memory etc. 505.

laudator temporis acti; mediaevalist, pre-Raphaelite; antiqu-ary, -arian; archaeologist etc.; Oldbuck, Dryasdust.

ancestry etc. (*paternity*) 166.

V. be -past etc. *adj.;* have -expired etc. *adj.;* − run its course, − had its day; pass; pass −, go- - by, − away, − off; lapse, blow over.

look −, trace −, cast the eyes- back; exhume.

Adj. past, gone, gone by, over, passed away, bygone, foregone; elapsed, lapsed, preterlapsed, expired, no more, run out, blown over, that has been, whilom, extinct, never to return, exploded, forgotten, irrecoverable; obsolete etc. (*old*) 124; extinct as the dodo.

former, pristine, *quondam, ci-devant,* late; ancestral.

foregoing; last, latter; recent, overnight; past, preterite, preter-perfect, -pluperfect, past perfect.

looking back etc. *v.;* retro-spective, -active; archaelogical etc. *n.*

Adv. formerly; of -old, −yore; erst, whilom, erewhile, time was, ago, over; in -the olden time etc. *n.;* anciently, long -ago, − since; a long -while, − time- ago; years −, ages-ago; some time -ago, − since, − back.

yesterday, the day before yesterday; last -year, − season, − month etc.; *ultimo,* lately etc. (*newly*) 123.

retrospectively; ere −, before −, till- now; hitherto, heretofore; no longer; once, − upon a time; from time immemorial; in the memory of man; time out of mind; already, yet, up to this time; *ex post facto.*

Phr. time was; the time -has, − hath- been. **Whewell.*

123. Newness.—N. newness etc. *adj.;* neologism, neoterism; novelty, recency; immaturity; youth etc. 127; gloss of novelty.

innovation; renovation etc. (*restoration*) 660.

modernist, neologist, neoteric.

modernism, modernity; mushroom; latest fashion, *dernier cri.*

upstart, *parvenu, nouveau riche.*

V. renew etc. (*restore*) 660; modernize.

Adj. new, novel, recent, fresh, green; young etc. 127; evergreen; raw, immature; virgin; untried, -handseled, -used, -trodden, -beaten; fledgling. -

late, modern, neoteric; new-born, -fashioned, -fangled, -fledged; of yesterday; just out, brand −, span-new, up to date, topical; vernal, renovated; innovatory.

fresh as -a rose, − a daisy, − paint; spick and span.

Adv. newly etc. *adj.;* afresh, anew, lately, just now, only yesterday, the other day; latterly, of late.

not long −, a short time- ago.

124. Oldness.—N. oldness etc. *adj.;* age, antiquity; cobwebs of antiquity.

maturity, ripeness; decline, decay; senility etc. 128.

seniority, eldership, primogeniture.

archaism etc. (*the past*) 122; thing −, relic- of the past; megatherium.

tradition, prescription, custom, folklore, immemorial usage, common law.

V. be -old etc. *adj.;* have -had, − seen- its day; become -old etc. *adj.;* age, fade.

Adj. old, olden, ancient, antique; of long standing, time-honored, venerable; eld-er, -est; first-born.

prime; prim-itive, -eval, -igenous; primordi-al, -nate; aboriginal etc. (*beginning*) 66; diluvian, antediluvian; pre-historic; patriarchal, preadamite; paleocrystic; fossil, paleozoic, pre-glacial, ante-mundane; archaic, classic, mediaeval, pre-Raphaelite, ancestral, black-letter.

immemorial, traditional, prescriptive, customary, whereof the memory of man runneth not to the contrary; inveterate, rooted.

antiquated, of other times, rococo, of the old school, after-age, obsolete; fusty, moth-eaten; out of -date, − fashion; stale, old-fashioned, behind the -age, − times; exploded; gone out, − by; *passé,* outworn, run out; disused; senile etc. 128; time-worn; crumbling etc. (*deteriorated*) 659; second-hand.

old as -the hills, − Methuselah, − Adam, − history.

Adv. since the -world was made, − year one, − days of Methuselah.

125. Morning. [Noon.]—N. morning, morn, matins, forenoon, *a.m.,* prime, dawn, daybreak, daylight, sun-up, peep −, break- of day; aurora,

Eos; first blush −, prime- of the morning; twilight, crepuscule, sunrise, cockcrow.

spring; vernal equinox.

noon; mid-, noon-day; noontide, meridian, prime.

summer, midsummer; summer solstice.

Adj. matin, matutinal; vernal, aestival.

Adv. at -sunrise etc. *n.*; with the lark, when the morning dawns.

126. Evening. [Midnight.]—N. evening, eve; decline −, fall −, close- of day; eventide, evensong, vespers; candlelight; nightfall, curfew, dusk, twilight, blind man's holiday; eleventh hour; sun-set, -down; going down of the sun, cock-shut, dewy eve, gloaming, bed-time.

afternoon, *post meridiem, p.m.*

autumn; fall, − of the leaf; autumnal equinox, Indian summer, harvest-time.

midnight; dead −, witching time- of night; winter, − solstice.

Adj. vespertine, autumnal, nocturnal, wintry, brumal, hiemal.

127. Youth.—N. youth; juven- -ility, -escence; juniority; infancy; baby-, child-, boy-, girl-, youth-hood; *incunabula;* minority, immaturity, nonage, teens, tender age, bloom.

cradle, nursery, leading-strings, pupilage, puberty, *pucelage.*

prime −, flower −, spring-tide −, seedtime −, golden season of life; heyday of youth, school days; rising generation, younger generation.

Adj. young, youthful, juvenile, green, callow, budding, sappy, *puisné,* beardless, unfledged, unripe, under age, in one's teens; *in statu pupillari;* younger, junior.

128. Age.—N. age; oldness etc. *adj.;* old −, advanced- age; sen-ility, -escence; years, anility, grey hairs, climacteric, grand climacteric, declining years, decrepitude, hoary age, caducity, superannuation; second childhood, -ishness; dotage; vale of years, decline of life, 'sear and yellow leaf;' three-score years and ten; green old age, ripe old age; longevity; time of life.

seniority, eldership; elders etc. (*veteran*) 130; firstling; *doyen,* dean, father; primogeniture; nostology.

V. be -aged etc. *adj.;* grow −, get- old etc. *adj.;* age; decline, wane.

Adj. aged; old etc. 124; elderly, senile; matronly, anile; in years; ripe, mellow, run to seed, declining, waning, past one's prime; grey, -headed; hoar, -y; venerable, time-worn, anti-quated, *passé,* effete, doddering, decrepit, super-annuated; advanced in -life, − years; stricken in years; wrinkled, marked with the crow's foot; having one foot in the grave; doting etc. (*imbecile*) 499.

old-, eld-er, -est; senior; first-born.

turned of, years old; of a certain age, no chicken, old as Methuselah; gerontic; ancestral; patriarchal etc. (*ancient*) 124.

129. Infant.—N. infant, babe, baby; nurse-, suck-, year-, wean-ling; *papoose, bambino.*

child, bairn, little- one, − tot, − mite, chick, brat, chit, pickaninny, kid, urchin; bant-, brat-ling; elf.

youth, boy, lad, slip, sprig, stripling, youngster, cub, unlicked cub, younker, callant, whipster, whipper-snapper, schoolboy, hobbledehoy, hopeful, cadet, minor, master.

scion; sap-, seed-ling; tendril, olive branch, nestling, chicken, duckling; larva, caterpillar, chrysalis, cocoon; tadpole, whelp, cub, pullet, fry, callow; codlin, -g; *foetus,* calf, colt, pup, foal, kitten; lamb, -kin.

girl; lass, -ie; wench, miss, damsel, *demoiselle,* damozel; maid, -en; virgin; nymph; colleen; minx, baggage, school-girl; tomboy, flapper, hoyden.

Adj. infant-ine, -ile; puerile; boy-, girl-, child-, baby-, kitten-ish; baby; new-born, unfledged, new-fledged, callow.

in -the cradle, − swaddling clothes, − long clothes, − arms, − leading strings; at the breast; in one's teens; young etc. 127.

130. Veteran.—N. veteran, old man, seer, patriarch, greybeard, dugout, grand-father, -sire; grandam, beldam; gaffer, gammer; hag, crone; pantaloon; sexage-, octoge-, nonage-, cente-nar-ian; old stager; dotard etc. 501.

preadamite, Methuselah, Nestor, Rip van Winkle, old Parr; elders; forefathers etc. (*pater-*nity) 166.

131. Adolescence.—N. adolescence, pubes-cence, majority; adultness etc. *adj.;* manhood, virility, maturity; flower of age; prime −, meridian- of life.

man etc. 373; woman etc. 374; adult, no chicken.

V. come -of age, − to man's estate, − to years of discretion; attain majority, assume the *toga virilis;* have -cut one's eye-teeth, − sown one's wild oats, settle down.

Adj. adolescent, pubescent, of age; of -full, − ripe- age; out of one's teens, grown up, mature, full- blown, − grown, in one's prime, in full bloom, manly, virile, adult; womanly, matronly; marriageable, nubile.

132. Earliness.—N. earliness etc. *adj.;* mor-ning etc. 125.

punctuality; promptitude etc. (*activity*) 682; haste etc. (*velocity*) 274; suddenness etc. (*instan-*taneity) 113.

prematurity, precocity, precipitation, an-ticipation; prevenience, a stitch in time.

V. be -early etc. *adj.;* − beforehand etc. *adv.;* keep time, take time by the forelock, anticipate, forestall; have −, gain- the start; steal a march upon; gain time, draw on futurity; bespeak, secure, engage, pre-engage.

accelerate; expedite etc. (*quicken*) 274; make haste etc. (*hurry*) 684.

Adj. early, prime, timely, in time, punctual, forward; prompt etc. (*active*) 682; summary.

premature, precipitate, precocious; pre-venient, anticipatory; rathe.

sudden etc. (*instantaneous*) 113; unexpected etc. 508; impending, imminent; near, − at hand; immediate.

Adv. early, soon, anon, betimes, rathe; eft, - soons; ere −, before- long; punctually etc. *adj.;* to the minute; in time; in -good, − military, − pudding, − due- time; time enough.

beforehand; prematurely etc. *adj.;* precipitately etc. (*hastily*) 684; too soon; before -its, − one's- time; in anticipation; unexpectedly etc. 508.

suddenly etc. (*instantaneously*) 113; before one can say 'Jack Robinson,' at short notice, extempore; on the spur of the -moment, − occasion; at once; on the -spot, − instant; at sight; off −, out of- hand; *à vue d'oeil;* straight, - way, -forth; forthwith, incontinently, summarily, instanter, immediately, briefly, shortly, quickly, speedily, apace, before the ink is dry, almost immediately, presently, at the first opportunity, in no long time, by and by, in a while, directly.

Phr. touch and go, no sooner said than done.

133. Lateness.—N. lateness etc. *adj.;* tardiness etc. (*slowness*) 275.

de-lay, -lation; cunctation, procrastination; detention; deferring etc. *v.;* filibuster, postponement, adjournment, prorogation, retardation, respite, reprieve, stay; protraction, prolongation, moratorium; contango; demurrage; remand; Fabian policy, *médecine expectante,* chancery suit; leeway; high time.

V. be -late etc. *adj.;* tarry, wait, stay, bide, take time; dawdle etc. (*be inactive*) 683; linger, loiter, saunter, lag behind; bide −, take- one's time; hang -about, −. around, − back, − in the balance; gain time; hang fire; stand −, lie-over.

put off, defer, delay, lay over, suspend; shift −, stave- off; waive, retard, remand, postpone, adjourn; procrastinate; dally; prolong, protract; spin −, draw −, lengthen- out; prorogue; keep back; tide over; push −, drive- to the last; let the matter stand over; reserve etc. (*store*) 636; temporize; consult one's pillow, sleep upon it.

shelve, table, lay on the table.

lose an opportunity etc. 135; be kept waiting, dance attendance; kick −, cool- one's heels; *faire antichambre;* wait impatiently; await etc. (*expect*) 507; sit up, − at night.

Adj. late, tardy, slow, behindhand, belated, postliminious, posthumous, backward, unpunctual; dilatory etc. (*slow*), overdue 275; delayed etc. *v.;* in abeyance.

Adv. late; late-, back-ward; late in the day; at - sunset, − the eleventh hour, − length, − last, − long; ultimately; after −, behind- time; too late; too late for etc. 135.

slowly, leisurely, deliberately, at one's leisure; *ex post facto; sine die.*

Phr. *nonum prematur in annum.*

134. Occasion.—N. occasion, opportunity, opening, room, scope, field; suitable −, proper- - time, − season; high time; opportuneness etc. *adj.;* tempestivity.

crisis, turn, juncture, emergency, conjuncture; turning point; given time.

nick of time; golden −, well-timed −, fine −, favorable- opportunity; clear stage, fair field; *mollia tempora; fata Morgana;* spare time etc. (*leisure*) 685.

V. seize etc. (*take*) 789 −, use etc. 677 −, give etc. 784- an -opportunity, − occasion; improve the occasion.

suit the occasion etc. (*be expedient*) 646.

strike the iron while it is hot, *battre le fer sur l'enclume,* make hay while the sun shines, take time by the forelock, *prendre la balle au bond.*

Adj. opportune, timely, well-timed, timeous, timeful, seasonable.

providential, lucky, fortunate, happy, favorable, propitious, auspicious, critical; suitable etc. 23; *obiter dicta.*

Adv. opportunely etc. *adj. ;* in -proper, − due- -time, − course, − season; for the nonce; in the - nick, − fulness- of time; all in good time; just in time, at the eleventh hour, now or never.

by the -way, − by; *en passant, à propos; pro - re natâ,* − *hac vice; par parenthèse,* parenthetically, by way of parenthesis; while-speaking of, − on this subject; *ex tempore;* on the spur of the -moment, − occasion; on the spot etc. (*early*) 132.

Phr. *carpe diem; occasionem cognosce;* one's hour is come, the time is up; that reminds me.

135. Intempestivity.—N. intempestivity; unseasonableness; unsuitable −, improper-time; unreasonableness etc. *adj.;* evil hour; *contretemps;* intrusion; anachronism etc. 115.

V. be -ill timed etc. *adj.;* mistime, intrude, come amiss, break in upon; have other fish to fry; be -busy, − engaged, − tied up, − occupied.

lose −, throw away −, waste −, neglect etc. 460- an opportunity; allow −, suffer- the - opportunity, − occasion- to -pass, − slip, − go by, − escape, − lapse; waste time etc. (*be inactive*) 683; let slip through the fingers, lock the stable door when the steed is stolen.

Adj. ill-, mis-timed; untimely, intrusive, unseasonable; out of -date, − season; inopportune, timeless, untoward, *mal à propos,* unlucky, inauspicious, unpropitious, unfortunate, unfavorable; unsuited etc. 24; inexpedient etc. 647.

unpunctual etc. (*late*) 133; too late for; premature etc. (*early*) 132; too soon for; wise after the event.

Adv. inopportunely etc. *adj.;* as ill luck would have it, in an evil hour, the time having gone by, a day after the fair.

Phr. after meat mustard, after death the doctor.

136. Frequency.—N. frequency, oftness; repetition, etc. 104.

V. recur etc. 104; do nothing but; keep, − on.

Adj. frequent, many times, not rare, thickcoming, incessant, perpetual, continual, constant, recurrent, repeated etc. 104; habitual etc. 613; hourly, etc. 138.

Adv. often, often to be met with, oft; oft-, often-times; frequently; repeatedly etc. 104; unseldom, not unfrequently; in -quick, − rapid-succession; many a time and oft; daily, hourly etc.; every -day, − hour, − moment etc.

perpetually, continually, constantly, incessantly, without ceasing, at all times, daily and hourly, night and day, day and night, day after day, morning, noon and night, ever and anon.

most often; commonly etc. (*habitually*) 613.

sometimes, occasionally, at times, now and then, from time to time, there being times when, *toties quoties*, often enough, again and again etc. 104.

137. Infrequency. —N.

infrequency, infrequence, rareness, rarity; fewness etc. 103; seldomness, uncommonness.

V. be -rare etc. *adj.*

Adj. un-, in-frequent; uncommon, sporadic, rare, − as a blue diamond; few etc. 103; scarce; almost unheard of, unprecedented, which has not occurred within the memory of the oldest inhabitant, not within one's previous experience.

Adv. seldom, rarely, scarcely, hardly; not often, unfrequently, infrequently, unoften; scarcely −, hardly- ever; once in a blue moon.

once; once -for all, − in a way; *pro hac vice;* like angels' visits, few and far between.

138. Regularity of recurrence. Periodicity. —N.

periodicity, intermittence; beat; oscillation etc. 314; pulse, pulsation; rhythm; alternation, -nateness, -nativeness, -nity.

bout, round, revolution, rotation, turn.

anniversary, birthday, jubilee, centenary, bi-, ter-centenary.

[Regularity of return] rota, cycle, period, stated time, routine; days of the week; Sunday, Monday etc.; months of the year; January etc.; feast, fast, saint's day etc.; Christmas, Easter, New Year's Day etc. 998; quarter-, Lady-, Midsummer-, Michaelmas-day; May Day, the King's Birthday; leap year, seasons.

punctuality, regularity, steadiness.

V. recur in regular -order, − succession; return, revolve, rotate; come -again, − in its turn; come round, − again; beat, pulsate; alternate; intermit..

Adj. periodic, -al; serial, recurrent, cyclic-, -al, rhythmic-, -al, even; recurring etc. *V.;* inter-, remittent; alternate, every other.

hourly; diurnal, daily; quotidian, tertian, weekly; hebdomad-al, -ary; bi-weekly, fortnightly; monthly, menstrual, catamenial; yearly, annual; biennial, triennial, etc.; bissextile; centennial, secular; paschal, lenten, etc.

regular, steady, punctual, constant, methodical, regular as clockwork.

Adv. periodically etc. *adj.;* at -regular intervals, − stated times; at -fixed, − established-periods; punctually etc. *adj.; de die in diem;* from day to day, day by day.

by turns, in -turn, − rotation; alternately, every other day, off and on, ride and tie, round and round.

139. Irregularity of recurrence. —N.

irregularity, uncertainty, unpunctuality; fitfulness etc. *adj.*

Adj. irregular, uneven, uncertain, unpunctual, capricious, erratic, desultory, fitful, flickering; rambling, rhapsodical; spasmodic, unsystematic, unequal, variable, halting.

Adv. irregularly etc. *adj.;* by fits and starts etc. (*discontinuously*) 70..

140. Change. [Difference at different times.]—N.

change, alteration, mutation, permutation, variation, modification, modulation, inflexion, mood, qualification, innovation, *metastasis,* deviation, shift, turn; diversion; break.

transformation, transfiguration; metamorphosis; metabolism; transmutation; trans-substantiation; metagenesis, transanimation, transmigration, metempsychosis; version, metathesis, transmogrification; catalysis; *avatar;* alterative.

conversion etc. (*gradual change*) 144; revolution etc. (*sudden or radical change*) 146; inversion etc. (*reversal*) 218; displacement etc. 185; transference etc. 270.

changeableness etc. 149; tergiversation etc. (*change of mind*) 607.

V. change, alter, vary, wax and wane; modulate, diversify, qualify, tamper with; turn, shift, veer, jibe, tack, chop, shuffle, swerve, dodge, warp, deviate, turn aside, evert, intervert; pass to, take a turn, turn the corner, resume.

work a change, modify, vamp, revamp, super-induce; trans-form, −mute, -ume, -figure etc. *n.;* metamorphose, ring the changes; convert, resolve; revolutionize; chop and change; patch, re-shape.

innovate, introduce new blood, shuffle the cards, spin the wheel; give a -turn, − color- to; influence, turn the scale; shift the scene, turn over a new leaf.

recast etc. 146; reverse etc. 218; disturb etc. 61; convert into etc. 144.

Adj. changed etc. *v.;* new-fangled; changeable etc. 149; transitional; modifiable; alterative.

Adv. *mutatis mutandis.*

Int. *quantum mutatus!*

Phr. 'a change came o'er the spirit of my dream;' *nous avons changé tout cela; tempora mutantur et nos mutamur in illis; non sum qualis eram.*

141. Permanence. [Absence of change.]—N.

stability etc. 150; quiescence etc. 265; obstinacy etc. 606.

permanence, -cy, persistence, fixity, fixity of purpose, endurance, durability; standing, *status quo;* maintenance, preservation, conservation; conservatism; *laissez-faire;* law of the Medes and Persians; standing dish.

V. let -alone, − be; persist, remain, stay, tarry, rest; hold, − on; last, endure, bide, abide, aby, dwell, maintain, keep; stand, − still, − fast; subsist, live, outlive, survive; hold −, keep- one's ground, − footing; hold good.

Adj. stable etc. 150; persisting etc. *v.;* permanent; established, fixed; durable; unchanged etc. (change etc. 140); unrenewed; intact, inviolate; persistent; monotonous, uncheckered; unfailing.

un-destroyed, -repealed, -suppressed; conservative, *qualis ab incepto;* prescriptive etc. (*old*) 124; stationary etc. 265.

Adv. *in statu quo;* for good, finally; at a stand, -still; *uti possidetis;* without a shadow of turning.

Phr. as you were!; *j'y suis j'y reste; esto perpetua; nolumus leges Angliae mutari;* let sleeping dogs lie.

142. Cessation. [Change from action to

rest.]—N. cessation, discontinuance, desistance, desinence.

inter-, re-mission; sus-pense, -pension, interruption, hitch; hartal; stop; stopping etc. *v.;* closure, stoppage, halt; arrival etc. 292.

pause, rest, lull, respite, truce, armistice, drop; interregnum, abeyance.

closure etc. 261.

dead -stop, — stand, — lock; checkmate; comma, colon, semicolon, period, full stop; end etc. 67; death etc. 360; *caesura.*

V. cease, discontinue, desist, stay; break —, leave- off; hold, stop, pull up, stall, stop short, check; stick, deadlock, hand fire; halt; pause, rest.

have done with, give over, surcease, shut up shop; give up etc. (*relinquish*) 624.

hold —, stay- one's hand; rest on one's oars, repose on one's laurels.

come to a -stand, — standstill, — dead lock, — full stop; arrive etc. 292; go out, die away, peter out; wear -away, — off; pass away etc. (*be past*) 122; be at an end.

intromit, interrupt, suspend, interpel; inter-, re-mit; put -an end, — a stop, — a period- to; bring to a stand, -still; stop, cut out, cut short, arrest, avast; stem the -tide, — torrent; pull the check string; switch off.

Int. halt! hold! stop! enough! avast! have done! a truce to! soft! leave off! shut up! give over! chuck it!

143. Continuance in action.—N. continu-ance, -ation; run; extension, prolongation; maintenance, perpetuation; persistence etc. (*perseverance*) 604a; repetition etc. 104.

V. continue, persist; go —, jog —, keep —, carry —, run — hold- on; abide, keep, pursue, stick to; endure; take —, maintain- its course; keep up.

sustain, uphold, hold up, keep on foot; follow up, perpetuate. prolong; maintain; preserve etc. 604a; harp upon etc. (*repeat*)104.

keep -going, — alive, — at it, — the pot boiling, — the ball rolling, — up the ball; plod-, plug-along; slog on; die in harness; hold on —, pursue- the even tenor of one's way.

let be; *stare super antiquas vias; quieta non movere;* let things take their course.

Adj. continuing etc. *v.;* uninterrupted, unintermitting, unremitting, unvarying, unshifting; unreversed, unstopped, unrevoked, unvaried; sustained; undying etc. (*perpetual*) 112; inconvertible.

follow-up.

Int. carry on! right away!

Phr. *vestigia nulla retrorsum, labitur et labetur.*

144. Conversion. [Gradual change to something different.]—N. conversion, reduction, transmutation, transformation, development, resolution, assimilation; assumption; naturalization.

chemistry, alchemy; progress, growth, lapse, flux.

passage; transit, -ion; transmigration, shifting etc. *v.;* conjugation; convertibility.

crucible, alembic, caldron, retort, test tube etc.

convert, neophyte, proselyte, pervert, renegade, deserter, apostate, turncoat.

V. be converted into; become, get, wax; come —, turn- -to, — into; turn out, lapse, shift; run —, fall —, pass —, slide —, glide —, grow —, ripen —, open —, resolve itself —, settle —, merge- into; melt, grow, come round to, mature, mellow; assume the -form, — shape, — state, — nature, — character- of; illapse; assume a new phase, undergo a change.

convert —, resolve- into; make, render; mold, form etc. 240; remodel, new model, refound, reform, reorganize; assimilate —, bring —, reduce- to; transform.

Adj. converted into etc. *v.;* convertible, resolvable into; transitional; naturalized.

Adv. gradually etc. (*slowly*) 275; *in transitu* etc. (*transference*) 270.

145. Reversion.—N. reversion, return; revulsion; reaction.

turning point, turn of the tide; *status quo ante bellum;* calm before a storm.

alternation etc. (*periodicity*) 138; inversion etc. 219; recoil etc. 277; regression etc. 283; restoration etc. 660; relapse etc. 661; vicinism, atavism, throwback.

V. revert, turn back, return; relapse etc. 661; recoil etc. 277; retreat etc. 283; restore etc. 660; undo, unmake; turn the -tide, — scale; escheat.

Adj. reverting etc. *v.;* revulsive, reactionary.

Adv. *à rebours,* wrong side out.

146. Revolution. [Sudden or violent change.]—N. revolution, *bouleversement,* subversion. break up; destruction etc. 162; sudden —, radical —, sweeping —, organic- change; clean sweep, *coup d'état,* overthrow, *débâcle;* counter-revolution, rebellion etc. 742.

transilience, jump, leap, plunge, jerk, start; explosion; spasm, convulsion, throe, revulsion; storm, earthquake, eruption, upheaval, cataclysm.

legerdemain etc. (*trick*) 545.

V. revolutionize; new model, remodel, recast; strike out something new, break with the past; change the face of, unsex; revert etc. 742.

Adj. unrecognizable.

Revolutionary, Bolshevik etc. 742.

147. Substitution. [Change of one thing for another.]—N. substitution, subrogation, commutation; supplanting etc. *v.;* supersession, metonymy etc. (*figure of speech*) 521.

[Thing substituted.] substitute, *succedaneum,* make-shift, temporary expedient, shift, *pis aller,* stop-gap, jury-mast, *locum tenens,* warming-pan, dummy, goat, scape-goat; double; change-ling; *quid pro quo,* alternative; remount; representative etc. (*deputy*) 759; palimpsest.

price, purchase-money, consideration, equivalent.

V. substitute, put in the place of, change for; make way for, give place to; supply —, take- the -place of; supplant, supersede, replace, cut out, serve as a substitute; step into —, stand in- the shoes of; make a shift —, put up- with; borrow of Peter to pay Paul; commute, redeem, compound for.

Adj. substituted etc. *v.;* vicarious, subdititious; substitutional.

Adv. instead; in -place, − lieu, − the stead, − the room- of; *faute de mieux.*

148. Interchange. [Double or mutual change.]—N. inter-, ex-change; com-, per-, intermutation; reciprocation, transposal, transposition, shuffling; reciprocity, castling [at chess]; hocus-pocus.

interchange-ableness, -ability.

barter etc. 794; tit for tat etc. (*retaliation*) 718; cross fire, battledore and shuttlecock; *quid pro quo.*

V. inter-, ex-, counter-change; bandy, transpose, shuffle, change hands, swap, trade, permute, reciprocate, commute; give and take, return the compliment; play at -puss in the corner, − battledore and shuttlecock; retaliate etc. 718; barter etc. 794.

Adj. interchanged etc. *v.;* reciprocal, mutual, commutative, interchanged etc. *v.;* interchangeable, intercurrent.

Adv. in exchange, *vice versâ, mutatis mutandis,* backwards and forwards, by turns, turn and turn about, turn about; each −, every one- in his turn.

149. Changeableness.—N. changeableness etc. *adj.;* mutability, inconstancy; versatility, mobility; instability, unstable equilibrium; vacillation etc. (*irresolution*) 605; fluctuation, vicissitude; alternation etc. (*oscillation*) 314.

restlessness etc. *adj.;* fidgets, disquiet; dis-, inquietude; unrest; agitation etc. 315.

moon, Proteus, chameleon, kaleidoscope, quicksilver, shifting sands, weathercock, harlequin, Cynthia of the minute, April showers; wheel of Fortune; transientness etc. 111.

V. fluctuate, vary, waver, flounder, flicker, flitter, flit, flutter, shift, shuffle, shake, totter, tremble, vacillate, wamble, turn and turn about, ring the changes; sway −, shift- to and fro; change and change about; oscillate etc. 314; vibrate −, oscillate- between two extremes; alternate; have as many phases as the moon.

Adj. change-able, -ful; changing etc. 140; mutable, variable, checkered, ever changing, kaleidoscopic, prote-an, -iform; versatile.

unstaid, inconstant; un-steady, -stable, -fixed, -settled; fluctuating etc. *v.;* restless; mercurial; agitated etc. 315; erratic, fickle; irresolute etc. 605; capricious etc. 608; touch-and-go; inconsonant, fitful, spasmodic; vibratory; afloat; alternating; alterable, plastic, mobile; fleeting, transient etc. 111.

Adv. see-saw etc. (*oscillation*) 314; off and on.

150. Stability.—N. stability; immutability etc. *adj.;* unchangeableness etc. *adj.;* constancy; stable equilibrium, immobility, soundness, vitality, stabiliment, stabilization, stiffness, ankylosis, solidity, *aplomb.*

establishment, fixture; rock, pillar, tower, foundation, leopard's spots, Ethiopian's skin, law of the Medes and Persians.

stabilimeter, stabilizator.

permanence etc. 141; obstinacy etc. 606.

V. be -firm etc. *adj.;* stick fast; stand −, keep −, remain- firm; weather the storm.

settle, establish, stablish, ascertain, fix, set, stabilitate, stabilize; retain, stet, keep hold; make -good, − sure; fasten etc. (*join*) 43; set on its legs, float; perpetuate.

settle down; strike −, take- root; take up one's abode etc. 184; build one's house on a rock.

Adj. unchangeable, immutable; unalter-ed, -able; not to be changed; constant; permanent etc. 141; invariable, undeviating; stable, durable; perennial etc. (*diuturnal*) 110.

fixed, steadfast, firm, fast, steady, balanced; confirmed, valid, fiducial, immovable, irremovable, riveted, rooted; settled, established etc. *v.;* vested; incontrovertible, stereotyped, indeclinable.

tethered, anchored, moored, at anchor, on a rock, firm as a rock; firmly -seated, − established etc. *v.;* deep-rooted, ineradicable; inveterate; obstinate etc. 606.

transfixed, stuck fast, aground, high and dry, stranded.

indefeasible, irretrievable, intransmutable, incommutable, irresoluble, irrevocable, irreversible, reverseless, inextinguishable, irreducible; indissol-uble, -vable; indestructible, undying, imperishable, indelible, indeciduous; insusceptible, − of change.

Int. *stet.*

151. Eventuality.—N. eventuality, event, occurrence, incident, affair, transaction, proceeding, fact; matter of −, naked- fact; phenomenon; advent.

business, concern; circumstance, particular, casualty, happening, accident, adventure, passage, crisis, pass, emergency, contingency, consequence etc. 154.

the world, life, things, doings, affairs, matters; things −, affairs- in general; the times, state of affairs, order of the day; course −, tide −, stream −, current −, run −, march- of -things, − events; ups and downs of life; chapter of accidents etc. (*chance*) 156; situation etc. (*circumstances*) 8.

V. happen, occur; take -place, − effect; come, become of; come -off, − about, − round, − into existence, − forth, − to pass, − on; pass, present itself; fall; fall −, turn- out; run, be on foot, fall in; be-fall, -tide, -chance; prove, eventuate, draw on; turn −, crop −, spring −, cast- up; super-, sur-vene; issue, emanate, arrive, ensue, arise, start, hold, take its course; pass off etc. (*be past*) 122.

meet with; experience; fall to the lot of; be one's -chance, − fortune, − lot; find; encounter, undergo; pass −, go- through; endure etc. (*feel*) 821.

Adj. happening etc. *v.;* going on, doing, current; in the wind, afloat; on -foot, − the *tapis;* at issue, in question; incidental.

eventful, momentous, signal; stirring, bustling, full of incident.

Adv. eventually, ultimately, in -the event of, − case; in the course of things; in the -natural, − ordinary- course of things; as -things, − times- go; as the world -goes, − wags; as the -tree falls, − cat jumps; as it may -turn out, − happen.

Phr. the plot thickens.

152. Destiny.—N. destiny etc. (*necessity*) 601; hereafter, future −, post- existence; future state, next world, world to come, after life; futurity etc. 121; everlasting -life, − death; prospect etc. (*expectation*) 507.

V. impend; hang −, lie −, hover- over; threaten, loom, await, come on, approach, stare one in the face; fore-, pre-ordain; predestine, doom, foredoom, foreshadow, have in store for.

Adj. impending etc. *v.*; destined; about to -be, − happen; coming, in store, to come, going to happen, instant, at hand, near; near −, close- at hand; overhanging, hanging over one's head, imminent; brewing, preparing, forthcoming; in the wind, on the cards, in reserve; that -will, − is to-be; in prospect etc. (*expected*) 507; looming in the -distance, − horizon, − future; unborn, in embryo; in the womb of -time; − futurity; on the knees of the gods; pregnant etc. (*producing*) 161.

Adv. in -time, − the long run; all in good time; eventually etc. 151; whatever may happen etc. (*certainly*) 474; as -chance etc. 156- would have it.

153. Cause. [Constant antecedent.]—N. cause, origin, source, principle, element; occasioner, prime mover, engine, turbine, motor, *primum mobile; vera causa;* author etc. (*producer*) 164; main-spring, agent; dynamo, generator, battery (electric); leaven; groundwork, foundation etc. (*support*) 215.

spring, fountain, well, font; fountain −, spring- head; *fons et origo,* genesis; descent etc. (*paternity*) 166; remote cause; influence.

pivot, hinge, turning-point, lever; key; kernel, core; proximate cause, *causa causans;* last straw that breaks the camel's back.

ground; reason, − why; why and wherefore, rationale, occasion, derivation; final cause etc. (*intention*) 620; *le dessous des cartes;* undercurrents.

rudiment, egg, germ, embryo, fetus, bud, root, *radix,* radical, etymon, nucleus, seed, stem, stalk, stock, *stirps,* trunk, tap-root; latent organism.

nest, cradle, nursery, womb, *nidus,* birth-, breeding-place, hot-bed.

caus-ality, -ation; origination; production etc. 161.

V. be the -cause etc. *n.*- of; originate; give - origin, − rise, − occasion- to; cause, occasion, sow the seeds of, kindle, suscitate; bring -on, − to pass, − about; produce; create etc. 161; set - up, − afloat, − on foot; found, broach, institute, lay the foundation of, inaugurate; lie at the root of.

procure, induce, draw down, open the door to, superinduce, evoke, entail, operate; elicit, provoke.

conduce to etc. (*tend to*) 176; contribute; promote; have a -hand in, − finger in- the pie; determine, decide, turn the scale, give the casting vote; have a common origin; derive its origin etc. (*effect*) 154.

Adj. caused etc. *v.*; causal, original; prim-ary, - itive, -ordial; aboriginal; radical; inceptive, embry-onic, -otic; *in -embryo, − ovo;* seminal, germinal; formative, productive etc. 168; at the bottom of; connate, having a common origin.

Adv. because etc. 155; behind the scenes.

154. Effect. [Constant sequent.]—N. effect,

consequence, sequela; derivative, -tion; result; result-ant, -ance; upshot, issue, *dénouement;* outcome; termination, end etc. 67; development, outgrowth, fruit, crop, harvest, product, bud, blossom, florescence, ear.

production, produce, product, finished product, work, handiwork, fabric, performance; creature, creation; offspring, -shoot; first-fruits, - lings; *prémices.*

V. be the -effect etc. *n.*- of; be -due, − owing-to; originate -in, − from; rise −, arise −, take its rise −, spring −, proceed −, emanate −, come −, grow −, bud −, sprout −, germinate −, issue −, flow −, result −, follow −, derive its origin −, accrue- from; come -to, − of, − out of; depend −, hand −, hinge −, turn- upon.

take the consequences, sow the wind and reap the whirlwind.

Adj. owing to; resulting from etc. *v.*; resultant; derivable from; due to; caused etc. by, 153; dependent upon; derived −, evolved- from; derivative; hereditary.

Adv. of course, it follows that, naturally, consequently; as a −, in- consequence; through all, all along of, necessarily, eventually.

Phr. *cela va sans dire,* thereby hangs a tale.

155. Attribution. [Assignment of cause.]—N. attribution, theory, etiology, ascription, reference to, rationale; accounting for etc. *v.*; imputation, derivation from.

fil-, affil-iation; pedigree etc. (*paternity*) 166. explanation etc. (*interpretation*) 522; reason why etc. (*cause*) 153.

V. attribute −, ascribe −, impute −, refer −, lay −, point −, trace −, bring home- to; put −, set- down- to; charge −, ground- on; invest with, assign as cause, charge with, blame, lay at the door of, father upon; saddle with; affiliate; account for, derive from, point out the -reason etc. 153; theorize; tell how it comes; put the saddle on the right horse.

Adj. attributed etc. *v.*; attributable etc. *v.*; refer-able, -rible; due to, derivable from; owing to etc. (*effect*) 154; putative.

Adv. hence, thence, therefore, for, since, on account of, because, owing to; on that account; from -this, − that- cause; thanks to, forasmuch as; whence, *propter hoc.*

why? wherefore? whence? how -comes, − is, − happens- it? how does it happen?

in -some, − some such- way; somehow, − or other.

Phr. that is why; *hinc illae lachrymae; cherchez la femme.*

156. Chance.† [Absence of assignable cause.]—N. chance, indetermination, accident, fortune, hazard, hap, haphazard, chance-medley, random, luck, *raccroc,* casualty, fortuity, contingence, coincidence, adventure, hit; fate etc. (*necessity*) 601; equal chance; lottery, raffle, tombola, sweepstake; toss up etc. 621; turn of the - table, − cards; hazard of the die, chapter of accidents; cast −, throw- of the dice; heads or tails, wheel of Fortune, whirligig of chance; *sortes; − Virgilianae.*

probability, possibility, contingency, odds, long odds, run of luck; main- chance.

theory of -probabilities, − chances; book-making; assurance; speculation, gamble, gaming etc. 621.

V. chance, hap, turn up; fall to one's lot; be one's -fate etc. 601; stumble on, light −, blunder −, hit- upon; take one's chance etc. 621.

Adj. casual, fortuitous, accidental, haphazard, random, stray, adventitious, adventive, causeless, incidental. contingent, uncaused, undetermined, indeterminate; possible etc. 470; unintentional etc. 621.

Adv. by -chance, − accident; casually; perchance etc. (*possibly*) 470; for aught one knows; as -good, − bad, − ill-luck etc. *n.*- would have it; as it may -be, − chance, − turn·up, − happen; as the case may be.

†The word *Chance* has two distinct meanings: the first, the absence of assignable *cause*, as above; and the second, the absence of *design*—for the latter see 621.

157. Power.—N. power; poten-cy, -tiality; puissance, might, force; energy etc. 171; dint; right -hand, − arm; ascendency, sway, control; pre-potency, -pollence; almightiness, omnipotence; authority etc. 737; strength etc. 159.

ability; ableness etc. *adj.;* competency; efficiency, -cacy; validity, cogency; enablement; vantage ground; influence etc. 175; horse power; dynamometer.

pressure; elasticity; gravity; attraction, repulsion; *vis -inertiae,* − *mortua,* − *viva;* friction, suction.

electricity, magnetism, galvanism, voltaic electricity, voltaism, electro-magnetism, electro-statics, electrification; electric − current, − power; potential −, dynamic −, kinetic −, electrical −, chemical −, atomic- energe; electric field, circuit, charge, discharge, shock, polarity, pole; amperage, voltage, wattage, resistance, conduction, induction, electrification, electrolysis.

electronics, radionics, electron physics, electrophysics, avionics, radiometry, photoelectronics; electron, negatron, positron, photoelectron, thermion, barytron; electronic effect; electron emission; electron −, cathode −, anode −, positive − ray; electron − current, − flow − stream, − beam, − volt; electronic circuit; conductance; electron tube, tube, vacuum tube, photoelectric tube, call; transistor.

capability, capacity; *quid valeant humeri quid ferre recusent;* faculty, quality, attribute, endowment, virtue, gift, property, qualification, susceptibility.

V. be -powerful etc. *adj.;* gain -power etc. *n.* belong −, pertain- to; lie −, be- in one's power; can.

electrify, generate, magnetize.

give −, confer −, exercise- power etc. *n.;* empower, enable, invest; in-, en-due; endow, arm; strengthen etc. 159; compel etc. 744.

Adj. powerful, puissant; potent, -ial; capable, able; equal −, up- to; cogent, valid; effect-ive, -ual; efficient, efficacious, adequate, competent; multi-, pleni-, omni-, armi- potent; mighty, ascendent; almighty.

electric, electrical, electronic etc.

forcible etc. *adj.* (*energetic*) 171; influential etc. 175; productive etc. 168.

Adv. powerfully etc. *adj.;* by -virtue, − dint-of.

158. Impotence.—N. impotence; in-, dis-ability; disablement, impuissance, imbecility, caducity; incapa-city, -bility; inapt-, inept-itude; indocility; invalidity, inefficiency, incompetence, disqualification.

telum imbelle, brutum fulmen, blank cartridge, flash in the pan, *vox et praeterea nihil,* dead letter, bit of waste paper, dummy; scrap of paper.

inefficacy etc. (*inutility*) 645; failure etc. 732.

helplessness etc. *adj.;* prostration, paralysis, palsy, ataxia, apoplexy, syncope, sideration, *deliquium,* collapse, exhaustion, softening of the brain, e nasculation, inanition, senility etc. 128; castrato, eunuch.

cripple, old woman, muff, molly-coddle, milk-sop.

V. be -impotent etc. *adj.;* not have a leg to stand on.

vouloir -rompre l'anguille au genou, − *prendre la lune avec les dents.*

collapse, faint, swoon, fall into a swoon, drop; go by the board; end in smoke etc. (*fail*) 732.

render -powerless etc. *adj.;* deprive of power; decontrol; dis-able, -enable; disarm, incapacitate, disqualify, unfit, invalidate, undermine, deaden, cramp, tie the hands; double up, prostrate, paralyze, muzzle, cripple, be-cripple, maim, lame, hamstring, draw the teeth of; throttle, strangle, *garrotte;* ratten, silence, sprain, clip the wings of, render *hors de combat,* spike the guns; take the wind out of one's sails, scotch the snake, put a spoke in one's wheel; break the -neck, − back; un-hinge, -fit; put out of gear.

unman, unnerve, devitalize, attenuate, enervate; emasculate, spay, caponize, castrate, geld; effeminize.

shatter, exhaust; weaken etc. 160.

Adj. powerless, impotent, unable, incapable, incompetent; ineff-icient, -ective; inept; un-fit, -fitted; un-, dis-qualified; unendowed; in-, un-apt; crippled, decrepit; disabled etc. *v.;* armless.

harmless, unarmed, weaponless, defenceless, *sine ictu,* unfortified, indefensible, vincible, pregnable, untenable.

para-lytic, -lyzed; palsied, imbecile; nerve-, sinew-, marrow-, pith-, lust-less; emasculate, disjointed, out of -joint, − gear; un-nerved, -hinged; water-logged, on one's beam ends, rudderless; laid on one's back; done up, dead beat, exhausted, shattered, demoralized; gravelled etc. (*in difficulty*) 704; helpless, unfriended, fatherless; without a leg to stand on, *hors de combat,* laid on the shelf.

null and void, nugatory, imoperative, good for nothing; dud; invertebrate; ineffectual etc. (*failing*) 732; inadequate etc. 640; inefficacious etc. (*useless*) 645.

159. Strength. (Degree of power.]—N. strength; power etc. 157; energy etc. 171; vigor, force; main −, physical −, brute- force; spring, elasticity, tone, tension, tonicity.

stoutness etc. *adj.;* lustihood, stamina, nerve,

muscle, sinew, thews and sinews, *physique;* pith, - iness; virility, vitality.

athlet-ics, -icism; gymnastics, feats of strength.

adamant, steel, iron, oak, heart of oak; iron grip; grit, bone.

athlete, gymnast, tumbler, acrobat; Atlas, Hercules, Antaeus, Samson, Cyclops, Goliath, Titan; tower of strength; giant refreshed.

strengthening etc. *v.;* invigoration, refreshment, refocillation.

[Science of forces] dynamics, statics.

V. be -strong etc. *adj.,* − stronger; overmatch.

render -strong etc. *adj.;* give -strength etc. *n.;* strengthen, invigorate, brace, nerve, fortify, buttress, sustain, harden, case-harden, steel; gird; screw −, wind −, set- up; gird −, brace- up one's loins; recruit, set on one's legs; vivify; refresh etc. 689; refect; reinforce etc. *(restore)* 660.

Adj. strong, mighty, vigorous, forcible, hard, adamantine, stout, robust, sturdy, hardy, powerful, potent, puissant, valid.

resistless, irresistible, invincible, proof against, impregnable, unconquerable, indomitable, inextinguishable, unquenchable; incontestable; more than a match for; over-powering, - whelming; all-powerful; sovereign.

able-bodied; athletic, gymnastic; Herculean, Cyclopean, Atlantean; muscular, husky, brawny, wiry, well-knit, broad-shouldered, sinewy, strapping, stalwart, gigantic.

man-ly, -like, -ful; masculine, male, virile, in the prime of manhood.

un-weakened, -allayed, -withered, -shaken, - worn, -exhausted; in full -force, − swing; in the plenitude of power.

stubborn, thick-ribbed, made of iron, deep-rooted; strong as -a lion, − a horse, − brandy; sound as a roach; in -fine, − high- feather; in fine fettle; like a giant refreshed.

Adv. strongly etc. *adj.;* by -force etc. *n.;* by main force etc. *(by compulsion)* 744.

Phr. 'our withers are unwrung.'

160. Weakness.—**N.** weakness etc. *adj.;* debility, atony, relaxation, languor, enervation; impotence etc. 158; infirmity, effeminacy, feminality; fragility, flaccidity; inactivity etc. 683.

declension −, loss −, failure- of strength; delicacy, invalidation, decrepitude, asthenia, adynamy, cachexy, *cachexia,* anemia, bloodlessness, sprain, strain.

reed, thread, rope of sand, broken reed, house -of cards, − built on sand.

soft-, weak-ling; infant etc. 129; youth etc. 127.

V. be -weak etc. *adj.;* drop, crumble, give way, totter, tremble, shake, halt, limp, fade, languish, decline, flag, fail, have one foot in the grave.

render -weak etc. *adj.;* weaken, enfeeble, debilitate, shake, deprive of strength, relax, enervate; un-brace, -nerve; cripple, unman, etc. *(render powerless)* 158; cramp, reduce, sprain, strain, blunt the edge of; dilute, impoverish; decimate; extenuate; reduce -in strength, − the strength of; invalidate; *mettre de l'eau dans son vin.*

Adj. weak, feeble, debile; impotent etc. 158; relaxed, unnerved etc. *v.;* sap-, strength-, power-less; weakly, unstrung, flaccid, adynamic, asthenic; nervous.

soft, effeminate, feminate, womanish.

frail, fragile, shattery, frangible, brittle etc. 328; flimsy, unsubstantial, gimcrack, gingerbread; rickety, cranky; creachy; drooping, tottering etc. *v.;* broken, lame, halt, game, withered, shattered, shaken, crazy, shaky, tumble-down; palsied etc. 158; decrepit; C3.

languid, poor, poorly, infirm; faint, -ish; sickly etc. *(disease)* 655; dull, slack, evanid, spent, short-winded, effete; weatherbeaten; decayed, rotten, worn, seedy, languishing, wasted, washy, wishy-washy, laid low, pulled down, the worse for wear.

un-strengthened etc. 159, -supported, -aided, - assisted; aidless, defenceless etc. 158.

on its last legs; weak as a -child, − baby, − chicken, − cat, − rat; weak as -water, − water gruel, − gingerbread, − milk and water; colorless etc. 429.

Phr. *non sum qualis eram.*

161. Production.—**N.** production, creation, construction, formation, fabrication, manufacture; building, architecture, erection, edification; coinage; organization; *nisus formativus;* putting togeher etc. *v.;* establishment; workmanship, performance; achievement etc. *(completion)* 729; effect etc. 154.

flowering, fructification fruition.

bringing forth etc. *v.;* parturition, birth, birth-throe, child-birth, delivery, confinement, *accouchement,* travail, labour, midwifery, obstetrics; geniture; gestation etc. *(maturation)* 673; evolution, development, growth; genesis, fertilization, breeding, conception, germination, generation, *epigenesis,* pro-creation, -generation, -pagation; fecundation, impregnation; spontaneous generation; *arche-genesis, -biosis; bio-, abio-, homo-, xeno-genesis.*

authorship, publication; works, *oeuvre, opus.*

edifice, building, structure, fabric, erection, pile, tower, flower, fruit.

V. produce, perform, operate, do, make, gar, form, construct, fabricate, frame, contrive, manufacture; weave, forge, coin, carve, chisel; build, raise, edify, rear, erect, put together; set −, run- up; establish, constitute, compose, organize, institute, get up; achieve, accomplish etc. *(complete)* 729.

flower, sprout, blossom, burgeon, bear fruit, fructify, spawn, teem, ean, yean, farrow, drop, calf, pup, whelp, kitten, kindle; bear, lay, bring forth, give birth to, lie in, be brought to bed of, evolve, pullulate, usher into the world.

make productive etc. 168; create; beget, conceive, get, generate, fecundate, impregnate; pro-create, -generate, -pagate; engender; bring −, call- into -being, − existence; breed, hatch, develop, bring up.

induce, superinduce; suscitate; cause etc. 153; acquire etc. 775.

Adj. produc-ed, -ing etc. *v.;* productive of; prolific etc. 168; creative; formative; gen-etic, -ial, -ital; fertile; pregnant; *enceinte,* big −, fraught-with; with child, in the family way, teeming, parturient, in the straw, brought to bed of; puerper-al, -ous.

architectonic; constructive.

162. Destruction. [Non-production.]—N. destruction; waste, dissolution, breaking up; di-, dis-ruption; consumption; disorganization.

fall, downfall, ruin, perdition, crash, smash, havoc, *délabrement, débâcle;* break -down, − up; prostration; desolation, *bouleversement,* wreck, crack-up, crash, wrack, shipwreck, cataclysm; Caudine Forks, Sedan.

extinction, annihilation; destruction of life etc. 361; knock-out, knock-down blow; doom, crack of doom.

destroying etc. *v.*; demo-lition, -lishment; biblioclasm; overthrow, subversion, suppression; abolition etc. (*abrogation*) 756; sacrifice; ravage, devastation, *sabotage, razzia;* incendiarism; revolution etc. 146; extirpation etc. (*extraction*) 301; *commencement de la fin,* road to ruin; dilapidation etc. (*deterioration*) 659.

V. be -destroyed etc.; perish; fall, − to the ground; tumble, topple; go −, fall- to pieces; break up; crumble, − to dust; go to -the dogs, − the wall, − smash, − shivers, − wreck, − pot, − wrack and ruin; go -by the board, − all to smash, − to pieces, − under; be all -over, − up- with; totter to its fall.

destroy; do −, make- away with; nullify; annul etc. 756; sacrifice, demolish; tear up; over-turn, -throw, -whelm; upset, subvert, put an end to; seal the doom of, do for, dish, undo; break -, cut- up; break −, cut −, pull −, mow −, blow −, beat-down; suppress, quash, put down; cut short, take off, blot out; dispel, dissipate, dissolve; consume.

smash, − to smithereens, quell, squash, squelch, crumple up, shatter, shiver; batter; tear −, crush −, cut −, shake −, pull −, pick- to pieces; nip; tear to -rags, − tatters; crush −, knock- to atoms; pulverize; ruin; strike out; throw −, knock- -down, − over; lay by the heels; fell, sink, swamp, scuttle, wreck, crash, shipwreck, engulf, submerge; lay in -ashes, − ruins; sweep away, erase, expunge, strike out, delete, efface, raze; level, − with the -ground, − dust.

deal destruction, lay waste, ravage, gut; dis-organize; dismantle etc. (*render useless*) 645; devour, swallow up, desolate, devastate, sap, mine, blast, confound; exterminate, extinguish, quench, annihilate; snuff −, put −, stamp −, trample- out; lay −, trample- in the dust; prostrate; tread −, crush −, trample- under foot; lay the axe to the root of; make -short work, − a clean sweep, − mincemeat- of; cut up root and branch; fling −, scatter- to the winds; throw overboard; strike at the root of, sap the foundations of, spring a mine, blow up; ravage with fire and sword; cast to the dogs; eradicate etc. 301.

Adj. destroyed etc. *v.;* perishing etc. *v.;* trembling −, nodding −, tottering- to its fall; in course of destruction etc. *n.;* extinct.

destructive, subversive, ruinous, incendiary, deletory; destroying etc. *v.*; suicidal; deadly etc. (*killing*) 361.

Adv. with -crushing effect, − a sledge-hammer.

Phr. *delenda est Carthago.*

163. Reproduction.—N. reproduction, renovation; restoration etc. 660; renewal; new edition, reprint etc. 21; revival, regeneration, palingenesia, revivification; apotheosis; resuscitation, reanimation, resurrection, resurgence, re-appearance, atavism; Phoenix; reincarnation.

generation etc. (*production*) 161; multiplication.

V. reproduce; restore etc. 660; revive, renovate, renew, regenerate, revivify, resuscitate, reanimate, refashion, stir the embers, put into the crucible; multiply, repeat, resurge.

crop up, spring up like mushrooms.

Adj. reproduced etc. *v.;* renascent, reappearing; reproductive; resurgent; progenitive; Hydra-headed.

164. Producer.—N. producer, creator, deviser, designer, originator, inventor, author, founder, generator, mover, architect; grower, constructor, maker etc. (*agent*) 690.

165. Destroyer.—N. destroyer etc. (*destroy* etc. 162); cankerworm etc. (*bane*) 663; iconoclast; assassin etc. (*killer*) 361; executioner etc. (*punish*) 975; Hun, Vandal, nihilist, anarchist.

166. Paternity.—N. paternity; parentage; fatherhood; consanguinity etc. 11.

parent, father, sire, dad, daddy, papa, governor, *pater, paterfamilias, abba;* genitor, progenitor, procreator, begetter; ancestor; grand-sire, -father; great-grandfather.

house, stem, truck, tree, stock, *stirps,* pedigree, lineage, line, family, tribe, sept, race, clan; genealogy, descent, extraction, birth, ancestry; forefathers, forbears, patriarchs.

motherhood, maternity; mother, dam, mamma, *materfamilias;* grand-mother; matriarch.

Adj. paternal, parental; maternal; family, ancestral, linear, matrilinear, patrilineal, patriarchal.

167. Posterity.—N. posterity, progeny, breed, issue, offspring, brood, litter, seed, farrow, spawn, spat; family, children, grandchildren, heirs; great-grandchild.

child, son, daughter; kid; infant etc. 129; bantling, scion; shoot, sprout, olive branch, sprit, branch; off-shoot, -set; ramification; descendant; heir, -ess; heir -apparent, − presumptive; chip of the old block; heredity; rising generation.

straight descent, sonship, line, lineage, filiation, promogeniture.

Adj. filial.

168. Productiveness.—N. productiveness etc. *adj.;* fecundity, fertility, luxuriance, uberty.

pregnancy, pullulation, fructification, multiplication, propagation, procreation; superfetation.

milch cow, rabbit, hydra, warren, seed-plot, land flowing with milk and honey; second crop, after-crop, -growth, -math; fertilization.

V. make -productive etc. *adj.;* fructify; pro-create, generate, fertilize, spermatize, impregnate; fecund-ate, -ify; teem, pullulate, multiply; produce etc. 161; conceive.

Adj. productive, prolific; teem-ing, -ful; fertile, fruitful, frugiferous, fruit-bearing; fructiferous; fecund, luxuriant; pregnant, uberous.

procre-ant, -ative; generative, life-giving, spermatic; originative; multiparous; omnific; propagable.

parturient etc. (*producing*) 161; profitable etc. (*useful*) 644.

169. Unproductiveness.—N. unproductiveness etc. *adj.;* infertility, steril; ity, infecundity; impotence etc. 158- unprofitableness etc. (*inutility*) 645.

waste, desert, Sahara, wild, wilderness, howling wilderness.

V. be -unproductive etc. *adj.;* hang fire, flash in the pan, come to nothing.

Adj. unproductive, inoperative, barren, addle, unfertile, unprolific, arid, sterile, unfruitful, acarpous, infecund; *sine prole;* fallow; teem-, issue-, fruitless; unprofitable etc. (*useless*) 645; null and void, of no effect.

170. Agency.—N. agency, operation, force, working, strain, function, office, maintenance, exercise, work, swing, play; inter-working, -action, procuration, procurement.

causation etc. 153; instrumentality etc. 631; influence etc. 175; action etc. (*voluntary*) 680; *modus operandi* etc. 627.

quickening —, maintaining- power; home stroke.

V. be -in action etc. *adj.;* operate, work; act, — upon; perform, play, support, sustain, strain, maintain, take effect, quicken, strike.

come —, bring- into -operation, — play; have -play, — free play; bring to bear upon.

Adj. operative, efficient, efficacious, practical, effectual.

at work, on foot; acting etc. (*doing*) 680; in -operation, — force, — action, — play, — exercise; acted —, wrought- upon.

Adv. by the -agency etc. *n.-* of; through etc. (*instrumentality*) 631; by means of etc. 632.

171. Physical Energy.—N. energy, physical energy, force; keenness etc. *adj.;* intensity, vigor, strength, elasticity; go; pep, live wire, high pressure; backbone, mettle, fire, vim.

acri-mony, -tude, -dity; causticity, virulence, poignancy; harshness etc. *adj.;* severity, edge, point; pungency etc. 392.

cantharides; Spanish fly; seasoning etc. (*condiment*) 393, stimulant, excitant.

activity, agitation, effervescence; ferment, -ation; ebullition, splutter, perturbation, stir, bustle; voluntary energy etc. 682; quicksilver.

resolution etc. (*mental energy*) 604; exertion etc. (*effort*) 686; excitation etc. (*mental*) 824.

V. give -energy etc. *n.;* energize, stimulate, kindle, excite, activate, exert; sharpen, pep up, intensify; inflame etc. (*render violent*) 173; wind up etc. (*strengthen*) 159.

strike, — into, — hard, — home; make an impression.

Adj. strong, energetic, forcible, active; strenuous, forceful, mettlesome, enterprising, go ahead; intense, deep-dyed, severe, keen, vivid, sharp, acute, incisive, trenchant, brisk, vigorous, live.

rousing, irritating; poignant; virulent, caustic, corrosive, mordant, harsh, stringent; double-edged, — shotted, — distilled; drastic, escharotic; racy etc. (*pungent*) 392; sarcastic etc. 932.

potent etc. (*powerful*) 157; radio-active.

Adv. strongly etc. *adj.; fortiter in re;* with telling effect.

Phr. the steam is up; *vires acquirit eundo.*

172. Physical Inertness.—N. inertness, dulness etc. *adj.;* inertia, *vis inertiae,* inertion, inactivity, torpor, languor; dormancy, quiescence etc. 265; latency, inaction, passivity.

mental inertness; sloth etc. (*inactivity*) 683; inexcitability etc. 826; irresolution etc. 605; obstinacy etc. 606; permanence etc. 141.

V. be -inert etc. *adj.;* hang fire, smoulder.

Adj. inert, inactive, passive, pacific; torpid etc. 683; sluggish, stagnant, dull, heavy, flat, slack, tame, slow, blunt; lifeless, dead, uninfluential.

latent, dormant, smouldering, unexerted.

Adv. inactively etc. *adj.;* in -suspense, -abey-ance.

173. Violence.—N. violence, inclemency, vehemence, might, impetuosity; boisterousness etc.; *adj.;* effervescence, ebullition; turbulence, bluster; uproar, riot, row, rumpus, *le diable à quatre,* devil to pay, all the fat in the fire.

severity etc. 739; ferocity, rage, berserk, fury; exacerbation, exasperation, malignity; fit, paroxysm, orgasm; force, brute force; outrage; *coup de main;* strain, shock, shog; spasm, convulsion, throe; hysterics, passion etc. (*state of excitability*) 825.

out-break, -burst; burst, bounce, dissilience, discharge, volley, explosion, blow up, blast, detonation, rush, eruption, displosion, torrent.

turmoil etc. (*disorder*) 59; ferment etc. (*agitation*) 315; storm, tempest, rough weather; squall etc. (*wind*) 349; earthquake, volcano, thunderstorm.

fury, dragon, demon, tiger, beldame, Tisiphone, Megaera, Alecto, madcap, wild beast; fire-eater etc. (*blusterer*) 887.

V. be -violent etc. *adj.;* run high; ferment, effervesce; romp, rampage; run -wild, — riot; break the peace; rush, tear; rush head-long, -foremost; run amuck, raise a storm, make a riot; make —, kick up- a row, — a fuss; bluster, rage, roar, riot, storm; boil, — over; fume, foam, come in like a lion, wreak, bear down, ride roughshod, out-Herod Herod; spread like wildfire.

break -, fly —, burst- out; bounce, shock, strain; break-, pry-, force-, prize- open.

render -violent etc. *adj.;* sharpen, stir up, quicken, excite, incite, urge, lash, stimulate; irritate, inflame, exacerbate, kindle, suscitate, foment; accelerate, aggravate, exasperate, convulse, infuriate, madden, lash into fury; fan —, add fuel to- the flame; *oleum addere camino.*

explode, go off, displode, fly, detonate, thunder, blow up, flash, flare, erupt, burst; let - off, − fly; discharge, detonize, fulminate.

Adj. violent, vehement, forcible; warm; acute, sharp; rough, rude, ungentle, bluff, boisterous, wild, vicious; brusque, abrupt, waspish; impetuous; rampant.

turbulent; disorderly; blustering, raging etc. *v.;* troublous, riotous; tumultu-ary, -ous; obstreperous, uproarious; extravagant; unmitigated; ravening, tameless; frenzied etc. *(insane)* 503; desperate etc. *(rash)* 863; infuriate, towering, furious, outrageous, frantic, hysteric, in hysterics.

fiery, flaming, scorching, hot, red-hot, ebullient.

savage, fierce, ferocious, fierce as a tiger.

excited etc. *v.;* un-quelled, -quenched, -extinguished, -repressed, -bridled, -ruly; headstrong; un-governable, -appeasable, -mitigable; un-, in-controllable; insup-, irre-pressible.

spasmodic, convulsive, explosive; detonating etc. *v.;* volcanic, meteoric; stormy etc. *(wind)* 349.

Adv. violently etc. *adj.;* amain; by -storm, − force, − main force; with might and main; tooth and nail; *vi et armis,* at the point of the -sword, − bayonet; at one fell swoop; with a high hand, through thick and thin; in desperation, with a vengeance; *à −, à touteoutrance;* head-long, - foremost, -first; like a bull at a gate.

174. Moderation.

N. moderation; lenity etc. 740; temperance,-temperateness, gentleness etc. *adj.;* sobriety; quiet; mental calmness etc. *(inexcitability)* 826.

moderating etc. *v.;* relaxation, remission, mitigation etc. 834; tranquilization, alleviation, assuagement, appeasement, contemporation, pacification.

measure, *juste milieu,* golden mean etc. 29.

moderator; lullaby, sedative, lenitive, demulcent, rose-water, balm, soothing syrup, poppy, opiate, anodyne, milk, opium, laudanum, 'poppy or mandragora;' wet blanket; palliative, calmative.

V.-be -moderate etc. *adj.;* keep within -bounds, − compass; sober −, settle- down; keep the pease, remit, relent; take in sail.

moderate, soften, mitigate, temper, accoy; at-, con-temper; mollify, lenify, dull, take off the edge, blunt, obtund, sheathe, subdue, chasten; sober −, tone −, smooth- down; censor, blue-pencil, weaken etc. 160; lessen etc. *(decrease)* 36; check; palliate.

tranquilize, assuage, appease, dulcify, swage, lull, soothe, compose, still, calm, cool, quiet, hush, quell, sober, pacify, tame, damp, lay, allay, rebate, slacken, smooth, alleviate, rock to sleep, deaden, smother; throw -cold water on, − a wet blanket over; slake; curb etc. *(restrain)* 751; tame etc. *(subjugate)* 749; smooth over; pour oil on the -waves, − troubled waters; pour balm into, *mettre de l'eau dans son vin.*

go out like a lamb, 'roar you as gently as any sucking dove.'

Adj. moderate; lenient etc. 740; gentle, mild; cool, sober, temperate, reasonable, measured; tempered etc. *v.;* calm, unruffled, quiet, tranquil,

still; slow, smooth, untroubled; tame; peaceful, - able; pacific, halcyon.

un-exciting, -irritating; soft, bland, oily, demulcent, lenitive, anodyne; hypnotic etc. 683; sedative; assuaging.

mild as mother's milk; milk and water; gentle as a lamb.

Adv. moderately etc. *adj.;* gingerly; *piano;* under easy sail, at half speed; within -bounds, − compass; in reason.

Phr. *est modus in rebus.*

175. Influence.

N. influence; importance etc. 642; weight, pressure, preponderance, prevalence, sway, pull; predomi-nance, -nancy; ascendency; control, dominance, reign; authority etc. 737; capability etc. *(power)* 157; interest; spell, magic, magnetism.

footing; purchase etc. *(support)* 215; play, leverage, vantage ground.

tower of strength, host in himself; protection, patronage, auspices.

V. have -influence etc. *n.;* be -influential etc. *adj.;* carry weight, actuate, sway, bias, weigh, tell; have a hold upon, magnetize, bear upon, gain a footing, work upon; take -root, − hold; strike root in.

run through, pervade, prevail, dominate, predominate, subject; out-, over-weigh; over-ride, - bear, − come; gain head; rage; be -rife etc. *adj.;* spread like wildfire; have −, get −, gain- -the upper hand, − full play.

be -recognized, − listened to; make one's voice heard, gain a hearing; play a -part, − leading part- in; lead, control, rule, master; get the mastery over; make one's influence felt, cut ice with; take the lead, pull the strings; turn −, throw one's weight into- the scale; set the fashion, lead the dance.

Adj. influential; important etc. 642; weighty; prevailing etc. *v.;* prevalent, rife, rampant; dominant, regnant, predominant, in the ascendant, hegemonical; authoritative, recognized, telling, with authority.

Adv. with telling effect.

175a. Absence of Influence.

N. impotence etc. 158; inertness etc. 172; irrelevancy etc. 10.

V. have no -influence etc. 175.

Adj. uninfluential; unconduc-ing, -ive, -ting to; powerless etc. 158; irrelevant etc. 10.

176. Tendency.

N. tendency; apt-ness, -itude; proneness, proclivity, bent, turn, tone, bias, set, warp, leaning to, predisposition, inclination, conatus, propensity, susceptibility; liability etc. 177; quality, nature, temperament; characteristic, idio-crasy, -syncrasy; cast, vein, grain; humor, mood; drift etc. *(direction)* 278; conduciveness, -ducement; applicability etc. *(utility)* 644; subservience etc. *(instrumentality)* 631.

V. tend, contribute, conduce, lead, dispose, incline, verge, bend to, warp, turn, trend, affect, carry, redound to, bid fair to, gravitate towards; promote etc. *(aid)* 707.

Adj. tending etc. *v.;* conducive, working to-

wards, in a fair way to, calculated to; liable etc.
177; subservient etc. (*instrumental*) 631; useful
etc. 644; subsidiary etc. (*helping*) 707.
Adv. for, whither.

177. Liability.—N. lia-bility, -bleness; possibility, contingency; suscepti-vity, -bility.
V. be -liable etc. *adj.;* incur, lay oneself open
to; run the —, stand a- chance; lie under, expose
oneself to, open a door to.
Adj. liable, subject; in danger etc. 665; open —,
exposed —, obnoxious- to; answerable, responsible, accountable, amenable; unexempt from; apt
to; dependent on; incident to.
contingent, incidental, possible, on the cards,
within range of, at the mercy of.

178. Concurrence.—N. concurrence, co-
operation, coagency; coincidence, consilience;
union; agreement etc. 23; consent etc. (*assent*)
488; alliance; concert etc. 709; partnership etc.
712; collaboration, conformity.
V. con-cur, -duce, -spire, -tribute; agree, unite,
harmonize; hang —, pull- together etc. (*co-
operate*) 709; help to etc. (*aid*) 707.
keep pace with, run parallel to; go —, go along
—, go hand in hand- with.
Adj. concurring etc. *v.;* concurrent, conformable, joint, co-operative, concordant, coincident, concomitant, harmonious; in alliance with,
banded together, of one mind, at one with;
parallel.
Adv. with one consent.

179. Counteraction.—N. counteraction, opposition; contrariety etc. 14; antagonism, polarity; clashing etc. *v.;* collision, interference,
resistance, renitency, friction; reaction; retro-
action; repercussion etc. (*recoil*) 277; counterblast; neutralization etc. (*compensation*) 30; *vis
inertiae;* check etc. (*hindrance*) 706.
voluntary -opposition etc. 708, — resistance
etc. 719; repression etc. (*restraint*) 751.
V. counteract; run counter, clash, cross; interfere —, conflict- with; jostle; go —, run —, beat
—, militate- against; stultify; antagonize, frustrate, oppose etc. 708; withstand etc. (*resist*) 719;
hinder etc. 706; repress etc. (*restrain*) 751; react
etc. (*recoil*) 277.
undo, neutralize, cancel; counterpoise etc.
(*compensate*) 30; overpoise.
Adj. counteracting etc. *v.;* antagonistic, conflicting, retroactive, renitent, reactionary; contrary etc. 14.
Adv. although etc. 30; in spite of etc. 708;
malgré; against.

180. Space. [Indefinite space.]—N. space,
extension, extent, superficial extent, expanse,
stretch; capacity, volume, room, accommodation,
scope, range, latitude, field, way, expansion, compass, sweep, play, swing, spread.
dimension, fourth dimension; relativity, geo-
metry.

spare —, elbow —, house- room; stowage,
roomage, margin; opening, sphere, arena; lee-,
sea-, head-way.
open —, free- space; wide open spaces, void etc.
(*absence*) 187; waste; wild-, wilder-ness; up-, bot-
tom-, moor -land; *campagna, veldt,* prairie,
steppe.
abyss etc. (*interval*) 198; unlimited space;
infinity etc. 105; world, wide world; ubiquity etc.
(*presence*) 186; length and breadth of the land.
proportions, acreage; acres, — roods and
perches; square -inches, — yards etc.
V. reach, extend, stretch, sweep, spread,
range, cover, thrust out, reach forth.
Adj. spacious, roomy, extensive, expansive,
capacious, ample; wide-spread, vast, world-wide,
uncircumscribed; boundless etc. (*infinite*) 105;
shore-, track-, path-less; large etc. 192.
spatial, dimensional, proportional; two-,
three-, four-dimensional; stereoscopic.
Adv. extensively etc. *adj.;* wherever; everywhere; far and -near, — wide; right and left, all
over, all the world over; throughout the -world,
— length and breadth of the land; under the sun,
in every quarter; in all -quarters, — lands; here,
there and everywhere; from -pole to pole, —
China to Peru, — Indus to the pole, — Dan to
Beersheba, — end to end; on the face of the earth,
in the wide world, from all points of the compass; to the -four winds, — uttermost parts of the
earth.

180a. Inextension.—N. in-, non-extension;
point; atom etc. (*smallness*) 32; pinprick; limitation etc. 229.

181. Region. [Definite space.]—N. region,
sphere, sphere of influence, corridor, ground,
soil, area, realm, hemisphere, quarter district,
beat, orb, orbit, zone, belt, circuit, circle; pale etc.
(*limit*) 233; com-, department; domain, tract,
territory, terrain, country, canton, county, shire,
province, *arrondissement,* diocese, parish, town-
ship, borough, constituency, *commune,* ward,
wapentake, hundred, riding, lathe, garth, soke,
tithing, bailiwick; empire, kingdom, principality,
duchy, grand —, arch- duchy, palatinate, republic,
commonwealth, dominion, colony, state, island.
arena, precincts, *enceinte,* walk, march; patch,
plot, enclosure, etc. 232; close, *enclave,* field,
court; street etc. (*abode*) 189.
clime, climate, zone, meridian, latitude.
Adj. territorial, local, parochial, provincial,
insular.

182. Place. [Limited space.]—N. place, lieu,
spot, point, dot; niche, nook, etc. (*corner*) 244;
hole; pigeonhole etc. (*receptacle*) 191; compartment; premises, precinct, station, confine; area,
court, yard, quadrangle, square, compound;
abode etc. 189; locality etc. (*situation*) 183.
ins and outs; every hole and corner.
Adv. somewhere, in some place, wherever it
may be, here and there, in various places,
passim.

183. Situation.—N. situation, position, locality, *locale, status,* latitude and longitude; footing, standing, standpoint, post; stage, aspect, attitude, posture, *pose.*

place, site, base, station, seat, *venue,* whereabouts, environment, neighborhood; bearings etc. (*direction*) 278; spot etc. (*limited space*) 182.

top-, ge-, chor-ography; map etc. 554.

V. be -situated, — situate; lie; have its seat in.

Adj. situ-ate, -ated; local, topical, topographical etc. *n.*

Adv. *in -situ. — loco;* here and there, *passim;* here-, there-, whereabouts; in place, here, there. in —, amidst- such and such- -surroundings, — *environs. — entourage.*

184. Location.—N. loca-tion, -lization; lodgement; de-, re-position; stow-, pack-age; collocation; packing, lading; establishment, settlement, installation; fixation; insertion etc. 300.

anchorage, roadstead, mooring, mooring mast, encampment, camp, bivouac.

plantation, colony, settlement, cantonment, encampment, reservation; colonization, domestication, situation; habitation etc. (*abode*) 189; cohabitation; 'a local habitation and a name;' indenization, naturalization.

V. place, situate, locate, localize, make a place for, put, lay, set, seat, station, lodge, quarter, post, install; storehouse, stow; extablish, fix, pin, root; graft; plant etc. (*insert*) 300; shelve, pitch, camp, lay down, deposit, reposit; cradle; moor, tether, picket; pack, tuck in; embed; vest, invest in.

billet on, quarter upon, saddle with; load, lade, freight; pocket, put up, bag.

inhabit·etc. (*be present*) 186; domesticate, colonize, populate, people; take —, strike-root; anchor; cast —, come to an- anchor; sit —, settle-down; settle; take up one's -abode, — quarters; plant —, establish —, locate- oneself; squat, perch, hive, *se nicher,* bivouac, burrow, get a footing; encamp, pitch one's tent; put up -at, — one's horses at; keep house.

indenizen, naturalize, adopt.

put back, replace etc. (*restore*) 660.

Adj. placed etc. *v.;* situate, posited, ensconced, embedded, embosomed, rooted; domesticated; vested in unremoved; settled, stationed, established.

moored etc. *v.;* at anchor.

185. Displacement.—N. displacement, elocation, transposition.

ejectment etc. 297; exile etc. (*banishment*) 893; removal etc. (*transference*) 270; unshipment.

misplacement, dislocation etc. 61; fish out of water.

V. dis-place, -plant, -lodge, -nest, -establish; misplace, unseat, disturb; exile etc. (*seclude*) 893; ablegate, set aside, remove; take —, cart- away; take —, draft- off; lade etc. 184, unship.

unload, empty etc. (*eject*) 297; transfer etc. 270; dispel.

vacate; depart etc. 293.

Adj. displaced etc. *v.;* un-placed, -housed, -harbored, -established, -settled; house-, homeless; out of -place, — a situation.

misplaced, out of its element.

186. Presence.—N. presence; occupancy, -ation; attendance; whereness.

permeation, pervasion; diffusion etc. (*dispersion*) 73.

ubi-ety, -quity, -quitariness; omnipresence.

bystander etc. (*spectator*) 444.

V. exist in space, be -present etc. *adj.;* assist at; make one -of, — at; look on, attend, remain; find —, present- oneself; show one's face; fall in the way of, occur in a place; lie, stand; occupy.

people; inhabit, dwell, reside, stay, sojourn, live, room, abide, bunk, lodge, nestle, roost, perch; take up one's abode etc. (*be located*) 184; tenant, occupy.

resort to, frequent, haunt; revisit.

fill, pervade, permeate; be -diffused, — disseminated- through; over-spread, -run; run through; meet one at every turn.

Adj. present; occupying, inhabiting etc. *v.;* moored etc. 184; residential, resi-ant, -dent, -dentiary; domiciled.

ubiquit-ous, -ary; omnipresent.

peopled, populous, full of people, inhabited.

Adv. here; there, where, everywhere, aboard, on board, at home, afield; on the spot; here, there and everywhere etc. (*space*) 180; in presence of, before; under the -eyes, —nose- of; in the face of; *in propriâ personâ.*

187. Absence. [Nullibiety.]—N. absence; inexistence etc. 2; non-residence, absenteeism; non-attendance, *alibi*

emptiness etc. *adj.;* void, *vacuum;* vac-uity, -ancy; *tabula rasa;* exemption; *hiatus* etc. (*interval*) 198; no man's land.

truant, absentee.

nobody; nobody -present, — on earth; no one; not a soul; *âme qui vive.*

V. be -absent etc. *adj.;* keep -away, — out of the way; play truant, absent oneself, stay away.

withdraw, make oneself scarce, vacate; go away, slip out, slip away, retreat etc. 293.

Adj. absent, not present, away, nonresident, gone, from home; missing; lost; wanted, wanting; omitted; nowhere to be found; inexistent etc. 2.

empty, void; blank, vac-ant, -uous; unten-anted, -occupied, -inhabited; tenantless; desert, -ed; devoid; un-, uninhabitable.

exempt from, not having.

Adv. without, *minus,* nowhere; elsewhere; neither here nor there; in default of; *sans;* behind one's back.

Phr. the bird has flown, *non est inventus.*

188. Inhabitant.—N. inhabitant; habitant, resident, -iary; dweller, in-dweller; occup-ier, -ant, farmer, planter; householder, lodger, boarder, paying guest; inmate, tenant, renter, incumbent, sojourner, *locum tenens,* commorant; settler, squatter, backwoodsman, colonist; islander; denizen, citizen; burgher, oppidan, cockney, cit, townsman, burgess; villager; cottager, -tier, -ter; compatriot.

native, indigene, aboriginal, aborigines, autochthones; Briton, Englishman, John Bull; new comer etc. (*stranger*) 57.

garrison, crew; population; people etc. (*mankind*) 372; colony, settlement; household.

V. inhabit etc. (*be present*) 186; indenizen etc. (*locate oneself*) 184.

Adj. indigenous; enchorial; national, nat-ive, -al; autochthonous; British, English; colonial; domestic, domiciliated, -ed; naturalized, vernacular, domesticated; domiciliary.

in the occupation of; garrisoned —, occupied-by.

189. Abode. [Place of habitation, or resort.]—**N.** abode, dwelling, lodging, -s; diggings, domicile, residence, address, habitation, where one's lot is cast, local habitation, berth, seat, lap, sojourn, housing, quarters, headquarters, resiance, tabernacle, throne, ark.

home, fatherland, mother country, country etc. 181; home-stead, -stall; fireside, chimney corner; hearth — stone; household gods, *lares et penates*, roof, household, housing, *dulce domum*, paternal domicile; native -soil, — land, blighty.

nest, *nidus*, snuggery; arbor, bower etc. 191; lair, den, cave, hole, hidingplace, cell, *sanctum sanctorum*, aerie, eyry, rookery, hive; *habitat*, haunt, covert, resort, retreat, perch, roost; nidification.

bivouac, camp, encampment, cantonment; castrametation; barrack, casemate, casern.

tent etc. (*covering*) 223; building etc. (*construction*) 161; chamber etc. (*receptacle*) 191.

tenement, messuage, farm, farmhouse, grange, *hacienda*.

cot, cabin, log cabin, shack, hut, *châlet*, croft, shed, booth, stall, hovel, bothy, shanty, igloo, tepee, wigwam; pen etc. (*inclosure*) 232; barn, bawn; kennel, sty, dog-hole, cote, coop, hutch, byre; cowhouse, -shed; stable, dove-cote, shippen.

house, mansion, place, villa, cottage, box, lodge, hermitage, *rus in urbe*, folly, rotunda, tower, *château*, castle, pavilion, hotel, court, manor-house, capital messuage, hall, palace, alcazar; country seat; kiosk, bungalow; temple etc. 1000; home of rest, alms-, poor-, work-house, asylum; boarding-, lodging-house; flat, maisonette, duplex, penthouse, suite of rooms, apartments, rooms, room building etc. 161; Mansion House, town hall, Capitol.

assembly-room, auditorium, coliseum, meeting-house, pump-room, spa, health resort, watering-place; club; theatre etc. 840; drill hall, gymnasium, church etc. 1000; Houses of Parliament etc. 696; school etc. 542; inn; hostel, -ry; hotel, tavern, caravansary, khan, hospice; public-, ale-, pot-, mug-house; gin-palace, gin mill; coffee-, eating-house; canteen, *restaurant*, *rotisserie*, cafeteria, grill-room, *buffet, café, estaminet*, *posada, bodega;* bar; saloon, speakeasy, shebeen.

hamlet, village, thorp, dorp, ham, kraal; borough, burgh, town, county-seat, — town, city, capital, metropolis; suburb, quarter, parish etc. 181; ghetto; province, country.

street, place, terrace, parade, esplanade, promenade, pier, embankment, road, villas, row, walk, lane, alley, court, quadrangle, quad, wynd, close, yard, passage, rents, mansions, buildings, mews.

square, polygon, circus, crescent, mall, *piazza*, arcade, colonnade, peristyle, cloister; gardens, grove, residences; block of buildings, market-place, *place.*

anchorage, roadstead, roads; dock, basin, wharf, quay, port, harbor; dry-, graving-, floating-dock.

garden, park, pleasure-ground, pleasance, demesne.

V. take up one's abode etc. (*locate oneself*) 184; inhabit etc. (*be present*) 186.

Adj. urban, oppidan, metropolitan; suburban; provincial, rural, rustic; countrified; regional, parochial, domestic; cosmopolitan; palatial.

190. Contents. [Things contained.]—**N.** contents; cargo, lading, freight, shipment, load, bale, burden; cart-, ship-load; cup —, basket —, etc. (*receptacle*) 191 - of; inside etc. 221; stuffing, ullage.

V. load, lade, ship, charge, fill, stuff.

191. Receptacle.—**N.** receptacle, container; inclosure etc. 232; recipient, receiver, reservatory.

compartment; cell, -ule; follicle; hole, corner, niche, recess, nook; crypt, stall, pigeon-hole, cove, oriel; cave etc. (*concavity*) 252.

capsule, vesicle, cyst, pod, calyx, *cancelli*, utricle, bladder, udder.

stomach, paunch; *venter*, abdomen, ventricle, crop, craw, ingluvies, maw, gizzard, bread-basket, belly, little Mary; mouth.

pocket, pouch, fob, sheath, scabbard, socket, bag, vanity bag, compact, sac, sack, saccule, despatch —, attaché-, tachy- case, wallet, scrip, card-, note-, case, billfold, poke, knit, knap-, haver-, ruck-sack, sachel, satchel, reticule, budget, net; ditty-, -box, -bag, kitbag; portfolio; saddlebags, holster; quiver etc. (*magazine*) 636.

chest, box, coffer, caddy, case, casket, pyx, pix, *caisson*, desk, *bureau*, reliquary, shrine; trunk, portmanteau, band-box, *valise*, suitcase, hand-, traveling-, overnight-, Gladstone-, carpet-bag, brief case; boot, imperial; *vache*; cage, manger, rack.

vessel, vase, bushel, barrel; canister, jar; pottle, basket, punnet, pannier, buck-basket, hopper, maund, creel, cran, crate, cradle, bassinet, wisket, whisket, *jardinière, corbeille*, hamper, wastepaper basket, dosser, dorser, tray, hod, scuttle, utensil, spittoon, cuspidor.

[For liquids] cistern etc. (*store*) 636; vat, caldron, barrel, cask, puncheon, keg, rundlet, tun, butt, firkin, hogshead, kilderkin, carboy, amphora, ampulla, bottle, jar, leather bottle, decanter, ewer, cruse, carafe, crock, kit, canteen, flagon; demijohn; flask, -et; stoup, noggin, vial, phial, ampoulé, cruet, caster; gourd; urn, *épergne*, salver, *patella, tazza, patera*; pig-, big-gin; tea-, coffee-pot, percolator, *samovar*; tyg, nipperkin, pocket-pistol; tub, bucket, pail, skeel, pot, tankard, jug, pitcher, toby, mug, pipkin; gal-, gall-ipot, pannikin; matrass, receiver, retort, alembic, bolthead, can, kettle; bowl, basin, jorum, punch-bowl, cup, goblet, chalice, tumbler, glass, wineglass, rummer, beaker, tass, horn, saucepan, skillet, posnet, tureen, terrine, *casserole*, sauce-, gravy-boat.

plate, platter, paten, dish, vegetable —, *entrée*-dish, trencher, calabash, porringer, potager, saucer, pan, crucible.

shovel, trowel, spoon; table-, dessert-, tea-, egg-,

salt-spoon; spatula, ladle; dipper; baler; watch-glass, thimble.

closet, commode, cupboard, cellaret, *chiffonnière*, locker, bin, bunker, *buffet*, press, safe, sideboard, drawer, chest of drawers, till, *scrutoire*, *secrétaire*, *éscritoire*, davenport, book-case, cabinet, canterbury; corner cupboard, wardrobe.

chamber, apartment, room, cabin; office, court, hall, atrium; suite of rooms, flat, story; saloon, *salon*, parlor; presence-chamber; sitting-, drawing-, reception-, state-, living-, work-room; gallery, cabinet, closet, cubicle; pew, box; *boudoir*; *adytum*, *sanctum*; bed-room, dormitory, dressing-room; refectory, dining-room, *salle-à-manger*; nursery, schoolroom; library, study; *studio*; billiard-, bath-, smoking-room; den, canteen, mess, officers' mess; gun-, ward-, mess-room.

attic, loft, garret, cockloft, clerestory; cellar, vault, hold, cockpit; *entre-sol*; mezzanine floor; ground-floor, *rez-de-chaussée*; basement, kitchen, cook-house, galley, pantry, scullery, offices; store-room etc. (*depository*) 636; lumber-room; dust-hole, -bin; dairy, laundry, coachhouse; *garage*; *hangar*; out-, pent-house; lean-to.

portico, porch, piazza, verandah, lobby, court, hall, vestibule, corridor, passage; ante-room, chamber; lounge; *foyer*, *loggia*.

conservatory, green-house, glass-house, vinery, bower, arbor, summer-house, alcove, grotto, hermitage, pergola.

lodging etc. (*abode*) 189; bed etc. (*support*) 215; carriage etc. (*vehicle*) 272.

Adj. capsular, saccu-lar, -lated; recipient; ventricular, cystic, vascular, vesicular, cellular, camerated, locular, multilocular, poly-gastric; marsupial; siliqu-ose, -ous.

192. Size.—N. size, magnitude, dimension, bulk, volume; largeness etc. *adj.*; greatness etc. (*of quantity*) 31; expanse etc. (*space*) 180; amplitude, mass; proportions.

capacity; ton-, tun-nage; caliber, scantling.

turgidity etc. (*expansion*) 194; corpulence, obesity; plumpness, etc. *adj.*; *embonpoint*, corporation, flesh and blood, lustihood.

hugeness etc. *adj.*; enormity, immensity, monstrosity.

giant, Brobdingnagian, Antaeus, Goliath, Gog and Magog, Gargantua, monster, mammoth, Cyclops; whale, porpoise, behemoth, leviathan, elephant, hippopotamus; colossus; tun, lump, bulk, block, loaf, mass, clod, nugget, bushel, thumper, whopper, spanker, strapper; Triton among the minnows.

mountain, mound; heap etc. (*assemblage*) 72.

largest portion etc. 50; full-, life-size.

V. ve- large etc. *adj.*; become -large etc. (*expand*) 194.

Adj. large, big; great etc. (*in quantity*) 31; considerable, bulky, voluminous, ample, massive, massy; capacious, comprehensive; spacious etc. 180; mighty, towering, fine, magnificent.

corpulent, stout, fat, plump, squab, full, lusty, strapping, bouncing; portly, burly, well-fed, full-grown; stalwart, brawny, fleshy; goodly; in good -case, — condition; in condition; chopping, jolly; chub-, chubby-faced.

lubberly, hulky, unwieldy, lumpish, gaunt, spanking, whacking, whopping, thumping, thundering, hulking; overgrown; puffy etc. (*swollen*) 194.

huge, immense, enormous, mighty; vast, -y; amplitudinous, stupendous; monst-er, -rous; gigantic, elephantine; giant, -like; colossal, Cyclopean, Brobdingnagian, Garguantuan, Titanic; infinite etc. 105.

large as life; plump as a dumpling, — partridge; fat as -a pig, — a quail, — butter, — brawn, — bacon.

193. Littleness.—N. littleness etc. *adj.*; smallness etc. (*of quantity*) 32; exiguity, inextension; parvi-tude, -ty; duodecimo; Elzevir edition, epitome, microcosm; rudiment; vanishing point; thinness etc. 203.

dwarf, pigmy, atomy, Liliputian, midget, chit, pigwidgeon, urchin, elf; doll, puppet; Tom Thumb, Hop-o'-my thumb, Humpty-dumpty; man-, mannikin; *homunculus*, dapperling, fingerling, dandiprat, cock-sparrow, scalawag.

animalcule, monad, mite, insect, emmet, fly; midge, gnat, shrimp, minnow, worm, maggot, entozoon; *bacillus*, microbe, micro-organism, *bacteria*; *infusoria*; microbe; grub; tit, tomtit, runt, mouse, small fry; millet-, mustard-seed; barleycorn; pebble, grain of sand; mole-hill, button, bubble.

point; atom etc. (*small quantity*) 32; fragment etc. (*small part*) 51; powder etc. 330; point of a pin, mathematical point; *minutiae* etc. (*unimportance*) 643.

micro-graphy, -meter, -scope; vernier; scale.

V. be -little etc. *adj.*; lie in a nutshell; become small etc. (*decrease*) 36, (*contract*) 195.

Adj. little; small etc. (*in quantity*) 32; minute, diminutive, microscopic; inconsiderable etc. (*unimportant*) 643; exiguous, puny, tiny, wee, petty, minikin, miniature, pigmy, elfin; under sized; dwarf, -ed, -ish; spare, stunted, limited; cramp, -ed; pollard, Liliputian, dapper, pocket; port-ative, -able; duodecimo; dumpy, squat; compact, handy; short etc. 201.

impalpable, intangible, evanescent, imperceptible, invisible, inappreciable, infinitesimal, homeopathic; atomic, corpuscular, molecular; rudiment-ary, -al; embryonic.

weazen, scant, scraggy, scrubby; thin etc. (*narrow*) 203; granular etc. (*powdery*) 330; shrunk etc. 195.

Adv. in a -small compass, — nutshell; on a small scale.

194. Expansion.—N. expansion; increase etc. 35 -of size; enlargement, extension, augmentation; ampli-fication, -ation; aggrandizement, spread, increment, growth, development, pullulation, swell, dilation, dilatation, rarefaction; turg-escence, -idness, -idity; obesity etc. (*size*) 192; dropsy, tumefaction, intumescence, swelling, tumor, *diastole*, distension; puff-ing, -iness; inflation; pandiculation.

dilatability, expansibility.

germination, growth, upgrowth; accretion etc. 35.

over-growth, -distension; hypertrophy, tympany.

bulb etc. (*convexity*) 250; plumper; superiority of size.

V. become -larger etc. (large etc. 192); expand, widen, enlarge, extend, grow, increase, incrassate, swell, gather; fill out; deploy, take open order, dilate, stretch, spread; mantle, was; grow —, spring- up; bud, bourgeon, shoot, sprout, germinate, put forth, vegetate, pullulate, open, burst forth, flower, blow etc. 734; gain —, gather- flesh; outgrow; spread like wildfire, overrun.

be larger than; surpass etc. (*be superior*) 33.

render -larger etc. (large etc. 192); expand, spread, extend, aggrandize, distend, develop, amplify, spread out, widen, magnify, rarefy, inflate, puff, puff out, blow up, stuff, pad, cram; exaggerate; fatten.

Adj. expanded etc. *v.*; larger etc. (large etc. 192); swollen; expansive; wide-open, -spread; fan-shaped; flabelliform; overgrown, exaggerated, bloated, fat, turgid, tumid, hypertrophied, dropsical; pot-, swag-bellied; edematous, obese, puffy, pursy, blowzy, distended; patulous; bulbous etc. (*convex*) 250; full-blown, -grown, -formed; big etc. 192.

195. Contraction.—N. contraction, reduction, diminution; decrease etc. 36- of size; defalcation, decrement; lessening, shrinkage; collapse, emaciation, attenuation, tabefaction, comsumption, marasmus, atrophy; systole, neck, hour-glass.

condensation, compression, constraint, compactness; compendium etc. 596; squeezing etc. *v.*; strangulation; corrugation; astringency, constringency; astringents, sclerotics; contractility, compressibility; coarctation.

inferiority in size.

V. become -small, — smaller; lessen, decrease etc. 36; grow less, dwindle, shrink, contract, narrow, shrivel, collapse, wither, lose flesh, wizen, fall away, waste, wane, ebb; decat etc. (*deteriorate*) 659.

be smaller than, fall short of; not come up to etc. (*be inferior*) 34.

render smaller, lessen, diminish, contract, draw in, shrink, shrivel, narrow, coarctate; constrict, constringe; condense, compress, boil down, deflate, exhaust, empty; squeeze, corrugate, crush, crumple up, warp, purse up, pack, stow; pinch, tighten, strangle; cramp; dwarf, bedwarf; shorten etc. 201; circumscribe etc. 229; restrain etc. 751; fold etc. 258.

pare, reduce, attenuate, rub down, scrape, file, grind, chip, shave, shear.

Adj. contracting etc. *v.*; astringent; shrunk, contracted etc. *v.*; strangulated, tabid, wizened, stunted, tabescent; marasmic; waning etc. *v.*; neap; compact; shriveled, preshrunk.

unexpanded etc. (expand etc. 194); inswept; contractile; compressible; smaller etc. small etc. 193).

196. Distance.—N. distance; space etc. 180; remoteness, farness; far- cry to; longinquity, elongation; offing; background; removedness; parallax; reach, span, stride; drift.

out-post, -skirt; horizon, sky-line; aphelion; foreign parts, *ultima Thule*, *ne plus ultra*, antipodes; long range, giant's stride.

dispersion etc. 73.

V. be -distant etc. *adj.*; extend —, stretch —, reach —, spread —, go —, get —, stretch away- to; range, outrange, outreach.

remain at a distance; keep —, stand- -away, — off, — aloof, — clear of.

Adj. distant; far -off, away; remote, telescopic, distal, wide of; stretching to etc. *v.*; yon, -der; ulterior; trans-marine, -pontine, -atlantic, -pacific, -continental, -polar, -equatorial, -alpine; tramontane; ultra-montane, -mundane; hyperborean, antihodean; inaccessible, out of the way; unapproached, -able; incontiguous.

Adv. far -off, — away; afar, -off; off; away; a -long, — great, — good- way off; wide away, aloof; wide —, clear- of; out of -the way, — reach; abroad, yonder, farther, further, beyond; *outre mer*, over the border, far and wide, over the hills and far away; from pole to pole etc. (*over great space*) 180; to the -uttermost parts, — ends- of the earth; out of -hearing, — range, nobody knows where, *à perte de vue*, out of the sphere of, wide of the mark; a far cry to.

apart, asunder; wide -apart, — asunder; *longo intervallo*; at arm's length.

197. Nearness.—N. nearness etc. *adj.*; proximity, propinquity; vicinity, -age; neighborhood, adjacency; contiguity etc. 199.

short -distance, — step, — cut; earshot, close quarters, brief span; stone's throw; bow —, gun —, pistol- shot; hair's breadth, span; close-up.

purlieus, neighborhood, vicinage, *environs*, *alentours*, suburbs, confines, *banlieue*, borderland; whereabouts.

bystander; neighbor, borderer.

approach etc. 286; convergence etc. 290; perihelion.

V. be -near etc. *adj.*; adjoin, hang about, trench on; border-, verge upon; stand by, approximate, tread on the heels of, cling to, clasp, hug; cuddle, huddle; hang about the skirts of, hover over; burn; abut.

bring —, draw- -near etc. 286; converge etc. 290; crowd etc. 72; place -side by side etc. *adv.*

Adj. near, nigh; close-, near- at hand; close, neighboring, propinquent, bordering upon; adjacent, adjoining, limitrophe; proxim-ate, ~al; at hand, handy; near the mark, near run; home, intimate.

Adv. near, nigh; hard —, fast- by; close -to, upon, — up; at the point of; next door to; within -reach, — call, — hearing, — earshot, — range; within an ace of; but a step, not far from, at no great distance; on the -verge, — brink, — skirts- of; in the -environs etc. *n.*; at one's -door, — feet, — elbow, — finger's end, — side; on the tip of one's tongue; under one's nose; within a -stone's throw etc. *n.*; in -sight, — presence- of; at close quarters; cheek by -jole, — jowl; beside, alongside, side by side, *tête-à-tête*; in juxtaposition etc. (*touching*) 199; yard-arm to yard-arm; at the heels of; on the confines of, at the threshold, bordering upon, verging to; in the way.

about; here-, there-abouts; roughly, in round

numbers; approxim- -ately, – atively; as good as, well nigh.

198. Interval.—N. interval, interspace; separation etc. 44; break gap, opening; hole etc. 260; chasm, *hiatus,* caesura; inter-ruption,-regnum; interstice, *lacuna,* cleft, mesh, crevice, chink, rime, creek, cranny, crack, chap, slit, slot, fissure, scissure, rift, flaw, breach, fracture, rent, gash, cut, leak, dike, ha-ha.

gorge, defile, ravine, canon, *crevasse,* abyss, abysm; gulf; inlet, frith, strait, gully, gulch, nullah; pass; notch; furrow etc. 259; yawning gulf; *hiatus - maxime, — valde- deflendus*; parenthesis etc. (*interjacence*) 228; void etc. (*absence*) 187; incompleteness etc. 530.

V. gape etc. (*open*) 260; part, remove.

Adj. with an interval, far between; separated, spaced, split.

Adv. at intervals etc. (*discontinuously*) 70; *longo intervallo.*

199. Contiguity.—N. contiguity, contact, proximity, apposition, juxtaposition, touching etc. *v.*; abutment, osculation; meeting, appulse, appulsion, *rencontre,* rencounter, syzygy, coincidence, conjunction, coexistence; adhesion etc. 46.

border-land; frontier etc. (*limit*) 233; tangent.

V. be -contiguous etc. *adj.*; join, adjoin, abut on, march with, border; tick, graze, touch, meet, osculate, kiss, come in contact; coincide; coexist; adhere etc. 46.

Adj. contiguous; touching etc. *v.*; in -contact etc. *n.*, conterminous, end to end, osculatory; pertingent; tangential.

hand to hand; close to etc. (*near*) 197; with no - interval etc. 198.

200. Length.—N. length, longitude, span, extent, mileage.

line, bar, rule, stripe, streak, spoke, radius.

lengthening etc. *v.*; pro-longation, -duction, -traction; ten-sion, -sure; extension.

[Measures of length] line, nail, inch, hand, palm, foot, cubit, yard, ell, fathom, rod, pole, perch, furlong, mile, league; chain, meter, kilo-, centi-, milli- etc meter.

pedometer, perambulator, odometer, odograph, speedometer, cyclometer, log, telemeter, range finder; scale etc. (*measurement*) 466.

V. be -long etc. *adj.*; stretch out, sprawl; extend –, reach –, stretch -to; make a long arm, 'drag its slow length along.'

render -long etc. *adj.*; lengthen, extend, elongate; stretch; pro-long, -duce, -tract; let –, pay –, draw –, spin- out; drawl.

enfilade, look along, view in perspective.

Adj. long, -some; lengthy, lank, wiredrawn, outstretched; stretched, drawn out, lengthened etc. *v.*; sesquipedalian etc. (*words*) 577; interminable, no end of.

line-ar, -al; longitudinal, oblong.

as long as -my arm, —to-day and to-morrow; unshortened etc. (shorten etc. 201).

Adv. lengthwise, at length, longitudinally, endlong, along; *tandem*; in a line etc. (*continuously*) 69; in perspective.

from -end to end; —stem to stern, —head to foot, —the crown of the head to the sole of the foot, — top to toe, —head to heels; fore and aft.

201. Shortness.—N. shortness etc. *adj.*; brevity; littleness etc. 193; a span.

shortening etc. *v.*; abbrevia-tion, -ture; abridgment, concision, retrenchment, curtailment, decurtation; reduction etc. (*contraction*) 195; epitome etc. (*compendium*) 596.

abridger, abstractor, epitomiser.

elision, ellipsis; conciseness etc. (*in style*) 572.

V. be -short etc. *adj.*; render -short etc. *adj.*; shorten, curtail, abridge, abbreviate, take in, reduce; compress etc. (*contract*) 195; epitomize etc. 596.

retrench, cut short, obtruncate; scrimp, cut, chop up, hack, hew; cut –, pare- down; clip, snip, dock, lop, prune; shear, shave, mow, reap, crop; snub; truncate, pollard, stunt, nip, nip in the bud, check the growth of; [in drawing] foreshorten.

Adj. short, brief, curt; compendious, compact; stubby, scrimp; shorn, stubbed; stumpy, thickset, podgy, stocky, pug; squab, -by; squat, dumpy; little etc. 193; curtailed of its fair proportions; short by; oblate; concise etc. 572; summary.

Adv. shortly etc. *adj.*; in short etc. (*concisely*) 572.

202. Breadth. Thickness.—N. breadth, width, latitude, amplitude; diameter, bore, calibre, radius; superficial extent etc. (*space*) 180.

thickness, crassitude; corpulence etc. (*size*) 192; dilatation etc. (*expansion*) 194.

V. be -broad etc. *adj.*; become –, render- -broad etc. *adj.*; expand etc. 194; thicken, widen.

Adj. broad, wide, ample, extended; discous; fanlike; out-spread, -stretched; wide as a church-door.

thick, dumpy, squab, squat, thickset, tubby; thick as a rope, stubby etc. 201.

203. Narrowness. Thinness.—N. narrowness etc. *adj.*; closeness, exility; exiguity etc. (*little*) 193.

line; hair's –, finger's -breadth; strip, streak, vein.

thinness etc. *adj.*; tenuity; emaciation, slenderness, macilency, *marcor.*

shaving, slip etc. (*filament*) 205; threadpaper, skeleton, shadow, scrag, anatomy, spindle-shanks, barebones, lantern jaws, mere skin and bone.

middle construction, stricture, neck, waist, isthmus, wasp, hour-glass; ridge, *ghaut,* pass; ravine etc. 198.

narrowing, coarctation, angustation, tapering; contraction etc. 195.

V. be-narrow etc. *adj.*; narrow, taper, diminish; contract etc. 195; render -narrow etc. *adj.*

Adj. narrow, close; slender, thin, fine; *svelte;* thread-like etc. (*filament*) 205; finespun, taper, slim, gracile, slight, slight-made; scant, -y; spare, delicate, incapacious; contracted etc. 195; unexpanded etc. (expand etc. 194); slender as a thread, capillary.

emaciated, lean, meager, gaunt, macilent; lank, - y; weedy, skinny, scrawny, scraggy; starv-ed, -eling; attenuated, shrivelled; wizened, pinched, peaky, skeletal, spindling, spindle- -legged, -shanked; ex- tenuated, tabid, marcid, bare-bone, raw-boned; herring-gutted; worn to a shadow, lean as a rake; thin as a -lath,—whipping post,—wafer; hatchet- faced; lantern-jawed.

204. Layer.—N. layer, stratum, course, bed, zone, *substratum,* floor, flag, stage, story, tier, slab, escarpment, table, tablet, panel, plaque; board, plank; trencher, platter.

plate; lam-ina, -ella; sheet, flake, foil, wafer, scale, coat, peel, pellicle, ply, thickness, mem- brane, film, leaf, slice, shive, cut, rasher, shaving, integument etc. (*covering*) 223.

V. slice, shave, pare, peel; plate, coat, veneer; cover etc. 223.

Adj. lamell-ar, -ated, -iform; laminated, -iferous; micaceous; schist-ose, -ous; scaly; filmy, mem- branous, flaky, squamous; folia-ted, -ceous; stratified, -form; tabular, discoid, spathic.

205. Filament.—N. filament, line; fiber, fibril; funicle, vein, hair, capillament, *cilium,* tendril, gossamer; hair-stroke; harl.

wire, string, thread, packthread, cotton, sewing- silk, twine, twist, whip-cord, cord, rope, cable, yarn, hemp, oakum, jute, wool, worsted.

strip, shred, slip, spill, list, band, fillet, *fascia,* ribbon, riband, tape, roll, lath, slat, strake, splinter, shiver, shaving.

beard etc. (*roughness*) 256; ramification; strand.

Adj. fil-amentous, -aceous, -iform; fibr-ous, - illous; thread-like, wiry, stringy, ropy; capill-ary, - iform; funicular, wire-drawn; anguilliform; flagelliform; hairy etc. (*rough*) 256; ligulate.

206. Height.—N. height, altitude, elevation, ceiling; eminence. pitch; loftiness etc. *adj.*; sublimity.

tallness etc. *adj.*; stature, procerity; prominence etc. 250.

colossus etc. (*size*) 192; giant, grenadier, giraffe.

mount, -ain; hill, butte, monticle, fell, knap; cape; head-, fore-land; promontory; ridge, hog's back, dune; rising -, vantage- ground; down; moor, -land; Alp; up-, table-, high-lands; heights etc. (*summit*) 210; knoll, hummock, hillock, barrow, mound, mole, *kopje;* steeps, bluff, cliff, craig, tor, peak, pike, clough; escarpment, edge, ledge, brae; dizzy height.

tower, pillar, column, pylon, obelisk, monument, steeple, spire, minaret, *campanile,* belfry, turret, roof, dome, cupola, pagoda, pyramid; sky scraper; Eiffel tower.

pole, pikestaff, maypole, flagstaff; mast, top—, topgallant- mast.

ceiling etc. (*covering*) 223.

high water; high—, flood—, spring-tide.

altimetry etc. (*angle*) 244; altimeter, height- finder, hypsometer, barograph.

V. be -high etc. *adj.*; tower, soar, command; hover; cap, culminate; overhang, hang over, im- pend, beetle; bestride, ride, mount; perch, sur- mount; cover etc. 233; overtop etc. (*be superior*) 33; stand on tiptoe.

become -high etc. *adj.*; grow, − higher, − taller; upgrow; rise etc. (*ascend*) 305.

render -high etc. *adj.*; heighten etc. (*elevate*) 307.

Adj. high, elevated, eminent, exalted, lofty, supernal; tall; gigantic etc. (*big*) 192; Patagonian; towering, beetling, soaring, hanging [gardens]; elevated etc. 307; upper; highest etc. (*topmost*) 210; monticulous, perching, hill-dwelling.

up-, moor-land; hilly, mountainous, alpine, sub- alpine, heaven-kissing; cloud-topt, -capt, -touching; aerial.

overhanging etc. *v.*; incumbent, overlying; super-incumbent, -natant, -imposed; prominent etc. 250.

tall as a -maypole; −poplar,—steeple; lanky etc. (*thin*) 203.

Adv. on high, high up, aloft, up, above, aloof, overhead; up—, above- stairs; in the clouds; on - tiptoe, —stilts,—the shoulders of; over head and ears; breast high.

over, upwards; from top to bottom etc. (*com- pletely*) 52.

207. Lowness.—N. lowness etc. *adj.*; debasement, depression; prostration etc. (*horizon- tal*) 213; depression etc. (*concave*) 252.

molehill; lowlands; bottomlands; basement- ground-floor; *rez de chaussee* etc. 211; hold; feet, heels.

low water; low—, ebb—, neap—, spring- tide.

V. be -low etc. *adj.*; lie -low, —flat; underlie; crouch, slouch, wallow, grovel; lower etc. (*depress*) 308.

Adj. low, neap, debased; nether, -most; flat, level with the ground; lying low, etc. *v.*; crouched, subjacent, squat, prostrate etc. (*horizontal*) 213.

Adv. under; be-, under-neath; below; down, - wards; adown, at the foot of; under-foot, -ground; down—, below-stairs; at a low ebb; below par.

208. Depth.—N. depth; deepness etc. *adj.*; profundity, depression etc. (*concavity*) 252.

hollow, pit, shaft, well, crater, abyss; gulf etc. 198; bowels of the earth, bottomless pit, hell.

soundings, sonar, depth of water, water, draught, submersion; plummet, sound, probe; sounding - rod, − line, − machine; lead; submarine, diving bell, bathysphere; diver.

V. be -deep etc. *adj.*; render -deep etc. *adj.*; deepen.

plunge etc. 310; sound, heave the lead, take soundings; dig etc. (*excavate*) 252.

Adj. deep, -seated; profound, sunk, buried; sub- merged etc. 310; sub-aqueous, -marine, -terranean, -terrene; underground.

bottom-, sound-, fathom-less; unfathom-ed, - able; abysmal; deep as a well, deep-sea.

knee-, ankle-deep.

Adv. beyond—, out of- one's depth; over head and ears, over one's head.

209. Shallowness.—N. shallowness etc. *adj.*; shoals; mere scratch; veneer, gloss, pinprick.

Adj. shallow, superficial; skin—, ankle—, knee-deep; just enough to wet one's feet; shoal, -y.

V. shallow, shoal, skim— over, —the surface, touch on.

210. Summit.—N. summit, -y; top, vertex, apex, zenith, pinnacle, acme, acropolis, culmination, meridian, utmost height, *ne plus ultra,* height, pitch, maximum, climax, apogee; culminating —, crowning —, turning- point; turn of the tide, fountain head; water-shed, -parting; sky, pole.

tip, -top; crest, crow's nest, cap, truck, peak, nib; end etc. 67; crown, brow; head, nob, noddle, pate, skull, cranium.

high places, heights.

top-, top-gallant mast, sky scraper; quarter —, hurricane- deck.

architrave, frieze, cornice, coping, coping-stone, zoophorus, capital, headpiece, capstone, epistyle, sconce, pediment, entablature; tympanum; ceiling etc. (*covering*) 223.

attic, loft, garret, house-top, upper story, roof.

topping, icing, frosting.

V. culminate, cap, crown, top; overtop etc. (*be superior to*) 33.

Adj. highest etc. (high etc. 206); top; top-, upper-most; tip-top; culminating etc. *v.*; meridi-an, -onal; capital, head, ,polar, supreme, supernal, top-gallant.

Adv. a-top, at the top of — the tree, — the heap.

211. Base.—N. base, -ment; plinth, dado, wainscot, baseboard; foundation etc. (*support*) 215; substructure, sub · stratum, sump, ground, earth, pavement, floor, paving, flag, carpet, ground-floor, deck; footing, groundwork, basis; hold, bilge, orlop deck.

bottom, nadir, foot, sole, toe, hoof, keel, kelson, root.

Adj. bottom; under-, nether-most; fundamental; founded —, based —, grounded —, built- on.

212. Verticality.—N. verticality; erectness etc. *adj.*; perpendicularity; right angle, normal; azimuth circle.

wall, palisade, precipice, cliff, steep, bluff.

elevation, erection; square, plumb-line, plummet.

V. be -vertical etc. *adj.*; stand -up, — on end, — erect, — upright; stick —, cock-up.

render -vertical etc. *adj.*; set —, stick —, raise —, cock- up; erect, rear, raise, pitch, raise on its legs.

Adj. vertical, upright, erect, perpendicular, normal, plumb, straight, bolt upright; rampant; straight —, standing- up etc. *v.*; rectangular, orthogonal.

Adv. vertically etc. *adj.*; up, on end; up —, right- on end; *à plomb,* endwise; on one's legs; at right angles.

213. Horizontality.—N. horizontality; flatness; level, plane; stratum etc. 204; dead -level, — flat; level plane.

recumbency; lying down etc. *v.*; reclination, decumbence; de-, discumbency; proneness etc. *adj.*; accubation, supination, resupination, prostration; azimuth.

plain, floor, platform, bowling-green; cricket--ground; court; gridiron; base-ball diamond; hockey rink; tennis-, croquet-ground, — lawn; billiard table; terrace, estrade, esplanade, *parterre,* table-land, *plateau,* ledge.

spirit-, level; T-square.

V. be -horizontal etc. *adj.*; lie, recline, couch; lie -down, — flat, — prostrate; sprawl, loll; sit down.

render -horizontal etc. *adj.*; lay, — down, — out; level, flatten, even, raze, equalize, smooth, align; prostrate, knock down, floor, fell, ground.

Adj. horizontal, level, even, plane; flat etc. 251; flat as a -billiard table, — bowling green; alluvial; calm, — as a mill-pond; smooth, —as glass.

re-, de-, pro-, ac-cumbent; lying etc. *v.*; prone, supine, couchant, jacent, prostrate.

Adv. horizontally etc. *adj.*; on -one's back. —all fours. — its beam ends.

214. Pendency.—N. pend-, dependency; suspension, hanging etc. *v.*

pendant, drop, tippet, tassel, lobe, tail, train, flap, lappet, skirt, pig-tail, queue, pendulum, hanger, suspender, supporter.

peg, knob, button, hook, nail, stud, ring, staple, tenterhook; davit; fastening etc. 45; spar, horse, chande-, gase-, electro-lier.

V. be -pendent etc. *adj.*; hang, depend, swing, dangle, droop, sag; swag; daggle, flap, trail, flow.

suspend, hang, sling, hook up, hitch, fasten to, append.

Adj. pend-ent, -ulous; pensile; hanging etc. *v.*; dependent; suspended etc. *v.*; lowering, overhanging, beetling, decumbent; loose, flowing.

having a -peduncle etc. *n.*; pedunculate, tailed, caudate.

215. Support.—N. support, backing, ground, foundation, base, basis; *terra firma;* bearing, fulcrum, *point d'appui,* caudex, purchase, footing, hold, -locus standi; landing, — stage, — place; stage, platform; block; rest, resting-place; ground--work, *substratum,* sustentation, subvention; floor etc. (*basement*) 211.

supporter; aid etc. 707; prop, stand, anvil, fulciment; hod, stay, shore, skid, rib, sprag, truss, bandage; sleeper; stirrup, stilts, shoe, sole, heel, splint, lap; bar, rod, boom, sprit, outrigger.

staff, stick, crutch, alpenstock, bourdon; *bâton,* maulstick, colstaff, cowlstaff, staddle; stalk, ped-icel, -icle, — uncle.

post, pillar, shaft, column, pilaster; pediment, pedestal; plinth, shank, leg, socle, zocle; buttress, jamb, mullion, abutment; pile, baluster, banister, stanchion, king post; balustrade.

frame, -work, body, *chassis, fuselage;* scaffold, skeleton, beam, rafter, girder, lintel, joist, cantilever, travis, trave, corner-stone, summer, transom; rung, round, step, sill.

columella, back-bone; key-stone; axle, -tree; axis; arch, ogive, mainstay.

trunnion, pivot, rowlock; peg etc. (*pendency*)

214; tie-beam etc. (*fastening*) 45; thole pin.

board; ledge, shelf, hob, bracket, trevet, trivet, arbor, rack, hatrack; mantel, -piece, -shelf; slab, console; counter, dresser; flange, corbel; table, trestle, teapoy; shoulder; perch; horse; easel, desk; retable, predella.

seat, throne, dais; divan, musnud; chair, bench, form, stool, camp-stool, sofa, settee, davenport, stall, miserere, arm —, easy —, elbow —, rocking-chair; couch, day bed, *fauteuil*, woolsack, ottoman, settle, squab, bench, box, dicky; saddle, pannel, pillion; side —, pack- saddle; pommel.

bed, berth, pallet, tester, crib, cot, bassinet, hammock, shakedown, camp bed, bunk, truckle-bed, cradle, litter, stretcher, bedstead; four-poster, French bed; bedding, mattress, *paillasse;* pillow, bolster; mat, rug, cushion.

stool, footstool, hassock, faldstool, *prie-dieu;* tabouret; tripod:

Atlas, Persides, Atlantes, Caryatides, Hercules.

V. be -supported etc.; lie —, sit —, recline —, lean —, loll —, rest —, stand —, step —, repose —, abut —, beat —, be based etc.- on; have at one's back; be-stride, -straddle.

support, bear, carry, hold, sustain, shoulder; hold —, back —, bolster —, shore- up; up-hold, - bear; prop; under-prop, -pin, -set; bandage, etc. 43; brace, truss; cradle, pillow.

give —, furnish —, afford —, supply —, lend- -, support, — foundations; bottom, found, base, ground, embed.

maintain, keep on foot; aid etc. 707.

Adj. support-ing, -ed, etc.*v.*; atlantean, columellar; sustentative, fundamental, basal.

Adv. astride on, astraddle; pick-a-back.

216. Parallelism.—N. parallelism; coextension, concentricity, collimation.

V. be —, lie- parallel to; collimate; equate, match.

Adj. parallel; coextensive, collateral, concentric, concurrent, abreast, aligned.

Adv. alongside, abreast etc. (*laterally*) 236.

217. Obliquity.—N. obliquity, inclination, skew, slope, slant; crookedness etc. *adj.*; slopeness; leaning etc. *v.*; bevel, bezel, ramp, tilt; bias, list, twist, warp, swag, cant, lurch; distortion etc. 243; bend etc. (*curve*) 245; tower of Pisa.

acclivity, rise, ascent, grade, gradient, *glacis,* rising ground, hill, bank, declivity, downhill, dip, fall, devexity; gentle —, rapid- slope; easy -ascent, — descent; shelving beach; *talus; montagne Russe; facilis descensus Averni.*

steepness etc. *adj.*; cliff, precipice etc. (*vertical*) 212; escarpment, scarp.

[Measure of inclination]clinometer, theodolite, level, sextant, quadrant, protractor; angle, sine, cosine, tangent etc. hypothenuse.

diagonal; zigzag, chevron.

V. be -oblique etc. *adj.*; slope, slant, lean, incline, shelve, stoop, decline, descent, bend, heel, careen, sag, swag, seel, slouch, cant, sidle.

render -oblique etc. *adj.*; sway, bias; slope, slant; incline, bend, crook; cant, tilt; distort etc. 243.

Adj. oblique, inclined; sloping etc. *v.*; tilted etc.

v.; recumbent, clinal, skew, askew, slant, aslant, bias, plagiedral, indirect, wry, awry, ajee, crooked; knock-kneed etc. (*distorted*) 243; bevel, out of the perpendicular.

uphill, rising, ascending, acclivous; downhill, falling, descending; declining, declivous, devex, anticlinal; steep, abrupt, precipitous, breakneck.

diagonal; trans-verse, -versal; athwart, antiparallel; curved etc. 245.

Adv. obliquely etc. *adj.*; on —, all on- one side; askew, askant, askance, aslope, asquint, edgewise, at an angle; side-long, -ways; slope-, slant-wise; by a side wind.

218. Inversion.—N. in-, e-, sub-, re-, retro-, intro-version; contraposition etc. 237; contrariety etc. 14; reversal; turn of the tide.

overturn; upset, capsize; somer-sault, -set; summerset; *culbute;* revulsion; *pirouette.*

transposition, transposal, anastrophy, *metastasis, hyperbaton, anastrophe, hysteron--proteron,* hypallage, *synchysis, tmesis,* parenthesis; *metathesis;* palindrome; Spoonerism.

pronation and supination.

V. be -inverted etc.; turn —, go —, wheel- -round, — about, — to the right about; turn —, go —, tilt —, topple-over; capsize, turn turtle.

in-, sub-, retro-, intro-vert; reverse; up-, overturn, -set; turn -topsy turvy etc. *adj.*; *culbuter;* transpose, put the cart before the horse, turn the tables.

Adj. inverted etc. *v.*; wrong side -out, — up; inside out, upside down; bottom —, keel- upwards; supine, on one's head, topsy turvy, *sens dessus sens dessous.*

inverse; reverse etc. (*contrary*) 14; opposite etc. 237.

topheavy, unstable.

Adv. inversely etc.*adj.*; hirdie-girdie; heels over head, head over heels.

219. Crossing.—N. crossing etc. *v.*; intersection, — lacement, — twinement, -digitation; decussation, transversion; convolution etc. 248.

reticulation, meshwork, network; inosculation, anastomosis, inter-texture, mortise.

net, *plexus,* web, mesh, twill, skein, sleeve, felt, lace; wicker; mat, -ting; plait, trellis, wattle, lattice, grating, *grille,* gridiron, tracery, fretwork, filigree, reticle; tissue, netting, mokes.

cross, crucifix, rood, crisscross, ⁎ crux; chain, wreath, braid, cat's cradle, knot; entanglement etc. (*disorder*) 59.

[woven fabrics] cloth, linen, muslin, cambric, drill, homespun, tweed, broadcloth etc.

V. cross, decussate; inter-sect, -lace, -twine, - twist, -weave, -digitate, -link.

twine, entwine, weave, inweave, twist, wreathe; anastomose, inosculate, dovetail, splice, link.

mat, plait, plat, braid, felt, twill; tangle, entangle, ravel, net, knot; dishevel, raddle.

Adj. crossing etc.*v.*; crossed, matted etc. *v.*; transverse.

cross, cruciform, crucial; reti-form, -cular, -culated; arcolar, cancellated, mullioned, latticed, grated, barred, streaked; textile, secant, plexal; interfretted.

Adv. across, thwart, athwart, transversely, crosswise.

220. Exteriority.—N. exteriority; outside, exterior; surface, superficies; skin etc. (*covering*) 223; superstratum; disk, disc; face, facet, external, the open.

excentricity; circumjacence etc. 227.

V. be -exterior etc. *adj.*; lie around etc. 227.

place -exteriorly, — outwardly, — outside; put —, turn- out.

Adj. exter-ior, -nal; extraneous, outer, -most; out-ward, -lying, -side, -door; round about etc. 227; extramural.

superficial, skin-deep; frontal, discoid.

extraregarding; eccentric; outstanding; extrinsic etc. 6.

Adv. externally etc. *adj.*; out, without, over, outwards, *ab extra*, out of doors; *extra muros*.

in the open air; *sub -Jovè*, — *dio*; *à la belle étoile*, *al fresco*.

221. Interiority.—N. interiority; inside, -land, interior, endocrine; interspace, subsoil, *substratum*.

contents etc. 190; substance, pith, marrow; backbone etc. (*center*) 222; heart, bosom, breast, abdomen; vitals, viscera, entrails, bowels, belly, intestines, guts, chitterlings, womb, lap; gland, cell; internal organs, *penetralia*, recesses, innermost recesses; cave etc. (*concavity*) 252.

inhabitant etc. 188.

V. be -inside etc. *adj.*, — within etc. *adv.*

place —, keep- within, enclose etc. (*circumscribe*) 229; intern; embed etc. (*insert*) 300.

Adj. inter-ior, -nal; inner, inside, intimate, inward, intraregarding; in-, inner-most; deep-seated; visceral, intestine, -tinal; inland; subcutaneous; interstitial etc. (*interjacent*) 228; inwrought etc. (*intrinsic*) 5; enclosed etc. *v.*

home, domestic, indoor, intramural, vernacular; endemic.

Adv. internally etc. *adj.*; inwards, within, in, inly; here-, there-, where-in; *ab intra*, withinside; in —, within- doors; at home, in the bosom of one's family.

222. Centrality.—N. centrality, centricalness; center; middle etc. 68; focus etc. 74.

core, kernel; nucleus, nucleolus; heart, pole, axis, pivot, fulcrum, bull's eye; hub, nave, navel; *umbilicus*, spine, backbone, marrow, pith; hot-bed; concentration etc. (*convergence*) 290; centralization; symmetry.

center of -gravity, — pressure, — percussion, — oscillation, — buoyancy etc. metacenter.

V. be -central etc. *adj.*; converge etc. 290.

render central, centralize, concentrate; bring to a focus.

Adj. centr-al, -ical; middle etc. 68; axial, pivotal, focal, umbilical, concentric; middlemost, nuclear, centric, centraidal; spinal, vertebral.

Adv. middle; midst; centrally etc. *adj.*

223. Covering.—N. covering, cover; canopy, tilt, awning, baldachin, tent, marquee, *tente d'abri*, umbrella, parasol, sunshade; veil (*shade*) 424; shield etc. (*defense*) 717; hall.

roof, dome, cupola, mansard roof; ceiling; thatch, tile; pan-, pen-tile; tiling, shingles, slates, slating, leads; shed etc. (*abode*) 189.

top, lid, covercle, door, *operculum*, eyelid, blind, curtain.

bandage, plaster, lint, wrapping, dossil, finger stall.

coverlet, counterpane, sheet, quilt, comforter, eiderdown; tarpaulin, blanket, rug, drugget, linoleum, oilcloth; housing.

in-, tegument; skin, pellicle, fleece, fell, fur, ermine, miniver, sable, sealskin etc.; fabrikoid; leather, morocco, calf, pigskin, elk, kid, cowhide etc.; shagreen, hide; pelt, -ry; cuticle, *dermis*, scarfskin, *epidermis*.

clothing etc. 225; mask etc. (*concealment*) 530.

peel, crust, bark, rind, *cortex*, husk, shell, coat.

capsule; ferrule; sheath, -ing; pod, cod; casing, case, theca; *elytron*; *involucrum*; wrapp-ing, -er; cellophane; envelope, vesicle; dermatology, conchology.

armor, -plate, armoring; veneer, facing; pavement; scale etc. (*layer*) 204; coating, paint, stain; varnish etc. (*resin*) 356a; anointing etc. *v.*; inunction; incrustation, superposition, obduction, ground, enamel, whitewash, plaster, stucco, rough cast, pebble dash, compo; rendering; cerement; ointment etc. (*grease*) 356.

V. cover; super-pose, -impose; over-lay, -spread; wrap etc. 225; incase; face, case, veneer, pave, paper; tip, cap, bind, revet.

coat, paint, varnish, pay, incrust, stucco, cement, dab, plaster, tar; wash; be-, smear; be-, daub; anoint, do over; gild, plate, electroplate, japan, laquer, lacker, enamel, whitewash; lay it on thick.

over-lie, -arch; conceal etc. 528.

Adj. covering etc. *v.*; cutaneous, dermal, cortical, cuticular, tegumentary, skinny, scaly, squamous; covered etc. *v.*; imbricated, loricated, armor-plated, iron-clad; under cover, hooded, cloaked, cowled.

224. Lining.—N. lining, inner coating; coating etc. (*covering*) 223; stalactite, -agmite.

filling, stuffing, wadding, padding, bushing.

wainscot, *parietes*, wall brattice.

V. line, stuff, incrust, wad, pad, fill.

Adj. lined etc. *v.*

225. Investment.—N. investment; covering etc. 223; dress, clothing, raiment, drapery, costume, attire, guise, toilet, *toilette*, trim; habiliment; vesture, -ment; garment, garb, palliament, apparel, wardrobe, wearing apparel, clothes, things.

array; tailoring, millinery; best bib and tucker; finery etc. (*ornament*) 847; full dress etc. (*show*) 882; garniture; theatrical properties.

outfit, equipment, *trousseau*; uniform, khaki, regimentals; academicals, canonicals etc. 999; livery, gear, harness, turn out, accoutrement, caparison, suit, rigging, trappings, traps, slops, togs, toggery; masquerade.

dishabille, morning dress, lounge suit, tea-gown, *kimono*, *négligé*, dressing-gown, *peignoir*, wrapper, undress; shooting-coat; smoking jacket, mufti; rags, tatters, old clothes; mourning, weeds; duds; slippers.

robe, tunic, dolman, *paletot*, habit, gown, coat, coatee, frock, blouse, *pelisse*, middy, sagum, *toga*, smock-frock; frock-, dress-, morning-, tail- coat; dress-suit, — clothes, swallow-tail coat, dinner-, Eton-jacket.

cloak, pall; mantle, mantlet, mantua, shawl, *pelisse*, veil, yashmak; cape, tippet, kirtle, plaid, muffler, comforter, Balaclava helmet, haik, huke, chlamys, mantilla, tabard, housing, horse-cloth, burnous, *roquelaure*, *houppelande*; sur-, top-, over-, great-coat; *surtout*, spencer, cardigan, sweater, blazer; mackintosh, waterproof, slicker, raincoat, oilskin, trench coat, ulster, monkey-, pea-, pilot-jacket, redingote; wraprascal, poncho, cardinal, pelerine, talma.

jacket, jumper, vest, jerkin, waistcoat, doublet, *camisole*, gabardine; stays, *corsage*, corset, corselet, bodice; stomacher; skirt; petticoat, slip, farthingale, kilt, jupe, crinoline, bustle, hobble skirt, *panier*, apron, pinafore; loin cloth.

trousers; breeches, trews, pantaloons, unmentionables, inexpressibles, overalls, pajamas, smalls, small-clothes; tights, pants, shorts, drawers; knickerbockers, knickers, plus fours, bloomers, divided skirt; phil-, fill-ibeg.

head-dress, -gear; cap, *béret*, tam o' shanter, glengarry, topee, sombrero; hat; cocked —, high —, tall —, top —, silk —, opera —, crush - hat, *gibus*, beaver, castor, bonnet, tile, wideawake, billy-cock; bowler; soft felt —, straw —, leghorn- hat, panama; toque; wimple; night-, mob-, skull-cap, biretta; hood, cowl, coif; capote, calach; skull-cap; kerchief, snood; head, *coiffure*; crown etc. (circle) 247; *chignon*, pelt, wig, front, peruke, periwig; caftan, turban, fez, *tarboosh*, taj, shako, csako, busby; *képi*, forage cap, bearskin; helmet etc. 717; mask, domino.

body clothes; linen; shirt, sark, smock, shift, *chemise*, *lingerie*; night-gown, -shirt; bed-gown, *sac de nuit*; jersey, guernsey; underclothing, -waistcoat.

neck-erchief, -cloth; tie, ruff, collar, cravat, stock, handkerchief, bandana, scarf; bib, tucker; dicky; boa; girdle etc. (circle) 247; cummerbund.

shoe, pump, brogue, boot, slipper, sandal, galoche, galoshes, arctics, rubber boots, overshoes, patten, clog, sabot; high-low; Blucher —, Wellington —, Hessian —, jack —, top- boot; Balmoral; legging, puttee, buskin, greave, galligaskin, moccasin, *gamache*, gambado, gaiter, spatter-dash, spat, antigropeles; stocking, hose, gaskins, trunk-hose, sock, hosiery.

glove, gauntlet, mitten, cuff, muffettee, wristband, sleeve.

swaddling cloth, baby-linen, *layette*; pocket-handkerchief.

shroud, etc. 363.

clothier, tailor, milliner, *costumier*, sempstress, seamstress, snip; dress-, habit-, breeches-, shoe-maker; cordwainer, cobbler, Crispin, hosier, hatter; draper, linendraper, haberdasher, mercer.

V. invest; cover etc. 223; envelop, lap, involve; in-, en-wrap; wrap; fold —, wrap —, lap —, muffle-up; overlap; sheathe, swathe, swaddle, roll up in, shroud, circumvest.

vest, clothe, array, dress, dight, drape, robe, enrobe, attire, tire, garb, habilitate, apparel, accouter, rig, fit out; bedizen, deck etc. (ornament) 847; perk; equip, harness, caparison; dress up.

wear; don; put —, huddle —, slip- on; mantle.
Adj. invested etc. *v.*; habited; dight, -ed; clad, *costumé*, shod, *chaussé*; *en grande tenue* etc. (show) 882.
sartorial.

226. Divestment.—N. divestment; taking off, stripping, removal etc. *v.*
nudity; bareness etc. *adj.*; undress; dishabille etc. 225, altogether; nu-, denu-dation; decortication, depilation, excoriation, desquamation; molting; exfoliation.
baldness, alopecia, acomia.
V. divest; uncover etc. (cover etc. 223); denude, bare, strip; undress, unclothe, disrobe etc. (dress, enrobe, etc. 225); uncoif; dismantle; uncase; put —, take —, cast- off; shed, doff; husk, peel, pare, decorticate, desquamate; excoriate, skin, scalp, flay, bark, expose, lay open; exfoliate, molt, mew; cast the skin.
Adj. divested etc. *v.*; bare, naked, nude; undressed, -draped, -clad, -clothed, -appareled; exposed; in dishabille; *décolleté*; bald, threadbare, ragged, callow, roofless.
in -a state of nature, — nature's garb, — buff, — native buff, — birthday suit; *in puris naturalibus*; with nothing on, stark naked; bald as a coot, bare as the back of one's hand; out at elbows; barefoot; bareback; leaf-, nap-, hairless, shaved, clean shaven, tonsured, beardless, bald-headed, acomous.

227. Circumjacence.—N. circumjacence, -ambience; environment, encompassment; atmosphere, medium; surroundings, entourage.
outpost; border etc. (edge) 231; girdle etc. (circumference) 230; outskirts, *boulevards*, suburbs, purlieus, precincts, *faubourgs*, *environs*, *banlieue*, neighborhood, vicinity.
V. lie -around etc. *adv.*; surround, beset, compass, encompass, environ, inclose, enclose, encircle, circle, embrace, circumvent, lap, gird; begird, girdle, engird; skirt, twine round; hem in etc. (circumscribe) 229; besiege, invest, blockade.
Adj. circum-jacent, -ambient, -fluent; ambient; surrounding etc. *v.*; circumferential, suburban.
Adv. around, about; without; on -every side, — all sides; right and left, all round, round about; in the neighborhood.

228. Interjacence.—N. inter-jacence, -currence, -venience, -location, -digitation, -penetration; permeation.
inter-jection, -polation, -lineation, -spersion, -calation; embolism.
inter-vention, -ference, -position; in-, ob-trusion; insinuation; insertion etc. 300; dovetailing; infiltration; intromission.
intermedi-um, -ary; go-between, agent, middleman, medium, bodkin, intruder, interloper; parenthesis, episode; fly-leaf.
partition, *septum*, diaphragm, mid-riff; partywall, panel, vail, bulkhead, brattice, *cloison*; halfway house.
V. lie —, come —, get- between; intervene, slide in, interpenetrate, permeate.

put between, introduce, intromit, import; throw –, wedge –, edge –, jam –, worm –, foist –, run –, plough –, work- in; interpose, -ject, -calate. -polate, -line, -leave, -sperse, -weave, -lard, -digitate; let in, dovetail, splice, mortise; insinuate, smuggle; infiltrate, ingrain.

interfere, put in an oar, thrust one's nose in; intrude, obtrude; have a finger in the pie; introduce the thin end of the wedge; thrust in etc. (*insert*) 300.

Adj. inter-jacent, -current, -venient, -vening etc. *v.*, -mediate, -mediary, -calary, -sitital, -costal, - mural, -planetary, -stellar; embolismal.

parenthetical, episodic: mediterranean; intrusive; embosomed; merged, mean, middle, medium, median.

Adv. between, betwixt; 'twixt; among, -st; amid, st; 'mid, -st, in the thick of; betwixt and between; sandwich-wise; parenthetically, *obiter dictum*.

229. Circumscription.—N. circumscription, limitation, inclosure; confinement etc. (*restraint*) 751; circumvallation, encincture; envelope etc. 232.

V. circumscribe, limit, bound, confine, restrict, enclose; surround etc. 227; compass about; imprision etc. (*restrain*) 751; hedge –, wall –, railin; fence –, hedge- round; embar; picket, corral.

enfold, bury, incase, pack up, enshrine, inclasp; wrap up etc. (*invest*) 225; embosom.

Adj. circumscribed etc. *v.*; begirt, lapt; circumambient; buried –, immersed- in; embosomed, in the bosom of, imbedded, encysted, mewed up; imprisoned etc. 751; land-locked, in a ring fence.

230. Outline.—N. outline, circumference; perimeter, -phery; ambit, circuit, lines, *tournure*, *contour*, profile, *silhouette*, lineaments; bounds, coastline.

zone, belt, girth, band, baldric, zodiac, girdle, tire, cingle, clasp, girt; *cordon* etc. (*inclosure*) 232; circlet etc. 247.

V. outline, delineate, *silhouette*, circumscribe etc. 229; profile, block out.

Adj. outlined etc. *v.*; circumferential, perimetric, peripheral.

231. Edge.—N. edge, verge, brink, brow, brim, margin, border, confines, skirt, rim, felloe, felly, flange, side, mouth; jaws, chops, chaps, *fauces*; lip, muzzle.

threshold, door, porch; portal etc. (*opening*) 260; coast, shore, strand, beach, bank, wharf, quay, dock.

frame, fringe, flounce, frill, list, trimming, edging, skirting, hem, selvedge, welt; furbelow, valance, exergue.

Adj. border, marginal, skirting; labial; labiated, marginated.

232. Inclosure.—N. inclosure, enclosure, envelope; package, box, crate, case etc. (*receptacle*) 191; wrapper; girdle etc. 230.

pen, fold, croft, sty; pen-, in-, sheep-'fold; paddock, pound, corral, kraal; yard, compound; net, seine net.

wall; hedge, -row; *espalier*; fence etc. (*defence*) 717; pale, paling, balustrade, rail, railing, gunwale; quickset hedge, park paling, circumvallation, *enciente*, ring fence.

barrier, barricade; gate; -way; door, hatch, *cordon*; prison etc. 752.

dike, dyke, ditch, fosse, moat, trench.

V. inclose; circumscribe etc. 229.

233. Limit.—N. limit, boundary, bounds, confine, *enclave*, term, bourn, verge, kerb-stone, curbstone, but, pale; termin-ation, -us; stint, frontier, precinct, marches.

boundary line, landmark; line of -demarcation, – circumvallation; pillars of Hercules; Rubicon, turning-point; *ne plus ultra*; sluice, flood-gate.

V. limit, bound, confine, define, circumscribe, demarcate, delimit, encompass.

Adj. definite; contermin-ate, -able, terminable, limitable; terminal, frontier, border, bordering, boundary.

Adv. thus far, – and no further.

234. Front.—N. front; fore, – part: foreground; forefront, face, disk, disc, frontage, *façade*, *proscenium*, facia, frontispiece; priority, anteriority; obverse [of a medal].

fore –, front- rank, first line; van, -guard; advanced guard; outpost, scout.

brow, forehead, visage, physiognomy, phiz, features, countenance, map, mug; rostrum, beak, bow, stem, prow, prore, jib, bowsprit; forecastle.

pioneer etc.(*precursor*) 64; metoposcopy.

V. be –, stand- in front etc. *adj.*; front, face, confront, breast, brave; bend forwards; come to the -front, – fore.

Adj. fore, forward, anterior, front, frontal, head-on, leading, first, primary.

Adv. before; in -front, – the van, – advance; ahead, right ahead; fore-, head-most; in the foreground; before one's -face, – eyes; face to face, *vis-à-vis*.

235. Rear.—N. rear, back, posterior-ity; rear - rank, – guard; background, *hinterland*.

occiput, nape, scruff, chine, heels; tail, rump, croup, buttock, posteriors, bottom, seat, backside, scut, breech, *dorsum*, loin; dorsal –, lumbar-region; hind quarters.

stern poop, after-part, counter; postern, heel-, tail-piece, crupper.

wake; train etc. (*sequence*) 281.

reverse; other side of the shield.

V. be -behind etc. *adv.*; fall astern; bend backwards; bring up the rear; follow etc. 622; tail, shadow.

Adj. back, rear; hind. -er, -most, -ermost; postern. -erior; dorsal, after; caudal, lumbar; mizzen.

Adv. behind; in the -rear, – ruck, – background; behind one's back; at the -heels, — tail. — back- of; back to back.

after, -most, aft, abaft, astern, stern- most, aback, rear-, hind-, back-ward.

236. Laterality.—N. laterality; side, flank, beam, quarter, lee; hand; cheek, jowl, jole, wing; profile; temple, *parietes*, loin, haunch, hip.

gable, -end; broadside; lee side.

points of the compass; East, Orient, Levant; West, occident; orientation.

V. be -on one side etc. *adv.*; flank, outflank; sidle; skirt, border.

Adj. lateral, sidelong; collateral; parietal, flanking, skirting; flanked; sideling.

many-sided; multi-, bi-, tri-, quadri- lateral.

East-ern, -ward, -erly; orient, -al, auroral, Levantine; West-ern, -ward, -erly; occidental, Hesperian; equatorial.

Adv. side-ways, -long; broadside on; on one side, abreast, abeam, alongside, beside, aside; by, — the side of; side by side; cheek by jowl etc. (*near*) 197; to -windward, — leeward; laterally etc. *adj.*; right and left; on her beam ends.

237. Contraposition.—N. contraposition, opposition; polarity; inversion etc. 218; opposite side; antithesis; reverse, inverse; counterpart; antipodes; opposite poles, North and South.

V. be -opposite etc. *adj.*; subtend.

Adj. opposite; reverse, inverse; antipodal, subcontrary; fronting, facing, diametrically opposite.

Northern, Septentrional, Boreal, arctic; Southern, Austral, antarctic, polar.

Adv. over, — the way, — against; against; face to face, vis-à-vis; as poles asunder.

238. Dextrality.—N. dextrality; right, — hand; dexter, offside, starboard.

Adj. dextral, right-handed; ambidextral; dexterous, dextrorsal etc.

239. Sinistrality.—N. sinistrality; left, — hand; *sinister*, nearside, larboard, port.

Adj. sinistral, sinister, sinistrorsal etc., left-handed, sinistromanual, sinistrous.

240. Form.—N. form, figure, shape, physique; con-formation, -figuration; make, formation, frame, construction, design, cut, set, build, trim, cut of one's jib; stamp, type, cast, mold; fashion; contour etc. (*outline*) 230; structure etc. 329.

feature, lineament, outline, turn; phase etc. (*aspect*) 448; posture, attitude, *pose*.

[Science of form] morphology.

[Similarity of form] isomorphism.

forming etc. *v.*; form-, figur-, efform- ation; sculpture.

V. form, shape, figure, fashion, efform, carve, cut, chisel, hew, cast; rough-hew, -cast; sketch; block —, hammer- out; trim; lick —, put- into

shape; model, knead, work up into, set, mold, sculpture; cast, stamp; built etc. (*construct*) 161.

Adj. formed etc. *v.*

[Receiving form] plastic, fictile, full- fashioned etc.

[Giving form] plasmic, etc.

[Similar in form] isomorphous etc.

241. Amorphism. [Absence of form.]—N. amorphism, informity, uncouthness; unlicked cub, rough diamond; *rudis indigestaque moles*; disorder etc. 59; deformity etc. 243.

disfigure-, deface-ment, deformation; mutilation.

V. [Destroy form] deface, disfigure, deform, mutilate, truncate; derange etc. 61.

Adj. shapeless, amorphous, malformed, formless; un-formed, -hewn, -fashioned, -shapen; rough, rude, Gothic, barbarous, rugged, in the rough; misshapen etc. 243.

242. Symmetry. [Regularity of form.]—N. symmetry, shapeliness, finish; beauty etc. 845; proportion, eurythmy, eurythmic, uniformity, parallelism; bi-, tri-, multi-lateral symmetry; centrality etc. 222.

arborescence, branching, ramification.

Adj. symmetrical, shapely, well set, finished; beautiful etc. 845; classic, chaste, severe.

regular, uniform, balanced; equal etc. 27; parallel, coextensive.

arbor-escent, -iform; dendr-iform, -oid; branching; ramous, ramose.

243. Distortion. [Irregularity of form.]—N. dis-, de-, con-tortion; knot, mop, warp, buckle, screw, twist; crookedness etc. (*obliquity*) 217; grimace; deformity; mal-, malcon-formation; monstrosity, misproportion, want of symmetry, *anamorphosis*; ugliness etc. 846; teratology.

V. distort, contort, twist, warp etc. *n.*; wrest, writhe, make faces, deform, misshape.

Adj. distorted etc. *v.*; out of shape, irregular, unsymmetric, awry, wry, askew, crooked, sinuous; anamorphous; not -true, — straight; on one side, crump, deformed; mis-shapen, -begotten; mis-, ill-proportioned; ill-made; grotesque, crooked as a ram's horn; hump-, hunch-, bunch-, crook-backed; bandy; bandy-, bow-legged; bow-, knock-kneed; splay-, club-footed; taliped; round-shouldered; snub-nosed; curtailed of one's fair proportions; scalene, stumpy etc. (*short*) 201; gaunt etc. (*thin*) 203; bloated etc. 194.

Adv. all manner of ways.

244. Angularity.—N. angular-ity, -ness; aduncity; angle, cusp, bend; fold etc. 258; notch etc. 257; fork, bifurcation.

elbow, knee, knuckle, ankle, groin, crotch, crane, fluke, scythe, sickle, zigzag, kimbo.

corner, nook, recess, niche, oriel.

right angle etc. (*perpendicular*) 212; obliquity etc. 217; angle of 45 degrees, miter; acute —, obtuse —, salient —, re-entrant —, spherical —, solid —, dihedral- angle.

angular -measurement, − elevation, − distance, − velocity; trigon-, goni-ometry; altimetry; clin-, graph-, goni-ometer; theodolite; transit circle; sextant, quadrant; dichotomy.

triangle, trigon, wedge; rectangle, square, lozenge, diamond; rhomb, -us; quadr-angle, -ilateral; parallelogram; quadrature; poly-, penta-, hexa-, hepta-, octa-, deca-gon.

Platonic bodies; cube, rhomboid; tetra-, penta-, hexa-, octa-, dodeca-, icosa-hedron; prism, pyramid; parallelopiped.

V. bend, fork, bifurcate, crinkle, divaricate, branch, ramify.

Adj. angular, bent, crooked, aduncous, uncinated, aquiline, jagged, serrated; falc-iform, -ated; furcular, furcated, forked, bifurcate, crotched; zigzag; dovetailed; knock-kneed, crinkled, akimbo, kimbo, geniculated; oblique etc. 217.

fusiform, wedge-shaped, cuneiform; tri-angular, -gonal, -lateral; quadr-angular, -ilateral; rectangular, square, foursquare, multilateral; polygonal etc. *n.*; cubical, rhomboidal, pyramidal.

245. Curvature.—N. curv-ature, -ity, -ation; incurv-ity, -ation; bend; flex- ure, -ion; conflexure; crook, hook, bought, bending; de-, inflexion; arcuation, devexity, turn; deviation, *détour*, sweep; curl, -ing; bough; recurv-ity, -ation; sinuosity etc. 248; aduncity.

curve, arc, arch, arcade, vault, dome, bow, crescent, *meniscus*, half-moon, lunule, horse-shoe, loop, crane-neck; para-, hyper-bola; catenary, festoon; conch-, cardi-oid; caustic, instep; tracery.

V. be -curved etc. *adj.*; sweep, swag, sag; deviate etc. 279; turn; re-enter.

render -curved etc. *adj.*; bend, curve, incurvate; de-, in-flect; crook; turn, round, arch, arcuate, arch over, loop the loop, concamerate; bow, coil, curl, recurve, frizzle.

Adj. curved etc. *v.*; curvi-form, -lineal, -linear; devex, devious; recurv-ed, -ous; *retroussé*; crump; bowed etc. *v.*; vaulted; hooked; falc-iform, -ated; semicircular, crescentic; lun-iform, -ular; semilunar, meniscal; cord-iform, -ated; cardioid; heart-, bell-, pear-, fig-shaped; reniform; lenti-form, -cular; bow-legged etc. (*distorted*) 243; oblique etc. 217; circular etc. 247.

246. Straightness.—N. straightness, rectilinearity, directness; inflexibility etc. (*stiffness*) 323; straight −, right −, direct-, bee- line; short cut.

V. be -straight etc. *adj*; have no turning; not -incline, − bend, − turn, − deviate- to either side; go straight; steer for etc. (*direction*) 278.

render straight, straighten, rectify; set −, putstraight; un-bend, -fold, -curl etc. 248, -ravel etc. 219, -wrap.

Adj. straight; rectiline-ar, -al; direct, even, right, true, in a line; unbent etc. *v.*; un-deviating, -turned, -distorted, -swerving; straight as an arrow etc. (*direct*) 278; inflexible etc. 323.

247. Circularity. [Simple circularity.]—**N.** circularity, roundness; rotundity etc. 249.

circle, circlet, ring, washer, areola, hoop, roundlet, *annulus*, annulet, bracelet, armlet, armilla; ringlet; eye, loop, wheel; cycle, orb, orbit, rundle, zone, belt, *cordon*, band; sash, girdle, cestus, cincture, baldric, fillet, *fascia*, wreath, garland; crown, corona, coronet, chaplet, snood, necklace, collar; noose, lasso, lariat.

ellipse, oval, ovule; ellipsoid, cycloid; epicycloid, -cycle; semi-circle; quadrant, sextant, sector.

V. make -round etc. *adj.*; round.

go round; encircle etc. 227; describe -a circle etc. 311.

Adj. round, rounded, circular, annular, orbicular; oval, ovate; elliptic, -al; ovoid, egg-shaped; pear-shaped etc. 245; cycloidal etc. *n.*; spherical etc. 249.

248. Convolution. [Complex circularity.]—**N.** winding etc. *v.*; con-, in-, circum-volution; wave, undulation, tortuosity, anfractuosity; sinu-osity, -ation, sinuousness; meandering, circuit, circumbendibus, twist, twirl, windings and turnings, *ambages*; torsion; inosculation; reticulation etc. (*crossing*) 219.

coil, roll, curl, buckle, spire, spiral, helix, corkscrew, worm, volute, whorl, rundle; tendril; scollop, scallop, escalop; kink.

serpent, snake, eel, maze, labyrinth.

V. be -convoluted etc. *adj.*; wind, twine, turn and twist, twirl, wave, undulate, meander; inosculate; entwine, intwine; twist, coil, roll; wrinkle, curl, crisp, twill; frizz, -le; crimp, crape, indent, scollop, scallop; wring, intort; contort; wreathe etc. (*cross*) 219.

Adj. convoluted; winding, twisted etc. *v.*; tortile, tortive; wavy; und-ated, -ulatory; circling, snaky, snake-like, serpentine; serpent-, anguill-, vermiform; vermicular; mazy, tortuous, anfractuous, sinuous, flexuous, wavy, sigmoidal.

involved, intricate, complicated, perplexed; labyrinth-ic, -ian, -ine; circuitous; peristaltic; daedalian, curly.

wreathy, frizzly, *crêpé*, buckled; ravelled etc. (*in disorder*) 59.

spiral, coiled, helical, turbinated.

Adv. in and out, round and round.

249. Rotundity.—N. rotundity; roundness etc. *adj.*; cyclindricity; spher-icity, -oidity; globosity.

cylin-der, -droid; barrel, drum; roll, -er; *rouleau*, column, rolling-pin, rundle; chimney-pot, drain-pipe.

cone, conoid; pear-, egg-, bell-shape.

sphere, globe, orb, orbit, ball, boulder, bowlder; spher-, ellips-, ge-, glob-oid, oblong −, oblatespheroid; drop, spherule, globule, vesicle, bulb, bullet, pellet, *pelote*, clew, pill, marble, pea, knob, pommel, knot.

V. render -spherical etc. *adj.*; form into a sphere, sphere, roll into a ball; give -rotundity etc. *n.*; round.

Adj. rotund; round etc. (*circular*) 247; cylindric, -ical, -oid; columnar, lumbriciform; conic, -al; spher-ical, -oidal; glob-ular, -ated, -ous, -ose; egg-, bell-, pear-shaped; ov-oid, -iform; gibbous; campaniform, -ulate, -iliform; fungiform, bead-like, moniliform, pyriform, bulbous; *teres atque rotundus*; round as -an orange, — an apple, — a ball, — a billiard ball, — a cannon ball.

250. Convexity.—N. convexity, prominence, projection, swelling, gibbosity, bilge, bulge, protuberance, protrusion; excrescency, camber.

intumescence; tumor; tubercle, -osity; excrescence; hump, hunch, bunch, gnarl.

tooth, knob, elbow, process, *apophysis*, condyle, bulb, node, nodule, nodosity, tongue, *dorsum*, boss, embossment, bump, clump; sugar-loaf etc. (*sharpness*) 253; bow; mamelon.

pimple, wen, wheal, *papula*, postule, pock, proud flesh, growth, goiter, *sarcoma*, caruncle, corn, bunion, wart, furnuncle, polypus, adenoid, fungus, fungosity, *exostosis*, bleb, blister, blain; boil etc. (*disease*) 655; bubble, blob.

papilla, nipple, teat, pap, breast, dug, mammilla; proboscis, .ose, neb, beak, snout, nozzle, snozzle; Adam's apple; belly, paunch, corporation; withers, back, shoulder, lip, flange.

peg, button, stud, ridge, rib, jutty, trunnion, snag.

cupola, dome, bee-hive; arch, balcony, eaves; pilaster.

relief, relievo, *cameo*; *basso-*, *mezzo-*, *alto-rilievo*; low-, bas-, high-relief.

hill etc. (*height*) 206; cape, promontory, mull; fore-, head-land; point of land, naze, ness, mole, jetty, hummock, ledge, spur.

V. be -prominent etc. *adj.*; project, bulge, protrude, bag, belly, pout, bouge, bunch; jut —, stand —, stick —, poke- out; stick —, bristle —, start —, cock —, shoot- up; swell —, hang —, bend-over; beetle.

render*-prominent etc. *adj.*; raise 307; emboss, chase.

Adj. convex, prominent, protuberant, underhung, undershot; projecting etc. *v.*; bossed, bossy, nodular, bunchy; clav-ate, -ated; hummocky, *moutonné*, mammiform; papul-ous, -ose; hemispheric, bulbous; bowed, arched; bold; bellied; tuber-ous, -culous; tumorous; cornute, knobby, odontoid; lenti-form, -cular; gibbous.

salient, in relief, raised, *repoussé*; bloated etc. (*expanded*) 194.

251. Flatness.—N. flatness etc. *adj.*; smoothness etc. 255.

plane; level etc. 213; plate, platter, table, tablet, slab.

V. render flat, flatten, squash; level etc. 213.

Adj. flat, plane, even, flush, scutiform, discoid; level etc. (*horizontal*) 213; smooth; flat as -a pancake, — a fluke, — a flounder, — a board, — my hand.

252. Concavity.—N. concavity, depression, dip; hollow, -ness; indentation, *intaglio*, cavity, antrum, dent, dint, dimple, follicle, pit, *sinus*, *alveolus*, *lacuna*; excavation, trench, shaft, sap, mine, tunnel, burrow; trough etc. (*furrow*) 259; honeycomb.

cup, basin, crater, punch-bowl; cell etc. (*receptacle*) 191; socket, faucet.

valley, vale, dale, dell, gap, dingle, combe, bottom, slade, strath, glade, grove, glen, cave, cavern, cove; grot, -to; alcove, *cul-de-sac*, blind alley; gully etc. 198; arch etc. (*curve*) 245; bay etc. (*of the sea*) 343.

excavator, sapper, miner.

V. be -concave etc. *adj.*; retire, cave in.

render -concave etc. *adj.*; depress, hollow; scoop, — out; gouge, dig, delve, excavate, dent, dint, mine, sap, undermine, burrow, tunnel, stave in.

Adj. depressed etc. *v.*; concave, hollow, stove in; dished; spoon-like; retiring; retreating; cavernous; porous etc. (*with holes*) 260; cellular, spongy, spongious; honeycombed, alveolar; infundibul-ar, -iform; funnel-, bell-shaped; campaniform, capsular; vaulted, arched.

253. Sharpness.—N. sharpness etc. *adj.*; acuity, acumination; spinosity.

point, spike, spine, *spiculum*, tine; needle, pin; tack, nail; prick, -le; spur, rowel, barb; spit, cusp; horn, antler; snag; tag; thorn, bristle.

nib, tooth, incisor, tusk; spoke, cog, ratchet.

crag, crest *arête*, cone, peak, sugar-loaf, pike, *aiguille*; spire, pyramid, steeple.

beard, *chevaux de frise*, porcupine, hedgehog, brier, bramble, thistle; comb, awn, bur.

wedge; knife-, cutting- edge; blade, edge-tool, cutlery, knife, penknife, whittle, razor; scalpel, bistoury, lancet; chisel; ploughshare, coulter; hatchet, axe, pick-axe, mattock, pick, adze, bill; billhook, cleaver, cutter; skiver; scythe, sickle, scissors, shears; sword etc. (*arms*) 727; bodkin etc. (*perforator*) 262.

sharpener, hone, strop; grind-, whet-stone; steel, emery.

V. be -sharp etc. *adj.*; taper to a point; bristle with.

render -sharp etc. *adj.*; sharpen, point, aculeate, acuminate, whet, barb, spiculate, set, strop, grind.

cut etc. (*sunder*) 44.

Adj. sharp, keen; acute; aci-cular, -form; aculeated, -minated; pointed; tapering; conical, pyramidal; mucron-ate, -ated; spindle-, needle-shaped; spiked, spiky, ensiform, peaked, salient, cusp-ed; -idate, -idated; corn-ute, -uted, -iculate; prickly; spiny, spinous; thorny, bristling, muricated, pectinated, studded, thistly, briery; craggy etc. (*rough*) 256; snaggy; digitated, two-edged, fusiform; denti-form, -culated; toothed; odontoid; star-like; stell-ated, -iform; arrow-headed; arrowy, barbed, spurred, sagittal; spear-shaped, hastate; horned; conical.

cutting; sharp-, knife-edged; sharp —, keen-as a razor; sharp as a needle; sharpened etc. *v.*; set.

254. Bluntness.—N. bluntness etc. *adj.*; abruptness, dullness.

V. be —, render- blunt etc. *adj.*; obtund, dull; take off the -point, — edge; turn.

Adj. blunt, obtuse, dull, bluff.

255. Smoothness.—N. smoothness etc. *adj.*; polish, gloss; lubric-ity, -ation.

down, velvet, silk, satin; slide; bowling green etc. (*level*) 213; glass, ice; asphalt, pavement, flags.

roller, steam-roller; iron, flat-iron, tailor's goose; sand-, emery-paper; burnisher, turpentine and bees-wax.

V. smooth, -en; plane; file; mow, shave; level, roll; macadamize; polish, burnish, planish, levigate, calender, glaze; iron, hot-press, mangle; lubricate etc. (*oil*) 332.

Adj. smooth; polished etc. *v.*; even; level etc. 213; plane etc. (*flat*) 251; sleek, glossy; silken, silky; lanate, downy, velvety; glabrous, slippery, glassy, lubricous, oily, soft; unwrinkled; smooth as -glass, — ice, — velvet, — oil; slippery as an eel; wooly etc. (*feathery*) 256.

256. Roughness.—N. roughness etc. *adj.*; tooth, grain, texture, ripple; asperity, rugosity, salebrosity, corrugation, nodosity; arborescence etc. 242.

brush, hair, beard, shag, mane, whisker, mutton-chops, *moustache*, *mustachio*, imperial, Van Dyke, tress, lock, curl, ringlet, *fimbriae*, *cilia*, *villi*; eye-lashes, eye-brows, love-lock.

plum-age, -osity; plume, *panache*, crest; feather, tuft, tussock, fringe, toupee.

wool, velvet, plush, nap, pile, floss, fluff, fur, down; byssus, moss, bur.

V. be -rough etc. *adj.*; go against the grain.

render -rough etc. *adj.*; roughen, rough cast, knurl; ruffle, crisp, crumple, crinkle, corrugate, engrail, set on edge, stroke —, rub- the wrong way, rumple.

Adj. rough, uneven; scabrous, knotted; nodular; rug-ged, -ose, -ous; asperous, crisp, salebrous, gnarled, unpolished, unsmooth, rough-hewn; knurled, cross-grained, crag-gy, -ged; crankling, scraggy, jagged, unkempt, prickly etc. (*sharp*) 253; arborescent etc. 242; leafy, well-wooded; feathery, plum-ose, -igerous; tufted, fimbriated, hairy, bristly, ciliated, filamentous, hirsute; crin-ose, -ite; bushy, hispid, villous, pappous, bearded, pilous, shaggy, shagged; fringed, befringed; set-ous, -ose, -aceous; 'like quills upon the fretful porcupine;' rough as a -nutmeg grater, — bear.

downy, velvety, flocculent, wolly; lan-ate, -ated; lanugin-ous, ose; tomentous.

Adv. against the grain, in the rough, on edge.

257. Notch.—N. notch, dent, nick, cut; indent, -ation; serration; dimple.

embrasure, battlement, machicolation; saw, tooth, crenelle, scallop, scollop, vandyke.

V. notch, nick, cut, pink, mill, score, dent, in-dent, jag, scarify, scotch, crimp, scollop, crenulate, vandyke.

Adj. notched etc. *v.*; crenate, -d; dentate, -d; denticulate, -d; toothed, palmated, serrated.

258. Fold.—N. fold, plicature, pleat, plait, ply, crease; tuck, gather; flexion, flexure, joint, elbow, doubling, duplicature, wrinkle, rimple, crinkle, crankle, crumple, rumple, rivel, ruck, ruffle, dog's ear, corrugation, frounce, flounce, lapel; pucker, crow's feet.

V. fold, double, plicate, pleat, plait, crease, wrinkle, crinkle, crankle, curl, smock, cockle up, crocker, rimple, rumple, frizzle, frounce, rivel, twill, corrugate, ruffle, crimple, crumple, pucker; turn —, double- -down, — under; tuck, ruck, hem, gather.

Adj. folded etc. *v.*

259. Furrow.—N. furrow, groove, rut, *sulcus*, scratch, streak, *striae*, crack, score, incision, slit; chamfer, fluting.

channel, gutter, trench, ditch, dike, dyke, moat, fosse, trough, kennel; ravine etc. (*interval*) 198.

V. furrow etc. *n.*; flute, groove, carve, corrugate, plough; incise, chase, enchase, grave, engrave, etch, bite in, cross-hatch.

Adj. furrowed etc. *v.*; ribbed, straited, sulcated, fluted, canaliculated; biscule-ous, -ate; trisulcate; corduroy.

260. Opening.—N. hole, foramen; puncture, blow-out, perforation; pin-, key-, loop-, port-, peep-, mouse-, pigeon-hole; eye, — of a needle; eyelet; slot.

opening; apert-ure, -ness; hiation, yawning, oscitancy, dehiscence, patefaction, pandiculation; gap, chasm etc. (*interval*) 198.

embrasure, window, casement, light; sky-, fan-light; lattice; bay, bow-window; oriel, dormer, lantern.

out-, in-let; vent, vomitory; *embouchure*; orifice, mouth, sucker, muzzle, throat, gullet, placket, weasand, wizen, nozzle, *esophagus*.

portal, porch, gate, ostiary, postern, wicket, trap-door, hatch, door; arcade; gate-, door-, hatch-, gang-way; lych-gate.

way, path etc. 627; thoroughfare; channel, passage, tube, pipe; waterpipe etc. 350; air-pipe etc. 351; vessel, tubule, canal, gut, fistula; adjutage, ajutage; chimney, smoke stack, flue, tap, funnel, gully, tunnel, main; mine, pit, adit, shaft; gallery, alley, aisle, glade, lane, vista.

bore, caliber; pore; blind orifice.

por-ousness, -osity; sieve, cullender, colander; grater, shredder; cribble, riddle, screen; honeycomb.

apertion, perforation; piercing etc. *v.*; terebration, empalement, pertusion, puncture, acupuncture, penetration.

opener, corkscrew, can opener, key, master-key, *passe-partout*.

V. open, ope, gape, dehisce, yawn, bilge; fly open.

perforate, pierce, empierce, tap, bore, drill; mine etc. (*scoop out*) 252; tunnel; trans-pierce, -fix; en-filade, impale, spike, spear, gore, spit, stab, pink, puncture, lance, trepan, trephine, stick, prick, rid-dle, punch; stave in.

cut a passage through; make -way, — room- for, un-cover, -close, -rip; lay —, cut —, rip —, throw-open.

Adj. open; perforated etc. *v.*; perforate; wide open, agape, ajar; un-closed, -stopped; oscitant, gaping, yawning; patent.

tubular, cannular, fistulous; per-vious, -meable; foraminous; vesi-, vas-cular; porous, follicular, cribriform, honeycombed, infundibular, riddled; tubul-ous, -ated, piped.

opening etc. *v.*; aperient.

Int. *open sesame!*

261. Closure.—N. closure, occlusion, blockade; shutting up etc. *v.*; obstruction etc. (*hindrance*) 706; gag; embolism; contraction etc. 195; infarction; con-, ob-stipation; blind -alley, — corner; *cul-de-sac, caecum*; imperforation, -viousness etc. *adj.*; -meability; stopper etc. 263; *operculum*.

V. close, occlude, plug; block —, stop —, fill —, bung —, cork —, button —, stuff —, shut —, dam-up, obturate; blockade; obstruct etc. (*hinder*) 706; bar, bolt, stop, seal, plumb; choke, throttle; ram down, tamp, dam, cram; trap, clinch; put to —, shut- the door; batten down the hatches.

Adj. closed etc. *v.*; shut, operculated; unopened.

unpierced, imporous, caecal; imperforate, - vious, -meable; impenetrable; un-, im-passable; invious; path-, way-less; untrodden.

unventilated; air-, water-tight; hermetically sealed; tight, snug.

262. Perforator.—N. perforator, piercer, borer, auger, gimlet, stylet, drill, wimble, awl, bradawl, scoop, terrier, corkscrew, dibble, trocar, trepan, trephine, probe, bodkin, needle, stiletto, broach, reamer, rimer, warder, lancet; punch, - eon; spikebit, gouge; spear etc. (*weapon*) 727.

263. Stopper.—N. stopper, stopple; plug, cork, bung, spike, spill, stop-cock, tap; rammer; ram, -rod; piston; stopgap; wadding, stuffing, padding, stopping, dossil, pledget, tompion, tourniquet, obturator; wad.

cover etc. 223; valve, slide valve; vent-peg, spigot.

janitor, door —, gate- keeper, porter, commissionaire, *concierge*, warder, beadle, Cerberus, usher, guard, sentry, sentinel; ostiary.

264. Motion. [Successive change of place.*]—N.** motion, movement, move; motivity, motility, going etc. *v.*; unrest.

stream, current, flow, flux, run, course, stir; conduction, evolution; kinematics.

step, rate, pace, tread, stride, gait, clip, port, footfall, cadence, carriage, velocity, angular velocity; progress, locomotion; journey etc. 266; voyage etc. 267; transit etc. 270.

restlessness etc. (*changeableness*) 149; mobility; movableness, motive power; laws of motion; mobilization.

V. be -in motion etc. *adj.*; move, go, hie, gang, budge, stir, pass, flit; hover -round, — about; shift, slide, slither, glide; roll, — on; flow, stream, run, drift, sweep along; wander etc. (*deviate*) 279; walk etc. 266; change —, shift- one's -place, — quarters; dodge; keep -going, — moving.

put —, set- in motion; move; impel etc. 276; propel etc. 284; render movable, mobilize.

Adj. moving etc. *v.*; in- motion; motile, transitional; motory, motive; shifting, movable, mobile, mercurial, unquiet; restless etc. (*changeable*) 149; nomadic etc. 266; erratic etc. 279.

Adv. under way; on the -move, — wing, — tramp, — march.

*A thing cannot be said to *move* from one place to another, unless it passes in succession through every intermediate place; hence motion is only such a change of place as is *successive*. 'Rapid, swift, etc., as thought' are therefore incorrect expressions.

265. Quiescence.—N. rest; stillness etc. *adj.*; quiescence; stag-nation, -nancy; fixity, immobility, catalepsy; indisturbance; quietism.

quiet, tranquillity, calm; repose etc. 687; peace; dead calm, anticyclone; statue-like repose; silence etc. 403; not a -breath of air, — mouse stirring; sleep etc. (*inactivity*) 683.

pause, lull etc. (*cessation*) 142; stand, — still; standing still etc. *v.*; lock; dead -lock, — stop, — stand; full stop; fix; embargo.

resting-place; bivouac; home etc. (*abode*) 189; pillow etc. (*support*) 215; haven etc. (*refuge*) 666; goal etc. (*arrival*) 292.

V. be -quiescent etc. *adj.*; stand —, lie- still; keep quiet, repose, hold the breath.

remain, stay; stand, lie to, ride at anchor, remain *in situ*, mark time, tarry; bring —, heave —, lay- to; pull —, draw- up; hold, halt; stop, — short; rest, pause, anchor; cast —, come to an- anchor; rest on one's oars; repose on one's laurels, take breath; stop etc. (*discontinue*) 142.

stagnate, vegetate; *quieta non movere*; let - alone, — well alone; abide, rest and be thankful; keep within doors, stay at home, go to bed.

dwell etc. (*be present*) 186; settle etc. (*be located*) 184; alight etc. (*arrive*) 292.

stick, — fast; stand, — like a post; not stir a -peg, — step; be at a -stand etc. *n.*

quell, becalm, hush, stay, lull to sleep, lay an embargo on; put the brake on.

Adj. quiescent, still; motion-, move-less; fixed; stationary; at -rest, — a stand, — a stand-still, — anchor; stock-still; immotile; standing still etc. *v.*; sedentary, untravelled, stay-at-home; becalmed, stagnant, quiet; un-moved, -disturbed, -ruffled; calm, restful; cataleptic; immovable etc. (*stable*) 150; sleeping etc. (*inactive*) 683; silent etc. 403; still as a -statue; — a post, — a mouse, — death.

Adv. at a stand etc. *adj.*; *tout court*; at the halt.

Int. stop! stay! avast! halt! hold, — hard! whoa!

Phr. *requiescat in pace.*

266. Journey. [Locomotion by land.]—N.** travel; traveling etc. *v.*; wayfaring, campaigning.

journey, excursion, expedition, tour, trip, grand tour, circuit, peregrination, discursion, ramble, pilgrimage, *trek*, course, ambulation, march, walk, hike, promenade, constitutional, stroll, saunter, tramp, jog-trot, turn, stalk, perambulation; noctambulation; somnambulism, sleep walking; outing, ride, drive, airing, jaunt.

equitation, horsemanship, riding, *manège*, ride and tie.

roving, vagrancy, pererration; marching and countermarching; nomadism; vagabond-ism, -age; gadding; flit, -ting; migration; e-, im-, de-, inter-migration.

plan, itinerary, guide; hand-, road- book; Baedeker, Murray, Bradshaw, time table.

procession, parade, cavalcade, caravan, file, *cortege*, column.

[Organs and instruments of locomotion] vehicle etc. 272; locomotive etc. 271; legs, feet, pegs, pins, trotters.

traveler etc. 268.

V. travel, journey, course; tour; take —, go- a journey, take —, go out for- -a walk etc. *n.*; have a run; take the air.

flit, take wing; migrate, emigrate, *trek*; rove, prowl, roam, range, patrol, pace up and down, traverse; scour —, traverse- the country; peragrate; per-, circum-ambulate; nomadize, wander, ramble, stroll, saunter, hover, go one's rounds, straggle; gad; — about; expatiate.

walk, march, step, tread, pace, plod, wend; promenade; trudge, tramp; stalk, stride, straddle, strut, foot it, stump, bundle, bowl along, toddle; paddle; tread —, follow —, pursue- a path.

take horse, ride, drive, trot, amble, canter, prance, fisk, frisk, *caracoler*; gallop etc. (*move quickly*) 274; motor, cycle, taxi; go by -car, — train, — tram, — bus, — plane.

peg —, jog —, wag —, shuffle- on; stir one's stumps; bend one's -steps, — course; make —, find —, wend —, pick —, thread —, plough-one's way; coast, slide, glide, skim, skate, ski; march in procession, file off, defile.

go —, repair —, resort —, hie —, betake oneself-to.

Adj. traveling etc. *v.*; ambulatory, itinerant, peripatetic, perambulatory, roving, rambling, gad-ding, discursive, vagrant, migratory, nomadic; cir-cumforane-an, -ous; somnambular, nocti-, mundi-vagant; locomotive, automotive, self-moving.

way-faring, -worn; travel-stained.

Adv. on -foot, — horseback, — Shanks's mare; by the Marrowbone stage; *in transitu* etc. 270; *en route* etc. 282.

Int. come along!

---

267. Navigation. [Locomotion by water, or air.]—**N.** navigation; aquatics; boating, cruising, yachting; ship etc. 273; oar, scull, sweep, punt pole, paddle, — wheel, screw, propeller, stern wheel, sail, canvas.

natation, swimming; fin, flipper, fish's tail.

aeronautics, aviation, flying, winging, cruising, gliding, ballooning; blind —, instrument — flying; avigation, take-off.

flight, trip, run; solo —, nolo (pilotless) —, super-sonic —, test — flight; air -lift, -drop; shuttle, recon-naisence, mission, dry run (coll.), search mission, combat flight, sortie, air raid, bombing mission; air — support, — cover, — umbrella; formation flying, maneuvers, aerobatics, stunt flying (coll.), diving, rolling, barrel roll, spin, tail spin, loop, buzzing.

landing, instrument —, crash — landing.

angle, center, axis, stability, load, pressure, tor-sion, torque, thrust, propulsion, jet propulsion, pitch, lift, dray, yaw, resistance, drift, flow, wash.

course, heading, altitude; air -route, -lane.

voyage, sail. cruise, passage, circumnavigation, *periplus*; head-, stern-, lee-way.

astro-, cosmo- nautics; space —, in-terplanetary — travel; space — exploration, — flight.

mariner, aeronaut etc. 269.

V. sail; put to sea etc. (*depart*) 293; take ship, get under way; spread -sail, — canvas; gather way, have way on; make —, carry- sail; plough the -waves, — deep, — main, — ocean; walk the waters.

navigate, warp, luff, scud, boom, kedge; drift, course, cruise, coast; hug the -shore, — land; cir-cumnavigate.

ply the oar, row, paddle, pull, scull, punt, steam, swim, float; buffet the waves, ride the storm, skim, *effleurer*, dive, wade.

fly, pilot, copilot, astronavigate, solo, take off, taxi, ascend, climb, stunt, spin, loop, roll, dive, buzz, land, descend, level off, bail out, parachute.

Adj. sailing etc. *v.*; seafaring, nautical, maritime, naval; sea-going, coasting, afloat; navigable, aquatic, natatory.

volitant, volant, aerostatic, aerial, aeronautic; alar, alate, pennate.

Adv. under -way, — sail, — canvas, — steam; on the wing.

---

268. Traveler.—**N.** traveler, wayfarer, voyager, itinerant, passenger.

tourist, excursionist, globe-trotter; explorer, ad-venturer, mountaineer, Alpine Club; peregrinator, wanderer, rover, straggler, rambler; bird of passage; gad-about, -ling; vagrant, scatterling, land-loper, waifs and estrays, wastrel, stray; loafer; tramp, -er, hobo, beachcomber, vagabond, nomad, Bohemian, gipsy, Arab, Wandering Jew, Hadji, pilgrim, palmer; peripatetic; somnambulist; sleep walker, noctambulist; emigrant, fugitive, refugee, *émigré*.

runner, courier, King's messenger; Mercury, Iris, Ariel, comet.

pedestrian, walker, foot-passenger; cyclist; wheelman.

rider, horseman, equestrian, cavalier, jockey, rough rider, trainer, breaker, huntsman.

driver, coachman, whip, Jehu, charioteer, postilion, post-boy, carter, wagoner, drayman, truckman; cab-man, -driver; *voiturier*, *vetturino*, *condottiere*; engine-driver; stoker, fireman, guard, brakeman, conductor; chauffeur, automobilist, motorist, motor —, truck —, taxi- driver.

---

269. Mariner.—**N.** sailor, mariner, navigator, argonaut; sea-man, -farer, -faring man; yachtsman; tar, jack tar, salt, gob, sea-dog, shellback, able seaman, A.B.; man-of-war's man, bluejacket, marine, jolly; midshipman, middy, reefer; captain, commander, master mariner, skipper, mate; ship-boat-, ferry-, water-, lighter-, barge-, longshore-man, hoveller; bargee, gondolier; oar-, -sman; rower; boat-, cock-swain; coxswain; steersman, helmsman, pilot; crew; lascar.

aerial navigator, navigator; aero-, astro-, cosmo-naut; balloonist, Icarus, aviator, pilot, flyer, copilot, spaceman; fighter —, bomber — pilot; bombardier, gunner; meteorologist; stewardess, aviatrix, aviatress; ground crew, aeromechanic, aeronautical engineer; parachutist, paratrooper.

270. Transference.—**N.** transfer, -ence; trans-, e-location; displacement; *meta-stasis*, *-thesis*; removal; re-, a-motion; relegation; de-, asportation; extradition, conveyance, draft; carrying, carriage; convection, -duction, -tagion; infection; transfusion; transfer etc. (*of property*) 783.

transit, transition; passage, ferry, gestation; portage, porterage, carting, cartage; shoveling etc. *v.*; vect-ion, -ure, -itation; shipment, freight, wafture; trans-mission, -port, -portation, -umption, -plantation, -lation; shift-, dodg-ing; dispersion etc. 73; transposition etc. (*interchange*) 148; traction etc. 285.

[Thing transferred] drift, alluvium, detritus, *moraine*; gift, legacy, bequest, lease; freight, mails, cargo, luggage, baggage, goods.

V. trans-fer, -mit, -port, -place, -plant; convey, assign, carry, bear, fetch and carry; carry —, ferry-over; hand, pass, forward; shift; conduct, convoy, bring, fetch, reach.

send, delegate, consign, mail post, relegate, turn over to, pass the buck, deliver; ship, embark; waft; switch, shunt; transpose etc. (*interchange*) 148; displace etc. 185; throw etc. 284; drag etc. 285.

shovel, lade, dip, ladle, bale, decant, draft off, transfuse.

Adj. transferred etc. *v.*; drifted; movable, portable, -ative; conductive; contagious, infectious.

transferable, assignable, conveyable, devisable, negotiable, transmissible.

Adv. from -hand to hand, — pillar to post. on —, by- the way; on the -road, — wing; as one goes; *in transitu*, *en route*, *chemin faisant*, *en passant*, in mid-progress.

271. Carrier.—**N.** carrier, porter, red cap, bearer, messenger, postman, tranter, conveyer; stevedore; coolie; conductor, locomotive, tractor, caterpillar tractor, motor.

beast of burden, cattle, horse steed, nag, palfrey, Arab, blood horse, thorough-bred, galloway, charger, courser, racer, hunter, jument, pony, filly, colt, foal, barb, roan, jade, hack, *bidet*, pad, cob, tit, punch, roadster, goer; race-, pack-, draft-, cart-, dray-, post-horse, mount; Shetland pony, sheltie; garran, jennet, genet, bayard, mare, stallion, gelding; stud.

Pegasus, Bucephalus, Rozinante.

ass, donkey, jackass, mule, hinny; sumpter - horse, — mule; reindeer; camel, dromedary, mehari, llama, elephant; carrier pigeon.

carriage etc. (*vehicle*) 272; ship etc. 273.

Adj. equine, asinine.

272. Vehicle.—**N.** vehicle, conveyance, carriage, car, caravan, van, furniture van, pantechnicon; wagon, wain, dray, cart, lorry.

carriole; sledge, sled, sleigh, bob-sleigh, toboggan, *luge*, truck, tram; limber, tumbrel, pontoon; barrow; wheel-, hand- -barrow, — cart, trolley; perambulator; Bath —, wheel —, sedanchair, jinriksha, rickshaw; ekka; chaise; palankeen, -quin; litter, horse-litter, brancard, crate, hurdle, stretcher, ambulance; velocipede, hobbyhorse, coaster, scooter, go-cart; cycle; bi-, tri-, quadri-cycle; tandem, safety; skate, roller —, ice — skate; sled, sleigh; ski, snow-shoe.

equipage, turn-out; coach, chariot; *quadriga*, chaise, phaëton, break, brake, mail-phaëton, wagonette, drag, curricle, tilbury, whisky, landau, *barouche*, victoria, brougham, clarence, calash, *calèche*, britzska, *araba*, kibitka; berlin; sulky, *désobligeant*, sociable, *vis-à-vis*, *dormeuse*; jaunting —, outside- car; *tarantass*; runabout; shay.

post-chaise; diligence; stage; stage —, mail —, hackney —, glass- coach; stage-wagon; car, omnibus, bus, fly, *cabriolet*, cab, hansom, shofle, fourwheeler, growler, *droshki*, drosky.

dog-cart, trap, gig, whitechapel, buggy, four-in-hand, unicorn, random, tandem; shandredhan, *char-à-banc*.

automobile, motor-, auto-, touring-, racing-, cycle-, side-, steam-, electric- car; motor — cycle, — bike; motorized vehicle; bus, minibus; buggy, crate, tub, flivver, jalopy, wreck, clunker, dog, heap (all. slang); coupe, coup, sedan, convertible, hard-top; camper, trailer, mobile home; limosine, landaulette, cabriolet, *coupé*, *voiturette*, runabout, electromobile, taxi, -cab.

train; passenger —, express —, freight —, subway —, special —, corridor —, parliamentary —, luggage —, goods- train, *train de luxe*; 1st-, 2nd-, 3rd- class- -train, — carriage, — compartment; Pullman —, sleeping-, club-, observation-, dining-, restaurant-car; mail-, luggage-, brake-van, coach, car, carriage; rolling stock; horse-box, cattle- truck.

273. Ship.—**N.** ship, vessel, sail; craft, bottom, navy, marine, fleet, flotilla, squadron; shipping, man of war etc. (*combatant*) 726; transport, tender, store-ship; merchant ship, merchantman; packet, liner; whaler, slaver, collier, coaster, tanker, freighter, freight steamer, cargo boat, lighter; fishing-, pilot- boat; trawler, drifter; cable ship; hulk; yacht; floating palace, ocean greyhound.

ship, bark, barque, brig, snow, hermaphrodite brig; brigantine, barquentine; schooner; topsail —, fore and aft —, three masted- schooner; *chassemarée*; sloop, cutter, corvette, clipper, foist, yawl, dandy, ketch, smack, lugger, barge, hoy, cat-, - boat, buss; sail-er, -ing vessel, wind jammer; steamer, -boat, -ship; mail—, paddle —, screw —, sternwheel- steamer; tug; train-ferry; line of steamers etc.

boat, pinnace, launch, motor-boat, picket-boat; hydroplane; life-, long-, jolly-, bum-, fly-, cock-, ferry-, canal- boat, dory, dugout, galliot; shallop, gig, funny, skiff, dingy, scow, cockleshell, wherry, coble, punt, cog, lerret; eight-, four-, pair- oar; randan; out- rigger; float, raft, pontoon; prame, ice-yacht.

state barge, bucentaur.

catamaran, coracle, gondola, carvel, caravel; felucca, caique, canoe; trireme; galley, — foist; bilander, dogger, hooker, howker; argosy, carack; galliass, galleon; galliot, polacca, polacre, corsair, tartane, junk, lorcha, praam, proa, prahu, saick, sampan, xebec, dhow; dahabeah; nuggar, cayak, piroque; trireme.

submarine, submersible.

aircraft (*combatant*) etc. 726; flying machine, air mail, aero-, air-, mono-, bi-, tri-, hydro aeroplane, plane, cabin —, transport —, propeller — plane; *avion*, flying boat, glider; helicopter, rotor —, gyro-plane, whirlybird, autogyro, gyrodine; sea-, hydro-plane; amphibian; jet. — plane; turbo-, ram-, pulse-, subsonic —, supersonic —, strato- jet; rocket – plane, – ship; space ship; war-, combat — plane; kamikaze, fleet, armada; trainer, flight simulator; aerostat, dirigible, blimp (coll.), zeppelin; parachute, chute (coll.); kite.

rocket, flying —, ballistic —, guided — missile; projectile; rocket —, robot —, buzz-bomb; multistage —, step —, test — rocket; booster; satellite; flying saucer, unidentified flying object. (UFO).

nacelle, car, gondola, aileron; hangar, airport, landing field, airdrome; catwalk, controls, rudder, tail.

Adj. marine, maritime, naval, nautical, seafaring, sea-, ocean-going, sea-worthy.

aerial, aeronautical, air-worthy, flying etc. *n.*

Adv. afloat, aboard; on -board, — ship board, — board ship.

274. Velocity.—N. velocity, speed, celerity; swiftness etc. *adj.*; rapidity, eagle speed; expedition etc. (*activity*) 682; pernicity; acceleration; haste etc. 684.

spurt, rush, dash, race, steeplechase; smart —, lively —, swift etc. *adj.* —, rattling —, spanking —, strapping- -rate — pace; round pace; flying, flight.

gallop, canter, trot, round trot, run, scamper; hand —, full- gallop, swoop.

lightning, light, electricity, wind; cannon-ball, rocket, arrow, dart, quicksilver; telegraph, express train; torrent; swallow flight.

eagle, antelope, courser, race-horse, gazelle, greyhound, hare, doe, squirrel.

Mercury, Ariel, Camilla, Harlequin.

[Measurement of velocity.] speedometer, log, - line, tachometer.

air speed, speed of sound, sonic —, subsonic —, supersonic —, ultrasonic —, hypersonic —, transonic — speed.

V. move quickly, trip, fisk; speed, hie, hasten; sprint, spurt, post, spank, scuttle; scud, -dle, scurry; scour, — the plain; scamper, sprint, dash, run, — like mad; fly, race, run a race, cut away, cut and run, shoot, tear, whisk, whiz, sweep, skim, brush; cut —, bowl- along; rush etc. (*be violent*) 173; dash -on, — off, — forward; bolt; trot, gallop, bound, flit, spring, dart, boom; march in -quick, — double-time; ride hard; et over the ground, scorch.

hurry etc. (*hasten*) 684; accelerate, put on; quicken; quicken —, mend- one's pace; clap spurs to one's horse; make-haste, — rapid strides, — forced marches, — the best of one's way; put one's best leg foremost, stir one's stumps, wing one's way, set off at a score; carry —, crowd- sail; go off like a shot, go ahead, gain ground; outstrip the wind, fly on the wings of the wind.

keep -up, — pace- with; outstrip etc. 303.

Adj. fast, speedy, swift, rapid, quick, fleet; nimble, agile, expeditious; express; active etc. 682; flying, galloping etc. *v.*; light- nimble-footed; winged; eagle-winged, mercurial, electric telegraphic; light-legged; light of heel; swift as -an arrow etc. *n.*; quick as -lightning etc. *n.*, — thought. *

Adv. swiftly etc. *adj.*; with -speed etc. *n.*; apace; at -a great rate, — full speed, — railway speed; full - drive, — gallop; post-haste, in full sail, tantivy; trippingly; instantaneously etc. 113; like a shot.

under press of -sale, — canvas, — sail and steam; *velis et remis*, on eagle's wing, in double quick time; with -rapid, — giant- strides; *à pas de géant*; in seven league boots; whip and spur; *ventre à terre*; as fast as one's -legs, — heels- will carry one; as fast on one can lay feet to the ground, at the top of one's speed; by leaps and bounds; with haste etc. 684; in- high — gear, — speed.

Phr. *vires acquirit eundo.*

*See note on 274.

275. Slowness.—N. slowness etc. *adj.*; languor etc. (*inactivity*) 683; drawl; creeping etc. *v.*, lentor.

retardation; slackening etc. *v.*; delay etc. (*lateness*) 133; claudication.

jog-, dog-trot, walk; mincing steps; slow -march, — time.

slow -goer, — coach, — back; lingerer, loiterer, sluggard, tortoise, snail; dawdle etc. (*inactive*) 683.

V. move -slowly, etc. *adv.*; creep, crawl, lag, slug, walk, drawl, linger, loiter, saunter; plod, trudge, stump along, lumber; trail; drag; dawdle etc. (*be inactive*) 683; grovel, worm one's way, steal along; jog —, rub —, bundle- on; toddle, waddle, wabble, slug; traipse, slouch, shuffle, halt, hobble, limp, claudicate, shamble; flag, falter, totter, stagger; mince, step short; march in -slow time, — funeral procession; take one's time; hang fire etc. (*be late*) 133.

retard, relax; slacken, check, moderate, rein in, curb; reef; strike —, shorten —, take in- sail; put on the drag, apply the brake; clip the wings; reduce the speed, decelerate; slacken -speed, — one's pace, lose ground; back -water, — pedal, put the engines astern, throttle down.

Adj. slow, slack; tardy; dilatory etc. (*inactive*) 683; gentle, easy; leisurely; deliberate, gradual; insensible, imperceptible; languid, sluggish, apathetic; phlegmatic; slow-paced, tardigrade, snail-like; creeping etc. *v.*

Adv. slowly etc. *adj.*; leisurely; *piano, adagio*; *largo, larghetto*; at half speed, under easy sail; at a -foot's, — snail's, — funeral- pace; slower than molasses in January; in slow time; with -mincing steps, — clipped wings; *haud passibus aequis*; in-low —, gear, — speed.

gradually etc. *adj.*; *gradatim*; by -degrees, — slow degrees, — inches, — little and little; step by step; inch by inch, bit by bit, little by little, *seriatim*; consecutively.

276. Impulse.—N. impulse, impulsion, impetus; momentum; push, pulsion, thrust, shove, jog, jolt, brunt, booming, boost, throw; explosion etc. (*violence*) 173; propulsion etc. 284, jet propulsion; firing, launching, projection, trajection.

percussion, concussion, collision, occursion, clash, encounter, cannon, *carambole*, appulse, shock, crash, bump; impact; *élan*; charge etc. (*attack*) 716; beating etc. (*punishment*) 972.

blow, dint, stroke, knock, tap, rap, slap, smack, pat, dab; fillip; slam, bang, hit, whack, thwack, clout; cuff etc. 972; squash, dowse, whap, swap, punch, thump, swipe, jab, pelt, kick, punce, calcitration; *ruade*; arietation; cut, thrust, lunge, yerk.

hammer, sledge-hammer, mall, maul, mallet, flail; ram, -mer; battering-ram, monkey, pile-driver; punch, bat, tamper, tamping iron; cudgel etc. (*weapon*) 727; axe etc. (*sharp*) 253.

[Science of mechanical forces] mechanics, dynamics etc.

V. give an -impetus etc. *n.*; impel, push; start, give a start to, set going; drive, urge, boom; thrust, prod, foin; cant; elbow, shoulder, jostle, justle, hustle, hurtle, shove, jog, jolt, bean, encounter; run –, bump –; butt- against; knock –, run- one's head against; impinge.

fire, launch, project, traject, propel, 284.

strike, knock, hit, bash, tap, rap, bat, slap, flap, dab, pat, thump, beat, bang, slam, dash; punch, thwack, whack; hit –, strike- hard; swap, batter, dowse, baste; pelt, patter, skelter, buffet, belabor, tamp; fetch one a blow, swat; poke at, pink, lunge, yerk; kick, calcitrate; butt; strike at etc. (*attack*) 716; whip etc. (*punish*) 972; propel etc. 284.

come –, enter- into collision; collide; foul; fall –, run- foul of.

throw etc.

Adj. impelling etc. *v.*; im-pulsive, -pellent; booming; dynamic, -al; impelled etc. *v.*

277. Recoil.—N. recoil; re-, retro-action; revulsion; rebound, *ricochet*; re-percussion, -calcitration; kick, *contre-coup*; springing back etc. *v.*; elasticity etc. 325; reflexion, reflex, reflux; reverberation etc. (*resonance*) 408; rebuff, repulse; return.

ducks and drakes; boomerang; spring; reactionist, reactionary.

V. recoil, resile, react; spring –, fly –, bound- back; rebound, reverberate, repercuss, recalcitrate, echo, *ricochet*.

Adj. recoiling etc. *v.*; re-fluent, -percussive, -calcitrant, -actionary; retroactive.

Adv. on the -recoil etc. *n.*

278. Direction.—N. direction, bearing, course, set, drift, tenor; tendency etc.176; incidence; bending, trending etc *v.*; dip, tack, aim, collimation; steer-ing, -age.

point of the compass, cardinal –, half –, quarter- points; North, East, South, West; N by E, ENE, NE by N, NE etc; rhumb, azimuth, line of collimation.

line, path, road, range, quarter, line of march; alignment; straight shot, bee-line.

course, bearing, heading, altitude, air -route, - lane, angle, center, axis, torsion, torque, pitch, lift, drift, flow, wash.

V. tend –, bend –, point- towards; conduct –, go- to; point -to, – at; bend, trend, verge, incline, dip, determine.

steer –, make- -for, – towards; aim –, level- at; take aim; keep –, hold- a course; be bound for; bend one's steps towards; direct –, steer –, bend –, shape- one's course; align –, align- one's march; go straight, – to the point; march -on, – on a point.

ascertain one's -direction etc. *n.*; *s'orienter*, see which way the wind blows; box the compass.

Adj. directed etc. *v.*, – towards; pointing towards etc. *v.*; bound for; aligned –, with; direct, straight; un-deviating, -swerving; straightforward; North, -ern, -erly, etc. *n.*

directable etc. *v.*

Adv. towards; on the -road, – high road- to; versus, to; hither, thither, whither; directly; straight, – forwards, – as an arrow; point blank; in a direct, – straight- line -to, – for, – with; in a line with; full tilt at, as the crow flies.

before –, near –, close to –, against- the wind; windwards, in the wind's eye.

through, *via*, by way of; in all -directions, – manner of ways; *quaqua-versum*, from the four winds.

279. Deviation.—N. deviation; swerving etc. *v.*; obliquation, warp, refraction; flection, flexion; sweep; de-flection, -flexure; declination.

diversion, digression, departure from, aberration, drift, sheer; divergence etc. 291; zigzag; *détour* etc. (*circuit*) 629.

[Desultory motion] wandering etc. *v.*; vagrancy, evagation; by-paths and crooked ways.

[Motion sideways, oblique motion] sidling etc. *v.*; *échelon*, leeway; knight's move (at chess).

V. alter one's course, deviate, depart from, turn, trend; bend, curve, etc. 245; swerve, heel, bear off. intervert; deflect; divert, – from its course; put on a new scent, shift, shunt, switch, wear, draw aside, crook, warp, short circuit.

stray, straggle; sidle, edge; diverge etc. 291; tralineate, digress, divagate, wander; wind, twist, meander, meander around Robin Hood's barn; veer, tack, sheer; turn -aside, – a corner, – away from; wheel, steer clear of; ramble, rove, drift; go astray, – adrift; yaw, dodge; step aside, ease off, make way for, shy.

fly off at a tangent; glance off; turn, wheel –; face- about; turn –, face- to the right about; wabble etc. (*oscillate*) 314; go out of one's way etc. (*perform a circuit*) 629; lose one's way.

Adj. deviating etc. *v.*; aberrant, errant; ex-, dis-cursive; devious, desultory, loose; rambling; stray, erratic, vagrant, undirected; circuitous, indirect, zigzag; crab-like.

Adv. astray from, round about, wide of the mark; to the right about; all manner of ways; circuitously etc. 629.

obliquely, sideling, like the move of the knight on a chessboard.

280. Precession. [Going before.]—**N.** precession, leading, heading; precedence etc. 62; priority etc. 116; the lead, *le pas*; van etc. (*front*) 234; precursor etc. 64.

V. go -before, – ahead, – in the van, – in advance; precede, forerun; usher in, introduce, herald; head, take the lead; lead, – the way, – the dance; get –, have- the start; steal a march; get -before, – ahead, – in front of; outstrip etc. 303; take precedence etc. (*first in order*) 62.

Adj. foremost, first, leading etc. *v.*

Adv. in advance, before, ahead, in the van; fore-head-most; in front.

Phr. *seniores priores.*

281. Sequence. [Going after.]—**N.** sequence, run; coming after etc. (*order*) 63; (*time*) 117; following; pursuit etc. 622.

follower, attendant, satellite, shadow, dangler, train.

V. follow; pursue etc. 622; go –, fly- after.

attend, beset, dance attendance on, dog, be-dog; tread -in the steps of, – close upon; be –, go –, follow- in the -wake, – trail, – rear- of; trail, follow as a shadow, hang on the skirts of; tread –, follow- on the heels of, tag after.

lag, get behind.

Adj. following etc. *v.*

Adv. behind; in the -rear etc. 235, – train of, wake of; after etc. (*order*) 63, (*time*) 117.

282. Progression. [Motion forwards; progressive motion.]—**N.** progress, -ion, -iveness; advancing etc. *v.*; advance, -ment; ongoing; flood-tide, headway; march etc. 266; rise; improvement etc. 658.

V. advance; proceed, progress; get -on, – along, – over the ground; gain ground; jog –, rub –, wag-on; go with the stream; keep –, hold on- one's course; go –, move –, come –, get –, pass –, push –, press- -on, – forward, – forwards, – ahead; press onwards, step forward; make –, work –, carve –, push –, force –, edge –, elbow- one's way; make -progress, – head, – way, – headway, – advances, – strides, – rapid strides etc. (*velocity*) 274; go –, shoot- ahead; distance; make up leeway.

Adj. advancing etc. *v.*; pro-gressive, -fluent; advanced.

Adv. forward, onward; forth, on ahead, under way, *en route* for, on -one's way, – the way, – the road, – the high road- to; in -progress, – mid progress; *in transitu* etc. 270.

Phr. *vestigia nulla retrorsum.*

283. Regression. [Motion backwards.]—**N.** regress, -ion; retro-cession, -gression, -gradation, -action; *reculade*; retreat, withdrawal, retirement, remigration; recession etc. (*motion from*) 287; recess; crab-like motion.

re-fluence, -flux; backwater, regurgitation, ebb, return; resilience; reflexion (*recoil*) 277; volte-face.

counter -motion, – movement, – march; veering, tergiversation, recidivation, backsliding, fall, relapse; deterioration etc. 659.

turning point etc. (*reversion*) 145.

V. re-cede, -grade, -turn, -vert, -treat, -tire; retro-grade, -cede; back, – down, – out, crawl; withdraw; rebound etc. 277; go –, come – turn –, hark –, draw –, fall –, get –, put –, run- back; lose ground; fall –, drop- astern; back water, put about; veer, – round; double, wheel, counter-march; ebb, regurgitate; *jib*, shrink, shy.

turn -tail, – round, – upon one's heel, – one's back upon; retrace one's steps, dance the back step; sound –, beat- a retreat; go home.

Adj. receding etc. *v.*; retro-grade, -gressive; re-gressive, -fluent, -flex, -cidivous, -silient; crab-like; reactionary etc. 277; counter-clockwise.

Adv. back, -wards; reflexively, to the right about; *à reculons, à rebours.*

Phr. *revenons à nos moutons,* as you were.

284. Propulsion. [Motion given to an object situated in front.]—**N.** pro-pulsion, -jection; *vis a tergo*; push etc. (*impulse*) 276; e-, jaculation; ejection etc. 297; throw, fling, toss, shot, discharge, shy.

[Science of propulsion] steam –, gas –, diesel –, jet –, rocket – propulsion, gunnery, ballistics, archery.

missile, projectile, ball, *discus*, javelin, hammer, quoit, brickbat, shot, bullet; arrow, shaft, gun etc. (*arms*) 727.

shooter, shot; gunner, gun-layer; archer, toxophilite; bow-, rifle-, marks- man; good –, crack- shot; sharpshooter etc. (*combatant*) 726.

V. propel, project, throw, fling, cast, pitch, chuck, toss, jerk, heave, shy, hurl; flirt, fillip.

dart, lance, tilt; e-, jaculate; fulminate, bolt, drive, sling, pitchfork.

send; send –, let –, fire- off; discharge, shoot; launch, send forth, let fly; dash.

put –, set- in motion; set agoing, start; give -a start, – an impulse- to; push, impel etc. 276; trundle etc. (*set in rotation*) 312; expel etc. 297.

carry one off one's legs; put to flight.

Adj. propelled etc. *v.*; propelling etc. *v.*; pro-pulsive, -jectile.

285. Traction. [Motion given to an object situated behind.]—**N.** traction; drawing etc. *v.*; draft, pull, tug, haul; rake; 'a long pull, a strong pull and a pull all together;' towage, haulage.

V. draw, pull, haul, lug, rake, drag, draggle, tug, tow, trail, trawl, train; take in tow.

wrench, jerk, twitch.

Adj. drawing etc. *v.*; tractive, tractile; ductile; pulling, hauling, tugging, towing.

286. Approach. Motion towards.]—**N.** approach, approximation, appropinquation; access; appulse; afflux, -ion; advent etc. (*approach of time*) 121; pursuit etc. 622; convergence etc. 290.

V. approach, approximate; near; get –, go –, draw- near; come, – near, – to close quarters; move –, set in- towards; drift; make up to; gain upon; pursue etc. 622; tread on the heels of; bear up; make the land; hug the -shore, – land.

Adj. approaching etc. *v.*; approximative; convergent; affluent; impending, imminent etc. (*destined*) 152.

Adv. on the road.

Int. come hither! approach! here! come! come near!

287. Recession. [Motion from.]—**N.** recession, retirement, withdrawal; retreat; retrocession etc. 283; departure etc. 293; recoil etc. 277; flight etc. (*avoidance*) 623.

V. recede, go, move from, retire, ebb, withdraw, shrink; come –, move –, go –, get –, drift-away; depart etc. 293; retreat etc. 283; move –, stand –, sheer- off; swerve from; fall back, stand aside; run away etc. (*avoid*) 623.

remove, shunt, side track, switch off.

Adj. receding etc. *v.*

288. Attraction. [Motion towards, actively.]—**N.** attract-ion, -iveness; pull; drawing to, pulling towards, adduction, magnetism, gravity, attraction of gravitation; lure, bait, decoy.

lode-stone, -star; magnet, siderite, magnetite.

V. attract; draw —, pull —, drag- towards; adduce.

lure, bait, decoy.

Adj. attracting etc. *v.*; attrahent, attractive, adducent, adductive, alluring.

289. Repulsion. [Motion from, actively.]—**N.** repulsion; driving from etc. *v.*; repulse; abduction.

V. repel; push —, drive — etc. 276; from; chase, dispel; retrude; abduce, abduct; send away, repulse, dismiss.

keep at arm's length, turn one's back upon, give the cold shoulder; send packing; send -off, — away- with a flea in one's ear, — about one's business.

Adj. repelling etc. *v.*; repellant, repulsive; abducent, abductive.

290. Convergence. [Motion nearer to.]—**N.** con-vergence, -fluence, -course, -flux, -gress, -currence, -centration; appulse, meeting; corradiation.

assemblage etc. 72; resort etc. (*focus*) 74; asymptote.

V. converge, concur; come together, unite, meet, fall in with; close -with, — in upon; center - round, — in; enter in; pour in.

gather together, unite, concentrate, bring into a focus.

Adj. converging etc. *v.*; con-vergent, -fluent, -current; centripetal; asymptotical.

291. Divergence. [Motion further off.]—**N.** diverg-ence, -ency; divarication, ramification, radiation; separation etc. (*disjunction*) 44; dispersion etc. 73; deviation etc. 279; aberration, declination.

V. diverge, divaricate, radiate; ramify; branch —, glance —, file- off; fly off, — at a tangent; spread, scatter, disperse etc. 73; deviate etc. 279; part etc. (*separate*) 44; splay apart.

Adj. diverging etc. *v.*; divergent, radiant, centrifugal; aberrant.

292. Arrival. [Terminal motion at.]—**N.** arrival, advent; landing; de-, disem-barkation; reception, welcome, *vin d'honneur*.

home, goal, bourn; landing-place, -stage; resting —, stopping -place; destination, harbor, haven, port; terminal, terminus, railway station, depot, airport; halt, halting -place, — ground; anchorage etc. (*refuge*) 666.

return, recursion, remigration; meeting; ren-, encounter.

completion etc. 729.

V. arrive; get to, come to; come; reach, attain; come up, — with, — to; overtake; make, fetch; complete etc. 729; join, rejoin.

light, alight, dismount; land, go ashore; debark, disembark; put -in, — into; visit, cast anchor, pitch

one's tent; sit down etc. (*be located*) 184; get to one's journey's end; make the land; be in at the death; come —, get- -back, — home; return; come in etc. (*ingress*) 294; make one's appearance etc. (*appear*) 446; drop in; detrain; outspan.

come to hand; come -at, — across; hit; come —, light —, pop —, bounce —, plump —, burst —, pitch- upon; meet; en- ren-counter; come in contact.

Adj. arriving etc. *v.*; homewardbound; terminal.

Adv. here, hither.

Int. welcome! hail! all hail! good- day, — morrow; greetings! hullo! well!

293. Departure. [Initial motion from.]—**N.** departure, decession, decampment; embarkation; take-off; outset, start; removal; exit etc. (*egress*) 295; exodus, Hejira, flight.

leave-taking, *congé*, valediction, valedictory, adieu, farewell, good-bye, stirrup-cup.

starting -point, — post; point —, place- of - departure, — embarkation; port of embarkation.

V. depart; go, — away; take one's departure, set out; set —, march —, put —, start —, be —, move —, get —, whip —, pack —, go —, take oneself- off; start, issue, march out, debouch; go —, sally-forth; sally, set forward; be gone.

leave a place, quit, vacate, evacuate, abandon; go off the stage, make ones' exit; retire, withdraw, remove; go -one's way, — along, — from home; take -flight, — wing; spring, fly, flit, wing one's flight; fly —, whip- away; take off, hop off; embark; go -on board, — aboard; set sail; put —, go- to sea; sail, take ship; hoist blue Peter; get under way, weigh anchor; strike tents, break camp, decamp; walk one's chalks, make tracks, cut one's stick; cut and run; take leave; say —, bid- -good-bye etc. *n.*; disappear etc. 449; abscond etc. (*avoid*) 623; entrain, embus, emplane; saddle —, harness —, hitch- up; inspan.

Adj. departing etc. *v.*; valedictory; outward bound.

Adv. whence, hence, thence; with a foot in the stirrup; on the wing, — move.

Int. begone! etc. (*ejection*) 297; to horse! all aboard! farewell! adieu! good-bye, — day! *au revoir! auf wiedersehen!* fare you well! so long! God -bless you, — speed! *bon voyage!*

294. Ingress. [Motion into.]—**N.** ingress; entrance, entry; introgression; influx; intrusion, inroad, incursion, invasion, irruption; pene-, interpene- tration; illapse, import, importation, infiltration; immigration; admission etc. (*reception*) 296; insinuation etc. (*interjacence*) 228; insertion etc. 300.

inlet; way in; mouth, door etc. (*opening*) 260; path etc. (*way*) 627; conduit etc. 350; immigrant, visitor, incomer, newcomer, colonist.

V. have the *entrée*; enter; go —, come —, pour —, flow —, creep —, slip —, pop —, break —, burst- -into, — in; set foot on; burst —, break-in upon; invade, intrude, butt in, horn in, crash; insinuate itself; inter-, penetrate; infiltrate; find one's way —, wriggle —, worm oneself- into.

give entrance to etc. (*receive*) 296; insert etc. 300.

Adj. incoming, ingressive etc. *n.*; inward bound.

Adv. inward.

295. Egress. [Motion out of.]—N. egress, exit, issue; emer-sion, -gence; disemboguement; out-break, -burst; e-, pro-ruption; emanation; evacuation; ex, trans-udation; extravasation, per-spiration, sweating, leakage, percolation, distillation, oozing; gush etc. (*water in motion*) 348; outpour, -ing; effluence, effusion; efflux, -ion; drain; dribbling etc. *v.*; defluxion; drainage; out-come, -put; discharge etc. (*excretion*) 299.

export; expatriation; e-, re-migration; *débouche*; exodus etc. (*departure*) 293; emigrant, migrant, *émigré*, colonist.

outlet, vent, spout, tap, sluice, floodgate; pore; vomitory, out-gate, sally-port; way out; mouth, door etc. (*opening*) 260; path etc. (*way*) 627; con-duit etc. 350; air-pipe etc. 351.

V. emerge, emanate, issue; go −, come −, move −, pass −, pour −, flow- out of; pass off, evacuate; migrate.

ex-, trans-ude; leak; run, − out, − through; per-, trans-colate; seep; strain, distil; perspire, sweat, drain, ooze; filter, filtrate; dribble, gush, spout, flow out; well, − out; pour, trickle etc. (*water in motion*) 348; effuse, extravasate, disem-bogue, discharge itself, debouch; come −, break-forth; burst- out, − through; find vent, escape etc. 671.

Adj. effused etc. *v.*; outgoing, outward bound.

Adv. outward.

296. Reception. [Motion into, actively.]—N. reception; admission, admittance, *entrée*, im-portation; initiation; intro-duction, -mission, -ception; immission, ingestion, imbibition, ab-sorption, ingurgitation, inhalation; suction, sucking; eating, drinking etc. (*food*) 298; insertion etc. 300; interjection etc. 228.

V. give -entrance to, − admittance to, − the *entrée*; intro-duce, -mit; usher, admit, receive, im-port, initiate, bring in, open the door to, throw open, ingest, absorb, imbibe, inhale, infiltrate; let −, take −, suck- in; re-admit, -sorb, -absorb; snuff up; swallow, ingurgitate; enfulf, engorge; gulp; eat, drink etc. (*food*) 298.

Adj. admit-ting etc. *v.*, -ted etc. *v.*; admissible; absorbent; introductory, introceptive, intromittent, initiatory.

297. Ejection. [Motion out of, actively.]—N. ejection, emission, effusion, rejection, expulsion, eviction, extrusion, trajection; discharge.

egestion, evacuation, vomition, disgorgement, voidance, eruption, eruptiveness; ruc-, cruc-tation; blood-letting, venesection, phlebotomy, paracen-tesis; tapping, drainage; clear-ance, -age, voidance; vomiting, excretion. 299.

deportation; banishment etc. (*punishment*) 972; rogue's march; relegation, extradition; dislodgment.

V. give -exit, − vent- to; let −, give −, pour −, send- out; des-, dis-patch; exhale, excern, ex-crete, disembogue, secrete, secern; extravasate,

shed, void, evacuate, egest, emit; open the -sluices, − floodgates; turn on the tap; extrude, detrude; ef-fuse, spend, expend; pour forth; squirt, spirt, spill, slop; perspire etc. (*exude*) 295; breathe, blow etc. (*wind*) 349.

tap, draw off; bale −, lade- out; let blood, broach.

eject, reject; expel, discard; cut, send to Coven-try, boycott, ostracize; *chasser*; banish etc. (*punish*) 972; throw etc. 284 -out, − up, − off, − away, − aside; push etc. 276 -out, − off, − away, − aside; shovel −, sweep- -out, − away; brush −, whisk −, turn −, send- -off, − away; discharge; send −, turn −, cast- adrift; turn −, bundle- out; throw overboard; give the sack to; send -packing, − about one's business, − to, the right about; strike off the roll etc. (*abrogate*) 756; turn out-neck and heels, − head and shoulders, − neck and crop; pack off; send away with a flea in the ear; send to Jericho; bow out, show the door to, dismiss, fire, sack.

turn out of -doors, − house and home; evict, oust; exorcise, un-house, -kennel; dislodge; un-, dis-people; depopulate; relegate, deport.

empty; drain, − to the dregs; sweep off; clear, − off, − out, − away; such, draw off, extract; clean out, make a clean sweep of, clear decks, purge.

em-, dis-, disem-bowel; eviscerate, gut; unearth, root -out, − up; averruncate; weed −, get out; eliminate, get rid of, do away with, shake off; exen-terate.

vomit, spew, puke, keck, retch; belch, − out, eruct, eructate; cast −, bring- up; disgorge; ex-pectorate, salivate, clear the throat, hawk, spit, sputter, splutter, slobber, drool, drivel, slaver, slab-ber.

unpack, unlade, unload, unship; break bulk.

be let out; ooze etc. (*emerge*) 295.

Adj. emitt-ing, -ed etc. *v.*

begone! get you gone! get −. go- away, − along, − along with you! go your way! away, − with! off with you! go, − about your business! be off! avaunt! aroynt! get out!

298. Food. [Eating.]—N. eating etc. *v.*; deglutition, gulp, epulation, mastication, man-ducation, rumination, gastronomy, gastrology; panto-, hippo-, ichthyo-phagy etc.; gluttony etc. 957; carnivorousness, vegetarianism.

mouth, jaws, mandible, mazard, chops.

drinking etc. *v.*; potation, draught, libation; carousal etc. (*amusement*) 840; drunkenness etc. 959.

food, *pabulum*; aliment, nourishment, nutriment; susten-ance, -tation; nurture, sub-sistence, provender, feed, fodder, provision, ration, keep, commons, board; commissariat etc. (*provision*) 637; prey, forage, pasture, pasturage; fare, cheer; diet, -ary; regimen; belly timber, staff of life; bread, −and cheese; proteins, carbohydrates, vitamines.

comestibles, eatables, victuals, edibles, *ingesta*; grub, prog, tack, hard tack, meat; bread, -stuffs; cereals; viands, cates, delicacy, dainty, creature comforts, contents of the larder, flesh-pots; festal board; ambrosia; good -cheer, − living.

hors-d'oeuvre; soup, pottage, *potage*, broth,

bouillon, consommé, purée, borsch, stock, skilly, gumbo; fish, − cakes, − pie; joint, rôti, pièce de résistance, relevé, hash, réchauffé, stew, ragoût, fricassee, mince, salim, goulash, bouillabaisse, remove, entrée, croquette, rissole, sausage, curry, bubble and squeak; haggis, collops, giblets; poultry, game etc.; biscuit, bun, scone, rusk, pancake, pie, pastry, pasty, patty, patisseria, tart, turnover, vol-au-vent, soufflé, dumpling, pudding, duff, compote, fritters, cake, napoleon, blancmange, custard, jelly, jam, sweets etc. 396; entremet; oatmeal, porridge, hasty pudding, gruel; eggs, omelet, cheese, matzoon, savory; vegetable, salad, mayonnaise, fruit; sauce, condiment etc. 393; kickshaws.

table, cuisine, bill of fare, menu, table d'hôte, ordinary, à la carte; cover.

meal, repast, feed, spread; mess; dish, plate, course, side dish; regale; regale-, refresh-, entertain-ment; refection, collation, picnic, feast, banquet, junket; breakfast; lunch, -eon, déjeuner, bever, tiffin, tea, dinner, supper, snack, whet, bait, dessert; pot-luck, table d'hôte, déjeuner à la fourchette; hearty −, square −, substantial −, full-meal; blow out; light refreshment; pemmican.

mouthful, bolus, gobbet, tit-bit, morsel, sop, sippet.

drink, beverage, liquor, broth, soup; potion, dram, draft, drench, swill; nip, peg, sip, sup, gulp.

wine, champagne, spirits, liqueur beer, porter, stout, ale, malt liquor, julep, Sir John Barleycorn, stingo, heavy wet, bitter, lager-beer, cider; grog, toddy, flip, purl, punch, negus, cup, bishop, posset, wassail; bitters, apéritif, high-ball, cocktail; whisky, rum, absinthe; gin etc. (intoxicating liquor) 959; coffee, chocolate, cocoa, tea, maté, the cup that cheers but not inebriates.

eating-house etc. 189.

V. eat, feed, fare, devour, swallow, take; gulp, bolt, snap; fall to; despatch, dispatch; discuss; take −, get −, gulp-down; lay −, tuck- in; lick, pick, peck; gormandize etc. 957; bite, champ, munch, cranch, craunch, crunch, chew, masticate, nibble, gnaw, mumble.

live on; batten −, fatten −, feast- upon; browse, graze, crop, regale; carouse etc. (make merry) 840; eat heartily, do justice to, play a good knife and fork, banquet.

break -bread, − one's fast; breakfast; lunch, dine, take tea, sup.

drink, − in, − up, − one's fill; quaff, sip, sup; suck, − up; lap; swig; swill, tipple etc. (be drunken) 959; empty one's glass, drain the cup; toss -off, − one's glass; wash down, crack a bottle, wet one's whistle.

cater, purvey etc. 637.

Adj. eatable, edible, esculent, comestible, alimentary; cereal, cibarious, dietetic; culinary; nutri-tive, -tious; succulent; drinkable, pot-able, - ulent; bibulous.

omn-, carn-, herb-, frug-, gran-, gramin-, phyt, ivorous; ichthyophagous.

prandial.

299. Excretion.—N. excretion, discharge, emanation; ejection etc. 297; exhalation, exudation, extrusion, secretion, effusion, extravasation, ecchymosis, evacuation, cacation, defecation, dysentery, dejection, feces, excrement;

perspiration, sweat; sub-, exud-ation; diaphoresis; sewage.

saliva, spittle, rheum; ptyalism, salivation, catarrh, distemper; diarrhea; ejecta, egesta, sputum, sputa; excreta; lava; exuviae etc. (uncleanness) 653.

hemorrhage, bleeding; catamenia, menses; outpouring etc. (egress) 295; leucorrhea.

V. excrete etc. (eject) 297; emanate etc. (come out) 295.

Adj. excretory, fecal, secretory; ejective, eliminant.

300. Insertion. [Forcible ingress.]—N. insertion, implantation, intercalation, embolism, introduction; interpolation, insinuation etc. (intervention) 228; planting etc. v.; injection, inoculation, importation, infusion; forcible -ingress etc. 294; immersion; submersion, -gence; dip, plunge; bath etc. (water) 337; interment etc. 363.

V. insert; intro-duce, -mit; put −, run- into; import; inject; interject; interject etc. 228; infuse, instil, inoculate, impregnate, imbue, imbrue.

graft, ingraft, bud, plant, implant; dovetail.

obtrude; thrust −, stick −, ram −, stuff −, tuck −, press −, drive −, pop −, whip −, drop −, put- in; impact; empierce etc. (make a hole) 260.

embed; immerse, immerge, merge; bathe, soak etc. (water) 337; dip, plunge etc. 310.

bury etc. (inter) 363.

insert etc. -itself; plunge in medias res.

Adj. inserted etc. v.

301. Extraction. [Forcible egress.]—N. extraction; extracting etc. v.; removal, elimination, extrication, eradication, evolution.

evulsion, avulsion; wrench; expression, squeezing; extirpation, extermination; ejection etc. 297; export etc. (egress) 295; distillation.

extractor, corkscrew, forceps, pliers.

V. extract, draw, pit; take −, draw −, pull −, tear −, pluck −, pick −, get- out; wring from, wrench; extort; root −, weed −, grub −, rakeup, − out; eradicate; pull −, pluck- up by the roots; averruncate; unroot; uproot, pull up, extirpate, dredge.

remove; educe, elicit; evolve, extricate; eliminate etc. (eject) 297; eviscerate etc. 297.

express, squeeze −, press- out; distil.

Adj. extracted etc. v.

302. Passage. [Motion through.]—N. passage, transmission; permeation; pene-, interpene-tration; transudation, infiltration; osmosis, osmose, endos-, exos-mose; intercurrence; ingress etc. 294; egress etc. 295; path etc. 627; conduit etc. 350; opening etc. 260; journey etc. 266; voyage etc. 267.

V. pass, − through; perforate etc. (hole) 260; penetrate, permeate, thread, thrid, enfilade; go -through, − across; go −, pass- over; cut across; ford, cross; pass and repass, work; make −, thread −, worm −, force- one's way; make −, force- a passage; cut one's way through; find its -way, −

vent; transmit, make way, clear the course; traverse, go over the ground.

Adj. passing etc. *v.*; intercurrent; osmotic etc. *n.*

Adv. *en passant* etc. (*transit*) 270.

303. Overstep. [Motion beyond.]—**N.** transcursion, -ilience, -gression: infraction, intrusion; trespass; encroach-, infringe-ment; extravagation, transcendence; redundance etc. 641; ingress etc. 294.

V. transgress, surpass, pass; go- beyond, – by; show in –, come to the- front; shoot ahead of; steal a march –, gain- upon.

over-step, -pass, -reach, -go, -ride- -leap, -jump, - skip, -lap, -shoot the mark; out-strip, -leap, -jump, -go, -step, -run, -ride, -rival, -do; beat, – hollow; distance; leave in the -lurch, – rear; go one better, throw into the shade; exceed, transcend, surmount; soar etc. (*rise*) 305.

encroach, intrude, trespass, infringe, invade, trench upon, intrench on; strain; stretch –, strain- a point; pass the Rubicon.

Adj. surpassing etc. *v.*

Adv. beyond the mark, ahead.

304. Shortcoming. [Motion short of.]—**N.** shortcoming, failure; delinquency; falling short etc. *v.*; de-fault, -falcation; leeway; labor in vain, no go.

incompleteness etc. 53; imperfection etc. 651; insufficiency etc. 640; noncompletion etc. 730; failure etc. 732.

V. come –, fall –, stop- -short, – short of; not reach; want; keep within -bounds, – the mark, – compass.

break down, stick in the mud, collapse, come to nothing; fall -through, – to the ground, – down; cave in; end in smoke, fizzle out, miss the mark, fail; lose ground; miss stays, slump.

Adj. unreached; deficient; short, – of; *minus*; out of depth; perfunctory etc. (*neglect*) 460.

Adv. within -the mark, – compass, – bounds; behindhand; *re infectâ*; to no purpose; far from it.

Phr. the bubble burst.

305. Ascent. [Motion upwards.]—**N.** ascent, ascension; rising etc. *v.*; rise, upgrowth; leap etc. 309; acclivity, hill etc. 217; stair, stairs, stair-case, - way, flight of -steps, – stairs; ladder, companion, – way; lift, elevator etc. 307.

rocket, lark; sky-rocket, -lark; Alpine Club.

V. ascend, rise, mount, arise, uprise; go –, get –, work one's way –, start –, spring –, shoot-up; zoom; aspire.

climb, clamber, ramp, scramble, swarm, *escalade*, surmount; scale, – the heights.

tower, soar, hover, spire, plane, swim, float, surge; leap etc. 309.

Adj. rising etc. *v.*; scandent, buoyant; super-natant, -fluitant; excelsior.

Adv. uphill.

306. Descent. [Motion downwards.]—**N.** descent, descension, declension, declination; fall;

falling etc. *v.*; drop, cadence; subsidence, lapse; come-down, downfall, tumble, slip, tilt, trip, lurch; cropper, *culbute*; titubation, stumble; fate of Icarus; dive, nose-dive, *volpané*.

avalanche, débâcle, landslip, slide.

V. descend; go –, drop –, come-down; fall, gravitate, drop, slip, slide, glissade, dive, plunge, settle; decline, slump, set, sink, droop, come down a peg.

dismount, alight, light, get down; swoop; stoop etc. 308; fall prostrate, precipitate oneself; let fall etc. 308.

tumble, trip, stumble, titubate, lurch, pitch, swag, topple; tumble –, tumble- -down, – over; tilt, sprawl, plump down, come a cropper.

Adj. descending etc. *v.*; descendent, declivitous; downcast; decur-rent, sive; labent, deciduous; nodding to its fall.

Adv. down, -hill, -wards.

307. Elevation.—**N.** elevation; raising etc. *v.*; erection, lift; sublevation, upheaval; sublimation, exaltation; prominence etc. (*convexity*) 250.

lever etc. 633; crane, derrick, windlass, capstan, winch, dredger, lift, elevator, escalator, dumb waiter.

V. heighten, elevate, raise, lift, erect; set –, stick –, perch –, perk –, tilt- up; rear, hoist, heave; up-lift, -raise, -rear, -bear, -cast, -hoist, - heave; buoy, weigh, mount, give a lift; exalt, sublimate; place –, set- on a pedestal.

take –, drag –, fish- up; dredge.

stand –, rise –, get –, jump- up; spring to one's feet; hold -oneself, – one's head- up; draw oneself up to his full height.

Adj. elevated etc. *v.*; standing up; stilted, at-tollent, rampant.

Adv. on -stilts, – the shoulders of, – one's legs, – one's hind legs.

308. Depression.—**N.** lowering etc. *v.*; depression; dip etc. (*concavity*) 252; abasement; detrusion; reduction.

over-throw, -set, -turn; upset; prostration, sub-version, precipitation.

bow; courtesy, curtsy; genuflexion, *kowtow*, obeisance, *salaam*.

V. depress, lower; let –, take- -down, – down a peg; cast; let -drop, – fall; sink, debase, bring low, abase, slash, reduce, detrude, pitch, precipitate.

over-throw, -turn, -set; upset, subvert, prostrate, level, fell; cast –, take –, throw –, fling –, dash –, pull –, cut –, knock –, hew- down; raze, – to the ground; humiliate, trample in the dust, pull about one's ears.

sit, – down; couch, squat, crouch, stoop, bend, bow, courtesy, curtsy; bob, duck, dip, genuflect, kneel; *kowtow, salaam*, make obeisance, prostrate oneself; bend, bow- the -head, – knee; incline the head; bow down; cower; recline etc. (*be horizontal*) 213.

Adj. depressed etc. *v.*; at a low ebb; prostrate etc. (*horizontal*) 213; detrusive.

309. Leap.—**N.** leap, jump, hop, spring, bound, vault, saltation.

dance, caper, gambol; curvet, caracole; *gam-bade*, *-bado*; capriole, demivolt; buck, – jump; hop, skip and jump.

kangaroo, jerboa, chamois, goat, frog, grasshopper, flea.

V. leap; jump -up, – over the moon; hop, spring, bound, vault, ramp, cut capers, gambol, trip, skip, dance, caper, curvet, *caracole*; foot it, bob, bounce, flounce, start, frisk etc. (*amusement*) 840; jump about etc. (*agitation*) 315; trip it on the light fantastic toe, dance oneself off one's legs.

Adj. leaping etc. *v.*; saltatory, frisky.

Adv. on the light fantastic toe.

310. Plunge.—N. plunge, dip, dive, header; ducking etc. *v.*; submergence, immersion, diver.

V. plunge, dip, souse, duck; dive, plump; take a -plunge, – header, make a plunge; bathe etc. (*water*) 337.

sub-merge, -merse; immerse, douse, sink, engulf, send to -the bottom, – Davy Jones' locker.

get out of one's depth; go -to the bottom, – down like a stone; founder, welter, wallow.

311. Circuition. [Curvilinear motion.]—**N.** circuition, circulation; turn, curvet; excursion; circum-vention, -navigation, -ambulation; north-west passage; ambit, gyre, lap, circuit etc. 629.

turning etc. *v.*; wrench; evolution; coil, helix, spiral; corkscrew.

V. turn, bend, wheel; go –, put- about; heel; go –, turn -round, – to the right about; turn on one's heel; make –, describe- a -circle, – complete circle; encircle; go –, pass- through -180°. – 360°.

circum-navigate, -aviate, -ambulate, -vent; put a girdle round the earth, go the round, make the round of.

turn –, round- a corner; double a point.

wind, circulate, meander; whisk, twirl; twist etc. (*convolution*) 248; make a *détour* etc. (*circuit*) 629.

Adj. turning etc. *v.*; circuitous; circum-foraneous, -fluent; devious, roundabout, circum-ambient, -flex, -navigable.

Adv. round about.

312. Rotation. [Motion in a continued circle.]—**N.** rotation, revolution, gyration, circulation, roll; circum-rotation, -volution, -gyration; volutation, circination, turbination, *pirouette*, convolution.

verticity; whir, whirl, swirl, eddy, vortex, whirlpool, gurge; cyclone, tornado; surge; *vertigo*, dizzy round; Maelstrom, Charybdis; Ixion; wheel of Fortune.

wheel, screw, propeller, whirligig, rolling stone, windmill; top, teetotum, merry-go-round; roller; cog-, fly-wheel; spit; jack; caster.

axis, axle, spindle, spool, pivot, pin, hinge, pole, swivel, gimbals, arbor, bobbin, mandrel, shaft.

[Science of rotatory motion] trochilics, gyrostatics.

V. rotate; roll, – along; revolve, spin; turn, – round; circumvolve; circulate; gyre, gyrate, wheel,

whirl, swirl, twirl, trundle, troll, bowl; slew round.

roll up, furl; wallow, welter; box the compass; spin like a -top, – teetotum.

Adj. rotating etc. *v.*; rota-tory, -ry; circumrotatory, trochilic, vertiginous, gyratory; vortic-al, -ose.

Adv. head over heels, round and round, like a horse in a mill.

313. Evolution. [Motion in a reverse circle.]—**N.** evolution, unfolding, development; eversion etc. (*inversion*) 218.

V. evolve; un-fold, -roll, -wind, -coil, -twist, - furl, -twine, -ravel; disentangle; develop.

Adj. evolving etc. *v.*; evolved etc. *v.*

314. Oscillation. [Reciprocating motion, motion to and fro.]—**N.** oscillation; vibration, libration; motion of a pendulum; nutation; undulation; pulsation; pulse; throb; seismic disturbance.

alternation; coming and going etc. *v.*; ebb and flow, flux and reflux, ups and downs; wave, vibratiuncle, swing, beat, shake, wag, see-saw, dance, lurch, dodge; fluctuation; vacillation etc. (*irresolution*) 605.

seismometer, vibroscope, seismograph.

V. oscillate; vi-, li-brate; alternate, undulate, wave; sway, rock, swing; pulsate, beat; wag, -gle; nod, bob, courtesy, curtsy; tick; play; chatter, wamble, wabble; teeter, dangle, swag.

fluctuate, dance, curvet, reel, quake; quiver, quaver, shake, flicker; wriggle; roll, toss, pitch; flounder, stagger, totter, waddle; move –, bob- up and down etc. *adv.*; pass and repass, ebb and flow, come and go, shuttle; vacillate etc. 605.

brandish, shake, flourish.

Adj. oscillating etc. *v.*; oscill-, undul-, puls-, libr-atory; vibrat-ory, -ile; pendulous, shutterwise, seismic.

Adv. to and fro, up and down, backwards and forwards, see-saw, zigzag, wibble-wabble, in and out, from side to side, like buckets in a well.

315. Agitation. [Irregular motion.]—**N.** agitation, stir, tremor, shake, ripple, jog, jolt, jerk, shock, succession, trepidation, quiver, quaver, dance; jactit-ation, -ance; shuffling etc. *v.*; twitter, flicker, flutter.

disquiet, perturbation, commotion, turmoil, turbulence; tumult, -uation; hubbub, rout, bustle, fuss, racket, *subsultus*, staggers, megrims, epilepsy, fits, twitching, vellication; St. Vitus's dance.

spasm, throe, throb, palpitation, convulsion, paroxysm; tetanus.

disturbance etc. (*disorder*) 59; restlessness etc. (*changeableness*) 149.

ferment, -ation; ebullition, effervescence, hurly burly, *cahotage*; tempest, storm, ground swell, heavy sea, whirlpool, vortex etc. 312; whirlwind etc. (*wind*) 349.

V. be -agitated etc.; shake; tremble, – like an aspen leaf; quiver, quaver, quake, shiver, twitter, twire, dither, dodder; twitch, writhe, toss, shuffle, tumble, stagger, bob, reel, sway; wag, -gle, wiggle; wriggle, – like an eel; squirm; dance, stumble, shamble, flounder, totter, flounce, flop, curvet, prance.

throb, pulsate, beat, palpitate, go pit-a-pat; flutter, flitter, flicker, bicker; bustle.

ferment, effervesce, foam; boil, – over; bubble, – up; simmer.

toss –, jump- about; jump like a parched pea; shake like an aspen leaf; shake to its -center, – foundations; be the sport of the winds and waves; reel to and fro like a drunken man; move –, drive-from post to pillar and from pillar to post; keep between hawk and buzzard.

agitate, shake, convulse, toss, tumble, bandy, wield, brandish, flap, flourish, whisk, jerk, hitch, jolt; jog, -gle; hostle, buffet, hustle, disturb, stir, shake up, churn, jounce, wallop, whip, vellicate.

Adj. shaking etc. *v.*; agitated, tremulous; de-, sub-sultory; shambling; giddy-paced, saltatory, convulsive, jerky, unquiet, restless, all of a twitter.

Adv. by fits and starts; subsultorily etc. *adj.*; *per saltum*; hop, skip and jump; in -convulsions, – fits, pit-a-pat.

316. Materiality.—N. material-ity, -ness; materialization; corpor-eity, -ality; substantiality, material existence, incarnation, flesh and blood, *plenum*; physical condition.

matter, body, substance, brute matter, stuff, element, principle, protoplasm, plasma, *parenchyma*, material, *substratum*, hyle, *corpus*, *pabulum*; frame.

object, article, thing, something; still life; stocks and stones; materials etc. 635.

[Science of matter] physics; somatology, -ics, natural –, experimental- philosophy; physical science, *philosophie positive*, materialism, hylism; applied –, micro-, molecular –, nuclear – physics.

atomics, atomic science, nucleonics, quantum mechanics, radiology.

atom, radical, tracer, isotope, pleiad; atomic – nucleus, – cluster; nuclear particle, neutron, protron, shell, valence electron.

materialist, physicist, atomic scientist, radiologist.

V. materialize, incorporate, incarnate, substantiate, embody.

atomize, split –, smash – the atom; radio-activate.

Adj. material, bodily; corpor-eal, -al; physical; somat-ic, -oscopic; sensible, tangible, ponderable, palpable, substantial; fleshly, incarnate.

physical, bio-, electro-, geo-physical; atomic, nuclear, thermonuclear, radio-active.

objective, impersonal, neuter, unspiritual, materialistic.

317. Immateriality.—N. immaterial-ity, -ness; incorporeity, dematerialization, unsubstantiality, spirituality; inextension; astral plane.

personality; I, myself, me; *ego*, spirit etc. (*soul*) 450; astral body; immaterialism; spiritual-ism, -ist; subliminal –, subconscious- self.

V. disembody, spiritualize, dematerialize.

Adj. immateri-al, -ate; incorpor-eal, -al; asomatous, unextended; un-, dis-embodied; extramundane, supersensible, unearthly;

pneumatoscopic; spiritual etc. (*psychical*) 450; aery.

personal, subjective.

318. World.—N. world, creation, nature, universe; earth, globe, wide world; *cosmos*; terraqueous globe, sphere; macro-, mega-cosm; music of the spheres; strato-, tropo-sphere.

heavens, sky, welkin, empyrean; starry -heaven, – host; firmament; vault –, canopy- of heaven; celestial spaces.

heavenly bodies, stars, luminaries, nebulae; galaxy, milky way, galactic circle, *via lactea*.

sun, orb of day, Apollo, Phoebus; photo-, chromo-sphere; solar system; planet, -oid, asteroid; comet; satellite; moon, orb of night, Diana, Luna; aerolite, meteor; falling –, shooting-star; meteorite.

constellation, zodiac, signs of the zodiac, Charles's wain, Great Bear, Southern Cross, Orion's belt, Cassiopeia's chair, Pleiades etc.

colures, equator, ecliptic, orbit.

[Science of heavenly bodies] astronomy; uranography, -logy; cosmo-logy, -graphy, -gony; *eidouranion*, orrery; geography; geodesy etc. (*measurement*) 466; star-gazing, -gazer; astronomer; cosmogonist, geodesist, geographer; observatory.

Adj. cosmic, cosmical, mundane; terr-estrial, -estrious, -aqueous, -ene, -eous; telluric, earthly, geotic, geodetic, cosmogonal, under the sun; sublunary, -astral.

solar, heliacal; lunar; celestial, heavenly, empyreal, sphery; starry, stellar; sider-eal, -al; astral; nebular.

Adv. in all creation, on the face of the globe, here below, under the sun.

319. Gravity.—N. gravi-ty, -tation; weight; heaviness etc. *adj.*; specific gravity; ponderosity, pressure, load; bur-den, -then; ballast, counterpoise; lump –, mass –, weight- of.

lead, millstone, mountain, Ossa on Pelion.

weighing, ponderation, trutination; weights; avoirdupois –, troy –, apothecaries'- weight; grain, scruple, drachm, ounce, pound, lb., load, stone, hundredweight, cwt., ton, quintal, carat, pennyweight, tod, gram, kilogram etc.

[Weighing instrument] balance, scales, steelyard, beam, weighbridge, spring balance, weighing machine.

[Science of gravity] statics.

V. be -heavy etc. *adj.*; gravitate, weigh, press, cumber, load.

[Measure the weight of] weigh, poise.

Adj. weighty; weighing etc. *v.*; heavy, – as lead; ponder-ous, -able; lump-ish, -y; cumber-, burden-some; cumbrous, unwieldy, massive.

in-, superin-cumbent.

320. Levity.—N. levity; lightness etc. *adj.*; imponderability, imponderables, buoyancy, volatility.

feather, dust, mote, down, thistledown, flue, cobweb, gossamer, straw, cork, bubble; float, bouy; ether, air.

leaven, ferment, barm, yeast, enzyme.

V. be -light etc. *adj.*; float, swim, be buoyed up.
render -light etc. *adj.*; lighten, levitate; leaven.

Adj. light, subtile, subtle, airy; imponder-ous, -able; astatic, weightless, ethereal, sublimated; uncompressed, volatile; buoyant, floating etc. *v.*; barmy, frothy; portable.

light as -a feather, − thistle down, − air.
fermenting etc. *n.*

321. Density.—N. density, solidity; solidness etc. *adj.*; impenetra-, impermea-bility; incompressibility; imporosity; cohesion etc. 46; constipation, consistence, spissitude.

specific gravity; hydro-, areo-meter.

condensation; solid-ation, -ification; consolidation; concretion, caseation, coagulation; petrifaction etc. (*hardening*) 323; crystallization, precipitation; deposit, precipitate, silt; inspissation; thickening etc. *v.*

indivisibility, indiscerptibility, indissolvableness.

solid body, mass, block, knot, lump; con-cretion, -crete, -glomerate; cake, clot, stone, curd, coagulum, grume; bone, gristle, cartilage.

V. be -dense etc.; become −, render- solid etc. *adj.*; solid-ify, -ate; concrete, set, take a set, consolidate, congeal, coagulate; curd, -le; fix, clot, cake, candy, precipitate, deposit, cohere, crystallize; petrify etc. (*harden*) 323.

condense, thicken, inspissate, incrassate; compress, squeeze, ram down, constipate.

Adj. dense, solid, solidified etc. *v.*; cohe-rent, -sive etc. 46; compact, close, serried, thickset; substantial, massive, lumpish; impenetrable, impermeable, imporous; incompressible; constipated; concrete etc. (*hard*) 323; knot-ted, -ty; gnarled; crystal-line, -lizable; thick, grumous, stuffy.

un-dissolved, -melted, -liquified, -thawed.

in-divisible, -discerptible, -frangible, -dissolvable, -dissoluble, -soluble, -fusible.

322. Rarity.—N. rarity; tenuity; absence of - solidity etc. 321; subtility; sponginess, compressibility.

rarefaction, expansion, dilatation, inflation, subtilization.

ether etc. (*gas*) 334.

V. rarefy, expand, dilate, subtilize, attenuate, thin.

Adj. rare, subtile, thin, fine, tenuous, compressible, flimsy, slight; light etc. 320; cavernous, spongy etc. (*hollow*) 252.

rarefied etc. *v.*; unsubstantial; uncom-pact, -pressed.

323. Hardness.—N. hardness etc. *adj.*; rigidity, renitence, inflexibility, temper, callosity, durity.

induration, petrifaction; lapid-ification, -escence; vitri-, ossi-, corni-fication; crystallization.

stone, pebble, flint, marble, rock, fossil, crag, crystal, quartz, granite, adamant; bone, cartilage; heart of oak, block, board, deal board; iron, steel; cast −, wrought- iron; nail; brick, concrete; cement.

V. render -hard etc. *adj.*; harden, stiffen, indurate, petrify, temper, ossify, vitrify.

Adj. hard, rigid, stubborn, stiff, firm; starch, -ed; stark, unbending, unlimber, unyielding; inflexible, tense; indurate, -d; gritty, proof.

adamant-ine, -ean; concrete, stony, rocky, lithic, granitic, vitreous; crystalline; horny, corneous; bony; oss-eous, -ific; cartilaginous; hard as a -stone etc. *n.*; stiff as -buckram, − a poker.

324. Softness.—N. softness, pliableness etc. *adj.*; flexibility; pli-ancy, -ability; sequacity, malleability; flabbiness; duct-, tract-ility; extend-, extensibility; plasticity; inelasticity; flaccidity, laxity.

clay, wax, butter, dough, pudding; cushion, pillow, feather-bed, pad, down, padding, wadding.

mollification; softening etc. *v.*

V. render -soft etc. *adj.*; soften, mollify, mellow, relax, temper; mash, knead, squash, *massage*.

bend, yield, relent, relax, give.

Adj. soft, tender, supple; pli-ant, -able; flex-ible, -ile; lithe, -some; lissom, limber, plastic; ductile; tract-ile, -able; malleable, extensile, sequacious, inelastic, mollient.

yielding etc. *v.*; flabby, limp, flimsy.

flaccid, flocculent, downy; spongy, edematous, medullary, doughy, argillaceous, mellow.

soft as -butter, − down, − silk; yielding as wax; tender as a chicken.

325. Elasticity.—N. elasticity, springiness, spring, resilience, renitency, buoyancy.

india-rubber, caoutchouc, gutta-percha, whalebone, gum elastic.

V. be -elastic etc. *adj.*; spring back etc. (*recoil*) 227.

Adj. elastic, tensile, springy, ductile, resilient, renitent, buoyant.

326. Inelasticity.—N. want of −, absence of- elasticity etc. 325; inelasticity etc. (*softness*) 324.

Adj. inelastic etc. (*soft*) 324.

327. Tenacity.—N. tenacity, toughness, strength; cohesion etc. 46; sequacity; stubbornness etc. (*obstinacy*) 606; viscidity etc. 352.

leather; gristle, cartilage.

V. be -tenacious etc. *adj.*; resist fracture.

Adj. tenacious, tough, cohesive, adhesive, strong, resisting, sequacious, stringy, gristly, cartilaginous, leathery, coriaceous, tough as whit-leather; stubborn etc. (*obstinate*) 606.

328. Brittleness.—N. brittleness etc. *adj.*; frag-, friab-, frangib-, fiss-ility; frailty; house of -cards, − glass.

V. be -brittle etc. *adj.*; live in a glass house.

break, crack, snap, split, shiver, splinter, crumble, break short, burst, fly, give way; fall to pieces; crumble -to, − into- dust.

Adj. breakable, brittle, frangible, fragile, frail, friable, delicate, gimcrack, shivery, fissile; splitting etc. *v.*; lacerable, splintery, crisp, crimp, short, brittle as glass.

329. Texture. [Structure.]—**N.** structure, organization, anatomy, frame, mold, fabric, construction; frame-work, carcass, architecture; stratification, cleavage.

substance, stuff, *compages*, *parenchyma*; constitution, staple, organism.

[Science of structures]organ-, oste-, my- splanchn-. neur-, angi-, aden-ology; angi-, aden-ography.

texture; inter-, con-texture; tissue, grain, web, surface; warp and -woof, – weft; tooth, nap etc. (*roughness*) 256; fineness –, coarseness- of grain.

[Science of textures] histology.

Adj. structural, organic; anatomic, -al.

text-ural, -ile; fine-, coarse-grained; fine, delicate, subtile, gossamery, filmy; coarse; homespun; linsey-woolsey.

330. Pulverulence. [State of powder.]—**N.** pulverulence; sandiness etc. *adj.*; efflorescence; friability.

powder, dust, sand, shingle; sawdust; grit; attrition; meal, bran, flour, *farina*, spore, sporule; crumb, seed, grain; particle etc. (*smallness*) 32; thermion; limature, filings, *débris*, *detritus*, scobs, magistery, fine powder; *flocculi*.

smoke; cloud of -dust, – sand, – smoke; puff –, volume -of smoke; sand –, dust- storm.

[Reduction to powder] pulverization, comminution, attenuation, granulation, disintegration, subaction, contusion, trituration, levigation, abrasion, detrition, multure; limation; filing etc. *v.*

[Instruments for pulverization] mill, millstone, grater, rasp, file, pestle and mortar, nutmeg grater, teeth, molar, grinder, chopper, grindstone, kern, quern, muller.

V. come to dust; be -disintegrated, – reduced to powder etc.

reduce –, grind- to powder; pulverize, comminute, granulate, triturate, levigate; scrape, file, abrade, rub down, grind, grate, rasp, pound, bray, bruise; con-tuse, -tund; beat, crush, cranch, craunch, crunch, muller, scranch, crumble, disintegrate; attenuate etc. 195.

Adj. powdery, pulverulent, granular, mealy, floury, farinaceous, branny, furfuraceous, flocculent, dusty, sandy, sabulous; aren-ose, -arious, - aceous; gritty; efflorescent, impalpable.

pulverizable; friable, crumbly, shivery; pulverized etc. *v.*; attrite; in pieces.

331. Friction.—**N.** friction, attrition; rubbing etc. *v.*; erasure; con-frication, -trition; affriction, abrasion, arrosion, limature, frication, rub; elbowgrease; rosin; *massage*.

V. rub, scratch, abrade, scrape, scrub, fray, rasp, graze, curry, scour, polish, rub out, erase, gnaw; file, grind etc. (*reduce to powder*) 330; *massage*. set one's teeth on edge; rosin.

Adj. anatriptic, abrasive.

332. Lubrication. [Absence of friction. Prevention of friction.]—**N.** smoothness etc. 255; unctuousness etc. 355.

lubri-cation, -fication; anointment; oiling etc. *v.* synovia; lubricant, graphite, glycerine, oil etc. 356; saliva; lather.

V. lubri-cate, -citate; oil, grease, lather, soap; wax.

Adj. lubricated etc. *v.*

333. Fluidity.—**N.** fluidity, liquidity; liquidness etc. *adj.*; gaseity etc. 334; liquefaction etc. 334.

fluid, inelastic fluid; liquid, liquor; lymph, humor, juice, sap, serum, blood, serosity, gravy, rheum, ichor, sanies.

solu-bility, -bleness.

[Science of liquids] hydro-logy, -statics, - dynamics, hydraulics. etc.

V. be -fluid etc. *adj.*; flow etc. (*water in motion*) 348; liquefy etc. 335.

Adj. liquid, fluid, serous, juicy, succulent, sappy; fluent etc. (*flowing*) 348.

liquefied etc. 335; uncongealed; soluble, hydrostatic etc. *n.*

334. Gaseity.—**N.** gaseity, gaseousness, vapourousness etc. *adj.*; flatulence, -lency; volatility, aeration, gasification.

elastic fluid, gas, air, vapor, ether, steam, fume, reek, *effluvium*, *flatus*; cloud etc. 353.

[Science of elastic fluids] pneumat-ics, -ostatics; aero-statics, -dynamics etc.

gas-, gaso-meter.

V. gassify, aerate, aerify; emit vapor etc. 336.

Adj. gaseous, aeriform, ethereal, aerial, airy, vaporous, volatile, evaporable; flatulent; aerostatic etc. *n.*

335. Liquefaction.—**N.** liquefaction; liquescen-ce, -cy, deliquescence; melting etc. (*heat*) 384; colliqu-ation, -efaction; thaw; de-, liquation; lixiviation, dissolution.

solution, apozem, lixivium, infusion, decoction, flux.

solvent, diluent, menstruum, alkahest, *aqua fortis*.

V. render -liquid etc 333; liquefy, run, deliquesce; melt etc. (*heat*) 384; solve; dissolve, resolve; liquate; hold in solution; leach, lixiviate.

Adj. lique-fied etc. *v.*, -scent, -fiable; deliquescent, soluble, colliquative; solvent.

336. Vaporization.—**N.** vapor-, volatilization; gasification; e-, vaporation; distillation, cohobation, sublimation; exhalation; volatility.

vaporizer, still, retort, spray, atomizer; fumigation, steaming.

V. render -gaseous etc. 334; vaporize, volatilize; distil, sublime; evaporate, exhale, smoke, transpire, emit vapor, fume, reek, steam, fumigate.

Adj. volatilized etc. *v.*; reeking etc. *v.*; volatile; evaporable, vaporizable.

337. Water.—N. water; serum, serosity; lymph; rheum; diluent.

dilution, maceration, lotion; washing etc. *v.*; im-, mersion; humectation, infiltration, spargefaction, affusion, irrigation, *douche*, balneation, bath.

deluge etc. (*water in motion*) 348; high water, flood-. spring-tide.

V. be -watery etc. *adj.*; reek.

add water, water, wet; moisten etc. 339; dilute, dip, immerse; merge; im-, sub-merge; plunge, souse, duck, drown; soak, steep, macerate, pickle, wash, sprinkle, sparge, lave, bathe, affuse, splash, swash, douse, slosh, drench; dabble, slop, slobber, irrigate, inundate, deluge; syringe, inject, gargle; infiltrate, percolate.

Adj. watery, aqueous, aquatic, lymphatic; balneal, diluent; drenching etc. *v.*; diluted etc. *v.*; weak; wet etc. (*moist*) 339.

Phr. the waters are out.

338. Air.—N. air etc. (*gas*) 334; common —, atmospheric- air; atmosphere, stratosphere, isothermal layer, troposphere, Heaviside layer.

open; — air; sky, welkin; blue, — sky; cloud etc. 353.

weather, climate, rise and fall of the barometer, isobar.

[Science of air] pneumatics, aero-logy, -scopy, - graphy; meteorology, climatology; eudio-, baro-, aero-meter; aneroid, baro-graph, -scope; weather-gauge, -glass, -cock.

exposure to the -air, — weather; ventilation; aero-station; -nautics; -naut etc. 265 and 269.

V. air, ventilate; fan etc. (*wind*) 349.

Adj. containing air, flatulent, effervescent; windy etc. 349.

atmospheric, airy; aeri-al, -form; pneumatic; meteorological; weather-wise.

Adv. in the open air, out of doors, *à la belle étoile, al fresco; sub -Jove, — dio.*

339. Moisture.—N. moisture; moistness etc. *adj.*; hum-idity, -ectation; madefaction, dew; *serein*; marsh etc. 345; Hygromet-ry, -er.

V. moisten, wet; humect, -ate; sponge, damp, dampen, bedew; imbue, imbrue, infiltrate, saturate; seethe, sop; soak, drench etc. (*water*) 337.

be -moist etc. *adj.*; not have a dry thread; perspire etc. (*exude*) 295*:*

Adj. moist, damp; watery etc. 337; undried, humid, wet, dank, muggy, dewy; roric; roscid; juicy.

wringing wet; wet -through, — to the skin; saturated etc. *v.*

swashy, soggy, dabbled; reeking, seething, dripping, soaking, soft, sodden, sloppy, muddy; swampy etc. (*marshy*) 345; irriguous.

340. Dryness.—N. dryness etc. *adj.*; siccity, aridity, drought, ebb-, neap-tide, low water.

drying, ex-, de-siccation; evaporation; dehydration; arefaction, dephlegmation, drainage.

drier, desiccator.

V. be -dry etc. *adj.*; render -dry etc. *adj.*; dry;

dry —, soak- up; sponge, swab, wipe; ex-, de-siccate, dehydrate,, anhydrate; drain, parch.

be fine, hold up.

Adj. dry, anhydrous, arid, waterless; dried etc. *v.*; undamped; juice-, sap- less; -sear; husky; rainless, without rain, fine; dry as -a bone, — dust, — a stick, — a mummy, — a biscuit; disiccated; dehydrated; water-proof, -tight.

341. Ocean.—N. sea, ocean, main, deep, brine, salt water, waters, waves, billows, high seas, offing, great waters, watery waste, 'vasty deep,' briny ocean, herring pond, steamer track, the seven seas; wave, tide etc. (*water in motion*) 348.

hydrograph-y, -er, oceanography; Neptune, Thetis, Triton, Naiad, Nereid; sea-nymph, Siren, mer-maid, -man; trident, dolphin.

Adj. oceanic; mar-ine, -itime; pleagic, -ian; sea-going, -worthy; hydrographic.

Adv. at —, on- sea; afloat, on the high seas.

342. Land.—N. land, earth, ground, dry land, *terra firma.*

continent, mainland, peninsula, delta; tongue —, neck- of land; isthmus; oasis; promontory etc. (*projection*) 250; highland etc. (*height*) 206.

coast, shore, scar, strand, beach; bank, lea; seaboard, -side, -shore, -bank, -coast, -beach; rock-, iron- bound coast; loom of the land; derelict; innings; *alluvium*, alluvion.

soil, glebe, clay, loam, marl, clodge, chalk, gravel, mold, subsoil, clod, clot; rock, crag, cliff.

acres; real estate etc. (*property*) 780; landsman, land-lubber, farmer.

geography etc. 318; agriculture etc. 371.

V. land, come to land; set foot on -the soil, — dry land; come —, go- ashore.

Adj. earthy; continental, midland; littoral, riparian, ripuarian; alluvial; terrene etc. (*world*) 318; landed, predial, territorial.

Adv. ashore; on -shore, — land.

343. Gulf. Lake.—N. land covered with water, gulf, gulph, bay, inlet, bight, estuary, arm of the sea, fiord, armlet; frith, firth, ostiary, mouth; lagune, lagoon; indraught; cove, creek; natural harbor; roads; strait, narrows; Euripus; sound, belt, gut, kyles.

lake, loch, lough, mere, tarn, plash, broad, pond, pool, lin, puddle, well, artesian well, tank, sump; standing —, dead —, sheet of- water; fish —; mill-pond; race, ditch, dike, dyke, dam; reservoir etc. (*store*) 636.

Adj. lacustrine; land locked.

344. Plain.—N. plain, table land, mesa, face of the country; open —, champaign-country; basin, downs, waste, weary waste, desert, tundra, wild, steppe, pampas, savanna, prairie, champaign, heath, common, wold, veld; moor, -land, uplands, fell; bush; *plateau* etc. (*level*) 213; *campagna.*

meadow, mead, haugh, pasturage, park, field,

lawn,. green, plat, plot, grass-plat, greensward, sward, grass, turf, sod, heather; lea, ley, lay; grounds.

Adj. campestrian, champaign, alluvial.

345. Marsh.—N. marsh, swamp, morass, marish, moss, fen, bog, quagmire, slough, sump, wash; mud, squash, slush.

Adj. marsh, -y; swampy, boggy, plashy, poachy, quaggy, soft; muddy, sloppy, squashy, spongy; paludal; moor-ish, -y; fenny.

346. Island.—N. island, isle, islet, eyot, ait, holm, reef, atoll, breaker; archipelago; islander.

Adj. insular, sea-girt.

347. Stream. [Fluid in motion.]—**N.** stream etc. (*of water*) 348, (*of air*) 349.

V. flow etc. 348; blow etc. 349.

348. River. [Water in motion.]—**N.** running water.

jet, spirt, squirt, spout, splash, swash, rush, gush, *jet d'eau*; sluice, chute.

water-spout, -fall, fall, cascade, force, foss, lin, - n, ghyll, Niagara; cata-ract, -dupe, -clysm; *débâcle*, inundation, deluge.

rain, -fall; *serein*; shower, scud; downpour, cloud burst; driving −, pouring −, drenching-rain; hycto-logy, -graphy; rainy season, monsoon; predominance of Aquarius, reign of St. Swithin; mizzle, drizzle, *stilliciduim*, plash; dropping etc. *v.*

stream, course, flux, flow, profluence; effluence etc. (*egress*) 295; defluxion; flowing etc. *v.*; current, tide, race.

spring; fount, -ain; rill, rivulet, gill, gullet, rillet; stream-, brook-let; runnel, sike, burn, beck, brook, stream, river; reach; tributary.

body of water, torrent, rapids, flush, flood, swash, spate; spring −, high −, full-tide; bore; eagre, *hugre*; fresh, -et; undertow, indraught, reflux, undercurrent, eddy, vortex, gurge, whirlpool, Maelstrom, regurgitation, overflow; confluence, corrivation.

wave, billow, surge, swell, ripple; roller, ground swell, surf, breaker, white horses; comber, beach-comber; rough −,. heavy −, cross −, long −, short −,. chopping −, choppy- sea, choppiness; tidal wave.

[Science of fluids in motion] Hydrodynamics; Hydraul-ics etc.; raingauge etc.

water-bearer, − carrier, Aquarius.

irrigation etc. (*water*) 337; pump; watering-pot, − cart; hydrant, standpipe, hose, sprinkler, drencher; fire engine, squirt, syringe.

V. flow, run; meander; gush, pour, spout, roll, jet, well, issue; drop, drip, dribble, plash, squirt, spurt, spirtle, trill, trickle, distil, percolate; stream, overflow, inundate, deluge, flow over, splash, swash; guggle, murmur, babble, bubble, purl, gurgle, sputter, regurgitate; ooze, flow out etc. (*egress*) 295.

rain, − hard, − in torrents, − cats and dogs, − pitchforks; come down in sheets; pour with rain, drizzle, mizzle, spit, sprinkle, set in.

flow −, fall −, open −, drain- into; discharge itself, desembogue.

[Cause a flow] pour; pour out etc. (*discharge*) 297; shower down; irrigate, drench etc. (*wet*) 337; spill, splash.

[Stop a flow] stanch; dam, -up etc. (*close*) 261; obstruct etc. 706.

Adj. fluent; dif-, pro-, af-fluent; tidal; flowing etc. *v.*; meand-ering, -ry, -rous; fluvi-al, -atile; streamy, showery, rainy, drizzly, drizzling, pluvial, pluviose, stillicidous.

349. Wind. [Air in motion.]—**N.** wind, draught, *flatus*, *afflatus*, air; breath, − of air; puff, whiff, zephyr; blow, drift; *aura*; stream, current; under-current.

gust, blast, breeze,. squall, gale, half a gale, storm, tempest, hurricane, whirlwind, tornado, samiel, cyclone, typhoon; simoon; harmattan, monsoon, trade wind, sirocco, *mistral*, *bise*, *föhn*, tramontane, levanter; capful of wind; fresh −, stiff- breeze; keen blast; blizzard.

windiness etc. *adj.*; ventosity; rough −, dirty −, ugly −, stress of- weather; dirty-, windy-, mackerel- sky; mare's tail; thick −, black −, white- squall.

anemography, aerodynamics; windgauge, anemometer, weather-cock, vane.

suf-, insuf-, per-, in-, af-flation; blowing, fanning etc. *v.*; ventilation.

sneezing etc. *v.*; sternutation; hic-cup, -cough; catching of the breath; breathing etc.

Eolus, Eurus, Boreas, Zephyr, cave of Eolus.

air-pump, lungs, bellows, blow-pipe, fan, blower; pulmotor, ventilator, punkah, aspirator, exhauster, ejector.

V. blow, waft; blow -hard, − great guns, − a hurricane etc. *n.*; whistle, roar, howl, ring in the shrouds; stream, issue.

respire, breathe, in-, ex-hale, puff; whif, -fle; gasp, wheeze; snuff, -le; sniff, -le; sneeze, cough, belch.

fan, ventilate; in-, per-flate; blow −, pump- up.

Adj. blowing etc. *v.*; windy, airy, aeolian, flatulent; breezy, gusty, squally; stormy, tempestuous, blustering; boisterous etc. (*violent*) 173. pulmon-ic, -ary.

350. Conduit. [Channel for the passage of water.]—**N.** conduit, channel, duct, watercourse, race; head −, tail- race; adit, aqueduct, canal, trough, flume, gutter, pantile; dike, canyon, ravine, gorge, hollow, main, gully, moat, ditch, drain, sewer, culvert, *cloaca*, sough, kennel, siphon, *piscina*; pipe etc. (*tube*) 260; funnel; tunnel etc. (*passage*) 627; water −, waste- pipe; emunctory, gully-hole, artery, aorta, vein, blood vessel; lymphatic; throat, alimentary canal, intestine; pore, spout, scupper; ad-, a-jutage; hose; gar-, gur-goyle; penstock, weir; flood-, water-gate; sluice, lock, valve; rose; waterworks.

Adj. vascular etc. (*with holes*) 260.

351. Air-pipe. [Channel for the passage of air.]—**N.** air-pipe, − shaft, − way, − passage, −

tube; shaft, flue, chimney, funnel, vent, blow-hole, nostril, nozzle, throat, weasand, *trachea*; *bronchus, -ia*; larynx, tonsils, wind-pipe, spiracle; ventiduct, -lator; louvre, Venetian blinds; blow-pipe etc. (*wind*) 349; pipe etc. (*tube*) 260.

352. Semiliquidity.—N. semiliquidity; stickiness etc. *adj.*; visc-idity, -osity; gumm-, glûtin-, muc-osity; spiss-, crass-itude; lentor; adhesiveness etc. (*cohesion*) 46.

inspiss-, incrass-ation; thickening, coagulation.

jelly, aspic, mucilage, gelatin, isinglass; colloid, mucus, phlegm; pituite, lava; glair, starch, gluten, albumen, milk, cream, protein; syrup, treacle; gum, size, glue, paste; wax, bee's-wax; emulsoid, emulsion, soup; squash, mud, slush, slime, ooze; moisture etc. 339; marsh etc. 345.

V. inspiss-ate; coagulate, gelatinize, gelatinify, gel, jell, emulsify, thicken; mash, squash, churn, beat up.

Adj. semi-fluid, -liquid; half-melted, -frozen; milky, muddy etc. *n.*; lact-eal, -ean, -eous, -escent, -iferous; emulsive, curdled, thick, succulent, uliginous.

gelat-, album-, mucilag-, glut-inous; gelatine, mastic, amylaceous, ropy, clammy, clotted; vis-cid, -cous; sticky, tacky; slab, -by; lentous, pituitous; mu-cid, -culent, -cous.

353. Bubble. [Mixture of air and water.] [Cloud.]—N. bubble; foam, froth, head, fume, spume, lather, suds, spray, surf, yeast, barm, spindrift.

cloud, vapor, fog, mist, haze, steam; scud, rack, *nimbus*; *cumulus*, woolpack, *cirrus*, *stratus*; *cirro-, cumulo-stratus*; *cirro-cumulus*; mackerel sky, mare's tail, dirty sky.

[Science of clouds] nephelognosy, nephology.

effervescence, fermentation; bubbling etc. *v.*

nebula; cloudiness etc. (*opacity*) 426; nebulosity etc. (*dimness*) 422.

V. bubble, boil, foam, froth, spume, mantle, sparkle, guggle, gurgle; effervesce, ferment, fizzle; aerate; cloud, overcast, befog.

Adj. bubbling etc. *v.*; frothy, nappy, effervescent,- sparkling, *mousseux*, up, fizzy, with a head on.

cloudy etc. *n.*; vaporous, nebulous, overcast; nubiferous, nephological; foggy, brumous.

354. Pulpiness.—N. pulpiness etc. *adj.*; pulp, paste, dough, sponge, curd, pap, rob, jam, pudding, mush, fool, poultice, grume.

Adj. pulpy etc. *n.*; pultaceous, grumous.

V. pulp, pulpify, mash.

355. Unctuousness.—N. unctuousness etc. *adj.*; unctuosity, lubricity; ointment etc. (*oil*) 356; anointment; lubrication etc. 332.

V. oil etc. (*lubricate*) 332.

Adj. unctuous, oily, oleaginous, adipose, sebaceous; fat, -ty; greasy; waxy, butyraceous; soapy, saponaceous, pinguid, lardaceous; slippery.

356. Oil.—N. oil, fat, butter, cream, grease, tallow, suet, lard, dripping, margarine, oleomargarine, exunge, blubber; glycerine, stearine, elaine, oleagine; soap; soft soap, wax, cerement; paraffin, spermaceti, adipocere; petroleum, mineral -, rock -, crystal- oil; kerosene, vegetable -, colza -, olive -, linseed -, cotton seed -, rape -, nut -, fusel- oil; animal -, neat's foot -, signal -, train- oil; ointment, unguent, liniment, salve, pomade, pomatum, brilliantine, spike -, nard.

356a. Resin.—N. resin, rosin, colophony; gum; lac, shellac, sealing-wax; amber, -gris; bitumen, pitch, tar, asphalt, -e, -um; varnish, copal, mastic, magilp, lacquer, japan.

V. varnish etc. (*overlay*) 223.

Adj. resinous, bituminous, pitchy, tarry.

357. Organization.—N. organized -world, - nature; living -, animated- nature; living beings; organic remains, organism; fossils; animal and vegetable kingdom; *fauna* and *flora*, biota.

prot-oplasm, -ein; albumen; structure etc. 329; organ-ization, -ism.

[Science of living beings] biology; natural history,[*] organic -, bio-chemistry, anatomy, physiology, embryology, morphology, evolution, Darwinism, Lamarkism, zoology etc. 368; botany etc. 369; naturalist, biologist etc.

Adj. organ-ic, -ized.

[*]The term *Natural History* is also used as relating to all the objects in Nature whether organic or inorganic, and including therefore *Mineralogy, Geology, Meteorology,* etc.

358. Inorganization.—N. mineral -world, - kingdom; unorganized -, inorganic -, brute -, inanimate- matter.

[Science of the mineral kingdom] mineralogy; geo-logy, -gnosy, -scopy; metall-urgy, -ography; lithology; orycto-logy, -graphy.

V. turn to dust, pulverize.

Adj. in-organic, -animate; unorganized; azoic; mineral.

359. Life.—N. life; vi-tality, -ability; animation; vital -spark, - flame, - force.

respiration, wind; breath -of life, - of one's nostrils; life-blood; Archeus; existence etc. 1.

vivification, vitalization; revivification etc. 163; Prometheus; life to come etc. (*destiny*) 152.

[Science of life] physiology, etiology, embryology, biology; animal economy.

nourishment, staff of life etc. (*food*) 298.

V. be -alive etc. *adj.*; live, breathe, respire; subsist etc. (*exist*) 1; walk -the earth; strut and fret one's hour upon a stage; be spared.

see the light, be born, come into the world; fetch -, draw- -breath, - the breath of life; quicken; revive; come to, - life.

give birth to etc. (*produce*) 161; bring to life, put into life, vitalize, vivi-fy, -ficate; reanimate etc. (*restore*) 660; keep -alive, - body and soul together, - the wolf from the door; support life.

have nine lives like a cat.

Adj. living, alive; in -life, — the flesh, — the land of the living; on this side of the grave, above ground, breathing, quick, animated, viable; lively etc. (*active*) 682; alive and kicking; tenacious of life.

vital; vivi-fying; -fied etc. *v.*; Promethean.

Adv. *vivendi causâ.*

---

360. Death.—N. death, dying etc. *v.*; de-cease, -mise; dissolution, departure, *obit*, release, rest, *quietus*, fall; loss, bereavement.

end etc. 67 —, cessation etc. 142 —, loss —, extinction —, ebb- of -life etc. 359.

death-warrant, -watch, -rattle, -bed; stroke —, agonies —, shades —, valley of the shadow —, jaws —, hand- of death; last -breath, — gasp, — agonies; dying -day, — breath, — agonies; swan song, *chant du cygne*; *rigor mortis*; Stygian shore; crossing the bar, the great adventure.

King -of terrors, — Death; Death, Angel of Death; mortality; doom etc. (*necessity*) 601.

euthanasia; happy release; break up of the system; natural -death, — decay; sudden —, violent- death; untimely end, watery grave; suffocation, *asphyxia*; heart failure; fatal disease etc. (*disease*) 655; death-blow etc. (*killing*) 361.

necrology, bills of mortality, obituary; death-song etc. (*lamentation*) 839.

V. die, expire, perish; meet one's -death, — end; pass away, be taken; yield —, resign- one's breath; resign one's -being, — life; end one's -days, — life, — earthly career; breathe one's last; cease to -live, — breathe; depart this life; be -no more etc. *adj.*; go —, drop —, pop -off; lose —, lay down —, relinquish —, surrender- one's life; drop —, sink- into the grave; close one's eyes; fall —, drop- dead, — down dead; break one's neck; give —, yield- up the ghost; be all over with one.

pay the debt to nature, shuffle off this mortal coil, take one's last sleep; go the way of all flesh; join the -greater number, — majority, — choir invisible, to life immortal awake; come —, turn- to dust; cross the Stygian ferry; go to -one's long account, — one's last home, — Davy Jones's locker, — the wall; receive one's death warrant, make one's will, die a natural death, go out like the snuff of a candle; come to an untimely end; catch one's death; go off the hooks, kick the bucket, pet out; go West; hop the twig, turn up one's toes; die a violent death etc. (*be killed*) 361; make the supreme sacrifice.

Adj. dead, lifeless; deceased, demised, departed, defunct; late, gone, no more; ex-, in-animate; out of the world, taken off, released; departed this life etc. *v.*; dead and gone; bereft of life, stone dead, dead as -a door nail, — a door post, — mutton, — a herring, — nits; launched into eternity, gathered to one's fathers, numbered with the dead, gone to a better land, behind the veil, beyond the grave, — mortal ken.

dying etc. *v.*; mori-bund, -ent, Acherontic; hippocratic; in -articulo, — extremis; in the -jaws, — agony- of death; going, — off; *aux abois*; on one's -last legs, — death bed; at -the point of death, — death's door, — the last gasp; near one's end, given over, booked, fey; with one foot in —, tottering on the brink of- the grave.

---

still-born; mortuary; deadly etc. (*killing*) 361.

Adv. *post -obit, — mortem.*

Phr. life -ebbs, — fails, — hangs by a thread; one's -days are numbered, — hour is come, — race is run, — doom is sealed; Death -knocks at the door, — stares one in the face; the breath is out of the body; the grave closes over one; *sic itur ad astra.*

---

361. Killing. [Destruction of life; violent death.]—**N.** killing etc. *v.*; homicide, manslaughter, murder, assassination, trucidation, occision; lynching, effusion of blood; blood, -shed; gore, slaughter, carnage, butchery; *battue*, gladiatorial combat.

massacre; *fussillade, noyade, pogrom*; thuggism; racketeering.

death blow, finishing stroke, *coup de grâce*, *quietus*; execution etc. (*capital punishment*) 972; judicial murder; martyrdom.

butcher, slayer, murderer, Cain, assassin, cut-throat, garrotter, *bravo*, thug, racketeer, gunman, mobster, gangster, Moloch, *matador, sabreur; guet-à-pens*; gallows, executioner etc. (*punishment*) 975; man-eater.

regicide, parricide, fratricide, infanticide, aborticide etc.

suicide, *felo de se, suttee, hara kiri*, Juggernaut; immolation, holocaust.

suffocation, strangulation, *garrotte*; hanging etc. *v.*

deadly weapon etc. (*arms*) 727; Aceldama; the potter's field, the field of blood.

fatal accident, violent death, casualty.

[Destruction of animals] slaughtering; phthiozoics;[*] sport, -ting; the chase, venery; hunting, coursing, shooting, fishing; pig-sticking; sports-, hunts-, fisher-man; hunter, Nimrod; slaughterer, knacker, slaughter-house, shambles, *abattoir.*

V. kill, put to death, slay, shed blood; murder, assassinate, butcher, slaughter; victimize, immolate; massacre; take away —, deprive of- life; make away with, put an end to; despatch, dispatch; burke settle, do, — to death, — for.

strangle, garrotte, hang, lynch, throttle, choke, stifle, suffocate, stop the breath, smother, asphyxiate, drown.

saber; cut -down, — to pieces, — the throat; jugulate; stab, run through the body, bayonet; put to the -sword, — edge of the sword.

shoot, — dead; blow one's brains out; brain, knock on the head; stone, lapidate; give —, deal- a death blow; give a -quietus, — coup de grâce.

behead, bowstring etc. (*execute*) 972.

hunt, shoot etc. *n.*

cut off, nip in the bud; launch into eternity, send to one's last account, bump off, rub out, sign one's death warrant, strike the death knell of.

give no quarter, pour out blood like water; decimate; run amuck, wade knee-deep —, imbrue one's hands- in blood.

die a violent death, welter in one's blood; dash —, blow- out one's brains; commit suicide; kill —, -make away with —, put an end to- oneself.

Adj. killing etc. *v.*; murd-, slaught-erous; sanguin-ary, -olent; blood-stained, -thirsty;

homicidal, red-handed; bloody, -minded; en-sanguined, gory, sanguineous.

mortal fatal, lethal; dead-, death-ly; mort-, leth-iferous; unhealthy etc. 657; internecine; suicidal.

sporting; piscator-ial, -y.

Adv. in at the death.

*Bentham, 'Chrestomathia.'

362. Corpse.—**N.** corpse, corse, carcass, bones, skeleton, dry-bones; defunct, relics, *relinquiae*, remains, mortal remains, dust, ashes, earth, clay; mummy; carrion; food for- worms, − fishes; tenement of clay, this mortal coil.

shade, ghost, *manes*, apparition etc. 980.

organic remains, fossils.

Adj. cadaverous, corpse-like; unburied etc. 363.

363. Interment.—**N.** interment, burial, inhumation, sepulture, entombment; in-, humation; obs-, ex-equies; funeral, wake, pyre, funeral pile; cremation.

funeral -rite, − solemnity; knell, passing bell, tolling; dirge etc. (*lamentation*) 839; cypress; *obit*, dead march, muffled drum; coroner, mortician, undertaker, mute, mourner, professional mourner, pallbearer; elegy; funeral -oration, − sermon; epitaph.

grave clothes, shroud; winding-sheet, cere-cloth; cerement.

coffin, shell, sarcophagus, urn, pall, bier, hearse, catafalque, cinerary urn.

grave, pit, sepulcher, tomb, vault, crypt, catacomb, mausoleum, *Golgotha*, house of death, narrow house, long home; cemetery, necropolis, boneyard; burial-place, -ground; grave-, church-yard; God's acre; mortuary, tope, cromlech, dolmen, menhir, barrow, tumulus, cairn; ossuary; bone-, charnel-, dead-house; *Morgue*; lich-gate; crematorium.

sexton, grave-digger.

monument, memorial, cenotaph, shrine; grave-head-, tomb-stone; *memento mori*; hatchment, stone, cross.

exhumation, disinterment; necropsy, autopsy, *post mortem* examination.

V. inter, bury, lay in −, consign to- the -grave, − tomb; en-, in-tomb; inhume; lay out, prepare for burial, embalm, mummify; conduct a funeral, hold services; toll the knell; put to bed with a shovel.

exhume, disinter, unearth.

Adj. buried etc. *v.*; burial; fune-real, -brial; mor-tuary, sepulchral, cinerary; elegiac; necroscopic.

Adv. *in memoriam*; *post-obit*, *-mortem*; beneath −, under- the sod.

Phr. *hic jacet, ci-git, requiescat in pace.*

364. Animality.—**N.** animal life; anima-tion, -lity, -lization; breath.

flesh, − and blood; corporeal nature; *physique*; strength etc. 159.

V. animalize, incorporate.

Adj. fleshly, incarnate, carnal, corporeal, human.

365. Vegetability.—**N.** vegetable life; vegeta-tion, -bility; herbage.

V. vegetate, germinate, sprout, shoot; cultivate.

Adj. vegetable etc. 367; rank, lush.

366. Animal.—**N.** animal, − kingdom; *fauna*; brute creation.

beast, brute, creature, created being; creeping −, living- thing; dumb -animal, − creature.

flocks and herds, live stock; domestic −, wild-animals; game, *ferae naturae*; beasts of the fields, fowls of the air, denizens of the day.

vertebrate, bi-, quadru-ped, mammal, marsupial, bird, reptile, batrachian, amphibian, fish, crus-tacean, shell fish, articulate, mollusc, worm, insect, zoophyte; protozoon, animalcule etc. 193.

horse etc. (*beast of burden*) 271; cattle, kine, ox; bull, -ock; steer, stot; cow, milch-cow, calf, heifer, shorthorn; sheep; lamb, -kin; ewe −, pet-lamb; ewe, ram, tup; pig, swine, boar, hog, shoat, sow; tag, teg, wether.

dog, bitch, hound; pup, -py; whelp, cur, mutt, mongrel; house-, watch-, sheep-, shepherd's, sport-ing-, fancy-, lap-, toy-, bull-, badger-dog; mastiff; blood-, grey-, stag-, deer-, fox-, otter-, hound; harrier, beagle, spaniel, pointer, setter, retriever; Newfoundland; water -dog, − spaniel; pug, poodle; dachshund; Pinscher; turnspit; terrier; fox −, Skye- terrier; Dandie-Dinmont; colley.

cat; puss,-y; kitten; grimalkin; gib-, tom-cat; mouser; fox, Reynard, vixen, stag, deer, hart, buck, doe, roe, antelope.

bird; poultry, fowl, cock, hen, chicken, chan-ticleer, partlet, rooster, dunghill cock, barn-door fowl; feathered -tribes, − songster; singing −, dicky- bird; canary; finch; auk, dodo, moa, roc, phoenix.

snake, serpent, viper, adder; newt, eft; asp, ver-min.

Adj. animal, zoological.

equine, bovine, vaccine, canine, feline; fishy; piscator-y, -ial; molluscous, vermicular.

*Extended lists of names of specific varieties of animals, vegetables, etc., are beyond the scope of this work.

367. Vegetable.—**N.** vegetable, − kingdom; *flora*, verdure.

plant; tree, shrub, bush; creeper; vine; herb, -age; grass.

annual; per-, bi-, tri-ennial; exotic.

timber; primeval −, virgin- forest; wood, -lands; hurst; frith, holt, weald, park, chase, greenwood, brake, grove, copse, coppice, *bocage*, *tope*, clump of trees, thicket, spinet, spinney; under-, brush-wood; boscage, scrub; the oak and the ash and the bonny ivy tree.

bush, jungle, prairie; heath, -er; fern, bracken, furze, gorse, whin, broom; grass, turf, grassland, greensward, green, lawn, meadow; pas-ture, -turage; turbary; sedge, rush, weed; fungus, mushroom, toadstool; lichen, moss, conferva, mold; seaweed etc.; growth, crop.

foliage, leafage, branch, bough, ramage; spray etc. 51; leaf, frond, flag, petal, shoot, tendril.

flower, blossom, bud, bloom, bine; flowering plant; tree, sapling, pollard; timber-, fruit-tree; palm-, gum-tree; pulse, legume.

Adj. veget-able, -ous; herb-aceous, -al; botanic; sylvan, silvan; arbor- ary, -eous, -escent, -ical; dendritic, dendriform; woody, grassy; ver-dant, - durous; floral, mossy; lign-ous, -eous; wooden, leguminous; end-, ex-ogenous.

*Extended lists of names of specific varieties of animals, vegetables, etc., are beyond the scope of this work.

368. Zoology. [The science of animals.]—**N.** zoo-logy, -nomy, -graphy, -tomy; anatomy; comparative anatomy; animal —, comparative-physiology; morphology.

anthrop-, ornith-, ichthy-, herpet-, ophi-, malac-, helminth-, entom-, oryct-, paleont-ology; ichthy-etc. -otomy; taxidermy.

zo- etc. -ologist.

Adj. zoological etc. *n.*

369. Botany. [The science of plants.]—**N.** botany; phyto-graphy, -logy, -tomy; vegetable physiology, herborization, dendr-, myc-, fung-, alg-ology; flora, pomona; botanist etc.; botanic garden etc. (*garden*) 371; *hortus siccus, herbarium*, herbal.

herb-ist, -arist, -alist, -orist, -arian etc.

V. botanize, herborize.

Adj. botanical etc. *n.*

370. Cicuration. [The economy or management of animals.]—**N.** taming etc. *v.*; cicuration, zoohygiantics, domestication, -lty; *manège*; veterinary art; breeding, pisciculture, apiculture etc.

menagery, vivarium, zoological garden, zoo; bear-pit; aviary, apiary, hive; aquarium, fishery, fish hatchery; duck-, fish-pond; stud-farm; stock farm, dairy.

[Destruction of animals] phthisozoics etc. (*killing*) 361.

neat-, cow-, shep-herd, shepherdess; grazier; drover, cowboy, cowkeeper; trainer, breeder, groom, ostler etc. 746; veterinary surgeon, vet, horse doctor; farrier; keeper; game keeper.

cage etc. (*prison*) 752; hen-coop, bird-cage, cauf; sheep-fold etc. (*inclosure*) 232.

V. tame, domesticate, acclimatize, breed, tend, break in, train, corral, round up; cage, bridle etc. (*restrain*) 751; ride etc. 266.

drive, yoke, harness, hitch; groom, curry-comb; milk; shear; hatch; incubate.

Adj. pastoral, bucolic; tame, domestic, domesticated, broken in, gentle, docile.

371. Agriculture. [The economy or management of plants.]—**N.** agriculture, cultivation, husbandry, farming; georgics, geoponics; tillage, tilth, agronomy, gardening; spade husbandry, vintage; hort-, arbor-, silv-, citr-, vit-, flor-iculture; intensive culture; landscape gardening; forestry, afforestation.

husbandman, horticulturist, citriculturist, gardener, florist; agricult-or, -urist; yeoman, farmer, cultivator, tiller of the soil, ploughman, sower, reaper; woodcutter, backwoodsman, forester; vine grower, vintager; Boer; Triptolemus.

field, meadow, garden; botanic —, winter —, or-

namental —, flower —, kitchen —, truck —, market —, hop- garden; nursery; green-, hot-, glass-house; conservatory, cucumber frame, *cloche*, bed, border, seed-plot; grass-plat, lawn; park etc. (*pleasure ground*) 840; *partere*, shrubbery, plantation, avenue, *arboretum*, pinery, *pinetum*, orchard, vineyard, vinery; orangery; farm etc. (*abode*) 189.

V. cultivate; till, – the soil; farm, garden; sow, plant; reap, mow, cut; manure, dress the ground, dig, delve, dibble, hoe, plough, plow, harrow, rake, weed, lop and top, force, transplant, thin out, bed out, prune, graft.

Adj. agr-icultural, -airan, -estic.

arable; predial, rural, rustic, country, bucolic, Boeotian; horticultural.

372. Mankind.—**N.** man, -kind; human -race, – species, – nature; humanity, mortality, flesh, generation.

[Science of man] anthropo-logy, -graphy, -sophy; ethno-logy, -graphy; humanitarianism.

human being; person, -age; individual, creature, fellow creature, mortal, body, somebody, one; such a —; someone; soul, living soul; earthling; party, head, hand; *dramatis personae*.

people, persons, folk, public, society, world; community, – at large; general public; nation, -ality; state, realm; common-weal, -wealth; republic, body politic; million etc. (*commonalty*) 876; population etc. (*inhabitant*) 188.

cosmopolite, lords of the creation, ourselves.

Adj. human, mortal, personal, individual, national, civic, public, cosmopolitan; anthropoid.

373. Man.—**N.** man, male, he; manhood etc. (*adolescence*) 131; gentleman, sir, master; yeoman, wight, swain, fellow, guy, blade, *beau*, chap, gaffer, good man; husband etc. (*married man*) 903; Mr., mister, *monsieur, sahib, Herr, señor, signor*; boy etc. (*youth*) 129; Adonis.

[Male animal] cock, drake, gander, dog, boar, stag, hart, buck, horse, entire horse, stallion; gib-, tom-cat; he-, Billy-goat; ram, tup; bull, -ock; capon, ox, gelding; steer, stot.

Adj. male, he, masculine; manly, virile; un-womanly, -feminine.

374. Woman.—**N.** woman, she, female, petticoat, skirt, moll, broad.

feminality, feminity, muliebrity; womanhood etc. (*adolescence*) 131; feminism; gynecology, gyniatrics, gynics.

womankind; the -sex, – fair; fair –, softer- sex; weaker vessel; the distaff side.

dame, madam, *madame*, mistress, Mrs., lady, *mem-sahib, Frau, señora, signora, donna, belle*, matron, dowager, goody, gammer; good -woman, – wife; squaw; wife etc. (*marriage*) 903; matron-age, -hood.

Venus, nymph, wench, *grisette*; little bit of fluff; girl etc. (*youth*) 129.

inamorata (love) etc. 897; courtesan etc. 962.

spinster, old maid, virgin, bachelor girl, new woman, amazon.

[Female animal] hen, slut, bitch, sow, doe, roe, mare; she-, Nanny-goat; ewe, cow; lioness, tigress; vixen.

gynecaeum, harem, seraglio, zenana, purdah.

Adj. female, she; feminine, womanly, ladylike, matronly, maidenly; womanish, effeminate, unmanly, gynecic.

375. Physical Sensibility.—N. sensibility; sensitiveness etc. adj.; physical sensibility, feeling, perceptivity, anaphylaxis, susceptibility, esthetics; moral sensibility etc. 882.

sensation, impression, effect; consciousness etc. (knowledge) 490.

external senses.

V. be -sensible etc. adj. -of; feel, perceive.

render, -sensible etc. adj.; excite, stir, sharpen, cultivate, tutor.

cause sensation, impress; excite –, produce- an impression.

Adj. sens-ible, -itive, -uous; esthetic, perceptive, sentient; conscious etc. (aware) 490; impressionable, responsive, alive to.

acute, sharp, keen, vivid, lively, impressive, thinskinned.

Adv. to the quick.

376. Physical Insensibility.—N. insensibility, physical insensibility; obtuseness etc. adj.; palsy, paralysis, anesthesia, analgesia, narcosis, hypnosis, twilight sleep, stupor, coma, trance, catalepsy; sleep etc. (inactivity) 683; moral insensibility etc. 823; numbness etc. 381.

anesthetic agent, general –, local- anesthetic, opium, ether, chloroform, cocaine, novocaine, chloral; nitrous oxide, laughing gas; refrigeration.

V. be -insensible etc. adj.; have a -thick skin, – rhinoceros hide.

render -insensible etc. adj.; blunt, pall, obtund, benumb, deaden, paralyze; anesthetize, drug, dope; put under the influence of -chloroform etc. n.; hypnotize; stupefy, stun, narcotize.

Adj. insensible, unfeeling, senseless, comatose, dazed, impercipient, callous, thick-skinned, pachydermatous; hard, -ened; case-hardened; proof; obtuse, dull; anesthetic; paralytic, palsied, numb, dead.

377. Physical Pleasure.—N. pleasure; physical –, sensual –, sensuous- pleasure; bodily enjoyment, animal gratification, sensuality; hedonism, luxuriousness etc. adj.; dissipation, round of pleasure; titillation, gusto, creature comforts, comfort, ease; pillow etc. (support) 215; luxury, lap of luxury; purple and fine linen; bed of -down, – roses; velvet, clover; cup of Circe etc. (intemperance) 954.

treat; diversion, divertisement, entertainment; refreshment, regale; feast; délice; dainty etc. 394; bonne bouche.

source of pleasure etc. 829; happiness etc. (mental enjoyment) 827.

V. feel –, experience –, receive- pleasure; enjoy, relish; luxuriate –, revel –, riot –, bask –, swim –, wallow-' in; feast on; gloat -over, – on; smack the lips.

live -on the fat of the land, – in comfort etc. adv.; bask in the sunshine, faire ses choux gras.

give pleasure etc. 829.

Adj. enjoying etc. v.; luxurious, voluptuous, sensual, hedonistic, comfortable, cosy, snug, in comfort, at ease.

agreeable etc. 829; grateful, refreshing, comforting, cordial, genial; sensuous; palatable etc. 394; sweet etc. (sugar) 396; fragrant etc. 400; melodious etc. 413; lovely etc. (beautiful) 845.

Adv. in -comfort etc. n.; on -a bed of roses etc. n.; at one's ease.

378. Physical Pain.—N. pain; suffering, -ance; bodily – physical -pain; – suffering; mental suffering etc. 828; dolor, ache; aching etc. v.; smart; shoot, -ing; twinge, twitch, gripe, head-, ear-, toothache; migraine, neuralgia, neuritis, lumbago, gout, sciatica; hurt, cut; sore, -ness; discomfort, malaise; tic douloureux.

spasm, cramp; nightmare, ephialtes; crick, stitch, kink; thrill, convulsion, throe; throb etc. (agitation) 315; pang.

sharp –, piercing –, throbbing –, shooting –, gnawing –, burning- pain; anguish, agony.

torment, torture; rack; cruci-ation, -fixion; martyrdom; martyr, toad under a harrow, vivisection.

V. feel –, experience –, suffer –, undergo-pain etc. n.; suffer, ache, smart, bleed; tingle; shoot; twinge, twitch, lancinate; writhe, wince, make a wry face; sit on -thorns, – pins and needles.

give –, inflict- pain; pain, hurt, chafe, sting, bite, gnaw, gripe, stab, grind; pinch, tweak; grate, gall, fret, prick, pierce, wring, convulse; torment, torture; rack, agonize; crucify; excruciate; break on the wheel, put to the rack; flag etc. (punish) 972; grate on the ear etc. (harsh sound) 410.

Adj. in -pain etc. n.; – a state of pain; pained etc. v.

painful; aching etc. v.; biting, poignant; sore, raw, tender, with exposed nerve.

379. Touch. [Sensation of pressure.] **—N.** touch; tact, -ion, -ility; feeling; palp-ation, -ability; manipulation; brush, tick, graze, contact etc. 199.

[Organ of touch] hand, finger, fore-finger, thumb, paw, feeler, antenna.

V. touch, feel, handle, finger, thumb, paw, fumble, grope, grabble; twiddle, tweedle; pass –, run-the fingers over, massage, rub, knead; palpate, stroke, manipulate, wield; throw out a feeler.

Adj. tact-ual, -ile; tangible, palpable; lambent.

380. Sensations of Touch.—N. itching etc. v.; titillation, formication, aura.

V. itch, tingle, creep, thrill, sting; prick, -le; tickle, titillate.

Adj. itching etc. v.

381. Numbness. [Insensibility to touch.] **—N.**

numbness etc. (*physical insensibility*) 376; pins and needles.
   local anesthetic,cocaine novocaine etc.; morphia.
   V. benumb etc. 376; freeze, dull, deaden.
   Adj. numb; benumbed etc. *v.*; intangible, impalpable.

382. Heat.—N. heat, caloric; temperature, warmth, fervor, calidity; incal-, incand-, recal-, decal-escence; glow, flush, blush; fever, hectic.
   phlogiston; fire, spark, scintillation, flash, flame, blaze; arc; bonfire; firework, pyrotechny; wild-fire; sheet of fire, lambent flame; devouring element; conflagration.
   summer, dog-days, canicule; baking etc. 384 —, white —, tropical —, Afric —, Bengal —, summer —, blood- heat; heat wave, sirocco, simoon; broiling sun; isolation; warming etc. 384.
   sun etc. (*luminary*) 423; fire worshipper etc. 991; furnace etc. 386.
   geyser, hot spring, volcano.
   : Science of heat, pyrology; thermology, -otics; thermometer etc. 389.
   V. be -hot etc. *adj.*; glow, incandesce, flush, sweat, swelter, bask, smoke, reek, stew, simmer, seethe, boil, burn, singe, scorch, scald, grill, broil, blaze, flame; smoulder; parch, fume, pant.
   heat etc. (*make hot*) 384; thaw, fuse, melt, give.
   Adj. hot, heated, warm, mild, genial, tepid, lukewarm, unfrozen; therm-al, -ic; calorific; fervent, -id; ardent; aglow.
   sunny, torrid, tropical, estival, canicular; close, sultry, stifling, stuffy, suffocating, oppressive; reeking etc. *v.*; baking etc. 384.
   red —, white —, smoking —, bruning etc. *v.* —, piping- hot; like -a furnace, — an oven; hot as -fire, — pepper; hot enough to roast an ox.
   fiery; incand-, incal-escent; candent, ebullient, glowing, smoking; on fire; blazing etc. *v.*; in -flames, — a blaze; alight, afire, ablaze; unquenched, -extinguished; smouldering; in a -heat, — glow, — fever, — perspiration, — sweat; sudorific; swelter-ing, -ed; blood-hot, -warm; warm as -a toast, — wool; recalescent, thermogenic, pyrotechnic, feverish, febrile, inflamed.
   volcanic, plutonic, igneous; isother-mal, -mic, -al.
   Phr. Not a breath of air.

383. Cold.—N. cold, -ness etc. *adj.*; frigidity, gelidity, algidity, inclemency, *fresco.*.
   winter; depth of —, hard- winter; Siberia, Nova Zembla; Ant-, arctic, North —; South- Pole.
   ice; snow, — flake, — crystal — drift; sleet; hail, -stone; rime, frost; hoar —, white —, hard —, sharp- frost; icicle, thick-ribbed ice; fall of snow, snow storm; heavy fall, *avalanche*; ice-berg, -floe; floe, berg; *glacier*; *nevée, serac*.
   [Sensation of cold] chilliness etc. *adj.*; chill shivering etc. *v.*; goose- skin, -flesh; *rigor*, horripilation, chattering of teeth; frostbite, chilblain.
   V. be -cold etc. *adj.*; shiver, starve, quake, shake, tremble, shudder, didder, quiver; perish with cold; chill etc. (*render cold*) 385.
   Adj. cold, cool; chill, -y; gelid, frigid, algid; fresh, keen, bleak, raw, inclement, bitter, biting,

niveous, cutting, nipping, piercing, pinching; claycold; starved etc. (*made cold*) 385; shivering etc. *v.*; aguish, *transi de froid*; frost- bitten, -bound, -nipped.
   cold as -a stone, — marble, — lead, — iron, — a frog, — charity, — Christmas; cool as -a cucumber, — custard.
   icy, glacial, frosty, freezing, wintry, brumal, hibernal, boreal, arctic, antarctic, polar, Siberian, hyemal; hyperbore-an, -al; ice-bound; frozen out.
   un-warmed, -thawed, -heated; isocheimal, -chimenal.
   Adv. coldly, bitterly etc. *adj.*; *à pierre fendre*.

384. Calefaction.—N. increase of temperature; heating etc. *v.*; cale-, tepe-, torre-faction; melting, fusion; liquefaction etc. 335; burning etc. *v.*; kindling, combustion; in-, ac-cension; con-, cremation; scorification; cauter-y, -ization; ustulation, calcination; in-, cineration; cupellation; carbonization.
   ignition, inflammation, adustion, flagration; de-, con-flagration; empyrosis, incendiarism; arson; *auto da fé*; suttee.
   boiling etc. *v.*; coction, ebullition, estuation, elixation, decoction.
   furnace etc. 386; blanket, flannel, fur, muffler, wrap; wadding etc. (*lining*) 224; clothing etc. 225.
   match etc. (*fuel*) 388; incendiary, pyromaniac; *pétroleur, pétroleuse*; cauterant, caustic, lunar caustic, apozem, moxa.
   sunstroke, *coup de soleil*; insolation, sunburn.
   pottery, ceramics, crockery, porcelain, china; earthen-, stone-ware; pot, mug, *terra-cotta*, brick, clinker; cinder, ash, *scoriae*; embers, dross, slag, products of combustion, coke, carbon, charcoal.
   inflamma-, combusti-bility.
   [Transmission of heat] diathermancy, transcalency, diathermy.
   V. heat, warm, chafe, stive, foment; make -hot etc. 382; sun oneself, bask in the sun.
   fire; set -fire to, — on fire; kindle, enkindle, light, ignite, strike a light; apply the -match, — torch- to; re-kindle, -lume; fan —, add fuel to- the flame; poke —, stir —, blow- the fire; make a bonfire of; burn at the stake.
   melt, thaw, fuse; liquefy etc. 335.
   burn, inflame, roast, toast, fry, grill, singe, parch, bake, torrefy, scorch; brand, cauterize, sear, burn in; corrode, char, carbonize, calcine, incinerate; smelt, cupel, scorify; reduce to ashes; burn to a cinder; commit —, consign- to the flames.
   boil, digest, stew, cook, seethe, scald, parboil, simmer; do to rags.
   take —, catch- fire; blaze etc. (*flame*) 382.
   Adj. heated etc. *v.*; molten, sodden; réchauffe; heating etc. *v.*
   inflammable, burnable, inflammatory, combustible; diatherm-al, -anous; burnt etc. *v.*; volcanic.

386. Refrigeration.—N. refrigeration, infrigidation, reduction of temperature; cooling etc. *v.*; con-gelation, -glaciation; ice etc. 383; solidification etc. (*density*) 321; refrigerator etc. 387.

extincteur; fire, – engine, – extinguisher, –
annihilator, – brigade, – man; sprinkler, hose,
hydrant, standpipe.
    incombusti-bility, -bleness etc. *adj.*
    V. cool, fan, refrigerate, refresh, ice; congeal,
freeze, glaciate; benumb, starve, pinch, chill,
petrify, chill to the marrow, nip, cut, pierce, bite,
make one's teeth chatter; damp, slack; quench; put
–, stamp- out; extinguish.
    go –, burn- out.
    Adj. cooled etc. *v.*; frozen out; cooling etc. *v.*;
.frigorific.
    incombustible; un-, unin-flammable; fire-proof.

386. Furnace.—N. furnace, blast furnace, fire-
box, stove, incinerator, destructor, crematorium,
crematory, kiln, oven, oast-house; hot-, bake-,
wash-house; laundry; conservatory; hearth, focus;
athanor, hypocaust, reverberatory; volcano; forge,
fiery furnace; *tuyère*, brasier, salamander, heater,
warming-pan, foot-warmer, hot-water bottle;
radiator; boiler, geyser, caldron, seething caldron,
pot; urn, kettle; chafing-dish; retort, crucible, alembic, still; saggar.
    fire-place, -dog, -irons; hearth, ingle, grate,
range, kitchener; kitchen range; oil-, gas-, electric,
-cooker, -stove; fireless cooker; fire; galley; ca-,
cam-boose; poker, tongs, shovel, hob, trivet; and-,
grid-iron; frying-, stew-pan etc.
    hot –, Turkish –, Russian –, vapor –, shower
–, warm- bath; *calidarium*, *tepidarium*,
sudatorium, sudatory; *hammam*.

387. Refrigerator.—N. refrigerator, -y;
frigidarium; cold storage; refrigerating-plant, –
machine; ice-house, -pail, -bag, -chest, -pack;
cooler, damper; wine-cooler, freezing mixture.

388. Fuel.—N. fuel, firing, combustible, coal,
wallsend, anthracite, bituminous coal, slack, culm,
cannel coal, lignite, briquette, coke, carbon, charcoal; turf, peat, fire-wood, bobbing, faggot, log,
yule log, ember, cinder etc. (*products of combustion*) 384; kindling wood, tinder, touch-wood;
fumigator, sulphur, brimstone; incense; port-fire;
fire-barrel, -ball, -brand.
    fuel oil, gas, gasoline, electricity.
    brand, torch, fuse; wick; spill, match, safety
match, light, lucifer, congreve, vesuvian, vesta,
fusee, locofoco; linstock; illuminant.
    candle etc. (*luminary*) 423; oil etc. (*grease*) 356;
petrol, gasoline, methylated –, spirit; gas,
acetylene.
    Adj. carbonaceous; combustible, inflammable.
    V. stoke, fire, feed, add fuel to the flames.

389. Thermometer.—N. thermo-meter, -scope,
-stat, -pile, differential thermometer; pyro-, calori-
meter; radio micrometer etc.

390. Taste.—N. taste, flavor, gust, *gusto*, relish,
savor; sapor, sapidity; twang, smack, smatch; after-
taste, tang.

tasting; de-, gustation.
    palate, tongue, tooth, stomach.
    V. taste, savor, smatch, smack, flavor, twang;
tickle the palate etc. (*savory*) 394; smack the lips.
    Adj. sapid, saporific; gusta-ble, -tory; strong;
flavored, spiced, savory; palatable etc. 394.

391. Insipidity.—N. insipidity; tastlessness etc.
adj.
    V. be -tasteless etc. *adj.*
    Adj. void of -taste etc. 390; insipid; jejune; taste-
gust-, savor-less; ingustible, mawkish, milk and
water, weak, stale, flat, vapid, *fade*, wishy-washy,
mild; untasted.

392. Pungency.—N. pungency, piquancy,
poignancy, *haut-goût*, strong taste, twang, race,
tang.
    sharpness etc. *adj.*; acrimony, acridity; roughness
etc. (*sour*) 397; unsavoriness etc. 395.
    niter, saltpeter; mustard, cayenne, caviar;
seasoning etc. (*condiment*) 393; brine.
    dram, cordial, nip, pick-me-up, bracer, potion.
    nicotine, tobacco, snuff, quid; segar; cigar, -ette,
gasper, fag; cheroot; weed; fragrant –, Indian-
weed; pipe, clay pipe, churchwarden, brier, meer-
schaum, hookah, hubble-bubble.
    V. be -pungent etc. *adj.*; bite the tongue.
    render -pungent etc. *adj.*; season, spice, salt,
pepper, pickle, brine, devil, curry.
    smoke, chew, take snuff.
    Adj. pungent, strong; high-, full-flavored; high-
tasted, -seasoned; gamy; sharp, stinging, rough,
piquant, racy; biting, mordant; spicy; seasoned etc.
v.; hot, – as pepper; peppery, vellicating,
escharotic, meracious; acrid, acrimonious, bitter;
rough etc. (*sour*) 397; unsavory etc. 395.
    salt, saline, brackish, briny; salt as -brine, – a
herring, – Lot's wife.

393. Condiment.—N. condiment, flavoring,
salt, mustard, pepper, cayenne, curry, seasoning,
sauce, spice, cinnamon, chillies, relish, *sauce
piquante*, caviare, pot-herbs, onion, garlic, pickle,
chutney, nutmeg etc.
    V. season etc. (*render pungent*) 392.

394. Savoriness.—N. savoriness etc. *adj.*;
relish, zest.
    tit-bit, dainty, delicacy, ambrosia, nectar, *bonne
bouche*; game, turtle, venison.
    V. taste good, be -savory etc. *adj.*; tickle the -
palate, – appetite; flatter the palate.
    render -palatable etc. *adj.*
    relish, like, smack the lips.
    Adj. savory, well-tasted, to one's taste, tasty,
good, palatable, nice, dainty, delectable; tooth-ful,
-some; gustful, appetizing, lickerish, delicate,
delicious, exquisite, rich, luscious, ambrosial.
    Adv. *per amusare la bocca.*
    Phr. *cela se laisse manger.*

395. Unsavoriness.—**N.** unsavoriness etc. *adj.*; amaritude; acri-mony, -tude; roughness etc. (*sour*) 397; acerbity, austerity; gall and worm-wood, rue, quassia, aloes; sickener.

V. be -unpalatable etc. *adj.*; sicken, disgust, nauseate, pall, turn the stomach.

Adj. un-savory, -palatable, -sweet; ill-flavored, un-appetizing, -eatable, inedible; bitter, − as gall; acrid, acrimonious; rough.

offensive, repulsive, nasty; sickening etc. *v.*; nauseous; loath-, ful-some; unpleasant etc. 830.

396. Sweetness.—**N.** sweetness, dulcitude, saccharinity.

sugar, cane-, beet-sugar; saccharine, glucose, syrup, treacle, molasses, honey, manna; confection, -ary; sweets, grocery, conserve, preserve, *confiture*, jam, marmalade, julep; sugar-candy, -plum; licorice, liquorice, plum, lollipop, *bon bon*, *jujube*, comfit, sweetmeat, caramel, toffee, butterscotch.

nectar; hydromel, mead, metheglin, honeysuckle, *liqueur*, sweet wine.

pastry, pie, tart, puff, pudding, cake.

dulc-ification, -oration.

V. be sweet etc. *adj.*

render -sweet etc. *adj.*; sugar, saccharize, sweeten; edulcorate; dulc-orate, -ify; candy; mull.

Adj. sweet, sugary; sacchar-ine, -iferous; dulcet, honied, candied, luscious, nectarious, melliferous; sweetened etc. *v.*

sweet as -a nut, − sugar, − honey.

397. Sourness.—**N.** sourness etc. *adj.*; acid, -ity; acetous fermentation; acerbity.

vinegar, verjuice, crab, alum.

V. be −, turn- -sour etc. *adj.*; set the teeth on edge.

render -sour etc. *adj.*; acid-ify, -ulate.

Adj. sour; acid, -ulous, -ulated; acerb; tart, crabbed; acet-ous, -ose; sour as vinegar, sourish, acescent, sub-acid; styptic, hard, rough; unripe, green.

398. Odor.—**N.** odor, smell, odorament, scent, effluvium; eman-, exhal-ation; fume, essence, trail, nidor, redolence.

sense of smell; scent; act of -smelling etc. *v.*

V. have an -odor etc. *n.*; smell, − of, − strong of; exhale; give out a -smell etc. *n.*; scent.

smell, scent; snuff, − up; sniff, nose, inhale.

Adj. odor-ous, -iferous; smelling, strong-scented; redolent, graveolent, nidorous, pungent.

[Relating to the sense of smell] olfactory, quick-scented..

399. Inodorousness.—**N.** inodorousness; absence −, want- of smell.

V. be -inodorous etc. *adj.*; not smell.

deodorize.

Adj. inodor-ous, -ate; scentless; without −, wanting- smell etc. 398.

deodoriz-ed, -ing.

400. Fragrance.—**N.** fragrance, aroma, redolence, perfume, *bouquet*; sweet smell, aromatic perfume.

perfumery; incense; musk, frankincense; pastil, -le; myrrh, perfumes of Arabia, chypre; otto, ottar, attar; bergamot, balm, civet, *pot-pourri*, pulvil; nosegay, *boutonnière*; scent, -bag; *sachet*, scent-bottle, smelling bottle, *vinaigrette*; toilet water, *eau de Cologne*; thurible, censer, thurification.

perfumer; incense bearer.

V. be -fragrant etc. *adj.*; have a -perfume etc. *n.*; smell sweet, scent, perfume, thurify, embalm.

Adj. fragrant, aromatic, redolent, spicy, balmy, scented; sweet-smelling, -scented; perfum-ed, -atory; thuriferous; fragrant as a rose, muscadine, ambrosial.

401. Fetor.—**N.** fetor, fetidness; bad etc. *adj.*; -smell, − odor; stench, stink; mephitis, foul −, mal- odor; *empyreuma*; mustiness etc. *adj.*; rancidity; foulness etc. (*uncleanness*) 653.

stoat, polecat, skunk; asafetida; fungus, garlic; stink-pot, -bomb.

V. have a -bad smell etc. *n.*; smell; stink, − in the nostrils, − like a polecat; smell -strong etc. *adj.*; − offensively.

Adj. fetid; strong-smelling; high, bad, strong, fulsome, offensive, noisome, rank, rancid, reasty, tainted, musty, fusty, frouzy; olid, -ous; nidorous; smelling, stinking; putrid etc. 653; suffocating, mephitic; empyreumatic.

402. Sound.—**N.** sound, noise, strain; accent, twang, intonation, tone, tune; cadence; sonority, sonorousness etc. *adj.*; audibility; resonance etc. 408; voice etc. 580.

[Science of sound] acou-, acu-stics; catacoustics; cataphonics; phon-ics, -etics, -ology, -ography; diacoustics, -phonics.

telephone, phonograph etc. 418.

V. produce sound; sound, make a noise; give out −, emit- sound; phonetize, phonate; resound etc. 408.

Adj. sounding; soniferous; sonorific; resonant, audible, acoustic, auditory, distinct; stertorous; phonic, sonant; phonetic.

403. Silence.—**N.** silence; stillness etc. (*quiet*) 265; peace, hush, lull, rest; muteness etc. 581; solemn −, awful −, dead −, deathlike- silence.

V. be -silent etc. *adj.*; hold one's tongue etc. (*not speak*) 585.

render -silent etc. *adj.*; silence, still, hush; stifle, muffle, gag, stop; muzzle- put to silence etc. (*render mute*) 581.

Adj. silent; still, -y; calm, quiet; noise-, sound-, speech-less; hushed etc. *v.*; mute etc. 581; aphonic.

soft, solemn, awful, deathlike, silent as the grave; inaudible etc. (*faint*) 405.

Adv. silently etc. *adj.*; *sub silentio*; in perfect silence.

Int. hush! 'sh! silence! soft! whist! tush! chut! tut! *pax!* mum's the word! hold your tongue! shut up! be silent! be quiet! stop that noise! hold your row! dry up! peace, be still!

Phr. one might hear a -feather, − pin- drop.

404. Loudness.—N. loudness, power; loud noise, din; clang, -or; clatter, noise, bombilation, roar, uproar, racket, static,, grinders, hubbub, *fracas, charivari*, trumpet blast; blare, flourish of trumpets, fanfare, *tintamarre*, peal, swell, blast, alarum, boom; resonance etc. 408.

vociferation; pandemonium, hullaballoo etc. 411; lungs; Stentor; megaphone; siren.

artillery, cannon, gunfire, shellburst, bomb; thunder.

V. be -loud etc. *adj.*; peal, swell, clang, boom, thunder, fulminate, roar; resound etc. 408; speak up, shout etc. (*vociferate*) 411; bellow etc. (*cry as an animal*) 412; give tongue.

rend the -air, − skies; fill the air; din −, ring −, thunder- in the ear; pierce −, split −, rend-the-ears, − head; deafen, stun; *faire le diable a quatre*; make one's windows shake; awaken −, startle- the echoes; make the welkin ring.

Adj. loud, sonorous; high-, big- sounding; blatant; deep, full, powerful, noisy, clangorous, multisonous, *fortisimo*; thundering, deafening etc. *v.*; trumpet-tongued; ear-splitting, -rending, − deafening; piercing; obstreporous, rackety, uproarious; enough to wake the -dead, − seven sleepers.

shrill etc. 410; clamorous etc. (*vociferous*) 411; stentor-ian, -ophonic.

Adv. loudly etc. *adj.*; aloud; at the top of one's voice, lustily, in full cry.

Phr. the air rings with.

405. Faintness.—N. faintness etc. *adj.*; faint sound, whisper, breath; under-tone, -breath; murmur, hum, rustle, buzz, purr; plash; sough, moan, sigh, susurration; tinkle; 'still small voice.'.

hoarseness etc. *adj.*; raucity.

silencer, soft pedal, damper, mute, *sourdine*.

V. whisper, breathe, murmur, purl, hum, gurgle, ripple, babble, flow; tinkle; mutter etc. (*speak imperfectly*) 583.

steal on the ear; melt in −, float on- the air. muffle, mute, deaden, damp, stifle.

Adj. inaudible; scarcely −, just- audible; low, dull; stifled, muffled; hoarse, husky; gentle, soft, faint; floating; purling, flowing etc. *v.*; whispered etc. *v.*; liquid; soothing; dulcet etc. (*melodious*) 413.

Adv. in a whisper, with bated breath, *sotto voce*, between the teeth, aside; *pian-o, -issimo; a la sourdine; con sourdine*; out of earshot, inaudibly etc. *adj.*

406. Snap. [Sudden and violent sounds.]—**N.** snap etc. *v.*; rapping etc. *v.*; de−, crepitation; smack, clap, report; thud; burst, explosion, discharge, detonation, blow-out, back-fire, firing, salvo, volley, pistol-shot.

squib, cracker, gun, rifle, pop-gun.

V. rap, snap, tap, knock; click; clash; crack, -

le; crash; pop; slam, bang, clap, thump, plump; toot; back-fire, explode, burst on the ear.

Adj. rapping etc. *v.*

Int. crash! bang!

407. Roll. [Repeated and protracted sounds.]—**N.** roll etc. *v.*; drumming etc. *v.*; tattoo; ding-dong; tantara; rataplan; whirr; rat-a-tat; rub-a-dub; pit-a-pat; quaver, clutter, *charivari*, racket; cuckoo; repetition etc. 104; peal of bells, devil's tattoo; reverberation etc. 408.

drumfire, barrage.

machine gun.

V. roll, drum, rumble, rattle, clatter, rustle, roar, drone, patter, clack.

hum, trill, shake; chime, peal, toll; tick, beat. drum −, din- in the ear.

Adj. rolling etc. *v.*; monotonous etc. (*repeated*), 104; like a bee in a bottle.

408. Resonance.—N. resonance; ring etc. *v.*; ringing etc. *v.*; tintinnabulation; reflection, reverberation, clangor.

low −, base −, bass −, flat −, grave −, deep −, pedal- note; bass; *basso, − profondo*; bari-, bary-tone; *contralto*.

V. re-sound, -verberate. -echo; ring. ding. sing. jingle, gingle, chink, clink; tink. -le; chime; gurgle etc. 405; plash. guggle. echo. ring in the ear.

Adj. resounding etc. *v.*; resonant, tinnient; tintinnabulary; deep-toned, -sounding, -mouthed; hollow, sepulchral; gruff etc. (*harsh*) 410.

408a. Non-resonance.—N. thud, thump, dead sound; non-resonance; muffled drums, cracked bell; silencer, damper; mute, *sourdine*.

V. sound dead; stop −, damp- the -sound, − reverberations; deaden, muffle.

Adj. non-resonant, dead, muted, muffled.

409. Sibilation. [Hissing sounds.]—**N.** sibilation; hiss etc. *v.*; sternutation; high note etc. 410.

goose, serpent, snake.

V. hiss, buzz, whiz, rustle; fizz, -le, sizzle, swish; wheeze, whistle, snuffle; squash; sneeze.

Adj. sibilant; hissing etc. *v.*; wheezy.

410. Stridor. [Harsh sounds.]—**N.** creak etc. *v.*; creaking etc. *v.*; discord etc. 414; stridor; harshness, roughness, sharpness etc. *adj.*; cacophony.

acute −, high- note; *soprano*, treble, tenor, *alto*, falsetto, *voce di testa*; shriek, cry etc. 411.

piccolo, fife, penny -whistle, − trumpet.

V. creak, grate, jar, burr, pipe, twang, jangle, clank, clink; scream etc. (*cry*) 411; yelp etc. (*animal sound*) 412; buzz etc. (*hiss*) 409.

set the teeth on edge, écorcher les orielles; pierce −, split- the -ears, − head; offend −, grate upon −, jar upon- the ear.

Adj. creaking etc. *v.*; strident, stridulous, harsh,

coarse, hoarse, horrisonous, raucous, metallic, rough, gruff, grum, sepulchral.

sharp, high, acute, shrill, high-pitched; trumpet-toned; piercing, ear-piercing; cracked; discordant etc. 414; cacophonous.

411. Cry.—N. cry etc. *v.*; voice etc. (*human*) 580; bark etc. (*animal*) 412.

vociferation, outcry, hullaballoo, chorus, clamor, hue and cry, plaint; lungs; stentor.

V. cry, roar, shout, bawl, brawl, halloo, halloa, hail, hoop, whoop, yell, bellow, howl, scream, screech, screak, shriek, shrill, squeak, squeal, squall, whine, whinny, pule, pipe, yaup.

cheer, hurrah; hoot; grumble, maon, groan.

snore, snort; grunt etc. (*animal sounds*) 412.

vociferate; raise —, lift up- the voice; call —, sing —, cry- out; exclaim; rend the air; thunder —, shout- at the -top of one's voice, — pitch of one's breath; *s'égosiller*; strain the -throat, — voice, — lungs; give a -cry etc.

Adj. crying etc. *v.*; clam-ant, -orous; vociferous; stentorian etc. (*loud*) 404; open-mouthed.

412. Ululation. [Animal sounds.]—**N.** cry etc. *v.*; crying etc. *v.*; ululation, latration, belling; reboation; call, note; bark, howl, yelp; twittering, woodnote; insect cry, fritinancy, drone; screech; cuckoo.

V. cry, ululate, howl, roar, bellow, blare, rebellow, bark, yelp; bay, — the moon; yap, growl, yarr, yawl, snarl, howl; grunt, -le; snort, squeak; neigh, bray; mew, mewl; purr, caterwaul, pule; bleat, low, moo; troat, croak, crow, screech, caw, coo, gobble, quack, cackle, gaggle, guggle; chuck, -le; cluck; clack; cheep, chirp, chirrup, twitter, sing, cuckoo; pout, wail, hum, buzz; hiss, blatter; hoot.

Adj. crying etc. *v.*; blatant, latrant; re-, mugient; deep-, full-mouthed.

Adv. in full cry.

413. Melody. Concord.—N. melody, rhythym, measure; rhyme etc. (*poetry*) 597.

pitch, *timbre*, intonation, tone, overtone.

scale, gamut; diapason; diatonic —, chromatic —, enharmonic- scale; key, clef, chords.

modulation, temperament, syncope, syncopation, preparation, suspension, resolution.

staff, stave, line, space, brace; bar, rest; *appogiato*, *-tura*; acciaccatura, shake, *arpeggio*.

note, musical note, notes of a sclae; sharp, flat, natural; high note etc. (*shrillness*) 410; low note etc. 408; interval; semitone; second, third, fourth etc.; diatessaron.

breve, semibreve, minim, crotchet, quaver; semi-, demisemi- quaver; sustained note, drone, burden.

tonic; key-, leading-, fundamental-, note; supertonic, mediant, dominant; sub-mediant, -dominant; organ-, pedal-point; octave, tetrachord; major —, minor- -mode, — scale, — key; Doric mode, passage, phrase.

concord, harmony; unison, -ance; chime, homophony; euphon-y, -ism; tonality; consonance; concent; part.

orchestration; harmonization, — phrasing.

[Science of harmony] harmon-y, -ics; thorough-, fundamental- bass; counterpoint; faburden.

piece of music etc. 415; composer, harmonist, contrapuntist.

V. be -harmonious etc. *adj.*; harmonize, chime, symphonize, transpose; put in tune, tune, accord, string; score, arrange, orchestrate.

Adj. harmoni-ous, -cal; in -concord etc. *n.*, — tune, — concert; unisonant, concentual, symphonizing, isotonic, homophonous, assonant, consonant.

measured, rhythmical, diatonic, chromatic, enharmonic.

melodious, musical; tuneful, tunable; sweet, dulcet, canorous; mell-ow, -ifluous; soft; clear, — as a bell; silvery; euphon-ious, -ic, -ical; symphonious; enchanting etc. (*pleasure-giving*) 829; fine-, full-, silver-toned.

Adv. harmoniously etc. *adj.*

414. Discord.—N. discord, -ance; dissonance, cacaphony, caterwauling; harshness etc. 410; consecutive fifths.

[Confused sounds] Babel, pandemonium; Dutch —, cat's- concert; marrow-bones and cleavers.

V. be -discordant etc. *adj.* ; jar etc. (*sound harshly*) 410.

Adj. discordant; dis-, ab-sonant; out of tune, tuneless; un-musical, -tunable; un-, im-melodious; un-, in-harmonious; sing-song; cacophonous; jarring, harsh etc. 410.

415. Music.—N. music, classical —, modern —, descriptive- music; concert, recital; strain, tune, air, *motif*; melody etc. 413; *aria*, *arietta*; piece of music, *sonata*; *rond-o, -eau*; *pástorale*, *cavatina*, roulade, *fantasia*, *toccata*, *concerto*, overture, symphony, symphonic poem, tone poem, prelude, voluntary, *intermezzo*, variations, *cadenza*; cadence; fugue, canon, serenade, *nocturne*, *notturno*, rhapsody, romance, *aubade*, dithyramb; opera, operetta; oratorio; composition, movement, stave.

instrumental music; full-, orchestral- score; minstrelsy, tweedledum and tweedledee, band, orchestra etc. 416; concerted piece, *potpourri*, medley, *capriccio*, incidental music; improvisation; peal.

vocal music, vocalism; chaunt, chant; psalm, -ody; hymn; song etc. (*poem*) 597; canticle, canzonet, *cantata*, *bravura*, *coloratura*; lay, ballad, ditty, carol, barcarolle, pastoral, recitative, *recitativo*, *solfeggio*, tonic sol-fa.

Lydian measures; slow -music, — movement; *adagio* etc. *adv.*; minuet; siren strains, soft music, lullaby; *berceuse*, cradle song, dump; dirge etc. (*lament*) 839; pibroch; martial music, march, funeral-, dead- march; dance music; waltz etc. (*dance*) 840; rag-time, syncopation, jazz.

solo, duet, *duo*, *trio*; quartet; quintet, sextet, septet; part song, descant, glee, madrigal, catch, round, chorus, *chorale*; antiphon, -y; accompaniment, second —, alto —, tenor —, bass-part; score, thorough bass; counterpoint.

composer etc. 413; musician etc. 416.

V. compose, perform etc. 416; attune.

Adj. musical; instrumental, orchestral, vocal, choral, lyric, operatic; harmonious etc. 413.

Adv. *adagio; largo, larghetto, andan-te, -tino; alla capella; maestoso, moderato; allegr-o, -etto; spiritoso, vivace, veloce; prest-o, -issimo; pian-o, -issimo, fort-e, -issimo, sforzando; con brio; capriccioso; scherz-o, -ando; legato, sostenuto, staccato, crescendo,* diminuendo, *rallentando, affettuoso, arioso; parlante, cantabile; obbligato; pizzacato, tremolo, vibrato.*

416. Musician. [Performance of Music.]—**N.** musician, *artiste, virtuoso,* performer, player, minstrel; bard etc. (*poet*) 597; instrumental-, organ-, accompan-, pian-, violin-, flaut-, harp-ist; harper, fiddler, fifer, trumpeter, piper, drummer; eatgut scraper.

band, orchestra, waits.

vocal-, melod-ist; singer, warbler; songst-, chaunt-er, -ress; *diva, cantatrice,* coloratura, soprano, mezzo-soprano, alto, contralto, tenor, baritone, bass, *basso, -profundo.*

choir, quire, chorister; chorus, − singer; choral society, festival, *eisteddfod.*

nightingale, philomel, thrush; siren; Orpheus, Apollo, the Muses, Erato, Euterpe, Terpsichore; tuneful -nine, − quire.

composer etc. 413.

performance, virtuosity, execution, touch, expression, solmization.

V. play, pipe, strike −, tune-up, sweep the chords, tickle −, paw- the ivories, vamp, tweedle, fiddle; strike the lyre, beat the drum; blow −, sound −, wind- the horn; grind the organ; touch the -guitar etc. (*instruments*) 417; thrum, strum, twang, drum, beat −, keep- time, conduct.

execute, perform; accompany; sing −, play- a second; compose, write music, set to music, arrange, harmonize, orchestrate.

sing, chaunt, chant, hum, warble, carol, chirp, chirrup, lilt, purl, quaver, trill, shake, twitter, whistle; sol-fa; intone.

have -an ear for music, − a musical ear, − a correct ear, − absolute pitch.

Adj. playing etc. *v.*; musical, lyric.

Adv. *adagio,* andante etc. (*music*) 415.

417. Musical Instruments.—**N.** musical instruments; band; string-, brass-, drum and fife-, military-, bugle-, German-, dance-, jazz-band; orchestra, string quartet; orchestration, orchestrelle.

[Stringed instruments] mono-, poly-chord; harp, lyre, lute, archlute, thearbo; mandol-a, -in, -ine; guitar; *ukulele;* psaltery, zither; bandore, cither, -in; gittern, rebeck, *bandurria,* banjo, zither banjo, *balalaika, samisen;* plectrum.

viol, -in, Cremona, Stradivarius; fiddle; kit; *vielle, viola, − d'amore, − di gamba;* tenor, *violoncello,* cello; bass, bass-, bass-viol; double-bass, *contrabasso, violone,* hurdy-gurdy; strings, catgut; bow, fiddlestick.

piano, -forte; grand −, concert grand −, baby −, upright −, cottage- piano; pianino, pianette; harpsi-, clavi-, clari-, mani-chord; *clavier,* spinet, virginals; dulcimer, *cymbalo;* Eolian harp; piano-

organ, -player, electric piano, player-piano, pianola.

[Wind instruments] organ, church −, pipe −, American- organ; harmoni-um, -phon; accordion, seraphina, concertina; melodeon; barrel- organ; humming top.

flute, fife, piccolo, flageolet, penny-whistle, reed instrument; clari-net, -onet; bass clarionet; saxophone; basset horn, *corno di bassetto;* musette, shawm, oboe, hautboy, *cor Anglais, corno Inglese,* bassoon, double bassoon, *contrafagotto;* bag-, union-pipes; ocarina, Pandean pipes; calliope; sirene, pipe, pitch-pipe; sourdet; whistle, catcall.

horn, bugle, key bugle, cornet, *cornet-à-pistons,* cornopean, clarion, trumpet, trombone, ophicleide, serpent; English-, French-, bugle-, sax-, flugel-, alt-, helicon-, post-horn; sackbut, euphonium, bombardon, tuba, bass tuba.

[Vibrating surfaces] cymbal, bell, gong, peal of bells, *carillon;* tambour, -ine; drum, tom-tom, tabor, -ret, -ourine, -orin; *sistrum, grand caisse,* bass-, big-, side-, kettle-drum; *tympani;* war drums; tymbal, timbrel, castanet, bones; musical-glasses, -stones; harmonica, sounding- board, rattle; gramophone, phonograph.

[Vibrating bars] reed, tuning-fork, triangle, Jew's harp, musical box, harmonicon, xylophone, marimba, *celeste.*

sord-ine, -et; *sourd-ine, -et;* mute.

418. Hearing. [Sense of sound.]—**N.** hearing etc. *v.*; audition, auscultation; eavesdropping; audibility; acoustics etc. 402.

acute −, nice −, delicate −, quick −, sharp −, correct −, musical -ear; ear for music.

ear, auricle, lug, acoustic organs, auditory apparatus, ear-drum, tympanum; ear-, speaking-trumpet, megaphone; telephone, radiophone, stethoscope, phonograph, gramophone, microphone.

hearer, auditor, listener, eavesdropper; audi-tory, -ence.

V. hear, overhear; hark, -en; list, -en; give −, lend −, bend- an ear; give attention; catch a sound, prick up one's ears; give -a hearing, − audience -to.

hang upon the lips of, be all ear, listen with both ears, monitor.

become audible; meet −, fall upon −, catch −, reach- the ear; be heard; ring in the ear etc. (*resound*) 408.

Adj. hearing etc. *v.*; auditory, auricular, aural, auditive, acoustic.

Adv. *arrectis auribus.*

Int. hark, − ye! hear! list, -en! *Oyez!* attention! lend me your ears!

419. Deafness.—**N.** deafness, hardness of hearing, surdity; inaudibility.

V. be -deaf etc. *adj.*; have no ear; shut −, stop −, close- one's ears; turn a deaf ear to.

render deaf, stun, deafen.

Adj. deaf, earless, surd; hard −, dull- of hearing; deaf-mute, stunned, deafened; stone deaf; deaf as -a post, − an adder, − a beetle, − a trunk-maker.

inaudible etc. 405; out of hearing.

420. Light.—N. light, ray, beam, stream, gleam, streak, pencil; sun-, moon-beam; dawn, aurora.

day; sunshine; light of -day, − heaven; sun etc. (*luminary*) 432, day-, broad day-, noontide- light; noon-tide, -day; glare.

glow etc. *v.*; afterglow, sunset; glimmering etc. *v.*; glint; play −, flood- of light; phosphorescence, flush, halo, glory, nimbus, aureole, *aureola*.

spark, *scintilla*; *facula*; sparkling etc. *v.*; emication, scintillation, flash, blaze, coruscation, fulguration; flame etc. (*fire*) 382; lightning, *ignis fatuus*, etc. (*luminary*) 423, radio-activity.

luster, sheen, shimmer, reflection; gloss, tinsel, spangle, brightness, brilliancy, splendor; ef-, refulgence; ful-gor, -gidity; dazzlement, resplendence, transplendency; luminousness etc. *adj.*; luminosity; lucidity; renitency; radi-ance, -ation; irradiation, illumination, phosphorescence, luminescence.

radiation, radiant heat, infra-red rays, visible radiation, ultra-violet −, actinic- rays, actinism; X −, Roentgen- rays; phot-, heli-ography; optical instruments etc. 445.

[Science of light] optics; photo-logy, -metry; di-, cat-optrics.

[Distribution of light] chiaroscuro, *clairobscur*, clear obscure, breadth, light and shade, black and white, tonality, half-tone, mezzotint.

reflection, refraction, dispersion, double refraction, polarization, diffraction, interference.

illuminant etc. 423.

V. shine, glow, glitter, phosphoresce; glis-ter, -ten; twinkle, gleam; flare, − up; glare, beam, shimmer, glimmer, flicker, sparkle, scintillate, coruscate, flash, fulgurate, blaze; be -bright etc. *adj.*; reflect light, daze, dazzle, bedazzle, raidate, shoot out beams.

clear up, brighten.

lighten, enlighten; light, − up; irradiate, shine upon; give −, hang out- a light; cast −, throw −, shed- -luster, − light- upon; illum-e, -ine, -inate; relume, strike a light; kindle etc. (*set fire to*) 384.

Adj. shining etc. *v.*; lumin-ous, -iferous; luc-id, -cnt, -ulent, -ific, -iferous; illuminating, light, -some; bright, vivid, splendent, nitid, lustrous, shiny, brilliant, beamy, scintillant, radiant, lambent; sheen, -y; glossy, burnished, glassy, sunny, orient, meridian; noon-day, -tide; cloudless, clear; unclouded, -obscured.

garish; re-, tran-splendent; re-, effulgent; ful-gid, -gent; relucent, splendid, blazing, in a blaze, ablaze, rutilant, meteoric, phosphorescent; aglow.

bright as silver; light −, bright- as -day, − noonday, − the sun at noonday.

optical, actinic, photo-genic, -graphic; heliographic, radioactive.

421. Darkness.—N. darkness etc. *adj.*; blackness etc. (*dark color*) 431; obscurity, gloom, murk; dusk etc. (*dimness*) 422; tenebrosity, umbrageousness.

Cimmerian −, Stygian −, Egyptian- darkness; night; midnight; dead of −, witching time of-night; blind man's holiday; darkness -visible; − that can be felt; palpable, obscure; Erebus.

shade, shadow, umbra, penumbra; sciagraphy; *silhouette*; radiograph, skiagraph.

obscuration; ad-, ob-umbration; obtenebration, offuscation, caligation; extinction; eclipse, total eclipse; gathering of the clouds.

shading; distribution of shade; *chiaroscuro* etc. (*light*) 420.

noctivagation, noctograph, noctuary.

obscurantist.

V. be -dark etc. *adj.*

darken, obscure, shade; dim; tone down, lower; over-cast, -shadow; cloud, eclipse; ob-, of-fuscate; ob-, ad-umbrate, cast into the shade; be-cloud, -dim, -darken; cast −, throw −, spread- a -shade, − shadow, − gloom.

extinguish; put −, blow −, snuff- out; doubt.

Adj. dark, -some, -ling; obscure, tenebrous, tenebrious, sombrous, pitch dark, pitchy, caliginous; black etc. (*in color*) 431.

sunless, lightless etc. (*see* sun, light etc. 423); somber, dusky; unilluminated etc. (*see* illuminate etc. 420); nocturnal; dingy, lurid, gloomy; murk-y, -some; shady, umbrageous; overcast etc. (*dim*) 422; cloudy etc. (*opaque*) 426; darkened etc. *v.*

dark as -pitch, − a pit, − Erebus.

benighted; noctivag-ant, -ous.

Adv. in the -dark, − shade; at night.

422. Dimness.—N. dimness etc. *adj.*; darkness etc. 421; paleness etc. (*light color*) 429.

half-light, *demi-jour*; partial -shadow, − eclipse; shadow of a shade; glimmer, -ing; nebulosity; cloud etc. 353; eclipse.

aurora, dusk, twilight, gloaming, blind man's holiday, shades of evening, crepuscule, cockshut time; break of day, daybreak, dawn.

moon-light, -beam, -shine; star- owl's-, candle-, rush-, fire-light; farthing candle.

V. be −, grow- -dim etc. *adj.*; flicker, twinkle, glimmer; loom, lower; fade; darken; pale, − its ineffectual fire.

render -dim etc. *adj.*; dim, bedim, obscure.

Adj. dim, dull, lack-luster, dingy, darkish, shorn of its beams; dark 421.

faint, shadowed forth; glassy; bleary; cloudy; misty etc. (*opaque*) 426; muggy, fuliginous; nebulous, -ar; obnubilated, overcast, crepuscular, twilight, muddy, lurid, leaden, dun, dirty; looming etc. *v.*

pale etc. (*colorless*) 429; confused etc. (*invisible*) 447.

423. Luminary. [Source of light.]—N. luminary; light etc. 420; flame etc. (*fire*) 382.

spark, *scintilla*; phosphorescence.

sun, orb of day, day star, Phoebus, Apollo, Helios, Phaethon, Hyperion, Ra, Aurora; star, orb, meteor; falling −, shooting- star; blazing −, dog-star; Sirius, canicula, Aldebaran; morning star, Lucifer, Phosphor, evening star; Hesperus, Venus, planet, moon etc. 318; constellation, galaxy; northern light, *aurora -borealis*, − *australis*, zodiacal light; mock sun, parhelion.

lightning; fork −, sheet −, summer- lightning, St. Elmo's fire; phosphorus; *ignis fatuus*; Jack o' − Friar's- lantern; Will o' the wisp, fire-drake, *Fata Morgana*.

glow-worm, fire-fly.

radium, luminous paint.

[Artificial light] gas; gas – , lime – , electric – , head – , search – , spot – , flash – , flood – , footlight; lamp, oil – , gas – , arc – , incandescent-lamp; flare; lant-ern, -horn; dark lantern, bull's eye, projector; candle, *bougie*, tallow – , wax- candle; dip, farthing dip; taper, rush-light; oil etc. (*grease*) 356; wick, burner; Argand, moderator, duplex; torch, *flambeau*, link, brand; cresset; gase-, chande-, electro-lier; candelabrum, *girandole*, sconce, luster, candle-stick.

firework, fizgig; pyrotechnics; Roman candle, Very light, star shell, parachute light; rocket, lighthouse etc. (*signal*) 550.

V. illuminate etc. (*light*) 420.

Adj. self-luminous, incandescent; phosphor-ic, -escent; luminescent, fluorescent, radiant etc. (*light*) 420.

424. Shade.—N. shade; awning etc. (*cover*) 223; parasol, sunshade, umbrella; screen, curtain, shutter, blind, gauze, veil, mantle, mask; cloud, mist, gathering of clouds; smoke screen; smoked glasses, colored spectacles; blinkers, blinders.

umbrage, glade; shadow etc. 421.

V. draw a curtain; put up – , close- a shutter; veil etc. *v.*; cast a shadow etc. (*darken*) 421; screen, obstruct the view.

Adj. shady, umbrageous, bowery.

425. Transparency.—N. transparen-ce, -cy; translucen-ce, -cy; diaphaneity; luc-, pelluc-, limp-idity.

transparent medium, glass, crystal, mica; lymph, water.

v. be -transparent etc. *adj.*; transmit light.

Adj. transparent, pellucid, lucid, diaphanous; trans-, tra-lucent; limpid, clear, serene, crystalline, clear as crystal, vitreous, transpicuous, glassy, hyaline.

426. Opacity.—N. opacity; opaqueness etc. *adj.*

film; cloud etc. 353.

V. be -opaque etc. *adj.*; obstruct the passage of light; ob-, of-fuscate.

Adj. opaque, impervious to light.

dim etc. 422; turbid, thick, muddy, opacous, obfuscated, fuliginous, cloudy, hazy, foggy, vaporous, nubiferous, muggy.

smoky, fumid, murky, dirty.

427. Semitransparency.—N. semitransparency, opalescence, milkiness, pearliness; gauze, muslin; film; mist etc. (*cloud*) 353; frosted glass.

Adj. semi-transparent, -pellucid, -diaphanous, -opacous, -opaque; opal-escent, -ine; pearly, milky, frosted, mat; misty.

428. Color.—N. color, hue, tint, tinge, dye, complexion, shade, tincture, cast, livery, coloration, chromatism, glow, flush; tone, key.

pure – , positive – , primary – , primitive – , complementary- color; three primaries; spectrum, chromatic dispersion; broken – , secondary –, tertiary- color.

local color, coloring, keeping, tone, value, aerial perspective.

[Science of color] chromatics, spectrum analysis; prism, spectroscope.

pigment, coloring matter, paint, dye, wash, distemper, stain; medium; mordant; oil-paint etc. (*painting*) 556.

V. color, dye, tinge, stain, tint, tinct, tone, paint, wash, ingrain, grain, illuminate, emblazon, imbue; paint etc. (*fine art*) 556; daub.

Adj. colored etc. *v.*; colorific, tingent, tinctorial; chormatic, prismatic; full-, high-, deep-colored; doubly-dyed; polychromatic.

bright, vivid, intense, deep; fresh, unfaded; rich, gorgeous; highly colored; gay; variegated etc. 440.

gaudy, florid; garish; showy, flaunting, flashy; raw, crude; glaring, flaring; discordant, inharmonious.

mellow, harmonious, pearly, sweet, delicate, tender, refined.

429. Achromatism. [Absence of color.]—**N.** achromatism; de-, dis-coloration; pall-or, -idity; paleness etc. *adj.*; etiolation; neutral tint, monochrome, black-and-white.

V. lose -color etc. 428; fade, fly, go; become -colorless etc. *adj.*; turn pale, pale, whiten.

deprive of color, decolorize, bleach, tarnish, achromatize, blanch, etiolate, wash out, tone down.

Adj. uncolored etc. (*see* color etc. 428); colorless, achromatic, hueless, pale, pallid; pale-, tallow-faced; faint, dull, cold, muddy, leaden, dun, wan, sallow, dead, dingy, ashy, ashen, ghastly, cadaverous, glassy, lack-luster; discolored etc. *v.* light-colored, fair, *blond*; white etc. 430.

pale as -death, – ashes, – a witch, – a ghost, – a corpse.

430. Whiteness.—N. whiteness etc. *adj.*; argent.

albification, albescence, albinism, etiolation.

snow, paper, chalk, milk, lily, ivory, silver, alabaster; white lead, chinese – , flake – , ivory – , zinc- white, white-wash, -ning, whiting.

V. be -white etc. *adj.*

render -white etc. *adj.*; whiten- bleach, blanch, etiolate, whitewash, silver, frost.

Adj. white; milky, milk-, snow-white; snowy, niveous, candid, chalky; hoar, -y; frosted, silvery; argent, -ine; canescent.

whitish, creamy, pearly, ivory, fair, *blond*, ash-blond, platinum blond; blanched etc. *v.*; high in tone, light.

white as -a sheet, – driven snow, – a lily, – silver; like -ivory etc. *n.*

431. Blackness.—N. blackness etc. *adj.*; darkness etc. (*want of light*) 421; swarthness, lividity, dark color, tone, color; *chiaroscuro* etc. 420.

nigrification, infuscation, denigration.

jet, ink, ebony, coal, pitch, soot, smudge, charcoal, sloe, raven, crow; black.

[Pigments] lamp –, ivory –, blue-black; writing –, printing –, printer's –, Indian- ink.

V. be -black etc. *adj.*

render -black etc. *adj.*; blacken, infuscate, denigrate; blot, -ch; smutch; smirch; darken etc. 421.

Adj. black, sable, swarthy, somber, dark, inky, ebon, atramentous, jetty; coal-, jet-black; fuliginous, pitchy, sooty, swart, dusky, dingy, murky, low-toned, low in tint; of the deepest dye.

black as -jet etc. *n.*, – my hat, – a shoe, – a tinker's pot, – November, – thunder, – midnight; nocturnal etc. (*dark*) 421; nigrescent; gray etc. 432; obscure etc. 421.

Adv. in mourning.

432. Gray.—N. gray etc. *adj.*; neutral tint, silver, pepper and salt, *chiaroscuro*, *grisaille*, grayness.

[Pigments] Payne's gray; black etc. 431.

Adj. gray, grey; steel –, iron- gray, dun, drab, dingy, leaden, livid, somber, sad, pearly; silver, -y, -ed; ash-en, -y; ciner-eous, -itious; grizzl-y, -ed; dove-, slate-, stone-, mouse-, ash-colored; mole; cool.

433. Brown.—N. brown etc. *adj.*

[Pigments] bister, ocher, sepia, Vandyke brown.

Adj. brown, adust, bay, dapple, auburn, chestnut, nutbrown, cinnamon, hazel, fawn, puce, *écru*, russet, tawny, fuscous, chocolate, maroon, foxy, tan, brunette, whitey-brown; snuff-, liver-colored; brown as -a berry, – mahogany; reddish brown; copper-, rust- colored; henna, bronze, khaki; russet, roan, sorrel.

sub-burnt; tanned etc. *v.*

V. render -brown etc. *adj.*; tan, embrown, bronze.

434. Redness.—N. red, scarlet, vermilion, cardinal, Post Office, red, carmine, crimson, pink, lake, *cerise*, cherry red, maroon, carnation, *couleur de rose*, *rose du Barry*; magenta, damask; flesh -color, – tint; color; fresh –, high- color; warmth; gules.

ruby, garnet, carbuncle; rose; rust, iron-mold.

[Dyes and pigments] cinnabar, cochineal; fuchsine; ruddle, madder, redlead; light –, Venetian- red; red ink, annotto.

redness etc. *adj.*; rub-escence, -icundity, -ification; erubescence, blush.

V. be –, become- -red etc. *adj.*; blush, flush, color up, mantle, redden.

render- red etc. *adj.*; redden, rouge; rub-ify, -ricate; incarnadine; ruddle.

Adj. red etc. *n.*; -dish; rufous, ruddy, florid, incarnadine, sanguine, bloody, gory; ros-y, -eate; blowz-y, -ed; brunt; rubi-cund, -form; lurid, stammel, blood-red; russet, murrey, carroty, sorrel, lateritious.

rose-, ruby-, cherry-, claret-, wine-, plum-,

flame-, flesh-, peach-, salmon-, brick-, brickdust-colored, reddish brown etc. 433.

red as -fire, – blood, – scarlet, – a turkeycock, – a lobster; warm, hot; foxy.

435. Greenness.—N. green etc. *adj.*; blue and yellow; vert.

emerald, verd antique, verdigris, malachite, beryl, aquamarine, reseda.

[Pigments] *terre verte*, verditer, bice, chlorophyl.

greenness, verdure, verdancy; viridity, -escence.

Adj. green, verdant; glaucous, olive; porraceous; green as grass.

emerald –, pea –, grass –, apple –, sea – olive –, bottle –, leaf- green.

greenish; vir-ent, -escent.

436. Yellowness.—N. yellow etc. *adj.*; or.

[Pigments] gamboge; cadmium –, chrome –, Indian –, lemon- yellow; orpiment, yellow ocher, Claude tint, aureolin.

crocus, saffron, topaz, gold.

jaundice; London fog; yellowness etc. *adj.*

Adj. yellow, aureate, gold, golden, gilt, gilded, flavous, citrine, fallow; fulv-ous, -id; sallow, luteous, fawny, creamy, sandy; xanth-ic, -ous; jaundiced.

gold-, citron-, saffron-, lemon-, sulphur-, amber-, straw-, primrose-, cream-colored; flazen, yellowish, buff.

yellow as a -quince, – guinea, – crow's foot.

437. Purple.—N. purple etc. *adj.*; blue and red, bishop's purple; aniline dyes, gridelin, amethyst; purpure.

livid-ness, -ity.

V. empurple.

Adj. purple, violet, plum-colored, lavender, lilac, puce, *mauve*; livid.

438. Blueness.—N. blue etc. *adj.*; garter-blue; watchet.

[Pigments] ultramarine, smalt, cobalt, cyanogen; Prussian –, syenite- blue; bice, indigo, woad.

lapis lazuli, sapphire, turquoise.

blue-, bluish-ness; bloom

Adj. blue, azure, cerulean; sky-blue, -colored, -dyed; navy-blue, aquamarine, electric blue, royal blue, cyanic; bluish; atmospheric, retiring; cold.

439. Orange.—N. orange, red and yellow; gold; or; flame etc. color, *adj.*

[Pigments] ochre, Mars orange, cadmium.

V. gild, warm.

Adj. orange; ocherous; orange-, gold-, flame-, copper-, brass-, apricot-colored; warm, hot, glowing.

440. Variegation.—N. variegation; di-, tri-chromism; iridescence, irisation, play of colors, polychrome, maculation, spottiness, striae.

spectrum, rainbow, iris, tulip, peacock, chameleon, butterfly, tortoiseshell; mackerel, - sky; zebra, leopard, mother-of-pearl, nacre, opal, marble, batik.

check, plaid, tartan, patchwork; mar-, par-quetry; mosiac, *tesserae*, tesselation, chess-board, checkers, chequers; harlequin; Joseph's coat; tricolor; patches, bands, stripes, spots etc of color.

V. be -variegated etc. *adj.*; variegate, stripe, streak, checker, chequer; be-, speckle, fleck; be-, sprinkle; stipple, maculate, dot, bespot; tattoo, inlay, tesselate, damascene; embroider, braid, quilt.

Adj. variegated etc. *v.*; many-colored, -hued; divers-, parti-colored; di-, poly-chromatic; bi-, tri-, versi-color; of all -the colors of the rainbow, — manner of colors; kaleidoscopic.

iridescent; opal-ine, -escent; prismatic, nacreous, pearly, shot, *gorge de pigeon*, *chatoyant*, irisated.

pied, piebald, skewbald; motley; mottled, mar-bled; pepper and salt, paned, dappled, clouded, cymophanous.

mosiac, tesselated, chequered, plaid; tortoiseshell etc. *n.*

spott-ed, -y; punctuated, powdered; speckled etc. *v.*; freckled, fleabitten, studded; fleck-ed, -ered; striated, barred, veined; brind-ed, -led; tabby; watered; grizzled; listed; embroidered etc. *v.*; daedal.

441. Vision.—N. vision, sight, optics, eye-sight.

view, look, espial, glance, ken, *coup d'oeil*; glimpse, peep, glint; gaze, stare, leer; perlustration, contemplation; conspect-ion, -uity; regard, survey; in-, intro-spection; *reconnaissance*, speculation, watch, espionage, *espionnage*, autopsy; ocular - inspection, — demonstration; sight-seeing.

macrography, micrography.

point of view; view-, stand- point; gazebo, loop-hole, *belvedere*, watchtower.

field of view; theater, amphitheater, arena, vista, horizon; commanding —, bird's eye —, panoramic- view; periscope.

visual organ, organ of vision; eye; naked —, unassisted- eye; eye-ball, retina, pupil, iris, cornea, white; optics, orbs; saucer —, goggle —, gooseberry-eyes.

short sight etc. 443; clear —, sharp —, quick —, eagle —, piercing-, —, penetrating- -sight, — glance, — eye; perspicacity, discernment; catopsis.

eagle, hawk, cat, lynx, Argus.

evil eye; basilisk, cockatrice.

spectacles, telescope etc. 445.

V. see, behold, discern, perceive, have in sight, descry, sight, make out, discover, distinguish, recognize, spy, espy, ken; get —, have —, catch- a -sight, — glimpse- of; command of view of; witness, contemplate, speculate; cast —, set- the eyes on; be a -spectator of, 444- of; look on etc. (*be present*) 186; see sights etc. (*curiosity*) 445; see at a glance etc. (*intelligence*) 498.

look, view, eye; lift up the eyes, open one's eye; look -at, — on, — upon, — over, — about one, — round; survey, scan, inspect; run the eye -over, — through; reconnoiter, glance -round, — on, — over; turn —, bend- one's looks upon; direct the

eyes to, turn the eyes on, cast a glance, make eyes at.

observe etc. (*attend to*) 457; watch etc. (*care*) 459; see with one's own eyes; watch for etc. (*expect*) 507; peek, peep, peer, pry, take a peep; play at bo-peep.

look -full in the face, — hard at, — intently; strain one's eyes; fix —, rivet- the eyes upon; stare, gaze; pore over, gloat -over, — on; leer, ogle, glare; goggle; cock the eye, squint, gloat, look askance; give the glad eye.

Adj. seeing etc. *v.*; visual, ocular, -al; ophthalmic.

far-, clear-sighted etc. *n.*; eagle-, hawk-, lynx-, keen-, Argus-eyed.

visible etc. 446.

Adv. visibly etc. 446; in sight of, with one's eyes open.

at -sight, — first sight, — a glance, — the first blush; *primâ facie*.

Int. look! etc. (*attention*) 457.

Phr. the scales falling from one's eyes.

442. Blindness.—N. blindness, anopsia, cecity, excecation, *amaurosis*, cataract, ablepsy, prestriction; dim-sightedness etc. 443.

V. be -blind etc. *adj.*; not see; lose sight of; have the eyes bandaged; grope in the dark.

not look; close —, shut —, turn away —, avert-the eyes; look another way; wink etc. (*limited vision*) 443; shut the eyes —, be blind- to; wink —, blink- at.

render -blind etc. *adj.*; blind, -fold; hoodwink, dazzle; put one's eyes out; throw dust into one's eyes; *jeter de la poudre aux yeux*; screen from sight etc. (*hide*) 528.

Adj. blind; eye-, sight-, vision-less; dark; stone-, sand-, stark-blind; undiscerning; dim-sighted etc. 443.

blind as -a bat, — a buzzard, — a beetle, — a mole, — an owl; wall-eyed.

blinded etc. *v.*

Adv. blind-ly, -fold; darkly.

443. Dim-sightedness. [Imperfect vision.] [Fallacies of vision.]—N. dim —, dull —, half —, short —, near —, long —, double -, astigmatic-—, failing- sight; dim etc -sightedness; snow blindness; purblindness, lippitude; my-, presby-opia; confusion of vision; astigmatism; nystagmus; color-blindness, dichromism, chromato-pseudo-blepsis, Daltonism; nyctalopy; *strabismus*, strabism, squint, cast in the eye, swivel eye, goggle eyes; obliquity of vision.

winking etc. *v.*; nictitation; blinkard, albino.

dizziness, swimming, scotomy; cataract; ophthalmia.

[Limitation of vision] eye shade, blinker, blinder; screen etc. (*hider*) 530.

[Fallacies of vision] *deceptio visûs*; refraction, distortion, illusion, false light, *anamorphosis*, virtual image, *spectrum*, *mirage*, looming, phasma; phant-asm, -asma, -om; vision; specter, apparition; ghost; *ignis fatuus* etc. (*luminary*) 423; specter of the Brocken; magic mirror; magic lantern etc. (*show*) 448; mirror, lens etc. (*instrument*) 445.

V. be -dim-sighted etc. *n.*; see double; have a - mote in the eye, − mist before the eyes, − film over the eyes; see through a -prism, − glass darkly; wink, blink, nictitate; squint; look ask-ant, -ance; screw up the eyes, glare, glower.

dazzle, glare, blur, swim, loom.

Adj. dim-sighted etc. *n.*; my-, presby-opic; astigmatic; moon-, mope-, blear-, goggle-, gooseberry-, one-eyed; blind of one eye, monoculous; half-, pur-, color-blind; dichromatic.

blind as a bat etc. (*blind*) 442; winking etc. *v.*

---

444. Spectator.—N. spectator, beholder, observer, inspector, viewer, looker-on, onlooker, witness, eye-witness, bystander, passer by; sight-seer.

spy, scout; sentinel etc. (*warning*) 668.

v. witness, behold etc. (*see*) 441; look on etc. (*be present*) 186.

---

445. Optical Instruments.—N. optical instruments; lens, meniscus, magnifier, reading −, burning- glass; micro-, mega-, teino-scope; spectacles, glasses, barnacles, goggles, giglamps, eyeglass, *pince-nez*, monocle; periscopic lens; telescope, glass, lorgnette, binocular; spy-, opera-, field-glass, periscope, range finder.

mirror, reflector, speculum; looking-, pier-, cheval-, hand-glass.

prism; camera, *camera-lucida*, *obscura*; projector, stereopticon, magic lantern etc. (*show*) 448; chro-, thau-matrope; stereo-, pseudo-, poly-, kaleido-scope.

photo-, opto-, erio-, actino-, luci-, radio-, spectro-meter; polari-, polemo-, spectro-scope, diffraction grating.

optics, optician, optometry, optometrist; microscop-y, -ist; photometry, photography; photographer.

---

446. Visibility.—N. visibility, perceptibility; conspicuousness, distinctness etc. *adj.*; conspicuity; appearance etc. 448; exposure; manifestation etc. 525; ocular -proof, − evidence, − demonstration; field of view etc. (*vision*) 441.

V. be −, become- -visible etc. *adj.*; appear, emerge, open to the view; meet −, catch- the eye; present −, show −, manifest −, produce −, discover −, reveal −, expose −, betray- itself; stand -forth, − out; show; arise; peep −, peer −, crop- out; start −, spring −, show −, turn −, crop- up; glimmer, glitter, glow, loom; glare; burst forth, scintillate; burst upon the -view, − sight; heave in sight; come -in sight, − into view, − out, − forth, − forward; see the light of day; break through the clouds; make its appearance, show its face, materialize, appear to one's eyes, come upon the stage, enter; float before the eyes, speak for itself. etc. (*manifest*) 525; attract the attention etc. 457; reappear; live in a glass house.

expose to view etc. 525.

Adj. visible, perceptible, perceivable, discernible, apparent; in -view, − full view, − sight; exposed to view, *en évidence*; unclouded.

obvious etc. (*manifest*) 525; plain, clear,

distinct, definite; well-defined, -marked; in focus; recognizable, palpable, autoptical; glaring, staring, conspicuous; stereoscopic; in -bold, − strong, − high- relief.

periscopic, panoramic.

before −, under- one's eyes; before one, *à vue d'oeil*, in one's eye, *oculis subjecta fidelibus*.

Adv. visibly etc. *adj.*; in sight of; before one's eyes etc. *adj.*; *veluti in speculum*.

---

447. Invisibility.—N. invisibility, nonappearance, imperceptibility; indistinctness etc. *adj.*; mystery, delitescence.

concealment etc. 528; latency etc. 526.

V. be -invisible etc. *adj.*; be hidden etc. (*hide*) 528; lurk etc. (*lie hidden*) 526; escape notice.

render -invisible etc. *adj.*; conceal etc. 528; put out of sight.

not see etc. (*be blind*) 442; lose sight of.

Adj. invisible, imperceptible, un-, in-discernible; un-, non-apparent; out of −, not in- sight; *à perte de vue*; behind the -scenes, − curtain; view-, sight-less; in-, un-conspicuous; unseen etc. (*see* see etc. 441); covert etc. (*latent*) 526; eclipsed, under an eclipse.

dim etc. (*faint*) 422; mysterious, dark, obscure, confused; indistin-ct, -guishable; shadowy, indefinite, undefined; ill-defined, -marked; blurred, fuzzy, out of focus; misty etc. (*opaque*) 426; veiled etc. (*concealed*) 528; delitescent.

---

448. Appearance.—N. appearance, phenomenon, sight, spectacle, show, premonstration, scene, species, view, *coup d'oeil*; look-out, out-look, prospect, vista, perspective, bird's-eye view, scenery; landscape, picture, *tableau*; display, exposure, *mise en scène*; scenery, *décor*; rising of the curtain.

phant-asm, -om etc. (*fallacy of vision*) 443.

pageant, *spectacle*; peep-, raree-, gallanty-show; *ombres chinoises*; projector, optical −, magic-lantern, phantasmagoria, dissolving views; cinema, -tograph; bio-scope, -graph; moving pictures, movies, film, screen etc.; pan-, di-, cosm-, georama; *coup* −, *jeu- de théâtre*; pageantry etc. (*ostentation*) 882; insignia etc. (*indication*) 550.

aspect, phase, *phasis*, seeming; shape etc. (*form*) 240; guise, look, complexion, color, image, mien, air, cast, carriage, port, demeanor; presence, expression, first blush, face of the thing; point of view, light.

lineament, feature, trait, lines; out-line, -side; contour, *silhouette*, face, countenance, physiognomy, visage, phiz, mug, cast of countenance, profile, *tournure*, cut of one's jib, metoposcopy; outside etc. 220.

V. appear; be −, become- visible etc. 446; seem, look, show; present −, wear −, carry −, have −, bear −, exhibit −, take −, take on −, assume- the -appearance, − semblance- of; look like; cut a figure, figure; present to the view; show etc. (*make manifest*) 525.

Adj. apparent, seeming, ostensible; on view.

Adv. apparently; to all -seeming, − appearance; ostensibly, seemingly, as it seems, on the face of it, *primâ facie*; at the first blush, at first sight; in the eyes of; to the eye.

449. Disappearance.—N. disappearance, evanescence, eclipse, occultation.

departure etc. 293; exit, vanishing point; dissolving views.

V. disappear, vanish, dissolve, fade, melt away, pass, go, avaunt; be -gone etc. *adj.*; leave -no trace, – 'not a rack behind;' go off the stage etc. (*depart*) 293; suffer – , undergo- an eclipse; be lost to – , retire from- -sight, – view.

lose sight of.

efface etc. 552.

Adj. disappearing etc. *v.*; evanescent; missing, lost; lost to -sight, – view; gone; *spurlos versenki.*

Int. vanish! disappear! avaunt! etc. (*ejection*) 297.

450. Intellect.—N. intellect, mind, understanding, reason, thinking principle; rationality; cogitative – , cognitive – , intellectual- faculties; faculties, senses, consciousness, observation, percipience, apperception, mentality, intelligence, intellection, intuition, association of ideas, instinct, flair, conception, judgment, wits, parts, capacity, intellectuality, reasoning power, brains, genius; wit etc. 498; ability etc. (*skill*) 698; wisdom etc. 498.

soul, spirit, ghost, inner man, heart, breast, bosom, *penetralia mentis, divina particula aurae,* heart's core; ego, psyche, pneuma, subconsciousness, subconscious, subliminal self; dual personality.

organ – , seat- of thought; *sensorium*, sensory, brain, gray matter; head, -piece; pate, noddle, skull, scull, *pericranium, cerebrum, cranium,* brain-pan, -box; sconce, upper story.

[Science of mind] metaphysics; psychics, psycho-logy, -metry, -genesis, -analysis, -physics, psychi-atry, -cal research, thought reading etc. 992; ideology; mental – , moral- philosophy; philosophy of the mind; pneumat-, phren-ology; no – , craniology, -scopy.

ideal-ity, -ism; transcendental-, spiritual-ism; immateriality etc. 317.

metaphysician, psychologist etc.

V. note, notice, mark; take -notice, – cognizance- of; be -aware, – conscious- of; realize; appreciate; ruminate etc. (*think*) 451; fancy etc. (*imagine*) 515; conceive, reason, understand.

Adj. [Relating to intellect] intellectual, mental, rational, subjective, metaphysical, nooscopic, spiritual; ghostly; psych-ical, -ological; cerebral.

immaterial etc. 317; endowed with reason.

Adv. *in petto.*

450a. Absence or want **of Intellect.—N.** absence – , want- of -intellect etc. 450; imbecility etc. 499; brutality; brute -instinct, – force.

Adj. unendowed with reason.

451. Thought.—N. thought; exercitation – , exercise- of the intellect; reflection, cogitation, consideration, meditation, study, lucubration, speculation, deliberation, pondering; head-, brainwork; cerebration; mentation, deep reflection; close study, application etc. (*attention*) 457.

abstract thought, abstraction, contemplation, musing; brown study etc. (*inattention*) 458; reverie, Platonism; depth of thought, workings of the mind, thoughts, inmost thoughts; self-counsel, communing, -consultation.

association – , succession – , flow – , train – , current- of -thought; – ideas.

after – , mature- thought; reconsideration, second thoughts; retrospection etc. (*memory*) 505; excogitation; examination etc. (*inquiry*) 461; invention etc. (*imagination*) 515.

thoughtfulness etc. *adj.*

V. think, reflect, reason, cogitate, excogitate, consider, deliberate; bestow -thought, – consideration- upon; speculate, contemplate, meditate, ponder, muse, dream, ruminate; brood – , conover; animadvert, study; bend–, apply- the mind etc. (*attend*) 457; digest, discuss, hammer at, weigh, perpend; realize, appreciate; fancy etc. (*imagine*) 515; trow.

take into consideration; take counsel etc. (*be advised*) 695; commune with – , bethink- oneself; collect one's thoughts; revolve – , turn over –, run over- in the mind; chew the cud –, sleep- upon; take counsel of – , advise with- one's pillow.

rack – , ransack – , crack- , beat – , cudgelone's brains; set one's -brain, – wits- to work.

harbor – , entertain – , cherish – , nurture- an idea etc. 453; take into one's head; bear in mind; reconsider.

occur; present – , suggest- itself; come –, getinto, one's head; strike one, flit across the view, come uppermost, run in one's head; enter – , pass in – , cross – , flash on – , flash across – , float in – , fasten itself on – , be uppermost in –, occupy- the mind; have in one's mind.

make an impression; sink – , penetrate- into the mind; engross the thoughts.

Adj. thinking etc. *v.*; thoughtful, pensive, meditative, reflective, cogitative, museful, wistful, contemplative, speculative, deliberative, studious, sedate, introspective, Platonic, philosophical.

lost – , engrossed – , rapt – , absorbed- in thought etc. (*inattentive*) 458; deep musing etc. (*intent*) 457.

in the mind, under consideration, in contemplation.

Adv. all things considered; taking everything into account.

Phr. the mind being on the stretch; the -mind, – head- -turning, – running- upon.

452. Incogitancy. [Absence or want of thought.]—**N.** incogitancy, vacancy, inunderstanding; inanity, fatuity etc. 499; thoughtlessness etc. (*inattention*) 458.

V. not -think etc. 451; not think of; dismiss from the -mind, – thoughts etc. 451.

indulge in reverie etc. (*be inattentive*) 458.

put away thought; unbend – , relax –, divert- the mind.

Adj. vacant, unintellectual, unideal, unoccupied, unthinking, inconsiderate, thoughtless; absent etc. (*inattentive*) 458; diverted; irrational etc. 499; narrow-minded etc. 481.

un-thought of, -dreamt of, -considered; off one's mind; incogitable, not to be thought of, inconceivable.

453. Idea. [Object of thought.]—**N.** idea, notion, conception, thought, apprehension, impression, perception, image, sentiment, reflection, observation, consideration; abstract idea, principle; archetype.

view etc. (*opinion*) 484; theory etc. 514; conceit, fancy; phantasy etc. (*imagination*) 515.

point of view etc. (*aspect*) 448; field of view.

454. Topic. [Subject of thought.]—**N.** subject of –, material for- thought; food for the mind, mental *pabulum*.

subject, -matter; matter, theme, topic, what it is about, *thesis*, text, business, affair, matter in hand, argument; motion, resolution; head, chapter; case, point; proposition, theorem; field of inquiry; moot point, problem, etc. (*question*) 461.

V. float –, pass- in the mind etc. 451.

Adj. thought of; uppermost in the mind; *in petto*.

Adv. under -discussion, – consideration, – advisement; in -question, – the mind; on -foot, – the carpet, – the *tapis*; before the house., relative to etc. 9.

455. Curiosity. [The desire of knowledge.]—**N.** interest, thirst for knowledge; curi-osity, -ousness; inquiring mind; inquisitiveness.

sight-seer, quidnunc, newsmonger, Paul Pry, peeping Tom, eavesdropper; gossip etc. (*news*) 532; questioner, *enfant terrible*.

V. be -curious etc. *adj.*; take an interest in, stare, gape; prick up the ears, see sights, lionize; pry, speer; dig up.

Adj. curious, inquisitive, burning with curiosity, overcurious, nosey; inquiring etc. 461; prying; inquisitorial; agape etc. (*expectant*) 507; attentive etc. 457.

Phr. what's the matter? what next?

456. Incuriosity. [Absence of curiosity.]—**N.** incuriosity; incuriousness etc. *adj.*; *insouciance* etc. 866; indifference, apathy.

V. be -incurious etc. *adj.*; have no -curiosity etc. 455; take no interest in etc. 823; mind one's own business.

Adj. incurious, uninquisitive, uninterested, indifferent, bored; impassive etc. 823.

457. Attention.—**N.** attention; mindfulness etc. *adj.*; intent-ness, -iveness; thought etc. 451; adverten-ce, -cy; observ-ance, -ation; consideration, reflection, perpension; heed; particularity; notice, regard etc. *v.*; circumspection etc. (*care*) 459; study, scrutiny, once-over; in-, intro-spection; revision, -al.

active –, diligent –, exclusive –, minute –, close –, intense –, deep –, profound –, abstract –, labored –, deliberate- -thought, – attention, – application, – study.

minuteness, attention to detail etc. 459.

absorption of mind etc. (*abstraction*) 458.

indication, calling attention to etc. *v.*

V. be -attentive etc. *adj.*; attend, advert to, observe, look, see, view, remark, notice, regard, take notice, mark; give –, pay- -attention. – heedto; listen in, incline –, lend- an ear to; trouble one's head about; give a thought –, animadvert- to; occupy oneself with; contemplate etc (*think of*) 451; look -at, – to, – after, – into, – over; see to; turn –, bend –, apply –, direct –, give- the -mind, – eye, – attention- to; have -an eye to, – in one's eye; bear in mind; take into -account, – consideration; keep in -sight, – view; have regard to, heed, mind, take cognizance of, be engaged in, entertain, recognize; make –, take- note of; note.

examine cursorily; glance -at, – upon, – over; cast –, pass- the eyes over; run over, turn over the leaves, dip into, perstringe; skim etc. (*neglect*) 460; take a cursory view of.

examine, – closely, – intently; scan, scrutinize, consider; give –, bend- one's mind to; overhaul, revise, pore over; inspect, review, pass under review; take stock of; fix –, rivet –, focus –, devote- the -eye, – mind, – thoughts, – attention-on or to; hear –, think- out; mind one's business.

revert –, hark back- to; watch etc. (*expect*) 507, (*take care of*) 459; hearken –, listen- to; prick up the ears; have –, keep- the eyes open; come to the point.

meet with attention; fall under one's -notice, – observation; be -under consideration etc. (*topic*) 454.

catch –, strike- the eye; attract notice; catch –, awaken –, wake –, invite –, solicit –, attract –, claim –, excite –, engage –, occupy –, strike –, arrest –, fix –, engross –, absorb –, rivet-the-attention, – mind, – thoughts, be -present to, – uppermost in- the mind.

bring under one's notice; point -out, – to, – at, – the finger at; lay the finger on, indigitate, indicate; direct –, call- attention to; show; put a -mark etc. (*sign*) 550- upon; call soldiers to 'attention;' bring forward etc. (*make manifest*) 525.

Adj. attentive, mindful, heedful, observant, regardful; alive –, awake- to, alert; observing etc. *v.*; taken up –, occupied- with; engaged –, engrossed –, interested –, wrapped- in; absorbed, rapt; breathless; pre-occupied etc. (*inattentive*) 458; watchful etc. (*careful*) 459; intent on, open-eyed, breathless, undistracted, upon the stretch; on the watch etc. (*expectant*) 507.

steadfast.

Int. see! look, – here, – out, – alive, – you, – to it! mark! lo! behold! soho! hark, – ye! mind ! halloo! observe! lo and behold! attention! *nota bene*; N.B.; `*`, `†`; I'd have you to know; notice! take notice! O yes! *Oyez!*

Phr. this is –, these are- to give notice.

458. Inattention.—**N.** in-attention, -consideration; inconsiderateness etc. *adj.*; oversight; inadverten-ce, -cy; non-observance, disregard.

supineness etc. (*inactivity*) 683; *étourderie*; want of thought; heedlessness etc. (*neglect*) 460; *insouciance* etc. (*indifference*) 866.

abstraction; absence —, absorption- of mind; preoccupation, distraction, reverie, brown study, deep musing, fit of abstraction, woolgathering.

V. be -inattentive etc. *adj.*; overlook, disregard; pass by etc. (*neglect*) 460; not -observe etc. 457; think little of.

close —, shut- one's eyes to; wink at; pay no attention to; dismiss —, discard —, discharge- from one's -thoughts, — mind; drop the subject, think no more of; set —, turn —, put- aside; turn -away from, — one's attention from, — a deaf ear to, — one's back upon.

abstract oneself, dream, indulge in reverie.

escape -notice, — attention; come in at one ear and go out at the other; forget etc. (*have no remembrance*) 506.

call off —, draw off —, call away —, divert —, distract- the -attention, — thoughts, — mind; put out of one's head; dis-concert, -compose; put out, confuse, perplex, bewilder, fluster, muddle, dazzle; throw a sop to Cerberus.

Adj. inattentive; un-observant, -mindful, -heeding, -discerning; inadvertent; mind-, regard-, respect-less; listless etc. (*indifferent*) 866; blind, deaf; flighty, hand over head; cur-, percur-sory; giddy-, scatter-, hare-brained; unreflecting, *écervelé*, inconsiderate, off-hand, thoughtless, dizzy, muzzy, brainsick; giddy, — as a goose; wild, harum-scarum, ranipole, high-flying; heed-, care-less etc. (*neglectful*) 460.

absent, absent-minded, abstracted, *distrait*; lost; lost —, wrapped- in thought, woolgathering; rapt, in the clouds, bemused; dreaming —, musing- on other things; pre-occupied; engrossed etc. (*attentive*) 457; in a -reverie etc. *n.*; off one's guard etc. (*inexpectant*) 508; napping; dreamy.

disconcerted, put out etc. *v.*; rattled.

Adv. inattentively, inadvertently etc. *adj.*; *per incuriam, sub silentio.*

Int. stand -at ease, — easy!

Phr. the attention wanders; one's wits gone a -woolgathering — bird's nesting; it never entered into one's head; the mind running on other things; one's thoughts being elsewhere; had it been a bear it would have bitten you.

---

459. Care. [Vigilance.]—**N.** care, solicitude, heed; heedfulness etc. *adj.*; scruple etc. (*conscientiousness*) 939.

watchfulness etc. *adj.*; vigilance, *surveillance*, eyes of Argus, watch, vigil, look out, watch and ward, *l'oeil du maître.*

alertness etc. (*activity*) 682; attention etc. 457; prudence etc., circumspection etc. (*caution*) 864; forethought etc. 510; precaution etc. (*preparation*) 673; tidiness etc. (*order*) 58, (*cleanliness*) 652; accuracy etc. (*exactness*) 494; minuteness, attention to detail; meticulousness, nicety, circumstantiality.

V. be -careful etc. *adj.*; reck; take care etc. (*be cautious*) 864; pay attention to etc. 457; take care of; look —, see- -to, — after; keep -an eye, — a sharp eye- upon; keep -watch, — watch and ward; mount guard, set watch, watch; keep in -sight, — view; chaperon, play gooseberry; mind, — one's business.

look -sharp, — about one; look with one's own eyes; keep a -good, — sharp- look-out; have all one's -wits, — eyes- about one; watch for etc. (*ex-*

pect) 507; stand to; keep one's eyes —, have the eyes —, sleep with one eye- open.

take precautions etc. 673; protect etc. (*render safe*) 664.

do one's best etc. 682; mind one's Ps and Qs, speak by the card, pick one's steps.

Adj. care-, regard-, heed-ful; taking care etc. *v.*; particular; prudent etc. (*cautious*) 864; considerate; thoughtful etc. (*deliberative*) 451; provident etc. (*prepared*) 673; alert etc. (*active*) 682; sure-footed.

guarded, on one's guard; on the -qui vive, — alert, — watch, — look-out; awake, broad awake, vigilant; watch-, wake-, wist-ful; Argus-, lynx-eyed; wide awake etc. (*intelligent*) 498; on the watch for etc. (*expectant*) 507.

tidy etc. (*orderly*) 58, (*clean*) 652; accurate etc. (*exact*) 494; scrupulous etc. (*conscientious*) 939; *cavendo tutus* etc. (*safe*) 664.

Adv. carefully etc. *adj.*; with care, gingerly.

Phr. *quis custodiet ipsos custodes?*

---

460. Neglect.—N. neglect; carelessness etc. *adj.*; trifling etc. *v.*; negligence; omission, laches, default; remissness, slackness, procrastination; supineness etc. (*inactivity*) 683; inattention etc. 458; *nonchalance* etc. (*insensibility*) 823; improvidence, recklessness etc. 863; slovenliness etc. (*disorder*) 59; (*dirt*) 653; improvidence etc. 674; non-completion etc. 730; inexactness etc. (*error*) 495.

paraleipsis [in rhetoric].

trifler, slacker, waster, waiter on Providence; Micawber.

V. be -negligent etc. *adj.*; take no care of etc. (take care of etc. 459); neglect; let -slip, — go; lay —, set —, cast —, put- aside; keep —, leave- out of sight; lose sight of.

overlook, disregard; pass -over, — by; let pass; blink; wink —, connive- at; gloss over; take no -note, — notice, — thought, — account- of; pay no regard to; *laisser aller*; allow to lie on the table.

scamp; trifle, fribble; do by halves; skimp; cut; slight etc. (*despise*) 930; play —, trifle- with; slur; skim, — the surface; *effleurer*; take a cursory view of etc. 457.

slur —, slip —, skip —, jump- over; pretermit, miss, skip, jump, omit, give the go-by to, push aside, throw into the background, shelve, sink; ignore, shut one's eyes to, refuse to hear, turn a deaf ear to; leave out of one's calculation; not -attend to etc. 457, — mind; not trouble -oneself, — one's head- -with, — about; forget etc. 506; be caught napping etc. (*not expect*) 508; leave a loose thread; let the grass grow under one's feet.

render -neglectful etc. *adj.*; put —, throw- off one's guard.

Adj. neglecting etc. *v.*; unmindful, negligent, neglectful; heedless, careless, thoughtless; perfunctory, remiss, slack.

inconsiderate; un-, in-circumspect; off one's guard; un-wary, -watchful, -guarded; offhand.

supine etc. (*inactive*) 683; inattentive etc 458; *insouciant* etc. (*indifferent*) 823; imprudent, reckless etc. 863; slovenly etc. (*disorderly*) 59, (*dirty*) 653; inexact etc. (*erroneous*) 495; improvident etc. 674.

neglected etc. *v.*; un-heeded, -cared for, -

perceived, -seen, -observed, -noticed, -noted, -marked, -attended to, -thought of, -regarded, -remarked, -missed; shunted, shelved.

un-examined, -studied, -searched, -scanned, -weighed, -sifted, -explored.

Adv. negligently etc. *adj.*; hand over head, anyhow; in an unguarded moment etc. (*unexpectedly*) 508; *per incuriam*.

Int. never mind, no matter, let it pass; it will be all the same a hundred years hence.

461. Inquiry. [Subject of Inquiry. Question.]—**N.** inquiry; request etc. 765; search, research, quest; pursuit etc. 622.

examination, review, scrutiny, investigation, indagation; per-quisition, -scrutation, -vestigation; inqu-est, -isition; exploration; *exploitation*, ventilation.

sifting; calculation, analysis, dissection, resolution, induction; Baconian method.

strict –, close –, searching –, exhaustive- inquiry; narrow –, strict- search; study etc. (*consideration*) 451.

scire facias, ad referendum; trial.

questioning etc. *v.*; interroga-tion, -tory; third degree; interpellation; challenge, examination, cross-examination, catechism; feeler, Socratic method, zetetic philosophy; leading question; discussion etc. (*reasoning*) 476; questionnaire, questionary.

reconnoitering, *reconnaissance*; prying etc. *v.*; espionage, *espionnage*; domiciliary visit, peep behind the curtain; lantern of Diogenes.

question, query, problem, *desideratum*, point to be solved, porism; subject –, field- of -inquiry, – controversy; point –, matter- in dispute; moot-point; issue, question at issue; bone of contention etc. (*discord*) 713; plain –, fair –, open- question; enigma etc. (*secret*) 533; knotty point etc. (*difficulty*) 704; *quod-libet*; threshold of an inquiry.

inquirer, investigator, experimenter, inquisitor, inspector, querist, examiner, catechist; scrut-ator, -ineer; analyst; quidnunc etc. (*curiosity*) 455.

V. make -inquiry etc. *n.*; inquire, seek, search, frisk, speer, look -for, – about for, – out for; scan, reconnoiter, explore, sound, rummage, ransack, pry, peer, look round; look –, go- -over, – through; spy, over-haul.

scratch the head, slap the forehead.

look –, peer –, pry- into every hole and corner; look behind the scenes; trace up; hunt –, fish –, dig –, ferret- out; unearth; leave no stone unturned.

seek a -clue, – clew; hunt, track, trail, shadow, mouse, dodge, trace; follow the -trail, – scent; pursue etc. 622; beat up one's quarters; fish for; feel for etc. (*experiment*) 463.

investigate; take up –, institute –, pursue –, follow up –, conduct –, carry on –, prosecute- -an inquiry etc. *n.*; look -at, – into; pre-examine; discuss, canvass, agitate.

examine, study, consider, calculate; dip –, dive –, delve –, go deep- into; make sure of, probe, sound, fathom; probe to the -bottom, – quick; scrutinize, analyze, anatomize, dissect, parse, resolve, sift, winnow; view –, try- in all its phases; thresh out.

bring in question, subject to examination; put to

the proof etc. (*experiment*) 463; audit, tax, pass in review; take into consideration etc. (*think over*) 451; take counsel etc. 695.

ask, question, demand; put –, pop –, propose –, propound –, moot –, start –, raise –, stir –, suggest –, put forth –, ventilate –, grapple with –, go into- a question.

put to the question, interrogate, catechize, pump, grill; cross-question, -examine; dodge; require an answer; pick –, suck- the brains of; feel the pulse.

be -in question etc. *adj.*; undergo examination.

Adj. inquiry etc. *v.*; inquisitive etc. (*curious*) 455; requisit-ive, -ory; catechetical, inquisitorial, analytic; in -search, – quest- of; on the look-out for, interrogative, zetetic; all-searching.

un-determined, -tried, -decided; in -question, – dispute, – issue, – course of inquiry; under - discussion, – consideration, – investigation etc. *n.*, *sub judice*, moot, proposed; doubtful etc. (*uncertain*) 475.

Adv. what? why? wherefore? whence? whither? where? *quaere*? how -comes, – happens, – is- it? what is the reason? what's -the matter, – up, in the wind? what on earth? when? who?

462. Answer.—N. answer, response, reply, replication, *riposte*, rejoinder, surrejoinder, rebutter, surrebutter, counter-evidence etc. 468, counter-charge, defence, plea; retort, repartee; contradiction etc. 536; rescript, -ion; antiphon, -y; acknowledgment; password; echo.

discovery etc. 480*a*; solution etc. (*explanation*) 522; rationale etc. (*cause*) 153; clue etc. (*indication*) 550.

Oedipus; oracle, etc. 513; return etc. (*record*) 551.

V. answer, respond, reply, rebut, retort, rejoin; give –, return for- answer; acknowledge, echo.

explain etc. (*interpret*) 522; solve etc. (*unriddle*) 522; discover etc. 480*a*; fathom, hunt out etc. (*inquire*) 461; satisfy, set at rest, determine.

Adj. answering etc. *v.*; respon-sive, -dent; oracular; antiphonal; conclusive.

Adv. because etc. (*cause*) 153; on the -scent, – right scent.

Int. *eureka!*

463. Experiment.—N. experiment; essay etc. (*attempt*) 675; research etc. (*investigation*) 461; trial, tentative method, *tâtonnement*.

verification, probation, *experimentum crucis*, proof, criterion, diagnostic test, tryout, crucial test, acid test.

crucible, reagent, check, touchstone, pix; assay, ordeal; ring.

empiricism, rule of thumb.

feeler; pilot –, messenger- balloon, *ballon d'essai*; pilot engine; scout; straw to show the wind.

speculation, random shot, leap in the dark.

analy-zer, -st; adventurer, explorer, sourdough, prospector; experiment-er, -ist, -alist; assayer.

V. experiment; essay etc. (*endeavor*) 675; try, assay, sample; make -an experiment, – trial of; give a trial to; put upon –, subject to- trial; experiment upon; rehearse; put –, bring –, submitto the -test, — proof; prove, verify, test, touch, practise upon, try one's strength.

grope; feel —, grope- -for, — one's way; fumble; *tâtonner, aller à tâtons*; put —, throw- out a feeler; send up a pilot balloon; see how the -land lies, — wind blows; consult the barometer; feel the pulse; fish —, bob- for; cast —, beat- about for; angle, trawl, cast one's net, beat the bushes.

venture, try one's fortune etc. (*adventure*) 675; explore etc. (*inquire*) 461.

Adj. experimental; probat-ive, ory, -ionary; analytic, docimastic; tentative; empirical]; speculative, tentive.

under probation, on one's trial, on trial, on approval.

464. Comparison.—N. comparison, collation, contrast; identification.

sim-ile, -ilitude; allegory etc. (*metaphor*) 521.

V. compare -to, — with; collate, confront; place side by side etc. (*near*) 197; set —, pit- against one another; contrast balance.

identify, draw a parallel, parallel.

compare notes; institute a comparison; *parva componere magnis*.

Adj. comparative, relative; metaphorical etc. 521.

compared with etc. *v.*; comparable.

Adv. relatively etc. (*relation*) 9; as compared with etc. *v.*

465. Discrimination.—N. discrimination, distinction, differentiation, diagnosis, diorism; nice perception; perception —, appreciation- of difference; acuteness; estimation etc. 466; nicety, refinement; taste etc. 850; *critique*, judgement, tact; insight, discernment etc. (*intelligence*) 498; nuances.

V. discriminate, distinguish, differentiate, severalize; separate; draw the line, sift; separate —, winnow- the chaff from the wheat; split hairs.

estimate etc. (*measure*) 466; know -which is which, — one's stuff, — one's way about, — what is what, — 'a hawk from a handsaw.'

take into -account, — consideration; give —, allow- due weight to; weigh carefully.

Adj. discriminating etc. *v.*; dioristic, discriminative, critical, distinctive; nice.

Phr. *il y a fagots et fagots*; *rem acu tetigisti*.

465a. Indiscrimination.—N. indiscrimination; promiscuity; indistinctness, -ion; uncertainty etc. (*doubt*) 475; obtuseness.

V. not -indiscriminate etc. 465; overlook etc.' (*neglect*) 460- a distinction; con-found, -fuse, jumble; swallow whole.

Adj. indiscriminate, undiscriminating, promiscuous; undistinguish-ed, -able, -ing; unmeasured.

466. Measurement.—N. measurement, ad-measurement, mensuration, survey, valuation, ap-

praisment, assessment, assize; estim-ate, -ation; dead reckoning; reckoning etc. (*numeration*) 85; gauging etc. *v.*

metrology, weights and measures, compound arithmetic.

measure, yard measure, standard, rule, foot-rule, chain, tape, staff, compass, callipers; dividers; gage, gauge, planimeter; meter, line, rod, check.

volt, kilowatt, ampere, candle power; horse power; axle load; foot pound.

flood —, high water- mark; Plimsoll mark; index etc. 550.

scale; gradu-ation, -ated scale; nonius; vernier etc. (*minuteness*) 193; pedo (*length*)- 200, sounding line etc. (*depth*) 208, thermo (*heat* etc. 398)-, baro (*air* etc. 338)-, dynamo (*power*)- 276, anemo (*wind* 349)-, gonio (*angle* 244)- meter; landmark etc. (*limit*) 233; balance etc. (*weight*) 310; optical instruments etc. 445.

co-ordinates, ordinate and abscissa, polar coordinates, latitude and longitude, declination and right ascension, altitude and azimuth.

geo-, stereo-, hypso-metry; metage; surveying, land surveying; geo-desy, -detics, -desia; ortho-, alti-metry; *cadastre*.

astrolabe, armillary sphere.

land, -surveyor; geometer, topographer, cartographer, hydrographer.

V. measure, meter, mete; value, assess, rate, appraise, estimate, form as estimate, set a value on; appreciate; standardize.

span, pace, step; apply the -compass etc. *n.*; gauge, plumb, probe, calliper, sound, fathom etc. 208; heave the -log, — lead; weigh etc. 319; survey.

take an average etc. 29; graduate.

Adj. measuring etc. *v.*; metric, -al; measurable; geodetical, cadastral, topographical.

467. Evidence. [on one side]**—N.** evidence; facts, premises, *data, praecognita*, grounds.

indication etc. 550; criterion etc. (*test*) 463.

testi-mony, -fication; attestation; deposition etc. (*affirmation*) 535; examination.

admission etc. (*assent*) 488; authority, warrant, credential, diploma, voucher, certificate, docket; record etc. 551; document, muniments; *pièce justificative*; deed, warranty etc. (*security*) 771; signature, seal etc. (*identification*) 550; exhibit, citation, reference.

witness, indicator; eye-, ear-witness; deponent; sponsor.

oral —, documentary —, hearsay —, external —, extrinsic —, internal —, intrinsic —, circumstantial —, cumulative —, *ex parte* —, presumptive —, collateral —, constructive- evidence; proof etc. (*demonstration*) 478; evidence in chief; finger prints, dactylogram.

secondary evidence; confirmation, corroboration, adminicle, support; ratification etc. (*assent*) 488; authentication, verification; compurgation, wager of law, comprobation.

citation, reference.

V. be -evidence etc. *n.*; evince, show, betoken, tell of; indicate etc. (*denote*) 550; imply, involve, argue, bespeak, breathe.

have —, carry- weight; tell, speak volumes; speak for itself etc. (*manifest*) 525.

rest –, depend- upon; repose on.

bear -witness etc. *n.*; give -evidence etc. *n.*; testify, depose, witness, vouch for; sign, seal, undersign, set one's hand and seal, sign and seal, deliver as one's act and deed, certify, attest; acknowledge etc. (*assent*) 488.

make absolute, confirm, ratify, corroborate, endorse, countersign, support, bear out, vindicate, uphold, warrant.

adduce, attest, cite, quote; refer –, appeal- to; call, – to witness; bring -forward, – into court; allege, plead; produce –, confront- witnesses; collect –, bring together –, rake up- evidence.

have –, make out- a case; establish, circumstantiate, authenticate, substantiate, verify, make good, quote chapter and verse; bring -home to, – to book.

Adj. showing etc. *v.*; evidential, indica-tive, -tory; deducible etc. 478; grounded –, founded –, based- on; first hand, authentic, verifiable; corroborative, confirmatory; significant, conclusive.

Adv. by inference; according to, witness, *a fortiori*; still -more, – less; *raison de plus*; in corroboration etc. *n.* of; *valeat quantum*; under -seal, – one's hand and seal.

468. Counter-evidence. [Evidence on the other side, on the other hand.]—**N.** counter-evidence; evidence on the other -side, – hand; disproof; refutation etc. 479; negation etc. 536, conflicting evidence.

plea etc. 617; vindication etc. 937; counter-protest; *tu quoque* argument; other side –, reverse-of the shield.

V. countervail, oppose; run counter; rebut etc. (*refute*) 479; subvert etc. (*destroy*) 162; check, weaken; contravene; contradict etc. (*deny*) 536; tell another story, turn the -tables, – scale; alter the case; cut both ways; prove a negative.

audire alteram partem.

Adj. countervailing etc. *v.*; contradictory, in rebuttal.

un-attested, -authenticated, -supported by evidence; supposititious, trumped up.

Adv. *per contra*, conversely, on the other hand.

469. Qualification.—**N.** qualification, limitation, modification, coloring.

allowance, grains of allowance, consideration, extenuating circumstances.

condition, proviso, exception; exemption; salvo, saving clause; discount etc. 813.

V. qualify, limit, modify, affect, temper, leaven, give a color to, introduce new conditions.

allow –, make allowance- for; admit exceptions, take into account.

take exception, object.

Adj. qualifying etc. *v.*; conditional; extenuatory; exceptional etc. (*unconformable*) 83.

hypothetical etc. (*supposed*) 514; contingent etc. (*uncertain*) 475.

Adv. provided, – always; if, unless, but, yet; according as; conditionally, admitting, supposing; on the supposition of etc. (*theoretically*) 514; with the understanding, even, although, though, for all that, after all, at all events.

with grains of allowance, *cum grano salis*; *exceptis excipiendis*; wind and weather permitting; if possible etc. 470.

subject to; with this -proviso etc. *n.*

470. Possibility.—**N.** possibility, potentiality; what -may be, – is possible etc. *adj.*; compatibility etc. (*agreement*) 23.

practicability, feasibility; practicableness etc. *adj.*

contingency, chance etc. 156.

V. be -possible etc. *adj.*; stand a chance, have a leg to stand on; admit of, bear.

render -possible etc. *adj.*; put in the way of.

Adj. possible; on the -cards, – dice; *in posse*, within the bounds of possibility, conceivable, credible, imaginable; compatible etc. 23.

practicable, feasible, workable, performable, achievable; within -reach, – measurable distance; accessible, superable, surmountable; at-, obtainable; contingent etc. (*doubtful*) 475.

Adv. possibly, by possibility; perhaps, -chance, -adventure; may be, haply, mayhap.

if possible, wind and weather permitting, God willing, *Deo volente*, D.V.

471. Impossibility.—**N.** impossibility etc. *adj.*; what -cannot, – can never- be; sour grapes; infeasibility, impracticability, hopelessness etc. 859.

V. be -impossible etc. *adj.*; have no chance whatever.

attempt impossibilities; square the circle; discover the -philosopher's stone – elixir of life, – secret of perpetual motion; wash a blackamoor white; skin a flint; make -a silk purse out of a sow's ear, – bricks without straw; have nothing to go upon; weave a rope of sand, build castles in the air, *prendre la lune avec les dents*, extract sunbeams from cucumbers, set the Thames on fire, milk a he-goat into a sieve, catch a weasel asleep, *rompre l'anguille au genou*, be in two places at once.

Adj. impossible; not -possible etc. 470; absurd, contrary to reason; unlikely, at variance with facts; unreasonable etc. 477; incredible etc. 485; beyond the bounds of -reason, – possibility; from which reason recoils; visionary; inconceivable etc. (*improbable*) 473; prodigious etc. (*wonderful*) 870; un-, in-imaginable, unthinkable, not a Chinaman's chance.

impracticable, unachievable; un-, in-feasible; insuperable; un-, in-surmountable; unat-, unobtainable; out of -reach, – the question; not to be -had, – thought of; beyond control; desperate etc. (*hopeless*) 859; incompatible etc. 24; inaccessible, uncomeatable, impassable, impervious, innavigable, inextricable.

out of –, beyond- one's -power, – depth, – reach, – grasp; too much for; *ultra crepidam*.

Phr. the grapes are sour; *non possumus*; *non nostrum tantas componere lites*.

472. Probability.—**N.** probability, likelihood; likeliness etc. *adj.*

vraisemblance, verisimilitude, plausibility;

color, semblance, show of; presumption; presumptive –, circumstantial- evidence; credibility.

reasonable –, fair –, good –, favorable- -chance, – prospect; prospect, well-grounded hope; chance etc. 156.

V. be -probable etc. *adj.*; give –, lend- color to; point to; imply etc. (*evidence*) 467; bid fair etc. (*promise*) 511; stand fair for; stand –, run- a good chance.

presume, infer, suppose, take for granted.

think likely, dare say, flatter oneself; expect etc. 507; count upon etc. (*believe*) 484.

Adj. probable, likely, hopeful, to be expected, in a fair way.

plausible, specious, ostensible, colorable, *ben trovato*, well-founded, reasonable, credible, easy of belief, presumable, presumptive, apparent.

Adv. probably etc. *adj.*; belike; in all - probability, – likelihood; very –, most- likely; as likely as not; like enough; ten etc. to one; apparently, seemingly, according to every reasonable expectation; *primâ facie*; to all appearance etc. (*to the eye*) 448.

Phr. the -chances, – odds- are; appearances –, chances- are in favor of; there is reason to -believe, – think, – expect; I dare say; all Lombard Street to a China orange.

473. Improbability.—N. improbability, unlikelihood; unfavorable –, bad –, little –, small –, poor –, scarcely any –, no –, not a ghost of a-chance; bare possibility; long odds; incredibility etc. 485.

V. be -improbable etc. *adj.*; have a -small chance etc. *n.*

Adj. improbable, unlikely, contrary to all reasonable expectation, implausible.

rare etc. (*infrequent*) 137; unheard of, inconceivable; un-, in-imaginable; incredible etc. 485; more than doubtful.

Int. not likely! no fear!

Phr. the chances are against.

474. Certainty.—N. certainty; necessity etc. 601; certitude, certainness, surety, assurance, sureness; dead –, moral- certainty; infallibleness etc. *adj.*; infallibility, reliability.

gospel, scripture, church, pope, court of final appeal; *res judicata, ultimatum.*

positiveness; dogmat-ism, -ist, -izer; *doctrinaire,* know-all, bigot, -ry; opinionist, Sir Oracle; *ipse dixit*; zealot.

fact; positive –, matter of- fact; *fait accompli.*

V. be -certain etc. *adj.*; stand to reason.

render -certain etc. *adj.*; in-, en-, as-sure; clinch, make sure; determine, decide, set at rest, 'make assurance double sure;' know etc. (*believe*) 484; dismiss all doubt.

dogmatize, lay down the law.

Adj. certain, sure; assured etc. *v.*; solid, well-founded.

unqualified, absolute, positive, determinate, definite, clear, unequivocal, categorical, unmistakable, decisive, decided, ascertained.

inevitable, unavoidable, ineluctable, avoidless,

unerring, infallible; unchangeable etc. 150; to be depended on, trustworthy, reliable, bound.

un-impeachable, -deniable, -questionable; indisputable, -contestable, -controvertible, - defeasible, -dubitable; irrefutable etc. (*proven*) 478; conclusive, without power of appeal, final.

indubious; without –, beyond a –, without a shade or shadow or- -doubt – question; past dispute; beyond all -question, – dispute; undoubted, -contested, -questioned, -disputed; question-, dount-less.

bigoted, fanatical, dogmatic, opinionat-ed, -ive, *doctrinaire.*

authoritative, authentic; official.

sure as -fate, – death and taxes, – a gun.

evident, self-evident, axiomatic; clear, – as day, – as the sun at noonday; obvious.

Adv. certainly etc. *adj.*; for certain, certes, sure, no doubt, doubtless, and no mistake, *flagrante delicto*, sure enough, to be sure, of course, as a matter of course, *à coup sur*, to a certainty, undoubtedly; in truth etc. (*truly*) 494; at -any rate, – all events; without fail; *coûte que coûte*; whatever may happen, if the worst come to the worst; come –, happen- what -may, – will; sink or swim; rain or shine.

Phr. *cela va sans dire*; there is -no question, – not a shadow of doubt; the die is cast etc. (*necessity*) 601.

475. Uncertainty.—N. uncertainty, incertitude, doubt; doubtfulness etc. *adj.*; dubi-ety, -tation, -tancy, -ousness.

hesitation, suspense; perplexity, embarrassment, dilemma, quandary, Morton's fork, bewilderment; timidity etc. (*fear*) 860; indecision, vacillation etc. 605; *diaporesis*, indetermination.

vagueness etc. *adj.*; haze, fog; obscurity etc. (*darkness*) 421; ambiguity etc. (*double meaning*) 520; contingency, double contingency, possibility upon a possibility; conjecture; open question etc. (*question*) 461; *onus probandi*; blind bargain, pig in a poke, leap in the dark, something or other; needle in a bottle of hay; roving commission.

fallibility, unreliability, untrustworthiness, precariousness.

V. be -uncertain etc. *adj.*; wonder whether.

lose the -clue, – clew, – scent; miss one's way.

not know -what to make of etc. (*unintelligibility*) 519, – which way to turn, – whether one stands on one's head or one's heels; float in a sea of doubt, hesitate, flounder; lose -oneself, – one's head, – one's way, wander aimlessly; muddle one's brains.

render -uncertain etc. *adj.*; put out, pose, puzzle, perplex, embarrass; confuse, -found; bewilder, mystify, bother, nonplus, addle the wits, throw off the scent; *ambiguas in vulgus spargere voces*; keep in suspense.

doubt etc. (*disbelieve*) 485; hang –, tremble- in the balance; depend.

Adj. uncertain; casual; random etc. (*aimless*) 621; changeable etc. 149.

doubtful, dubious; indecisive; unsettled, -decided, -determined; in suspense, open to discussion; controvertible; in question etc. (*inquiry*) 461; insecure, unstable.

vague; in-determinate, -definite; ambiguous, equivocal; undefin-ed, -able; confused etc. (*indistinct*) 447; mystic, mysterious, veiled, obscure, cryptic, oracular.

perplexing etc. *v.*; enigmatic, paradoxical; apocryphal, problematical, hypothetical; experimental etc. 463.

fallible, questionable, precarious, slippery, ticklish, debatable, disputable; un-reliable, -trustworthy.

contingent, — on, dependent on; subject to; dependent on circumstances; occasional; provisional.

unauth-entic, -enticated, -oritative; un-ascertained, -confirmed; undemonstrated; un-told, -counted.

in a -state of uncertainty, — cloud, — maze; ignorant etc. 491; on the horns of a dilemma; afraid to say; out of one's reckoning, astray, adrift; as -sea, — fault, — a loss, — one's wit's end, — a *nonplus*; puzzled etc. *v.*; lost abroad, *désorienté*; dis-tracted, -traught.

Adv. *pendente lite*; *sub spe rati*.

Phr. Heaven knows; who can tell? who shall decide when doctors disagree?

476. Reasoning.—N. reasoning; ratio-cination, -nalism; dialectics, induction, generalization.

discussion, comment; ventilation; inquiry etc. 461.

argumentation, controversy, debate; polemics, wrangling; contention etc. 720; logomachy; disputation, -ceptation; paper war.

art of reasoning, logic.

process —, train —, chain- of reasoning; de-, induction; systhesis, analysis.

argument; case, plea, *plaidoyer*, opening; *lemma*, proposition, terms, premises, postulate, *data*, starting point, principle; inference etc. (*judgment*) 480.

pro-, syllogism; enthymeme, sorites, dilemma, *perilepsis*, *a priori* reasoning, *reductio ad absurdum*, horns of a dilemma, *argumentum ad hominem*, comprehensive argument.

reasoner, logician, dialectician; disputant; controver-sialist, -tist; wrangler, arguer, debater, polemic, casuist, rationalist; scientist.

logical sequence; good case; correct —, just —, sound —, valid —, cogent —, logical —, forcible —, persuasive —, persuasory —, consectary —, conclusive etc. 478 —, subtle- reasoning; force of argument; strong -point, — argument.

arguments, reasons, pros and cons.

V. reason, argue, discuss, debate, dispute, wrangle; bandy -words, — arguments; chop logic; hold —, carry on- an argument; controvert etc. (*deny*) 536; canvass; comment —, moralize-upon; consider etc. (*examine*) 461.

open a -discussion, — case; join —, be at- issue; moot; come to the point; stir —, agitate —, ventilate —, torture- a question; try conclusions; take up a -side, — case.

contend, take one's stand upon, insist, lay stress on; infer etc. 480.

follow from etc. (*demonstration*) 478.

Adj. rational; reasoning etc. *v.*; rationalistic; argumentative, controversial, dialectic, polemical; discurs-ory, -ive; disputations.

debatable, controvertible.

logical; in-, de-ductive; synthetic, analytic; relevant etc. 23.

Adv. for, because, hence, whence, seeing that, since, sith, then, thence, so; for -that, — this, — which- reason; for-, inasmuch as; whereas, *ex concesso*, considering, in consideration of; there-, where-fore; consequently, *ergo*, thus, accordingly; *a fortiori*.

in -conclusion, — fine; finally, after all, *au bout du compte*, on the whole, taking one thing with another.

rationally etc. *adj.*

477. Sophistry. [The absence of reasoning.] **Intuition.** [False or vicious reasoning; show of reason.]—**N.** intuition, instinct, association; presentiment; rule of thumb.

sophistry, paralogy, perversion, casuistry, jesuitry, equivocation, evasion, mental reservation; chicane, -ry; quiddit, quiddity; mystification; special pleading; speciousness etc. *adj.*; nonsense etc. 497; word-, tongue-fence.

false —, vicious- reasoning; *petitio principii*, *ignoratio elenchi*; *post hoc ergo propter hoc*; *non sequitur*, *ignotum per ignotius*.

misjudgment etc. 481; false teaching etc. 538.

sophism, solecism, paralogism; quibble, quirk, *elenchus*, elench, fallacy, *quodlibet*, subtertuge, subtlety, quillet, inconsistency, antilogy; 'a mockery, a delusion and a snare;' claptrap, mere words; 'lame and impotent conclusion.'

meshes —, cobwebs- of sophistry; flaw in an argument; weak point, bad case.

over-refinement; hair-splitting etc. *v.*

sophist, casuist, paralogist.

V. judge -intuitively, — by intuition; hazard a proposition, talk at random.

reason -ill, — falsely etc. *adj.*; paralogize; misjudge etc. 481.

pervert, quibble; equivocate, mystify, evade, elude; gloss over, varnish; misteach etc. 538; mislead etc. (*error*) 495; cavil, refine, subtilize, split hairs; misrepresent etc. (*lie*) 544.

beg the question, reason in a circle, cut blocks with a razor, beat about the bush, play fast and loose, blow hot and cold, prove that black is white and white black, travel out of the record, *parler à tort et à travers*, put oneself out of court, not have a leg to stand on.

Adj. intuitive, instinctive, impulsive; independent of —, anterior to- reason; gratuitous; hazarded; unconnected.

unreasonable, illogical, false, unsound, invalid; unwarranted, not following; inconsequent, -ial; inconsistent, incongruous; abson-ous, -ant; un-scientific; untenable, inconclusive, incorrect; fall-acious, -ible; groundless, unproved.

deceptive, sophistical, sophisticated, casuistical, jesuitical; illus-ive, -ory; specious, hollow, plausible, *ad captandum*, evasive; irrelevant etc. 10.

weak, feeble, poor, flimsy, loose, vague, irrational; nonsensical etc. (*absurd*) 497; foolish etc. (*imbecile*) 499; frivolous, pettifogging, quibbling; finespun, over-refined.

at the end of one's tether, *au bout de son latin*.

Adv. intuitively etc. *adj.*; by intuition; illogically etc. *adj.*

Phr. *non constat*; that goes for nothing.

478. Demonstration.—N. demonstration, proof; conclusiveness etc. *adj.*; *apodixis*, probation, comprobation.

logic of facts etc. (*evidence*) 467; *experimentum curcis* etc. (*test*) 463; argument etc. 476; irrefragability.

V. demonstrate, prove, establish, make good; show; evince etc. (*be evidence of*) 467; verify etc. 467; settle the question, reduce to demonstration, set the question at rest.

make out, — a case; prove one's point, have the best of the argument; draw a conclusion etc. (*judge*) 480.

follow, — of course; stand to reason; hold -good, — water.

Adj. demonstra-ting etc. *v.*, -tive, -ble; probative, unanswerable, conclusive; apodictic, -al; irre-sistible, -futable, -fragable, undeniable.

categorical, decisive, crucial.

demonstrated etc. *v.*; proven; unconfuted, -answered, -refuted; evident etc. 474.

deducible, consequential, consectary, inferential, following.

Adv. of course, in consequence, consequently, as a matter of course.

Phr. *probatum est*; there is nothing more to be said, Q.E.D., it must follow.

479. Confutation.—N. con-, re-futation; answer, complete answer; disproof, conviction, redargution, invalidation; expos-ure, -ition; clincher; retort; *reductio ad absurdum*; knock down — , *tu quoque-* argument.

V. con-, re-fute; parry, negative, disprove, redargue, expose, show the fallacy of, rebut, defeat; demolish etc. (*destroy*) 162; over-throw, -turn; scatter to the winds, explode, invalidate; silence; put —, reduce- to silence; clinch -an argument, — a question; give one a set down, stop the mouth, shut up; have, — on the hip; get the better of; confound, convince.

not leave a leg to stand on, cut the ground from under one's feet.

be confuted etc.; fail; expose —, show- one's weak point.

Adj. confut-ing, -ed etc. *v.*; capable of refutation; re-, con-futable.

condemned -on one's own showing, — out of one's own mouth.

Phr. the argument falls to the ground, *cadit quaestio*, it does not hold water, `suo sibi gladio hunc jugulo.`

480. Judgment. [Conclusion. **]—N.** result, conclusion, upshot; deduction, inference, ergotism, illation; corollary, porism; moral.

estimation, valuation, appreciation, judication; di-, ad-judication; arbitr- ament, -ement, -ation; assessment, ponderation.

award, estimate; review, criticism, *critique*, notice, report.

decision, determination, judgment, finding, verdict, sentence, decree, — nisi, — absolute, — interlocutory; dictum; *res judicata*.

plébiscite, referendum, voice, casting vote; vote etc. (*choice*) 609; opinion etc. (*belief*) 484; good judgment etc. (*wisdom*) 498.

judge, jurist, umpire; arbi-ter, -trator; assessor, referee; censor, reviewer, critic; *connoisseur*; commentator etc. 524; inspector, inspecting officer.

V. judge, conclude; come to —, draw — , arrive at- a conclusion; ascertain, determine, make up one's mind.

deduce, derive, gather, collect, draw an inference, make a deduction, weet, ween.

form an estimate, estimate, size up; appreciate, value, count, assess, rate, rank, account; regard, consider, think of; look upon etc. (*believe*) 484.

settle; pass —, give- an opinion; decide, try, pronounce, rule; pass -judgment, — sentence; sentence, doom; find; give —, deliver- judgment; ad-jud-ge, -icate; arbitrate, award, report; bring in a verdict; make absolute, set a question ar rest; confirm etc. (*assent*) 488.

comment, criticize; review, pass under review etc. (*examine*) 457; investigate etc. (*inquire*) 461.

hold the scales, sit in judgment; try —, hear- a cause.

Adj. judging etc. *v.*; judicious etc. (*wise*) 498; determinate, conclusive, censorious, critical etc. 932.

Adv. on the whole, all things considered.

480a. Discovery. [Result of search or inquiry. **]—N.** discovery, invention, detection, disenchantment, disclosure, find, ascertainment, revelation.

trover etc. 775.

V. discover, find, determine, evolve; fix upon; find —, trace —, make —, hunt —, fish —, worm —, ferret —, root-out; fathom; bring —, draw-out; educe, elicit, bring to light, invent; dig —, grub —, fish- up; unearth, disinter.

solve, resolve; un-riddle, -ravel, -lock; pick —, open- the lock; find a -clue, — clew- to; interpret etc. 522; disclose etc. 529.

trace, get at; hit it, have it; lay one's -finger, — hands- upon; spot; get —, arrive- at the -turth etc. 494; put the saddle on the right horse, hit the right nail on the head.

be near the truth, burn; smoke, scent, sniff, smell a rat.

open the eyes to; see -through, — daylight, — in its true colors, — the cloven foot; detect; catch, — tripping.

pitch —, fall —, light —, hit —, stumble —, pop- upon; come across; meet —, fall in- with.

recognize, realize, verify, make certain of, identify.

Int. *eureka!*

481. Misjudgment.—N. misjudgment, obliquity of —, warped- judgment; mis-calculation, -computation, -conception etc. (*error*) 495; hasty conclusion.

prejud-gment, -ication, -ice; foregone conclusion; pre-notion, -vention, -conception, -dilection, -possession, -apprehension, -sumption, -sentiment; fixed –, preconceived- idea; *idée fixe*; *mentis gratissimus error*; fool's paradise.

esprit de corps, party spirit, race –, class-prejudice, partisanship, clannishness, *prestige*.

bias, warp, twist; hobby, fad, whim, *craze*, quirk, crotchet, partiality, infatuation, blind side, mote in the eye.

one-sided –, partial –, narrow –, confined –, superficial- –views, – ideas,– conceptions, – notions; narrow mind; bigotry etc. (*obstinacy*) 606; *odium theologicum*; pedantry; hypercriticism. *doctrinaire* etc. (*positive*) 474.

V. mis-judge, -estimate, -think, -conjecture, -conceive etc. (*error*) 495; fly in the face of facts; mis-calculate, -reckon, -compute.

overestimate etc. 482; underestimate etc. 483.

pre-, fore-judge; pre-suppose, -sume, -judicate; dogmatize; have a -bias etc. *n*.; have only one idea; *jurare in verba magistri*, run away with the notion; jump –, rush- to a conclusion; look only at one side of the shield; view -with jaundiced eye, – through distorting spectacles; not see beyond one's nose; *dare pondus fumo*; get the wrong sow by the ear etc. (*blunder*) 699.

give a -bias, – twist; bias, warp, twist; pre-judice, -possess.

Adj. misjudging etc. *v.*; ill-judging, wrong-headed; prejudiced, prejudicial, etc. *v.*; jaundiced; short-sighted, pur-blind; partial, one-sided, super-ficial.

narrow-minded; confined, insular, provincial, parochial, illiberal, intolerant, narrow, besotted, infatuated, fanatical, cracked, warped, *entêté*, positive, dogmatic, dictatorial; conceited; opin-, opini-ative; opinion-ed, -ate, -ative, -ated; self-opinioned, wedded to an opinion, *opinâtre*; bigoted etc. (*obstinate*) 606; crotchety, fussy, impracticable; unreason-able, -ing; stupid etc. 499; credulous etc. 486.

misjudged etc. *v.*

Adv. *ex parte*.

Phr. nothing like leather; the wish the father to the thought.

482. Overestimation.—N. overestimation etc. *v.*; exaggeration etc. 549; vanity etc. 880; optim-, pessim-ism, -ist; megalomania.

much -cry and little wool, – ado about nothing; storm in a teacup; fine talking, rodomontade, gush, hot air, gas, bombast.

egotism etc. 880; boasting etc. 884.

V. over-estimate, -rate, -value, -prize, -weigh, -reckon, -strain, -praise; estimate too highly, attach too much importance to, make mountains of molehills, catch at straws; strain, magnify; exaggerate etc. 549; set too high a value upon; think –, make- -much, – too much- of; outreckon.

extol, – to the skies; make the -most, – best, – worst- of, eulogize, panegyrize, gush, puff, boost; make two bites of a cherry.

have too high an opinion of oneself etc. (*vanity*) 880.

Adj. overestimated etc. *v.*; oversensitive etc.

(*sensibility*) 822; inflated, puffed up, exaggerated etc. 549.

Phr. all his geese are swans; *parturiunt montes*.

483. Underestimation.—N. underestimation; depreciation etc. (*detraction*) 934; pessim-ism, -ist; undervaluing etc. *v.*; modesty etc. 881.

V. under-rate, -estimate, -value, -reckon; depreciate; disparage etc. (*detract*) 934; not do justice to; mis-, dis-prize; ridicule etc. 856; slight etc. (*despise*) 930; neglect etc. 460; slur over, under-state.

make -light, – little, – nothing, – no account- of; minimize, belittle, run down, think nothing of; set -no store by, – at naught; shake off as dewdrops from the lion's mane.

Adj. depreciat-ing, -ed, -ive, -ory, etc. *v.*; unappreciated, -valued, -prized; pejorative.

484. Belief.—N. belief; credence; credit; assurance; faith, trust, troth, confidence, presumption, sanguine expectation etc. (*hope*) 858; dependence on, reliance on.

persuasion, conviction, convincement, plerophory, self-conviction; certainty etc. 474; opinion, mind, view; conception, thinking; impression etc. (*idea*) 453; surmise etc. 514; conclusion etc. (*judgment*) 480.

tenet, dogma, principle, way of thinking; popular belief etc. (*assent*) 488.

firm –, implicit –, settled –, fixed –, rooted –, deep-rooted –, staunch –, unshaken –, steadfast –, inveterate –, calm –, sober –, dispassionate –, impartial –, well-founded- -belief, – opinion etc.; *uberrima fides*.

system of opinions, school, doctrine, articles, canons; declaration –, profession- of faith; tenets, *credenda*, creed; thirty-nine articles etc. (*orthodoxy*) 983a; catechism; assent etc. 488; *propaganda* etc. (*teaching*) 537.

credibility etc. (*probability*) 472.

V. believe, credit; give -faith, – credit, – credence- to; see, realize; assume, receive; set down –, take- for; have –, take- it; consider, esteem, presume.

count –, depend –, calculate –, pin one's faith –, reckon –, lean –, build –, rely –, rest- upon; lay one's account for; make sure of.

make oneself easy -about, – on that score; take on -trust, – credit; take for -granted, – -gospel; allow –, attach- some weight to.

know, – for certain; have –, make- no doubt; doubt not; be – rest- -assured etc. *adj.*; persuade –, assure –, satisfy- oneself; make up one's mind.

give one credit for; confide –, believe –, put one's trust- in; place –, repose- implicit confidence in; take -one's word for, – at one's word; place reliance on, rely upon, swear by, regard to.

think, hold; take, – it; opine, be of opinion, conceive, trow, ween, fancy, apprehend; have –, hold –, possess –, entertain –, adopt –, imbibe –, embrace –, get hold of –, hazard –, foster –, nurture –, cherish- -a belief, – an opinion etc. *n*.

view –, consider –, take –, hold –, conceive –, regard –, esteem –, deem –, look upon –, account –, set down- as; surmise etc. 514.

get −, take- it into one's head; come round to an opinion; swallow etc. (*credulity*) 486.

cause to -be believed etc. *v.*; satisfy, persuade, have the ear of, gain the confidence of, assure; convince, -vict, -vert; put across, sell; wean, bring round; bring −, put −, win- over; indoctrinate etc. (*teach*) 537; cram down the throat; produce −, carry- conviction; bring −, drive- home to.

go down, find credence, pass current; be - received etc. *v.*, − current etc. *adj.*; possess −, take hold of −, take possession of- the mind.

Adj. believing etc. *v.*; certain, sure, assured, positive, cocksure, satisfied, confident, unhesitating, convinced, secure.

under the impression; impressed −, imbued −, penetrated- with.

confiding, trustful, suspectless; unsusp-ecting, -icious; void of suspicion; credulous etc. 486; wedded to.

believed etc. *v.*; accredited, putative; unsuspected.

worthy of −, deserving of −, commanding- -belief, − confidence; credible, reliable, trusted, trustworthy, to be depended on, undoubted; satisfactory; probable etc. 472; fiduci-al, -ary; persuasive, impressive.

relating to belief, doctrinal.

Adv. in the -opinion, − eyes- of; *me judice*; me-seems, -thinks; to the best of one's belief; I - dare say, − doubt not, − have no doubt, − am sure; in my opinion; sure enough etc. (*certainty*) 474; depend −, rely- upon it; be −, rest- assured; I'll warrant you etc. (*affirmation*) 535.

485. Unbelief. Doubt.—N. un-, dis-, mis-belief; discredit, miscreance; infidelity etc. (*irreligion*) 989; dissent etc. 489; change of -opinion etc. 484; retraction etc. 607.

doubt etc. (*uncertainty*) 475; skepticism, misgiving, demur; dis-, mis-trust; misdoubt, suspicion, jealousy, scruple, qualm; *onus probandi*.

incredib-ility, -leness; incredulity; unbeliever etc. 487.

V. dis-believe, -credit; not -believe etc. 484; misbelieve; refuse to admit etc. (*dissent*) 489; refuse to believe etc. (*incredulity*) 487.

doubt; be -doubtful etc. (*uncertain*) 475; doubt the truth of; be -skeptical as to etc. *adj.*; diffide; dis-, mis-trust; suspect, smoke, scent, smell a rat; have −, harbor −, entertain- -doubts, − suspicions; have one's doubts.

demur, stick at, pause, hesitate, scruple, waver, stop and consider.

hang in -suspense, − doubt.

throw doubt upon, raise a question; bring −, call- in question; question, challenge, query; dispute; deny etc. 536; cavil; cause −, raise −, start −, suggest −, awake- a -doubt, − suspicion; ergotize.

startle, stagger; shake −, stagger- one's faith, − belief.

Adj. unbelieving; incredulous −, skeptical- as to; distrustful −, shy −, suspicious- of; doubting etc. *v.*

doubtful etc. (*uncertain*) 475; disputable; un-worthy −, undeserving- of -belief etc. 484; questionable; sus-pect, -picious; open to -suspicion,

− doubt; staggering, hard to believe, incredible, not to be believed, inconceivable.

fallible etc. (*uncertain*) 475; undemonstrable; controvertible etc. (*untrue*) 495.

Adv. *cum grano salis.*

Phr. *fronti nulla fides*; *nimium ne crede colori*; *'timeo Danaos et dona ferentes;'* *credat Judaeus Apella*; let those believe who may.

486. Credulity.—N. credul-ity, -ousness etc. *adj.*; gull-, cull-ibility; gross credulity, infatuation; self-delusion, -deception; blind reasoning; superstition; one's blind side; bigotry etc. (*obstinacy*) 606; hyper-orthodoxy etc. 984; misjudgment etc. 481.

credulous person etc. (*dupe*) 547.

V. be -credulous etc. *adj.*; *jurare in verba magistri*; follow implicitly; swallow, − whole, gulp down; take on trust; take for -granted, − gospel; run away with -a notion, − an idea; jump −, rush-to a conclusion; think the moon is made of green cheese; take −, grasp- the shadow for the substance; catch at straws.

impose upon etc. (*deceive*) 545.

Adj. credulous, gullible; easily -deceived etc. 545; simple, green, soft, childish, silly, stupid; over-credulous, -confident; infatuated, superstitious; confiding etc. (*believing*) 484.

Phr. the wish the father to the thought; *credo quia impossibile.*

487. Incredulity.—N. incredul-ous-ness, -ity; skepticism, pyrrhonism; want of faith etc. (*irreligion*) 989.

suspiciousness etc. *adj.*; scrupulosity; suspicion etc. (*unbelief*) 485; dissent etc. 489.

unbeliever, skeptic, aporetic; atheist, agnostic, infidel, disbeliever, misbeliever, pyrrhonist etc. 989; heretic etc. (*heterodox*) 984.

v. be -incredulous etc. *adj.*; distrust etc. (*disbelieve*) 485; refuse to believe; shut one's -eyes, − ears- to; turn a deaf ear to; hold aloof; ignore; *nullis jurare in verba magistri,*

Adj. incredulous, skeptical, unbelieving, in-convincible; hard −, shy- of belief; suspicious, scrupulous, distrustful, heterodox etc. 984.

488. Assent.—N. assent, -ment; acquiescence, admission; nod; ac-, con-cord, -cordance; agreement etc. 23; affirm-ance, -ation; recognition, acknowledgment, avowal; confession, − of faith.

unanimity, common consent, *consensus*, ac-clamation, chorus, *vox populi*; popular −, current- -belief, − opinion; public opinion; concurrence etc. (*of causes*) 178; co-operation etc. (*voluntary*) 709.

ratification, confirmation, corroboration, ap-proval, acceptance, *visa*; indorsement etc. (*record*) 551.

consent etc. (*compliance*) 762.

affirmant, consenter, covenantor, subscriber, en-dorser, upholder.

V. assent; give −, yield −, not- assent; acquiesce; agree etc. 23; receive, accept, accede, accord, concur, lend oneself to, consent, coincide, reciprocate, go with; be -at one with etc. *adj.*; go along −, chime in −, strike in −, close- with; echo, enter into one's views, agree in opinion; vote −, give one's voice- for; recognize; subscribe −, conform −, defer- to; say -yes, − ditto, − amen; − aye- to.

acknowledge, own, admit, allow, avow, confess; concede etc. (*yield*) 762; come round to; abide by; permit etc. 760.

come to −, arrive at- -an understanding, − terms, − an agreement.

con-, af-firm; ratify, approve, endorse, countersign; visa; corroborate etc. 467.

go −, swim- with the stream, float with the current; be in the fashion, join in the chorus; be in every mouth.

Adj. assenting etc. *v.*; of one -accord, − mind; of the same mind, at one with, agreed, acquiescent, content; willing etc. 602.

un-contradicted, -challenged, -questioned, -controverted.

carried −, agreed- *-nem. con.* etc. *adv.*; unanimous; agreed on all hands, carried by acclamation.

affirmative etc. 535.

Adv. yes, yea, ay, aye, true; good; well; very -well, − true; well and good; granted; *placet*; even −, just- so; to be sure, surely, 'thou hast said;' truly, exactly, precisely, that's just it, indeed, certainly, certes, *ex concesso*; of course, unquestionably, assuredly, no doubt, doubtless, undoubtedly.

be it so; so -be it, − let it be, so mote it be; amen; with all my heart; willingly etc. 602.

with one -consent, − voice, − accord; unanimously, *unâ voce*, by common consent, in chorus, to a man, *nem. con.*; *nemine contradicente*, − *dissentiente*; without a dissentient voice; as one man, one and all, on all hands.

489. Dissent.—N. dissent; discordance etc. (*disagreement*) 24; difference −, diversity- of opinion.

non-conformity etc. (*heterodoxy*) 984; protestantism, recusancy, schism; disaffection; secession etc. 624; recantation etc. 607.

dissension etc. (*discord*) 713; discontent etc. 832; cavilling.

protest; contradiction etc. (*denial*) 536; noncompliance etc. (*rejection*) 764; disapprobation etc. 932; hartal.

dissent-ient, -er; non-juror, -content; recusant, sectary, schismatic, protestant, non-conformist, separatist, non-co-operator, conscientious objector, passive resister.

V. dissent, demur; call in question etc. (*doubt*) 485; differ in opinion, disagree; say -no etc. 536; refuse -assent, − to admit; cavil, protest, raise one's voice against, make bold to differ; repudiate; contradict etc. (*deny*) 536; agree to differ.

have no notion of, differ *toto caelo*; revolt -at, − from the idea.

shake the head, shrug the shoulders; look -askance, − askant.

secede; recant etc. 607.

Adj. dissenting etc. *v.*; negative etc. 536; dissident, -entient; unconsenting etc. (*refusing*) 764;

non-content, -juring; protestant, recusant; unconvinced, -verted.

unavowed, unacknowledged; out of the question.

discontented etc. 832; unwilling etc. 603; extorted.

sectarian, denominational, schismatic, heterodox, intolerant.

Adv. no etc. 536; at -variance, − issue- with; under protest; *non placet.*

Int. God forbid! not for the world; not on your life; I beg to differ; I'll be hanged if; never tell me; your humble servant, pardon me; tell that to the marines.

Phr. many men many minds; *quot homines tot sententiae; tant s'en faut; il s'en faut bien.*

490. Knowledge.—N. knowledge; cogn-izance, -ition, -oscence; acquaintance, experience, ken, privity, insight, familiarity; com-, ap-prehension; recognition; appreciation etc. (*judgment*) 480; intuition; consci-ence, -ousness; preception, precognition; acroamatics.

light, enlightenment; glimpse, inkling; side light; glimmer, -ing; dawn; scent, suspicion; impression etc. (*idea*) 453; discovery etc. 480*a*.

system −, body- of knowledge; science, philosophy, pansophy; theory, Etiology; circle of the sciences; pandect, doctrine, body of doctrine; cy-, ency-clopedia; school etc. (*system of opinions*) 484.

tree of knowledge; republic of letters etc. (*language*) 560.

erudition, learning, lore, scholarship, reading, letters; literature; booklearning, bookishness; biblio-mania, -latry; information, general information; store of -knowledge etc.; education etc. (*teaching*) 537; culture, attainments; acquirements, -sitions; accomplishments, proficiency; practical knowledge etc. (*skill*) 698; higher education, liberal education; dilettantism; rudiments etc. (*beginning*) 66.

deep −, profound −, solid −, accurate −, acroatic −, acroamatic −, vast −, extensive −, encyclopedical- knowledge, − learning; omniscience, pantology.

march of intellect; progress −, advance- of -science, − learning; schoolmaster abroad.

V. know, ken, scan, wot; wot −, be aware etc. *adj.*- of; ween, weet, trow, have, possess.

conceive; ap-, com-prehend; take, realize, understand, appreciate; fathom, make out; recognize, discern, perceive, see, get a sight of, experience.

know full well; have −, possess- some knowledge of; be -au *courant* etc. *adj.*; have -in one's head, − at one's fingers' ends; know by -heart, − rote; be master of; *connaître le dessous des cartes*, know what's what etc. 698.

see one's way; learn, discover etc. 480*a*.

come to one's knowledge etc. (*information*) 527.

Adj. knowing etc. *v.*; cognitive; acroamatic.

aware −, cognizant −, conscious- of; acquainted −, made acquainted- with; privy −, in the secret; up −, alive- to; sensible of; behind the -scenes, − curtain; let into; apprized −, informed- of; undeceived.

proficient −, versed −, read −, forward −,

strong –, at home- in; conversant –, familiar-with.

erudite, instructed, learned, lettered, educated; high-brow; well-conned, -informed, -read, -grounded, -educated; enlightened, shrewd, insightful, *savant*, blue, bookish, scholastic, solid, profound, deep-read, book-learned; accomplished etc. (*skilful*) 698; omniscient; self-taught, -educated.

known etc. *v.*; ascertained, well-known, recognized, received, notorious, noted; proverbial; familiar, – as household words, to every schoolboy; hackneyed, trite, commonplace.

knowable, cogn-oscible, -izable.

Adv. to –, to the best of- one's knowledge.

Phr. one's eyes being opened etc. (*disclosure*) 529.

491. Ignorance.—N. ignorance, nescience, *tabula rasa*, crass ignorance, *ignorance crasse*; unacquaintance; unconsciousness etc. *adj.*; dark-, blind-ness; incomprehension, inexperience, simplicity.

unknown quantities, *x*, *y*, *z*.

sealed book, *terra incognita*, virgin soil, unexplored ground; dark ages.

[Imperfect knowledge] smattering, superficiality, half-learning, sciolism, glimmering; bewilderment etc. (*uncertainty*) 475; incapacity.

[Affectation of knowledge] pedantry; charlatanry, -ism.

V. be -ignorant etc. *adj.*; not -know etc. 490; know -not, – not what, – nothing of; have no -idea, – notion, – conception; not have the remotest idea; not know chalk from cheese.

ignore, be blind to; keep in ignorance etc. (*conceal*) 528.

see through a glass darkly; have a -film over the eyes, – glimmering etc. *n.*; wonder whether; not know what to make of etc. (*unintelligibility*) 519; not pretend –, not take upon oneself- to say.

Adj. ignorant, nescient; un-knowing, -aware, -acquainted, -apprized, -witting, -weeting, -conscious; wit-, weet-less; a stranger to; unconversant.

un-informed, -cultivated, -versed, -instructed, -taught, -initiated, -tutored, -schooled, -guided, -enlightened; Philistine; behind the age.

shallow, superficial, green, rude, empty, half-learned, illiterate; un-read, -informed, -educated, -learned, -lettered, -bookish; empty-headed; lowbrow; pedantic.

in the dark; be-nighted, -lated; blind-ed, -fold; hoodwinked; misinformed; *au bout de son latin*, at the end of his tether; at fault; at sea etc. (*uncertain*) 475; caught tripping.

un-known, -apprehended, -explained, -ascertained, -investigated, -explored, -heard of, -perceived; concealed etc. 528; novel.

Adv. ignorantly etc. *adj.*; unawares; for -anything, – aught- one knows; not that one knows.

Int. God –, Heaven –, the Lord –, nobody-knows.

Phr. a little learning is a dangerous thing.

492. Scholar.—N. scholar, *connoisseur*, *savant*, pundit, schoolman, professor, graduate,

wrangler, moonshee; academ-ician, -ist; fellow, don, post graduate, advanced student; master –, bachelor- of arts; doctor, licentiate, gownsman; philo-sopher, -math; scientist, clerk; soph, -ist, -ister; linguist, classicist; glosso-, etymo-, philologist; philologer; lexico-, glosso-grapher; scholiast, commentator. annotator, grammarian; *littérateur*, *literati*, *dilettanti*, *illuminati*; Mezzofanti, admirable Crichton, Maecenas.

book-worm, *helluo librorum*, biblio-phile, -maniac; blue-stocking, *bas-bleu*; big-wig, learned Theban.

learned –, literary- man; *homo multarum literarum*; man of -learning, – letters, – education; high-brow, intelligentsia.

antiquar-ian, -y; archeologist; sage etc. (*wise man*) 500.

pendant, *doctrinaire*; pedagogue, Dr. Pangloss; pantologist.

teacher etc. 540; schoolboy etc. (*learner*) 541.

Adj. learned etc. 490; brought up at the feet of Gamaliel.

493. Ignoramus.—N. ignoramus, illiterate, moron, dunce, numskull; wooden spoon; no scholar.

sciolist, smatterer, dabbler, half-scholar; *charlatan*; wiseacre.

novice, griffin; greenhorn etc. (*dupe*) 547; tyro etc. (*learner*) 541.

lubber etc. (*bungler*) 701; fool etc. 501; pedant etc. 492.

Adj. bookless, shallow, simple, dense, dumb, thick, dull, ignorant etc. 491.

494. Truth. [Object of knowledge.]—**N.** fact, reality etc. (*existence*) 1; plain matter of fact; nature etc. (*principle*) 5; truth, verity; gospel; orthodoxy etc. 983a; authenticity; veracity etc. 543.

accuracy, exactitude; exact-, precise-ness etc. *adj.*; precision, delicacy; rigor, mathematical precision, punctuality; clockwork precision etc. (*regularity*) 80.

orthology; *ipsissima verba*; letter of the law, realism.

plain –, honest –, sober –, naked –, unalloyed –, unqualified –, stern –, exact –, intrinsic- truth; *nuda veritas*; the very thing; not an -illusion etc. 495; real Simon Pure; unvarnished tale; the truth, the whole truth and nothing but the truth; just the thing.

V. be -true etc. *adj.*, – the case; stand the test; have the true ring; hold -good, – true, – water; conform to rule.

render –, prove- -true etc. *adj.*; substantiate etc. (*evidence*) 467.

get at the truth etc. (*discover*) 480a.

Adj. real, actual etc. (*existing*) 1; veritable, true; certain etc. 474; substantially –, categorically-true etc; true -to the letter, – to life, – to scale, – the facts, – as gospel; unimpeachable; veracious etc. 543; unre-, uncon-futed; un-ideal -imagined; realistic.

exact, accurate, definite, precise, well defined, just, right, correct, strict, severe; close etc. (*similar*) 17; literal; rigid, rigorous; scrupulous etc. (*con-*

scientious) 939; religiously exact, punctual, mathematical, scientific; faithful, constant, unerring; curious, particular, punctilious, meticulous, nice, delicate, fine.

genuine, authentic, legitimate, pukka; orthodox etc. 983*a*; official, *ex officio*.

pure, natural, sound, sterling; un-sophisticated, -adulterated, -varnished, -colored; in its true colors.

well-grounded, -founded; solid, substantial, tangible, valid; undis-torted, -guised; un-affected, -exaggerated, -romantic, -flattering.

Adv. truly etc.*adj*.; verily, indeed, in reality; as a matter of fact; beyond -doubt, – question; with truth etc. (*veracity*) 543; certainly etc. (*certain*) 474; actually etc. (*existence*) 1; in effect etc. (*intrinsically*) 5.

exactly etc. *adj.* ; *ad amussim*; *verbatim, – et literatim*; word for word, literally, *literatim, totidem verbis, sic*, to the letter, chapter and verse, *ipsissimis verbis; ad unguem*; to an inch; to a -nicety, – hair, – tittle, – turn, – T; *au pied de la lettre*; neither more nor less; in -every respect, – all respects; *sous tous les rapports*; at -any rate, – all events; strictly speaking.

Phr. the -truth, – fact- is; *rem acu tetigisti*.

495. Error.—N. error, fallacy; misconception, -apprehension, -understanding; inexactness etc. *adj.*; laxity; misconstruction etc. (*misinterpretation*) 523; miscomputation etc. (*misjudgment*) 481; *non-sequitur* etc. 477; misstatement, -report; anachronism; malapropism.

mistake; miss, fault, blunder, boner, bloomer, howler, *quid pro quo*, cross purposes, oversight, misprint, *erratum, corrigendum*, slip, blot, flaw, loose thread; trip, stumble etc. (*failure*) 732; botchery etc. (*want of skill*) 699; slip of the -tongue, – pen; *lapsus -linguae, – calami*, clerical error; bull etc. (*absurdity*) 497.

il-, de-lusion; false -impression, – idea; bubble; self-deceit, -deception; warped notion; mists of error; superstition, exploded notion.

heresy etc. (*heterodoxy*) 984; hallucination etc. (*insanity*) 503; false light etc. (*fallacy of vision*) 443; dream etc. (*fancy*) 515; fable etc. (*untruth*) 546; bias etc. (*misjudgment*) 481; misleading etc. *v.*

V. be -erroneous etc. *adj.*

cause error; mis-lead, -guide; lead -astray, – into error; beguile, misinform etc. (*misteach*) 538; delude; give a false -impression, – idea; falsify, garble, mistate; deceive etc. 545; lie etc. 544.

err; be -in error etc. *adj.*; – mistaken etc. *v.*; be deceived etc. (*duped*) 547; mistake, receive a false impression, deceive oneself; fall into –, lie under –, labor under -an error etc. *n.*; be in the wrong, blunder; mis-apprehend, -conceive, -understand, -reckon, -count, -calculate etc. (*misjudge*) 481.

play –, be- at cross purposes etc. (*misinterpret*) 523.

trip, stumble; lose oneself etc. (*uncertainty*) 475; go astray; fail etc. 732; take the wrong sow by the ear etc. (*mismanage*) 699; put the saddle on the wrong horse; reckon without one's host; take the shadow for the substance etc. (*credulity*) 486; dream etc. (*imagine*) 515.

Adj. erroneous, untrue, false, devoid of truth, fallacious, faulty, apocryphal, unreal, ungrounded,

groundless; unsubstantial etc. 4; heretical etc. (*heterodox*) 984; unsound; illogical etc. 477; wrong.

in-, un-exact; in-accurate, -correct; indefinite etc. (*uncertain*) 475.

illus-ive, -ory; delusive; mock; ideal etc. (*imaginary*) 515; spurious etc. 545; deceitful etc. 544; perverted.

controvertible, unsustain-able, -ed; unauthenticated, untrustworthy.

exploded, refuted, discarded.

in –, under an- error etc. *n.*; mistaken etc. *v.*; tripping etc. *v.*; out, – in one's reckoning; aberrant; beside –, wide of the- -mark, – truth; astray etc. (*at fault*) 475; on -a false, – the wrongscent; in the wrong box; at cross purposes, all in the wrong, all abroad, at sea.

Adv. more or less.

496. Maxim.—N. maxim, aphorism; apo-, apoph-thegm; *dictum*, saying, gnome, adage, saw, proverb, epigram; sentence, *mot*, motto, word, byword, precept, moral, phylactery, *protasis*, brocard.

axiom, postulate, theorem, *scholium*, truism.

reflection etc. (*idea*) 453; conclusion etc. (*judgment*) 480; golden rule etc. (*precept*) 697; principle, *principia*; profession of faith etc. (*belief*) 484; formula.

wise –, sage –, received –, admitted –, recognized- maxim etc.; true –, common –, hackneyed –, trite –, commonplace- saying etc.

Adj. aphoristic, proverbial, phylacteric; axiomatic, gnomic.

Adv. as -the saying is, – they say.

497. Absurdity.—N. absurd-ity, -ness etc. *adj.*; imbecility etc. 499; alogy, nonsense, paradox, inconsistency; stultiloqu-y, -ence, futility.

blunder, muddle, bull; Irish-, Hibernic-ism; slip-slop; anti climax; bathos; sophism etc. 477.

farce, burlesque, *galimatias, amphigouri*, rhapsody; farrago etc. (*disorder*) 59; extravagance, romance; sciomachy.

joke, catch, sell, pun, verbal quibble, macaronic, jargon, fustian, twaddle etc. (*no meaning*) 517; exaggeration etc. 549; moonshine, stuff; mare's nest.

vagary, tomfoolery, mummery, monkey trick, practical joke, *boutade, escapade*.

V. play the fool etc. 499; stultify, blunder, muddle; joke; talk nonsense, *parler à tort et à travers; battre la campagne*; be -absurd etc. *adj.*

Adj. absurd, nonsensical, preposterous, egregious, senseless, farcical, inconsistent, ridiculous, extravagant, quibbling, futile; macaronic, punning, paradoxical.

foolish etc. 499; sophistical etc. 477; unmeaning etc. 517; without rhyme or reason; fantastic.

Int. fiddle-de-dee! pish! pish and tush! pho! stuff and nonsense! rubbish! !rot! bosh! in the name of the Prophet—figs!

Phr. *credat Judaeus Apella*; tell it to the marines.

498. Intelligence. Wisdom.—N. intelligence, capacity, comprehension, understanding, intellect etc. 450; nous, parts, sagacity, mother wit, wit, *esprit*, gumption, quick parts, grasp of intellect; acuteness etc. *adj.*; acumen, subtlety, penetration; perspica-cy, -city; discernment; long-headedness, due sense of, good judgment; discrimination etc. 465; craftiness, cunning etc. 702; refinement etc. (*taste*) 850.

head, brains, gray matter, headpiece, upper story, long head; eagle -eye, − glance; eye of a - lynx, − hawk.

wisdom, sapience, sense; good −, common −, plain −, horse- sense; clear thinking; rationality, reason; reasonableness etc. *adj.*; judgment; solidity, depth, profundity, caliber; enlarged views; reach −, compass- of thought; enlargement of mind.

genius, inspiration, *geist*, fire of genius, heaven-born genius, soul; talent etc. (*aptitude*) 698.

[Wisdom in action] prudence etc. 864; vigilance etc. 459; tact etc. 698; foresight etc. 510; sobriety, self-possession, *aplomb*, ballast, mental - poise, − balance.

a bright thought, inspiration, brainwave, not a bad idea.

V. be -intelligent etc. *adj.*; have all one's wits about one; understand etc. (*intelligible*) 518; catch −, take in- an idea; take a -joke, − hint.

. see -through, − at a glance, − with half an eye, − far into, − through a millstone; penetrate; discern etc. (*descry*) 441; foresee etc. 510.

discriminate etc. 465; know what's what etc. 698; listen to reason.

Adj. [Applied to persons] intelligent, quick of apprehension, keen, acute, alive, brainy, awake, bright, quick, sharp; quick-, keen-, clear-, sharp-eyed, -sighted, -witted; wide awake; canny, shrewd, astute; clear-headed; far-sighted etc. 510; discerning, perspicacious, penetrating, piercing; argute nimble-, needle-witted; sharp as a needle; alive to etc. (*cognizant*) 490; clever etc. (*apt*) 698; arch etc. (*cunning*) 702; *pas si bête*; acute etc. 682.

wise, sage, sapient, sagacious, reasonable, rational, sound, in one's right mind, sensible, *abnormis sapiens*, judicious, strong-minded.

un-prejudiced, -biassed, -bigoted, -prepossessed; un-dazzled, -perplexed; of unwarped judgment, impartial, equitable, fair, broad-minded.

cool; cool-, long-, hard-, strong-headed; long-sighted, calculating, thoughtful, reflecting; solid, deep, profound.

oracular; heaven-directed, -born.

prudent etc. (*cautious*) 864; sober, staid, solid; considerate, politic, wise in one's generation; watchful etc. 459; provident etc. (*prepared*) 673; in advance of one's age; wise as -a serpent, − Solomon, − Solon.

[Applied to actions] wise, sensible, reasonable, judicious; well-judged, -advised; prudent, politic; expedient etc. 646.

499. Imbecility. Folly.—N. want of - intelligence etc. 498, − intellect etc. 450; shallow-, silli-, foolish-ness etc. *adj.*; imbecility, incapacity, vacancy of mind, poverty of intellect, clouded perception, poor head, apartments to let; stup-, stolidity; hebetude, dull understanding, meanest capacity; short-sightedness; incompetence etc. (*unskilfulness*) 699.

one's weak side; bias etc. 481; infatuation etc. (*insanity*) 503.

simplicity, puerility, babyhood; dotage, anility, second childishness, senile dementia, fatuity; idio-cy, -tism; driveling.

folly, frivolity, desipience, irrationality, trifling, ineptitude, nugacity, inconsistency, lip-wisdom, conceit; sophistry etc. 477; giddiness etc. (*inattention*) 458; eccentricity etc. 503; extravagance etc. (*absurdity*) 497; rashness etc. 863.

act of folly etc. 699.

V. be -imbecile etc. *adj.*; have no -brains, − sense etc. 498.

trifle, drivel, *radoter*, dote; ramble etc. (*madness*) 503; play the -fool, − monkey, − goat, take leave of one's senses; not see an inch beyond one's nose; stultify oneself etc. 699; talk nonsense etc. 497.

Adj. [Applied to persons] un-intelligent, -intellectual, -reasoning; mind-, wit-, reason-, brain-less; having no -head etc. 498; not -bright etc. 498; inapprehensible.

weak-, addle-, puzzle-, blunder-, muddle-, muddy-, pig-, beetle-, maggotty-, gross-headed; beef-, fat- -witted, -headed.

weak, feeble-minded; dull-, shallow-, rattle-, lack-brained; half-, nit-, short-, dull-, blunt-witted; shallow-, clod-, addle-pated; dim-, short-sighted; thick-skulled; weak in the upper story.

shallow, *borné*, weak, wanting, soft, nutty, sappy, spoony; dull, − as a beetle; stupid, heavy, insulse, obtuse, blunt, stolid, doltish, asinine; inapt etc. 699; prosaic etc. 843.

child-ish, -like; infant-ine, -ile; baby-, bab-ish; puerile; anile; simple etc. (*credulous*) 486.

fatuous, idiotic, imbecile, moronic, driveling; blatant, babbling; vacant; sottish; bewildered etc. 475.

blockish, unteachable; Boeot-ian, -ic; bovine; ungifted, -discerning, -enlightened, -wise, - philosophical; spiritless.

foolish, silly, senseless, irrational, insensate, nonsensical, inept; maudlin.

narrow-minded etc. 481; bigoted etc. (*obstinate*) 606; giddy etc. (*thoughtless*) 458; rash etc. 863; eccentric etc. (*crazed*) 503.

[Applied to actions] foolish, unwise, indiscreet, injudicious, improper, unreasonable, without reason, ridiculous, silly, stupid, asinine; ill-imagined, -advised, -judged, -devised; inconsistent, irrational, unphilosophical; extravagant etc. (*nonsensical*) 497; sleeveless, idle, useless etc. 645; inexpedient etc. 647; frivolous etc. (*trivial*) 643; absurd etc. 497.

Phr. *Davis ṣum non Oedipus.*

500. Sage.—N. sage, wise man; pundit; master-mind, − spirit of the age; longhead, thinker, philosopher.

authority, oracle, mentor, luminary, shining light, *esprit fort, magnus Apollo*, Solon, Solomon, Nestor, Magi, 'second Daniel.'

man of learning etc. 492; expert etc. 700; wizard etc. 994.

[Ironically] wiseacre, bigwig.

Adj. wise, learned; authoritative, oracular; erudite etc. 490; venerable, reverenced, revered, *emeritus*.

501. Fool.—N. fool, idiot, tomfool, wiseacre, simpleton, Simple Simon, nit-wit, witling, dizzard, donkey, ass; ninny, -hammer; moron, dolt, booby, Tom Noddy, looby; hoddy-doddy, noddy, nonny, noodle, nizy, owl; goose, -cap; *imbécile*; gaby, *radoteur*, nincompoop, *badaud*, zany; trifler, babbler; pretty fellow; natural, *niais*.

child, baby, infant, innocent, milksop, sop.

oaf, lout, loon, lown, dullard, doodle, calf, colt, buzzard, block, put, stick, stock, numps, tony.

bull-, dunder-, addle-, block-, dull-, logger-, jolt-, jolter-, beetle-, gross-, thick-, giddy-head; num-, thick- skull; lack-, shallow-brain; half-, lack-wit; dunder-pate; fat-head, poor stick.

sawney, gowk; clod, -hopper; clod-, clot-poll, - pate; bull-calf; men of Boeotia, wise men of Gotham.

un sot à triple étage, sot; jobbernowl, changeling, mooncalf, *gobemouche*.

dotard, driveller; old -fogey, — woman; crone, grandmother.

greenhorn etc. (*dupe*) 547; dunce etc. (*ignoramus*) 493; lubber etc. (*bungler*) 701; madman etc. 504.

one who -will not set the Thames on fire, — did not invent gunpowder; *qui n'a pas inventé la poudre*; no conjuror.

502. Sanity.—N. sanity; soundness etc. *adj.*; rationality, normality, sobriety, lucidity, lucid interval; senses, sober senses, sound mind, *mens sana*.

V. be -sane etc. *adj.*; retain one's senses, — reason.

become -sane etc. *adj.*; come to one's senses, sober down.

render -sane etc. *adj.*; bring to one's senses, sober.

Adj. sane, rational, reasonable, *compos mentis*, of sound mind; sound, -minded.

self-possessed; sober, -minded.

in one's -sober senses, — right mind; in possession of one's faculties.

Adv. sanely etc. *adj.*

503. Insanity.—N. disordered -reason, — intellect; diseased —, unsound —, abnormal- mind; derangement, unsoundness.

insanity, lunacy; madness etc. *adj.*; mania, *rabies*, *furor*, mental aliénation, paranoia, aberration; *amentia*, dementation, -tia, -cy; *dementia praecox*; *morosis*, idiocy, phrenitis, frenzy, raving, incoherence, wandering, delirium, calenture of the brain, delusion, hallucination; lycanthropy, brain storm, *delirium tremens*, D.T.'s.

vertigo, dizziness, swimming; sunstroke, *coup de soleil*, siriasis.

fanatisism, infatuation, craze; oddity, eccentricity, twist, monomania; klepto-, dipso-manià; hypochondriasis etc. (*low spirits*) 837; *melancholia*, hysteria.

screw —, tile —, slate- loose; bee in one's bonnet, rats in the upper story.

dotage etc. (*imbecility*) 499.

V. be —, become- -insane etc. *adj.*; lose one's senses, — reason, — faculties, — wits; go —, run-

mad, run amuck; rave, dote, ramble, wander; drivel etc. (*be imbecile*) 499; have a -screw loose etc. *n.*, — devil; *avoir le diable au corps*; lose one's head etc. (*be uncertain*) 475.

derange, render —, drive- -mad etc. *adj.*; madden, dementate, addle the wits, derange the head, infatuate, befool; turn -the brain, — one's head.

Adj. insane, mad, lunatic; crazy, crazed, *aliéné*, *non compos mentis*; not right, cracked, touched; bereft of reason; unhinged, deranged, unsettled in one's mind; insensate, reasonless, beside oneself, demented, daft; phren-, fren-zied. -etic; possessed, — with a devil; far gone, maddened, moonstruck; shatterpated; barmy; mad-, scatter-, shatter-, crackbrained, off one's head; bug-house, *loco*.

maniacal; manic, manic-depressive; delirious, light-headed, incoherent, rambling, doting, wandering; frantic, raving, stark staring mad, amok, amuck.

corybantic, dithyrambic; rabid, giddy, vertiginous, dizzy, wild, haggard, mazed; flighty; distracted, -aught; bewildered etc. (*uncertain*) 475.

mad as a -March hare, — hatter; of -unsound mind etc. *n.* touched —, wrong —, not right- in one's -head, — mind, — wits, — upper story; out of one's -mind, — senses, — wits; not in one's right mind.

fanatical, infatuated, odd, eccentric; hypp-ed, -ish.

imbecile, silly etc. 499.

Adv. like one possessed.

Phr. the mind having lost its balance; the reason under a cloud; *tête -exaltée, -montée*.

504. Madman—N. madman, lunatic, maniac, bedlamite, candidate for Bedlam, raver, madcap; energumen; paranoiac; auto-, mono-, pyro-, megalo-, dipso-, klepto-maniac; hypochondriac etc. (*low spirit*) 837.

dreamer etc. 515; rhapsodist, seer, high-flier, enthusiast, crank, eccentric, nut, fanatic, *fanatico*, *exalté*; knight errant, Don Quixote.

idiot etc. 501.

505. Memory.—N. memory, remembrance; reten-tion, -tiveness; tenacity; *veteris vestigia flammae*; tablets of the memory; readiness.

reminiscence, recognition, recurrence, recollection, rememoration; retrospect, -ion; after-thought.

suggestion etc. (*information*) 527; prompting etc. *v.*; hint, reminder, token of remembrance, *memento, souvenir*, keepsake, relic, *memorandum*; remembrancer, flapper; memorial etc. (*record*) 551; commemoration etc. (*celebration*) 883.

things to be remembered, *memorabilia*.

art of —, artificial- memory; *memoria technica*; mnemo-nics, -technics; phrenotypics; Mnemosyne; memorandum-, note-, engagement-, prompt-book.

retentive —, tenacious —, green —, trustworthy —, capacious —, faithful —, correct —, exact —, ready —, prompt- memory.

V. remember, mind; retain the -memory, — remembrance- of; keep in view.

have —, hold —, bear —, carry —, keep —, retain- in *or* in the -thoughts, — mind, — memory, — remembrance; be in —, live in —, remain in —, dwell in – , haunt – , impress- one's -memory, – thoughts, – mind.

sink in the mind; run in the head; not be able to get it out of one's head; be deeply impressed with; rankle etc. (*revenge*) 919.

recur to the mind; flash -on the mind, – across the memory.

recognize, recollect, bethink oneself, recall, call up, conjure up, retrace; look – , trace- -back, – backwards; think – , look back- upon; review; call – , recall – , bring- to mind; remembrance; carry one's thoughts back; rake up the past.

suggest etc. (*inform*) 527; prompt; put – , keep- in mind; remind; fan the embers; call – , summon – , rip- up; renew; *infandum renovare dolorem*; task – , tax – , jog – , flap – , refresh – , rub up – , awaken- the memory; pull by the sleeve; bring back the memory, put in remembrance, memorialize.

get – , have – , learn – , know – , say – , repeat- by -heart, – rote; drive – , get- into -one's head; say one's lesson; repeat, – as a parrot; have at one's finger's ends.

_commit to memory; memorize; con, – over; fix – , rivet – , imprint – , impress – , stamp – , grave – , engrave – , store – , treasure up – , bottle up – , embalm – , enshrine- in the memory; load – , store – , stuff – , burden- the memory with.

redeem from oblivion; keep the memory -alive, – green; *tangere ulcus*; keep up the memory of; commemorate etc. (*celebrate*) 883.

make a note of etc. (*record*) 551.

Adj. remember-ing, -ed etc. *v.*; mindful, reminiscential; retained in the memory etc. *v.*; pent up in one's memory; fresh; green, – in remembrance, still vivid; unforgotten, present to the mind; within one's -memory etc. *n.*; indelible; not to be forgotten, unforgettable, enduring; uppermost in one's thoughts; memorable etc. (*important*) 642.

Adv. by -heart, – rote; without book, *memoriter*.

in memory of; *in memoriam*; suggestive.

Phr. *manet altâ mente repostum*; *forsan et haec olim meminisse juvabit*.

506. Oblivion.—N. oblivion; forgetfulness etc. *adj.*; obliteration etc. 552, of – , insensibility etc. 823 to- the past.

short – , treacherous – , loose – , slippery – , failing- memory; decay – , failure – , lapse- of memory; memory like a sieve; waters of -Lethe, – oblivion, *amnesia*.

pardon, acquittal, amnesty, oblivion; absolution.

V. forget; be -forgetful etc. *adj.*; fall – , sink- into oblivion; have -a short memory etc. *n.* – no head.

forget one's own name, have on the tip of one's tongue, come in at one ear and go out at the other.

slip – , escape – , fade from – , die away from- the memory; lose, – sight of.

unlearn; efface etc. 552 – , discharge- from the memory; consign to -oblivion, – the tomb of the Capulets; think no more of etc. (*turn the attention from*) 458; cast behind one's back, wean one's thoughts from; let bygones be bygones etc. (*forgive*) 918.

Adj. forgotten etc. *v.*; unremembered, past recollection, bygone, out of mind; buried – , sunk-

in oblivion; clean forgotten; gone out of one's -head, – recollection.

forgetful, oblivious, mindless, heedless, Lethean; insensible etc. 823- to the past.

Phr. *non mi ricordo*; the memory -failing, – deserting one, – being at (*or* in) fault.

507. Expectation.—N. expect-ation, -ance, -ancy; anticipation, reckoning, calculation; contingency; foresight etc. 510.

contemplation, prospection, look out; prospect, perspective, horizon, vista; destiny etc. 152.

suspense, waiting, abeyance; curiosity etc. 455; anxious – , ardent – , eager – , breathless – , sanguine- expectation; torment of Tantalus.

presumption, hope etc. 858; trust etc. (*belief*) 484; prognostication, auspices etc. (*prediction*) 511.

V. expect; look -for, – out for, – forward to; hope for, anticipate; have in -prospect, – contemplation; keep in view; contemplate, promise oneself; not -wonder etc. 870 -at, – if.

wait – , tarry – , lie in wait – , watch – , bargain- for; keep a -good, – sharp- look-out for; await; stand at 'attention,' abide, bide one's – , mark- time, watch.

foresee etc. 510; prepare for etc. 673; forestall etc. (*be early*) 132; count upon etc. (*believe in*) 484; think likely etc. (*probability*) 472; make one's mouth water.

lead one to expect etc. (*predict*) 511; have in store for etc. (*destiny*) 152.

prick up one's ears, hold one's breath.

Adj. expectant; expecting etc. *v.*; in -expectation etc. *n.*; on the watch etc. (*vigilant*) 459; open- eyed, -mouthed; agape, gaping, all agog; on -tenterhooks, – tiptoe, – the tiptoe of expectation; *aux aguets*; ready; curious etc. 455; looking forward to; prepared for; on the rack.

expected etc. *v.*; long expected, foreseen; in prospect etc. *n.*; prospective; in -one's eye, – view, – the horizon; impending etc. (*destiny*) 152.

Adv. expectantly; in the event of; on the watch etc. *adj.*; with -breathless expectation etc. *n.*; – bated -breath, – eyes, – ears strained; *arrectis auribus*; on edge.

Phr. we shall see; *nous verrons*.

508. Inexpectation.—N. in-, non-expectation; false expectation etc. (*disappointment*) 509; miscalculation etc. 481; unforeseen contingency, the unforeseen, the unexpected.

surprise, sudden burst, thunderclap, blow, shock; bolt out of the blue; eye-opener; wonder etc. 870.

V. not -expect etc. 507; be taken by surprise; start; miscalculate etc. 481; not bargain for; come – , fall- upon.

be -unexpected etc. *adj.*; come -unawares etc. *adv.*; turn up, pop, drop from the clouds; come – , burst – , flash – , bounce – , steal – , creep- upon one; come – , burst- like a thunder-clap; -bolt; take – , catch- -by surprise, – unawares, – napping.

pounce – , spring a mine- upon.

_surprise, startle, take aback, electrify, stun, stagger, take away one's breath, throw off one's guard; astonish etc. (*strike with wonder*) 870.

Adj. non-expectant; surprised etc. *v.*; un-warned, -aware; off one's guard; inattentive etc. 458.

un-expected, -anticipated, -prepared for, -looked for, -foreseen, -hoped for; dropped from the clouds; beyond – , contrary to – , against- expectation; out of one's reckoning; unheard of etc. (*exceptional*) 83; startling; sudden etc. (*instantaneous*) 113.

Adv. abruptly, unexpectedly, plump, pop, *à l'improviste*, unawares; without -notice, – warning, – saying 'by your leave;' like a -thief in the night, – thunderbolt; in an unguarded moment; suddenly etc. (*instantaneously*) 113.

Int. heyday! etc. (*wonder*) 870.

Phr. little did one -think, – expect; nobody would ever -suppose, – think, – expect; who would have thought?'

509. Disappointment. [Failure of ex-pectation.]—**N.** disappointment, disillusionment; blighted hope, balk; blow; slip 'twixt cup and lip; non-fulfilment of one's hopes; sad – , bitter- disap-pointment; trick of fortune; afterclap; false – , vain- expectation; miscalculation etc. 481; fool's paradise; much cry and little wool.

V. be disappointed; look -blank, – blue; look – , stand- -aghast etc. (*wonder*) 870; find to one's cost; laugh on the wrong side of one's mouth; find one a false prophet.

disappoint; crush – , dash – , balk – , disap-point – , blight – , falsify – , defeat – , not realize- one's -hope, – expectation; balk, jilt, bilk; play one -false, – a trick; dash the cup from the lips; tantalize; dumb-found, -founder; disillusion, -ize; dissatisfy, disgruntle.

Adj. disappointed etc. *v.*; disconcerted, aghast; out of one's reckoning; disgruntled.

Phr. the mountain brought forth a mouse; *nascitur ridiculus mus*; *parturiunt montes*; *diis aliter visum*, the bubble burst; one's countenance falling.

510. Foresight.—**N.** foresight, prospicience, prevision, longsightedness; anticipation; providence etc. (*preparation*) 673.

fore-thought, -cast; pre-deliberation, -surmise; foregone conclusion etc. (*prejudgment*) 481; prudence etc. (*caution*) 864.

foreknowledge; *prognosis*; pre-cognition, - science, -notion, -sentiment; second sight; sagacity etc. (*intelligence*) 498.

prospect etc. (*expectation*) 507; foretaste; prospectus etc. (*plan*) 626.

V. foresee; look -forwards to, – ahead, – beyond; scent from afar; feel in one's bones; look – , pry – , peep into the future.

see one's way; see how the -land lies, – wind blows, – cat jumps.

anticipate; expect etc. 507; be beforehand etc. (*early*) 132; predict etc. 511; fore-know, -judge, -cast; surmise; have an eye to the -future, – main chance; *respicere finem*; keep a sharp look-out etc. (*vigilance*) 459; forewarn etc. 668.

Adj. foreseeing etc. *v.*; prescient; anticipatory; far-seeing, -sighted; sagacious etc. (*intelligent*) 498; weather-wise; provident etc. (*prepared*) 673; prospective etc. 507.

Adv. against the time when.

511. Prediction.—N. prediction, an-nouncement; program, programme etc. (*plan*) 626; premonition etc. (*warning*) 668; *prognosis*, prophecy, vaticination, Mantology, prognostication, premonstration, augur-y, -ation; a-, ha-riolation; fore-, a-boding; bode-, abode-ment; omin-ation, -ousness; auspices, forecast; sign, presage, prognostic; omen etc. 512; horoscope, nativity; sooth, -saying; fortune-telling; divination; crystal gazing, necromancy etc. 992; prophet etc. 512.

[Divination by the stars] astrology, horoscopy, astromancy, judicial astrology.*

[Place of prediction] *adytum.*

prefigur-ation, -ement; prototype, type.

V. predict, prognosticate, prophesy, vaticinate, divine, foretell, soothsay, augurate, tell fortunes; cast a -horoscope, – nativity; advise; forewarn etc. 668.

presage, augur, bode; a-, fore-bode, -cast; fore-, be-token; pre-figure, -show; portend; fore-show, -shadow, shadow forth, typify, ominate, signify, point to, precurse.

usher in, herald, premise, announce; lower.

hold out – , raise – , excite- -expectation, – hope; bid fair, promise, lead one to expect; be the -precursor etc. 64.

Adj. predicting etc. *v.*; predictive, prophetic, fatidical, vaticinal, oracular, Sibylline, haruspical, weatherwise.

ominous, presageful, portentous; augur-ous, -al, -ial, auspici-al, -ous; prescious, monitory, ex-tispicious, premonitory, precursory, significant of, pregnant with, big with the fate of.

Phr. 'coming events cast their shadows before.'

*The following terms, expressive of different forms of divination, have been collected from various sources, and are here given as a curious illustration of bygone super-stitions:

Divination *by oracles,* Theomancy; *by the Bible,* Bibliomancy; *by ghosts,* Psychomancy; *by spirits seen in a magic lens,* Cristallomantia; *by shadows or manes,* Sciomancy; *by appearances in the air,* Aeromancy, Chaomancy, *by the stars at birth,* Genethliacs; *by meteors,* Meteoromancy; *by winds,* Austromancy, *by sacrificial ap-pearances,* Aruspicy (or Haruspicy), Hieromancy, Hieroscopy; *by the entrails of animals sacrificed,* Hieromancy; *by the entrails of a human sacrifice,* An-thropomancy; *by the entrails of fishes,* Ichthyomancy; *by sacrificial fire,* Pyromancy; *by red-hot iron,* Sideromancy; *by smoke from the alter,* Capnomancy; *by mice,* Myomancy; *by birds,* Orniscopy, Ornithomancy; *by a cock picking up grains,* Alectryomancy (or Alectoromancy); *by fishes,* Ophiomancy; *by herbs,* Botanomancy; *by water,* Hydromancy; *by fountains,* Pegomancy; *by a wand,* Rhab-domancy; *by dough of cakes,* Crithomancy; *by meal,* Aleuromancy, Alphitomancy; *by salt,* Halomancy; *by dice,* Cleromancy; *by arrows,* Belomancy; *by a balanced hatchet,* Axinomancy; *by a balanced sieve,* Coscinomancy; *by a suspended ring,* Dactyliomancy; *by dots made at random on paper,* Geomancy; *by precious stones,* Lithomancy; *by pebbles,* Pessomancy; *by pebbles drawn from a heap,* Psephomancy; *by mirrors,* Catoptromancy; *by writings in ashes,* Tephramancy; *by dreams,* Oneiromancy; *by the hand,* Palmistry, Chiromancy; *by nails reflecting the sun's rays,* Onychomancy; *by finger rings,* Dactylomancy; *by numbers,* Arithmancy; *by drawing lots,* Sortilege; *by passages in books,* Stichomancy; *by the letters forming the name of the person,* Onomancy, Nomancy; *by the*

features. Anthroposcopy; *by the mode of laughing.*
Geloscopy; *by ventriloquism.* Gastromancy; *by walking in
a circle.* Gyromancy: *by dropping melted wax into water.*
Ceromancy: *by currents.* Bletonism.

512. Omen.—N. omen, portent, presage,
prognostic, augury, auspice; sigh etc. (*indication*)
550; herald, forerunner, harbinger etc. (*precursor*)
64.

bird of ill omen, signs of the times; gathering
clouds; warning etc. 668.

prefigurement etc. 511.

513. Oracle.—N. oracle; prophet, -ess; seer,
soothsayer, augur, fortune-teller, palmist, medium,
clairvoyant, crystal gazer, witch, geomancer,
aruspex; a-, ha-ruspice; Sibyl; Python, -ess; Pythia,
Pythian —, Delphian- oracle; Monitor, Sphinx,
Tiresias, Cassandra, Sibylline leaves; Zadkiel, Old
Moore; sorcerer etc. 994; interpreter etc. 524.

514. Supposition.—N. supposition, assumption, postulation, condition, pre-supposition,
hypothesis, postulate, *postulatum*, theory, *data*;
pro-, position; *thesis*, theorem; proposal etc. (*plan*)
626.

bare —, vague —, loose- -supposition, —
suggestion; conceit; conjecture; guess, — work;
rough guess, shot; conjecturality; surmise,
suspicion, inkling, suggestion, suggestiveness,
association of ideas, hint; presumption etc. (*belief*)
484; divination, speculation.

theorist, speculator, doctrinarian, hypothesist.

V. suppose, conjecture, surmise, suspect, guess,
divine; theorize; pre-sume, -surmise, -suppose;
assume, fancy, wis, take it; give a guess, speculate,
believe, dare say, take it into one's head, take for
granted.

put forth; pro-pound, -pose; moot; hypothesize;
start, put a case, submit, move, make a motion;
hazard —, throw out —, put forward- a -
suggestion, — conjecture.

allude to, suggest, hint, put it into one's head.

suggest itself etc. (*thought*) 451; run in the head
etc. (*memory*) 505; marvel —, wonder- -if, —
whether.

Adj. supposing etc. *v.*; given, mooted,
postulatory; assumed etc. *v.*; supposit-ive, -itious;
gratuitous, speculative, conjectural, hypothetical,
suppositional, theoretical, academic, supposable,
presumptive, putative.

suggestive, allusive, stimulating.

Adv. if, — so be; an; on the -supposition etc. *n.*;
ex hypothesi; in -case, — the event of; *quasi*, as if,
provided; perhaps etc. (*by possibility*) 470; for
aught one knows.

515.   Imagination.—N.   imagination;
originality; invention; fancy; inspiration; *verve*;
empathy.

warm —, heated —, excited —, sanguine —, ardent —, fiery —, boiling —, wild —, bold —,

daring —, playful —, lively —, fertile- -
imagination, — fancy.

'mind's eye;' 'such stuff as dreams are made of.'

ideal-ity, -ism; romanticism, utopianism, castle-
building; dreaming; frenzy; ecs-, ex-tasy; calenture
etc. (*delirium*) 503; reverie, brown study, trance;
somnambulism.

conception, *vorstellung*, ercogitation, 'a fine
frenzy,' poetic frenzy, divine afflatus; cloud-,
dream-land; flight —, fumes- of fancy; 'thickcoming fancies;' creation —, coinage- of the brain;
imagery, word painting.

conceit, maggot, figment, myth, dream, vision,
shadow, chimera; phan-tasm, -tasy; fantasy, fancy;
whim, -sey; vagary, rhapsody, romance, *extravaganza*; air-drawn dagger, bugbear, nightmare;
flying Dutchman, great sea-serpent, man in the
moon, castle in the air, *château en Espagne*;
Utopia, Atlantis, happy valley, millennium, fairy
land; land of Prester John, kingdom of Micomicon;
work of fiction etc. (*novel*) 594; poetry etc. 597;
drama etc. 599; Arabian nights; *le pot au lait*;
dream of Alnaschar etc. (*hope*) 858; day —,
golden- dream

illusion etc. (*error*) 495; phantom etc. (*fallacy
of vision*) 443; *Fata Morgana* etc. (*ignis fatuus*)
423; vapor etc. (*cloud*) 353; stretch of the
imagination etc. (*exaggeration*) 549.

idealist, romanticist, visionary; mopus; romancer, dreamer; somnambulist; rhapsodist etc.
(*fanatic*) 504.

V. imagine, fancy, conceive; ideal-, real-ize;
dream, — of; 'give to airy nothing a local
habitation and a name.'

create, originate, devise, invent, coin, fabricate;
improvise, strike out something new.

set one's wits to work; strain —, crack- one's invention; rack —, ransack —, cudgel- one's brains;
excogitate.

give -play, — the reins, — a loose- to the -
imagination, — fancy; empathize; indulge in
reverie.

conjure up a vision; fancy —, represent —, picture —, figure- to oneself; envisage.

float in the mind; suggest itself etc. (*thought*)
451.

Adj. imagined etc. *v.*; *ben trovato*; air-drawn, -
built.

imagin-ing etc. *v.*, -ative; original, inventive,
creative, fertile, productive; ingenious.

romantic, high-flown, flighty, extravagant,
fanatic, enthusiastic, Utopian, Quixotic;
preposterous, rhapsodical.

ideal, unreal; in the clouds, *in nubibus*; unsubstantial etc. 4; illusory etc. (*fallacious*) 495; fictitious, theoretical, hypothetical.

fabulous, legendary; myth-ic, -ological;
chimerical; imagin-, vision-ary; notional; fan-cy, -
ciful, -tastic, -tastical; whimsical; fairy, -like.

dreamy, entranced, vaporous.

516. Meaning. [Idea to be conveyed.] [Thing
signified.]—**N.** meaning; signific-ation, -ance;
sense, expression; im-, pur-port; drift, tenor, implication, connotation, essence, force, spirit
bearing, coloring; scope.

matter; subject, -matter; argument, text, sum and
substance; gist etc. 5.

general –, broad –, substantial – colloquial
–, literal –, plain –, simple –, accepted –,
natural –, unstrained –, true etc. (*exact*) 494 –,
honest etc. 543 –, *primâ facie* etc. (*manifest*)
525- meaning.

literality; literal interpretation; after acceptation;
allusion etc. (*latency*) 526; suggestion etc. (*information*) 527; synonym; figure of speech etc.
521; acceptation etc. (*interpretation*) 522.

V. mean, signify, express, connote, denote; im-,
pur-port; convey, imply, breathe, indicate, bespeak,
bear a sense; tell –, speak- of; touch on; point –,
allude- to; drive at; involve etc. (*latency*) 526;
delcare etc. (*affirm*) 535.

understand by etc. (*interpret*) 522.

Adj. meaning etc. *v.*; expressive, suggestive,
meaningful, allusive; signific-ant, -ative, -atory;
pithy; full of –, pregnant with- meaning.

declaratory etc. 535; intelligible etc. 518; literal,
metaphrastic; synonymous; tantamount etc.
(*equivalent*) 27; implied etc. (*latent*) 526; explicit
etc. 525; literal etc. 562.

Adv. to that effect; that is to say etc. (*being interpreted*) 522.

literally; evidently, from the context.

517. Unmeaningness. [Absence of
meaning.]—**N.** unmeaningness etc. *adj.*; scrabble,
scribble, scrawl, daub, (*painting*), strumming
(*music*).

empty sound, dead letter, *vox et praeterea nihil*;
'a tale told by an idiot, full of sound and fury,
signifying nothing;' 'sounding brass and a tinkling
cymbal.'

nonsense, jargon, gibberish, jabber, mere words,
hocus-pocus, fustian, rant, bombast, balderdash,
palaver, patter, flummery, *verhiage*, habble, *bavardage*, *baragouin*, platitude, *niaiserie*; inanity;
rigmarole, rodomontade; truism; *nugae canorae*;
twaddle, twattle, fudge, trash; stuff, – and nonsense; bosh, rubbish, rot, drivel, moonshine, wish-
wash, fiddle-faddle, flapdoodle; absurdity etc. 497;
vagueness etc. (*unintelligibility*) 519.

V. mean nothing; be -unmeaning etc. *adj.*;
twaddle, quibble, rant, gabble, scrabble etc. *n.*

Adj. unmeaning; meaning-, sense-less; nonsensical; void of -sense etc. 516.

in-, un-expressive; vacant, fatuous; not
significant; insignificant,.

trashy, washy, inane, vague, trumpery, trivial,
fiddle-faddle, twaddling, quibbling.

unmeant, not expressed; tacit etc. (*latent*) 526.
inexpressible, undefinable, incommunicable.

Int. rubbish! etc. 497.

518. Intelligibility.—**N.** intelligibility, clearness, clarity, explicitness etc. *adj.*; lucidity, perspicuity; legibility, plain speaking etc.
(*manifestation*) 525; precision etc. 494; a word to
the wise.

V. be -intelligible etc. *adj.*; speak -for itself, –
volumes; tell its own tale, lie on the surface.

render -intelligible etc. *adj.*; popularize, simplify, clear up; elucidate etc. (*explain*) 522.

understand, comprehend; take, – in; catch,
grasp, recognize, follow, collect, master, make out;

see -with half an eye, – daylight, – one's way; enter into the ideas of; come to an understanding.

Adj. intelligible; clear, – as -day, – crystal, –
noonday; lucid; per-, tran-spicuous; luminous,
transparent; comprehensible.

easily understood, easy to understand, for the
million, intelligible to the meanest capacity,
popularized.

plain, distinct, explicit, clear-cut; positive;
definite etc. (*precise*) 494.

graphic, vivid, telling; expressive etc. (*meaning*)
516; illustrative etc. (*explanatory*) 522.

un-ambiguous, -equivocal, -mistakable etc.
(*manifest*) 525, -confused; legible, recognizable;
obvious etc. 525.

Adv. in plain -terms, – words, – English.

Phr. he that runs may read etc. (*manifest*) 525.

519. Unintelligibility.—**N.** unintelligibility,
incomprehensibility, imperspicuity; in-
conceivableness, vagueness etc. *adj.*; obscurity; ambiguity etc. 520; doubtful meaning; uncertainty etc.
475; perplexity etc. (*confusion*) 59; spinosity; *ob-
scurum per obscurius*; mystification etc. (*concealment*) 528; latency etc. 526; tran-
scendentalism.

paradox; enigma, riddle etc. (*secret*) 533; *dignus
vindice nodus*; sealed book; steganography,
freemasonry.

pons asinorum, asses' bridge; double –, high-
Dutch, Greek, Hebrew; jargon etc. (*unmeaning*).
517.

obscurantist.

V. be -unintelligible etc. *adj.*; require -
explanation etc. 522; have a doubtful meaning,
pass comprehension.

render -unintelligible etc. *adj.*; conceal etc. 528;
darken etc. 421; confuse etc. (*derange*) 61; perplex
etc. (*bewilder*) 475.

not -understand etc. 518; lose, – the clue; miss;
not know what to make of, be able to make
nothing of, give it up; not be able to -account for,
– make either head or tail of; be at sea etc. (*uncertain*) 475; wonder etc. 870; see through a glass
darkly etc. (*ignorance*) 491.

not understand one another; play at cross purposes etc. (*misinterpret*) 523.

Adj. un-intelligible, -accountable, -decipherable,
-discoverable, -knowable, -fathomable; in-
cognizable, -explicable, -scrutable; inap-, incomprehensible; insol-vable, -uble; impenetrable.

illegible, indecipherable, as Greek to one,
unexplained, paradoxical; enigmatic, -al; puzzling,
baffling.

obscure, dark, muddy, clear as mud, seen
through a mist, dim, nebulous, shrouded in
mystery; undiscernible etc. (*invisible*) 447; misty
etc. (*opaque*) 426; hidden etc. 528; latent etc. 526.

indefinite etc. (*indistinct*) 447; perplexed etc.
(*confused*) 59; undetermined, vague, loose, ambiguous; mysterious; mystic, -al; transcendental; occult, recondite, esoteric, abstruse, crabbed.

incon-ceivable, -ceptible; searchless; above –,
beyond –, past- comprehension; beyond one's
depth; unconceived.

inexpressible, undefinable, incommunicable,
unutterable, ineffable, unpronounceable.

520. Equivocalness. [Having a double sense.]—**N.** equivocalness etc. *adj.*; double - meaning etc. 516; ambiguity, *double entendre*, pun, paragram, *calembour*, quibble, *équivoque*, anagram; conundrum etc. (*riddle*) 533; word-play etc. (*wit*) 842; homonym, -y; amphibo-ly, -logy; ambiloquy.

Sphinx, Delphic oracle.

equivocation etc. (*duplicity*) 544; white lie, mental reservation etc. (*concealment*) 528.

V. be -equivocal etc. *adj.*; have two -meanings etc. 516; equivocate etc. (*palter*) 544.

Adj. equivocal, ambiguous, amphibolous, homonymous; double-tongued etc. (*lying*) 544.

521. Metaphor.—N. figure of speech; *facon de parler*, way of speaking, colloquialism.

phrase etc. 566; figure, trope, metaphor, tralatition, metonymy, enallage, *catachresis*, synecdoche, *autonomasia*; irony, satire, figurativeness etc. *adj.*; image, -ry; *metalepsis*, type, anagoge, simile, personification, *prosopopaeia*, allegory, apologue, parable, fable; allusion, adumbration; application; euphemism; euphuism.

V. employ -metaphor etc. *n.*; personify, allegorize, adumbrate, shadow forth, apply, allude –, refer- to.

Adj. metaphorical etc. *n.*; figurative, catachrestical, typical, tralatitious, parabolic, allegorical, allusive, anagogical; ironical; colloquial.

Adv. so to -speak, – say, – express oneself; as it were.

Phr. *mutato nomine de te fabula nattatur.*

522. Interpretation.—N. interpretation, definition; explan-, explic-ation; solution, answer; rationale; plain –, simple –, strict- interpretation; meaning etc. 516.

translation; rend-ering, -ition; reddition; literal –, free- translation; key, crib; secret; clew etc. (*indication*) 550; Rosetta stone.

exegesis; ex-pounding, -position; Hermeneutics; comment, -ary; inference etc. (*deduction*) 480; illustration, exemplification; gloss, annotation, *scholium*, note; e-, di-lucidation, enucleation; *éclaircissement*, *mot de l'énigme*.

symptomat-, semei-ology; metoposcopy, physiognomy; diagnosis, prognosis; paleography etc. (*philology*) 560.

accept-ion, -ation, -ance; light, reading, lection, construction, version.

equivalent, – meaning etc. 516; synonym; para-, meta-phrase; convertible terms, apposition; dictionary etc. 562; polyglot.

V. interpret, explain, define, construe, translate, render; do –, turn- into; transfuse the sense of. find out etc. 480a- -the meaning etc. 516- of; read; spell –, figure –, make- out; decipher, decode, unravel, disentangle, puzzle out; find the key of, enucleate, resolve, solve; read between the lines.

account for; find –, tell- the cause etc. 153- of; throw –, shed- -light, – new light, – a fresh light- upon; clear up, elucidate.

illustrate, exemplify; unfold, expound, comment upon, annotate; popularize etc. (*render intelligible*) 518.

take –, understand –, receive –, accept- in a particular sense; understand by, put a construction on, be given to understand.

Adj. explanatory, expository; explica-tive, -tory; exegetical; hermeneutic, interpretive, illustrative, elucidative, annotative, scholiastic.

polyglot; literal; para-, meta-phrastic; cosignificative, synonymous; equivalent etc. 27.

Adv. in -explanation etc. *n.*; that is to say, *id est*, *videlicet*, to wit, namely, in other words.

literally, strictly speaking; in -plain, – plainer- - terms, – words, – English; more simply.

523. Misinterpretation.—N. misinterpretation, -apprehension, -understanding, - acceptation, -construction, -application; *catachresis*; cross -reading, – purposes; mistake etc. 495.

misrepresentation, perversion, exaggeration etc. 549; false -coloring, – construction; abuse of terms; parody, travesty; falsification etc. (*lying*) 544.

V. mis-interpret, -apprehend, -understand, - conceive, -judge, -doubt, -spell, -translate, - construe, -apply; mistake etc. 495.

misrepresent, pervert; garble etc. (*falsify*) 544; distort; detort; travesty, play upon words; stretch –, strain –, wrest- the -sense, – meaning; explain away; put a -bad, – false- construction on; give a false coloring, look through -rose colored –, – dark – spectacles.

be –, play- at cross purposes.

Adj. misinterpreted etc. *v.*; untranslat-ed, -able.

Adv. at cross purposes.

524. Interpreter.—N. interpreter, translator, ex-positor, -pounder, -ponent, -plainer; demonstrator.

scholiast, commentator, annotator; meta-, para-phrast.

spokesman, speaker, mouthpiece, prolocutor; diplomat etc. 758.

guide, courier, dragoman, *valet de place*, cicerone, showman; oneirocritic; Oedipus; oracle etc. 513.

525. Manifestation.—N. manifestation; unfolding; plainness etc. *adj.*; plain speaking; expression; showing etc. *v.*; exposition, demonstration, *séance*; exhibition, production; display, showing off etc. 882; premonstration. [Thing shown] exhibit, show.

indication etc. (*calling attention to*) 457; publicity etc. 531; disclosure etc. 529; openness etc. (*honesty*) 543, (*artlessness*) 703; *épachement*, prominence.

V. make –, render- -manifest etc. *adj.*; bring forth, – forward, – to the front, – into view; give notice, express; represent, set forth, exhibit; show,

\- up; expose; produce; hold up −, expose- to view; set −, place −, lay- before -one, − one's eyes; tell to one's face; trot out, put through one's paces, unfold, show off, show forth, unveil, bring to light, display, demonstrate, unroll; lay open; draw −, bring- out; bring out in strong relief; call −, bring- into notice; hold up the mirror; wear one's heart upon his sleeve; show one's -face, − colors; manifest oneself; speak out; make no -mystery, − secret- of; unfurl the flag; proclaim etc. (*publish*) 531.

indicate etc. (*direct attention to*) 457; disclose etc. 529; elicit etc. 480a; interpret etc. 522.

be -manifest etc. *adj.*; appear etc. (*be visible*) 446; transpire etc. (*be disclosed*) 529; speak for itself, stand to reason; stare one in the face; loom large, appear on the horizon, rear its head; give - token, − sign, − indication of; tell its own tale etc. (*intelligible*) 518; go without saying.

Adj. manifest, apparent; salient, striking, demonstrative, prominent, in the foreground, notable, pronounced.

flagrant; notorious etc. (*public*) 531; arrant; stark staring; unshaded, glaring.

defin-ed, -ite; distinct, conspicuous etc. (*visible*) 446; obvious, evident, incontestable, unmistakable, not to be mistaken, plain, clear, palpable, self-evident, autoptical; intelligible etc. 518; clear as -day, − daylight, − noonday; plain as -a pikestaff, − the sun at noonday, − the nose on one's face, − the way to the parish church.

ostensible; open, − as day; overt, patent, express, explicit; naked, bare, literal, downright, undisguised, exoteric.

unreserved; frank, plain spoken etc. (*artless*) 703; barefaced, brazen, bold, shameless, daring, flaunting, loud.

manifested etc. *v.*; disclosed etc. 529; expressible, capable of being shown, producible; in-, un-concealable.

Adv. manifestly, openly etc. *adj.*; before one's eyes, under one's nose, to one's face, face to face, above board, *cartes sur table*, on the stage, in plain sight, in open court, in the open, − streets; at the cross roads; in market overt; in the face of -day, − heaven; in -broad −, open- daylight; without reserve; at first blush, *primâ facie*, on the face of; in set terms.

Phr. *cela saute aux yeux*; he that runs may read; you can see it with half an eye; it needs no ghost to tell us; the meaning lies on the surface; *cela va sans dire*; *res ipsa loquitur*.

526. Latency.—**N.** latency, inexpression; hidden −, occult- meaning; occultness, occultism, mysticism, mystery, cabala, symbolism, anagoge; silence etc. (*taciturnity*) 585; concealment etc. 528; more than meets the -eye, − ear; Delphic oracle; *les dessous des cartes*, undercurrent.

allusion, insinuation, implication; innuendo etc. 527; adumbration; 'something rotten in the state of Denmark.'

snake in the grass etc. (*pitfall*) 667; secret etc. 533.

darkness, invisibility, impreceptibility.

latent influence, power behind the throne; friend at court, wire puller.

V. be -latent etc. *adj.*; lurk, smoulder, underlie,

make no sign; escape -observation, − detection, − recognition; lie hid etc. 528.

laugh in one's sleeve; keep back etc. (*conceal*) 528.

involve, imply, implicate, connote, import, understand, allude to, infer, leave an inference; symbolize; whisper etc. (*conceal*) 528.

Adj. latent; lurking etc. *v.*; secret etc. 528; occult, symbolic, mystic; implied etc. *v.*; dormant.

un-apparent, -known, -seen etc. 441; in the background; invisible etc. 447; indiscoverable, dark; impenetrable etc. (*unintelligible*) 519; unspied, -suspected.

un-said, -written, -published, -breathed, -talked of, -told etc. 527, -sung, -exposed, -proclaimed, -disclosed etc. 529, -pronounced, -mentioned, -expressed; not expressed, tacit.

un-developed, -solved, -explained, -traced, -discovered etc. 480a, -tracked, -explored, -invented.

indirect, crooked, inferential; by -inference, − implication; implicit; constructive; allusive, covert, muffled; steganographic; under-stood, -hand, -ground; concealed etc. 528; delitescent.

Adv. by a side wind; *sub silentio*; in the background; behind -the scenes, − one's back, − the veil; below the surface; on the tip of one's tongue; secretly etc. 528; between the lines; by a mutual understanding.

Phr. 'thereby hangs a tale.' 'that is another story.'

527. Information.—**N.** information, enlightenment, acquaintance, knowledge etc. 490; publicity etc. 531.

communication, intimation; not-ice, -ification; e-an-nunciation; announcement; representation, round robin, presentment.

case, estimate, specification, report, advice, monition; news etc. 532; return etc. (*record*) 551; account etc. (*description*) 594; statement etc. (*affirmation*) 535.

mention; acquainting etc. *v.*; instruction etc. (*teaching*) 537; outpouring; intercommunication, communicativeness.

informant, authority, teller, announcer, annunciator, harbinger, herald, intelligencer, commentator, columnist, reporter, exponent, mouthpiece; informer, keek, eavesdropper, delator, detective, sleuth; *mouchard*, spy, stool pigeon, newsmonger; messenger etc. 534; *amicus curiae*.

valet de place, *cicerone*, pilot, guide; guide-, hand-book; *vade mecum*; manual; map, plan, chart, gazetteer; itinerary etc. (*journey*) 266.

hint, suggestion, wrinkle, innuendo, inkling, whisper, passing word, word in the ear, subaudition, cue, by-play; gesture etc. (*indication*) 550; gentle − broad- hint; *verbum sapienti*; word to the wise; insinuation etc. (*latency*) 526.

V. tell; inform, − of; acquaint, − with; impart, − to; make acquainted with, bring to the ears of, apprise, advise, enlighten, awaken.

let fall, mention, express, intimate, represent, communicate, make known; publish etc 531; notify, signify, specify, convey the knowledge of.

let one −, have one to- know; serve notice, give one to understand; give notice; set −, lay −, put-before; point out, put into one's head; put one in possession of; instruct etc. *(teach)* 537; direct the attention to etc. 457.

an-nounce, -nunciate; report, – progress; bring –, send –, leave –, write- word; tele-graph, - phone; ring –, call- up; wire; retail, render an account; give an account etc. *(describe)* 594; state etc. *(affirm)* 535.

disclose etc. 529; show cause; explain etc. *(interpret)* 522.

hint; give an inkling of; give –, drop –, throw out- a hint; insinuate; allude –, make allusion- to; glance at; tip off, tip the wink etc. *(indicate)* 550; suggest, prompt, give the cue, breathe; whisper, – in the ear.

give a bit of one's mind; tell one plainly, – once for all; speak volumes.

un-deceive, -beguile; set right, correct, open the eyes of, disabuse.

be -informed of etc.; know etc. 490; learn etc. 539; get scent of, gather from; awaken –, open one's eyes- to; become -alive, – awake- to; keep posted; hear, overhear, understand.

come to one's -ears, – knowledge; reach one's ears.

Adj. informed etc. *v.*; *communiqué*; reported etc. *v.*; published etc. 531; advisory.

expressive etc. 516; explicit etc. *(open)* 525, *(clear)* 518; plain-spoken etc. *(artless)* 703.

declara-, nuncupa-, exposi-tory; declarative, enunciative, communicat-ive, -ory; oral.

Adv. from information received; according to - rumor, – report; in the air; from what one can gather.

Phr. a little bird told me.

---

528. Concealment.—N. concealment; hiding etc. *v.*; occultation, mystification.

seal of secrecy; screen etc. 530; disguise etc. 530; masquerade; masked battery; hiding place etc. 530; cipher, code, crypt-, stegan-ography; invisible –, sympathetic- ink; palimpsest; freemasonry.

stealth, -iness; obreption; slyness etc. *(cunning)* 702.

latit-ancy, -ation; seclusion etc. 893; privacy, secrecy, secretness; *incognita*.

reticence; reserve; mental –, reservation, aside; *arrière pensée*, suppression, evasion, white lie, misprision; silence etc. *(taciturnity)* 585; suppression of truth etc. 544; underhand dealing; close-, secretive-ness etc. *adj.*; mystery.

latency etc. 526; snake in the grass; secret etc. 533.

V. conceal, hide, secrete, stow away, put out of sight; lock –, seal –, bottle- up.

cover, screen, cloak, veil, shroud; screen from - sight, – observation; draw the veil; draw –, close- the curtain; curtain, shade, eclipse, throw a veil over; be-cloud, -fog, -mask; mask, disguise; ensconce, muffle, smother; whisper.

keep -from, – back, – to oneself; keep -snug, – close, – secret, – dark; bury; sink, suppress; keep -from, – out of -view, – sight; keep in –, throw into- the -shade, – background; cover up one's tracks; stifle, hush up, withhold, reserve; fence with a question; ignore etc. 460.

code, codify, use a cipher.

keep -a secret, – one's own counsel; hold one's

---

tongue etc. *(silence)* 585; make no sign, not let it go further; not breathe a -word, – syllable- about; not let the right hand know what the left is doing; hide one's light under a bushel, bury one's talent in a napkin.

keep –, leave- in -the dark, – ignorance; blind, – the eyes; blindfold, hoodwink, mystify; puzzle etc. *(render uncertain)* 475; bamboozle etc. *(deceive)* 545.

be -concealed etc. *v.*; suffer an eclipse; retire from sight, couch; hide oneself; lie -hid, – in ambush, – low, – *perdu*, – snug, – close; seclude oneself etc. 893; lurk, sneak, skulk, slink, pussyfoot, prowl; steal -into, – out of, – by, – along; play at -bopeep, – hind and seek; hide in holes and corners.

Adj. concealed etc. *v.*; hidden; veiled, secret, recondite, mystic, cabalistic, occult, dark; cryptic, -al, private, privy, *in petto*, auricular, clandestine, close, inviolate.

behind a -screen etc. 530; under -cover, – an eclipse; in -ambush, – hiding, – disguise; in a -cloud, – fog, – mist, – haze, – dark corner; in the -shade, – dark; clouded, wrapt in clouds; invisible etc. 447; buried, underground, *perdu*; incommunicado; secluded etc. 893.

un-disclosed etc. 529; -told etc. 527; covert etc. *(latent)* 526; mysterious etc. *(unintelligible)* 519.

irrevealable, inviolable; confidential; esoteric; not ot be spoken of.

obreptitious, furtive, stealthy, feline, skulking etc. *v.*; surreptitious, underhand, hole and corner; sly etc. *(cunning)* 702; secretive, evasive, noncommittal, reserved, reticent, uncommunicative, buttoned up; close, – as wax; taciturn etc. 585.

Adv. secretly etc. *adj.*; in -secret, – private, – one's sleeve, – holes and corners; in the dark etc. *adj.*

janius clausis, with closed doors, *à huis clos*; hugger-mugger, *à la dérobée*; under the -cloak of, – rose, – table; *sub rosâ*, *en tapinois*, in the background, aside, on the sly, with bated breath, *sotto voce*, in a whisper, without beat of drum, *à la sourdine*.

in –, strict- confidence; confidentially etc. *adj.*; between -ourselves, – you and me; *entre nous, inter nos*, under the seal of secrecy; in -code, – cipher.

underhand, by stealth, like a thief in the night; stealthily etc. *adj.*; behind -the scenes, – the curtain, – one's back, – a screen etc. 530; *incognito; in camerâ*.

Phr. it -must, – will- go no further; 'tell it not in Gath,' nobody the wiser.

---

529. Disclosure.—N. disclosure; retection; unveiling etc. *v.*; deterration, revealment, revelation; divulgence, expos-ition, -ure; *exposé*; whole truth; tell-tale etc. *(news)* 532.

acknowledgment, avowal; confession, -al; shrift. bursting of a bubble; *dénouement*.

V. dis-close, -cover, -mask; draw –, draw aside –, lift –, raise –, lift up –, remove –, tear- the -veil, – curtain; un-mask, -veil, -fold, -cover, -seal, -kennel; take off –, break- the seal; lay -open, – bare; expose; open, – up; bare, bring to light; evidence; make -clear, – evident, – manifest; evince.

divulge, reveal, break; let into the secret; reveal the secrets of the prison-house; tell etc. (*inform*) 527; breathe, utter, blab, peach; let -out, – fall, – drop, – the cat out of the bag; betray; tell tales, – out of school; come out with; give -vent, – utterance- to; open the lips, blurt out, vent, whisper about; speak out etc. (*make manifest*) 525; make public etc. 531; unriddle etc. (*find out*) 480*a*; split; blow the gaff; break the news.

acknowledge, allow, concede, grant, admit, own, confess, avow, throw off all disguise, turn inside out, make a clean breast; show one's -hand, – cards; unburden –, disburden- one's -mind, – conscience, – heart; open –, lay, bare –, tell a piece of- one's mind; unbosom oneself, own to the soft impeachment; say –, speak- the truth; turn -King's, – Queen's, – States's- evidence.

raise –, drop –, lift –, remove –, throw off- the mask; expose; debunk; lay open; un-deceive, - beguile; disabuse, set right, correct, open the eyes of; *désillusionner*.

be -disclosed etc.; transpire, come to light; come in sight etc. (*be visible*) 446; become known, escape the lips; come –, ooze –, creep –, leak –, peep –, crop- out; show its -face, – colors; discover etc. itself; break through the clouds, flash on the mind.

Adj. disclosed etc. *v.*

Int. out with it!

Phr. the murder is out; a light breaks in upon one; the scales fall from one's eyes; the eyes are opened.

530. Ambush. [Means of concealment.]—**N.** hiding-place; secret -place, drawer; recess, hole, funk hole, holes and corners; closet, crypt, *adytum*, abditory, *oubliette*, safe, – deposit.

ambush, -buscade; stalking horse; lurking-hole, -place; secret path, backstairs; retreat etc. (*refuge*) 666.

screen, cover, shade, blinder; veil, curtain, blind, *purdah*, cloak, cloud.

mask, vizor, visor, disguise, masquerade dress, domino; *camouflage*.

pitfall etc. (*source of danger*) 667; trap etc. (*snare*) 545.

v. ambush, ambuscade, lie in ambush etc. (*hide oneself*) 528; lie in wait for; set a trap for etc. (*deceive*) 545.

Adv. *aux aguets.*

531. Publication.—**N.** publication; public - announcement etc. 527; promulgation, propagation, proclamation, pronouncement, encylical, *pronunciamento*; circulation, indiction, edition, imprint, impression, printing; hue and cry.

publicity, notoriety, currency, flagrancy, cry, *bruit*; *vox populi*; report etc. (*news*) 532.

the Press, fourth estate, public press, newspaper, periodical, journal, gazette; house organ, trade publication, tabloid, daily, weekly, monthly, quarterly, annual, magazine, monograph, book; review; news sheet, special edition, supplement, feature, rotogravure, comic strips; leaflet, pamphlet; telegraphy; publisher etc. *v.*

circular, – letter; manifesto, advertisement,

puff, placard, bill, *affiche*, broadside, poster; notice etc. 527; program.

V. publish; make -public, – known etc. (*information*) 527; speak –, talk- of; broach, utter; put forward; circulate, propagate, promulgate; spread –, abroad; rumor, diffuse, disseminate, evulgate; put –, give –, send- forth; emit, edit, get out; issue; cover, report; bring –, lay –, drag- before the public; give -out, – to the world; put –, bandy –, hawk –, buzz –, whisper –, bruit –, blaze- about; drag into the -open day, – limelight; voice.

proclaim, herald, blazon, blaze –, noise- abroad; sound a trumpet; trumpet –, thunder- forth; give tongue; announce with -beat of drum, – flourish of trumpets; proclaim -from the housetops, – at Charing Cross, at the cross roads; declare, declaim.

advertise, placard, post, – up; *afficher*, publish in the Gazette, send round the crier.

raise a -cry, – hue and cry, – report; set news afloat.

telegraph, cable, wireless, broadcast.

be -published etc; be –, become- public etc. *adj.*; come out; go –, fly –, buzz –, blow- about; get -about, – abroad, – afloat, – wind; find vent; see the light; go forth, take air, acquire currency, pass current; go -the rounds, – the round of the newspapers, – through the length and breadth of the land; *virum volitare per ora*; pass from mouth to mouth; spread; run –, spread- like wildfire.

Adj. published etc. *v.*; current etc. (*news*) 532; in circulation, public; notorious; flagrant, arrant; open etc. 525; trumpet-tongued; encyclical, promulgatory; exoteric.

Adv. publicly etc. *adj.*; in open court, with open doors; in the limelight.

Int. *Oyez!* O yes! notice!

Phr. notice is hereby given; this is –, these are- to give notice.

532. News.—**N.** news; information etc. 527; piece –, budget- of -news, – information; report, story, yarn, copy, filler, intelligence, tidings; stop press news.

word, advice, *aviso*, message; dis-, des-patch; telegram, cable, wireless telegram, radio-gram, marconi-gram, communication, errand, embassy; *bulletin*.

microphone; public address system, P.A.; walkie talkie, radio -telephone, -phone.

radio, wireless (Eng.), high fidelity, hi fi, radio set, transistor, receiver; speaker, loudspeaker, amplifier, tweeter, woofer; transmitter, broadcaster; AM –, FM –, short wave – transmitter; radio station, studio, control room, network, hookup, circuit; frequency, kilocycles, megacycles; band, channel, modulation, amplification; broadcast, program, newscast, network show, commerical announcement, serial, sound effects; signature, station – identification, – break; radio listener, audiophile.

television, TV, video, color television; television –, live – broadcast, telecast, TV show; televising, telecasting, transmission, television channel, video, audio, beam, reception, image, test pattern; rain, snow, ghost; television –, TV – station, mobile unit, TVmobile, transmitter, televisor, boost, camera; set, monitor, tube, screen.

rumor, hearsay, *on dit*, flying rumor, news stirring, cry, buzz, *bruit*, fame; talk, *ouï-dire*, scandal, eavesdropping; town –, table- talk; tittle-tattle; *canard*, topic of the day, idea afloat.

fresh –, stirring –, old – stale- news; glad tidings; old –, stale- story.

narrator etc. (*describe*) 594; news-, scandal-monger; tale-bearer; tell-tale, gossip, tattler, busybody, chatterer; informer.

broad-, news-, sports-caster; commentator, announcer, master of ceremonies, M.C., programmer, sound man, radioman, ham, radioperator.

television technician, TV man, cameraman, soundman.

V. transpire etc. (*be disclosed*) 529; rumor etc. (*publish*) 531.

broadcast, radio, transmit, send, release, beam; sign – on, – off; go on –, go off – the air, monitor; listen –, tune – in.

tele-vise, -cast; color cast.

Adj. many-tongued; rumored; publicly –, currently- -rumored, – reported; rife, current, floating, afloat, going about, in circulation, in everyone's mouth, all over the town.

Adv. as the story -goes, – runs; as they say, it is said.

533. Secret.—N. secret; dead –, profound-secret; *arcanum*, mystery; latency etc. 526; Asian mystery; sealed book, secrets of the prison-house; *le dessous des cartes*.

enigma, riddle, puzzle, nut to crack, conundrum, charade, rebus, logogriph; mono-, ana-gram; acrostic, cross-word puzzle; Sphinx; *crux criticorum*.

maze, labyrinth, Hyrcynian wood.

problem etc. (*question*) 461; paradox etc. (*difficulty*) 704; unintelligibility etc. 519; *terra incognita* etc. (*ignorance*) 491.

Adj. secret etc. (*concealed*) 528.

534. Messenger.—N. messenger, envoy, emissary, legate; nuncio, internuncio; intermediary; ambassador etc. (*diplomatist*) 758.

marshal, flag-bearer, herald, crier, trumpeter, bellman, pursuivant, *parlementaire*, *apparitor*.

courier, runner, dawk, *estafette*; Hermes, Mercury, Iris, Ariel.

postman, letter carrier, telegraph boy, messenger boy, district messenger; despatch rider, commissionaire, erand-boy.

mail; post, -office; letter-bag; mail -boat, - train, – coach, – van, aerial mail; tele-graph, -phone; cable, wire; carrier-pigeon; wireless telegraph, -phone; radiotele-graph, -phone.

journalist, newspaperman, reporter; gentleman –, representative- of the press; sob sister; penny-a-liner; special –, war –, own- correspondent; spy, scout; informer etc. 527.

535. Affirmation.—N. affirm-ance, -ation; statement, allegation, assertion, predication, declaration, word, averment.

asseveration, adjuration, swearing, oath, af-

fidavit; deposition etc. (*record*) 551; avouchment, assurance; protest, -ation; profession; acknowledgment etc. (*assent*) 488; pledge.

vote, voice, suffrage, ballot.

remark, observation; position etc. (*proposition*) 514; saying, *dictum*, sentence, *ipse dixit*.

emphasis, positiveness, peremptoriness; dogmatism etc. (*certainty*) 474; dogmatist etc. 887.

V. assert; make -an assertion etc. *n.*; have one's say; say, affirm, predicate, declare, state, represent; protest, profess.

put -forth, – forward; advance, allege, propose, propound, enunciate, enounce, broach, set forth, hold out, maintain, contend, pronounce, pretend.

depose, depone, aver, avow, avouch, asseverate, swear; make –, take one's- oath; make –, swear –, put in- an affidavit; take one's Bible oath, kiss the book, vow, *vitam impendere vero*; swear till one is black in the face, – all's blue; be sworn, call Heaven to witness; vouch, warrant, certify, assure, swear by bell, book and candle.

swear by etc. (*believe*) 484; insist –, take one's stand- upon; emphasize, lay stress on; assert – roundly, – positively; lay down, – the law; raise one's voice, dogmatize, have the last word; rap out; repeat; re-assert, -affirm.

announce etc. (*information*) 527; acknowledge etc. (*assent*) 488; attest etc. (*evidence*) 467; adjure etc. (*put to one's oath*) 768.

Adj. asserting etc. *v.*; declaratory, predicatory, pronunciative, affirmative, *soi-disant*; positive; certain etc. 474; express, explicit etc. (*patent*) 525; absolute, emphatic, flat, broad, round, pointed, marked, distinct, decided, confident, assertive, insistent, trenchant, dogmatic, definitive, formal, solemn, categorical, peremptory; unretracted; predicable, affirmable.

Adv. affirmatively etc. *adj.*; in the affirmative, with emphasis, *ex cathedrâ*, without fear of contradiction.

I must say, indeed, i' faith, let me tell you, why, give me leave to say, marry, you may be sure, I'd have you to know; upon my -word, – honor; by my troth, egad, I assure you; by -jingo, – Jove, – George, – etc.; troth, seriously, sadly; in –, in sober- -sadness, – truth, – earnest; of a truth, truly, pardi, perdy; in all conscience, upon oath; be assured etc. (*belief*) 484; yes etc. (*assent*) 488; I'll -warrant, – warrant you, – engage, – answer for it, – be bound, – venture to say, – take my oath; in fact, as a matter of fact, forsooth, joking apart; so help me God; not to mince the matter.

Phr. quoth he; *dixi*.

536. Negation.—N. ne-, abne-gation; denial; dis-avowal, -claimer; abjuration; contra-diction, -vention; recusation, protest, rebuttal; recusancy etc. (*dissent*) 489; flat –, emphatic- -contradiction, – denial; *démenti*.

qualification etc. 469; repudiation etc. 610; retraction etc. 607; confutation etc. 479; refusal etc. 764; prohibition etc. 761.

V. deny; contra-dict, -vene; controvert, give denial to, gainsay, negative, shake the head.

dis-own, -affirm, -claim, -avow; recant etc. 607; revoke etc. (*abrogate*) 756.

dispute, impugn, traverse, rebut, join issue upon; bring –, call- in question etc. (doubt) 485.

deny -flatly, – peremptorily, – emphatically, – absolutely, – wholly, – entirely; give the lie to, belie.

repudiate etc. 610; set aside, ignore etc. 460; rebut etc. (confute) 479; qualify etc. 469; refuse etc. 764.

Adj. denying etc. v.; denied etc. v.; contradictory; negat-ive, -ory; revocatory; recusant etc. (dissenting) 489; at issue upon.

Adv. no, nay, not, nowise; not a -bit, – whit, – jot; not -at all, – in the least, – so; no such thing; nothing of the -kind, – sort; quite the contrary, tout au contraire, far from it; tant s'en faut; on no account, in no respect; by -no, – no manner of-means; negatively.

phr. there never was a greater mistake; I know better; non haec in foedera.

537. Teaching.—N. teaching etc. v.; instruction; edification; education; pedagogy; tuition; tutor-, tutel-age; direction, guidance.

qualification, preparation; train-, school-ing etc. v.; discipline; exer-cise, -citation; drill, practice.

persuasion, proselytism, propagandism, propaganda; in-doctrination, -culcation, oculation.

explanation etc. (interpretation) 522; lesson, lecture, sermon, homily; apologue, parable; discourse, prelection, preachment, disquisition.

exercise, task; curriculum; course, – of study; grammar, three R's, initiation, A.B.C etc. (beginning) 66.

elementary –, primary –, secondary –, grammar school –, high school –, college –, university –, technical –, liberal –, classical –, religious –, denominational –, moral –, secular-education; technical –, vocational- training; university extension lectures; propaedeutics, moral tuition; evening classes, correspondence course.

physical education, gymnastics, calisthenics, eurythmics; sloyd.

V. teach, instruct, edify, school, tutor; cram, prime, coach; enlighten etc. (inform) 527.

in-culcate, -doctrinate, -oculate, -fuse, -stil, -fix, – graft, -filtrate; im-bue, -pregnate, -plant; graft, sow the seeds of, disseminate, propagandize.

give an idea of; put -up to, – in the way of; set right.

sharpen the wits, enlarge the mind; give new ideas, open the eyes, bring forward, 'teach the young idea how to shoot;' improve etc. 658.

expound etc. (interpret) 522; lecture; prelect; read –, give- a -lesson, – lecture, – sermon, – discourse; hold forth, preach; sermon-, moral-ize; point a moral.

train, discipline; bring up, – to; educate, form, ground, prepare, qualify, drill, exercise, practice, habituate, familiarize with, nurture, dry-nurse, breed, rear, take in hand; break, – in; tame; pre-instruct; initiate; inure etc. (habituate) 613.

put to nurse, send to school.

direct, guide; direct attention to etc. (attention) 457; impress upon the -mind, – memory; beat into, – the head; convince etc. (belief) 484.

Adj. teaching etc. v.; taught etc. v.; educational;

scholastic, academic, doctrinal; disciplinal; instructive, didactic, hortative, pedagogic, tutorial.

Phr. the schoolmaster abroad.

538. Misteaching—N. mis-teaching, -information, -intelligence, -guidance, -direction, -persuasion, -instruction, -leading etc. v.; perversion, false teaching; sophistry etc. 477; college of Laputa; the blind leading the blind.

V. mis-inform, -teach, -direct, -guide, -instruct, -correct; pervert; put on a false –, throw off the-scent; deceive etc. 545; mislead etc. (error) 495; misrepresent; lie etc. 544; ambiguas in vulgum spargere voces, preach to the wise, teach one's grandmother to suck eggs.

render unintelligible etc. 519; bewilder etc. (uncertainty) 475; mystify etc. (conceal) 528; unteach.

Adj. mjsteaching etc. v.; unedifying.

Phr. piscem natare doces.

539. Learning.—N. learning; acquisition of -knowledge etc. 490, – skill etc. 698; acquirement, attainment; edification, scholarship, erudition; lore; information; self-instruction; study, reading, perusal; inquiry etc. 461.

ap-, prenticeship; pupil-age, -arity; tutelage, novitiate, matriculation.

docility etc. (willingness) 602; aptitude etc. 698.

V. learn; acquire –, gain –, receive –, take in –, drink in –, imbibe –, pick up –, gather –, get –, obtain –, collect –, glean- -knowledge, – information, – learning.

acquaint oneself with, master; make oneself master of, – acquainted with; grind, cram; get –, coach- up; learn by -heart, – rote.

read, spell, peruse; con –, pore –, thumb- over; wade through; dip into; run the eye -over, – through; turn over the leaves.

study; be -studious etc. adj.; consume the midnight oil, mind one's book.

go to -school, – college, – the university; serve -an (or one's) apprenticeship, – one's time; learn one's trade; be -informed etc. 527; be -taught etc. 537.

Adj. studious; schol-astic, -arly; teachable; docile etc. (willing) 602; apt etc. 698; industrious etc. 682; learned erudite.

Adv. at one's books; in statu pupillari etc. (learner) 541.

540. Teacher.—N. teacher, trainer, instructor, institutor, master, tutor, don, director, Corypheus, dry nurse, coach, grinder, crammer; governor, bear-leader; governess, duenna; disciplinarian.

professor, lecturer, reader, prelector, prolocutor; preacher; Boanerges; pastor etc. (clergy) 996; schoolmaster, dominie, usher, pedagogue, abecedarian; schoolmistress, dame, monitor, proctor, pupil-teacher.

expositor etc. 524; preceptor, guide; mentor etc. (adviser) 695; pioneer, apostle, missionary, propagandist, moonshee; example etc. (model for imitation) 22.

professorship etc. (school) 542.

tutelage etc. (teaching) 537.

Adj. professorial, tutorial etc. 537.

541. Learner.—N. learner, scholar, student, *alumnus*, *élève*, pupil; ap-, prentice; articled clerk; school-boy, -girl, beginner, tyro, abecedarian, alphabetarian.

recruit, novice, neophyte, tenderfoot, inceptor, *débutant*, catechumen, probationer; undergraduate; freshman, frosh; sophomore, junior, senior; junior −, senior- soph; sophister, questionist, fellow-, commoner, pensioner, exhibitioner, sizar, scholar, fellow, advanced −, post graduate −, research- student.

class, form, grade, standard, remove; pupilage etc. (*learning*) 539.

disciple, follower, apostle, proselyte; fellow student, school-mate, -fellow, class mate, condisciple.

Adj. *in statu pupillari*, in leading strings, sophomoric.

542. School.—N. school, academy, university, *alma mater*, college, seminary, Lyceum; instit-ute, -ution, *conservatoire*; *palaestra*, *gymnasium*.

day −, boarding −, public −, preparatory −, elementary −, primary −, nursery −, dame's −, grammar −, Board −, County −, Council −, parochial −, denominational −, Sunday −, religious −, collegiate −, secondary −, continuation −, night −, correspondence −, secretarial −, military −, law −, medical −, business −, technical- school; technical −, training- college; Polytechnic; training ship; *Kindergarten*, nursery, *crèche*, reformatory.

pulpit, desk, reading desk, ambo, class-, lectureroom, theater, amphitheater, forum, stage, rostrum, platform, hustings, tribune.

school −, horn −, text-book; grammar, primer, abecedary, rudiments, manual, *vade mecum*, Lindley, Murray, Cocker.

professor-, lecture-, reader-ship; chair; schoolmaster etc. 540.

School Board, Council of Education; *propaganda*.

Adj. scholastic, academic, collegiate; educational.

Adv. *ex cathedrâ*.

543. Veracity.—N. veracity; truthfulness, frankness etc. *adj.*; truth, sooth, sincerity, candor, honesty, fidelity; plain dealing, *bona fides*; love of truth; probity etc. 939; ingenuousness etc. (*artlessness*) 703.

the truth the whole truth and nothing but the truth; honest −, sober- truth etc. (*fact*) 494; unvarnished tale; light of truth.

V. speak −, tell- the truth; speak by the card; paint in its −, show oneself in ones -true colors; make a clean breast of it. (*disclose*) 529; speak one's mind etc. (*be blunt*) 703; not -lie etc. 544, − deceive etc. 545.

Adj. truthful, true; ver-acious, -edical; scrupulous etc. (*honorable*) 939; sincere, candid, frank, open, straightforward, unreserved; open-, true-, simple- hearted; honest, trustworthy; undissembling etc. (dissemble etc. 544); guileless, pure; unperjured, ture blue, as good as one's word;

unaffected, unfeigned, *bonâ fide*; outspoken, ingenuous etc. (*artless*) 703; undisguised etc. (*real*) 494.

Adv. truly etc. (*really*) 494; on oath; in plain words etc. 703; in −, with −, of a −, in good −, very- truth; as the -dial to the sun, − needle to the pole; honor bright; troth; in good -sooth, − earnest; unfeignedly, with no nonsense, in sooth, sooth to say, *bonâ fide*, in *foro conscientiae*; without equivocation; *cartes sur table*, from the bottom of one's heart; by my troth etc. (*affirmation*) 535.

544. Falsehood.—N. false-hood, -ness; fals-ity, -ification; misrepresentation; deception etc. 545; untruth etc. 546; guile; bad faith; lying etc. *v.*; misrepresentation; mendacity, perjury, false swearing; forgery, invention, fabrication; subreption; covin.

perversion −, suppression- of truth; *suppressio veri*; perversion, distortion, false coloring; exaggeration etc. 549; prevarication, equivocation, shuffling, fencing, evasion, fraud; *suggestio falsi* etc. (*lie*) 546; mystification etc. (*concealment*) 528; simulation etc. (*imitation*) 19; dis-simulation, -sembling; deceit.

sham; pretence, pretending, malingering.

lip-homage, − service; mouth honor; hollowness; mere -show, − outside, eye-wash, window dressing; duplicity, double dealing, insincerity, hypocrisy, cant, humbug, casuistry; jesuit-ism, -ry; pharisaism; Machiavelism, 'organized hypocrisy;' crocodile tears, mealy-mouthedness, quackery; charlatan-ism, -ry; gammon; bun-kum, -come; flam, ban, flim-flam, cajolery, flattery; Judas kiss; perfidy etc. (*bad faith*) 940; *il volto sciolto i pensieri stretti*.

unfairness etc. (*dishonesty*) 940; artfulness etc. (*cunning*) 702; misstatement etc. (*error*) 495.

V. be -false etc. *adj.*, − a liar etc. 548; speak -falsely etc. *adv.*; tell a -lie etc. 546; lie, fib; lie like a trooper; swear falsely, forswear, perjure oneself, bear false witness.

mis-state, -quote, -cite, -report, -represent; belie, falsify, pervert, distort; put a false construction upon etc. (*misinterpret*) 523.

prevaricate, equivocate, quibble; palter, − to the understanding; *répondre en Normand*; trim, shuffle, fence, mince the truth, beat about the bush, blow hot and cold, play fast and loose.

garble, gloss over, disguise, give a color to; give −, put- a -gloss, − false coloring- upon; color, varnish, cook, dress up, embroider; varnish right and puzzle wrong; exaggerate etc. 549.

invent, fabricate; trump −, get- up; forge, hatch, concoct; romance etc. (*imagine*) 515; cry 'wolf!'

dis-semble, -simulate; feign, assume, put on, pretend, make believe; play -false, − a double game; coquet; act −, play- a part; affect etc. 855; simulate, pass off for; counterfeit, fake, sham, make a show of; malinger; swing the lead; say the grapes are sour.

cant, play the hypocrite, sham Abraham, *faire pattes de velours*, put on the mask, clean the outside of the platter, lie like a conjuror; hang out −, hold out −, sail under- false colors; 'commend the poisoned chalice to the lips;' *ambiguas in vulgus spargere voces*; deceive etc. 545.

Adj. false, deceitful, mendacious, unveracious,

fraudulent, untruthful, dishonest; faith-, truth-, troth-less; un-fair, -candid; evasive; un-, disingenuous; hollow, insincere, *Parthis mendacior*; forsworn.

canting; hypocrit-, jesuit-, pharisa-ical; tartuffish; Machiavelian; double-tongued, -faced, -handed, -minded, -hearted, -dealing; two-faced, bare-faced; Janus-faced; smooth-faced, -spoken, -tongued; plausible; mealy-mouthed; affected etc. 855.

collus-ive, -ory; artful etc. (*cunning*) 702; perfidious etc. 940, spurious etc. (*deceptive*) 545; untrue etc. 546; falsified etc. *v.*; covinous.

Adv. falsely etc. *adj.*; *à la Tartufe*, with a double tongue; out of whole cloth; slily etc. (*cunning*) 702.

545. Deception.—N. deception; falseness etc. 544; untruth etc. 546; impos-ition, -ture; fraud, deceit, guile; fraudulen-ce, -cy; covin; knavery etc. (*cunning*) 702; misrepresentation etc. (*falsehood*) 544.

delusion, gullery, bluff, spoof, *blague*; juggl-ing, -ery; sleight of hand, legerdemain; presti-giation, -digitation; magic etc. 992; conjur-ing, -ation; hocus pocus, jockeyship; trickery, coggery, hanky-panky, chicanery, pettifogging, sharp practice; *supercherie*, cozenage, circumvention, ingannation; collusion; treachery etc. 940; practical joke.

trick, cheat, wile, ruse, blind, feint, plant, bubble fetch, catch, chicane, juggle, reach, hocus, bite, thimble-rig, card-sharping, artful dodge, machination, swindle, hoax; tricks upon travellers; confidence trick; strategem etc. (*artifice*) 702; theft etc. 791.

snare, trap, pitfall, decoy, gin; sprin-ge, -gle; noose, hook; bait, decoy-duck, tub to the whale, baited trap, *guet-à-pens*; cobweb, net, meshes, toils, mouse-trap, bird-lime; ambush etc. 530; trapdoor, sliding panel, false bottom; spring-net, -gun; mask, -ed battery; mine; booby trap.

Cornish hug; wolf in sheep's clothing etc. (*deceiver*) 548; disguise, -ment; false colors, masquerade, mummery, borrowed plumes; *pattes de velours*.

mockery etc. (*imitation*) 19; copy etc. 21; counterfeit, sham, brummagem, make-believe, forgery, fraud, fake; lie etc. 546; 'a mockery, a delusion, and a snare,' hollow mockery.

whited –, painted- sepulcher; tinsel, paste, false jewelry, scagliola, ormolu, German silver, Britannia metal, paint; jerry building; man of straw.

illusion etc. (*error*) 495; *ignis fatuus* etc. 423; *mirage* etc. 443.

V. deceive, take in; defraud, cheat, jockey, do, cozen, diddle, nab, gyp, chouse, double cross, play one false, bilk, cully, jilt, bite, pluck, swindle, victimize; abuse; mystify; blind one's eyes; blindfold, hoodwink, spoof, bluff; throw dust into the eyes, 'keep the word of promise to the ear and break it to the hope,' 'draw a herring across the trail.'

impose –, practice –, play –, put –, palm –, foist- upon; snatch a verdict.

circumvent, overreach; out-reach, -wit; maneuvre; steal a march upon, give the go-by to, leave in the lurch.

set –, lay- a -trap, – snare- for; bait the hook, forlay, spread the toils, lime; decoy, waylay, lure,

beguile, delude, inveigle; tra-, tre-pan; kidnap; let-, hook-in; trick; en-, in-trap, -snare, entoil, benet; nick, springe; catch, – in a trap; sniggle, entangle, illaqueate, hocus, practice on one's credulity, dupe, gull, hoax, fool, befool, bamboozle; hum, -bug; gammon, stuff up, dope, sell; play a -trick, – practical joke- upon one; balk, trip up, throw a tub to a whale; fool to the top of one's bent, send on -a wild goose chase, – a fool's errand; make -game, – a fool, – an April fool, – an ass- of; trifle with, cajole, flatter; come over etc. (*influence*) 615; gild the pill, make things pleasant, divert, put a good face upon; dissemble etc. 544.

cog, – the dice, play with marked cards; live by one's wits, play at hide and seek; obtain money under false pretences etc. (*steal*) 791; conjure, juggle, practice chicanery; gerrymander.

play –, palm –, foist –, fob- off.

lie etc. 544; misinform etc. 538; mislead etc. (*error*) 495; betray etc. 940; be -deceived etc. 547.

Adj. deceived etc. *v.*; deceiving etc. *v.*; cunning etc. 702; prestigi-ous, -atory; decept-ive, -ious; deceitful, covinous; delus-ive, -ory; illus-ive, -ory; elusive, insidious, *ad captandum vulgus*.

untrue etc. 546; mock, sham, make-believe, counterfeit, faked, pseudo, spurious, so-called; pretended, feigned, trumped up, bogus, scamped, fraudulent, tricky, factitious, artificial, bastard; surreptitious, illegitimate, contraband, adulterated, sophisticated; unsound, rotten at the core; colorable; disguised; meretricious; tinsel, pinch-beck, plated; catch-penny; Brummagem; simulated etc. 544.

Adv. under -false colors, – the garb of, – cover of; over the left.

Phr. *fronti nulla fides.*

546. Untruth.—N. untruth, falsehood, lie, story, thing that is not, fib, bounce, crammer, taradiddle, whopper.

forgery, fabrication, invention; mis-statement, -representation; perversion, falsification, gloss, *suggestio falsi*; exaggeration etc. 549.

fiction; fable, nursery tale; romance etc. (*imagination*) 515; untrue –, false –, trumped up- -story, – statement; thing devised by the enemy; *canard*; shave, sell, hum, yarn, traveler's tale, Canterbury tale, cock and bull story, fairy tale, clap-trap.

myth, moonshine, bosh, all my eye, -and Betty Martin, mare's nest, farce.

irony; half truth, white lie, pious fraud; mental reservation etc. (*concealment*) 528.

pretence, pretext; false -plea etc. 617; subterfuge, evasion, shift, shuffle, make-believe; sham etc. (*deception*) 545.

profession, empty words; Judas kiss etc. (*hypocrisy*) 544; disguise etc. (*mask*) 530.

V. have a false meaning; not ring true.

pretend, sham, feign, counterfeit, make believe.

Adj. untrue, false, trumped up; void of –, without- foundation; far from the truth, false as dicer's oaths; unfounded, *ben trovato*, invented, fabulous, fabricated, forged; fict-, fact-, supposit-, surrept-itious; e-, il-lusory; ironical; satirical; evasive; *soi-disant* etc. (*misnamed*) 565.

Phr. *se non e vero e ben trovato.*

547. Dupe.—N. dupe, gull, gudgeon, *gobemouche*, cull, cully, victim, sucker, pigeon, April fool; laughing stock etc. 857; Cyclops, simple Simon, flat, mug, greenhorn; fool etc. 501; puppet, cat's paw.

V. be -deceived etc. 545, – the dupe of; fall into a trap; swallow –, nibble at- the bait; bite; catch a Tartar.

Adj. credulous etc. 486; mistaken etc. (*error*) 495.

548. Deceiver.—N. deceiver etc. (deceive etc. 545); dissembler, hypocrite; sophist, Pharisee, Jesuit, Mawworm, Pecksniff, Joseph Surface, Tartufe, Janus; serpent, snake in the grass, cockatrice, Judas, wolf in sheep's clothing; Molly Maguire; jilt; shuffler.

liar etc. (lie etc. 544; story-teller, perjurer, false-witness, *mentuer à triple étage*, Scapin.

imposter, pretender, capper, decoy, fraud, *soi-disant*, humbug; adventurer; Cagliostro, Fernam Mendez Pinto; ass in lion's skin etc. (*bungler*) 701; actor etc. (*stage player*) 599.

quack, *charlatan*, mountebank, saltimbanco, *saltimbanque*, empiric, quacksalver, medicaster.

conjuror, juggler, magician, necromancer, trickster, prestidigitator, medium, jockey; crimp; decoy-duck, stool pigeon; rogue, knave, cheat; swindler etc. (*thief*) 792; jobber.

549. Exaggeration.—N. exaggeration; expansion etc. 194; hyperbole, stretch, strain, coloring; high coloring, caricature, *caricatura*; extravagance etc. (*nonsense*) 497; Baron Munchausen; men in buckram, yarn, fringe, embroidery, traveler's tale; Pelion upon Ossa.

storm in a teacup; much ado about nothing etc. (*over-estimation*) 482; puffery etc. (*boasting*) 884; rant etc. (*turgescence*) 577.

figure of speech, *façon de parler*; stretch of fancy, – the imagination; flight of fancy etc. (*imagination*) 515.

false coloring etc. (*falsehood*) 544; aggravation etc. 835.

V. exaggerate, magnify, pile up, aggravate; amplify etc. (*expand*) 194; overestimate etc. 482; hyperbolize; over-charge, -state, -draw, -lay, -shoot the mark, -praise; make -much, – the most- of; strain, – a point; stretch, – a point; go great lengths; spin a long yarn; draw –, shoot with- a long-bow; deal in the marvelous.

out -Herod Herod, run riot, talk at random.

heighten, overcolor; color -highly, – too highly; embroider, *broder*; flourish; color etc. (*misrepresent*) 544; puff etc. (*boast*) 884.

Adj. exaggerated etc. v.; overwrought; bombastic etc. (*magniloquent*) 577; hyperbolical, on stilts; fabulous, extravagant, preposterous, egregious, *outré*, high-flying.

Adv. hyperbolically etc. *adj.*

550. Indication.—N. indication; symbol-ism, -ization; semeio-logy, -tics; sign of the times.

lineament, feature, *trait*, characteristic, trick,

diagnostic; divining-rod; cloven hoof; footfall; means of recognition; earmark.

sign, symbol; ind-ex, -ice, -icator; point, -er; marker; exponent, note, token, symptom.

type, figure, emblem, cipher, device; representation etc. 554; epigraph, motto, posy.

gest-ure, -iculation; pantomime; wink, glance, leer; nod, shrug, beck; touch, nudge; grip; dactylology, -nomy; freemasonry, telegraphy, chirology, by-play, dumb-show; cue; hint etc. 527; clue, clew, key, scent, tract etc. 551.

signal, -post; rocket, blue light; watch-fire, -tower; telegraph, semaphore, flag-staff; cresset, fiery cross; calumet; heliograph, signal-, flash-lamp; radar, radar signal, pulse –, microwave –, radar; tracing, blips, pips.

mark, line, stroke, dash, score, stripe, streak, scratch, tick, dot, point, notch, nick, blaze; asterisk, red letter, Italics, heavy type, inverted commas, quotation marks, sublineation, underlining, jotting; print; impr-int, -ess, ession; note, annotation, mark of exclamation.

[For identification] badge, criterion; counter-check, -mark, -sign, -foil, duplicate, tally; label, tab, ticket, stub, billet, letter, counter, *tessera*, card, bill, check; witness, voucher; stamp; *cachet*; trade –, Hall- mark; broad arrow; signature; address –, visiting- card; *carte de visite*; credentials etc. (*evidence*) 467; passport, identity book; attestation; hand, – writing, sign-manual; cipher; monogram, – mark, seal, sigil, signet; autograph, -y, paraph, brand; superscription; in-, en-dorsement; title, heading, rubric, docket; *mot -de passe*, – *du guet*; *passe-parole*; shibboleth; watch-, catch-, password; open *sesame*.

insignia, banner, -et, -ol; bandrol; flag, colors, streamer, standard, eagle, labarum, oriflamb, *oriflamme*; figure-head; ensign; pen-non, -nant, -dant; burgee, blue Peter, jack, ancient, gonfalon, union-jack; tricolor, stars and stripes; bunting.

heardlry, crest; coat of –, arms; armorial bearings, hatchment; e-, scutcheon; shield, supporters; livery, uniform; cockade, *epaulette*, brassard, chevron; garland, chaplet, love-knot, fillet, favor.

[Of locality] beacon, cairn, post, staff, flagstaff, hand, pointer, vane, cock, weathercock; guide-, hand-, finger-, directing-, sign-post; pillars of Hercules, pharos, signal fire; land-, sea-mark; lighthouse, balize; pole-, load-, lode-star; cynosure, guide; address, direction, name; sign, -board.

[Of the future] warning etc. 668; omen etc. 512; prefigurement etc. 511. [Of the past] trace record etc. 551. [Of danger] warning etc. 668; alarm etc. 669. [Of authority] scepter etc. 747. [Of triumph] trophy etc. 733. [Of quantity] gauge etc. 466. [Of distance] mile-stone, -post. [Of disgrace] brand, fool's cap, stigma, mark of Cain. [For detection] check, tell-tale; test etc. (*experiment*) 463.

notification etc. (*information*) 527; advertisement etc. (*publication*) 531.

word of command, call; bugle-, trumpet-call; reveille, taps; bell, alarum, cry; battle –, rallying-cry.

church, bell, angelus, sacring bell; muezzin.

exposition etc. (*explanation*) 522; proof etc. (*evidence*) 463; pattern etc. (*prototype*) 22.

V. indicate; be the -sign etc. *n.*- of; denote,

betoken; argue, testify etc. (*evidence*) 467; bear the -impress etc. *n.*- of; con-note, -notate.

represent, stand for; typify etc. (*prefigure*) 511; symbolize.

put -an indication, – a mark, – etc. *n.*; note, mark, tick, blaze, stamp, earmark; set one's seal upon; label, ticket, docket; dot, spot, score, dash, trace, chalk; print; im-print, -press, surprint; engrave, stereotype, electrotype.

signal, transmit, send, radiate, beam, deflect, echo, bounce back, return.

make a -sign etc. *n.*; signalize; give –, hang out-a signal; beck, -on; gesture; not; wink, glance, leer, nudge, shrug, tip the wink; gesticulate; raise –, hold up- the-finger, – hand; saw the air, suit the action to the word.

wave –, unfurl –, hoist –, hang out- a banner etc. *n.*; wave -the hand, – a kerchief; give the cue etc. (*inform*) 527; show one's colors; give –, sound- an alarm; beat the drum, sound the trumpets, raise a cry.

sign, seal, attest etc. (*evidence*) 467; underline etc. (*give importance to*) 642; call attention to etc. (*attention*) 457; give notice etc. (*inform*) 527.

Adj. indicat-ing etc. *v.*; -ive, -ory; de-, connotative; diacritical, representative, typical, symbolic, pantomimic, pathognomonic, symptomatic, ominous, characteristic, demonstrative, diagnostic, exponential, emblematic, armorial; individual etc. (*special*) 79.

known –, recognizable- by; indicated etc. *v.*; pointed, marked.

[Capable of being denoted] denotable; indelible.

Adv. in token of; symbolically etc. *adj.*; in dumb show.

Phr. *ecce signum*; *ex ungue leonem*, *ex pede Herculem*.

551. Record.—N. trace, vestige, relic, remains; scar, *cicatrix*; foot-step, -mark, -print; track, mark, wake, trail, spoor, scent, *piste*.

monument, hatchment, escutcheon, slab, tablet, trophy, achievement; obelisk, pillar, column, monolith, cromlech, dolmen; memorial; *memento* etc. (*memory*) 505; testimonial, medal, ribbon, order; commemoration etc. (*celebration*) 883.

record, note, minute; *dossier*; register, -try; census, roll etc. (*list*) 86; cartulary, diptych, Domesday book; entry, memorandum, indorsement, inscription, copy, duplicate, docket; notch etc. (*mark*) 550; muniment, deed etc. (*security*) 771; document; deposition, *procès-verbal*; affidavit; certificate etc. (*evidence*) 467.

note-, memorandum-, pocket-, commonplace-book; portfolio; scoring-board, -sheet; bulletin board; card index, file; pigeon-holes, *excerpta*, *adversaria*, jottings, dottings.

gazette, -er; newspaper, magazine etc. 531; alman-ac, -ack; calendar, ephemeris, noctuary, diary, log, journal, account-, cash-, day-book, ledger.

archive, scroll, state-paper, Congressional Record, return, blue-book; statistics etc. 86; *compte rendu*; Acts –, Transactions –, Proceedings- of; Hansard's Debates; chronicle, annals; legend; history, biography etc. 594.

registration; en-, in-rolment; tabulation; entry,

booking; signature etc. (*identification*) 550; recorder etc. 553; journalism.

drawing, photograph etc. 554; phonograph –, gramophone- record; music roll.

V. record; put –, place- upon record; go on record; chronicle, calendar, hand down to posterity; keep up the memory of etc. (*remember*) 505; commemorate etc. (*celebrate*) 883; report etc. (*inform*) 527; commit to –, reduce towriting; put –, set down- -in writing, – in black and white; put –, jot –, take –, write –, note –, set-down; note, minute, put on paper; take –, make- a -note, – minute, – memorandum; make a return.

mark etc. (*indicate*) 550; sign etc. (*attest*) 467.

enter, book; post, – up; insert, make an entry of; mark –, tick- off; register, list, docket, enroll, inscroll; file etc. (*store*) 636.

Adv. on record.

552. Obliteration. [Suppression of sign.]—**N.** obliteration; erasure, rasure; effacement; interference; cancel, -lation; cassation; circumduction; deletion, blot; *tabula rasa*.

V. efface, obliterate, erase, rase, expunge, cancel; blot –, take –, rub –, scratch –, strike –, wipe –, wash –, sponge- out; wipe –, rub- off; wipe away; deface, render illegible; draw the pen through, apply the sponge.

interfere, jam, black-, block-out; clutter, screen.

be -effaced etc.; leave no -trace etc. 449; 'leave not a rack behind.'

Adj. obliterated etc. *v.*; out of print; printless; leaving no trace; intestate; un-recorded, -registered, -written.

Int. *dele*; out with it!

553. Recorder.—N. recorder, notary, clerk; regis-trar, -trary, -ter; prothonotary; amanuensis, secretary, scribe, stenographer, remembrancer, book-keeper, *custos rotulorum*, Master of the Rolls.

annalist; histori-an, -ographer; chronicler, journalist, reporter, columnist; biographer etc. (*narrator*) 594; antiquary etc. (*antiquity*) 122; memorialist.

draughtsman etc. 559; engraver 558; photographer, cinematographer, camera man.

Recording instrument, recorder, camera, phonograph, gramophone, dictaphone, telegraphone, telautograph, printing telegraph, tape recorder, ticker, time recorder, cash register, turnstile, speedometer, voting machine, seismograph, radar, oscilloscope, teletypewriter, pari-mutuel, photostat.

554. Representation.—N. represent-ation, -ment; imitation etc. 19; illustration, delineation, depictment, portrayal; imagery, portraiture, iconography; design, -ing; art, fine arts; painting etc. 556; sculpture etc. 557; engraving etc. 558; photography, radiography, skiagraphy.

person-ation, -ification; impersonation; drama etc. 599.

picture, drawing, sketch, draught, draft; tracing; copy etc. 21; photo-, helio-graph; daguerreo-, talbo-, calo-, helio-type; cabinet, *carte-de-visite,* snapshot; X-ray photograph; radio-gram, -graph, skia-graph, -gram.

image, likeness, icon, portrait; striking –, speaking- likeness; very image; effigy, fac-simile.

figure, – head; puppet, doll, *figurine,* aglet, manikin, lay-figure, model, *marionnette, fantoccini,* bust; waxwork, statue, -tte, automaton, Robot.

hieroglyphic, anaglyph; dia-, mono-gram, graph.

map, plan, chart; ground plan, projection, elevation; ichno-, carto-graphy; atlas; outline, scheme; view etc. (*painting*) 556.

artist, draughtsman etc. 559.

V. represent, delineate; depict, -ure; portray; picture; take –, catch- a likeness etc. *n.*; hit off, photograph, daguerreotype; figure; shadow -forth, – out; adumbrate; body forth; describe etc. 594; trace, copy; mold.

dress up; illustrate, symbolize.

paint etc. 556; carve etc. 557; engrave etc. 558.

person-ate, -ify; impersonate; assume a character; pose as; act; play etc. (*drama*) 599; mimic etc. (*imitate*) 19; hold the mirror up to nature.

Adj. represent-ing etc. *v.,* -ative; illustrative; represented etc. *v.*; imitative, figurative.

like etc. 17; graphic etc. (*descriptive*) 594.

555. Misrepresentation.—N.
misrepresentation, distortion, exaggeration; daubing etc. *v.*; bad likeness, daub, sign-painting; scratch, caricature; *anamorphosis.*

V. misrepresent, distort, overdraw, travesty, parody, burlesque, exaggerate, caricature, daub.

Adj. misrepresented etc. *v.*

556. Painting.—N.
painting; depicting; drawing etc. *v.*; design; perspective, skiagraphy; *chiaroscuro* etc. (*light*) 420; composition; treatment, values, atmosphere, tone, technique.

historical –, portrait –, miniature –, land-scape –, marine –, flower –, scene- painting; scenography.

school, style; the grand style, high art, *genre,* portraiture; ornamental art etc. 847.

mono-, poly-chrome; *grisaille.*

pallet, palette; easel; brush, pencil, stump; blacklead, charcoal, crayons, chalk, pastel; paint etc. (*coloring matter*) 428; water-, body-, oil-color; oils, oil-paint; varnish etc. 356a; *gouache,* tempera, distemper, fresco, water-glass; enamel; encaustic painting; *graffito, gesso;* mosiac; tapestry.

picture, painting, piece, *tableau,* canvas; oil etc.- painting; fresco, cartoon; easel –, cabinet- picture; drawing, draught, draft; pencil etc. –, watercolor-drawing; sketch; outline; study.

portrait etc. (*representation*) 554; whole –, full –, half- length; kitcat, head; miniature; shade, *silhouette;* profile.

landscape, sea-piece, -scape; view, scene, prospect; interior; bird's- eye view; pan-, di-orama; still life.

picture –, art- gallery; *studio, atelier.*

V. paint, design, limn, draw, sketch, pencil, scratch, shade, stipple, hatch, dash off, chalk out, square up; color, dead-color, wash, varnish; draw in -pencil etc. *n.*; paint in -oils etc. *n.*; stencil; depict etc. (*represent*) 554.

Adj. painted etc. *v.*; pictorial, graphic, picturesque, decorative; classical, romantic, pre-Raphaelite, modern, cubist, futurist, vorticist. pencil, oil etc. *n.*

Adv. in -pencil etc. *n.*

Phr. *fecit, delineavit.*

557. Sculpture.—N.
sculpture, insculpture; carving etc. *v.*; statuary, ceramics, plastic arts.

high –, low –, bas- relief; relievo; *basso-, alto-, mezzo-relievo; intaglio,* anaglyph; medal, -lion; *cameo.*

marble, bronze, *terra cotta;* ceramic ware, pottery, porcelain, china, earthenware, faïence, enamel, *cloisonné.*

statue etc. (*image*) 554; cast etc. (*copy*) 21; glyptotheca.

V. sculpture, carve, cut, chisel, model, mold; cast.

Adj. sculptured etc. *v.*; in relief, anaglyptic, ceroplastic, ceramic; parian; marble etc. *n.*

558. Engraving.—N.
engraving, chalcography; line –, mezzotint –, stipple –, chalk- engraving; dry-point, bur; etching, aquatinta; plate –, copper-plate –, steel –, wood-, process-, photo-engraving; xylo-, ligno-, glypto-, cero-, litho-, chromolitho-, photolitho-, zinco-, glypho- -graphy, -graph.

impression, print, engraving, plate; steel-, copper-plate; etching; mezzo-, aqua-, litho-tint; cut, woodcut, block; stereo-, grapho-, auto-, helio-type; half-tone; *photogravure, rotogravure.*

graver, *burin,* etching-point, style; plate, stone, wood-block, negative; die, punch, stamp.

printing; plate –, copper-plate –, intaglio –, anastatic –, lithographic –, color –, three color-printing; type-printing etc. 591.

illustr-, illumin-ation; *vignette,* initial letter, *cul de lampe,* tail-piece.

V. engrave, grave, stipple, scrape, etch; bite, – in; lithograph etc. *n.*; print.

Adj. insculptured; engraved etc. *v.*

Phr. *sculpsit, imprimit.*

559. Artist.—N.
artist; painter, limner, drawer, sketcher, delineator; cartoon-, caricatur-ist, designer, engraver; draughtsman; copyist; enameller, -list.

historical –, landscape –, genre –, marine –, flower –, portrait –, miniature –, scene –, sign-painter; engraver; Apelles; sculptor, carver, chaser, modeller, lapidary, *figuriste,* statuary; Phidias, Praxiteles; Royal Academician.

photographer, retoucher.

560. Language.—N. language; phraseology etc.
569; speech etc. 582; tongue, lingo, vernacular,
slang; mother –, vulgar –, native- tongue;
household words; King's or Queen's English;
idiom; dialect etc. 563.

volapuk, esperanto, ido, occidental, Ro.

confusion of tongues, Babel, *pasigraphie*; pantomime etc. (*signs*) 550; *onomatopaeia*.

phil-, gloss-, glott-ology; linguistics,
chrestomathy; paleo-logy; -graphy; comparative
grammar.

literature, letters, polite literature, *belles lettres*,
muses, humanities, *literae humaniores*, republic of
letters, dead languages, classics; genius of a
language; scholarship etc. (*knowledge*) 490.

linguist etc. (*scholar*) 492.

V. speak, say, express by words etc. 566.

Adj. lingu-al, -istic; dialectic; vernacular,
current, colloquial, slangy; bilingual, polyglot;
literary.

561. Letter.—N. letter; character; hieroglyphic
etc. (*writing*) 590; type etc. (*printing*) 591;
capitals; majus-, minus-cule; alphabet, ABC,
abecedary, christcross row, chrisscross row.

consonant, vowel, diphthong; mute, surd;
sonant, liquid, labial, dental, palatal, gutteral.

syllable; mono-, dis-, poly-syllable; affix, prefix,
suffix.

spelling, orthography; phon ography, ctic
spelling; ana-, meta-grammatism.

cipher, monogram, anagram; double – acrostic.

V. spell.

Adj. literal; alphabetical, abecedarian; syllabic;
uncial etc. (*writing*) 590; phonetic, voiced, mute
etc. *n.*

562. Word.—N. word, term, vocable; name
etc. 564; phrase etc. 566; root, etymon; derivative;
part of speech etc. (*grammar*) 567.

dictionary, vocabulary, word book, lexicon, index, glossary, thesaurus, *gradus, delectus*, concordance.

etymology, lexicology, derivation; phonology,
orthoepy; gloss-, termin-, orism-ology; paleology
etc. (*philology*) 560; comparative philology.

lexicograph-er, -y; glossographer etc. (*scholar*)
492; etymologist; logolept.

verbosity, verbiage, loquacity etc. 584.

Adj. verbal, literal; titular, nominal. [Similarly
derived] conjugate, paraonymous; derivative.

Adv. verbally etc. *adj.*; *verbatim* etc. (*exactly*)
494.

563. Neology.—N. neolo-gy; -gism; new-
fangled expression; barbarism; caconym; archaism,
black letter, monkish Latin; corruption; missaying,
antiphrasis.

paronomasia, play upon words; wordplay etc.
(*wit*) 842; *double-entente* etc. (*ambiguity*) 520;
palindrome, paragram, clinch; abuse of -language,
– terms.

dialect, brogue, *patois*, provincialism, broken
English, *lingua franca*; Brit-, Gall-, Scott-, Hibern-
icism; American-ism; Gipsy lingo, Romany, pidgin
English.

dog Latin, macaronics, gibberish, confusion of
tongues, Babel; jargon.

colloquialism etc. (*figure of speech*) 521; by-
word; technicality, lingo, slang, cant, *argot*, St.
Giles's Greek, thieves' Latin, peddler's French,
flash tongue, Billingsgate, Wall Street slang.

pseudonym etc. (*misnomer*) 565; Mr. So-and-so;
what d'ye call 'em, what's his name; thingum-my, -
bob; *je ne sais quoi*.

neologist, coiner of words.

V. coin words.

Adj. neologic, -al; rare; archaic; obsolete etc.
(*old*) 124; colloquial, dialectic, slang, cant.

564. Nomenclature.—N. nomenclature;
naming etc. *v.*; nuncupation, nomination, baptism;
orismology; *onomatopaeia*; antonomasia.

name; appella-tion, -tive; designation; title;
head, -ing, caption; denomination; by-name,
epithet.

style, proper name; prae-, ag-, cog-nomen;
patronymic, surname; cognomination; compellation, description; empty -title, – name; handle to one's name; namesake, eponym.

synonym, antonym.

term, expression, noun; by-word; convertible
terms etc. 522; technical term; cant etc. 563.

V. name, call, term, denominate, designate,
style, entitle, intitule, clepe, dub, christen, baptize,
nickname, characterize, specify, define, distinguish
by the name of; label etc. (*mark*) 550.

be -called etc. *v.*; take –, bear –, go (or be
known) by –, go (or pass) under –, rejoice in- the
name of.

Adj. named etc. *v.*; hight, yclept, known as;
what one may -well, – fairly, – properly, – fitly-
call.

nuncupa-tory, -tive; cognominal, titular,
nominal; orismological.

565. Misnomer.—N. misnomer; *lucus a non
lucendo*; Mrs. Malaprop; what d'ye call 'em etc.
(*neologism*) 563.

nickname, *sobriquet*, by-name, handle,
moniker; assumed -name, – title; *alias*; *nom de -
guerre*, – *plume*, – *theâtre*; pseudonym, pen
name, stage name.

V. mis-name, -call, - term; nickname; assume -a
name, – an alias.

Adj. misnamed etc. *v.*; pseudonymous; *soi-
disant*; self-called, -styled, -christened; so-called.

nameless, anonymous; without a –, having no-
name; innominate, unnamed.

Adv. in no sense.

566. Phrase.—N. phrase, expression, set
phrase; sentence, paragraph; figure of speech etc.
521; idi-om, -otism; turn of expression.

paraphrase etc. (*synonym*) 522; periphrase etc. (*circumlocution*) 573; motto etc. (*proverb*) 496. phraseology etc. 569.

V. express, phrase; word, – it; give -words, – expression- to; voice; arrange in –, clothe in –, put into –, express by- words; couch in terms; find words to express; speak by the card.

Adj. expressed etc. *v.*; idiomatic.

Adv. in -round, – set, – good, set- terms; in set phrases.

567. Grammar.—N. grammar, accidence, syntax, *praxis*, analysis, paradigm, punctuation; parts of speech, inflexion, case, declension, conjugation; *jus et norma loquendi*; Lindley Murray etc. (*school-book*) 542; correct style; philology etc. (*language*) 560.

V. parse, analyze; decline, conjugate; punctuate.

Adj. grammatical; syntactic; inflexional.

568. Solecism.—N. solecism; bad –, false –, faulty- grammar; slip, error; slip of the -pen, – tongue; *lapsus calami*-, – *linguae*; *faux pas*; slip-slop; bull.

V. use -bad, – faulty- grammar; solecize, commit a solecism; murder the -King's, – Queen's- English; break Priscian's head.

Adj. ungrammatical; in-correct, -accurate; faulty, improper, incongruous, abnormal.

569. Style.—N. style, diction, phraseology, wording; manner, strain; composition; mode of expression, choice of words, literary power, ready pen, pen of a ready writer; command of language etc. (*eloquence*) 582; authorship; *la morgue littéraire*.

V. express by words etc. 566; write.

570. Perspicuity.—N. perspicuity etc. (*intelligibility*) 518; plain speaking etc. (*manifestation*) 525; defin-iteness, -ition; exactness etc. 494; perspicuousness, logical acuteness.

Adj. lucid etc. (*intelligible*) 518; explicit etc. (*manifest*) 525; exact etc. 494.

571. Obscurity.—N. obscurity etc. (*unintelligibility*) 519; involution; hard words; ambiguity etc. 520; vagueness etc. 475, inexactness etc. 495; what d'ye call 'em etc. (*neologism*) 563; cloudiness, confusion.

Adj. obscure etc. *n.*; crabbed, involved, confused.

572. Conciseness.—N. conciseness etc. *adj.*; brevity, 'the soul of wit,' laconism; Tacitus; ellipsis; syncope; abridgment etc. (*shortening*) 201; compression etc. 195; epitome etc. 596; monostich; portmanteau word, telescope word, protogram.

V. be -concise etc. *adj.*; condense etc. 195; abridge etc. 201; abstract etc. 596; come to the point.

Adj. concise, brief, short, terse, close; to the point, exact; neat, compact, condensed, pointed; laconic, curt, pithy, trenchant, summary; pregnant; compendious etc. (*compendium*) 596; succinct; elliptical, epigrammatic, crisp, sententious.

Adv. concisely etc. *adj.*; briefly, summarily; in brief, – short, – a word, – few words, – a nutshell; for shortness sake; to -come to the point, – make a long story short, – cut the matter short, – be brief; it comes to this, the long and short of it is.

573. Diffuseness.—N. diffuseness etc. *adj.*; amplification etc. *v.*; dilating etc. *v.*; verbosity, *verbiage*, wordiness, cloud of words, *copia verborum*; flow of words etc. (*loquacity*) 584.

poly-, tauto-, batto-, perisso-logy; pleonasm, exuberance, redundance; thrice-told tale; prolixity; circumlocution, *ambages*; periphra-se, -sis; round-about phrases; episode; expletive; penny-a-lining; padding, drivel, twaddle, rigmarole; richness etc. 577.

V. be -diffuse etc. *adj.*; run out on, descant, expatiate, enlarge, dilate, amplify, expand, inflate, pad; launch –, branch- out; rant.

maunder, prose; harp upon etc. (*repeat*) 104; dwell on, insist upon.

digress, ramble, *battre la campagne*, beat about the bush, perorate, spin a long yarn, protract; spin –, swell –, draw- out, drivel.

Adj. dif-, pro-fuse; wordy, verbose, largiloquent, copious, exuberant, effusive, pleonastic, lengthy; long, -some, -winded, -spun, -drawn out; diffusive, spun out, protracted, prolix, prosing, maundering; circumlocutory, periphrastic, ambagious, round-about; digressive; dis-, ex-cursive; rambling, episodic; flatulent, frothy.

Adv. diffusely etc. *adj.*; at large, *in extenso*; about it and about it.

574. Vigor.—N. vigor, power, force; boldness, raciness etc. *adj.*; spirit, point, antithesis, piquancy; verve, glow, fire, warmth, ardor, enthusiasm; 'thoughts that breathe and words that burn;' strong language; punch; gravity, sententiousness; elevation, loftiness, sublimity.

eloquence; command of -words, – language.

Adj. vigorous, nervous, powerful, forcible, trenchant, mordant, biting, incisive, impressive; sensational.

spirited, lively, glowing, sparkling, racy, bold, slashing; pungent, *piquant*, full of point, pôinted, pithy, antithetical; sententious.

lofty, elevated, sublime, grand, weighty, ponderous; eloquent; vehement, petulant, impassioned; poetic.

Adv. in -glowing, – good set, – no measured- terms.

575. Feebleness.—N. feebleness etc. *adj.*;

Adj. feeble, bald, tame, meager, insipid, nerve-les, jejune, vapid, trashy, cold, frigid, poor, dull, dry, languid; pros-ing, -y, -aic; unvaried, monotonous, weak, frail, washy, wishy-washy, sloppy; sketchy, slight; careless, slovenly, loose, lax; slip-shod, -slop; inexact; dis-jointed, - connected; puerile, childish; flatulent; rambling etc. (*diffuse*) 573.

576. Plainness.—N. plainness etc. *adj.*; simplicity, severity; plain -terms, – English; Saxon English; household words.

V. speak plainly; call a spade 'a spade;' plunge *in medias res*; come to the point.

Adj. plain, simple; un-ornamented, -adorned, - varnished; home-ly, -spun; neat; severe, chaste, pure, Saxon; commonplace, matter of fact, natural, prosaic, sober, unimaginative.

dry, unvaried, monotonous etc. 575.

Adv. in plain -terms, – words, – English, – common parlance; point blank.

577. Ornament.—N. ornament; floridity etc. *adj.*; turg-idity, -escence; altiloquence etc. *adj.*; orotundity; declamation, teratology; well-rounded periods; elegance etc. 578.

inversion, antithesis, alliteration, *paronomasia*; figurativeness etc. (*metaphor*) 521.

flourish; flowers of speech, – rhetoric; euphuism, -emism.

big-, high-sounding words; macrology, *sesquipedalia verba*, sesquipedalianism; Alexandrine; inflation, pretension; rant, bombast, fustian, bunkum, balderdash, prose run mad; fine writing; Minerva press.

phrasemonger; euph-uist, -emist.

V. ornament, overlay with ornament, overcharge; smell of the lamp.

Adj. ornamented etc. *v.*; beautified etc. 847; ornate, florid, rich, flowery; euph-uistic, -emistic; sonorous; high-, big-sounding; inflated, swelling, tumid; turg-id, -escent; pedantic, pompous, stilted; high-flown, -flowing; sententious, rhetorical, declamatory; grandiose; grand-, magn-, altiloquent; sesquipedal, -ian; Johnsonian, mouthy; bombastic; fustian; frothy, flashy, flaming, flamboyant.

antithetical, alliterative; figurative etc. 521; artificial etc. (*inelegant*) 579.

Adv. ore rotundo; with rounded phrase.

578. Elegance.—N. elegance, purity, grace, ease, felicity, distinction, gracefulness, refinement, readiness etc. *adj.*; concinnity, euphony, numerosity, balance, rythum, symmetry, proportion; restraint; good taste, propriety.

well rounded –, well turned –, flowing-periods; the right word in the right place; antithesis etc. 577.

purist, stylist.

V. point an antithesis, round a period.

Adj. elegant, polished, classical, Attic, correct, Ciceronian, artistic; chaste, pure, Saxon, academical.

graceful, easy, readable, fluent, flowing, tripping; unaffected, natural, unlabored; melliflous; euph-onious, -emistic; rhythmical, balanced, symmetrical.

felicitous, happy, neat; well –, neatly- -put, – expressed.

579. Inelegance.—N. inelegance; vulgarity, bad taste; stiffness etc. *adj.*; unlettered Muse; barbarism; slang etc. 563; solecism etc. 568; mannerism etc. (*affectation*) 855; euphuism; fustian etc. 577; cacophony; want of balance; words that - break the teeth, – dislocate the jaw.

V. be -inelegant etc. *adj.*

Adj. inelegant, graceless, ungraceful, unpolished; harsh, abrupt; dry, stiff, cramped, formal, *guindé*; forced, labored, awkward; artificial, mannered, ponderous; turgid etc. 577; affected, euphuistic; barbarous, uncouth, grotesque, rude, crude, halting; vulgar, offensive to ears polite.

580. Voice.—N. voice; vocality; organ, lungs, bellows; good –, fine –, powerful etc. (*loud*) 404 –, musical etc. 413- voice; intonation; tone etc. (*sound*) 402- of voice.

vocalization; cry etc. 411; strain, utterance, prolation; exclam-, ejacul-, vocifer-ation; enunci-, articul-ation; articulate sound; distinctness; clearness, – of articulation; stage whisper; delivery; attack.

accent, -uation; emphasis, stress; broad –, strong –, pure –, native –, foreign- accent; pronunciation.

[Word similarly pronounced] homonym.

orthoepy; euphony etc. (*melody*) 413.

gastri-, ventri-loquism; ventriloquist; polyphon-ism, -ist.

[Science of voice] phonology etc. (*sound*) 402.

V. sing, speak, utter, breathe, voice; give - utterance, – tongue; cry etc. (*shout*) 411; ejaculate, rap out; vocalize, prolate, articulate, enunciate, enounce, pronounce, accentuate, aspirate, deliver, mouth; emit, murmur, whisper, – in the ear, croon, yodel.

Adj. vocal, phonetic, oral; ejaculatory, articulate, distinct, stertorous; enunciative; accentuated, aspirated; euphonious etc. (*melodious*) 413.

581. Aphony—N. aphony, *aphonia*; dumbness etc. *adj.*; obmutescence; absence –, want- of voice; dysphony; silence etc. (*taciturnity*) 585; raucity; harsh etc. 410 –, unmusical etc. 414- voice; *falsetto*, 'childish treble;' mute, dummy, deaf mute.

V. keep silence etc. 585; speak -low, – softly; whisper etc. (*faintness*) 405.

silence; render -mute, – silent etc. 403; muzzle, muffle, suppress, smother, gag, strike dumb, dumbfound, -founder; drown the voice, put to silence, stop one's mouth, cut one short.

stick in the throat.

Adj. aphon-ous, -ic, dumb, mute; deaf-mute, –

and dumb; mum; tongue-tied; breath-, tongue-, voice-, speech-, word-less; mute as a -fish, – stock-fish, – mackerel; silent etc. (*taciturn*) 585; muzzled; in-articulate, -audible.

croaking, raucous, hoarse, husky, dry, hollow, sepulchral, hoarse as a raven.

Adv. with -bated breath, – the finger on the lips; *sotto voce*; in a -low tone, – cracked voice, – broken voice; in an aside.

Phr. *vox faucibus haesit.*

582. Speech.—N. speech, faculty of speech; locution, talk, parlance, verbal intercourse, prolation, oral communication, word of mouth, *parole*, palaver, prattle; effusion.

oration, recitation, delivery, say, address, speech, lecture, harangue, sermon, *tirade*, screed, formal speech, salutatory, peroration; prelection; speechifying; soliloquy etc. 589; allocution etc. 586; interlocution etc. 588.

oratory; elo-cution, -quence; rhetoric, declamation; grandi-, multi-loquence; burst of eloquence; facundity; talkativeness; flow –, command- of -words, – language; *copia verborum*; power of speech, gift of the gab; *usus loquendi.*

speaker etc. *v.*; spokesman, pro-, inter-locutor; mouthpiece, Hermes; ora-tor, -trix, -tress; Demosthenes, Cicero; rhetorician; stump –, platform- orator, tub-thumper; elocutionist; speech-maker, patterer, *improvisatore.*

V. speak, – of; say, utter, pronounce, deliver, give utterance to; utter –, pour- forth; breathe, let fall, come out with; rap –, blurt- out; have on one's lips; have at the -end, – tip- of one's tongue.

break silence; open one's -lips, – mouth; lift –, raise- one's voice; give –, wag the- tongue; talk, outspeak; put in a word or two.

hold forth; make –, deliver- -a speech etc. *n.*; speechify, harangue, declaim, stump, flourish, spout, rant, recite, lecture, preach, sermonize, discourse, be on one's legs; have –, say- one's say; expatiate etc. (*speak at length*) 573; speak one's mind.

soliloquize etc. 589; tell etc. (*inform*) 527; speak to etc. 586; talk together etc. 588.

be -eloquent etc. *adj.*; have -a tongue in one's head, – the gift of the gab etc. *n.*

pass –, escape- one's lips; fall from the -lips, – mouth.

Adj. speaking etc., spoken etc. *v.*; oral, lingual, phonetic, not written, unwritten, outspoken; eloquent, -cutionary; orat-, rhetorical; declamatory; grandiloquent etc. 577; talkative etc. 584.

Adv. orally etc. *adj.*; by word of mouth, *vivâ voce*, from the lips of.

Phr. quoth –, said- he etc.

583. Stammering. [Imperfect Speech.]**—N.** inarticulateness; stammering etc. *v.*; hesitation etc. *v.*; impediment in one's speech; aphasia, titubancy, traulism; whisper etc. (*faint sound*) 405; lisp, drawl, tardiloquence; nasal -tone, – accent; twang; *falsetto* etc. (*want of voice*) 581; broken -voice, – accents, – sentences.

brogue etc. 563; slip of the tongue, *lapsus linguae.*

V. stammer, stutter, hesitate, falter, hammer; balbu-tiate, -cinate; haw, hum and haw, be unable to put two words together.

mumble; mutter; maund, -er; whisper etc. 405; mince, lisp; jabber, gabble, gibber; sp-, spl-utter; muffle, mump; drawl, mouth; croak; speak -thick, – through the nose; snuffle, clip one's words; murder the -language, – King's (*or* Queen's) English; mis-pronounce, -say.

Adj. stammering etc. *v.*; inarticulate, guttural, nasal; tremulous.

Adv. *sotto voce* etc. (*faintly*) 405.

584. Loquacity.—N. loquac-ity, -iousness; talkativeness etc. *adj.*; garrulity; multiloquence, much speaking, effusion, wordiness.

jaw; gab, -ble; jabber, chatter; prate, prattle, cackle, clack; twaddle, trattle, rattle; *caquet, -terie*; blabber, *bavardage*, bibble-babble, gibble-gabble; small talk etc. (*converse*) 588.

fluency, flippancy, volubility, flowing tongue; flow –, of words; *flux de -bouche, – mots, – paroles*; *copia verborum, cacoëthes loquendi*; verbosity etc. (*diffuseness*) 573; gift of the gab etc. (*eloquence*) 582.

talker; chatter-er, -box; babbler etc. *v.*; rattle; ranter; sermonizer, proser, driveller; wind bag; gossip etc. (*converse*) 588; magpie, jay, parrot, poll, Babel; *moulin à paroles.*

V. be -loquacious etc. *adj.*; talk glibly, pour forth, patter; prate, palaver, prose, chatter, prattle, clack, jabber, jaw; rattle, – on; twaddle, twattle; babble, gabble; out-talk; talk oneself -out of breath, – hoarse; maunder, gush, blatter; talk a donkey's hind leg off; expatiate etc. (*speak at length*) 573; gossip etc. (*converse*) 588; din in the ears etc. (*repeat*) 104; talk -at random, – nonsense etc. 497; be hoarse with talking.

Adj. loquacious, talkative, conversational, garrulous, linguacious, multiloquous; chattering etc. *v.*; chatty etc. (*sociable*) 892; declamatory etc. 582; open-mouthed.

fluent, voluble, glib, flippant; long-tongued, -winded etc. (*diffuse*) 573.

Adv. trippingly on the tongue; glibly etc. *adj.*

Phr. the tongue running -fast, – loose, – on wheels.

585. Taciturnity.—N. silence, muteness, ob-mutescence; taciturnity, pauciloquy, costiveness, curtness; reserve, reticence etc. (*concealment*) 528; *aposiopesis.*

man of few words.

V. be -silent etc. *adj.*; keep silence; hold one's -tongue, – peace, – jaw; not speak etc. 582; say nothing; seal –, close –, put a padlock on- the -lips, – mouth; put a bridle on one's tongue; keep one's tongue between one's teeth; make no sign, not let a word escape one; keep a secret etc. 528; not have a word to say; lay –, place- the finger on the lips; render mute etc. 581.

stick in one's throat.

Adj. silent, mute, mum; silent as -a post, – a stone, – the grave etc. (*still*) 403; dumb etc. 581.

taciturn, sparing of words; close, – mouthed, –

tongued; laconic, costive, inconversable, curt; reserved; reticent etc. (*concealing*) 528.

Int. tush! silence! mum! hush! *chut!* hist! tut! etc. 403.

586. Allocution.—N. allocution, alloquy, address; speech etc. 582; apostrophe, interpellation, appeal, invocation, salutation; word in the ear. [Feigned dialogue] dialogism.

platform etc. 542; audience etc. (*interview*) 588.

V. speak to, address, accost, make up to, apostrophize, appeal to, invoke; hail, salute; call to, halloo.

take -aside, — by the button, button-hole; talk to in private.

lecture etc. (*make a speech*) 582.

Int. soho! halloo! hey! hist! hi!

587. Response etc.; *see* Answer 462.

588. Interlocution.—N. interlocution; collocution, colloquy, converse, conversation, confabulation, talk, discourse, verbal intercourse; communion, oral communication, commerce; dia-, duo-, tria-logue.

causerie, chat, chit-chat; small —, table —, teatable —, town —, village —, idle- talk; tattle, gossip, tittle-tattle; babble, -ment; *tripotage*, cackle, prittle-prattle, *on dit*; talk of the -town, — village.

conference, parley, interview, audience, *pourparler*; *tête-à-tête*; reception, *conversazione*; congress etc. (*council*) 696; pow-wow.

hall of audience, *durbar*, coliseum, assembly hall, auditorium.

palaver, debate, logomachy, war of words, controversy.

talker, gossip, tattler; Paul Pry, tabby, chatterer etc. (*loquacity*) 584; interlocutor etc. (*spokesman*) 582; conversation-ist, -alist; dialogist.

'the feast of reason and the flow of soul;' *mollia tempora fandi*.

V. talk together, converse, confabulate; hold —, carry on —, join in —, engage in- a conversation; put in a word; shine in conversation; bandy words; parley; palaver; chat, gossip, tattle; prate etc. (*loquacity*) 584.

discourse —, confer —, commune —, commerce- with; hold -converse, — conference, — intercourse; talk it over; be closeted with; talk with one -in private, — *tête-à-tête*.

Adj. conversing etc. *v.*; interlocutory; conversational, -able; discursive, -coursive; chatty etc. (*sociable*) 892; colloquial, *tête-à-tête*, confabulatory.

589. Soliloquy.—N. soliloquy, monologue, apostrophe.

solilo-quist, -quizer, monologist.

V. soliloquize; say —, talk- to oneself; say aside, think aloud, apostrophize.

Adj. soliloquizing etc. *v.*

Adv. aside.

590. Writing.—N. writing etc. *v.*; chiro-, stelo-, cero-graphy, graphology; stylography; pen-craft, -script, -manship; quill-driving; typewriting.

writing, manuscript, MS., *literae scriptae*; these presents.

stroke —, dash- of the pen; *coup de plume*; line; pen and ink.

letter etc. 561; uncial writing, cuneiform character, arrow-head, Ogham, Runes, futhorc; hieroglyphic, hieratic, demotic; script; contraction.

short-hand; steno-, brachy-, tachy-graphy; secret writing, writing in cipher; crypt-, stegan-ography; phono-, pasi-, poly-, logo-graphy.

copy; tran-, re-script; draft, rough —, fair- copy; handwriting; signature, sign-manual; auto-, mono-, holo-graph; hand, fist; mark.

calligraphy; good —, running —, flowing —, cursive —, legible —, copperplate —, round —, bold-hand.

cacography, *griffonage, barbouillage*; bad —, cramped —, crabbed —, illegible- hand; scribble etc. *v.*; *pattes de mouche*; ill-formed letters; pothooks and hangers.

stationery; pen, quill, goose-quill, reed; stylographic-, fountain-pen; pencil, style, stylus; paper, foolscap, parchment, vellum, papyrus, pad, tablet, block, note book, slate, marble, pillar, table, black board.

ink-bottle, -pot, -stand, -well, -horn; typewriter.

transcription etc. (*copy*) 21; inscription etc. (*record*) 551; superscription etc. (*indication*) 550.

composition, authorship; *cacoethes scribendi*.

writer, scribe, amanuensis, scrivener, secretary, clerk, penman, copyist, transcriber, quill-driver; writer for the press etc. (*author*) 593.

shorthand writer, stenographer; typewriter, typist.

V. write, pen; copy, engross; write out, — fair; transcribe; scribble, scrawl, scrabble, scratch; interline; stain paper; write down etc. (*record*) 551; sign etc. (*attest*) 467; take down, — in shorthand; typewrite, type.

compose, indite, draw up, redact, draft, formulate; dictate; inscribe, throw on paper, dash off; concoct.

take -up the pen, — pen in hand; shed —, spill —, dip one's pen in- ink.

Adj. writing etc. *v.*; written etc. *v.*; in -writing, — black and white; under one's hand.

uncial, Runic, cuneiform, hieroglyphical etc. *n.*

Adv. *currente calamo*; pen in hand.

591. Printing.—N. printing; block —, type-printing, lino-, mono-type; plate printing etc. (*engraving*) 558; the press etc. (*publication*) 531; composition.

print, letterpress, text, matter, standing type; context, note, page, column; over-running; head-, foot-line, title.

typography; stereo-, electro-, apro-type; type,

black letter, heavy type, font, fount; pi, pie; capitals etc. (*letters*) 561; diamond, pearl, nonpareil, minion, brevier, bourgeois, long primer, small pica, pica, english, great primer.

folio etc. (*book*) 593; copy, impression, pull, proof, galley –, author's –, page- proof, revise.

printer, compositor, reader; printer's devil.

V. print; compose; put –, go- to press; pass –, see- through the press; publish etc. 531; bring out; appear in –, rush into- print.

Adj. printed etc. *v.*; in type; typographical etc. *n.*

---

592. Correspondence.—N. correspondence, letter, epistle, note, *billet*, post-, letter-card, missive, circular, form letter; favor, *billet-doux*; des-, dis-patch; *bulletin*, communication etc. 532; these presents; rescript, -ion; post etc. (*messenger*) 534; letter writer, correspondent.

V. correspond, – with; write –, send a letter- to; keep up a correspondence; drop a line to; despatch; communicate with; circularize.

Adj. epistolary.

---

593. Book.—N. book, -let; writing, work, volume, tome, opuscule; tract, -ate; *livret*; *brochure, libretto*, handbook, treatise, text-book, codex, manual, pamphlet, monograph, enchiridion, circular, publication; book of poems; novel; chap-book.

part, issue, number, *livraison*; album, portfolio; periodical, serial, magazine, *ephemeris*, annual, journal.

paper, bill, sheet, broadsheet, screed; leaf, -let; fly-leaf, page; quire, ream.

chapter, section, head, article, paragraph, passage, clause, supplement, appendix; *feuilleton*.

folio, quarto, octavo; duo-, sexto-, octo-decimo.

en-, cyclopedia, dictionary, lexicon, thesaurus, concordance, anthology, bibliography; compilation, compendium, catalogue etc. 86; library, bibliotheca; the press etc. (*publication*) 531.

writer, author, *littérateur*, essayist, journalist, publicist; scribe, penman, war –, special –, correspondent; pen, scribbler, the scribbling race; ghost, hack, literary hack, Grub-street writer; writer for –, gentlemen of –, representative of- the press; reporter, penny-a-liner; editor, sub-editor; playwright etc. 599; poet etc. 597.

bookseller, publisher; biblio-pole, -polist, -grapher; librarian; book -collector, – worm.

book -shop, – club, circulating –, lending –, public- library; publishing house.

knowledge of books, bibliography; book-learning etc. (*knowledge*) 490.

---

594. Description.—N. description, account, statement, report; *exposé* etc. (*disclosure*) 529; specification, particulars, scenario, plot; state –, summary- of facts; brief etc. (*abstract*) 596; return etc. (*record*) 551; *catalogue raisonné* etc. (*list*) 86; guide-book etc. (*information*) 527.

delineation etc. (*representation*) 554; sketch, vignette; monograph; minute –, detailed –, particular –, circumstantial –, graphic- account; narration, recital, rehearsal, relation.

histori-, chron-ography; historic Muse, Clio; history; bi-, autobi-ography; necrology, obituary.

narrative, history; memoir, memorials; annals etc. (*chronicle*) 551; tradition, legend, saga, epic, epos, story, tale, historiette; personal narrative, journal, letters, life, adventures, fortunes, experiences, confessions; anecdote, ana, *trait*.

work of fiction, short story, novelette, novel, romance, penny dreadful, shilling, shocker, Minerva press; fairy –, nursery- tale; fable, allegory, parable, apologue.

relator etc. *v.*; *raconteur*; historian etc. (*recorder*) 553; biographer, fabulist, novelist, story teller, romancer, teller of tales, spinner of yarns, anecdotist.

V. describe; set forth etc. (*state*) 535; draw a picture, picture; portray etc. (*represent*) 554; characterize, particularize; narrate, relate, recite, recount, sum up, run over, recapitulate, rehearse, fight one's battles over again.

unfold etc. (*disclose*) 529- a tale; tell; give –, render- an account of; report, make a report, draw up a statement.

detail; enter into –, descend to- -particulars, – details.

Adj. descriptive, graphic, narrative, epic, suggestive, well-drawn; historic; auto-, biographical, realistic, expository, tradition-al, -ary; legendary; fabulous, mythical; anecdotic, storied; described etc. *v.*

---

595. Dissertation.—N. dissertation, treatise, essay; *thesis*, theme; tract, -ate, -ation, excursus; discourse, memoir, disquisition, lecture, sermon, homily, pandect.

commentary, review, *critique*, criticism, article; lead-er, -ing article, editorial; argument, running commentary.

investigation etc. (*inquiry*) 461; study etc. (*consideration*) 451; discussion etc. (*reasoning*) 476; exposition etc. (*explanation*) 522.

commentator, critic, essayist, pamphleteer; publicist, reviewer, leader writer, editor, annotator.

V. dissert –, descant –, write –, touch- upon a subject; dissertate; treat of –, take up –, ventilate –, discuss –, deal with –, go into –, canvass –, handle –, do justice to- a subject; comment, criticize, interpret etc. 522.

Adj. dis-cursive, -coursive; disquisitional, disquisitionary; expository, critical.

---

596. Compendium.—N. compend, -ium; abstract, *précis*, epitome, *multum in parvo*, analysis, pandect, digest, sum and substance, brief, abridgment, summary, *aperçu*, draft, minute, note; synopsis, textbook, *conspectus*, outlines, syllabus, contents, heads, prospectus.

album; scrap –, note –, memorandum –, commonplace- book; extracts, *excerpta*, cuttings; fugitive -pieces, – writings; *spicilegium*, flowers, anthology, miscellany, *collectanea*, *analecta*; compilation.

recapitulation, *résumé*, review.

abbrevia-tion, -ture; contraction; shortening etc. 201; compression etc. 195.

V. abridge, abstract, epitomize, summarize; make –, prepare –, draw –, compile- an abstract etc. *n.*

recapitulate, review, skim, run over, sum up.

abbreviate etc. (*shorten*) 201; condense etc. (*compress*) 195; compile etc. (*collect*) 72; edit, blue pencil.

Adj. compendious, synoptic, analectic, analytical; abridged etc. *v.*

Adv. in -short, – epitome, – substance, – few words.

Phr. it lies in a nutshell.

597. Poetry.—**N.** poetry, poetics, poesy, Muse, Calliope, tuneful Nine, Parnassus, Helicon, Pierides, Pierian spring, afflatus, inspiration.

versification, rhyming, making verses; prosody, scansion, orthometry.

poem; epic, – poem; epopee, *epopaea*, ode, epode, idyl, lyric, eclogue, pastoral, bucolic, georgic, dithyramb, anacreontic, sonnet, roundelay, *rondel, rondoletto, rondeau, rondo,* triolet, madrigal, canzonet, *cento,* monody, elegy, palinode; rhapsody.

dramatic –, lyric- poetry; opera; posy, anthology.

song, ballad, lay; love –, drinking –, war –, folk –, sea- song; lullaby; music etc. 415; nursery rhymes.

[Bad poetry] doggerel, Hudibrastic verse, prose run mad; macaronics; macaronic –, leonine-verse; runes.

canto, stanza, distich, verse, line, couplet, triplet, quatrain, sestet; *strophe, antistrophe,* refrain, chorus, burden.

verse, rhyme, assonance, crambo, meter, measure, foot, numbers, strain, rhythm; accentuation etc. (*voice*) 580; iambus, dactyl, spondee, trochee, anapaest etc.; hex-, pent-ameter; Alexandrine; blank verse, alliteration.

elegiacs etc. *adj.*; elegiac etc. *adj.* -verse, – meter, – poetry.

poet, – laureate; laureate; minor poet, bard, lyrist, scald, troubadour, *trouvère;* mistrel; minne-, meister-singer; *improvisatore;* versifier, sonneteer; ballad monger; rhym-er, -ist, -ester; poetaster.

V. poetize, sing, versify, make verses, rhyme, scan.

Adj. poetic, -al; lyric, -al; tuneful; epic; dithyrambic etc. *n.*; metrical; a-, catalectic; elegiac, iambic, trochaic, spondaic, anapest; Ionic, Sapphic, Alcaic, Pindaric.

598. Prose.—**N.** prose, – writer, pros-aism, -aist, -er.

V. prose, write prose.

write -prose, – in prose.

Adj. pros-y, -aic; unpoetical.

rhymeless, unrhymed, in prose, not in verse.

599. Drama.—**N.** drama, the -drama, – stage,

– theater, – play; theatricals, dramaturgy, histrionic art, buskin, sock, *cothurnus,* Melpomene and Thalia, Thespis.

play, stage-play, piece, five-act play, tragedy, comedy, opera, comic opera, *vaudeville, comedietta, lever de rideau,* curtain raiser, interlude, afterpiece, exode, farce, *divertissement, extravaganza,* burletta, harlequinade, pantomime, mimodrama, burlesque, *opéra bouffe,* musical comedy, review, revue, intimate revue, variety, cabaret entertainment, *ballet, spectacle,* masque, *drame, comédie drame;* melo-drama, -drame; *comédie larmoyante,* emotional drama, sensation drama, tragi-, farcical-comedy; mono-drame, -logue; duologue; trilogy; charade, *proverbe;* mystery, miracle –, morality- play.

act, scene, *tableau;* in-, intro-duction; pro-, epilogue, curtain; *libretto,* book, script.

performance, representation, show, *mise en scène,* stagery, *jeu de théâtre,* stage-craft; acting; gesture etc. 550; impersonation etc. 554; stage business, gag, patter, buffoonery.

theater; play-, opera-house; house; music hall; *cabaret;* amphitheater, circus, hippodrome; puppet-show, *fantoccini; marionnettes,* Punch and Judy.

cinema, -tograph-, picture –, theater, the pictures, the movies, the talkies.

auditory, *auditorium,* front of the house, stalls, boxes, balcony, dress –, upper- -circle, – boxes, amphitheater, pit, gallery; *foyer;* greenroom; dressing rooms, *coulisses.*

flat; drop, – scene; wing, screen, side-scene; transformation scene, curtain, act-drop, safety –, fire- curtain; *proscenium,* forestage.

stage, revolving stage, scene, the boards; star –, grave –, trap, mezzanine floor; flies; gridiron, floats, battens, footlights; lime –, spot –, flood –, bunch-lights; scenery, set, *décor;* orchestra.

theatrical '-costume, – properties, props.

part, *rôle,* character, cast, *dramatis personae; répertoire.*

actor, player; stage –, strolling- player; old –, stager, performer; mime, -r; *artiste;* com-, tragedian, straight man; *tragédienne,* Thespian, Roscius, star.

pantomimist, clown, harlequin, *buffo,* buffoon, *farceur, grimacier,* pantaloon, columbine; *Pierrot, Pierrette;* punch, -inello; *pulcinell-o, -a;* mute, *figurante,* general utility; super, -numerary, extra.

mummer, guiser, guisard, gysart, masque.

mountebank, Jack Pudding; tumbler, posture-master, acrobat, equilibrist, juggler, contortionist; *danseuse, ballerina,* ballet -dancer, – girl, *coryphée; bayadère, geisha;* chorus -singer, – girl.

company; first tragedian, *prima donna,* lead, leading lady, protagonist; *jeune premier;* juvenile lead, *débutant, -e;* light –, genteel –, low- -comedy, – comedian; *soubrette,* walking gentleman, *amoroso,* heavy, heavy father, *ingénue, jeune veuve, commère, compère.*

property man, *costumier,* machinist, stage hand, electrician, prompter, call-boy; director, manager; stage –, acting –, business- manager; *entrepreneur, impresario,* producer, press agent.

dramatic -author, – writer; play-writer, -wright; dramatist, mimographer; dramatic critic.

V. act, play, perform; stage, produce, put on the stage; personate etc. 554; mimic etc. (*imitate*) 19; enact; play –, act –, go through –, perform- a part; rehearse, spout, gag, rant; 'strut and fret one's hour upon a stage;' tread the -stage, — boards; come out;, star.

Adj. dramatic; theatric, -al; scenic, histrionic, anctorial, comic, tragic, buskined, farcical, tragicomic, melodramatic, operatic; stagey spectacular; stagestruck.

Adv. on the -stage, — boards; before -the floats, — an audience; in the limelight, behind the footlights; behind the scenes.

600. Will.—N. will, volition, conation, velleity; will and pleasure, free-will; freedom etc. 748; discretion; choice, inclination, intent, purpose, option etc. (*choice*) 609; voluntariness; spontane-ity, -ousness; originality.

pleasure, wish, desire, mind; frame of mind etc. (*inclination*) 602; intention etc. 620; predetermination etc. 611; self-control etc. determination etc. (*resolution*) 604; will-power.

V. will, list; see —, think- -fit; determine etc. (*resolve*) 604; settle etc. (*choose*) 609; volunteer.

have a will of one's own; do what one chooses etc. (*freedom*) 748; have it all one's own way; have one's -will, — own way.

use —, exercise- one's discretion; take -upon oneself, — one's own course, — the law into one's own hands; do -of one's own accord, — upon one's own -responsibility, — authority; take the bit between one's teeth; take responsibility; originate etc. (*cause*) 153.

Adj. voluntary, volitive, volitional, wilful; free etc. 748; optional; discretion-al, -ary; volitient; dictatorial.

minded etc. (*willing*) 602; prepense etc, (*predetermined*) 611; intended etc. 620; autocratic; unbidden etc. (bid etc. 741); spontaneous; original etc. (*causal*) 153.

Adv. voluntarily etc. *adj.*; at -will. – pleasure; *à -volonté*, — *discrétion*; *al piacere*; *ad -libitum*, — *arbitrium*; as -one thinks proper, — it seems good to.

of one's own -accord, — free will; *proprio –*, *suo –*, *ex mero- motu*; out of one's own head; by choice etc. 609; purposely etc. (*intentionally*) 620; deliberately etc. 611.

Phr. *stet pro ratione voluntas*; *sic volo sic jubeo.*

601. Necessity.—N. involuntariness; instinct, blind —, natural- impulse; inborn —, innate-proclivity; the force of circumstances.

necessi-ty, -tation, necessarianism; obligation; compulsion etc. 744; subjection etc. 749; stern —, hard —, dire —, imperious —, inexorable —, iron —, adverse- -necessity, — fate; what must be.

desti-ny, -nation; fatality, fate, *kismet*, doom, foredoom, election, predestination; pre-, foreordination; lot, fortune; fatalism, determinism; inevitableness etc. *adj.*; spell etc. 993.

star, -s; planet, -s; astral influence; sky, Fates, Norns, *Parcae*, Sisters three, Clotho, Lachesis, Atropos; book of fate; God's will, will of Heaven; wheel of Fortune, Ides of March, Hobson's choice.

last -shift, — resort; *dernier ressort*; *pis aller*

etc. (*substitute*) 147; necessaries etc. (*requirement*) 630.

necess-arian, -itarian; fatalist, determinist; automaton.

V. lie under a necessity; be -fated, — doomed, — destined etc., — in for, — under the necessity of; have no -choice, — alternative; be- obliged —, forced —, driven —, one's -fate etc. *n*.- to; be -pushed to the wall, — driven into a corner, — unable to help, — drawn irresistibly.

destine, doom, foredoom, devote; pre-destine, -ordain; cast a spell etc. 992; necessitate; compel etc. 744.

Adj. necessary; needful etc. (*requisite*) 630.

fated; destined etc. *v.*; fateful; elect; spell-bound.

compulsory etc. (*compel*) 744; uncontrollable, inevitable, unavoidable, irrestible, irrevocable, inexorable, binding; avoid-, resist-less; written in the book of fate.

involuntary, instinctive, automatic, blind, mechanical; un-conscious, -witting, -thinking; unintentional etc. (*undesigned*) 621; impulsive etc. 612.

Adv. necessarily etc. *adv.*; of -necessity, — course; *ex necessitate rei*; needs must; perforce etc. 744; *nolens volens*; will he nil he, willy nilly, *bon gré mal gré*, willing or unwilling, *coûte que coûte*, forcefully.

faute de mieux; by stress of; if need be.

Phr. it cannot be helped; there is no- help for, — helping- it; it -will, — must, — must needs- be, — be so, — have its way; the die is cast; *jacta est alea*; *che sarà sarà*; 'it is written;' one's- days are numbered, — fate is sealed; *Fata obstant*; *diis aliter visum.*

602. Willingness.—N. willingness, voluntariness etc. *adj.*; willing mind, heart.

disposition, inclination, leaning, *animus*; frame of mind, humor, mood, vein; bent etc. (*turn of mind*) 820; *penchant* etc. (*desire*) 865; aptitude etc. 698.

doc-ility, -ibleness, tractability; persuasi-bleness, -bility; pliability etc. (*softness*) 324.

geniality, cordiality; goodwill; alacrity, readiness, earnestness, forwardness, enthusiasm; zeal, eagerness etc. (*desire*) 865.

assent etc. 488; compliance etc. 762; pleasure etc. (*will*) 600.

labor of love, self-appointed task; volunteer, -ing, gratuitous service; unpaid worker, amateur.

V. be -willing etc. *adj.*; incline, lean to, mind, propend; had as lief; lend —, give —, turn- a willing ear; have -a, — half a, — a great- mind to; hold —, cling- to; desire etc. 865.

see —, think- -good, — fit, — proper; acquiescence etc. (*assent*) 488; comply with etc. 762.

swallow —, nibble at- the bait; gorge the hook; swallow hook, line and sinker; have —, make- no scruple of; make no bones of; jump —, catch- at; meet half way; volunteer, offer oneself etc. 763.

Adj. willing, minded, fain, disposed, inclined, favorable, favorably- minded, -inclined, -disposed; nothing loth; in the -vein, — mood, — humor, — mind.

ready, forward, enthusiastic, earnest, eager; bent upon etc. (*desirous*) 865; predisposed, propense.

docile; persua-dable, -sible; suasible, easily persuaded, facile, easy-going; amenable; tractable etc. (*pliant*) 324; genial, gracious, cordial, hearty; content etc. (*assenting*) 488.

voluntary, gratuitous, spontaneous; unasked etc. (ask etc. 765); unforced etc. (*free*) 748.

Adv. willing etc. *adj.*; fain, freely, as lief, heart and soul; with -pleasure, – all one's heart, – open arms; with -good, – right good- will; *de bonne volonté*, *ex animo*; *con amore*, heart in hand, nothing loth, without reluctance, of one's own accord, graciously, with a good grace, without demur.

à la bonne heure; by all -means, – manner of means; to one's heart's content; yes etc. (*assent*) 488.

Int. sure, -ly! of course!

603. Unwillingness.—**N.** unwillingness etc. *adj.*; indispos-ition, -edness; disinclination, aversation, aversion; nolleity, nolition; renitence; reluctance; indifference etc. 866; backwardness etc. *adj.*; slowness etc. 275; want of -alacrity, – readiness; indocility etc. (*obstinacy*) 606.

scrupul-ousness, -osity; qualms of conscience, delicacy, demur, scruple, qualm, shrinking, recoil; hesitation etc. (*irresolution*) 605; fastidiousness etc. 868.

averseness etc. (*dislike*) 867; dissent etc. 489; refusal etc. 764.

slacker, scrimshanker, *embusqué*, unwilling worker, forced labor.

V. be -unwilling etc. *adj.*; nill; dislike etc. 867; grudge, begrudge; not be able to find it in one's heart to, not have the stomach to.

demur, stick at, scruple, stickle; hang fire, run rusty, slack, shirk, scamp, give up, fight shy of, not pull fair; recoil, shrink, swerve; hesitate etc. 605; avoid etc. 623.

oppose etc. 708; dissent etc. 489; refuse etc. 764.

Adj. unwilling; not in the vein, loth, shy of, disinclined, indisposed, averse, reluctant, not content; adverse etc. (*opposed*) 708; laggard, backward, remiss, slack, slow to; renitent; indifferent etc. 866; scrupulous; squeamish etc. (*fastidious*) 868; repugnant etc. (*dislike*) 867; rest-iff, -ive; demurring etc. *v.*; unconsenting etc. (*refusing*) 764; involuntary etc. 601; grudging, irreconcilable.

Adv. unwilling etc. *adj.*; grudgingly, with a heavy heart; with -a bad, – an ill- grace; against –, sore against- -one's wishes, – one's will, – the grain; *invitâ Minervâ*; *à contre coeur*; *malgré soi*; in spite of -one's teeth, – oneself; *nolens volens* etc. (*necessity*) 601; perforce etc. 744; under protest; no etc. 536; not for the world, far be it from me; not if I can help it; if I must I must.

604. Resolution.—**N.** determination, will; iron –, unconquerable- will; will of one's own, decision, resolution, backbone, grit; strength of - mind, – will; resolve etc. (*intent*) 620; *intransigeance*; firmness etc. (*stability*) 150; energy, manliness, vigor; game, pluck; resoluteness etc. (*courage*) 861; zeal etc. 682; *aplomb*; desperation; devot-ion, -edness.

mastery over self; self-control, -command, -

mastery, -possession, -reliance, -government, -restraint, -conquest, -denial; moral -courage, – strength, – fiber; perseverance etc. 604a; tenacity; obstinacy etc. 606; bull-dog; British lion.

V. have -determination etc. *n.*; know one's own mind; be -resolved etc. *adj.*; make up one's mind, will resolve, determine; decide etc. (*judgment*) 480; form –, come to- a -determination, – resolution, – resolve; conclude, fix, seal, determine once for all, bring to a crisis, drive matters to an extremity; take a decisive step etc. (*choice*) 609; take upon oneself etc. (*undertake*) 676.

devote oneself –, give oneself up- to; throw away the scabbard, kick down the ladder, nail one's colors to the mast, set one's back against the wall, set one's teeth, put one's foot down, burn one's bridges, take one's stand; stand firm etc. (*stability*) 150; steel oneself; stand no nonsense, not listen to the voice of the charmer.

buckle to; put –, lay –, set- one's shoulder to the wheel; put one's heart into; run the gantlet, make a dash at, take the bull by the horns; beard the lion in his den; rush –, plunge- *in medias res*; go in for; insist upon, make a point of; set one's heart, – mind- upon.

stick at nothing; make short work of etc. (*activity*) 682; not stick at trifles; go -all lengths, – the whole hog; persist etc. (*persevere*) 604a; go down with colors flying, die game; go through fire and water, ride in the whirlwind and direct the storm.

Adj. resolved etc. *v.*determined; strong-willed, -minded; resolute etc. (*brave*) 861; self-possessed, plucky, tenacious; decided, definitive, peremptory; un-hesitating, -flinching, -shrinking; firm, cast iron, indomitable, game to the backbone; inexorable, relentless, not to be -shaken, – put down; *tenax propositi*; inflexible etc. (*hard*) 323; obstinate etc. 606; steady etc. (*persevering*) 604a; unbending, unyielding, irrevocable; firm as a rock; grim.

earnest, serious; set –, bent –, intent- upon. steeled –, proof- against; *in utrumque paratus*.

Adv. resolutely etc. *adj.*; in –, in good- earnest; seriously, joking apart, earnestly, heart and soul; on one's metal; manfully, like a man, with a high hand; with a strong hand etc. (*exertion*) 686.

at any -rate, – risk, – hazard, – price, – cost, – sacrifice; at all -hazards, – risks, – events; cost what it may; *coûte que coûte*; *à tort et à travers*; once for all; neck or nothing; rain or shine; with colors nailed to the mast.

Phr. *spes sibi quisque*.

604a. Perseverance. —**N.** perseverance; continuance etc. (*inaction*) 143; permanence etc. (*absence of change*) 141; firmness etc. (*stability*) 150.

constancy, steadiness; singleness –, tenacity- of purpose; persistence, plodding, patience; sedulity etc. (*industry*) 682; pertina-cy, -city, -ciousness; iteration etc. 104.

bottom, game, pluck, stamina, backbone, grit; indefatiga-bility, -bleness; bulldog courage.

V. persevere, persist; hold -on, – out; die in the last ditch, be in at the death; stick –, cling –, adhere- to ; stick to one's text, keep on; keep to –, maintain- one's -course, – ground; bear –, keep –, hold-up; plod; stick to work etc. (*work*) 686;

continue etc. 143; follow up; die -in harness, – at one's post.

Adj. persevering, constant; stead-y, -fast; un-deviating, -wavering, -faltering, -swerving, - flinching, -sleeping, -flagging, -drooping; steady as time; uninter-, un-remitting; plodding; industrious etc. 682; strenuous etc. 686; pertinacious; persist-ing, -ent.

solid, sturdy, staunch, stanch, ture to oneself; un-changeable etc. 150; unconquerable etc. (*strong*) 159; indomitable, game to the last, indefatigable, untiring, unwearied, never tiring.

Adv. through -evil report and good report, – thick and thin, – fire and water; *per fas et nefas*; without fail, sink or swim, at any price, *vogue la galère*; in sickness and in health.

Phr. never say die; *vestigia nulla retrorsum*.

605. Irresolution.—N. irresolution, infirmity of purpose, indecision; in-, un-determination, loss of will power; unsettlement; uncertainty etc. 475; demur, suspense; hesi-tating etc. *v.*, -tation, -tancy; vacillation; ambivalence; changeableness etc. 149; fluctuation; alternation etc. (*oscillation*) 314; caprice etc. 608; lukewarmness.

fickleness, levity, *légèreté*; pliancy etc. (*softness*) 324; weakness; timidity etc. 860; cowardice etc. 862; half measures.

waverer, ass between two bundles of hay; shut-tlecock, butterfly; timeserver, opportunist, turn coat.

V. be -irresolute etc. *adj.*; hang –, keep- in suspense; heave 'ad referendum;' think twice about, pause; dawdle etc. (*inactivity*) 683; remain neuter; dilly dally. hesitate, boggle, hover, wobble, shilly-shally, hum and haw, demur, not know one's own mind; debate, balance; dally –, coquet- with; will and will not, *chasser-balancer*; go half-way, compromise, make a compromise; be thrown off one's balance, stagger like a drunken man; be afraid etc. 860; let 'I dare not' wait upon 'I would;' falter, waver.

vacillate etc. 149; change etc. 140; retract etc. 607; fluctuate; alternate etc. (*oscillate*) 314; keep off and on, play fast and loose; blow hot and cold etc. (*caprice*) 608.

shuffle, palter, blink; trim.

Adj. irresolute, infirm of purpose, double-minded, half-hearted; un-decided, -resolved, - determined; drifting; shilly-shally; fidgety, tremulous; wobbly; hesitating etc. *v.*; off one's balance; at a loss etc. (*uncertain*) 475.

vacillating etc. *v.*; unsteady etc. (*changeable*) 149; unsteadfast, fickle, unreliable, irresponsible, unstable, without ballast; capricious etc. 608; volatile, frothy; light, -some, -minded; giddy; fast and loose.

weak, feeble-minded, frail; timid etc. 860; cowardly etc. 862; facile; pliant etc. (*soft*) 324; unable to say 'no,' easy-going.

revocable, reversible.

Adv. irresolutely etc. *adj.*; irresolvedly; in faltering accents; off and on; from pillar to post; see-saw etc. 314.

Int. 'how happy could I be with either!'

606. Obstinacy.—N. obstinateness etc. *adj.*; obstinacy, tenacity; perseverance etc. 604*a*; im-movability; old school; inflexibility etc. (*hardness*) 323; obdur-acy, -ation; dogged resolution; resolution etc. 604; ruling passion; blind side.

self-will, contumacy, perversity; pervica-cy, -city; indocility.

bigotry, intolerance, dogmatism; opinia-try, -tiveness; fixed idea etc.; intractibility, in-corrigibility; (*prejudgment*) 481; fanaticism, zealotry, infatuation, monomania, opinionativeness.

mule; opin-ionist, -ionatist, -iator, -ator; stickler; dogmatist, die-hard, bitter-ender; bigot; zealot, en-thusiast, fanatic.

V. be -obstinate etc. *adj.*; stickle, take no denial, fly in the face of facts; opinionate, be wedded to an opinion, hug a belief; have one's own way etc. (*will*) 600; persist etc. (*persevere*) 604*a*; have –, insist on having- the last word.

die -hard, – fighting, fight -against destiny, – to the last ditch; not yield an inch, stand out.

Adj. obstinate, tenacious,. stubborn, obdurate, case-hardened; inflexible etc. (*hard*) 323; im-movable, not to be moved; inert etc. 172; un-changeable etc. 150; inexorable etc. (*determined*) 604; mulish, obstinate as a mule, pig-headed.

dogged; sullen, sulky; un-moved, -influenced, -affected.

wilful, self-willed, perverse; res-ty, -tive, -tiff; pervicacious, wayward, refractory, unruly; head-y, -strong; *entete*; contumacious; cross-grained.

arbitrary, dogmatic, opinionated, positive, bigoted; prejudiced etc. 481; prepossessed, in-fatuated; stiff-backed, -necked, -hearted; hard-mouthed, hidebound; unyielding; im-pervious, - practicable, -persuasible; unpersuadable; in-, un-tractable; incorrigible, deaf to advice, impervious to reason; crotchety etc. 608.

Adv. obstinately etc. *adj.*

Phr. *non possumus*; no surrender.

607. Tergiversation.—N. change of -mind, – intention, – purpose; afterthought.

tergiversation, recantation; palinode, -ody; renunciation; abjur-ation, -ement; defection etc. (*relinquishment*) 624; going over etc. *v.*; apostasy; retract-ion, -ation; withdrawal, disavowal etc. (*negation*) 536; revo-cation, -kement; reversal; repentance etc. 950; *redintegratio amoris*.

coquetry, flirtation; vacillation etc. 605; back-sliding, recidivation.

turn-coat, | -tippet; rat, apostate, - renegade, mugwump; con-, per-vert; proselyte, deserter; backslider, recidivist; black leg.

time-server, -pleaser; timist, Vicar of Bray, trim-mer, ambidexter; weathercock etc. (*changeable*) 149; Janus.

V. change one's -mind, – intention, – purpose, – note; abjure, renounce; withdraw from etc. (*relinquish*) 624; wheel –, turn –, veer- round; turn a *pirouette*; go over –, pass –, change –, skip- from one side to another; go to the right about; box the compass, shift one's ground, go upon another tack; back down, crawl, crawfish.

apostatize, change sides, go over, rat; recant, retract; revoke; rescind etc. (*abrogate*) 756; recall, forswear, abjure, unsay; come -over, – round- to an opinion.

draw in one's horns, eat one's words; eat –,

swallow- the leek; swerve, flinch, back out of, retrace one's steps, think better of it; come back –, return- to one's first love; turn over a new leaf etc. (*repent*) 950.

trim, shuffle, play fast and loose, blow hot and cold, coquet, flirt, hold with the hare but run with the hounds; straddle; *nager entre deux eaux*; wait to see how the -cat jumps, – wind blows.

Adj. changeful etc. 149; irresolute etc. 605; ductile, slippery as an eel, trimming, ambidextrous, timeserving; coquetting etc. *v.*

revocatory, reactionary.

Phr. 'a change came o'er the spirit of my dream.'

608. Caprice.—N. caprice, fancy, humor; whim, -sey, -wham; crotchet, *capriccio*, quirk, freak, maggot, fad, vagary, prank, fit, flim-flam, *escapade*, *boutade*, wild-goose chase; capriciousness etc. *adj.*; kink.

V. be -capricious etc. *adj.*; have a maggot in the brain; take it into one's head, strain at a gnat and swallow a camel; blow hot and cold; play -fast and loose, – fantastic tricks.

Adj. capricious; erratic, eccentric, fitful, hysterical; full of -whims etc. *n.*; maggoty; inconsistent, fanciful, fantastic, whimsical, crotchety, particular, humorsome, freakish, skittish, wanton, wayward; contrary; captious; arbitrary; unrestrained, undisciplined; not amenable to reason; uncomfortable etc. 83; penny wise and pound foolish; fickle etc. (*irresolute*) 605; frivolous, sleeveless, giddy, volatile.

Adv. by fits and starts, without rhyme or reason, at one's own sweet will.

Phr. *nil fuit unquam six impar sibi*; the deuce is in him.

609. Choice.—N. choice, option; discretion etc. (*volition*) 600; preoption; alternative; dilemma; *ambarras de choix*; adoption, cooptation; novation; decision etc. (*judgment*) 480.

election, poll, ballot, vote, voice, suffrage, plumper, cumulative vote; *plebiscitum*, *plébiscite*, *vox populi*; *referendum*, electioneering; voting etc. *v.*; franchise; ballot box; slate; ticket.

selection, excerption, gleaning, eclecticism; *excerpta*, gleanings, cuttings, scissors and paste; pick etc. (*best*) 650.

preference, prelation; predilection etc. (*desire*) 865.

V. offer for one's choice, set before; hold out –, present –, offer- the alternative; put to the vote.

use –, exercise –, one's- -discretion, – option; adopt, take up, embrace, espouse; choose, elect, coopt; take –, make- one's choice; make choice of, fix upon.

vote, poll, hold up one's hand; divide.

settle; decide etc. (*adjudge*) 480; list etc. (*will*) 600; make up one's mind etc. (*resolve*) 604.

select; pick, – and choose; pick –, single- out, excerpt; cull, glean, winnow; sift –, separate –, winnow- the chaff from the wheat; pick up, pitch upon; pick one's way; indulge one's fancy.

set apart, reserve, mark out for; mark etc. 550.

prefer; have -rather, – as lief; fancy etc. (*desire*) 865; be persuaded etc. 615.

take a -decided, – decisive- step; commit oneself to a course; pass –, cross- the Rubicon; cast in one's lot with; take for better or for worse.

Adj. optional; co-optative; discretional etc. (*voluntary*) 600; on approval.

ecletic; choosing etc. *v.*; preferential; chosen etc. *v.*; choice etc. (*good*) 648.

Adv. optionally etc. *adj.*; at pleasure etc. (*will*) 600; either, – the one or the other; or; at the option of; whether or not; once for all; for one's money.

by -choice, – preference; in preference; rather, before.

609a. Absence of Choice.—N. no –, Hobson's- choice; first come, first served; necessity etc. 601; not a pin to choose etc. (*equality*) 27; any, the first that comes.

neutrality, indifference; indecision etc. (*irresolution*) 605.

V. be -neutral etc. *adj.*; have no choice; waive, not vote; abstain –, refrain- from voting; leave undecided; make a virtue of necessity.

Adj. neu-tral, -ter; indifferent; undecided etc. (*irresolute*) 605.

Adv. either etc. (*choice*) 609.

610. Rejection.—N. rejection, repudiation, exclusion; declination; refusal etc. 764.

V. reject; set –, lay- aside; give up; decline etc. (*refuse*) 764; exclude, except, eliminate; pluck, spin; cast.

repudiate, scout, set at naught; fling –, cast –, thrown –, toss- -to the winds, – to the dogs, – overboard, – away; send to the right about; disclaim etc. (*deny*) 536; discard etc. (*eject*) 297, (*have done with*) 678.

Adj. rejected etc. *v.*; reject-aneous, -itious; not - chosen etc. 609, – to be thought of; out of the question.

Adv. neither, – the one nor the other; no etc. 536.

Phr. *non haec in foedera.*

611. Predetermination.—N. premeditation, deliberation, -determination, -destination; foreordination; foregone conclusion; *parti pris*; resolve, propendency; intention etc. 620; project etc. 626.

V. pre-determine, -destine, -meditate, -resolve, - concert; foreordain; resolve beforehand.

Adj. pre-pense, -meditated etc. *v.*, -designed; advised, studied, designed, calculated; aforethought; intended etc. 620; foregone.

well-laid, -devised, -weighed; maturely considered; cut and dried; cunning.

Adv. advisedly etc. *adj.*; with premeditation, deliberately, all things considered, with eyes open, in cold blood; intentionally etc. 620.

612. Impulse.—N. impulse, sudden thought; *impromptu*, improvisation; inspiration, hunch, flash, spurt.

improvisatore, *improvisatrice*, improviser, extemporizer; creature of impulse.

V. flash on the mind.

say what comes uppermost; improvise, extemporize; rise to the occasion; spurt.

Adj. extemporaneous, impulsive, indeliberate; improvis-ed, -ate, -atory; un-, unpre-meditated; *improvisé*; unprompted, -guided; natural, unguarded; spontaneous etc. (*voluntary*) 600; instinctive etc. 601.

Adv. extem-pore, -poraneously; offhand, *impromptu, à l'improviste*; improviso; on the spur of the -moment, − occasion.

613. Habit.—N. habit, -ude; assuetude, -faction; wont; run, way.

common −, general −, natural −, ordinary −, habitual- -course, − run, − state- of things; matter of course; beaten -path, − track, − ground.

prescription, custom, use, usage, immemorial usage, practice; tradition; prevalence, observance; conventionalism, -ity; mode, fashion, vogue; *etiquette* etc. (*gentility*) 852; order of the day, cry; conformity etc. 82.

habitué, addict.

one's old way, old school, consuetude, *veteris vestigia flammae*; *laudator temporis acti*.

rule, standing order, precedent, routine; red-tape, -tapism; pipe-clay; rut, groove.

cacoëthes; bad −, confirmed −, inveterate −, intrinsic etc. 5- habit; addiction, trick.

training etc. (*education*) 537; seasoning, hardening, inurement; radication; second nature, acclimatization; knack etc. (*skill*) 698.

V. be -wont etc. *adj.*

fall into a custom etc. (*conform to*) 82; tread −, follow- the beaten -track, − path; *stare super antiquas vias*; move in a rut, run on in a groove, go round like a horse in a mill, go on in the old jobtrot way.

habituate, inure, harden, season, caseharden; accustom, familiarize; naturalize, acclimatize; keep one's hand in; train etc. (*educate*) 537.

get into the -way, − knack- of; learn etc. 539; cling −, adhere- to; repeat etc. 104; acquire −, contract −, fall into- a -habit, − trick; addict oneself −, take- to; accustom oneself to.

be -habitual etc. *adj.*; prevail; come into use, become a habit, take root; gain −, grow- upon one.

Adj. habitual; ac-, customary; prescriptive; accustomed etc. *v.*; traditional; of -daily, − everyday- occurrence; wonted, usual, general, ordinary, common, frequent, every-day, household, jog-trot; well-trodden, -known; familiar, vernacular, trite, commonplace, banal, bromidic, conventional, regular, set, stock, officinal, established, stereotyped; pre-vailing, -valent; current, received, acknowledged, recognized, accredited; of course, admitted, understood.

conformable etc. 82; according to - -use, − custom, − routine; in -vogue, − fashion; fashionable etc. (*genteel*) 852.

wont; used − given − addicted −, attuned −, habituated etc. *v.*- to; in the habit of; *habitué*; at home in etc. (*skilful*) 698; seasoned; permeated −, imbued- with; devoted −, wedded- to; never free from.

hackneyed, fixed, rooted, deep-rooted, ingrafted, permanent, inveterate, besetting; naturalized; ingrained etc. (*intrinsic*) 5.

Adv. habitually etc. *adj.*; always etc. (*uniformly*) 16.

as -usual, − is one's wont, − things go, − the world goes, − the sparks fly upwards; *more -suo, − solito*.

as a rule, for the most part; generally etc. *adj.*; most often, − frequently.

Phr. cela s'entend.

614. Desuetude.—N. desuetude, disusage; disuse etc. 678; want of -habit, − practice; inusitation; newness to; new brooms.

infraction of usage etc. (*unconformity*) 83; non-prevalence; 'a custom more honored in the breach than the observance.'

V. be -unaccustomed etc. *adj.*; leave off −, cast off −, break off −, wean oneself of −, violate −, break through −, infringe- -a habit, − a custom, − a usage; break one's fetters; disuse etc. 678; wear off.

Adj. un-accustomed, -used, -wonted, -seasoned, -inured, -habituated, -trained; new; green etc. (*unskilled*) 699; fresh, original, unhackneyed.

unusual etc. (*unconformable*) 83; un-conventional, non-observant; disused etc. 678.

Adv. just for once.

615. Motive.—N. motive, springs of action.

reason, ground, call, principle; mainspring, *primum mobile*, key-stone; the why and the wherefore; *pro* and *con*, reason why; secret −, ulterior- motive, *arrière-pensée*; intention etc. 620.

inducement, consideration; attraction etc. 288; loadstone; magnet, -ism, -ic force; allect-ation, -ive; temptation, enticement, *agacerie*, allurement, witchery; bewitch-ment, -ery; charm; spell etc. 993; fascination, blandishment, cajolery; seduc-tion, -ement; honeyed words, voice of the tempter, son of the Sirens; forbidden fruit, golden apple.

persuasi-bility, -bleness; attractability; impress-, suscept-ibility; softness; persuas-, attract-iveness; tantalization.

influence, prompting, dictate, instance; impuls-e, -ion; incit-ement, -ation; press, instigation; provocation etc. (*excitation of feeling*) 824; in-spiration; per-, suasion; encouragement, advocacy; exhortation, advice etc. 695; solicitation etc. (*request*) 765; lobbying.

incentive, stimulus, spur, fillip, whip, goad, rowel, provocative, whet, dram.

bribe, lure; decoy, − duck; bait, trail of a red herring; bribery and corruption; sop, − for Cerberus.

prompter, tempter; seduc-er, -tor; suggester; coaxer, wheedler; instigator, firebrand, incendiary; Siren, Circe; *agent provocateur*; lobbyist.

V. induce, move; draw, − on; bring in its train, give an -impulse etc. *n.*- to; inspire; put up to, prompt, call up; attract, beckon.

stimulate etc. (*excite*) 824; spirit up, inspirit; a-, rouse; ecphorize; animate, incite, provoke, instigate, set on, actuate; act −, work −, operate-upon; encourage; pat –, clap- on the -back, – shoulder.

influence, weigh with, bias, sway, incline, dispose, predispose, turn the scale, inoculate; lead, – by the nose; have –, exercise- influence- -with, – over, – upon; go –, come- round one; turn the head, magnetize.

persuade; prevail -with, – upon; overcome, carry; bring -round, – to one's senses; draw –, win –, gain –, come –, talk- over; procure, enlist, engage; invite, court.

tempt, seduce, overpersuade, entice, allure, captivate, fascinate, intrigue, bewitch, carry away, charm, conciliate, wheedle, coax, lure, suggest; inveigle; tantalize; cajole etc. (*deceive*) 545.

tamper with, bribe, suborn, grease the palm, bait with a silver hook, gild the pill, make things pleasant, put a sop into the pan, throw a sop to, bait the hook.

enforce, force; impel etc. (*push*) 276; propel etc. 284; whip, lash, goad, spur, prick, urge; egg –, hound –, hurry- on; drag etc. 285; exhort; advise etc. 695; call upon etc.; press etc. (*request*) 765; advocate.

set -an example, – the fashion; keep in countenance; back up.

be -persuaded etc.; yield to temptation, come round; concede etc. (*consent*) 762; obey a call; follow -advice, – the bent, – the dictates of; act on principle.

-**Adj.** impulsive, motive; suas-, persuas-, hortative, -ory; protreptical; inviting, tempting etc. *v.*; seductive, attractive, irresistible; fascinating etc. (*pleasing*) 829; provocative etc. (*exciting*) 824.

induced etc. *v.*; disposed; persuadable etc. (*docile*) 602; spellbound; instinct –, smitten- with; inspired etc. *v.*- by.

Adv. because, therefore etc. (*cause*) 155; from -this, – that- motive; for -this, – that- reason; for; by reason –, for the sake –, on the score –, on account- of; out of, from, as, forasmuch as.

for all the world; on principle.

615a. Absence of Motive.—**N.** absence of motive; caprice etc. 608; chance etc. (*absence of design*) 621.

V. have no motive; scruple etc. (*be unwilling*) 603.

Adj. without rhyme or reason; aimless etc. (*chance*) 621.

Adv. capriciously; out of mere caprice.

616. Dissuasion.—**N.** dissuasion, dehortation, expostulation, remonstrance; deprecation etc. 766.

discouragement, damper, wet blanket; warning.

cohibition etc. (*restraint*) 751; curb etc. (*means of restraint*) 752; check etc. (*hindrance*) 706.

reluctance etc. (*unwillingness*) 603; contraindication.

V. dissuade, dehort, cry out against, remonstrate, expostulate, warn, contraindicate.

disincline, indispose, shake, stagger; dispirit; discourage, -hearten, -enchant; deter; hold –, keep-back etc. (*restrain*) 751; render -averse etc. 603;

repel; turn aside etc. (*deviation*) 279; wean from; act as a drag etc. (*hinder*) 706; throw cold water on, damp, cool, chill, blunt, calm, quiet, quench; deprecate etc. 766.

Adj. dissuading etc. *v.*; dissuasive; dehortatory, expostulatory; monit-ive, -ory.

dissuaded etc. *v.*; uninduced etc. (induce etc. 615); unpersuadable etc. (*obstinate*) 606; averse etc. (*unwilling*) 603; repugnant etc. (*dislike*) 867.

617. Plea. [Ostensible motive, ground, or reason assigned.]—**N.** plea, pretext; allegation, advocation; ostensible -motive, – ground, – reason; excuse etc. (*vindication*) 937; color; gloss, guise.

loop-, starting-hole; how to creep out of, salvo, come off.

handle, peg to hang on room, *locus standi*; stalking horse, *cheval de bataille*, cue.

pretence etc. (*untruth*) 546; put off, subterfuge, dust thrown in the eyes; blind; moonshine; mere –, shallow- pretext; lame -excuse, – apology, tub to a whale; flase plea, sour grapes; makeshift, shift, white lie; special pleading etc. (*sophistry*) 477; soft sawder etc. (*flattery*) 933.

V. plead, allege; shelter oneself under the plea of; excuse etc. (*vindicate*) 937; gloss over; lend a color to; furnish a -handle etc. *n.*; make a -pretext, – handle- of; use as a plea etc. *n.*; take one's stand upon, make capital out of, pretend etc. (*lie*) 544.

Adj. ostensible etc. (*manifest*) 525; excusing; alleged, apologetic; pretended etc. 545.

Adv. ostensibly; under -color, – the plea, – the pretence- of.

618. Good.—**N.** good, benefit, advantage; improvement etc. 658; interest, service, behoof, behalf; weal; main chance, *summum bonum*, common weal; 'consummation devoutly to be wished;' gain, boot; profit, harvest.

boon etc. (*gift*) 784; good turn; blessing, benison; world of good; piece of good -luck, – fortune; nuts, prize, windfall, godsend, waif, treasure trove.

good fortune etc. (*prosperity*) 734; happiness etc. 827.

[Source of good] goodness etc. 648; utility etc. 644; remedy etc. 662; pleasure-giving etc. 829.

Adj. commendable etc. 931; useful etc. 644; good etc., beneficial etc. 648.

V. benefit, profit, advantage, serve, help, avail; do good to, gain, prosper, flourish.

Adv. well, aright, satisfactorily, favorably, not amiss; all for the best; to one's -advantage etc. *n.*; in one's -favor, – interest etc. *n.*

Phr. so far so good.

619. Evil.—**N.** evil, ill, harm, hurt, mischief, nuisance; machinations of the devil, Pandora's box, ills that flesh is heir to.

blow, buffet, stroke, scratch, bruise, wound, gash, mutilation; mortal -blow, – wound; *im-*

medicabile vulnus; damage, loss etc. (*deterioration*) 659.

disadvantage, prejudice, drawback.

disaster, accident, casualty; mishap etc. (*misfortune*) 735; bad job, devil to pay; calamity, bale, woe, catastrophe, tragedy; ruin etc. (*destruction*) 162; adversity etc. 735.

mental suffering etc. 828. [Evil spirit] demon etc. 980. [Cause of evil] bane etc. 663. [Production of evil] badness etc. 649; painfulness etc. 830; evil doer etc. 913.

outrage, wrong, injury, foul play; bad —, ill-turn; disservice; spoliation etc. 791; grievance, crying evil.

V. be in trouble etc. (*adversity*) 735; harm, injure, hurt, do disservice to.

Adj. disastrous, bad etc. 649; awry, out of joint; disadvantageous, injurious, harmful.

Adv. amiss, wrong, ill, to one's cost.

620. Intention.—N. intent, -ion, -ionality; purpose; *quo animo*; project etc. 626; undertaking etc. 676; predetermination etc. 611; design, ambition.

contemplation, mind, *animus*, view, purview, proposal; study; look out.

final cause; *raison d'être*; *cui bono*; object, aim, end; 'the be all and the end all;' drift etc. (*meaning*) 516; tendency etc. 176; destination, mark, point, butt, goal, target, bull's-eye, quintain; prey, quarry, game.

decision, determination, resolve; set —, settled-purpose; *ultimatum*; resolution etc. 604; wish etc. 865; *arrière-pensée*; motive etc. 615.

[Study of final causes] teleology.

V. intend, purpose, design, mean; have to; propose to oneself; harbor a design; have in -view, — contemplation, — one's eye, — *petto*; have an eye to.

bid —, labor- for; be —, aspire —, endeavour-after; be —, aim —, drive —, point —, level- at; take aim; set before oneself; study to.

take upon oneself etc. (*undertake*) 676; take into one's head; meditate, contemplate; think —, dream —, talk- of; premeditate etc. 611; compass, calculate; dest-ine, -inate, propose.

project etc. (*plan*) 626; have a mind to etc. (*be willing*) 602; desire etc. 865; pursue etc. 622.

Adj. intended etc. *v.*; intentional, advised, express, determinate; prepense etc. 611; bound for; intending etc. *v.*; minded, disposed, inclined; bent upon etc. (*earnest*) 604; at stake, on the -anvil, -tapis; in -view; — prospect, — the breast of; *in petto*; teleological.

Adv. intentionally etc. *adj.*; advisedly, wittingly, knowingly, designedly, purposely, on purpose, by design, studiously, pointedly; with -intent etc. *n.*; deliberately etc. (*with premeditation*) 611; with one's eyes open, in cold blood.

for; with -a view, — an eye- to; in order -to, — that; to the end —, with the intent- that; for the purpose —, with the view —, in contemplation —, on account- of.

in pursuance of, pursuant to; *quo animo*; to all intents and purposes.

621. Chance.†[Absence of purpose in the succession of events.]**—N.** chance etc. 156; lot, fate etc. (*necessity*) 601; luck; good luck etc. (*good*) 618; bad luck etc. 735; wheel of fortune; mascot; swastika.

speculation, venture, stake, flutter, flier, gamble, game of chance; mere —, random- shot; blind bargain, leap in the dark; pig in a poke etc. (*uncertainty*) 475; fluke, pot-luck.

drawing lots; sorti-legy, -tion; *sortes*, — *Virgilianae*; *rouge et noir*, hazard, *roulette*, pitch and toss, chuck-farthing, cup-tossing, heads or tails, cross and pile, wager; bet, -ting; risk, stake, plunge; gambling; the turf.

stock exchange, bourse, board of trade, curb exchange.

gaming-, gambling-, betting-house; hell; betting ring, totalizator; dice, — box; dicer; gam-bler, -ester, plunger, stock operator, manipulator, punter; man of the turf; adventurer, speculator; bookmaker, layer, backer.

V. chance etc. (*hap*) 156; stand a chance etc. (*be possible*) 470.

toss up; cast —, draw- lots; leave —, trust- -to chance, — to the chapter of accidents; tempt fortune; chance it, take one's chance; run —, incur —, encounter- the -risk, — chance; stand the hazard of the die.

speculate, try one's luck, set on a cast, raffle, put into a lottery, buy a pig in a poke, shuffle the cards.

risk, venture, hazard, stake; lay, — a wager; make a bet, wager, bet, gamble, game, play for; play at chuck-farthing.

Adj. fortuitous etc. 156; unintentional, -ded; accidental; not meant; un-designed, -purposed; unpremeditated etc. 612; never thought of.

indiscriminate, promiscuous; undirected, random; aim-, drift-, design-, purpose-, cause-less; without purpose.

possible etc. 470.

Adv. casually etc. 156; unintentionally etc. *adj.*; unwittingly.

en passant, by the way, incidentally; as it may happen; at -random, — a venture, — haphazard; as luck would have it, by -chance, — good fortune; un-, -luckily.

† See note on 156.

622. Pursuit. [Purpose in action.]**—N.** pursuit, pursuing etc. *v.*; prosecution; pursuance; enterprise etc. (*undertaking*) 676; business etc. 625; adventure etc. (*essay*) 675; quest etc. (*search*) 461; scramble, hue and cry, game; hobby.

chase, hunt, *battue*, race, steeplechase, hunting, coursing; ven-ation, -ery; fox-chase; sport, -ing; shooting, angling, fishing, hawking.

pursuer; hunt-er, -sman; sportsman, Nimrod, the field; hound etc. 366.

V. pursue, prosecute, follow; run —, make —, be —, hunt —, prowl- after; shadow; carry on etc. (*do*) 680; engage in etc. (*undertake*) 676; set about etc. (*begin*) 66; endeavor etc. 675; court etc. (*request*) 765; seek etc. (*search*) 461; aim at etc. (*intention*) 620; follow the trail etc. (*trace*) 461; fish for etc. (*experiment*) 463; press on etc. (*haste*) 684; run a race etc. (*velocity*) 274.

chase, give chase, course, dog, hunt, hound, stalk; tread —, follow- on the heels of etc. (*sequence*) 281.

rush upon; rush headlong etc. (*violence*) 173;

ride −, run- full tilt at; make a leap −, jump −, snatch- at; run down; start game.

tread a path; take −, hold- a course; shape −, direct −, bend- one's -steps, − course; play a game; fight −, elbow- one's way; follow up; take -to, − up; go in for; ride one's hobby.

Adj. pursuing etc. *v.*; in quest of etc. (*inquiry*) 461; in -pursuit, − full cry, − hot pursuit; on the scent.

Adv. in pursuance of etc. (*intention*) 620; after.

Int. tally-ho! yoicks! so-ho!

623. Avoidance. [Absence of pursuit.]—**N.** abst-ention, -inence; forbearance; refraining etc. *v.*; inaction etc. 681; neutrality.

avoidance, evasion, elusion; seclusion etc. 893.

avolation, flight; escape etc. 671; retreat etc. 287; recoil etc. 277; departure etc. 293; rejection etc. 610.

shirker etc. *v.*; slacker; truant; fugitive, refugee; runa-way, -gate; renegade; deserter.

V. abstain, refrain, spare, not attempt; not do etc. 681; maintain the even tenor of one's way.

eschew, keep from, let alone, have nothing to do with; keep −, stand −, hold- -aloof, − off; take no part in, have no hand in.

avoid, shun; steer −, keep- clear of; fight shy of; keep -one's, − at a respectful- distance; keep −, get- out of the way; evade, elude, turn away from; set one's face against etc. (*oppose*) 708; deny oneself.

shrink; hang −, hold −, draw- back; recoil etc. 277; retire etc. (*recede*) 287; flinch, blink, blench, shy, shirk, dodge, parry, make way for, give place to.

beat a retreat; turn -tail, − one's back; take to one's heels; run, -away, − for one's life; cut and run; be off, − like a shot; fly, flee; fly −, flee −, run away- from; take −, take to- flight; desert, elope; make −, scamper −, sneak −, shuffle −, sheer- off; break −, burst −, tear oneself −, slip −, slink −, steal- -away, − away from; slip cable, part company, turn on one's heel; sneak out of, play truant, give one the go by, give leg bail, take French leave, slope, decamp, flit, bolt, abscond, levant, skedaddle, absquatulate, cut one's stick, walk one's chalks, show a light pair of heels, make oneself scarce; escape etc. 671; go away etc. (*depart*) 293; abandon etc. 624; reject etc. 610.

lead one a -dance, − a merry chase, − pretty dance; throw off the scent, play at hide and seek.

Adj. unsought, unattempted; avoiding etc. *v.*; neutral; shy of etc. (*unwilling*) 603; elusive, evasive, distant; fugitive, runaway; shy, wild.

Adj. lest, in order to avoid.

Int. forebear! keep −, hands- off! *sauve qui peut!* devil take the hindmost.

624. Relinquishment.—**N.** relinquish-, abandon-ment; desertion, defection, secession, withdrawal; cave of Adullam; *nolle prosequi.*

discontinuance etc. (*cessation*) 142; renunciation etc. (*recantation*) 607; abrogation etc. 756; resignation etc. (*retirement*) 757; desuetude etc. 614; cession etc. (*of property*) 782.

V. relinquish, give up, abandon, desert, forsake, leave in the lurch; depart −, secede −, withdraw-from; back − out of, − down from, leave, go back on one's word, quit, − take leave of, bid a long farewell; vacate etc. (*resign*) 757.

renounce etc. (*abjure*) 607; forego, have done with, drop; write off; disuse etc. 678; discard etc. 782; wash one's hands of; drop all idea of; *nolle-pros.*; lose interest in.

break −, leave- off; desist; stop etc. (*cease*) 142; hold −, stay- one's hand; quit one's hold; give over, shut up shop.

throw up the -game, − cards; give up the -point, − argument; pass to the order of the day, move the previous question, table the motion.

Adj. unpursued; relinquished etc. *v.*; relinquishing etc. *v.*

Int. avast etc.! (*stop*) 142.

625. Business.—**N.** business, occupation, employment; pursuit etc. 622; what one is doing-, − about; affair, concern, matter, case, undertaking.

matter in hand, irons in the fire; thing to do, *agendum*, task, work, job, chore, errand, transaction, commission, mission, charge, care; duty etc. 926.

part, *rôle*, cue; province, function, look-out, department, capacity, sphere, orb, field, line; walk, − of life; beat, round, routine; race, career.

office, place, post, incumbency, living situation, appointment, billet, berth, employ; service etc. (*servitude*) 749; engagement; undertaking etc. 676.

vocation, calling, profession, *métier*, cloth, faculty; industry, art; industrial arts; craft, mystery, handicraft; trade etc. (*commerce*) 794.

exercise; work etc. (*action*) 680; avocation; press of business etc. (*activity*) 682.

V. pass −, employ −, spend- one's time in; employ oneself -in, − upon; occupy −, concern-oneself with; make it one's -business etc. *n.*; undertake etc. 676; enter a profession; betake oneself to, turn one's hand to; have to do with etc. (*do*) 680.

drive a trade; carry on −, do −, transact- -business, − a trade etc. *n.*; keep a shop; ply one's task, − trade; labor in one's vocation; pursue the even tenor of one's way; attend to -business, − one's work.

officiate, serve, act; act −, play- one's part; do duty; serve −, discharge −, perform- the -office, − duties, − functions- of; hold −, fill- -an office, − a place, − a situation; hold a portfolio.

be -about, − doing, − engaged in, − employed in, − occupied with, − at work on; have one's hands in, have in hand; have on one's -hands, − shoulders; bear the burden; have one's hands full etc. (*activity*) 682.

be -in the hands of, − on the stocks, − on the anvil; pass through one's hands.

Adj. business-like; work-a-day; professional; official, functional; busy etc. (*actively employed*) 682; on −, in -hand, − one's hands; afoot; on -foot, − the anvil; going on; acting.

Adv. in the course of business, all in a day's work; professionally etc. *adj.*

626. Plan.—**N.** plan, scheme, design, project; propos-al, -ition; suggestion; resolution, motion;

precaution etc. (*provision*) 673; deep-laid etc. (*premeditated*) 611- plan etc.; racket.

system etc. (*order*) 58; organization etc. (*arrangement*) 60; germ etc. (*cause*) 153; Five Year Plan.

sketch, skeleton, outline, draught, draft, *ébauche, brouillon*; rough-cast, – draft, – draught, – copy; proof, revise.

forecast, *programme*, prospectus, scenario; *carte du pays*; card; bill, protocol; order of the day, list of agenda, *memorandum*; bill of fare etc. (*food*) 298; base of operations; platform, plank.

rôle; policy etc. (*line of conduct*) 692.

contrivance, invention, expedient, receipt, nostrum, artifice, device, gadget; stratagem etc. (*cunning*) 702; trick etc. (*deception*) 545; alternative, loophole, shift etc. (*substitute*) 147; last shift etc. (*necessity*) 601.

measure, step; stroke, – of policy; master stroke; trump-, court-card; *chaval de bataille*, great gun; *coup*, – *d'état*; clever –, bold –, good- -move, – hit, – stroke; bright -thought, – idea, great idea.

intrigue, cabal, plot, frame-up, conspiracy, complot, machination; under-, counter-plot.

schem-ist, -atist; strategist, machinator, schemer; projector, author, builder, artist, promoter, designer etc. *v.*; conspirator; *intrigant* etc. (*cunning*) 702.

V. plan, scheme, design, frame, contrive, project, forecast, sketch; conceive, devise, invent etc. (*imagine*) 515; set one's wits to work etc. 515; spring a project; fall –, hit- upon; strike –, chalk –, cut –, lay –, map-out; lay down a plan; shape –, mark- out a course; predetermine etc. 611; concert, preconcert, preestablish; prepare etc. 673; hatch, – a plot; concoct; take -steps, – measures.

cast, recast, systematize, organize; arrange etc. 60; digest, mature.

plot; counter-plot, -mine; dig a mine; lay a train; intrigue etc. (*cunning*) 702.

Adj. planned etc. *v.*; strategic, -al; planning etc. *v.*; in course of preparation etc. 673; under consideration; on the -*tapis*, – carpet, – table.

627. Method. [Path.]—**N.** method, way, manner, wise, gait, form, mode, fashion, tone, guise; *modus operandi*; procedure etc. (*line of conduct*) 692.

path, road, route, course; line of -way, – road; trajectory, orbit, track, beat, tack.

steps; stair, -case; flight of stairs, ladder, stile.

bridge, viaduct, gauntry, pontoon, stepping stone, plank, gangway, catwalk, drawbridge; pass, ford, ferry, tunnel, subway, elevated; pipe etc. 260.

door; gateway etc. (*opening*) 260; channel, passage, avenue, means of access, approach, perron, adit, entrance; artery, lane, alley, aisle, lobby, corridor, cloister; back- door, -stairs; secret passage; covert-way.

road-, path-, stair-way; thoroughfare; highway, pike, turnpike, trail, parkway, *boulevard*; turnpike –, royal –, coach- road; broad –, King's –, Queen's- highway; beaten -track, – path; horse –, bridle- road, – track, – path; pathway; walk, *trottoir*, foot-path, pavement, flags, side-walk; by –, cross- -road, – path, – way; cut; short -cut

etc. (*mid-course*) 628; *carrefour*; private –, occupation- road; highways and byways; rail-, tramroad, -way; funicular, ropeway, causeway; defile, cutting; canal etc. (*conduit*) 350; street etc. (*abode*) 189.

Adv. how; in what -way, – manner; by what mode; so, in this way, after this fashion, on these lines.

one way or another, anyhow; somehow or other etc. (*instrumentality*) 631; by way of; *viâ*; *in transitu* etc. 270; on the high road to.

Phr. *hae tibi erunt artes.*

628. Mid-course.—**N.** middle-, mid-course; moderation, mean etc. 29; middle etc. 68; *juste milieu*, *mezzo termine*, golden mean, *aurea mediocritas*.

straight etc. (*direct*) 278 -course, – path; short –, cross- cut; short- circuit; great circle sailing.

neutrality; half –, half and half- measures; compromise.

V. keep in –, steer –, preserve- -a middle, – an even- course; go straight etc. (*direct*) 278.

go half way, compromise, make a compromise.

Adj. neutral, average, even, impartial, moderate, straight etc. (*direct*) 278.

629. Circuit.—**N.** circuit, round-about way, digression, divagation, *détour*, circum-ambience, -ambulation, bendibus, *ambages*, loop; winding etc. (*circuition*) 311; zigzag etc. (*deviation*) 279.

V. perform –, make- a circuit; go -round about, – out of one's way; make a *détour*; meander etc. (*deviate*) 27; circumambulate.

lead a pretty dance; beat about, – the bush; make two bites of a cherry.

adj. circuitous, indirect, round-about; zig-zag etc. (*deviating*) 279; circum-ambient, -ambulatory.

Adv. by -a side wind, – an indirect course; in a roundabout way; from pillar to post.

630. Requirement.—**N.** requirement, need, wants, necessities; necessaries, – of life; stress, exigency, pinch, *sine quâ non*, matter of necessity; case of -need, – life or death.

needfulness, essentiality, necessity, indispensability, urgency, prerequisite.

requisition etc. (*request*) 765, (*exaction*) 741; run upon; demand –, call- for.

desideratum etc. (*desire*) 865; want etc. (*deficiency*) 640.

charge, claim, command, injunction, requisition, mandate, order, *ultimatum.*

V. require, need, want, have occasion for; entail; not be able to -do without, – dispense with; prerequire.

render necessary, necessitate, create a necessity for, call for, put in requisition; make a requisition etc. (*ask for*) 765, (*demand*) 741,

stand in need of; lack etc. 640; desiderate; desire etc. 865; be -necessary etc. *adj.*

Adj. required etc. *v.*; requisite, needful,

necessary, imperative, essential, indispensable, prerequisite; called for; in -demand, — request.

urgent, exigent, pressing, instant, crying, absorbing.

in want of; destitute of etc. 640.

Adv. *ex necessitate rei* etc. (*necessarily*) 601; of —, out of stern- necessity; at a pinch.

Phr. there is no time to lose; it cannot be -spared, — dispensed with.

631. Instrumentality.—N. instrumentality; aid etc. 707; subservien-ce, -cy; mediation, intervention, -mediacy, medium, inter-medium, -mediary, vehicle, hand; agency etc. 170.

minister, handmaid, servant, slave, maid, valet; midwife, *accoucheur*, obstetrician; go-between; cat's paw; stepping-stone.

key; master —, pass —, latch- key; 'open seseme;' passport, *passe partout*, safe-conduct; influence.

instrument etc. 633; expedient etc. (*plan*) 626; means etc. 632.

V. subserve, minister, tend, mediate, intervene; come —, go- between, interpose; pull the strings; be -instrumental etc. *adj.*; pander to.

Adj. instrumental; useful etc. 644; ministerial, subservient, mediatorial; inter-mediate, -vening; conducive.

Adv. through, by, *per*; where-, there-, here-by; by the -agency etc. 170- of; by dint of; by —, in-virtue of; through the -medium etc. *n.*- of; along with; on the shoulders of; by means of etc. 632; by —, with- -the aid etc. (*assistance*) 707- of.

per fas et nefas, by fair means or foul; somehow, — or other; by hook or by crook.

632. Means.—N. means, resources, revenue, wherewithal, ways and means, income; capital etc. (*money*) 800; stock in trade etc. 636; provision etc. 637; a shot in the locker; appliances etc. (*machinery*) 633; means and appliances; conveniences; cards to play; expedients etc. (*measures*) 626; two strings to one's bow; sheet anchor etc. (*safety*) 666; aid etc. 707; medium etc. 631.

V. find —, have —, possess- means etc. *n.*; provide the wherewithal.

Adj. instrumental etc. 631; mechanical etc. 633.

Adv. by means of, with; by -what, — all, — any, — some- means; where-, here-, there-with; wherewithal.

how etc. (*in what manner*) 627; through etc. (*by the instrumentality of*) 631; with —, by- the aid etc. (*assistance*) 707- of; by the -agency etc. 170- of.

633. Instrument.—N. machinery, mechanism, engineering.

instrument, organ, tool, implement, utensil, contrivance, machine, motor, engine, lathe, gin, mill, pump.

gear; tack-le, -ling, trice, rigging, gear, apparatus, appliances; plant, *matériel*; harness, trap-

pings, fittings, accouterments; equip-ment, -age; appointments, furniture, upholstery; chattels; paraphernalia etc. (*belongings*) 780; *impedimenta*.

mechanical powers; lever, -age; mechanical advantage; crow, -bar; handspike, gavelock, jemmy, arm, limb, wing; oar, paddle; pulley, sheave; parbuckle; wheel and axle; wheel-, clock-work; wheels within wheels; pinion, gear wheel, spur —, bevel-gearing, chains, belting, crank, winch, capstan, windlass, crane, derrick, hoist, lift etc. 307; cam; pedal; wheel etc. (*rotation*) 312; inclined plane; wedge; screw; jack; spring, mainspring.

handle, hilt, haft, shaft, heft, shank, blade, trigger, tiller, helm, treadle, key; turnscrew, screwdriver, spanner, wrench.

hammer etc. (*impulse*) 276; edge tool etc. (*cut*) 253; borer etc. 262; vice, teeth etc. (*hold*) 781; nail, rope etc. (*join*) 45; peg etc. (*hang*) 214; support etc. 215; spoon etc. (*vehicle*) 272; arms etc. 727; oar etc. (*navigation*) 267.

Adj. instrumental etc. 631; mechanical, machinal, automatic, self-acting; brachial.

634. Substitute.—N. substitute etc. 147; deputy etc. 759; proxy, alternative, understudy.

635. Materials.—N. material, raw material, stuff, stock, staple; building materials, bricks and mortar; metal; stone; clay, brick; crockery etc. 384; compo, -sition; reinforced —, ferro-, concrete; cement; wood, ore, timber; gravel, cobbles, macadam, asphalt, tarmac.

materials; supplies, munition, fuel, grist, household stuff; *pabulum* etc. (*food*) 298; ammunition etc. (*arms*) 727; contingents; relay, reinforcement; baggage etc. (*personal property*) 780; means etc. 632.

Adj. raw etc. (*unprepared*) 674; wooden etc. *n.*

636. Store.—N. stock, fund, mine, vein, lode, quarry; spring; fount, -ain; well, -spring; milch-cow.

stock in trade, supply; heap etc. (*collection*) 72; treasure; reserve, *corps de réserve*, reserve fund, nest-egg, savings, *bonne bouche*.

crop, harvest, mow, vintage; yield, product, gleanings.

store, accumulation, hoard, rick, stack; lumber; relay etc. (*provision*) 637.

store-house, -room, -closet; depository, *dépôt*, *cache*, safe deposit, vault, pantechnicon, repository, -servatory, -pertory; *repertorium*; promptuary, warehouse, *entrepôt*, magazine, dump, buttery, larder, pantry, panary, lanary, still-room, spence; crib, garner, granary, silo, barn; bunker; thesaurus; bank etc. (*treasury*) 802; armoury; arsenal; dock; gallery, museum, library, conservatory, hot-house; manag-ery, -erie, aquarium, zoological gardens.

reservoir, cistern, tank, sump, pond, mill-pond; gasometer.

budget, quiver, bandolier, portfolio; coffer etc. (*receptacle*) 191.

conservation; storing etc. *v.*; storage.
dictionary etc. 562; list etc. 86.

V. store; put –, lay –, set- by; stow away; set
–, lay- apart; store –, hoard –, treasure –, lay
–, heap –, put –, garner –, save- up; *cache*; accumulate, amass, hoard, fund, garner, save, bank.

conserve, reserve; keep –, hold- back; husband,
– one's resources.

deposit; stow, stack, load, dump; harvest; heap,
collect etc. 72; lay -in, – down, – by, store etc.
adj.; keep, file [papers] lay in etc. (*provide*) 637;
preserve etc. 670; put by for a rainy day.

Adj. stored etc. *v.*; in -store, – reserve, – ordinary; spare, supernumerary.

637. Provision.—N. provision, supply; grist, –
to the mill; subvention etc. (*aid*) 707; resources etc.
(*means*) 632.

provising etc. *v.*; purveyance; reinforcement;
commissary, commissariat.

rations; iron –, emergency- rations; provender
etc. (*food*) 298; *viaticum*; ensilage.

caterer, purveyor, commissary, quartermaster,
steward, housekeeper, manciple, feeder, batman,
victualler, storekeeper, grocer, provision merchant,
green-, grocer, *comprador*, *restaurateur*; sutler etc.
(*merchant*) 797; innkeeper, publican, confectioner,
baker, butcher, wine merchant, vintner.

V. provide; make -provision, – due provision
for; lay in, – a stock, – a store.

sup-ply, -peditate; furnish; find, – one in; arm.

cater, victual, provision, purvey, forage; beat up
for; stock, – with; make good, replenish; fill, –
up; recruit, feed, ration.

have in -store, – reserve; keep, – by one, – on
foot; have to fall back upon; store etc. 636; provide
against a rainy day etc. (*economy*) 817.

638. Waste.—N. consumption, expenditure,
exhaustion; dispersion etc. 73; ebb; leakage etc.
(*exudation*) 295; loss etc. 776; wear and tear;
waste; prodigality etc. 818; misuse etc. 679;
wasting etc. *v.*; rubbish etc. (*useless*) 645.

mountain in labor.

v. spend, expend, use, consume, swallow up,
exhaust, deplete; impoverish; spill, drain, empty;
disperse etc. 73.

cast –, throw –, fling –, fritter- away; burn the
candle at both ends, waste; squander etc. 818.

'waste its sweetness on the desert air;' cast -one's
bread upon the waters, – pearls before swine; employ a steam engine to crack a nut, waste powder
and shot, break a butterfly on a wheel; labor in
vain etc. (*useless*) 645; cut a whetstone with a
razor, pour water into a sieve; tilt at windmills.

leak etc. (*run out*) 295; run to waste; ebb; melt
away, run dry, dry up.

Adj. wasted etc. *v.*; at a low ebb.

wasteful etc. (*prodigal*) 818; penny wise and
pound foolish.

Phr. *magno conatu magnas nugas; le jeu n'en
vaut pas la chandelle.*

639. Sufficiency.—N. sufficiency, adequacy,
enough, withal, *quantum sufficit*, satisfaction, competence; no less.

mediocrity etc. (*average*) 29.

fill; fullness etc (*completeness*) 52; plen-itude, -
ty; abundance; copiousness etc. *adj.*; amplitude,
galore, lots, profusion; full measure; 'good measure
pressed down, shaken together and running over.'

luxuriance etc. (*fertility*) 168; affluence etc.
(*wealth*) 803; fat of the land; 'a land flowing with
milk and honey;' cornucopia; horn of -plenty, –
Amalthæa; mine etc. (*stock*) 636.

outpouring; flood etc. (*great quantity*) 31; tide
etc. (*river*) 348; repletion etc. (*redundance*) 641;
satiety etc. 869; rich man etc. 803.

V. be -sufficient etc. *adj.*; suffice, do, just do,
satisfy, pass muster; have -enough etc. *n.*; eat –,
drink –, have- one's fill; roll –, swim- in; wallow
in etc. (*superabundance*) 641.

abound, exuberate, teem, flow, stream, rain,
shower down; pour, – in; swarm; bristle with.

render -sufficient etc. *adj.*; replenish etc. (*fill*)
52.

Adj. sufficient, enough, adequate, up to the
mark, commensurate, competent, satisfactory,
valid, tangible.

measured; moderate etc. (*temperate*) 953.

full etc. (*complete*) 52; ample; plen-ty, -tiful, -
teous; plenty as blackberries; copious, abundant;
abounding etc. *v.*; replete, enough and to spare,
flush; choke-full; well-stocked, -provided; liberal;
unstint-ed, -ing; stintless; without stint; un-sparing,
-measured; lavish etc. 641; wholesale.

rich, luxuriant etc. (*fertile*) 168; affluent etc.
(*wealthy*) 803; wantless; big with etc. (*pregnant*)
161.

un-exhausted,   -wasted;   exhaustless,
inexhaustible.

Adv. sufficiently, amply etc. *adj.*; full; in -
abundance etc. *n.*; with no sparing hand; to one's
heart's content, *ad libitum*, without stint.

Phr. cut and come again.

640. Insufficiency.—N. insufficiency;
inadequa-cy, -teness; incompetence etc. (*impotence*) 158; deficiency etc. (*incompleteness*) 53;
imperfection etc. 651; shortcoming etc. 304;
paucity; stint; scantiness etc. (*smallness*) 32; none
to spare; bare subsistence.

scarcity, dearth; want, need, lack, poverty,
exigency; inanition, starvation, famine, drought.

dole, pittance, mite; short -allowance, – commons; half-rations; banyan –, fast- day, Lent.

emptiness, poorness etc. *adj.*; depletion,
vacancy, flaccidity; ebb-tide; low water; 'a beggarly
account of empty boxes;' indigence etc. (*poverty*)
804; insolvency etc. (*non-payment*) 808; poor man
etc. 804; bankrupt etc. 808.

V. be -insufficient etc. *adj.*; not -suffice etc. 639;
come short of etc. 304; run dry.

want, lack, need, require; *caret*; be in want etc.
(*poor*) 804; live from hand to mouth.

render- insufficient etc. *adj.*; drain of resources;
impoverish etc. (*waste*) 638; stint etc. (*begrudge*)
819; put on short -commons, – allowance.

do -insufficiently -etc. *adv.*; scotch the snake.

Adj. insufficient, inadequate; too -little etc. 32;
not -enough etc. 639; incompetent; incompetent etc.
(*impotent*) 158; 'weighed in the balance and found
wanting;' perfunctory etc. (*neglect*) 460; deficient

etc. (*incomplete*) 53; wanting etc. *v.*; imperfect etc.
651; ill-furnished, -provided, -stored, -off.

slack, at a low ebb; empty, vacant, bare; short
—, out —, destitute —, devoid —, bereft etc. 789
—, denuded- of; dry, drained.

un -provided, -supplied, -furnished; unreplenished, -fed; un-stored, -treasured; empty-
handed.

meager, poor, thin, scrimp, sparing, spare, stint-
ed, stunted; skimpy; starv-ed, -eling; half-starved,
emaciated, famine-stricken, famished, underfed,
undernourished; jejune.

scant etc. (*small*) 32; scarce; not to be had, —
for love or money, — at any price; scurvy; stingy
etc. 819; at the end of one's tether; without -
resources etc. 632; in want etc. (*poor*) 804; in debt
etc. 806.

Adv. insufficiently etc. *adj.*; in default —, for
want- of; failing.

641. Redundance.—N. redundance; too -
much, — many; superabundance, -fluity, -fluence,
-saturation; nimiety, transcendency, exuberance,
profuseness; profusion etc. (*plenty*) 639; repletion,
enough in all conscience, *satis superque*, lion's
share; more than -enough etc. 639; plethora,
engorgement, congestion, load, surfeit, sickener;
turgescence etc. (*expansion*) 194; over-dose, -
measure, -supply, -flow; inundation etc. (*water*)
348; *avalanche.*

accumulation etc. (*store*) 636; heap etc. 72;
drug, — in the market; glut; crowd; burden.

excess; sur-, over-plus, epact; margin; remainder
etc. 40; duplicate; surplusage; expletive; work of
—, supererogation; *bonus, bonanza.*

luxury; intemperance etc. 954; extravagance etc.
(*prodigality*) 818; exorbitance, lavishness.

pleonasm etc. (*diffuseness*) 573; too many irons
in the fire; embarassment of riches; money to burn.

V. super-, over-abound; know no bounds,
swarm; meet one at every turn; creep —, bristle-
with; overflow; run —, flow —, well —, brim-over;
run riot; over-run, -stock, -lay, -charge, -dose, -
feed, -burden, -load, -do, -whelm, -shoot the mark
etc. (*go beyond*) 303; surcharge, supersaturate,
gorge, glut, load, drench, whelm, inundate, deluge,
flood; drug, — the market.

choke, cloy, accloy, suffocate; pile up, lay it on,
— with a trowel, lay on thick; impregnate with;
lavish etc. (*squander*) 818.

send —, carry- coals to Newcastle, — owls to
Athens; teach one's grandmother to suck eggs;
pisces natare docere; kill the slain, 'gild refined
gold,' 'paint the lily;' butter one's bread on both
sides, put butter upon bacon; employ a steam-
engine to crack a nut etc. (*waste*) 638.

exaggerate etc. 549; wallow in; roll in etc.
(*plenty*) 639; remain on one's hands, hang heavy
on hand, go a begging.

Adj. redundant; too -much, — many; exuberant,
inordinate, superabundant, excessive, overmuch,
replete, profuse, lavish; prodigal etc. 818; exorbitant; overweening; extravagant; overcharged etc.
v.; supersaturated, drenched, overflowing; running
-over, — to waste, — down.

crammed —, filled- to overflowing; gorged, stuff-
ed, ready to burst; dropsical, turgid, plethoric,
full-blooded; obese etc. 194; voluminous.

superfluous, unnecessary, needless, super-
vacaneous, uncalled for, to spare, in excess; over
and above etc. (*remainder*) 40; *de trop*;
adscititious etc. (*additional*) 37; supernumerary
etc. (*reserve*) 636; on one's hands, spare, duplicate,
supererogatory, expletive; *un peu fort.*

Adj. over, too, over and above; over —, too-
much; too far; without —, beyond — out of-
measure; with ... to spare; over head and ears; up to
one's eyes, — ears; *extra*; beyond the mark etc.
(*transcursion*) 303; over one's head.

Phr. It never rains but it pours.

642. Importance.—N. importance,
consequence, moment, prominence, consideration,
mark, materialness.

import, significance, concern; emphasis, interest.

greatness etc. 31; superiority etc. 33; notability
etc. (*repute*) 873; weight etc. (*influence*) 175;
value etc. (*goodness*) 648; usefulness etc. 644.

gravity, seriousness, solemnity; no -joke, —
laughing matter; pressure, urgency, stress; matter of
life and death.

memorabilia, notabilia, great doings; red-letter
day.

great -thing, — point; main chance, 'the be all
and end all,' cardinal point, outstanding feature;
substance, gist etc. (*essence*) 5; sum and substance,
gravamen, head and front; important —, principal
—, prominent —, essential- part; half the battle;
sine quâ non; breath of one's nostrils etc. (*life*)
359; cream, salt, core, kernel, heart, nucleus; key,
note, -stone; corner stone; trumpcard etc. (*device*)
626; salient points.

top-sawyer, first fiddle, *prima donna*, chief, big-
wig; triton among the minnows.

V. be -important etc. *adj.*, — somebody, —
something; import, signify, matter, be an object;
carry weight etc. (*influence*) 175; make a figure
etc. (*repute*) 873; be in the ascendant, come to the
front, lead the way, take the lead, play first fiddle,
throw all else into the shade; lie at the root of;
deserve —, merit —, be worthy- -of notice, —
regard, — consideration.

attach —, ascribe —, give- importance etc. *n.*-
to; value, care for; set store -upon, — by; mark etc.
550; mark with a white stone, underline; write —,
put —, print- in -italics, — capitals, — large letters,
— large type, — letters of gold; accentuate, emphasize, lay stress on.

make a fuss, — a stir, — a piece of work, —
much ado- about; make -of, — much of.

Adj. important; of -importance etc. *n.*; momentous, material; to the point; not to be -overlooked,
— despised, — sneezed at; egregious; weighty etc.
(*influential*) 175; of note etc. (*repute*) 873;
notable, prominent, salient, signal; memorable,
remarkable; worthy of -remark, — notice; never to
be forgotten; stirring, eventful.

grave, serious, earnest, noble, grand, solemn, impressive, commanding, imposing.

urgent, pressing, critical, instant.

paramount, essential, vital, all-absorbing;
radical, cardinal, chief, main, prime, primary, principal, leading, capital, foremost, overruling; of vital
etc. importance.

in the front rank, first-rate, A1; superior etc. 33;
considerable etc. (*great*) 31; marked etc. *v.*; rare
etc. 137.

significant, telling, trenchant, emphatic, pregnant; *tanti*.

Adv. materially etc. *adj.*; in the main; above all, *par excellence*, to crown all.

643. Unimportance.—N. unimportance, insignificance, nothingness, immateriality.

triviality, trivia, fribble, levity, frivolity; paltriness etc. *adj.*; poverty; smallness etc. 32; vanity etc. (*uselessness*) 645; matter of - indifference etc. 866; no object; side issue.

nothing, – to signify, – worth speaking of, – particular, – to boast of, – to speak of; small –, no great –, trifling etc. *adj.*-matter; mere -joke, – nothing; hardly –, scarcely- anything; nonentity, cipher, figurehead; no great shakes, *peu de chose*; child's play; small beer.

toy, plaything, popgun, paper pellet, gimcrack, geegaw, bauble, trinket, *bagatelle*, kickshaw, knicknack, whim-wham, trifle, 'trifles light as air.'

trumpery, trash, rubbish, stuff, *fatras*, frippery; 'leather or prunello;' chaff, drug, froth, bubble, smoke, cobweb; weed; refuse etc. (*inutility*) 645; scum etc. (*dirt*) 653.

joke, jest, snap of the fingers; fudge etc. (*unmeaning*) 517; fiddlestick, – end; pack of nonsense, mere farce.

straw, pin, fig, continental, button, rush; bulrush, feather, halfpenny, farthing, brass farthing, doit, peppercorn, jot, rap, pinch of snuff, old song.

minutiae, details, minor details, small fry; dust in the balance, feather in the scale, drop in the ocean, fléa-bite, molehill; fingle-fangle.

nine days' wonder, *ridiculus mus*; flash in the pan etc. (*impotence*) 158; much ado about nothing etc. (*overestimation*) 482; storm in a teacup.

V. be -unimportant etc. *adj.*; not -matter etc. 642; go for –, matter –, signify- -little, – nothing, – little or nothing; not matter a -straw etc. *n.*

make light of etc. (*underestimate*) 483; catch at straws etc. (*overestimate*) 482.

Adj. unimportant; of -little, – small, – no- - account, – importance etc. 642; immaterial; un-, non-essential; not vital; irrelevant, incidental, indifferent.

subordinate etc. (*inferior*) 34; *médiocre* etc. (*average*) 29; passable, fair, respectable, tolerable, commonplace; uneventful, mere, common; ordinary etc. (*habitual*) 613; inconsiderable, so-so, insignificant, inappreciable, nugatory.

trifling, trivial; slight, slender, light, flimsy, frothy, idle; puerile etc. (*foolish*) 499; airy, shallow; weak etc. 160; powerless etc. 158; frivolous, petty, niggling; pid-, ped-dling; fribble, inane, ridiculous, farcical; fini-cal, -kin; fiddlefaddle, namby-pamby, wishy-washy, milk and water.

poor, paltry, pitiful; contemptible etc. (*contempt*) 930; sorry, mean, meager, shabby, miserable, wretched, vile, scrubby, scrannel, weedy, niggardly, scurvy, putid, beggarly, worthless, twopenny-half penny, cheap, trashy, catchpenny, gimcrack, trumpery, one-horse; toy.

not worth -the pains, – while, – mentioning, – speaking of, – a thought, – a curse, – a straw, – rap etc. *n.*; beneath –, unworthy of- -notice, –

regard, – consideration, – contempt; *de lanâ caprinâ*; vain etc. (*useless*) 645.

Adv. slightly etc. *adj.*; rather, somewhat, pretty well, fairly well, tolerably.

for aught one cares.

Int. no matter! pish! tush! tut! pshaw! pugh! pooh, -pooh! fudge! bosh! humbug! fiddle-stick, – end! fiddlededee! never mind! *n'importe!* what - signifies, – matter, – boots it, – of that, – 's the odds! a fig for! stuff! nonsense! stuff and nonsense!

Phr. *magno conatu magnas nugas*; *le jeu n'en vaut pas la chandelle*; it -matters not, – does not signify; it is of no -consequence, – importance.

644. Utility.—N. utility; usefulness etc. *adj.*; efficacy, efficiency, adequacy; service, use, stead, avail; help etc. (*aid*) 707; applicability etc. *adj.*; subservience etc. (*instrumentality*) 631; function etc. (*business*) 625; value; worth etc. (*goodness*) 648; money's worth; productiveness etc. 168; *cui bono* etc. (*intention*) 620; utilization etc. (*use*) 677; step in the right direction.

common weal, public good; utilitarianism etc. (*philanthropy*) 910.

V. be -useful etc. *adj.*; avail, serve; subserve etc. (*be instrumental to*) 631; conduce etc. (*tend*) 176; answer –, serve- -one's turn, – a purpose.

act a part etc. (*action*) 680; perform –, discharge- -a function etc. 625; do –, render- -a service, – good service, – yeoman's service; bestead, stand one in good stead; be the making of; help etc. 707.

bear fruit etc. (*produce*) 161; bring grist to the mill; profit, remunerate; benefit etc. (*do good*) 648.

find one's -account, – advantage- in; reap the benefit of etc. (*be better for*) 658.

render useful etc. (*use*) 677.

Adj. useful; of -use etc. *n.*; serviceable, usable, proficuous, good for; subservient etc. (*instrumental*) 631; conducive etc. (*tending*) 176; subsidiary etc. (*helping*) 707.

advantageous etc. (*beneficial*) 648; profitable, gainful, remunerative, worth one's salt; in-, valuable; prolific etc. (*productive*) 168.

adequate; ef-ficient, -ficacious; effect-ive, -ual; practicable, expedient etc. 646.

applicable, available, ready, handy, at hand, tangible; commodious, adaptable; of all work.

Adv. usefully etc. *adj.*; *pro bono publico*.

645. Inutility.—N. inutility; uselessness etc. *adj.*; inefficacy, futility; inep-, inap-titude; unsubservience; inadequacy etc. (*insufficiency*) 640; inefficiency etc. (*incompetence*) 158; unskilfulness etc. 699; disservice; unfruitfulness etc. (*unproductiveness*) 169; labor -in vain, –. lost, – of Sisyphus; lost -trouble, – labor; work of Penelope; sleeveless errand, wild goose chase, mere farce.

tautology etc. (*repetition*) 104; supererogation etc. (*redundance*) 641.

vanitas vanitatum, vanity, inanity, worthlessness, nugacity; triviality etc. (*unimportance*) 643.

caput mortuum, waste paper, dead letter; blunt tool.

litter, rubbish, lumber, odds and ends, cast-off clothes; button-top; shoddy; rags, orts, trash, refuse, sweepings, scourings, off-scourings, dross, slag, waste, rubble, dottle, drast, *débris*; stubble, leavings; broken meat; dregs etc. (*dirt*) 653; weeds, tares; rubbish heap, dust hole; *rudera*, deads.

fruges consumere natus etc. (*drone*) 683.

V. be -useless etc. *adj.*; go a begging etc. (*redundant*). 641; fail etc. 732.

seek −, strive- after impossibilities; use vain efforts, labor in vain, roll the stone of Sisyphus, beat the air, lash the waves, *battre l'eau avec un bâton*, *donner un coup d'épée dans l'eau*, fish in the air, milk the ram, drop a bucket into an empty well, sow the sand; bay the moon; preach −, speak- to the winds; whistle jigs to a milestone; kick against the pricks, *se battre contre des moulins*; lock the stable door when the steed is stolen etc. (*too late*) 135; hold a farthing candle to the sun; cast pearls before swine etc. (*waste*) 638; carry coals to Newcastle etc. (*redundance*) 641; wash a blackamoor white etc. (*impossible*) 471.

render -useless etc. *adj.*; dis-mantle, -mast, -mount, -qualify, -able; unrig; cripple, lame etc. (*injure*) 659; spike guns, clip the wings; put out of gear.

Adj. useless, inutile, inefficacious, futile, unavailing, bootless; inoperative etc. 158; inadequate etc. (*insufficient*) 640; in-, un- subservient: inept, inefficient etc.(*impotent*) 158; of no -avail etc. (*use*) 644; ineffectual etc. (*failure*) 732; incompetent etc. (*unskilful*) 699; 'stale, flat and unprofitable:' superfluous etc. (*redundant*) 641; dispensable; thrown away etc. (*wasted*) 638; abortive etc. (*immature*) 674.

worth-, value-less; unsaleable; not worth a straw etc. (*trifling*) 643; dear at any price.

vain, empty, inane; gain-, profit-, fruit-less; un-serviceable, -profitable; ill-spent; unproductive etc. 169; *hors de combat*; barren, sterile, impotent, un-productive; effete, past work etc. (*impaired*) 659; obsolete etc. (*old*) 124; fit for the -dust-hole, − wastepaper basket; good for nothing; of no earthly use; not worth -having, − powder and shot; leading to no end, uncalled for; un-necessary, -needed, superfluous.

Adv. uselessly etc. *adj.*; to -little, − no, − little or no- purpose.

Int. *cui bono?* what's the good!

646. Expedience. [Specific subservience.]—**N.** expedien-ce, -cy; desirableness, -bility etc. *adj.*; fitness etc. (*agreement*) 23; utility etc. 644; propriety; advantage; opportunism, pragmatism.

high time etc. (*occasion*) 134.

V. be -expedient etc. *adj.*; suit etc. (*agree*) 23; befit; suit −, befit- the -time, − season, − occasion.

conform etc. 82.

Adj. expedient; desir-, advis-, accept-able; convenient; worth while, meet; fit, -ting; due, proper, eligible, seemly, becoming; befitting etc. *v.*; opportune etc. (*in season*) 134; *in loco*; suitable etc. (*accordant*) 23; applicable etc. (*useful*) 644; practical, effective, pragmatical; suitable, handy.

Adv. in the right place; conveniently etc. *adj.*; in the nick of time.

Phr. *operae pretium est.*

647. Inexpedience.—**N.** enexpedien-ce, -cy; undesira-bleness, -bility etc. *adj.*; discommodity, impropriety; unfitness etc. (*disagreement*) 24; inutility etc. 645; inconvenience, inadvisability; disadvantage.

V. be -inexpedient etc. *adj.*; come amiss etc. (*disagree*) 24; embarrass etc. (*hinder*) 706; put to inconvenience; pay too- dear for one's whistle.

Adj. inexpedient, undesirable; un-, in-advisable; objectionable; troublesome, in-apt, -eligible, -admissable, -convenient; in-, dis-commodious; disadvantageous; inappropriate, unsuitable, unfit etc. (*inconsonant*) 24.

ill-contrived, -advised; unsatsifactory; un-profitable etc., unsubservient etc. (*useless*) 645; inopportune etc. (*unseasonable*) 135; out of −, in the wrong- place; improper, unseemly.

clumsy, awkward; cum-brous, -bersome; lumbering, unwieldy, hulky; unmanageable etc. (*impracticable*) 704; impedient (*in the way*) 706.

unnecessary etc. (*redundant*) 641.

Phr. it will never do.

648. Goodness. [Capability of producing good. Good qualities.]—**N.** goodness etc. *adj.*; excellence, merit; virtue etc. 944; value, worth, price.

super-excellence, -eminence; superiority etc. 33; perfection etc. 650; *coup de maître*; master-piece, *chef d'oeuvre*, prime, flower, cream, *élite*, pick, A1, none such, *nonpareil*, *crème de la crème*, flower of the flock, cock of the roost, salt of the earth; champion.

tid-bit; gem, − of the first water; *bijou*, precious stone, jewel, pearl, diamond, ruby, brilliant, treasure; good thing; *rara avis*, one in a thousand.

beneficence etc. 906; good man etc. 948.

V. be -beneficial etc. *adj.*; produce −, do- good etc. 618; profit etc. (*be of use*) 644; benefit; confer a -benefit etc. 618.

be the making of, do a world of good, make a man of.

produce a good effect; do a good turn, confer an obligation; improve etc. 658.

do no harm, break no bones.

be -good etc. *adj.*; excel, transcend etc. (*be superior*) 33; bear away the bell.

stand the -proof, − test; pass -muster, − an examination.

challenge comparison, vie, emulate, rival.

Adj. harm-, hurt-less; unobnoxious; in-nocuous, -nocent, -offensive.

beneficial, valuable, of value; serviceable etc. (*useful*) 644; advantageous, profitable, edifying; salutary etc. (*healthful*) 656.

favorable; propitious etc. (*hopegiving*) 858; fair.

good, − as gold; excellent; better; superior etc. 33; above par; nice, fine; genuine etc. (*true*) 494.

best, choice, select, picked, elect, eximious, *recherché*, rare, priceless; unpara-goned, -lleled etc. (*supreme*) 33; superlatively etc. 33- good; super-fine, -excellent; bonzer; of the first water; first-rate, -class; high-wrought; exquisite, very best, crack, prime, tip-top, gilt-edged, capital, cardinal; standard etc. (*perfect*) 650; inimitable.

admirable, estimable; praiseworthy etc. (*approve*) 931; pleasing etc. 829; *couleur de rose*, precious, of great price; costly etc. (*dear*) 814; worth -its weight in gold, − a Jew's eye, − a king's ransom; matchless, peerless, invaluable, inestimable, precious as the apple of the eye.

tolerable etc. (*not very good*) 651; up to the mark, un-exceptionable, -objectionable; satisfactory, tidy.

in -good, – fair- condition; fresh; unspoiled; sound etc. (*perfect*) 650.

Adv. beneficially etc. *adj.*; well etc. 618.

649. Badness. [Capability of producing evil. Bad qualities.]—**N.** hurtfulness etc. *adj.*; virulence.

evil doer etc. 913; bane etc. 663; plague-spot etc. (*insalubrity*) 657; evil star, ill wind; snake in the grass, skeleton in the closet; *amari aliquid*, thorn in the side; Jonah, jinx, hoodoo.

malignity; malevolence etc. 907; tender mercies [ironically].

ill-treatment, annoyance, molestation, abuse, oppression, persecution, outrage; misusage etc. 679; injury etc. (*damage*) 659.

badness etc. *adj.*; peccancy, abomination; painfulness etc. 830; pestilence etc. (*disease*) 655; guilt etc. 947; depravity etc. 945.

V. be -hurtful etc. *adj.*; cause –, produce –, inflict –, work –, do- evil etc. 619; damnify, endamage, hurt, harm, scathe; injure etc. (*damage*) 659; pain etc. 830.

wrong, aggrieve, oppress, persecute; trample –, tread –, bear hard –, put-upon; overburden; weigh -down, – heavy on; victimize; run down; molest etc. 830.

maltreat, abuse; ill-use, -treat; thwart, buffet, bruise, scratch, maul; smite etc. (*scourge*) 972; do -violence, – harm, – a mischief; stab, pierce, outrage.

do –, make- mischief; bring –, get- into trouble.

destroy etc. 162.

Adj. hurt-, harm-, scath-, bane-, bale-ful; injurious, deleterious, detrimental, noxious, pernicious, mischievous, full of mischief, mischiefmaking, malefic, malignant, nocuous, noisome; prejudicial; dis-serviceable, advantageous; wide-wasting.

unlucky, sinister; obnoxious, untoward, disastrous.

oppressive, burdensome, onerous; malign etc. (*malevolent*) 907.

corrupting etc. (corrupt etc. 659) virulent, venomous, envenomed, corrosive; poisonous etc. (*morbific*) 657; deadly etc. (*killing*) 361; destructive etc. (*destroying*) 162; inauspicious etc. 859.

bad, ill, arrant, as bad bad can be, dreadful; horrid, -rible; dire; rank, peccant, foul, fulsome; rotten, – at the core.

vile, base, villainous; mean etc. (*paltry*) 643; injured etc., deteriorated etc. 659; unsatisfactory, exception, -able, indifferent; below par etc. (*imperfect*) 651; ill-contrived, -conditioned; wretched, sad, grievous, deplorable, lamentable; piti-ful, -able, woeful etc. (*painful*) 830.

evil, wrong; depraved etc. 945; shocking; reprehensible etc. (*disapprove*) 932.

hateful, – as a toad; abominable, detestable, execrable, cursed, accursed, confounded; damn-ed, -able; infernal; diabolic etc. (*malevolent*) 907.

inadvisable etc. (*inexpedient*) 647; unprofitable etc. (*useless*) 645; incompetent etc. (*unskilful*) 699; irremediable etc. (*hopeless*) 859.

Adv. badly etc. *adj.*; wrong, ill; to one's cost; where the shoe pinches.

Phr. bad is the best; the worst come to the worst.

650. Perfection.—**N.** perfection; perfectness etc. *adj.*; indefectibility; inpecc-ancy, -ability.

pink, *beau idéal*, phoenix, paragon; pink –, acme- of perfection; *ne plus ultra*; summit etc. 210.

cygne noir; philosopher's stone; chrysolite, Koh-i-noor, black tulip.

model, standard, pattern, mirror, admirable Chrichton; trump; very prince of.

master-piece, -stroke, super-excellence etc. (*goodness*) 648; transcendence etc. (*superiority*) 33.

V. be -perfect etc. *adj.*; transcend etc. (*be supreme*) 33.

bring to perfection, perfect, ripen, mature; consummate, complete etc. 729; put in trim etc. (*prepare*) 673; put the finishing touch to.

Adj. perfect, faultless, ideal; indefective, -ficient, -fectible; immaculate, spotless, impeccable; free from -imperfection etc. 651; un-blemished, -injured etc. 659; sound, – as a roach; in perfect condition; scathless, intact, harmless; seaworthy etc. (*safe*) 644; right as a trivet; *in seipso totus teres atque rotundus*; consummate etc. (*complete*) 52; finished etc. 729; complete in itself.

best etc. (*good*) 648; model, standard; inimitable, unparagoned, unparalleled etc. (*supreme*) 33; superhuman, divine; beyond all praise etc. (*approbation*) 931; *sans peur et sans reproche*.

Adj. to perfection, to the limit; perfectly etc. *adj.*; *ad unguem*; clean, – as a whistle.

651. Imperfection.—**N.** imperfection; imperfectness etc. *adj.*; deficiency; inadequacy etc. (*insufficiency*) 640; peccancy etc. (*badness*) 649; immaturity etc. 674.

fault, defect, weak point; screw loose; rift within the lute; fly in the ointment; flaw etc. (*break*) 70; gap etc. 198; twist etc. 243; taint, attainder; bar sinister, hole in one's coat; blemish etc. 848; weakness etc. 160; half-blood, touch of the tar brush; shortcoming etc. 304; drawback; seamy side.

mediocrity; no great -shakes, – catch; not much to boast of.

V. be -imperfect etc. *adj.*; have a -defect etc. *n.*; lie under a disadvantage; spring a leak.

not –, barely- pass muster; fall short etc. 304.

Adj. imperfect; not -perfect etc. 650; de-ficient, -fective; faulty, unsound, mutilated, tainted; out of -order, – tune; cracked, leaky; sprung; warped etc. (*distort*) 243; lame; injured etc. (*deteriorated*) 659; peccant etc. (*bad*) 649; frail etc. (*weak*) 160; inadequate etc. (*insufficient*) 640; crude etc. (*unprepared*) 674; incomplete etc. 53; found wanting; below par; shorthanded; below –, under- its full -strength, – complement.

indifferent, middling, ordinary, mediocre; average etc. 29; so-so; *così-così*, milk and water; tolerable, fair, passable; pretty -well, − good; rather −, moderately- good; good −, well-enough; decent; not -bad, − amiss; inobjectionable, admissable, bearable, only better than nothing.

secondary, inferior; second-rate, -best, one-horse.

Adv. almost etc.; to a limited extent, rather etc. 32; pretty, moderately; only; considering, all things considered, enough.

Phr. *surgit amari aliquid.*

652. Cleanness.—N. cleanness etc. *adj.*; purity; cleaning etc. *v.*; purification, defecation etc. *v.*; purgation, lustration; de-, abs-tersion; epuration, mundation, ablution, lavation, colature; disinfection etc. *v.*; drain-, sewerage.

lavatory, bath, -room; swimming pool, natatorium; public baths; hot −, cold −, Turkish −, Swedish −, Russian − vapor- bath; *hammam*, laundry, washhouse; washerwoman, laundress, laundryman; scavenger, cleaner, sweeper, goodie; crossing sweeper, white wings, dustman, sweep.

brush; broom, besom, carpet-sweeper, vacuum-cleaner, mop, squilgee, rake, shovel, sieve, riddle, screen, filter; scraper, strigil.

napkin, *serviette*, cloth, table-, carving-cloth, table-linen, napery, maukin, handkerchief, towel, sudary; doyley, doily, duster, sponge, mop, swab.

cover, drugget, mat, doormat.

soap, wash, lotion, detergent, cathartic, purgative; purifier etc. *v.*, dentifrice, tooth-powder, -paste; mouth wash; disinfectant.

V. be −, render- clean etc. *adj.*

clean, -se; mundify, rinse, wring, flush, full, wipe, mop, sponge, scour, swab, scrub, holystone, brush up.

wash, shampoo, lave, launder, buck; abs-, de-terge; clear, purify; de-purate, ⟶spumate, -fecate; purge, expurgate; Bowdlerize; elutriate, lixiviate, edulcorate, clarify, refine, rack; fil-ter, -trate; drain, strain.

disinfect, sterilize, pasteurize, fumigate, ventilate, deodorize; whitewash.

sift, winnow, screen, riddle, pick, weed, comb, rake, brush, sweep.

rout −, clear −, sweep etc.- out; make a clean sweep of.

Adj. clean, -ly; pure; immaculate; spot-, stain-, taint-less; without a stain, un-stained, -spotted, -soiled, -sullied, -tainted, -infected, -adulterated; aseptic; sweet, − as a nut.

neat, spruce, tidy, trim, gimp, clean as a new penny, like a cat in pattens; cleaned etc. *v.*; kempt.

Adv. neatly etc. *adj.*; clean as a whistle.

653. Uncleanness.—N. uncleanness etc. *adj.*; impurity; immundi-ty, -city; impurity etc. [of mind] 961.

defilement, contamination etc. *v.*; defedation; soil-ure, -iness; abomination; leaven; taint, -ure; fetor etc. 401.

decay; putre-scence, -faction; corruption; mold, must, mildew, dry-rot, *mucor*, rubigo, caries.

slovenry; slovenliness etc. *adj.*; squalor.

dowdy, drab, slut, malkin, slattern, sloven, slam-merkin, scrub, draggletail, mudlark, dustman, sweep; beast.

dirt, filth, soil, slop; dust, cobweb, flue; smoke, soot, smudge, smut, grime, raff.

sordes, dregs, grounds, lees; sedi-, settle-ment; heel-tap; dross, -iness; mother, precipitate, *scoria*, ashes, cinders, recrement, slag; scum, froth.

hog-wash, swill, ditch-, dish-, bilge-water; rins-ings, cheese-parings; sweepings etc. (*useless refuse*) 645; off-, out-scourings; off-scum; *caput mortuum*, *residuum*, sprue, feculence, clinker, draff; scurf, -iness; *exuviae*, morphew; fur, -fur; dandruff; tartar.

riffraff; vermin, louse, cootie, flea, bug.

mud, mire, quagmire, *alluvium*, silt, sludge, slime, slush, slosh.

spawn, offal, garbage, carrion; *excreta* etc. 299; slough, peccant humor, pus, matter, suppuration, *lienteria*; *feces*, excrement, ordure, dung; sew-, sewer-age; muck, coprolite; guano, manure, compost.

dunghill, *coluvies*, mixen, midden, bog, laystall, sink, w.c., water-, earth-closet, latrine, privy, jakes, John's, cess, -pool; sump, sough, *cloaca*, drain, sewer, common sewer; Cloacina; dust-hole.

sty, pig-sty, lair, den, Augean stable, sink of corruption; slum, rookery.

V. be −, become- unclean etc. *adj.*; rot, putrefy, fester, rankle, reek; stink etc. 401; mold, -er; go - bad etc. *adj.*

render -unclean etc. *adj.*; dirt. -y; soil, smoke, tarnish, slaver, spot, smear, daub, blot, blur, smudge, smutch, smirch; d-, dr-abble, -aggle; spat-ter, slubber; be-smear etc.; -mire, -slime, -grime, - foul; splash, stain, distain, maculate, sully, pollute, defile, debase, contaminate, taint, leaven; corrupt etc. (*injure*) 659; cover with -dust etc. *n.*; drabble in the mud.

wallow in the mire; slob-, slab-ber.

Adj. unclean, dirty, filthy, grimy; soiled etc. *v.*; not to be handled with kid gloves; dusty, snuffy, smutty, sooty, smoky; thick, turbid, dreggy; slimy.

uncleanly, slovenly, untidy, sluttish, dowdy, slat-ternly, draggletailed; un-combed, -kempt, -scoured, -swept, -wiped, -washed, -strained, -purified; squalid.

nasty, coarse, foul, impure, offensive, abominable, beastly, reeky, reechy; fetid etc. 401.

moldy, lentiginous, musty, mildewed, rusty, moth-eaten, mucid, rancid, bad, gone bad, touched, fusty, reasty, rotten, corrupt, tainted, high, fly-blown, maggoty; putr-id, -escent, -efied; purulent, carious, peccant, fec-al, -ulent; ster-coraceous, excrementitious; scurfy, impetiginous; gory, bloody; rotting etc. *v.*; rotten as -a pear, − cheese.

crapulous etc. (*intemperate*) 954; gross etc. (*impure in mind*) 961.

654. Health.—N. health, sanity; soundness etc. *adj.*; vigor; good −, perfect −, excellent −, rude −, robust- health; bloom, *mens sana in corpore sano*; Hygeia; incorrupti-on, -bility; good state −, clean bill- of health, eupepsia.

V. be in health etc. *adj.*; bloom, flourish.

keep -body and soul together, − on one's legs; enjoy -good, − a good state of - health; have a clean bill of health.

return to health; recover etc. 660; get better etc. (*improve*) 658; take a -new, – fresh- lease of life; convalesce, be convalescent, recruit; restore to health; cure etc. (*restore*) 660.

Adj. health-y, -ful; in -health etc. *n.*; well, sound, strong, fit, hearty, hale, fresh, blooming, green, whole; florid, flush, hardy, stanch, staunch, brave, robust, vigorous, weather-proof; convalescent.

un-scathed, -injured, -maimed, -marred, - tainted; sound of wind and limb, safe and sound; without a scratch.

on one's legs; sound as a -roach, – bell; fresh as -a daisy, – a rose, – April; picture of health; bursting with health; fit as a fiddle; hearty as a buck; in -fine, – high- feather; in -good case, – full bloom; in fine fettle; pretty bobbish, tolerably well, as well as can be expected.

sanitary etc. (*health-giving*) 656; sanatory etc. (*remedial*) 662.

655. Disease.*—N. disease, illness, sickness etc. *adj.*; ailing etc. *v.*; 'the ills that flesh is heir to;' morb-idity, -osity; infirmity, ailment, indisposition; complaint, disorder, malady; distemper, -ature.

visitation, attack, seizure, stroke, fit, epilepsy, apoplexy, shock, shell-shock.

delicacy, loss of health, valetudinarianism, invalidism, cachexy; *cachexia*, atrophy, *marasmus*; indigestion, *dyspepsia*; decay etc. (*deterioration*) 659; malnutrition, decline, consumption, palsy, paralysis, prostration; occupational diseases.

taint, pollution, infection, contagion, septicity, septicaemia, blood poisoning, pyaemia, epi-, endemic; murrain, plague, pestilence, virus, pox.

sore, ulcer, abscess, fester, boil; pimple etc. (*swelling*) 250; carbuncle, gathering, whitlow, imposthume, peccant humor, issue; rot, canker, cancer, *carcinoma*, *caries*, mortification, corruption, gangrene, *sphacelus*, leprosy, eruption, rash, breaking out, venereal disease.

fever, calenture; inflammation.

fatal etc. (*hopeless*) 859- -disease etc.; dangerous illness, galloping consumption, churchyard cough; general breaking up, break up of the system.

[Disease of the mind] neurasthenia; idiocy etc. 499; insanity etc. 503.

martyr to disease; cripple; 'the halt, the lame and the blind;' valetudinar-y, -ian; invalid, patient, case; sick-room, -chamber, hospital etc. 662.

[Science of disease] path-, eti-, nos-ology, therapeutics, diagnosis, prognosis.

V. be -ill etc. *adj.*; ail, suffer, labor under, be affected with, complain of; droop, flag, languish, halt; sicken, peak, pine, waste away, fail, lose strength; gasp.

keep one's bed; feign sickness etc. (*falsehood*) 544; malinger.

lay -by, – up; take –, catch- -a disease etc. *n.*, – an infection; be stricken by; break out.

Adj. diseased; ailing etc. *v.*; ill, – of; taken ill, seized with; indisposed, unwell, sick, squeamish, poorly, seedy; affected –, afflicted- with illness; laid up, confined, bed-ridden, invalided, in hospital, on the sick list; out of -health, – sorts; valetudinary.

un-sound, -healthy; sickly, morbose, healthless,

infirm, chlorotic, unbraced, drooping, flagging, lame, halt, crippled, halting.

morbid, tainted, vitiated, peccant, contaminated, poisoned, septic, tabid, mangy, leprous, cankered; rotten, – to, – at- the core; withered, palsied, paralytic, tuberculous; dyspeptic.

touched in the wind, broken-winded, spavined, gasping; *hors de combat* etc. (*useless*) 645.

weak-ly, -ened etc. (*weak*) 160; decrepit; decayed etc. (*deteriorated*) 659; incurable etc. (*hopeless*) 859; in declining health; cranky; in a bad way, in danger, prostrate; moribund etc. (*death*) 360.

morbific, epidemic etc. 657.

*Extended lists of different diseases are beyond the scope of this work.

656. Salubrity.—N. salubrity, salubriousness; healthiness etc. *adj.*

fine -air, – climate; eudiometer.

[Preservation of health] *hygiène*; valetudinarian, -ism, preventorium, sanitarian; *sanitarium*, *sanitorium*, immunity.

V. be -salubrious etc. *adj.*; agree with, be good for; assimilate etc. 23.

Adj. salu-brious, -tary, -tiferous, wholesome; health-y, -ful; sanitary, prophylactic, benign, bracing, tonic, invigorating, good for, nutritious, hyg-eian, -ienic.

in-noxious, -nocuous, -nocent; harmless, uninjurious, uninfectious; immune.

sanative etc. (*remedial*) 662; restorative etc. (*reinstate*) 660; useful etc. 644.

657. Insalubrity.—N. insalubrity, unhealthiness etc. *adj.*; non-naturals; plague spot; malaria etc. (*poison*) 663; death in the pot, contagion.

Adj. insalubrious; un-healthy, -wholesome; noxious, noisome, foul; morbi-fic, -ferous; mephitic, septic, azotic, deleterious; pesti-lent, -ferous, -lential; virulent, venomous, envenomed, poisonous, toxic, narcotic.

contagious, infectious, catching, taking, communicable, epidemic, zymotic, sporadic, endemic, pandemic, epizoötic.

innutritious, indigestible, ungenial; uncongenial etc. (*disagreeing*) 24.

deadly etc. (*killing*) 361.

658. Improvement.—N. improvement; a-, melioration; betterment; mend, amendment, emendation; mending etc. *v.*; advancement; advance etc. (*progress*) 282; ascent etc. 305; promotion, preferment; elevation etc. 307; increase etc. 35.

cultiv-, civiliz-ation; menticulture, culture, march of intellect; eugenics, euthenics, meliorism, telesis.

reform, -ation; revision, radical reform; second thoughts, correction, *limae labor*, refinement, elaboration; purification etc. 652; repair etc. (*restoration*) 660; recovery etc. 660.

revise; revised –, new- edition.

reformer, radical, progressive.

V. improve; be −, become −, get- better; mend, amend.

advance etc. (*progress*) 282; ascend etc. 305; increase etc. 35; fructify, ripen, mature; pick up, come about, rally, take a favorable turn; turn -over a new leaf, − the corner; raise one's head, sow one's wild oats; recover etc. 660.

be -better etc. *adj.*, − improved by; turn to - right, − good, − best- account; profit by, reap the benefit of; make -good use of, − capital out of; place to good account; take advantage of.

render better, improve, emend, make over, better; a-, meliorate; correct.

improve −, refine- upon; rectify; enrich, mellow, elaborate, fatten.

promote, cultivate, advance, forward, enhance; bring -forward, − on; foster etc. 707; invigorate etc. (*strengthen*) 159.

touch −, rub −, brush −, furbish −, bolster −, vamp −, brighten −, warm- up; polish, cook, make the most of, set off to advantage; prune; repair etc. (*restore*) 660; put in order etc. (*arrange*) 60.

review, revise, edit, redact; make -corrections, − improvements etc. *n.*; doctor etc. (*remedy*) 662; purify etc. 652.

relieve, refresh, revive, infuse new blood into, recruit, re-invigorate, renew, revivify, freshen, build -afresh, − anew; uplift, inspire.

re-form, -model, -organize; new model, civilize.

view in a new light, think better of, appeal from Philip drunk to Philip sober.

palliate, mitigate; lessen etc. 36- an evil.

Adj. improving etc. *v.*; progressive, improved etc. *v.*; better, − off, − for; all the better for, better advised.

reform-, emend-atory; reparatory etc. (*restorative*) 660; remedial etc. 662.

corrigible; improvable, curable, accultural.

Adv. on -consideration, − reconsideration, − second thoughts, − better advice; *ad melius inquirendum*; on the -mend, − up grade.

659. Deterioration.—N. deterioration, debasement; want, ebb; recession etc. 287; retrogradation etc. 283; decrease etc. 36.

degenera-cy, -tion, -teness; degradation; depravation, -ement; depravity etc. 945; demoralization, retrogression.

impairment, inquination, injury, damage, loss, detriment, delaceration, outrage, havoc, inroad, ravage, scath; perversion, prostitution, vitiation, discoloration, oxidation, pollution, defedation, poisoning, venenation, leaven, contamination, canker, corruption, adulteration, alloy.

decl-ine, -ension, -ination; decadence, -cy; falling off etc. *v.*; caducity, decrepitude, senility.

decay, dilapidation, ravages of time, wear and tear; cor-, e-rosion; mouldi-, rotten-ness; moth and rust, dry-rot, blight, marasmus, atrophy, collapse; disorganization; *délabrement* etc. (*destruction*) 162.

wreck, mere wreck, honeycomb, *magni nominis umbra*.

V. be −, become- -worse, − deteriorated etc. *adj.*; have seen better days, deteriorate, degenerate,

fall off; wane etc. (*decrease*) 36; ebb; retrograde etc. 283; decline, droop; go down etc. (*sink*) 306; go -downhill, − on from bad to worse, − farther and fare worse; jump out of the frying pan into the fire.

run to -seed, − waste; swale, sweal; lapse, be the worse for; break, − down; spring a leak, crack, start; shrivel etc. (*contract*) 195; fade, go off, wither, molder, rot, rankle, decay, go bad; go to - fall into- decay; 'fall into the sear and yellow leaf,' rust, crumble, shake; totter, − to its fall; perish etc. 162; die etc. 360.

[Render less good] deteriorate; weaken etc. 160; put back; taint, infect, contaminate, poison, empoison, envenom, canker, corrupt, exulcerate, pollute, vitiate, inquinate; de-, em-base; denaturalize, leaven; de-flower, -bauch, -file, - prave, -grade; stain etc. (*dirt*) 653; discolor; alloy, adulterate, sophisticate, tamper with, prejudice.

pervert, prostitute, demoralize, brutalize; render vicious etc. 945; compromise.

embitter, ex-, acerbate, aggravate.

injure, impair, labefy; damage, harm, hurt, shend, scathe, spoil, mar, despoil, dilapidate, waste; overrun; ravage; pillage etc. 791.

wound, stab, pierce, maim, lame, surbate, cripple, hough, hamstring, hit between the wind and water, scotch, mangle, mutilate, disfigure, blemish, deface, warp.

blight, rot; cor-, e-rode, eat away; wear -away, − out; gnaw, − at the root of; sap, mine, undermine, shake, sap the foundations of, break up; dis-organize, -mantle, -mast; destroy etc. 162.

damnify etc. (*aggrieve*) 649; do one's worst; knock down; deal a blow to; play -havoc, − sad havoc, − the mischief, − the deuce, − the very devil- -with, − among; decimate.

Adj. unimproved etc. (improve etc. 658); deteriorated etc. *v.*; altered, − for the worse; injured etc. *v.*; sprung; withering, spoiling, etc. *v.*; on the -wane, − decline; tabid; degenerate; worse; the −, all the- worse for; out of -repair, − tune; imperfect etc. 651; the worse for wear; battered; weather-ed, -beaten; stale, *passé*, shaken, dilapidated, frayed, faded, wilted, shabby, secondhand, second-rate, threadbare; worn, − to- -a thread, − a shadow, − the stump, rags; reduced, − to a skeleton, skeletonized; far gone.

decayed etc. *v.*; moth-, worm-eaten; mildewed, rusty, moldy, spotted, seedy, time-worn, mossgrown; discolored; effete, wasted, crumbling, moldering, rotten, cankered, blighted, tainted; depraved etc. (*vicious*) 945; decrep-id, -it; broken down; done, − for, − up; worn out, used up; fit for the -dust-hole, − wastepaper basket; past work etc. (*useless*) 645.

at a low ebb, in a bad way, on one's last legs, washed -up; − out; undermined, deciduous; nodding to its fall etc. (*destruction*) 162; tottering etc. (*dangerous*) 665; past cure etc. (*hopeless*) 859; fatigued etc. 688; backward; retrograde etc. (*retrogressive*) 283; deleterious etc. 649; behind the times.

Adv. on the down grade; beyond hope.

Phr. out of the frying pan into the fire; *aegrescit medendo*.

660. Restoration.—N. restor-ation, -al; re-instatement, -placement, -habilitation, -

establishment, -construction; reporduction etc. 163; re-novation, -newal; reviv-al, -escence; refreshment etc. 689; re-suscitation, -animation, - vivification, -viction; Phoenix; reorganization.

renaissance, renascence, rebirth, second youth, rejuvenation, rejuvenescence, new birth; regeneration, -cy, -teness; palingenesis, reconversion, resurgence, resurrection.

redress, retrieval, reclamation, recovery; convalescence; resumption, *résumption*.

recurrence etc. (*repetition*) 104; *réchauffé, rifacimento.*

cure, recure, sanation; healing etc. *v.*; redintegration; rectification, instauration.

repair, reparation, mending; recruiting etc. *v.*; cicatrization; disinfection; tinkering.

reaction; redemption etc. (*deliverance*) 672; restitution etc. 790; relief etc. 834.

mender, repairer, renewer; tinker, cobbler; doctor etc. 662; *vis medicatrix* etc. (*remedy*) 662. curableness.

V. return to the original state; recover, rally, revive; come -to, – round, – to oneself; pull through, weather the storm, be oneself again; get - well, – round, – the better of, – over, – about; rise from -one's ashes, – the grave; resurge, resurrect; survive etc. (*outlive*) 110; resume, reappear; come to, – life again; live –, rise- again; relive.

heal, skin over, cicatrize; right itself.

restore, put back, place *in statu quo*; re-instate, - place, -seat, -habilitate, -establish, -estate, -install.

re-construct, -build, -organize, -constitute; reconvert; re-new, -novate; recondition; regenerate; rejuvenate.

re-deem, -claim, -cover, -trieve; rescue etc. (*deliver*) 672.

redress, recure; cure, heal, remedy, doctor, physic, medicate; break of; bring round, set on one's legs.

re-suscitate, -vive, -animate, -vivify, -call to life; reproduce etc. 163; warm up; reinvigorate, refresh etc. 689.

redintegrate, make whole; recoup etc. 790; make -good, – all square; rectify; put –, set- -right, – to rights, – straight; set up, correct; put in order etc. (*arrange*) 60; refit, recruit; fill up, – the ranks; reinforce.

repair, mend; put in -repair, – thorough repair, – complete repair; retouch, botch, vamp, tinker, doctor, cobble; do –, patch –, plaster –, vamp-up; darn, fine-draw, heel-piece; stop a gap, stanch, staunch, caulk, calk, careen, splice, bind up wounds.

Adj. restored etc. *v.*; *redivivus*, convalescent; in a fair way; none the worse; rejuvenated, renascent.

restoring etc. *v.*; restorative, recuperative; sana-, repara-tive, -tory; curative, remedial.

restor-, recover-, san-, remedi-, retriev-, cur-able.

Adv. *in statu qho*; as you were.

Phr. *revenons à nos moutons.*

661. Relapse.—N. relapse, lapse; falling back etc. *v.*; retrogradation etc. (*retrogression*) 283; deterioration etc. 659.

[Return to, or recurrence of a bad state] backsliding, recidivation, recrudescence.

V. relapse, lapse; fall –, slide –, sink- back;

have a relapse; return; retrograde etc. 283; recidivate; fall off etc. 659- again.

662. Remedy.—N. remedy, help, redress; antidote, anti-toxin, -biotic; anti-, counter-poison, prophylactic, antiseptic, germicide, bactericide, corrective, restorative, stimulant, pick-me-up, tonic; sedative etc. 174; palliative; febrifuge; alterant, -ative; specific; emetic, carminative; narcotic etc. *adj.*; Nepenthe, Mithridate.

cure; radical –, perfect –, certain- cure; sovereign remedy.

physic, medicine, patent medicine, Galenicals, simples, drug, wonder –, miracle – drugs; potion, draught, dose, pill, bolus, lozenge, tablet, tabloid, capsule; electuary; linct-us, -ure; medicament.

nostrum; receipt, recipe, prescription; catholicon, panacea, elixir, *elixir vitae*, philosopher's stone; balm, balsam, cordial, theriac, ptisan.

salve, ointment, cerate, oil, lenitive, lotion, cosmetic; plaster; epithem, embrocation, liniment, cataplasm, sinapism, arquebusade, traumatic, vulnerary, pepastic, poultice, collyrium, depilatory.

compress, pledget; bandage etc. (*support*) 215.

treatment, medical treatment, regimen; diet-ary, -etics; *vis medicatrix*, – *naturae*; *médicine expectante*; seton, blood-letting, bleeding, venesection, phlebotomy, cupping, leeches; operation, surgical operation; tonsillectomy, appendectomy; injection, electrolysis, massage.

pharma-cy, -cology, -ceutics; acology; materia medica, pharmacopoeia, therapeutics, therapy, posology, pathology etc. 655; home-, hetero-, all-, hydr-opathy; cold water –, open air- cure; dietetics; sur-, chirur-gery, osteopathy; healing art, leechcraft, practice of medicine; ortho-paedy, - praxy; dentistry, midwifery, obstetrics, gynecology.

faith -cure, – healing, Christian science; psycho-therapy, -analysis, psychiatry.

hospital, infirmary, clinic; pest-, lazar-house; lazaretto, lazaret; lock hospital; *maison de santé; ambulance*; dispensary; *sanatorium, sanitarium,* spa, baths, pump-room, well; *hospice*; Red Cross; nursing home; asylum.

doctor, physician, surgeon; medical –, general-practitioner, consultant, specialist; medical attendant; medical student, medico; chemist, apothecary, pharmacopolist, druggist; leech; Aesculapius, Hippocrates, Galen; *accoucheur*, gynecologist, midwife, oculist, aurist, dentist; operator; osteopath, bonesetter; nurse, monthly nurse, sister; dresser; *masseur, masseuse*.

V. apply a -remedy etc. *n.*; doctor, dose, physic, nurse, minister to, attend, dress the wounds, plaster, bandage, poultice; heal, cure, work a cure, kill or cure, remedy, stay (disease), snatch from the jaws of death; prevent etc. 706; relieve etc. 834; palliate etc. 658; restore etc. 660; drench with physic; consult, operate, extract, deliver; bleed, cup, let blood, transfuse; electrolyse; psycho-analyse.

Adj. remedial; restorative etc. 660; corrective, palliative, healing; sana-tory, -tive; prophylactic; salutiferous etc. (*salutary*) 656; medic-al, -inal; therapeutic, surgical, chirurgical, orthopedic, epulotic, paregoric, tonic, corroborant, analeptic, balsamic, anodyne, hypnotic, neurotic, narcotic, sedative, lenitive, demulcent, emollient; depuratory; deter-sive, -gent; abstersive, disinfectant, febrifugal, alternative; traumatic, vulnerary.

dietetic, alimentary; nutrit-ious, -ive; peptic; alexi-pharmic, -teric; remedi-, cur-able.

663. Bane. —N.
bane, curse, thorn in the -side, -flesh, bugbear, *bête noire*; evil etc. 619; hurtfulness etc. (*badness*) 649; painfulness etc. (*cause of pain*) 830; scourge etc. (*punishment*) 975; *damnosa hereditas*; white elephant.

sting, fang, thorn, tang, bramble, briar, nettle.

poison, leaven, virus, venom; intoxicant; arsenic, Prussic acid, antimony, tartar emetic, strychnine, nicotine, cyanide of potassium, corrosive sublimate; curare; hyoscine etc.; poison-, mustard-. tear-gas; carbon di-, mon-oxide; ptomaine poisoning, botulism; miasm, mephitis, malaria, azote, sewer gas; pest, stench etc. 401.

rust, worm, moth, moth and rust, fungus, mildew; dry-rot; canker, -worm; cancer; torpedo; viper etc. (*evil-doer*) 913; demon etc. 980.

hemlock, hellebore, nightshade, *belladonna*, henbane, aconite; Upas tree.

drugs, dope, opium, morphia, morphine, cocaine, heroin, hashish, bhang.

[*Science of poisons*] Toxicology.

Adj. baneful etc. (*bad*) 649; poisonous etc. (*unwholesome*) 657.

664. Safety.—N.
safety, security, impregnability; invulnera-bility, -bleness etc. *adj.*; danger -past, — over; storm blown over; coast clear; escape etc. 671; means of escape, safetyvalve; safeguard, palladium, sheet anchor, rock, tower of strength.

guardian, ward-, warden-ship; tutelage, custody, safe keeping; preservation etc. 670; protection, auspices.

safe-conduct, escort, convoy; guard, sheild etc. (*defense*) 717; guardian angel, tutelary -god, — deity, — saint; *genius loci*.

protector, guardian; ward-en, -er; preserver, custodian, *duenna chaperon*, third person.

watch-, ban-dog; Cerberus; watch-, patrol-, police-man, constable, peeler, bobby, copper, cop, bull, flat-foot, detective, armed guard; sentinel, sentry, scout etc. (*warning*) 668; garrison; guardship.

[Means of safety] refuge etc., anchor etc. 666; precaution etc. (*preparation*) 673; quarantine, *cordon sanitaire*. [Sense of security] confidence etc. 858.

V. be -safe etc. *adj.*; keep one's head above water, tide over, save one's bacon; ride out —, weather- the storm; light upon one's feet; bear a charmed life; escape etc. 671; possess nine lives.

make —, render- -safe etc. *adj.*; protect, watch over; take care of etc. (*care*) 459; preserve etc. 670; cover, screen, shelter, shroud, flank, ward; guard etc. (*defend*) 717; secure etc. (*restrain*) 751; intrench, fence round etc. (*circumscribe*) 229; house, nestle, ensconce; take charge of.

escort, convoy; garrison; watch, mount guard, patrol, scout, spy.

make assurance double sure etc. (*caution*) 864; take up a loose thread; take precautions etc. (*prepare for*) 673; take in a reef; double reef topsails.

seek safety; take —, find- shelter etc. 666; run into port.

Adj. safe, secure, sure; in -safety, — security; have an anchor to windward; on the safe side; under the -shield of, — shade of, — wing of, — shadow of one's wing; under -cover, — lock and key; out of -danger, — the meshes, — harm's way; in -harbor, — port; on sure ground, at anchor, high and dry, above water, on *terra firma*; unthreatened, -molested; protected etc. *v.*; cavendo tutus; panoplied etc. (*defended*) 717.

snug, sea-, air-worthy; weather-, water-, fire-, bomb-proof.

defensible, tenable, proof against, invulnerable; un-assailable, -attackable; im-pregnable, -perdible; founded on a rock; inexpugnable.

safe and sound etc. (*preserved*) 670; harmless; scathless etc. (*perfect*) 650; unhazarded; not -dangerous etc. 665.

protecting etc. *v.*; guardian, tutelary; perservative etc. 670; trustworthy etc. 939.

Adv. *ex abundanti cautela*; with impunity.

Phr. all's well; all clear; *salva res est*; *suave mari magno*; safety first.

665. Danger. N.
danger, peril, insecurity, jeopardy, risk, hazard, venture, precariousness, slipperiness; instability etc. 149; defenselessness etc. *adj.*

exposure etc. (*liability*) 177; vulnerability; vulnerable point, heel of Achilles; forlorn hope etc. (*hopelessness*) 859.

[Dangerous course] leap in the dark etc. (*rashness*) 863; road to ruin, *facilis descensus Averni*, hair-breadth escape.

cause for alarm; source of danger etc. 667. [Approach of danger] rock —, breakers- ahead; storm brewing; clouds -in the horizon, — gathering; warning etc. 668; alarm etc. 669. [Sense of danger] apprehension etc. 860.

V. be -in danger etc. *adj.*; be exposed to —, run into —, incur —, encounter- -danger etc. *n.*; run a risk; lay oneself open to etc. (*liability*) 177; lean on —, trust to- a broken reed; feel the ground sliding from under one, have to run for it; have the -chances, — odds- against one.

hang by a thread, totter; tremble on the -verge, — brink; sleep — stand -on a volcano; sit on a barrel of gunpowder, live in a glass house.

bring —, place —, put- in -danger etc. *n.*; endanger, expose to danger, imperil, jeopard, -ize, compromise; sail too near the wind etc. (*rash*) 863; put one's head in the lion's mouth.

adventure, risk, hazard, venture, stake, set at hazard; run the gauntlet etc. (*dare*) 861; engage in a forlorn hope.

threaten etc. 909- danger; run one hard; lay a trap for etc. (*deceive*) 545.

Adj. in -danger etc. *n.*; endangered etc. *v.*; fraught with danger; danger-, hazard-, peril-, parl-, pericul-ous; unsafe, unprotected etc. (*safe, protect* etc. 664); insecure, untrustworthy, unreliable; built upon sand, on a sandy basis.

defence-, fence-, guard-, harbor-less; unshielded; vulnerable, expugnable, unsheltered, exposed; open to etc. (*liable*) 177.

aux abois, at bay; on -the wrong side of the wall, - a lee shore, - the rocks.

at stake, in question; precarious, aleatory, critical, ticklish; slip-pery, -py; hanging by a thread etc. *v.*; with a halter round one's neck; between - the hammer and the anvil, — Scylla and Charybdis, — two fires; on the -edge, — brink, — verge of a- -precipice, — volcano; in the lion's den, on slippery ground, under fire; not out of the wood.

un-warned, -admonished, -advised; unprepared etc. 674; off one's guard etc. (*inexpectant*) 508.

tottering; un-stable, -steady; shaky, top-heavy, tumble-down, ramshackle, crumbling, waterlogged; help-, guide-less; in a bad way; reduced to —, at- the last extremity; trembling in the balance; nodding to its fall etc. (*destruction*) 162.

threatening etc. 909; ominous, ill-omened; alarming etc. (*fear*) 860; explosive; poisonous etc. 657.

adventurous etc. (*rash*) 863, (*bold*) 861.

Int. stop! look out! beware! take care!

Phr. *incidit in Scyllam qui vult vitare Charybdim; nam tua res agitur paries dum proximus ardet.*

666. Refuge. [Means of safety.]—**N.** refuge, sanctuary, retreat, fastness; stronghold, keep, last resort; ward; prison etc. 752; asylum, ark, home, almshouse, refuge for the destitute; hiding-place etc. (*ambush*) 530; *sanctum sanctorum* etc. (*privacy*) 893.

roadstead, anchorage; breakwater, mole, port, haven; harbor, — of refuge; sea-port; pier, jetty, embankment, quay.

covert, shelter, abri, screen, lee-wall, wing, shield, umbrella; splash-, dash-board, mudguard.

wall etc. (*inclosure*) 232; fort etc. (*defence*) 717.

anchor, kedge; grap-nel, -pling iron; sheet-, mushroom-anchor, main-stay; support etc. 215; check etc. 706; ballast.

jury-mast; vent-peg; safety -valve, — lamp; lightning conductor.

means of escape etc. (*escape*) 671; life-boat, swimming belt, cork jacket; life preserver, breeches buoy; parachute, plank, stepping-stone.

safeguard etc. (*protection*) 664.

V. seek —, take —, find- refuge etc. *n.*; seek —, find- safety etc. 664; throw oneself into the arms of; claim sanctuary; take to the -hills, — woods; make port, reach shelter, bar —; bolt —, lock -the door, — gete; let the portcullis down; raise the drawbridge.

667. Pitfall. [Source of danger.]—**N.** rocks, reefs, coral reef, sunken rocks, snags; sands, quicksands, Goodwin sands, sandy foundation; slippery ground; breakers, shoals, shallows, bank, shelf, flat, lee shore, iron-bound coast; rock —, breakers- ahead; derelict.

precipice; abyss, chasm, pit, crevasse; maelstrom, whirlpool, eddy, vortex, rapids, current, bore, tidal wave; storm, squall, hurricane, whirlwind; volcano;

ambush etc. 530; pitfall, trap-door; trap etc. (*snare*) 545.

sword of Damocles; wolf at the door, snake in the grass, viper in one's bosom, death in the pot; latency etc. 526.

ugly customer, dangerous person, *le chat qui dort*; firebrand, hornet's nest.

Phr. *latet anguis in herbâ; proximus ardet Ucalegon.*

668. Warning.—N. warning, caution, *caveat*; notice etc. (*information*) 527; premoni-tion, - shment; prediction etc. 511; contraindication; symptom; lesson, dehortation; admonition, monition; alarm etc. 669.

handwriting on the wall, *tekel upharsin*, yellow flag; fog-signal, -horn; siren; monitor, warning voice, Cassandra, signs of the times, Mother Carey's chickens, stormy petrel, bird of ill omen, gathering clouds, clouds in the horizon, cloud no bigger than a man's hand, death-watch.

watch-tower, beacon, signal-post; light-house etc. (*indication of locality*) 550.

sent-inel, -ry; watch, -man; watch and ward; watch-, ban-, house-dog; patrol, vedette, picket, bivouac, scout, spy, spial; advanced —, rear-guard, lookout, flagman.

cautiousness etc. 864.

V. warn, caution; fore-, pre-warn; ad-, premonish; give -notice, — warning; menace etc. (*threaten*) 909; put on one's guard; sound the alarm etc. 669; croak.

beware, ware; take -warning, — heed at one's peril; watch out for; keep watch and ward etc. (*care*) 459.

Adj. warning etc. *v.*; premonitory, monitory, cautionary; admonitory, -tive; ominous, threatening, lowering, minatory, symptomatic.

warned etc. *v.*; on one's guard etc. (*careful*) 459; (*cautious*) 864.

Adv. *in terrorem* etc. (*threat*) 909.

Int. beware! ware! take care! mind! — take care-what you are about; mind! look out!

Phr. *ne reveillez pas le chat qui dort*; *foenum habet in cornu.*

669. Alarm. [Indication of danger.]—**N.** alarm; alarum, larum, alarm bell, tocsin, *alerte*; beat of drum, sound of trumpet, note of alarm, hue and cry, signal of distress, S.O.S.; blue-lights; war-cry, -whoop; warning etc. 668; fog-signal, -horn; siren; yellow flag; danger signal; red -light, — flag; fire -bell, — alarm; burglar alarm, police whistle, watchman's rattle.

false alarm, cry of wolf; bug-bear, -aboo.

V. give —, raise —, sound —, beat- the *or* an -alarm etc. *n.*; alarm; warn etc. 668; ring the tocsin; *battre la générale*; cry wolf.

Adj. alarming etc. *v.*

Int. *sauve qui peut! qui vive?* who goes there?

670. Preservation.—N. preservation; safe keeping; conservation etc. (*storage*) 636; maintenance, upkeep, support, sustentation, conservatism; *vis conservatrix*; salvation etc. (*deliverance*) 672; drying etc. *v.*

[Means of preservation] prophylaxis; preserv-er, -ative; canned goods; cold pack; hygi-astics, -antics; cover, durgget; *cordon sanitaire.*

[Superstitious remedies] charm etc. 993.

V. preserve, maintain, keep, sustain, support; keep -up, – alive; not willingly let die; shore –, bank- up; nurse; save, rescue; be –, make- safe etc. 664; take care of etc. (*care*) 459; guard etc. (*defend*) 717.

stare super antiquas vias; hold one's own; hold –, stand- -one's ground etc. (*resist*) 719.

embalm, dry, cure, smoke, salt, pickle, season, kyanize, bottle, pot, tin, can; husband etc. (*store*) 636.

Adj. preserving etc. *v.*; conservative; prophylatic; preserva-tory, -tive; hygienic.

preserved etc. *v.*; un-impaired, -broken, -injured, -hurt, -singed, -marred; safe, – and sound; intact, with a whole skin, without a scratch.

Phr. *nolumus leges Angliae mutari.*

671. Escape.—N. escape, scape; avolation, elopment, flight, get-away; evasion etc. (*avoidance*) 623; retreat; narrow –, hairbreadth- escape; close –, near- shave; come off, impunity.

[Means of escape] loophole etc. (*opening*) 260; path etc. 627; secret -door, – passage; refuge etc. 666; vent, – peg; safety-valve; drawbridge, fire-escape.

reprieve etc. (*deliverance*) 672; liberation etc. 750.

refugee etc. (*fugitive*) 623.

V. escape, scape; make –, effect –, make good- one's escape, make a get-away; get -off, – clear off, – well out of; *échapper belle*, save one's bacon; weather the storm etc. (*safe*) 664; escape scot-free.

elude etc., make off etc. (*avoid*) 623; march off etc. (*go away*) 293; give one the slip; slip through the -hands, – fingers; slip the collar, wriggle out of; break -loose, – from prison; break –, slip –, get- away; find -vent, – a hole to creep out of.

Adj. escap-ing, -ed etc. *v.*; stolen away, fled.

Phr. the bird has flown.

672. Deliverance.—N. deliverance, extrication, rescue; repriev-e, -al; respite; ransom; liberation etc. 750; truce, armistice; redemption, salvation; riddance; gaol delivery; exemption, day of grace; redeemableness.

V. deliver, extricate, rescue, save, redeem, ransom,.free, liberate, release, set free, redeem, emancipate; bring -off, – through; *tirer d'affaire*, get the wheel out of the rut; snatch from the jaws of death, come to the rescue; rid; retrieve etc. (*restore*) 660; be –, get- rid of.

Adj. saved etc. *v.*; extric-able, redeem-, rescu-able.

Phr. to the rescue!

673. Preparation.—N. preparation; providing etc. *v.*; provi-sion, -dence; anticipation etc. (*foresight*) 510; precaution, -concertation,

disposition; forecast etc. (*plan*) 626; rehearsal, not of preparation.

[Putting in order] arrangement etc. 60; clearance; adjustment etc. 23; tuning; equipment, outfit, accoutrement, armament, array.

ripening etc. *v.*; maturation, evolution; elaboration, concoction, digestion; gestation, hatching, incubation, sitting.

groundwork, datum, first stone, cradle, stepping-stone; foundation, scaffold etc. (*support*) 215; scaffolding, *échafaudage.*

[Preparation -of men] training etc. (*education*) 537; inurement etc. (*habit*) 613; novitiate; [– of food] cook-ing, -ery; brewing, culinary art; [– of the soil] till-, plough-, sow-ing; semination, cultivation.

[State of being prepared] prepared-, readi-, ripe-, mellow-ness; maturity; *un impromptu fait à loisir.*

[Preparer] preparer, teacher, coach, trainer, pioneer; *avant-courrier, -coureur*; sappers and miners, paver, navvy; packer, stevedore; warming-pan; precursor etc. 64.

V. prepare; get –, make- ready; make preparations, settle preliminaries, get up, sound the note of preparation; address oneself to.

set –, put- in order etc. (*arrange*) 60; forecast etc. (*plan*) 626; prepare –, plough –, dress- the ground; till –, cultivate- the soil; predispose, sow the seed, lay a train, dig a mine; lay –, fix- the foundations, – basis, -groundwork; dig the foundations, erect the scaffolding; lay the first stone etc. (*begin*) 66.

rough hew; cut out work; block –, hammer-out; lick into shape etc. (*form*) 240.

elaborate, mature, ripen, mellow, season, bring to maturity; nurture etc.

(*aid*) 707; hatch, cook, brew; temper; anneal, smelt; dry, cure etc. 670.

equip, arm, man; fit-out, -up; furnish, rig, dress, garnish, betrim, accouter, array, fettle, fledge; dress –, furbish –, brush –, vamp- up; refurbish; sharpen one's tools, trim one's foils, set, prime, attune; whet the -knife, – sword; wind –, screw- up; adjust etc. (*fit*) 27; put in- trim, – train, – gear, – working order, – tune, – a groove for, – harness; pack, stow away, store.

train etc. (*teach*) 537; inure etc. (*habituate*) 613; breed; prepare etc.- for; rehearse; make provision for; take -steps, – measures, – precautions; provide, – against; beat up for recruits; open the door to etc. (*facilitate*) 705.

set one's house in order, make all snug; clear - decks, – for action; close one's ranks; shuffle the cards.

prepare oneself; serve an apprenticeship etc. (*learn*) 539; lay oneself out for, get into harness, gird up one's loins, buckle on one's armor, *reculer pour mieux sauter*, prime and load, shoulder arms, get the steam up, put the horses to.

guard –, make sure- against; forearm, make sure, prepare for the evil day, have a rod in pickle, provide against a rainy day, feather one's nest; lay in provisions etc. 637; make investments; keep on foot.

be -prepared, – ready etc. *adj.*; hold oneself in readiness, watch and pray, keep one's powder dry; lie in wait for etc. (*expect*) 507; anticipate etc. (*foresee*) 510; *principiis obstare*; *veniente occurrere morbo.*

Adj. preparing etc. *v.*; in -preparation, – course

of preparation, – agitation, – embryo, – hand, – train; afoot, afloat; on -foot, – the stocks, – the anvil; under consideration etc. (*plan*) 626; brewing, hatching, forthcoming, brooding; in -store for, – reserve.

precautionary, provident; prepara-tive, -tory; provisional, inchoate, under revision; preliminary etc. (*precedent*) 62.

prepared etc. *v.*; in readiness; ready, – to one's hand, – made, cut and dried; ready for use, reach me down; made to one's hand, handy, on the table, made to order; in gear; in working -order, – gear; snug; in practice.

ripe, mature, mellow; practiced etc. (*skillet*) 698; labored, elaborate, highly-wrought, smelling of the lamp, worked up.

in -full feather, – best bib and tucker; in – , at-harness; in – the saddle, – arms, – battle array; – war paint; up in arms; armed -at all points, – to the teeth, – *cap-à-pie*; sword in hand; booted and spurred.

in utrumque – , *semper- paratus*; on the alert etc. (*vigilant*) 459; at one's post.

Adv. in -preparation; – anticipation of; afoot, astir, abroad; abroach.

674. Non-preparation.—N. non-, absence of –, want of- preparation; unpreparedness; in-culture, inconcoction, improvidence.

immaturity, crudity; rawness etc. *adj.*; abortion; disqualification.

[Absence of art] nature, state of nature; virgin soil, unweeded garden; rough diamond, neglect etc. 460.

rough copy etc. (*plan*) 626; germ etc. 153; raw material etc. 635.

improvisation etc. (*impulse*) 612.

V. be -unprepared etc. *adj.*; want – . lack-preparation; lie fallow; *s'embarquer sans biscuits*; live from hand to mouth.

[Render unprepared] dismantle etc. (*render useless*) 645;. undress etc. 226.

extemporize, improvise.

surprise, pay a surprise visit, take by surprise, drop in upon, take unawares; take pot-luck.

Adv. un-prepared etc. prepare etc. 673] without -preparation etc. 673; incomplete etc. 53; rudimental, embryonic, abortive; immature, unripe, raw, green, crude; coarse; rough, -cast, -hewn; in the rough; un-hewn, -formed, -fashioned, -wrought, - labored, -blown, -cooked, -boiled, -concocted, - cút, -polished.

callow, un-hatched, -fledged, -nurtured, -licked, -taught, -educated, -cultivated, -trained, -tutored, - drilled, -exercised; precocious, premature; un-, in-digested; un-mellowed, -seasoned, -leavened.

fallow; un-sown, -tilled; natural, in a state of na-ture; undressed; in dishabille, *en déshabille, en négligé.*

un-, dis-qualified; unfitted; ill-digested; un-begun, -ready, -arranged, -organized, -furnished, - provided, -equipped, -trimmed; out of -gear, – or-der; dismantled etc. *v.*

shiftless, improvident, unthrifty, ¡thoughtless, unguarded; happy-go-lucky; caught napping etc. (*inexpectant*) 508; unpremeditated etc. 612.

Adv. extempore etc. 612.

675. Essay.—N. essay, trial, endeavor, aim, at-tempt; venture, adventure, speculation, *coup d'essai, début*; probation etc. (*experiment*) 463.

V. try, essay; experiment etc. 463; endeavor, strive; tempt, tackle, take on, attempt, make an at-tempt; venture, adventure, speculate, take one's chance, tempt fortune; try one's -fortune, – luck, – hand; use one's endeavor; feel –, grope – , pick- one's way.

try hard, push, make a bold push, use one's best endeavor; do one's best etc. (*exertion*) 686.

Adj. essaying etc. *v.*; experimental etc. 463; tentative, empirical, probationary.

Adv. experimentally etc. *adj.*; on trial, at a ven-ture; by rule of thumb.

if one may be so bold.

676. Undertaking.—N. undertaking, compact etc. 769; engagement etc. (*promise*) 768; enter-, em-prise; venture etc. 675; pilgrimage; matter in hand etc. (*business*) 625; move; first move etc. (*beginning*) 66.

V. undertake; engage – , embark- in; launch – ; plunge- into;. volunteer; apprentice oneself to; engage etc. (*promise*) 768; contract etc. 769; take upon -oneself, – one's shoulders; devote oneself to etc. (*determination*) 604.

take -up, – in hand; tackle; set – , go- about; set –, fall- -to, – to work; launch forth; set up shop; put in -hand, – execution; set forward; break the neck of a business, be in for; put one's hand to; betake oneself to, turn one's hand to, go to do; begin etc. 66; broach, institute, etc. (*originate*) 153; put – , lay- one's -hand to the plough, – shoulder to the wheel.

have in hand etc. (*business*) 625; have many irons in the fire etc. (*activity*) 682.

Adj. undertaking etc. *v.*; on the anvil etc. 625; adventurous, venturesome.

Int. here goes!

677. Use.—N. use; employ, -ment; exer-cise, - citation; appli-cation, -ance; adhibition, disposal; consumption; agency etc. (*physical*) 170; usufruct; usefulness etc. 644; recourse, resort, avail, pragmatism.

[Conversion to use] utilization, service, wear. [Way of using] usage.

V. use, make use of, employ, put to use; apply, put in -action, – operation, – practice; set -in motion, – to work.

ply, work, wield, handle, manipulate; play, – off; exert, exercise, practice, avail oneself of, profit by; resort – , have recourse – , recur – , take – , betake oneself- to; take -up with, – advantage of; lay one's hands on, try.

render useful etc. 644; mold; turn to -account, – use; convert to use, utilize, administer; work up; call – , bring- into play; put into requisition; call –, draw- forth; press – , enlist- into the service; bring to bear upon, devote, dedicate, consecrate, apply, adhibit, dispose of; make a -handle, – cat's paw- of.

fall beak upon, make a shift with; make the -most, – best- of.

use – , swallow- up; consume, absorb, expend; tax, task, wear, put to task.

Adj. in use; used etc. *v.*; well-worn, -trodden. useful etc. 644; subservient etc. (*instrumental*) 631; utilitarian; pragmatical.

678. Disuse.—N. forbearance, abstinence; disuse; relinquishment etc. 782; desuetude etc. (*want of habit*) 614.

V. not use; do without, dispense with, let alone, not touch, forbear, abstain, spare, waive, neglect; keep back, reserve.

lay -up, − by, − on the shelf, − up in a napkin; shelve; set −, put −, lay- aside; disuse, leave off, have done with; supersede; discard etc. (*eject*) 297; dismiss, give warning.

throw aside etc. (*relinquish*) 782; make away with etc. (*destroy*) 162; cast −, heave −, throw-overboard; cast to the -dogs, − winds; dismantle etc. (*render useless*) 645.

lie −, remain- unemployed etc. *adj.*

Adj. not used etc. *v.*; un-employed, -applied, -disposed of, -spent, -exercised, -touched, -trodden, -essayed, -gathered, -culled; uncalled for, not required.

disused etc. *v.*; done with; run down, used up, cast off.

679. Misuse.—N. mis-use, -usage, - employment, -application, -appropriation.

abuse, profanation, prostitution, desecration; waste etc. 638.

V. mis-use, -employ, -apply, -appropriate.

desecrate, abuse, profane, prostitute; waste etc. 638; over-task, -tax, -work; squander etc. 818.

cut a whetstone with a razor, employ a steam-engine to crack a nut; catch at a straw.

Adj. misused etc. *v.*

680. Action.—N. action, performance; doing etc. *v.*; perpetration; exercise, -citation; movement, operation, evolution, work; labor etc. (*exertion*) 686; *praxis*, execution; procedure etc. (*conduct*) 692; handicraft; business etc. 625; agency etc. (*power at work*) 170.

deed, act, overt act, stitch, touch, gest; trans-action, job, doings, dealings, proceeding, measure, step, maneuver, bout, passage, move, stroke, blow; *coup*, − de main, − d'état; *tour de force* etc. (*display*) 882; feat, exploit, stunt; achievement etc. (*completion*) 729; handiwork, workmanship, crafts-manship; manufacture; stroke of policy etc. (*plan*) 626.

actor etc. (*doer*) 690.

V. do, perform, execute; achieve etc. (*complete*) 729; transact, enact; commit, perpetrate, inflict; exercise, prosecute, carry on, work, practice, play.

employ oneself, ply one's task; officiate, have in hand etc. (*business*) 625; labor etc. 686; be at work; pursue a course; shape one's course etc. (*conduct*) 692.

act, operate; take -action, − steps; strike a blow, lift a finger, stretch forth one's hand; take in hand etc. (*undertake*) 676; put oneself in motion; put in practice; carry into execution etc. (*complete*) 729; act upon.

be -an actor etc. 690; take −, act −, play −, perform- a part in; participate in; have a -hand in, − finger in the pie; have to do with; be a -party to,− participator in; bear −, lend- a hand; pull an oar, run in a race; mix oneself up with etc. (*meddle*) 682.

be in action; come into operation etc. (*power at work*) 170.

Adj. doing etc. *v.*; acting; in action; in harness; on duty; at work; in operation etc. 170; up to one's ears in work, in the midst of things.

Adv. in the -act, − midst of, − thick of; red-handed, *in flagrante delicto*; while one's hand is in.

681. Inaction.—N. inaction, passiveness, ab-stinence from action; non-interference; Fabian −, conservative- policy; neglect etc. 460; stagnation, vegetation; loafing.

inactivity etc. 683; rest etc. (*repose*) 687; quiescence etc. 265; want of −, in- occupation; unemployment; idle hours, time hanging on one's hands, *dolce far niente*; sinecure.

V. not -do, − act, − attempt; be -inactive etc. 683; abstain from doing, do nothing, hold, spare; not -stir, − move, − lift- a -finger, − foot, − peg; fold one's -arms, −. hands; leave −, let- alone; let -be, − pass, − things take their course, − it have its way, − well alone; *quieta non movere*; *stare super antiquas vias*; rest and be thankful, live and let live; lie −, rest- upon one's oars; *laisser -aller*, − *faire*; stand aloof; refrain etc. (*avoid*) 623; keep oneself from doing; remit −, relax- one's efforts; desist etc. (*relinquish*) 624; stop etc. (*cease*) 142; pause etc. (*be quiet*) 265.

wait, lie in wait, bide one's time, take time, tide it over.

cool −, kick- one's heels; loaf, while away the -time, − tedious hours; pass −, fill −, beguile- the time; talk against time; waste time etc. (*inactive*) 683.

lie -by, − on the shelf, − in ordinary, − idle, − to, − fallow; keep quiet, slug; have nothing to do, whistle for want of thought; twiddle one's thumbs.

undo, do away with; take -down, − to pieces; destroy etc. 162.

Adj. not doing etc. *v.*; not done etc. *v.*; undone; passive; un-occupied, -employed; out of -employ, − work, − a job; fallow; *désoeuvré*.

Adv. *re infectâ*, at a stand, *les bras croisés*, with folded arms; with the hands -in the pockets, − behind one's back; *pour passer le temps*.

Int. so let it be! stop! etc. 142; hands off!

Phr. nothing doing; *cunctando restituit rem*.

682. Activity.—N. activity; briskness, liveliness etc. *adj.*; animation, life, vivacity, spirit, verve, dash, energy, go.

nimbleness, agility; smartness, quickness etc. *adj.*; velocity etc. 274; alacrity, promptitude; des-, dis-patch; expedition; haste etc. 684; punctuality etc. (*early*) 132.

eagerness, zeal, ardor, *perfervidum ingenium*, *empressement*, earnestness, intentness; *abandon*; vigor etc. (*physical energy*) 171; devotion etc. (*resolution*) 604; exertion etc. 686.

industry, assiduity; assiduousness etc. *adj.*; sedulity; laboriousness; drudgery etc. (*labor*) 686; painstaking, diligence; perseverance etc. 604*a*; indefatigation; habits of business.

vigilance etc. 459; wakefulness; sleep-, restlessness; *pervigilium, insomnia*; racketing.

movement, bustle, hustle, stir, fuss, ado, bother, pottering; fidget, -iness; flurry etc. (*haste*) 684.

officiousness; dabbling, meddling; inter-ference, -position, -meddling, butting in, intrusiveness; tampering with, intrigue.

press of business, no sinecure, plenty to do, many irons in the fire, great doings, busy hum of men, battle of life, thick of -things, — the action; the madding corwd.

housewife, busy bee; new brooms; sharp fellow, blade; hustler, devotee, enthusiast, fan, zealot, fanatic; meddler, intermeddler, intriguer, busybody, kibitzer, pickthank.

V. be -active etc. *adj.*; busy oneself in; stir, -about, — one's stumps; bestir —, rouse- oneself; speed, hasten, peg away, lay about one, bustle, fuss; raise —, kick up- a dust; push; make a -push, — fuss, — stir; go ahead, push forward; flight —, elbow- one's way; make progress etc. 282; toil etc. (*labor*) 686; drudge, plod, persist etc. (*persevere*) 604*a*; keep -up the ball, — the pot boiling.

look sharp; have all one's eyes about one etc. (*vigilance*) 459; rise, arouse oneself, get up early, hustle, push; be about, keep moving, steal a march, kill two birds with one stone; seize the opportunity etc. 134; lose no time, not lose a moment, make the most of one's time, not suffer the grass to grow under one's feet, improve the shining hour, make short work of; dash off; make haste etc. 684; do one's best, take pains etc. (*exert oneself*) 686; do —, work- wonders.

have -many irons in the fire, — one's hands full, — much on one's hands; have other -things to do, — fish to fry; be busy; not have a moment -to spare, — that one can call one's own.

have one's fling, run the round of; go all lengths, stick at nothing, run riot.

outdo; over-do, -act, -lay, -shoot the mark; make a toil of a pleasure.

have a hand in etc. (*act in*) 680; take an active part, put in one's oar, have a finger in the pie, mix oneself up with, trouble one's head about, intrigue; agitate.

tamper with, meddle, moil; inter-meddle, -fere, -pose; obtrude; poke —, thrust- one's nose in, butt in.

Adj. active; brisk, — as a lark, — as a bee; lively, animated, vivacious; alive, — and kicking; frisky, spirited, stirring.

nimble, — as a squirrel; agile; light-, nimble-footed; featly, tripping.

quick, prompt, yare, instant, ready, alert, spry, sharp, smart, slick, go-ahead; fast etc. (*swift*) 274; quick as a lamplighter, expeditious; awake, broad awake; wide awake etc. (*intelligent*) 498.

forward, eager, ardent, strenuous, zealous, enterprising, pushing, in earnest; resolute etc. 604.

industrious, assiduous, diligent, sedulous, notable, painstaking; intent etc. (*attention*) 457; indefatigable etc. (*persevering*) 604*a*; unwearied; unsleeping, sleepless, never tired; plodding, hard-working etc. 686; business-like, workaday.

bustling; restless, -- as a hyena; fussy, fidgety; pottering; busy, — as a hen with one chicken.

working, laboring, at work, on duty, in harness; up in arms; on one's- legs, at call; up and -doing, — stirring.

busy, occupied; hard at -work, — it; up to one's ears, in full of business, busy as a bee.

meddling etc. *v.*; meddlesome, pushing, officious, overofficious, *intrigant*.

astir, stirring; a-going, -foot; on foot; in full swing; eventful; on the alert etc. (*vigilant*) 459.

Adv. actively etc. *adj.*; with -life and spirit, — might and main etc. 686, — haste etc. 684, — wings; full tilt, *in mediis rebus.*

Int. be — , look- -alive, — sharp! move —, push-on! keep moving! go ahead! stir your stumps! *age quod agis!*

Phr. *carpe diem* etc. (*opportunity*) 134; *nulla dies sine lineâ; nec mora nec requies;* no sooner said than done etc. (*early*) 132; catch a weasel asleep.

683. Inactivity.—N. inactivity; inaction etc. 681; inertness etc. 172; obstinacy etc. 606.

lull etc. (*cessation*) 142; quiescence etc. 265; rust, -iness.

idle-, remiss-ness etc. *adj.*; sloth, indolence, indiligence; otiosity, dawdling etc. *v.*

dullness etc. *adj.*; languor; segni-ty, -tude; lentor; sluggishness etc. (*slowness*) 275; procrastination etc. (*delay*) 133; torp-or, -idity, -escence; stupor etc. (*insensibility*) 823; somnolence; drowsiness etc. *adj.*; nodding etc. *v.*; oscitation, -ancy; pandiculation, hypnotism, lethargy; heaviness, heavy eye-lids, sand in the eyes.

sleep, slumber; sound —, heavy —, balmy-sleep; Morpheus, dreamland; coma, trance, catalepsy, hypnosis, *ecstasis*, dream, hibernation, nap, doze, snooze, *siesta*, wink of sleep, forty winks, snore; Hypnology.

dull work; pottering; relaxation etc. (*loosening*) 47; Castle of Indolence.

[Cause of inactivity] lullaby, *berceuse*; anesthetic, sedative etc. 174; torpedo.

idler, drone, droil, dawdle, mopus; do-little, *fainéant*, dummy, sleeping partner; afternoon farmer; truant etc. (*runaway*) 623; lounger, *lazzarone*, floater, loafer, tramp, beggar, cadger; lubber, -bard; slow-coach etc. (*slow*) 275; opium —, lotus- eater; slug; lag-, slug-gard, lie-abed; slumberer, dormouse, marmot; waiter on Providence, *fruges consumere natus.*

V. be -inactive etc. *adj.*; do nothing etc. 681; move slowly etc. 275; let the grass grow under one's feet; take one's time, dawdle, poke, drawl, droil, lag, hang back, slouch; loll, -op; lounge, loaf, loiter; go to sleep over; sleep at one's post; *ne battre que d'une aile.*

take -it easy, — things as they come; lead an easy life, vegetate, swim with the stream, eat the bread of idleness; loll in the lap of -luxury, — indolence; waste —, consume —, kill —, lose time; burn daylight, waste the precious hours.

idle —, trifle —, fritter —, fool- away time; spend —, take- time in; ped-, pid-dle; potter, putter, dabble, faddle, fribble, fiddle-faddle; dally, dilly-dally.

sleep, slumber, be asleep; hibernate; oversleep; sleep like a -top, — log, — dormouse; sleep -soundly, — heavily; doze, drowze, snooze, nap; take a -nap etc. *n.*; dream; snore; settle —, go —,

go off- to sleep; drop off; fall − , drop- asleep; close
− , seal up- -the -eyes, − eyelids; weigh down the
eyelids; get sleepy, nod, yawn; go to bed, turn in.

languish, expend itself, flag, hang fire; relax.

render -idle etc. *adj.*; sluggardize; mitigate etc.
174.

Adj. inactive; motionless etc. 265; unoccupied
etc. (*doing nothing*) 681.

indolent, lazy, slothful, idle, otiose, lusk, remiss,
slack, inert, torpid, sluggish, languid, supine,
heavy, dull, leaden, lumpish; exanimate, soulless;
listless; dron-y, -ish; lazy as Ludlam's dog.

dilatory, laggard; lagging etc. *v.*; slow etc. 275;
rusty, flagging; lackadaisical, maudlin, fiddle-
faddle; pottering etc. *v.*; shilly-shally etc.
(*irresolute*) 605.

sleeping etc. *v.*; alseep; fast − , dead − , sound-
alseep; in a sound sleep; sound as a top, dormant,
comatose; in the -arms, − lap- of Morpheus.

sleep-y, -ful; dozy, drowsy, somnolent, tor-
pescent; lethargic, -al; heavy, − with sleep; napping; somni-fic, -ferous; sopor-ous, -ific, -iferous;
hypnotic; balmy, dreamy; un-, una-wakened.

sedative etc. 174.

Adv. inactively etc. *adj.*; at leisure etc. 685.

Phr. the eyes begin to draw straws.

684. Haste.—N. haste, urgency; des-, dis-patch;
acceleration, spurt, spirt, forced march, rush, dash;
velocity etc. 274; precipit-ancy, -ation, -ousness
etc. *adj.*; impetuosity; *brusquerie*; hurry, scurry,
scuttle, drive, scramble, push, hustle, bustle,- fuss,
fidget, flurry, flutter, splutter.

V. haste, hasten; make -haste, − a dash etc. *n.*;
hurry −, dash − , whip − , push − , press- -on, −
forward; hurry, skurry, scuttle along, bundle on,
dart to and fro, bustle, flutter, scramble; plunge, −
headlong; run, race, speed; dash off; rush etc.
(*violence*) 173.

bestir oneself etc. (*be active*) 682; lose -no time,
− not a moment, − not an instant; make short
work of; make the best of one's -time, − way.

be -precipitate etc. *adj.*; jump at; be in -haste, −
a hurry etc. *n.*; have -no time, − not a moment- -
to lose, − to spare; work -under pressure, −
against time.

quicken etc. 274; accelerate, expedite, put on,
precipitate, urge, whip, spur, flog, goad.

Adj. hasty, hurried, *brusque*; scrambling, cursory, precipitate, headlong, furious, boisterous, impetuous, hot-headed; feverish, fussy; pushing.

in -haste, − a hurry etc. *n.*; in -hot, − all- haste;
breathless, pressed for time, hard pressed, urgent.

Adv. with -haste, − all haste, − breathless
speed; in haste etc. *adj.*; apace etc. (*swiftly*) 274;
amain; all at once etc. (*instantaneously*) 113; at
short notice etc., immediately etc. (*early*) 132;
posthaste; by -express, − telegraph, − wire, −
wireless, − air mail.

hastily, precipitately etc. *adj.*; helter-skelter,
hurry-skurry, holusbolus; slap-dash, -bang; full-tilt,
-drive; heels over head, head and shoulders,
headlong, *à corps perdu*.

by -fits and starts, − spurts; hop, skip and jump.

Phr. *sauve qui peut*, devil take the hindmost, no
time to be lost; no sooner said than done etc.
(*early*) 132; a word and a blow.

Int. hurry up! look alive! get a move on! buck
up! double march! rush! urgent!

685. Leisure.—N. leisure; spare -time, −
hours, − moments; vacant hour; time, − to spare,
− on one's hands; holiday etc. (*rest*) 687; *otium
cum dignitate*, ease.

V. have -leisure etc. *n.*; take one's -time, −
leisure, − ease; repose etc. 687; move slowly etc.
275; while away the time etc. (*inaction*) 681; be -
master of one's time, − an idle man; *desipere in
loco*.

Adj. leisurely; slow etc. 275; deliberate, quiet,
calm, undisturbed; at -leisure, − one's ease, − a
loose end.

Phr. time hanging heavy on one's hands.

686. Exertion.—N. exertion, effort, strain, tug,
pull, stress, force, pressure, throw, stretch, struggle,
spell, spurt, spirt; stroke − , stitch- of work.

'a stong pull, a long pull and a pull all together;'
dead lift; heft; gymnastics, sports; exer-cise, -
citation; wear and tear; ado; toil and trouble; uphill
− , hard − , warm- work; harvest time.

labor, work, toil, travail, manual labor, sweat of
one's brow, swink, operoseness, drudgery, slavery,
fagging; hammering; *limae labor*.

trouble, pains, duty; resolution etc. 604; energy
etc. (*physical*) 171.

V. exert oneself; exert − , tax- one's energies;
use exertion.

labor, work, toil, moil, sweat, fag, drudge, slave,
drag a lengthened chain, wade through, strive,
strain; make − , stretch- a long arm; pull, tug, ply;
ply − , tug at- the oar; do the work; take the
laboring oar.

bestir oneself (*be active*) 682; take trouble,
trouble oneself.

work hard; rough it; put forth -one's strength, −
a strong arm; fall to work, bend the bow; buckle to,
set one's shoulder to the wheel etc. (*resolution*)
604; work like a -Briton, − horse, − carthorse, −
galley-slave, − coalheaver; labor − , work-day and
night; redouble one's efforts; do double duty; work
double -hours, − tides; sit up, burn the -midnight
oil, − candle at both ends; stick to etc. (*persevere*)
604*a*; work − , fight- one's way; lay about one,
hammer at.

take pains;- do one's -best, − level best, − utmost; do -the best one can, − all one can, − all in
one's power, − as much as in one lies, − what lies
in one's power; use one's -best, − utmost- endeavor; try one's -best, − utmost; play one's best
card; put one's -best, − right- leg foremost; have
one's whole soul in one's work, put all one's
strength into, strain every nerve; spare no -efforts,
− pains; go all lengths; go through fire and water
etc. (*resolution*) 604; move heaven and earth,
leave no stone unturned.

Adj. laboring etc. *v.*

laborious, operose, elaborate; strained; toil-,
trouble-, burden-, weari-some; uphill; herculean,
gymnastic, athletic, palestric.

hardworking, painstaking, strenuous, energetic,
hard at work, on the stretch.

Adv. laboriously etc. *adj.*; lustily; with -might
and main, − all one's might, − a strong hand, −
sledge-hammer, − much ado; to the best of one's
abilities, *totis viribus, vi et armis, manibus
pedibusque*, tooth and nail, *unguibus et rostro*,

hammer and tongs, heart and soul; through thick
and thin etc. (*perseverance*) 604a.
by the sweat of one's brow, *suo Marte*.

687. Repose.—N. repose, rest, silken repose;
sleep etc. 683.
relaxation, breathing time; halt, pause etc.
(*cessation*) 142; respite.
day of rest, *dies non*, Sabbath, Lord's day,
holiday, red-letter day, vacation, recess.
V. repose; rest, – and be thankful; take -rest, –
one's ease.
relax, unbend, slacken; take breath etc. (*refresh*)
689; rest upon one's oars; pause etc. (*cease*) 142;
stay one's hand.
lie down; recline, – on a bed of down, – on an
easy chair; go to -rest, – bed, – sleep etc. 683.
take a holiday, shut up shop; lie fallow etc.
(*inaction*) 681.
Adj. reposing etc. *v.*; unstrained.
Adv. at rest.

688. Fatigue.—N. fatigue; weariness etc. 841;
yawning, drowsiness etc. 683; lassitude, tiredness,
fatigation, exhaustion; sweat.
anhelation, shortness of breath, panting; faintness; collapse, prostration, swoon, fainting,
deliquium, syncope, lipothymy.
V. be -fatigued etc. *adj.*; yawn etc. (*get sleepy*)
683; droop, sink, flag; lose -breath, – wind; gasp,
pant, puff, blow, drop, swoon, faint, succumb.
fatigue, tire, weary, bore, irk, fag, jade, harass,
exhaust, knock up, wear out, prostrate.
tax, task, strain; over-task, -work, -burden, -tax,
-strain.
Adj. fatigued etc. *v.*; weary etc. 841; drowsy etc.
683; drooping etc. *v.*; haggard; toil-, way-worn;
footsore, surbated, weatherbeaten; faint; done –,
used –, knock- up; exhausted, prostrate, spent;
over-tired, -spent, -fatigued; forspent; unre-freshed,
-stored.
worn, – out; battered, shattered, pulled down,
seedy, altered.
breath-, wind-less; short of –, out of -breath, –
wind; blown, puffing and blowing; short-breathed;
anhelous; broken-, short-winded.
ready to drop, more dead than alive, dog -tired,
– weary, walked off one's legs, tired to death, on
one's last legs, played out, *hors de combat*.
fatiguing etc. *v.*; tire-, irk-, weari-some; weary;
trying.

689. Refreshment.—N. bracing etc. *v.*;
recovery of -strength etc. 159; restoration, revival
etc. 660; repair, refection, refocillation, refreshment, regalement, bait; relief etc. 834.
V. brace etc. (*strengthen*) 159; reinvigorate; air,
freshen up, refresh, recruit; repair etc. (*restore*)
660; fan, revocillate.
breathe, respire; draw –, take –, gather –,
take a long –, regain –, recover- breath; get better, raise one's head; recover –, regain –, renew-
one's strength etc. 159; perk up.

come to oneself etc. (*revive*) 660; feel like a
giant refreshed.
Adj. refreshing etc. *v.*; recuperative etc. 660;
refreshed etc. *v.*; un-tired, -wearied.

690. Agent.—N. doer, actor, agent, performer,
perpetrator, operator; execu-tor, -trix; practitioner,
worker, stager.
bee, ant, working bee, laboring oar, shaft horse,
servant –, maid- of all work, general servant, factotum.
workman, artisan; crafts-, handicrafts-man;
mechanic, operative; working –, laboring- man;
hewers of wood and drawers of water, laborer,
navvy; hand, man, day laborer, journeyman, hack;
mere -tool etc. 633; porter, docker, stevedore,
beast of burden, drudge, fag.
maker, artificer, artist, wright, manufacturer,
architect, contractor, builder, mason, bricklayer,
smith, forger, Vulcan; black-, tin-smith; carpenter;
ganger, platelayer.
machinist, mechanician, engineer, electrician,
plumber, gasfitter etc.
semp-, sem-, seam-stress; needle-, char-, work-
woman; tailor, cordwainer.
minister etc. (*instrument*) 631; servant etc. 746;
representative etc. (*commissioner*) 758; (*deputy*)
759.
co-worker, fellow-worker, party to, participator
in, co-operator, colleague, associate, collaborator,
particeps criminis, dramatis personae; personnel.
Phrs. '*quorum pars magna fui.*'

691. Workshop.—N. work-shop, -house;
laboratory; manufactory, mill, factory, armory, arsenal, mint, forge, loom; cabinet, *studio*, *bureau*,
atelier; hive, – of industry; nursery; hot-house, -
bed; kitchen, kitchenette; dock, -yard; slip, yard,
wharf; found-ry, -ery; furnace; vineyard, orchard,
farm, kitchen garden.
melting pot, crucible, alembic, caldron, mortar,
matrix.

692. Conduct.—N. dealing, transaction etc.
(*action*) 680; business etc. 625.
tactics, game, policy, polity; general-, statesman-
, seaman-ship; strate-gy, -gics; plan etc. 626.
husbandry; house-keeping, -wifery; stewardship;
ménage; regimen, *régime*; econom-y, -ics; political
economy; management; government etc. (*direction*) 693.
execution, manipulation, treatment, campaign,
career, life, course, walk, race.
conduct; behavior; de-, com-portment; carriage,
maintien, demeanor, guise, bearing, manner, mien,
air, observance.
course –, line- of -conduct, – action, – –
proceeding; *rôle*; process, ways, practice,
procedure, *modus operandi*; method etc., path etc.
627.
V. transact, execute; des-, dis-patch; proceed
with, discharge; carry -on, – through, – out, –
into effect; work out; go –, get- through; enact; put
into practice; officiate etc. 625.

behave –, comport –, demean –, carry –, bear –, conduct –, acquit- oneself.

run a race, lead a life, play a game; take –, adopt- a course; steer –, shape- one's course; play one's- part, – cards; shift for oneself; paddle one's own canoe.

conduct; manage etc. (*direct*) 693.

deal –, have to do- with; treat, handle a case; take -steps, – measures.

Adj. conducting etc. *v.*; strategical, business-like, practical, economic, executive.

693. Direction.—N. direction; manage-ment, -ry; government, gubernation, conduct, legislation, regulation, guidance; steer-, pilot-age; reins, – of government; helm, rudder, controls, joy stick, needle, compass, binnacle; guiding –, load –, lode –, pole- star; cynosure.

super-vision, -intendence; *surveillance*, oversight; eye of the master; control, charge, auspices; board of control etc. (*council*) 696; command etc. (*authority*) 737.

premier-, senator-ship; director etc. 694; chair, seat, portfolio.

statesmanship; state-, king-craft.

minis-try, -tration; administration; steward-, proctor-ship; agency.

V. direct, manage, govern, conduct; order, prescribe, cut out work for; head, lead; lead –, show- the way; take the lead, lead on; regulate, guide, steer, pilot, take –, be at- the helm; have –, handle –, hold –, take- the reins, handle the ribbons; drive, tool; tackle.

super-intend, -vise; overlook, control, keep in order, look after, see to, oversee, legislate for; ad-minister, ministrate; patronize; have the -care, – charge- of; have –, take- the direction; pull the -strings, – wires; rule etc. (*command*) 737; have –, hold- -office, – the portfolio; preside, – at the board; take –, occupy –, be in- the chair; pull the stroke oar.

Adj. directing etc. *v.*; executive, supervisory, hegemonic.

Adv. at the -helm, – head of, in charge of; un-der the auspices of.

694. Director.—N. director, manager, gover-nor, rector, comptroller; super-intendent, -visor; intendant; over-seer, -looker; foreman, boss, straw boss; supercargo, husband, inspector, visitor, ranger, surveyor, aedile, moderator, monitor, task-master; master etc. 745; leader, ringleader, demagogue, corypheus, conductor, fugleman, precentor, bellwether, agitator.

guiding star etc. (*guidance*) 693; adviser etc. 695; guide etc. (*information*) 527; pilot; helms-man; steers-man, -mate; man at the wheel; wire-puller.

driver, whip, Jehu, charioteer; coach-, car-, cab-man, jarvey; postilion, *vetturino*, muleteer, team-ster; whipper in; engineer, engine driver, motor-man, *chauffeur*.

head, – man; principal, president, speaker; chair, -man; captain etc. (*master*) 745; superior; dean; mayor etc. (*civil authority*) 745; vice-president, prime minister, premier, vizier, grand vizier; dictator.

officer, functionary, minister, official, red-tapist, bureaucrat; man –, Jack- in office; office-bearer; person in authority etc. 745.

statesman, strategist, legislator, lawgiver, politi-cian, administrator, statist, statemonger; Minos, Draco; arbiter etc. (*judge*) 967; king maker, power behind the throne.

board etc. (*council*) 696.

secretary, – of state; Reis Effendi; vicar etc. (*deputy*) 759; steward, factor; agent etc. 758; bailiff, middleman; ganger, clerk of works; land-reeve; factotum, major-domo, seneschal, house-keeper, shepherd, *croupier*; proctor, procurator, curator, librarian.

Adv. *ex officio.*

695. Advice.—N. advice, counsel, adhortation; word to the wise; suggestion, submonition, recom-mendation, advocacy, consultation.

exhortation etc. (*persuasion*) 615; expostulation etc. (*dissuasion*) 616; admonition etc. (*warning*) 668; guidance etc. (*direction*) 693.

instruction, charge, injunction.

adviser, prompter; counsel, -lor; monitor, men-tor, Nestor, *magnus Apollo*, senator; teacher etc. 540.

guide, manual, chart etc. (*information*) 527.

physician, leech, archiater; arbiter etc. (*judge*) 967.

refer-ence, -ment; consultation, conference, parley, *pourparler* etc. 696.

V. advise, counsel; give -advice, – counsel, – a piece of advice; suggest, prompt, submonish, recommend, prescribe, advocate; exhort etc. (*per-suade*) 615.

enjoin, enforce, charge, instruct, call; call upon etc. (*request*) 765; dictate.

expostulate etc. (*dissuade*) 616; admonish etc. (*warn*) 668.

advise with; lay heads –, consult- together; compare notes; hold a council, deliberate, be closeted with.

confer, consult, refer to, call in; take –, follow-advice; follow implicitly; be advised by, have at one's elbow, take one's cue from.

Adj. recommendatory; hortative etc. (*per-suasive*) 615; dehortatory etc. (*dissuasive*) 616; ad-monitory etc. (*warning*) 668; consultative.

Int. go to!

696. Council.—N. council, committee, sub-committee, *comitia*, court, chamber, cabinet, board, bench, staff; consultation.

senate, *senatus*, parliament, house, – of Lords, – Peers, – Commons, legislature, legislative assembly, federal council, chamber of deputies, directory, *reichsrath, rigsdag, cortes*, storthing, witenagemote, *junta*, divan, *musnud, sanhedrim*, Amphictyonic council; *duma, zemstvo, soviet, cheka, ogpu; Dail Eireann*; caput, consistory, chapter, syndicate; court of appeal etc. (*tribunal*) 966; board of -control, – works; vestry; county –, borough –, district –, parish –, town- council; local board.

cabinet −, privy- council, royal commission; cockpit, convocation, synod, congress, congregation, convention, diet, states-general, aulic council.

League of Nations, assembly, *caucus*, conclave, *clique*, conventicle; meeting, sitting, *séance*, conference, session, hearing, palaver, *pourparler*, *durbar*, pow-wow, house; *quorum*.

senator; member, − of parliament; councilor, M.P., representative of the people.

Adj. senatorial, curule, parliamentary.

697. Precept.—N. precept, direction, instruction, charge; prescript, -ion; *recipe*, receipt; golden rule; maxim etc. 496.

commandment, rule, ruling, canon, law, code, *corpus juris*, *lex scripta*, common −, unwritten −, canon- law; the Ten Commandments; act, statute, convention, rubric, stage direction, regulation; form, -ula, -ulary; technicality; nice point.

order etc. (*command*) 741.

698. Skill.—N. skill, skilfulness, address; dexter-ity, -ousness; adroitness, expertness etc. *adj* ; proficiency, competence, craft, callidity, facility, knack, trick, sleight; master-y, -ship; excellence, panurgy; ambidext-erity, -rousness; sleight of hand etc. (*deception*) 545.

sea-, air-, marks-, horse-manship; tight-, rope-dancing.

accomplish-, acquire-, attain-ment; art, science; techn-icality, -ology, -ique; practical −, technical knowledge; technocracy; finish, technic.

knowledge of the world, world wisdom, *savoir-faire*; tact; mother wit etc. (*sagacity*) 498; discretion etc. (*caution*) 864; *finesse*; craftiness etc. (*cunning*) 702; management etc. (*conduct*) 692; *ars celare artem*; self-help.

cleverness, talent, ability, ingenuity, capacity, parts, talents, faculty, endowment, *forte*, turn, gift, genius, flair, feeling; intelligence etc. 498; sharpness, readiness etc. (*activity*) 682; invention etc. 515; apt-ness, -itude; turn −, capacity −, genius-for; felicity, capability, *curiosa felicitas*, qualification, habilitation.

proficient etc. 700.

masterpiece, *coup de maître,· chef- d'oeuvre, tour de force*; good stroke etc. (*plan*) 626.

V. be -skilful etc. *adj* ; excel in, be master of; have -a turn for etc. *n*.

know -what's what, − a hawk from a handsaw, − what one is about, − on which side one's bread is buttered, − what's o'clock, − a thing or two; have cut one's -eye, − wisdom- teeth.

see -one's way, − where the wind lies, − which way the wind blows; have -all one's wits about one, − one's hand in; *savoir vivre*; *scire quid valeant humeri quid ferre recusent*

look after the main chance; cut one's coat according to one's cloth; live by one's wits; exercise one's discretion, feather the oar, sail near the wind; stoop to conquer etc. (*cunning*) 702; play one's -cards well, − best card; hit the right nail on the head, put the saddle on the right horse.

take advantage of, make the most of; profit by etc. (*use*) 677; make a hit etc. (*succeed*) 731; make a virtue of necessity; make hay while the sun shines etc. (*occasion*) 134.

Adj. skilful, dexterous, adroit, expert, apt, slick, handy, quick, deft, ready, resourceful, gain; smart etc. (*active*) 682; proficient, good at, up to, at home in, master of, a good hand at, *au fait*, thoroughbred, masterly,· crack, accomplished; conversant etc. (*knowing*) 490.

experienced, practiced, skilled; up −, well up-in; in -practice, − proper cue; competent, efficient, qualified, capable, fitted, fit for, up to the mark, trained, initiated, prepared, primed, finished. .

clever, able, ingenious, felicitous, gifted, talent-ed, endowed, cute, inventive etc. 515; shrewd, sharp etc. (*intelligent*) 498; cunning etc. 702; alive to, up to snuff, not to be caught with chaff; discreet.

neat-handed, fine-fingered, ambidextrous, sure-footed; cut out −, fitted- for.

technical, artistic, scientific, daedalian, ship-shape; workman-, business-, statesman-like.

Adv. skilfully etc. *adj* ; well etc. 618; artistically; with -skill, − consummate skill; *secundum artem, suo Marte*; to the best of one's abilities etc. (*exertion*) 686; like a machine.

699. Unskillfulness.—N. unskillfulness etc. *adj* ; want of -skill etc. 698; incompeten-ce, -cy; inability, -felicity, -dexterity, -experience; clumsiness; disqualification, unproficiency; quackery.

folly, stupidity etc. 499; indiscretion etc. (*rashness*) 863; thoughtlessness etc. (*inattention*) 458, (*neglect*) 460.

mis-management, -conduct; impolicy; malad-ministration; mis-rule, -government, -application, -direction, -feasance.

absence of rule, rule of thumb; bungling etc. *v* ; failure etc. 732; screw loose; too many cooks.

blunder etc. (*mistake*) 495; *étourderie, gaucherie*, act of folly, *balourdise*; botch, -ery; bad job, sad work.

sprat sent out to catch a whale, much ado about nothing, wildgoose chase.

bungler etc. 701; fool etc. 501.

layman, amateur.

V. be -unskillful etc. *adj*; not see an inch beyond one's nose; blunder, bungle, boggle, fumble, muff, botch, bitch, flounder, loppet, stumble, trip; hobble etc. 275; put one's foot in it; make a -mess, − hash, − sad work- of; overshoot the mark.

play -tricks with, − Puck; mismanage, -conduct, -direct, -apply, -send.

stultify −, make a fool of −, commit- oneself; act foolishly; play the fool; put oneself out of court; lose one's -head, − cunning.

begin at the wrong end; do things by halves etc. (*not complete*) 730; make two bites of a cherry; play at cross purposes; strain at a gnat and swallow a camel etc. (*caprice*) 608; put the cart before the horse; lock the stable door when the horse is stolen etc. (*too late*) 135.

not know -what one is about, − one's own interest, − on which side one's bread is buttered; stand in one's own light, quarrel with one's bread and butter, throw a stone in one's own garden, kill the goose which lays the golden eggs, pay dear for one's whistle, cut one's own throat, burn one's fingers; knock –, run- one's head against a stone wall; fall into a trap, catch a Tartar, bring the house about one's ears; have too many -eggs in one basket (*imprudent*) 863, – irons in the fire.

mistake etc. 495; take the shadow for the substance etc. (*credulity*) 486; be in the wrong box, aim at a pigeon and kill a crow; take –, get- the wrong sow by the ear, – the dirty end of the stick; put -the saddle on the wrong horse, – a square peg into a round hole, – new wine into old bottles.

cut a whetstone with a razor; hold a farthing candle to the sun etc. (*useless*) 645; fight with –, grasp at- a shadow; catch at straws, lean on a broken reed, reckon without one's host, pursue a wildgoose chase; go on a fool's –, sleeveless-errand; go further and fare worse; loose –, miss-one's way; fail etc. 732.

Adj. un-skillful etc. 698; unskilled, inexpert; bungling etc. *v.*; awkward, clumsy, unhandy, lubberly, *gauche*, *maladroit*, left-, heavy-handed; slovenly, slatternly; gawky.

adrift, at fault.

in-, un-apt; inhabile; un-tractable, -teachable; giddy etc. (*inattentive*) 458; inconsiderate etc. (*neglectful*) 460; stupid etc. 499; inactive etc. 683; incompetent; un-, dis-, ill-qualified; unfit; quackish; raw, green, inexperienced, rusty, out of practice.

un-accustomed, -used, -trained etc. 537; -initiated, -conversant etc. (*ignorant*) 491; shiftless; unbusinesslike, unpractical; unstatesmanlike.

un-, ill-, mis-advised; ill-devised, -imagined, -judged, -contrived, -conducted; un-, mis-guided; misconducted, foolish, wild; infelicitous; penny wise and pound foolish etc. (*inconsistent*) 608.

Phr. one's fingers being all thumbs; the right hand forgets its cunning.

il se noyerait dans une goutte d'eau.

incidit in Scyllam qui vult vitare Charybdim; out of the frying pan into the fire.

700. Proficient.—N. proficient, expert, adept, dab; *connoisseur* etc. (*scholar*) 492; master, -hand; top-sawyer, *prima donna,* first fiddle, *chef de cuisine*; protagonist; past master; profess-or, -ional, specialist.

picked man; medalist, prizeman.

veteran; old -stager, – campaigner, – soldier, – file, – hand; man of -business, – the world.

nice –, good –, clean- hand; practised –, experienced- -eye, – hand; marksman; good –, dead –, crack- shot; rope-dancer, funambulist, acrobat, contortionist; cunning man; conjuror etc. (*deceiver*) 548; wizard etc. 994.

genius; master-mind, – head, – spirit.

cunning –, sharp -blade, – fellow; jobber; cracksman etc. (*thief*) 792; politician, tactician, diplomat, -ist, strategist.

pantologist, admirable Crichton, Jack of all trades; prodigy of learning; walking encyclopedia; mine of information.

701. Bungler.—N. bungler; blunderer, -head; marplot, fumbler, lubber, lout, oaf, duffer, stick, clown; bad –, poor- -hand, – shot; butter-fingers.

no conjuror, flat, muff, slow coach, looby, lub-

ber, swab; clod, yokel, hick, awkward squad, novice, greenhorn, jaywalker, *blanc-bec*.

land lubber; fresh water –, fair weather- sailor; horse-marine; fish out of water, ass in lion's skin, jackdaw in peacock's feathers; quack etc. (*deceiver*) 548; Lord of Misrule.

sloven, slattern, trapes.

Phr. *il n'a pas inventé la poudre*; he will never set the Thames on fire.

702. Cunning.—N. cunning, craft; cunningness, craftiness etc. *adj.*; subtlety, artificiality; maneuvring etc. *v.*; temporization; circumvention.

chicane, -ry; sharp practice, knavery, jugglery; concealment etc. 528; nigger in the woodpile; guile, duplicity etc. (*falsehood*) 544; foul play.

diplomacy, politics; Machiavellism; jobbery, back-stairs influence, gerrymandering.

art, -ifice; device, machination; plot etc. (*plan*) 626; maneuver, stratagem, dodge, artful dodge, wile; trick, -ery etc. (*deception*) 545; ruse, – *de guerre*; *finesse*, side-blow, thin end of the wedge, shift, go by, subterfuge, evasion; white lie etc. (*untruth*) 546; juggle, *tour de force*; tricks -of the trade, – upon travelers; imposture, deception; *expié-glerie*, net, trap etc. 545.

Ulysses, Machiavel, sly boots, fox, reynard; Scotch-, Yorkshire-man; Jew, Yankee; intriguer, *intrigant*, schemer, trickster.

V. be -cunning etc. *adj.*; have cut one's eye-teeth; contrive etc. (*plan*) 626; live by one's wits; maneuver; intrigue, gerrymander, *finesse*, double, temporize, stoop to conquer, *reculer pour mieux sauter*, circumvent, steal a march upon; overreach etc. 545; throw off one's guard; surprise etc. 508; outdo, get the better of, snatch from under one's nose; snatch a verdict; waylay, undermine, introduce the thin end of the wedge; play -a deep game, – tricks with; have an axe to grind; *ambiguas in vulgum spargere voces*; flatter, make things pleasant.

Adj. cunning, crafty, artful; skilful etc. 698; subtle, feline, vulpine; cunning as a -fox, – serpent; deep, – laid; profound; designing, contriving; intriguing etc. *v.*; strategic, diplomatic, politic, Machiavellian, time-serving; artificial; trick-y, -sy; wily, sly, slim, insidious, stealthy, foxy; underhand etc. (*hidden*) 528; subdolous; deceitful etc. 545; double-tongued, -faced; shifty; crooked; arch, pawky, shrewd, acute; sharp, – as a needle; canny, astute, leery, knowing, up to snuff, too clever by half, not to be caught with chaff.

Adv. cunningly etc. *adj.*; slily, on the sly, by a side wind.

Phr. diamond cut diamond.

703. Artlessness.—N. artlessness etc. *adj.*; nature, simplicity; innocence etc. 946; *bonhomie*, *naïveté*, *abandon*, candor, sincerity; singleness of -purpose, – heart; honesty etc. 939; plain speaking; *épanchement*.

rough diamond, matter of fact man; *le palais de vérité*; *enfant terrible*.

V. be -artless etc. *adj.*; look one in the face; wear one's heart upon his sleeves for daws to peck

at; think aloud; speak -out, − one's mind; be free
with one, call a, spade a spade.

Adj. artless, natural, pure, native, simple, plain,
inartificial, untutored, unsophisticated, *ingénu*,
unaffected, *naïve*; sincere, frank; open, − as day;
candid, ingenuous, guileless, unsuspicious,
childlike; honest etc. 939; innocent etc. 946; Arcadian; undesigning, straightforward; unreserved,
unvarnished, above-board; simple-, single-minded;
frank-, open-, single-, simple-hearted; open and
above-board.

free-, plain-, out-spoken; blunt, downright,
direct, matter of fact, unpoetical; unflattering.

Adv. in plain -words, − English; without mincing the matter; not to mince the matter etc. (*affirmation*) 535.

Phr. *Davus sum non Oedipus; liberavi animam
meam.*

704. Difficulty.—N. difficulty; hardness etc.
adj.; impracticability etc. (*impossibility*) 471;
tough −, hard −, uphill- work; hard −, Herculean −, Augean- task; task of Sisyphus,
Sisyphean labor, tough job, teaser, rasper, dead lift.

dilemma, embarrassment; perplexity etc. (*uncertainty*) 475; involvement; intricacy; entanglement etc. 59; cross fire; awkwardness,
delicacy, ticklish card to play, deadlock, knot,
Gordian knot, *dignus vindice nodus*, net, meshes,
maze; coil etc. (*convolution*) 248; crooked path.

nice −, delicate −, subtle −, knotty-point;
vexed question, *vexata quaestio*, poser; puzzle etc.
(*riddle*) 533; paradox; hard −, nut to crack; bone
to pick, *crux, pons asinorum*, where the shoe pinches.

nonplus, quandary, strait, pass, pinch, pretty
pass, stress, brunt; critical situation, crisis; trial,
rub, emergency, exigency, scramble.

scrape, hobble, slough, quagmire, hot water, hornet's nest; sea −, peck- of troubles; pretty kettle of
fish; pickle, stew, *imbroglio*, mess, muddle, botch,
fuss, bustle, ado; false position; set fast, stand; dead
-lock, − set; fix, horns of a dilemma, *cul de sac*;
hitch; stumbling block etc. (*hindrance*) 706.

V. be -difficult etc. *adj.*; run one hard, go
against the grain, try one's patience, put one out;
put to one's -shifts, − wit's end; go hard with −,
try- one; pose, perplex etc. (*uncertain*) 475; bother,
nonplus, gravel, bring to a dead lock; be -
impossible etc. 471; be in the way of etc. (*hinder*)
706.

meet with −, labor under −, get into −, plunge
into −, struggle with −, contend with −, grapple
with- difficulties; labor under a disadvantage; be -in
difficulty etc. *adj.*

fish in troubled waters, buffet the waves, swim
against the stream, scud under bare poles.

have -much ado with, − a hard time of it; come
to the -push, − pinch; bear the brunt.

grope in the dark, lose one's way, weave a
tangled web, walk among eggs.

get into a -scrape etc. *n.*; bring a hornet's nest
about one's ears; be put to one's shifts; flounder,
boggle, struggle; not know which way to turn etc.
(*uncertain*) 475; get -tangled up, − wound up;
perdre son latin; stick - at, − in the mud, − fast;
come to a -stand, − dead lock; hold the wolf by
the ears.

render -difficult etc. *adj.*; encumber, embarrass,
ravel, entangle; put a spoke in the wheel etc. (*hinder*) 706; lead a pretty dance.

Adj. difficult, not easy, hard, tough; trouble-,
toil-, irk-some; operose, laborious, onerous, arduous, Herculean, formidable; sooner −, more
easily- said than done; difficult −, hard- to deal
with; ill-conditioned, crabbed; not -to be handled
with kid gloves, − made with rosewater.

awkward, unwieldy, unmanageable; intractable,
stubborn etc. (*obstinate*) 606; perverse, refractory,
plaguy, trying, thorny, rugged; knot-ted, -ty; invious; path-, track-less; labyrinthine etc. (*convoluted*) 248; intricate, complicated etc. (*tangled*)
59; impracticable etc. (*impossible*) 471; not -
feasible etc. 470; desperate etc. (*hopeless*) 859.

embarrassing, perplexing etc. (*uncertain*) 475;
delicate, ticklish, critical; beset with −, full of −,
surrounded by −, entangled by −, encompassed
with- difficulties.

under a difficulty; in -difficulty, − hot water, −
the suds, − a cleft stick, − a fix, − the wrong
box, − a scrape etc. *n.*; − deep water, − a fine
pickle; *in extremis*; between -two stools, − Scylla
and Charybdis; surrounded by -shoals, − breakers,
− quicksands; at cross purposes; not out of the
wood.

reduced to straits; hard −, sorely- pressed; run
hard; pinched, put to it, straitened; hard -up, − put
to it, − set; put to one's shifts; puzzled, at a loss
etc. (*uncertain*) 475; at -the end of one's tether, −
one's wit's end, − a nonplus, − a standstill;
graveled, nonplussed, stranded, aground; stuck −,
set- fast; up a tree, at bay, *aux abois*, driven -into a
corner, − from post to pillar, − to extremity, −
to one's wit's end, − to the wall; *au bout de son
latin*; out of one's -depth, − reckoning; put −,
thrown -out.

accomplished with difficulty; hard-fought, -
earned.

Adv. with -difficulty, − much ado; hardly etc.
adj.; uphill; against the -stream, − grain; *à
rebours*; *invitâ Minervâ*; in the teeth of; at −,
upon- a pinch; at long odds.

Phr. ay there's the rub; *hic labor hoc opus*;
things are come to a pretty pass.

705. Facility.—N. facility, ease; easiness etc.
adj.; capability; feasibility etc. (*practicability*) 470;
flexibility, pliancy etc. 324; smoothness etc. 255;
convenience.

plain −, smooth −, straight- sailing; mere
child's play, holiday task.

smooth water, fair wind; smooth − royal- road;
clear -coast, − stage; *tabula rasa; full play* etc.
(*freedom*) 748.

disen-cumbrance, -tanglement; deoppilation;
permission etc. 760.

V. be -easy etc. *adj.*; go on −, run- smoothly;
have -full play etc. *n.*; go −, run- on all fours; obey
the helm, work well.

flow −, swim −, drift −, go- with the- -stream,
− tide; see one's way; have -it all one's own way,
− the game in one's own hands; walk over the
course, win -at a canter, − hands down; make -
light of, − nothing of; be at home in etc. (*skilful*)
698.

render -easy etc. *adj.*; facilitate, smooth, ease; popularize; lighten, - the labor; free, clear; disencumber, -embarrass, -entangle, -engage; deobstruct, unclog, extricate, unravel; untie -, cut- the knot; disburden, unload, exonerate, emancipate, free from, deoppilate; humor etc. (*aid*) 707; lubricate etc. 332; relieve etc. 834.

leave -a hole to creep out of, - a loophole, - the matter open; give -the reins to, - full play, - full swing; make way for; open the -door to, - way; prepare -, smooth -, clear- the -ground, - way, - path, - road; pave the way, bridge over; permit etc. 760.

Adj. easy, facile; feasible etc. (*practicable*) 470; easily -managed, - accomplished; within reach, accessible, easy of access, for the million, open to.

manageable, wieldy; towardly, tractable; submissive; yielding, ductile; pliant etc. (*soft*) 324; glib, slippery; smooth etc. 255; on -friction wheels, - velvet; convenient.

un-, dis-burdened, -encumbered, -embarrassed; exonerated; un-loaded, -obstructed, -trammeled, -impeded, -restrained etc. (*free*) 748; at ease, light.

at -, quite at- home; in -one's element, - smooth water.

Adv. easily etc. *adj.*; readily, smoothly, swimmingly, *ad lib.*, on easy terms, single-handed.

Phr. touch and go.

Int. all clear!

706. Hindrance.—N. prevention, preclusion, obstruction, stoppage; prohibition; inter-ruption, -ception, -clusion; hindrance, impedition; retardment, -ation; constriction; embarrassment, oppilation; coarctation, stricture, restriction; anchor etc. 666; restraint etc. 751 & 752; inhibition etc. 761; blockade etc. (*closure*) 261; picketing.

inter-ference, -position; obtrusion; discouragement, -countenance, -approval, -approbation; opposition etc. 708.

impedimen·, let, obstacle, obstruction, knot, knag; check, hitch, *contretemps, impasse,* screw loose, grit in the oil.

bar, stile, barrier; turn-stile, -pike; gate, portcullis; bulwark, parapet, barricade etc. (*defence*) 717; wall, dead wall, breakwater, groyne; bulkhead, block, buffer; stopper etc. 263; boom, dam, weir, burrock.

drawback, objection; stumbling-block, -stone; lion in the path; snag; snags and sawyers.

en-, in-cumbrance; clog, skid, shoe, spoke; brake, drag, - chain. - weight; stay, stop; preventive, prophylactic; contraception; load, burden, fardel, *onus,* millstone round one's neck, *impedimenta;* dead weight; lumber, pack; nightmare, Ephialtes, incubus, old man of the sea; remora.

difficulty etc. 704; insuperable etc. 471- obstacle; estoppel; ill wind; head wind etc. (*opposition*) 708; trammel, tether etc. (*means of restraint*) 752; hold back, counterpoise; damper, wet blanket, hinderer, marplot, kill-joy, dog in the manger, interloper; trail of a red herring; opponent etc. 710.

V. hinder, impede, impedite, embarrass.

keep -, stave -, ward- off; picket; obviate; a-, ante-vert; turn aside, draw off, prevent, forefend, nip in the bud; retard, slacken, check, let; counteract, -check; preclude, debar, foreclose, estop;

inhibit etc. 761; shackle etc. (*restrain*) 751; restrict, restrain, cohibit.

obstruct, filibuster, stop, stay, bar, bolt, lock; block, - up; belay, barricade; block -, stop- the way; dam up etc. (*close*) 261; put on the -brake etc. *n.*; scotch -, lock -, put a spoke in- the wheel; put a stop to etc. 142; traverse, contravene; inter-rupt, -cept; oppose etc. 708; hedge -in, - round; cut off; interclude.

inter-pose, -fere, -meddle etc. 682.

cramp, hamper; clog, - the wheels; cumber; en-, in-cumber; handicap; choke; saddle -, load-with; overload, lay; lumber, trammel, tie one's hands, put to inconvenience; in-, discommode; discompose; hustle, drive into a corner; choke off.

run -, fall- foul of; cross the path of, break in upon.

thwart, frustrate, disconcert, balk, foil, baffle, snub, override, circumvent; defeat etc. 731; spike guns etc. (*render useless*) 645; spoil, mar, clip the wings of; cripple etc. (*injure*) 659; put an extinguisher on; damp; dishearten etc. (*dissuade*) 616; discountenance, throw cold water on, spoil sport; lay -, throw- a wet blanket on; cut the ground from under one, take the wind out of one's sails, undermine; be -, stand- in the way of; act as a drag; hang like a millstone round one's neck.

Adj. hindering etc. *v.*; obstr-uctive, -uent; impedi-tive, -ent; intercipient; prophylactic etc. (*remedial*) 662.

in the way of, unfavorable; onerous, burdensome; cumb-rous, -ersome; obtrusive.

hindered etc. *v.*; wind-bound, water-logged, heavy laden; hard pressed.

unassisted etc. (*see* assist etc. 707); single-handed, alone; deserted etc. 624.

707. Aid.—N. aid, -ance; assistance, help, opitulation, succor; support, lift, advance, furtherance, promotion; coadjuvancy etc. (*co-operation*) 709.

patronage, championship, countenance, favor, interest, advocacy, auspices.

sustentation, subvention, subsidy, bounty, alimentation, nutrition, nourishment, maintenance; manna in the wilderness; food etc. 298; means etc. 632.

ministr-y, -ation; subministration; accomodation.

relief, rescue; help at a dead lift; supernatural aid; *deus ex machinâ.*

supplies, reinforcements, succors, contingents, recruits; support etc. (*physical*) 215; adjunct, ally etc. (*helper*) 711.

V. aid, assist, help, succor, lend one's aid; come to the aid etc. *n.*- of; contribute, subscribe to; bring -, give -, furnish -, afford -, supply- -aid etc. *n.*; render assistance; give -, stretch -, lend -, bear -, hold out- a -hand, - helping hand; give one a -lift, - cast, - turn; take -by the hand, - in tow; help a lame dog over a stile, lend wings to.

relieve, rescue; set -up, - agoing, - on one's legs; bear -, pull- through; give new life to, be the making of; reinforce, recruit; set -, put -, push-forward; give -a lift, - a shove, - an impulse- to; promote, further, forward, advance; speed, expedite, quicken, hasten.

support, sustain, uphold, prop, hold up, bolster.

cradle, nourish; nurture, nurse, dry nurse, suckle, put out to nurse; manure, cultivate, force; foster; cherish, foment; feed –, fan- the flame.

serve; do service to, tender to, pander to; ad-, sub-, minister to; tend, attend, wait on; take care of etc. 459; entertain; smooth the bed of death.

oblige, accomodate, consult the wishes of; humor, cheer, encourage.

second, stand by; back, – up; pay the piper, abet; work –, make interest –, stick up –, take up the cudgels- for; take up –, espouse –, adopt- the cause of; advocate, beat up for recruits, press into the service; squire, give moral support to, keep in countenance, countenance, patronize; lend - oneself, – one's countenance- to; smile –, shine- upon; favor, befriend, take up, take in hand, enlist under the banners of; side with etc. (*co-operate*) 709.

be of use to; subserve etc. (*instrument*) 631; benefit etc. 648; render a service etc. (*utility*) 644; conduce etc. (*tend*) 176.

Adj. aiding etc. *v* ; auxiliary, adjuvant, helpful; coadjuvant etc. 709; subservient, ministrant, ancillary, accessory, subsidiary.

at one's beck; friendly, amicable, favorable, propitious, well-disposed; neighborly; obliging etc. (*benevolent*) 906.

Adv. with –, by- -the aid etc. *n.*- of; on –, in-behalf of; in -aid, – the service, – the name, – favor, – furtherance- of; on account of; for the sake of, on the part of; *non obstante*.

Int. help! save us! to the rescue! S.O.S.!

708. Opposition.—N. opposition, antagonism, oppug-nancy, -nation; impugnation; contravention; counteraction etc. 179; counterplot.

cross-fire, under-current, head-wind.

clashing, collision, conflict, lack of harmony, contest.

competition, two of a trade, rivalry, emulation. race; war to the knife.

absence of -aid etc. 707; resistance etc. 719; restraint etc. 751; hindrance etc. 706.

V. oppose, conteract, run counter to; withstand etc. (*resist*) 719; control etc. (*restrain*) 751; hinder etc. 706; antagonize, oppugn, fly in the face of, go dead against, kick against, fall foul of; set –, pit-against; face, confront, cope with; make a -stand, – dead set- against; set -oneself, one's face-against; protest –, vote –, raise one's voice-against; disfavor, turn one's back upon; set at naught, slap in the face, slam the door in one's face.

be –, play- at cross purposes; counter-work, - mine; thwart, overthwart.

stem, breast, encounter; stem –, breast- the - tide, – current, – flood; buffet the waves; beat up –, make head- against; grapple with; kick against the pricks etc. (*resist*) 719; contend etc. 720 –, do battle etc. (*warfare*) 722- -with, – against.

contra-dict, -vene; belie; go –, run –, beat –, militate- against; come in conflict with.

emulate etc. (*compete*) 720; rival, spoil one's trade.

Adj. oppos-ing, -ed etc. *v* ; adverse, antagonistic; ambivalent; contrary etc. 14; at variance etc. 24; at issue, at war with; in opposition; 'agin the Government.'

un-favorable, -friendly; hostile, inimical, cross, unpropitious.

in hostile array, front to front, with crossed bayonets, at daggers drawn; up in arms; resistant etc. 791.

competitive, emulous.

Adv. against, *versus*, counter to, in conflict with, at cross purposes.

against the -grain, – current, – stream, – wind, – tide; with a headwind; with the wind - ahead, – in one's teeth.

in spite, in despite, in defiance; in the -way, – teeth, – face- of; across; a-, over-thwart; where the shoe pinches.

though etc. 30; even; *quand même*; *per contra*.

Phr. *nitor in adversum*.

709. Co-operation.—N. co-operation; coadju-vancy, -tancy; coagency, coefficiency; concert, con-currence, complicity, participation; union etc. 43; amalgamation, combination etc. 48; collusion.

association, alliance, colleagueship, jointstock, copartnership, trust, cartel, pool, ring, combine, interlocking directorate; confederation etc. (*party*) 712; federation, coalition, fusion; a long pull, a strong pull and a pull all together; log-rolling, freemasonry.

unanimity etc. (*assent*) 488; *esprit de corps*, party spirit; clan-, partisan-ship; reciprocity, concord etc. 714.

V. co-operate, co-adjute, concur; conduce etc. 178; combine, cartelize, unite one's efforts; keep –, draw –, pull –, club –, hang –, hold –, league –, band –, be banded- together; stand –, put- shoulder to shoulder; act in concert, join forces, fraternize, cling to one another, conspire, concert, lay one's heads together; confederate, be in league with; collude, understand one another, play into the hands of, hunt in couples.

side –, take side –, go along –, go hand in hand –, join hands –, make common cause –, strike in –, unite –, join –, mix oneself up –, take part –, play along –, cast in one's lot- with; join –, enter into- partnership with; rally round, follow the lead of; come to, pass over to, come into the views of; be –, row –, sail- in the same boat; sail on the same tack.

be a party to, lend oneself to; participate; have a -hand in, – finger in the pie; take –, bear- part in; second etc. (*aid*) 707; take the part of, play the game of; espouse a -cause, – quarrel.

Adj. co-operating etc. *v* ; in -co-operation etc. *n.*, – league etc. (*party*) 712; coadju-vant, -tant; hand and glove with.

favorable etc. 707- to; un-opposed etc. 708.

Adj. as one man etc. (*unanimously*) 488; shoulder to shoulder; in co-operation with.

710. Opponent.—N. opponent, antagonist, ad-versary; adverse party, opposition; enemy etc. 891; assailant.

oppositionist, obstructive; obscurantist; brawler; wrangler, brangler, disputant, extremist, irreconcilable, diehard; bitter-ender.

malcontent; Jacobin, Fenian etc. 742; demagogue, reactionist.

passive resister, conscientious objector.

rival, competitor, contestant.

711. Auxiliary.—N. auxiliary; recruit; assistant; adju-vant, -tant; adjunct; help, er, -mate, -ing hand; midwife; colleague, partner, mate, con-*frère*, co-operator; coadju-tor, -trix; collaborator.

ally; friend etc. 890; confidant, *fidus Achates*, pal, chum, buddy, *alter ego*.

confederate; ac-, complice; accessory, – after the fact; *particeps criminis*.

aide-de-camp, secretary, clerk, associate, marshal; right-hand; candle-, bottle-holder; hand-maid; servant etc. 746; puppet, cat's-paw; stooge, dependent, creature, jackal; tool, *âme damnée*; satellite, adherent, parasite.

votary, disciple; secta-rian, -ry; seconder, backer, upholder, supporter, abettor, advocate, partisan, champion, patron, friend at court, mediator.

friend in need, Jack at a pinch, *deus ex machinâ*, guardian angel, fairy godmother; special providence, tutelary genius.

712. Party.—N. party, faction, side, denomination, class, communion, set, crowd, crew, band, horde, posse, phalanx; regiment etc. 726; family, clan etc. 166.

Tories, Conservatives, Unionists, Whigs, Liberals, Radicals, Labour party, Socialists, Communists etc.; Republicans, Democrats, Farmer-Labor; *Fascisti*, Revolutionaries etc. 742.

community, body, fellowship, sodality, solidarity; con-, fraternity; sorority; brother-, sisterhood.

Freemasons, Knights Templars, Odd Fellows, Ku Klux Klan etx.

knot, gang, *clique*, ring, circle; *coterie*, club, *casino*.

corporation, corporate body, guild; establishment, company, copartnership, firm, house, joint concern, joint-stock company, trust, investment trust, combine etc. 709.

society, association; instit-ute, -ution; union; trade-union; league, syndicate, alliance, *Verein*, *Bund*, *Zollverein*, combination; league –, alliance- offensive and defensive; coalition; federation; confedera -tion, -cy; junto, cabal, *camarilla*, *camorra*, *brigue*; freemasonry; party spirit etc. (*co-operation*) 709.

staff; cast, *dramatis personae*.

V. unite, join; club together etc. (*co-operate*) 709; cement –, form- a party etc. *n.*; associate etc. (*assemble*) 72.

Adj. in -league, – partnership, – alliance etc. *n.*

bonded –, banded –, linked etc. (*joined*) 43- together; embattled; confederated, federative, joint, corporate, leagued, fraternal, masonic, cliquish.

Adv. hand in hand, side by side, shoulder to shoulder, *en masse*, in the same boat.

713. Discord.—N. disagreement etc. 24; discord, -accord, -sidence, -sonance; jar, clash, shock; jarring, jostling etc. *v*; screw loose.

variance, difference, dissension, misunderstanding, cross purposes, odds, *brouillerie*; division, split, rupture, disruption, division in the camp, house divided against itself, rift within the lute; disunion, breach; schism etc. (*dissent*) 489; feud, faction.

quarrel, dispute, rippet, spat, tiff, *tracasserie*, squabble, altercation, words, high words; wrangling etc. *v*; jangle, brabble cross questions and crooked answers, snip-snap; family jars.

polemics; litigation; strife etc. (*contention*) 720; warfare etc. 722; outbreak, open rupture; breaking off of negotiations, recall of ambassadors; declaration of war.

broil, brawl, row, racket, hubbub, rixation; embroilment, embranglement, *imbroglio*, *fracas*, breach of the peace, piece of work, scrimmage, rumpus; breeze, squall; riot, disturbance etc. (*disorder*) 59; commotion etc. (*agitation*) 315; bear garden, Donnybrook Fair.

subject of dispute, ground of quarrel, battle ground, disputed point; bone -of contention, – to pick; apple of discord, *casus belli*; question at issue etc. (*subject of inquiry*) 461; vexed question, *vexata quaestio*, brand of discord.

troublous times; cat-and-dog life; contentiousness etc. *adj*; enmity etc. 889; hate etc. 898; Kilkenny cats; disputant etc. 710; strange bedfellows.

V. be -discordant etc. *adj*; disagree, come amiss etc. 24; clash, jar, jostle, pull different ways, conflict, have no measures with, misunderstand one another; live like cat and dog; differ; dissent etc. 489; have a -bone to pick, – crow to pluck- with.

fall out, quarrel, dispute; litigate; controvert etc. (*deny*) 536; squabble, wrangle, jangle, brangle, bicker, nag; spar etc. (*contend*) 720; have -words etc. *n*. with; fall foul of.

split; break –, break squares –, part company- with; declare war, try conclusions; join –, put in- issue; pick a quarrel, fasten a quarrel on; sow –, stir up- -dissension etc. *n.*; embroil, estrange, entangle, disunite, widen the breach; set -at odds, – together by the ears; set –, pit- against; rub up the wrong way.

get into hot water, fish in troubled waters, brawl; kick up a -row, – dust; turn the house out of window.

Adj. discordant; disagreeing etc. *v*; out of tune, dissonant, inharmonious, harsh, grating, jangling, ajar, on bad terms; dissentient etc. 489; inconsistent, contradictory, incongruous, discrepant; un- reconciled, -pacified.

quarrelsome, unpacific; gladiatorial, controversial, polemic, disputatious; factious; liti-gious, -gant; pettifogging.

at odds, at loggerheads, at daggers drawn, at variance, at issue, at cross purposes, at sixes and sevens, at feud, at high words; up in arms, together by the ears, in hot water, embroiled.

torn, disunited.

Phr. *quot homines tot sententiae*; no love lost between them, *non nostrum tantas componere lites*.

714. Concord.—N. concord, accord, harmony, symphony, homology; agreement etc. 23; sympathy etc. (*love*) 897; response; union, unison, unity; bonds of harmony; peace etc. 721; unanimity etc. (*assent*) 488; league etc. 712; happy family.

rapprochement; réunion; amity etc. (*friendship*) 888; reciprocity; alliance, *entente cordiale*, good understanding, conciliation, arbitration, peacemaker etc. 724.

V. agree etc. 23; accord, harmonize with; fraternize; be -concordant etc. *adj.* ; go hand in hand; blend −, tone in- with; run parallel etc. (*concur*) 178; understand one another; pull together etc. (*co-operate*) 709; put up one's horses together, sing in chorus.

side −, sympathize −, go −, chime in −, fall in- with; come round; be pacified etc. 723; assent etc. 488; enter into the -ideas, − feelings- of; reciprocate.

hurler avec les loups; go −, swim- with the stream.

pour oil on troubled waters, keep in good humor, render accordant, put in tune; come to an understanding, meet half-way; keep the −, remain at- peace.

Adj. concordant, congenial; agreeing etc. *v.*; in-accord etc. *n.*; harmonious, united, cemented; banded together etc. 712; allied; friendly etc. 888; fraternal; conciliatory; at one with; of one mind etc. (*assent*) 488.

at peace, in still water; tranquil etc. (*pacific*) 721.

Adv. with one voice etc. (*assent*) 488; in concert with, hand in hand; on one's side, unanimously.

715. Defiance.—N. defiance; daring etc. *v.*; dare, challenge, *cartel*; threat etc. 909; war-cry, -whoop.

V. defy, dare, beard; brave etc. (*courage*) 861; bid defiance to; set at -defiance, − naught; hurl defiance at; dance the war dance; snap the fingers at, laugh to scorn; disobey etc. 742.

show -fight, − one's teeth, − a bold front; bluster, look big, stand akimbo; double −, shake-the fist; threaten etc 909.

challenge, call out; throw −, fling- down the -gauntlet, − gage, − glove.

Adj. defiant; defying etc. *v.*; with arms akimbo; rebellious, insolent; reckless, greatly daring.

Adv. in -defiance, − the teeth- of; under one's very nose.

Int. do your worst! come if you dare! come on! marry come up! hoity toity!

Phr. *noli me tangere*; *nemo me impune lacessit*.

716. Attack.—N. attack; assault, − and battery; onset, onslaught, charge.

aggression, drive, offence; incursion, inroad; invasion; irruption; outbreak; *estrapade*, *ruade*; *coup de main*, sally, *sortie*, *camisade*, raid, foray; run -at, − against; dead set at.

storm, -ing; boarding, *escalade*; siege, investment, obsession, bombardment, cannonade; air raid.

fire, volley; platoon −, file −, rapid-fire; *fusillade*; sharp-shooting, sniping; broadside; raking −, cross −, machine gun- fire; − volley of grapeshot, *feu d'enfer*; salvo.

cut, thrust, lunge, pass, *passado*, *carte* and

tierce, home thrust, *coup de pied*; kick, punch, etc. (*impulse*) 276.

battue, razzia, Jacquerie, dragonnade; devastation etc. 162.

assailant, aggressor, invader.

base of operations, point of attack.

V. attack, assault, assail; set −, fall- upon; charge, impugn, break a lance with, enter the lists.

assume −, take- the offensive; be −, become-the aggressor; strike the first blow, fire the first shot, throw the first stone at; lift a hand −, draw the sword- against; take up the cudgels; advance −, march- against; march upon, invade, harry; come on, show fight.

strike at, poke at, thrust at; aim −, deal- a blow at; give −, fetch- one a -blow, − kick; have a -cut, − shot, − fling, − shy- at; be down −, pounce-upon; fall foul of, pitch into, launch out against; bait, slap on the face; make a -thrust, − pass, − set, − dead set- at; dunt; bear down upon.

close with, come to close quarters, bring to bay.

ride full tilt against; let fly at, dash at, run a tilt at, rush at, tilt at, run at, fly at, hawk at, have at, let out at; make a -dash, − rush at; attack tooth and nail; strike home; drive −, press- one hard; be hard upon, run down, strike at the root of.

lay about one, run amuck.

fire -upon, − at, − a shot at; shoot at, pop at, level at, let off a gun at; open fire, pepper, bombard, shell, pour a broadside into; fire -a volley, − red-hot shot; spring a mine.

throw -a stone, − stones- at; stone, lapidate, pelt; hurl -at, − against, − at the head of.

beset, besiege, beleaguer; lay siege to, invest, open the trenches, plant a battery, sap, mine; storm, board, scale the walls.

cut and thrust, bayonet, butt; kick, strike etc. (*impulse*) 276; whip etc. (*punish*) 972.

Adj. attacking etc. *v.*; aggressive, offensive, obsidional.

up in arms; on the warpath; over the top.

Adv. on the offensive.

Int. 'up and at them!'

717. Defense.—N. defense, protection, guard, ward; shielding etc. *v.*; propugnation; preservation etc. 670; guardianship.

self-defense, -preservation; resistance etc. 719. safeguard etc. (*safety*) 664; screen etc. (*shelter*) 666, (*concealment*) 530; barrage; fortification; muni-tion, -ment; bulwark, fosse, moat, ditch, in-trenchment, trench, dugout, gas mask; dike, dyke; parapet, parados, sunk fence, embankment, mound, mole, bank; earth- field-work, gabions; fence, wall, dead wall, contravallation; paling etc. (*inclosure*) 232; palisade, haha, stockade, *stoccado*, *laager*, *sangar*; barri-er, -cade; boom; port-cullis, *chevaux de frise*; aba-, abat-, abba-tis; *vallum*, circumvallation, battlement, rampart, scarp; e-, counter-scarp; glacis, casemate.

mine, countermine.

buttress, abutment, shore etc. (*support*) 215.

breastwork, *banquette*, curtain, mantlet, bastion, demilune, redan, ravelin; advanced −, horn −, out- work, lunette, barb-acan, -ican; redoubt; fort-elage, -alice; lines; coast defense.

loop-hole, machicolation; sally-port, postern gate.

hold, stronghold, fastness; asylum etc. (*refuge*) 666; keep, donjon, fortress, citadel; capitol, castle; tower, – of strength; fort, barracoon, pah, sconce, martello tower, peel-house, block-house, rath; wooden walls; turret, barbette.

buffer, corner-stone, fender, apron, mask, gauntlet, thimble, carapace, armor, shield, buckler; target, targe, aegis, breastplate, cuirass, plastron, habergeon, mail, coat of mail, brigandine, hauberk, lorication, helmet, helm, basinet, sallet, salade, heaume, morion, murrion, armet, cabaset, vizor, casquetel, siege-cap, head-piece, casque, steel helmet, tin hat; *pickelhaube*, csako; shako etc. (*dress*) 225; bearskin; panoply; truncheon etc. (*weapon*) 727.

garrison, picket, piquet; defender, protector; guardian etc. (*safety*) 664; trabant, body guard, champion; knight-errant, Paladin; propugner.

V. defend, forfend, fend; shield, screen, shroud; fence round etc. (*circumscribe*) 229; fence, intrench; guard etc. (*keep safe*) 664; guard against; take care of etc. (*vigilance*) 459; bear harmless; keep –, ward –, beat- off; hinder etc. 706.

parry, repel, propugn, put to flight; give a warm reception to [*ironical*]; hold –, keep- at -bay, – arm's length.

stand –, act- on the defensive; show fight; maintain –, stand- one's ground; stand by; hold one's own; bear –, stand- the brunt; fall back upon, hold, stand in the gap.

Adj. defending etc. *v.*; defensive; mural; armed, – at all points, – *cap-à-pie*, – to the teeth; panoplied; accoutred, harnessed; iron-plated, -clad, loop-holed, castellated, machicolated; casemated; defended etc. *v.*; proof against, bomb-, bullet-proof; protective.

Adv. defensively; on the -defense, – defensive; in defense; at bay, *pro aris et focis*.

Int. no surrender! *il ne passeront pas!*

Phr. defense not defiance.

718. Retaliation.—N. retaliation, reprisal, retort; counter-stroke, -blast, -plot, -project; retribution, *lex talionis*; reciprocation etc. (*reciprocity*) 12.

requital, desert, tit for tat, give and take, blow for blow, *quid pro quo*, a Roland for an Oliver, measure for measure, an eye for an eye, diamond cut diamond, the biter bit, a game at which two can play; boomerang.

recrimination etc. (*accusation*) 938; revenge etc. 919; compensation etc. 30; reaction etc. (*recoil*) 277.

V. retaliate, retort, turn upon; pay -off, – back; pay in -one's own, – the same- coin; cap; reciprocate etc. 148; turn the tables upon, return the compliment; give -a *quid pro quo* etc. *n.*, – as much as one takes; give and take, exchange -blows, – fisticuffs; be -quits, – even- with; pay off old scores.

serve one right, be hoist on one's own petard, throw a stone in one's own garden, cathch a Tartar.

Adj. retaliating etc. *v.*; retalia-tory, -tive; retributive, recriminatory, reciprocal.

Adv.. in retaliation; *en revanche*.

Phr. *mutato nomine de te fabula narratur; par pari refero; tu quoque*; you're another; *suo sibi gladio hunc jugulo.*

719. Resistance.—N. resistance, stand, front, oppugnation; opposition etc. 708; renitence, reluctation, recalcitration, recalcitrance; repugnance; kicking etc. *v.*

repulse, rebuff.

insurrection etc. (*disobedience*) 742; strike; turn –, lock –, barring- out; *levée en masse, Jacquerie*; riot etc. (*disorder*) 59.

V. resist; not -submit etc. 725; repugn, reluctate, withstand; stand up –, strive –, bear up –, be proof –, make head- against; stand, – firm, – one's ground, – the brunt of, – out; hold -one's ground, – one's own, – out.

breast the -wave, – current; stem the -tide, – torrent; face, confront, grapple with; show a bold front etc. (*courage*) 861; present a front; make a –, take one's- stand.

kick, – against; recalcitrate, kick against the pricks; oppose etc. 708; fly in the face of; lift the hand against etc. (*attack*) 716; rise up in arms etc. (*war*) 722; strike, turn out; draw up a round robin etc. (*remonstrate*) 932; revolt etc. (*disobey*) 742; make a riot.

prendre le mors aux dents; take the bit between the teeth; sell one's life dearly, die hard, keep at bay; repel, repulse.

Adj. resisting etc. *v.*; resist-ive, -ant; refractory etc. (*disobedient*) 742; recalcitrant, re-nitent, -pulsive, -pellant; up in arms.

proof against; unconquerable etc. (*strong*) 159; stubborn, unconquered; indomitable etc. (*persevering*) 604a; unyielding etc. (*obstinate*) 606.

Int. hands off! keep off!

720. Contention.—N. contention, strife; contest, -ation; struggle; belligerency; opposition etc. 708.

controversy, polemics; debate etc. (*discussion*) 476; war of words, logomachy, litigation; paper war, ink slinging; high words etc. (*quarrel*) 713; sparring etc. *v.*

competition, rivalry; corrival-ry, -ship; agonism, *concours*, match, race, horse-racing, heat, steeple chase, point-to-point race, handicap; boat race, regatta; field-day; sham fight, Derby day; turf, sporting, bull-fight, tauromachy, *gymkhana*, rodeo, Olympiad.

wrestling, *ju-jitsu*, pugilism, boxing, fisticuffs, spar, mill, set-to, scrap, round, bout, event; prize-fighting; quarter-staff, single stick; gladiatorship, gymnastics; athletic-s, – sports; games of skill etc. 840.

shindy; *fracas* etc. (*discord*) 713; clash of arms; tussle, scuffle, broil, fray; affray, -ment; velitation; col-, luctation; brabble, *brique*, scramble, *mêlée*, scrimmage, stramash, bush-fighting.

free –, stand up –, hand to hand –, running-fight.

conflict, skirmish; ren-, en-counter; *rencontre*, collision, affair, brush, fight; battle, – royal; combat, action, engagement, joust, tournament; tilt, -ing; tourney, list; pitched battle, guerilla warfare.

death-struggle, struggle for life or death, Armageddon; hard knocks, sharp contest, tug of war.

naval -engagement, – battle; *naumachia*, sea-fight.

duel, -lo; single combat, monomachy, satisfaction, *passage d'armes*, passage of arms, affair of honor; triangular duel; hostile meeting, digladiation; appeal to arms etc. (*warfare*) 722.

deeds –, feats- of arms; pugnacity; combativeness etc. *adj.*; bone of contention etc. 713.

V. contend; contest, strive, struggle, scramble, wrestle; spar, square; exchange -blows, – fisticuffs; scrap, mix with, fib, justle, tussle, tilt, box, stave, fence; skirmish; fight etc. (*war*) 722; wrangle etc. (*quarrel*) 713.

contend etc. –, grapple –, engage –, close –, buckle –, bandy –, try conclusions –, have a brush etc. *n.* –, tilt- with; encounter, fall foul of, pitch into, clapperclaw, run a tilt at; oppose etc. 708; reluct.

join issue, come to blows, be at loggerheads, set-to, come to the scratch, exchange shots, measure swords, meet hand to hand; take up the -cudgels, – glove, – gauntlet; enter the lists; couch one's lance; give satisfaction; appeal to arms etc. (*warfare*) 722.

lay about one; break the peace.

compete –, cope –, vie –, race- with; outvie, emulate, rival; run a race; contend etc. –, stipulate –, stickle- for; insist upon, make a point of.

Adj. contending etc. *v.*; together by the ears, at loggerheads, at war, at issue.

competitive, rival; belligerent; contentious, combative, bellicose, unpeaceful; warlike etc. 722; quarrelsome etc. 901; pugnacious; pugilistic, gladiatorial; palestric, -al.

Phr. *a verbis ad verbera*; a word and a blow.

721. Peace.—N. peace; amity etc. (*friendship*) 888; harmony etc. (*concord*) 714; tranquility etc. (*quiescence*) 265; truce etc. (*pacification*) 723; pacificism; pipe –, calumet- of peace.

piping time of peace, quiet life; neutrality.

V. be at peace; keep the peace etc. (*concord*) 714; make peace etc. 723.

Adj. pacific; peace-able, -ful; calm, tranquil, untroubled, halcyon; bloodless; neutral.

Phr. the storm blown over; the lion lies down with the lamb.

722. Warfare.—N. warfare; fighting etc. *v.*; hostilities; war, arms, the sword; Mars, Bellona, grim visaged war, *horrida bella*, Armageddon.

appeal to -arms, – the sword; ordeal –, wager-of battle; *ultima ratio regum*, arbitrament of the sword.

battle array, campaign, crusade, expedition; mobilization; state of siege; battle-field etc. (*arena*) 728; warpath.

art of war, tactics, strategy, castrametation; general-, soldier-ship; aerial –, submarine –, naval –, chemical-, atomic-, guerila- warfare; military evolutions, ballistics, gunnery; chivalry; poison gas; gun-powder, shot, – and shell.

battle, tug of war etc. (*contention*) 720; service, campaigning; active service, tented field; fiery cross, trumpet, clarion, bugle, pibroch, slogan; war-cry, -whoop; battle cry, beat of drum, rappel, tom-tom; word of command; pass-, watch-word.

war to the -death, – knife; *guerre à -mort*, – *outrance*; open –, internecine –, civil- war.

V. arm; raise –, mobilize- troops; raise up in arms; take up the cudgels etc. 720; take up –, fly to –, appeal to- -arms, – the sword; draw –, unsheathe- the sword; dig up the hatchet; go to –, declare –, wage –, let slip the dogs of- war; cry havoc; kindle –, light- the torch of war; raise one's banner, send round the fiery cross; hoist the black flag; throw –, fling- away the scabbard; enrol, enlist, join up; take the field; take the law into one's own hands; do –, give –, join –, engage in –, go to- battle; flesh one's sword; set to, fall to, engage, measure swords with, draw the trigger, cross swords; come to -blows, – close quarters; fight; combat; contend etc. 720; battle –, break a lance- with.

serve; see –, be on- -service, – active service; campaign; wield the sword, shoulder a musket, smell powder, be under the fire; spill –, imbrue the hands in- blood; be on the warpath.

carry on -war, – hostilities; keep the field; fight the good fight; go over the top; cut one's way through; fight -it out, – like devils, – one's way, – hand to hand; sell one's life dearly.

Adj. conten-ding, -tious etc. 720; armed, – to the teeth, – cap-à-pie; sword in hand; in –, under –, up in- arms; at war with; bristling with arms; in -battle array, – open arms, – the field; embattled.

unpacific, unpeaceful; belligerent, combative, armigerous, bellicose, martial, warlike; mili-tary, - tant; soldier-like, -ly; chivalrous; strategical, internecine.

Adv. *flagrante bello*, in the -thick of the fray, – cannon's mouth; at the -swords's point, – point of the bayonet.

Int. *vae victis!* to arms! to your tents O Israel!

Phr. the battle rages.

723. Pacification.—N. pacification, conciliation; reconcil-iation, -ement; shaking of hands, accomodation, arrangement; adjustment; terms, compromise; amnesty, deed of release.

peace-offering; olive-branch; overtures; pipe –, calumet –, preliminaries- of peace.

truce, armistice; suspension of -arms, – hostilities; breathing-time; convention; *modus vivendi*; flag of truce, white flag, *parlementaire*, *cartel*.

hollow truce, *pax in bello*; drawn battle.

V. pacify, tranquilize, compose; allay etc. (*moderate*) 174; reconcile, propitiate, placate, conciliate, meet half-way, hold out the olive-branch, heal the breach, make peace, restore harmony, bring to terms.

settle –, arrange –, accommodate- -matters, – differences; set straight; make up a quarrel, *tantas componere lites*; come to -an understanding, – terms; bridge over, hush up; make -it, – matters-up; shake hands.

raise a siege; put up –, sheathe- the sword; bury the hatchet, lay down one's arms, turn swords into ploughshares; smoke the calumet of peace, close the temple of Janus; keep the peace etc. (*concord*) 714; be -pacified etc.; come round.

Adj. conciliatory, pacificatory; composing etc *v.*; pacified etc. *v.*

Phr. *requiescat in pace*.

724. Mediation.—N. media-tion, -torship, -tization; inter-vention, -position, -ference, -meddling, -cession; parley, negotiation, arbitration; flag of truce etc. 723; good offices, peace -offering; diploma-tics, -cy; compromise etc. 774.

mediator, intercessor, peacemaker, make-peace, negotiator, go-between; diplomatist etc. (*consignee*) 758; moderator, propitiator, umpire, arbitrator.

V. media-te, -tize; inter-cede, -pose, -fere, -vene; step in, negotiate; meet half-way; arbitrate; *magnas componere lites.*

Adj. mediatory, propitiatory, diplomatic.

725. Submission.—N. submission, yielding, acquiescence, compliance; non-resistance; obedience etc. 743; submissiveness, deference.

surrender, cession, capitulation, resignation.

obeisance, homage, kneeling, genuflexion, courtesy, curtsy, *salaam, kowtow,* prostration.

V. succumb, submit, yield, bend, resign, defer to, accede.

lay down –, deliver up- one's arms; hand over one's sword; lower –, haul down –, strike- one's flag, – colors; deliver the keys of the city.

surrender, – at discretion; cede, capitulate, come to terms, retreat, beat a retreat; draw in one's horns etc. (*humility*) 879; give -way, – ground, – ✱ in, – up; cave in; suffer judgment by default; bend, – to one's yoke; – before the storm; reel back; bend –, knuckle- -down, – to, – under; knock under.

humble oneself; eat -dirt, – the leek, – humble pie; bite –, lick- the dust; be –, fall- at one's feet; craven; crouch before, throw oneself at the feet of; swallow the -leek, – pill; kiss the rod; turn the other cheek; *avaler des couleuvres,* gulp down.

obey etc. 743; kneel to, bow to, pay homage to, cringe to, truckle to; bend the -neck, – knee; kneel, fall on one's knees, bow submission, courtesy, curtsy, *kowtow*; make obeisance.

pocket the affront; make -the best of, – a virtue of necessity; grin and abide, shrug the shoulders, resign oneself; submit with a good grace etc. (*bear with*) 826.

Adj. surrendering etc. *v.*; submissive, resigned, crouching; down-trodden; down on one's marrow bones; on one's bended knee; weak-kneed, un-, non-resisting; pliant etc. (*soft*) 324; undefended.

untenable, indefensible; humble etc. 879.

Phr. have it your own way; it can't be helped; amen etc. (*assent*) 488.

726. Combatant.—N. combatant; disputant, controversialist, polemic, litigant, belligerent; competitor, rival, corrival; fighter, assailant, aggressor; champion, Paladin; moss-trooper, swashbuckler, fire-eater, duellist, bully, bludgeon-man, rough, fighter, fighting-man, prize-fighter, pugilist, pug, boxer, bruiser, the fancy, gladiator, athlete, wrestler; fighting-, game-cock; swordsman, *sabreur.*

warrior, soldier, Amazon, man-at-arms, armigerent; campaigner, veteran; red-coat, military man, *rajpoot,* brave.

armed force, troops, soldiery, military, forces, sabaoth, the army, standing army, regulars, the line, troops of the line, militia, territorials, yeomanry, volunteers, trainband, fencible; auxiliary –, reserve- forces; reserves, *posse comitatus,* national guard, *gendarme,* beefeater; guards, -man; yeoman of the guard, life guards, household troops.

janissary; myrmidon; Mama-, Mame-luke; spahee, *spahi,* Cossack, Croat, Pandour; irregular, free lance, *franc-tireur, bashi-bazouk, guerilla, condottiere;* mercenary.

levy, draught, commando; *Land-wehr, -sturm;* conscript, recruit, rookie, cadet, raw levies.

private, – soldier; Tommy Atkins, rank and file, peon, trooper, doughboy, sepoy, *askari, legionnaire,* legionary, food for powder, cannon fodder; officer etc. (*commander*) 745; subaltern, ensign, shave-tail, standard bearer, non-com; spear-pike-man; halberdier, lancer; musketeer, carabineer, rifleman, sharpshooter, yager, skirmisher; grenadier, fusileer; archer, bowman.

horse and foot; horse –, foot- soldier; cavalry, horse, artillery, horse –, field –, heavy –, mountain- artillery, infantry, light horse, *voltigeur, Uhlan,* mounted rifles, dragoon, hussar, trooper; light –, heavy- dragoon; heavy; *cuirassier;* gunner, cannoneer, bombardier, artillery-man, matross; sapper, – and miner; engineer; light infantry, rifles, *chasseur, zouave*; military train, supply and transport, coolie.

army, – corps, *corps d'armée,* host, division, column, wing, detachment, *escadrille,* garrison, flying column, brigade, regiment, *corps,* battalion, squadron, company, platoon, battery, subdivision, section, squad; piquet, picket, guard, rank, file; legion, phalanx, cohort; cloud of skirmishers; impi.

war-horse, charger, *destrier.*

armored -train, – car; tank.

marine, man of war's man etc. (*sailor*) 269; navy, first line of defense, wooden walls; naval forces, fleet, flotilla, armada, squadron.

man-of-war, warship; H.M.S., U.S.S.; capital ship; line-of-battle ship, battle ship; super-, dreadnought, battle –, armored –, protected – light-cruiser; scout, flotilla leader; destroyer, torpedo boat; submarine, submersible, U-boat; submarine chaser, eagle boat, mystery ship, Q-boat; mine-layer, -sweeper; ship of the line, iron-clad, turret-ship, ram, Monitor, floating battery; first-rate, frigate, sloop of war, corvette, gunboat, bomb-vessel, fire-boat; flag ship, guard ship, cruiser; air-plane carrier; privateer; tender; depôt –, parent-ship; store –, troop- ship; transport, catamaran.

aircraft etc. 273; air force, scout, fighter, bomber, troop carrier, aerial patrol, seaplane, flying boat, torpedo plane; airship, Zeppelin; rigid –, semi-rigid –, non-rigid- airship; dirigible –, free –, captive –, kite –, observation- balloon.

anti-aircraft guns, searchlights, sound locators; catapult.

727. Arms.—N. arm, -s; weapon, deadly weapon; arma-ment, -ture; panoply, stand of arms; armor etc. (*defense*) 717; armory etc. (*store*) 636.

ammunition; powder, – and shot; explosive; propellant; gun-powder, -cotton; dynam-, melin-cord-, lydd-ite; trinitrotoluene, T.N.T.; ammonal; cartridge; ball cartridge, *cartouche,* fire-ball; dud, black Marie; 'villainous saltpeter;' poison –, mustard –, lachrymatory –, tear- gas.

sword, saber, broadsword, cutlass, falchion, scimitar, cimeter, brand, whinyard, bilbo, glaive, glave, rapier, skean, Toledo, Ferrara, tuck, claymore, creese, kris, *kukri*, dagger, dirk, hanger, poniard, stiletto, stylet, dudgeon, bayonet; sword-bayonet, -stick; side arms, foil, blade, steel; axe, bill; pole-, battle-axe; gisarm, halberd, partisan, tomahawk, bowie-knife; at-, att-, yat-aghan; yatachan; good –, trusty –, naked- sword; cold –, naked-steel.

club, mace, truncheon, staff, bludgeon, cudgel, life-preserver, shillelagh, sprig; hand-, quarter-staff; bat, cane, stick, knuckle-duster, sand bag.

gun, piece; fire-arms; artillery, ordnance; siege –, battering-train; park, battery; cannon, gun of position, heavy –, siege –, field –, mountain –, anti-aircraft –, breech loading –, quick firing-gun; field piece, mortar, trench mortar; mine –, flame- -thrower, napalm; howitzer, carronade, culverin, basilisk; falconet jingal, swivel, *pederero*, *bouche à feu*; smooth bore, rifled cannon; Armstrong –, Lancaster –, Paixhan –, Whitworth –, Parrott –, Krupp –, Gatling –, Maxim –, Vickers –, Hotchkiss –, Lewis –, machine- gun; tommy gun, Thompson's submachine gun; *mitrailleu-r, -se*; pompom; blow pipe.

small arms; musket, -ry, firelock, flintlock, fowling-piece, shot gun, rifle, *fusil*, caliver, carbine, blunderbuss, musketoon, Brown Bess, matchlock, harquebuss, *arquebuse*, haguebut; petronel; smallbore; breech-, muzzle-loader; Minié –, Enfield –, Westly Richards –, Snider –, Springfield –, Martini-Henry –, Lee-Metford –, Lee-Enfield –, Mauser –, Männlicher –, magazine –, repeating- rifle; needle-gun, *chassepot*; pis-tol, -et; revolver, automatic pistol, automatic; wind-, air-gun; flame –, gas- projector.

bow, cross-bow, arbalest, balister, catapult, sling; battering-ram etc. (*impulse*) 276; gunnery; ballistics etc. (*propulsion*) 284.

missile, bolt, projectile, shot, pellet, ball; grape; grape –, canister –, bar –, cannon –, langrel –, langrage –, round –, chain- shot; explosive; incendiary –, expanding –, soft-nosed –, dum-dum- bullet; slug, stone, brickbat; hand –, rifle-grenade; high explosive –, incendiary –, stink-, A-, H-, atomic –, hydrogen – bomb; petard, torpedo, carcass, rocket; congreve, – rocket; shrapnel, *mitraille*; thunderbolt; mine, land mine, infernal machine.

pike, lance, spear, spontoon, javelin, assagai, throwing stick, dart, djerrid, arrow, reed, shaft, bolt, boomerang, harpoon, gaff.

728. Arena.—N. arena, field, platform; scene of action, theater; walk, course; hustings; stage, boards etc. (*playhouse*) 599; amphitheater; Coli-, Colos-seum; Flavian amphitheater, hippodrome, circus, race-course, track, *stadium*, *corso*, turf, cockpit, bear-garden, play-ground, playing fields, *gymnasium*, *palaestra*, ring, lists; tilt-yard, -ing ground; *Campus Martius*, *Champ de Mars*; aerodrome, airport, air base, flying field.

theater –, seat- of war; battle-field, -ground; field of -battle, – slaughter; no man's land; Aceldama, camp; the enemy's camp; trysting- place etc. (*place of meeting*) 74.

729. Completion.—N. completion; ac-complish-, achieve-, fulfil-ment; performance, execution; des-, dis-patch; consummation, culmination, climax; finish, conclusion, ef-fectuation; close etc. (*end*) 67; terminus etc. (*arrival*) 292; winding up; *finale*, *dénouement*, catastrophe, issue, upshot, result; final –, last –, crowning –, finishing- -touch, – stroke; last finish, *coup de grâce*; crowning of the edifice; coping-, keystone; missing link etc. 53; super-structure, *ne plus ultra*, work done, *fait accompli*.

elaboration; finality; completeness etc. 52.

V. effect, -uate; accomplish, achieve, compass, consummate, hammer out; bring to -maturity, – perfection; perfect, complete; elaborate.

do, execute, make; go –, get- through; work out, enact; bring -about, – to bear, – to pass, – through, – to a head.

des-, dis-patch; knock –, finish –, polish- off; make short work of; dispose of, set at rest; perform, discharge, fulfil, realize; put in -practice, – force; carry -out, – into effect, – into execution; make good; be as good as one's word.

. do thoroughly, not do by halves, go the whole hog; drive home; be in at the death etc. (*persevere*) 604*a*; carry through, play out, exhaust, deliver the goods, fill the bill.

finish, bring to a close etc. (*end*) 67; wind up, stamp, clinch, seal, set the seal on, put the seal to; give the -final touch etc. *n*. to; put the -last, – finishing- hand to; crown, – all; cap.

ripen, culminate; come to a -head, – crisis; come to its end; die -a natural death, – of old age; run -its course, – one's race; touch –, reach –, attain- the goal; reach etc. (*arrive*) 292; get in the harvest.

Adj. completing, final; conclu-ding, -sive; crowning etc. *v.*; exhaustive, complete, mature, perfect, consummate.

done, completed etc. *v.*; done for, sped, wrought out; highly wrought etc. (*preparation*) 673; thorough etc. 52; ripe etc. (*ready*) 673.

Adv. completely etc. (*thoroughly*) 52; to crown all, out of hand.

Phr. the race is run; *actum est*; *finis coronat opus*; *consummatum est*; *c'en est fait*; it is all over; the game is played out, the bubble has burst.

730. Non-Completion.—N. non-completion, -fulfilment; shortcoming etc. 304; incompleteness etc. 53; drawn -battle, – game; work of Penelope, task of Sisyphus.

non-performance, inexecution; neglect etc. 460.

V. not -complete etc. 729; leave -unfinished etc. *adj.*, – undone; neglect etc. 460; let -alone, – slip; lose sight of.

fall short of etc. 304; do things by halves; scotch the snake, not kill it; hang fire; be slow to; collapse etc. 304.

Adj. not completed etc. *v.*; incomplete etc. 53; uncompleted, unfinished; unaccomplished; un-performed, unexecuted; sketchy, addle.

in progress, in hand; going on, proceeding; on one's hands; on the fire; on the stocks; in preparation; lacking the finishing touch.

Adv. *re infectâ*.

731. Success.—N. success, -fulness; speed; advance etc. (*progress*) 282.

trump card; hit, stroke; lucky –, fortunate –, good- -hit, – stroke; bold –, master- stroke; *coup de maître*, checkmate; half the battle, prize; profit etc. (*acquisition*) 775; best seller.

continued success; good fortune etc. (*prosperity*) 734; time well spent.

advantage over; edge; upper-, whiphand; ascendancy, mastery; expugnation, conquest, victory, subdual; subjugation etc. (*subjection*) 749.

triumph etc. (*exultation*) 884; proficiency etc. (*skill*) 698; conqueror, victor, winner, champion; master of the -situation, – position.

V. succeed; be -successful etc. *adj.*; gain one's -end, – ends; crown with success.

gain –, attain –, carry –, secure –, win- -a point, – an object; put over; make a go of; manage to, contrive to; accomplish etc. (*effect, complete*) 729; do –, work- wonders.

come off -well, – successfully, – with flying colors; make short work of; take –, carry- by storm; bear away the bell; win -one's spurs, – the battle; win –, carry –, gain- the -day, – prize, – palm; climb on the bandwagon; have -the best of it, – it all one's own way, – the game in one's own hands, – the ball at one's feet, – one on the hip; walk over the course; carry all before one, remain in possession of the field; score a success, win hands down.

speed; make progress etc. (*advance*) 282; win –, make –, work –, find- one's way; strive to some purpose; prosper etc. 734; drive a roaring trade; make profit etc. (*acquire*) 775; reap –, gather- the -fruits, – benefit of, – harvest; make one's fortune, get in the harvest, turn to good account; turn to account etc. (*use*) 677.

triumph, be triumphant; gain –, obtain- -a victory, – an advantage; chain victory to one's car.

surmount –, overcome –, get over- -a difficulty, – an obstacle etc. 706; *se tirer d'affaire*; make head against; stem the -torrent, – tide, – current; weather the storm, – a point; turn a corner, keep one's head above water, tide over; master; get –, have –, gain- the -better of, – best of, – upper hand, – ascendancy; whip hand, – start of; distance; surpass etc. (*superiority*) 33.

defeat, conquer, vanquish, discomfit; over-come, throw, -power, -master, -match, -set, -ride, -reach; out-wit, -do, -flank, -maneuver, -general, -vote; take the wind out of one's adversary's sails; beat, – hollow; rout, lick, drub, floor, worst; put -down, – to flight, – to the rout, – *hors de combat*; – out of court.

silence, quell, nonsuit, checkmate, upset, confound, nonplus, trump; baffle etc. (*hinder*) 706; circumvent, elude; trip up – the heels of; drive -into a corner, – to the wall; run hard, put one's nose out of joint.*

settle, do for; break the -neck of, – back of; capsize, sink, shipwreck, drown, swamp; subdue; subjugate etc. (*subject*) 749; reduce; make the enemy bite the dust; victimize, roll in the dust, trample under foot, put an extinguisher upon.

answer, – the purpose; avail, prevail, take effect, do, turn out well, work well, take, tell, bear fruit; hit -it, – the mark, – the right nail on the head; nick it; turn up trumps, make a hit; find one's account in.

Adj. succeeding etc. *v.*; successful; prosperous

etc. 734; triumphant; flushed –, crowned- with success; victorious; set up; in the ascendant; unbeaten etc. (*see* beat etc. *v.*); well-spent; felicitous, effective, in full swing.

Adv. successfully etc. *adj.*; with flying colors, in triumph, swimmingly; *à merveille*, beyond all hope; to some –, good- purpose; to one's heart's content.

Phr. *veni vidi vici,* the day being one's own, one's star in the ascendant; *omne tulit punctum.*

732. Failure.—N. failure; non-success, -fulfilment; dead failure, successlessness; abortion, miscarriage; *brutum fulmen* etc. 158; labor in vain etc. (*inutility*) 645; no go; inefficacy; inefficaciousness etc. *adj.*; vain –, ineffectual –, abortive- -attempt, – efforts; flash in the pan, 'lame and impotent conclusion;' frustration; slip 'twixt cup and lip etc. (*disappointment*) 509.

blunder etc. (*mistake*) 495; fault, omission, miss, oversight, slip, trip, stumble, claudication, footfall; false –, wrong- step; *faux pas*, titubation, *bévue*, *faute*, lurch; botchery etc. (*want of skill*) 699; scrape, jam, mess, muddle, foozle, *fiasco*, break-down.

mishap etc. (*misfortune*) 735; split, collapse, smash, blow, explosion.

repulse, rebuff, defeat, rout, overthrow, discomfiture; beating, drubbing; *quietus*, nonsuit, subjugation; check-, fool's-mate.

fall, downfall, ruin, perdition, wreck etc. (*destruction*) 162; death-blow; bankruptcy etc. (*non-payment*) 808.

losing game, *affaire flambée*.

victim, prey; bankrupt.

V. fail; be -unsuccessful etc. *adj.*; not -succeed etc. 731; make -vain efforts etc. *n.*; do –, labor –, toil- in vain; lose one's labor, take nothing by one's motion; bring to naught, make nothing of; wash a blackamoor white etc. (*impossible*) 471; roll the stone of Sisyphus etc. (*useless*) 645; do by halves etc. (*not complete*) 730; lose ground etc. (*recede*) 283; flunk; fall short of etc. 304.

miss, – one's aim, – the mark, – one's footing, – stays; slip, trip, stumble; make a -slip etc. *n.*, – blunder etc. 495, – mess of, – botch of; bitch it, miscarry, abort, go up like a rocket and come down like the stick, reckon without one's host; get the wrong sow by the ear etc. (*blunder, mismanage*) 699.

limp, halt, hobble, titubate; fall, tumble; lose one's balance; fall -to the ground, – between two stools; flounder, falter, stick in the mud, run aground, split upon a rock; run –, knock –, dash-one's head against a stone wall; break one's back; break down, sink, drown, founder, have the ground cut from under one; get into -trouble, – a mess, – a scrape; come to grief etc. (*adversity*) 735; go to -the wall, – the dogs, – pot; lick –, bite- the dust; be -defeated etc. 731; have the worst of it, lose the day, come off second best, lose; fall a prey to; succumb etc. (*submit*) 725; not have a leg to stand on.

come to nothing, end in smoke; fall -to the ground, – through, – dead, – still-born, – flat; slip through one's fingers; hang –, miss- fire; flash in the pan, collapse; topple down etc. (*descent*) 305; go to wrack and ruin etc. (*destruction*) 162.

go amiss, go wrong, go cross, go hard with, go on a wrong tack; go on –, come off –, turn out

−, work- ill; take -a wrong, − an ugly- turn; gang agley.

be all -over with, − up with; explode; dash one's hopes etc. (*disappoint*) 509; defeat the purpose; upset the apple cart; sow the wind and reap the whirlwind, jump out of the frying pan into the fire.

Adj. unsuccessful, successless; failing, tripping etc. *v.*; at fault; unfortunate etc. 735.

abortive, addle, still-born; fruitless, sterile, bootless; ineffect-ual, -ive; inefficient etc. (*impotent*) 158; inefficacious; lame, hobbling, décousu; insufficient etc. ʻ640; unavailing etc. (*useless*) 645; of no effect.

aground, grounded, swamped, stranded, cast away, wrecked, foundered, capsized, shipwrecked, non-suited; foiled; defeated etc. 731; struck −, borne −, broken- down; down-trodden; overborne, -whelmed; all up with; beaten to a frazzle.

lost, undone, ruined, broken; bankrupt etc. (*not paying*) 808; played out; done -up. − for; dead beat, ruined root and branch, *flambé*, knocked on the head; destroyed etc. 162.

frustrated, thwarted, crossed, unhinged, disconcerted, dashed; thrown -off one's balance, − on one's back, − on one's beam ends; unhorsed, in a sorry plight; hard hit.

stultified, befooled, dished, hoist on one's own petard, victimized, sacrificed.

wide of the mark etc. (*error*) 495; out of one's reckoning etc. (*inexpectation*) 508; left in the lurch; thrown away etc. (*wasted*) 638; unattained; uncompleted etc. 730.

Adv. unsuccessfully etc. *adj.*; to little or no purpose, in vain, *re infectâ*.

Phr. the bubble has burst, the game is up, all is lost; the devil to pay; *parturiunt montes* etc. (*disappointment*) 509.

---

733. Trophy.—N. trophy; medal, prize, palm; ribbon, blue ribbon, *cordon bleu*; citation; cup, laurel, -s; bays, crown, chaplet, wreath, civic crown; Victoria Cross, V.C., *Croix de Guerre*, Iron Cross; Distinguished Service Cross, Medal of Honor, Congressional Medal; insignia etc. 550; feather in one's cap etc. (*honor*) 873; decoration etc. 877; garland, triumphal arch.

triumph etc. (*celebration*) 883; flying colors etc. (*show*) 882.

monumentum aere perennius.

---

734. Prosperity.—N. prosperity, welfare, well-being; affluence etc. (*wealth*) 803; success etc. 731; thrift, roaring trade; chicken in every pot, the full dinner paid; good −, smiles of- fortune; blessings, godsend.

luck; good −, run of- luck; sunshine; fair -weather, − wind; palmy −, bright −, halcyondays; piping times, tide, flood, high tide.

Saturnia regna, Saturnian age; golden -time, − age; bed of roses; fat of the land, milk and honey, loaves and fishes, fleshpots of Egypt.

made man, lucky dog, *enfant fâté,* spoiled child of fortune.

upstart, *parvenu, nouveau riche,* profiteer, skipjack, mushroom.

V. prosper, thrive, flourish; be -prosperous etc. *adj.*; drive a roaring trade; go on -well, − smoothly, − swimmingly; sail before the wind, swim with the tide; run -smooth, − smoothly, − on all fours.

rise −, get on- in the world; work −, make-one's way; look up; lift −, raise- one's head, make one's -fortune, − pile, feather one's nest.

flower, blow, blossom, bloom, fructify, bear fruit, fatten, batten.

keep oneself afloat; keep −, hold- one's head above water; light −, fall- on one's -legs, − feet; drop into a good thing; bear a charmed life; bask in the sunshine; have a -good, − fine- time of it; have a run, − of luck; have the -good fortune etc. *n.* to; take a favorable turn; live -on the fat of the land, − in clover.

Adj. prosperous; thriving etc. *v.*; in a fair way, buoyant; well -off, − to do, − to do in the world; set up, at one's ease; rich etc. 803; in good case; in -full, − high- feather; fortunate, lucky, in luck; born -with a silver spoon in one's mouth, − under a lucky star; on the sunny side of the hedge.

auspicious, propitious, providential.

palmy, halcyon; agreeable etc. 829; *couleur de rose.*

Adv. prosperously etc. *adj.*; swimmingly; as good luck would have it; beyond all -expectation, − hope, − one's wildest dreams.

Phr. one's star in the ascendant, all for the best, one's course runs smooth.

---

735. Adversity.—N. adversity, evil etc. 619; failure etc. 732; bad −, ill −, evil −, adverse −, hard- -fortune, − hap, − luck, − lot; frowns of fortune; evil -dispensation, − star, − genius; ups and downs of life, broken fortunes; hard -case, − lines, − life; sea −, peck- of troubles; hell upon earth; slough of despond; jinx.

trouble, humiliation, hardship, curse, blight, blast, load, pressure.

pressure of the times, iron age, evil day, time out of joint; hard −, bad −, sad- times; rainy day, cloud, dark cloud, gathering clouds, ill wind; visitation, infliction; affliction etc. (*painfulness*) 830; bitter -pill, − cup; care, trial; the sport of fortune.

mis-hap, -chance, -adventure, -fortune; disaster, calamity, catastrophe; accident, casualty, cross, reverse, check, *contretemps*, rub, pinch, setback.

losing game; falling etc. *v.*; fall, down-fall, come-down; ruin -ation, -ousness; undoing; extremity; ruin etc. (*destruction*) 162.

V. be -ill off etc. *adj.*; go hard with; fall on evil, − days; go on ill; not -prosper etc. 734.

go -downhill, − to rack and ruin etc. (*destruction*) 162, − to the dogs; fall, − from one's high estate; decay, sink, decline, go down in the world; have seen better days; bring down one's grey hairs with sorrow to the grave; come to grief; be all -over, − up- with; bring a -wasp's, − hornet's- nest about one's ears.

Adj. unfortunate, unblest, unhappy, unlucky; im-, un-prosperous; luck-, hap-less; out of luck; in trouble, in a bad way, in an evil plight; under a cloud; clouded; ill −, badly- off; in adverse circumstances; poor etc. 804; behindhand, down in the world, decayed, undone; on the road to ruin, on its last legs, on the wane; in one's utmost need.

planet-struck, devoted; born -under an evil star, — with a wooden ladle in one's mouth; ill-fated, - starred, -omened; inconspicuous, ominous, doomed, unpropitious.

adverse, untoward; disastrous, calamitous, ruinous, dire, deplorable.

Adv. if the worst come to the worst, as ill luck would have it, from bad to worse, out of the frying pan into the fire.

Phr. one's star is on the wane; one's luck -turns, — fails; the game is up, one's doom is sealed, the ground crumbles under one's feet, *sic transit gloria mundi, tant va la cruche à l'eau qu'à la fin elle se casse.*

736. Mediocrity.—N. moderate —, average- circumstances; respectability; middle classes, *bourgeoisie*; mediocrity; golden mean etc. (*mid- course*) 628, (*moderation*) 174.

V. jog on; go —, get on- -fairly, — quietly, — peaceably, — tolerably, — respectably; steer a middle course etc. 628.

Adj. middling, so-so, fair, medium, moderate, mediocre, second-, third- etc. -rate.

737. Authority.—N. authority; influence, patronage, power, preponderance, credit, *prestige,* prerogative, jurisdiction; right etc. (*title*) 924.

divine right, dynastic rights, authoritativeness; absolut-eness, -ism; despotism, tyranny; *jus nocendi.*

command, empire, sway, rule; domin-ion, - ation; sovereignty, supremacy, suzerainty; lord-, head-ship; chiefdom; seignior-y, -ity, hegemony, patriarchate, patriarchy; master-y, -ship, -dom; government etc. (*direction*) 693; dictation, control.

hold, grasp; grip, -e; reach; iron sway etc. (*severity*) 739; fangs, clutches, talons; rod of em- pire etc. (*scepter*) 747.

reign, regnancy, *régime,* dynasty; director-, dic- tator-ship; protector-ate, -ship; caliphate, pashalic, electorate; presiden-cy, -tship; administration; pro-, consulship; prefecture; seneschalship; magistra-ture, -cy; raj.

empire; monarchy; king-hood, -ship; royalty, regality, autocracy, monocracy, arist-archy, - ocracy; oligarchy, democracy, demogogy; republic, -anism, federalism; socialism, collectivism; com- munism, bolshevism, syndicalism; mob law, mobocracy, ochlocracy, ergatocracy; *vox populi, imperium in imperio*; bureaucracy; beadle-, bum- ble-dom; stratocracy; martial law, military -power, — government; feodality, feudal system, feudalism.

Thearchy, diarchy; du-, tri-, heter-archy; du-, tri- umvirate; auto-cracy, -nomy; limited monarchy; constitutional -government, — monarchy; home rule, autonomy; self-government, -determination; representative government; Soviet government.

gyn-archy, -ocracy, -aeocracy; petticoat govern- ment, matriarchate, matriarchy.

[Vicarious authority] commission etc. 755; deputy etc. 759; permission etc. 760.

country, state, realm, commonwealth, canton,

constituency, toparchy, municipality, polity, body politic, *posse comitatus.*

person in authority etc. (*master*) 745; judicature etc. 965; cabinet etc. (*council*) 696; usurper; seat of -government, — authority; head-quarters.

[Acquisition of authority] accession; installation etc. 755; usurpation.

V. authorize etc. (*permit*) 760; warrant etc. (*right*) 924; dictate etc. (*order*) 741; have —, hold —, possess —, exercise —, exert —, wield- - authority etc. *n.*

be -at the head of etc. *adj.*; hold —, be in —, fill an- office; hold —, occupy- a post; be -master etc. 745.

rule, sway, command, control, administer; govern etc. (*direct*) 693; lead, preside over, reign; possess —, be seated on —, occupy- the throne; sway —, wield- the scepter; wear the crown.

have —, get- the -upper, — whip- hand; gain a hold upon, preponderate, dominate, boss, rule the roost; over-ride, -rule, -awe; lord it over, hold in hand, keep under, make a puppet of, lead by the nose, hold in the hollow of one's hand, turn round one's little finger, bend to one's will, hold one's own, wear the breeches; have -the ball at one's feet, — it all one's own way, — the game in one's own hand, — on the hip, — under one's thumb; be master of the situation; take the lead, play first fid- dle, set the fashion; give the law to; carry with a high hand; lay down the law; 'ride in the whirlwind and direct the storm;' rule with a rod of iron etc. (*severity*) 739.

ascend —, mount- the throne, take the reins, — into one's hand; assume -authority etc. *n.*, — the reins of government; take —, assume the- com- mand.

be -governed by, — in the power of; be under - the rule of, — the domination of.

Adj. ruling etc. *v.*; regnant, at the head, dominant, paramount, supreme, predominant, preponderant, in the ascendant, influential; guber- natorial; imperious; authoritative, executive, ad- ministrative, clothed with authority, official, *ex of- ficio,* ministerial, bureaucratic, departmental, im- perative, peremptory, overruling, absolute; hegemonic, -al; arbitrary; compulsory etc. 744; stringent.

regal, sovereign; royal, -ist; monarchical, kingly; imperial, -istic; princely; feudal; aristo-, auto-cratic; oligarchic etc. *n.*; democratic, republican, dynastic.

at one's command; in one's -power, — grasp; un- der control; authorized etc. (*due*) 924.

Adv. in the name of, by the authority of, *de par le Roi,* in virtue of; under the auspices of, in the hands of.

at one's pleasure; by a -dash, — stroke- of the pen; *ex mero motu; ex cathedrâ.*

Phr. the grey mare the better horse; 'every inch a king.'

738. Laxity. [Absence of authority.]—**N.** laxity; lax-, loose-, slack-ness; toleration etc. (*lenity*) 740; freedom etc. 748.

anarchy, interregnum; relaxation; loosening etc. *v.*; remission; dead letter, *brutum fulmen,* misrule; license, licentiousness; insubordination etc. (*disobedience*) 742; lynch law etc. (*illegality*) 964; nihilism.

[Deprivation of power.] dethronement, deposition, usurpation, abdication.

V. be -lax etc. *adj.*; *laisser -faire*, − *aller*; hold a loose rein; give -the reins to, − rope enough, − a loose to; tolerate; relax; misrule.

go beyond the length of one's tether; have one's -swing, − fling; act without -instructions, − authority; act on one's own responsibility, usurp authority.

dethrone, depose; abdicate.

Adj. lax, loose; slack; remiss etc. (*careless*) 460; weak.

relaxed; licensed; reinless, unbridled; anarchical; unauthorized etc. (*unwarranted*) 925.

739. Severity.—N. severity; strictness, formalism, harshness etc. *adj.*; rigor, stringency, austerity; inclemency etc. (*pitilessness*) 914a; arrogance etc. 885.

arbitrary power; absolut-, despot-ism; dictatorship, autocracy, tyranny, domineering, oppression; assumption, usurpation; inquisition, reign of terror, martial law; iron -heel, − rule, − hand, − sway; tight grasp; brute -force, − strength; coercion etc. 744; strong −, tight- hand.

hard -lines, − measure; tender mercies [ironical.]; sharp practice; bureaucracy, red tape; pipe-clay, officialism.

tyrant, disciplinarian, martinet, stickler, formalist, bashaw, despot, hard master, Draco, oppressor, inquisitor, extortioner, harpy, vulture, bird of prey.

V. be -severe etc. *adj.*

assume, usurp, arrogate, take liberties; domineer, bully etc. 885; tyrannize, inflict, wreak, stretch a point, put on the screw; be hard upon; bear −, lay a heavy hand on; be −, come- down upon; illtreat; deal-hardly with, − hard measure to; rule with a rod of iron, chastise with scorpions; dye with blood; oppress, override; trample −, tread- -down, − upon, − under foot; crush under an iron heel, ride roughshod over; rivet the yoke; hold −, keep a tight hand; force down the throat; coerce etc. 744; give no quarter etc. (*pitiless*) 914a.

Adj. severe; strict, hard, harsh, dour, rigid, stiff, stern, rigorous, uncompromising, exacting, exigent, *exigeant*, inexorable, inflexible, obdurate, austere, relentless, Spartan, Draconian, stringent, strait-laced, puritanical, prudish, searching, unsparing, ironhanded, hard-headed, peremptory, absolute, positive, arbitrary, imperative; coercive etc. 744; tyrannical, despotic, masterful, extortionate, grinding, withering, oppressive, inquisitorial; inclement etc. (*ruthless*) 914a; cruel etc. (*malevolent*) 907; haughty, arrogant etc. 885.

Adv. severely etc. *adj.*; with a -high, − strong, − tight, − heavy-hand.

at the point of the -sword, − bayonet.

Phr. *Delirant reges plectuntur Achivi.*

740. Leniency.—N. leni-ency, -ence, -ty; moderation etc. 174; toler-ance, -ation; mildness, gentleness; favor; indulgen-ce, -cy; clemency, mercy, forbearance, quarter; compassion etc. 914.

V. be -lenient etc. *adj.*; tolerate, bear with; *parcere subjectis*, give quarter.

indulge, allow one to have his own way, spoil.

Adj. lenient; mild, − as milk; gentle, soft; tolerant, indulgent, easy-going; clement etc. (*compassionate*) 914; forbearing; complaisant, longsuffering.

741. Command.—N. command, order, ordinance, act, *fiat*, bidding, *dictum*, hest, behest, call, beck, nod.

des-, dis-patch; message, direction, injunction, charge, instructions; appointment, fixture.

demand, exaction, imposition, requisition, claim, reclamation, revendication; *ultimatum* etc. (*terms*) 770; request etc. 765; requirement.

dictation; dict-, mand-ate; *caveat*, decree, decree -nisi, − absolute, *senatus consultum*; precept; pre-, re-script; writ, ordination, bull, edict, decretal, dispensation, prescription, brevet, placet, ukase, *firman*, hatti-sheriff, warrant, passport, *mittimus*, *mandamus*, summons, subpoena, *nisi prius*, interpellation, citation; word, − of command; *mot d'ordre*; bugle −, trumpet- call; beat of drum, tattoo; order of the day; enactment etc. (*law*) 963; *plébiscite* etc. (*choice*) 609.

V. command, order, decree, enact, ordain, dictate, direct, give orders.

prescribe, set, appoint, mark out; set −, prescribe −, impose- a task; set to work, put in requisition etc. 926.

bid, enjoin, charge, call upon, instruct; require, − at the hands of; exact, impose, tax, task; demand; insist on etc. (*compel*) 744.

claim, lay claim to, revendicate, reclaim.

cite, summon; call −, send- for; subpoena; beckon.

issue a command; make −, issue −, promulgate- -a requisition, − a decree, − an order etc. *n.*; give the -word of command, − word, − signal; call to order; give −, lay down- the law; assume the command etc. (*authority*) 737; remand.

be -ordered etc.; receive an order etc. *n.*

Adj. commanding etc. *v.*; authoritative etc. 737; decret-ory, -ive, -al; imperative, jussive, decisive, final.

Adv. in a commanding tone; by a -stroke, − dash- of the pen; by order, at beat of drum, on the first summons; at the word of command.

Phr. the decree is gone forth; *sic volo sic jubeo; le Roi le veut.*

742. Disobedience.—N. disobedience, insubordination, contumacy; infraction, -fringement; violation, non-compliance; non-observance etc. 773.

revolt, rebellion, mutiny, outbreak, rising, uprising, putsch, insurrection, *émeute*; riot, tumult etc. (*disorder*) 59; strike etc. (*resistance*) 719; barring out; defiance etc. 715.

mutinousness etc. *adj.*; mutineering; sedition, treason; high −, petty −, misprison of- treason; *premunire*; *lèse- majesté*; violation of law etc. 964; defection, secession, revolution, *sabotage*, bolshevism, *Sinn Fein.*

insurgent, mutineer, rebel, revolter, rioter, traitor, *carbonaro*, *sansculottes*, red republican, communist, Fenian, chartist, *frondeur*; seceder, runagate, brawler, anarchist, demagogue; suffragette; Spartacus, Masaniello, Wat Tyler, Jack Cade; bolshevist, bolshevik, maximalist, ringleader.

V. disobey, violate, infringe; shirk; set at defiance etc. (*defy*) 715; set authority at naught, run riot, fly in the face of, bolt, take the law into one's own hands; kick over the traces.

turn –, run- restive; champ the bit; strike etc. (*resist*) 719; rise, – in arms; secede; mutiny, rebel.

Adj. disobedient; uncompl-ying, -iant; unsubmissive; unruly, ungovernable; insubordinate, impatient of control; rest-iff, -ive; refractory, contumacious; recusant etc. (*refuse*) 764; recalcitrant; resisting etc. 719; lawless, mutinous, seditious, insurgent, riotous, revolutionary.

disobeyed, unobeyed; unbidden.

743. Obedience.—N. obedience; observance etc. 772; compliance; submission etc. 725; subjection etc. 749; non-resistance; passiveness, passivity, resignation.

allegiance, loyalty, fealty, homage, deference, devotion, fidelity, constancy.

submiss-ness, -iveness; ductility etc. (*softness*) 324; obsequiousness etc. (*servility*) 886.

V. be -obedient etc. *adj.*; obey, bear obedience to; submit etc. 725; comply, answer the helm, come at one's call; do -one's bidding, – what one is told, – suit and service; attend to orders, serve -devotedly, ∠, loyally, – faithfully.

follow, – the lead of, – to the world's end; serve etc. 746; play second fiddle.

Adj. obedient; compl-ying, -iant; law-abiding, loyal, faithful, leal, devoted; at one's -call, – command, – orders, – beck and call; under -beck and call, – control.

restrainable; resigned, passive; submissive etc. 725; henpecked; pliant etc. (*soft*) 324.

unresist-ed, -ing.

Adv. obediently etc. *adj.*; in compliance with, in obedience to.

Phr. to hear is to obey; as –, if- you please; at your service.

744. Compulsion.—N. compulsion, coercion, coaction, constraint, eminent domain, duress, enforcement, press, conscription.

force; brute –, main –, physical- force; the sword, *ultima ratio*; club –, mob –, lynch- law; *argumentum baculinum*, *le droit du plus fort*, martial law.

restraint etc. 751; necessity etc. 601; *force majeure*; Hobson's choice; the spur of necessity.

V. compel, force, make, drive, coerce, constrain, enforce, necessitate, oblige.

force upon, press; cram –, thrust –,. forcedown the throat; say it must be done, make a point of, insist upon, take no denial; put down, dragoon.

extort, wring from; put –, turn- on the screw; drag into; bind, – over; pin –, tie- down; require, tax, put in force; commandeer; restrain etc. 751.

Adj. compelling etc. *v.*; coercive, coactive; inexorable etc. 739; compuls-ory, -atory; obligatory, stringent, peremptory, binding.

forcible, not to be trifled with; irresistible etc. 601; compelled etc. *v.*; fain to.

Adv. by -force etc. *n.*, – force of arms; on compulsion, perforce; *vi et armis*, under the lash; at the point of the -sword, – bayonet; forcibly; by a strong arm.

under protest, in spite of one's teeth; against one's will etc. 603; *nolens volens* etc. (*of necessity*) 601; by stress of -circumstances, – weather; under press of; *de rigueur*.

745. Master.—N. master, *padrone*; lord, – paramount; command-er, -ant; captain; chief, -tain; *sahib*, sirdar, sachem, sheik, head, senior, governor, *duce*, ruler, dictator; leader etc. (*director*) 694.

lord of the ascendant; cock of the -walk, – roost; grey mare; mistress.

potentate; liege, – lord; suzerain, sovereign, monarch, autocrat, despot, tyrant, oligarch, overlord.

crowned head, emperor, king, anointed king, majesty, *imperator*, protector, president, stadtholder, judge.

caesar, kaiser, czar, sultan, grand Turk, caliph, imaum, shah, padishah, sophi, mogul, great mogul, khan, cham; lama, tycoon, mikado, inca, cazique; domn; vaivode; wai-, way-wode; landamman; seyyid, cacique.

prince, duke etc. (*nobility*) 875; arch-duke, doge, elector; scignior; mar-, land-grave; rajah, emir, nizam, nawab, negus.

empress, queen, sultana, czarina, princess, infanta, duchess, margravine, begum, maharani.

regent, viceroy, exarch, palatine, khedive, hospodar, beglerbeg, three-tailed bashaw, pasha, pashaw, bashaw, bey, beg, dey, scherif, tetrarch, satrap, mandarin, subhadar, nabob, maharajah; burgrave; laird etc. (*proprietor*) 779; High Commissioner.

the -authorities, – powers that be, – government; staff, *état major*, aga, official, man in office, person in authority.

[Naval authorities] admiral, -ty, – of the fleet; rear-, vice-, port-admiral; senior-, naval officer, S.N.O., commodore, captain, commander, lieutenant-commander, lieutenant, sub-lieutenant, midshipman, warrant –, petty- officer, leading seaman; skipper, mate, master.

[Military authorities] marshal, field-marshal, *maréchal*; general, -issimo; commander-in-chief, *seraskier*, *hetman*; lieutenant-, major-general; commandant; colonel, lieutenant-colonel, major, captain, centurion, skipper, lieutenant, second-lieutenant, officer, staff-officer, *aide de camp*, brigadier, brigade-major, adjutant, *jemidar*, ensign, cornet, cadet, subaltern, warrant officer, quartermaster, noncommissioned officer, N.C.O.; sergeant, -major; top-sergeant, color sergeant; corporal, -major; lance-, acting-corporal; drum major; shavetail.

[Air authorities] air -marshal, – commodore; group captain, squadron leader, wing commander, flight lieutenant, flying –, pilot- officer.

[Civil authorities] judge etc. 967; mayor, -alty; prefect, chancellor, archon, provost, magistrate, syndic; alcalde, alcaid; burgomaster, *corregidor*, seneschal, alderman, warden, constable, portreeve; lord mayor, sheriff; officer etc. (*executive*) 965.

746. Servant.—N. subject, liegeman; servant, retainer, follower, henchman, servitor, domestic, menial, help, lady help, *employé*, *attaché*; official.

retinue, suite, *cortège*, staff, court.

attendant, squire, usher, page, buttons, donzel, footboy; dog robber; train-, cup-bearer; waiter, busboy, tapster, butler, livery servant, lackey, foot-man, flunkey, valet, *valet de chambre*; boots; scout, gyp; equerry, groom; jockey, hostler, ostler, tiger, orderly, messenger, cad, gillie, caddie; *wallah*; journeyman, herdsman, swineherd.

bailiff, castellan, seneschal, chamberlain, *major-domo*, groom of the chambers.

secretary; under —, assistant- secretary; clerk; clerical staff, stenographer, subsidiary; agent etc. 758; subaltern; under-ling, -strapper; man.

maid, -servant, waitress; handmaid; *confidente*, lady's maid, abigail, *soubrette*; nurse, *bonne*, *ayah*; nurse-, nursery-, house-, parlor-, waiting-, chamber-, kitchen-, scullery-, between —, laundry —, dairy-maid; *femme —*, *fille- de chambre*; *camarista*; *chef de cuisine*, *cordon bleu*, cook, scullion, Cinderella; maid —, servant- of all work, tweeny, general servant, girl, slavey; laundress, bed-maker, goodie, char-woman etc. (*worker*) 690.

serf, vassal, slave, negro, helot; bondsman, -woman; bondslave; *âme damnée*, *odalisque*, ryot, *adscriptus glebae*; vill-ain, -ein; bead-, bede-sman; sizar; pension-er, -ary; client; dependant, -ent; hanger on, stooge, satellite; parasite etc. (*servility*) 886; led captain; *protégé*, ward, hireling, mercenary, puppet, creature.

badge of slavery; bonds etc. 752.

V. serve; minister to, wait —, attend —; dance attendance —, pin oneself- upon; squire, tend, hang on the sleeve of, char, do for; fag; valet.

Adj. in the train of; in one's -pay, — employ; at one's call etc. (*obedient*) 743; in bonds.

747. Scepter. [Insignia of authority.]—**N.** scepter, regalia, rod of empire, sword of state, mace, *fasces*, wand; staff, — of office; *bâton*, truncheon; flag etc. (*insignia*) 550; ensign —, emblem —, badge —, insignia- of authority, rank marks, brassard, badge, sash; cocked —, brass- hat.

epaulette, aiguilette, crown, star, eagle, bar, double bar, pip, stripe, chevron, curl, ring, anchor, shoulder-strap, tab.

throne, chair, musnud, divan, dais, woolsack.

toga, pall, mantle, robes of state, ermine, purple.

crown, coronet, diadem, tiara, triple crown, miter, crozier, cardinal's hat etc.; cap of maintenance; decoration; title etc. 877; portfolio.

key, signet, seals, talisman; helm; reins etc. (*means of restraint*) 752.

748. Freedom.—N. freedom, liberty, independence; license etc. (*permission*) 760; facility etc. 705.

scope, range, latitude, play; free —, full- -play, — scope; free stage and no favor; swing, full swing, elbow-room, margin, rope, wide berth; Liberty Hall.

franchise, denization; free —, freed-, liveryman; denizen.

autonomy, self-government, homerule, self-determination, liberalism, free trade; non-interference etc. 706.

immunity, exemption; emancipation etc. (*liberation*) 750; en-, af-franchisement; rights, privileges.

free land, freehold; allodium; frankalmoigne, mortmain.

independent, free-lance, -thinker, -trader.

V. be -free etc. *adj.*; have -scope etc. *n.*, — the run of, — one's own way, — a will of one's own, — one's fling; do what one -likes, — wishes, — pleases, — chooses; go at large, feel at home, paddle one's own canoe; stand on one's -legs, — rights; shift for oneself.

take a liberty; make -free with, — oneself quite at home; use a freedom; take -leave, — French leave.

set free etc. (*liberate*) 750; give the reins to etc. (*permit*) 760; allow —, give- scope etc. *n.* to; give a horse his head.

make free of; give the -freedom of, — franchise; en-, af-franchise.

laisser -faire, — *aller*; live and let live; leave to oneself; leave —, let- alone; mind one's own business.

Adj. free, — as air; out of harness, independent, at large, loose, scot free; left -alone, — to oneself.

in full swing; uncaught, unconstrained, unbuttoned, unconfined, unrestrained, unchecked, unprevented, unhindered, unobstructed, unbound, uncontrolled, untrammeled.

unsubject, ungoverned, unenslaved, unenthralled, unchained, unshackled, unfettered, unreined, unbridled, uncurbed, unmuzzled, unimpeded.

unrestricted, unlimited, unconditional; absolute; discretionary etc. (*optional*) 600.

unassailed, unforced, uncompelled.

unbiassed, unprejudiced, uninfluenced, spontaneous.

free and easy; at —, at one's- ease; *dégagé*, quite at home; wanton, rampant, irrepressible, unvanquished.

exempt; freed etc. 750; freeborn; autonomous, freehold, allodial; *gratis* etc. 815.

unclaimed, going a begging.

Adv. freely etc. *adj.*; ad libitum etc. (*at will*) 600.

749. Subjection.—N. subjection; depend-ence, -ance, -ency; subordination; thrall, thraldom, enthralment, subjugation, bondage, serfdom; feudal--ism, -ity; vassalage, villenage; slavery, enslavement, involuntary servitude.

service; servi-tude, -torship; tendence, employ, tutelage, clientship; liability etc. 177; constraint etc. 751; oppression etc. (*severity*) 739; yoke etc. (*means of restraint*) submission etc. 725; obedience etc. 743.

V. be -subject etc. *adj.*; be —, lie- at the mercy of; depend —, lean —, hang- upon; fall -a prey to, — under; play second fiddle.

be a -mere machine, — puppet, — football; not dare to say one's soul is his own; drag a chain.

serve etc. 746; obey etc. 743; submit etc. 725.

break in, tame; subject, subjugate; master etc. 731; tread -down, — under foot; weigh down; drag at one's chariot wheels; reduce to -subjection, —

slavery; en-, in-, be-thral; enslave, lead captive; take into custody etc. (*restrain*) 751; rule etc. 737; drive into a corner, hold at the sword's point; keep under; hold in -bondage, – leading strings, – swaddling clothes.

Adj. subject, dependent, subordinate; feud-al, -atory; in subjection to, under control; in -leading strings, – harness; subjected, enslaved etc. *v.*; con-strained etc. 751; subservient, servile, fawning, slavish, obsequious, cringing; down-trodden; over-borne, -whelmed; under the lash, on the hip, led by the nose, henpecked; the -puppet, – sport, – plaything- of; under one's -orders, – command, – thumb; like dirt under one's feet; a slave to; at the mercy of; in the -power, – hands, – clutches- of; at the feet of; at one's beck and call etc. (*obedient*) 743; liable etc. 177; parasitical; stipendiary.

Adv. under.

750. Liberation.—N. liberation, disengagement, release, disenthrallment, enlargement, emancipation; af-, en-franchisement; manumission; discharge, dismissal.

deliverance etc. 672; redemption, extrication, acquittance, absolution; acquittal etc. 970; escape etc. 671.

V. liberate, free; set -free, – clear, – at liberty; render free, emancipate, release; en-, af-franchise; manumit; enlarge; dis-band, -charge, -miss, – enthral; let -go, – loose, – out, – slip; cast –, turn- adrift; deliver etc. 672; absolve etc (*acquit*) 970; reprieve.

unfetter etc. 751; untie etc. 44; loose etc. (*disjoin*) 44; loosen, relax; un-bolt, -bar, -close, -cork, -clog, -hand, -bind, -latch, -chain, -harness; dis-engage, -entangle; clear, extricate, unloose.

gain –, obtain –, acquire- one's -liberty etc. 748; get -rid, – clear- of; deliver oneself from; shake off the yoke, slip the collar; break -loose, – prison; tear asunder one's bonds, cast off trammels; escape etc. 671.

Adj. at -liberty, – large, free, liberated etc. *v.*; out of harness etc. 748; adrift.

Int. unhand me! let me go!

751. Restraint.—N. restraint; hindrance etc. 706; coercion etc. (*compulsion*) 744; cohibition, constraint, repression; discipline, control, self-restraint etc. 604.

confinement; durance, duress; im-, prisonment; incarceration, coarctation, entombment, man-cipation, durance vile, thrall, -dom, limbo, cap-tivity; blockade; quarantine; detention.

arrest, -ation; custody, keep, care, charge, ward, restringency.

curb etc. (*means of restraint*) 752; *lettres de cachet.*

limitation, restriction, protection, monopoly; prohibition etc. 761; economic pressure.

prisoner etc. 754.

V. restrain, check; put –, lay- under restraint; en-, in-, be-thral; restrict; debar etc. (*hinder*) 706; constrain; coerce etc. (*compel*) 744; curb, control; hold –, keep- -back, – from, – in, – in check, – within bounds; hold in -leash, – leading strings; withhold.

keep under; repress, suppress; smother; pull in, rein in; hold, – fast; keep a tight hand on; prohibit etc. 761; in-, co-hibit.

enchain; fasten etc. (*join*) 43; fetter, shackle; en-, trammel; bridle, muzzle, gag, pinion, manacle, handcuff, tie one's hands, hobble, bind hand and foot; swathe, swaddle; pin –, peg- down; tether, picket; tie, – up, – down; secure; forge fetters.

confine; shut –, clap –, lock –, box –, mew –, bottle –, cork –, seal –, button- up; shut –, hem –, bolt –, wall –, rail- in; impound, pen, coop; enclose etc. (*circumscribe*) 229; cage; in-, en-cage; close the door upon, cloister; imprison, immure; incarcerate, entomb; clap –, lay- under hatches; put in -irons, – a strait waistcoat; throw –, cast- into prison; put into bilboes.

arrest; take -up, – charge of, – into custody; take –, make- -prisoner, – captive; captivate; lead -captive, – into captivity; send –, commit- to prison; commit; give in -charge, – custody; subjugate etc. 749.

Adj. re-, con-strained; imprisoned etc. *v.*; pent up; jammed in, wedged in; under -restraint, – lock and key, – hatches; serving –, doing- time; in swaddling clothes; on *parole*; in custody etc. (*prisoner*) 754; cohibitive; coactive etc. (*compulsory*) 744.

stiff, restringent, straitlaced, hide-bound.

ice-, wind-, weather-bound; 'cabined, cribbed, confined;' in Lob's pound, laid by the heels.

Adv. in captivity, under arrest, behind the bars, in -prison, – jail, – durance vile.

752. Prison. [Means of restraint.]**—N.** prison, -house; jail, gaol, cage, coöp, den, death house, condemned –, cell; stronghold, fortress, keep, donjon, dungeon, *Bastille, oubliette,* bridewell, house of correction, hulks, tool-booth, panopticon, penitentiary, guard-room, clink, can, stir, tronk, jug, lock-up, hold; round –, watch –, station –, sponging-house; station; house of detention, black hole, pen, fold, pound; enclosure etc. 232; penal settlement; chain gang; debtors' prison; reform-atory; federal penitentiary, state prison; criminal lunatic asylum; bilboes, stocks, limbo, quod.

Dartmoor, Newgate, Fleet, Marshalsea; King's (*or* Queen's) Bench; Sing Sing, Dannemora.

bond; strap, bandage, splint, tourniquet; irons, pinion, gyve, fetter, shackle, trammel, manacle, handcuff, bracelets, darbies, strait waistcoat, strait-jacket.

yoke, collar, halter, harness; muzzle, gag, bit, brake, curb, snaffle, bridle; rein, -s; ribbons, lines, bearing-rein; martingale, leading string; tether, picket, band, guy, chain; cord etc. (*fastening*) 45.

bolt, bar, lock, padlock, rail, wall; paling, palisade; fence; barrier, barricade.

brake, drag etc. (*hindrance*) 706.

753. Keeper.—N. keeper, custodian, *custos,* ranger, warder, jailer, gaoler, turnkey, castellan, guard; watch, -dog, -man; Charley; sen-try, -tinel; watch and ward; *concierge,* coast-guard, *guarda costa,* gamekeeper.

escort, body guard, convoy.

protector, governor, duenna; guardian; gover-ness etc. (*teacher*) 540; nurse, *bonne, ayah, amah.*

754. Prisoner.—N. prisoner, captive, *détenu*, close prisoner.

jail-bird, ticket-of-leave man.

V. stand committed; be -imprisoned etc. 751.

Adj. imprisoned etc. 751; in -prison, – quod, – durance vile, – limbo, – custody, – charge, – chains; under -lock and key, – hatches; on *parole*; detained at his Majesty's pleasure.

755. Commission. [Vicarious authority.]—**N.** commission, delegation; con-, as-signment; procuration; deputation, legation, mission, embassy; agency, agentship; power of attorney, proxy; clerkship.

errand, charge, *brevet*, diploma, *exequatur*, permit etc. (*permission*) 760.

appointment, nomination, return; charter; ordination; installation, inauguration, investiture; accession, coronation, enthronement.

vicegerency; regency, regentship.

viceroy etc. 745; consignee etc. 758; deputy etc. 759.

V. commission, delegate, depute; consign, assign; charge; in-, en-trust; turn over to; commit, – to the hands of; authorize etc. (*permit*) 760.

put in commission, accredit, engage, hire, bespeak, appoint, name, nominate, return, ordain; install, induct, inaugurate, invest, crown; en-roll, -list.

employ, empower; give power of attorney to; set –, place- over; send out.

be commissioned, be accredited; represent, stand for; stand in the -stead, – place, – shoes- of.

Adj. commissioned etc. *v.*

Adv. per procuratione.

756. Abrogation.—N. abrogation, annulment, nullification; cancelling etc. *v.*; cancel; revo-cation, -kement; repeal, rescission, defeasance.

dismissal, *congé*, demission; depos-al, -ition; sack, dethronement; disestablish-, disendow-ment; deconsecration.

aboli-tion, -shment; dissolution.

counter-order, -mand; repudiation, retractation; recantation etc. (*tergiversation*) 607.

V. abrogate, annul, cancel; destroy etc. 162; abolish; revoke, repeal, rescind, reverse, retract, recall; over-rule, -ride; set aside; disannul, dissolve, quash, nullify, declare null and void; dis-establish, -endow; deconsecrate.

disclaim etc. (*deny*) 536; ignore, repudiate; recant etc. 607; divest oneself, break off.

counter-mand, -order; do away with; sweep –, brush- away; throw -overboard, – to the dogs; scatter to the winds, cast behind.

dismiss, discard; cast –, turn- -off, – out, – adrift, – out of doors, – aside, – away; send -off, – away, – about one's business; discharge, get rid of, fire out, fire etc. (*eject*) 297; jilt.

cashier; break; oust; set down, unseat, -saddle; un-, de-, disen-throne; depose, uncrown; unfrock, strike off the roll; dis-bar, -bench.

be -abrogated etc.; receive its quietus.

Adj. abrogated etc. *v.*; *functus officio*.

Int. get along with you! begone! go about your business! away with!

757. Resignation.—N. resignation, retirement, abdication, renunciation, abjuration, disclaimer, abandonment, relinquishment.

V. resign; give –, throw- up; lay down, throw up the cards, wash one's hands of, abjure, renounce, forego, disclaim, abandon, relinquish, retract, demit; deny etc. 536.

abrogate etc. 756; desert etc. (*relinquish*) 624; get rid of etc. 782.

abdicate; vacate, – one's seat; accept the stewardship of the Chiltern Hundreds; retire; tender –, send in –, hand in- one's resignation.

Adj. abdicant, renunciatory etc. *v.*

Phr. 'Othello's occupation's gone.'

758. Consignee.—N. consignee, trustee, nominee, committee.

delegate; commiss-ary, -ioner; emissary, envoy, commissionaire; messenger etc. 534.

diplomatist, diplomat, *corps diplomatique*, embassy; am-, em-bassador; representative, resident, consul, legate, nuncio, internuncio, *chargé d' affaires, attaché*.

vicegerent etc. (*deputy*) 759; plenipotentiary.

functionary, placeman, curator; treasurer etc. 801; agent, factor, bailiff, steward, clerk, secretary, attorney, solicitor, proctor, broker, underwriter, commission agent, auctioneer, one's man of business; factotum etc. (*director*) 694; caretaker.

negotiator, go between; middleman; under agent, *employé*; servant etc. 746.

salesman; commercial, – traveler; bagman, *commis-voyageur*, touter.

newspaper –, own –, war –, special-correspondent; reporter.

759. Deputy.—N. deputy, substitute, vice, proxy, *locum tenens*, delegate, representative, next friend, surrogate, secondary.

regent, vicegerent, vizier, minister, vicar; premier etc. (*director*) 694; chancellor, prefect, provost, warden, lieutenant, archon, consul, proconsul; viceroy etc. (*governor*) 745; commissioner etc. 758; plenipotentiary, *alter ego*.

team, eight, eleven; champion.

V. be -deputy etc. *n.*; stand –, appear –, hold a brief –, answer- for; represent; stand –, walk- in the shoes of; stand in the stead of.

substitute, ablegate, accredit; commission, empower, delegate etc. 755.

Adj. acting; vice, -regal; accredited to.

Adv. in behalf of, by proxy.

760. Permission.—N. permission, leave; allow-, suffer-ance; toler-ance, -ation; liberty, law, license, concession, grace; indulgence etc. (*lenity*) 740; favor, dispensation, exemption, release; connivance; vouchsafement.

authorization, warranty, accordance, admission.

permit, warrant, *brevet*, precept, sanction, authority, *firman*; pass, -port; furlough, license, *carte blanche*, ticket of leave; grant, charter, patent.

V. permit; give -permission etc. *n.*, – power;

let, allow, admit; suffer, bear with, tolerate, recognize; concede etc. 762; accord, vóuchsafe, favor, humor, gratify, indulge, stretch a point; wink at, connive at; shut one's eyes to.

grant, empower, charter, enfranchise, privilege, confer a privilege, license, authorize, warrant; sanction; entrust etc. (*commission*) 755.

give -*carte blanche*, – the reins to, – scope to etc. (*freedom*) 748; leave -alone, – it to one, – the door open; open the -door to, – floodgates; give a loose to.

let off; absolve etc. (*acquit*) 970; release, exonerate, dispense with.

ask –, beg –, request- -leave, – permission.

Adj. permitting etc. *v.*; permissive, indulgent; permitted etc. *v.*; patent, chartered, permissible, allowable, lawful, legitimate, legal; legalized etc. (*law*) 963; licit; unforbid,' -den; unconditional.

Adv. permissibly; by –, with –, on- -leave etc. *n.*; *speciali gratiā*; under favor of; *pace*; *ad libitum* etc. (*freely*) 748, (*at will*) 600; by all means etc. (*willingly*) 602; yes etc. (*assent*) 488.

761. Prohibition.—N. pro-, in-hibition; *veto*, disallowance; interdict, -ion; injunction; embargo, ban, *verboten*, taboo, proscription; *index expurgatorius*; restriction etc. (*restraint*) 751; hindrance etc. 706; forbidden fruit.

V. pro-, in-hibit; forbid, put one's *veto* upon, disallow; bar; debar etc. (*hinder*) 706, forefend.

keep -in, – within bounds; restrain etc. 751; cohibit, withhold, limit, circumscribe, clip the wings of, restrict, narrow; interdict, taboo; put –, place- under -an interdiction, – the ban; proscribe, censor; exclude, shut out; shut –, bolt –, show- the door; warn off; dash the cup from one's lips; forbid the banns.

Adj. prohibit-ive, -ory; interdictive; proscriptive; restrictive, exclusive; forbidding etc. *v.*

prohibited etc. *v.*; not -permitted etc. 760; unlicensed, contraband, under the ban of; illegal etc. 964; unauthorized, not to be thought of.

Adv. on no account etc. (*no*) 536.

Int. forbid it heaven! etc. (*deprecation*) 766. hands –, keep- off! hold! stop! avast!

Phr. that will never do.

762. Consent.—N. consent; assent etc. 488; acquiescence; approval etc. 931; compliance, agreement, concession; yield-ance, -ingness; accession, acknowledgment, acceptance, agnition.

settlement, ratification, confirmation, adjustment.

permit etc. (*permission*) 760; promise etc. 768.

V. consent; assent etc. 488; yield assent, admit, allow, concede, grant, yield; come -over, – round; give in to, acknowledge, agnize, give consent, comply with, acquiesce, agree to, fall in with, accede, accept, embrace an offer, close with, take at one's word, have no objection.

satisfy, meet one's wishes, settle, come to terms etc. 488; not -refuse etc. 764; turn a willing ear etc. (*willingness*) 602; jump at; deign, vouchsafe; promise etc. 768.

Adj. consenting etc. *v.*; agreeable, compliant; agreed etc. (*assent*) 488; unconditional.

Adv. yes etc. (*assent*) 488; by all means etc. (*willingly*) 602; if –, as- you please; be it so, so be it, well and good, of course.

763. Offer.—N. offer, proffer, presentation, tender, bid, overture; propos-al, -ition; motion, invitation; candidature; offering etc. (*gift*) 784.

V. offer, proffer, present, tender; bid; propose, move; make -a motion, – advances; start; invite, hold out, place- at one's disposal, – in one's way, put forward.

hawk about; offer for sale etc. 796; press etc. (*request*) 765; lay at one's feet.

offer –, present- oneself; volunteer, come forward, be a candidate; stand –, bid- for; seek; be at one's service; go a begging; bribe etc. (*give*) 784.

Adj. offer-ing, -ed etc. *v.*; in the market, for sale, to let, disengaged, on hire.

764. Refusal.—N. refusal, rejection; non-, incompliance; denial; declining etc. *v.*; declension; peremptory –, flat –, point blank- refusal; repulse, rebuff; discountenance.

recusancy, renunciation, abnegation, negation, protest, disclaimer; dissent etc. 489; revocation etc. 756.

V. refuse, reject, deny, decline; nill, negative; refuse –, withhold- one's assent; shake the head; close the -hand, – purse; grudge, begrudge, be slow to, hang fire.

be deaf to; turn -a deaf ear to, – one's back upon; set one's face against, discountenance, not hear of, have nothing to do with, wash one's hands of, stand aloof, forswear, set aside, cast behind one; not yield an inch etc. (*obstinacy*) 606.

resist, cross; not -grant etc. 762; repel, repulse; shut –, slam- the door in one's face; rebuff; send -back, – to the right about, – away with a flea in the ear; deny oneself, not be at home to; discard etc. (*repudiate*) 610; rescind etc. (*revoke*) 756; disclaim, protest; dissent etc. 489.

Adj. refusing etc. *v.*; rest-ive, -iff; recusant; uncomplying, noncompliant, unconsenting, uncomplaisant, protestant; not willing to hear of, deaf to.

refused etc. *v.*; ungranted, out of the question, not to be thought of, impossible.

Adv. no etc. 536; on no account, not for the world; no thank you.

Phr. *non possumus*; [ironically] your humble servant; *bien obligé*.

765. Request.—N. requ-est, -isition; claim etc. (*demand*) 741; petition, suit, prayer; begging letter, round-robin.

motion, overture, application, canvass, address, appeal, apostrophe; imprecation; rogation; proposal, proposition.

orison etc. (*worship*) 990; incantation etc. (*spell*) 993.

mendicancy; asking, panhandling, begging etc. *v.*; postulation, solicitation, invitation, entreaty, importunity, supplication, instance, impetration, imploration, obsecration, obtestation, invocation, interpellation.

V. request, ask; beg, crave, sue, pray, petition, solicit, invite, pop the question, make bold to ask; beg -leave, – a boon; apply to, call to, put to; call -upon, – for; make –, address –, prefer –, put up- a -request, – prayer, – petition; make - application, – a requisition; ask –, trouble- one for; claim etc. (*demand*) 741; offer up prayers etc. (*worship*) 990; whistle for.

beg hard, entreat, beseech, plead, supplicate, implore, apostrophize; conjure, adjure; obtest; cry to, kneel to, appeal to; invoke, evoke; impetrate, imprecate, ply, press, urge, beset, importune, dun, tax, clamor for; cry -aloud, – for help; fall on one's knees; throw oneself at the feet of; come down on one's marrow-bones.

beg from door to door, send the hat round, go a begging; mendicate, mump, cadge, panhandle, beg one's bread.

dance attendance on, besiege, knock at the door.

bespeak, canvass, tout, make interest, court; seek, bid for etc. (*offer*) 763; publish the banns.

Adj. requesting etc. *v.*; precatory; suppli-ant, -cant, -catory; invoc-, imprec-, rog-atory; postulant, mendicant.

importunate, clamorous, urgent; solicitous; cap in hand; on one's -knees, – bended knees, – marrow-bones.

Adv. prithee, do, please, pray; be so good as, be good enough; have the goodness, vouchsafe, will you, I pray thee, if you please.

Int. for -God's, – heaven's, – goodness', – mercy's- sake.

766. Deprecation. [Negative request.]—**N.** deprecation, expostulation; remonstrance; intercession, mediation.

V. deprecate, protest, expostulate, enter a protest, intercede for.

Adj. deprecatory, expostulatory, intercessory, mediatorial.

deprecated, protested.

un-, unbe-sought; unasked etc. (*see* ask etc. 765).

Int. cry you mercy! God forbid! forbid it Heaven! Heaven -forefend, – forbid! far be it from! hands off! etc. (*prohibition*) 761.

767. Petitioner.—**N.** petitioner, solicitor, applicant; suppli-ant, -cant; suitor, candidate, claimant, postulant, aspirant, competitor, bidder; place –, pot- hunter; prizer.

beggar, mendicant, mumper, sturdy beggar, cadger, panhandler.

canvasser, barker, touter etc. 768.

sycophant, parasite etc. 886.

768. Promise.—**N.** promise, undertaking, word, troth, plight, pledge, *parole*, word of honor, vow; oath etc. (*affirmation*) 535; profession, assurance, warranty, guarantee, insurance, obligation; contract etc. 769.

engagement, pre-engagement; affiance; betroth, -al, -ment; marriage -compact, – vow.

V. promise; give a -promise etc. *n.*; undertake, engage; make –, form- an engagement; enter -into, – on- an engagement; bind –, tie –, pledge –, commit –, take upon- oneself; vow; swear etc. (*affirm*) 535; give –, pass –, pledge –, plight-one's -word, – honor, – credit, – troth; betroth, plight faith; take the vows.

assure, warrant, guarantee, vouch for, avouch, covenant etc. 769; attest etc. (*bear witness*) 467.

hold out an expectation; contract an obligation; become -bound to, – sponsor for; answer –, be answerable- for; secure; give security etc. 771; underwrite.

adjure, administer an oath, put to one's oath, swear a witness.

Adj. promising etc. *v.*; promissory; votive; under hand and seal; upon -oath, – affirmation.

promised etc. *v.*; affianced, pledged, bound; committed, compromised; in for it.

Adv. as one's head shall answer for; upon my honor.

Phr. in for a penny, in for a pound.

768a. Release from engagement.—**N.** release etc. (*liberation*) 750.

Adj. absolute; unconditional etc. (*free*) 748.

769. Compact.—**N.** compact, contract, agreement, bargain, deal, transaction; affidation; pact, -ion; bond, covenant, indenture.

stipulation, settlement, convention; compromise, *cartel*.

protocol, treaty, *concordat*, *Zollverein*, *Sonderbund*, charter, *Magna Charta*, Pragmatic Sanction.

negotiation etc. (*bargaining*) 794; diplomacy etc. (*mediation*) 724; negotiator etc. (*agent*) 758.

ratification, completion, signature, seal, sigil, signet.

V. contract, covenant, agree for, engage etc. (*promise*) 768.

treat, negotiate, stipulate, make terms; bargain etc. (*barter*) 794.

make –, strike- a bargain; come to -terms, – an understanding; compromise etc. 774; seat at rest; close, – with; conclude, complete, settle; confirm, ratify, clench, subscribe, underwrite; en-, in-dorse; put the seal to; sign, seal etc. (*attest*) 467; indent.

take one at one's word, bargain by inch of candle.

Adj. contractual, agreed etc. *v.*; conventional; under hand and seal; signed, sealed and delivered.

Phr. *caveat emptor.*

770. Conditions.—**N.** conditions, terms; articles, – of agreement.

clauses, provisions; proviso etc. (*qualification*) 469; covenant, stipulation, obligation, *ultimatum*, *sine quâ non*; *casus foederis*.

V. make –, come to- -terms etc. (*contract*) 769; make it a condition, stipulate, insist upon, make a point of; bind, tie up.

Adj. conditional, provisional, guarded, fenced, hedged in.

Adv. conditionally etc. (*with qualification*) 469; provisionally, *pro re natâ*; on condition; with a reservation.

771. Security.—N. security; guaran-ty, -tee; gage, waranty, bond, tie, pledge, plight, mortgage, debenture, hypothecation, bill of sale, lien, pignus, pawn, pignoration; real security; bottomry; collateral, vadium.

stake, deposit, earnest, handsel, caution.

promissory note; bill, − of exchange; I.O.U.: personal security, covenant, specialty; *parole* etc. (*promise*) 768.

acceptance, indorsement, signature, execution, stamp, seal.

spon-sor, -sion, -sorship; surety, bail; mainpernor, hostage.

recognizance; deed −, covenant- of indemnity.

authentication, verfication, warrant, certificate, voucher, docket, doquet; record etc. 551; probate, attested copy.

receipt; ac-, quittance; discharge, release.

muniment, title-deed, instrument; deed, − poll; assurance, insurance, indenture; charter etc. (*compact*) 769; charter-poll; paper, parchment, settlement, will, testament, last will and testament, codicil.

V. give -security, − bail, − substantial bail; go bail; pawn, impawn, hock, spout, mortgage, hypothecate, impignorate.

guarantee, warrant, assure; accept, indorse, underwrite, insure.

execute, stamp; sign, seal etc. (*evidence*) 467.

let, set; grant −, take −, hold- a lease; hold in pledge; lend on security etc. 787.

Adj. secure, -ed; pledged etc. *v.*; in pawn, on deposit.

772. Observance.—N. observance, performance, compliance; obedience, etc. 743; fulfilment, satisfaction, discharge; acquit-tance, - tal.

adhesion, acknowledgment; fidelity etc. (*probity*) 939; exact etc. 494- observance.

V. observe, comply with, respect, acknowledge, abide by; cling to, adhere to, be faithful to, act up to; meet, fulfil, carry -out, − into execution; execute, perform, keep, satisfy, discharge; do one's office.

perform −, fulfill −, discharge −, acquit oneself of- an obligation; make good; make good −, keep- one's -word, − promise; redeem one's pledge; keep faith with, stand to one's engagement.

Adj. observant, faithful, true, loyal; honorable etc. 939; true as the -dial to the sun, − needle to the pole; punct-ual, -ilious; meticulous; literal etc. (*exact*) 494; as good as one's word.

Adv. faithfully etc. *adj.*

773. Non-observance.—N. non-observance etc. 772; evasion, inobservance, failure, omission, neglect, laches, laxity, informality.

infringement, infraction; violation, transgression.

retractation, repudiation, nullification; protest; forfeiture.

lawlessness; disobedience etc. 742; bad faith etc. 940.

V. fail, neglect, omit, elude, evade, give the go by to, cut, set aside, ignore; shut −, close- one's eyes to, avoid.

infringe, transgress, pirate, violate, break, trample under foot, do violence to, drive a coach and six through.

discard, protest, repudiate, fling to the winds, set at naught, nullify, declare null and void; cancel etc. (*wipe off*) 552.

retract, go back from, be off, forfeit, go from one's word, palter; stretch −, strain- a point.

Adj. violating etc. *v.*; lawless, transgressive; elusive, evasive; lax, casual; non-observant.

unfulfilled etc. (*see* fulfil etc. 772).

774. Compromise.—N. com-promise, - mutation, -position; middle term, *mezzo termine*; compensation etc. 30; adjustment, mutual concession.

V. com-promise, -mute, -pound; take the mean; split the difference, meet one half way, give and take; come to terms etc. (*contract*) 769; submit to −, abide by- arbitration; patch up, bridge over, fix up, arrange; adjust, − differences; agree; make -the best of, − a virtue of necessity; take the will for the deed.

775. Acquisition.—N. acquisition; gaining etc. *v.*; obtainment; procur-ation, -ement; purchase, descent, inheritance; gift etc. 784.

recovery, retrieval, revendication, replevin; redemption, salvage, trover; find, *trouvaille*, foundling.

gain, thrift; money-making, -grubbing; lucre, filthy lucre, loaves and fishes, the main chance, pelf; emolument etc. 973; wealth etc. 803.

profit, earnings, winnings, innings, clean-up, pickings, perquisite, net profit; income etc. (*receipt*) 810; pro-ceeds, -duce, -duct; out-come, - put; return, fruit, crop, harvest, tilth; second crop, aftermath; benefit etc. (*good*) 618.

sweepstakes, trick, prize, pool.

[Fraudulent acquisition] subreption; theft, stealing etc. 791.

V. acquire, get, gain, win, earn, obtain, procure, gather, annex; collect etc. 72; pick, − up; glean, take etc. 789.

find; come −, pitch −, light- upon; scrape -up, − together; get in, reap and carry, net, bag, sack, bring home, secure, come across, derive, draw, get in the harvest.

profit; make −, draw- profit; turn to -profit, − account; make -capital out of, − money by; obtain a return, reap the fruits of; reap − , gain- an advantage; turn -a penny, − an honest penny; make the pot boil, bring grist to the mill; make −, coin −, raise- money; raise -funds, − the wind; fill one's pocket etc. (*wealth*) 803.

treasure up etc. (*store*) 636; realize, clear; produce etc. 161; take etc. 789.

get back, recover, regain, retrieve, revendicate, replevy, redeem, come by one's own.

come -by, – in for; receive etc. 785; inherit; step into, – a fortune, – the shoes of; succeed to.

get -hold of, – between one's finger and thumb, – into one's hand, – at; take – , come into – , enter into- possession.

be -profitable etc. *adj.*; pay, answer.

accrue etc. (*be received*) 785.

Adj. acquir-ing, -ed etc. *v.*; acquisitive; productive, profitable, advantageous, gainful, remunerative, paying, lucrative.

776. Loss.—N. loss; de-, perdition; forfeiture, lapse.

privation, bereavement; deprivation etc. (*dispossession*) 789; riddance.

V. lose; incur – , experience – , meet with- a loss; miss; mislay, let slip, allow to slip through the fingers, squander; be without etc. (*exempt*) 777a; forfeit.

get rid of etc. 782; waste etc. 638.

be lost, lapse.

Adj. losing etc. *v.*; not having etc. 777a.

shorn of, deprived of; denuded, bereaved, bereft, *minus*, cut off; dispossessed etc. 789; rid of, quit of; out of pocket.

lost etc. *v.*; long lost; irretrievable etc. (*hopeless*) 859; irredentist; off one's hands.

Int. farewell to! adieu to! good riddance! -

777. Possession.—N. possession, seisin; ownership etc. 780; occupancy; hold, -ing; tenure, tenancy, feodality, dependency; villenage; socage, chivalry, knight service.

exclusive possession, impropriation, monopoly, corner; retention etc. 781; pre-possession, - occupancy; nine points of the law.

future possession, heritage, inheritance, heirship, reversion, fee, seigniority, feud, fief.

bird in hand, *uti possidetis*, *chose* in possession.

V. possess, have, hold, occupy, enjoy; be - possessed of etc. *adj.*; have -in hand etc. *adj.*; own etc. 780; command.

inherit; come -to, – in for.

engross, monopolize, forestall, regrate, impropriate, have all to oneself, corner; have a firm hold of etc. (*retain*) 781; get into one's hand etc. (*acquire*) 775.

belong to, appertain to, pertain to; be -in one's possession etc. *adj.*; vest in.

Adj. possessing etc. *v.*; worth; possessed of, seized of, master of, in possession of; endowed – , blest – , instinct – , fraught – , laden – , charged – , instilled – , with.

possessed etc. *v.*; on hand, by one; in hand, in store, in stock; in one's -hands, – grasp, – possession; at one's -command, – disposal; one's own etc. (*property*) 780.

unsold, unshared.

777a. Exemption.—N. exemption; exception, immunity, privilege, release etc. 927a; absence etc. 187.

V. not -have etc. 777; be -without etc. *adj.*

Adj. exempt from, devoid of, without, unpossessed of, unblest with, immune from.

not -having etc. 777; unpossessed; untenanted etc. (*vacant*) 187; without an owner.

unobtained, unacquired.

778. Participation. [Joint possession.]—**N.** participation; co-, joint-tenancy; possession – , tenancy- in common; joint – , common- stock; co-, partnership; communion; community of - possessions, – goods; communalism, communism, socialism, collectivism; co-operation etc. 709; profit sharing.

snacks, co-portion, picnic, hotchpotch; co-heirship, -parceny, -parcenary; gavelkind.

participator, sharer; co-, partner; shareholder; co-, joint-tenant; tenants in common; co-heir, -parcener.

communist, socialist.

V. par-ticipate, -take; share, – in; come in for a share; go -shares, – snacks, – halves; share and share alike.

have – , possess – , be seized- -in common, – as joint tenants etc. *n.*

join in; have a hand in etc. (*co-operate*) 709.

Adj. partaking etc. *v.*; communistic, socialistic, co-operative, profit sharing.

Adv. share and share alike.

779. Possessor.—N. possessor, holder; occupant, -ier; tenant; person – , man- -in possession etc. 777; renter, lodger, lessee, under-lessee; zemindar, ryot; tenant -on sufferance, – at will, – from year to year, – for years, – for life.

owner; propriet-or, -ress, -ary; impropriator, master, mistress, lord.

land-holder, -owner, -lord, -lady; lord -of the manor, – paramount; heritor, laird, vavasor, landed gentry, mesne lord.

cestui-que-trust,. beneficiary, mortgagor.

grantee, feoffee, relessee, devisee; legat-ee, -ary.

trustee; holder etc.- of the legal estate; mortgagee.

right – , rightful- owner.

[Future possessor] heir, – apparent; – presumptive; heiress; inherit-or, -ress, -rix; reversioner, remainder-man.

780. Property.—N. property, possession, *suum cuique, meum et tuum*.

owner-, proprietor, lord-ship; seignority; empire etc. (*dominion*) 737.

interest, stake, estate, right, title, claim, demand, holding; tenure etc. (*possession*) 777; vested – , contingent – , beneficial – , equitable- interest; use, trust, benefit; legal – , equitable- estate; seisin.

absolute interest, paramount estate, freehold; fee, – simple, – tail; estate -in fee, – in tail, – tail; estate in tail -male, – female, – general.

limitation, term, lease, settlement, strict settlement, particular estate; estate -for life, – for years, – *pur autre vie*; remainder, reversion, expectancy, possibility.

dower, dowry, *dot*, jointure, marriage portion, appanage, inheritance, heritage, patrimony, alimony; legacy etc. (*gift*) 784.

assets, belongings, means, resources, circumstances; wealth etc. 803; money etc. 800; what one -is worth, — will cut up for; estate and effects.

landed —, real- -estate, — property; realty; land, -s; subdivision; plot, site; tenements; hereditaments; corporeal —, incorporeal- hereditaments; acres; ground etc. (*earth*) 342; acquest; messuage.

territory, state, kingdom, principality, realm, empire, protectorate, margravate, dependancy, colony, sphere of influence, mandate.

manor, honor, domain, demesne; farm, ranch, plantation, *hacienda*; allodium etc. (*free*) 748; fieff, feoff, feud, zemindary, dependency.

free-, copy-, lease-holds; chattels real; fixtures, plant, heirloom easement; folkland; right of - common, — user.

personal -property, — estate, — effects; personalty, chattels, goods, effects, movables; stock, — in trade; things, traps, rattle-traps, paraphernalia; equipage etc. 633.

parcels, appurtenances.

impedimenta; lug-, bag-gage; bag and baggage; pelf; cargo, lading.

rent-roll; income etc. (*receipts*) 810.

patent, copyright; *chose* in action; credit etc. 805; debt etc. 806.

V. possess etc. 777; be the -possessor etc. 779- of own; have for one's own, — very own; come in for, inherit; enfeoff.

favor of the realty.

be one's own -property etc. *n.*; belong to; appertain to.

Adj. one's own; landed, predial, manorial, allodial, seignorial; free-, copy-, lease-hold; feu-feo-dal; hereditary, entailed, personal.

Adv. to one's -credit, — account; to the good.

to one and -his heirs for ever, — the heirs of his body, — his heirs and assigns, — his executors, administrators and assigns.

781. Retention.—N. retention; retaining etc. *v.*; keep, detention, custody; tenacity, firm hold, grasp, gripe, grip, iron grip.

fangs, teeth, claws, talons, nail, hook, tentacle, *tenaculum*; bond etc. (*vinculum*) 45.

clutches, tongs, forceps, pincers, nippers, pliers, tweezers, vise.

paw, hand, finger, wrist, fist, neaf, neif.

bird in hand; captive etc. 754.

V. retain, keep; hold, — fast, — tight, — one's own, — one's ground; clinch, clench, clutch, grasp, gripe, hug, have a firm hold of.

secure, withold, detain; hold —, keepback; keep close; husband etc. (*store*) 636; reserve; have —, keep- in stock etc. (*possess*) 777; enfail, tie up, settle.

Adj. retaining etc. *v.*; retentive, tenacious, unforfeited, undeprived, undisposed, uncommunicated.

incommunicable, inalienable; in mortmain; in strict settlement.

Phr. *uti possidetis*.

782. Relinquishment.—N. relinquishment, abandonment etc. (*of a course*) 624; renunciation,

expropriation, dereliction; cession, surrender, dispensation; resignation etc. 757; riddance.

derelict etc. *adj.*; jetsam; waif, foundling, orphan.

v. relinquish, give up, surrender, yield, cede; let -go, — slip; spare, drop, resign, forego, renounce, abjure, abandon, expropriate, give away, dispose of, part with; lay -aside, — apart, — down, — on the shelf etc. (*disuse*) 678; set —, put- aside; make away with, cast behind; discard, cast off, dismiss; maroon.

give -notice to quit, — warning; supersede; be —, get- -rid of, — quit of; eject etc. 297.

rid —, disburden —, divest —, djspossess- oneself of; wash one's hands of; divorce, desert; disinherit, cut off.

cast —, throw —, pitch —, fling- -away, — aside, — overboard, — to the dogs; cast —, throw —, sweep- to the winds; put —, turn —, sweep- away; jettison.

quit one's hold.

Adj. relinquished etc. *v.*; cast off, derelict; unowned, unappropriated, unculled; left etc. (*residuary*) 40; divorced; disinherited.

Int. away with!

783. Transfer.—N. transfer, conveyance, assignment, alienation, abalienation; demise, limitation; conveyancing; transmission etc. (*transference*) 270; enfeoffment, bargain and sale, lease and release; exchange etc. (*interchange*) 148, barter etc. 794; substitution etc. 147.

succession, reversion; shifting -use, — trust; devolution.

V. transfer, convey; alien, -ate; assign; grant etc. (*confer*) 784; consign; make —, hand- over; pass, hand, transmit, negotiate; hand down; exchange etc. (*interchange*) 148.

change -hands, — from one to another; devolve, succeed; come into possession etc. (*acquire*) 775; take over.

abalienate; disinherit; dispossess etc. 789; substitute etc. 147.

Adj. alienable, negotiable, transferable, reversional.

Phr. estate coming into possession.

784. Giving.—N. giving etc. *v.*; bestowal, donation; present-ation, -ment; accordance; con-, cession; delivery, consignment, dispensation, communication; endowment; invest-ment, -iture; award.

almsgiving, charity, liberality, generosity; philanthropy etc. 910.

[Thing given] gift, donation, present, *cadeau*; fairing; free gift, boon, favor, benefaction, grant, offering, oblation, sacrifice, immolation.

grace, act of grace, *bonus, bonanza*.

allowance, contribution, subscription, subsidy, tribute, subvention.

bequest, legacy, devise, will, dotation, appanage; dowry; voluntary -settlement, — conveyance etc. 783; amortization.

alms, largess, bounty, dole, sportule, donative, help, oblation, offertory, Peter's pence, *honorarium*, gratuity, Maundy money, Christmas box, Easter offering, vail, tip, *douceur*, drink money, *pourboire, trinkgeld, backsheesh*; fee etc. (*recompense*) 973; consideration.

bribe, bait, ground-bait; peace-offering, handsel.

giver, grantor etc. *v.*; donor, feoffer, settlor; almoner; testator; investor, subscriber, contributor; fairy godmother; Santa Claus, benefactor etc. 816.

V. deliver, hand, pass, put into the hands of; hand –, make –, deliver –, pass –, turn- over.

present, give away, dispense, dispose of; give –, deal –, dole –, mete –, fork –, shell –, squeeze- out.

pay etc. 807; render, impart, communicate.

concede, cede, yield, part with, shed cast; spend etc. 809.

give, bestow, confer, grant, accord, award, assign.

entrust, consign, vest in.

make a present; allow, contribute, subscribe, donate, furnish its quota.

invest, endow, settle upon; bequeath, leave, devise.

furnish, supply, help; ad-, minister to; afford, spare; accommodate –, indulge –, favor- with; shower down upon; lavish, pour on, thrust upon; tip, bribe; tickle –, grease- the palm; offer etc. 763; sacrifice, immolate.

Adj. giving etc. *v.*; given etc. *v.*; allow-ed, -able; concessional; communicable; charitable, eleemosynary, sportulary, tributary; *gratis* etc. 815.

785. Receiving.—N. receiving etc. *v.*; acquisition etc. 775; reception etc. (*introduction*) 296; suscipiency, acceptance, admission.

re-, ac-cipient; assignee, devisee; lega-tee, -tary; grantee, feoffee, donee, relessee, lessee.

sportulary, stipendiary; beneficiary; pension-er, -ary; almsman.

income etc. (*receipt*) 810.

v. receive; take etc. 789; acquire etc. 775; admit.

take in, catch, touch; pocket; put into one's pocket, – purse; accept; take off one's hands.

be received; come -in, – to hand; pass –, fall- into one's hand; go into one's pocket; fall to one's lot, – share; come –, fall- to one; accrue; have -given etc. 784 to one.

Adj. receiving etc. *v.*; re-, suscipient.

received etc. *v.*; given etc. 784; second-hand.

not given, unbestowed etc. (*see* give, bestow etc. 784).

786. Apportionment.—N. apportion-, allot-, consign-, assign-, appoint-ment; appropriation; dispensation, -tribution; allocation, division, deal; repartition; administration.

dividend, portion, contingent, share, allotment, lot, cut, split, measure, dose; dole, meed, pittance; *quantum*, ration; ratio, proportion, quota, *modicum*, mess, allowance.

V. apportion, divide; cut, split, divvy; distribute, administer, dispense; billet, allot, detail, cast, share, mete; portion –, parcel –, dole- out; deal, carve.

partition, assign, appropriate, appoint.

come in for one's share etc. (*participate*) 778.

Adj. apportioning etc. *v.*; respective.

Adv. respectively, each to each.

787. Lending.—N. lending etc. *v.*; loan, advance, accommodation, feneration; mortgage etc. (*security*) 771; investment.

mont de piété, pawnshop, hock shop, spout, my uncle's.

lender, pawnbroker, money lender, usurer, Jew, Shylock.

V. lend, advance, loan, accommodate with; lend on security; pawn etc. (*security*) 771.

intrust, invest; place –, put- out to interest; sink, risk.

let, demise, lease, set, under-, sub-let.

Adj. lending etc. *v.*; lent etc. *v.*; unborrowed etc. (*see* borrowed etc. 788).

Adv. in advance; on -loan, – security.

788. Borrowing.—N. borrowing, pledging, pawning.

borrowed plumes; plagiarism etc. (*thieving*) 791.

replevin.

V. borrow, desume; pawn.

hire, rent, farm; take a -lease, – demise; take –, hire- by the -hour, – mile, – year etc.

raise –, take up- money; float bonds; raise the wind; fly a kite, borrow of Peter to pay Paul; run into debt etc. (*debt*) 806.

make use of, plagiarize, pirate.

replevy.

789. Taking.—N. taking etc. *v.*; reception etc. (*taking in*) 296; deglutition etc. (*taking food*) 298; appropriation, prehension, prensation; capture, caption; ap-, de-prehension; abreption, seizure; abduction, -lation; subtraction etc. (*subduction*) 38; abstraction, ademption.

dispossession; depriv-ation, -ement; bereavement; divestment; disherison; distraint, distress; sequestration, confiscation, attachment, execution; eviction etc. 297.

rapacity, extortion, vampirism, predacity, blood-sucking; theft etc. 791.

resumption; repris-e, -al; recovery etc. 775.

clutch, swoop, wrench; grip etc. (*retention*) 781; haul, take, catch; scramble.

taker, captor, capturer; vampire; extortioner.

V. take, catch, hook, nab, bag, sack, pocket, put into one's pocket, scrounge; receive; accept.

reap, crop, cull, pluck; gather etc. (*get*) 775; draw.

ap-, im-propriate; assume, possess oneself of; take possession of; commandeer; lay –, clap- one's hands on; help oneself to; make free with, dip one's hands into, lay under contribution; intercept; scramble for; deprive of.

take –, carry –, bear- -away, – off; abstract; hurry off –, run away- with; abduct; steal etc. 791; ravish; seize; pounce –, spring- upon; swoop -to, – down upon; take by -storm, – assault; snatch, reave.

snap up, nip up, whip up, catch up; kidnap, crimp, capture, lay violent hands on.

get −, lay −, take −, catch −, lay fast −, take firm- hold of; lay by the heels, take prisoner; fasten upon, grip, grapple, embrace, gripe, clasp, grab, clutch, collar, throttle, take by the throat, claw, clinch, clench, make sure of.

catch at, jump at, make a grab at, snap at, snatch at; reach, make a long arm, stretch forth one's hand.

take -from, − away from; deduct etc. 38; retrench etc. (*curtail*) 201; dispossess, ease one of, snatch from one's grasp; tear −, tear away −, wrench −, wrest −, wring- from; extort; deprive of, bereave; disinherit, cut off with a shilling.

oust etc. (*eject*) 297; divest; levy, distrain, confiscate; sequest-er, -rate, accroach; usurp; despoil, strip, fleece, shear, displume, impoverish, eat out of house and home; drain, − to the dregs; gut, dry, exhaust, swallow up; absorb etc. (*suck in*) 296; draw off; suck, − like a leech, − the blood of.

retake, resume; recover etc. 775.

Adj. taking etc. *v.*; privative, prehensile; predaceous, -al, -atory, -atorial; rap-acious, -torial; ravenous; parasitic; all-devouring, -engulfing.

bereft etc. 776.

Adv. at one fell swoop.

Phr. give an inch and take an ell.

790. Restitution.—N. restitution, return; ren-, red-dition; reinstatement, restoration; reinvestment, recuperation; repatriation; rehabilitation etc. (*reconstruction*) 660; reparation, atonement, indemnity, compensation, recompense.

release, replevin, redemption; recovery etc. (*getting back*) 775; remitter, reversion.

V. return, restore; recondition; give −, carry −, bring- back; render, − up; give up; let go, unclutch; dis-, re-gorge; regurgitate; recoup, reimburse, repay, indemnify, reinvest, remit, rehabilitate; repair etc. (*make good*) 660.

redeem, recover etc. (*get back*) 775; take back again; revest, revert.

Adj. restoring etc. *v.*; recuperative etc. 660; in full restitution, to compensate for.

Phr. *suum cuique*.

791. Stealing.—N. stealing etc. *v.*; theft, thievery, robbery, latrociny, direption; abstraction, appropriation; plagiar-y, -ism; rape, kidnapping, depredation; raid, hold up.

spoliation, plunder, pillage; sack, -age; rapine, *brigandage*, highway robbery, foray, *razzia*; blackmail; piracy, privateering, buccaneering; filibustering, -ism; burglary; house-breaking; cattle-stealing, -rustling, -lifting.

peculation, embezzlement; fraud etc. 545; larceny, petty larceny, pilfering, shop-lifting.

thievishness; rapacity, kleptomania, Alsatia; den of -Cacus, − thieves.

license to plunder, letters of marque.

V. steal, thieve, rob, purloin, pilfer, filch, lift, prig, bag, nim, crib, cabbage, palm; abstract; appropriate, plagiarize.

convey away, carry off, abduct, kidnap, shanghai, impress, crimp; make −, walk −, run-off with; run away with; spirit away; seize etc. (*lay violent hands on*) 789.

plunder, pillage, rifle, sack, loot, ransack, spoil, spoliate, despoil, strip, sweep, gut, forage, levy black-mail, pirate, pickeer, maraud, lift cattle, rustle, poach, smuggle, run.

stick −, hold- up.

swindle, peculate, embezzle; sponge, mulct, rook, bilk, pluck, pigeon, skin, fleece, diddle; defraud etc. 545; obtain under false pretences; live by one's wits

rob −, borrow of- Peter to Paul; set a thief to catch a thief.

disregard the distinction between *meum* and *tuum*.

Adj. thieving etc. *v.*; thievish, light-fingered; furacious, -tive; piratical; pred-aceous, -al, -atory, -atorial; raptorial etc. (*rapacious*) 789.

stolen etc. *v.*

Phr. *sic vos non vobis*.

792. Thief.—N. thief, robber, *homo trium literarum*, pilferer, rifler, filcher, plagiarist.

spoiler, depredator, pillager, marauder; harpy, shark, land-shark, falcon, moss-trooper, bushranger, Bedouin, brigand, freebooter, bandit, thug, dacoit, pirate, corsair, viking, Paul Jones; buccan-eer, -ier; piqu-, pick-eerer; rover, ranger, privateer, filibuster; rapparee, wrecker, picaroon; smuggler, poacher, plunderer; racketeer.

highwayman, Dick Turpin, Claude Duval, Macheath, knight of the road, footpad, sturdy beggar; abductor, kidnapper.

cut-, pick-purse; pick-pocket, light-fingered gentry; sharper; card-, skittle-sharper; crook; thimble-rigger; rook, Greek, blackleg, leg, welsher, defaulter; Autolycus, Cacus, Barabbas, Jeremy Diddler, Robert Macaire, artful dodger, trickster; swell mob, *chevalier d'industrie*; shop-lifter.

swindler, peculator; forger, coiner, counterfeiter; shoful; fence, receiver of stolen goods, duffer; smasher.

burglar, housebreaker; cracks-, mags-man; Bill Sikes, Jack Sheppard, Jonathan Wild, Raffles, cat burglar.

793. Booty.—N. booty, spoil, plunder, price, loot, graft, swag, pickings, boodle; *spolia opima*, prey; blackmail; stolen goods.

Adj. looting etc. *n.*; manubial, spoliative.

794. Barter.—N. barter, exchange, scorse, truck system; interchange etc. 148.

a Roland for an Oliver; *quid pro quo*; commutation, -position.

trade, commerce, mercature, buying and selling, bargain and sale; traffic, business, nundination, custom, shopping; commercial enterprise, speculation, jobbing, stock-jobbing, *agiotage*, brokery, arbitrage.

dealing, transaction, negotiation, bargain.

free trade.

V. barter, exchange, truck, scorse, swop; interchange etc. 148; commutate etc. (*substitute*) 147; compound for.

trade, traffic, buy and sell, give and take, nundinate; carry on −, ply −, drive- a trade; be in -

business, – the city; keep a shop, deal in, employ one's capital in.

trade –, deal –, have dealings- with; transact –, do- business with; open –, keep- an account with.

bargain; drive –, make- a bargain; negotiate, bid for; dicker, haggle, higgle; chaffer, huckster, cheapen, beat down; stickle, – for; out-, underbid; ask, charge; strike a bargain etc. (*contract*) 769.

speculate, give a sprat to catch a herring; buy in the cheapest and sell in the dearest market; rig the market.

Adj. commercial, mercantile, trading; interchangeable, marketable, staple, in the market, for sale.

wholesale, retail.

Adv. across the counter; on 'change.

795. Purchase.—N. purchase, emption; buying, purchasing, shopping; pre-emption, refusal.

coemption, bribery; slave trade.

buyer, purchaser, *emptor*, vendee; patron, employer, client, customer, *clientèle*.

V. buy, purchase, invest in, procure; rent etc. (*hire*) 788; repurchase, buy in.

keep in one's pay, bribe, suborn; pay etc. 807; spend etc. 809.

make –, complete- a purchase; buy over the counter; pay cash for.

shop, market, go a shopping.

Adj. purchased etc. *v.*

Phr. *caveat emptor.*

796. Sale.—N. sale, vent, disposal; auction, roup, Dutch auction; custom etc. (*traffic*) 794.

vendi-bility, -bleness.

seller, salesman; peddler, smous; vender, vendor, consignor; merchant etc. 797; auctioneer.

V. sell, vend, dispose of, effect a sale; sell -over the counter, – by auction etc. *n.*; dispense, retail; deal in etc. 794; sell -off, – out; turn into money; realize; bring -to, – under- the hammer; put up to auction; auction, offer –, put up- for sale; hawk, peddle, bring to market; offer etc. 763; undersell; dump, unload.

let; mortgage etc. (*security*) 771.

Adj. under the hammer, in the market, for sale.

saleable, marketable, vendible, in demand, having a ready sale; unsaleable etc., unpurchased, unbought; on one's hands.

797. Merchant.—N. merchant, trader, dealer, monger, chandler, salesman; changer; regrater; shop-keeper, -man; trades-man, -people, -folk.

retailer; chapman, hawker, huckster, higgler; peddler, smous, pedlar, *colporteur*, cadger, Autolycus; sutler, *vivandière*; coster-man, -monger; market woman; cheap jack; caterer etc. 637; tallyman.

money-broker, -changer, -lender; stock-broker, -jobber; cambist, usurer, moneyer, banker.

jobber; broker etc. (*agent*) 758; buyer etc. 795; seller etc. 796.

concern; firm etc. (*partnership*) 712.

798. Merchandise.—N. merchandise, ware, commodity, effects, goods, article, stock, produce, staple commodity; stock in trade etc. (*store*) 636; cargo etc. (*contents*) 190.

799. Mart.—N. mart; market, -place, *forum*; fair, bazaar, staple; stock –, exchange; 'change, *bourse*, Wall Street, Rialto, hall, guildhall; tollbooth, custom-house; Tattersalls.

shop, stall, booth; wharf; office, chambers, counting-house, *bureau*; coun-, comp-ter.

ware-house, -room; *dépôt*, interposit, *entrepôt*, *emporium*, establishment; store etc. 636.

open market, market-overt.

800. Money.—N. money -matters, – market; finance; accounts etc. 811; funds, treasure; capital, stock; assets etc. (*property*) 780; wealth etc. 803; supplies, ways and means, wherewithal, sinews of war, almighty dollar, needful, cash.

sum, amount; balance, -sheet; sum total; proceeds etc. (*receipts*) 810.

currency, circulating medium, specie; coin, – of the realm; piece, hard cash, dollar, sterling coin; pounds, shillings and pence; L s. d., guineas; pocket, breeches pocket, purse; money in hand; the best, ready, – money; filthy lucre, shekels, roll, jack, rhino, blunt, dust, bawbees, brass, dibs, dough, mopus, tin, salt, chink, oof, spondulics, pile, wads.

precious metals, gold, silver, copper, nickel; bullion, bar, ingot, nugget.

petty cash; pocket-, pin-money; small –, change; small coin, loose cash; doit, stiver, rap, mite, farthing, *sou*, penny, shilling, bob, tanner, tester, groat, guinea, ducat; *rouleau*; *wampum*; good –, round –, lump- sum; power –, mint –, tons- of money; plum, lac of rupees, millions, money-bags, miser's hoard, stocking, mine of wealth etc. 803.

[Science of coins] numismatics, chrysology.

paper-money; money –, postal –, Post Office-order; note, – of hand; bank –, treasury- note; Bradbury; promissory note; I.O.U., bond; bill, – of exchange; draft, check, order, warrant, *coupon*, debenture, exchequer bill, *assignat*, greenback, gold –, silver- certificate.

copper, nickel, dime, quarter, two bits, half a dollar, dollar, buck, simoleon, fiver, tenner, a twenty, a sawbuck, a century, a grand; eagle, double eagle.

gold standard, bimetallism, fiat money; rate of –, exchange; in-, de-flation.

remittance etc. (*payment*) 807; credit etc. 805; liability etc. 806; solvency etc. 803.

draw-er, -ee; oblig-or, -ee; moneyer, coiner, counterfeiter, forger.

false –, bad- money; base –, counterfeit- coin, flash note, slip, kite; Bank of Elegance.

argumentum ad crumenam.

V. amount to, come to, mount up to; touch the pocket; draw, – upon; endorse etc. (*security*) 771; issue, utter, circulate; discount etc. 813.

forge, counterfeit, coin, circulate, – pass- bad money.

Adj. monetary, pecuniary, crumenal, fiscal, financial, sumptuary, numismatical; sterling; solvent etc. 803.

801. Treasurer.—N. treasurer; bursar, -y; purser, purse-bearer; cash-keeper, banker; depositary; questor, receiver, steward, trustee, chartered –, accountant; Accountant-General, almoner, liquidator, paymaster, cashier, teller; cambist; money-changer etc. (*merchant*) 797.

financier, Chancellor of the Exchequer, minister of finance; Secretary of the Treasury, Director of the Budget, Controller of Currency.

802. Treasury.—N. treasury, bank, exchequer, almonry, fisc, hanaper, bursary; safe; strong-box, -hold, -room; coffer; chest etc. (*receptacle*) 191; depository etc. 636; till, -er; cash-box, -register, purse, pocketbook, wallet; money-bag, -belt, -box, *porte-monnaie*.

purse-strings; pocket, breeches pocket.

sinking fund; stocks; government –, public –, parliamentary- -stocks, – funds, – securities, bonds; gild-edged securities; Consols, Liberty bonds, government bonds, *crédit mobilier*.

803. Wealth.—N. wealth, riches, fortune, handsome fortune, opulence, affluence; good –, easy- circumstances; independence; competence etc. (*sufficiency*) 639; solvency, soundness, solidity.

provision, livelihood, maintenance; alimony, dowry, means, resources, substance; property etc. 780; command of money.

income etc. 810; capital, money; round sum etc. (*treasure*) 800; mint of money, mine of wealth, *El Dorado*, Pactolus, Golconda, Potosi, *bonanza*; philosopher's stone.

long –, full –, well lined –, heavy- purse; purse of Fortunatus.

pelf, Mammon, lucre, filthy lucre; loaves and fishes; fleshpots of Egypt.

rich –, moneyed –, warm- man; man of substance; capitalist, millionaire, Nabob, Croesus, Midas, Plutus, Dives, Timon of Athens; Timo-, Pluto-cracy; Danaë.

V. be -rich etc. *adj.*; roll –, wallow- in -wealth, – riches; have money to burn.

afford, well afford; command -money, – a sum; make both ends meet, hold one's head above water.

become -rich etc. *adj.*; fill one's -pocket etc. (*treasury*) 802; feather one's nest, clean up –, make- a fortune; make money etc. (*acquire*) 775.

enrich, imburse.

worship -Mammon, – the golden calf.

Adj. wealthy, rich, affluent, opulent, moneyed, monied, worth -a great deal, – much; well -to do, – off; warm; well –, provided for.

made of money; rich as Croesus; rolling in -riches, – wealth.

flush, – of -cash, – money, – tin; in -funds, – cash, – full feather; solvent, solid, sound, pecunious, out of debt, all straight; able to pay 20s in the L.

Phr. one's ship coming in.

804. Poverty.—N. poverty, indigence, penury, pauperism, destitution, want; need, -iness; lack,

necessity, privation, distress, difficulties, wolf at the door.

bad –, poor –, needy –, embarrassed –, reduced –, straitened- circumstances; slender –, narrow- means; straits; hand to mouth existence, *res angusta domi*, low water, impecuniosity.

beggary; mendi-cancy, -city; broken –, loss of-fortune; insolvency etc. (*non-payment*) 808.

empty -purse, – pocket; light purse; beggarly account of empty boxes.

poor man, pauper, mendicant, mumper, beggar, starveling; *pauvre diable*.

V. be -poor etc. *adj.*; want, lack, starve, live from hand to mouth, have seen better days, go down in the world, be on one's uppers, come upon the parish; go to -the dogs, – wrack and ruin; not have a -penny etc. (*money*) 800, – shot in one's locker; beg one's bread; *tirer le diable par la queue*; run into debt etc. (*debt*) 806.

render -poor etc. *adj.*; impoverish; reduce, – to poverty; pauperize, fleece, ruin, bring to the parish.

Adj. poor, indigent; poverty-striken; badly –, poorly –, ill- off; poor as -a rat, – a church mouse, – Job's turkey, – Job; fortune-, dower-, money-, penni-less; unportioned, unmoneyed; impecunious; broke, flat; out –, short- of -money, – cash; without –, not worth- a rap etc. (*money*) 800; *qui n'a pas le sou*, out of pocket, hard up; out at -elbows, – heels; seedy, bare-footed; beggar-ly, -ed; destitute; fleeced, strapped, stripped; bereft, bereaved; reduced.

in -want etc. *n.*; needy, necessitous, distressed, pinched, straitened; put to one's -shifts, – last shifts; unable to -keep the wolf from the door, – make both ends meet; embarrassed, under hatches; involved etc. (*in debt*) 806; insolvent etc. (*not paying*) 808.

Adv. in formâ pauperis.

Phr. zonam perdidit.

805. Credit.—N. credit, trust, tick, score, tally, account.

letter of credit, circular note; duplicate; mortgage, lien, debenture, paper credit, floating capital; draft; securities.

creditor, lender, lessor, mortgagee; dun; usurer.

V. keep –, run up- an account with; entrust, credit, accredit.

place to one's -credit, – account; give –, take-credit; fly a kite.

Adj. credit-ing, -ed; accredited.

Adv. on -credit etc. *n.*; to the -account, – credit- of.

806. Debt.—N. debt, obligation, liability, indebtment, debit, score.

arrears, deferred payment, deficit, default; insolvency etc. (*non-payment*) 808; bad debt.

interest; usance, usury; premium; floating -debt, – capital.

debtor, debitor; mortgagor; defaulter etc. 808; borrower.

V. be -in debt etc. *adj.*; owe; incur –, contract- a debt etc. *n.*; run up -a bill, – a score, – an account; go on tick, put on the cuff; borrow etc. 788; run –, get- into debt; outrun the constable.

answer –, go bail- for; back one's note.

Adj. indebted; liable, chargeable, answerable for.

in -debt, – embarrassed circumstances, – difficulties; incumbered, involved; involved –, plunged –, deep –, over head and ears- in debt; deeply involved; fast tied up; insolvent etc. (*not paying*) 808; *minus*, out of pocket.

unpaid; unrequieted, unrewarded; owing, due, in arrear, outstanding.

807. Payment.—N. pay-, defray-ment; discharge; ac-, quittance; settlement, clearance, liquidation, satisfaction, reckoning, arrangement.

acknowledgment, release; receipt, – in full, – in full of all demands; voucher.

repayment, reimbursement, retribution; pay etc. (*reward*) 973; money paid etc. (*expenditure*) 809.

ready money etc. (*cash*) 800; stake, remittance, instalment.

payer, liquidator etc. 801.

V. pay, defray, make payment; pay -down, – on the nail, – ready money, – at sight, – in advance; cash, honor a bill, acknowledge; redeem; pay in kind.

pay one's -way, – shot, – footing; pay -the piper, – sauce for all, – costs; do the needful; come across; shell –, fork- out; come down with, – the dust; tickle –, grease- the palm; expend etc. 809; put –, lay- down.

discharge, settle, quit, acquit oneself of; account –, reckon –, settle –, be even –, be quits- with; strike a balance; settle –, balance –, square- accounts with; quit scores; foot the bill; wipe –, clear- off old scores; satisfy; pay in full; satisfy –, pay in full of- all demands; clear, liquidate; pay - up, – old debts.

disgorge, make repayment; repay, refund, reimburse, retribute; make compensation etc. 30.

Adj. paying etc., paid etc. *v.*; owing nothing, out of debt, all straight, clear of -debt, – encumbrance; unowed, never indebted.

Adv. to the tune of; on the nail; money –, cash-down; cash on delivery.

808. Non-payment.—N. non-payment; default, defalcation; protest, repudiation; application of the sponge; whitewashing.

insolvency, bankruptcy, failure; overdraft, overdrawn account; insufficiency etc. 640; run upon a bank.

waste paper bonds; dishonored –, protested-bills; bogus cheque.

bankrupt, insolvent debtor, lame duck, man of straw, welsher, stag, defaulter, absconder, levanter.

V. non -pay etc. 807; fail, break, stop payment; become -insolvent, – bankrupt; be gazetted.

protest, dishonor, repudiate, nullify.

pay under protest; button up one's pockets, draw the purse strings; apply the sponge; pay over the left shoulder, get whitewashed; swindle etc. 791; run up bills, fly kites.

Adj. not paying; in debt etc. 806; behindhand, in arrear; beggared etc. (*poor*) 804; unable to make both ends meet; *minus*; worse than nothing.

insolvent, bankrupt, in the gazette, gazetted, ruined.

unpaid etc. (*outstanding*) 806; *gratis* etc. 815; unremunerated.

809. Expenditure.—N. expenditure, money going out; out-goings, -lay; expenses, disbursement; prime cost etc. (*price*) 812; circulation; run upon a bank.

[Money paid] payment etc. 807; pay etc. (*remuneration*) 973; bribe etc. 973; fee, footing, garnish; subsidy; tribute, Peter's pence; contingent, quota; donation etc. 784.

pay in advance, earnest, handsel, deposit, instalment.

investment; purchase etc. 795.

V. expend, spend; run –, get- through; pay, disburse; open –, loose –, untie- the purse strings; lay –, shell –, fork- out; bleed; make up a sum, invest, sink money.

fee etc. (*reward*) 973; pay one's way etc. (*pay*) 807; subscribe etc. (*give*) 784; subsidize, bribe.

Adj. expend-ing, -ed etc. *v.*; sumptuary, liberal etc. 816; openhanded, lavish etc. 818; extensive etc. 814.

810. Receipt—N. receipt, accountable –, conditional –, binding –, return- receipt; value received, money coming in; income, incomings, innings, revenue, return, proceeds; gross receipts, net profit; earnings etc. (*gain*) 775.

rent, – roll; rent-al, -age; rack-rent.

premium, *bonus*; sweepstakes, tontine, prize, drawing.

pension, annuity, jointure etc. (*property*) 780; alimony, pittance; emolument etc. (*remuneration*) 973.

V. receive etc. 785; take money; draw –, derive- from; get, be in receipt of, acquire etc. 775; take etc. 789.

bring in, yield, afford, pay, return; accrue etc. (*be received from*) 785.

Adj. receiv-ing, -ed etc. *v.*; profitable etc. (*gainful*) 775.

811. Accounts.—N. accounts, accompts; commercial –, monetary- arithmetic; statistics etc. (*numeration*) 85; money matters, finance, budget, bill, score, reckoning, account.

books, account book, ledger; day –, cash –, pass- book; journal; debtor and creditor –, cash –, petty cash –, running- account; account-current; balance, – sheet; *compte rendu*, account settled.

book-keeping, audit; double –, single- entry; reckoning etc. 85.

chartered –, certified public –, accountant; auditor, actuary, bookkeeper; financier etc. 801; accounting party.

V. keep accounts, enter, post, book, credit, debit, carry over; take stock; balance –, make up –, square –, settle –, wind up –, cast up –, add up –, tot up- accounts; make accounts square.

bring to book, audit, tax, surcharge and falsify.

falsify –, garble –, cook –, doctor- an account.

Adj. monetary etc. 800; account-able, -ing; statistical.

812. Price.—N. price, amount, cost, expense, prime cost, charge, figure, demand, damage, fare, hire; wages etc. (*remuneration*) 973.

dues, duty, toll, tax, impost, cess, sess, tallage, levy, capitation-, poll-, income-, sur-, sales-, super-tax; gabel, *gabelle*; gavel, *octroi*, custom, tariff, excise, assessment, taxation, benevolence, tithe, tenths, exactment, ransom, salvage; broker-, wharf-, lighter-, ton-, freight-age.

worth, rate, value, valuation, appraisement, money's worth, par value; penny etc. -worth; price current, market price, quotation; what it will -fetch etc. *v.*

bill etc. (*account*) 811; shot.

V. bear −, set −, fix- a price; appraise, assess, price, charge, demand, ask, require, exact, run up; distrain; run up a bill etc. (*debt*) 806; have one's price; liquidate.

amount to, come to, mount up to; stand one in. fetch, sell for, cost, bring in, yield, afford.

Adj. priced etc. *v.*; to the tune of, *ad valorem*; mercenary, venal.

Phr. no penny, no paternoster; *point d'argent, point de Suisse*, no longer pipe, no longer dance, no song, no supper.

one may have it for.

813. Discount.—N. discount, abatement, concession, reduction, depreciation, allowance, qualification, set off, drawback, poundage, *agio*, percentage; rebate, -ment; backwardation, contango; salvage; tare and tret.

V. discount, bate; a-, re-bate; deduct, reduce, mark down, take off, allow, give, make allowance; tax, depreciate.

Adj. discounting etc. *v.*

Adv. at a discount, below par.

814. Dearness.—N. dearness etc. *adj.*; high −, famine −, fancy- price; overcharge; extravagance; exorbitance, extortion; heavy pull upon the purse; Pyrrhic victory.

V. be -dear etc. *adj.*; cost -much, − a pretty penny; rise in price, look up.

overcharge, bleed, fleece, skin, extort.

pay -too much, − through the nose, −, too dear for one's whistle.

Adj. dear; high, -priced; of great price, expensive, costly, precious, worth a Jew's eye, dear bought; unreasonable, extravagant, exorbitant, extortionate.

at a premium; not to be had, − for love or money; beyond −, above- price; priceless, of priceless value.

Adv. dear, -ly; at great −, heavy- cost; *à grands frais*.

Phr. prices looking up; *le jeu ne vaut pas la chandelle*.

815. Cheapness.—N. cheapness, low price; depreciation; bargain; good penny etc.- worth, *bon marché*.

[Absence of charge] gratuity; free -quarters, − seats, − admission, − warren; pass, Annie Oakley; run of one's teeth; nominal price, peppercorn rent; labor of love.

drug in the market.

V. be -cheap etc. *adj.*; cost little; come down −, fall- in price.

buy for -a mere nothing, − an old song; have one's money's worth; cheapen, beat down.

Adj. cheap; low, − priced; moderate, reasonable; in-, un-expensive; well −, worth the money; *magnifique et pas cher*; good −, cheap- at the price; dirt −, dog- cheap; cheap, -as dirt, − and nasty; catchpenny.

reduced, marked down, half-price, depreciated, unsaleable.

gratuitous, *gratis*, free, for love, − nothing; cost-, expense-less; without charge, not charged, untaxed; scot −, shot −, rent- free; free of -cost, − expense; honorary, unbought, unpaid, complimentary.

Adv. for a mere song; at -cost price, − prime cost, − a reduction, − a bargain; on the cheap.

816. Liberality.—N. liberality, generosity, munificence; bount-y, -eousness, -ifulness; hospitality; charity etc. (*beneficence*) 906.

benefactor, free giver, Lady Bountiful.

V. be -liberal etc. *adj.*; spend −, bleed- freely; shower down upon; open one's purse strings etc. (*disburse*) 809; spare no expense, give -with both hands, − carte blanche.

Adj. liberal, free, generous; charitable etc. (*beneficent*) 906; hospitable; bount-iful, -eous; handsome; unsparing, ungrudging; open-, free-, full-handed; open-, large-, free-hearted; munificent, princely, unstinting.

overpaid.

Adv. liberally, ungrudgingly, with open hand.

817. Economy.—N. economy, frugality; thrift, -iness; prudence, care, husbandry, good housewifery, savingness, retrenchment.

savings; prevention of waste, save-all; cheese parings and candle ends; parsimony etc. 819.

V. be -economical etc. *adj.*; economize, save; retrench; cut- down expenses, − one's coat according to one's cloth, make both ends meet, keep within compass, meet one's expenses, pay one's way; keep one's head above water; husband etc. (*lay by*) 636; save −, invest- money; put out to interest; provide −, save- -for, − against- a rainy day; feather one's nest; look after the main chance.

Adj. economical, frugal, careful, thrifty, saving, chary, spare, sparing; parsimonious etc. 819.

underpaid.

Adv. sparingly etc. *adj.*; *ne quid nimis*.

818. Prodigality.—N. prodi-gality, -gence; unthriftiness, waste, -fulness; profus-ion, -eness; extravagance; squandering etc. *v.*; lavishness; malversation.

prodigal; spend-, waste-thrift; losel, play-boy, spender, squanderer, locust.

V. be -prodigal etc. *adj.*; squander, lavish, sow broadcast; pour forth like water; pay through the nose etc. (*dear*) 814; spill, waste, dissipate, exhaust, drain, eat out of house and home, overdraw, outrun the constable; run -out, − through; misspend; throw -good money after bad, − the helve after the hatchet; burn the candle at both ends; make ducks and drakes of one's money;

squander one's substance, spend money like water; fool –, potter –, muddle –, fritter –, throw-away one's money; pour water into a sieve, kill the goose that lays the golden eggs; *manger son blé en herbe.*

Adj. prodigal, profuse, thriftless, unthrifty, im-provident, wasteful, losel, extravagant, lavish, dissipated, over liberal; full-handed etc. (*liberal*) 816.

penny wise and pound foolish.

Adv. with an unsparing hand; money burning one's pocket; recklessly profuse.

Int. hang the expense!

819. Parsimony.—N. parsimony, parcity; par-simoniousness, stinginess etc. *adj.*; stint; illiberality, avarice, tenacity, avidity, rapacity, extortion, venality, cupidity; selfishness etc. 943; *auri sacra fames.*

miser, niggard, churl, screw, tightwad, skinflint, crib, codger, muckworm, money-grubber, pinch-fist, scrimp, lickpenny, hunks, curmudgeon, *Harpagon,* Silas Marner, harpy, extortioner, Jew, usurer.

V. be -parsimonious etc. *adj.*; grudge, begrudge, stint, skimp, pinch, gripe, screw, dole out, hold back, withhold, starve, famish, live upon nothing, skin a flint.

drive a -bargain, – hard bargain; cheapen, beat down; stop one hole in a sieve; have an itching palm, grasp, grab.

Adj. parsimonious, penurious, stingy, miserly, mean, shabby, peddling, scrubby, pennywise, near, niggardly, frugal to excess; close; fast-, close-, strait-handed; close-, hard-, tight-fisted; tight, sparing; chary; grudging, griping etc. *v.*; illiberal, ungenerous, churlish, hidebound, sordid, mer-cenary, venal, covetous, usurious, avaricious, greedy, extortionate, rapacious.

Adv. with a sparing hand.

820. Affections.—N. affections, character, qualities, disposition, nature, spirit, tone; temper, -ament; *diathesis,* idiosyncrasy; cast –, habit –, frame- of -mind, – soul; predilection, turn; natural –, turn of mind; bent, bias, predisposition, proneness, proclivity; propen-sity, -sedness, -sion, -dency; vein, humor, mood, grain, mettle; sympathy etc. (*love*) 897.

soul, heart, breast, bosom, inner man; heart's -core, – strings, – blood; heart of hearts, *penetralia mentis*; secret and inmost recesses of the –, cockles of one's- heart; inmost -heart, – soul; back-bone.

passion, pervading spirit; ruling –, master-passion; *furore*; fulness of the heart, heyday of the blood, flesh and blood, flow of soul, force of character.

V. have –, possess- -affections etc. *n.*; be of a -character etc. *n.*; be -affected etc. *adj.*; breathe.

Adj. affected, characterized, formed, molded, cast; at-, tempered; framed; pre-, disposed; prone, inclined; having a -bias etc. *n.*; tinctured –, im-bued –, penetrated –, eaten up- with.

inborn, inbred, ingrained, in the grain, congenital, inherent, bred in the bone; deep-rooted, ineffaceable, inveterate; pathoscopic.

Adv. in one's -heart etc. *n.*; at heart; heart and soul etc. 821; in the -vein, – mood.

821. Feeling.—N. feeling; suffering etc. *v.*; en-durance, tolerance, sufferance, supportance, ex-perience, response; sympathy etc. (*love*) 897; im-pression, inspiration, affection, sensation, emotion, pathos, deep sense.

fire, warmth, glow, unction, *gusto,* vehemence; ferv-or, -ency; heartiness, cordiality; earnestness, eagerness; *empressment,* ardor, zeal, passion, en-thusiasm, *verve, furore,* fanaticism; excitation of feeling etc. 824; fulness of the heart etc. (*disposition*) 820; passion etc. (*state of ex-citability*) 825; ecstasy etc. (*pleasure*) 827.

blush, suffusion, flush; hectic; tingling, thrill, kick, turn, shock; agitation etc. (*irregular motion*) 315; quiver, heaving, flutter, flurry, fluster, twitter, tremor; throb, -bing; pulsation, palpitation, paint-ing; trepid-, perturb-ation; ruffle, hurry of spirits, pother, stew, ferment.

V. feel; receive an -impression etc. *n.*; be -impressed with etc. *adj.*; entertain –, harbor –, cherish- -feeling etc. *n.*

respond; catch the -flame, – infection; enter the spirit of.

bear, suffer, support, sustain, endure, brook, thole, aby; abide etc. (*be composed*) 826; ex-perience etc. (*meet with*) 151; taste, prove; labor –, smart- under; bear the brunt of, brave, stand.

swell, glow, warm, flush, blush, change color, mantle; turn -color, – pale, – red, – black in the face; blench, crimson, whiten, pale, tingle, thrill, heave, pant, throb, palpitate, go pit-a-pat, tremble, quiver, flutter, twitter; stagger, reel; shake etc. 315; be -agitated, – excited etc. 824; look -blue, – black; wince, draw a deep breath.

impress etc. (*excite the feelings*) 824.

Adj. feeling etc. *v.*; sentient; sensuous; sensor-ial, -y; emo-tive, -tional; of –, with- feeling etc. *n.*

warm, quick, lively, smart, strong, sharp, acute, cutting, piercing, incisive, keen, – as a razor; trench-ant, pungent, racy, *piquant,* poignant, caustic.

impressive, deep, profound, indelible; deep-, home-, heart-felt; swelling, soul-stirring, deep-mouthed, heart-expanding, electric, thrilling, rap-turous, ecstatic.

earnest, wistful, eager, breathless; fer-vent, -vid; gushing, passionate, warmhearted, hearty, cordial, sincere, zealous, enthusiastic, glowing, ardent, burning, red-hot, fiery, flaming; boiling, – over.

pervading, penetrating, absorbing; rabid, raving feverish, fanatical, hysterical; impetuous etc. (*ex-citable*) 825; overmastering.

impressed –, moved –, touched –, affected –, penetrated –, seized –, imbued etc. 820-with; devoured by; wrought up etc. (*excited*) 824; struck all of a heap; rapt; in a -quiver etc. *n.*; enraptured etc. 829.

Adv. heart and soul, from the bottom of one's heart, *ab imo pectore, de profundis,* at heart, *con amore,* heartily, devoutly, over head and ears.

Phr. the heart -big, – full, – swelling, – beating, – pulsating, – throbbing, – thumping, – beating high, – melting, – overflowing, – bursting, – breaking.

822. Sensibility.—N. sensi-bility, -bleness, -tiveness; moral sensibility; impress-, affect-ibility; suscepti-bleness, -bility, -vity; mobility; viva-city, -ciousness; tender-, soft-ness; sentimental-ity, -ism. excitability etc. 825; fastidiousness etc. 868; physical sensibility etc. 375.

sore -point, – place; where the shoe pinches.
V. be -sensible etc. *adj.*; have a -tender, –
warm, – sensitive- heart.

take to – , treasure up in the- heart; shrink.
'die of a rose in aromatic pain;' touch to the
quick.

Adj. sensi-ble, -tive; impressi-ble, -onable;
suscepti-ve, -ble; alive to, impassion-able, -ed;
gushing; warm-, tender-, soft-hearted; tender – , as
a chicken; soft, sentimental, romantic; enthusiastic,
highflying, spirited, mettlesome, vivacious, lively,
expressive, mobile, tremblingly alive; excitable etc.
825; over-sensitive, without skin, thin-skinned;
fastidious etc. 868.

Adv. sensibly etc. *adj.*; to the -quick, – inmost
core.

823. Insensibility.—N. insensi-bility, -bleness;
moral insensibility; inertness, *inertia, vis inertiae*;
impassi-bility, -bleness; inappetency, apathy,
phlegm, dulness, hebetude, supineness, lukewarmness, insusceptibility, unimpressibility.

cold -fit, – blood, – heart; cold-, cool-ness;
frigidity, *sang-froid*; stoicism, imperturbation etc.
(*inexcitability*) 826; *nonchalance*, unconcern, dry
eyes; *insouciance* etc. (*indifference*) 866;
recklessness etc. 863; callousness; heart of stone,
stock and stone, marble, deadness.

torp-or, -idity; obstupefaction, lethargy, coma,
trance; sleep etc. 683; suspended animation; stup-
or, -efaction; paralysis, palsy; numbness etc.
(*physical insensibility*) 376.

neutrality; quietism, vegetation.

V. be -insensible etc. *adj.*; have a rhinoceros
hide; show -insensibility etc. *n.*; not -mind, – care,
– be affected by; have no desire for etc. 866; have
–, feel –, take- no interest in; *nil admirari*; not care
a -straw etc. (*unimportance*) 643 for; disregard etc.
(*neglect*) 460; set at naught etc. (*make light of*)
483; turn a deaf ear to etc. (*inattention*) 458;
vegetate.

render -insensible, – callous; blunt, obtund,
numb, benumb, paralyze, chloroform, deaden,
hebetate, stun, stupefy; brut-ify, -alize.

inure; harden, – the heart; steel, case-harden,
sear.

Adj. insensible, unconscious; impassi-ve, -ble;
blind to, deaf to, dead to; un-, in-susceptible; unim-
press-ionable, -ible; passion-, spirit-, heart-, soulless; unfeeling, unmoral.

apathetic; leuco-, phlegmatic; dull, frigid; cold, -
blooded, -hearted; unemotional; cold as charity;
flat, obtuse, inert, supine, sluggish, torpid; sleepy
etc. (*inactive*) 683; languid, half-hearted, tame;
numb, -ed; comatose; anesthetic etc. 376;
stupefied, chloroformed, palsy-stricken.

indifferent, lukewarm; Laodicean; careless, mindless, regardless; inattentive etc. 458; neglectful
etc. 460; disregarding.

unconcerned, *nonchalant, pococurante,* in-
souciant, sans souci; unambitious etc. 866.

un-affected, -ruffled, -impressed, -inspired, -
excited, -moved, -stirred, -touched, -shocked, -
struck; unblushing etc. (*shameless*) 885;
unanimated; vegetative.

callous, thick-skinned, pachydermatous, impervious; hard, -ened; inured, case-hardened;
steeled – , proof- against; imperturbable etc. (*inexcitable*) 826; unfelt.

Adv. insensibly etc. *adj.*; *aequo animo*: without
being -moved, – touched, – impressed: in cold
blood; with -dry eyes, – withers unwrung.

Phr. never mind; it is of no consequence etc.
(*unimportant*) 643; it cannot be helped: nothing
coming amiss; it is all -the same, – one- to.

824. Excitation.—N. excitation of feeling;
mental –, excitement; suscitation, galvanism,
stimulation, piquancy, provocation inspiration,
calling forth, infection; interest, animation,
agitation, perturbation; subjugation, fascination,
intoxication; en-, ravishment; entrancement, high
pressure.

unction, impressiveness etc. *adj.*; emotional appeal; melodrama; psychological moment, crisis;
sensationalism.

trail of temper, *casus belli*; irritation etc. (*anger*)
900; passion etc. (*state of excitability*) 825; thrill
etc. (*feeling*) 821; repression of feeling etc. 826.

V. excite, affect, touch, move, impress, strike, interest, intrigue, animate, inspire, impassion, smite,
infect; stir – , fire – , warm- the blood; set astir; a-
wake; a-, waken; call forth; e-, pro-voke; raise up,
summon up, call up, wake up, blow up, get up,
light up; raise; get up steam, rouse, arouse, stir, fire,
kindle, enkindle, apply the torch, set on fire, inflame, illuminate.

stimulate; ex-, suscitate; inspirit; spirit up, stir up,
work up; infuse life into, five new life to; bring – ,
introduce- new blood; quicken; sharpen, whet;
work upon etc. (*incite*) 615, hurry on, give a fillip,
put on one's mettle.

fan the -fire, – flame; blow the coals, stir the
embers; fan, – into a flame; foster, heat, warm,
foment, raise to a fever heat; keep -up, – the pot
boiling; revive, rekindle; rake up, rip up.

stir – , play on – , come home to- the feelings;
touch -a string, – a chord, – the soul, – the
heart; go to one's heart, penetrate, pierce, go
through one, touch to the quick, open the wound;
possess – , pervade – , penetrate – , imbrue – ,
absorb – , affect – , disturb- the soul.

absorb, rivet the attention; sink into the -mind,
– heart; prey on the mind; intoxicate; over-whelm,
-power; *bouleverser*, upset, turn one's head.

fascinate; enrapture etc. (*give pleasure*) 829.

agitate, perturb, ruffle, fluster, flutter, shake,
disturb, faze, startle, shock, stagger; give one a -
shock, – turn; strike -dumb, – all of a heap; stun,
astound, electrify, galvanize, petrify.

irritate, sting; cut, – to the -heart, – quick; try
one's temper; fool to the top of one's bent; pique;
infuriate, madden, make one's blood boil; lash into
fury etc. (*wrath*) 900.

be -excited etc. *adj.*; flash up, flare up; catch the
infection; thrill etc. (*feel*) 821; mantle; work
oneself up; seethe, boil, simmer, foam, fume,
flame, rage, rave; run mad etc. (*passion*) 825.

Adj. excited etc. *v.*; wrought up, on the *qui vive*,
astir, sparkling; in a -quiver etc. 821, – fever, –
ferment, – blaze, – state of excitement; in
hysterics; black in the face, over-wrought; hot, red-
hot, flushed, feverish; all -of a twitter, – of a flutter, – of a dither, – in a pucker; with -quivering
lips, – tears in one's eyes.

flaming; boiling, – over; ebullient, seething;
foaming, – at the mouth; fuming, raging, carried
away by passion, wild, raving, frantic, mad, dis-

tracted, distraught, beside oneself, out of one's wits, amuck, ready to burst, *bouleversé*, demoniacal.

lost, *eperdu*, tempest-tossed; haggard; ready to sink.

stung to the quick, up, on one's high ropes.

exciting etc. *v.*; impressive, warm, glowing, fervid, swelling, imposing, spirit-stirring, thrilling; high-wrought; soul-stirring, -subduing; heart-swelling, -thrilling; agonizing etc. (*painful*) 830; telling, sensational, melodramatic, hysterical; overpowering, -whelming; more than flesh and blood can bear.

piquant etc. (*pungent*) 392; spicy, appetizing, provocative, *provaquant*, tantalizing.

Adv. till one is black in the face.

Phr. the heart -beating high, − going pit-a-pat, − leaping into one's mouth; the blood -being up, − boiling in one's veins; the eye -glistening, − 'in a fine frenzy rolling;' the head turned.

825. Excitability. [Excess of sensitiveness.] — **N.** excitability, impetuosity, vehemence; boisterousness etc. *adj.*; turbulence; impatience, intolerance, non-endurance; irritability etc. (*irascibility*) 901; itching etc. (*desire*) 865; wincing; disquiet, -ude; restlessness; fidge-ts, - tiness; agitation etc. (*irregular motion*) 315.

trepidation, perturbation, ruffle, hurry, -skurry, fuss, flurry; fluster, flutter; pother, stew, ferment; whirl; thrill etc. (*feeling*) 821; state −, fever- of excitement; transport.

passion, excitement, flush, heat; fever, -heat; fire, flame, fume, blood boiling; tumult; effervescence, ebullition; boiling, − over; whiff, gust, storm, tempest; scene, breaking out, burst, fit, paroxysm, explosion; out-break, -burst; agony.

violence etc. 173; fierceness etc. *adj.*; rage, fury, *furor*, *furore*, desperation, madness, distraction, raving, delirium, brain storm; frenzy, hysterics; intoxication; tearing −, raging- passion, towering rage; anger etc. 900.

fascination, infatuation, fanaticism; Quixot-ism, -ry; *tête montée*.

V. be -impatient etc. *adj.*; not be able to -bear etc. 826; bear ill, wince, chafe, champ the bit; be in a -stew etc. *n.*; be out of all patience, fidget, fuss, not have a wink of sleep; toss, − on one's pillow.

lose one's temper etc. 900; break −, burst −, fly- out; go −, fly- -off, − off the handle, − off at a tangent; explode; flare up, flame up, fire up, burst into a flame, take fire, fire, burn; boil, − over; foam, fume, rage, rave, rant, tear; go −, run- − wild, − mad; go into hysterics; run -riot, − amuck; *battre la campagne, faire le diable à quatre*, play the deuce; raise -Cain, − the devil.

Adj. excitable, easily excited, in an excitable state; high strung; irritable etc. (*irascible*) 901; impatient, intolerant.

feverish, febrile, hysterical; delirious, mad, moody, maggoty-headed.

unquiet, mercurial, electric, galvanic, hasty, hurried, restless, fidgety, fussy; chafing etc. *v.*

startlish, mettlesome, high mettled, skittish.

vehement, demonstrative, violent, wild, furious, fierce, fiery, hot-headed, mad-cap.

over-zealous, enthusiastic, impassioned, fanatical; rabid etc. (*eager*) 865.

rampant, clamorous, uproarious, turbulent, tempestuous, tumultuary, boisterous.

impulsive, impetuous, passionate; uncontroll-ed, -able; ungovernable, irrepressible, stanchless, inextinguishable, burning, simmering, volcanic, ready to burst forth.

excit-ed, -ing etc. 824.

Int. pish! pshaw!

Phr. *noli me tangere.*

826. Inexcitability. [Absence of excitability, or of excitement.] — **N.** inexcit-, imperturb-, inirritability; even temper, tranquil mind, dispassion; tolerance, toleration, patience.

passiveness etc. (*physical inertness*) 172; hebetude, -ation; impassibility etc. (*insensibility*) 823; stupefaction.

coolness, calmness etc. *adj.*; composure, placidity, indisturbance, imperturbation, *sang-froid*, tranquility, serenity; quiet, -ude; peace of mind, mental calmness.

staidness etc. *adj.*; gravity, sobriety, Quakerism; philosophy, equanimity, stoicism, command of temper; self-possession, -control, -command, - restraint; presence of mind.

submission etc. 725; resignation; suffer-, support-, endur-, long-suffer-, forbear-ance; longanimity; fortitude; patience -of Job, − 'on a monument,' − 'sovereign o'er transmuted ill;' moderation; repression −, subjugation- of feeling; restraint etc. 751.

tranquilization etc. (*moderation*) 174.

V. be -composed etc. *adj.*

laisser -faire, − aller; take things -easily, − as they come; take it easy, run on, live and let live; take -easily, − cooly, − in good part; *aequam serva e mentem*.

bear, − well, − the brunt; go through, support, endure, brave, disregard.

tolerate, suffer, stand, bide, abide, aby; bear −, put up −, abide- with; acquiesce; submit etc. (*yield*) 725; submit with a good grace; resign −, reconcile- oneself to; brook, digest, eat, swallow, pocket, stomach; make -light of, − the best of, − a virtue of necessity; put a good face on, keep one's countenance; carry -on, − through; check etc. 751- oneself.

compose, appease etc. (*moderate*) 174; propitiate; repress etc. (*restrain*) 751; render insensible etc. 823; overcome −, allay −, repress-one's -excitability etc. 825; master one's feelings.

make -oneself, − one's mind- easy; set one's mind at -ease, − rest.

calm −, cool- down; thaw, grow cool.

be -borne, − endured; go down.

Adj. in-, un-excitable; imperturbable; unsusceptible etc. (*insensible*) 823; un-, dispassionate; cold-blooded, inirritable; enduring etc. *v.*; stoical, Platonic, philosophic, staid, stayed; sober, − minded; grave; sober −, grave- as a judge; sedate, demure, cool-, level-headed; steady.

easy-going, peaceful, placid, calm; quiet, − as a mouse; tranquil, serene; cool, − as -a cucumber, − custard; undemonstrative.

temperate etc. (*moderate*) 174; composed, collected; un-excited, -stirred, -ruffled, -disturbed, - perturbed, -impassioned; unoffended; unresisting.

meek, tolerant; patient, − as Job; submissive etc. 725; tame; content, resigned, chastened, subdued, lamblike; gentle, − as a lamb; *suaviter in modo*; mild, − as mother's milk; soft as peppermint; armed with patience, bearing with, clement, forbearant, long-suffering.

Adv. 'like patience on a monument smiling at grief;' *aequo animo*, in cold blood etc. 823; more in sorrow than in anger.

Int. patience! and shuffle the cards.

827. Pleasure.—**N.** pleasure, gratification, enjoyment, fruition; ob-, de-lectation; relish, zest; *gusto* etc. (*physical pleasure*) 377; satisfaction etc. (*content*) 831; complacency.

well-being; good etc. 618; snugness, comfort, ease; cushion etc. 215; *sans souci*, mind at ease.

joy, gladness, delight, glee, cheer, sunshine; cheerfulness etc. 836.

treat, refreshment; frolic, fun, lark, gambol, merry-making; amusement etc. 840; luxury etc. 377; hedonism.

mens sana in corpore sano.

happiness, felicity, bliss; beati-tude, -fication; enchantment, transport, rapture, ravishment, ecstasy; *summum bonum*; paradise, elysium etc. (*heaven*) 981; third –, seventh- heaven; unalloyed - happiness etc.

honeymoon; palmy –, halcyon- days; golden - age, – time; *Saturnia regna*, Eden, Arcadia, happy valley, Agapemone; Cockaigne.
V. be pleased etc. 829; feel –, experience-pleasure etc. *n.*; joy; enjoy –, hug- oneself; be in-clover etc. 377, – elysium etc. 981; tread on enchanted ground; fall –, go- into raptures.

feel at home, breathe freely, bask in the sunshine.

be -pleased etc. 829- with; receive –, derive-pleasure etc. *n.*- from; take -pleasure etc. *n.*- in; delight in, rejoice in, indulge in, luxuriate in; gloat over etc. (*physical pleasure*) 377; enjoy, relish, like; love etc. 897; take -to, – a fancy to; have a liking for; enter into the spirit of.

take in good part.

treat oneself to, solace oneself with.

Adj. pleased etc. 829; not sorry; glad, -some; pleased as Punch.

happy, blest, blessed, blissful, beatified; happy as -a king, – the day is long; thrice happy, *ter quaterque beatus*; enjoying etc. *v.*; joyful etc. (*in spirits*) 836; hedonic.

in -a blissful state, – paradise etc. 981; – raptures, – ecstasies, – a transport of delight.

comfortable etc. (*physical pleasure*) 377; at ease; content etc. 831; *sans souci*, in clover.

overjoyed, entranced, enchanted; enraptured; en-, ravished; transported; fascinated, captivated.

with -a joyful face, – sparkling eyes.

pleasing etc. 829; ecstatic, beat-ic, -ific; painless, unalloyed, without alloy, cloudless.

Adv. happily etc. *adj.*; with pleasure etc. (*willingly*) 60; with -glee etc. *n.*

phr. one's heart leaping with joy.

828. Pain.—**N.** mental suffering, pain, dolor; suffer-ing, -ance; ache, smart etc. (*physical pain*) 378; passion.

displeasure, dissatisfaction, discomfort, discomposure, disquiet; *malaise*; inquietude, uneasiness, vexation of spirit; taking; discontent etc. 832.

dejection etc. 837; weariness etc. 841.

annoyance, irritation, worry, infliction, visitation; plague, bore; bother, -ation; stew, vexation, mortification, chagrin, *esclandre*; *mauvais quart d'heure.*

care, anxiety, solicitude, trouble, trial, ordeal, fiery ordeal, shock, blow, cark, dole, fret, burden, load.

concern, grief, sorrow, distress, affliction, woe, bitterness, gloom, heartache; heavy –, aching –, bleeding –, broken- heart; heavy affliction, gnawing grief; unhappiness, infelicity, misery, tribulation, wretchedness, desolation; despair etc. 859; extremity, prostration, depth of misery.

nightmare, *ephialtes*, incubus.

anguish, agony; throe, tor-ture, -ment; crucifixion, martyrdom; pang, twinge, stab; the rack, the stake; purgatory etc. (*hell*) 982.

hell upon earth; iron age, reign of terror; slough of despond etc. (*adversity*) 735; peck –, sea- of troubles; ills that flesh is heir to, (*evil*) 619; miseries of human life; unkindest cut of all.

sufferer, victim, prey, martyr, object of compassion, wretch, shorn lamb.

V. feel –, suffer –, experience –, undergo –, bear –, endure- pain etc. *n.*; smart, ache etc. (*physical pain*) 378; suffer, bleed, ail; be the victim of; bear – take up- the cross.

labor under afflictions; quaff the bitter cup, have a bad time of it; fall on evil days etc. (*adversity*) 735; go hard with, come to grief, fall a sacrifice to, drain the cup of misery to the dregs, sup full of horrors.

sit on thorns, be on pins and needles, wince, fret, chafe, worry oneself, be in a taking, fret and fume, take -on, – to heart.

grieve; mourn etc. (*lament*) 839; yearn, repine, pine, droop, languish, sink; give way; despair etc. 859; break one's heart; weigh upon the heart etc. (*inflict pain*) 830.

Adj. in –, in a state of –, full of- pain etc. *n.*; suffering etc. *v.*; pained, afflicted, worried, displeased etc. 830; aching, griped, sore etc. (*physical pain*) 378; on the rack; in limbo; between hawk and buzzard.

un-comfortable, -easy; ill at ease; in a -taking, – way; disturbed; discontented etc. 832; out of humor etc. 901a; weary etc. 841.

heavy laden, stricken, crushed, a prey to, victimized, ill-used.

unfortunate etc. (*hapless*) 735; to be pitied, doomed, devoted, accursed, undone, lost, stranded.

unhappy, infelicitous, poor, wretched, miserable, woe-begone; cheerless etc. (*dejected*) 837; careworn.

concerned, sorry; sorrow-ing, -ful; cut up, chagrined, horrified, horror-stricken; in –, plunged in –, a prey to- grief etc. *n.*; in tears etc. (*lamenting*) 839; steeped to the lips in misery; heart-stricken, -broken, -scalded; broken-hearted; in despair etc. 859.

Phr. 'the iron entered into our soul;' *haeret lateri lethalis arundo;'* one's heart bleeding.

829. Pleasurableness. [Capability of giving pleasure; cause or source of pleasure.]—**N.** pleasurable-, pleasant-, agreeable-ness etc. *adj.*; pleasure giving, jocundity, delectability; amusement etc. 840.

attraction etc. (*motive*) 615; attractiveness, -

ability; invitingness etc. *adj.*; charm, fascination, captivation, enchantment, witchery, seduction, winsomeness, winning ways, amenity, amiability, sweetness.

loveliness etc. (*beauty*) 845; sunny –, brightside; sweets etc. (*sugar*) 396; goodness etc. 648; manna in the wilderness, land flowing with milk and honey.

treat; regale etc. (*physical pleasure*) 377; dainty; tit-, tid-bit; nuts, *sauce piquante.*

V. cause –, produce –, create –, give –, afford –, procure –, offer –, present –, yield-pleasure etc. 827.

please, charm, delight; gladden etc. (*make cheerful*) 836; take, captivate, fascinate; enchant, entrance, enrapture, transport, bewitch; en-, ravish.

bless, beatify; satisfy; gratify –, desire etc. 865; slake, satiate, quench; indulge, humor, flatter, tickle; tickle the palate etc. (*savory*) 394; regale, refresh; enliven; treat; amuse etc. 840; take –, tickle –, hit- one's fancy; meet one's wishes; win –, gladden –, rejoice –, warm the cockles of- the heart; do one's heart good.

attract, allure etc. (*move*) 615; stimulate etc. (*excite*) 824; interest, intrigue.

make things pleasant, popularize, gild the pill, sweeten.

Adj. causing pleasure etc. *v.*; pleasure-giving; pleas-ing, -ant, -urable; agreeable, cushy; grat-eful, -ifying; leef, lief, acceptable; welcome, – as the roses in May; welcomed; favorite; to one's -taste, – mind, – liking, – heart's content; satisfactory etc. (*good*) 648.

refreshing; comfortable; cordial; genial; glad, -some; sweet, delectable, nice, dainty; delic-ate, -ious; dulcet; luscious etc. 396; palatable etc. 394; luxurious, voluptuous; sensual etc. 377.

attractive etc. 615; inviting, prepossessing, engaging; win-ning, -some; taking, fascinating, captivating, killing; seduc-ing, -tive; alluring, enticing; appetizing etc. (*exciting*) 824; cheering etc. 836; bewitching; interesting, absorbing, enchanting, entrancing, enravishing.

charming; delightful, felicitous, exquisite; lovely etc. (*beautiful*) 845; ravishing, rapturous; heartfelt, thrilling, ecstatic; beat-ic, -ific; seraphic; empyrean; elysian etc. (*heavenly*) 981.

palmy, halcyon, Saturnian.

Phr. *decies repetita placebit.*

830. Painfulness. [Capability of giving pain; cause or source of pain.]—**N.** painfulness etc. *adj.* ; trouble, care etc. (*pain*) 828; trial; af-, in-fliction; cross, blow, stroke, burden, load, curse; bitter -pill, – draught, – cup; waters of bitterness.

annoyance, grievance, nuisance, vexation, mortification, sickener; bore, bother, pother, hot water, sea of troubles, hornet's nest, plague, pest.

cancer, ulcer, sting, thorn; canker etc. (*bane*) 663; scorpion etc. (*evil-doer*) 913; dagger etc. (*arms*) 727; scourge etc. (*instrument of punishment*) 975; carking –, canker worm of- care; mishap, misfortune etc. (*adversity*) 735; *désagrément, esclandre,* rub.

source of -irritation, – annoyance; wound, sore subject, skeleton in the closet; thorn in -the flesh, – one's side; where the shoe pinches, gall and wormwood.

sorry sight, heavy news, provocation; affront etc. 929; head and front of one's offending.

infestation, molestation; malignity etc. (*malevolence*) 907.

V. cause –, occasion –, give –, bring –, induce –, produce –, create –, inflict- pain etc. 828; pain, hurt, wound.

pinch, prick, gripe etc. (*physical pain*) 378; pierce, lancinate, cut.

hurt –, wound –, grate upon –, jar upon- the feelings; wring –, pierce –, lacerate –, break –, rend- the heart; make the heart bleed; tear –, rend- the heart-strings; draw tears from the eyes.

sadden; make unhappy etc. 828; plunge into sorrow, grieve, fash, afflict, distress; cut -up, – to the heart.

displease, annoy, incommode, discommode, discompose, trouble, disquiet, disturb, thwart, cross, perplex, molest, tease, rag, tire, irk, vex, mortify, wherret, worry, plague, bother, pester, bore, pother, harass, harry, badger, heckle, bait, beset, infest, persecute, importune, be troublesome.

wring, harrow, torment, torture; put to the -rack, – question; break on the wheel, rack, scarify; cruci-ate, -fy; convulse, agonize; barb the dart; plant a -dagger in the breast, – thron in one's side.

irritate, provoke, sting, nettle, try the patience, pique, fret, rile, tweak the nose, chafe, gall; sting –, wound –, cut- to the quick; aggrieve, affront, enchafe, enrage, ruffle, sour the temper; give offence etc. (*resentment*) 900.

maltreat, bite, snap at, assail, bully; smite etc. (*punish*) 972.

sicken, disgust, revolt, nauseate, disenchant, repel, offend, shock, stink in the nostrils; go against –, turn- the stomach; make one sick, set the teeth on edge, go against the grain, grate on the ear; stick in one's -throat, – gizzard; rankle, gnaw, corrode, horrify, appal, freeze the blood; chill the spine; make the -flesh creep, – hair stand on end; make the blood -curdle, – run cold; make one shudder.

haunt, – the memory; weigh –, prey- on the -heart, – mind, – spirits; bring one's grey hairs with sorrow to the grave; add a nail to one's coffin.

Adj. causing pain, hurting etc. *v.*; hurtful etc. (*bad*) 649; painful; dolor-ific, -ous; unpleasant; un-, dis-pleasing; disagreeable, unpalatable, bitter, distasteful; uninviting; unwelcome; undesir-able, -ed; obnoxious; unacceptable, unpopular, thankless.

unsatisfactory, untoward, unlucky, uncomfortable.

distressing; afflict-ing, -ive; joy-, cheer-, comfortless; dismal, disheartening; depress-ing, -ive; dreary, melancholy, grievous, piteous; woeful, rueful, mournful, deplorable, pitiable, lamentable; sad, affecting, touching, pathetic.

irritating, provoking, stinging, annoying, aggravating, mortifying, galling; unaccommodating, invidious, vexatious; trouble-, tire-, irk-, weari-some; plagu-ing, -y; awkward.

importunate; teas-, pester-, bother-, harass-, worry-, torment-, cark-ing.

in-toler-, -suffer-, -support-able; un-bear-, – endur-able; past bearing; not to be -borne, – endured; more than flesh and blood can bear; enough to -drive one mad, – provoke a saint, – make a parson swear, – try the patience of Job.

shocking, terrific, grim, appalling, crushing; dreadful, fearful, frightful; thrilling, tremendous, dire; heart-breaking, -rending, -wounding, -corroding, -sickening; harrowing, rending.

odious, hateful, execrable, repulsive, repellent, abhorrent; horri-d, -ble, -fic, -fying; offensive; nause-ous, -ating; disgust-, sicken-, revolt-ing; nasty; loath-some, -ful; fulsome; vile etc. (*bad*) 649; hideous etc. 846.

sharp, acute, sore, severe, grave, hard, harsh, cruel, biting, acrimonious, caustic; cutting, corroding, consuming, racking, excruciating, searching, searing, grinding, grating, agonizing; envenomed.

ruinous, disastrous, calamitous, tragical; desolating, withering; burdensome, onerous, oppressive; cumb-rous, -ersome.

Adv. painfully etc. *adj.*; with -pain etc. 828; deuced.

Int. *hinc illae lachrymae!* woe is me!

Phr. *surgit amari aliquid*; the place being too hot to hold one; the iron entering the soul.

831. Content.—N. content, -ment, -edness; complacency, satisfaction, entire satisfaction, ease, heart's ease, peace of mind; serenity etc. 826; cheerfulness etc. 836; ray of comfort; comfort etc. (*well-being*) 827.

re-, conciliation; resignation etc. (*patience*) 826. waiter on Providence.

V. be -content etc. *adj.*; rest -satisfied, — and be thankful; take the good the gods provide, let well alone, feel oneself at home, hug oneself, lay the flattering unction to one's soul.

take -up with, — in good part; assent etc. 488; be reconciled to, make one's peace with; get over it; take -heart, — comfort; put up with etc. (*bear*) 826.

render -content etc. *adj.*; set at ease, comfort; set one's -heart, — mind- at -ease, — rest; speak peace; conciliate, reconcile, win over, propitiate, disarm, beguile; content, satisfy; gratify etc. 829.

be -tolerated etc. 826; go down, — with; do.

Adj. content, -ed; satisfied etc. *v.*; at -ease, — one's ease, — home; with the mind at ease, *sans souci, sine curâ*, easy-going, not particular; conciliatory; unrepining, of good comfort; resigned etc. (*patient*) 826; cheerful etc. 836.

un-afflicted, -vexed, -molested, -plagued; serene etc. 826; at rest; snug, comfortable; in one's element.

satisfactory, satisfying, ample, sufficient, adequate, tolerable.

Adv. to one's heart's content; *à la bonne heure*; all for the best.

Int. amen etc. (*assent*) 488; very well, so much the better, well and good; it —, that- will do; it cannot be helped.

Phr. nothing comes amiss.

832. Discontent.—N. discontent, -ment; dissatisfaction; dissent etc. 489; labor unrest.

disappointment, mortification; cold comfort; regret etc. 833; repining, taking on etc. *v.*; inquietude, vexation of spirit, soreness; heart-burning, -grief; querulousness etc. (*lamentation*) 839; hypercriticism.

malcontent, grumbler, growler, croaker, *laudator temporis acti*; censurer, complainer,

faultfinder, murmurer, Adullamite, Diehard, Bitterender.

the Opposition, cave of Adullam, indignation meeting, 'winter of our discontent.'

V. be -discontented etc. *adj.*; quarrel with one's bread and butter; repine; regret etc. 833; wish one at the bottom of the Red Sea; take -on, — to heart; shrug the shoulders; make a wry —, pull a long-face; knit one's brows; look -blue, — black, — black as thunder, — blank, — glum.

take -in bad part, — ill; fret, chafe, make a piece of work; grumble, croak, grouse; lament etc. 839.

cause -discontent etc. *n.*; dissatisfy, disappoint, mortify, put out, disconcert; cut up; dishearten.

Adj. discontented; dissatisfied etc. *v.*; unsatisfied, ungratified; dissident; dissentient etc. 489; malcontent, exigent, exacting, hypercritical.

repining etc. *v.*; regretful etc. 833; down in the mouth etc. (*dejected*) 837.

in -high dudgeon, — a fume, — the sulks, — the dumps, — bad humor; glum, sulky; sour, — as a crab; soured, sore; out of -humor, — temper.

disappointing etc. *v.*; unsatisfactory.

Int. so much the worse!

Phr. that —, it- will never do.

833. Regret.—N. regret, repining; home sickness, nostalgia; *mal —, maladie- du pays*; lamentation etc. 839; contrition, compunction, penitence etc. 950.

bitterness, heart-burning.

laudator temporis acti etc. (*discontent*) 832.

V. regret, deplore; bewail etc. (*lament*) 839; repine, cast a longing lingering look behind; rue, — the day; repent etc. 950; *infandum renovare dolorem*.

prey —, weigh —, have a weight- on the mind; leave an aching void.

Adj. regretting etc. *v.*; regretful; home-sick.

regretted etc. *v.*; much to be regretted, regrettable; lamentable etc. (*bad*) 649.

Int. what a pity! hang it!

Phr. 'tis -pity, — too true.

834. Relief.—N. relief; deliverance; refreshment etc. 689; easement, softening, alleviation, mitigation, palliation etc. 174; soothing, lullaby; cradle song, *berceuse*.

solace, consolation, comfort, encouragement.

lenitive, restorative etc. (*remedy*) 662; poultice etc. *v.*; cushion etc. 215; crumb of comfort, balm in Gilead; aspirin.

V. relieve, ease, alleviate, mitigate, palliate, soothe, addulce; salve; soften, — down; foment, stupe, poultice; assuage, allay.

cheer, comfort, console; encourage, bear up, pat on the back, give comfort, set at ease; enliven, gladden —, cheer- the heart.

remedy; cure etc. (*restore*) 660; refresh; pour -balm into, — oil on.

smoothe the ruffled brow of care, temper the wind to the shorn lamb, lay the flattering unction to one's soul.

disburden etc. (*free*) 705; take off a load of care.

be relieved; breathe more freely, draw a long breath; take comfort; dry —, wipe- the -tears, — eyes.

Adj. relieving etc. *v.*; consolatory, soothing; assua-ging, -sive; bal-my, -samic; lenitive, palliative; anodyne etc. (*remedial*) 662; curative etc. 660.

---

835. Aggravation.—N. aggravation, heightening; exacerbation; exasperation; overestimation etc. 482; exaggeration etc. 549.

V. aggravate, render worse, heighten, embitter, sour; ex-, acerbate; exasperate, envenom; tease, provoke, enrage.

add fuel to the -fire, − flame; fan the flame etc. (*excite*) 824; go from bad to worse etc. (*deteriorate*) 659.

Adj. aggravated etc. *v.*; worse, unrelieved; aggravable; aggravating etc. *v.*

Adv. out of the frying pan into the fire, from bad to worse, worse and worse.

Int. so much the worse!

---

836. Cheerfulness.—N. cheerfulness etc. *adj.*; geniality, gaiety, *l'allegro*, cheer, good humor, spirits; high −, animal −, flow of- spirits; glee, high glee, light heart; sunshine of the -mind, − breast; *gaieté de coeur, bon naturel*.

liveliness etc. *adj.*; life, alacrity, vivacity, animation, *allégresse*; jocundity, joviality, jollity; levity; jocularity etc. (*wit*) 842.

mirth, merriment, hilarity, exhilaration; laughter etc. 838; merry-making etc. (*amusement*) 840; heyday, rejoicing etc. 838; marriage bells.

nepenthe, Euphrosyne.

optimism etc. (*hopefulness*) 858; self-complacency.

V. be -cheerful etc. *adj.*; have the mind at ease, smile, put a good face upon, keep up one's spirits; view -the bright side of the picture, − things *en couleur de rose*; *ridentem dicere verum*, cheer up, brighten up, light up, bear up; chirp, take heart, cast away care, drive dull care away, perk up.

rejoice etc. 838; carol, chirrup, lilt; frisk, rollick, give a loose to mirth.

cheer, enliven, elate, exhilarate, gladden, in-spirit, animate, raise the spirits, inspire; put in good humor; cheer −, rejoice- the heart; delight etc. (*give pleasure*) 829.

Adj. cheerful; happy etc. 827; cheer-y, -ly; of good cheer, smiling; blithe; in −, in good- spirits; in high -spirits, − feather; happy as -the day is long, − a king; gay, − as a lark; *allegro*; light, -some, -hearted; buoyant, *débonnaire*, bright, free and easy, airy; janty, jaunty, canty; spright-ly, -ful; spry; spirit-ed, -ful; lively; animated, breezy; vivacious; brisk, − as a bee; sparkling; sportive; full of -play, − spirit; all alive.

sunny, palmy; hopeful etc. 858.

merry, − as a -cricket, − grig, − marriage bell; joyful, joyous, jocund, jovial; jolly, − as a thrush, − as a sandboy; blithesome; glee-ful, -some; hilarious, rattling.

winsome, bonny, hearty, buxom.

play-ful, -some; *folâtre*, playful as a kitten, tricksy, frisky, frolicsome; gamesome; jocose, jocular, waggish; mirth-, laughter-loving; mirthful, rollicking.

elate, -d; exulting, jubilant, flushed; rejoicing etc. 838; cock-a-hoop.

cheering, inspiriting, exhilarating; cardiac, -al; pleasing etc. 829; flourishing, halcyon.

Adv. cheerfully etc. *adj.*

Int. never say die! come! cheer up! hurrah! etc. 838; 'hence loathed melancholy!' begone dull care! away with melancholy!

---

837. Dejection.—N. dejection; dejectedness etc. *adj.*; depression, prosternation; lowness −, depression- of spirits; weight −, oppression −, damp- on the spirits; low −, bad −', drooping −, depressed- spirits; heart sinking; heaviness −, failure- of heart.

heaviness etc. *adj.*; infestivity, gloom; weariness etc. 841; *taedium vitae*, disgust of life; *mal du pays* etc. (*regret*) 833.

melancholy; sadness etc. *adj.*; *il penseroso*, melancholia, dismals, mumps, mopes, lachrymals, dumps, blues, blue devils, doldrums, vapors, megrims, spleen, horrors, hypochondriasis, pessimism; despondency, slough of Despond; disconsolateness etc. *adj.*; hope deferred, blank despondency.

prostration, − of soul; broken heart; despair etc. 859; cave of -despair, − Trophonius.

demureness etc. *adj.*; gravity, solemnity; long −, grave- face.

hypochondriac, seek-sorrow, self-tormentor, *heautontimorumenos*, *malade imaginaire*, *médecin tant pis*; croaker, pessimist; mope, mopus.

[Cause of dejection] affliction etc. 830; sorry sight; *memento mori*; damper, wet blanket, Job's comforter; death's head, skeleton at the feast.

V. be -dejected etc. *adj.*; grieve; mourn etc. (*lament*) 839; take on, give way, lose heart, despond, droop, sink.

lower, look downcast, frown, pout; hang down the head; pull −, make- a long face; laugh on the wrong side of the mouth; grin a ghastly smile; look -blue, − like a drowned man; lay −, take- to heart.

mope, brood over; fret; sulk; pine, − away; yearn; repine etc. (*regret*) 833; despair etc. 859.

refrain from laughter, keep one's countenance; be −, look- grave etc. *adj.*; repress a smile, keep a straight face.

depress; dis-courage, -hearten; dis-pirit; damp, dull, deject, lower, sink, dash, knock down, un-man, prostrate, break one's heart; frown upon; cast a -gloom, − shade- on; sadden; damp −, dash −, wither- one's hopes; weigh −, lie heavy −, prey-on the -mind, − spirits; damp −, depress- the spirits.

Adj. cheer-, joy-, spirit-less; uncheer-ful, -y; unlively; unhappy etc. 828; melancholy, dismal, somber, dark, gloomy, adust, *triste*, clouded, murky, lowering, frowning, lugubrious, Acherontic, funereal, mournful, lamentable, dreadful.

dreary, flat; dull, − as -a beetle, − ditchwater; depressing etc. *v.*

'melancholy as a gib cat;' oppressed with −; a prey to- melancholy; down-cast, -hearted; down -in the mouth, − on one's luck; heavy-hearted; in the -dumps, − suds, − sulks, − doldrums; in doleful dumps, in bad humor; sullen; mumpish, dumpish; mopish, moping; moody, glum; sulky etc. (*discontented*) 832; out of -sorts, − humor, − heart, − spirits; ill at ease, low-spirited, in low spirits, a cup too low; weary etc. 841; dis-couraged, -heartened; desponding; chop-, jaw-, crest-fallen.

sad, pensive, *penseroso*, tristful; dole-some, -ful; woebegone, lachrymose, in tears, melancholic, hypped, hypochondriacal, bilious, jaundiced, atrabilious, saturnine, splenetic; lackadaisical.

serious, sedate, staid, stayed; grave, − as -a judge, − an undertaker, − a mustard pot; sober, solemn, demure; grim; grim-faced, -visaged; rueful, wan, long-faced.

disconsolate; un-, in-consolable; forlorn, comfortless, desolate, *désolé*, sick at heart; soul-, heartsick; *au désepoir*; in despair etc. 859; lost.

overcome; broken-, borne-, bowed-down; heartstricken etc. (*mental suffering*) 828; cut up, dashed, sunk; unnerved, unmanned; down-fallen, -trodden; broken-hearted; care-worn.

Adv. with -a long face, − tears in one's eyes; sadly etc. *adj*.

Phr. the countenance falling; the heart -failing, − sinking within- one.

838. Rejoicing. [Expression of pleasure.]—**N.** rejoicing, exultation, triumph, jubilation, heyday, flush, revelling; merry-making etc. (*amusement*) 840; jubilee etc. (*celebration*) 883; *paean, Te Deum* etc. (*thanksgiving*) 990; congratulation etc. 896; applause etc. 971.

smile, simper, smirk, grin; broad −, sardonicgrin.

laughter, giggle, titter, crow, cheer, chuckle, snicker, snigger, shout, Homeric laughter, horse −, hearty- laugh; guffaw; burst −, fit −, shout −, roar −, peal- of laughter; cachinnation.

risibility; derision etc. 856.

Momus; Democritus the Abderite; rollicker; Laughter holding both his sides.

V. rejoice; thank −, bless- one's stars; congratulate −, hug- oneself; rub −, clap- one's hands; smack the lips, fling up one's cap; dance, skip, caleer; sing, carol, chirrup, chirp; hurrah; cry for −, leap with- joy; exult etc. (*boast*) 884; triumph; hold jubilee etc. (*celebrate*) 883; make merry etc. (*sport*) 840; sing a paean of joy.

smile, simper, smirk; grin, − like a Cheshire cat; mock, laugh in one's sleeve; laugh, − outright; giggle, titter, snigger, crow, smicker, chuckle, snicker, cackle; burst -out, − into a fit of laughter; shout, split, roar.

-shake −, split −, hold both- one's sides; roar −, die- with laughter.

raise laughter etc. (*amuse*) 840.

Adj. rejoicing etc. *v.*; jubilant, exultant, triumphant; flushed, elated; laughing etc. *v.*; risible; ready to -burst, − split, − die with laughter; convulsed with laughter.

laughable etc. (*ludicrous*) 853.

Int. hip, hip, -hurrah! huzza! aha! hail! tolderolloll! tra-la la! Heaven be praised! *io triumphe! tant mieux!* so much the better.

Phr. the heart leaping with joy.

839. Lamentation. [Expression of pain.]—**N.** lament, -ation; wail, complaint, plaint, murmur, mutter, grumble, groan, moan, whine, whimper, sob, sigh, suspiration, heaving, deep sigh.

cry etc. (*vociferation*) 411; scream, howl; outcry, wail of woe, frown, scowl.

tear; weeping etc. *v.*; flood of tears, fit of crying, lachrymation, melting mood, weeping and gnashing of teeth.

plaintiveness etc. *adj.*; languishment; condolence etc. 915.

mourning, weeds, willow, cypress, crêpe, crape, deep mourning; sackcloth and ashes; knell etc. 363; dump, deathsong, dirge, coronach, keen, *nenia*, requiem, elegy, *epicedium*; threne; mon-, thren-ody; jeremiad; ululation.

mourner, professional mourner, keener; grumbler etc. (*discontent*) 832; Niobe; Heraclitus.

V. lament, mourn, deplore, grieve, weep over; be-wail, -moan; keen; condole with etc. 915; fret etc. (*suffer*) 828; wear −, go into −, put onmourning; wear -the willow, − sackcloth and ashes; *infandum renovare dolorem* etc. (*regret*) 833; give sorrow words.

sigh; give −, heave −, fetch- a sigh; 'waft a sigh from Indus to the pole;' sigh 'like furnace;' wail.

cry, weep, sob, greet, blubber, pipe, snivel, bibber, whimper, pule; pipe one's eye; drop −, shed- -tears, − a tear; melt −, burst- into tears; *fondre en larmes*; cry -oneself blind, − one's eyes out.

scream etc. (*cry out*) 411; mew etc. (*animal sounds*) 412; groan, moan, whine, yammer; roar; roar −, bellow- like a bull; cry out lustily, rend the air, yell.

frown, scowl, make a wry face, grimace, gnash one's teeth, wring one's hands, tear one's hair, beat one's breast, roll on the ground, burst with grief.

complain, murmur, mutter, grumble, growl, clamor, make a fuss about, croak, grunt, maunder; deprecate etc. (*disapprove*) 932.

cry out before one is hurt, complain without cause.

Adj. lamenting etc. *v.*; in mourning, in sackcloth and ashes; crying, sorrowing, -ful etc. (*unhappy*) 828; mourn-, tear-ful; lachrymose; plaint-ive, -ful, quer-ulous, -imonious; in the melting mood.

in -tears, with tears in one's eyes; with -moistened, − watery- eyes; bathed −, dissolvedin tears; 'like Niobe all tears.'

elagiac, epicedial, threnetic.

Adv. *de profundis; les larmes aux yeux*.

Int. heigh-ho! alas! alack! O dear! ah −, woe isme! lackadaisy! well −, lack −, alack- a day! wella-way! alas the day! *O tempora! O mores!* what a pity! *miserabile dictu!* O lud lud! too true!

Phr. tears -standing in, − starting from- the eyes; eyes -suffused, − swimming, − brimming −, over- flowing- with tears.

840. Amusement.—**N.** amuse-, entertain-ment; diver-sion, -tissement; reaction, relaxation, solace; pastime, *passetemps*, sport; labor of love; pleasure etc. 827.

fun, frolic, merriment, whoopee, jollity; joviality, -ness; heyday; laughter etc. 838; jocos-ity, -eness; droll-, buffoon-, tomfool-ery; mummery, masquing, pleasantry; wit etc. 842; quip, quirk.

play; game, − at romps; gambol, romp, prank, antic, rig, lark, spree, skylarking, vagary, trick, monkey trick, *gambade, fredaine, escapade, échappée*, bout, *espièglerie*; practical joke etc. (*ridicule*) 856.

dance; round −, square −, solo −, step −, tap −, clog −, skirt −, sand −, folk −, morris-dance, *pas seul*, step, turn, *chassé*, cut, shuffle, double shuffle; hop, reel, rigadoon, saraband, hornpipe, bolero, fandango, pavan, tarantella, minuet, waltz, polka; galop, -ade; Schottische, *pas de quatre*, Boston, one-, two-step, rumba, tango, maxixe, fox-, turkey-trot, shimmy, ragtime, cakewalk, jazz, blues, Charleston; jig, breakdown, fling, strathspey; *allemande*; gavot, -te; mazurka, morisco; quadrille, lancers, country dance, *cotillon*, polonaise, Sir Roger de Coverley, Swedish dance; *ballet* etc. (*drama*) 599; ball; *bal*, — *masqué*, — *costumé*; masquerade, fancy dress ball; *thé dansant*; Terpsichore, choreography, Russian ballet, classical dancing; eurythmics; nautch dance, *danse du ventre*, cancan.

festivity, merry-making; party etc. (*social gathering*) 892; *fête*, festival, gala, *ridotto*; revel-s, -ry, -ling; carnival, brawl, saturnalia, high jinks; feast, banquet etc. (*food*) 298; regale, *symposium*, wassail; carous-e, -al; jollification, junket, wake, pic-nic, *fête champêtre*, garden party, gymkhana, regatta, track meet, field day, jamboree, treat.

round of pleasures, dissipation, a short life and a merry one, racketing, holiday making, high jinks.

rejoicing etc. 838; jubilee etc. (*celebration*) 883.

bonfire, fireworks, *feu-de-joie*, rocket, catherine wheel, roman candle etc.

holiday; gala —, red letter —, play- day; high days and holidays; high —, Bank- holiday; May —, Derby- day; Saint —, Easter —, Whit- Monday; King's birthday, Empire Day; *mi-carême*; Bairam; wayzgoose, bean feast, beano.

place of amusement, theater etc. 599; concert-, ball-, assembly-room; music-hall, cinema, movies, talkies, vaudeville; hippodrome, circus, rodeo; *casino*, *kursaal*; winter garden; park, pleasance, arbor; garden etc. 371; pleasure-, play-, cricket-, football-, polo-, croquet-, archery-, hunting-ground; golf links, race course, stadium, gridiron, bowl, speedway, racing track, ring; gymnasium, swimming pool; shooting gallery; tennis-, racket-court;- bowling-green, -alley; croquet-lawn, rink, skating rink; roller-coaster, roundabout, carousel, merry-go-round; swing; *montagne russe*; switchback, scenic railway etc.

game, — of -chance, — skill; athletic sports, gymnastics; fencing; archery, rifle-shooting; tournament, pugilism etc. (*contention*) 720; sporting etc. 622; horse-racing, the turf; aquatics etc. 267; skating, roller skating; ski-running, -joring, - jumping, bobsleighing, luging, tobogganing, winter sports; sliding; cricket, tennis, lawn —, table —, deck-tennis, rackets, fives, squash, ping pong, trap bat and ball, battledore and shuttlecock, badminton, *la grâce*; pall mall, tip-cat, croquet, golf, curling, hockey, basketball, soccer, football, Rugby, Association, *pallone*, polo; tent-pegging, tilting at the ring, quintain, greasy pole; quoits, *discus*; throwing the hammer, putting the -weight, — shot, tossing the caber; knurr and spell; leap-frog; hop, skip and jump; French and English, tug of war; blind man's buff, hunt the slipper, hide-and-seek, kiss in the ring; snapdragon; cross questions and crooked answers; jig-saw puzzle; rounders, base-ball, *la crosse* etc.; angling; swimming, diving, water-polo.

billiards, pool, pyramids, snooker, bagatelle; bowls, skittles, ninepins, kail, American bowls.

cards; bridge, auction, contract, whist, rubber; round game, coon-can, loo, cribbage, *bésique*, pinocle, euchre, drole, *écarté*, skat, picquet, all-fours, quadrille, ombre, reverse, Pope Joan, commit; bo-, boa-ston; *vingt-et-un*; *quinze*, thirty-one, put-and-take, speculation, connections, brag, cassino, lottery, commerce, snip-snap-snorem, lift smoke, blind hookey, Polish bank, poker, banker; faro; Earl of Coventry, Napoleon, nap, patience, pairs; old maid, fright, beggar-my-neighbor; *baccarat*, *chemin de fer*, *monté*, roulette.

chess, draughts, backgammon, dominoes, checkers, mah jong, merelles, nine men's morris, go-bang, solitaire; game of —, fox and-goose; lotto; etc.

morra; gambling etc. (*chance*) 621.

toy, plaything, bauble; doll etc. (*puppet*) 554; teetotum; knick-knack etc. (*trifle*) 643; magic lantern etc. (*show*) 448; peep-, puppet-, raree-, gallanty-show; marionettes, Punch and Judy; toyshop; 'quips and cranks and wanton wiles, nods and becks and wreathed smiles.'

sportsman, gamester, gambler etc. 621; reveler, master of the -ceremonies, — revels; *arbiter elegantiarum*.

V. amuse, entertain, divert, eliven; tickle, — the fancy; titillate, raise a smile, put in good humor; cause —, create —, occasion —; raise —, excite —, produce —, convulse with- laughter; set the table in a roar, be the death of one.

recreate, solace, cheer, rejoice; please' etc. 829; interest; treat, regale.

amuse oneself; game; play, — a game, — pranks, — tricks; sport, disport, toy, wanton, revel, junket, feast, carouse, banquet, make merry; drown care; drive dull care away; frolic, gambol, frisk, romp; caper; dance etc. (*leap*) 309; keep up the ball; run a rig, sow one's wild oats, have one's fling, paint the town red, take one's pleasure; see life; *desipere in loco*, play the fool.

make —, keep- holiday; go a Maying.

while away —, beguile- the time; kill time, dally.

Adj. amusing, entertaining, diverting etc. *v.*; recreative, lusory; pleasant etc. (*pleasing*) 829; laughable etc. (*ludicrous*) 853; witty etc. 842; festive, -al; jovial, jolly, jocund, roguish, rompish; sporting; playful — as a kitten; sportive, ludibrious.

amused etc. *v.*; 'pleased with a feather, tickled with a straw.'

Adv. 'on the light fantastic toe,' at play, in sport.

Int. *vive la bagatelle! vogue la galère!*

Phr. *Deus nobis haec otia fecit; dum vivimus vivamus.*

841. Weariness.—N. weariness, defatigation, boredom, *ennui*; lassitude etc. (*fatigue*) 688; drowsiness etc. 683.

disgust, nausea, loathing, sickness; satiety etc. 869; *taedium vitae* etc. (*dejection*) 837.

wearisome-, tedious-ness etc. *adj.*; dull work, tedium, monotony, twice told tale.

bore, button-hole, proser, wet blanket; heavy hours, 'the enemy' [time].

V. weary, tire etc. (*fatigue*) 688; bore; bore —, weary —, tire- -to death, — out of one's life, — -out of all patience; set —, send- to sleep.

pall, sicken, nauseate, disgust.

harp on the same string; drag its -slow, — weary-length along.

never hear the last of; be -tired etc. *adj.* -of, – with; yawn; died with *ennui*.

Adj. wearying etc. *v.*; wearing; weari-, tire-, irksome; uninteresting, stupid, bald, devoid of interest, dry, monotonous, dull, arid, tedious, humdrum, mortal, flat; pros-y, -ing; slow; soporific, somniferous, dormitive.

disgusting etc. *v.*; unenjoyed.

weary; tired etc. *v.*; drowsy etc. (*sleepy*) 683; uninterested, flagging, used up, worn out, *blasé*, life-weary, weary of life; sick of.

Adv. wearily etc. *adj.*; *usque ad nauseam*.

Phr. time hanging heavily on one's hands; *toujours perdrix*; *crambe repetita*.

842. Wit.—N. wit, -tiness; attic -wit, – salt; atticism; salt, *esprit*, point, fancy, whim, humor, drollery, pleasantry.

farce, buffoonery, fooling, tomfoolery; harlequinade etc. 599; broad -farce, – humor; fun, *espiéglerie*; *vis comica*.

jocularity; jocos-ity, -eness; facetiousness; waggery, -ishness; whimsicality; comicality etc. 853.

smartness, ready wit, banter, *badinage*, *persiflage*, retort, repartee, *quid pro quo*; ridicule etc. 856.

facetiae, quips and cranks; jest, joke, capital joke; standing -jest, – joke; conceit, quip, quirk, crank, quiddity, *concetto*, *plaisanterie*, brilliant idea; merry –, bright –, happy- thought; sally; flash, – of wit, – of merriment; scintillation; *mot*, – pour rire; witticism, smart saying, *bon mot*, *jeu d'esprit*, epigram; jest book; dry joke, *quodlibet*, cream of the jest.

word-play, *jeu de mots*; play -of, – upon-words; pun, -ning; *double entente* etc. (*ambiguity*) 520; quibble, verbal quibble; conundrum etc. (*riddle*) 533; anagram, acrostic, double acrostic, *nugae canorae*, trifling, idle conceit, *turlupinade*.

old joke, Joe Miller, chestnut, hoary-headed jest.

V. joke, jest, cut jokes; crack a joke; perpetrate a -joke, – pun; make -fun of, – merry with; set the table in a roar etc. (*amuse*) 840; scintillate.

retort, flash back; banter etc. (*ridicule*) 856; *ridentem dicere verum*; joke at one's expense.

Adj. witty, attic, salty; quick-, nimble-witted; keen, clever, smart, brilliant, pungent, jocular, jocose, funny, waggish, facetious, whimsical, humorous, gilbertian; playful etc. 840; merry and wise; pleasant, sprightly, *spirituel*, sparkling, epigrammatic, full of point, *ben trovato*; comic etc. 853.

Adv. in joke, in jest, in sport, in play.

843. Dullness.—N. dullness, heaviness, flatness; infestivity etc. 837; stupidity etc. 499; want of originality, dearth of ideas.

prose, matter of fact; heavy book, *conte à dormir debout*; platitude.

V. be -dull etc. *adj.*; prose, platitudinize, take *au sérieux*, be caught napping.

render -dull etc. *adj.*; damp, depress, throw cold water on, lay a wet blanket on; fall flat upon the ear; hang fire.

Adj. dull, – as ditch water; dry, insipid, jejune; unentertaining, uninteresting, unlively,

unimaginative; heavisome, heavy-gaited; insulse; dry as dust; pros-y, -ing, -aic; matter of fact, commonplace, banal, pointless; 'weary, flat, stale and unprofitable.'

stupid, slow, flat, sluggish, ponderous, humdrum, monotonous; melancholic etc. 837; stolid etc. 499; plodding.

Phr. *Davus sum non Oedipus*.

844. Humorist.—N. humorist, wag, wit, reparteeist, epigrammatist, gag man, punster; *bel esprit*, life of the party; wit-snapper, -cracker, -worm; joker, jester, jokesmith, Joe Miller, *drôle de corps*, *gaillard*, spark, *persiffleur*, banterer.

buffoon, *farceur*, merry-andrew, mime, tumbler, acrobat, mountebank, charlatan, posturemaster, harlequin, punch, *pulcinella*, scaramouch, clown; wearer of the -cap and bells, – motley; motley, fool; pantaloon, gipsy; jack -pudding, – in the green, – a dandy; zany; mad-cap, pickle-herring, witling, caricaturist, *grimacier*.

845. Beauty.—N. beauty, the beautiful, *le beau ideal*, loveliness.

[Science of the perception of beauty] Callaesthetics.

form, elegance, grace, beauty unadorned; symmetry etc. 242; comeliness, fairness etc. *adj.*; pulchritude, polish, gloss; good -effect, – looks; *belle tournure*; bloom, brilliancy, radiance, splendor, gorgeousness, magnificence; sublimi-ty, -fication.

concinnity, delicacy, refinement; charm, *je ne sais quoi*, style, chic, swank.

Venus, – of Milo; Aphrodite, Hebe, the Graces, Peri, Houri, Cupid, Apollo, Hyperion, Adonis, Antinous, Narcissus; Helen of Troy.

peacock, butterfly; flower, flow'ret gay, rose, lily, asphodel; garden; flower of, pink of; *bijou*; jewel etc. (*ornament*) 847; work of art.

pleasurableness etc. 829.

beautifying; landscape gardening; decoration etc. 847; calisthenics.

V. be -beautiful etc. *adj.*; shine, beam, bloom; become one etc. (*accord*) 23; set off, grace, flatter one.

render -beautiful etc. *adj.*; beautify; polish, burnish; gild etc. (*decorate*) 847; set out.

'snatch a grace beyond the reach of art.'

Adj. beaut-iful, -eous; handsome; pretty; lovely, graceful, elegant; delicate, dainty, refined, exquisite; fair, personable, comely, seemly; bonny; good-looking; well-favored, -made, -formed, -proportioned; proper, shapely; symmetrical etc. (*regular*) 242; harmonious etc. (*color*) 428; sightly.

fit to be seen, passable, not amiss.

goodly, dapper, tight, jimp; gimp; janty, jaunty; natty, quaint, trim, tidy, neat, spruce, smart, tricksy.

bright, -eyed; rosy-, cherry-cheeked; rosy, ruddy; blooming, in full bloom.

brilliant, shining, beam-y, -ing; sparkling, swanky, splendid, resplendent, dazzling, glowing; glossy, sleek.

showy, specious; rich, gorgeous, superb, magnificent, grand, fine, sublime, imposing; majestic 873.

artistic, -al; aesthetic; pict-uresque, -orial; *fait à piendre*, paintable; well-composed, -grouped, -varied; curious.

enchanting etc. (*pleasure-giving*) 829; attractive etc. (*inviting*) 615; becoming etc. (*accordant*) 23; ornamental etc. 847.

undeformed, undefaced, unspotted; spotless etc. (*perfect*) 650.

846. Ugliness.—N. ugliness etc. *adj.*; deformity, inelegance; disfigurement etc. (*blemish*) 848; want of symmetry, inconcinnity; distortion etc. 243; squalor etc. (*uncleanness*) 653.

forbidding countenance, vinegar aspect, hanging look, wry face, '*spretae injuria formae.*'

eyesore, object, figure, sight, fright, specter, scarecrow, hag, harridan, satyr, witch, toad, baboon, monster, Caliban, Aesop, '*monstrum horrendum informe ingens cui lumen ademptum.*'

V. be -ugly etc. *adj.*; look ill, grin horribly a ghastly smile, make faces.

render -ugly etc. *adj.*; deface; dis-, de-figure; deform, spoil, distort etc. 243; blemish etc. (*injure*) 659; soil. etc. (*render unclean*) 653.

Adj. ugly, - as -sin, - a toad, - a scarecrow, - a dead monkey; plain, bald etc. 226; homely etc. (*unadorned*) 849; ordinary, unornamental, inartistic; unsightly, unseemly, uncomely, unshapely, unlovely; sightless, seemless; not fit to be seen; unbeaut-eous, -iful; beautiless; shapeless etc. (*amorphous*) 241; course; garish, over-decorated etc. 882.

mis-shapen, -proportioned; monstrous; gaunt etc. (*thin*) 203; dumpy etc. (*short*) 201; curtailed of its fair proportions; ill-made, -shaped, -proportioned; crooked etc. (*distorted*) 243; hard-featured, -visaged; ill-, hard-, evil-favored; ill-looking; unprepossessing.

graceless, inelegant; ungraceful, ungainly, uncouth; stiff; rugged, rough, gross, rude, awkward, clumsy, slouching, rickety; gawky; lump-ing, -ish; lumbering; hulk-y, -ing; unwieldy.

squalid, haggard; grim, -faced, -visaged; grisly, ghastly; ghost-, death-like; cadaverous, gruesome.

frightful, hideous, odious, uncanny, forbidding, repellant, repulsive; horri-d, -ble; shocking etc. (*painful*) 830.

foul etc. (*dirty*) 653; dingy etc. (*colorless*) 429; gaudy etc. (*color*) 428; disfigured etc. *v.*; discolored (*blemished*) etc. 848.

847. Ornament.—N. ornament, -ation, -al art; ornat-ture, -eness; adorn-ment, decoration, embellishment; architecture.

garnish, polish, varnish, French polish, gilding, japanning, lacquer, ormolu, enamel.

cosmetics, rouge, powder, lipstick, lip salve, mascara; manicure, nail polish; permanent -, Marcel -, finger-wave.

pattern, diaper, powdering, panelling, graining, pargeting, inlay, detail; texture etc. 329; richness; tracery, molding, beading, reeding, fillet, listel, strapwork, *coquillage*, flourish, *fleur-de-lis*; arabesque, fret, *anthemion*; egg and -tongue, -dart; *astragal*, zigzag, *acanthus, cartouche*; pilaster etc. (*projection*) 250; cyma, ogee.

em-, broidery, needlework; knitting, crochet, tatting, brocade, *brocatelle*, beads, bugles; galloon, lace, gimp, *guipure*, fringe, trapping, border, edging, insertion, *motif*, trimming; *passementerie*; drapery, hanging, tapestry, arras; millinery, ermine.

wreath, festoon, garland, lei, chaplet, flower, nosegay, *bouquet*, posy, 'daisies pied and violets blue.'

tassle, knot; shoulder-knot, *épaulette*, epaulet, aigulet, *aiguilette*, frog; star, rosette, bow; feather, plume, *panache, aigrette*.

jewel, -ry, -lery; bijoutry; *bijou, -terie*; diadem, tiara; pendant, trinket, locket, necklace, armilla, bracelet, bangle, armlet, anklet, ear-, nose- ring, carcanet, chain, *châtelaine*, albert, brooch; torque.

gem, precious stone; diamond, brilliant, beryl, aquamarine, alexandrite, cat's eye, emerald, calcedony, chrysoprase, cornelian, jasper, bloodstone, agate, heliotrope; girasol, -e; onyx, plasma; sard, -onyx; garnet, lapis-lazuli, opal, peridot, chrysolite, sapphire, ruby; spinel, -le; balais; oriental –, topaz; turquois, -e; zircon, jacinth, hyacinth, carbuncle, amethyst; moonstone; pearl, coral.

finery, frippery, gewgaw, gimcrack, knick-knack, tinsel, spangle, sequin, *clinquant*, pinch-beck, paste; excess of ornament etc. (*vulgarity*) 851; gaud, pride, ostentation; frills and furbelows.

illustration, illumination, *vignette; fleuron*; head-, tail-piece; *cul-de-lampe*; flowers of rhetoric etc. 577; work of art, article of vertu, bric-à-brac, curio, *bibelot*.

V. ornament, embellish, enrich, decorate, adorn, beautify, adonize.

smarten, furbish, polish, gild, varnish, whitewash, enamel, japan, lacquer, paint, grain.

garnish, trim, dizen, bedizen, prink, prank; trick –, fig- out; deck, bedeck, dight, bedight, array; dress, - up. preen, spruce up, titivate; spangle, bespangle, powder; embroider, work; chase, tool, emboss, fret; emblazon, blazon, illuminate; illustrate.

become etc. (*accord with*) 23.

Adj. ornamented, beautified etc. *v.*; ornate, rich, gilt, begilt, tesselated, enamelled, inlaid; festooned; topiary.

smart, gay, tricksy, flowery, glittering; new-gilt, -spangled; fine, - as -a Mayday queen, - fivepence, - a carrot fresh scraped; pranked out, bedight, well-groomed.

showy, flashy; gaudy etc. (*vulgar*) 851; garish; gorgeous.

ornamental, decorative; becoming etc. (*accordant*) 23.

848. Blemish.—N. blemish, disfigurement, deformity; defect etc. (*imperfection*) 651; flaw; injury etc. (*deterioration*) 659; spots on the sun; eyesore.

stain, blot, slur; spot, -tiness; speck, -le; blur, freckle, mole, *macula*, patch, blotch, birthmark, blain, maculation, tarnish, smudge, smear; dirt etc. 653; bruise, black eye, scar, wem; pustule; excrescence, pimple etc. (*protuberance*) 250.

V. disfigure etc. (*injure*) 659; speckle; render ugly etc. 846.

Adj. pitted, freckled, discolored, bloodshot, bruised, disfigured; stained etc. *n.*; imperfect etc. 651; injured etc. (*deteriorated*) 659.

849. Simplicity.—N. simplicity; plain-, homeli-ness; undress, nudity, nakedness, beauty unadorned, chastity, chasteness.

V. be -simple etc. *adj.* -
render -simple etc. *adj.*; simplify, chasten, strip of ornament.

Adj. simple, plain; home-ly, -spun; ordinary, household.

natural, unaffected; free from -affectation, — ornament; *simplex munditiis*; *sans façon, en déshabillé*, nude, naked.

chaste, inornate, severe.
un-adorned, -ornamented, -decked, -garnished, -arranged, -trimmed, -varnished.
bald, flat, dull, blank.

850. Taste. [Good taste.]—**N.** taste; good — , refined — , cultivated- taste; delicacy, refinement, fine feeling, gust, *gusto*, tact, *finesse*; nicety etc. (*discrimination*) 465; polish, elegance, grace.

virtu; dilettanteism, virtuosity; fine art; cul-ture, -ivation.

[Science of taste] esthetics.

man of -taste etc.; *connoisseur*, judge, critic, *conoscente, virtuoso, amateur, dilettante*, Aristarchus, Corinthian, *arbiter elegantiarum*, stagirite, euphemist.

'caviar to the general.'

V. appreciate, judge, criticize, discriminate etc. 465.

Adj. in good taste; tasteful, tasty; unaffected, pure, chaste, classical, attic; cultivated, refined; dainty; esthetic, artistic; elegant etc. 578; euphemistic.

to one's -taste, — mind; after one's fancy; *comme il faut; tiré à quatre épingles*.

Adv. elegantly etc. *adj.*

Phr. *nihil tetigit quod non ornavit*.

851. Vulgarity. [Bad taste.]—**N.** vulgar-ity, -ism; barbar-, Vandal-, Gothic-ism; *mauvais goût*, bad taste; Babbittry; *gaucherie*, awkwardness, want of tact; ill-breeding etc. (*discourtesy*) 895; ungentlemanly behavior.

coarseness etc. *adj.*; indecorum, misbehavior.

low-, homeli-ness; low life, *mauvais ton*, rusticity; boorishness etc. *adj.*; brutality; rowdy-, ruffian-, blackguard-ism; ribaldry; slang etc. (*neology*) 563.

bad joke, *mauvaise plaisanterie*.

[Excell of ornament] gaudi-, tawdri-ness; false ornament; finery, frippery, trickery, tinsel, gewgaw, *clinquant*.

rough diamond, tomboy, hoyden, cub, unlicked cub; clown etc. (*commonalty*) 876; Hun, Goth, Vandal, Boeotian; vulgarian; snob, cad, bounder, gent; *parvenu* etc. 876; frump, dowdy; slattern etc. 653.

V. be -vulgar etc. *adj.*; misbehave; talk — , smell of the- shop.

Adj. in bad taste, vulgar, unrefined, gutter.
coarse, indecorus, ribald, gross; unseemly, un-

beseeming, unpresentable; *contra bonos mores*; ungraceful etc. (*ugly*) 846.

dowdy, slovenly etc. (*dirty*) 653; ungenteel, shabby genteel; low etc. (*plebeian*) 876;uncourtly; uncivil etc. (*discourteous*) 895; ill-bred, -mannered; underbred; ungentleman-ly, -like; unladylike, unfeminine; wild, — as an unbacked colt.

unkempt, uncombed, untamed, unlicked, unpolished, uncouth, plebeian; incondite; heavy, rude, awkward; home-ly, -spun, -bred; provincial, hick, countrified, rustic, uncultivated, freshwater; boorish, clownish; savage, brutish, blackguard, rowdy, snobbish; barbar-ous, -ic; Gothic, unclassical, doggerel, heathenish, tramontane, outlandish; Bohemian.

obsolete etc. (*antiquated*) 124; unfashionable, old-fashioned, out of date; new-fangled etc. (*unfamiliar*) 83; fantastic, odd etc. (*ridiculous*) 853.

particular; affected etc. 855; meretricious; extravagant, monstrous, horrid; shocking etc. (*painful*) 830.

gaudy, tawdry, bedizened, tricked out, gingerbread; obtrusive, flaunting, loud, flashy, garish, showy.

852. Fashion.—N. fashion, style, *ton, bon ton*, society; good — , polite- society; drawing room, civilized life, civilization, town, *beau monde*, high life, court; world; fashionable — , gay- world; Vanity Fair; show etc. (*ostentation*) 822.

manners, breeding etc. (*politeness*) 894; air, demeanor etc. (*appearance*) 448; *savoir faire*; gentlemanliness, gentility, decorum, propriety, *bienséance*; conventions — , dictates- of society; Mrs. Grundy; convention, -ality; punctilio; form, -ality; etiquette, point of etiquette; custom etc. 613; mode, vogue, style, go; rage etc. (*desire*) 865; prevailing taste, *dernier cri*, dress etc. 225.

man — , woman- of -fashion, — the world; height — , pink — , star — , glass — , leader- of fashion; *arbiter elegantiarum* etc. (*taste*) 850; upper ten thousand etc. (*nobility*) 875; *élite* etc. (*distinction*) 873.

V. be -fashionable etc. *adj.*, — the rage etc. *n.*; have a run, pass current.

follow — , conform to — , fall in with- the fashion etc. *n.*; go with the stream etc. (*conform*) 82; *savoir -vivre, — faire*; keep up appearances, behave oneself.

set the — , bring into- fashion; give a tone to — , cut a figure in- society, rub shoulders with nobility, keep one's carriage.

Adj. fashionable; in -fashion etc. *n.*; *à la mode, comme il faut*; admitted — , admissible- in -society etc. *n.*; presentable, decorous, punctilious, conventional etc. (*customary*) 613; genteel; well-bred, -mannered, -behaved, -spoken; gentleman-like, -ly; ladylike; civil, polite etc. (*courteous*) 894.

polished, refined, thoroughbred, courtly; *distingué*, aristocratic, unembarrassed, poised, *dégagé*; ja-, jau-nty; dashing, fast, showy, high toned, toney.

modish, stylish, in the latest style, *recherché*; new-fangled etc. (*unfamiliar*) 83.

in -court, — full, — evening- dress; *en grande tenue* etc. (*ornament*) 847.

Adv. fashionably etc. *adj.*; for fashion's sake.

853. Ridiculousness.—N. ridiculousness etc.
adj.; comical-, odd-ity etc. *adj.*; extravagance,
drollery.

farce, comedy; burlesque etc. (*ridicule*) 856;
buffoonery etc. (*fun*) 840; frippery; doggerel verses;
Irish bull, Hibernianism, Hibernicism; Spoonerism;
absurdity etc. 497; bombast etc. (*unmeaning*) 517;
anticlimax, bathos; monstrosity etc. (*unconformity*) 83; laughing stock etc. 857.

V. be -ridiculous etc. *adj.*; pass from the sublime
to the ridiculous; make one laugh; play the fool,
make a fool of oneself, commit an absurdity.

play a joke on, make a -fool of, – sucker of, –
monkey of.

Adj. ridiculous, ludicrous; comic, -al; droll,
funny, laughable, *pour rire*, grotesque, farcical,
odd; whimsical, – as a dancing bear; fanciful, fantastic, queer, rum, quizzical, waggish, quaint,
bizarre; eccentric etc. (*unconformable*) 83;
strange, outlandish, out of the way, *baroque*,
rocaille, rococo; awkward etc. (*ugly*) 846.

absurd, extravagant, *outré*, monstrous,
preposterous, bombastic, inflated, stilted,
burlesque, mock heroic.

drollish; serio-, tragic-comic; gimcrack, contemptible etc. (*unimportant*) 643; doggerel;
ironical etc. (*derisive*) 856; risible.

Phr. *'risum teneatis amici?'* *rideret Heraclitus.*

854. Fop.—N. fop, fine gentleman; swell;
dand-y, -iprat; exquisite, coxcomb, toff, beau,
macaroni, blade, blood, buck, man about town,
fast man; fribble, jemmy, spark, popinjay, puppy,
prig, *petit maître*; jacka-napes, -dandy; man
milliner; Jemmy Jessamy, carpet-knight, masher,
Dundreary, Johnnie, dude.

belle, fine lady, *coquette*, flirt.

855. Affectation.—N. affectation; affectedness
etc. *adj.*; acting a part etc. *v.*; pretence etc.
(*falsehood*) 544; (*ostentation*) 882; boasting etc.
884.

charlatanism, quakery, shallow profundity, humbug, pretension, airs, pedantry, purism,
precisianism, euphuism, prunes and prisms;
teratology etc. (*altiloquence*) 577.

mannerism, *simagrée*, grimace.

conceit, foppery, dandyism, man millinery, cox-
combry, puppyism.

stiffness, formality, buckram; prudery,
demureness, coquetry, mock modesty, *minauderie*,
sentimentalism; *mauvaise honte*, false shame.

affector, performer, actor; pedant, pedagogue,
doctrinaire, purist, euphuist, mannerist; shoneen;
grimacier; lump of affectation, *précieuse ridicule*,
bas bleu, blue stocking, poetaster; prig, hypocrite;
charlatan etc. (*deceiver*) 548; *petit maître* etc.
(*fop*) 854; flatterer etc. 935; *coquette*, prude,
puritan; precisian, formalist.

V. affect, act a part, put on; give oneself airs etc.
(*arrogance*) 885; boast etc. 884; coquet; simper,
mince, attitudinize, strike a pose, pose; flirt a fan;
over-act, -play, -do.

Adj. affected, full of affectation, pretentious,
pedantic, stilted, stagey, theatrical, big-sounding,
ad captandum, canting, insincere.

not natural, unnatural; self-conscious; *maniéré*;
artificial; over-wrought, -done, -acted; euphuistic
etc. 577.

stiff, starch, formal, prim, smug, demure, *tiré à*
quatre épingles, quakerish, puritanical, prudish,
pragmatical, priggish, conceited, coxcomical, fop-
pish, dandified; fini-cal, -kin, -cky, mincing,
simpering, namby-pamby, sentimental,
languishing.

856. Ridicule.—N. ridicule, derision; sardonic
-smile, – grin; irrision; snigger; scoffing etc.
(*disrespect*) 929; mockery, quiz, banter, irony,
persiflage, raillery, chaff, *badinage*; quizzing etc.
v.

squib, satire, skit, quip, quib, grin.

parody, burlesque, travesty; farce etc. (*drama*)
599; caricature, take-off.

buffoonery etc. (*fun*) 840; practical joke, horse-
play.

V. ridicule, deride; laugh at, grin at, smile at;
snigger; laugh in one's sleeve; banter, rally, chaff,
joke, twit, quiz, poke fun at, jolly, roast, rag; fleer;
play –, play tricks upon; fool, – to the top of
one's bent; show up.

satirize, parody, caricature, burlesque, travesty.

turn into ridicule; make merry with; make -fun,
– game, – a fool, – an April fool- of; rally; scoff
etc. (*disrespect*) 929.

raise a laugh etc. (*amuse*) 840; play the fool,
make a fool of oneself.

be ridiculous etc. 853.

Adj. deris-ory, -ive; mock; sarcastic, ironical,
quizzical, burlesque, Hudibrastic; scurrilous etc.
(*disrespectful*) 929.

Adv. in -ridicule etc. *n.*

857. Laughing-stock. [Object and cause of
ridicule.]—**N.** laughing-, jesting-, gazing-stock;
butt, game, fair game; April fool etc. (*dupe*) 547.

original, oddity; queer –, odd- fish; quiz, square
toes; old –, fogey *or* fogy..

monkey; buffoon etc. (*jester*) 844; pantomimist
etc. (*actor*) 599.

jest etc. (*wit*) 842.

858. Hope.—N. hope, -s; desire etc. 865; fervent hope, sanguine expectation, trust, confidence,
reliance; faith etc. (*belief*) 484; affiance, assurance,
secur-eness, -ity; reassurance.

good -omen, – auspices; promise; well-
grounded hopes; good –, bright- prospect; clear
sky.

as-, pre-sumption; anticipation etc. (*expectation*)
507.

hopefulness, buoyancy, optimism, enthusiasm,
heart of grace, aspiration; optimist, utop-ian, -ist;
Pollyanna.

castles in the air, *châteaux en Espagne*, hope
chest, *le pot au lait*, Utopia, millennium; day –,
golden- dream; dream of Alnaschar; airy hopes,
fool's paradise; *mirage* etc. (*fallacies of vision*)
443; fond hope.

beam –, ray –, gleam –, glimmer –, dawn
–, flash –, star- of hope; cheer; bit of blue sky,

silver lining of the cloud, bottom of Pandora's box, balm in Gilead.

anchor, sheet-anchor, main-stay; staff etc. (*support*) 215; heaven etc. 981.

V. hope, trust, confide, rely on, put one's trust in, lean upon; pin one's -hope, — faith- upon etc. (*believe*) 484.

feel —, entertain —, harbor —, indulge —, cherish —, feed —, foster —, nourish —, encourage —, cling to —, live in- hope etc. *n.*; see land; feel —, rest- -assured, — confident etc. *adj.*

presume; promise oneself; expect etc. (*look forward to*) 507.

hope for etc. (*desire*) 865; anticipate.

be -hopeful etc. *adj.*; look on the bright side of, view on the sunny side, make the best of it, hope for the best; put -a good, — a bold, — the best-face upon; keep one's spirits up; take heart, — of grace; be of good -heart, — cheer; flatter oneself, lay the flattering unction to one's soul.

catch at a straw, hope against hope, count one's chickens before they are hatched.

give —, inspire —, raise —, hold out- hope etc. *n.*; raise expectations; encourage, hearten, cheer, assure, reassure, buoy up, embolden; promise, bid fair, augur well, be in a fair way, look up, flatter, tell a flattering tale.

Adj. hoping etc. *v.*; in -hopes etc. *n.*; hopeful, confident; secure etc. (*certain*) 484; sanguine, in good heart, buoyed up, buoyant, elated, flushed, exultant, enthusiastic; utopian.

unsus-pecting, -picious; fearless, free —, exempt from- -fear, — suspicion, — distrust, — despair; undespairing, self-reliant.

probable, on the high road to; within sight of -shore, — land; promising, propitious; of —, full of-promise; of good omen; auspicious, *de bon augure*; reassuring; encouraging, cheering, inspiriting, looking up, bright, roseate, *couleur de rose*, rose-colored.

Adv. hopefully etc. *adj.*

Phr. *nil desperandum*; never say die, *dum spiro spero*, *latet scintillula forsan*, all is for the best, *spero meliora*; the wish being father to the thought; 'hope told a flattering tale;' *rusticus expectat dum defluat amnis*.

859. Hopelessness. [Absence, want, or loss of hope.]—**N.** hopelessness etc. *adj.*; despair; desperation; despondency etc. (*dejection*) 837; pessimism.

hope deferred, dashed hopes; vain expectation etc. (*disappointment*) 509.

airy hopes etc. 858; forlorn hope; bad -job, — business; *enfant perdu*; gloomy —, black spots in the- horizon; slough of Despond, cave of Despair.

Job's comforter; bird of -bad, — ill-omen.

V. despair; lose —, give up —, abandon —, relinquish- -all hope, — the hope of; give -up, — over; yield to despair; falter; despond etc. (*be dejected*) 837; *jeter le manche après la cognée.*

inspire —, drive to- despair etc. *n.*; disconcert; dash —, crush —, shatter —, destroy- one's hopes; hope against hope.

Adj. hopeless, desperate, despairing, in despair, *au désespoir*, forlorn; inconsolable etc. (*dejected*) 837; broken-hearted.

out of the question, not to be thought of; im-

practicable etc. 471; past -hope, — cure, — mending, — recall; at one's last gasp etc. (*death*) 360; given -up, — over.

incurable, cureless, immedicable, remediless, beyond remedy; incorrigible; irre-parable, -mediable, -coverable, -versible, -trievable, -claimable, -deemable, -vocable; ruined, undone; immitigable.

unpromising, unpropitious; inauspicious, ill-omened, threatening, clouded over, lowering, ominous.

Phr. '*lasciate ogni speranza voi ch' entrate*;' its days are numbered; the worst come to the worst.

860. Fear.—N. fear, timidity, diffidence, want of confidence; apprehensive-, fearful-ness etc. *adj.*; solicitude, anxiety, care, apprehension, misgiving; mistrust etc. (*doubt*) 485; suspicion, qualm; hesitation etc. (*irresolution*) 605.

nervous-, restless-ness etc. *adj.*; in-, dis-quietude; flutter, trepidation, fear and trembling, perturbation, tremor, quivering, shaking, trembling, throbbing heart, palpitation, ague fit, cold sweat; abject fear etc. (*cowardice*) 862; mortal funk, heart-sinking, despondency; despair etc. 859.

fright; affright, -ment; alarm, pavor, dread, awe, terror, horror, dismay, consternation, panic, scare, stampede [of horses].

intimidation, terrorism, reign of terror.

[Object of fear] bug-bear, -aboo; scarecrow; hobgoblin etc. (*demon*) 980; daymare, nightmare, Gorgon, Medusa, mormo, ogre, Hurlothrumbo, raw head and bloody bones, fee faw fum, *bête noire*, *enfant terrible*.

alarmist etc. (*coward*) 862.

V. fear, stand in awe of; be -afraid etc. *adj.*; have -qualms etc. *n.*; apprehend, sit upon thorns, eye askance; distrust etc. (*disbelieve*) 485.

hesitate etc. (*be irresolute*) 605; falter, funk, cower, crouch; skulk etc. (*cowardice*) 862; let 'I dare not' wait upon 'I would;' take -fright, — alarm; start, wince, flinch, shy, shrink; fly etc. (*avoid*) 623.

tremble, shake; shiver, — in one's shoes; shudder, flutter; shake —, tremble- -like an aspen leaf, — all over; quake, quaver, quiver, quail; get the wind up.

grow —, turn- pale; blench; stand aghast; not dare to say one's soul is one's own.

inspire —, excite- -fear, — awe; raise apprehensions; give —, raise —, sound- an alarm; alarm, startle, scare, cry 'wolf,' disquiet, dismay; fright, -en; affright, terrify; astound; frighten from one's propriety; frighten out of one's -wits, — senses, — seven senses; awe; strike -all of a heap, — an awe into, — terror; harrow up the soul, appal, unman, petrify, horrify.

make one's -flesh creep, — hair stand on end, — blood run cold, — teeth chatter; chill one's spine; take away —, stop- one's breath; make one -tremble etc.

haunt, obsess, beset; prey —, weigh- on the mind.

put in -fear, — bodily fear; terrorize, intimidate, cow, daunt, over-awe, abash, deter, discourage; browbeat, bully; threaten etc. 909.

Adj. fearing etc. *v.*; frightened etc. *v.*; in -fear, — a fright etc. *n.*; haunted with the -fear etc. *n.*- of.

afraid, fearful; tim-id, -orous; nervous, diffident, coy, faint-hearted, tremulous, shaky, afraid of one's shadow, apprehensive, restless, fidgety; more frightened than hurt.

aghast; awe-, horror-, terror-, panic- -struck, - stricken; frightened to death, white as a sheet; pale, — as -death, — ashes, — a ghost; breathless, in hysterics.

inspiring fear etc. *v.*; alarming; formidable, redoubtable; perilous etc. (*danger*) 665; portentous; fear-ful, -some; dread, -ful; fell; dire, -ful; shocking; terri-ble, -fic; tremendous; horri-d, -ble, -fic; ghastly; awful, awe-inspiring, eerie, weird; revolting etc. (*painful*) 830.

Adv. *in terrorem.*

Int. 'angels and ministers of grace defend us!'

Phr. *ante tubam trepidat*; *horresco referens*, one's heart failing one, *obstupui steteruntque comae et vox faucibus haesit.*

861. Courage. [Absence of fear.]—N. courage, bravery, valor; resolute-, bold-ness etc. *adj.*; spirit, daring, gallantry, intrepidity; contempt —, defiance- of danger; derring-do; audacity; rashness etc. 863; dash; defiance etc. 715; confidence, self-reliance.

man-liness, -hood; nerve, pluck, mettle, game; heart, — of grace; spunk, gameness, grit, face, virtue, hardihood, fortitude; firmness etc. (*stability*) 150; heart of oak; ' bottom, backbone etc. (*perseverance*) 604*a.*

resolution etc. (*determination*) 604; tenacity, bull-dog courage.

prowess, heroism, chivalry.

exploit, feat, achievement; heroic -deed, — act; bold stroke.

man, — of mettle; hero, demigod, paladin, heroine, Amazon, Hector, Joan of Arc; lion, tiger, panther, bulldog; game-, fighting-cock; bully, fire-eater etc. 863; dare-devil.

V. be -courageous etc. *adj.*; dare, venture, make bold; face —, front —, affront —, confront —, brave —, defy —, despise —, mock- danger; look in the face; look -full, — boldly, — danger- in the face; face; meet, — in front; brave, beard; defy etc. 715.

take —, muster —, summon up —, pluck up-courage; nerve oneself, take heart; take —, pluck up- heart of grace; hold up one's head, screw one's courage to the sticking place; come -to, — up to-the scratch; stand, — to one's guns, — fire, — against; bear up — against; hold out etc. (*persevere*) 604*a.*

put a bold face upon; show —, present- a bold front, face the music; envisage; show fight.

bell the cat, take the bull by the horns, beard the lion in his den, march up to the cannon's mouth, go through fire and water, run the gauntlet, go over the top.

give —, infuse —, inspire- courage; reassure, encourage, embolden, inspirit, cheer, hearten, nerve, put upon one's mettle, rally, raise a rallying cry; pat on the back, make a man of, keep in countenance.

Adj. courageous, brave; val-iant, -orous; gallant, intrepid; spirit-ed, -ful; high-spirited, -mettled; mettlesome, game, plucky; man-ly, -ful; resolute; stout, -hearted; iron-, lion-hearted; heart of oak; Penthesilean.

bold, — spirited; daring, audacious; fear-, daunt-, dread-, awe-less; un-daunted, -appalled, -dismayed, -awed, -blenched, -abashed, -alarmed, -flinching, -shrinking, -blenching; apprehensive; confident, self-reliant; bold as -a lion, — brass.

enterprising, adventurous; ventur-ous, -esome; dashing, chivalrous; soldierly etc. (*warlike*) 722; heroic.

fierce, savage; pugnacious etc. (*bellicose*) 720.

strong-minded, hardy, doughty; firm etc. (*stable*) 150; determined etc. (*resolved*) 604; dogged, indomitable etc. (*persevering*) 604*a.*

up to, — the scratch; upon one's mettle; reassured etc. *v.*; unfeared, undreaded.

Phr. one's blood being up.

862. Cowardice. [Excess of fear.]—N. cowardice, pusillanimity; cowardliness etc. *adj.*; timidity, effeminacy.

poltroonery, baseness; dastard-ness, -y; abject fear, funk; Dutch courage; fear etc. 860; white feather, faint heart.

coward, poltroon, dastard, sneak, recreant; shy —, dunghill- cock; coistril, milksop, white-liver, nidget, cur, craven, one that cannot say 'Boo' to a goose; Bob Acres, Jerry Sneak.

alarm-, terror-, pessim-ist; runagate etc. (*fugitive*) 623; shirker.

V. quail etc. (*fear*) 860; be -cowardly etc. *adj.*, — a coward etc. *n.*; funk; cower, skulk, sneak; flinch, shy, fight shy, slink, turn tail; run away etc. (*avoid*) 623; show the white feather, have cold feet, show a yellow streak.

Adj. coward, -ly; fearful, shy; tim-id, -orous; skittish; poor-spirited, spirit-less, soft, effeminate.

weak-minded; infirm of purpose etc. 605; weak-, faint-, chicken-, lily-, pigeon-hearted; yellow; white-, lily-, milk-livered; milksop, smock-faced; unable to say 'Boo' to a goose.

dastard, -ly; base, craven, sneaking, dunghill, recreant; unwar-, unsoldier-like.

'in face a lion but in heart a deer.'

unmanned; frightened etc. 860.

Int. *sauve qui peut!* devil take the hindmost!

Adv. in fear and trembling, in fear of one's life, in a blue funk.

Phr. *ante tubam trepidat*, one's courage oozing out.

863. Rashness.—N. rashness etc. *adj.*; temerity, want of caution, imprudence, indiscretion; over-confidence, presumption, audacity.

precipit-ancy, -ation; impetuosity; levity; foolhardi-hood, -ness; heed-, thought-lessness etc. (*inattention*) 458; carelessness etc. (*neglect*) 460; desperation; Quixotism, knight-errantry; fire-eating.

gam-ing, -bling; blind bargain, leap in the dark, fool's paradise; too many eggs in one basket.

desperado, rashling, mad-cap, dare-devil, Hotspur, fire-eater, bully, *bravo*, Hector, scapegrace, *enfant perdu*; Don Quixote, knight-errant, Icarus; adventurer; gam-bler, -ester; dynamitard.

V. be -rash etc. *adj.*; stick at nothing, play a desperate game; run into danger etc. 665; play with -fire, — edge tools.

carry too much sail, sail too near the wind, ride
at single anchor, go out of one's depth.

take a leap in the dark, buy a pig in a poke.

donner tête baissée; knock one's head against a
wall etc. (*be unskilful*) 699; rush on destruction;
kick against the pricks, tempt Providence, go on a
forlorn hope.

count one's chickens before they are hatched;
reckon without one's host; catch at straws; trust to
– , lean on- a broken reed.

Adj. rash, incautious, indiscreet, injudicious; imprudent, improvident, temerarious; uncalculating;
heedless; careless etc. (*neglectful*) 460; without
ballast, heels over head; giddy etc. (*inattentive*)
458; wanton, reckless, wild, madcap; desperate,
devil-may-care.

hot-blooded, -headed, -brained; head-long, -
strong; break-neck; fool-hardy; harebrained;
precipitate, impulsive.

over-confident, -weening; ventur-esome, -ous;
adventurous, Quixotic; fire-eating, cavalier; free-
and-easy.

off one's guard etc. (*inexpectant*) 508.

Adv. post haste, *à corps perdu*, hand over head,
tête baissée, head- foremost; happen what may.

Phr. neck or nothing, the devil being in one.

864. Caution.—N. caution; cautiousness etc.
adj.; discretion, prudence, cautel, heed, circumspection, calculation, deliberation; safety first.

foresight etc. 510; vigilance etc. 459; warning
etc 668.

coolness etc. *adj.*; self-possession, -command;
presence of mind, *sang froid*; well-regulated mind;
worldly wisdom, Fabian policy.

V. be -cautious etc. *adj.*; take -care, – heed, –
good care; have a care; mind, – what one is about;
be on one's guard etc. (*keep watch*) 459; make
assurance double sure; ca' canny.

bespeak etc. (*be early*) 132.

think twice, look before one leaps, keep one's
weather eye open, count the cost, look to the main
chance, cut one's coat according to one's cloth; feel
one's -ground, – way; see how the land lies etc.
(*foresight*) 510; wait to see how the cat jumps;
bridle one's tongue; *reculer pour mieux sauter* etc.
(*prepare*) 673; let well alone, let sleeping dogs lie,
ne pas réveiller le chat qui dort.

keep out of -harm's way, – troubled waters;
keep at a respectful distance, stand aloof; keep –,
be- on the safe side.

husband one's resources etc. 636.

caution etc. (*warn*) 668.

Adj. cautious, wary, guarded; on one's guard
etc. (*watchful*) 459; *cavendo tutus*; *in medio
tutissimus*.

care-, heed-ful; cautelous, stealthy, chary, shy of,
circumspect, prudent, canny, safe, non-committal,
discreet, politic; sure-footed etc. (*skilful*) 698.

unenterprising, unadventurous, cool, steady, self-
possessed; over-cautious.

suspicious, leery, vigilant.

Adv. cautiously, gingerly etc. *adj.*

Int. have a care! look out! *cave canem!*

Phr. *timeo Danaos*; *festina lente*.

865. Desire.—N. desire, wish, fancy, fantasy;
want, need, exigency.

mind, inclination, leaning, bent, *animus*, partiality, *penchant*, predilection; propensity etc. 820;
willingness etc. 602; liking, love, fondness, relish.

longing, hankering; solicitude, anxiety; yearning,
coveting; aspiration, ambition, vaulting ambition;
eagerness, zeal, ardor, *empressement*, breathless
impatience, over-anxiety; solicitude, impetuosity
etc. 825.

appet-ite, -ition, -ence, -ency; sharp appetite,
keenness, hunger, stomach, twist; thirst, -iness;
drouth, mouth-watering; itch, -ing; prurience,
cacoëthes, cupidity, lust, concupiscence.

edge of -appetite, – hunger; torment of Tantalus; sweet – , lickerish- tooth; itching palm;
longing – , wistful – , sheep's-eye.

avidity; greed, -iness; covetous-, ravenous-ness
etc. *adj.*; grasping, craving, canine appetite,
rapacity; voracity etc. (*gluttony*) 957.

passion, rage, *furore*, mania, *manie*; inextinguishable desire; dips-, klept-, mon-omania.

[Person desiring] desirer, lover, *amateur*,
votary, devotee, aspirant, solicitant, candidate; cormorant etc. 957; sycophant.

[Object of desire] *desideratum*; want etc.
(*requirement*) 630; 'consumation devoutly to be
wished;' attraction, magnet, allurement, fancy,
temptation, seduction, lure, fascination, *prestige*,
height of one's ambition, idol; whim, -sey; maggot;
hobby, -horse.

Fortunatus's cap, wishing cap, love potion.

V. desire; wish, – for; be -desirous etc. *adj.*;
have a -longing etc. *n.*; hope etc. 858.

care for, affect, like, list; take to, cling to, take a
fancy to; fancy; prefer etc. (*choose*) 609.

have -an eye, – a mind- to; find it in one's heart
etc. (*be willing*) 602; have a fancy for, set one's
eyes upon; cast a sheep's eye – , look sweet- upon;
take into one's head, have a heart, be bent upon;
set one's -cap at, – heart upon, – mind upon;
covet.

want, miss, need, lack, desiderate, feel the want
of; would fain -have, – do; would be glad of.

be -hungry etc. *adj.*; have a good appetite, play a
good knife and fork; hunger – , thirst – , crave – ,
lust – , itch – , hanker – , run mad- after; raven
–, die- for; burn to.

desiderate; sigh – , cry – , gape – , gasp – , pine
–, pant – , languish – , yearn – , long – , be on
thorns – , hope- for; aspire after; catch at, grasp at,
jump at.

woo, court, solicit; fish – , spell – , whistle – ,
put up- for; ogle.

cause – , create – , raise – , excite – , provoke-
desire; whet the appetite; appetize, titillate, allure,
attract, take one's fancy, tempt; hold out -
temptation, – allurement; tantalize, make one's
mouth water, *faire venir l'eau à la bouche*.

gratify desire etc. (*give pleasure*) 829.

Adj. desirous; desiring etc. *v.*; orectic, ap-
petitive; inclined etc. (*willing*) 602; partial to; fain,
wishful, optative; anxious, wistful, curious; at a loss
for, sedulous, solicitous.

craving, hungry, sharp-set, peckish, ravening,
with an empty stomach, esurient, lickerish, thirsty,
athirst, parched with thirst, pinched with hunger,
famished, dry, drouthy; hungry as a -hunter, –
hawk, – horse, – church mouse.

greedy, – as a hog; over-eager, voracious;
ravenous, – as a wolf; open-mouthed, covetous,
rapacious, grasping, extortionate, exacting, sordid,

alieni appetens; insati-able, -ate; unquenchable, quenchless; omnivorous.

unsatisfied, unsated, unslaked.

eager, avid, keen; burning, fervent, ardent; agog; all agog; breathless; impatient etc. (*impetuous*) 825; bent –, intent –, set- -on, – upon; mad after, *enragé*, rabid, dying for, devoured by desire.

aspiring, ambitious, vaulting, sky-aspiring.

desirable; popular; desired etc. *v.*; in demand; pleasing etc. (*giving pleasure*) 829; appeti-zing, -ble; tantalizing.

Adv. wistfully etc. *adj.*; fain.

Int. would -that, – it were! O for! *esto perpetua!* if only!

Phr. the wish being the father to the thought; *sua cuique voluptas*; *hoc erat in votis*, the mouth watering, the fingers itching; *aut Caesar aut nullus.*

866. Indifference.—N. indifference, neutrality; coldness etc. *adj.*; unconcern, *insouciance, nonchalance*; want of -interest, – earnestness; anorexy, inappetency; apathy etc. (*insensibility*) 823; supineness etc. (*inactivity*) 683; disdain etc. 930; recklessness etc. 863; inattention etc. 458.

V. be -indifferent etc. *adj.*; stand neuter; take no interest in etc. (*insensibility*) 823; have no -desire etc. 865, – taste, – relish- for; not care for; care nothing -for, – about; not care a -straw etc. (*unimportance*) 643 -about, – for; not mind.

set at naught etc. (*make light of*) 483; spurn etc. (*disdain*) 930.

Adj. indifferent, cold, frigid, lukewarm; cool, – as a cucumber; unconcerned, *insouciant*, phlegmatic, *pococurante*, easy-going, devil-may-care, careless, listless, lackadaisical, feckless; half-hearted; un-ambitious, -aspiring, -desirous, -solicitous, -attracted.

un-attractive, -alluring, -desired, -desirable, -cared for, -wished, -valued, all one to.

insipid etc. 391; vain.

Adv. for aught one cares.

Int. never mind.

867. Dislike.—N. dis-like, -taste, -relish, -inclination, -placency.

reluctance; backwardness etc. (*unwillingness*) 603.

repugnance, disgust, queasiness, turn, nausea, loathing; avers-eness, -ation, -ion; abomination, antipathy, abhorrence, horror; mortal –, rooted- -antipathy, – horror; hatred, detestation; hate etc. 898; animosity etc. 900; hydrophobia.

sickener; gall and wormwood etc. (*unsavory*) 395; shuddering, cold sweat.

V. dis-, mis-like; mind, object to; have rather not, not care for; have –, conceive –, entertain –, take- -a dislike, – an aversion- to; have no -taste, – stomach- for.

shun, avoid etc. 623; eschew; withdraw –, shrink –, recoil- from; not be able to -bear, – abide, – endure; shrug the shoulders at, shudder at, turn up the nose at, look askance at; make a -mouth, – wry face, – grimace; make faces.

loathe, nauseate, abominate, detest, abhor; hate etc. 898; take amiss etc. 900; have enough of etc. (*be satiated*) 869.

cause –, excite- dislike; disincline, repel, sicken; make –, render- sick; turn one's stomach, nauseate, wamble, disgust, shock, stink in the nostrils; go against the -grain, – stomach; stick in the throat; make one's blood run cold etc. (*give pain*) 830; pall.

Adj. disliking etc. *v.*; averse to, loth, adverse; shy of, sick of, out of conceit with; disinclined; heart-, dog-sick; queasy.

disliked etc. *v.*; uncared for, unpopular; out of favor; repulsive, repugnant, repellent; abhorrent, insufferable, fulsome, nauseous; loath-some, -ful; offensive; disgusting etc. *v.*; disagreeable etc. (*painful*) 830; unsavory etc. 395.

Adv. *usque ad nauseam.*

Int. faugh! foh! ugh!

868. Fastidiousness.—N. fastidiousness etc. *adj.*; nicety, meticulosity, hypercriticism, difficulty in being pleased, *friandise*, epicurism *omnia suspendens naso.*

discrimination, discernment, good taste, perspicacity.

epicure, gourmet.

[Excess of delicacy] prudery, prudishness, primness.

V. be -fastidious etc. *adj.*; split hairs, discriminate, have a sweet tooth.

mince the matter; turn up one's nose at etc. (*disdain*) 930; look a gift horse in the mouth, see spots on the sun.

Adj. fastidious, meticulous, exacting, nice, delicate, *délicat*, finical, finicky, difficult, dainty, lickerish, squeamish, thin-skinned; s-, queasy; hard –, difficult- to please; querulous, particular, over-particular, straitlaced, prudish, prim, scrupulous; censorious etc. 932; hypercritical, discriminating, discerning, perspicacious.

Phr. *noli me tangere.*

869. Satiety.—N. satiety, satisfaction, saturation, repletion, glut, surfeit; weariness etc. 841.

spoiled child; *enfant gâté*; too much of a good thing, *toujours perdrix*; *crambe repetita.*

V. sate, satiate, satisfy, saturate; cloy, quench, slake, pall, glut, gorge, surfeit; bore etc. (*weary*) 841; tire etc. (*fatigue*) 688; spoil.

have -enough of, – quite enough of, – one's fill, – too much of; be -satiated etc. *adj.*

Adj. satiated etc. *v.*; overgorged; *blasé*, used up, sick of, heart-sick.

Int. enough! hold! *eheu jam satis!*

870. Wonder.—N. wonder, marvel; astonish-, amaze-, wonder-, bewilder-ment; amazedness etc. *adj.*; admiration, awe; stup-or, -efaction; stound, fascination; sensation; surprise etc. (*inexpectation*) 508; cynosure.

note of admiration; thaumaturgy etc. (*sorcery*) 992.

V. wonder, marvel, admire; be -surprised etc. *adj.*; start; stare; open –, rub –, turn up- one's eyes; gloar; gape, open one's mouth, hold one's breath; look –, stand- -aghast, – agog; look blank etc. (*disappointment*) 509; *tomber des nues*; not believe one's -eyes, – ears, – -senses.

not be able to account for etc. (*unintelligible*) 519; not know whether one stands on one's head or one's heels.

surprise, astonish, amaze, astound; dumbfound, -er; startle, dazzle; strike, – with -wonder, – awe; electrify; stun, stupefy, petrify, confound, bewilder, flabbergast; stagger, throw on one's beam ends, fascinate, turn the head, take away one's breath, strike dumb; make one's -hair stand on end, – tongue cleave to the roof of one's mouth; make one stare.

take by surprise etc. (*be unexpected*) 508.

be -wonderful etc. *adj.*; beggar – , baffle-description; stagger belief.

Adj. surprised etc. *v.*; aghast, all agog, breathless, agape; open-mouthed; awe-, thunder-, moon-, planet-struck; spell-bound; lost in -amazement, – wonder, – astonishment; struck all of a heap, unable to believe one's senses, like a duck in thunder.

wonderful, wondrous; surprising etc. *v.*; unexpected etc. 508; unheard of; mysterious etc. (*inexplicable*) 519; miraculous; *foudroyant*.

in-describable, -expressible, -effable; un-utterable, -speakable.

monstrous, prodigious, stupendous, marvelous; in-conceivable, -credible; in-, un-imaginable; strange etc. (*uncommon*) 83; passing strange.

striking etc. *v.*; over-whelming; wonder-working.

Adv. wonderfully etc. *adj.*; fearfully; for a – , in the name of- wonder, strange to say; *mirabile -dictu*, – visu; to one's great surprise.

with -wonder etc. *n.*, – gaping mouth, – open eyes, – upturned eyes; eyes starting out of one's head.

Int. lo, – and behold! O! hey-day! halloo! what! indeed! really! surely! humph! hem! good -lack, – heavens, – gracious! – lord! by jove! gad so! well a day! dear me! only think! lack-a-daisy! my -stars, – goodness! gracious goodness! goodness gracious! mercy on us! heavens and earth! God bless me! bless -us, – my heart! odzookens! *O gemini!* ad-zooks! hoity-toity! strong! Heaven save – , bless-the mark! can such things be! zounds! 'sdeath! what -on earth, – in the world! who would have thought it! etc. (*inexpectation*) 508; fancy! did you ever? you don't say so! what do you say to that! how now! where am I? well I'm blowed! etc.

Phr. *vox faucibus haesit*; one's hair standing on end.

871. Expectance. [Absence of wonder.]—**N.** expectan-ce, -cy etc. (*expectation*) 507; calmness, composure, tranquillity, serenity, coolness, im-perturbability etc. 826.

nine days' wonder.

V. expect etc. 507; not -be surprised, – wonder etc. 870; *nil admirari*, make nothing of.

Adj. expecting etc. *v.*; unamazed, astonished at nothing; *blasé* etc. (*weary*) 841; unimaginative, calm, serene, imperturbable etc. 826; expected etc. *v.*; foreseen.

common, ordinary etc. (*habitual*) 613.

Int. no wonder; of course; why not?

872. Prodigy.—**N.** prodigy, phenomenon; wonder, -ment; genius, marvel, miracle; freak, monster etc. (*unconformity*) 83; curiosity, lion, infant prodigy, sight, spectacle; *jeu* – , *coup- de théâtre*; gazing-stock; sign; portent etc. 512.

bursting of a -shell, – bomb; volcanic eruption, peal of thunder; thunder-clap, -bolt.

what no words can paint; wonders of the world; *annus mirabilis*; *dignus vindice nodus*.

873. Repute.—N. distinction, mark, name, figure; repute, reputation, character; good – , high-repute; note, notability, notoriety, *éclat*, 'the bubble reputation,' vogue, celebrity; fame, famousness; renown; populairty, *aura popularis*; esteem, approval, approbation etc. 931; credit, *succès d'estime, prestige*, talk of the town; name to conjure with.

glory, honor; luster etc. (*light*) 420; illustriouness etc. *adj.*

account, regard, respect; reputableness etc. *adj.*; respectability etc. (*probity*) 939; good -name, – report; fair name.

dignity; stateliness etc. *adj.*; solemnity, grandeur, splendor, nobility, majesty, sublimity.

rank, standing, brevet rank, precedence, *pas*, station, place, *status*; position, – in society; order, degree, *locus standi*, caste, condition.

greatness etc. *adj.*; eminence; height etc. 206; importance etc. 642; pre-, super-eminence; high mightiness, primacy; top of the -ladder, – tree.

elevation; ascent etc. 305; super-, ex-altation; dignification, aggrandizement.

dedication, consecration, enthronement, canonization, apotheosis, deification, celebration, enshrinement, glorification.

hero, man of mark, great card, celebrity, worthy, lion, *rara avis*, notability, somebody; man of rank etc. (*nobleman*) 875; pillar of the -state, – society, – church.

chief etc. (*master*) 745; first fiddle etc. (*proficient*) 700; scholar etc. 492; cynosure, mirror; flower, pink, pearl; paragon etc. (*perfection*) 650; choice and master spirits of the age; *élite*; star, sun, constellation, galaxy.

ornament, honor, feather in one's cap, halo, aureole, nimbus; halo – , blaze- of glory; blushing honors; laurels etc. (*trophy*) 733.

memory, posthumous fame, niche in the temple of fame; immor-tality, -tal name; *magni nominis umbra*.

V. be conscious of glory; be proud of etc. (*pride*) 878; exult etc. (*boast*) 884; be vain of etc. (*vanity*) 880.

be -distinguished etc. *adj.*; shine etc. (*light*) 420; shine forth, figure; make – , cut- a -figure, – dash, – splash.

rival, surpass; out-shine, -rival, -vie, -jump; emulate, vie with, eclipse; throw – , cast- into the shade; overshadow.

live, flourish, glitter, scintillate, flaunt; gain – , acquire- honor etc. *n.*; play first fiddle etc. (*be of importance*) 642; bear the -palm, – bell; lead the way; take -precedence, – the wall of; gain – , win-laurels, – spurs, – golden opinions etc. (*approbation*) 931; graduate, take one's degree, pass one's examination, win a -scholarship, – fellowship.

make -a, – some- -noise, – noise in the world; leave one's mark, exalt one's horn, star, have a run, be run after; enjoy popularity, come -into vogue, – to the front; raise one's head.

enthrone, signalize, immortalize, deify, exalt to the skies; hand one's name down to posterity.

consecrate; dedicate to, devote to; enshrine, inscribe, blazon,. lionize, blow the trumpet, crown with laurel.

confer −, reflect- honor etc. *n.* on; shed a luster on; redound to one's honor, ennoble.

give −, do −, pay −, render- honor to; honor, accredit, pay regard to, dignify, glorify; sing praises to etc. (*approve*) 931; look up to; exalt, aggrandize, elevate, nobilitate.

Adj. distinguished, *distingué*, noted; of -note etc. *n.*; honored etc. *v.*; popular; fashionable etc. 852.

in good odor; in −, in high- favor; reput-, respect-, credit-able.

remarkable etc. (*important*) 642; notable, notorious; celebrated, renowned, in every one's mouth, talked of; fam-ous, -ed; far-famed; conspicuous, to the front; foremost; in the -front rank, − ascendant.

imperishable, deathless, immortal, never fading, *aere perennius*; time-honored.

illustrious, glorious, splendid, brilliant, radiant; bright etc. 420; full-blown; honorific.

eminent, prominent; high etc. 206; in the zenith; at the -head of, − top of the tree; peerless, of the first water; superior etc. 33; super-, pre-eminent.

great, dignified, proud, noble, honorable, worshipful, lordly, grand, stately, august, princely, imposing, solemn, transcendent, majestic, sacred, sublime, heaven-born, heroic, *sans peur et sans reproche*; sacrosanct.

Int. hail! all hail! *ave! viva! vive!* long life to! glory −, honor- be to!

Phr. one's name -being in every mouth, − living for ever; *sic itur ad astra, fama volat, aut Caesar aut nullus*; not to know him argues oneself unknown; none but himself could be his parallel, *palmam qui meruit ferat.*

874. Disrepute.—N. disrepute, discredit; ill-, bad- -repute, -name, -odor, -favor; disapprobation etc. 932; in-gloriousness, derogation; a-, debasement; abjectness etc. *adj.*; degradation, dedecoration; 'a long farewell to all one's greatness;' odium, obloquy, opprobrium,· ignominy.

dishonor, disgrace; shame, humiliation; scandal, baseness, vileness; perfidy, turpitude etc. (*improbity*) 940; infamy.

tarnish, taint, defilement, pollution.

stain, blot, spot, blur, stigma, brand, reproach, imputation, slur.

crying −, burning- shame; *scandalum magnatum*, badge of infamy, blot in one's escutcheon; bend −, bar- sinister; champain, point champain; by- word of reproach; Ichabod.

argumentum ad verecundiam; sense of shame etc. 879.

V. be -inglorious etc. *adj.*; incur -disgrace etc. *n.*; have −, earn- a bad name; put −, wear- a halter round one's neck; disgrace −, expose- oneself.

play second fiddle; lose caste; pale one's ineffectual fire; recede into the shade; fall from one's high estate; keep in the background etc. (*modesty*) 881; be conscious of disgrace etc. (*humility*) 879; look -blue, − foolish, − like a fool; cut a -poor,

− sorry- figure; laugh on the wrong side of the mouth; make a sorry face, go away with a flea in one's ear, slink away.

cause -shame etc. *n.*; shame, disgrace, put to shame, dishonor; throw −, cast −, fling −, reflect- dishonor etc. *n.* upon; be a -reproach etc. *n.* to; derogate from.

tarnish, stain, blot, sully, taint; discredit, degrade, debase, defile; beggar; expel etc. (*punish*) 972.

impute shame to, brand, post, stigmatize, vilify, defame, slur, cast a slur upon, hold up to shame, send to Coventry; tread −, trample- under foot; show up, drag through the mire, heap dirt upon; reprehend etc. 932.

bring low, put down, snub; take down a peg, − lower, − or two.

obscure, eclipse, outshine, take the shine out of; throw −, cast- into the shade; overshadow; leave −, put- in the background; push into a corner, put one's nose out of joint; put out, − of countenance.

upset, throw off one's center; discompose, disconcert; put to the blush etc. (*humble*) 879.

Adj. disgraced etc. *v.*; blown upon; shorn of -its beams, − one' glory; overcome, down-trodden; loaded with -shame etc. *n.*; in -bad repute etc. *n.*; out of -repute, − favor, − fashion, − countenance; at a discount; under -a cloud, − an eclipse; unable to show one's face; in the -shade, − background; out at elbows, down in the world, down and out.

inglorious; nameless, renownless, obscure, unknown to fame; un-noticed, -noted, -honored, -glorified.

shameful; dis-graceful, -creditable, -reputable; despicable; questionable; unbecoming, unworthy; derogatory; degrading, humiliating, *infra dignitatem*, dedecorous; scandalous, infamous, too bad, unmentionable; ribald, opprobrious; arrant, shocking, outrageous, notorious, shady.

ignominious, scrubby, dirty, abject, vile, beggarly, pitiful, low, mean, shabby; base etc. (*dishonorable*) 940.

Adv. to one's shame be it spoken.

Int. fie! shame! for shame! *proh pudor! O tempora! O mores!* ough! *sic transit gloria mundi!*

875. Nobility.—N. nobility, rank, condition, distinction, optimacy, blood, *pur sang*, birth, high descent, order; quality, gentility; blue blood of Castile; *ancien régime*.

high life, *haut monde*; upper -classes, − ten thousand; *élite*, aristocracy, great folks; fashionable world etc. (*fashion*) 852; salariat.

peer, -age; house of -lords, − peers; lords, − temporal and spiritual; *noblesse*; baronage, knightage; noble, -man; lord, -ling; grandee, *magnifico*, hidalgo; don, -ship; aristocrat, swell, three-tailed bashaw; gentleman, squire, squireen, patrician, laureate.

gentry, gentlefolk; squirarchy, better sort, *magnates, primates, optimates*.

king etc. (*master*) 745; prince, crown prince, *Dauphin*; duke; marquis, -ate; earl, viscount, baron, thane, banneret; baronet, -cy; knight, -hood; count, armiger, laird; sig-, seig-nior; esquire, boyar, margrave, vavasor, sheik, emir, ameer, scherif, *pasha*, effendi, sahib.

queen etc. 745; princess, begum, duchess, marchioness; countess etc.; lady, dame.

personage –, man- of -distinction, – mark, – rank; nota-bles, -bilities; celebrity, big-wig, magnate, great man, star; *magni nominis umbra*; 'every inch a king;' grand Panjandrum

V. be -noble etc. *adj.*

Adj. noble, exalted; of -rank etc. *n.*; princely, titled, patrician, aristocratic; high-, well-born; of gentle blood; genteel, *comme il faut*, gentlemanlike, courtly etc. (*fashionable*) 852; highly respectable.

Adv. in high quarters.

876. Commonalty.—N. commonalty, democracy; obscurity; low -condition, – life, – society, – company; *bourgeoisie*; mass of -the people, – society; Brown, Jones, and Robinson; Tom, Dick, and Harry; lower –, humbler- -classes, – orders; vulgar –, common- herd; rank and file, *hoc genus omne*; the -many, – general, – crowd, – people, – populace, – multitude, – million, – masses, – mobility, – peasantry; king Mob; proletariat, *fruges consumere nati*, great unwashed; man in the street

mob; rabble, – rout; chaff, rout, horde, *canaille*; scum –, *residuum* –, dregs- of -the people, – society; swinish multitude, *faex populi*; *profanum* –, *ignobile- vulgus*; vermin, riff-raff, tag-rag and bobtail; small fry.

commoner, one of the people, democrat, plebeian, republican, proletary, *prolétaire*, *roturier*, Mr. Snooks, *bourgeois*, *épicier*, Philistine, cockney; *grisette*, *demi-monde*.

peasant, countryman, boor, carle, churl; vill-ain, -ein; serf, kern, tyke, tike, chuff, ryot, fellah; longshoreman; swain, clown, hind; clod, -hopper; hobnail, yokel, hick, rube, cider squeezer, hog-trotter, bumpkin; ploughman, -boy; rustic, chawbacon, tiller of the soil; hewers of wood and drawers of water, groundling; gaffer, loon, put, cub, Tony Lumpkin, looby, lout, under-ling; *gamin*, guttersnipe, street arab, mudlark; rough, rowdy, ruffian, roughneck; pot-wallopper, slubberdegullion; vulgar –, low- fellow; cad, curmudgeon.

upstart, *parvenu*, *nouveau-riche*, skipjack; nobody, – one knows; *hesterni quirites*, *pessoribus orti*; *bourgeois gentilhomme*, *novus homo*, snob, gent, mushroom, no one knows who, adventurer; man of straw.

beggar, panhandler, gaberlunzie, muckworm, mudlark, *sans-culotte*, raff, tatterdemalion, caitiff, ragamuffin, Pariah, outcast of society, tramp, weary Willie, bum, vagabond, *chiffonaier*, rag-picker, Cinderella, cinderwench, scrub, jade; boots, gossoon.

Goth, Vandal, Hottentot, savage, barbarian, Yahoo; unlicked cub, rough diamond.

barbar-ousness, -ism; Boeotia.

V. be -ignoble etc. *adj.*, – nobody etc. *n.*

Adj. ignoble, common, mean, low, base, vile, sorry, scrubby, beggarly, below par; no great shakes etc. (*unimportant*) 643; home-ly, -spun; vulgar, low-minded; snobbish, *parvenu*.

plebeian, proletarian; of -low, – mean- -parentage, – origin, extraction; low-, base-, earth-born, low bred; mushroom, dunghill, risen from the ranks; unknown to fame, obscure, untitled.

rustic, uncivilized; lout-, boor-, clown-, churl-, brut-, raff-ish; rude, unlicked, unpolished.

barbar-ous, -ian, -ic, -esque; cockney, born within sound of Bow bells.

underling, menial, servile, subaltern.

Adv. below the salt.

877. Title.—N. title, honor; knighthood etc. (*nobility*) 875.

royal –, serene- highness, excellency, grace; lordship, worship, Rt. Hon., rever-ence, -end; esquire, sir; madam, *madame*; master, mistress, Mr., Mrs., *signor, señor; Mein Herr, mynheer*; your –, his- honor; handle to one's name.

decoration, laurel, palm, wreath, garland, bays, medal, ribbon, riband, blue ribbon, *cordon*, cross, crown, coronet, star, garter; feather, – in one's cap; chevron, epaulet, *épaulette*, colors, cockade; livery; order, arms, armorial bearings, shield, scutcheon, crest, reward etc. 973.

878. Pride.—N. dignity, self-respect, *mens sibi conscia recti*.

pride; haughtiness etc. *adj.*; high notions, *hauteur*; vainglory, crest; arrogance etc. (*assumption*) 885; pomposity etc. 882.

proud man, highflier; fine -gentleman, – lady; *grande dame*,

V. be proud etc. *adj.*; put a good face on, look one in the face; stalk abroad, perk oneself up; presume, swagger, strut; rear –, lift up –, hold up- one's head; hold one's head high, look big, take the wall, 'bear like the Turk no rival near the throne,' carry with a high hand; ride the –, mount on one's- high horse; set one's back up, bridle, toss the head; give oneself airs etc. (*assume*) 885; boast etc. 884.

pride oneself on; glory in, take pride in; pique –, plume –, hug- oneself; stand upon, be proud of; put a good face on; not -hide one's light under a bushel, – put one's talent in a napkin; not think small beer of oneself etc. (*vanity*) 880.

Adj. dignified; stately; proud, -crested; lordly, baronial; lofty-minded; high-souled, -minded, -mettled, -handed, -plumed, -flown, -toned.

haughty, paughty, insolent, lofty, high, mighty, swollen, puffed up, flushed, blown; vain-glorious; purse-proud, fine; proud as -a peacock, Lucifer; bloated with pride.

supercilious, disdainful, bumptious, magisterial, imperious; high-handed, – and mighty; overweening, consequential; arrogant etc. 885; unblushing etc. 880.

stiff, -necked; starch; perked –, stuck- up; in buckram, straitlaced; prim etc. (*affected*) 855.

on one's -high horses, – tight ropes, – high ropes; on stilts; *en grand seigneur*.

Adv. with head erect, with one's nose in the air.

Phr. *odi profanum vulgus et arceo.*

879. Humility.—N. hum-ility, -bleness; meek-, low-ness; lowli-ness, -hood; abasement, self-abasement, -effacement; submission etc. 725; resignation.

condescension; affability etc. (*courtesy*) 894.

modesty etc. 881; verecundity, blush, suffusion, confusion; sense of -shame, — · disgrace; humiliation, mortification; let —, set- down.

V. be -humble etc. *adj.*; deign, vouchsafe, condescend; humble —, demean- oneself; stoop, — to conquer; carry coals; submit etc. 725; submit with a good grace etc. (*brook*) 826; yield the palm.

lower one's -tone, — note; sing small, draw in one's horns, sober down; hide one's -face, — diminished head; not dare to show one's face, take shame to oneself, not have a word to say for oneself; feel —, be conscious of- -shame, — disgrace; drink the cup of humiliation to the dregs; eat -humble pie, — one's words, — dirt; be humiliated, receive a snub.

blush -for, — up to the eyes; redden, change color; color up; hang one's head, look foolish, feel small.

render humble; humble, humiliate; let —, set —, take —, tread —, frown- down; snub, abash, abase, make one sing small, strike dumb; teach one -his distance, — his place; take down a peg. — lower; throw —, cast- into the shade etc. 874; stare —, put- out of countenance; put to the blush; confuse, ashame, mortify, disgrace, crush; send away with a flea in one's ear.

get a set down.

Adj. humble, lowly, meek; modest etc. 881; humble-, sober-minded; unoffended; submissive etc. 725; servile etc. 886.

condescending; affable etc. (*courteous*) 894.

humbled etc. *v.*; bowed down, resigned; abashed, ashamed, dashed; out of countenance; down in the mouth; down on one's -knees, — marrow-bones; humbled in the dust, brow-beaten; chap-, crest-fallen; dumbfoundered, flabbergasted, struck all of a heap.

shorn of one's glory etc. (*disrepute*) 874.

Adv. with -downcast eyes, — bated breath, — bended knee; on all fours, on one's feet.

under correction, with due deference.

Phr. I am your -obedient, — very humble- servant; my service to you.

880. Vanity.—N. vanity; conceit, -edness; self-conceit, -complacency, -confidence, -sufficiency, - esteem, -love, -approbation, -praise, -glorification, - laudation, -gratulation, -applause, -admiration; *amour-propre*; selfishness etc. 943.

airs, pretensions, mannerism; egotism; prigg-ism, -ishness; coxcombery, gaudery, vainglory, elation; pride etc. 878; ostentation etc. 882; assurance etc. 885.

vox et praeterea nihil; *cheval de bataille*.

ego-ist, -tist; peacock, coxcomb etc. 854; Sir Oracle etc. 887.

V. be -vain etc. *adj.*, — vain of; pique oneself etc. (*pride*) 878; lay the flattering unction to one's soul.

have -too high, — an overweening- opinion of - oneself, — one's talents; blind oneself as to one's own merit; not think -small beer, — *vin ordinaire*- of oneself; put oneself forward; fish for compliments; give oneself airs etc. (*assume*) 885; boast etc. 884.

render -vain etc. *adj.*; inspire with -vanity etc. *n.*; inflate, puff up, turn up, turn one's head.

Adj. vain, — as a peacock; conceited, assured, overweening, pert, forward, perky; vain-glorious, high-flown; ostentatious etc. 882; puffed up, inflated, flushed.

self-satisfied, -confident, -sufficient, -flattering, - admiring, -applauding, -glorious, -opinionated; *entêté* etc. (*wrong-headed*) 481; wise in one's own conceit, pragmatical, overwise, pretentious, priggish; egotistic, -al; *soi-disant* etc. (*boastful*) 884; arrogant etc. 885.

un-abashed, -blushing; un-constrained, - ceremonious; free and easy.

Adv. vainly etc. *adj.*

Phr. how we apples swim!

881. Modesty.—N. modesty; humility etc. 879; diffidence, timidity; retiring disposition, unobtrusiveness, bashfulness etc. *adj.*; *mauvaise honte*; blush, -ing; verecundity; self-knowledge.

reserve, constraint; demureness etc. *adj.*; blushing honors.

V. be -modest etc. *adj.*; retire, reserve oneself; give way to; draw in one's horns etc. 879; hide one's face.

keep -private, — in the background, — one's distance; pursue the noiseless tenor of one's way, 'do good by stealth and blush to find it fame,' hide one's light under a bushel, cast a sheep's eye.

Adj. modest, diffident; humble etc. 879; timid, timorous, bashful; shy, nervous, skittish, coy, sheepish, shamefaced, blushing, over-modest.

unpreten-ding, -tious; un-obtrusive, -assuming, - ostentatious, -boastful, -aspiring; poor in spirit.

out of countenance etc. (*humbled*) 879.

reserved, constrained, demure.

Adv. humbly etc. *adj.*; quietly, privately; without -ceremony, — beat of the drum; *sans façon*.

882. Ostentation.—N. ostentation, display, show, flourish, parade, *étalage*, pomp, array, state, solemnity, dash, splash, glitter, strut, swank, side, swagger, pomposity; preten-se, -sions; showing off; fuss.

magnificence, splendor; *coup d'oeil*; grand doings.

coup de théâter; stage -effect, — trick; clap-trap; *mise en scène; tour de force; chic*.

demonstration, flying colors; tomfoolery; flourish of trumpets etc. (*celebration*) 883; pageant, -ry; spectacle, exhibition, procession; turn —, set- out; grand function; *fête*, gala, field-day; review, march past, promenade, insubstantial pageant.

dress; court —, full —, evening —, ball —; fancy- dress; tailoring, millinery, man-millinery, frippery; foppery, equipage.

ceremon-y, -ial; ritual; form, -ality; etiquette; punct-o, -ilio, -ilious-ness; starched-, stateli-ness.

mummery, solemn mockery, mouth honor.

attitudinarian; fop etc. 854.

V. be -ostentatious etc. *adj.*; come —, put oneself- forward; attract attention, star it.

make —, cut- a -figure, — dash, — splash; strut, blow one's own trumpet; figure, — away; make a show, — display; glitter.

show -off, — one's paces; parade, march past;

display, exhibit, put forward, hold up; trot −, hang- out; sport, brandish, blazon forth; dangle, − before the eyes.

cry up etc. (*praise*) 931; *prôner*, flaunt, emblazon, prink, set off, mount, have framed and glazed.

put a good, − smiling- face upon; clean the outside of the platter etc. (*disguise*) 544.

Adj. ostentatious, showy, dashing, pretentious, ja-, jau-nty; grand, pompous, palatial; high-sounding; turgid etc. (*big-sounding*) 577; garish, gorgeous; gaudy, − as a -peacock, − butterfly, − tulip; flaunting, flashing, flaming, glittering; gay etc. (*ornate*) 847; colorful.

splendid, magnificent, sumptuous.

theatrical, dramatic, spectacular, scenic, ceremonial, ritual, -istic.

solemn, stately, majestic, formal, stiff, ceremonious, punctilious, starch-ed, -y.

en grande tenue, in best bib and tucker, in Sunday best, *endimanché*.

Adv. with -flourish of trumpet, − beat of drum, − flying colors, − a brass band.

ad captandum vulgus.

883. Celebration.—N. celebration, solemnization, jubilee, diamond jubilee, commemoration, ovation, paean, triumph, jubilation.

triumphal arch, bonfire, salute; salvo, − of artillery; *feu de joie*, flourish of trumpets, *fanfare*, colors flying, illuminations, fireworks.

inauguration, installation, presentation; *début*, coming out, birthday anniversary, bi-, ter-, centenary; silver −, golden −, diamond- wedding, - day; coronation; Lord Mayor's show; harvest home, red letter day, festival; trophy etc. 733; *Te Deum* etc. (*thanksgiving*) 990; fête etc. 882; holiday etc. 840.

V. celebrate, keep, signalize, do honor to, commemorate, solemnize, hallow, mark with a red letter, hold high festival, maffick.

pledge, drink to, toast, hob and nob.

inaugurate, install, instate, induct, chair.

rejoice etc. 838; kill the fatted calf, hold jubilee, roast an ox, fire a salute.

Adj. celebrating etc. *v.*; commemorative, celebrated, immortal.

Adv. in -honor, − commemoration, − celebration of.

Int. hail! all hail! *io -paean*, − *triumphe!* 'see the conquering hero comes!'

884. Boasting.—N. boasting etc. *v.*; boast, vaunt, crake; preten-ce, -sions; puff, -ery; flourish, *fanfaronnade*; gasconade; bluff, swank, brag, - gardism'; bravado, bunkum, Buncombe; high-falutin; jact-itation, -ancy; bounce, rant, bluster; venditation, vaporing, rodomontade, bombast, fine talking, tall talk, magniloquence, teratology, heroics; jingoism, Chauvinism; exaggeration etc. 549; gas, hot air.

vanity etc. 880; *vox et praeterea nihil*; much cry and little wool, *brutum fulmen*.

exultation; glorification; flourish of trumpets; triumph etc. 883.

boaster; bragg-art, -adocio; hot air merchant;

Gascon, *fanfaron*, pretender, fourflusher, *soi-disant*; windbag, blowhard, bluffer; chauvinist; blusterer etc. 887; charlatan, jack-pudding, trumpeter; puppy etc. (*fop*) 854.

V. boast, make a boast of, brag, vaunt, puff, show off, flourish, crake, crack, trumpet, strut, swagger, vapor, bluff; draw the long bow.

exult, crow over, neigh, chuckle, triumph; glory, gloat, jubilate; throw up one's cap; talk big, *se faire valoir*, *faire claquer son fouet*, take merit to oneself, make a merit of, sing *Io triumphe*, holloa before one is out of the wood.

Adj. boasting etc. *v.*; magniloquent, flaming, Thrasonic, stilted, gasconading, braggart, boastful, pretentious, *soi-disant*; vain-glorious etc. (*conceited*) 880.

elate, -d; jubilant, triumphant, exultant; in high feather; flushed, − with victory; cock-a-hoop; on stilts.

vaunted etc. *v.*

Adv. vauntingly etc. *adj.*; with a brass band.

Phr. 'let the galled jade wince.'

885. Insolence. [Undue assumption of superiority.]—N. insolence; haughtiness etc. *adj.*; arrogance, airs; overbearance, brashness, bumptiousness, contumely, disdain; domineering etc. *v.*; tyranny etc. 739.

impertinence; cheek, nerve, sauce; sauciness etc. *adj.*; flippancy, dicacity, petulance, procacity, bluster; swagger, -ing etc. *v.*; bounce; terrorism, jingoism, chauvinism.

as-, pre-sumption; beggar on horseback; usurpation.

impudence, assurance, audacity, self-assertion, hardihood, front, face, brass; shamelessness etc. *adj.*; effrontery, hardened front, face of brass.

assumption of infallibility.

malapert, saucebox etc. (*blusterer*) 887.

V. be -insolent etc. *adj.*; bluster, vapor, swagger, swell, give oneself airs; snap one's fingers, kick up a dust; swear etc. (*affirm*) 535; rap out oaths; roister.

arrogate; as-, pre-sume; make -bold, − free; take a liberty, give an inch and take an ell.

domineer, bully, dictate, hector; lord it over, bulldoze; *traiter de haut*, *regarder de haut en bas*; exact; snub, huff, beard, fly in the face of; put to the blush; bear- - -, beat- down; browbeat, intimidate; trample −, tread- -down, − under foot; dragoon, ride roughshod over, terrorize.

out-face, -look, -stare, -brazen, -brave; stare out of countenance; brazen out; lay down the law; teach one's grandmother to suck eggs; assume a lofty bearing; talk −, look- big; put on big looks, act the *grand seigneur*; mount −, ride- the high horse; toss the head, carry with a high hand.

tempt Providence, want snuffing.

Adj. insolent, haughty, arrogant, imperious, magisterial, dictatorial, arbitrary; high-handed, high and mighty; contumelious, supercilious, overbearing, intolerant, domineering, overweening, high-flown.

flippant, pert, cavalier, saucy, forward, impertinent, fresh, malapert.

precocious, assuming, would-be, bumptious.

bluff; brazen-, browed-faced, shameless, aweless, unblushing, unabashed; bold-, bare-faced; dead −, lost- to shame.

impudent, audacious, presumptuous, free and easy, devil-may-care, rollicking; janty, jaunty; roistering, blustering, hectoring, swaggering, vaporing; thrasonic, fire-eating, 'full of sound and fury.'

Adv. insolently, with a high hand; *ex cathedrâ*.

Phr. one's bark being worse than his bite.

886. Servility.—N. servility; slavery etc. (*subjection*) 749; obsequiousness etc. *adj.*; subserviency; abasement; pros-tration, -ternation; genuflexion etc. (*worship*) 990; fawning etc. *v.*; tuft-hunting, time-serving, flunkeyism; sycophancy etc. (*flattery*) 933; humility etc. 879.

sycophant, parasite, yes-man; toad, -y, -eater; tuft-hunter; snob, flunkey, lap-dog, spaniel, lickspittle, smell-feast, *Graeculus esuriens*, hanger on, stooge, *cavaliere servente*, led captain, carpet knight; time-server, fortune-hunter, Vicar of Bray, Sir Pertinax Mac Sycophant, pick-thank; flatterer etc. 935; doer of dirty work; *âme damnée*, tool; reptile; slave etc. (*servant*) 746; courtier; sponge, jackal; truckler.

V. cringe, bow, stoop, kneel, bend the knee; fall on one's knees, prostrate oneself; worship etc. 990.

sneak, crawl, crouch, cower, truckle to, grovel, fawn, toady, lick the feet of, kiss the hem of one's garment.

pay court to; feed –, fatten –, batten- on; dance attendance on, pin oneself upon, hang on the sleeve of, *avaler des couleuvres*, keep time to, fetch and carry, do the dirty work of.

go with the stream, follow the crowd, worship the rising sun, hold with the hare and run with the hounds.

Adj. servile, obsequious; supple, – as a glove; soapy, oily, pliant, cringing, fawning, slavish, groveling, sniveling, mealy-mouthed; beggarly, sycophantic, parasitical; abject, prostrate, down on one's marrow-bones; base, mean, sneaking; crouching etc. *v.*

Adv. hat –, cap- in hand.

887. Blusterer.—N. bluster-, swagger-, vapor-, roister-, brawl-er; brazen-face; *fanfaron*; braggart etc. (*boaster*) 884; bully, terrorist, rough, roughneck; hooligan, hoodlum, larrikin, ruffian; Mohock, -hawk; drawcansir, swashbuckler, Captain Boabdil, Sir Lucius O'Trigger, Thraso, Pistol, Parolles, Bombastes Furioso, Hector, Chrononhotonthologos; jingo; desperado, dare-devil, fire-eater; fury etc. (*violent person*) 173; rowdy.

puppy etc. (*fop*) 854; prig; Sir Oracle, dogmatist, *doctrinaire*, stump orator, jack-in-office; saucebox, malapert, jackanapes, minx; bantam-cock.

888. Friendship.—N. friendship, amity; friendliness etc. *adj.*; brotherhood, fraternity, sodality, confraternity, sorosis, sisterhood; harmony etc. (*concord*) 714; peace etc. 721.

firm –, staunch –, intimate –, familiar –, bosom –, cordial –, tried –, devoted –, lasting –, fast –, sincere –, warm –, ardent- friendship.

cordiality, fraternization, *entente cordiale*, good understanding, *rapprochement*, sympathy, fellowfeeling, response, welcomeness; *camaraderie*.

affection etc. (*love*) 897; favoritism; goodwill etc. (*benovolence*) 906; partiality.

acquaintance, familiarity, intimacy, intercourse, fellowship, knowledge of; introduction.

V. be -friendly etc. *adj.*, – friends etc. 890; – acquainted with etc. *adj.*; know; have the ear of; keep- company with etc. (*sociality*) 892; hold communication –, have dealings –, sympathize- with; have a leaning to; bear good will etc. (*benevolence*) 906; love etc. 897; make much of; befriend etc. (*aid*) 707; introduce to.

set one's horses together; hold out –, extend the right hand of -friendship; – fellowship; become -friendly etc. *adj.*; make -friends etc. 890 with; break the ice, be introduced to; make –, pick –, scrape- acquaintance with; get into favor, gain the friendship of.

shake hands with, fraternize, embrace; receive with open arms, throw oneself into the arms of; meet half way, take in good part.

Adj. friendly, amic-able, -al; well affected, unhostile, neighborly, brotherly, fraternal, sisterly, sympathetic, harmonious, hearty, cordial, warmhearted, devoted.

friends –, well –, at home –, hand in handwith; on -good, – friendly, – amicable, – cordial, – familiar, – intimate- -terms; – footing; on -speaking, – visiting- terms; in one's good -graces, – books.

acquainted, familiar, intimate, thick, hand and glove, hail fellow well met, free and easy; welcome.

Adv. amicably etc. *adj.*; with open arms; *sans cérémonie*; arm in arm.

889. Enmity.—N. enmity, hostility; unfriendliness etc. *adj.*; discord etc. 713.

alienation, estrangement; dislike etc. 867; hate etc. 898; antagonism.

heartburning; animosity etc. 900; malevolence etc. 907.

V. be -inimical etc. *adj.*; keep –, hold- at arm's length; be at loggerheads; bear malice etc. 907; fall out; take umbrage etc. 900; harden the heart, alienate, estrange.

Adj. inimical, unfriendly, hostile; at -enmity, – variance; – swords points, – daggers drawn, – open war with; up in arms against; in bad odor with.

on bad –, not on speaking- terms; cool; cold, -hearted; estranged, alienated, disaffected, irreconcilable.

890. Friend.—N. friend, – of one's bosom, intimate acquaintance, neighbor, well-wisher; *alter ego*; best –, bosom –, fast- friend; *amicus usque ad aras*; *fidus Achates*; *persona grata*.

favorer, *fautor*, patron, backer, Maecenas; tutelary saint, good genius, advocate, partisan, sympathizer; ally; friend in need etc. (*auxiliary*) 711.

associate, compeer, comrade, mate, companion, *confrère*, camarade, *confidante*, colleague; old –, crony; side-kick; chum, buddy, bunkie, roommate, pal; play-fellow, -mate; classmate, schoolfellow; bed-fellow, -mate; maid of honor.

compatriot; fellow −, countryman, − townsman.

shop-, ship-, mess-mate; fellow −, boon −, potcompanion; co-partner.

Arcades ambo, Pylades and Orestes, Castor and Pollux, Nisus and Euryalus, Damon and Pythias, *par nobile fratrum*.

host, Amphitryon, Boniface; guest, visitor, frequenter, *habitué*; *protégé*.

891. Enemy.—N. enemy; antagonist, foeman; open −, bitter- enemy; opponent etc. 710; back friend.

public enemy, enemy to society, traitor, anarchist etc. 743.

Phr. every hand being against one.

892. Sociality.—N. soci-ality, -ability, -ableness etc. *adj.*; social intercourse; consociation; intercourse, -community; consort-, companion-, fellow-, comrade-ship; clubbism; *esprit de corps*.

conviviality; good -fellowship, − company, *camaraderie*; joviality, jollity, *savoir -vivre*, festivity, festive board, merry-making; loving cup; hospitality, heartiness; cheer.

welcome, -ness; greeting; hearty −, warm −, welcome- reception; urbanity etc. (*courtesy*) 894; intimacy, familiarity.

good −, jolly- fellow, good mixer, Rotarian; *bon enfant*.

social −, family- circle; circle of acquaintance, *coterie*, society, company.

social -gathering, − *réunion*; assembly etc. (*assemblage*) 72; party, entertainment, reception, *levée*, at home, *conversazione*, *soirée*, *matinée*, evening −, morning −, afternoon −, garden −, dinner −, tea −, cocktail- party; symposium, singsong; kettle-, drum; *partie carrée*, dish of tea, *ridotto*, rout, housewarming; ball, prom, hop, dance, *thé dansant*; festival etc. (*amusement*) 840; wedding breakfast; 'the feast of reason and the flow of soul.'

visit, -ing; round of visits; call, morning call; interview etc. (*interlocution*) 588; assignation; tryst, -ing place; appointment.

club etc. (*association*) 712.

V. be -sociable etc. *adj.*; associate −, sort −, keep company −, walk hand in hand -with; eat off the same trencher, club together, consort, bear one company, join; make acquaintance with etc. (*friendship*) 888; make advances, fraternize, embrace; intercommunicate.

be −, feel −, make oneself- at home with; make free with; crack a bottle with; take pot luck with, receive hospitality, live at free quarters.

visit, pay a visit; interchange -visits, − cards; call -at, − upon; leave a card; drop in, look in; look one up, beat up one's quarters.

entertain; give a -party etc. *n.*; be at home, see one's friends, hang out, keep open house, do the honors; receive, − with open arms; welcome; give a warm reception etc. *n.* to; kill the fatted calf.

Adj. sociable, companionable, clubbable, clubby, conversable, cosy, cosey, chatty, conversational; homiletical.

convivial; fest-ive, -al; jovial, jolly, hospitable.

welcome, − as the roses in May; *fêté*, entertained.

free and easy, hail fellow well met, familiar, on visiting terms, acquainted.

social, neighborly; international, cosmopolitan, gregarious.

Adv. *en famille*, in the family circle; *sans -façon*, − *cérémonie*, arm in arm.

893. Seclusion. Exclusion.—N. seclusion, privacy; retirement; concealment; reclusion, recess; snugness etc. *adj.*; delitescence; rustication, *rus in urbe*; solitude; solitariness etc. (*singleness*) 87; isolation; loneliness etc. *adj.*; estrangement from the world, anchoritism, voluntary exile; aloofness.

cell, hermitage; convent etc. 1000; *sanctum sanctorum*; study, library, den; hide-out.

depopulation, desertion, desolation; wilderness etc. (*unproductive*) 169; howling wilderness; rotten borough, Old Sarum.

exclusion, excommunication, banishment, exile, ostracism, proscription; cut, − direct; dead cut.

inhospit-ality, -ableness etc. *adj.*; un-, dissociability; domesticity, Darby and Joan.

recluse, hermit, eremite, cenobite; anchor-et, -ite; Simon Stylites; Troglodyte, Timon of Athens, Santon, *solitaire*, ruralist, disciple of Zimmermann, closet cynic, Diogenes; outcast, Pariah, castaway, outsider, pilgarlic; wastrel, foundling, orphan.

V. be −, live- secluded etc. *adj.*; keep −, stand −, hold oneself- -aloof, − in the background; keep snug; shut oneself up; deny −, secludeoneself; creep into a corner, rusticate, *aller planter ses choux*; retire, − from the world; hermetize, take the veil; abandon etc. 624.

cut, − dead; refuse to -associate with, − acknowledge; look cool −, turn one's back −, shut the door- upon; repel, blackball, excommunicate, exclude, exile, expatriate; banish, outlaw, maroon, ostracize, proscribe, cut off from, send to Coventry, keep at arm's length, draw a cordon round; boycott, blockade, lay an embargo on, isolate.

depopulate; dis-, un-people.

Adj. secluded, sequestered, retired, delitescent, private, bye; out of the -world, -way; in a backwater; 'the world forgetting by the world forgot.' snug, domestic, stay-at-home.

unsociable; un-, dis-social; inhospitable, cynical, inconversable, unclubbable, *sauvage*, eremetic.

solitary; lone-ly, -some; isolated, single.

excluded, estranged; unfrequented; uninhabitable, -ed; tenantless; un-tenanted, -occupied; abandoned; deserted, − in one's utmost need; unfriended; kith-, friend-, home-less; lorn, forlorn, desolate.

un-visited, -introduced, -invited, -welcome; under a cloud, left to shift for oneself, derelict, outcast, outside the gates.

banished etc. *v.*; under an embargo.

Phr. *noli me tangere*.

894. Courtesy.—N. courtesy; respect etc. 928; good -manners, − behavior, − breeding; manners; politeness etc. *adj.*; *bienséance*, urbanity, comity, gentility; gentle −, breeding; polish, presence, cultivation, culture; civili-ty, -zation; amenity, suavity; good -temper, — humor; amiability, easy temper, complacency, soft tongue, mansuetude; condescension etc. (*humility*) 879; affability, complaisance, *prévenance*, amiability, gallantry, chivalry; pink of -politeness, — courtesy.

compliment; fair —, soft —, sweet- words; honeyed phrases, flattering remarks, ceremonial; salutation, reception, presentation, introduction, *accueil*, greeting, recognition; welcome, *abord*, respects, *devoir*, regards, remembrances; kind -regards, — remembrances; love, best love, duty; deference.

obeisance etc. (*reverence*) 928; bow, courtesy, curtsy, scrape, *salaam*, *kow-tow*, bowing and scraping; kneeling; genuflexion etc. (*worship*) 990; obsequiousness etc. 886; capping, shaking hands etc. *v.*; grip of the hand, embrace, hug, squeeze, *accolade*, loving cup, *vin d'honneur*, pledge; love token etc. (*endearment*) 902; kiss, buss, salute.

mark of recognition, not; 'nods and becks and wreathed smiles;' valediction etc. 293; condolence etc. 915.

V. be -courteous etc. *adj.*; show -courtesy etc. *n.*

mind one's P's and Q's, behave oneself, be all things to all men, conciliate, speak one fair, take in good part; make —, do- the amiable; look as if butter would not melt in one's mouth; mend one's manners.

receive, do the honors, usher, greet, hail, bid welcome; welcome, — with open arms; shake hands; hold out —, press —, squeeze- the hand; bid God speed; speed the parting guest; cheer, serenade.

salute; embrace etc. (*endearment*) 902; kiss, — hands; drink to, pledge, hob and nob; move to, nod to; smile upon.

uncover, cap; touch —, take off- the hat; doff the cap; pull the forelock; present arms; make way for; bow; make one's bow; scrape, curtsy, courtesy; bob a -curtsy, — courtesy; kneel; bow —, bend- the knee; salaam, *kowtow*.

visit, wait upon, present oneself, pay one's respects, pay a visit etc. (*sociability*) 892; dance attendance on etc. (*servility*) 886; pay attentions to; do homage to etc. (*respect*) 928.

prostrate oneself etc. (*worship*) 990.

give —, send- one's duty etc. *n.* to.

render -polite etc. *adj.*; polish, civilize, humanize.

Adj. courteous, polite, civil, mannerly, urbane; well-behaved, -mannered, -bred, -brought up, gently bred, of gentle -breeding, — manners, good-mannered, polished, civilized, cultivated; refined etc. (*taste*) 850; gentlemanlike etc. (*fashion*) 852; gallant, chivalrous, on one's good behavior.

fine —, fair —, soft- spoken; honey-mouthed, -tongued; oily, ûnctuous, bland, suave; obliging, conciliatory, complaisant, complacent; obsequious etc. 886.

ingratiating, winning; gentle, mild; good-humored, cordial, gracious, amiable, tactful, addressful, affable, genial, friendly, familiar; neighborly.

Adv. courteously etc. *adj.*; with a good grace; with -open, — outstretched- arms; *à bras ouverts*; *suaviter in modo*, in good humor.

Int. hail! welcome! well met! *ave!* all hail! good -day, — morning etc., — morrow! God speed! *pax vobiscum!* may your shadow never be less! *chin-chin!*

895. Discourtesy.—N. discourtesy; ill-breeding; ill —, bad —, ungainly- manners; insuavity; grouchiness; un-courteousness etc. *adj.*, tactlessness; rusticity, inurbanity; illiberality, incivility, displacency.

disrespect etc. 929; procacity, impudence; barbar-ism, -ity; misbehavior, brutality, blackguard--ism, conduct unbecoming a gentleman, *grossièreté, brusquerie*; vulgarity etc. 851.

churlishness etc. *adj.*; spinosity, perversity; moroseness etc. (*sullenness*) 901*a*.

bad-, ill-temper; sternness etc. *adj.*; austerity, moodishness, captiousness etc. 901; cynicism; tartness etc. *adj.*; acrimony, acerbity, virulence, asperity.

scowl, black looks, frown; short answer, rebuff; hard words, contumely; unparliamentary language, personality.

bear, bruin, brute, grouch, blackguard, beast; unlicked cub; frump, cross-patch; saucebox etc. 887.

V. be -rude etc. *adj.*; insult etc. 929; treat with discourtesy; take a name in vain; make -bold, — free- with; take a liberty; stare out of countenance, ogle, point at, put to the blush.

cut; turn -one's back upon, — on one's heel; give the cold shoulder; keep at -a distance, — arm's length; look -cool, — coldly, — black- upon; show the door to, send away with a flea in the ear.

lose one's temper etc. (*resentment*) 900; sulk etc. 901*a*; frown, scowl, glower, pout; snap, snarl, growl.

render -rude etc. *adj.*; brut-alize, -ify.

Adj. dis-, un-courteous; uncourtly; ill-bred, -mannered, -behaved, -conditioned; unbred; un-manner-ly, -ed; im-, un-polite; un-polished, -civilized, -genteel; ungentleman-like, -ly; unladylike; blackguard; vulgar etc. 851; dedecorous; foul-mouthed, -spoken; abusive.

un-civil, -gracious, -ceremonious; cool; pert, forward, obtrusive, impudent, rude, saucy, precocious; insolent etc. 885.

repulsive; un-complaisant, -accommodating, -neighborly, -gallant; inaffable; un-gentle, -gainly; rough, rugged, bluff, blunt, gruff; churl-, boor-, bear-ish; brutal, *brusque*; stern, harsh, austere; cavalier.

tart, sour, crabbed, sharp, short, trenchant, sarcastic, crusty, biting, caustic, virulent, bitter, acrimonious, venomous, contumelious; snarling etc., *v.*; surly, — as a bear; perverse; grim, sullen etc. 901*a*; peevish etc. (*irascible*) 901.

Adv. discourteously etc. *adj.*; with -discourtesy etc. *n.*, — a bad grace.

896. Congratulations.—N. con-, gratulation; felicitation; salute etc. 894; condolence etc. 915; compliments of the season; good —, best- wishes.

V. con-, gratulate; felicitate, compliment; give —, wish one- joy; tender —, offer- one's congratulations; wish -many happy returns of the day, — a merry Christmas and a happy new year.

congratulate oneself etc. (*rejoice*) 838.

Adj. con-, gratulatory.

897. Love.—N. love; fondness etc. *adj.*; liking; inclination etc. (*desire*) 865; regard, dilection, admiration, fancy.

affection, sympathy, fellow-felling; tenderness etc. *adj.*; heart, brotherly love; benevolence etc. 906; attachment.

yearning, tender passion, *affaire de coeur, amour,* gallantry, passion, flame, devotion, fervor, enthusiasm, transport of love, rapture, enchantment, infatuation, adoration, idolatry.

narcissism, Oedipus complex, Electra complex.

Cupid, Venus, Eros; myrtle; true lover's knot; love -token, — suit, — affair, — tale, — story; the old story, plighted love; courtship etc. 902; *amourette.*

maternal love.

attractiveness, charm; popularity; favorite etc. 899.

lover, suitor, follower, admirer, adorer, wooer, amoret, beau, sweetheart, inamorato, swain, young man, flame, love, truelove; leman, Lothario, gallant, paramor, *amoroso, cavaliere servente,* captive, *cicisbeo; caro sposo,* Don Juan, sheik, ladies' man, squire of dames, Knave of Hearts.

inamorata, lady-love, idol, darling, duck, Dulcinea, angel, goddess, *cara sposa;* mistress.

betrothed, affianced, *fiancée.*

flirt, *coquette;* amorette; pair of turtle doves; abode of love, *agapemone.*

V. love, like, affect, fancy, care for, take an interest in, be partial to, sympathize with; be -in love etc. *adj.*- with; have —, entertain —, harbor —, cherish a -love etc. *n.* for; regard, revere; take to, bear love to, be wedded to; set one's affections on; make much of, feast one's eyes on; hold dear, prize, treasure; hug, cling to, cherish, pet, caress etc. 902.

burn; adore, idolize, love to distraction, *aimer eperdument;* dote -on, — upon.

take a fancy to, fall for, be stuck on, look sweet upon; become -enamored etc. *adj.*; fall in love with, lose one's heart; desire etc. 865.

excite love; win —, gain —, secure —, engage- the -love, — affections, — heart; take the fancy of; have a place in —, wind round- the heart; attract, attach; endear, charm, fascinate, captivate, bewitch, seduce, enamor, enrapture, turn the head.

get into favor; ingratiate —, insinuate —, worm- oneself; propitiate, curry favor with, pay one's court to, make a date with, *faire l'aimable,* set one's cap at, flirt, coquet.

Adv. loving etc. *v.*; fond of; taken —, struck- with; smitten, bitten; attached to, wedded to; enamored; charmed etc. *v.*; in love; lovesick; over head and ears in love.

affectionate, tender, sweet upon, sympathetic, loving, fond, amorous, amatory; erotic, uxurious, ardent, passionate, rapturous, devoted, motherly.

loved etc. *v.*; beloved; well —, dearly- beloved; dear, precious, darling, pet, little; favorite, popular.

congenial; to —, after- one's -mind, — taste, — fancy, — own heart.

in one's good -graces etc. (*friendly*) 888; dear as the apple of one's eye, nearest to one's heart.

lovable, adorable; lovely, sweet; attractive, seductive, winning; charming, engaging, interesting, enchanting, captivating, fascinating, intriguing, bewitching; amiable, like an angel, angelic, seraphic.

898. Hate.—N. hate, hatred, vials of hate; Hymn of Hate.

dis-affection, -favor; alienation, estrangement, coolness; enmity etc. 889; animosity etc. 900.

umbrage, pique, grudge; dudgeon, spleen; bitterness, — of feeling; ill —, bad- blood; acrimony; malice etc. 907; implacability etc. (*revenge*) 919.

repugnance etc. (*dislike*) 867; odium, unpopularity; loathing, detestation, antipathy; object of -hatred, — execration; abomination, aversion, *bête noire;* enemy etc. 891; bitter pill; source of annoyance etc. 830.

V. hate, detest, abominate, abhor, loathe; recoil —, shudder- at; shrink from, view with horror, hold in abomination, revolt against, execrate; scowl etc. 895; disrelish etc. (*dislike*) 867.

owe a grudge; bear -spleen, — a grudge, — malice etc. (*malevolence*) 907; conceive an aversion to.

excite —, provoke- hatred etc. *n.*; be -hateful etc. *adj.*; stink in the nostrils; estrange, alienate, repel, set against, sow dissension, set by the ears, envenom, incense, irritate, rile, ruffle, vex; horrify etc. 830.

Adj. hating etc. *v.*; abhorrent; averse from etc. (*disliking*) 867; set against.

bitter etc. (*acrimonious*) 895; implacable etc. (*revengeful*) 919.

un-loved, -beloved, -lamented, -deplored, -mourned, -cared for, -endured, -valued; disliked etc. 867.

crossed in love, forsaken, rejected, love-lorn, jilted.

obnoxious, hateful, odious, abominable, repulsive, offensive, shocking; disgusting etc. (*disagreeable*) 830.

invidious, spiteful; malicious etc. 907.

insulting, irritating, provoking.

[Mutual hate] at -daggers drawn, — swords points; not on speaking terms etc. (*enmity*) 889.

Phr. no love lost between.

899. Favorite.—N. favorite, pet, cosset, minion, idol, jewel; spoiled child, *enfant gâté,* led captain; crony; fondling; apple of one's eye, man after one's own heart; *persona grata.*

love, dear, darling, duck, honey, jewel; mopsey, moppet; sweetheart etc. (*love*) 897.

general —, universal- favorite; idol of the people; matinée idol, movie —, radio- star.

900. Resentment.—N. resentment, displeasure, animosity, anger, wrath, indignation; vexation, exasperation, bitter resentment, wrathful indignation.

pique, umbrage, huff, miff, soreness, dudgeon, acerbity, virulence, bitterness, acrimony, asperity, spleen, gall; heart-burning, -swelling; rankling.

ill —, bad- -humor, — temper; irascibility etc. 901; ill blood etc. (*hate*) 898; revenge etc. 919.

excitement, irritation; warmth, bile, choler, ire, fume, pucker, dander, ferment, ebullition; towering -passion, — rage, *acharnement,* angry mood, taking, pet, tiff, passion, fit, tantrums.

burst, explosion, paroxysm, storm, rage, fury, desperation; violence etc. 173; fire and fury; vials of wrath; gnashing of teeth, hot blood, high words.

scowl etc. 895; sulks etc. 901a.

[Cause of umbrage] affront, provocation, offence; indignity etc. (*insult*) 929; grudge, crow to pluck, sore subject; red rag to a bull; *casus belli.*

Furies, Erinys, Eumenides, Alecto, Megaera, Tisiphone.

buffet, slap in the face, box on the ear, rap on the knuckles.

V. resent; take -amiss, − ill, − to heart, − offence, − umbrage, − huff, − exception; take in - ill part, − bad part, − dudgeon; *ne pas entendre raillerie*; breathe revenge, cut up rough.

fly −, fall −, get- into a -rage, − passion; bridle −, bristle −, froth −, fire −, flare- up; open −, pour out- the vials of one's wrath.

pout, knit the brow, frown, scowl, lower, snarl, growl, gnarl, gnash, snap; redden, color; look - black, − black as thunder, − daggers; bite one's thumb; show −, grind- one's teeth; champ the bit.

chafe, mantle, fume, kindle, fly out, take fire; boil, − over; boil with -indignation, − rage; rage, storm, foam; vent one's -rage, − spleen; lose one's temper, stand on one's hind legs, stamp the foot, kick up a row, fly off the handle, cut up rough; stamp −, quiver −, swell −, foam- with rage; burst with anger; raise Cain, breathe fire and fury.

have a fling at; bear malice etc. (*revenge*) 919.

cause −, raise- anger; affront, offend; give - offence, − umbrage; anger; hurt the feelings; insult, discompose, fret, ruffle, nettle, heckle, huff, pique; excite etc. 824; irritate, stir the blood, stir up bile; sting, − to the quick; rile, provoke, chafe, wound, incense, inflame, enrage, aggravate, add fuel to the flame, fan into a flame, widen the breach, envenom, embitter, exasperate, infuriate, kindle wrath; stick in one's gizzard; rankle etc. 919.

put out of humor; put one's -monkey, − backup; set −, get- one's back up; raise one's -gorge, − dander, − choler; work up into a passion; make - one's blood boil, − the ears tingle; throw into a ferment, madden, drive one mad; lash into -fury, − madness; fool to the top of one's bent; set by the ears.

bring a hornet's nest about one's ears.

Adj. angry, wrath, irate; ire-, wrath-ful; cross etc. (*irascible*) 901; sulky etc. 901a; bitter, virulent; acrimonious etc. (*discourteous*) etc. 895; violent etc. 173.

warm, burning; boiling, − over; fuming, raging; foaming, − at the mouth; convulsed with rage.

offended etc. *v.*; waxy, *acharné*; wrought, worked up; indignant, hurt, sore, peeved; set against.

fierce, wild, rageful, furious, mad with rage, fiery, infuriate, rabid, savage; relentless etc. 919.

flushed with -anger, − rage; in a -huff, − stew, − fume, − pucker, − passion, − rage, − fury; on one's high ropes, up in arms; in high dudgeon.

Adv. angrily etc. *adj.*; in the height of passion; in the heat of -passion, − the moment.

Phr. one's -blood, − back, − monkey- being up; *fervens difficili bile jecur*; the gorge rising, eyes flashing fire; the blood -rising, − boiling; *haeret lateri lethalis arundo.*

901. Irascibility.—N. irascibility, temper; crossness etc. *adj.*; susceptibility, procacity,

petulance, irritability, tartness, acerbity, protervity; pugnacity etc. (*contentiousness*) 720.

excitability etc. 825; bad −, fiery −, crooked −, irritable etc. *adj.*- temper; *genus irritabile*, hot blood.

ill humor etc. (*sullenness*) 901a; asperity etc., churlishness etc. (*discourtesy*) 895.

huff etc. (resentment) 900; a word and a blow.

Sir Fretful Plagiary; brabbler, Tartar; shrew, vixen, virago, termagant, dragon, scold, Xanthippe; porcupine; spit-fire; fire-eater etc. (*blusterer*) 887; fury etc. (*violent person*) 173.

V. be -irascible etc. *adj.*; have a -temper etc. *n.*, − devil in one; fire up etc. (*be angry*) 900.

Adj. irascible; bad-, ill-tempered; irritable, susceptible; excitable etc. 825; thin-skinned etc. (*sensitive*) 822; fretful, fidgety; on the fret.

hasty, over-hasty, quick, warm, hot, testy, touchy, techy, tetchy; like -touchwood, − tinder; huffy; pet-tish, -ulant; waspish, snapp-y, -ish, peppery, fiery, passionate, choleric, shrewish, 'sudden and quick in quarrel.'

querulous, captious, mood-y, -ish; quarrelsome, contentious, disputatious; pugnacious etc. (*bellicose*) 720; cantankerous, exceptious; restive etc. (*perverse*) 901a; churlish etc. (*discourteous*) 895.

cross, − as -crabs, − two sticks, − a cat, − a dog, − the tongs; like a bear with a sore head; fractious, peevish, *acariâtre*.

in a bad temper; sulky etc. 901a; angry etc. 900.

resent-ful, -ive; vindictive etc. 919.

Int. pish!

901a. Sullenness.—N. sullenness etc. *adj.*; morosity, spleen; churlishness etc. (*discourtesy*) 895; irascibility etc. 901.

moodiness etc. *adj.*; perversity; obstinacy etc. 606; torvity, spinosity; crabbedness etc. *adj.*

ill −, bad- -temper, − humor; sulks, dudgeon, mumps, doleful dumps, doldrums, fit of the sulks, *bouderie*, black looks, scowl, huff etc. (*resentment*) 900.

V. be -sullen etc. *adj.*; sulk; frown, scowl, lower, glower, grouse, grouch, crab, gloam, pout, have a hang-dog look, glout.

Adj. sullen, sulky; ill-tempered, -humored, - affected, -disposed; in -an ill, − a bad, − a shocking- -temper, − humor; out of -temper, − humor; knaggy, torvous, crusty, crabbed; sore as a boil; surly etc. (*discourteous*) 895.

moody; spleen-ish, -ly; splenetic, cankered.

cross, -grained; perverse, wayward, humorsome; restive; cantankerous, refractory, intractable, exceptious, sinistrous, deaf to reason, unaccommodating, rusty, crust, froward.

dogged etc. (*stubborn*) 606.

grumpy, glum, grim, grum, morose, frumpish; in the -sulks etc. *n.*; out of sorts; scowl-, glower-, growl-ing.

peevish etc. (*irascible*) 901.

902. Endearment. [Expression of affection or love.]**—N.** endearment, caress; blandish-, blandiment; *épanchement*, fondling, billing and cooing, dalliance.

embrace, salute, kiss, buss, smack, osculation,

deosculation; amorous glances; ogle, side glance, sheep's eyes.

courtship, wooing, suit, addresses, the soft impeachment; love-making; an affair; serenading; caterwauling.

flirting etc. v.; flirtation, gallantry; coquetry, spooning.

ture lover's knot, plighted love, engagement, bethrothal; love -tale, – token, – letter; *billet-doux*, valentine.

honeymoon; Strephon and Chloe, 'Arry and 'Arriet.

V. caress, fondle, pet, dandle, nurse; pat, – on the -head, – cheek; chuck under the chin, smile upon, coax, wheedle, cosset, coddle, cocker; make -of, – much of, pamper; cherish, foster, kill with kindness.

clasp, hug, cuddle; fold –, strain- in one's arms; nestle, nuzzle, neck, embrace, kiss, buss, smack, blow a kiss; salute etc. (*courtesy*) 894.

bill and coo, spoon, toy, dally, flirt, coquet; galli-, gala-vant; philander; make love; pay one's -court, – addresses, – attentions- to; serenade; court, woo; set one's cap at; be –, look- sweet upon; ogle, cast sheep's eyes upon; *faire les yeux doux.*

fall in love with, win the affections etc. (*love*) 897; die for.

propose; make –, have- an offer; pop the question; plight one's -troth, – faith; become - engaged, – betrothed.

Adj. caressing etc. v.; 'sighing like furnace;' love sick, spoony.

carressed etc. v.

903. Marriage.—N. marriage, matrimony, wedlock, union, intermarriage, *vinculum matrimonii*, nuptial tie, knot.

married state, coverture, bed, cohabitation.

match; betrothment etc. (*promise*) 768; wedding, nuptials, Hymen, bridal; e-, spousals; leading to the altar etc. v.; nuptial benediction, *epithalamium*,

torch –, temple- of Hymen; hymeneal altar; honeymoon.

bride, bridegroom; brides-maid; -man.

best –, grooms-man, page, usher.

married -man, – woman, – couple; neogamist, Benedick, partner, spouse, mate, yokemate; husband, man, consort, baron; old –, good- man; wife of one's bosom; help-meet, -mate, rib, better half, grey mare, old woman, good wife; feme, – coverte; squaw, lady; matron, -age, -hood; man and wife; wedded pair, Darby and Joan.

affinity, soul-mate.

mono-, bi-, di-, deutero-, tri-, poly-gamy; mormonism; poly-andry; Turk, Bluebeard.

unlawful –, left-handed –, companionate –, morganatic –, ill-assorted- marriage; *mésalliance*; *mariage de convenance*; an affair.

match-maker, marriage broker, matrimonial agent.

V. marry, wive, take to oneself a wife; be - married, – spliced; go –, pair- off; wed, espouse, lead to the hymeneal altar, take 'for better, for worse,' give one's hand to, bestow one's hand upon; remarry; intermarry.

marry, join, handfast; couple etc. (*unite*) 43; tie

the nuptial knot; give -away, – in marriage; affy, affiance; betroth etc. (*promise*) 768; publish –, bid- the banns; be asked in church.

Adj. married etc. v.; one, – bone and one flesh.

marriageable, nubile.

engaged, betrothed, affianced.

matrimonial, marital, conjugal, connubial, wedded; nuptial, hymeneal, spousal, bridal.

Phr. the gray mare the better horse.

904. Celibacy.—N. celibacy, singleness, single blessedness; bachelor-hood, -ship; miso-gamy, - gyny.

virginity, *pueelage*; maiden-hood, -head.

unmarried man, bachelor, agamist, old bachelor; miso-gamist, -gynist; celibate.

unmarried woman, spinster; maid, -en; virgin, *feme sole*, old maid; bachelor girl; nun etc.

V. live single; keep bachelor hall.

Adj. un-married, -wedded; wife-, spouse-less; single, virgin, celibate.

905. Divorce.—N. divorce, -ment; separation; judicial separation, separate maintenance; *separatio a -mensâ et thoro, – vinculo matrimonii.*

widowhood, viduage, viduity, weeds.

widow, -er; relict; dowager; *divorcée*; cuckold.

V. live -separately, – apart; separate, divorce, disespouse, put away; wear the horns.

906. Benevolence.—N. benevolence, Christian charity; God's -love, – grace; good-will; philanthropy etc. 910; unselfishness etc. 942.

good -nature, – feeling, – wishes; kind-, kindliness etc. *adj.*; lovingkindness, benignity, brotherly love, charity, humanity, fellow-feeling, sympathy; goodness –, warmth- of heart; *bon-homie*; kindheartedness; amiability, milk of human kindness, tenderness; love etc. 897; friendship etc. 888.

toleration, consideration, generosity; mercy etc. (*pity*) 914.

charitableness etc. *adj.*; bounty, alms-giving; good works, beneficence, the luxury of doing good.

acts of kindness, a good turn; good –, kind- offices, – treatment.

good Samaritan, sympathizer, well-wisher, philanthropist, *bon enfant*; altruist.

V. be -benevolent etc. *adj.*; have one's heart in the right place, bear good will; wish -well, – God speed; view –, regard- with an eye of favor; take in good part; take –, feel- an interest in; be –, feel- interested- in; sympathize with, feel for; fraternize etc. (*be friendly*) 888.

enter into the feelings of others, do as you would be done by, meet halfway.

treat well; give comfort, smooth the bed of death; do -good, – a good turn; benefit etc. (*goodness*) 648; render a service, be of use; aid etc. 707.

Adj. benevolent; kind, -ly; wellmeaning; amiable; obliging, accommodating, indulgent, considerate, gracious, complacent, good-humored.

warm-, soft-, kind-, tender-, large-, broadhearted; merciful etc. 914; philanthropic etc. 910; charitable, beneficent, humane, benign, benignant; bount-eous, -iful etc. 816.

good-, well-natured; spleenless; sympath-izing, -etic; complaisant etc. (*courteous*) 894; kindly, well-meant, -intentioned.

fatherly, motherly, brotherly, sisterly; pat-, mat-, frat-ernal; friendly etc. 888.

Adv. with -a good intention, – the best intentions.

Int. God speed! much good may it do!

907. Malevolence.—N.

malevolence; bad intent, -ion; un-, dis-kindness; ill -nature, – will, – blood; bad blood; enmity etc. 889; hate etc. 898; malignity; malice, – aforethought, – prepense; maliciousness etc. *adj.*; spite, despite; resentment etc. 900.

uncharitableness etc. *adj.*; incompassionateness etc. 914*a*; gall, venom, rancor, rankling, virulence, mordacity, acerbity; churlishness etc. (*discourtesy*) 895.

hardness of heart, heart of stone, obduracy; cruelty; cruelness etc. *adj.*; brutality, savagery; fer-ity, -ocity; barbarity, inhumanity, immanity, truculence, ruffianism; evil eye, cloven -foot, – hoof; Inquisition; torture.

ill –, bad- turn; affront etc. (*disrespect*) 929; outrage, atrocity; ill usage; intolerance, bigotry, persecution; tender mercies [ironical]; 'unkindest cut of all.'

V. be -malevolent etc. *adj.*; bear –, harbor- -spleen, – a grudge, – malice; betray –, show- the cloven foot.

hurt etc. (*physical pain*) 378; annoy etc. 830; injure, harm, wrong; do -harm, – an ill office- to; outrage; disoblige, malign, plant a thorn in the breast.

molest, worry, harass, haunt, harry, bait, tease, throw stones at; play the devil with; hunt down, dragoon, hound; persecute, oppress, grind; maltreat; ill-treat, -use.

wreak one's malice on, do one's worst, break a butterfly on the wheel; dip –, imbrue- one's hands in blood; have no mercy etc. 914*a*.

Adj. male-, unbene-volent; unbenign; ill-disposed, -intentioned, -natured, -conditioned, - contrived; evil-minded, -disposed.

malicious; malign, -ant; rancorous; de-, spiteful; mordacious, caustic, bitter, envenomed, acrimonious, virulent; un-amiable, -charitable; maleficent, venomous, grinding, galling.

harsh, disobliging; un-kind, -friendly, -gracious; treacherous; inofficious; invidious; uncandid; churlish etc. (*uncourteous*) 895; surly, sullen etc. 901*a*.

cold, -blooded, -hearted; hard-, flint-, marble-, stony-hearted; hard of heart, unnatural; ruthless etc. (*unmerciful*) 914*a*; relentless etc. (*revengeful*) 919.

cruel; brut-al, -ish; savage, – as a -bear, – tiger; ferine, feral, ferocious; inhuman; barbarous, fell, untamed, tameless, truculent, incendiary; blood-thirsty etc. (*murderous*) 361; atrocious.

fiend-ish, -like; demoniacal; diabolic, -al; devilish, infernal, hellish, Satanic.

Adv. malevolently etc. *adj.*; with -bad intent etc. *n.*

908. Malediction.—N.

malediction, malison, curse, imprecation, denunciation, execration,

anathema, ban, proscription, excommunication, commination, thunders of the Vatican, fulmination, *maranatha*, aspersion, vilification, vituperation, scurrility.

abuse; foul –, bad –, strong –, un-parliamentary- language, Limehouse; Billingsgate, sauce, evil speaking; cursing etc. *v.*; profane swearing, oath.

threat etc. 909; more bark than bite; invective etc. (*disapprobation*) 932.

V. curse, accurse, imprecate, damn, swear at; slang; curse with bell, book and candle; invoke –, call down- curses on the head of; devote to destruction.

execrate, beshrew, scold; anathematize etc. (*censure*) 932; hold up to execration, denounce, proscribe, excommunicate, fulminate, thunder against; threaten etc. 909; curse up hill and down dale.

curse and swear; swear, – like a trooper; fall a cursing, rap out an oath, damn, cuss.

Adj. curs-ing, -ed etc. *v.*; maledictory.

Int. woe to! beshrew! *ruat coelum!* ill –, woe-betide! confusion seize! damn! confound! blast! curse! devil take! hang! out with! a plague –, out-upon! aroynt! *honi 'soit!*

Phr. *delenda est Carthago.*

909. Threat.—N.

threat, menace; defiance etc. 715; abuse, minacity, intimidation; fulmination; commination etc. (*curse*) 908; gathering clouds etc. (*warning*) 668.

V. threat, -en; menace; snarl, growl, gnarl, mutter, bark, bully.

defy etc. 715; intimidate etc. 860; keep –, hold up –, hold out- *in terrorem*; shake –, double –, clinch- the fist at; thunder, talk big, fulminate, use big words, bluster, look daggers.

Adj. threatening, menacing; mina-tory, -cious; comminatory, abusive; *in terrorem*; ominous etc. (*predicting*) 511; defiant etc. 715; under the ban.

Int. *vae victis!* at your peril! do your worst!

910. Philanthropy.—N.

philanthropy; altruism, humanit-y, -arianism; universal benevolence; *deliciae humani generis;* cosmopolitanism, utilitarianism, the greatest happiness of the greatest number, social science, sociology.

common weal, public welfare, socialism, communism.

patriotism, civism, nationality, love of country, *amor patriae*, public spirit.

chivalry, knight errantry; generosity etc. 942.

philanthropist, altruist etc. 906; utilitarian, Ben-thamite, socialist, communist, cosmopolite, citizen of the world, *amicus humani generis;* knight errant; patriot.

Adj. philanthropic, altruistic, humanitarian, utilitarian, cosmopolitan; public-spirited, patriotic; humane, large-hearted etc. (*benevolent*) 906; chival-ric, -rous, generous etc. 942.

Adv. pro -bono publico, – aris et focis.

Phr. '*humani nihil a me alienum puto.*'

911. Misanthropy.—N.

misanthropy, incivism; egotism etc. (*selfishness*)- 943; moroseness etc. 901*a*; cynicism; defeatism.

misanthrope, misanthropist, egotist, cynic, man-
hater, Timon, Diogenes.

woman-hater, misogynist.

Adj. misanthropic, antisocial, unpatriotic;
egotistical etc. (*selfish*) 943; morose etc. 901*a*.

912. Benefactor.—N. benefactor, savior, good
genius, tutelary saint, patron, guardian angel, fairy
godmother, good Samaritan; *pater patriae*; salt of
the earth etc. (*good man*) 948; auxiliary etc. 711.

913. Evil-doer. [*Maleficent being.*]—**N.** evil-
-doer, — worker; wrong doer etc. 949; mischief
maker, marplot; oppressor, tyrant; firebrand, incendiary, pyromaniac, anarchist, destroyer, Hun,
Boche, Vandal, iconoclast; communist; terrorist,
apache, gunman, gangster, racketeer.

savage, brute, ruffian, barbarian, semi-barbarian,
caitiff, desperado; Mo-hock, -hawk; bludgeon man,
bully, rough, hooligan, larrikin, dangerous classes,
ugly customer; thief etc. 792.

cockatrice, scorpion, hornet; viper, adder; snake,
— in the grass; serpent, cobra, asp, rattlesnake,
anaconda; canker-, wire-worm; locust, Colorado
beetle; torpedo; bane etc. 663.

cannibal; Anthropophag-us, -ist; bloodsucker,
vampire, ogre, ghoul, gorilla; vulture; gyr-, ger-
falcon.

wild beast, tiger, hyaena, butcher, hangman; cut-
throat etc. (*killer*) 361; blood-, sleuth-, hell-hound.

hag, hellhag, beldam, Jezebel.

monster; fiend etc. (*demon*) 980; homicidal
maniac, devil incarnate, demon in human shape;
Frankenstein's monster.

harpy, siren, vampire; Furies, Eumenides etc.
,900.

Attila, scourge of the human race.

Phr. *foenum habet in cornu.*

914. Pity.—N. pity, compassion, com-
miseration; bowels, — of compassion; condolence
etc. 915; sympathy, fellow-feeling, tenderness,
yearning, forbearance, humanity, mercy, clemency,
exorability; leniency etc. (*lenity*) 740; charity, ruth,
long-suffering.

melting mood; *argumentum ad misericordiam*;
quarter, grace, *locus poenitentiae*.

sympathizer, champion, partisan.

V. pity; have —, show —, take- pity etc. *n.*;
commiserate, compassionate; condole etc. 915;
sympathize; feel —, be sorry —, yearn- for; weep,
melt, thaw, enter into the feelings of.

forbear, relent, relax, give quarter, wipe the
tears, *parcere subjectis*, give a *coup de grâce*, put
out of one's misery; be cruel to be kind.

raise —, excite- pity etc. *n.*; touch, soften; melt,
— the heart; appeal to one's better feelings;
propitiate, disarm.

ask for -mercy etc. *n.*; supplicate etc. (*request*)
765; cry for quarter, beg one's life, kneel;
deprecate.

Adj. pitying etc. *v.*; pitiful, compassionate, sympathetic, touched.

merciful, clement, ruthful; humane;
humanitarian etc. (*philanthropic*) 910; tender, —

hearted, — as a chicken; soft, — hearted; unhardened; lenient etc. 740; exorable, forbearing;
melting etc. *v.*; weak.

Int. for pity's sake! mercy! have —, cry you-
mercy! God help you! poor -thing, — dear, —
fellow! woe betide! *quis talia fando temperet a
lachrymis!*

Phr. one's heart bleeding for; *haud ignara mali
miseris succurrere disco.*

914a. Pitilessness.—N. pitilessness etc. *adj.*;
inclemency; inexorability, hardness of heart; inflexibility; severity etc. 739; malevolence etc. 907.

V. have no —, shut the gates of- mercy etc. 914;
give no quarter.

Adj. piti-, merci-, ruth-, bowel-less; unpitying,
unmerciful, inclement; in-, un-compassionate;
inexorable, inflexible; harsh etc. 739; cruel etc.
907; unrelenting etc. 919.

915. Condolence.—N. condolence; lamentation etc. 839; sympathy, consolation.

V. condole with, console, sympathize etc. 914;
share one's misery; feel for; express —, testify- pity;
afford —, supply- consolation; lament etc. 839-
with; send one's condolences.

916. Gratitude.—N. gratitude, thankfulness,
gratefulness, feeling of obligation.

acknowledgement, recognition, thanksgiving,
giving thanks.

thanks, praise, benediction; paean; *Te Deum*
etc. (*worship*) 990; grace, — before, — after-
meat; thank-offering.

requital.

V. be -grateful etc. *adj.*; thank; give —, render
—, return —, offer —; tender- thanks etc. *n.*;
acknowledge, requite.

feel —, be —, lie- under an obligation; *savoir
gré*; not look a gift horse in the mouth; never
forget, overflow with gratitude; thank —, bless-
one's stars; fall on one's knees.

Adj. grateful, thankful, obliged, beholden, indebted to, under obligation.

Int. thanks! many thanks! gramercy! much
obliged! thank you! thank Heaven! Heaven be
praised!

917. Ingratitude.—N. ingratitude,
thanklessness, oblivion of benefits; unthankfulness.

'benefits forgot;' thankless -task, — office.

V. be -ungrateful etc. *adj.*; forget benefits; look
a gift horse in the mouth.

Adj. un-grateful, -mindful, -thankful; thankless,
ingrate, wanting in gratitude, insensible of benefits.

forgotten; un-acknowledged, -thanked, -
requited, -rewarded; ill-requited.

Int. thank you for nothing! '*et tu Brute!*'

918. Forgiveness.—N. forgiveness, pardon,
condonation, grace, remission, absolution, amnesty, oblivion; indulgence; reprieve.

conciliation; reconciliation etc. (*pacification*) 723; propitiation.

excuse, exoneration, quittance, release, indemnity; bill –, act –, covenant –, deed- of indemnity; exculpation etc. (*acquittal*) 970.

longanimity, placability, forbearance; *amantium irae*; *locus poenitentiae*.

V. forgive, – and forget; pardon, condone, think no more of, let bygones be bygones, shake hands; forget an injury, bury the hatchet; clean the slate.

excuse, pass over, overlook; wink at etc. (*neglect*) 460; bear with; allow –, make allowances- for; let one down easily, not be too hard upon, pocket the affront; blot out one's transgression.

let off, remit, absolve, give absolution, reprieve; acquit etc. 970.

beg –, ask –, implore- pardon etc. *n.*; conciliate, propitiate, placate; make up a quarrel etc. (*pacify*) 723; let the wound heal.

Adj. forgiving, placable, conciliatory.

forgiven etc. *v.*; un-resented, -avenged, revenged.

Adv. cry you mercy.

Phr. *veniam petimusque damusque vicissim*; more in sorrow than in anger.

919. Revenge.—N. revenge, -ment; vengeance; avenge-ment, -ance; sweet revenge, *vendetta*, death-feud, eye for an eye, blood for blood, a Roland for an Oliver; retaliation etc. 718; day of reckoning.

rancor, vindictiveness, implacability; malevolence etc. 907; ruthlessness etc. 914*a*.

avenger, vindicator, Nemesis, Eumenides.

V. re-, a-venge; take –, have one's- revenge; breathe -revenge, – vengeance; wreak one's - vengeance, – anger; give no quarter.

have -accounts to settle, – a crow to pluck, – a rod in pickle; pay off old scores.

keep the wound green; harbor -revenge, – vindictive feeling; bear malice; rankle, – in the breast; have at one's mercy.

Adj. revenge-, venge-ful; vindictive, rancorous; pitiless etc. 914*a*; ruthless, rigorous, avenging, retaliative.

unforgiving, unrelenting; inexorable, stony-hearted, implacable; relent-, remorse-less.

aeternum servans sub pectore vulnus; rankling, immitigable.

Phr. *manet -cicatrix,– altâ mente repostum*. revenge is sweet.

920. Jealousy.—N. jealous-y, -ness; jaundiced eye, heartburning; green-eyed monster; yellows; Juno.

V. be -jealous etc. *adj.*; view with -jealousy, – a jealous eye.

Adj. jealous, – as a Barbary pigeon; jaundiced, yellow-eyed, horn-mad.

921. Envy.—N. envy; enviousness etc. *adj.*; rivalry; *jalousie de métier*.

V. envy, covet, lust after, crave, burst with envy, regard with envious eyes.

Adj. envious, invidious, covetous; *alieni appetens*.

922. Right.—N. right; what -ought to, – should- be; fitness etc. *adj.*; *summum jus*.

justice, equity; equitableness etc. *adj.*; propriety; fair play, impartiality, measure for measure, give and take, *lex talionis*, square deal.

Astraea, Nemesis, Themis.

scales of justice, even-handed justice, retributive justice, *suum cuique*; clear stage –, fair field- and no favor; Queensberry rules.

morals etc. (*duty*) 926; law etc. 963; honor etc. (*probity*) 939; virtue etc. 944.

V. be -right etc. *adj.*; stand to reason.

see -justice done, – one righted, – fair play; do justice to; recompense etc. (*reward*) 973; hold the scales even, give and take; serve one right, put the saddle on the right horse; give -every one, – the devil- his due; *audire alteram partem*.

deserve etc. (*be entitled to*) 924.

Adj. right, good; just, reasonable; fit etc. 924; equ-al, -able, -itable; evenhanded, fair, – and square.

legitimate, justifiable, rightful; as it -should, – ought to- be; lawful etc. (*permitted*) 760, (*legal*) 963.

deserved etc. 924.

Adv. rightly etc. *adj.*; in -justice, – equity, – reason.

without -distinction of, – regard to, – respect to- persons; upon even terms.

Int. all right!

923. Wrong.—N. wrong; what -ought not to, – should not- be; *malum in se*; unreasonableness, grievance; shame.

injustice; unfairness etc. *adj.*; iniquity, foul play, partiality, leaning; favor, -itism; nepotism, party spirit, partisanship; undueness etc. 925; unlawfulness etc. 964.

robbing Peter to pay Paul etc. *v.*; the wolf and the lamb; vice etc. 945.

a custom more honored in the breach than the observance.

V. be -wrong etc. *adj.*; cry to heaven for vengeance.

do -wrong etc. *n.*; be -inequitable etc. *adj.*; favor, lean towards; encroach; impose upon; reap where one has not sown; give an inch and take an ell; rob Peter to pay Paul.

Adj. wrong, -ful; bad, too bad; unjust, -fair; in-, un-equitable; unequal, partial, one-sided.

objectionable; un-reasonable, -allowable, -warrantable, -justifiable; not cricket, not playing the game; improper, unfit; unjustified etc. 925; illegal etc. 964; iniquitous, criminal; immoral etc. 945; injurious etc. 649.

in the wrong, – box.

Adv. wrongly etc. *adj.*

Phr. it will not do; this is too bad.

924. Dueness.—N. due, -ness; right, privilege, prerogative, prescription, title, claim, pretension, demand, birthright.

immunity, license, liberty, franchise; vested - interest, — right; licitness.

sanction, authority, warranty, charter; warrant etc. (*permission*) 760; constitution etc. (*law*) 963; tenure; bond etc. (*security*) 771.

deserts, merits, dues.

claimant, appellant; plaintiff etc. 938.

V. be -due etc. *adj*.to, — the due etc. *n*.of; have -right, — title, — claim- to; be entitled to; have a claim upon; belong to etc. (*property*) 780.

deserve, merit, be worthy of, richly deserve.

* demand, claim; call upon —, come upon —, appeal to- for; re-vendicate, -claim; exact; insist -on, — upon; challenge; take one's stand, make a point of, require, lay claim to, assert, assume, arrogate, make good; substantiate; vindicate a -claim, — right; make out a case.

give —, confer- a right; sanction, entitle; authorize etc. 760; sanctify, legalize, ordain, prescribe, allot.

give every one his due etc. 922; pay one's dues; have one's -due, — rights; stand upon one's rights.

use a right, assert, enforce, put in force, lay under contribution.

Adj. having a right to etc. *v*.; entitled to; claiming; deserving, meriting, worthy of.

privileged, allowed, sanctioned, warranted, authorized; ordained, prescribed, constitutional, chartered, enfranchised.

prescriptive, presumptive; absolute, indefeasible; un-, in-alienable.

imprescriptible, inviolable, unimpeachable, unchallenged; sacrosanct.

due to, merited, deserved, condign, richly deserved, *emeritus*.

allowable etc. (*permitted*) 760; lawful, licit, legitimate, legal; legalized etc. (*law*) 963.

square, unexceptionable, right; equitable etc. 922; due, *en règle*; fit, -ting; correct, proper, meet, befitting, becoming, seemly; decorous; creditable, up to the mark, right as a trivet; just —, quite- the thing; *selon les règles*.

Adv. duly, *ex officio*, *de jure*; by -right; — divine right; as is -fitting, — proper, — fitting and proper; *jure divino*, *Dei gratiâ*, in the name of.

Phr. *civis Romanus sum*.

925. Undueness. [Absence of right.]—N. undueness etc. *adj*.; *malum prohibitum*; impropriety; illegality. 964.

falseness etc. *adj*.; emptiness —, invalidity- of title; illegitimacy.

loss of right, disfranchisement, forfeiture.

usurpation, assumption, tort, violation, breach, encroachment, presumption, seizure, stretch, exaction, imposition, lion's share.

usurper, pretender, Carlist; imposter.

V. be -undue etc. *adj*.; not be -due etc. 924.

infringe, encroach, trench on, exact; arrogate, — to oneself; give an inch and take an ell; stretch —, strain- a point; usurp, violate, do violence to; sail under false colors.

dis-franchise, -entitle, -qualify; invalidate.

relax etc. (*be lax*) 738; misbehave etc. (*vice*) 945; misbecome.

Adj. undue; unlawful etc. (*illegal*) 964; unconstitutional, *ultra vires*; illicit; un-authorized, -warranted, -allowed, -sanctioned, -justified; un-, dis-entitled, -qualified; un-privileged, -chartered.

illegitimate, bastard, spurious, false; usurped, tortious.

un-deserved, -merited, -earned; unfulfilled. forfeited, disfranchised.

improper; un-meet, -fit, -befitting, -seemly; un-, mis-becoming; seemless; *contra bonos mores*; not the thing, out of the question, not to be thought of; preposterous, pretentious, would- be.

926. Duty.—N. duty, what ought to be done, moral obligation, accountableness, liability; *onus*, responsibility; bounden —, imperative- duty; call, — of duty.

allegiance, fealty, tie; engagement etc. (*promise*) 768; part; function, calling etc. (*business*) 625.

morality, morals, decalogue; case of conscience; conscientiousness etc. (*probity*) 939; conscience, inward monitor, still small voice within, sense of duty, tender conscience.

dueness etc. 924; propriety, fitness, seemliness, amenableness, decorum; the -thing, — proper thing; the -right, — proper- thing to do.

[Science of morals] eth-ics, -ology; deon-, aretology; moral —, ethical-philosophy; casuistry, polity.

observance, fulfilment, discharge, performance, acquittal, satisfaction, redemption; good behavior.

V. be -the duty of, — incumbent etc. *adj*.on, — responsible etc. *adj*.; behoove, become, befit, beseem; belong —, pertain- to; fall to one's lot; devolve on; lie -upon, — on one's head, — at one's door; rest with, — on the shoulders of.

take upon oneself etc. (*promise*) 768.

be —, become- -bound to, — sponsor for; be responsible for; incur a -responsibility etc. *n*.; be —, stand —, lie- under an obligation; have to answer for, owe it to oneself.

impose a -duty etc. *n*.; enjoin, require, exact; bind, — over; saddle with, prescribe, assign, call upon, look to, oblige.

enter upon —, perform —, observe —, fulfil —, discharge —, adhere to —, acquit oneself of —, satisfy- -a duty, — an obligation; act one's part, redeem one's pledge, do justice to, be at one's post; do duty; do one's duty etc. (*be virtuous*) 944.

be on one's good behavior, mind one's P's and Q's.

Adj. obligatory, binding; imperative, peremptory; stringent etc. (*severe*) 739; behooving etc. *v*.; incumbent —, chargeable- on; under obligation; obliged —, bound —, tied- by; saddled with.

due —, beholden —, bound —, indebted- to; tied down; compromised etc. (*promised*) 768; in duty bound.

amenable, liable, accountable, responsible, answerable.

right, meet etc. (*due*) 924; moral, ethical, casuistical, conscientious, ethological.

Adv. with a safe conscience, as in duty bound, on one's own responsibility, at one's own risk, *suo periculo*; *in foro conscientiae*; *quamdiu se bene gesserit*; at one's post, on duty.

Phr. *dura lex sed lex*.

927. Dereliction of Duty.—N. dere; liction of duty; fault etc. (*guilt*) 947- sin etc. (*vice*) 945; non-observance, -performance, -co-operation; neglect, carelessness, laziness, incompetence, eye-service, relaxation, infraction, violation, transgression, failure, evasion, indolence; dead letter.

slacker, loafer, striker, non-co-operator.

V. violate; break, – through; infringe; set - aside, – at naught; trample -on, – under foot; slight, neglect, evade, renounce, forswear, repudiate; wash one's hands of; escape, transgress, fail.

call to account etc. (*disapprobation*) 932.

927a. Exemption.—N. exemption, freedom, irresponsibility, immunity, liberty, license, release, exoneration, excuse, dispensation, absolution, franchise, renunciation, discharge; exculpation etc. 970; *aegrotat.*

V. be -exempt etc. *adj.*

exempt, release, acquit, discharge, quit-claim, remise, remit; free, set at liberty, let off, pass over, spare, excuse, dispense with, give dispensation, license; stretch a point; absolve etc. (*forgive*) 918; exonerate etc. (*exculpate*) 970; save the necessity.

Adj. exempt, free, immune, at liberty, scot free; released etc. *v.*; unbound, unencumbered; irresponsible, unaccountable, not answerable; excusable.

928. Respect.—N. respect, regard, consideration; courtesy etc. 894; attention, deference, reverence, honor, esteem, estimation, veneration, admiration; approbation etc. 931.

homage, fealty, obeisance, genuflexion, kneeling, prostration; obsequiousness etc. 886; salaam, *kowtow,* bow, presenting arms, salute.

respects, regards, duty, *devoirs, égards.*

devotion etc. (*piety*) 987.

V. respect, regard; revere, -nce; hold in reverence, honor, venerate, hallow; esteem etc. (*approve of*) 931; think much of; entertain –, bear- respect for; have a high opinion of; look up to, defer to; pay -attention, – respect etc. *n.*- to; do –, render- honor to; do the honors, hail; show courtesy etc. 894; salute, present arms; do –, pay- homage to; pay tribute to; kneel to, bow to, bend the knee to; fall down before, prostrate oneself, kiss the hem of one's garment; worship etc. 990.

keep one's distance, make room, observe due decorum, stand upon ceremony.

command –, inspire- respect; awe, impose, overawe, dazzle.

Adj. respecting etc. *v.*; respectful, deferential, decorous, reverential, obsequious, ceremonious, bare-headed, cap in hand, on one's knees; prostrate etc. (*servile*) 886.

respected etc. *v.*; in high -esteem, – estimation; time-honored, venerable, *emeritus.*

Adv. in deference to; with -all, – due, – the highest- respect; with submission.

saving your -grace, – presence; *salva sit reverentia; pace tanti nominis.*

Int. hail! all hail! *esto perpetua!* may your shadow never be less!

929. Disrespect.—N. dis-respect, -esteem, - estimation, -favor, -repute; low estimation; disparagement etc. (*dispraise*) 932; (*detraction*) 934.

irreverence; slight, neglect; *spretae injuria formae;* superciliousness etc. (*contempt*) 930.

vilipendency, contumely, affront, dishonor, insult, indignity, outrage, discourtesy etc. 895; practical joking; scurrility, scoffing, sibilation; ir-, derision; mockery; irony etc. (*ridicule*) 856; sarcasm.

hiss, hoot, gibe, flout, jeer, scoff, gleek, taunt, sneer, quip, fling, wipe, slap in the face.

V. hold in disrespect etc. (*despise*) 930; misprize, disregard, slight, undervalue, depreciate, trifle with, set at naught, pass by, push aside, overlook, turn one's back upon, laugh in one's sleeve; be -disrespectful etc. *adj.*, – discourteous etc. 895; treat with -disrespect etc. *n.*; set down, browbeat.

dishonor, desecrate; insult, affront, outrage.

speak slightingly of; disparage etc. (*dispraise*) 932; vilipend, call names; throw –, fling- dirt; drag through the mud, point at, indulge in personalities; make -mouths, – faces; bite the thumb; take –, pluck- by the beard; toss in a blanket, tar and feather.

have –, hold- in derision; deride, scoff, sneer, laugh at, snigger, ridicule, gibe, mock, jeer, taunt, twit, niggle, gleek, gird, flout, fleer; roast, turn into ridicule; guy, burlesque etc. 856; laugh to scorn etc. (*contempt*) 930; smoke; fool; make -game, – a fool, – an April fool- of; play a practical joke; rag; lead one a dance, run the rig upon, have a fling at, scout, hiss, hoot, mob.

Adj. disrespectful; aweless, irreverent; disparaging etc. 934; insulting etc. *v.*; supercilious etc. (*scornful*) 930; rude, derisive, contemptuous, sarcastic; scurri-le, -lous; contumelious.

un-respected, -worshipped, -envied, -saluted; un-dis-regarded.

Adv. disrespectfully etc. *adj.*

930. Contempt.—N. contempt, disdain, scorn, sovereign contempt; despi-sal, -ciency; vilipendency, contumely; slight, sneer, spurn, by-word.

contemptuousness etc. *adj.*; scornful eye; smile of contempt; derision etc. (*disrespect*) 929.

[State of being despised] despisedness.

V. despise, contemn, scorn, disdain, feel contempt for, view with a scornful eye, disregard, slight, not mind; pass by etc. (*neglect*) 460.

look down upon; hold -cheap, – in contempt, – in disrespect; think -nothing, – small beer- of; make light of; underestimate etc. 483; esteem - slightly, – of small or no account; take no account of, care nothing for; set no store by; not care a - straw etc. (*unimportance*) 643; set at naught, laugh in one's sleeve, snap one's fingers at, shrug one's shoulders, turn up one's nose at, pooh-pooh, damn with faint praise; sneeze –, whistle –, sneer- at; curl up one's lip, toss the head, *traiter de haut;* laugh at etc. (*be disrespectful*) 929.

point the finger of –, hold up to –, laugh to- scorn; scout, hoot, flout, hiss, scoff at.

turn -one's back, – a cold shoulder- upon; tread –, trample- upon; – under foot; spurn, kick; fling to the winds etc. (*repudiate*) 610; send away with a flea in the ear.

Adj. contemptuous; disdain-, scorn-ful; withering, contumelious, supercilious, cynical, haughty, bumptious, cavalier, derisive.

contemptible, despicable; pitiable; pitiful etc.
(*unimportant*) 643; despised etc. *v.*; down-
trodden; unenvied.

Adv. contemptuously etc. *adj.*

Int. a fig for etc. (*unimportant*) 643; bah! never
mind! away with! hang it! fiddle-de-dee!

931. Approbation.—N. approbation; approv-
al, -ement; sanction, advocacy; nod of approbation;
esteem, estimation, good opinion, golden opinions,
admiration; love etc. 897; appreciation, regard, account, popularity, *kudos*, credit; repute etc. 873.

commendation, praise; laud, -ation; good word;
meed −, tribute- of praise; encomium; eulog-y, -
ium; *éloge*, panegyric; homage, hero worship;
benediction, blessing, benison.

applause, plaudit, clap; clapping, − of hands;
accl-aim, -amation; cheer; paean, hosannah; shout
−, peal −, chorus −, thunders- of -applause etc.
Kentish fire; Prytaneum; blurb.

V. approve; think -good, − much of, − well of,
− highly of; esteem, value, prize; set great store -
by, − on.

do justice to, appreciate; honor, hold in esteem,
look up to, admire; like etc. 897; be in favor of,
wish God speed; hail, − with satisfaction.

stand −, stick- up for; uphold, hold up, countenance, sanction; clap −, pat- on the back; keep
in countenance, endorse, give credit, recommend;
mark with a white -mark, − stone.

commend, praise; be-, laud; compliment, pay a
tribute, bepraise; clap, − the hands; applaud,
cheer, acclaim, acclamate, encore; panegyrize,
eulogize, cry up, *prôner*, puff; extol, − to the
skies; magnify, glorify, exalt, boost, swell, make
much of; flatter etc. 933; bless, give a blessing to;
have −, say- a good word for; speak -well, −
highly, − in high terms- of; sing −, sound −,
chaunt −, resound- the praises of; sing praises to;
cheer −, applaud- to the -echo, − very echo.

redound to the -honor, − praise, − credit- of;
do credit to; deserve -praise etc. *n.*; recommend itself; pass muster.

be -praised etc.; receive honorable mention; be
in -favor, − high favor- with; ring with the praises
of, win golden opinions, gain credit, find favor
with, stand well in the opinion of; *laudari a
laudato viro*.

Adj. approving etc. *v.*; in favor of; lost in admiration.

commendatory, complimentary, benedictory,
laudatory, panegyrical, eulogistic, encomiastic, ac-
clamatory, lavish of praise, uncritical.

approved, praised etc. *v.*; un-censured, -
impeached; popular, in good odor; in high esteem
etc. (*respected*) 928; in −, in high- favor.

deserving −, worthy of- praise etc. *n.*;
praiseworthy, commendable, of estimation; good
etc. 648; meritorious, estimable, creditable,
plausible, unimpeachable; beyond all praise.

Adv. commendably, with credit, to admiration;
well etc. 681; with three times three.

Int. hear, hear! well done! *brav-o! -a! -i!*
bravissimo! euge! macte virtute! so far so good,
that's right, quite right; *optime!* one cheer more;
may your shadow never be less! *esto perpetua!*
long life to! *viva! enviva!* God speed! *valete et
plaudite! encore! bis!*

Phr. *probatum est.*

932. Disapprobation.—N. disappro-bation, -
val; improbation; dis-esteem, -valuation, -
placency; odium; dislike etc. 867; dissent etc. 489.

dis-praise, -commendation; blame, censure,
obloquy; detraction etc. 934; disparagement,
depreciation; denunciation; condemnation etc.
971; ostracism; boycott; black-list, -ball; *index -
expurgatorius, − librorum prohibitorum.*

animadversion, reflection, stricture, objection,
exception, criticism; sardonic -grin, − laugh; sarcasm, insinuation, innuendo; bad −, poor −, left-
handed- compliment.

satire; sneer etc. (*contempt*) 930; taunt etc.
(*disrespect*) 929; cavil, carping, censoriousness;
hypercriticism etc. (*fastidiousness*) 868.

reprehension, remonstrance, expostulation,
reproof, reprobation, admonition, increpation,
reproach; rebuke, reprimand, castigation, jobation,
lecture, curtain lecture, blow up, wigging, dressing,
− down; rating, scolding, trimming; correction, set
down, rap on the knuckles, *coup de bec*, rebuff;
slap, − on the face; home thrust; hit, frown, scowl,
black look.

diatribe; jeremiad; *tirade*, philippic.

clamor, outcry, hue and cry; hiss, -ing; sibilation,
cat-call; execration etc. 908.

chiding, upbraiding etc. *v.*; exprobration, abuse,
vituperation, invective, objurgation, contumely,
personal remarks; hard −, cutting −, bitter-
words.

evil-speaking; bad language etc. 908; personality.

V. disapprove; dislike etc. 867; lament etc. 839;
object to, take exception to; be scandalized at,
think ill of; view with -disfavor, − dark eyes, −
jaundiced eyes; *nil admirari*, disvalue, improbate.

frown upon, look grave; bend −, knit- the
brows; shake the head at, shrug the shoulders; turn
up the nose etc. (*contempt*) 930; look -askance, −
black upon; look with an evil eye; make a wry -
face, − mouth- at; set one's face against.

dis-praise, -commend, -parage; deprecate, speak
ill of, not speak well of, slate, condemn etc. (*find
guilty*) 971.

blame; lay −, cast- blame upon; censure, *fron-
der*, reproach, pass censure on, reprobate, impugn.
remonstrate, expostulate, recriminate.

reprehend, chide, admonish; bring −, call- -to
account, − over the coals, − to order; take to
task, reprove, lecture, bring to book; read a -lesson,
− lecture- to; rebuke, correct.

reprimand, chastise, castigate, lash, blow up,
trounce, trim, *laver la tête*, overhaul; give it one,
− finely; gibbet.

accuse etc. 938; impeach, denounce; hold up to -
reprobation, − execration; expose, brand, gibbet,
stigmatize; show −, pull −, take- up; cry 'shame'
upon; be outspoken; raise a hue and cry against.

execrate etc. 908; exprobrate, speak daggers,
vituperate; abuse, −, like a pickpocket; scold, rate,
objurgate, upbraid, fall foul of; jaw; rail, − at, − in
good set terms; bark at; anathematize, call names;
call by -hard, − ugly- names; a-, re-vile; vili-fy, -
pend; bespatter; backbite; clapperclaw; rave −,
thunder −, fulminate- against; load with
reproaches; lash with the tongue.

exclaim −, protest −, inveigh −, declaim −,
cry out −, raise one's voice- against.

decry; cry −, run −, frown- down; clamor, hiss,

hoot, mob, ostracize; draw up –, sing- a round robin; black-ball, -list.

animadvert –, reflect- upon; glance at; cast -reflection, – reproach, – a slur- upon; insinuate, damn with faint praise; 'hint a fault and hesitate dislike;' not to be able to say much for.

scoff at, point at; twit, taunt etc. (*disrespect*) 929; sneer at etc. (*despise*) 230; satirize, lampoon; defame etc. (*detract*) 934; depreciate, find fault with, criticize, cut up; pull –, pick- to pieces; take exception; cavil; peck –, nibble –, carp- at; be -censorious etc. *adj.*; pick -holes, – a hole, – a hole in one's coat; make a fuss about.

take –, set- down; snub, snap one up, give a rap on the knuckles; throw a stone -at, – in one's gar-den; have a -fling, – snap- at; have words with, pluck a crow with; give one a -wipe, – lick with the rough side of the tongue.

incur blame, excite disapprobation, scandalize, shock, revolt; get a bad name, forfeit one's good opinion, be under a cloud, come under the ferule, bring a hornet's nest about one's ears.

take blame, stand corrected; have to answer for.

Adj. disapproving etc. *v.*; scandalized.

disparaging, condemnatory, damnatory, denun-ciatory, reproachful, abusive, objurgatory, clamorous, vituperative; defamatory etc. 934.

satirical, sarcastic, sardonic, cynical, dry, sharp, cutting, biting, severe, virulent, withering, trench-ant, hard upon; censorious, critical, captious, carping, hypercritical; fastidious etc. 868; sparing of –, grudging- praise.

disapproved, chid etc. *v.*; in bad odor, blown upon, unapproved; unblest; at a discount, ex-ploded; weighed in the balance and found wanting.

blameworthy, reprehensible etc. (*guilt*) 947; to –, worthy of- blame, answerable, un-commendable, exceptionable, not to be thought of, bad etc. 649; vicious etc. 945.

un-lamented, -bewailed, -pitied.

Adv. with a wry face; reproachfully etc. *adj.*

Int. it is too bad! it -won't, – will never- do! marry come up! Oh! come! 'sdeath!

forbid it Heaven! God –, Heaven- forbid! out –, fie- upon it! away with! tut! *O tempora! O mores!* shame! fie, – for shame! out on you!

tell it not in Gath!

933. Flattery.—N. flattery, adulation, gloze; bland-ishment, -iloquence; cajolery; fawning, wheedling etc. *v.*; captation, coquetry, sycophancy, obsequiousness, flunkeyism, toad-eating, tuft-hunting; snobbishness.

incense, honeyed words, flummery; bun-kum, -combe; blarney, *placebo*, butter; soft -soap, – sawder; rose water.

voice of the charmer, mouth honor; lip-homage; euphemism; unctuousness etc. *adj.*

V. flatter, praise to the skies, puff; wheedle, cajole, glaver, coax; fawn, –, upon; humor, gloze, soothe, pet, coquet, slaver, butter; be-spatter, -slubber, -plaster, -slaver; lay it on thick, overpraise; earwig, cog, collogue; truckle –, pander *or* pandar –, pay court- to; court; creep into the good graces of; curry favor with, hang on the sleeve of; fool to the top of one's bent; lick the dust.

lay the flattering unction to one's soul, gild the pill, make things pleasant.

overestimate etc. 482; exaggerate etc. 549.

Adj. flattering etc. *v.*; adulatory; mealy-, honey-mouthed; honeyed; smooth, – tongued; soapy, oily, unctuous, blandiloquent, specious; fine-, fair-spoken; plausible, servile, sycophantic, fulsome; courtier-ly, -like.

Adv. *ad captandum*.

934. Detraction.—N. detraction, disparagement, depreciation, vilification, obloquy, scurrility, scandal, defamation, aspersion, traducement, slander, calumny, obtrectation, evil-speaking, backbiting, *scandalum magnatum*.

personality, libel, squib, lampoon, skit, pasquinade; *chronique scandaleuse*.

sarcasm, cynicism; criticism (*disapprobation*) 932; invective etc. 932; envenomed tongue; *spretae injuria formae*.

detractor etc. 936.

V. detract, derogate, decry, depreciate, disparage; run –, cry- down; minimize, make light of; belittle, sneer at etc. (*contemn*) 930; criticize, pull to pieces, pick a hole in one's coat, asperse, cast aspersions, blow upon, bespatter, blacken; vili-fy, -pend; avile; give a dog a bad name, brand, malign, backbite, libel, lampoon, traduce, slander, defame, calumniate, bear false witness against; speak ill of behind one's back.

'damn with faint praise, assent with civil leer; and without sneering, others teach to sneer.'

fling dirt etc. (*disrespect*) 929; anathematize etc. 932; dip the pen in gall, view in a bad light.

Adj. detracting etc. *v.*; defamatory, detractory, derogatory; disparaging, libellous; scurril-e, -ous; abusive; foul-spoken, -tongued, -mouthed; slan-derous; calumni-ous, -atory; sar-castic, -donic; satirical, cynical.

935. Flatterer.—N. flatterer, adulator; eu-logist, -phemist; optimist, encomiast, *laudator*, whitewasher, booster.

toad-y, -eater; sycophant, courtier, pickthank, Sir Pertinax MacSycophant; *flâneur, prôneur*; puffer, touter, *claqueur*; claw-back, ear-wig, doer of dirty work; parasite, hanger on etc. (*servility*) 886.

936. Detractor.—N. detractor, reprover; cens-or, -urer; cynic, critic, caviller, carper, word-catcher.

defamer, backbiter, slanderer, knocker, Sir Ben-jamin Backbite, lampooner, satirist, traducer, libeller, calumniator, dearest foe, dawplucker, Thersites; Zoilus; good-natured –, candid- friend [satirically]; reviler, vituperator, castigator; shrew etc. 901.

disapprover, *laudator temporis acti*.

937. Vindication.—N. vindication, justification, warrant; exoneration, exculpation; acquittal etc. 970; whitewashing.

extenuation; pallia-tion, -tive; softening, mitigation.

reply, defense; recrimination etc. 938.

apology, gloss, varnish; plea etc. 617; salvo; excuse, extenuating circumstances; allowance, − to be made; *locus poenitentiae.*

apologist, vindicator, justifier; defendant etc. 938.

justifiable charge, true bill.

V. justify, warrant; be an -excuse etc. *n.*- for; lend a color, furnish a handle; vindicate; ex-, disculpate; acquit etc. 970; clear, set right, exonerate, whitewash.

extenuate, palliate, excuse, soften, apologize, varnish, slur, gloze; put a -gloss, − good faceupon; mince; gloss over, bolster up, help a lame dog over a stile.

advocate, defend, plead one's cause; stand −, stick −, speak- up for; contend −, speak- for; bear out, keep in countenance, support; plead etc. 617; say in defense; plead ignorance; confess and avoid, propugn, put in a good word for.

take the will for the deed, make allowance for, do justice to; give -one, − the Devil- his due.

make good; prove -the truth of, − one's case; be justified by the event.

Adj. vindicat-ed, -ing etc. *v.*; vindicat-ive, -ory; palliative; exculpatory; apologetic.

excusable, defensible, pardonable; veni-al, -able; specious, plausible, justifiable.

Phr. *'honi soit qui mal y pense.'*

938. Accusation.—**N.** accusation, charge, imputation, slur, inculpation, exprobration, delation; crimination; in-, ac-, re-crimination; *tu quoque* argument; invective etc. 932.

de-nunciation, -nouncement; libel, challenge, citation, arraignment; im-, ap-peachment; indictment, bill of indictment, true bill; lawsuit etc. 969; condemnation etc. 971.

gravamen of a charge, head and front of one's offending, *argumentum ad hominem*; scandal etc. (*detraction*) 934; *scandalum magnatum.*

accuser, prosecutor, plaintiff, complainant, petitioner; relator, informer; appellant.

accused, defendant, prisoner, panel, co-, respondent; litigant.

V. accuse, charge, tax, impute, twit, taunt with, reproach.

brand with reproach; stigmatize, slur; cast a -stone at, − slur on; incriminate; inculpate, implicate; call to account etc. (*censure*) 932; take toblame, − task; put in the black book.

inform against, indict, denounce, arraign; im-, ap-peach; have up, show up, pull up, challenge, cite, lodge a complaint; prosecute, bring an action against etc. 969.

charge −, saddle- with; lay to one's -door, − charge; lay the blame on, bring home to; cast −, throw- in one's teeth; cast the first stone at.

have −, keep- a rod in pickle for; have a crow to pluck with.

trump up a charge.

Adj. accusing etc. *v.*; accusat-ory, -ive; imputative, denunciatory; re-, criminatory.

accused etc. *v.*; suspected; under -suspicion, − a cloud, − *surveillance*; in -custody, − detention; in the -lock up, − watch house, − house of detention.

accusable, imputable; in-defensible, -excusable; un-pardonable, -justifiable; vicious etc. 945.

Int. look at home; *tu quoque* etc. (*retaliation*) 718.

939. Probity.—**N.** probity, integrity, rectitude; uprightness etc. *adj.*; honesty, faith; honor; good faith, *bona fides*; purity, clean hands.

fairness etc. *adj.*; fair play, justice, equity, impartiality, principle; grace.

constancy; faithfulness etc. *adj.*; fidelity, loyalty; incorrupt-ion, -ibility.

trustworthiness etc. *adj.*; truth, candor, singleness of heart; veracity etc. 543; tender conscience etc. (*sense of duty*) 926.

punctil-iousness, -io; delicacy, nicety; scrupulosity, -ousness etc. *adj.*; scruple; point, − of honor; punctuality.

dignity etc. (*repute*) 873; respectability, -bleness etc. *adj.*; gentleman; man of -honor, − his word; *fidus Achates, preux chevalier; galantuomo*; truepenny, trump, brick; true Briton, white man, sportsman.

court of honor, a fair field and no favor; *argumentum ad verecundiam.*

V. be -honorable etc. *adj.*; deal -honorably, − squarely, − impartially, − fairly; speak the truth etc. (*veracity*) 543; tell the truth and shame the devil, *vitam impendere vero*; show a proper spirit, make a point of; do one's duty etc. 944; play the game.

redeem one's pledge etc. 926; keep −, be as good as- one's -promise, − word; keep faith with, not fail.

give and take, *audire alteram partem*, give the devil his due, put the saddle on the right horse.

redound to one's honor

Adj. upright; honest, − as daylight; veracious etc. 543; virtuous etc. 944; honorable; fair, right, just, equitable, impartial, even-handed, square; fair −, open- and aboveboard.

constant, − as the northern star; faithful, loyal, staunch; true, − blue, − to one's colors, − to the core, − as the needle to the pole; true-hearted, trust-y, -worthy; as good as one's word, to be depended on, incorruptible.

manly, straightforward etc. (*ingenuous*) 703; frank, candid, open-hearted.

conscientious, tender-conscienced, right-minded; high-principled, -minded; scrupulous, religious, strict; nice, punctilious, correct, punctual; respect-, reput-able; gentlemanlike.

inviol-able, -ate; un-violated, -broken, -betrayed; un-bought, -bribed.

innocent etc. 946; pure; stainless; un-stained, -tarnished, -sullied, -tainted, -perjured; uncorrupt, -ed; unde-filed, -praved, -bauched; *integer vitae scelerisque purus; justus et tenax propositi.*

chivalrous, jealous of honor, *sans peur et sans reproche*; high-spirited.

supra-mundane, unworldly, overscrupulous.

Adv. honorably etc. *adj.*; *bona fide*; on the square, in good faith, honor bright, *foro conscientiae*, with clean hands; by fair means.

940. Improbity.—**N.** improbity; dishon-esty, -our; deviation from rectitude; disgrace etc. (*disrepute*) 874; fraud etc. (*deception*) 545; lying etc. 544; bad −, Punic- faith; *mala −, Punica, fides*; infidelity; faithlessness etc. *adj.*; Judas kiss, betrayal; scrap of paper.

breach of -promise, − trust, − faith; prodition, disloyalty, divided allegiance, treason, high treason; apostacy etc. (*tergiversation*) 607; non-observance etc. 773.

shabbiness etc. *adj.*; villainy; baseness etc. *adj.*; abjection, debasement, turpitude, moral turpitude, laxity, trimming, shuffling.

perfidy; perfidiousness etc. *adj.*; treachery, double-dealing; unfairness etc. *adj.*; knavery, roguery, rascality, foul-play; jobb-ing, -ery; Tammany, graft; venality, nepotism; corruption, job, shuffle, fishy transaction, barratry; sharp practice, heads I win, tails you lose; mouth-honor etc. (*flattery*) 933.

V. be -dishonest etc. *adj.*; play false; break one's -word, − faith, − promise; jilt, betray, forswear; shuffle etc. (*lie*) 544; live by one's wits, sail near the wind; play with marked cards.

disgrace −, dishonor −, demean −, degrade-oneself; derogate, stoop, grovel, sneak, lose caste; sell oneself, go over to the enemy; seal one's infamy.

Adj. dishon-est, -orable; un-conscientious, - scrupulous; fraudulent etc. 545; knavish; disgraceful etc. (*disreputable*) 874; wicked etc. 945.

false-hearted, disingenuous; unfair, one-sided; double, -tongued, -faced; time-serving, crooked, tortuous, insidious, Machiavellian, dark, slippery; questionable; fishy; perfidious, treacherous, perjured.

infamous, arrant, foul, base, vile, low, ignominious, blackguard:

contemptible, abject, mean, shabby, little, paltry, dirty, scurvy, scabby, sneaking, groveling, scrubby, rascally, pettifogging; beneath one; not cricket.

low-minded, -thoughted; base-minded.

undignified, indign; unbe-coming, -seeming, fitting; de-rogatory, -grading; *infra dignitatem*; ungentleman-ly, -like; un-knightly, -chivalric, - manly, -handsome; recreant, inglorious.

corrupt, venal; debased, mongrel.

faithless, of bad faith, false, unfaithful, disloyal; untrustworthy; trust-, troth-less; lost to shame, dead to honor.

Adv. dishonestly etc. *adj.*; *malā fide*, like a thief in the night, by crooked paths; by foul means.

Int. *O tempora! O mores!*

941. Knave.—**N.** knave, rogue, villain; Seapin, rascal; Lazarillo de Tormes; bad man etc. 949; blackguard etc. 949.

traitor, betrayer, arch-traitor, conspirator, stool pigeon, Judas, Catiline; reptile, serpent, snake in the grass, wolf in sheep's clothing, sneak, Jerry Sneak, tell-tale, squealer, mischief-maker, trimmer; renegade etc. (*tergiversation*) 607; truant, recreant; sycophant etc. (*servility*) 886.

942. Disinterestedness.—**N.** disinterestedness etc. *adj.*; generosity; liberal-ity, -ism; altruism; benevolence etc. 906; elevation, loftiness of purpose, exaltation, magnanimity; chival-ry, -rous spirit; heroism, sublimity.

self-denial, -abnegation, -effacement, -sacrifice, - immolation, -control etc. (*resolution*) 604; stoicism, devotion, martyrdom, *suttee*.

labor of love.

V. be -disinterested etc. *adj.*; make a sacrifice, lay one's head on the block; put oneself in the place of others, do as one would be done by, do unto others as we would men should do unto us.

Adj. disinterested; unselfish; self-denying, - sacrificing, -devoted; generous.

handsome, liberal, noble; noble-, high-minded; princely, great, high, elevated, lofty, exalted, spirited, stoical, magnanimous; great-, large-hearted, chivalrous, heroic, sublime.

un-bought, -bribed; uncorrupted etc. (*upright*) 939.

943. Selfishness.—**N.** selfishness etc. *adj.*; self-love, -indulgence, -worship, -interest; ego-tism, - ism; egocentrism, narcissism; *amour propre* etc. (*vanity*) 880; nepotism.

worldliness etc. *adj.*; world wisdom.

illiberality; meanness etc. *adj.*

time-server; tuft-, fortune-hunter; self-seeker; jobber, worldling; egotist, egoist, monopolist, nepotist, profiteer; temporizer, trimmer; dog in the manger, charity that begins at home.

V. be -selfish etc. *adj.*; please −, indulge −, coddle- oneself; consult one's own -wishes, − pleasure; look after one's own interest; feather one's nest; take care of number one, have an eye to the main chance, know on which side one's bread is buttered; give an inch and take an ell; wangle.

Adj. selfish; self-seeking, -indulgent, -interested; wrapt up −, centered- in self; egotistic, -al; egoistical; egocentric.

illiberal, mean, ungenerous, narrowminded; mercenary, venal; covetous etc. 819.

unspiritual; earthly, -minded; mundane; worldly, -minded, -wise; time-serving.

interested; *alieni appetens sui profusus*.

Adv. ungenerously etc. *adj.*; to gain some private ends; from selfish −, interested- motives.

Phr. *après nous le déluge.*

944. Virtue.—**N.** virtue; virtuousness etc. *adj.*; morality; moral rectitude; integrity etc. (*probity*) 939; nobleness etc. 873.

morals; ethics etc. (*duty*) 926; cardinal virtues.

merit, worth, desert, excellence, credit; self-control etc. (*resolution*) 604; self-denial etc. (*temperance*) 953.

well-doing; good -actions, − behavior; discharge −, fulfilment −, performance- of duty; well spent life; innocence etc. 946.

V. be -virtuous etc. *adj.*; practice -virtue etc. *n.*; do −, fulfil −, perform −, discharge- one's duty; redeem one's pledge etc. 926; act well, − one's part; fight the good fight; acquit oneself well; command −, master- one's passions; keep -straight, − in the right path.

set -an, − a good- example; be on one's -good, − best- behavior.

Adj. virtuous, good; innocent etc. 946; meritorious, deserving, worthy, desertful; correct; dut-iful, -eous; moral; right, -eous, -minded; well-intentioned, creditable, laudable, commendable, praiseworthy; above −, beyond- all praise; excellent, admirable; sterling, pure, noble.

exemplary; match-, peer-less; saint-ly, -like; heaven-born, angelic, seraphic, godlike.

Adv. virtuously etc. *adj.*; *e merito*.

945. Vice.—N. vice; evil-doing, – courses; wrong doing; wickedness, viciousness etc. *adj.*; iniquity, peccability, demerit; sin, Adam; old – offending- Adam.

immorality, impropriety, indecorum, scandal, laxity, looseness of morals; want of -principle, – ballast; obliquity, backsliding, infamy, demoralization, pravity, depravity, pollution; hardness of heart; brutality etc. (*malevolence*) 907; corruption etc. (*debasement*) 659; knavery etc. (*improbity*) 940; profligacy; lust etc. 961; flagrancy, atrocity; cannibalism.

infirmity; weakness etc. *adj.*; weakness of the flesh, frailty, imperfection; error; weak side; foible; fail-ing, -ure; crying –, besetting- sin; defect, deficiency, shortcoming; cloven foot.

lowest dregs of vice, sink of iniquity, Alsatian den; *gusto picaresco.*

fault, crime; criminality etc. (*guilt*) 947.

sinner etc. 949.

V. be -vicious etc. *adj.*; sin, commit sin, do amiss, err, transgress; misdemean –, forget –, misconduct- oneself; mis-do, -behave; fall, lapse, slip, trip, offend, trespass; deviate from the -line of duty, – path of virtue etc. 944; take a wrong course, go astray; hug a -sin, – fault; sow one's wild oats.

render -vicious etc. *adj.*; demoralize, brutalize; corrupt etc. (*degrade*) 659.

Adj.* vicious; sinful; sinning etc. *v.*; wicked, iniquitous, bad, immoral, unrighteous, wrong, criminal; naughty, incorrect; undut-eous, -iful.

unprincipled, lawless, disorderly, *contra bonos mores*, indecorous, unseemly, improper; dissolute, profligate, scampish; unworthy; worth-, desert-less; disgraceful, recreant; reprehensible, blameworthy, uncommendable; dis-creditable, -reputable.

base, sinister, scurvy, foul, gross, vile, black, grave, facinorous, felonious, nefarious, shameful, scandalous, infamous, villainous, of a deep dye, heinous; flag-rant, -itious; atrocious, incarnate, accursed.

Mephistophelian, satanic, diabolic, hellish, infernal, stygian, fiend-ish, -like, hell-born, demoniacal, devilish.

mis-created, -begotten; demoralized, corrupt, depraved.

evil-minded, -disposed; ill-conditioned; malevolent etc. 907; heart-, grace-, shame-, virtue-less; abandoned, lost to virtue; unconscionable; sunk –, lost –, deep –, steeped- in iniquity.

incorrigible, irreclaimable, obdurate, reprobate, past praying for; culpable, reprehensible etc. (*guilty*) 947.

unjustifiable; in-defensible, -excusable; inexpiable, unpardonable, irremissible.

weak, frail, lax, infirm, imperfect, indiscreet; demoralizing, degrading.

Adv. wrong; sinfully etc. *adj.*; without excuse.

Int. *O tempora! O mores!*

*Most of these adjectives are applicable both to the act and to the agent.

946. Innocence.—N. innocence; guiltlessness etc. *adj.*; incorruption, impeccability.

clean hands, clear conscience, *mens sibi conscia recti.*

innocent, new born babe, lamb, dove.

V. be -innocent etc. *adj.*; *nil conscire sibi nullâ pallescere culpâ.*

acquit etc. 970; exculpate etc. (*vindicate*) 937.

Adj. innocent, not guilty, unguilty; guilt-, fault-, sin-, stain-, blood-, spot-less; clear, immaculate; *rectus in curiâ*; un-spotted, -blemished, -erring; undefiled etc. 939; unhardened, Saturnian; Arcadian etc. (*artless*) 703.

in-, un-culpable; unblam-ed, -able; blameless, inerrable, above suspicion; irrepr-oachable, -ovable, -ehensible; un-exceptionable, -objectionable, -impeachable; salvable; venial etc. 937.

harmless; in-offensive, -noxious, -nocuous; dove-, lamb-like; pure, harmless as doves; innocent as -a lamb, – the babe unborn; more sinned against than sinning.

virtuous etc. 944; un-reproved, -impeached, -reproached.

Adv. innocently etc. *adj.*; with clean hands; with a -clear, – safe- conscience.

947. Guilt.—N. guilt, -iness; culpability; crimin-ality, -ousness; deviation from rectitude etc. (*improbity*) 940; sinfulness etc. (*vice*) 945; peccability.

mis-conduct, -behavior, -doing, -deed; malpractice, fault, sin, error, transgression; dereliction, delinquency; indiscretion, lapse, slip, trip, *faux pas, peccadillo*; flaw, blot, omission; fail-ing, -ure.

offence, trespass, mis-demeanor, -feasance, prision, tort; mal-efaction, -feasance, -versation; crime, felony.

enormity, atrocity, outrage; deadly –, mortal –, unpardonable- sin; died without a name. *corpus delicti.*

Adj. guilty, to blame, culpable, peccable, in fault, censurable, reprehensible, blameworthy, uncommendable, illaudable; weighed in the balance and found wanting; exceptionable, objectionable.

Adv. *in flagrante delicto*; red-handed, in the very act.

948. Good Man.—N. good man, worthy.

good woman, goddess, *madonna*, virgin.

model, paragon etc. (*perfection*) 650; good example; hero, demigod, seraph, angel; innocent etc. 946; saint etc. (*piety*) 987; benefactor etc. 912; philanthropist etc. 910; Aristides.

brick, trump, rough diamond, ugly duckling.

salt of the earth; one in ten thousand; one of the best.

Phr. *si sic omnes!*

949. Bad Man.—N. bad man, wrongdoer, worker of iniquity; evil-doer etc. 913; sinner; the -wicked etc. 945; bad example.

rascal, scoundrel, villain, miscreant, caitiff; wretch, reptile, viper, serpent, cockatrice, basilisk, urchin; tiger, monster; devil etc. (*demon*) 980; devil incarnate; demon in human shape, Nana Sahib; hell-hound, -cat; rake-hell.

bad woman, jade, Jezebel, adultress, etc. 962.

scamp, scapegrace, rip, runagate, ne'er-do-well, reprobate, *roué*, rake; limb; one who has sold himself to the devil, fallen angel, *âme damnée*, *vaurien*, *mauvais sujet*, loose fish, sad, dog; lost —, black-sheep; castaway, recreant, defaulter; prodigal etc. 818; libertine etc. 962.

rough, rowdy, ugly customer, ruffian, hoodlum, bully; Jonathan Wild; hangman; incendiary; thief etc. 792; murderer etc. 361.

culprit, delinquent, criminal, melefactor, misdemeanant; felon; convict, jail-bird, ticket-of-leave man; outlaw.

blackguard, *polisson*, loafer, sneak; raps-, rascallion; cullion, mean wretch, varlet, kern, *âme-de-boue*, *drôle*; cur, dog, hound, whelp, mongrel; lown, loon, runnion, outcast, vagabond; rogue etc. (*knave*) 941; scum of the earth, riff-raff; *Arcades ambo*.

Int. sirrah!

950. Penitence.—N. penitence, contrition, compunction, repentance, remorse; regret etc. 833.

self-reproach, -reproof, -accusation, -condemnation, -humiliation; stings —, pangs —, qualms —, prickings —, twinge —, twitch —, touch —, voice- of conscience; compunctious visitings of nature.

acknowledgment, confession etc. (*disclosure*) 529; apology etc. 952; recantation etc. 607; penance etc. 952; resipiscence.

awakened conscience, deathbed repentance, *locus poenitentiae*, stool of repentance, cutty stool.

penitent, Magdalen, prodigal son, returned prodigal, a sadder and wiser man.

V. repent, be sorry for; be -penitent etc. *adj.*; rue; regret etc. 833; think better of; recant etc. 607; knock under etc. (*submit*) 725; plead guilty; sing -*miserere*, - *de profundis*; cry *peccavi*; own oneself in the wrong; acknowledge, confess etc. (*disclose*) 529; humble oneself; beg pardon etc. (*apologize*) 952; turn over a new leaf, put on the new man, turn from sin; reclaim; repent in sackcloth and ashes etc. (*do penance*) 952; learn by experience.

Adj. penitent; repenting etc. *v.*; repentant, contrite; conscience-smitten, -stricken; self-accusing, -convicted.

penitenti-al, -ary; chastened, reclaimed; not hardened; un-hardened.

Adv. *meâ culpâ*.

Phr. *peccavi*; *erubuit*; *salva res est*; *vous l'avez voulu, Georges Dandin*.

951. Impenitence.—N. impenitence, irrepentance, recusance.

hardness of heart, seared conscience, induration, obduracy.

V. be -impenitent etc. *adj.*; steel —, harden- the heart; die -game, — and make no sign.

Adj. impenitent uncontrite, obdurate; hard, -ened; seared, recusant; unrepentant; relent-, -remorse-, grace-, shrift-less.

lost, incorrigible, irreclaimable.

unre-claimed, -formed; unrepented, unatoned.

952. Atonement.—N. atonement, reparation; compromise, composition; compensation etc. 30; quittance, quits; indemni-ty, -fication; expiation,

redemption, reclamation, conciliation, propitiation.

amends, apology, *amende honorable*, satisfaction; peace —, sin —, burnt- offering; scapegoat, sacrifice.

penance, fasting, maceration, sackcloth and ashes, white sheet, shrift, flagellation, lustration; purga-tion, -tory.

V. atone, — for; expiate; propitiate; make - amends, — good; reclaim, redeem, repair, ransom, absolve, purge, shrive, do penance, stand in a white sheet, repent in sackcloth and ashes.

set one's house in order, wipe off old scores, make matters up; pay the -forfeit, — penalty.

apologize, beg pardon, express regret, *faire amende honorable*, give satisfaction; come —, fall-down on one's -knees, — marrow bones.

Adj. propitiatory, expiatory; sacrific, -ial, -atory; piacul-ar, -ous.

953. Temperance.—N. temperance, moderation, sobriety, soberness.

forbearance, abnegation; self-denial, -restraint, -control etc. (*resolution*) 604.

frugality; vegetarianism, teetotalism, total abstinence, prohibition; abst-inence, -emiousness, asceticism etc. 955; system of -Pythagoras, — Cornaro; Pythagorism, Stoicism.

vegetarian; Pythagorean, gymnosophist; teetotaler etc. 958; abstainer.

V. be -temperate etc. *adj.*; abstain, forbear, refrain, deny oneself, spare; know when one has had enough; take the pledge; look not upon the wine when it is red.

Adj. temperate, moderate, sober, frugal, sparing; abst-emious, -inent; within compass; measured etc. (*sufficient*) 639.

Pythagorean; vegetarian; teetotal, pussy-foot.

954. Intemperance.—N. intemperance; sensuality, animalism, carnality; pleasure; effeminacy, silkiness; luxur-y, -iousness; lap of -pleasure, — luxury.

indulgence; high-, free- living, in-abstinence, self-indulgence; voluptuousness etc. *adj.*; epicurism, -eanism; sybaritism.

dissipation; licentiousness etc. *adj.*; debauchery; crapulence.

revel-s, -ry; debauch, carousal, jollification, drinking bout, wassail, Saturnalia, orgies; excess, too much; intoxication etc. 959.

Circean cup; drug habit etc. 663.

V. be -intemperate etc. *adj.*; indulge, exceed; live -well, — high, — on the fat of the land; give a loose to -indulgence etc. *n.*; don not wisely but too well; wallow in -voluptuousness etc. *n.*; plunge into dissipation.

revel, rake, live hard, run riot, sow one's wild oats; slake one's -appetite, — thirst; swill; pamper.

Adj. intemperate, inabstinent, intoxicated etc. 958; sensual, self-indulgent; voluptuous, luxurious, licentious, wild, dissolute, rakish, fast, debauched.

brutish, crapulous, swinish, piggish, hoggish, bestial.

Paphian, Epicurean, Sybaritical; bred —, nursed- in the lap of luxury; indulged, pampered, full-fed.

954a. Sensualist.—N. Sybarite, voluptuary, Sardanapalus, man of pleasure, carpet knight; epicure, -an; *gourm-et, -and;* gormandizer, gutling, glutton, pig, hog; votary – , swine- of Epicurus; sensualist; Heliogabalus; free – , hard- liver; libertine etc. 962; hedonist.

955. Asceticism.—N. asceticism, puritanism, sabbatarianism; cynicism, austerity; total abstinence.

mortification, maceration, sackcloth and ashes, flagellation; penance etc. 952; fasting etc. 956; martyrdom.

ascetic; anchor-et, -ite; martyr; *Heautontimorumenos;* hermit etc. (*recluse*) 893; puritan, sabbatarian, cynic.

Adj. ascetic, austere, puritanical; cynical; over-religious.

956. Fasting.—N. fasting; exrophagy; famishment, starvation; banting.

fast, *jour maigre;* fast – , banyan-day; Lent, quadragesima; Rama-dan, -zan; spare – , meager-diet; lenten -diet, – entertainment; *soupe maigre,* short -rations, – commons; Barmecide feast; hunger strike.

V. fast, starve, clem, famish, perish with hunger; dine with Duke Humphrey; make two bites of a cherry.

Adj. lenten, quadragesimal; unfed; starved etc. *v.;* half-starved; fasting etc. *v.;* hungry etc. 865.

957. Gluttony.—N. gluttony; greed; greediness etc. *adj.;* voracity.

epicurism; good – , high- living; edacity, gulosity, crapulence; gutt-, guzz-ling; over-indulgence.

good cheer, blow out; feast etc. (*food*) 298; gastronomy.

epicure, *bon vivant, gourmand;* glutton, cormorant, hog, belly-god, Apicius, gastronome, gormandizer.

V. gormandize, gorge; over-gorge, -eat- oneself; engorge, eat one's fill, cram, stuff, stodge, glut, satiate; gutt-le, guzz-le; bolt, devour, gobble up; gulp etc. (*swallow food*) 298; raven, eat out of house and home.

have the stomach of an ostrich; play a good knife and fork etc. (*appetite*) 865.

Adj. gluttonous, greedy; gormandizing etc. *v.;* edacious, omnivorous, crapulent, swinish, voracious, devouring.

pampered; over-fed, -gorged.

958. Sobriety.—N. sobriety; teetotalism, temperance etc. 953.

water-drinker; teetotal-er, -ist; abstainer, Good Templar, Rechabite, band of hope; prohibitionist, pussyfoot.

V. take the pledge.

Adj. sober, – as a judge; dry, on the water wagon.

959. Drunkenness.—N. drunkenness etc. *adj.;* intemperance; drinking etc. *v.;* inebri-ety, -ation; ebri-ety, -osity; befuddlement; insobriety; intoxication; temulency, bibacity, wine-bibbing; com- , potation; deep potations, bacchanals, *bacchanalia,* libations.

oino-, dipso-mania; *delirium tremens,* d.t., alcohol, -ism.

drink; alcoholic drinks, alcohol, booze; gin, blue ruin, grog, brandy, port wine; punch, -bowl; cup, rosy wine, flowing bowl; drop, – too much; dram; beer, wine, spirits etc. (*beverage*) 298; cocktail, nip, peg; stirrup cup.

drunkard, sot, toper, tippler, bibber, wine-bibber; hard – , gin – , dram- drinker; soak, soaker, sponge, tun; love-, toss-pot; thirsty soul, reveller, carouser; Bacchanal, -ian; Bacch-al, -ante; devotee to Bacchus, dipsomaniac.

V. get – , be- drunk etc. *adj.;* see double; take a -drop, – glass- too much; drink, tipple, tope, booze, bouse, guzzle, swill, soak, sot, lush, bib, swig, carouse; sacrifice at the shrine of Bacchus; take to drinking; drink -hard, – deep, – like a fish; have one's swill, drain the cup, splice the main brace, take a hair of the dog that bit you.

liquor, – up; wet one's whistle, take a whet; lift one's elbow; crack a – , pass the- bottle; toss of etc. (*drink up*) 298; go to the -ale, – public house.

make one-drunk etc. *adj.;* inebriate, fuddle, fuzzle, get into one's head.

Adj. drunk, tipsy; intoxicated; inebri-ous, -ate, -ated; in one's cups; in a state of -intoxication etc. *n.;* temulent, -ive; fuddled, mellow, cut, boosy, fou, fresh, merry, elevated, squiffy; plastered, befuddled, sozzled; flush, -ed; flustered, disguised, groggy, beery; topheavy; potvaliant, glorious, potulent; over-come, -taken; whittled, screwed, tight, primed, oiled, corned, raddled, sewed up, lushy, nappy, muddled, muzzy, bosky, obfuscated, maudlin; crapulous, dead – , blind- drunk.

inter pocula; in – , the worse for- liquor, having had a drop too much, half seas over, three sheets in the wind; under the table, blind to the world, one over the eight.

drunk as -a piper, – a fiddler, – a lord, – Chloe, – an owl, – David's sow, – a wheelbarrow.

drunken, bibacious, bibulous, sottish; given – , addicted- to -drink, – the bottle; toping etc. *v.;* wet.

Phr. *nunc est bibendum.*

960. Purity.—N. purity; decency, decorum, delicacy; continence, chastity, honesty, virtue, modesty, shame; pudicity, *pucelage,* virginity.

vestal, virgin, Joseph, Hippolytus; Lucretia, Diana; prude.

Adj. pure, undefiled, modest, delicate, decent, decorous; *virginibus puerisque;* chaste, continent, virtuous, honest, Platonic.

961. Impurity.—N. impurity; uncleanness etc. (*filth*) 653; immodesty; grossness etc. *adj.;* indelicacy, indecency; impudicity; obscenity, ribaldry, smut, bawdry, *double entendre, équivoque;* Aretinism; pornography.

concupiscence, lust, carnality, flesh, salacity; pruriency, lechery, lasciviency, lubricity, lewdness.

incontinence, intrigue, *faux pas*; *amour*, *-ette*; gallantry; dabauchery, libertinism, *libertinage*, fornication; *liaison*; wenching, venery, dissipation.

seduction; defloration, defilement, abuse, violation, rape; incest.

social evil, harlotry, stupration, whoredom, concubinage, cuckoldom, adultery, advoutry, *crim. con.*; free love.

seraglio, harem, zenana; brothel, bagnio, stew, bawdy-house, *lupanar*, house of ill fame, *bordel*, kip.

V. be -impure etc. *adj.*; intrigue; debauch, defile, assault, attack, seduce; prostitute; abuse, violate, deflower; commit -adultery etc. *n.*

Adj. impure; unclean etc. (*dirty*) 653; not to be mentioned to ears polite; immodest, shameless; indecorous, -delicate, -decent; loose, suggestive, *risqué*, coarse, gross, broad, free, equivocal, smutty, fulsome, ribald, obscene, bawdy, pornographic.

concupiscent, prurient, lickerish, rampant, lustful; carnal, -minded; lewd, lascivious, lecherous, libidinous, erotic, ruttish, salacious; Paphian; voluptuous; incestuous.

· unchaste, -light, wanton, licentious, adulterous, debauched, dissolute; of -loose character, – easy virtue; frail, gay, riggish, incontinent, meretricious, rakish, gallant, dissipated; no better than she should be; on the -town, – streets, – *pavé*, – loose.

adulterous, incestuous, bestial.

962. Libertine.—N. libertine; voluptuary etc. 954*a*; rake, debauchee, loose fish, rip, rake-hell, fast man; *intrigant*, gallant, seducer, fornicator, lecher, satyr, goat, whoremonger, *paillard*, adulterer, gay deceiver, Lothario, Don Juan, Bluebeard.

adulteress, advoutress, courtesan, prostitute, strumpet, tart, hustler, chippy, broad, harlot, whore, punk, *fille de joie*; woman, – of the town; street-walker, Cyprian, miss, piece; frail sisterhood, fallen woman; demirep, wench, trollop, trull, baggage, hussy, drab, bitch, jade, skit, rig, quean, mopsy, slut, minx, harridan; woman -of easy virtue etc. (*unchaste*) 961; wanton, fornicatress; Jezebel, Messalina, Delilah, Thaïs, Phryne, Aspasia, Lais, *lorette*, *cocotte*, *petite dame*, *grisette*; demimonde; white slave.

concubine, mistress, fancy woman, kept woman, doxy, *chère amie*, *bona roba*.

pimp; pand-er, -ar; bawd, *conciliatrix*, procuress, mackerel; wittol.

963. Legality.—N. legality; legitima-cy, -teness, legitimization.

legislature; law, code, *corpus juris*, constitution, pandect, charter, act, enactment, statute, rule; canon etc. (*precept*) 697; ordinance, institution, regulation; by-, bye-law, rescript; decree etc. (*order*) 741; *ordonnance*; standing order; *plébiscite* etc. (*choice*) 609.

legal process; form, -ula, -ality; rite; arm of the law; *habeas corpus*.

[Science of law] jurisprudence, nomology; legislation, codification.

equity, common law; *lex* –, *lex nonscripta*, unwritten law; law of nations, international law, *jus gentium*; *jus civile*; civil –, criminal –, canon –, statute –, ecclesiastical- law; *lex mercatoria*.

constitutional-ism, -ity; justice etc. 922.

V. legalize, legitimize; enact, ordain; decree etc. (*order*) 741; pass a law; legislate; codify, formulate; authorize.

Adj. legal, legitimate; according to law; vested, constitutional, chartered, legalized; lawful etc. (*permitted*) 760; statut-able, -ory; legislat-orial, -ive.

Adv. legally etc. *adj.*; in the eye of the law; *de jure*.

964. Illegality. [Absence or violation of law.]—**N.** lawlessness; breach –, violation- of law; disobedience etc. 742; unconformity etc. 83.

arbitrariness etc. *adj.*; antinomy, violence, brute force, despotism, outlawry.

mob –, lynch –, club –, Lydford –, martial –, drumhead- law; *coup d'état*; *le droit du plus fort*; *argumentum baculinum*.

illegality, informality, unlawfulness, illegitimacy, bar sinister.

trover and conversion; smuggling, boot-legging, rum-running, poaching; simony.

speakeasy, speakie, blind pig.

V. offend against –, violate- the law; set the law at defiance, ride rough-shod over, drive a coach and six through a statute; make the law a dead letter, take the law into one's own hands.

smuggle, run, poach.

Adj. illegal; prohibited etc. 761; not allowed, unlawful, illegitimate, illicit, contraband, actionable.

unchartered, unconstitutional; unwarrant-ed, -able; unauthorized; informal, unofficial; in-, extra-judicial.

lawless, arbitrary; despotic, -al; summary, irresponsible; un-answerable, -accountable.

null and void; a dead letter.

Adv. illegally etc. *adj.*; with a high hand, in violation of law.

965. Jurisdiction. [Executive.]—**N.** jurisdiction, judicature, administration of justice, soc; executive, commission of the peace; magistracy etc. (*authority*) 737.

judge etc. 967; tribunal etc. 966; municipality, corporation, bailiwick, shrievalty; lord -lieutenant; lord –, mayor, city manager, alderman etc. 745; sheriff, bailie, shrieve, chief –, constable; police, – force; constabulary, bumbledom.

officer; proctor, high –, commissioner; bailiff, tipstaff, bum-bailiff, catchpoll, beadle; police-man, -constable, -sergeant; *sbirro*, *alguazil*, *gendarme*, kavass, *lictor*, macebearer, *huissier*, bedel.

press-gang; exciseman, gauger, custom-house officer, *douanier*.

coroner, edile, aedile, portreeve, paritor; *posse comitatus*.

V. judge, sit in judgment.

Adj. executive, administrative, municipal;

inquisitorial, causidical; judic-atory, -iary, -ial; juridical.

Adv. *coram judice.*

966. Tribunal.—N. tribunal, court, board, bench, judicatory, curia; court of -justice, - law, - arbitration; inquisition; guild.

justice - , judgment - , mercy- seat; woolsack; bar, - of justice; dock; forum, hustings, *bureau*, drum-head; jury-, witness-box.

senate-house, town-hall, theater; House of - Lords, - Commons.

assize, eyre; ward-, burgh-mote; superior courts of Westminster; court of -record, - oyer and terminer, - assize, - appeal - error; High court of -Judicature, - Appeal; Judicial Committee of the Privy Council; Star-Chamber; Court of -Chancery, - King's *or* Queen's Bench, - Exchequer, - Common Pleas, - Probate, - Arches, - Admiralty, - Criminal Appeal; Lords Justices' - , Rolls - , Vice Chancellor's - , Stannary - , Divorce - , Palatine - , ecclesiastical - , county - , police- court; sessions; quarter - , pettysessions; court -leet, - baron, - of pie poudre, - of common council; board of green cloth.

court-martial; drum-head court-martial; *durbar*, divan; Areopagus; *rota.*

Adj. judicial etc. 965; appellate; curial.

967. Judge.—N. judge, justi-ce, -ciar, ciary; chancellor; justice - , judge- of assize; recorder, common serjeant; puisne - , assistant - , county court- judge; conservator - , justice- of the peace, J.P.; court etc. (*tribunal*) 966; grand - , petty - , coroner's- jury; panel, juror, juryman; twelve men in a box; magistrate, police magistrate, stipendiary, the great unpaid, beak; his -worship, - honor, - lordship; deemster, moderator.

Lord -Chancellor, - Justice; Master of the Rolls, Vice-Chancellor; Lord Chief -Justice, - Baron; Mr. Justice; Baron, - of the Exchequer.

jurat, assessor; arbi-ter, -trator; umpire; refer-ee, -endary; revising barrister; domesman; censor etc. (*critic*) 480; official - , receiver.

archon, tribune, praetor, *ephor*, syndic, *podestà*, mullah, ulema, mufti, cadi, kadi; Rhadamanthus.

litigant etc. (*accusation*) 938.

V. adjudge etc. (*determine*) 480; try a -case, - prisoner.

Adj. judicial etc. 965.

Phr. 'a Daniel come to judgment.'

968. Lawyer.—N. lawyer, jurist, legist, civilian, pundit, publicist, jurisconsult, legal adviser, advocate; barrister, - at law; counsel, -lor; King's *or* Queen's counsel; K.C.; Q.C.; silk gown, leader; junior, - counsel; stuff gown, serjeant-at-law; bencher, tubman; judge etc. 967.

bar, legal profession, gentleman of the long robe; junior - , outer - , inner- bar; Inns of Court; equity draftsman, conveyancer, pleader, special pleader.

solicitor, attorney, proctor; notary, - public; scrivener, cursitor; writer, - to the signet; S.S.C.; limb of the law; pettifogger.

V. practice -at, - within- the bar; plead; call - , to called- -to, - within- the bar; take silk.

Adj. learned in the law; at the bar; forensic.

969. Lawsuit.—N. lawsuit, suit, action, cause, petition; litigation; dispute etc. 713.

citation, arraignment, prosecution, impeachment; accusation etc. 938; presentment, true bill, indictment.

apprehension, arrest; committal; imprisonment etc. (*restraint*) 751.

writ, summons, subpoena, *latitat*, *nisi prius*; *habeas corpus*.

pleadings; declaration, bill, claim; *procèsverbal*, bill of right, information, *corpus delicti*; affidavit, state of facts; answer, replication, plea, demurrer, rebutter, rejoinder; surre-butter, - joinder.

suitor, party to a suit; litigant etc. 938; libellant.

hearing, trial; verdict etc. (*judgment*) 480; appeal, - motion; writ of error; *certiorari*.

case, decision, precedent, ruling; decided case, reports.

V. go to - , appeal to the- law; bring to -justice, - trial, - the bar; put on trial, pull up; accuse etc. 938; prefer - , file- a claim etc. *n.*; take the law of, inform against.

serve with a writ, cite, apprehend, arraign, sue, prosecute, bring an action against, indict, impeach, attach, distrain, commit; arrest; summon, -s; give in charge etc. (*restrain*) 751.

empanel a jury, implead, join issue; close the pleadings; set down for hearing.

try, hear a cause; sit in judgment; adjudicate etc. 480.

Adj. litigious etc. (*quarrelsome*) 713; *qui tam*; *coram* - , *sub- judice.*

Adv. *pendente lite.*

Phr. *adhuc sub judice lis est.*

970. Acquittal.—N. acquit-tal, -ment; clearance, exculpation, exoneration; discharge etc. (*release*) 750; *quietus*, absolution, compurgation, reprieve, respite; pardon etc. (*forgiveness*) 918. [Exemption from punishment] impunity, immunity.

V. acquit, exculpate, exonerate, clear; absolve, whitewash, assoil, discharge; release; liberate etc. 750.

reprieve, respite; pardon etc. (*forgive*) 918; let off, - scot free.

Adj. acquitted etc. *v.*; un-condemned, - punished, -chastised; recommended to mercy.

971. Condemnation.—N. condemnation, conviction, proscription, damnation; death warrant; penalty etc. 974.

attain-der, -ture, -tment.

V. condemn, convict, cast, bring home to, find guilty, damn, doom, sign the death warrant, sentence, pass sentence on, attaint, confiscate, proscribe, sequestrate; non-suit.

disapprove etc. 932; accuse etc. 938.

stand condemned.

Adj. condem-, dam-natory; condemned etc. *v.*; non-suited etc. (*failure*) 732; self-convicted.

Phr. *mutato nomine de te fabula narratur.*

972. Punishment.—N. punishment, punition; chast-isement, -ening; correction, castigation.

discipline, infliction, trial; judgment; penalty etc. 974; retribution; thunderbolt, Nemesis; requital etc. (*reward*) 973; penology; retributive justice.

lash, scaffold etc. (*instrument of punishment*) 975; imprisonment etc. (*restraint*) 751; chain gang; transportation, banishment, expulsion, deportation, exile, involuntary exile, ostracism; penal servitude, hard labor; galleys etc. 975; beating etc. *v.*; flagellation, fustigation, gantlet, *strappado*, *estrapade*, *bastinado*, *argumentum baculinum*, stick law, rap on the knuckles, box on the ear; blow etc. (*impulse*) 276; stripe, cuff, kick, buffet, pummel; slap, – in the face; wipe, douse; *coup de grâce*; torture, rack; picket, -ing; *dragonnade*; capital punishment, extreme penalty; execution; hanging etc. *v.*; de-capitation, -collation; *garrot-te*, *-to*; electrocution, lethal chamber; crucifixion, impalement; martyrdom, *auto-da-fé*; *noyade*; *hara-kiri*, happy despatch.

V. punish; chast-ise, -en; castigate, correct, inflict punishment, administer correction, deal retributive justice.

visit upon, pay; pay –, serve- out; settle with, get even with, get one's own back; do for; make short work of, give a lesson to, strafe, serve one right, make an example of; have a rod in pickle for; give it one.

strike etc. 276; deal a blow to, administer the lash, smite; slap, – the face; smack, cuff, box the ears, spank, thwack, thump, beat, lay on, swinge, buffet; thresh, thrash, pummel, drub, leather, trounce, baste, belabor; lace, – one's jacket; dress, give a -dressing, – down; trim, warm, wipe, tund, cob, bang, strap, comb, lash, lick, larrup, whallop, whop, flog, scourge, whip, birch, cane, give the stick, switch, flagellate, horsewhip, *bastinado*, towel, rub down with an oaken towel, rib roast, dust one's jacket, fustigate, pitch into, lay about one, beat black and blue; beat to a -mummy, – jelly; give a black eye; hit on the head; sandbag.

tar and feather; pelt, stone, lapidate; mast-head, keelhaul.

execute; bring to the -block, – gallows; behead; de-capitate, -collate; guillotine; hang, turn off, gibbet, bowstring, hang, draw and quarter; shoot; decimate; burn; electrocute; break on the wheel, crucify; em-, im-pale; flay; lynch; put to death.

torture; put -on, – to- the rack; picket.

banish, exile; trans-, de-port; expel, ostracize; rusticate; drum out; dismiss, -bar, -bench; strike off the roll, unfrock; post.

suffer, – for, – punishment; be -flogged, – hanged etc.; come to the gallows, dance upon nothing, die in one's shoes; be rightly served.

Adj. punishing etc. *v.*; penal, puni-tory, -tive; inflictive, castigatory; punished etc. *v.*

Int. *à la lanterne!*

973. Reward.—N. reward, recompense, remuneration, prize, meed, guerdon, reguerdon; indemni-ty, -fication, price; quittance; compensation; reparation, *ersatz*, assythment, redress; retribution, reckoning, acknowledgment, requital, amends, sop; atonement; consideration, return, *quid pro quo*; salvage, perquisite; vail etc. (*donation*) 784; *douceur*, bribe, bait, baksheesh,

tip; hush-, smart-money; black-mail; carcelage; *solatium*.

allowance, salary, stipend, wages; pay, -ment; emolument; tribute; batta, shot, scot; premium, fee, *honorarium*; hire.

crown etc. (*decoration of honor*) 877.

V. re-ward, -compense, -pay, -quite; re-munerate; compensate; fee, tip, bribe; pay one's footing etc. (*pay*) 807; make amends, indemnify, atone; satisfy, acknowledge.

get for one's pains, reap the fruits of.

Adj. remunerat-ive, -ory; munerary, compensatory, retributive, reparatory.

974. Penalty.—N. penalty; retribution etc. (*punishment*) 972; pain, pains and penalties; *peine forte et dure*; penance etc. (*atonement*) 952; the devil to pay.

fine, mulct, amercement; forfeit, -ure; escheat, damages, deodand, sequestration, confiscation, *premunire*.

V. penalize, fine, mulct, amerce, sconce, confiscate; sequest-rate, -er; escheat; estreat, forfeit.

975. Scourge. [Instrument of punishment.]—**N.** scourge, rod, cane, stick; ra-, rat-tan; birch, – rod; rod in pickle; switch, ferule, cudgel, truncheon; rubber hose.

whip, lash, strap, thong, cowhide, knout; cat, – o'-nine-tails, *sjambok*, quirt; rope's end.

pillory, stocks, whipping-post; cuck-, duck-ing stool; brank; triangle, wooden horse, maiden, thumbscrew, boot, rack, wheel, iron heel; treadmill, crank, galleys.

scaffold; block, axe, *guillotine*; stake; cross; gallows, gibbet, Tyburn tree; drop, noose, rope, halter, bowstring; electric chair, lethal chamber.

house of correction etc. (*prison*) 752.

gaol-, jail-er; executioner; hang-, heads-man; Jack Ketch; lyncher.

976. Deity.—N. Deity, Divinity; God-head, -ship; Omnipotence, Providence.

[Quality of being divine] divin-eness, -ity.

God, Lord, Jehovah, *Deus*; The -Almighty, – Supreme Being, – First Cause; *Ens Entium*; Author –, Creator- of all things; Author of our being; The -Infinite, – Eternal; The All-powerfull, -wise, -merciful, -holy; The Omni-potent, -scient.

[Attributes and perfections] infinite -power, – wisdom, – goodness, – justice, – truth, – love, – mercy; omni-potence, -science, -presence; unity, immutability, holiness, glory, majesty, sovereignty, infinity, eternity.

The -Trinity, – Holy Trinity, – Trinity in Unity, – Triune God; Three in One and One in Three.

God the Father; The -Maker, – Creator, – Preserver.

[Functions] creation, preservation, divine government; The-ocracy, -archy; providence; ways –, dealings –, dispensations –, visitations- of Providence.

God the Son, Jesus, Christ; The -Messiah, – Anointed, – Savior, – Redeemer, – Mediator,

− Intercessor, − Advocate, − Judge; The Son of - God, − Man, − David; The Only Begotten; The Lamb of God, The Word; Em-, Im-manuel; The - King of Kings and Lord of Lords, − King of Glory, − Prince of Peace, − Good Shepherd, − Way, − Truth, − Life, − Bread of Life, − Light of the World; The -Lord our, − Sun of- Righteousness.
The -Incarnation, − Hypostatic Union, − Word made Flesh.
[Functions] salvation, redemption, atonement, propitiation, mediation, intercession, judgment.
God the Holy Ghost, The Holy Spirit, Paraclete; The -Comforter, − Consoler, − Spirit of Truth, − Dove.
[Functions] inspiration, unction, regeneration, sanctification, consolation.
eon, aeon, special providence, *Deus ex machinâ*; *Avatar*.
V. create, uphold, preserve, govern etc.
atone, redeem, save, propitiate, mediate etc.
predestinate, elect, call, ordain, bless, justify, sanctify, glorify etc.
Adj. almighty, holy, hallowed, sacred, divine, heavenly, celestial; messianic; sacrosanct; all- powerful, -wise, -seeing, -knowing; omnipotent, omniscient; supreme.
super-human, -natural; ghostly, spiritual, hyper- physical, unearthly; the-istic, -ocratic, deistic; anointed.
Adv. *jure divino*, by divine right; *Deo volente*, D.V.

977. Angel. [Beneficent spirits.]−N. angel, archangel; heavenly host, choir invisible, host of heaven, sons of God; Michael, Gabriel etc.; seraph, -im; cherub, -im; ministering spirit, morning star; saint, *Madonna*; Our Lady, the Blessed Virgin, the Virgin Mary.
Adj. angelic, seraphic, cherubic.

978. Satan. [Maleficent spirits.]−N. Satan, the Devil, Lucifer, Ahrimancs, Belial; Sammael, Zamiel, Beelzebub, the Prince of the Devils; Mephistopheles, his satanic majesty.
the tempter; the evil -one, − spirit; the -author of evil, − wicked one, − old Serpent; the Prince of -darkness, − this world, − the power of the air; the -foul, − arch- fiend; the devil incarnate; the - common enemy, − angel of the bottomless pit; Abaddon, Apollyon, Mammon.
fallen agnels, unclean spirits, devils; the -rulers, − powers- of darkness; inhabitants of Pàn- demonium; demon etc. 980.
diabolism; devil-ism, -ship, -dom, -ry, -worship; *diablerie*; satanism, manicheism; the cloven foot; black magic etc. 992.
Adj. satanic, diabolic, devilish, infernal, hell- born.

979. Jupiter.−N. god, -dess; heathen gods and goddesses; Pantheon; Jupiter, Jove, Zeus, Apollo, Mars, Mercury, Neptune, Vulcan, Bacchus, Pluto, Saturn, Cupid, Eros, Pan; Juno, Ceres, Proserpina, Dina, Minerva, Pallas, Athenae, Venus, Aphrodite, Vesta; The Fates etc. 601.

Allah, Brahma, Vishnu, Siva, Shiva, Krishna, Juggernaut, Buddha; Ra, Isis, Osiris; Belus, Bel, Baal, Asteroth etc.; Thor, Odin; Mumbo Jumbo; good −, tutelary- genius; demiurge, familiar, − spirit; Sibyl; fairy, fay; sylph, -id; Ariel, peri, nymph, nereid, dryad, oread, sea-maid, Banshee, Benshie, Ormuzd; Oberon, Titania, Mab, hamadryad, naiad, mermaid, kelpie, Ondine, nix, nixie, sprite; denizens of the air; pixy etc. (*bad spirit*) 980.
mythology; heathen −, fairy- mythology; Lem- prière, folklore.
Adj. fairy-, sylph-like; sylphic.

980. Demon.−N. demon, -ry, -ism, -ology; evil genius, fiend, familiar, − spirit, devil; bad −, un- clean- spirit; cacodemon; incubus, Frankenstein's monster, succubus and succuba, Titan, Shedim, Mephistopheles, Asmodeus, Moloch, Belial, Ahriman, fury, The Furies etc. 900; harpy; Friar Rush.
vampire, ghoul; af-, ef-freet; afrite; ogre, -ss; gnome, gin, djinn, imp, deev, *lamia*; bo-gie, -gle; nis, kobold, flibbertigibbet, fairy, brownie, pixy, elf, dwarf, urchin, Puck, Robin Goodfellow; lepre-, cluri-chaune; troll, dwerger, sprite, oaf, changeling, bad fairy, nixe, pigwidgeon, Will-o'-the-wisp; Erl King.
[Supernatural appearance] ghost, specter, ap- parition, genie, spirit, shade, shadow, vision, phan- tom etc. 443; materialization (*spiritualism*) 992, hob-, goblin; wraith, spook, werwolf, boggart, ban- shee, *loup-garou, lemures*; evil eye.
nisse, necks; mer-man, -maid, -folk; siren, Lorelei; satyr, faun.
Adj. supernatural, weird, uncanny, unearthly; spectral; ghost-ly, -like; elf-in, -like; fiend-ish, -like; impish, demoniacal; haunted.

981. Heaven.−N. heaven; kingdom of - heaven, − God; heavenly kingdom; throne −, presence- of God; inheritance of the saints in light.
Paradise, Eden, abode of the blessed; Holy City, New Jerusalem; celestial bliss, glory.
[Mythological -heaven] Olympus; [− paradise] Elysium, Elysian fields, Arcadia, bowers of bliss, garden of the Hesperides, Islands of the Blessed; happy hunting-ground; third −, seventh- heaven; Valhalla (Scandinavian); Nirvana (Bud- dhist).
future state, eternity, eternal life, life after death, eternal home, resurrection, translation; resuscitation etc. 660; apotheosis, deification.
Adj. heavenly, celestial, supernal, unearthly, from on high, paradisiacal, beatific, elysian, Olym- pian, Arcadian.

982. Hell.−N. hell, bottomless pit, place of torment; habitation of fallen angels; Pan- demonium, Abaddon, Domdaniel.
hell fire; everlasting -fire, − torment; lake of fire and brimstone; fire that is never quenched, worm that never dies.
purgatory, limbo, gehenna, abyss.
[Mythological hell] Tartarus, Hades, Avernus, Styx, Stygian creek, pit of Acheron, Cocytus,

Phlegethon, Lethe; infernal regions, *inferno*, shades below, realms of Pluto.
. Pluto, Rhadamanthus, Erebus, Charon, Cerberus; Tophet.
Adj. hellish, infernal, stygian.

983. Theology. [Religious Knowledge.]—**N.** Theology (natural and revealed); Theo-gony, -sophy; Divinity; Hagio-logy, -graphy; Caucasian mystery; monotheism; religion; religious -persuasion, − sect, − denomination; cult; creed etc. (*belief*) 484; articles −, declaration −, profession −, confession- of faith.
theolog-ue, -ian; divine, schoolman, canonist, monotheist.
Adj. theological, religious; canonical; denominational; sectarian etc. 984.

983a. Orthodoxy.—N. orthodoxy; strictness, soundness, religious truth, true faith; truth etc. 494.
Christian-ity, -ism; Catholic-ism, -ity; 'the faith once delivered to the saints;' hyperorthodoxy etc. 984; iconoclasm.
the Holy −, the Orthodox- Church; Catholic −, Universal −, Apostolic −, Established- Church; temple of the Holy Ghost; Church −, body −, members −, disciples −, followers- of Christ; Christian, − community; true believer; canonist etc. (*theologian*) 983; Christendom, collective body of Christians, the Church Militant.
canons etc. (*belief*) 484; thirty-nine articles; Apostles' −, Nicene −, Athanasian- Creed; Church Catechism; textuary.
Adj. orthodox, sound, literal, strict, faithful, catholic, schismless, Christian, evangelical, scriptural, divine, monotheistic; true etc. 494.

984. Heterodoxy. [Sectarianism.]—**N.** heterodoxy; error etc. 495; false doctrine, heresy, schism; schismatic-ism, -alness; recusancy, backsliding, apostasy; atheism etc. (*irreligion*) 989.
bigotry etc. (*obstinacy*) 606; fanaticism, iconoclasm; hyperorthodoxy, precisianism, bibliolatry, hagiolatry, sabbatarianism, puritanism; idolatry etc. 991; superstition etc. (*credulity*) 486; dissent etc. 489.
sectar-ism, -ianism; nonconformity; secularism; syncretism, religious sects; the clash of creeds.
protestant-, advent-, Arian-, Erastian-, Calvin-, quaker-, method-, anabapt-, Pusey-, tractarian-, ritual-, Origen-, Sabellian-, Socinian-, De-, The-, mon-, material-, positiv-, latitudinairan-ism etc.
High −, Low −, Broad −, Free- Church; ultramontanism; monasticism; pap-ism, -istry; papacy; Anglican-, Catholic-, Roman-ism; popery, Scarlet Lady, Church of Rome, Greek Church; Christian Science, The Church of Christ Scientist.
pagan-, heathen-, ethic-ism; mythology; animism; poly-, di-, tri-, pan-theism; dualism; heathendom.
Juda-, Gentil-, Mahometan-, Islam-, Turc-, Brahmin-, Hindoo-, Buddh-, Lama-, Confucian-, Shinto-, Sabian-, Gnostic-. Soofee-, Hylothe-, Mormon-ism.
Theosophy; Spiritualism, Occultism.

heretic, antichrist; pagan, heathen; pai-, pay-nim; *giaour*; gentile; pan-, poly-theist; idolator; misbeliever, apostate, backslider.
bigot etc. (*obstinacy*) 606; fanatic, dervish, abdal, iconoclast.
latitudinarian, limitarian, Deist, Theist, Unitarian; positivist, materialist; agnostic, sceptic etc. 989.
schismatic; sectar-y, -ian, -ist; seceder, separatist, recusant, dissenter; non-conformist, -juror; Huguenot, Protestant; orthodox dissenter, Congregationalist, Independent; Episcopalian, Presbyterian; Lutheran, Calvinist, Quaker, Methodist, Wesleyan; Ana-, Baptist; Dunker; Mormon, Latter-day Saint, Irvingite, Sandemanian, Glassite, Erastian; Sub-, Supra-lapsarian; Gentoo, Antinomian, Swedenborgian, Adventist, Plymouth Brother; Theosophist etc.
Catholic, Roman Catholic, Romanist, papist, ultramontane; Old Catholic, tractarian, Anglican, Puseyite, ritualist; Puritan.
Jew, Hebrew, Rabbist; Mahometan, Mohammedan, Mussulman, Moslem, Islamite, Osmanli; Brahm-in, -an; Parsee, Sofi, Soofee; Buddhist; Zoroastrian, Magi, Gymnosophist, fire-worshipper, Sabian, Gnostic, Sadducee, Rosicrucian etc.
Adj. heterodox, heretical; un-orthodox, -scriptural, -canonical; antiscriptural, apocryphal; un-, anti-christian; schismatic, recusant, iconoclastic; sectarian; dis-senting, -sident; secular etc. (*lay*) 997.
pagan; heathen, -ish; ethnic, -al; gentile, painim; pan-, poly-theistic; agnostic, sceptic.
Judaical, Mohammedan, Moslem, Brahminical, Buddhist etc. *n*.; Romish, Protestant etc. *n*.
bigoted etc. (*prejudiced*) 481; (*obstinate*) 606; superstitious etc. (*credulous*) 486; fanatical; idolatrous etc. 991; visionary etc. (*imaginative*) 515.

985. Revelation.—N. revelation, inspiration, *afflatus*.
Word, − of God; Scripture; the -Scriptures, − Bible, − Book of Books; Holy -Writ, − Scriptures; inspired writings, Gospel.
Old Testament, Septuagint, Vulgate, Pentateuch; Octateuch; the -Law, − Jewish Law, − Prophets; major −, minor- Prophets; Hagio-grapha, -logy; Hierographa; Apocrypha.
New Testament; Gospels, Evangelists, Acts, Epistles, Apocalypse, Revelations.
Talmud; Mishna, Masorah.
prophet etc. (*seer*) 513; evangelist, apostle, disciple, saint; the −, the Apostolical- fathers; Holy Men of old, inspired -writers, − penmen.
Adj. scriptural, biblical, sacred, prophetic; evangel-ical, -istic; apostolic, -al; inspired, theopneustic, apocalyptic, ecclesiastical, canonical, textuary.

986. Pseudo-Revelation.—N. the -Koran, − Alcoran; Ly-king, Shaster, Vedas, Zendavesta, Vedidad, Purana, Edda; Go-, Gau-tama; Book of Mormon.
[False prophets and religious founders] Buddha, Zoroaster, Zerdhusht, Confucius, Mahomet.
[Idols] golden calf etc. 991; Baal, Moloch, Dagon.

987. Piety.—N. piety, religion, theism, faith; religiousness, holiness etc. *adj.*; saintship; religionism; sanctimony etc. (*assumed piety*) 988; reverence etc. (*respect*) 928; humility, veneration, devotion; prostration etc. (*worship*) 990; grace, unction, edification; sancti-ty, -tude; consecration. spiritual existence, odor of sanctity, beauty of holiness.

theopathy, beatification, adoption, regeneration, conversion, justification, sanctification, salvation, inspiration, bread of life; Body and Blood of Christ.

believer, convert, theist, Christian, devotee, pietist; the -good, — righteous, — just, — believing, — elect; Saint, *Madonna*.

the children of -God, — the kingdom, — light. **V.** be -pious etc. *adj.*; have -faith etc. *n.*; believe, receive Christ; revere etc. 928; worship etc. 950; be -converted etc.

convert, edify, sanctify, hallow, keep holy, beatify, regenerate, inspire, consecrate, enshrine.

Adj. pious, religious, devout, devoted, reverent, godly, heavenly minded, humble; pure, — in heart; holy, spiritual, pietistic; saint-ly, -like; seraphic, sacred, solemn.

believing, faithful, Christian, Catholic.

elected, adopted, justified, sanctified, regenerated, inspired, consecrated, converted, unearthly, not of the earth.

988. Impiety.—N. impiety; sin etc. 945; irreverence; profan-eness etc. *adj.*, -ity, -ation; blasphemy, desecration, sacrilege; scoffing etc. *v.*

[Assumed piety] hypocrisy etc. (*falsehood*) 544; pietism, cant, pious fraud; lip-devotion, -service, -reverence; mis-devotion, formalism, austerity; sancti-mon-y, -iousness etc. *adj.*; pharisaism, precisianism; sabbat-ism, -arianism; *odium theologicum*, sacerdotalism; bigotry etc. (*obstinacy*) 606, (*prejudice*) 481.

hardening, backsliding, declension, perversion, reprobation apostacy, recusancy.

sinner etc. 949; scoffer, blasphemer; sacrilegist; worldling; hypocrite etc. (*dissembler*) 548; Scribes and Pharisees; Tartufe, Maw-worm.

bigot; saint [ironically]; Pharisee, sabbatarian, formalist, methodist, puritan, pietist, precisian, religionist, devotee, ranter, fanatic, wowser.

the -wicked, — evil, — unjust, — reprobate; son of -men, — Belial, — the wicked one; children of darkness.

V. be -impious etc. *adj.*; profane, desecrate, blaspheme, revile, scoff; swear etc. (*malediction*) 908; commit sacrilege.

snuffle; turn up the whites of the eyes; idolize.

Adj. impious; irreligious etc. 989; desecrating etc. *v.*; profane, irreverent, sacrilegious, blasphemous.

un-hallowed, -sanctified, -regenerate; hardened, perverted, reprobate.

hypocritical etc. (*false*) 544; canting, pietistical, sanctimonious, unctuous, pharisaical, over-righteous, righteous over much.

bigoted, fanatical etc. 481 and 606; priest-ridden.

Adv. under the -mask, — cloak, — pretence, — form, — guise- of religion.

989. Irreligion.—N. irreligion, indevotion; ungodliness etc. *adj.*; laxity, quietism, apathy, indifference, passivity.

scepticism, doubt; un-, dis-belief; incredul-ity, -ousness etc. *adj.*; want of -faith, — belief; pyrrhonism; doubt etc. 485; agnosticism.

atheism, deism; hylotheism; materialism; positivism; nihilism.

infidelity, freethinking, antichristianity, rationalism.

atheist, anti-christian, sceptic, unbeliever, deist, infidel, pyrrhonist; *giaour*, heathen, alien, gentile, Nazarene; *esprit fort*, freethinker, latitudinarian, rationalist; materialist, positivist, nihilist, agnostic.

V. be -irreligious etc. *adj.*; disbelieve, lack faith; doubt, question etc. 485.

dechristianize; serve Mammon, love darkness better than light.

Adj. irreligious; in-, un-devout; devout-, god-, grace-less; un-godly, -holy, -sanctified, -hallowed; atheistic, without God.

sceptical, free-thinking; un-believing, -converted; incredulous, faithless, lacking faith; deistical; un-, anti-christian.

worldly, mundane, earthly, carnal, unspiritual; worldly etc.- minded.

Adv. irreligiously etc. *adj.*

990. Worship.—N. worship, adoration, devotion, aspiration, latria, homage, service, humiliation; kneeling, genuflexion, prostration.

prayer, invocation, supplication, rogation, intercession, orison, holy breathing; petition etc. (*request*) 765; collect, litany, Lord's prayer, paternoster, *Ave Maria*, rosary; bead-roll; latria, dulia, hyperdulia, vigils; revival; cult.

thanksgiving; giving —, returning- thanks; grace, praise, glorification, benediction, doxology, hosanna; h-, allelujah; *Te Deum*, *non nobis Domine*, *nunc dimittis*; paean.

psalm, -ody; hymn, plainsong, chant, chaunt, response, anthem, motet; antiphon, -y.

oblation, sacrifice, incense, libation; burnt —, votive —, thank-offering, offertory, collection.

discipline; self-discipline, -examination, -denial; fasting.

divine service, office, duty; morning prayer; mass, matins, evensong, vespers, compline; holy day etc. (*rites*) 998.

worshipper, congregation, communicant, celebrant.

V. worship, lift up the heart, aspire; revere etc. 928; adore, do service, pay homage; humble oneself, kneel; bow —, bend- the knee; fall -down, — on one's knees; prostrate oneself, bow down and worship, recite the rosary.

pray, invoke, supplicate; put —, offer- up -prayers, — petitions; beseech etc. (*ask*) 765; say one's prayers, tell one's beads.

return —, give- thanks; say grace, bless, praise, laud, glorify, magnify, sing praises; give benediction, lead the choir, intone, chant, sing.

propitiate, offer sacrifice, fast, deny oneself; vow, offer vows, give alms.

work out one's salvation; go to church; attend -service, — mass; communicate etc. (*rite*) 998.

Adj. worshipping etc. *v.*; devout, devotional, reverent, pure, solemn; fervid etc. (*heartfelt*) 821.

Int. h-, allelujah! hosanna! glory be to God! O Lord! pray God that! God -grant, – bless, – save, – forbid! *sursum corda.*

991. Idolatry.—N. idol-atry, -ism; demon-ism, -olatry; idol –, demon –, devil –, fire- worship; zoolatry, fetishism, Mari-, Bibli-, ecclesi-, heliolatry.

deification, apotheosis, canonization; hero worship.

sacrifices, hecatomb, holocaust; human sacrifices, immolation, mactation, infanticide, self-immolation, *suttee.*

idol, golden calf, graven image, fetish, *avatar,* Juggernaut, joss, *lares et penates;* Baal etc. 986.
idolator etc. *n.*

V. worship -idols, – pictures, – relics; put on a pedestal, bow down to, prostrate oneself before, make sacrifice to; deify, canonize, idolize.

Adj. idolatrous.

992. Sorcery.—N. sorcery; superstition; occult -art, – sciences; black –, magic; the black art, necromancy, theurgy, thaumaturgy; demon-ology, -omy, -ship; *diablerie,* bedevilment; witch-craft, -ery; glamor; fetis-hism, -ism; ghost dance; hoodoo, voodoo; Shamanism [Esquimaux] , vampirism; conjuration; bewitchery, exorcism, enchantment, incantation, obsession, possession, mysticism, second sight, mesmerism, animal magnetism; od –, odylic- force; electro-biology, *clairvoyance;* spiritualism, spirit-rapping, table-turning; thought reading, telepathy, thought transference, automatic writing, *planchette,* ouija board; crystal gazing; spirit manifestation, materialization, astral body, ectoplasm etc.

divination etc. (*prediction*) 511; sortilege, ordeal, *sortes Virgiliance;* hocus-pocus etc. (*deception*) 545; oracle etc. 513.

V. practice -sorcery etc. *n.;* cast a -horoscope, – nativity; conjure, exorcise, charm, enchant; bewitch, -devil; overlook, look on with the evil eye; entrance, mesmerize, magnetize; fascinate etc. (*influence*) 615; taboo; wave a wand; rub the -ring, – lamp; cast a spell; call up spirits, – from the vasty deep; raise spirits from the dead; raise –, lay-ghosts; command genii.

Adj. magic, -al; mystic, weird, cabalistic, talismanic, phylacteric, incantatory; charmed etc. *v.*

993. Spell.—N. spell, charm, incantation, exorcism, weird, cabala, exsufflation, cantrap, runes, abracadabra, hocus-pocus, open *sesame,* counter-charm, Ephesian letters, bell, book and candle, Mumbo-jumbo, evil-eye, fee-faw-fum.

talisman, amulet, periapt, telesm, phylactery, philter, wish-bone, merry-thought, mascot, scarab, swastika; fetish; *agnus Dei.*

wand, caduceus, rod, divining rod, lamp of Aladdin, magic carpet, seven-league boots; magic ring; wishing –, Fortunatus's- cap.

994. Sorcerer.—N. sorcerer, magician; thaumat-, the-urgist; conjuror, necromancer, seer,

wizard, witch; fairy etc. 980; *lamia,* hag, warlock, charmer, exorcist, voodoo, mage, diviner, dowser; cunning| – , , medicine- ; man, witch doctor; Shaman, figure-flinger, ecstatica, medium, *clairvoyant,* mesmerist, hypnotist; *deus ex machinâ;* astrologer; soothsayer etc. 513.

Katerfelto, Cagliostro, Merlin, Comus, Mesmer, Rosicrucian; Hecate, Circe, Lilith, siren, weird sisters; witch of Endor.

995. Churchdom.—N. church, -dom; ministry, apostleship, priesthood, prelacy, hierarchy, church government, christendom, pale of the church.

clerical-, sacerdotal-, episcopalian-, ultramontan-ism; Theocracy; ecclesiolog-y, -ist; priestcraft, *odium theologicum.*

monach-ism, -y; monasticism, monkhood.

[Ecclesiastical offices and dignities] pontificate, primacy, archbishopric, archiepiscopacy; prelacy; bishop-ric, -dom; episcop-ate, -acy; see, diocese; deanery, stall; canon-ry, -icate; prebend, -aryship; benefice, incumbency, glebe, advowson, living, cure, – of souls; rectorship; vicar-iate, -ship; pastor-ate, -ship; deacon-ry, -ship; -curacy; chaplain, -cy, -ship; cardinal-ate, -ship; abbacy, presbytery.

holy orders, ordination, institution, consecration, induction, reading in, preferment, translation, presentation.

popedom, papacy, the -Vatican, – apostolic see, – see of Rome; religious sects etc. 984.

council etc. 696; conclave, college of cardinals, convocation, synod, consistory, chapter, vestry, presbytery; sanhedrim, *congé d'élire;* ecclesiastical courts, consistorial court, court of Arches.

V. call, ordain, induct, prefer, translate, consecrate, present, elect, bestow.

take -orders, – the veil, – vows.

Adj. ecclesi-astical, -ological; clerical, sacerdotal, priestly, prelatical, pastoral, ministerial, capitular, theocratic; hierarchical, archiepiscopal; episcopal, -ian; canonical; mon-astic, -achal; monkish; abbati-al, -cal; pontifical, papal, apostolic; untramontane, priest-ridden.

996. Clergy.—N. clergy, clericals, ministry, priesthood, presbytery, the cloth, the pulpit.

clergyman, divine, ecclesiastic, churchman, priest, presbyter, hierophant, pastor, shepherd, minister, clerk in holy orders; father, – in Christ; *padre, abbé, curé;* patriarch; reverend; black coat; confessor; sky pilot.

dignitaries of the church; ecclesi-, hier-arch; eminence, reverence, elder, primate, metropolitan, archimandrite, archbishop, bishop, prelate, diocesan, suffragan, dean, subdean, archdeacon, prebendary, canon, rural dean, rector, parson, vicar, perpetual curate, residentiary, beneficiary, incumbent, chaplain, curate, – in charge; deacon, -ess; preacher; lay reader, lecturer; capitular; missionary, propagandist, Jesuit, revivalist, field preacher.

churchwarden, sidesman; clerk, precentor, choir; almoner, *suisse;* verger, beadle, sexton, sacristan; acol-yth, -othyst, -yte; thurifer; chorister, choir boy.

[Roman Catholic priesthood] Pope, *Papa,* Holy

Father, pontiff, high priest, cardinal; ancient —,
flamen; confessor, penitentiary; spiritual director.

cenobite, conventual, abbot, prior, monk, friar,
lay brother, beadsman, mendicant, pilgrim,
palmer; canon-regular, -secular; Jesuit, Franciscan,
Friars minor, Minorites; Observant, Capuchin,
Dominican, Carmelite; Augustinian; Gilbertine;
Austin-, Black-, White-, Grey-, Crossed-, Crutch-
ed- Friars; Bonhomme, Carthusian, Benedictine,
Cistercian, Trappist, Cluniac, Premonstratensian,
Maturine; Templar, Hospitaller.

abb-, prior-, canon-ess; mother superior;
religieuse, nun, sister, beguine, novice, postulant.

[Under the Jewish dispensation] prophet, priest,
high priest, Levite; Rabbi, -n; scribe.

[Mohammedan etc.] mullah, ulema, imauam,
sheik; so-fi, -phi; mufti, hadji, muezzin, dervish; fa-
kir, -quir; brahmin, gooroo, druid, bonze, santon,
abdal, Lama, talapoin, caloyer etc.

V. take orders etc. 995.

Adj. the —, the very —, the Right- Reverend;
ordained, in orders, called to the ministry.

997. Laity.—N. laity, flock, fold, congregation,
assembly, brethren, people.

temporality, secularization.

layman, civilian; parishioner, catechumen;
secularist.

V. secularize.

Adj. secular, lay, laical, civil, temporal, profane.

998. Rite.—N. rite; ceremon-y, -ial; ordinance,
observance, function, duty; form, -ulary; solemnity,
sacrament; incantation etc. (spell) 993; service,
psalmody etc. (worship) 990; liturgies.

ministration; preach-ing, -ment; predication, sermon, homily, exhortation, lecture, discourse,
pastoral.

baptism, christening, chrism; immersion; bap-
tismal regeneration; font; circumcision.

confirmation; imposition —, laying on- of hands;
churching, purification, ordination etc. (churchdom) 995; excommunication.

Eucharist, Lord's supper, communion; the —,
the holy- sacrament; celebration, high celebration;
missa cantata; offertory; introit; consecration; con-
, tran-substantiation; real presence; elements, bread
and wine; mass; high —, low —, dry- mass.

matrimony etc. 903; burial etc. 363; visitation of
the sick.

seven sacraments, impanation, extreme unction,
last rites, viaticum, invocation of saints,
canonization, transfiguration, auricular confession;
fasting; maceration, flagellation, sackcloth and
ashes; penance etc. (atonement) 952; absolution;
telling of beads, reciting the rosary, processional;
thurification, incense, holy water, aspersion.

relics, rosary, beads, reliquary, host, cross, rood,
crucifix, pax, pix, pyx, agnus Dei, censer, thurible,
patera, urceole; chalice, patten, Holy Grail,
sangrail; seven-branch candle stick, monstrance,
sacring bell.

ritual, rubric, canon, ordinal; liturgy, prayer-
book, book of common prayer, pietas, euchology,

litany, lectionary; missal, breviary, mass-book,
bead-roll.

psalter; psalm —, hymn- book; hymn-al, -ology;
psalmody.

ritual-, ceremonial-ism; sabbat-ism, -arianism;
ritualist, sabbatarian.

holyday, feast, fast; Sabbath, Passover, Pentecost;
Advent, Christmas, Noel, Epiphany, Lent, Shrove
Tuesday, Ash Wednesday, Maundy Thursday;
Passion —, Holy- week; Good Friday, Easter,
Ascension Day, Whitsuntide; Trinity Sunday, Cor-
pus Christi; All-Saints' —, — Souls'- Day; Candle-,
Lam-, Martin-, Michael-mas; hogmanay; Rama-
dan, -zan; Bairam etc. etc.

V. perform service, do duty, minister, officiate,
baptize, dip, sprinkle; confirm, lay hands on; give
—, administer —, take —, receive —, attend —,
partake of- the -sacrament; — communion; communicate; celebrate mass; administer —, receive-
extreme unction; anele, shrive, absolve, confess; do
penance; genuflect; cross oneself, make the sign of
the cross.

excommunicate, ban with bell, book and candle.

preach, sermonize, predicate, lecture.

Adj. ritual, -istic; ceremonial, liturgic; bap-
tismal, eucharistical; paschal.

999. Canonicals.—N. canonicals, vestments;
robe, gown, Geneva gown, frock, pallium, surplice,
cassock, dalmatic, scapulary, cope, scarf, tunicle,
chasuble, alb, alba, stole; fan-on, -nel; tonsure,
cowl, hood; calo-te, -tte; bands; capouch, amice,
orarium, ephod; apron, lawn sleeves, pontificals,
pall; miter, tiara, triple crown; shovel —, cardinal's- hat; biretta; crosier; pastoral staff; costume
etc. 225.

1000. Temple.—N. place of worship; house of
-God, — prayer.

temple, cathedral, minister, church, kirk, chapel,
meeting-house, bethel, tabernacle, conventicle,
basilica, fane, holy place, chantry, oratory.

synagogue; mosque; marabout; pantheon;
pagoda, joss-house, dagobah, tope; kiosk.

parsonage, rectory, vicarage, manse, deanery,
glebe, church house; Vatican; bishop's palace;
Lambeth.

altar, shrine, sanctuary, Holy of Holies, sanctum
sanctorum, sacrarium, -isty; communion —, holy
—, Lord's- table; table of the Lord; pyx; baptistery,
font; piscina, stoup; aumbry; sedile; reredos; rood-
loft, — screen; jube.

chancel, quire, choir, nave, aisle, transept, lady
chapel, vestry, crypt, cloisters, porch; triforum,
clerestory, churchyard, golgotha, calvary, Easter
sepulcher; stall, pew, sitting; pulpit, ambo, lectern,
reading-desk, confessional; prothesis, credence,
baldachin, baldacchino; jesse, apse, belfry; chap-
ter-house; presbytery.

monastery, priory, abbey, friary, convent, nun-
nery, cloister.

Adj. claustral, cloistered; monast-ic, -erial; conventual.

INDEX

The numbers refer to the headings under which the words or phrases occur. When the same word or phrase may be used in various senses, the several headings under which it, or its synonyms, will be found, according to those meanings, are indicated by the words printed in Italics. These words in Italics are not intended to explain the meaning of the word or phrase to which they are annexed, but only to assist in the required reference.

When the word given in the Index is itself the title or heading of a category, the number of reference is printed in blacker type, thus: **abode 189.**

aedile 965
aegis 717
aegrescit medendo 659
aegrotat 927a
aeolian 349
— harp 417
aequam servare mentem 826
aequo animo 823 826
aerate 334, 353
aere perennius 873
aerial 273
elevated 206
flying 267
gas 334
air 338
— navigation 267
— navigator 269
— mail 534
— patrol 726
— perspective 428
— warfare 722
aerie 189
aerify 334
aerodonetics 267
aerodrome 728
aerodynamics 267, 334, 349
aerolite 318
aerology 338
aeromancy 511
aeromechanics 267
aerometer 338
aeronaut 269
aeronautical 273
aeronautics 267, 338
aeroplane 273
aerostat balloon 273
aerostatics 267, 334
aerostation 338
aery 317
Aesculapius 662
Aesop846
aesthetic
sensibility 375
beauty 845
taste 850
aestival 125
aeternum servans sub pectore vulnus 919
afar 196
affable 879, 894
affair event 151
topic 454
business 625
battle 720
love 902, 903
— of honour 720
affaires, charge d' - 758
affaire de coeur 897
affect relate to 9
tend to 176
qualify 469
feign 544
touch 824
desire 865
love 897
affectation 855
affected with
feeling 821
disease 655

affectibility 822
affecting 830
affection 821, 897
affections 820
affettuoso 415
affiance 768, 858
affianced 897, 903
affiche 531
affidation 769
affidavit
affirmation 535
record 551
lawsuit 969
affiliation
relation 9
kindred 11
attribution 155
affine 11
affinitive 9
affinity 9, 17
mate 905
affirmation 535, 488
affix add 37
sequel 39
fasten 43
letter 561
afflation 349
afflatus 349, 597, 985
afflict 830
— with illness 655
affliction pain 828
infliction 830
adversity 735
affluence
sufficiency 639
prosperity 734
wealth 803
affluent river 348
afflux 286
afford supply 784
wealth 803
yield 810
sell for 812
— aid &c. 707
afforestation 371
affranchise
make free of 748
liberate 750
affray 720
affreet 980
affriction 331
affright 860
affront molest 830
provocation 900
insult 929
— danger 861
affuse 337
afield 186
afire 382
afloat extant 1
unstable 149
going on 151
ship 273
navigation 267
ocean 341
news 532
preparing 673
keep oneself — 734
set — publish 531
afoot on hand 625
preparing 673
astir 682
afore 116
aforementioned116
aforesaid
preceding 62
repeated 104

prior 116
aforethought 611
aforetime 116
afraid 860
be — irresolute 605
— to say uncertain 475
afresh 104, 123
Afric heat 382
Afrikander 57
afrite 980
aft 235
after in order 63
in time 117
too late 135
rear 235
pursuit 622
be — intention 620
pursuit 622
go — follow 281
— all for all that 30
qualification 469
on the whole 476
— time 133
after acceptation 516
after-age 124
after-clap 509
after-crop 65, 168
after-dinner 117
after-glow 40, 65, 420
after-growth 65
after-life 152
aftermath
sequel 65
fertile 168
profit 775
aftermost 235
afternoon 126
— farmer 683
after-part 65, 235
after-piece 599
after-taste 65, 390
after-thought
thought 451
memory 505
change of mind 607
after-time 121
afterwards 117
age 745
agacerie 615
again 90, 104
— and again 136
come — periodic 138
fall off — 661
live — 660
against
counteraction 179
anteposition 237
provision 673
voluntary opposition 708
chances — 473
declaim — 932
false witness — 934
go — 708
set — actively 898
set one's face 764, 932
stand up — resist 719
raise &c. one's voice — 489
— one's will 744
— one's expectation 508

— the grain difficult 704
painful 830
dislike 867
— the stream 704
— the time when 510
— one's will 744
— one's wishes 603
agamist 904
agape open 260
curious 455
expectant 507
wonder 870
Agapemone 827, 897
agate 847
age time 106
period 108
long time 110
era 114
present time 118
oldness 124
advanced life 128
of — 131
from age to — 112
age quod agis! 682
agency
physical 170
instrumentality 631
means 632
employment 677
voluntary action 680
direction 693
commission 755
agenda 625, 626
agent physical 153
intermediary 228
voluntary 690
consignee 759
— provocateur 615
agentship 755
ages: for — 110
— ago 122
agglomerate 46, 72
agglutinate 46
aggrandize
in degree 35
in bulk 194
honor 873
aggravate
increase 35
vehemence 173
exaggerate 549
render worse 659
distress 835
exasperate 900
aggravating 830
aggravation 835
aggregate 50, 72, 84
aggregation 46
aggression 716
aggressor 726
aggrieve 649, 830
aggroup 72
aghast
disappointed 509
fear 860
wonder 870
agile 274, 682
agio 813
agiotage 794
agitate move 315
inquire 461
activity 682

824
— a question 476
agitation [see agitate]
changeableness 149
energy 171
motion 315
in — preparing 673
agitator leader 694
aglet 554
agley, gang — 732
aglow 382, 420
agnate 11
agnition 762
agnomen 564
agnostic 487
agnosticism 984, 989
agnus Dei 993, 998
ago 122
not long — 123
agog expectant 507
desire 865
wonder 870
agoing 682
set — 707
agonism 720
agonizing 824, 830
agony 378, 828
— of death 360
— of excitement 825
agrarian 371
agree accord 23
concur 178
assent 488
concord 714
consent 762
compact 769
compromise 774
— in opinion 488
— with salubrity 656
agreeable
comfortable 82
physically 377
mentally 829
agreeably to 82
agreement 23 [see agree]
compact 769
agrestic 371
agriculture 371
agronomy 371
aground fixed 150
in difficulty 704
failure 732
ague-fit 860
aguets, aux — expectation 507
ambush 530
aguish cold 383
ah me! 839
aha! rejoicing 838
ahead 234, 280
go — progression 282
shoot — transcursion 303
activity 682
rock — 665, 667
Ahrimanes 987, 980
aid 707, 906
by the — of 631, 632
aide-de-camp 711, 745

aidless 160
aigrette 847
aiguille 253
aiguillette 747, 847
aigulet 847
ail 655, 828
aileron 267, 273
ailment 655
aim 278, 620, 675
 – a blow at 716
aimable 894
faire l' – 897
aimer éperdument
897
aimless *without*
motive 615a
chance 621
air *unsubstantial* 4
broach 66
lightness 320
gas 334
atmospheric **338**
wind 349
tune 415
appearance 448
refresh 689
demeanor 692
fashionable 852
beat the – 645
fill the – 404
fine – *salubrity* 656
fish in the – 645
fowls of the – 366
in the – 527
rend the – 404
take – 531
air-balloon 273
air base 728
air-commodore 745
aircraft 273, 726
air-drawn 515
airdrome 273
air-force 726
air-gun 727
airing 266
air-mail 273
airman 269
airmanship 698
air-marshal 745
air-passage 351
air-pipe **351**
airport 273, 292,
728
air-pump 349
air-raid 716
airs *affectation* 855
pride 878
vanity 880
arrogance 885
air-shaft 351
air service 267
airship 273, 726
air-tight 261
airways 267
airworthy 273, 664
airy [*see* air]
windy 349
unimportant 643
gay 836
– *hopes* 858, 859
give to – *nothing*
a local habita-
tion &c. 515
aisle *passage* 260
way 627
in a church 1000
ait 346
ajar *open* 260

discordant 713
ajee 217
ajutage 260, 350
akimbo *angular* 244
stand – 715
akin *related* 9
*consanguineous*11
similar 17
al fresco 220 ˙
alabaster *white* 430
alack! 839
alacrity *willing* 602
active 682
cheerful 836
Aladdin's lamp 993
alar 267
alarm *warning* 668
notice of danger ˊ
669
fear 860
cause for – 665
give an – *indicate*
550
alarmist 862
alarum 114, 550, 669
alas! 839
alate 267
alb 999
albeit 30
albert
chain 847
albification 430
albinescence 430
albinism 430
albino 443
album 503, 506
albumen
semi-liquid 352
protein 357
Alcaic 597
alcaid 745
alcalde 745
alcazar 189
alchemy 144
alcohol 995
Alcoran 986
alcove 191, 252
Aldebaran 423
alderman 745
ale 298
alea, jacta est – 601
aleatory 665
Alecto 173
alectromancy 511
alehouse 189
go to the – 959
alembic
conversion 144
vessel 191
furnace 386
laboratory 691
alentours 197
alert *watchful* 457,
459
active 682
alerte 669
aleuromancy 511
Alexandrine
ornate style 577
verse 597
alexandrite 848
alexipharmic 662
alexiteric 662
algebra 85
algid 383
algology 369
algorithm 85
alguazil 965

alias
otherwise 18
pseudonym 565
alibi 187
alien *irrelevant* 10
foreign 57
transfer 783
gentile 989
alienable 783
alienate
transfer 783
estrange 44, 889
set against 898
alienation
mental – 503
alieni appetens
grasping 865
envious 921
selfish 943
alienism 54
align 278
alight *stop* 265
arrive 292
descend 306
on fire 382
alike 17
share and share –
778
aliment *food* 298
alimentary 662
– *canal* 350
alimentation
aid 707
alimony
property 780
provision 803
income 810
aliquot 51, 84
aliter visum, diis –
601
alive
living 359
intelligent 498
˙ *active* 682
cheerful 836
be – *with* 102
keep – *continue*
143
keep the memory
– 505
look – 684
– *to attention* 457
cognizant 490
informed 527
able 698
sensible 822
alkahest 335
all *whole* 50
complete 52
generality 78
– *absorbing* 642
in – *ages* 112
– *aboard* 495
– *agog* 865
– *in all* 50
– *along* 106
– *along of* 154
– *but* 32
– *colors* 440
– *considered* 451,
480
– *day long* 110
– *devouring* 190
in – *directions* 278
– *engrossing* 190
at – *events com-*
pensation 30
qualification 469

true 494
resolve 604
– *fours easy* 705
cards 840
– *in good time* 152
– *hail! welcome* 292
honor to 873
celebration 883
courtesy 894
– *hands everybody*
78
on – *hands* 488
– *of a dither* 824
– *of a heap* 72
– *knowing* 976
– *manner of differ-*
ence 15
multiform 81
with – *one's might*
686
– *at once* 113
– *one* 27, 866
– *out* 52
– *over end* 67
universal 78
destruction 162
space 180
at – *points* 52 ˙
– *in one's power*
686
– *powerful*
mighty 159
God 976
in – *quarters* 180
with – *respect* 928
in – *respects* 52,
494
– *right!* 922
– *Saints' day* 998
searching 461
– *seeing* 976
on – *sides* 227
– *sorts diverse* 16a
mixed 41
multiform 81
– *talk* 4
– *things to all*
men 894
– *the time* 106
at – *times* 136
– *together* 50
– *ways* 243, 279
– *wise* 976
– *the world and*
his wife 78
of – *work*
useful 644
maid - 746
Allah 979
allay
moderate 174
pacify 723
relieve 834
– *excitability* 826
allective 615
allege *evidence* 467
assert 535
plea 617
allegiance 743, 926
allegory 464, 521,
594
allegro *music* 415
cheerful 836
allelujah 990
allemande 840
all-embracing 76
alleviate 174, 834
alley *court* 189

passage 26
way 627
alliance *relation* 9
kindred 11
physical co-opera-
tion 178
voluntary co-oper-
ation 709
party 712
union 714
allied to *like* 17
alligation 43
align 278
alliteration
similarity 17
style in writing
577
poetry 597
allocation 60, 786
allocution 586
allodium *free* 748
property 780
allopathy 662
alloquy 586
allot *arrange* 60
distribute 786
due 924
allow *assent* 488
admit 529
permit 760
consent 762
give 784
– *to have one's*
own way 740
allowable 760, 924
allowance
qualification 469
gift 784
allotment 786
discount 813
salary 973
with grains of –
485
make – *for forgive*
918
vindicate 937
alloy *mixture* 41
combination 48
debase 659
allude *hint* 514
mean 516
refer to 521
latent 526
inform 527
allure *move* 615
create desire 865
alluring 829
allusive
relative 9 ˙
alluvial *level* 213
land 342
plain 344
alluvium
deposit 342
land 342
soil 653
ally *combine* 48
auxiliary 711
friend 891
alma mater 542
almanac
list 86
chronometry 114
record 551
almighty 157
Almighty, the – 976
almoner
treasurer 801

science 357
comparative – 368
anatriptic 331
ancestral
bygone 122
old 124
aged 128
ancestry 166
anchor
connection 45
stop 265
safeguard 666
badge 747
hope 858
at – fixed 150
stationed 184
safe 664
cast – settle 184
arrive 292
have an – to wind-
ward 664
sheet – means 632
anchorage
location 184
roadstead 189
refuge 866
anchored 150
anchorite 893, 955
ancien régime 875
ancient old 124
flag 550
– times 122
ancientness 122
ancillary 707
and 37, 88
andante 415
andiron 386
androgynous 83
anecdote 594
anele 998
anemia 160
anemography 349
ἀνεμώλια βάζειν 497
anemometer
wind 349
measure 466
anent 9
aneroid 338
anesthesia 376, 381, 683
anew again 104
newly 123
anfractuosity 248
angel
object of love 897
good person 948
supernatural
being 977
fallen –
bad man 949
devil 978
guardian –
safety 664
auxiliary 711
benefactor 912
– of Death 362
– 's visits 137
angelic 944
angels and minis-
ters of grace de-
fend us! 860
angelus 550
anger 900
more in sorrow
than in – 826, 918
angiology 329
angle 244

try 463
at an – 217
Anglicanism 984
angling 622, 840
anguille au genou,
rompre l' – 158, 471
anguilliform 205, 248
anguis in herbâ 667
anguish
physical 378
moral 828
angular 244
– velocity 264
angularity 244
angusta domi, res
– 804
angustation 203
anhelation 688
anhydrate 340
anhydrous 340
aniline dyes 437
anility 128, 499
animadvert
consider 451
attend to 457
reprehend 932
animal 366
female – 374
– cries 412
– economy 359
– gratification 377
– life 364
– physiology 368
– spirits 836
– and vegetable
kingdom 357
animalcule 193, 366
animalism
sensuality 954
animality 364
animate
induce 615
excite 824
enliven 836
animation
life 359
animality 364
activity 682
vivacity 836
suspended – 823
animism 984
animo, ex – 602
quo – 620
animosity
dislike 867
enmity 889
hatred 898
anger 900
animus
willingness 602
intention 620
desire 865
ankle 244
– deep 208, 209
anklet 847
ankylosis 150
annalist 114, 553
annals
chronology 114
record 551
account 594
anneal 673
annex
addition 37
adjunct 39
junction 43

acquire 775
Annie Oakley 815
annihilate 2, 162
anniversary 138
anno 106
Anno Domini
era 106
old age 124
annotation 522, 550
annotator 524
scholar 492
interpreter 524
editor 595
annotto 434
announce
predict 511
inform 527
publish 531
assert 535
announcer 527
annoy
molest 649, 907
disquiet 830
annoyance 828
source of – 830
annual periodic 138
plant 367
book 593
annuity 810
annul 162, 750
annular 247
annunciate 527
annus magnus 108
anodyne
lenitive 174
remedial 662
anoint coat 223
lubricate 332
oil 355
anointed
deity 976
king 745
anomaly 59, 83
disorder 59
irregularity 83
anon 132
anonymous 565
anopsia 442
anorexy 866
another
different 15
repetition 104
– story 468, 526
go upon – tack 607
– time 119
answer
to an inquiry 462
confute 479
solution 522
succeed 731
pecuniary profit 775
pleadings 969
require an – 461
– for deputy 759
promise 768
go bail 806
I'll – for it 535
– the helm 745
– the purpose 731
– to correspond 9
– one's turn 644
answerable
agreement 23
liable 177
bail 806
duty 926

censurable 932
ant 690
Antaeus 159, 192
antagonism
difference 14
physical 179
voluntary 708
enmity 889
antagonist 710, 891
antagonistic 24
antarctic 237
antecedence 62, 116
antecedent 64
antechamber 191
ante Christum 106
antedate 115
antediluvian 124
antelope 274
antemundane 124
antenna 379
anteposition 62
anterior
in order 62
in time 116
in place 234
– to reason 477
anteroom 191
antevert 706
anthem 990
anthemion 847
anthology
book 533
collection 596
poem 597
anthracite 388
anthropoid 372
anthropology
zoology 368
mankind 372
anthropomancy 511
anthropophagi 913
anthroposcopy 511
anthroposophy 372
antic 840
anti-aircraft gun 564, 727
antichambre,
faire – 133
antichristian 984, 989
antichronism 115
anticipate
anachronism 115
priority 116
future 121
early 132
expect 507
foresee 510
prepare 673
hope 858
in – 116
anticlimax
decrease 36
bathos 497, 853
anticlinal 217
anticyclone 265
antidote 662
antigropelos 225
antilogarithm 84
antilogy 477
antimony 663
Antinomian 984
antinomy 964
Antinous 845
antiparallel 217
antipathy 867, 898
antiphon music 415
answer 462

worship 990
antiphrasis 563
antipodes
difference 14
distance 196
contraposition 237
antipoison 660
antiquary
past times 122
scholar 492
historian 553
antiquas vias,
stare super – 613, 670
antiquated 128
antique 124
antiquity 122
antiscriptural 984
antiseptic 652, 662
antisocial 911
antistrophe 597
antithesis
contrast 14
difference 15
opposite 237
style 574, 577
antitoxin 662
antitype 22
antler 253
antonomasia
metaphor 521
nomenclature 564
antonym 14
antrum 252
anvil support 215
on the –
intended 620
in hand 625
preparing 673
anxiety pain 828
fear 860
desire 865
anxious expectation 507
any some 25
part 51
no choice 609a
at – price 604a
at – rate
certain 474
true 494
at all hazards 604
anybody 78
anyhow 460, 627
anything one
knows, for – 491
aorist 109, 119
aorta 350
apace early 132
swift 274
apache 913
apart 44, 87
set – 636
wide – 196
apartment 191
–s 189
–s to let
imbecile 499
apathetic 275
apathy
indifference 465
insensibility 823
irreligion 989
ape imitate 19
Apelles 559
aperçu 596
aperture 260

arctic *northern* 237
  cold 383
arctics 225
arcuation 245
ardent *fiery* 382
  eager 682
  feeling 821
  loving 897
  – expectation 507
  – imagination 515
ardet, proximus –
  665, 667
ardor *vigor* 574
  activity 821
  feeling 821
  desire 865
arduous 704
area 181, 182
arefaction 340
arena *space* 180
  region 181
  field of view 441
  field of battle **728**
arenaceous 330
areola 247
areolar 219
areometer 321
Areopagus 966
arête 253
aretinism 961
aretology 926
Argand lamp 423
argent 430
argillaceous 324
argosy 273
argot 563
argonaut 269
argue *evidence* 467
  reason 476
  indicate 550
  dissectation 595
argument *disagree-*
  ment 24
  topic 454
  discussion 476
  meaning 516
  have the best of
    an – 478
argumentum
  – baculinum
    compel 744
    lawless 964
    punish 972
  – ad crumenam
    800
  – ad hominem
    reasoning 476
    accuse 938
  – ad verecundiam
    939
Argus-eyed 441, 459
argute 498
aria 415
arianism 984
arid 340
  unproductive 169
  uninteresting 841
Ariel *courier* 268
  swift 274
  messenger 534
  spirit 979
arietation 276
arietta 415
aright *well* 618
Ariman [*see* Ahri-
  manes]
ariolation 511
arioso 415

aris et focis, pro –
  defence 717
  philanthropy 910
arise *exist* 1
  begin 66
  happen 151
  mount 305
  appear 446
  – from 154
Aristarchus 850
Aristides
  good man 948
aristocracy
  power 737
  fashion 852
  nobility 875
ἄριστον μέτρον 628
Arithmancy 511
arithmetic 85
ark *abode* 189
  asylum 666
arm *part* 51
  power 157
  instrument 633
  provide 637
  prepare 673
  war 722
  weapon 727
  make a long – 200
  – chair 215
  – in arm
  together 88
  friends 888
  sociable 892
  – of the law 963
  – of the sea 343
armada 726
Armageddon 720,
  722
armament 673, 727
armed 717
  – at all points 673
  – force 726
  – guard 664
armet 717
armful 25
armiger 875
armigerent 726
armigerous 722
armilla 247, 847
armillary sphere
  466
armipotent 157
armistice
  cessation 142
  respite 672
  pacification 723
armless 158
armlet *ring* 247
  gulf 343
  ornament 847
armor *cover* 223
  defence 717
  arms 727
  buckle on one's –
    673
  – plated 223
armored
  – car 726
  – cruiser 726
  – train 726
armorial bearings
  550, 877
armory *store* 636
  workshop 691
arm's length
  at – 196
  keep at –

repel 289
  defence 717
  enmity 889
  seclusion 893
  discourtesy 895
arms 727 [*see* arm]
  heraldry 550
  war 722
  honors 877
  clash of – 720
  deeds of – 720
  with folded – 681
  in – *infant* 129
  throw oneself into
    the – of 666, 880
  under – 722
  up in – *active* 682
  discord 713
  resistance 719
  resentment 900
  enmity 889
Armstrong gun 727
army *collection* 72
  multitude 102
  troops 726
aroma 400
around 227
  lie – 220
arouse *move* 615
  excite 824
  – oneself 682
aroynt *begone* 297
  malediction 908
arquebusade 662
arquebuse 727
arraign 938, 969
arrange
  set in order 60
  plan 626
  compromise 774
  – with creditors
    807
  – itself 58
arrange – matters
  pacify 723
  – music 413, 416
  – in a series 69
  – under 76
arrangement 23, 60
  [*see* arrange]
  order 58
  temporary – 111
arrant *identical* 31
  manifest 525
  notorious 531
  bad 649
  disreputable 874
  base 940
arras 847
array *order* 58, 60
  series 69
  assemblage 72
  multitude 102
  dress 225
  prepare 673
  adorn 847
  ostentation 882
  battle – 722
arrear, in – 53, 808
arrears *debt* 806
arrectis auribus
  hear 418
  expect 507
arrest *stop* 142
  restrain 751
  in law 969
  – the attention 457
arrière-pensée

after-thought 65
  mental reservation
    528
  motive 615
  set purpose 620
arrival 292
arrive *happen* 151
  reach 292
  complete 729
  – at a conclusion
    480
  – at the truth 480a
arrogant *severe* 739
  proud 878
  insolent 885
arrogate 885, 924
  – to oneself
  undue 925
arrondissement 181
arrosion 331
arrow *swift* 274
  missile 284
  arms 727
  broad – 550
arrow-head
  form 253
  writing 590
'Arry and 'Arriet
  902
ars celare artem
  698
arsenal *store* 636
  workshop 661
arsenic 663
arson 384
art *representation*
  554
  business 625
  skill 698
  cunning 702
  fine – 850
  work of – 845, 847
  – gallery 556
artery 350, 627
artes, hae tibi
  erunt – 627
artesian well 343
artful 544, 702
  – dodge 545, 702
article *thing* 3
  part 51
  matter 316
  chapter 593
  review 595
  goods 798
articled clerk 541
articles
  thirty-nine – 983a
  – of agreement
    770
  – of faith 484, 983
articulate 366
articulation
  junction 43
  speech 580
articulo, in –
  transient 111
  dying 360
artifice 626, 702
artificer 690
artificial
  fictitious 545
  cunning 702
  affected 855
  – language 579
artillery
  explosion 404
  arms 727

artilleryman 726
artisan 690
artist *painter &c.*
  559
  contriver 626
  agent 690
artiste *music* 416
  drama 599
artistic *skilful* 698
  beautiful 845
  taste 850
  – language 578
artlessness 703
aruspex 513
aruspicy 511
arundo, haeret
  lateri lethalis –
    828
as *motive* 615
  – broad as long 27
  – can be 52
  – good as 27
  – if *similar* 17
  suppose 514
  – little as may be
    32
  – it may be
  circumstance 8
  event 151
  chance 156
  – much again 90
  – soon as 120
  – they say 496, 532
  – things are 7
  – things go 151,
    613
  – to 9
  – usual 82
  – it were 17, 521
  – you were 141,
    283
  – well as 37
  – the world wags
    151
ascend *be great* 31
  increase 35
  rise 305
  improve 658
ascendancy
  power 157
  influence 175
  success 731
ascendant
  lord of the – 745
  in the –
  influence 175
  important 642
  success 731
  authority 737
  repute 873
  one's star in the –
  prosperity 734
ascension
  [*see* ascend]
  calefaction 384
  – Day 998
ascent
  [*see* ascend]
  gradient 217
  rise 305
  glory 873
ascertain *fix* 150
  determine 480
ascertained 474,
  490
ascertainment 480a
asceticism 955
ascititious

- la générale 669
se – contre des
  moulins 645
ne – que d'une aile
  683
battology
  repeat 104
  diffuse style 373
battue *pursuit* 622
  attack 716
  kill 361
bauble 643, 840
bavardage 517, 584
bawd 962
bawdy, – house 961
bawl 411
bawn 189
bay *concave* 252
  gulf 343
  cry 412
  brown 433
  at – *danger* 665
  difficulty 704
  defence 717, 719
  bring to – 716
  – the moon 645
  – window 260
bayadére 599
bayard 271
bayonet *kill* 361
  attack 716
  weapon 727
  crossed –s 708
  at the point of the
  – *war* 722
  severity 739
  coercion 744
bays *trophy* 733
  crown 877
bazaar 799
B.C. 106
be 1
  – all and end all
  whole 50
  intention 620
  importance 642
  – off *depart* 293
  eject 297
  retract 773
  – it so 488
  – that as it may 30
beach 231, 342
beach comber 268
beacon 550, 663
bead 249
beadle *janitor* 263
  law officer 965
  church 996
beadledom 737
beadroll *list* 86
  prayers 990
  ritual 998
beads
  ornament 847
  tell one's – 990,
  998
beadsman
  servant 746
  clergy 996
beagle 366
beak *face* 234
  nose 250
  magistrate 967
beaker 161
beam *support* 215
  plank 236
  weigh 319
  light 420

on – ends
powerless 158
horizontal 213
side 236
fail 732
wonder 870
beaming
beautiful 845
bean 276
beanfeast 840
bear *produce* 161
sustain 215
carry 270
admit of 470
suffer 821
endure 826
bring to – 677
more than flesh
  and blood can –
  824
unable to –
excited 825
dislike 867
– away 789
– away the bell
  648, 731
– the brunt 704,
  717
– the burden 625
– the cross 828
– company 88
– down 173, 885
– down upon 716
– false witness 544
– fruit *produce* 161
useful 644
success 731
prosper 734
– a hand 680
– hard upon 649
– harmless 717
– ill 825
– off *deviate* 279
– on 215
– oneself 692
– out *evidence* 467
vindicate 937
– pain 828
– the palm 33
– a sense 516
– through 707
– up *approach* 286
persevere 604a
relieve 834
cheerful 836
– up against 719,
  861
– upon
relevant 9, 23
influence 175
– with
tolerate 740
permit 760
take coolly 826
forgive 918
bear
savage 907
surly 895
had it been a – it
  would have bit-
  ten you 458
– garden
disorder 59
discord 713
arena 728
– leader 540
– pit 370
– skin *cap* 225

helmet 717
– with a sore back
  901
bearable 651
beard *hair* 205
prickles 253
rough 256
defy 715
brave 861
insolence 885
pluck by the –
disrespect 929
– the lion 604
beardless 127, 226
bearer 271, 363
bearing *relation* 9
support 215
direction 278
meaning 516
demeanor 692
– rein 706, 752
bearings
circumstances 8
situation 183
armorial – 550
beast *animal* 366
unclean 653
discourteous 895
– of burden 271,
  690
beat *be superior* 33
periodic 138
region 181
impulse 276
surpass 303
oscillate 314
agitation 315
crush 330
sound 407
line of pursuit 625
path 627
overcome 731
strike 972
– about
circuit 629
– the air 645
– against 708
– one's breast 839
– about the bush
try for 463
evade the point 477
prevaricate 544
diffuse style 573
– down *destroy* 162
cheapen 794, 819
insolent 885
– of drum
music 416
publish 531
alarm 669
wear 722
command 741
pomp 882
without – of
drum 528
– into *teach* 537
– off 717
– a retreat
retire 283
avoid 623
submit 725
– time *clock* 114
music 416
– up *churn* 352
– up against
oppose 708
– up for *cater* 637
– up one's quarters

seek 461
visit 892
– up for recruits
prepare 673
aid 707
beaten track
habit 613
way 627
leave the – 83
tread the – 82
beatic 827
beatific 829, 981
beatification 827,
  987
beating high
the heart – 824
beatitude 827
beau *man* 373
fop 854
admirer 897
– idéal 650, 845
– monde 852
beautify 845, 847
beautiless 846
beauty 845
beaver *hat* 225
becalm 265
because *cause* 153
attribution 155
answer 462
reasoning 476
motive 615
bechance 151
beck *rill* 348
sign 550
mandate 741
at one's – *aid* 707
obey 743
beckon *sign* 550
motive 615
call 741
becloud *dark* 421
hide 528
become
change to 144
accord with 23
behove 926
– of 151
becoming
accordant 23
proper 646
beautiful 845, 847
due 924
becripple 158
bed *lodgment* 191
layer 204
support 215
garden 371
marriage 903
brought to – 161
death – 360
smooth the – of
  death 707
go to – 265, 683
keep one's – 655
– of down 687
– gown 255
– maker 746
– out 371
– ridden 655
– room 191
– of roses 377, 734
put to – with a
  shovel 363
– time 126
bedarken 421
bedaub 223, 653
bedazzle 420

bedding 215
bedeck 847
bedel 965
bedesman
  [*see* beadsman]
bedevil *derange* 61
sorcery 992
bedew 339
bedight 847
bedim 421, 422
bedizen *clothe* 225
ornament 847
vulgar 851
Bedlam
– broke loose 59
candidate for –
  • 504
be-dog 281
Bedouin 792
bedraggled 59
bedwarf 195
bee 690
busy – 682
swarm like –s 102
– in one's bonnet
  503
– in a bottle 407
– line 246, 278
–'s wax 352
beef-eater 726
beef-headed 499
beehive 250
Beelzebub 978
beer 298
beery 959
beetle *overhang* 206,
  214
project 250
blind as a – 442
Colorado – 913
– head 501
befall 151
befit *agree* 23
expedient 646
due 924, 926
befog 353, 528
befool *mad* 503
deceive 545
befooled
victimized 732
before *in order* 62
in time 116
presence 186
in space 234
precession 280
preference 609
set – one 525
– Christ 106
– long 132
– mentioned 62,
  116
– now 122
– one's eyes 446,
  525
– one's time 132
– you could –turn
  round, – say
  Jack Robinson
  113
beforehand
prior 116
early 132
foresight 510
resolve – 611
befoul 653
befriend 707, 888
befuddlement 959
beg *Turk* 745

all for the –
  good 618
  prosper 734
  content 831
  hope 858
bad is the – 649
do one's –
  care 459
  try 675
  activity 682
  exertion 686
have the – of it 731
make the – of it
  over-estimate 482
  use 677
  submit 725
  compromise 774
  take easily 826
  hope 858
  the – 800
  to the – of one's
    belief 484
  – bib and tucker
    prepared 673
    ornament 847
    ostentation 882
  – friends 890
  – intentions 906
  – man 903
  – part 31, 50
  – seller 731
  make the – of
    one's time 684
bestead 644
bestial 954, 961
bestir oneself
  activity 682
  haste 684
  exertion 686
bestow 784
  – one's hand 903
  – thought 451
bestraddle 215
bestrew 73
bestride 206, 215
bet 621
betake oneself to
  journey 266
  business 625
  use 677
bête, pas si – 498
bête noire bane 663
  fear 860
  hate 898
bethel 1000
bethink 451, 505
bethral 749, 751
betide 151
betimes 132
betoken
  evidence 467
  predict 511
  indicate 550
betray disclose 529
  deceive 545
  dishonor 940
  – itself visible 446
betrayer 941
betrim 673
betroth 768, 903
betrothed 897
better good 648
  improve 658
  appeal to one's –
    feelings 914
  get – health 654
  improve 658
  refreshment 689

restoration 660
get the – of, 479,
  702, 731
think – of 658, 950
seen – days
  deteriorate 659
  adversity 735
  poor 804
  – half 903
  only – than noth-
    ing 651
  – sort 875
  for – for worse
    choice 609
    marriage 903
between 228
  – cup and lip 111
  far – 198
  lie – 228
  – the lines 526
vibrate – two ex-
  tremes 149
  – ourselves 528
  – two fires 665
  – maid 746
betwixt 228
bevel 217
  – gearing 653
bever 298
beverage 298
bévue 732
bevy 72, 102
bewail regret 833
  lament 839
beware 665, 668
bewilder
  put out 458
  uncertainty 475
  astonish 870
bewitch
  fascinate 615
  please 829
  excite love 897
  exorcise 992
bey 745
beyond superior 33
  distance 196
  go – 303
  – compare 31, 33
  – control 471
  – one's depth 208,
    519
  – expression 31
  – one's grasp 471
  – hope 731, 534
  – the mark 303,
    641
  – measure 641
  – possibility 471
  – praise
    perfect 650
    approbation 931
    virtue 944
  – price 814
  – question 474, 494
  – reason 471
  – remedy 859
  – seas 57
bezel 217
bhang 663
bias influence 175
  tendency 176
  slope 217
  prepossession 481
  disposition 820
bib pinafore 225
  drink 959
bibber weep 839

tope 959
bibble-babble 584
bibelot 847
bibendum, nunc
  est – 959
Bible 895
  – oath 535
biblioclasm 162
bibliography 593
bibliolatry
  learning 490
  heterodoxy 984
  idolatry 991
bibliomancy 511
bibliomania 490
bibliomaniac 492
bibliophile 492
bibliopole 593
bibliotheca 593
bibulous 298, 959
bicameral 90
bicapital 90
bice 435, 438
bicentenary 98,
  138, 883
bicker flutter 315
  quarrel 713
bicolor 440
biconjugate 91
bicuspid 91
bicycle 272
bid order 741
  offer 763
  – the banns 903
  – defiance 715
  – fair tend 176
  probable 472
  promise 511
  hope 858
  – a long farewell
    624
  – for intend 620
  offer 763
  request 765
  bargain 794
bidder 767
bide wait 133
  remain 141
  take coolly 806
  – one's time 133
  watch 507
  inactive 681
bidet 271
biennial
  periodic 138
  plant 367
bienséance 852, 894
bier 363
bifacial 90
bifarious 90
bifid 91
bifold 90
biform 90
bifurcate 91, 244
big in degree 31
  in size 192
  wide 194
  look – defy 715
  proud 878
  insolent 885
  talk – 885, 909
  – sounding
    loud 404
    words 577
    affected 855
  – swollen 194
  – with ≥1
  – with the fate of

511
bigamy 903
biggin 191
bight 343
bigot positive 474
  prejudice 481
  obstinate 606
  heterodox 984
  impious 988
bigotry 907
bigwig scholar 492
  sage 500
  nobility 875
bijou goodness 648
  beauty 845
  ornament 847
bilander 273
bilateral 90, 236
bilbao 727
bilboes 752
  put into – 751
bile 900
bilge base 211
  convex 250
  yawn 260
  – water 653
bilious 837
bilingual 560
bilk
  disappoint 509
  cheat 545
  steal 791
bill list 86
  hatchet 253
  placard 531
  ticket 550
  paper 593
  plan 626
  weapon 727
  money order 800
  money account
    811
  charge 812
  in law 969
  true – 969
  – and coo 902
  – of exchange 771
  – of fare food 298
  plan 626
  – of indictment
    938
  –s of mortality 360
  – of sale 771
billet locate 184
  ticket 550
  apportion 786
billet epistle 592
  – doux 902
billfold 191
billhook 253
billiard – ball 249
  – room 191
  – table flat 213
billiards 840
Billingsgate 563,
  908
billion 98
billow sea 348
  river 341
billy-cock 225
billy-goat 373
bimetallism 800
bin 191
binary 89
bind connect 43
  cover 223
  compel 744
  condition 770

obligation 926
  – hand and foot
    751
  – oneself 768
  – over 744
  – up wounds 660
binding 681, 744
bine 367
binnacle 693
binocular 445
binomial 89
biogenesis 161
biograph 448
biography 594
biology 357, 359
bioscope 448
biota 357
biparous 89
bipartite 44, 91
biplane 273
biplicity 89
biquadrate 96
birch flog 972
  – rod 975
bird 366
  kill two –s with
    one stone 682
  –'s eye view 441,
    448
  –s of a feather 17
  the – has flown
    187, 671
  – in hand 777, 781
  – of ill omen
    omen 512
    warning 668
    hopeless 859
  – of passage 268
  – of prey 739
  a little – told me
    527
birdcage 370
birdlime glue 45
  trap 545
biretta 999
birth beginning 66
  production 161
  paternity 166
  nobility 875
  – place 153
  – right 924
  – suit 226
birthday 138, 883
birthmark 848
bis repeat 104
  approval 931
biscuits, s'embar-
  quer sans – 674
bise 349
bisection 68, 91
bishop punch 298
  clergy 996
  –'s palace 1000
  –'s purple 437
bishopric 995
bisque 33
bissextile 138
bister 433
bistoury 253
bisulcate 259
bit
  small quantity 32
  part 51
  interval 106
  curb 752
  just a – 26
  – by bit
  by degrees 26

– setter 662
bonehouse 363
boner 495
bones [see bone]
  corpse 362
  music 417
break no – 648
make no – 602,
  705
boneyard 363
bonfire 382
  festivity 840
  celebration 883
make a – of 384
bonhomie 703, 906
bonhomme 996
Boniface 890
bonne 746, 753
– bouche end 67
  pleasant 377
  savory 394
  saving 636
à la – heure 602,
  831
de – volonté 602
bonnet 225
bonny 836, 845
bono: cui –
  intention 620
  utility 644
  inutility 645
pro – publico 644,
  910
bonus extra 641
  gift 784
  money 810
bony 323
bonze 996
bonzer 648
booby 501
– trap 545
boodle 793
book register 86
publication 531
  record 551
  volume 593
  script 599
  enter accounts 811
at one's –s 539
bring to –
  evidence 467
  account 811
  reprove 932
mind one's – 539
school – 542
without –
  by heart 505
– of Books 985
– club 593
– of fate 601
– learning 490
– shop 593
book-case 191
booked dying 360
bookish 490
bookkeeper 553
bookkeeping 811
bookless
  unlearned 493
bookmaking 156
bookseller 593
bookworm 492, 593
boom
  support 215
  sail 267
  rush 274
  impulse 276
  sound 404

obstacle 706
  defence 717
boomerang
  recoil 277
  retribution 718
  weapon 727
boon 784
  beg a – 765
– companion 890
boor clown 876
boorish 851, 895
boost 276, 482, 931
booster 935
boot box 191
  dress 225
  advantage 618
· punishment 975
to – added 37
– legging 964
booted and spurred
  673
booth 189, 799
bootless 645, 732
boots dress 225
  servant 746
  low person 876
what – it? 643
booty 793
booze 959
bo-peep 441, 528
bordel 961
border edge 231
  limit 233
  flower bed 371
  ornament 847
– upon 197, 199
bore diameter 202
  hole 260
  tide 348, 667
  fatigue 688
  trouble 828
  plague 830
  weary 841
bored 456
boreal
  Northern 237
  cold 383
Boreas 349
boredom 841
borer 262
born 359
– so 5
– under an evil
  star 735
– under a lucky
  star 734
borne 826
– down failure 732
  defection 837
borné 499
borough 181, 189
  rotten – 893
– council 696
borrow 19, 788
– of Peter &c. 147
borrowed plumes
  deception 545
borrower 806
borrowing 788
bosh absurdity 497
  unmeaning 517
  untrue 546
  trifling 643
bosky 959
bosom breast 221
  mind 450
  affections 820
in the – of 229

– of one's family
  221
– friend 890
boss 250, 694, 737
  straw – 694
boston 840
botanic garden 369,
  371
Botanomancy 511
Botany 367, 369
botch bungle 59
  mend 660
  unskilful 699
  difficulty 704
  fail 732
both 89
listen with – ears
  418
burn the candle at
  – ends 641
butter one's bread
  on – sides 641
bother
  uncertainty 475
  bustle 682
  difficulty 704
  trouble 828
  harass 830
bothy 189
bottle
  receptacle 191
  preserve 670
bee in a – 407
crack a – 298
pass the – 959
smelling – 400
– green 435
– holder
  auxiliary 177
  mediator 724
– up remember 505
  hide 528
  restrain 751
bottom
  lowest part 211
  support 215
  posterior 235
  combe 252
  ship 273
  pluck 604a
  courage 861
at – 5
at the – of
  cause 153
go to the – 310
probe to the – 461
from the – of one's
  heart veracity
  543
  feeling 821
– upwards 218
– land 180, 207
bottomless 208
– pit 982
angel of the – pit
  978
bottomry 771
botulism 663
bouche:
  bonne – end 67
  savory 394
  saving 636
  pleasant 829
– à feu 727
bouderie 901a
boudoir 191
bouffe, opera 599
bouge 250

bough part 51
  curve 245
  tree 367
bought flexure 245
bougie 423
boulder 249
boulevards 227
bouleversement
  revolution 146
  destruction 162
  excite 824
bouillabaise 298
bouillon 298
bounce violence 173
– jump 309
  lie 546
  boast 884
  insolence 885
– upon 292, 508
bouncing large 192
bound
  circumscribe 229
  swift 274
  leap 309
  certain 474
I'll be – 535
– back recoil 277
– by 926
– for direction 278
  destination 620
– to promise 768
  responsible 926
boundary 233
bounden duty 926
bounder 851
boundless 105, 180
bounds 230, 233
keep within –
  moderation 174
  shortcoming 304
  restrain 751
  prohibit 761
– of possibility 470
bountiful 816, 906
  Lady – 816
bounty gift 784
bouquet
  fragrant 400
  beauty 847
bourgeois
  middle class 29
  type 591
  commoner 876
bourdon 215
bourgeon 194
bourn 233
bourse 621, 799
bouse 959
bout turn 138
  job 680
  fight 720
  prank 840
  drinking – 954
bout
au – du compte
  476
au – de son latin
  sophistry 477
  ignorance 491
  difficulty 704
boutade 497, 608
boutonnière 400
bovine 366, 499
bow be inferior 34
  fore part 234
  curve 245
  projection 250
  stoop 308

fiddlestick 417
  weapon 727
  ornament 847
  servility 886
  reverence 894
  respect 928
bend the – 686
draw the long –
  884
– down worship
  990, 991
– out 297
– submission 725
– window 260
Bow bells
  born within sound
  of – 876
Bowdlerize 652
bowed down 837,
  879
bowelless 914a
bowels inside 221
– of compassion
  914
– of the earth 208
bower 189, 191
–s of bliss 981
bowery 424
bowie knife 727
bowl vessel 191
  rotate 312
  stadium 840
  flowing – 959
– along walk 266
  swift 274
bowlder 249
bowline 45
bowler hat 225
bow-legged 243
bowling-green 213,
  840
bowls 840
bowman 726
bowshot 197
bowsprit 234
bowstring execution
  972, 975
box house 189
  chest 191
  seat 215
  theater 599
  fight 720
  horse – 272
  musical – 417
  wrong – error 495
  unskilful 699
  dilemma 704
– the compass
  direction 278
  rotation 312
  change of mind
  607
– the ear 900, 972
– up 751
boxer 726
boy 129
– scout 534
boyar 875
boyhood 127
boycott 55, 297, 893
brabble 713, 720
brabbler 901
brace tie 43
  fasten 45
  two 89
  strengthen 159
  support 214
  music 413

hold a – for 759
 – case 191
briefly *anon* 132
brier
  sharp 253
  pipe 390
  bane 663
brig 273
brigade 726
brigadier 745
brigand 792
brigandage 791
brigandine 717
brigantine 273
bright *shine* 420
  color 428
  intelligent 498
  cheery 836
  beauty 845
  glory 873
  – days 734
  – eyed 845
  – prospect 858
  – side 829
look at the – side
  836, 858
  – thought
  sharp 498
  good stroke 626
  wit 842
brighten up
  furbish 658
brigue 712, 720
brilliant
  shining 420
  good 648
  wit 842
  beautiful 845
  gem 847
  glorious 873
  – idea 842
brilliantine 356
brim 231
  – over 641
brimful 52
brimstone 388
brindled 440
brine 341, 392
bring 270
  – about 153, 729
  – back 790
  – back to the
    memory 505
  – to bear upon
    relation 9
    action 170
  – into being 161
  – to a crisis 604
  – forth 161
  – forward
    evidence 467
    manifest 525
    teach 537
    improve 658
  – grey hairs to the
    grave 735, 830
  – grist to the mill
    644
  – home 775
  – home to 155
  – in *receive* 296
    income 810
    price 812
  – to life 359
  – to light 480a
  – low 874
  – to maturity 673,
    729

– to mind 505
– under one's
  notice 457
– off 672
– out
  discover 480a
  manifest 525
  publish 591
  – over
  persuade 484
  – to perfection
    677
  – into play 677
  – to a point 74
  – in question 461
  – up the rear 235
  – round
  persuade 615
  restore 660
  – to terms 723
  – to *convert* 144
  halt 265
  – together 72
  – in its train 88
  – to trial 969
  – up *develop* 161
  vomit 297
  educate 537
  – in a verdict 480
  – word 527
brink 231
  on the –
  almost 32
  coming 121
  near 197
  – of the grave 360
briny 392
  – ocean 341
brio *music* 415
  active 682
brisk *prompt* 111
  energetic 171
  active 682
  cheery 836
bristle 253
  – up *stick up* 250
  angry 900
  – with 639, 641
  – with arms 722
bristly 256
Britannia metal
  545
Briticism 563
British 188
  – lion 604
Briton, true – 939
  work like a – 686
brittleness 328
britzska 272
broach *begin* 66
  found 153
  reamer 262
  tap 297
  publish 531
  assert 535
broad *general* 78
  space 202
  lake 343
  emphatic 535
  indelicate 961,
    962
  – accent 580
  – awake 459, 682
  – daylight 420,
    525
  – farce 842
  – grin 838
  – highway 627

– hint 527
  – meaning 516
  – minded 498
broadcast
  disperse 73
  spread 78
  publish 531
  sow – 818
broadcloth 219
broadhearted 906
broadsheet 593
broad-shouldered
  159
broadside 236
  publication 531
  cannonade 716
broadsword 727
Brobdingnagian
  192
brocade 847
brochure 593
Brocken, specter of
  the 443
broder 549
brogue *boot* 225
  dialect 563
broidery 847
broil *heat* 382
  fry 384
  fray 713, 720
broke *poor* 804
broken
  discontinuous 70
  weak 160
  – color 428
  – down
  decrepit 659
  failing 732
  dejected 837
  – English 563
  – fortune 735, 804
  – heart 828, 837
  hopeless 859
  – reed 160, 665
  – meat 645
  – voice 581, 583
  – winded
  disease 655
  fatigue 688
broker 758, 797
brokerage *pay* 812
brokery 794
bromidic 613
bronchia 351
bronze *alloy* 41
  brown 433
  sculpture 557
brooch 847
brood 102, 167
  – over 451, 847
brooding
  preparing 673
brook *stream* 348
  bear 821, 826
broom 652
broth 298
brothel 961
brother *kin* 11
  similar 17
  equal 27
brotherhood 712
brotherly
  friendship 888
  love 897
  benevolence 906
brougham 272
brought to bed 161
brouillerie 713

brouillon 626
brow *top* 210
  edge 231
  front 234
browbeat
  intimidate 860
  swagger 885
  disrespect 929
  –en *humbled* 879
brown **433**
  – Bess 727
  – study 451, 458
Brown, Jones and
  Robinson 876
brownie 980
browse 298
bruin 895
bruise *powder* 330
  hurt 619
  injure 649
  blemish 848
bruiser 726
bruit
  report 531, 532
brumal 126, 383
brumous 353
Brummagem 545
brunette 433
brunt *beginning* 66
  impulse 276
  bear the –
  difficulty 704
  defence 717
  endure 821, 826
brush *rough* 250
  rapid motion 274
  graze 379
  clean 652
  fight 720
  paint – 556
  – away *reject* 297
  abrogate 756
  – up *clean* 652
  furbish 658
  prepare 673
brushwood 367
brusque *violent* 173
  haste 684
  discourtesy 895
brutal *vulgar* 851
  rude 895
  savage 907
brutalize
  [*see* brutal]
  corrupt 659
  deaden 823
  vice 945
brute *animal* 366
  rude 895
  maleficent 913
  – force
  strength 159
  violence 173
  animal 450a
  severe 739
  compulsion 744
  lawless 964
  – matter 316, 358
Brute, et tu 917
brutish [*see* brute]
  vulgar 851
  ignoble 876
  intemperate 954
brutum fulmen
  impotent 158
  failure 732
  lax 738
  boast 884

bubble
  unsubstantial 4
  transient 111
  little 193
  convexity 250
  light 320
  water 348
  air **353**
  error 495
  deceit 545
  trifle 643
  – burst
  fall short 304
  disappoint 509
  fail 732
  – reputation 873
  – and squeak 298
  – up *agitation* 315
buccaneer 791, 792
bucentaur 273
Bucephalus 271
buck *stag* 366
  male 373
  wash 652
  money 800
  fop 854
  – basket 191
  – jump 309
  – up 684
bucket 191
  kick the – 360
  drop – in empty
    well 645
  like –s in well 314
buckle *tie* 43
  fastening 45
  distort 243
  curl 248
  – on one's armor
    673
  – to 604, 686
  – with *grapple* 720
buckler 717
buckram 855, 878
  men in – 549
bucolic
  pastoral 370
  poem 597
bud 367
  beginning 66
  germ 153
  expand 194
  graft 300
  – from 154
Buddha 979, 986
Buddhism 984
budding *young* 127
buddy 711, 890
budge 264
budget *heap* 72
  bag 191
  store 636
  finance 811
  – of news 532
buff **436**
  blind man's – 840
  native – 226
buffer
  hindrance 706
  defence 717
buffet 191
  strike 276
  agitate 315
  evil 619
  bad 649
  affront 900
  smite 972
  – the waves 704,

bane 663
painful 830
candelabrum 423
candent 382
candid *white* 430
  sincere 543
  ingenuous 703
  honorable 939
candidate 767, 865
candidature 763
candle 423
  bargain by inch of
   – 769
  burn – at both
   ends 686
  not fit to hold a –
   to 34
  – ends 40, 817
  – holder 711
  – light 126, 422
  – power 466
  – stick 423, 998
  hold – to sun 645
Candlemas 998
candor
  veracity 543
  artlessness 705
  honor 939
candy *dense* 321
  sweet 396
cane *weapon* 727
  punish 972
  scourge 975
canescent 430
Canicula 423
canicular 382
caniculated 259
canine 366
  – *appetite* 865
canister 191
canker *disease* 655
  deterioration 659
  bane 663
  pain 830
canned goods 670
cannel coal 388
cankered
  sullen 901a
cankerworm 663
  evil-doer 913
  care 830
cannibal 913
cannibalism 945
cannon
  collision 276
  loud 404
  arms 727
  – fodder 726
  –'s mouth *war* 722
  courage 861
cannonade 716
cannonball 249, 274
cannoneer 726
cannot 271
cannular 260
canny 498, 702
  ca' – 864
canoe 273
  paddle one's own
   – 748
canon *rule* 80
  ravine 198
  music 415
  belief 484
  precept 697
  priest 996
  rite 998
  – law 697

canonical
  regular 82
  inspired 985
  ecclesiastical 995
canonicals 999
canonist 983
canonization
  repute 873
  deification 991
  rite 998
canonry 995
canopy 223
  – of heaven 318
canorous 413
cant *oblique* 217
  jerk 276
  hypocrisy 544
  neology 563
  impiety 988
cantabile 415
cantankerous 901,
  901a
cantata 415
  missa – 998
cantatrice 416
canteen 189, 191
canter 266, 274
  win at a – 705
canterbury
  receptacle 191
Canterbury tale
  546
cantharides 171
canticle 415
cantilever 215
canting 855
cantle 51
cantlet 32, 51
canto 597
canton 181, 737
cantonment 184,
  189
cantrap 993
canty 836
canvas *sail* 267
  picture 556
  under press of –
   274
canvass
  investigate 461
  discuss 476
  dissert 595
  solicit 765
canvasser 767
canyon 350
canzonet 415, 597
caoutchouc 325
cap *be superior* 33
  height 206
  summit 210
  cover 223
  hat 225
  retaliate 718
  complete 929
  salute 894
  fling up one's –
   838
  Fortunatus's – 993
  set one's – at 897,
   902
  – and bells 844
  – fits 23
  – in hand
   request 765
   servile 886
  – of maintenance
   747

capability
  endowment 5
  power 157
  skill 698
  facility 705
capacious *space* 180
  – *memory* 505
capacity
  endowment 5
  power 157
  space 180
  size 192
  intellect 450
  wisdom 498
  office 625
  talent 698
cap-à-pie
  complete 52
  armed –
   prepared 673
   defence 717
   war 722
caparison 225
cape *height* 206
  cloak 225
  projection 250
capella, alla – 415
caper *leap* 309
  dance 840
capful *quantity* 25
  small 32
  – of wind 349
capillament 205
capillary
  hairlike 205
  thin 203
capital *city* 189
  top 201
  letter 561
  important 642
  excellent 648
  money 800
  wealth 803
  make – out of
   pretext 617
   acquire 775
  print in –s 642
  – *messuage* 189
  – *punishment* 972
  ship 726
capitalist 803
capitation 85
  – tax 812
capitol 189, 717
capitular 995, 996
capitulate 725
capnomancy 511
capon 373
caponize 38, 158
capote 225
capouch 999
capper 548
capriccio *music* 415
  whim 608
caprice 608
  out of – 615a
capricious
  irregular 139
  changeable 149
  irresolute 605
  whimsical 608
capriole 309
capsize 218, 731
capsized 732
capstan 307, 633
capstone 210
capsular 252
capsule *vessel* 190

tunicle 223
  medicine 662
captain 269, 745
captandum, ad –
  sophistry 477
  deception 545
  affectation 855
  ostentation 882
  flattery 933
captation 933
captious
  capricious 608
  irascible 901
  censorious 932
caption
  taking 789
  beginning 66
  heading 564
captivate
  induce 615
  restrain 751
  please 829
captivated 827
captivating 829, 897
captive
  prisoner 754
  adorer 897
  lead – 749
  make – 751
  – balloon 273
captivity 751
capture 789
Capuchin 996
caput 696
  – mortuum 645,
   653
caquet 584
car 272
carabineer 726
carack 273
caracole 309
caracoler 266
carafe 191
caramel 396
carambole 276
carapace 717
cara sposa 897
carat 309
caravan 266, 272
caravansary 189
caravel 273
carbine 727
carbohydrates 298
carbon 388
  – dioxide 663
  – monoxide 663
carbonaro 742
carbonization 384
carboy 191
carbuncle *red* 434
  abscess 655
  jewel 847
carcanet 847
carcass
  structure 329
  corpse 362
  bomb 727
carcelage 973
carcinoma 655
card *unravel* 60
  ticket 550
  plan 626
  address – 550
  by the – 82
  great – 873
  house of –s 328
  leave a – 892
  on the –s 152, 177,

470
  play one's – 692
  play one's best –
   686
  play one's –s well
   698
  playing –s 840
  shuffle the –s
   begin again 66
   change 140
   chance 621
   prepare 673
  speak by the –
   care 459
   veracity 543
   phrase 566
  throw up the –s
   757
  ticklish – 704
  trump – 626
  – index 60, 86, 551
  –s to play 632
cardcase 191
cardiac 836
cardigan 225
cardinal *intrinsic* 5
  dress 225
  red 434
  important 642
  excellent 648
  priest 995, 996
  –'s hat 747
  – points 278
  – virtues 944
cardioid 245
card-sharper 792
card-sharping 545
care *attention* 459
  business 625
  adversity 735
  custody 751
  economy 817
  pain 828
  fear 860
  for aught one –s
   643, 866
  begone dull – 836
  drive – away 840
  have the – of 693
  take – 665, 864
  take – of 459
  – for *important*
   642
  desire 865
  love 897
careen *slope* 217
  repair 660
career 625, 692
careless
  inattentive 458
  neglectful 460,
   927
  feeble 575
  insensible 823
  indifferent 866
caress 897, 902
caret *incomplete* 53
  want 640
careworn 828, 837
cargo 270
  large quantity 31
  contents 190
  property 780
  goods 798
  – boat 273
caricature
  likeness 19
  copy 21

catalogue 60, 86
catalysis 49, 140
catamaran 273, 726
catemenial 138, 299
cataphonics 402
cataplasm 662
catapult 284, 726,
  727
cataract
  waterfall 348
  blindness 442,
  443
catarrh 299
catastrophe
  disaster 619
  finish 729
  misfortune 735
  end 67
catch imitate 19
  fastening 45
  song 415
  detect 480a
  joke 497
  gather the mean-
  ing 518
  cheat 545
  receive 785
  take 789
  by -es 70
  no great – 651
  – at willing 602
  desire 865
  – the attention
  457
  – one's death 360
  – a disease 655
  – the ear 418
  – the eye 446
  – fire 384
  – a glimpse of 441
  – an idea 498
  – the infection
  excitation 824
  – a likeness 554
  – a sound 418
  – at straws
  overrate 482
  credulous 486
  unskilful 699
  rash 863
  – by surprise 508
  – a Tartar dupe
  547
  retaliate 718
  – in a trap 545
  – tripping 480a
  – up 789
catching
  infectious 657
catchpenny
  deceiving 545
  trumpery 643
  cheap 815
catchpoll 965
catchword 550
catechism 461, 484
  church – 983a
catechize 461
catechumen 541,
  997
categorical
  positive 474
  demonstrative 478
  affirmative 535
categorically true
  494
category 7, 75
  in the same – 9

catena 69
catenary 245
catenation 69
cater 298, 637
caterpillar tractor
  271
caterwaul
  cat-cry 412
  discord 414
  courting 902
cates 298
catgut 417
  – scraper 416
cathartic 652
cathedrâ, ex –
  affirm 535
  school 542
  authority 737
  audacity 885
cathedral 1000
  Catherine wheel
  840
catholic
  universal 78
  religious 987
  – church 983a
  Roman – 984
catholicon 662
Catiline 941
catopsis 441
catoptrics 420
catoptromancy 511
cattle 271, 366
  – truck 272
catwalk 273, 627
Caucasian mystery
  983
caucus 696
caudal 67, 235
caudate 214
caudex 215
Caudine forks 162
cauf 370
caught tripping 491
caulk 660
cause source 153
  law-suit 969
  final – 620
  take up the – of
  707
  tell the – of 522
  –d by 154
causeless
  casual 156
  aimless 621
causerie 588
causeway 627
causidical 965
caustic
  energetic 171
  feeling 821
  painful 830
  gruff 895
  malevolent 907
  – curve 245
cautel 864
cautelâ, ex abun-
  danti – 664
cautery 384
caution warn 668
  prudence 864
  security 771
  want of – 863
cavalcade 69, 266
cavalier
  horseman 268
  rash 863
  insolent 885

discourteous 895
contemptuous 930
cavaliere servente
  servile 886
  lover 897
cavalry 726
cavatina 415
cave dwelling 189
  cell 191
  cavity 252
  – canem 864
  – of Adullam 624,
  832
  – in hollow 252
  submit 725
caveat
  warning 668
  command 741
  – emptor 769
cavendo tutus 664,
  864
cavern [see cave]
cavernous 252
caviar 392, 393
  – to the general
  850
cavil sophistry 477
  dissent 489
  censure 932
cavilier 936
cavity 252
caw 412
cayak 273
cayenne 392, 393
cazique 745
cease 142
  – to breathe 360
  – to exist 2
ceaseless 112
cecal 261
cecity 442
cecum 261
cede submit 725
  relinquish 782
  give 784
ceiling 206, 210, 223
celare artem, ars –
  698
cela va sans dire
  conformity 82
  consequence 154
celebrant 990
celebration 883, 998
celebrity 873, 875
celerity 274
celeste 417
celestial
  physical 318
  religious 976
  heaven 981
celibacy 904
cell abode 189
  receptacle 191
  cavity 221, 252
  prison 752
  hermitage 893
cellar 191
cellaret 191
cello 417
cellophane 223
cellular 191, 252
cement
  medium 45
  unite 43, 46, 48
  covering 223
  hard 323
  material 635
  – a party 712

cemented
  concord 714
cemetery 363
cenobite 893, 996
cenotaph 363
censer 998
censor
  moderate 174
  critic 480
  ban 761
  detractor 936
censorious 480, 932
censurable 947
censure 932
censurer 936
census 85, 86
  record 551
centaur 83, 366
centenarian 130
centenary
  hundred 98
  period 138
  celebration 883
center 68, 222
  – round 72, 290
centesimal 99
cento 597
centrality 222
centralize
  combine 48
centrifugal 291
centripetal 290
centroidal 222
centuple 98
centurion 745
century
  hundred 98
  period 108
  long time 110
  money 800
ceramic
  bake 384
  – ware 557
cerate 662
Cerberus
  janitor 263
  custodian 664
  hades 932
  sop for – 615
cereal 298
cerebration 451
cerebrum 450
cere-cloth 363
cerement
  covering 223
  wax 356
ceremonious 928
ceremony
  parade 882
  courtesy 894
  rite 998
Ceres 979
cerise 434
cerography 558,
  590
Ceromancy 511
ceroplastic 557
certain special 79
  indefinite number
  100
  sure 474
  belief 484
  true 494
  make – of 480a
  of a – age 128
  to a – degree 32
certainly yes 488

certainness 474
certainty 474
certes 474, 488
certificate
  evidence 467
  record 551
certify 467, 535
certiorari 969
certitude 474
cerulean 438
cess tax 812
  sewer 653
cessation 142
cession
  surrender 725
  of property 782.
  gift 784
cesspool 653
cestui-que trust 779
cestus 45, 247
chafe
  physical pain 378
  warm 384
  irritate 825
  mental pain 828,
  830
  discontent 832
  incense 900
chaff trash 643
  ridicule 856
  vulgar 876
  not to be caught
  with – 698, 702
  winnow – from
  wheat 609
chaffer 794
chafing-dish 386
chagrin 828
chain fasten 43
  vinculum 45
  series 69
  measure 200
  interlinking 219
  measure 466
  gearing 633
  imprison 752
  ornament 847
  drag a – 749
  drag a lengthened
  – 686
  in –s 754
chain gang 752, 972
chain-shot 727
chair support 215
  vehicle 272
  professorship 542
  throne 747
  celebration 883
  president 694
  in the – 693
chairman 694
chaise 272
chalcography 558
chalet 189
chalice 191, 998
chalk earth 342
  white 430
  mark 550
  drawing 556
  – from cheese 14,
  491
  – out plan 626
challenge
  question 461
  doubt 485
  claim 924
  defy 715

accuse 938
– comparison 648
cham 745
chamber *room* 191
council 696
mart 799
sick – 655
chamberlain 746
chambermaid 746
chameleon 149, 440
chamfer 259
chamois 309
champ 298
– the bit *disobedient* 742
chafe 825
angry 900
champagne 298
champaign 344
champain 874
Champ de Mars 728
champêtre, fête – 840
champion
best 648
auxiliary 711
defence 717
combatant 726
representative 759
sympathizer 914
championship 707
chance 156, 621
be one's – 151
game of – 840
great – 472
small – 473
stand a – 177, 470
take one's – 675
–s against one 665
whirligig of – 156
as – would have it 152
chancel 1000
chancellor
president 745
deputy 759
judge 967
– of the exchequer 801
chancery
court of – 966
– suit *delay* 133
chandelier 214, 423
chandelle, le jeu n'en vaut pas la – 638, 643
dear 814
chandler 797
change
alteration 140
mart 799
small coin 800
inter– 148
radical – 146
sudden – 146
– about 149
– color 821
– for 147
– hands 783
– of mind 607
– of opinion 485
– of place 264
changeableness 149, 605
changeful
fickle 607
changeling

substitute 147
fool 501
changeless 16
changer 797
channel
furrow 259
opening 260
conduit 350
way 627
chant *song* 415
sing 416
worship 990
chant du cygne 360
chanter 416
chanticleer 366
chantry 1000
chaomancy 511
chaos 59
chap *crack* 198
jaw 231
fellow 373
– *book* 593
chapel 1000
chaperon
accompany 88
watch 459
protect 664
chapfallen 878
chaplain 995, 996
chaplet *circle* 247
garland 550
trophy 733
ornament 847
chapman 797
chapter *part* 51
topic 454
book 593
council 696
church 995
– of accidents 156, 621
– *house* 1000
– and verse 467, 494
char *burn* 384
serve 746
char-à-banc 272
character
nature 5
state 7
class 75
oddity 83
letter 561
drama 599
disposition 820
reputation 873
characteristic
intrinsic 5
special 79
tendency 176
mark 550
characterize 564, 594
characterized 820
charade 533, 599
charcoal *fuel* 384, 388
black 431
drawing 556
charge *fill* 52
contents 190
business 625
requisition 630
direction 693
advice 695
precept 697
attack 716
order 741

custody 751
commission 755
bargain for 794
price 812
accusation 938
in – prisoner 754
justifiable – 937
take – of 664
take in – 751
– on *attribute* 155
– with 155, 777
chargé d'affaires 758
chargeable *debt* 806
– on *duty* 926
charger
carrier 271
fighter 726
Charing Cross, proclaim at – 531
chariot 272
drag at one's – wheels 749
charioteer 268, 694
charity *give* 784
liberal 816
beneficent 906
pity 914
Christian – 906
cold as – 823
– that begins at home 943
charivari 404, 407
charlatan
ignoramus 493
impostor 548
mountebank 844
boaster 884
charlatanism
ignorance 491
falsehood 544
affectation 855
Charles's wain 318
Charleston 840
Charley 753
charm *motive* 615
please 829
beauty 845
love 897
conjure 992
spell 993
bear a –ed life 644, 734
charmer 994
voice of the – 933
not listen to voice of – 604
charnel-house 363
Charon 982
chart 527, 554
charter
commission 755
permit 760
compact 769
security 771
privilege 924
chartered
legal 963
– *accountant* 801, 811
– *libertine* 962
Chartist 742
charwoman 690, 746
chary
economical 817
stingy 819
cautious 864

Charybdis 312, 665
chase *emboss* 250
furrow 259
drive away 289
killing 361
forest 367
pursue 622
ornament 847
wild goose – 645
chaser 559
chasm *interval* 198
opening 260
chassé 840
chassemarée 273
chassepot 727
chasser 297
– *balancer* 605
chasseur 726
chassis 215
chaste
shapely 242
language 576, 578
simple 849
good taste 850
pure 960
chasten
moderate 174
punish 972
chastened
subdued spirit 826
penitent 950
chastise 932, 972
– with scorpions 739
chasuble 999
chat 588
chat qui dort 667, 668
château 189
– en Espagne 858
chatelaine 847
chatoyant 440
chattels 633, 789
chatter 314, 584
chatterbox 584
chattering of teeth *cold* 383
chatty 584, 892
chauffeur 268
chaunt
song 415
sing 416
worship 990
chaussé 225
Chauvinism 884, 885
chawbacon 876
cheap 643, 815
hold – 930
– jack 797
cheapen *haggle* 794
begrudge 819
cheapness 815
cheat 545, 548
check
numerical 85
stop 142
moderate 174
counteract 179
slacken 275
plaid 440
experiment 463
measure 466
evidence 468
ticket 550
dissuade 616
hinder 706

misfortune 735
restrain 751
money order 800
– the growth 201
– oneself 826
checkered 149
checkers 440, 840
checkmate
stop 142
success 731
failure 732
check-roll 86
check-string
pull the – 142
cheek *side* 236
impertinence 885
– by jowl *with* 88
near 197
cheeks *dual* 89
cheep 412
cheer *repast* 298
cry 411
aid 707
pleasure 827
relief 834
mirth 836
rejoicing 838
amusement 840
courage 861
sociality 892
welcome 894
applaud 931
good – *hope* 858
high living 957
cheerfulness 836
cheerless 830, 837
cheeseparings
remains 40
dirt 653
economy 817
chef de cuisine
proficient 700
servant 746
chef-d'oeuvre 648, 698
cheka 696
chemin
– de fer
game 840
– faisant 270
chemise 225
chemist 662
Chemistry 144
organic – 357
cheque 800
chequer 440
– roll 86
cherchez la femme 155
chère amie 962
cherish *aid* 707
love 897
endearment 902
– a belief 484
– feelings &c. 821
– an idea &c. 451
cherry
– red 434
two bites of a – *overrate* 482
roundabout 629
clumsy 699
cherry-cheeked 845
cherry-colored 434
cheroot 392
cherub 977
Cheshire cat 838

- of thought 498
compassion 914
  object of - 828
compatible
  consentaneous 23
  possible 470
compatriot
  inhabitant 188
  friend 890
compeer *equal* 27_
  friend 890
compel 744
compellation 564
compendency 43
compendious 201
compendium 596
  book 593
compensate
  make up for 30
  requite 973
compensation 30
compère 599
competence
  power 157
  sufficiency 639
  skill 698
  wealth 803
competition
  opposition 708
  contention 720
competitor
  opponent 710
  combatant 726
  candidate 767
compilation
  collect 72
  book 593
  compendium 596
compile 54
complacent
  pleased 827
  content 831
  courteous 894
  kind 906
complain 839
complainant 938
complaint
  illness 655
  murmur 839
  lodge a - 938
  - *without cause* 839
complaisant
  lenient 740
  courteous 894
  kind 906
complement
  adjunct 39
  remainder 40
  part 52
  arithmetic 84
complementary
  correlation 12
  colour 428
complete
  entire 52
  accomplish 729
  compact 769
  - *answer* 479
  - *circle* 311
  in a - *degree* 31
completeness 52
completion 729
complex 59
complexion
  state 7
  color 428
  appearance 448

compliance
  conformity 82
  obedience 743
  consent 762
  observance 772
complicate
  derange 61
complicated
  disorder 59
  convolution 248
complice 711
complicity 709
compliment
  courtesy 894, 896
  praise 931
  poor - 932
  -s *of season* 896
complimentary
  free 815
complot 626
comply [see compli-
  ance]
compo *coating* 223
  material 635
component 56
componere lites
  723, 724
comport
  oneself 692
  - *with* 23
compos mentis 502
compose
  make up 54, 56
  produce 161
  moderate 174
  music 416
  write 590
  printing 591
  pacify 723
  assuage 826
composed
  self-possessed 826
composer
  music 413
composite 41
composition 54
  [see compose]
  combination 48
  piece of music 415
  picture 556
  style 569
  writing 590
  building material 635
  compromise 774
  barter 794
  atonement 952
compositor
  printer 591
compost 653
composure 826, 871
compotation 959
compote 298
compound
  mix 41
  combination 48
  limited space 182
  enclosure 232
  compromise 774
  - *arithmetic* 466
  - *for substitute* 147
  barter 794
comprador 637
comprehend
  compose 54
  include 76
  know 490
  understand 518

comprehension [see
  comprehend]
  intelligence 498
comprehensive 76
  complete 50
  general 78
  wide 192
  - *argument* 476
compress
  contract 195
  curtail 201
  condense 321
  remedy 662
compressible 322
comprise 76
comprobation
  evidence 467
  demonstration 478
compromise
  dally with 605
  mid-course 628
  taint 659
  danger 665
  pacify 723
  compact 769
  compound 774
  atone 952
compromised
  promised 768
compter 799
compte rendu
  record 551
  accounts 811
comptroller 694
compulsion 744
compunction 833, 950
compurgation
  evidence 467
  acquittal 970
compute 85
comrade 890
comradeship 892
con *think* 451
  get by heart 505
  learn 539
conation 600
conatu magnas
  nugas, magno -
  waste 638
  unimportance 643
conatus 176
concamerate 245
concatenation
  junction 43
  continuity 69
concavity 252
conceal
  invisible 447
  hide 528
  cunning 702
concealment 528, 893
concede
  assent 488
  admit 529
  permit 760
  consent 762
  give 784
conceit *idea* 453
  folly 499
  supposition 514
  imagination 515
  wit 842
  affectation 855
  vanity 880
conceited
  dogmatic 481

conceivable 470
conceive *begin* 66
  beget 161
  teem 168
  believe 484
  understand 490
  imagine 515
  plan 626
concent 413
concentrate
  assemble 72
  centrality 222
  converge 290
concentric 216, 222
conception
  [see conceive]
  intellect 450
  idea 453
concern
  relation 9
  event 151
  business 625
  importance 642
  firm 797
  grief 828
  - *oneself with* 625
concert
  agreement 23
  synchronism 120
  music 415
  act in - 709
  in - *musical* 413
  concord 714
  - *measures* 626
concertina 417
concerto 415
concert-room 840
concession
  permission 760
  consent 762
  compromise 774
  giving 784
  discount 813
concesso, ex -
  reasoning 476
  assent 488
concetto 842
conchoid 245
conchology 223
concierge 163, 753
conciliate
  talk over 615
  pacify 723
  satisfy 831
  courtesy 894
  atonement 952
conciliatory [see
  conciliate]
  concord 714
  forgiving 918
conciliatrix 962
concinnity
  agreement 23
  style 578
  beauty 845
conciseness 572
concision 201
conclave
  assembly 72
  council 696
  church 995
conclude
  end 67
  infer 480
  resolve 604
  complete 729
  compact 769
conclusion

[see conclude]
  sequel 65
  germination 161
  judgment 480
  try -s 476
  forgone - 611
  hasty - 481
conclusive
  [see conclude]
  answer 462
  evidence 467
  certain 474
  proof 478
  - *reasoning* 476
concoct *lie* 544
  write 590
  plan 626
  prepare 673
concomitant
  accompany 88
  same time 120
  concurrent 178
concord *agree* 23
  music 413
  assent 488
  harmony 714
concordance 562
  book 593
concordant 173
concordat 769
concordia discors
  24, 59
concours 720
concourse
  assemblage 72
  convergence 290
concremation 384
concrete *existent* 3
  mass 46
  definite 79
  density 321
  hardness 323
  materials 635
concubinage 961
concubine 926
concupiscence 865, 961
concur
  co-exist 120
  causation 178
  converge 290
  assent 488
  concert 709
concurrence 178, 216
concussion 276
condemnation 932, 971
condemned cell 752
condense
  compress 195
  dense 321
condensed
  concise 572
condescend 879
condign 924
condiment 393
condisciple 541
condition *state* 7
  modification 469
  supposition 514
  term 770
  repute 573
  rank 875
  in - *plump* 192
  in good - 648
  on - 770
  in perfect - 650

idea 453
attention 457
qualification 469
inducement 615
importance 642
gift 784
benevolence 906
respect 928
requital 973
deserve – 642
in – *of*
compensation 30
reasoning 476
on – 658
take into –
thought 451
attention 457
under –
topic 454
inquiry 461
plan 626
considered, all
things –
collectively 50
judgment 480
premeditation 611
imperfection 651
consign
transfer 270
commission 755
property 783
give 784
– to the flames 384
– to oblivion 506
– to the tomb 363
consignee 758
consignor 790
consignment
commission 755
gift 784
apportionment 786
consilience 178
consist
– in 1
– of 54
consistence
density 321
consistency
uniformity 16
agreement 23
consistently with 82
consistory
council 696
church 995
consolation
relief 834
condole 915
religious 976
console
table 215
Consoler
the – 976
consolidate
unite 46, 48
condense 321
consols 802
consommé 298
consonant
agreeing 23
musical 413
letter 561
consort
accompany 88
associate 892
spouse 903
– with 23

consortium 23
consortship 892
conspection 441
conspectus 596
conspicuous
visible 446
famous 873
conspiracy 626
conspirator 626
traitor 941
conspire
concur 178
co-operate 709
constable
policeman 664
governor 745
officer 965
constant
fixed 5
uniform 16
continuous 69
regular 80
continual 112
frequent 136
regular 138
immutable 150
exact 494
persevering 604a
obey 743
faithful 939
– *flow* 69
constellation
stars 318
luminary 423
glory 873
consternation 860
constipation
closure 261
density 321
constituency 181, 737
constituent 51, 56
constitute
compose 54, 56
produce 161
constitution
nature 5
state 7
composition 54
structure 329
charter 924
law 963
constitutional
walk 226
– government 737
constrain
compel 744
restrain 751
abash 881
constraint 195
constrict 195, 706
constringe 195
construct 161
construction 161
form 240
structure 329
meaning 522
put a false – upon 523
constructive
latent 526
– *evidence* 467
constructor 164
construe 522
consubstantiation 998
consuetude 618
consul 758, 759

consulship 737
consult 695
– one's pillow 133
– one's own wishes 943
– the wishes of 707
consultant 662
consultation 695, 696
consume
destroy 162
waste 638
use 677
– away 36
– time
time 106
inactivity 683
consumere natus, fruges – 683
consuming 830
consummate
great 31
complete 52
completed 729
– *skill* 698
consummation
end 67
completion 729
– devoutly to be wished
good 618
desire 865
consumption [*see consume*]
decrease 36
shrinking 195
disease 655
contact 199
come in –
arrive 292
contagion
transfer 270
disease 655
unhealthy 657
contain
be composed of 54
include 76
container 191
contaminate
soil 653
spoil 659
contaminated
diseased 655
contango 133, 813
contemn 930
contemper 174
contemplate
view 441
think 451
expect 507
purpose 620
contemporary 120
contemporation 174
contempt 930
– of danger 861
contemptible
unimportant 643
dishonorable 940
contend
reason 476
assert 535
fight 720
– with difficulties 704
– for
vindicate 937
content
assenting 488

willing 602
calm 826
satisfied **831**
to one's heart's –
sufficient 639
success 731
contention 720
contentious 901
contents
ingredients 56
list 86
components **190**
synopsis 596
conterminate
end 67
limit 233
conterminous 199
contesseration 72
contest 709, 720
contestant 710
context 591
from the – 516
contexture 329
contiguity 199
continence 960
continent
land 342
continental 643
contingency
event 151
uncertainty 475
expectation 507
contingent
conditional 8
casual 156
liable 177
possible 470
uncertain 475
supply 635
aid 707
allotted 786
donation 809
unforeseen 508
– duration **108a**
– interest 780
continual
perpetual 112
frequent 136
continuance 143
continuation
adjunct 39
sequence 63
sequel 65
– school 542
continue
endure 106, 110
persist 143
continued 69
– success 731
continuity 69
uniformity 16
contortion
distortion 243
convolution 248
contortionist 599, 700
contour
outline 230
appearance 448
contra 14
per – 708
– bonos mores
vulgar 851
improper 925
vice 945
contraband
deceitful 545
prohibited 761

illicit 964
contrabasso 417
contraception 706
contract
shrink 195
narrow 203
– *promise* 768
bargain 769
bridge 840
– a debt 806
– a habit 613
– an obligation 768
contractility 195
contraction 195
short-hand 590
compendium 596
contractor 690
contradict
contrary 14
answer 462
dissent 489
deny 536
oppose 708
contradictory
disagreement 24
evidence 468
discord 713
contradistinction 15
contraindicate
dissuade 616
warning 668
contraire, tout au – 536
contralto 408, 416
contraposition
inversion 218
reversion **237**
contrapuntist 413
contrariety 14
contrary
opposite 14
antagonistic 179
captious 608
opposing 708
quite the – 536
– to expectation
improbable 473
unexpected 508
– to reason 471
contrast
contrariety 14
difference 15
comparison 464
contravallation 717
contravene
contrary 14
counterevidence 468
deny 536
hinder 706
oppose 708
contre coeur, à – 603
contre-coup 277
contretemps
ill-timed 135
hindrance 706
misfortune 735
contribute
cause 153
tend 176
concus 178
aid 707
give 784
contribution 784
lay under – 789, 924

insignia 747
title 877
corporal
  corporeal 316
  officer 745
corporate 43
  – body 712
corporation
  bulk 192
  convex 250
  association 712
  jurisdiction 965
corporeal 3, 316, 364
  – hereditaments 780
corporeity 316
corps *assemblage* 72
  troops 726
  à – perdu
  haste 684
  rash 863
  – de reserve 636
corpse 362
corpulence 192
corpus 316
  – Christi 998
  – delicti
  guilt 947
  lawsuit 969
  – juris
  precept 697
  law 963
corpuscle
  small 32
  little 193
corradiation
  focus 74
  convergence 290
corral 232, 370
correct
  orderly 58
  true 494
  inform 527
  disclose 529
  improve 658
  repair 660
  due 924
  censure 932
  honorable 939
  virtuous 944
  punish 972
  – ear 416, 418
  – memory 505
  – reasoning 476
  – style
  grammatical 567
  elegant 578
correction
  [see correct]
  house of – 752
  under – 879
corrective 662
corregidor 745
correlation
  relation 9
  reciprocity 12
correspondence
  correlation 12
  similarity 17
  agreement 23
  writing 592
  – course 537
correspondent
  messenger 534
  journalist 593
  consignee 758
corresponding

similar 17
agreeing 23
corridor *region* 181
  place 191
  passage 627
  – train 272
corrigendum 495
corrigible 658
corrival 726
corrivalry 720
corrivation 348
corroborant 662
corroboration
  evidence 467
  assent 488
corrode *burn* 384
  erode 659
  afflict 830
corrosive
  [see corrode]
  acrid 171
  destructive 649
  – sublimate 663
corrugate
  derange 61
  constrict 195
  roughen 256
  rumple 258
  furrow 259
corruption
  decomposition 49
  neology 563
  foulness 653
  disease 655
  deterioration 659
  improbity 940
  vice 945
corrupting
  noxious 649
corsage 225
corsair 273, 792
corse 362
corselet 225
corset 225
corso 728
cortège
  adjunct 39
  continuity 69
  accompaniment 88
  journey 266
  suite 746
cortes 696
cortex
  cortical 223
coruscate 420
corvette 273, 726
corybantic 503
coryphée 599
Corypheus
  teacher 540
  director 694
coscinomancy 511
cosey 892
cosignificative 522
cosine 217
cosmetic
  remedy 662
  ornament 847
cosmic 318
cosmogony &c. 318
cosmopolitan
  abode 189
  mankind 372
  philanthropic 910
  sociality 892
cosmorama 448
cosmos 60, 318

Cossack 726
cosset
  darling 899
  caress 902
cost 812
  pay –s 807
  to one's –
  evil 619
  badness 649
  – what it may 604
  – price 815
costermonger 797
costless 815
costly 814
costive
  taciturn 585
costume 225
  theatrical – 599
costumé 225
  bal – 840
costumier 225
  theatrical 599
cosy *snug* 377
  sociable 892
cot *abode* 189
  bed 215
cote 189
cotenancy 778
coterie *class* 75
  junto 712
  society 892
coterminous 120
cothurnus 599
cotillon 840
cottage 189
  – piano 417
cottager 188
cotter 188
cotton 205
  – seed oil 356
couch *lie* 213
  bed 215
  stoop 308
  lurk 528
  – one's lance 720
  – in terms 566
couchant 213
couci-couci 651
cough 349
  churchyard – 655
couleur de rose
  good 648
  prosperity 734
  view en – 836
coulisses 599
coulter 253
council
  senate 696
  church 995
  hold a – 695
  – of education 542
  – school 542
councillor 696
counsel
  advice 695
  lawyer 968
  keep one's own – 528
  take – *think* 451
  inquire 461
  be advised 695
count *clause* 51
  item 79
  compute 85
  estimate 480
  lord 875
  – one's chickens before they are

hatched 858, 863
  – the cost 864
  – upon
  believe 484
  expect 507
  to be –ed on one's fingers 103
countenance
  face 234
  appearance 448
  favor 707
  approve 931
  keep in –
  conform 82
  induce 615
  encourage 861
  vindicate 937
  keep one's –
  brook 826
  not laugh 837
  out of –
  abashed 879
  put out of – 874
  stare out of – 885
  – falling
  disappointment 509
  dejection 837
counter *contrary* 14
  number 84
  table 215
  stern 235
  token 550
  shop-board 799
  over the –
  barter 794
  buy 795
  sell 796
  run – 179
  – to 708
counteract
  compensate 30
  physically 179
  hinder 706
  voluntarily 708
counteraction 14, 179
counterbalance 30
counterblast
  counteract 179
  retaliate 718
countercharge 462
counterchange
  correlation 12
  interchange 148
countercharm 993
countercheck
  mark 550
  hindrance 706
counterclaim 30
counter-evidence 468
counterfeit
  imitate 19
  copy 21
  simulate 544
  sham 545
  coinage 792
counterfoil 550
countermand 756
countermarch 266, 283
countermark 550
countermine
  plan 626
  oppose 708
countermotion 283

counterorder 756
counterpane 223
counterpart
  match 17
  copy 21
  reverse 237
counterplot
  plan 626
  oppose 708
  retaliate 718
counterpoint 415
counterpoise
  compensate 30
  weight 319
  hinder 706
counter-poison 662
counterpole 14
counter-project 718
counter-protest 468
counter-revolution 146
counterscarp 717
countersign
  evidence 467
  assent 488
  mark 550
counterstroke 718
countervail
  outweigh 28
  compensate 30
  evidence 468
counterwork 708
countess 875
counting-house 799
countless 105
countrified 189
  vulgar 851
country
  region 181
  abode 189
  rural 371
  authority 737
  love of – 910
country-dance 840
countryman
  commonalty 876
  friend 890
county 181
  – seat 189
  – town 189
  – school 542
  – council 696
  – court 966
coup
  instantaneous 113
  action 680
  – de bec
  attack 716
  censure 932
  – d'épée dans l'eau 645
  – d'essai 675
  – d'état
  revolution 146
  plan 626
  action 680
  lawless 964
  – de grâce
  end 67
  death-blow 361
  completion 729
  punishment 972
  – de main
  violence 173
  action 680
  attack 716
  – de maître
  excellent 648

642
best 648
– color
white 430
yellow 436
– of the jest 842
creamy 352
crease 258
create *cause* 153
produce 161
imagine 515
created being 366
creation
[*see* create]
effect 154
world 318
Creator 976
creator 164
creature *thing* 3
effect 154
animal 366
man 372
parasite 711
slave 746
– comforts
food 298
pleasure 377
crèche 542
credat Judaeus
Apella
unbelief 485
absurdity 497
credence *belief* 484
church 1000
credenda 484
credential 467
credible
possible 470
probable 472
belief 484
credit *belief* 484
influence 737
pecuniary 805
account 811
repute 873
approbation 931
desert 944
to one's –
property 780
crédit mobilier 802
creditable *right* 924
creditor 805
credo quia
impossibile 486
credulity 486
credulous person
dupe 547
creed *belief* 484
theology 983
Apostles' – 983a
creek *interval* 198
water 343
creel 191
creep *crawl* 275
tingle 380
(*inactivity* 683)
– in 294
– into a corner 893
– into the good
graces of 933
– out 529
– upon one 508
– with
multitude 102
redundance 641
creeper 367
creeping
sensation 380

– thing 366
creese 727
cremation
of corpses 363
burning 384
crematorium 363,
386
crematory 386
crème de la crème
648
Cremona 417
crenate 257
crenele 257
crenulate 257
creole 57
crêpé 248, 839
crepidam, ultra –
471
crepitation 406
crepuscule
dawn 125
. *dusk* 422
crescendo
increase 35
musical 415
crescent
growing 35
street 189
curve 245
cresset 423, 550
crest *supremacy* 33
summit 210
pointed 253
tuft 256
sign 550
armorial 877
pride 878
on the 33
crest-fallen
dejected 837
humble 879
crevasse 198, 667
crevice 198
crew *assemblage* 72
inhabitants 188
mariners 269
party 712
crib *bed* 215
key 522
granary 636
steal 791
parsimony 819
cribbage 840
cribbed, confined,
cabined – 751
cribble 260
cribriform 260
Crichton,
Admirable –
scholar 492
perfect 650
proficient 700
crick *pain* 378
cricket *game* 840
not – 940
– ground 213
crier 534
send round the –
531
crim. con. 961
crime 945, 947
criminal 923, 945
culprit 949
– law 963
court of – appeal
966
criminality 947
criminate 938

crimp *crinkle* 248
notch 257
brittle 328
deceiver 548
take 789
steal 791
crimple 258
crimson 434, 821
cringe *submit* 725
subject 749
servility 886
crinite 256
crinkle *angle* 244
convolution 248
roughen 256
fold 258
crinoline 225
cripple *disable* 158
weaken 160
injure 659
crippled
disease 655
crisis
conjuncture 8
present time 118
opportunity 134
event 151
strait 704
excitement 824
bring to a – 604
come to a – 729
crisp *rumpled* 248
rough 256
brittle 328
style 572
Crispin 225
criss-cross 219
oristallomantia 511
criterion *test* 463
evidence 467
indication 550
crithomancy 511
critic *judge* 480
taste 850
detractor 936
critical
contingent 8
opportune 134
discriminating
465
important 642
dangerous 665
difficult 704
censorious 932
criticism
judgment 480
dissertation 595
disapprobation
932
detraction 934
critique
[*see* criticism]
croak *cry* 412
hoarseness 581
stammer 583
warning 668
discontent 832
lament 839
croaker 832, 837
Croat 726
crochet 847
crock 191
crockery 384
crocodile tears 544
crocus *yellow* 436
Croesus 803
croft 189, 232
Croix de Guerre 733

cromlech 363, 551
crone *veteran* 130
fool 501
crony *friend* 890
favourite 899
crook *curve* 245
deviation 279
thief 792
crooked
sloping 217
distorted 243
angular 244
latent 526
crafty 702
ugly 846
dishonorable 940
– *path* 704
– temper 901
– ways 279
croon 580
crop
stomach 191
harvest 154
shorten 201
eat 298
vegetable 367
store 636
gather 775
take 789
second – 167, 775
– out *visible* 446
disclose 529
– up *begin* 66
take place 151
reproduction 163
cropper *fall* 306
croquet *game* 840
ground *level* 213
croquette 298
crosier 747, 999
cross *mix* 41
across 219
pass 302
grave 363
oppose 708
failure 732
disaster 735
refuse 764
pain 830
decoration 877
fretful 901
punishment 975
rites 998
fiery – 722
proclaim at the –
roads 531
red – 662
–ed bayonets 708
– breed 63
– cut 628
– fire *interchange*
148
difficulty 704
opposition 708
attack 716
–ed in love 898
– the mind 451
– the path of 706
– and pile 621
– purposes 14
disorder 59
error 495
misinterpret 523
unskilful 699
difficulty 704
opposition 708
discord 713
– oneself 998

– questions
inquiry 461
discord 713
– road 627
– the Rubicon 609
– sea 348
– swords 722
crossbow 727
cross-examine 461
cross-grained 256
obstinate 606
sulky 901a
crossing 219
– sweeper 652
crosspatch 895
crossroads 8
cross-word puzzle
533
crotch 244
crotchet
eccentric 83
music 413
misjudgment 481
obstinacy 606
caprice 608
crouch *lower* 207
stoop 308
fear 860
servile 886
– before 725
croup 235
croupier 694
crow *cry* 412
black 431
rejoice 838
boast 884
pluck a – with 932
as the – flies 278
–'s foot (*age*) 128
–'s nest 210
– to pluck
discord 713
anger 900
accuse 938
crowbar 633
crowd 72
multitude 102
close 197
redundance 641
party 712
vulgar 876
in the – *mixed* 41
madding – 682
crown *top* 210
circle 247
complete 729
trophy 733
scepter 747
install 755
decoration 877
reward 973
to – all 33, 642
–ed head 745
– with laurel 873
– with success 731
crowning
[*see* crown]
superior 33
end 67
– point 210
cruche à l'eau &c.
tant va la – 735
crucial
crossing 219
proof 478
– test 463
cruciate

physical *pain* 378
mental *pain* 830
crucible
 dish 191
 conversion 144
 furnace 386
 experiment 463
 laboratory 691
 put into the – 163
crucifix 219, 998
crucifixion 828
cruciform 219
crucify
 physical torture
  378
 mental agony 830
 execution 972
crucis, experimen-
 tum – 463
crude *color* 428
 - *style* 579
 unprepared 674
cruel
 painful 830
 inhuman 907
 – to be kind 914
cruelly *much* 31
cruet 191
cruise
 vessel 191
 navigation 267
cruiser 726
cruising 267
crumb *small* 32
 powder 330
 – of comfort 834
crumble
 decrease 36
 weak 160
 destruction 162
 brittle 328
 pulverize 330
 spoil 659
 – into dust
 decompose 49
 – under one's feet
  735
crumbling
 [*see* crumble]
 dangerous 665
crumenal 800
crump
 distorted 243
 curved 245
crumple
 ruffle 256
 fold 258
 – up *destroy* 162
 crush 195
crunch
 shatter 44
 chew 298
 pulverize 330
crupper 235
crusade 722 ·
crush *crowd* 72
 destroy 162
 compress 195
 pulverize 330
 humble 879
 – under an iron
  heel 739
 – one's hopes
 disappoint 509
 hopeless 859
crushed 828
crushing 830
crust 223

crustacean 366
crusty 895, 901*a*
crutch
 support 215
 angle 244
 –ed *Friars* 996
crux 219, 704
 – *criticorum* 533
cry *human* 411
 animal 41?
 publish 531, 532
 call 550
 voice 580
 vogue 613
 weep 839
 far – to 196
 full – *loud* 404
 raise a – 550
 – *aloud*
 implore 765
 – *out against*
 dissuade 616
 censure 932
 – *down* 932, 934
 – *for* 865
 – *before hurt* 839
 – *for joy* 838
 – *you mercy*
 deprecate 766
 pity 914
 forgive 918
 – *shame* 932
 – *to beseech* 765
 – *up* 931
 – *for vengeance*
  923
 – *wolf false* 544
 alarm 669
 – *and little wool*
 overrate 482
 boast 884
 disappoint 509
crying [*see* cry]
 urgent 630
 weary 841
 – *evil* 619
 – *shame* 874
 – *sin* 945
crypt *cell* 191
 grave 363
 ambush 530
 altar 1000
cryptic 475, 528
cryptography
 hidden 528
 writing 590
crystal *hard* 323
 transparent 425
 snow – 383
 – *gazer* 513
 – *gazing* 511, 992
 – *oil* 356
 clear *as* – 519
crystalline
 dense 321
 hard 323
 transparent 425
crystallization 321,
 323
csako 225, 717
cub *young* 129
 vulgar 851
 clown 876
 unlicked – 241
cubby-hole 191
cube
 three dimensions
  92, 93

form 244
cubicle 191
cubist 556
cubit 200
cucking stool 975
cuckold 905
cuckoldom 961
cuckoo
 imitation 19
 repetition 104
 sound 407
 cry 412
cuddle 196, 902
cudgel *beat* 276
 weapon 727
 punish 975
 take up the –s
 aid 707 ·
 attack 716
 contention 720
 – one's *brains*
 think 451
 imagine 515
cue *hint* 527
 watchword 550
 plea 617
 rôle 625
 take one's – *from*
  695
 in proper – 698
cuff *sleeve* 225
 blow 276
 punishment 972
cui bono 644, 645
cuique voluptas
 sui – 865
cuirass 717
cuirassier 726
cuisine 298
 batterie de – 957
culbute
 inversion 218
 fall 306
cul-de-lampe
 engraving 558
 ornament 847
cul-de-sac
 concave 252
 closed 261
 difficulty 704
culinary 298
 – *art* 673
cull *dupe* 547
 choose 609
 take 789
cullender 260
cullibility 486
cullion 949
cully *deceive* 545,
 547
culm 388
culminate
 maximum 33
 height 206
 top 210
 complete 729
culpability *vice* 945
 guilt 947
culprit 949
cult 983
cultivate *till* 365,
 371
 sharpen 375
 improve 658
 prepare 673
 aid 707
cultivated
 courteous 894

– *taste* 850
cultivator 371
culture
 knowledge 490
 improvement 658
 taste 850
 politeness 894
culverin 727
culvert 350
cum multis aliis 37,
 102
cumber *load* 319
 obstruct 706
cumbersome
 incommodious
  647
 disagreeable 830
cummerbund 225
cumulative 72
 increasing 35
 assembled 72
 – *evidence* 467
 – *vote* 609
cumulus 353
cunctando restituit
 rem 681
cunctation 133
 – *character* 590
cunning
 prepense 611 ·
 sagacious 698
 artful 702
 – *fellow* 700
 – *man* 994
cup *vessel* 191
 hollow 252
 beverage 298
 remedy 662
 trophy 733
 tipple 959
 between – and lip
  111
 in one's –s 959
 – that *cheers* &c.
  298
 – of *humiliation*
  879
 dash the – *from*
  one's *lips* 509
 – *too low* 837
cupbearer 746
cupboard 191
cupellation 384
Cupid *beauty* 845
 love 897
 gods 979
cupidity
 avarice 819
 desire 865
cupola *height* 206
 roof 223
 dome 250
cup-tossing 621
cur *dog* 366
 coward 862
 sneak 949
curable 658, 660,
 662
curacy 995
curare 663
curate 996
curative 660
curator 464, 758
curb *moderate* 174
 slacken 275
 dissuade 616
 restrain 751

shackle 752
curb exchange 621
curbstone 233
curd *density* 321
 pulp 354
 (*cohere* 46)
curdle *condense* 321
 (*cohere* 46)
 make the *blood* –
  830
curdled 352
cure *reinstate* 660
 remedy 662
 preserve 670
 benefice 995
curé 996
cureless 859
curfew 126
curia 966
curio 847
curiosa felicitas 698
curiosity
 unconformity 83
 inquiring **455**
 phenomenon 872
curious
 exceptional 83
 inquisitive 455
 true 494
 beautiful 845
 desirous 865
curiously *very* 31
curl *bend* 245
 convolution 248
 hair 256
 cockle up 258
 badge 747
 – up one's *lip* 930
curling *game* 840
curmudgeon
 miser 819
 plebeian 876
currency
 publicity 531
 money 800
current *existing* 1
 usual 78
 present 118
 happening 151
 flow 264
 of water 348
 of air 349
 rife 531, 532
 language 560
 habit 613
 danger 667
 account – 811
 against the – 708
 go with the – 82
 pass –
 believed 484
 fashion 852
 stem the – 708
 – *belief* 488
 – of *events* 151
 – of *ideas* 451
 – of *time* 109
currente calamo
 590
curricle 272
curriculum 537
curry *food* 298
 rub 331
 condiment 392,
  393
 – *favour with*
 love 897
 flatter 933

curry-comb 370
curse *bane* 663
  adversity 735
  painful 830
  malediction 908
cursed *bad* 649
cursitor 968
cursive 590
cursory
  transient 111
  inattentive 458
  hasty 684
  take a — view of
    457
  neglect 460
curst 901a
curt *short* 201
  concise 572
  taciturn 585
curtail *retrench* 38
  shorten 201
  —ed of its fair pro-
    portions
  distorted 243
  ugly 846
curtain 223
  shade 424
  hide 528, 530
  theatre 599
  fortification 717
  behind the —
  invisible 447
  inquiry 461
  knowledge 490
  close the — 528
  raise the — 529
  rising of the — 448
  — lecture 932
  — raiser 66, 599
curtsy
  stoop 308, 314
  submit 725
  polite 894
curule 696
curvature 245
curvet *leap* 309
  turn 311
  oscillate 314
  agitate 315
curvilinear 245
  — motion 311
cushion *pillow* 215
  soft 324
  relief 834
cushy 829
cusp *angle* 244
  sharp 253
cuspidor 191
cuss 908
custard 298
custodes? quis cus-
  todiet — 459
custodian 753
custody *safe* 664
  captive 751
  retention 781
  in — *prisoner* 754
  accused 938
  take into — 751
custom *old* 124
  habit 613
  barter 794
  sale 796
  tax 812
  fashion 852
  — honored in
    breach 614
customary

[*see custom*]
  regular 80
customer 795
custom-house 799
  — officer 965
custos 753
  — *rotulorum* 553
cut *divide* 44
  bit 51
  discontinuity 70
  interval 198
  curtail 201
  layer 204
  form 240
  notch 257
  blow 276
  eject 297
  reap 371
  physical pain 378
  cold 385
  neglect 460
  carve 557
  engraving 558
  road 627
  attack 716
  portion 786
  affect 824
  mental pain 830
  dance step 840
  *decline acquaint-
    ance* 893
  discourtesy 895
  tipsy 959
  — *short* 528
  unkindest — of all
    pain 828
  malevolence 907
  — across 302
  — adrift 44
  — along 274
  have a — at 716
  — away 274
  — a whetstone with
    a razor
    sophistry 477
    waste 638
    misuse 679
  — both ways 468
  — capers 309
  — according to
    cloth
    economy 817
    caution 864
  — and come again
    repeat 104
    enough 639
  — dead 893
  — direct 893
  — down *destroy* 162
    shorten 201
    fell 308
    kill 361
  — down expenses
    817
  — and dried
    arranged 60
    prepared 673
  — a figure
    appearance 448
    fashion 852
    repute 873
    display 882
  — the first turf 66
  — the ground from
    under one
    confute 479
    hinder 706
  — to the heart 824,

830
  — ice with
    influence 175
  — of one's jib 448
  — jokes 842
  — the knot 705
  — off *subduct* 38
    disjoin 44
    kill 361
    impede 706
    bereft 776
    secluded 893
  — off with a shil-
    ling 789
  — open 260
  — out *surpass* 33
    stop 142
    substitute 147
    plan 626
  — out for 698
  — out work
    prepare 673
    direct 693
  — to pieces
    destroy 162
    kill 361
  — a poor figure 874
  — to the quick 830
  — up root and
    branch 162
  — up rough 900
  — and run 274
  depart 293
  escape 623
  — short *stop* 142
  destroy 162
  shorten 201
  silence 581
  — one's stick
  depart 283
  avoid 623
  — one's own throat
    699
  — and thrust 716
  — in two 91
  — up *divide* 44
  destroy 162
  pained 828
  give pain 830
  discontented 832
  dejected 837
  censure 932
  what one will — up
    for 780
  — one's way
    through 302
cutaneous 223
cute 698
cuticle 223
cutlass 727
cutlery 253
cut-purse 792
cutter 273
cut-throat
  killer 361
  evil-doer 913
cutting *sharp* 253
  cold 383
  path 627
  affecting 821
  painful 830
  reproachful 932
cuttings
  excerpta 596
  selections 609
cutty stool 950
cwt. 98, 319
cyanogen 438

cyanide of potas-
  sium *poison* 663
cycle *time* 106
  period 138
  circle 247
  ride 266
  vehicle 272
  — car 272
cyclist 268
cycloid 247
cyclometer 200
cyclone
  rotation 312
  wind 349
Cyclopean
  ' *strong* 159
  huge 192
cyclopedia
  knowledge 490
  book 593
Cyclops
  monster 83
  mighty 159
  huge 192
  dupe 547
cygne
  chant du — 360
  — noir 650
cylindric 249
cyma 847
cymbal 417
cymbalo 417
cymophanous 440
cynic
  misanthrope 911
  detractor 936
  ascetic 955
  closet — 893
cynical
  contemptuous 930
  censorious 932
  detracting 934
cynicism
  discourtesy 895
  contempt 930
cynosure *sign* 550
  direction 693
  wonder 870
  repute 873
Cynthia of the
  minute 149
cypher [*see cipher*]
cypress
  interment 363
  mourning 839
Cyprian 962
cyst 191
czar 745

D

da capo 104
dab *small* 32
  paint 223
  slap 276
  clever 700
dabble *water* 337
  dirty 653
  meddle 682
  fribble 683
dabbled *wet* 339
dabbler 493
dachshund 366
dacoit 792
dactyl 597
dactylogram 467
dactyliomancy 511

dactylonomy
  numeration 85
  symbol 550
dad 166
daddy 166
dado 211
daedal
  variegated 440
daedalion
  convoluted 248
  artistic 698
daft 503
dagger 727
  look —s *anger* 900
  threat 909
  air drawn — 515
  plant — in breast
    give pain 830
  speak —s 932
  at —s drawn
    opposed 708
  discord 713
  enmity 889
  hate 898
daggle *hang* 214
  dirty 653
dagobah 1000
Dagon 986
daguerreotype
  represent 554
  paint 556
dahabeah 273
Dail Eireann 696
daily
  frequent 136
  periodic 138
  — occurrence
  normal 82
  habitual 613
  — paper 531
dainty *food* 298
  savory 394
  pleasing 829
  delicate 845
  tasty 850
  fastidious 868
dairy 191, 370
  — maid 946
dais *support* 215
  throne 747
daisy
  fresh as a — 654
  — pied 847
dale 252
dally *delay* 133
  irresolute 605
  inactive 683
  amuse 840
  fondle 902
dalmatic 999
Daltonism 443
dam *parent* 166
  close 261
  pond 343
  obstruct 706
damage *evil* 619
  injure, spoil 659
  price 812
damages 974
damascene 440
damask 434
dame
  woman 374
  teacher 540
  lady 875
damn
  malediction 908
  condemn 971

unnerve 158
spoil 659
vicious 945
Demosthenes 582
demotic 590
demulcent
  mild 174
  soothing 662
demur
  disbelieve 485
  dissent 489
  unwilling 603
  hesitate 605
  without – 602
demure
  grave 826
  sad 837
  affected 855
  modest 881
demurrage 132
demurrer 969
den *abode* 189
  study 191, 893
  sty 653
  prison 752
  – of thieves 791
denary 98
denaturalize
  corrupt 659
denaturalized
  abnormal 83
dendriform 242, 367
dendrology 369
denial
  negation 536
  refusal 764
  self – 953
denigrate 431
denization 748
denizen
  inhabitant 188
  freeman 748
  –s of the air 979
  –s of the day 366
Denmark, rotten in
  the state of –
  526
denomination
  class 75
  name 564
  sect 712
  religious – 983
denominational
  dissent 489
  theological 983
  – education 537
denominator 84
denote
  specify 79
  mean 516
  indicate 550
dénouement
  end 67
  result 154
  disclosure 529
  completion 729
denounce
  curse 908
  disapprove 932
  accuse 938
dense
  crowded 72
  ignorant 493
density 321
dent 252, 257
dental 561
denticulated 253,
  257

dentifrice 652
dentistry 662
denude 226
denuded *loss* 776
  – of
    insufficient 640
denunciation
  [*see* denounce]
deny *dissent* 489
  negative 556
  refuse 764
  – oneself
  avoid 623
  seclude 893
  temperate 953
  ascetic 990
Deo volente 470,
  976
deobstruct 705
deodand 974
deodorize 399
  clean 652
deontology 926
deoppilation 705
deorganization 61
deosculation 902
depart 293
  – from
  deviate 15, 279
  relinquish 624
  – this life 360
departed
  non-existent 2
department
  class 75
  region 181
  business 625
departure 293
  new – 66
  point of – 293
depend *hang* 214
  contingent 475
  – upon
  be the effect of 154
  evidence 467
  trust 484
  – on circumstan-
    ces 475
depended on, to
  be –
  certain 474
  reliable 484
  honorable 939
dependency 777,
  780
dependent
  effect 154
  liable 177
  hanging 214
  puppet 711
  servant 746
  subject 749
deperdition 776
dephlegmation 340
depict 554, 556
  describe 594
depilation 226
depilatory 662
depletion 638, 640
deplorable *bad* 649
  disastrous 735
  painful 830
deplore *regret* 833
  complain 839
  remorse 950
deploy 194
depone 535
deponent 467

depopulate
  eject 297
  desert 893
deportation
  removal 270
  emigration 297
  expulsion 972
deportment 692
depose
  evidence 467
  declare 535
  dethrone 738, 756
deposit *place* 184
  precipitate 321
  store 636
  security 771
  payment 809
depositary 801
deposition
  [*see* depose,
  deposit]
  record 551
depository 636
depôt *terminal* 292
  store 636
  shop 799
  – ship 726
deprave *spoil* 659
depraved *bad* 649
  vicious 945
deprecation 766
  pity 914
  disapprove 932
depreciation
  decrease 36
  underestimate 483
  discount 813
  cheap 815
  disrespect 929
  censure 932
  detraction 934
  accusation 938
depredation 791
depredator 792
deprehension 789
depression
  lowness 207
  depth 208
  concavity 252
  lowering 308
  dejection 837
  dulness 843
depressing
  painful 830
deprive *subduct* 38
  take 798
  – of life 361
  – of power 158
  – of property 789
  – of strength 160
deprived of 776
depth *physical* 208
  mental 498
  out of one's – 304
  310
  – bomb 727
  – of misery 828
  – of thought 451
  – of winter 383
depurate *clean* 652
  improve 658
depuratory 662
deputation 755
depute 755
deputies, chamber
  of – 696
deputy 759
dequantitate 36

derangement 61
  mental – 503
Derby-day 720
derelict *land* 342
  danger 667
  relinquish 782
  outcast 893
dereliction
  relinquishment
    624, 782
  guilt 947
  – of duty 927
deride
  ridicule 856
  disrespect 929
  contempt 930
derivation
  origin 153, 154,
    155
  verbal 562
derive
  attribute 155
  deduce 480
  acquire 775
  income 810
dermal 223
dermatology 223
dernier
  – cri 850
  – ressort 601
dérobée, à la – 528
derogate
  underrate 483
  disparage 934
  dishonor 940
  – from 874
derogatory
  shame 874
  dishonor 940
derrick 307, 633
derring-do 861
dervish 996
désagrément 830
descant *music* 415
  diffuseness 573
  loquacity 584
  dissert 595
descend *slope* 217
  go down 306
  – to particulars
  special 79
  describe 594
descendant 167
descension
  facilis Averni,
  facilis – 665
descent *lineage* 166
  fall 306
  inheritance 775
description
  kind 75
  name 564
  narration 594
descriptive music
  415
descry 441
desecrate
  misuse 679
  disrespect 929
  profane 988
desert
  unproductive 169
  empty 187
  plain 344
  run away 623
  relinquish 624,
    782
  merit 944
  waste sweetness

on *– air* 638
deserted
  outcast 893
deserter 144, 607,
  623
desertless 945
deserts 924
deserve
  be entitled to 924
  merit 944
  – notice 642
  – belief 484
désespoir, au –
  dejected 837
  hopeless 859
déshabillé, en –
  not dressed 226
  unprepared 674
  homely 849
desiccate 340
desiccator 340
desiderate *need* 630
  desire 865
desideratum
  inquiry 461
  requirement 630
  desire 865
design
  prototype 22
  form 240
  delineation 554
  painting 556
  intention 620
  plan 626
designate
  specify 79
  call 564
designation 75
designed
  aforethought 611
designer 164, 559
designing
  cunning 702
designless 621
désillusioner 529
desinence *end* 67
  discontinuance
    142
desipience 499
desipere in loco 840
desirable 646
desire 865
  will 600
  have no – for 866
desist
  discontinue 142
  relinquish 624
  inaction 681
desk *box* 191
  support 215
  school 542
  pulpit 1000
désobligeant 272
désoeuvré 681
desolate *alone* 87
  ravage 162
  afflicted 828
  dejected 837
  secluded 893
desolating
  painful 830
désorienté 475
despair *grief* 828,
  859
despatch *eject* 297
  kill 361
  news 532
  epistle 592

dolt 501
doltish 499
domain
  class 75
  region 181
  property 780
Domdaniel 982
dome *high* 206
  roof 223
  curvature 245
  convex 250
Domesday book
  list 86
  record 551
domesman 967
domestic
  inhabitant 188
  home 189
  interior 221
  servant 746
  secluded 893
  – *animals* 366
domesticate
  locate 184
  acclimatize 613
  – *animals* 370
domicile 189
domiciled 186
domiciliary 188
  – *visit* 461
dominant 175
  note in music 413
domination 737
dominical 998
domineer
  tyrannize 739
  insolence 885
Domini, anno – 106
Dominican 996
Dominie 540
dominion 181, 737
domino *dress* 225
  mask 530
  game 840
domn 745
don *put on* 225
  scholar 492
  teacher 540
  noble 875
Don Juan 897
donation 784
done *finished* 729
  work – 729
  – *for spoilt* 659
  failure 732
  – *up*
    impotent 158
    tired 688
  have – *with*
    cease 142
    relinquish 624
    disuse 678
donee 785
donjon 717, 752
donkey *ass* 271
  fool 501
  talk a –'*s hind leg
  off* 584
donna 374
Donnybrook Fair
  disorder 59
  discord 713
donor 784
donzel 746
doodle 501
doom *end* 67
  fate 152
  destruction 162

death 360
judgment 480
necessity 601
sentence 971
– *sealed*
death 360
adversity 735
doomed 735, 828
doomsday
  end 67
  future 121
  till – 112
door *entrance* 66
  cover 223
  brink 231
  barrier 232
  opening 260
  passage 627
  at one's – 197
  beg from door to –
    765
  bolt the – 666
  close the – *upon*
    751
  death's – 360
  keep within –*s* 265
  lie at one's – 926
  lock the – 666
  open a – *to*
    liable 177
  open the – *to*
    receive 296
    facilitate 705
    permit 760
  show the – *to*
    eject 297
    discourtesy 895
  – *mat* 652
doorkeeper 263
doorway 260
dope 376, 545, 663
doquet
  security 771
Dorado, El – 803
Doric mode 413
dormant
  inert 172
  latent 526
  asleep 683
dormer 260
dormeuse 272
dormir debout,
  conte à – 843
dormitive 841
dormitory 191
dormouse 683
dorp 189
dorsal 235
dorser 191
dorsum 235, 250
dory 273
dose *quantity* 25
  part 51
  medicine 662
  apportion 786
dosser 191
dossier *bundle* 72
  record 551
dossil 223, 263
dot *small* 32
  place 182
  little 193
  variegate 440
  mark 550
  dowry 780
  on the – 113
dotage 128, 499
dotard 130, 501

dotation 784
dottle 40, 645
dote *drivel* 499, 503
  – *upon* 897
douanier 965
double
  similar 17
  increase 35
  duplex 90
  substitute 147
  fold 258
  turn 283
  finesse 702
  march at the – 274
  see –
    dim sight 443
    drunk 959
  – *acrostic*
    letters 561
  – *dutch* 518
  – *entry* 811
  – *the fist* 909
  – *march* 684
  – *meaning* 520
  – *a point* 311
  in – *quick time*
    274
  – *reef topsails* 664
  – *sure* 474
  work – *tides* 686
  – *up*
    render powerless
    158
double bar 747
double-bass 417
doublecross 545
double-dealing
  lie 544
  cunning 940
double-distilled 171
double-dyed 428
double-eagle 800
double-edged 90,
  171
double entendre
  ambiguity 520
  impure 961
double-faced
  lie 544
  cunning 702, 940
double-headed 90
double-minded 605
double-shotted 171
doublet 225
double-tongued
  lie 544
  cunning 702, 940
doubt
  uncertain 475
  disbelieve **485**
  sceptic 989
doubtful 475
  more than – 473
  – *meaning*
    unintelligible 519
doubtless
  certain 474
  belief 484
  assent 488
douceur 784, 973
douche 337
dough 324, 354, 800
doughty 861
dour 739
douse
  immerse 310
  splash 337

blow 972
Dove
  Holy Ghost 976
dove
  innocent 946
  roar like sucking –
    174
dovecote 189
dovetail
  agree 23
  join 43
  intersect 219
  intervene 228
  angle 244
  insert 300
dowager 374, 905
dowdy 653, 851
dower 780, 803, 810
dowerless 804
down
  below 207
  light 320
  bear – *upon* 716
  bed of –
    pleasure 377
    repose 687
  come – 306
  get – 306
  go –
    sink 306
    calm 826
  keep – 36
  money – 807
  take –
    lower 308
    rebuff 874
    humble 879
  – *on one's mar-*
    row-bones 886
  – *in the mouth* 837
  – *and out* 874
  – *in price* 815
  go – *like a stone*
    310
  be – *upon*
    attack 716
    severe 739
downcast 306, 837
  – *eyes* 879
downfall
  destruction 162
  fall 306
  failure 732
  misfortune 735
downhill 217, 306
  go –
    adversity 735
downpour 348
downright
  absolute 31
  manifest 525
  sincere 703
downs 206, 344
down-trodden
  submission 725
  vanquished 732
  subject 749
  dejected 837
  disrepute 874
  contempt 930
downwards 306
downy
  smooth 255
  plumose 256
  soft 324
dowry 780, 784
dowse 276
dowser 994

doxology 990
doxy 897
doyer 128
doyley 652
doze 683
dozen 98
drab *color* 432
  slut 653
  hussy 962
drabble 653
drachm 319
Draco 694, 739
draff 653
draft [*see also*
  draught]
  multitude 102
  drawing 554, 556
  write 590
  abstract 596
  plan 626
  cheque 800
  credit 805
  – *off displace* 185
  transfer 270
draft-horse 271
drag *carriage* 272
  crawl 275
  traction 285
  impediment 706
  put on the – 275
  – *a chain*
    tedious 109, 110
    exertion 686
    subjection 749
  – *into*
    implicate 54
    compel 744
  – *through mire*
    disrepute 874
    disrespect 929
  – *on tedious* 110
  – *into open day*
    531
  – *towards*
    attract 288
  – *slow length*
    long 200
    weary 841
draggle 285, 653
  – *tail* 59
drag-net
  all sorts 78
dragoman 524
dragon *monster* 83
  violent 173
  animal 366
  irascible 901
dragonnade
  attack 716
  punish 972
dragoon
  soldier 726
  compel 744
  insolent 885
  worry 907
drain
  flow out 295 *
  empty 297
  dry 340
  conduit 350
  waste 638
  clean 652
  unclean 653
  exhaust 789
  dissipate 818
  – *the cup*
    drink 298
  drunken 959

sleepy 683
weary 841
drub
defeat 731, 732
punish 972
drudge *labour* 686
worker 682, 690
drug
render insensible
376 .
superfluity 641
trash 643
remedy 662
bane 663
- in the market
815
drugget
cover 223
clean 652
preserve 670
druggist 662
druid 996
drum
repeat 104
cylinder 249
sound 407
music 417
party 892
beat of -
signal 550
alarm 669
war 722
command 741
parade 882
ear - 418
muffled -
funeral 363
non-resonance
408a
- and fife band 417
- fire 407
- out 972
drum-head 964,
966
drum-major 745
drummer 416
drunken 959
reel like a - *man*
315
drunkenness 959
dry *arid* 340
style 575, 576, 579
hoarse 581
scanty 640
preserve 670
exhaust 789
tedious 841
dull 842
thirsty 865
cynical 932
teetotal 958
run - 640
with - *eyes* 823
- dock 189
- joke 842
- land 342
- the tears 834
- up 340, 638
dryad 979
dry-as-dust
antiquarian 122
dull 843
dryness 340
dry-nurse
teach 537
teacher 540
aid 707
dry-point 558

dry-rot
dirt 653
decay 659
bane 663
dualism 984
duality 89
duarchy 737
dub 564
dubious 475
ducat 800
duce 745
duchess 745, 875
duchy 181
duck *stoop* 308
plunge 310
water 337
darling 897, 899
play -*s and*
drakes
recoil 277
prodigality 818
-'s egg
zero 101
- in thunder 870
ducking-stool 975
duckling 127
duck-pond 370
duct 350
ductile
elastic 323
flexible 324
trimming 607
easy 705
docile 743
dud 158, 727
dude 854
duds 225
dudgeon
dagger 727
discontent 832
churlishness 895
hate 898
anger 900
sullenness 901a
due
expedient 646
owing 806
proper 924, 926
give his - *to*
right 922
vindication 937
fair 939
in - *course* 109
occasion 134
- respect 928
- sense of 498
- time
soon 132
- to
cause and effect
154, 155
give - *weight* 465
duel 720
duelist 726
dueness 924
duenna
teacher 540
guardian 664
keeper 753
dues 812
duet 415
duff 298
duffer
bungler 701
smuggler 792
dug 250
dug-out
old man 130

boat 273
defence 717
duke *ruler* 745
noble 875
dulce domum 189
dulcet
sweet 396
sound 405
melodious 413
agreeable 829
dulcify 174, 396
dulcimer 417
Dulcinea 897
dulcorate 396
dulia 990
dull *weak* 160
inert 172
moderate 174
blunt 254
insensible 376,
381
spund 405
dim 422
colorless 429
ignorant 493
stolid 499
style 575
inactive 683
unapt 699
callous 823
dejected 837
weary 841
prosing 843
simple 849
- of hearing 419
- sight 443
dullard 501
dullness 843
duly 924
duma 696
dumb 581
- animal 366
- show 550
- waiter 307
strike -
ignorant 493
astonish 870
humble 879
dumbfounder
disappoint 509
silence 581
astonish 870
humble 879
dummy
substitute 147
impotent 158
speechless 581
inactive 683
dump *music* 415
store 636
lament 839
undersell 796
dumpling 298
dumps
discontent 832
dejection 837
sulk 901a
dumpy *little* 193
short 201
thick 202
dun *dim* 422
colorless 429
grey 432
importune 765
creditor 805
dunce
ignoramus 493
fool 501

dunderhead 501
dune 206
dung 653
dungeon 752
dunghill
dirt 653
cowardly 862
baseborn 876
- cock 366
Dunker 984
dunt 716
duo 415
duodecimal 99
duodecimo
little 193
book 593
duodenary 98
duologue
interlocution 588
drama 599
dupe
credulous 486
deceive 545
deceived 547
duplex 90, 189
duplicate
imitate 19
copy 21
double 90
tally 550
record 551
redundant 641
pawn 805
duplication
imitation 19
doubling 90
repetition 104
duplicature
fold 258
duplicity
duality 89
falsehood 544
dura lex sed lex 926
durable
long time 110
stable 150
durance 141, 751
in - 754
duration 106
contingent - 108a
infinite - 112
durbar
conference 588
council 696
tribunal 966
duress
compulsion 744
restraint 751
during 106
- pleasure &c.
108a
durity 323
dusk
evening 126
half-light 422
dusky
dark 421
black 431
dust *levity* 320
powder 330
corpse 362
trash 643
dirt 653
money 800
come to -
die 360
come down with
the - 807

humbled in the -
879
kick up a - 885
level with the -
162
lick the -
submit 725
fail 732
make to bite the -
731
turn to -
deorganized 358
die 360
- in the balance
643
throw - *in the*
- *eyes*
blind 442
deceive 545
plead 617
- one's jacket 972
duster 652
dust-bin, dust-hole
191, 645
fit for the -
useless 645
dirty 653
spoilt 659
dustman
cleaner 652
dust-storm 330
dusty
powder 330
dirt 653
Dutch
double - 519
high - 519
- auction 796
- courage 862
Dutchman, flying
515
dutiful 944
duty
business 625
work 686
tax 812
courtesy 894
obligation 926
respect 928
worship 990
rite 998
do one's -
virtue 944
on - 680, 682
duumvirate 737
Duval, Claude -
792
D.V. 470, 976
dwarf
lessen 36
small 193
elf 980
dwell
reside 186
abide 265
- upon
descant 573
dweller 188
dwelling 184, 189
dwindle *lessen* 36
shrink 195
dyad 89
dye 428
dying 360
dyke [*see* dike]
dynamic energy
157
dynamics 276

complete 729
carry into – 692
with crushing –
162
in – 5
take – 731
to that – 516
effective
capable 157
useful 644
effectuation 729
expedient 646
effects 780, 798
effectual 731
effectually 52
effectuate 729
effeminate
weak 160
womenlike 374
timorous 862
sensual 954
effeminize 158
effendi 875
effervesce
energy 171
violence 173
agitate 315
bubble 353
excited 825
effervescent 338
effete *old* 128
weak 160
useless 645
spoiled 659
efficacious
[*see* efficient]
efficient
power 157
agency 170
utility 644
skill 698
effigy 21, 554
effleurer *skim* 267,
460
efflorescence 330
effluxion of time
109
effluence *egress* 295
flow 348
effluvium 334, 398
efflux 295
efformation 240
effort 686
effreet 980
effrontery 885
effulgence 420
effuse
pour out 295, 297
excrete 299
speech 582
loquacity 584
effusion of blood
361
effusive 573
eft 366
eftsoons 117
egad 535
égards 928
egesta 299
egestion 297
egg *beginning* 66
cause 153
food 298
walk among –s
704
too many –s in
one basket
unskilful 699

(*imprudent* 863)
– and dart
ornament 847
– on 615
egg-shaped 247,
249
ego *intrinsic* 5
speciality 79
immaterial 317
non – 6
egocentrism 943
egotism
vanity 880
cynicism 911
selfishness 943
egregious
exceptional 83
absurd 497
exaggerated 549
important 642
egregiously 31, 33
egress **295**
Egyptian darkness
421
eheu! fugaces
labuntur anni
111
eiderdown 223
eidouranion 318
Eiffel tower 206
eight *number* 98
boat 273
representative 759
eisteddfod 72, 416
eighty 98
either *choice* 609
happy with – 605
ejaculate
propel 284
utter 580
ejection 185, **297**
ejecta 299
ejector 349
eke *also* 37
– out *complete* 52
spin out 110
ekka 272
El Dorado 803
elaborate
improve 658
prepare 673
laborious 686
work out 729
elaine 356
élan 276
elapse 109, 122
elastic fluid 334
elasticity
power 157
strength 159
energy 171
spring **325**
elate *cheer* 836
rejoice 838
hope 858
vain 880
boast 884
elbow *angle* 244
projection 250
push 276
at one's –
near 197
advice 695
lift one's –
drink 959
out at –s
undress 226
poor 804

disrepute 874
– one's way
progress 282
pursuit 622
active 682
elbow-chair 215
elbow-grease 331
elbow-room 180,
748
elder *older* 124
aged 128
veteran 130
clergy 996
elect *choose* 609
good 648
predestinate 976
pious 987
clergy 996
election
numerical 84
necessity 601
electioneering 609
elector 745
electorate 737
Electra complex
897
electric
swift 274
sensation 821
excitable 825
car 272
– blue 438
– chair 974
– light 423
– piano 417
electrician 599, 690
electricity 157, 388
electrify
unexpected 508
excite 824
astonish 870
electro-biology 992
electrocution 972
electrolier 214, 423
electrolyze 49
electro-magnetism
157
electromobile 272
electron 32
electronics 157
electroplate 223
electrotype 21, 591
electuary 662
eleemosynary 784
elegance
in style 578
beauty 845
taste 859
Bank of – 800
elegy *interment* 363
poetry 597
lament 839
element
component 56
beginning 66
cause 153
matter 316
in one's –
facility 705
content 831
devouring – 382
out of its – 195
elementary 42
– education 537
– school 542
elements
Eucharist 998
elench 477

elephant
large 192
carrier 271
white – *bane* 663
elevated
tipsy 959
elevation
height 206
vertical 212
raising **307**
plan 554
– of style 574
improvement 658
glory 873
– of mind 942
angular – 244
élève 541
eleven 98
representative 759
eleventh hour
evening 126
late 133
opportune 134
elf *infant* 129
little 193
imp 980
elicit *cause* 153
draw out 301
discover 480a
manifest 525
eligible 646
Elijah's mantle 63
eliminant 299
eliminate
subduct 38
simplify 42
exclude 55
weed 103
extract 301
reject 610
elision 44, 201
élite *best* 648
distinguished 873
aristocratic 875
elixation 384
elixir 662
– of life 471
elk 223
ell 200
take an –
take 789
insolence 885
wrong 923
undue 925
selfish 943
ellipse 247
ellipsis *shorten* 201
style 572
ellipsoid 247, 249
elocation 185, 270
elocution 582
éloge 931
elongation 196, 200
elopement 623, 671
eloquence 572, 582
else 37
elsewhere 187
elucidate 522
elude
sophistry 477
avoid 623
escape 671
succeed 731
palter 773
elusive 545
elusory 546
elutriate 652
elysian 829, 981

Elysium 827, 981
elytron 223
Elzevir edition 193
emaciation 195,
203, 640
emanate 151
go out of 295
excrete 299
– from 544
emanation 398
emancipate
facilitate 705
free 748, 750
emasculate
impotent 158
embalm
interment 363
perfume 400
preserve 670
– in the memory
505
embankment
esplanade 189
refuge 666
fence 717
embar 229
embargo
stoppage 265
prohibition 761
exclusion 893
embark
transfer 270
depart 293
– in *begin* 66
engage in 676
embarquer sans
biscuits, s' – 674
embarras de
– choix 609
embarrass 641,
704, 706
embarrassed 804,
806
embarrassing 475
embase 659
embassy
errand 532
commission 755
consignee 758
embattled
arranged 60
leagued 712
war array 722
embed
locate 184
base 215
enclose 221
insert 300
embellish 847
embers 384
embezzle 791
embitter
deteriorate 659
aggravate 835
acerbate 900
emblazon
color 428
ornament 847
display 882
emblem 550, 747
embody
join 43
combine 48
form a whole 50
compose 54
embolden
hope 858
encourage 861

induce 615
undertake 676
do battle 722
commission 755
promise 768
compact 769
I'll –
  affirmation 535
  – the attention
  457
  – with 720
engaged
  marriage 903
  be – 135
  – in attention 457
engagement
  business 625
  battle 720
  betrothal 902
engaging
  pleasing 829
  amiable 897
engender 161
engine 153, 633
engine-driver 268
engineer 690, 694,
  726
engineering 633
engird 227
English 188
  broken – 563
  king's – 560
  murder the king's
  – 568
  plain –
  intelligible 518
  interpreted 522
  style 576
  – horn 417
engorge
  swallow 296
  gluttony 957
engorgement
  too much 641
engrail 256
engrave
  furrow 259
  mark 550
  – in the memory
  505
engraver 559
engraving 21, 22,
  558
engross write 590
  possess 777
  – the thoughts
  thought 451
  attention 457
engrossed in
  thought 451
engulf
  destroy 162
  plunge 310
  swallow up 296
enhance
  increase 35
  improve 658
enharmonic 413
enigma
  question 461
  secret 533
enigmatic
  uncertain 475
  unintelligible 517
  obscure 519
enigme, mot d' –
  522
enjoin advise 695

command 741
prescribe 926
enjoy
  physically 377
  possess 777
  morally 827
  – health 654
  – popularity 873
  – a state 7
enkindle heat 384
  excite 824
enlarge
  increase 35
  swell 194
  in writing 573
  liberate 750
  – the mind 537
enlarged views 498
enlighten
  illumine 420
  inform 527
  teach 537
enlightened
  knowledge 490
enlist engage 615
  war 722
  commission 755
  under the ban-
  ners of 707
  – into the service
  677
enliven
  delight 829
  cheer 836
  amuse 840
enmity 889
ennoble 873
ennui 841
enormity
  crime 947
enormous great 31
  big 192
  – number 102
enough much 31
  no more! 142
  sufficient 639
  moderately 651
  satiety 869
  know when one
  has had – 953
  – in all conscience
  641
  – to drive one
  mad 830
  – and to spare 639
enounce 535, 580
enrage 830, 900
enragé 865
enrapture
  excite 824
  beatify 829
  love 897
enraptured 827
enravish 829
enravished 827
enravishment 824
enrich
  improve 658
  wealth 803
  ornament 847
enrobe 225
enroll list 86
  record 551
  – troops 722
  commission 755
ens essence 1
Ens Entium 976
ensample 22

ensanguined 361
ensconce
  conceal 528
  safety 664
ensconced
  located 184
ensemble 50
enshrine
  circumscribe 229
  repute 873
  sanctify 987
  – in the memory
  505
ensiform 253
ensign
  standard 550
  officer 726
  master 745
  – of authority 747
ensilage 637
enslave 749
ensnare 545
ensue follow 63, 117
  happen 151
ensure 474
entablature 210
entail cause 153
  tie up property
  781
entangle
  interlink 43
  derange 61
  ravel 219
  entrap 545
  embroil 713
entangled
  disorder 59
  – by difficulties
  704
entend, cela s' – 613
entente
  agreement 23
  alliance 714
  friendship 888
enter go in 294
  appear 446
  note 551
  accounts 811
  – into the compo-
  sition of 56
  – into details
  special 79
  describe 594
  – into an engage-
  ment 768
  – into the feelings
  of 914
  – into the ideas of
  understand 518
  concord 714
  – in converge 290
  – the lists
  attack 716
  contention 720
  – the mind 451
  – a profession 625
  – into the spirit of
  feel 821
  delight 827
  – upon 66
  – into one's views
  488
enterprise
  pursuit 622
  undertaking 676
  commercial – 794
enterprising
  active 171, 682

courageous 861
entertain
  bear in mind 457
  support 707
  amuse 840
  sociality 892
  – doubts 485
  – feeling 821
  – an idea 451
  – an opinion 484
entertainment 840
  pleasure 377
  repast 298
entêté 481, 606
enthral
  subjection 749
  restraint 751
enthrone 873
enthronement 755
enthusiasm
  language 574
  willingness 602
  feeling 821
  hope 858
  love 897
enthusiast
  madman 504
  obstinate 606
  active 682
enthusiastic
  imaginative 515
  sensitive 822
  excitable 825
  sanguine 858
enthymeme 476
entice 615
enticing 829
entire whole 50
  complete 52
  continuous 69
  – horse 373
entirely much 31
entitle name 564
  give a right 924
entity 1
entoil 545
entomb inter 363
  imprison 751
Entomology 368
entourage 88, 183,
  227
entozoon 193
entrails 221
entrammel 751
entrance
  beginning 66
  ingress 294
  way 627
  enrapture 827,
  829
  magic 992
  give – to 296
entranced 515
entrancement 824
entrap 545
entrain 293
entre nous 528
entreat 765
entrée
  reception 296
  dish 298
  give the – 296
  have the – 294
  – dish 191
entremet 298
entrepôt 636, 799
entrepreneur 599
entre-sol 191

entrust
  commission 755
  give 784
  credit 805
entry beginning 66
  ingress 294
  record 551
entwine join 43
  intersect 219
  convolve 248
enucleate 522
enumerate 85
  – among 76
enumeration 86
enunciate
  inform 527
  affirm 535
  voice 580
envelop 225
envelope 223, 232
envenom
  deprave 659
  exasperate 835
  hate 898
  anger 900
envenomed
  bad 649
  insalubrious 657
  painful 830
  malevolent 907
  – tongue 934
environ 227
environment 183
environs 197
  in such and such –
  183
envisage 515, 861
envoy
  messenger 534
  consignee 758
envy 921
enwrap 225
enzyme 320
Eolian harp 417
Eolus 349
eon 976
épanchement
  manifest 525
  artless 703
  endearment 902
epact 641
épaulette
  badge 550, 747
  ornament 847
  decoration 877
éperdu 824
épergne 191
ephemeral 111
ephemeris
  calendar 114
  record 551
  book 593
Ephesian letters
  993
ephialtes
  physical pain 378
  hindrance 706
  mental pain 828
ephod 999
ephor 967
epic 594, 597
epicedium 839
epicene 81, 83
épicier 876
epicure
  fastidious 868
  sybarite 954a
  glutton 957

expose]
appearance 448
– to weather 338
expound
interpret 522
teach 537
expounder 524
express
rapid 274
squeeze out 301
mean 516
declare 525
inform 527
journal 531
intentional 620
by – haste 684
– train 272
– by words 566
expressed, well –
578
expressible 525
expression [see
express]
musical 416
aspect 448
nomenclature 564
phrase 566
mode of – 569
new fangled – 563
expressive
meaning 516
sensibility 822
exprobation 932,
938
expropriation 782
expugnable 665
expugnation 731
expulsion 55 [see
expel]-
expunge 162, 552
expurgate 38, 652
expurgatorious,
index – 761
exquisite
savory 394
excellent 648
pleasurable 829
beautiful 845
fop 854
exquisitely 31
exsiccate 340
exsudation 299
exsufflation 993
exsuscitate 824
extant 1
extasy [see ecstasy]
extemporaneous
[see extempore]
transient 111
extempore
instant 113
early 132
occasion 134
off-hand 612
unprepared 674
extend
expand 194
prolong 200
– to 196
extended 202
extensibility 324
extensile 324
extension [see
extend] 35, 142,
180
– of time 110
extensive 31, 180
– knowledge 490

extenso, in –
whole 50
diffuse 573
extent 26, 180
extenuate
decrease 36
weaken 160
excuse 937
extenuated 203
extenuating cir-
cumstances
469, 937
extenuatory 469
exteriority 220
exterminate 162
extermination 301
external 57, 220
– evidence 467
– senses 375
extinct
inexistent 2
past 122
destroyed 162
darkness 421
become – 4
extincteur 385
extinction of life
360
extinguish
destroy 162
blow out 385
darken 421
extinguisher 165
put an – upon
hinder 706
defeat 731
extirpate 301
extispicious 511
extol
over-estimate 482
praise 931
extort extract 301
compel 744
despoil 789
extorted
dissent 489
extortion 814, 819
extortionate 739,
865
extra 37, 599, 641
ab – 220
extract
draw off 297
take out 301
quotation 596
remedy 662
extraction 301\
paternity 166
– of roots 85
extractor 301
extradition 270, 297
extrajudicial 964
extramundane 317
extramural 220
extraneous
extrinsic 6
not related 10
foreign 57
outside 220
extraneousness 57
extraordinary
great 31
exceptional 83
extraregarding 220
extravagant
inordinate 31
violent 173
absurd 497

foolish 499
fanciful 515
exaggerated 549
excessive 641
high-priced 814
prodigal 818
vulgar 851
ridiculous 853
extravagation 303
extravaganza
fanciful 515
drama 599
extravasate 295,
297
extreme
inordinate 31
end 67
– unction 998
extremis, in –
dying 360
difficulty 704
extremist 710
extremity end 67-
adversity 735
tribulation 828
drive matters to
an – 604
at the last – 665
extricate
take out 301
deliver 672
facilitate 705
liberate 750
extrinsicality 6
extrinsic evidence
467
extrusion 297, 299
exuberant
– style 573
redundant 639
exudation 295, 299
exulcerate 659
exult 838, 884
exultant 858
exulting 836
exunge 356
exuviae 653
eye circle 247
opening 260
organ of sight 441
all my – and
Betty Martin
546
appear to one's
– 446
before one's –s
front 234
visible 446
manifest 525
cast the –s on
see 441
cast the –s over
attend to 457
catch the – 457
close the –s
blind 442
death 360
sleep 683
dry –s 823
fix the –s on 457
have an – to
attention 457
intention 620
desire 865
in one's –
visible 446
expectant 507
in the –s of

appearance 448
belief 484
keep an – upon
459
look with one's
own –s 459
make –'s at 441
mind's – 515
with moistened –s
839
open the –s to
480a
with open –s 870
set one's –s upon
865
shut one's –s to
inattention 458
permit 760
to the –s 448
under the –s of
186
up to one's –s
641
have one's –s
about one 459
– askance 860
–s draw straws 683
an – for an – 718,
919
– glistening 824
in the – of the law
963
– of the master
693
–'of a needle 260
–s open
attention 457
care 459
intention 620
–s opened
disclosure 529
–s out 442
eye-ball 441
eyebrows 256
eyeglass 445
eyelashes 256
eyeless 442
eyelet 260
eyelid 223
eye-shade 443
eye-sight 441
eyesore 846, 848
eye-teeth
have cut one's –
adolescence 131
skill 698
cunning 702
eye-wash 544
eye-witness
spectator 444
evidence 467
eyot 346
eyre 966
eyry 189

F

Fabian policy
delay 133
inaction 681
caution 864
fable error 495
metaphor 521
fiction 546
description 590
fabric state 7
effect 154

texture 329
fabricate
composition 54
make 161
invent 515
falsify 544
fabrication lie 546
fabula narratur, de
te – retaliate 718
condemn 971
fabulist 594
fabulous
enormous 31
imaginary 515
untrue 546
exaggerated 549
faburden 413
façade 234
face exterior 220
covering 223
front 234
aspect 448
oppose 708
resist 719
brave 861
impudence 885
change the – of
146
fly in the – of
disobey 742
put a good – upon
sham 545
calm 826
cheerful 836
hope 858
pride 878
display 882
vindicate 93
in the – of
presence 186
opposite 708
look in the –
see 441
proud 878
make –s
distort 243
ugly 846
disrespect 929
on the – of
manifest 525
show –
present 186
visible 446
not show –
disreputable 874
bashful 879
to one's – 525
wry – 378
– about 279
set one's – against
708
– of the country
344
on the – of the
earth
space 180
world 318
– to face front 234
contraposition
237
manifest 525
– of the thing
appearance 448
facet 220
facetiae 842
facetious 842
facia 234
facile willing 602

fame *greatness* 31
news 532
renown 873
familiar
known 490
habitual 613
sociable 892
affable 894
– *spirit* 979, 980
on – *terms* 888
familiarize
teach 537
habit 613
famille, en – 892
family
kin 11
class 75
ancestors 166
posterity 167
party 712
in the bosom of
one's – 221
happy – 714
– *circle* 892
– *jars* 713
– *likeness* 17
– *tie* 11
in the – *way* 161
famine 640
– *price* 814
famine-stricken
640
famish
stingy 819
fasting 956
famished
insufficient 640
hungry 865
famous 873
famously 31
fan *blow* 349
cool 385
refresh 689
stimulate 824
flirt a – 855
– the embers 505
– the flame
violence 173
heat 384
aid 707
excite 824
– into a flame
anger 900
–shaped 194
fanatic
madman 504
imaginative 515
zealot 682
religious – 988
fanatical
misjudging 481
insane 503
emotional 821
excitable 825
heterodox 984
over-righteous 988
fanaticism 606
fanciful
imaginative 515
capricious 608
ridiculous 853
fancy *think* 451
idea 453
believe 484
suppose 514
imagine 515
caprice 608

choice 609
pugilism 726
wit 842
desire 865
wonder 870
love 897
after one's – 850
indulge one's –
609
take a – to
delight in 827
desire 865
take one's –
please 829
– *dog* 366
– *dress* 840
– *price* 814
– *woman* 962
fandango 840
fandi, mollia tem-
pora – 588
fane 1000
fanfare *loudness*
404
celebration 883
fanfaron 887
fanfaronnade 884
fangs *venom* 663
rule 737
retention 781
fan-light 260
fan-like 202
fannel 999
fanon 999
fantasia 415
fantastic *odd* 83
absurd 497
imaginative 515
capricious 608
unfashionable 851
ridiculous 853
fantasy
imagination 515
desire 865
fantoccini 554, 599
faquir 996
far – *away* 196
– *be it from*
unwilling 603
deprecation 766
– *between*
disjunction 44
few 103
interval 198
– *from it*
unlike 18
shortcoming 304
no 536
– *from the truth*
546
– *and near* 180
– *off* 196
– *and wide* 31,
180, 196
farce
absurdity 497
untruth 546
drama 599
wit 842
ridiculous 853
mere –
unimportant 643
useless 645
farceur
actor 599
humorist 844
fardel

bundle 72
hindrance 706
fare *state* 7
food 298
price 812
bill of –
list 86
farewell
departure 293
relinquishment
624
loss 776
– *to greatness* 874
far-famed 873
far-fetched 10
far-flung 73
far-gone
much 31
insane 503
spoiled 654
farinaceous 330
farm *till* 371
property 780
rent 788
farmer 188, 342,
371
afternoon – 683
farm-house 189
Farmer-Labor 712
faro 840
farrago 59
farrier 370
farrow
produce 161
litter 167
multitude 102
far-sighted 442, 510
farther 196
[*and see* further]
farthing
quarter 97
worthless 643
coin 800
– *candle* 422
farthingale 225
fasces 747
fascia 205, 247
fascicle 51
fasciculated 72
fascinate
influence 615
excite 824
please 829
astonish 870
love 897
conjure 992
fascinated
pleased 827
fascination [*see*
fascinate]
infatuation 825
desire 870
fascine 72
Fascisti 712
fas et nefas, per –
604a, 631
fash 830
fashion
state 7
form 240
custom 613
method 627
ton **852**
after a –
middling 32
after this – 617
follow the – 82

be in the – 488
man of – 852
set the –
influence 175
authority 737
for –'s *sake* 852
fast *joined* 43
steadfast 150
rapid 274
fashionable 852
intemperate 954
not eat 956
worship 990
rite 998
stick – 704
– *asleep* 683
– *by* 197
– *day* 956
– *friend* 890
– *and loose*
sophistry 477
falsehood 544
irresolute 605
tergiversation 607
caprice 608
– *man fop* 854
libertine 962
fasten *join* 43
hang 214
restrain 751
– *on the mind* 451
– *a quarrel upon*
713
– *upon* 789
fastening 45
fast-handed 819
fastidious
censorious 932
fastidiousness 868
fasting
insufficiency 640
worship 990
penance 952
abstinence 956
fastness
asylum 666
defence 717
fat *corpulent* 192
expansion 194
unctuous 355
oleaginous 356
kill the –*ted calf*
celebration 883
sociality 892
– *in the fire*
disorder 59
violence 173
– *of the land*
pleasure 377
enough 639
prosperity 734
intemperance 95
fata – *Morgana*
occasion 134
ignis fatuus 423
– *obstant* 601
fatal 361
– *disease* 655
fatalism 601
fatality 601
fate *end* 67
necessity 601
chance 621
be one's – 156
sure as – 474
Fates 601, 979
fat-head 501

father *eldest* 128
paternity 166
priest 996
Apostolical –s 985
gathered to one's
–s 360
heavy – 599
– *upon* 155
Father, God the –
976
fatherland 189
fatherless 158
fatherly 906
fathom
length 200
investigate 461
solve 462
measure 466
discover 480a
knowledge 490
fathomless 208
fatidical 511
fatigation 688
fatigue **688**
fatras 643
fatten
expand 194
improve 658
prosperous 734
– *on parasite* 886
– *upon*
feed 298
fatuity 4, 499
fatuous 517
fat-witted 499
faubourg 227
fauces 231
faucet 252
faugh! 867
fault
break 70
error 495
imperfection 651
failure 732
vice 945
guilt 947
at –
uncertain 475
ignorant 491
unskilful 699
find – *with* 932
faultless 650, 946
faulty 495, 651
faun 980
fauna 366
faut: comme il –
taste 850
fashion 852
il s'en – *bien* 489
tant s'en – 536
faute 732
– *de mieux*
substitution 147
necessity 601
fauteuil 215
fautor 890
faux pas
error 568
failure 732
misconduct 947
intrigue 961
favor
resemble 16
badge 550
letter 592
aid 707
indulgence 740

permit 760
gift 784
partiality 923
appearances in –
of 472
get into –
friendship 888
love 897
in – repute 873
approbation 931
in – of
approve 931
under – of 760
view with – 906
– with 784
favorable
occasion 134
willing 602
good 648
aid 707
– prospect 472
– to 709
take a – turn
improve 658
prosperity 734
favorably
well 618
favorer 890
favorite
pleasing 829
beloved 897, **899**
favoritism
friendship 888
wrong 923
fawn color 433
cringe 749, 886
flatter 993
fay 979
fealty
obedience 743
duty 926
respect 928
fear **860**
fearful
painful 830
timid 862
fearfully 31, 870
fearless hope 858
courage 861
fearsome 860
feasible 470, 705
feast period 138
repast 298
pleasure 377
revel 840
rite 998
– one's eyes 897
feast of reason
conversation 588
– and flow of soul
sociality 892
feat action 680
courage 861
– of arms 720
– of strength 159
feather
class 75
tuft 256
light 320
trifle 643
ornament 847
decoration 877
in full –
prepared 673
prosperous 734
rich 803
hear a – drop 403

in high –
health 654
cheerful 884
pleased with a –
840
– in one's cap
honor 873
decoration 877
– one's nest
prepare 673
prosperity 734
wealth 803
economy 817
selfish 943
– the oar 698
– in the scale 643
feather-bed 324
feathered tribes
366
feathery 256
featly 682
feature
character 5
component 56
form 240
appearance 448
press 531
lineament 550
– in 56
features
face 234
febrifuge 662
febrile 382, 825
fecal 653
feces 299, 653
fecit 556
feckless 866
feculence 653
fecund 168
fecundate 161
federal council 696
– penitentiary 752
federalism 737
federation 48, 709,
712
fee possession 777
property 780
pay 809
reward 973
feeble weak 160
illogical 477
feeble-minded 497,
605
feebleness
style **575**
feed eat 298
supply 637
– the flame 707
fee-faw-fum
bugbear 860
spell 993
feel sense 375
touch 379
emotion 821
– for try 463
benevolence 906
pity 914
condole with 915
– the pulse 461
– the want of 865
– one's way
essay 675
caution 864
feeler 379
inquiry 461
experiment 463
feeling 698, **821**

feet low 207
walkers 266
at one's –
near 197
subjection 749
humility 879
fall at one's –
submit 725
fall on one's –
prosper 734
lick the – of
servile 886
light upon one's
safe 664
spring to one's –
307
throw oneself at
the – of
entreat 765
feign 544, 546
feigned 545
feint 545
felicitas, curiosa –
698
felicitate 896
felicitous
agreeing 23
- style 578
skilful 698
successful 731
pleasant 829
felicity 827
feline cat 366
stealthy 528
cunning 702
fell destroy 162
mountain 206
lay flat 21
skin 223
lay low 308
moor 344
dire 860
malevolent 907
fellah 876
felloe 231
fellow similar 17
equal 27
companion 88
dual 89
man 373
scholar 492, 541
fellow-commoner
541
fellow-companion
890
fellow-countryman
890
fellow-creature 372
fellow-feeling
friendship 888
love 897
benevolence 906
pity 914
fellowship
partnership 712
distinction 873
friendship 888
companionship
890
good – 892
fellow-student 541
fellow-worker 690
felly 231
felo-de-se 361
felon 949
felonious 945
felony 947

felt texture 219
heart– 821
felucca 273
female 374
feme coverte 903
feme sole 904
femininity
weakness 160
woman 374
feminine 374
feminism 374
femme de chambre
746
fen 345
fence enclose 232
evade 544
defence 717
fight 720
prison 752
thief 792
– round 229
– with a question
528
fenced 770
fenceless 665
fencible 726
fencing 840
feneration 787
fend 717
fender 717
Fenian 710, 742
fenum habet in
cornu 668, 913
feodal 780
feodality 737, 777
feoff property 780
feoffee 779, 785
feoffer 784
ferae naturae 366
feral 907
ferine 907
ferment
disorder 59
energy 171
violence 173
agitation 315
lightness 320
effervesce 353
emotion 821
excitement 824,
825
anger 900
fermentation,
acetous – 397
fern 367
ferocity 173, 907
Ferrara
sword 727
ferret out 461, 480a
ferro-concrete 635
ferrule 223
ferry 270, 627
ferry-boat 273
ferry-man 269
fertile 161, 168
– imagination 515
ferule 975
come under the –
932
fervent hot 382
desirous 865
– hope 858
fervid hot 382
heartfelt 821
excited 824
fervour heat 382
animation 821
love 897

festal eating 298
social 892
fester 653, 655
festina lente 864
festival
music 416
celebration 883
festivity 840, 892
festoon 245, 847
fetch bring 270
arrive 292
evasion 545
sell for 812
– one a blow
strike 276
attack 716
– and carry
servile 886
– a sigh 839
fête 840, 882
fêté 892
fetishism 992
fetid 401
fetish 991, 993
fetter 751, 752
fettle 673
state 5
prepare 673
in fine – 159, 654
fetus 129, 153
feu
– d'enfer 716
– de joie
amusement 840
celebration 883
feud discord 713
possess 777
property 780
death – 919
feudal 737, 780
feudatory 749
feuilleton 593
fever heat 382
disease 655
excitement 825
feverish hurry 684
animated 821
excited 824
few
a – 100
– and far between
70
– words
concise 572
taciturn 585
compendium 596
fewness **103**
fey 360
fez 225
fiancée 897
fiasco 732
fiat 741
– money 800
fib falsehood 544,
546
thump 720
fiber link 45
filament 205
moral – 60
fickle 149, 605
fictile 240
fiction untruth 546
work of – 594
fictitious 515, 546
fiddle 416, 417
fiddle-de-dee
absurd 497

impotent 158
unproductive 169
failure 732
– tongue 563
– up *excited* 824
– upon
unexpected 508
– of wit 842
flashing
ostentatious 882
flashy
gaudy color 428
style 577
ornament 847
vulgar 851
flask 191
flat *inert* 172
abode 189
story 191
low 207
horizontal 213
vapid 391
low tone 408
musical note 413
positive 535
dupe 547
back-scene 599
shoal 667
bungler 701
poor 804
insensible 823
dejected 837
weary 841
dull 843
simple 849
fall – 732
– contradiction
536
– iron 255
– refusal 764
flatfoot 664
flatness 251
flatter *deceive* 545
cunning 702
please 829
grace 845
encourage 858
approbation 931
adulation 933
– oneself
probable 472
hope 858
– the palate 394
flatterer 935
flattering
– remarks 894
– tale
hope 858
– unction to one's
soul
content 831
vain 880
flattery 933
flattery 544, **933**
flatulent
gaseous 334
air 338
wind 349
- *style* 573, 575
flatus 334, 349
flaunt 873, 882
flaunting *vulgar* 85
gaudy 428
unreserved 525
flautist 416
**Flavian amphi-
theater** 728

flavor 390
flavoring 393
flavous 436
flaw *break* 70
crack 198
error 495
imperfection 651
blemish 848
fault 947
– in an argument
477
flaxen 436
flay *divest* 226
punish 972
flea *jumper* 309
dirt 653
– in one's ear
repel 289
eject 297
refuse 764
disrepute 874
abashed 879
discourteous 895
contempt 930
flea-bite 643
flea-bitten 440
fleck 32
flecked 440
flection 279
fled *escaped* 671
fledge 673
fledgling 123
flee *avoid* 623
fleece *tegument* 223
strip 789
rob 791
impoverish 804
surcharge 814
insult 929
fleet *ridicule* 856
fleet *ships* 273
swift 274
navy 726
Fleet *prison* 752
fleeting 4, 111
flesh *bulk* 192
animal 364
mankind 372
carnal 961
gain – 194
ills that – is heir
to *evil* 619
disease 655
in the – 359
one – 903
way of all – 360
weakness of the –
945
– and blood
substance 3
materiality 316
animality 364
affections 820
make the – creep
pain 830
fear 860
flesh-color 434
flesh-pots 298
– of Egypt 734,
803
fleshly 316
fleur-de-lis 847
fleuron 847
flexible 324, 705
flexion
curvature 245
fold 258

deviation 279
flexuous 248
flexure 245, 258
flibbertigibbet 980
flicker
changing 149
waver 314
flutter 315
light 420
dim 422
flickering 139
flier 621
flies *theatre* 599
flight *flock* 102
volitation 267
swiftness 274
departure 293
avoidance 623
escape 671
– lieutenant 745
put to –
propel 284
repel 717
vanquish 731
– of fancy 515
– of stairs 305,
627
– of time 109
flighty *inattentive*
458
mad 503
fanciful 515
flim-flam 544, 608
flimsy *unsubstan-
tial* 4
weak 160
rarity 322
soft 324
sophistical 477
trifling 643
flinch *swerve* 607
avoid 623
fear 860
cowardice 862
fling *propel* 284
jig 840
jeer 929
have one's –
active 682
laxity 738
freedom 748
amusement 840
– aside 782
have a – at
attack 716
resent 900
disrespect 929
censure 932
– away *reject* 610
waste 638
relinquish 782
– down 308
– to the winds
destroy 162
not observe 773
flint *hard* 323
flint-hearted 907
flintlock 727
flip *beverage* 298
flippant *fluent* 584
pert 885
flipper *paddle* 267
flirt *propel* 284
coquet 607, 854
love 897
endearment 902
– a fan 855

flit *elapse* 109
changeable 149
move 264
travel 266
swift 274
depart 293
run away 623
flitter
small part 32
changeable 149
flutter 315
flitting 111
float *establish* 150
navigate 267
boat 273
buoy up 305
lightness 320
before the –s
on the stage 599
– on the air 405
– before the eyes
446
– bonds 788
– in the mind
thought 451
imagination 515
floater 683
floating
[*see* float]
rumoured 532
– battery 726
– capital 805
– debt 806
– dock 189
flocculent
woolly 256
soft 324
pulverulent 330
flock
assemblage 72
multitude 102
laity 997
–s and herds 366
– together 72
floe *ice* 383
flog 972
hasten 684
flood *much* 31
crowd 72
river 348
abundance 639
redundance 641
prosperity 734
stem the – 708
– of light 420
– of tears 839
flood-gate
limit 233
egress 295
conduit 350
open the –s
eject 297
permit 760
flood-light 423,
599
flood-mark 466
flood-tide
increase 35
complete 52
height 206
advance 282
water 337
floor *level* 204
base 211
horizontal 213
support 215
overthrow 731

ground – 191
flop 315
Flora 369
floral 367
florescence 154
floriculture 371
florid *color* 428
red 434
– *style* 577
health 654
florist 371
floss 256
flotilla 273, 726
flotsam and jetsam
73
flounce
trimming 231
jump 309
agitation 315
flounder
change 149
toss 315
uncertain 475
bungle 699
difficulty 704
fail 732
flour 330
flourish
brandish 314, 315
exaggerate 549
language 577
speech 582
prosper 618
healthy 654
prosperous 734
ornament 847
repute 873
display 882
boast 884
– of trumpets
loud 404
cheerfulness 836
publish 531
ostentation 882
celebrate 883
boast 884
flout 929, 936
flow *course* 109
hang 214
motion 264
stream 348
murmur 405
abundance 639
– from
result 154
– of ideas 451
– in 294
– into *river* 348
– out 295
– over 641
– of soul
conversation 588
affections 820
cheerful 836
social 892
– with the tide
705
– of time 109
– of words 582,
584
flower *essence* 5
produce 161
vegetable 367
prosper 734
beauty 845
ornament 847
repute 873

delight 827
globated 249
globe
　sphere 249
　world 318
　on the face of the
　－ 318
　－ trotter 268
globule 32, 249
glomeration 72
gloom 421, 827, 837
gloomy horizon 859
glorification 884
glorify
　honor 873
　approve 931
　worship 990
glorious
　illustrious 873
　tipsy 959
glory
　light 420
　honor 873
　heaven 981
　King of － 976
　－ in 878, 884
　－ be to God 990
gloss smooth 255
　sheen 420
　interpretation 522
　falsehood 546
　plea 617
　beauty 845
　－ of novelty 123
　－ over
　neglect 460
　sophistry 477
　falsehood 544
　vindicate 937
glossary 86, 562
glossographer 492
glossologist 492
glossology 560, 562
glossy [see gloss]
glottology 560
glout 901a
glove 225
　take up the － 720
　throw down the －
　　715
glow warm 382
　shine 420
　appear 446
　color 428
　style 574
　passion 821
glower
　glare 443
　discourteous 895
　sullen 901a
glowing
　[see glow]
　orange 439
　excited 824
　beautiful 845
　－ terms 574
glow-worm 423
gloze 933, 937
glucose 396
glue cement 45
　cementing 46
　semiliquid 352
glum
　discontented 832
　dejected 837
　sulky 901a
glut

redundance 641
satiety 869
gluttony 957
glutinous 352
glutton 954a, 957
gluttony 957
glycerine 332, 356
glyphography 558
glyptography 558
glyptotheca 557
gnarl protuberance
　250
　anger 900
　threat 909
gnarled 256, 321
gnash one's teeth
　839, 900
gnat little 193
　strain at a － &c.
　caprice 608
gnaw eat 298
　rub 331
　injure 659
gnawing
　－ grief 828, 830
　－ pain 378
gnome 496, 980
gnomic 496
gnomon 114
Gnostic 984
go
　cease to exist 2
　energy 171, 682
　move 264
　recede 287
　depart 293
　fade 429
　disappear 449
　fashion 852
　come and － 314
　as things － 613
　－ about
　turn round 311
　published 531
　undertake 676
　－ across 302
　－ after
　in time 117
　in motion 281
　－ ahead
　energetic 171
　precede 280
　advance 282
　active 682
　－ against 708
　－ astray 495
　－ away 293
　－ back 283, 624
　－ bad 659
　－ bail 771
　－ before 280
　－ between
　interjacent 228
　instrumental 631
　mediate 631, 724
　－ beyond 303
　－ by the board
　　158
　－ about your
　business
　ejection 297
　dismissal 756
　－ by
　conform to 82
　elapse 109
　past 122
　outrun 303

subterfuge 702
give the － by to
　neglect 460
　deceive 545
　avoid 623
　not observe 773
　－ by the name of
　　564
　－ deep into 461
　－ down sink 306
　decline 659
　－ down with
　believed 484
　tolerated 826
　content 831
　－ farther and fare
　worse 659
　－ forth depart 293
　publish 531
　－ halves 91
　－ hand in hand
　accompany 88
　same time 120
　－ hard 704
　－ on ill 735
　－ in 294
　－ in for
　resolution 604
　pursuit 622
　－ into
　ingress 294
　inquire 461
　dissert 595
　－ all lengths
　complete 52
　resolve 604
　exertion 686
　－ mad 503
　－ near 286
　－ no further
　keep secret 528
　－ for nothing
　sophistry 477
　unimportant 643
　－ off explode 173
　depart 293
　die 360
　wither 659
　marry 903
　－ on time 106
　continue 143
　advance 282
　－ on for ever 112
　－ one better 303
　－ out
　cease 142
　egress 295
　extinct 385
　－ out of one's
　head 506
　－ over
　passage 302
　explore 461
　apostate 607
　faithless 940
　－ to pieces 162
　－ on record 551
　－ round 311
　－ shares 778
　－ to sleep 683
　－ through
　meet with 151
　pass 302
　explore 461
　perform 599
　conduct 692
　complete 729

endure 826
　－ to extend 196
　travel 266
　direction 278
　remonstrance 695
　－ up 305
　－ to war 722
　－ with
　assent 488
　concord 714
　－ with the stream
　conform 82
　servile 886
　－ from one's word
　　773
goad 615
　hasten 684
goal end 67
　reach 292
　object 620
　reach the －
　complete 729
goat substitute 147
　jumper 309
　lecher 962
　he － male 373
　play the － 499
gob 269
gobang 840
gobbet
　small piece 32
　food 298
gobble cry 412
　gormandize 957
　eat 298
gobemouche 501,
　547
go-between 758
goblet 191
goblin 980
go-cart 272
GOD 976
　house of － 1000
　kingdom of － 981
　sons of － 977
　－'s acre 363
　－ bless me! 870
　－ bless you
　farewell 293
　－ forbid 766
　－'s grace 906
　－ grant 990
　－ knows 491
　－'s love 906
　for －'s sake 765
　－'s will 601
　－ willing 470
god 979
　household －s 189
　tutelary － 664
goddess love 897
　good woman 948
　heathen 979
Godhead 976
godlike 987
godly 944
godsend good 618
　prosperity 734
Godspeed
　farewell 293
　hope 858
　courtesy 894
　benevolence 906
　approbation 931
goer horse 271
goes [see go]
　as one － 270

here － 676
Gog and Magog 192
goggle 441
　－ eyes 443
goggles 445
going [see go]
　general 78
　rumor 532
　－ to happen 152
　－ on
　incomplete 53,
　　730
　current 151
　transacting 625
goiter 250
Golconda 803
gold yellow 436
　orange 439
　money 800
　write in letters
　of － 642
　worth its weight
　in － 648
gold certificate 800
golden [see gold]
　－ age
　prosperity 734
　pleasure 827
　－ apple 615
　－ calf
　wealth 803
　idol 985
　idolatry 991
　－ dream
　imagination 515
　hope 858
　－ mean
　moderation 174
　mid-course 628
　－ opinions 931
　－ opportunity 134
　－ rule
　precept 697
　－ season of life
　　127
　－ wedding 883
golf 840
Golgotha 363, 1000
Goliath 159, 192
goloshes 225
gondola 273
gondolier 269
gone [see go]
　past 122
　absent 187
　dead 360
　－ bad 653
　－ by
　antiquated 124
　－ out of one's rec-
　ollection 506
gonfalon 550
gong 417
goniometer 244,
　466
good
　complete 52
　palatable 394
　assent 488
　benefit 618
　beneficial 648
　right 922
　virtuous 944
　pious 987
　as － as 197
　be so － as 765
　do － 906

for –
  diuturnal 110
  permanent 141
make –
  evidence 467
  provide 637
  restore 660
  complete 729
  substantiate 924
  vindicate 937
  atone for 952
  so far so – 931
  think – 931
  to the – 780
  turn to – account
    731
what's the – 645
  – actions 944
  – at 698
  – auspices 858
  – behavior
    contingent 108a
    duty 926
    virtue 944
  in one's – books
    888
  – bye 293
  in – case 192
  – chance 472
  – cheer food 298
    cheerful 826
  – circumstances
    803
  – condition 192
  – day
    arrival 292
    departure 293
    courtesy 894
  – effect
    goodness 648
    beauty 845
  – enough
    not perfect 651
  be – enough 765
  put a – face upon
    cheerful 836
    proud 878
  – fellow 892
  – fight war 722
    virtue 944
  – for
    useful 644
    salubrious 656
  – fortune 734
  – Friday 998
  – genius
    friend 890
    benefactor 912
    god 979
  in one's – graces
    888
  – hand 700
  – humor
    concord 714
    cheerfulness 836
    amuse 840
    courtesy 894
    kindly 906
  – intention 906
  – judgment 498
  – lack! 870
  – living
    food 298
    gluttony 957
  – look-out 459
  – looks 845
  – luck 734

– man man 373
  husband 903
  worthy 948
  – manners 894
  much – may it do
    906
  – morrow 292
  – name 873
  – nature 906
  – night 293
  – for nothing
    impotence 158
    useless 645
  in – odor
    repute 873
    approbation 931
  – offices
    mediation 724
    kind 906
  – old time 122
  – omen 858
  – opinion 931
  take in – part
    pleased 827
    courteous 894
    kind 906
  – pennyworth 815
  – at the price 815
  to – purpose 731
  – repute 873
  – sense 498
  – society 852
  – taste 578, 850
  – temper 894
  – thing 648
  – time early 132
    opportune 134
    prosperous 73.
  – turn
    kindness 906
  – understanding
    714
  – wife
    woman 374
    spouse 903
  – will
    willingness 602
    benevolence 906
  – word
    approval 931
    vindication 937
  – as one's word
    veracity 543
    observance 772
    probity 939
  – works 906
goodie 652, 746
goodly
  great 31
  large 192
  handsome 845
good mixer 892
goodness
  [see good] 648
  virtue 944
  have the –
    request 765
  – gracious! 870
  – of heart 906
goods effects 270,
    780
  merchandise 798
good taste 868
Goodwin sands 667
goody 374
gooroo 996
goose hiss 409

game of – 840
giddy as a – 458
  tailor's – 255
kill the – with
  golden eggs
    699, 818
a wild – chase 545
gooseberry
  old – 978
  play – 459
  – eyes 411, 443
goosecap 501
goose egg 101
goosefiesh 383
goosequill 590
goose-skin 383
Gordian knot 59,
    704
gore stab 260
  blood 361
gorge ravine 198
  conduit 350
  fill 641
  satiety 869
  gluttony 957
  raise one's – 900
  – the hook 602
gorge de pigeon 440
gorgeous
  colour 428
  beauty 845
  ornament 847
  ostentation 882
Gorgon 860
gorilla 913
gormandize 298,
    954a, 957
gorse 367
gory red 434
  murderous 361
  unclean 653
gospel
  certainty 474
  truth 494
  take for – 484
Gospels 985
gossamer
  filament 205
  light 320
  texture 329
gossip news 532
  babbler 584
  conversation 588
gossoon 876
Gotama 986
Goth 851, 876
Gotham, wise men
  of – 501
gothic
  amorphous 241
gouache 556
gouge concave 252
  perforator 262
goulash 298
gourd 191
gourmand 954a,
    957
gourmet 868, 954a
gout 378
goût, haut – 392
goutte d'eau, il se
  noyerait dans
  une – 699
govern 693, 737
governess 540
  [see govern]
  ruling power 745

divine – 976
  petticoat – 699
governor
  tutor 540
  director 694
  ruler 745
  keeper 753
gowk 501
gown dress 225
  canonicals 999
gownsman 492
grab take 789
  miser 819
grabble 379
grace style 578
  permission 760
  concession 784
  elegance 845
  polish 850
  title 877
  pity 914
  forgiveness 918
  honor 939
  piety 987
  worship 990
  act of – 784
  God's – 906
  with a bad – 603
  with a good –
    willing 602
  · courteous 894
  in one's good –s
    888
  heart of – 861
  say – 990
  submit with a
    good – 826
  – before meat 916
grâce: coup de –
    914
  la – 840
graceless
  inelegant 579
  ugly 846
  vicious 945
  impenitent 951
  irreligious 989
Graces 845
gracile 203
gracious
  willing 602
  courteous 894
  kind 906
  good – 870
grade degree 26
  arrange 60
  term 71
  ascent 217
  on the down – 658
  on the up – 659
gradatim
  gradually 26
  in order 58
  continuous 69
  slow 275
gradation
  degree 26
  order 58
  continuity 69
gradient 217
gradual degree 26
  continuous 69
  slow 275
graduate
  adjust 23
  calibrate 26
  arrange 60
  series 69

  measure 466
  scholar 492, 873
graduated scale 466
gradus 86, 562
Graeculus esuriens
    886
graft join 43
  locate 184
  insert 300
  trees 371
  teach 537
  booty 794
  corruption 940
Grail
  holy – 998
grain essence 5
  small 32
  tendency 176
  little 193
  rough 256
  weight 319
  texture 329
  powder 330
  paint 428
  temper 820
  ornament 847
  against the –
    rough 256
    unwilling 603
    opposing 708
  in the – 820
  –s of allowance
    qualification 469
    doubt 485
  like –s of sand
    incoherent 47
gram 319
gramercy 916
graminivorous 298
grammar
  beginning 66
  teaching 537
  school 542
  language 567
  bad – 568
  comparative – 560
grammarian 492
gramophone 417,
    418, 553
granary 636
grand
  great 31
  style 574
  important 642
  money 800
  handsome 845
  glorious 873
  ostentatious 882
  – climacteric 128
  – doings 882
  – duchy 181
  – jury 967
  en – seigneur
    proud 878
    insolent 885
  en –e tenue
    ornament 847
    show 882
  – piano 417
  – style 556
  – tour 266
  – Turk 745
  – vizier 694
grandam 130
grandchildren 167
grandee 875
grande dame 878
grandeur 873

grandfather 130, 166
grandiloquent 577
grandiose 577
grandmother 166
  simple 501
  teach – 538
grandsire 130, 166
grange 189
granite 323
granivorous 298
grano salis, cum 469, 485
grant *admit* 529
  permit 760
  consent 762
  confer 784
  God – 990
  – a lease 771
granted 488
  take for –
  believe 484
  suppose 514
grantee
  possessor 779
  receiver 785
granular 330
granulate 330
granule 32
grapes, sour –
  unattainable 471
  falsehood 544
  excuse 617
grape-shot
  attack 716
  arms 727
graph 554
graphic
  intelligible 518
  painting 556
  descriptive 594
graphite 332
graphito 556
graphology 590
graphometer 244
graphotype 558
grapnel 666
grapple
  fasten 43
  clutch 789
  – with
  - *a question* 461
  - *difficulties* 704
  oppose 708
  resist 719
  contention 720
grappling-iron
  fastening 45
  safety 666
grasp
  comprehend 518
  power 737
  retain 781
  seize 789
  in one's – 737
  possess 777
  tight – *severe* 739
  – at 865
  – of intellect 498
grasping
  miserly 819
  covetous 865
grass 344, 367
  let the – grow under one's feet
  neglect 460
  inactive 683

not let the – &c.
  active 682
grasshopper 309
grass-plat 371
grate *rub* 330
  physical pain 378
  stove 386
  – on the ear
  harsh sound 410
  – on the feelings 830
grated
  barred 219
grateful
  physically pleasant 377
  agreeable 829
  thankful 916
grater 260, 330
gratification
  animal – 377
  moral – 827
gratify 829
  permit 760
  please 829
grating [*see* grate]
  lattice 219
  harsh 713
gratis 815
gratitude **916**
gratuitous
  inconsequent 477
  supposititious 514
  voluntary 602
  payless 815
gratuty
  gift 784
  gratis 815
gratulate 896
gravaman 642
  – of a charge 938
grave *great* 31
  engrave 259, 558
  tomb 363
  important 642
  composed 826
  distressing 830
  sad 837
  heinous 945
  beyond the – 360
  look –
  disapprove 932
  rise from the – 660
  silent as the – 403
  sink into the – 360
  on this side of the – 359
  – in the memory 505
  – note 408
  – trap 599
gravel
  earth 342
  material 635
  puzzle 704
graveolent 398
graven image 991
graver 558
graving dock 189
gravitate
  descend 306
  weigh 319
  – towards 176
gravity *force* 157
  weight **319**
  vigor 574

importance 642
sedateness 826
seriousness 827
  center of – 222
specific –
  weight 319
  density 321
gravy 333
  – *boat* 191
gray **432** [and *see* grey]
graze *touch* 199
  browse 298
  rub 331
  brush 379
grazier 370
gré, savoir – 916
grease
  lubricate 332
  oil 356
  – the palm
  tempt 615
  give 784
  pay 807
greasy 355
great *much* 31
  big 192
  glorious 873
  magnanimous 942
  (*important* 642)
  – bear 318
  – circle sailing 628
  – coat 225
  – doings
  importance 642
  bustle 682
  – folks 875
  – gun 626
  – hearted 942
  – Mogul 745
  – number 102
  – primer 591
  – quantity 31
greater 33
  – number 102
  – part 31
  nearly all 50
greatest 33
greatness **31**
greave 225
greed
  desire 865
  gluttony 957
greedy
  avaricious 819
green
  new 123
  young 127
  lawn 344
  grass 367
  color 435
  credulous 486
  novice 491
  unused 614
  healthy 654
  immature 674
  unskilled 699
  board of – cloth 966
  – memory 505
  – old age 128
greenback 800
green-eyed monster 920
greenhorn

novice 493
dupe 547
bungler 701
greenhouse
  receptacle 191
  horticulture 371
greenness **435**
green-room 599
greensward 344
Greenwich time 114
greenwood 367
Greek
  unintelligible 519
  sharper 792
  St. Giles's – 563
  – Church 984
  – Kalends 107
greet *weep* 839
  hail 894
greeting
  sociality 892
  –'s! 292
gregarious 892
grenade 727
grenadier
  tall 206
  soldier 726
grey 432
  – beard 130
  – friar 996
  – hairs 128
  bring – hairs to the grave
  adversity 735
  harass 830
  – mare
  ruler 737
  master 745
  wife 903
  – matter
  brain 498
  –hound
  swift 274
  animal 366
  ocean –hound 273
gridelin 437
gridiron
  flatness 213
  crossing 219
  stove 386
  stage 599
  stadium 840
grief 828
  come to – 735
grievance
  evil 619
  painful 830
  wrong 923
grieve *mourn* 828
  pain 830
  dejected 837
  complain 839
grievous 649, 830
grievously 31
griffin 83, 366, 493
griffo 41
griffonage 590
grig *merry* 836
grill 382, 384, 461
  – room 189
grille 219
grim
  resolved 604
  painful 830
  doleful 837
  ugly 846

discourteous 895
sullen 901a
–visaged war 722
grimace 243, 839, 855
grimacier
  actor 599
  humorist 844
  affected 855
grimalkin 366
grimy 652
grin *laugh* 838
  ridicule 856
  – and abide 725
  – a ghastly smile
  dejected 837
  ugly 846
grind
  reduce 195
  sharpen 253
  pulverize 330
  pain 378
  learn 539
  oppress 907
  – the organ 416
  – one's teeth 900
grinder
  teacher 330
  noise 404
grinding 739, 830
grindstone 253, 330
grip
  indication 550
  power 737
  retention 781
  clutch 789
  – of the hand 894
gripe [*see* grip]
  pain 378
  parsimony 819
grisaille
  grey 432
  painting 556
grisette
  woman 374
  commonalty 876
  libertine 962
grisly 846
grist
  materials 635
  provision 637
  – to the mill
  useful 644
  acquire 775
gristle 321, 327
grit
  strength 159
  powder 330
  stamina 604a
  courage 861
  – in the oil
  hindrance 706
gritty 323
grizzled
  grey 432
  variegated 440
groan 411, 839
groat 800
grocer 637
grocery 396
grog 298, 959
groin 244
groom 370, 746
  – well
  – of the chambers 746
  –'s man 903

groove
 furrow 259
 habit 613
 in a – 16
 move in a – 82
 put in a – for 673
grope
 feel 379
 experiment 463
 try 675
 in the dark 442,
 704
gross
 great 31
 whole 50
 number 98
 ugly 846
 vulgar 851
 vicious 945
 impure 961
 – *credulity* 486
 – *receipts* 810
grosshead 501
grossheaded 499
grossièreté 895
grot [*see* grotto]
grotesque
 odd 83
 distorted 243
 – *style* 579
 ridiculous 853
grotto
 alcove 191
 hollow 252
grouch 895, 901a
ground
 cause 153
 region 181
 base 211
 lay down 213
 support 215
 coating 223
 land 342
 plain 344
 evidence 467
 teach 537
 motive 615
 plea 617
 above – 359
 down to the – 52
 dress the – 371
 fall to the – 732
 get over the – 274
 go over the – 302
 level with the –
 162
 maintain one's –
 persevere 604a
 play– 840
 prepare the – 673
 stand one's –
 defend 717
 resist 719
 – *bait* 784
 – cut from under
 one 732
 – *floor*
 chamber 191
 low 207
 base 211
 – *on*
 attribute 155
 – *plan* 554
 – of quarrel 713
 – *sliding from*
 under one 665
 – *swell*

agitation 315
 waves 348
grounded
 stranded 732
 well– 490
 – *on basis* 211
 evidence 467
groundless
 unsubstantial 4
 illogical 477
 erroneous 495
groundling 876
grounds
 dregs 653
groundwork
 precursor 64
 cause 153
 basis 211
 support 215
 preparation 673
group
 marshal 60
 cluster 72
 – *captain* 745
grouping 60
grouse 852, 901a
grout 45
grove
 street 189
 glade 252
 wood 367
grovel
 below 207
 move slowly 275
 cringe 886
 base 940
grow
 increase 35
 become 144
 expand 194
 – *from*
 effect 154
 – *into* 144
 – *less* 195
 – *taller* 206
 – *together* 46
 – *up* 194
 – *upon one* 613
grower 164
growl *cry* 412
 complain 839
 discourtesy 895
 anger 900
 threat 909
growler *cab* 272
 discontented 832
 sulky 901a
grown up 131
growth [*see* grow]
 development 161
 – *in size* 194
 tumor 250
 vegetation 367
groyne 706
grub
 small animal 193
 food 298
 – *up*
 eradicate 301
 discover 480a
Grub-street writer
 593
grudge
 unwilling 603
 refuse 764
 stingy 819
 hate 898

anger 900
 bear a – 907
 owe a – 898
 grudging 603
 – *praise* 932
gruel 298
gruesome 846
gruff
 harsh sound 410
 discourteous 895
grum
 harsh sound 410
 morose 901a
grumble
 cry 411
 complain 832,
 839
grume 321, 354
grumous 321, 354
grumpy 901a
Grundy, Mrs. 852
grunt 412
 complain 839
guano 653
guarantee 768, 771
guard
 traveling 268
 safety 664
 defence 717
 soldier 726
 sentry 753
 advanced – 668
 mount –
 care 459
 safety 664
 off one's –
 inexpectant 508
 throw off one's –
 cunning 702
 on one's –
 careful 459
 cautious 864
 rear – 668
 – *against*
 prepare 673
 defence 717
 – *ship* 664, 726
guarda costa 753
guarded
 conditions 770
guardian
 safety 664
 defence 717
 keeper 753
 – *angel*
 helper 711
 benefactor 912
guardless 665
guard-room 752
gubernation 693
gubernatorial 737
gudgeon 547
guerdon 973
guernsey 229
guerre:
 nom de – 565
 – à outrance &c.
 722
guerilla 726
 – *warfare* 720
guess 514
guesswork 514
guest 890
 paying – 188
guet:
 mot de – 550
 –à-pens 545

guffaw 838
guggle
 gush 348
 bubble 353
 resound 408
 cry 412
guide
 pattern 22
 courier 524
 teach 537
 teacher 540
 indicate 550
 direct 693
 director 694
 advise 695
guide-book 527
guided by, be – 82
guideless 665
guide-post 550
guiding star 693
guild 712, 966
guildhall 799
guile
 deceit 544, 545
 cunning 702
guileless 543, 703
guillotine 972, 975
guilt 947
guiltless 946
guilty:
 find – 971
 plead – 950
guindé 579
guinea 800
guipure 847
guisard 599
guise
 state 7
 dress 225
 appearance 448
 plea 617
 mode 627
 conduct 692
guiser 599
guitar 417
gulch 198
gules 434
gulf
 interval 198
 deep 208
 lake 343
gull 545, 547
gullible 486
gullet *throat* 260
 rivulet 348
gully *gorge* 198
 hollow 252
 opening 260
 conduit 350
gulosity 957
gulp *swallow* 296
 take food 298
 – *down*
 credulity 486
 submit 725
gum *fastening* 45
 fasten 46
 resin 356a
 – *elastic* 325
 – *tree* 367
gumbo 298
gummy 352
gumption 498
gun *report* 406
 weapon 727
 great – 626
 blow great –s 349

sure as a – 474
gunboat 726
gunfire 404
gunman 361
gunner 776
gunnery
 warfare 722
 cannon 727
gunlayer 284
gunpowder
 warfare 722
 ammunition 727
 not invent – 665
 sit on barrel of –
 501
gunroom 193
gun-shot 197
gunwale 232
gurge 312, 348
gurgle
 flow 348
 bubble 353
 faint sound 405
 resonance 408
gurgoyle 350
gush
 flow out 295
 flood 348
 exaggeration 482
 talk 584
gushing
 emotional 821
 impressible 822
gusset 43
gust *wind* 349
 physical taste 390
 passion 825
 moral taste 850
gustation 390
gustful 394
gustless 391
gusto [*see* gust]
 physical pleasure
 377
 emotion 821
gut *destroy* 162
 opening 260
 strait 343
 eviscerate 297
 sack 789
 steal 791
gutling 954a
guts *inside* 221
guttapercha 325
gutter *groove* 259
 conduit 350
 vulgarity 851
guttersnipe 876
guttle 957
guttural
 letter 561
 inarticulate 583
guy
 fastening 45, 752
 fellow 373
 disrespect 929
 grotesque 853
guzzle
 gluttony 957
 drunkenness 959
gybe [*see* jibe]
gymkhana 720, 840
gymnasium 191
 school 542
 arena 728, 840
gymnast 159
gymnastics

training 537
exercise 686
contention 720
sport 840
gymnosophist
  abstainer 953
  sectarian 984
gynander 83
gynarchy 727
gynecaeum 374
gynecology 662
gyniatrics 374
gynics 374
gyp 545, 746
gyrate 312
gyrfalcon 913
gyromancy 511
gyrostat 312
gysart 599
gyve 752

H

habeas corpus 963, 969
haberdasher 225
habergeon 717
habiliment 225
habilitation 698
habit
  essence 5
  coat 225
  custom 613
  want of – 614
  –s of business 682
  – of mind 820
habitant 188
habitat 189
habitation 189
habit-maker 225
habitual
  unvariable 16
  orderly 58
  ordinary 82
  customary 613
habituate 537, 613
habitude
  state 7
  habit 613
habitué 613
hacienda 189, 780
hack cut 44
  shorten 201
  horse 271
  writer 594
  worker 690
  literary – 593
hackle 44
hackney-coach 272
hackneyed
  known 490
  trite 496
  habitual 613
Hades 982
Hadji
  traveler 268
  priest 996
hae tibi erunt artes 627
haeret lateri lethalis arundo
  displeasure 828
  anger 900
haft 633

hag age 128
  ugly 846
  wretch 913
  witch 994
haggard
  insane 503
  tired 688
  wild 824
  ugly 846
haggis 298
haggle cut 44
  chaffer 794
Hagiographa 985
Hagiolatry 984
Hagiology 983, 985
haguebut 727
ha-ha trench 198, 719
haik 225
hail welcome 292
  ice 383
  call 586
  rejoicing 838
  honor to 873
  celebration 883
  courtesy 894
  salute 928
  approve 931
  –fellow well met
  friendship 888
  sociality 892
hailstone 383
hair small 32
  filament 205
  roughness 256
  to a – 494
  –'s breadth
  near 197
  narrow 203
  –breadth escape
  danger 665
  escape 671
  –s on the head
  multitude 102
  make one's –
  stand on end
  distressing 830
  fear 860
  wonder 870
hairless 226
hairy rough 256
halberd 727
halberdier 726
halcyon calm 174
  peace 721
  prosperous 734
  joyful 827, 829
hale 654
half 91
  – the battle
  important 642
  success 731
  – distance 68
  – a dozen six 98
  several 102
  see with – an eye
  intelligent 498
  intelligible 518
  manifest 525
  – a gale 349
  – and half
  equal 27
  mixed 41
  incomplete 53
  – a hundred 98
  – light 422
  – measures

incomplete 53
vacillating 605
mid-course 628
– moon 245
– price 815
– rations 640
– scholar 493
– seas over 959
– sight 443
– speed
  moderate 174
  slow 275
– truth 546
half-blind 443
half-blood
  mixture 41
  unconformity 83
  imperfect 651
half-frozen 352
half-hearted
  irresolute 605
  insensible 823
  indifferent 866
half-learned 491
half-melted 352
halfpenny
  trifle 643
half-starved
  insufficient 640
  fasting 956
half-way
  small 32
  middle 68
  between 228
  go – irresolute 605
  mid-course 628
  meet –
  willing 602
  compromise 774
half-witted 499, 501
hall chamber 189
  receptacle 191
  mart 799
  music – 599
  – of audience 588
  – mark 550
hallelujah 990
halliard 45
halloo cry 411
  look here! 457
  call 586
  wonder 870
hallow
  celebrate 883
  respect 928
hallowed 976
hallucination
  error 495
  insanity 503
halo light 420
  glory 873
Halomancy 511
halser 45
halt cease 142
  weak 160
  rest 265
  go slowly 275
  lame 655
  fail 732
  at the – 265
halter rope 45
  restraint 752
  punishment 975
  wear a – 874
  with a – round one's neck 665
halting

style 579
– place 292
halve [see half]
halves
  do by –
  neglect 460
  not complete 730
  not do by – 729
  go – 778
ham house 189
hamadryad 979
hammam 386, 652
hamlet 189
hammer
  repeat 104
  knock 276
  stammer 583
  under the –
  auction 796
  between the – and the anvil 665
  – at think 451
  work 686
  – out form 240
  prepare 673
  complete 729
hammock 215
hamper basket 191
  obstruct 706
hamstring 158, 659
hanaper 802
hand
  measure of length 200
  side 236
  transfer 270
  man 372
  organ of touch 379
  indicator 550
  writing 590
  medium 631
  agent 690
  grasp 781
  transfer 783
  at – future 121
  destined 152
  near 197
  useful 644
  bad – 590
  bird in – 781
  come to – 292, 785
  fold one's –s 681
  give one's – to
  marry 903
  good –
  writing 590
  skill 698
  proficiency 700
  helping – 707, 711
  hold in – 737
  hold out the – 894
  hold up the –
  vote 609
  in –
  incomplete 53
  business 625
  preparing 673
  not finished 730
  possessed 777
  money 800
  in the –s of
  authority 737
  subjection 749
  lay –s on
  discover 480a
  use 677

take 789
rite 998
much on one's –s 682
on one's –s
  business 625
  redundant 641
  not finished 730
  for sale 796
on the other – 468
no – in 623
poor – 701
put into one's –s 784
put one's – to 676
ready to one's – 673
shake –s 918
stretch forth one's – 680
take by the – 707
take in –
  teach 537
  undertake 676
time hanging on one's –s
  inaction 681
  leisure 685
  weary 841
try one's – 675
turn one's – 675
turn one's – to 625
under one's
  in writing 590
  promise 768
  compact 769
  – back 683
  – cart 272
  – of death 360
  – down
  record 551
  transfer 783
have one's –s full 682
  – gallop 274
  – glass 445
  – and glove 709, 888
  – in hand
  joined 43
  accompanying 88
  same time 120
  concur 178
  co-operate 709
  party 712
  concord 714
  friend 888
  social 892
  – to hand
  touching 199
  transfer 270
  fight 720, 722
  – over head
  inattention 458
  neglect 460
  reckless 863
  have a – in
  cause 153
  act 680
  co-operate 709
  have one's – in
  skill 698
  keep one's – in 613
live from – to mouth
  insufficient 640

in action 680
active 682
subjection 749
– up 293
harp
  repeat 104
  musical instru-
  ment 417
  weary 841
Harpagon 819
harper 416
harpist 416
harpoon 727
harpsichord 417
harpy
  relentless 739
  thief 792
  miser 819
  evil-doer 913
  demon 980
harquebuss 727
harridan 846, 962
harrier 366
harrow
  agriculture 371
  – up the soul 860
harrowing 830
harry pain 830
  attack 716
  persecute 907
Harry, old – 978
harsh
  acrid 171
  'sound 410
  style 579
  discordant 713
  severe 739
  disagreeable 830
  morose 895
  malevolent 907
  – voice 581
hart 366, 373
hartal 142, 489
harum-scarum 59,
  458
haruspice 513
Haruspicy 511
harvest
  effect 154
  profit 618
  store 636
  acquisition 775
  get in the –
  complete 729
  succeed 731
  – home
  celebration 883
  – time
  autumn 126
  exertion 686
has been 122
hash mix 41
  cut 44
  confusion 59
  food 298
  make a – 699
hashish 863
hasp 43, 45
hassock 215
hastate 253
haste
  velocity 274
  activity 682
  hurry 684
hasten
  promote 707
hasty

transient 113
hurried 684
impatient 825
irritable 901
– pudding 298
hat 225
  cardinal's – 999
  send round the –
  765
  shovel – 999
  – in hand 886
hatch
  produce 161
  gate 232
  opening 260
  chickens 370
  fabricate 544
  shading 556
  plan 626
  prepare 673
  – a plot 626
hatches, under –
  restraint 751
  prisoner 754
  poor 804
hatchet
  cutting 253
  bury the – 918
  dig up the – 722
  throw the helve
  after the – 818
hatchet-faced 203
hatchment
  funeral 363
  arms 550
  round 551
hatchway 260
hate 867, 898
hateful 649, 830
hath been, the
  time – 122
hatrack 215
hatter 225
  mad as a – 503
hatti-sheriff 741
hatred [see hate],
  object of – 898
hauberk 717
haud passibus
  æquis 28, 275
haugh 344
haughty
  proud 878
  insolent 885
  contemptuous 930
haul drag 285
  catch of fish &c.
  789
  – down one's flag
  725
  – in 10
haunch 236
haunt focus 74
  presence 186
  abode 189
  alarm 860
  persecute 907
  – the memory
  remember 505
  trouble 830
haunted 980
haut
  traiter de –
  insolence 885
  contempt 930
hautboy 417
haut-goût 392

haut-monde 875
hauteur 878
have confute 479
  ken 49
  possess 777
  – the advantage
  28, 33
  – at 716
  – no choice 609a
  – done! 142
  – to do with 9
  – no end 112
  – other fish to fry
  135
  – it
  discover 480a
  believe 484
  – one to know 527
  – some knowledge
  of 490
  – nothing to do
  with 10
  – for one's own
  780
  – rather 609
  – one's rights 924
  – the start 116
  – in store 152, 637
  – to 620
  – up 638
  – it your own way
  submission 725
haven 292, 666
haversack 191
havoc
  destruction 162
  cry – war 722
  play – spoil 659
haw 583
hawk spit 297
  stammer 583
  eye of a – 498
  – about
  publish 531
  offer 763
  sell 796
  – at 716
  between – and
  buzzard 315,
  828
  know a – from a
  handsaw 465,
  698
hawker 796
hawk-eyed 441
hawking chase 622
hawser 45
hay while the sun
  shines, make –
  134
haycock 72
hazard
  chance 156, 621
  danger 665
  at all –s 604
  – a conjecture 514
  – a proposition
  477
haze mist 353
  uncertainty 475
  in a –
  hidden 528
hazel 433
hazy opaque 426
he 373
head precedence 62
  beginning 66

class 75
  summit 210
  coiffure 225
  lead 280
  froth 353
  person 372
  intellect 450
  topic 454
  wisdom 498
  picture 556
  nomenclature 564
  chapter 593
  direct 693
  director 694
  master 745
  at the – of
  direction 693
  authority 737
  repute 873
  bow the – 308
  bring to a – 729
  come into one's –
  451
  come to a – 729
  drive into one's –
  505
  gain – 175
  get into one's –
  thought 451
  learn 505
  belief 484
  intoxicate 959
  give a horse his –
  748
  hang one's – 879
  have in one's – 490
  from – to heels 52,
  200
  hit on the – 912
  knock on the –
  361
  knock one's –
  against
  impulse 276
  unskilful 699
  fail 732
  lie on one's – 926
  lift up one's – 878
  make – against
  oppose 708
  resistance 719
  success 731
  never entered
  into one's – 458
  have no – 506
  on one's – 218
  off one's – 503
  can't get out of
  one's – 505
  over – and ears
  deep 641
  debt 806
  love 897
  put into one's –
  supposition 514
  information 527
  put out of one's –
  458
  run in the – 505
  not know whether
  one stands on –
  or heels
  uncertain 475
  wonder 870
  take into one's –
  thought 451
  caprice 608

intention 620
  turn the – 824
  trouble one's –
  about 457
  as one's – shall
  answer for 768
  with – erect 878
  from – to foot 200
  – and front
  important 642
  – and front of
  one's offending
  provocation 830
  charge 938
  – over heels
  inversion 218
  rotation 312
  – light 423
  – line 591
  – and shoulders
  irrelevant 10
  complete 52
  haste 684
  make neither – nor
  tail of 519
  hold one's – up
  307
  – above water
  safe 664
  prosperous 743
  wealth 803
  with a – on 353
headache 378
head-dress 225
header 310
head-foremost
  violent 173
  rash 863
head-gear 225
heading prefix 64
  beginning 66
  indication 550
  title 564
headland
  height 206
  projection 250
headlong
  hurry 684
  rush 863
  rush –
  violence 173
headman 694
headmost
  front 234
  precession 280
head-piece
  summit 210
  intellect 450
  helmet 717
  ornament 847
head-quarters
  focus 74
  abode 189
  authority 737
head-race 350
head-stone 363
heads
  compendium 596
  – or tails 156, 621
  lay – together
  advice 695
  co-operate 709
  – I win tails you
  lose
  unfair 940
headship 737
headsman 975

high-brow 492
higher 33
highest 210
highfalutin 884
high-flavored 392
high-flier
  madman 504
  proud 878
high-flown
  imaginative 515
  style 577
  proud 878
  vain 880
  insolent 885
high-flying
  inattentive 458
  exaggerated 549
  ostentatious 822
highlands 206
high-low 225
high-mettled
  excitable 825
  brave 861
high-minded
  honorable 939
  magnanimous 942
highness *title* 877
high-pitched 410
high-seasoned 392
high-souled 878
high-sounding
  loud 404
  words 577
  display 882
high-spirited 861, 939
hight 564
high-toned 852
high-water
  completeness 52
  height 206
  crater 337
  – mark
  measure 466
highway 627
  –s and byways 627
  – robbery 791
highwayman 792
high-wrought
  good 648
  prepared 673
  excited 824
hike 266
hilarity 836
hill *height* 206
  convexity 250
  ascent 305
  descent 306
  take to the –s 666
  –dwelling 206
hillock 206
hilt 633
hinc illæ lachrymæ 155
hind *back* 235
  clown 876
  on one's – legs
  elevation 307
  anger 900
  – quarters 235
hinder 706
hindermost 67, 235
Hindooism 984
hindrance 706
hinge *fasten* 43

fastening 45
cause 153
depend upon 154
rotate 312
hinny 271
hint *reminder* 505
  suppose 514
  inform 527
  take a – 498
  – a fault &c. 932
hinterland 235
hip 236
  have on the –
  confute 479
  success 731
  authority 737
  subjection 749
  – hip, hurrah! 838
hipped [*see* hypped]
hippocentaur 80
Hippocrates 662
hippocratic 360
hippodrome
  drama 599
  arena 728
  amusement 840
hippogriff 83
Hippolytus 960
hippophagy 298
hippopotamus 192
hirdie-girdie 218
hire
  commission 755
  borrowing 788
  price 812
  reward 973
  on – 763
hireling 746
hirsute 256
hispid 256
hiss *sound* 409
  animal cry 412
  disrespect 929
  contempt 930
  disapprobation 932
hist! 585, 586
histology 329
historian 553
historic 594
historiette 594
historical:
  – painter 559
  – painting 556
historiographer 553
historiography 594
history *past* 122
  record 551
  narrative 594
History, Natural – 357
histrionic 599
hit *chance* 156
  strike 276
  reach 292
  succeed 731
  censure 932
  (*punish* 972)
  good – 626
  make a – 731
  – one's fancy 829
  – the mark 731
  – off 545
  – upon
  discover 480a
  plan 626
hitch

fasten 43
knot 45
stoppage 142
hang 214
jerk 315
harness 370
difficulty 704
hindrance 706
  – up 293
hither 278, 292
  come – 286
hitherto 122
hive
  multitude 102
  location 184
  abode 189
  bees 870
  workshop 691
H.M.S. 726
hoar *aged* 128
  white 430
  – frost 383
hoard 636
hoarse
  husky 405
  harsh 410
  voiceless 581
  talk oneself – 584
hoary [*see* hoar]
hoax 545
hob *support* 215
  stove 386
  – and nob
  celebration 883
  courtesy 894
hobble
  limp 275
  awkward 699
  difficulty 704
  fail 732
  shackle 751
  – skirt 225
hobbledehoy 129
hobby
  crotchet 481
  pursuit 622
  desire 865
hobby-horse 272
hobgoblin
  fearful 860
  demon 980
hobo 268
hobnail 876
Hobson's choice
  necessity 601
  no choice 609a
  compulsion 744
hoc genus omne 876
hock 771
hock shop 787
hockey 840
hockey rink 213
hocus 545
hocus-pocus
  interchange 148
  unmeaning 517
  cheat 545
  conjuration 992
  spell 993
hod
  receptacle 191
  support 215
  vehicle 272
hoddy-doddy 501
hodge-podge 41, 59
hoe 272, 371

hog *animal* 366
  sensualist 954a
  glutton 957
  (greedy as a – 865
  go the whole – 604
hog's back 206
hogmanay 998
hogshead 191
hog-wash 653
hoist 307
  – the black flag 722
  – a flag 550
  – on one's own petard
  retaliation 718
  failure 732
hoity-toity! 815, 870
hold *cohere* 46
  contain 54
  remain 141
  cease 142
  go on 143
  happen 151
  receptacle 191
  cellar 207
  base 211
  support 215
  halt 265
  believe 484
  be passive 681
  defend 717
  power 737
  restrain 751
  prison 752
  prohibit 761
  possess 777
  retain 781
  enough! 869
  have a firm – 781
  have a – upon 175
  gain a – upon 737
  get – of 789
  quit one's – 782
  take – 175
  – aloof
  stay away 187
  distrust 487
  avoid 623
  – an argument 476
  – authority 737
  – back *avoid* 623
  store 636
  hinder 706
  restrain 751
  retain 781
  miserly 819
  – one's breath
  wonder 870
  – converse 588
  – a council 695
  – fast 751, 781
  – forth *teach* 537
  speak 582
  – good 478, 494
  – one's ground 141
  – in hand 737
  – one's hand
  cease 142
  relinquish 624
  – hard 265
  – up one's head 861
  – a lease 771

– a meeting 72
– off 623
– office 693
– on
  continue 141, 143
  persevere 604a
  – out [*see below*]
  – one's own
  preserve 670
  defend 717
  resist 719
  – oneself in readiness 673
  – in remembrance 505
  – both one's sides 838
  – a situation 625
  – in solution 335
  – to 602
  – together 43, 709
  – one's tongue 403, 585
  – up [*see below*]
  – oneself up 307
hold out
  endure 106
  affirm 535
  persevere 604a
  resist 719
  offer 763
  brave 861
  – expectation
  predict 511
  promise 768
  – temptation 865
hold up
  continue 143
  support 215
  not rain 340
  aid 707
  rob 791
  display 882
  extol 931
  – one's hand
  sign 550
  threat 609
  – to execration
  cures 908
  censure 932
  – the mirror 525
  – to scorn 930
  – to shame 874
  – to view 525
holder 779
holdfast 45
holding
  tenancy 777
  property 780
hole *place* 182
  hovel 189
  receptacle 191
  opening 260
  ambush 530
  – in one's coat 651
  – and corner
  place 182
  peer into – 461
  hiding 528, 530
  – to creep out of
  plea 617
  escape 671
  facility 705
holiday *leisure* 685
  repose 687
  amusement 840
  – task *easy* 705

holiness *God* 976
 piety 987
holloa 411
 – before one is out
  of the wood 884
hollow
 unsubstantial 4
 . *completely* 52
 incomplete 53
 depth 208
 concavity 252
 channel 350
 – *sound* 408
 specious 477
 false 544
 voiceless 581
 beat – 731
 – truce 723
holm 346
holocaust
 kill 361
 sacrifice 991
 (*destruction* 162)
holograph 590
holster 191
holt 367
holus bolus 684
Holy *of God* 976
 pious 987
 keep – 987
 – breathing 990
 – Church 983*a*
 – City 981
 – day 998
 – Ghost 976
 temple of the –
  Ghost 983*a*
 – men of old 985
 – orders 995
 – place 1000
 – Scriptures 985
 – Spirit 976
 – water 998
 – week 998
holystone 652
homage
 submission 725
 fealty 743
 reverence 928
 approbation 931
 worship 990
home *focus* 74
 habitation 189
 near 197
 interior 221
 arrival 292
 refuge 666
 at – *party* 72
 present 186
 within 221
 at ease 705
 social gathering
  892
 be at –
 – *to visitors* 892
 feel at –
  freedom 748
  pleasure 827
  content 831
 look at –
  accusation 938
 make oneself at –
  free 748
  sociable 892
 not be at – 764
 stay at – 265
 at – in

knowledge 490
skill 698
at – with
 friendship 888
bring – to
 evidence 467
 belief 484
 accuse 938
 condemn 971
 come – 292
 eternal – 98
 from – 187
 get – 292 ,
 go – 283
 go from – 293
long – 363 .
strike –
 energy 171
 attack 716
 – stroke 170
 – thrust
  attack 716
 censure 932
home-bred 851
home-felt 821, 824
home-rule 737, 748
homeless
 unhoused 185
 banished 893
homely
 language 576
 unadorned 849
 common 851, 876
homeopathic
 small 32
 little 193
Homeopathy 662
Homeric
 – laughter 838
home-sick 833
home-spun
 texture 329
home-stall 189
homestead 189
homeward bound
  292
homicidal maniac
  913
homicide 361
homiletical 892
homily
 teaching 537
 advice 595
 sermon 998
hominem, argu-
  mentum ad –
  938
homogeneity
 relation 9
 identity 13
 uniformity 16
 simplicity 42
homogenesis 161
homologous 23
homology
 relation 9
 uniformity 16
 equality 27
 concord 714
homonym
 equivocal 520
 vocal sound 580
homophony 413
homunculus 193
Hon. 817
hone 253
honest

veracious 543
 honorable 939
 pure 960
 – *meaning* 516
 turn an – penny
  775
 – *truth* 494
honey
 sweet 396
 favorite 899
 milk and – 734
honeycomb
 concave 252
 opening 260
 deterioration 659
honeyed
 – *phrases* 894
 – *words*
 allurement 615
 flattery 933
honeymoon
 pleasure 827
 . *endearment* 902
 marriage 903
honey-mouthed
  894, 933
honeysuckle 396
honorarium 784,973
honorary 815
honor
 demesne 780
 glory 873
 title 877
 respect 928
 approbation 931
 probity 939
 affair of – 720
 do – to 883
 do the –s
  sociality 892
  courtesy 894
  respect 928
 his – *judge* 967
 in – of 883
 man of – 939
 upon my – 535,
  768
 word of – 768
 – be to 873
 – a bill 807
 – in the breach
  923
 – bright
  veracity 543
  probity 939
honte, mauvaise –
  881
hood 225, 999
hooded 223
hoodlum 887
hoodoo 649
hoodwink
 ignore 491
 blind 442
 hide 528
 deceive 545
hoof 211
 cloven – 907
hook *fasten* 43
 fastening 45
 hang 214
 curve 245
 deceive 545
 retain 781
 take 789
 by – or by crook
  631

hookah 392
hooker *ship* 273
hookey, blind – 840
hooks, go off the
  360
hooligan 887, 913
hoop *circle* 247
 cry 411
hoot *cry* 411, 412
 deride 929
 contempt 930
 censure 932
hop *leap* 309
 dance 840, 892
 – off 293
 – skip and jump
  leap 309
 agitation 315
 haste 684
 game 840
 – the twig 360
hope 858
 band of – 958
 beyond – 658, 734
 dash one's –s 837
 excite – 511
 foster – 858
 well-grounded –
  472
 – against hope 859
 – for the best 858
 – deferred
  dejection 837
  lamentation 859
 – for *expect* 507
 desire 865
hope chest 858
hopeful *infant* 129
 probable 472
 hope 858
hopelessness 471,
  859
Hop-o'-my-thumb
  193
hopper 191
horary 108
horde
 assemblage 72
 party 712
 commonalty 876
horizon
 distance 196
 view 441
 expectation 507
 appear on the –
  525
 gloomy – 859
horizontality 213
horn
 receptacle 191
 sharp 253
 music 417
 draw in one's –s
  recant 607
  submit 725
  humility 879
 exalt one's – 873
 wear the –s 905
 –s of a dilemma
  reasoning 476
  difficulty 704
 – in 294
 – mad 920
 – of plenty 639
hornbook 542
hornet
 evil-doer 913

–'s nest
 pitfall 667
 difficulty 704
 adversity 735
 painful 830
 resentment 900
 censure 932
hornpipe 840
hornwork 717
horny 323
Horny, old – 978
horology 114
horoscope 511, 992
horresco referens
  860
horrible *great* 31
 noxious 649
 dire 830
 ugly 846
 fearful 860
horrid [*see* horrible]
 vulgar 851
horrida bella 722
horrific [*see*
  horrible]
horrified 828, 860
horrify 830, 860
horripilation 383
horrisonous 410
horror 860, 867
 view with – 898
horrors 837
 sup full of – 828
horror-stricken 828
hors de combat
 impotent 158
 useless 645
 tired out 688
 put – 731
hors-d'œuvre 298
horse *hang on* 214
 stand 215
 carrier 271
 animal 366
 male 373
 cavalry 726
 ride the high –
  885
 put the –s to 673
 put up one's –s at
  184
 put up one's –s
  together
  concord 714
  friendship 888
 take – 266
 to – 293
 war – 726
 work like a – 686
 – artillery 726
 – of another color
  15
 – doctor 370
 – and foot 726
 – laugh 838
 – marine 701
 like a – in a mill
  613
 – racing
  pastime 840
  contention 720
 – soldier 726
 – track 627
horseback 266
horse-cloth 225
horseman 268
horsemanship

465a
indispensable 630
indispose
   dissuade 616
indisposed
   unwilling 603
   sick 655
indisputable 474
indissoluble,
   indissolvable
   joined 43
   whole 50
   stable 150
   dense 321
indistinct 447
indistinction 465a
indistinguishable
   identical 13
   invisible 447
indisturbance 265,
   826
indite 590
individual
   whole 50
   special 79
   unity 87
   person 372
indivisible *whole* 50
   dense 321
indocility 158, 606
indoctrinate 537
indolence 683, 927
indomitable
   strong 159
   determined 604
   persevering 604a
   resisting 719
   courage 861
indoor 221
indorse 769, 771
indorsement 550,
   551
indraught 343, 348
indubitable 474
induce *cause* 153
   power 157
   produce 161
   motive 615
induct 883
induction
   inquiry 461
   reasoning 476
   drama 599
   appointment 755
   - *of a priest* 995
indulge *lenity* 740
   allow 760
   please 829
   intemperance 954
   gluttony 959
   - one's fancy 609
   - in 827
   - oneself 943
   - in reverie
   inattention 458
   fancy 515
   - with *give* 784
indulgence
   [*see* indulge]
   absolution 918
indulgent *kind* 906
induration
   hardening 323
   impenitence 951
Indus to the pole,
   from – 180
industry 625, 682

hive of – 691
indweller 188
indwelling 5
inebriety 959
inedible 395
ineffable *great* 31
   inexpressible 521
   wonderful 870
ineffaceable 820
ineffectual
   incapable 158
   useless 645
   failing 732
   - attempt 732
   pale its – fire 422
inefficacious
   incapable 158
   useless 645
   failing 732
inefficient 158
inelastic *soft* 324
   - fluid 333
inelasticity 326
inelegance 579, 846
ineluctable 474
inept 24, 158, 645
inequality 28
inequitable 923
ineradicable
   intrinsic 5
   stable 150
inerrable 946
inertia 172
inertness
   physical 172
   inactive 683
   moral 823
inestimable 648
inevitable 474, 601
inexact
   erroneous 495
   feeble 575
inexcitability 826
inexcusable
   accusable 938
   vicious 45
inexecution 730
inexhaustible 105,
   639
inexistence 2
inexorable
   unavoidable 601
   resolved 604
   stern 739
   compelling 744
   pitiless 914a
   revengeful 919
inexpectation 508
inexpedience 647
inexpensive 815
inexperience 491,
   699
inexpert 699
inexpiable 945
inexplicable 519
inexpressible
   great 31
   unmeaning 517
   unintelligible 519
   wonderful 870
inexpressibles 225
inexpression
   latency 526
inexpensive 517
inexpugnable 664
inextension 180a
   littleness 193

immateriality 317
inextinguishable
   stable 150
   strong 159
   excitable 825
   - desire 865
inextricable
   coherent 46
   disorder 59
   impossible 471
infallibility 474
   assumption of –
   885
infamy *shame* 874
   dishonor 940
   vice 945
infancy 66, 127
infandum renovare
   dolorem 505,
   833
infant 129
   fool 501
   - prodigy 872
Infanta 745
infanticide 361, 991
infantine 129
   foolish 499
infantry 726
infarction 261
infatuation
   misjudgment 481
   credulity 486
   folly 499
   insanity 503
   obstinacy 606
   passion 825
   love 897
infeasible 471
infect *mix with* 41
   contaminate 659
   excite 824
infectâ, re –
   shortcoming 304
   non-completion
   730
   failure 732
infection
   transference 270
   disease 655
infectious 270, 657
infecund 169
infelicity
   inexpertness 699
   misery 828
infelicitous 24
infer 472
inference 476, 480
   by – 467
inferential
   demonstrative 478
   latent 526
inferiority
   in degree 34
   in size 195
   imperfection 651
   personal – 34
infernal *bad* 649
   malevolent 907
   wicked 945
   satanic 978
   - machine 727
   - regions 982
infertility 169
infest 830
infestivity 837, 843
infibulation 43
infidel 487, 989

infidelity
   dishonor 940
   irreligion 989
infiltrate *mix* 41
   intervene 228
   interpenetrate 294
   moisten 337, 339
   teach 537
infiltration
   passage 302
Infinite, the – 976
infinite 105
   - goodness 976
infinitely *great* 31
infinitesimal
   small 32
   little 193
   - calculus 85
infinity 105
infirm *weak* 160
   disease 655
   vicious 945
   - of purpose 605
infirmary 662
infirmity
   [*see* infirm]
infix 537
inflame
   render violent 173
   burn 384
   excite 824
   anger 900
inflamed 382
inflammable 384,
   388
inflammation
   heating 384
   disease 655
inflate *increase* 35
   expand 194
   blow 349
inflated
   overestimation
   482
   style 573, 577
   ridiculous 853
   vain 880
inflation
   [*see* inflate]
   rarefaction 322
   currency 800
inflect 245
inflexible *hard* 323
   resolved 604
   obstinate 606
   stern 739
   inexorable 914a
inflexion
   change 140
   curvature 245
   grammar 567
inflict *act upon* 680
   severity 739
   - evil 649
   - pain
   bodily pain 378
   mental pain 830
   - punishment 972
infliction
   adversity 735
   mental pain 828,
   830
   punishment 972
influence 153
   change 140
   physical – 175
   inducement 615

instrumentality
   631
   authority 737
   absence of – 175a
   sphere of – 780
   make one's – felt
   631
influx 294
infold 232
inform 527
   - against
   accuse 938
   go to law 969
informal 83, 964
informality 773
informant 527
information
   knowledge 490
   communication
   527
   learning 539
   lawsuit 969
pick up – 539
informer 532
informity 241
infra dignitatem
   874, 940
infraction
   trespass 303
   disobedience 742
   non-observance
   773
   exemption 927
   - of usage &c.
   unconformity 83
   desuetude 614
infrangible
   combined 46
   dense 321
infra-red rays 420
infrequency 137
infrigidation 385
infringe
   transgress 303
   disobey 742
   not observe 773
   undueness 925
   dereliction 927
   - a law &c. 83
infundibular 252,
   269
infuriate
   violent 173
   excite 824
   anger 900
infuscate 431
infuse *mix* 41
   insert 300
   teach 537
   - courage 861
   - life into 824
   - new blood 658
infusible 321
infusion [*see* infuse]
   liquefaction 335
infusoria 193
ingannation 545
ingathering 72
ingemination 90
ingenerate 5
ingenious 515, 698
ingenite 5
ingenium, per-
   fervidum – 682
ingénu *artless* 703
ingénue *actress* 599
ingenuity 698

- at the door
  death 360
  request 765
- down
  destroy 162
  lay flat 213
  lower 308
  injure 659
  dishearten 837
- on the head
  kill 361
- one's head
  against 699
- off complete 729
- out 162
- over 162
- under 725
- up 688
knock-down argument 479
knocked
- to atoms 162
- on the head
  failure 732
knocker 936
knock-kneed 243, 244
knoll 206
knot ligature 45
  entanglement 59
  group 72
  intersection 219
  round 249
  dense 321
  difficulty 704
  hindrance 706
  junto 712
  ornament 847
  marriage 903
  true lover's - love 897
  endearment 902
  tie the nuptial - 903
knotted rough 256
knout 975
know believe 484
  knowledge 490
  friendly 888
  associate 892
  I'd have you to - 457, 535
  not that one -s 491
- what one is about 698
- all 474
I - better 536
- no bounds great 31
  infinite 105
  redundance 641
- for certain 484
- by heart 505
- one's own mind 604
- one's stuff 465
- one's way about 465
- nothing of 491
- what's what 698
- which is which 465
knowing 702
knowingly 620
knowledge 490
  [and see know]

acquire - 539
come to one's - 527
practical - 698
- of the world 698
known:
  become - 529
  make - inform 527
  publish 531
  well - 490
  habitual 613
- as 564
- by 550
knuckle 244
- down 725
knuckle-duster 727
knurl 256
knurr and spell 840
kobold 980
Koh-i-noor 650
kopje 206
Koran 986
kowtow bow 308
  submission 725
  courtesy 894
  respect 928
kraal 189, 232
kraken 83
kris 727
Krishna 979
kudos 931
Ku klux klan 712
kursaal 840
kyanize 670
kyles 343

L

laager 717
labarum 550
labefy 659
label 39, 550
labent 306
labial lip 231
  letter 561
labitur et labetur 112, 143
labor
  parturition 161
  work 680
  exertion 686
  hard -
  punishment 972
  mountain in - 638
- for 620
- of love
  willing 602
  amusement 840
  disinterested 942
- party 712
- under state 7
  disease 655
  difficulty 704
  feeling 821
  affliction 828
- in vain
  fall short 304
  useless 645
- in one's vocation 625
- unrest 832
labor hoc opus, hic - 704
laboratory 691
labored - style 579
  prepared 673

- study 457
laborer 690
laboring
- man 690
- oar 686
laborious
  active 682
  exertion 686
  difficult 704
labyrinth
  disorder 59
  convolution 248
  secret 533
lac number 98
  resin 356a
- of rupees 800
lace stitch 43
  netting 219
  ornament 847
- one's jacket 972
lacerable 328
lacerate 44
- the heart 830
laches 460, 773
Lachesis 601
lachrymae, hinc
  illae - 830
lachrymatory gas 727
lachrymis, quis
  temperet a - 914
lachrymose 837
lack require 630
  insufficient 640
  destitute 804
  desire 865
- faith 989
- harmony 708
- preparation 674
- wit 501
lackadaisical
  inactive 683
  melancholy 837
  indifferent 866
lackadaisy! 839, 870
lack-brain 499, 501
lacker [see lacquer]
lackey 746
lack-luster 422, 429
laconic 572
lacquer
  covering 223
  resin 356a
  adorn 847
lacrosse 840
lacteal 352
lacuna 198, 252
lacustrine 343
lad 129
ladder 305, 627
  kick down the - 604
lade load 184
  transfer 185
  contents 190
  dip 270
- out 297
laden 52
  heavy - 828
- with 777
ladies' man 897
lading 190, 780
  bill of - list 86
ladle receptacle 191
  transfer 270
  vehicle 272

lady woman 374
  rank 875
  wife 903
  our - 977
- day 138
- help 746
- 's maid 746
lady chapel 1000
ladylike
  womanly 374
  fashionable 852
lady-love 897
lag linger 275
  follow 281
  dawdle 683
- behind 133
laggard 603, 683
lager beer 298
lagoon 343
laical 997
laid: - on one's
  back 158
- by the heels 751
- low 160
- up 655
lair 189, 653
laird master 745
  proprietor 779
  nobility 875
Lais 962
laisse manger, cela
  se - 394
laisser: - aller,
- faire
  permanence 141
  neglect 460
  inaction 681
  laxity 738
  freedom 748
  inexcitable 826
laity 997
lake water 343
  pink 434
- of fire and brim-
  stone 982
Lama 745, 996
Lamaism 984
Lamarkism 357
lamb infant 129
  animal 366
  gentle 826
  innocent 946
  go out like a - 174
  lion lies down
  with - 721
Lamb of God 976
lambent
  touching 379
- flame heat 382
  light 420
Lambeth 1000
lame incomplete 53
  impotent 158
  weak 160
  imperfect 651
  disease 655
  injury 659
  failing 732
- conclusion
  illogical 477
  failure 732
  help a - dog over
  a stile aid 707
  vindicate 937
- duck 808
- excuse 617
lamellar 204

lamentable bad 649
  painful 830
  sad 837
lamentably very 31
lamentation 839
lamia 980, 994
lamina 51, 204
lamination 204
Lammas 998
lamp 423
  rub the - 992
  safety - 666
  smell of the -
  style 577
  prepared 673
lamplighter
  quick 682
lampoon 932, 934
lampooner 936
lanâ caprinâ, de -
  643
lanary 636
lanate 25, 256
lance pierce 260
  throw 284
  spear 727
  break a - with
  attack 716
  warfare 722
  couch one's - 720
- corporal 745
lancer 726
- 's dance 340
lancet 253, 262
lancinate 378, 830
land arrive 292
  ground 342
  estate 780
  gone to a better -
  360
  hug the - 286
  make the - 286
  on - 342
  see - 858
- covered with
  water 343
- flowing with
  milk and honey
  168
  how the - lies
  circumstances 8
  experiment 463
  foresight 510
  in the - of the
  living 359
landamman 745
landau 272
landed
- gentry 779
- estate 780
landgrave 745
landholder 779
landing field 273
landing-place 215,
  292
landlady 779
land-locked 229,
  343
landloper 268
landlord 779
land-lubber 343,
  701
landmark
  limit 233
  indication 550
land-mine 727
landreeve 694

LAN–LAY

Landsturm 726

Landwehr 726

- style 575

- for 865

[see languid]

- of Diogenes 461

- jaws 203

Laodicean 822

- of luxury

- of memory 506

- of time 109

Laputa, college of – 538

- number 102

- type 642

- aux yeux 839

- into fury 909

- with the tongue 931

- the waves 645

- in order 67

- in time 122

- but one &c. 67

- for ever 112

- finish 729

- gasp 360

- resort 666

- rites 998

- shift 601

- sleep 360

- stage 67

- straw 153

- stroke 729

- touch 729

- word

- year &c. 122

- organism 153

Latin

- and longitude

Latter-day Saint 984

- temporis acti past 122

- at ridicule 856

(undervalue 483)

- to scorn defy 715

- in one's sleeve

- on the wrong side of one's mouth

- gas 376

- forth 676

- into 676

- into eternity 360, 361

- out 573

- out against 716

- maid 746

- man 652

- of praise 931

Jewish – 985

- of the Medes and Persians 80, 148

- sleeves 999

- tennis 840

- style 575

- about one

- one's account for

debauched 961
lichgate 363
lichen 367
licit 760, 924
lick *lap* 298
  conquer 731
  punish 972
  – the dust 933
  – into shape 240
lickerish
  savory 394
  desirous 865
  fastidious 868
  licentious 961
lickpenny 819
lickspittle 886
lictor 965
lid 223
lie *situation* 183
  presence 186
  recline 213
  falsehood 544
  untruth 546
  give the – to 536
  white – 617
  – abed 683
  – in ambush 528
  – by 681
  – at one's door 926
  – down *flat* 213
  rest 687
  – fellow 674
  – hid 528
  – in *be* 1
  give birth 161
  – low 528
  – under a necessity 601
  – in a nutshell 32
  – on 215
  – over *defer* 133
  destiny 152
  – in one's power 157
  – at the root of 153
  – still 265
  – to
  quiescence 265
  inaction 681
  – under 177
  – in wait for
  expect 507
  inaction 681
lief *pleasant* 829
  as – *willing* 602
  choice 609
liege 745
liegeman 746
lien 771, 805
lienteria 653
lieu 182
  in – of 147
lieutenant 745, 759
  lord – 965
life *essence* 5
  events 151
  vitality 359
  biography 594
  activity 682
  conduct 692
  cheerful 836
  animal – 364
  battle of – 682
  come to – 660
  infuse into

excite 824
  put – into 359
  recall to – 660
  see – 840
  support – 359
  take away – 361
  tenant for – 779
  – to come 152
  – after death 981
  – or death
  need 630
  important 642
  contention 720
  – and spirit 682
Life, the 976
life-blood 5, 359
life-boat 273, 666
life-giving 168
lifeguards 726
lifeless 172, 360
lifelike 17
lifelong 110
life-preserver 666, 727
life-size 192
lifetime 108
life-weary 841
lift *raise* 307
  aid 707
  steal 791
  – cattle 791
  – up the eyes 441
  – a finger 680
  – hand against 716
  – one's head 734
  – up the heart 990
  – the mask 529
  – the voice
  shout 411
  speak 582
lift-smoke 840
ligament 45
ligation 43
ligature 45
light *state* 7
  small 32
  window 260
  velocity 274
  arrive 292
  descend 306
  levity 320
  kindle 384
  watch 388
  luminosity 420
  luminary 423
  – *in colour* 429
  white 430
  aspect 448
  knowledge 490
  interpretation 522
  unimportant 643
  easy 705
  gay 836
  loose 961
  blue – *signal* 550
  bring to –
  discover 480a
  manifest 525
  disclose 529
  children of – 987
  come to – 529
  false – 443
  foot –s 599
  half – 422
  make – of
  underrate 483

easy 705
  inexcitable 826
  despise 930
  in one's own – 699
  obstruct the – 426
  side – 490
  see the – *life* 359
  publication 531
  transmit – 425
  throw – upon 522
  a – breaks in upon one 529
  – under a bushel
  hide 528
  not hide 878
  modesty 881
  – comedy 599
  – cruiser 726
  – fantastic toe 309
  – upon one's feet 664
  – heart 836
  – of heel 274
  – horse 726
  – infantry 726
  – purse 804
  – and shade 420
  – of truth 543
  – up *illumine* 420
  excite 824
  – upon *chance* 156
  arrive at 292
  discover 480a
  acquire 775
Light of the World 976
lighten
  make light 320
  illume 420
  facilitate 705
lighter *boat* 273
lighterage 812
lighterman 269
light-fingered 791, 792
light-footed 274, 682
light-headed 503
lighthouse 550
lightless 421
light-minded 605
lightning
  velocity 274
  flash 420
  spark 423
  like greased – 113
lightsome
  luminous 420
  irresolute 605
  cheerful 836
ligneous 367
lignite 388
lignography 558
ligulate 205
like *similar* 17
  relish 394
  enjoy 377, 827
  wish 865
  love 897
  do what one –s 748
  look – 448
  we shall not look upon his – again 33
  – master like man 19

– a pin in paper 58
  likely 472
  think – 507
  likeness 21, 554
  bad – 555
  likewise 37
  liking 865, 897
  have a – for 827
  to one's – 829
  lilac *color* 437
  Liliputian 193
  Lillith 994
  lilt 416, 836
  lily *white* 430
  beauty 845
  paint the – 641
  lily-livered 862
  limæ labor
  improve 658
  toil 686
  limature 330, 331
  limb *member* 51
  instrument 633
  scamp 949
  – of the law 968
  limber 272, 324
  limbo *prison* 751, 752
  pain 828
  purgatory 982
  lime *entrap* 545
  – light 423, 531, 599
  Limehouse 908
  limine, in – 66
  limit *complete* 52
  end 67
  circumscribe 229
  boundary 233
  qualify 469
  restrain 751
  prohibit 761
  limitarian 984
  limitation [*see* limit]
  estate 780, 783
  limited
  – *in quantity* 32
  – *in size* 393
  to a – extent
  imperfect 651
  limitless 105
  limitrophe 197
  limn 556
  limner 559
  limousine 272
  limp *weak* 160
  slow 275
  supple 324
  fail 732
  limpid 425
  lin 343, 348
  lincture 662
  line *fastening* 45
  continuous 69
  ancestors 166
  descendants 167
  length 200
  no breadth 203
  string 205
  lining 224
  outline 230
  straight 246
  of steamers 273
  direction 278
  music 413
  appearance 448

measure 466
  mark 550
  writing 590
  verse 597
  vocation 625
  army and navy 726
  boundary – 233
  draw the – 465
  drop a – to 526
  in a –
  continuous 69
  straight 246
  in a – with 278
  read between the –s 522
  sounding – 208
  straight – 246
  troops of the – 726
  – of action 692
  – of battle 69
  – of battle ship 726
  – engraving 558
  – of march 278
  – of road 627
  lineage *kindred* 11
  series 69
  ancestry 166
  posterity 167
  lineament
  outline 230
  feature 240
  appearance 448
  mark 550
  linear
  continuity 69
  pedigree 166
  length 200
  linen 225
  liner 273
  lines
  fortification 717
  hard –
  adversity 735
  severity 739
  reins 752
  linger *protract* 110
  delay 133
  loiter 275
  lingerie 225
  lingo 560, 563
  lingua franca 563
  linguacious 584
  lingual 560, 582
  linguist 492
  linguistics 560
  liniment 356, 662
  lining 224
  link *relation* 9
  connect 43
  connecting – 45
  part 51
  term 71
  crossing 219
  torch 423
  golf –s 840
  missing – 53, 729
  linked together
  party 712
  linoleum 223
  linotype 591
  linseed oil 356
  linsey-wolsey 41
  linstock 388
  lint 223
  lintel 215

serve – 989
mammoth 192
man *adult* 131
  mankind 372
  male 373
  prepare 673
  workman 690
  servant 746
  courage 861
  husband 903
  make a – of 648,
   861
  Son of – 976
  straight – 599
  to a – 488
  –at-arms 726
  one's – of business
   758
  –'s estate 131
  – in office 745
  – in the street 876
  –of-war 273, 726
  –of-war's man 269
  – at the wheel 694
  – and wife 903
manacle 751, 752
manage 693
  – to *succeed* 731
manageable 705
management
  conduct 692
  skill 698
manager
  stage – 599
  director 694
managery 693
manche après la
  cognée, jeter le
  – 859
mancible 637
mancipation 751
mandamus 741
mandarin 745
mandate 630, 741
mandible 298
mandolin 417
mandragora 174
mandrel 312
manducation 298
mane 256
man-eater 361
manège 266, 370
manes 362
manet: – altâmente
  repostum 505
  – cicatrix 919
maneuver 680, 702
manful *strong* 159
  resolute 604
  brave 861
manger 191
manger:
  cela se laisse –.394
  – son blé en herbe
   818
mangle
  separate 44
  smooth 255
  injure 659
mangled 53
mangy 655
man-hater 911
manhood 131, 861
mania *insanity* 503
  desire 865
maniac 504
manibus pedibus–

que 686
manic 503
manic-depressive
  503
manicure 847
manicheism-978
manichord 417
manie 865
maniéré 855
manifest
  list 86
  visible 446
  obvious 525
  disclose 529
manifestation 525
manifesto 531
manifold 81, 102
manikin *dwarf* 193
  image 554
maniple 103
manipulate
  handle 379
  use 677
  conduct 692
manipulator 621
mankind 372
manly
  adolescent 131
  strong 159
  male 373
  brave 861
  honest 939
manna *food* 396
  – in the wilderness
   aid 707
  pleasing 829
manner *kind* 75
  style 569
  way 627
  conduct 692
  in a – 32
  by all – of means
   536
  by no – of means
   602
  to the – born 5
mannered 579
mannerism
  special 79
  unconformity 83
  affectation 855
  vanity 880
mannerly 894
manners 852, 894
manor 780
  lord of the – 779
  – house 189
manorial 780
Mansard roof 223
manse 1000
mansion 189
manslaughter 361
mansuetude 894
mantelpiece 215
mantilla 225
mantle *spread* 194
  dress 225
  foam 353
  shade 424
  redden 434
  robes 747
  flush 821, 824
  anger 900
mantlet *cloak* 225
  defence 717
Mantology 511
manual *guide* 527

schoolbook 542
book 593
advice 695
– labor 686
manubial 793
manufactory 691
manufacture 161,
  680
manufacturer 690
manumission 750
manure
  agriculture 371
  dirt 653
  aid 707
manuscript 22, 590
many 102
  the – 876
  for – a day 110
  – irons in the fire
   682
  – men many
   minds 489
  – times
   repeated 104
   frequent 136
many-colored 440
many-sided 81, 236
many-tōngued 532
map 234, 527, 554
  – out 626
mar 659, 706
marabou 83
marabout 1000
maranatha 908
marasmus
  shrinking 195
  atrophy 655
  deterioration 659
maraud 791
marauder 792
marble *ball* 249
  hard 323
  sculpture 557
  tablet 590
  insensible 823
marble 440
marble-hearted 907
march *region* 181
  journey 266
  progression 282
  music 415
  dead – 363
  forced – 684
  on the – 264
  steal a –
  advance 280
  go beyond 303
  deceive 545
  active 682
  cunning 702
  – against 716
  – of events 151
  – of intellect
   knowledge 490
   improvement 658
  – off 293
  – on a point 278
  – past 882
  – of time 109
  – with 199
March, Ides of – 601
marches 233
marchioness 875
marcid 203
marconigram 523
marcor 203
mare *horse* 271

female 374
–'s nest 497, 546
–'s tail *wind* 349
  cloud 353
marechal 745
margarine 356
margin *space* 180
  edge 231
  redundance 641
  latitude 748
margravate 780
margrave 745, 875
marimba 417
marine *fleet* 273
  sailor 269
  oceanic 341
  soldier 726
  tell it to the –s
   489, 497
  – painter 559
  – painting 556
mariner 269
Mariolatry 991
marionnette
  representation
   554
  drama 599
  amusement 840
marish 345
marital 903
maritime 267, 341
mark *degree* 26
  term 71
  take cognizance
   of 450
  attend to 457
  indication 550
  record 551
  writing 590
  object 620
  importance 642
  repute 873
  beyond the – 303
  leave one's – 873
  man of – 873, 875
  near the – 197
  overshoot the –
   699
  put a – upon 457
  save the – 870
  up to the –
  enough 639
  good 648
  skill 698
  due 924
  wide of the – 196,
   495
  within the – 304
  – down 813
  – off 551
  – out *choose* 609
   plan 626
   command 741
  – of recognition
   894
  – with a red letter
   883
  – time
   chronometry 114
   halt 265
   wait 507
  – with a white
   stone 931
marked [*see* mark]
  great 31
  affirmed 535
  well– 446

  in a – degree 31
  play with – cards
   545
  – down 815
marker 550
market *buy* 795
  mart 799
  bring to – 796
  buy in the cheap-
   est &c. – 794
  in the –
  offered 763
  barter 794
  sale 796
  rig the – 794
  – garden 371
  – overt
  manifest 525
  mart 799
  – place *street* 189
  mart 799
  – price 812
  – woman 797
marketable 794,
  796
marksman 700
marksmanship 698
marl 342
marmalade 396
marmot 683
maroon
  color 433, 434
  abandon 782, 893
marplot
  bungler 701
  obstacle 706
  malicious 913
marque, letters of –
  791
marquee 223
marquetry 440
marquis 875
marriage 903
  companionate –
   903
  ill-assorted – 904
  – bells 836
  – portion 780
marriageable 131,
  903
marrow *essence* 5
  interior 221
  central 222
  chill to the – 385
marrow-bones, on
  one's –
  submit 725
  beg 765
  humble 879
  servile 886
  atonement 952
marrowless 158
marry *combine* 48
  assertion 535
  wed 903
  – come up
  defiance 715
  anger 900
  censure 932
Mars 722, 979
  – orange 439
marsh 345
marshal
  arrange 60
  messenger 534
  auxiliary 711
  officer 745

merged 228
meridian
region 181
room 125
summit 210
light 420
– of life 131
merit
goodness 648
due 924
virtue 944
make a – of 884
– notice 642
merito, e – 944
meritorious 931
Merlin 994
mermaid 341
monster 83
mythology 979, 980
merman 341
mero motu, ex – 600
merriment
cheerful 836
amusement 840
merry *cheerful* 836
drunk 959
make – *sport* 840
make – with
wit 842
ridicule 856
wish a – Christmas &c. 896
– and wise 842
merry-andrew 844
merry-go-round 312, 840
merry-making 827, 840, 892
merry-thought 842
mersion 337
meruit ferat, pal-mam qui – 873
merveille, à – 731
mesa 344
mésalliance 24, 903
meseems 484
mesh 198, 219
meshes *trap* 545
difficulty 704
– of sophistry 477
meshwork 219
mesial
middle 68
mesmerism 992
mesmerist 994
mesne lord 779
mess *mixture* 41
disorder 59
barracks 191
meal 298
difficulty 704
portion 786
make a –
unskilful 699
fail 732
message
intelligence 532
command 741
Messalina 962
messenger 271
envoy **534**
servant 746
– balloon 463
Messiah 976
messianic 976

messmate 890
messuage 189
messy 59
metabolism 140
metacenter 222
metachronism 115
metage 466
metagenesis 140
metagrammatism 561
metal 635
Brittania – 545
metallic *sound* 410
metalepsis 521
metallurgy 358
metamorphosis 140
metaphor
comparison 464
figure **521**
(*analogy* 17)
metaphrase 522
metaphrast 524
metaphrastic 516
metaphysics 450
metastasis, meta-thesis
change 140
inversion 218
displacement 270
mete *measure* 466
distribute 786
– out *give* 784
metempsychosis 140
meteor 318, 423
meteoric 173, 420
meteorology 338
meteoromancy 466
meter 466
meter
length 200
poetry 597
metheglin 396
methylated spirit 388
methinks 484
method *order* 58
way **627**
want of – 59
methodical 60
Methodist 984
methodist
journalist 988
methodize 60
Methuselah 130
old as – 12
since the days of – 124
meticulous 772
métier 625
métis 83
metonymy 521
metoposcopy
front 234
appearance 44
interpret 522
metrical
measured 466
verse 597
metrology 466
moderation 174
mid-course 628
metropolis 189
metropolitan
archbishop 996
mettle *spirit* 820
courage 861

man of – 861
on one's –
resolved 604
put on one's –
excite 824
encourage 861
mettlesome
energetic 171
sensitive 822
excitable 825
brave 861
mettre de l'eau
dans son vin 160
meum et tuum 780
disregard distinc-tion between – 791
mew *moult* 226
cry 412
– up 751
mewed up 229
mewl 412
mews 189
mezzanine floor 191, 599
mezzo rilievo
convex 250
sculpture 557
mezzo termine
middle 68
mid-course 628
compromise 774
Mezzofanti 492
mezzosoprano 416
mezzotint 420, 558
miasm 663
mica 425
micacious 204
mi-carême 840
Micawber 460
Michael 977
Michaelmas 998
Micomicon 515
microbe 163, 193
microcosm 193
micrography 193, 441
micrometer 193
micro-organism 193
microphone 418
microscope 193, 445
microscopic 32, 193
mid 68
Midas 803
mid-course 628
mid-day 125
midden 653
middle – *in degree* 29
– in order 68
– in space 222, 228
– classes 736
– constriction 203
– course 29, 628
– man *director* 694
agent 758
– point 29
– term 68
compromise 774
middlemost 222
middling 29, 32, 68, 651
middy 225, 269
midge 193
midget 193

midland 342
midnight *night* 126
dark 421
– oil 539, 689
mid-progress 282
midriff 68, 228
midshipman 269, 745
midships 68
midst – *in order* 68
central 222
interjacent 228
in the – of
mixed with 41
doing 680
midsummer 125
– day 138
midway 68
midwife
instrument 631
remedy 662
auxiliary 711
midwifery 161, 662
mien 448, 692
miff 900
might *power* 157
violence 173
energy 686
mightily 31
mighty *much* 31
strong 159
large 192
haughty 878
migraine 378
migrate 266, 295
mikado 745
milch cow
productive 168
animal 366
store 636
mild *moderate* 174
warm 382
insipid 391
lenient 740
calm 826
courteous 894
mildew 653, 663
mildewed
spoiled 659
mile 200
milestone 550
whistle jigs to a – 645
milieu, juste – 174, 628
militant 722
church – 983a
military
warfare 722
soldiers 726
– authorities 745
– band 417
– power 737
– time 132
– train 726
militate against 708
militia 726
milk *moderate* 174
semiliquid 352
cows &c. 370
white 430
mild 740
– a he-goat into a sieve 471
flow with – and honey *plenty* 639

prosperity 734
pleasant 829
– of human kind-ness 906
– the ram 645
– and water
weak 160
insipid 391
unimportant 643
imperfect 651
milk-livered 862
milksop
incapable 158
fool 501
coward 862
milky [see milk]
semitransparent 427
whiteness 430
– way 318
mill 330
notch 257
machine 633
workshop 691
fight 720
like a horse in a – 312
millennium
number 98
period 108
futurity 121
utopia 515
hope 858
millesimal 99
millet seed 193
milliard 98
milliner 225
man – 854
millinery *dress* 225
ornament 847
display 882
man – 855
million 98
multitude 102
people 372
populace 876
for the –
intelligible 518
easy 705
–s *money* 800
millionaire 803
mill-pond *level* 213
pond 343
store 636
mime 19, 599, 844
mimeograph 19
mimeotype 19
mimic 19
mimodrama 599
minacity 909
minaret 206
minatory 668
minauderie 855
mince *cut up* 44
slow 275
food 298
stammer 583
affected 855
extenuate 937
– the matter 868
not – the matter
affirm 525
artless 703
– the truth 544
mincemeat of
make – 162
mincing 855

greater – 536
misteaching **538**
mister 373
misterm 565
misthink 481
mistime 135
mistral 349
mistranslate 523
mistress *lady* 374
  master 745
  possessor 779
  title 877
  love 897
  concubine 962
mistrust 485
misty [*see* mist]
  semi-transparent 427
misunderstand
  misinterpret 523
misunderstanding 495, 713
misuse **679**
mite *bit* 32
  small 193
  insufficiency 649
  money 800
  little – 129
miter *junction* 43
  angle 244
  crown 747, 999
Mithridate 662
mitigate *abate* 174
  improve 658
  relieve 834
mitigation
  [*see* mitigate]
  extenuation 937
mitraille 727
mitrailleur 727
mitten 225
mittimus 741
mix 41
  – oneself up with
    meddle 682
  co-operate 709
  – with 720
mixen 653
mixture 41
  mere – 59
mix-up 59
mizzen 235
mizzle 348
mnemonics 505
Mnemosyne 505
moa 366
moan 405
  cry 411
  lament 839
moat *enclosure* 232
  ditch 259
  canal 350
  defence 717
mob *crowd* 72
  multitude 102
  vulgar 876
  hustle 929
  scold 932
  king – 876
  – cap 225
  – law
  authority 737
  illegality 964
mobile
  inconstant 149
  movable 264
  sensitive 822

mobility, the – 876
mobilize
  assemblage 72
  render movable 264
  – troops 722
mobocracy 737
mobster 361
moccasin 225
mock *imitate* 17, 19
  repeat 104
  erroneous 495
  deceptive 545
  chuckle 838
  ridicule 856
  disrespect 929
  – danger 861
  – modesty 855
  – sun 423
mockery
  [*see* mock]
  unsubstantial 4
  solemn – 882
  – delusion and
    snare
  sophistry 477
  deception 545
mocking-bird 19
modal 6, 7, 8
mode *state* 7
  music 413
  habit 613
  method 627
  fashion 852
  – of expression 569
  mode, à la – 852
model *copy* 21
  prototype 22
  rule 80
  form 240
  representation 554
  sculpture 557
  perfection 650
  good man 948
  new – 658
  – after 19
  – condition 80
modeller 559
moderate
  average 29
  small 32
  allay 174
  slow 275
  sufficient 639
  cheap 815
  temperate 953
  – circumstances
  mediocrity 736
moderately
  imperfect 651
moderation [*see*
  moderate] **174**
  mid-course 628
  inexcitability 826
moderato *music* 415
moderator 174
  lamp 423
  director 694
  mediator 724
  judge 967
modern 123
  music 415
  art 556
modest *small* 32
modesty

humility **881**
  purity 960
mock – 855
modicum *little* 32
  allotment 786
modification
  difference 15
  variation 20a
  change 140
  qualification 469
modish 852
modulation
  variation 20a
  change 140
  music 413
module 22
modulus 84
modus: – operandi
  method 627
  conduct 692
  – in rebus 174
  – vivendi 723
mogul 745
Mohammedan 984
Mohawk
  swaggerer 887
  evil-doer 913
moiety 51, 91
moil *active* 682, 686
  exertion 686
moisture *wet* 337
  humid 339
mokes 219
molar 330
molasses 396
mole *mound* 206
mold *condition* 7
  matrix 22
  convert 144
  form 240
  structure 329
  earth 342
  vegetation 367
  model 554
  carve 557
  decay 653
  turn to account 677
molded 820
  – on 19
molder 653, 659
molding 847
moldy 653, 659
  prominence 250
  color 432
  refuge 666
  defence 717
  spot 848
molecular 32
molecule 193
molehill *little* 193
  low 207
  trifling 643
molest *trouble* 830
molestation
  damage 649
  malevolence 907
mollia tempora 134
  – fandi 588
mollify *allay* 174
  soften 324
mollusk 366
mollycoddle 158
Molly Maguire 548
Moloch
  slaughter 361
  demon 980

heathen deity 986
molten 384
moment
  – of time 113
  importance 642
  for the – 111
  lose not a – 684
  not have a – 682
  on the spur of the – 612
momentous 152
momentum 276
Momus 838
monachism 995
monad 193
monarch 745
monarchy 737
monastery 1000
monastic 995
monasticism 984
monetary 800
  – arithmetic 11
money **800**
  wealth 803
  bad – 800
  command of – 803
  for one's – 609
  made of – 803
  make – 775
  raise – 788
  save – 817
  throw away one's – 818
  – to burn 641, 803
  – burning one's
    pocket 818
  – coming in 810
  – down 807
  – going out 809
  – market 800
  – matters 811
  – paid 809
  –'s worth
  useful 644
  price 812
  cheap 815
money-bag 800, 802
money-belt 800
money-broker 797
money-changer 797, 801
moneyed 803
moneyer 797
money-grubbing 775
moneyless 804
monger 797
mongrel
  mixture 41
  anomalous 83
  dog 366
  base 949
moniker 565
moniliform 249
monism 984
monition 527, 668
  information 527
  warning 668
monitor *hear* 418
  oracle 513
  pupil-teacher 540
  director 694
  adviser 695
  war-ship 726
  inward – 926
monitory

prediction 511
  dissuasion 616
  warning 668
monk 996
monkey
  imitative 19
  support 215
  catapult 276
  ridiculous 857
  play the – 499
  –jacket 225
  – trick
  absurdity 497
  sport 840
  – up 900
monkhood 995
monkish Latin 563
monochord 417
monochrome 429, 556
monocracy 737
monoculous 443
monode 445
monodrame 599
monody 597, 839
monogamist 904
monogamy 903
monogram
  sign 550
  cipher 533
  diagram 554
  letter 561
monograph
  publication 531
  writing 590
  book 593
  description 594
monolith 551
monolithic 983a
monologue
  soliloquy 589
  drama 599
monomachy 720
monomania 503
  obstinacy 606
  fanaticism 825
monomaniac 504
monomark 550
monoplane 273
monopolist 943
monopoly
  restraint 751
  possession 777
monostich 572
monosyllable 561
monotheism 983
monotonous
  uniform 16
  equal 27
  repetition 104
  permanent 141
  – style 575
  weary 841
  dull 843
monotype 591
monsoon 349
monsieur 370
monster
  exception 83
  large 192
  ugly 846
  prodigy 872
  evil-doer 913
  ruffian 949
monstrance 998
monstrosity
  [*see* monster]

forth – 509
not a – stirring 265
mouse-colored 432
mousehole 260
mouser 366
mousetrap 545
mousseux 353
moustache 256
mouth *entrance* 66
receptacle 191
brink 231
opening 260
eat 298
estuary 343
enunciate 580
drawl 583
deep –ed
resonant 408
bark 412
down in the – 879
make –s 929
open one's – 582
stop one's – 581
word of – 582
– honor
falsehood 544
show 882
flattery 933
pass from – to mouth 531
– wash 652
– watering 865
mouthful
quantity 25
small 32
food 298
mouthpiece
speaker 524
information 527
speech 582
mouthy *style* 577
moutonné 250
moutons, revenons à nos – 660
movable 264, 270
movables 780
move *begin* 66
motion 264
propose 514
induce 615
undertake 676
act 680
offer 763
excite 824
get a – on 684
good – 626
on the – 293
– forward 282
– from 287
– in a groove 82
– heaven and earth 686
– off 293
– on *progress* 282
activity 682
– out of 295
– quickly 274
– slowly 275
– to 894
moveless 265
movement
motion 264
music 415
action 680
activity 682

moved with 821
mover 164
movies 448, 599, 840
movie star 899
moving
keep – 682
self – 266
– pictures 448
mow *shorten* 201
smooth 255
agriculture 371
store 636
– down
destroy 162
moxa 384
M.P. 696
Mr. 373, 877
Mrs. 374
MS. 22, 590.
much 31
make – of
importance 642
friends 888
love 897
endearment 902
approval 931
not say – for 932
think – of 928, 931
– ado *exertion* 686
difficulty 704
– ado about nothing
over-estimate 482
exaggerate 549
unimportant 643
unskilful 699
– cry and little wool 884
– the same
identity 13
similarity 17
equality 27
– speaking 584.
mucid 352, 653
mucilage 352
muck 653
run a – *kill* 361
attack 716
excitement 825
muckle 31
muckworm 819, 876
mucor 653
mucosity 352
mucronate 253
muculent 352
mud *marsh* 345
semiliquid 352
dirt 653
clear as – 519
stick in the – 704
– guard 666
muddle *disorder* 59
derange 61
inattention 458
absurd 497
difficulty 704
failure 732
– one's brains 475
muddled 959
muddle-headed 499
muddy *moist* 339
dim 422
opaque 426
color 429
stupid 499

mudlark *dirty* 653
commonalty 876
muezzin 550, 996
muff *incapable* 158
dress 225
bungle 699
bungler 701
muffettee 225
muffle *wrap* 225
silent 403
deaden 408a
conceal 528
voiceless 581
stammer 583
muffled *faint* 405
latent 526
– drums
funeral 363
non-resonance 408a
muffler 225, 384
mufti *undress* 225
judge 967
priest 996
mug *cup* 191
face 234, 448
pottery 384
dupe 547
mug-house 189
muggy *moist* 339
dim 422
opaque 426
mugient 412
mugwump 607
mulatto
mixture 41
exception 83
mulct *steal* 791
fine 974
mule *mongrel* 83
beast of burden 271
obstinate 606
muleteer 694
muliebrity 374
mull
prominence 250
sweeten 396
mullah 967, 996
muller 330
mullion 215
mullioned 219
multifarious
irrelevant 10
diverse 16a
multiform 81
multiferous 102
multifid
divided 51
multifold 81
multiformity 81
multigenerous 81
multilateral 236, 244
multilocular 191
multiloquence 582, 584
multinomial 102
multiparous 168
multipartite 44
multiple 84, 102
multiplex 81
multiplicand 84
multiplicate 81
multiplication
increase 35
arithmetic 85

multitude 102
reproduction 163
productiveness 168
multiplicator 84
multiplicity 102
multiplier 84
multiply 35
multipotent 157
multisonous 404
multitude 72, 102
the – 876
multum in parvo 596
multure 330
mum 581, 585
–'s the word 403
mumble *chew* 298
mutter 583
Mumbo Jumbo 979, 993
mummer 599
mummery
absurdity 497
imposture 545
masquerade 840
parade 882
mummify 363
mummy *dry* 340
corpse 362
beat to a – 972
mump *mutter* 583
beg 765
mumper 767, 804
mumpish *sad* 837
mumps 837, 901a
munch 298
Munchausen 549
mundane
world 318
selfish 943
irreligious 989
mundation 652
mundivagant 266
munerary 973
munerate 973
municipal 965
municipality 737
munificent 816
muniment
evidence 465
record 551
defence 717
security 771
munition
materials 635
defence 717
mural 717
murder 361
– the King's English
solecism 568
stammering 583
the – is out 529
murderer 361
muricated 253
murky *dark* 421
opaque 426
black 431
gloomy 837
murmur *purl* 348
sound 405
voice 580
complain 839
murmurer 832
murrain 655
Murray *travel* 266

Lindley – 542
murrey 434
murrion 717
mus, nascitur ridiculus – 509, 643
muscadine 400
muscle 159
muscular 159
muse 451
[*and see* musing]
Muse *poetry* 597
historic – 594 ·
unlettered – 579
musette 417
Muses, the – 416
museum
collection 72
store 636
mush 354
mushroom
new 123
fungus 367
upstart 734
low-born 876
spring up like –s 163
– anchor 666
music **415**
face the – 861
set to – 416
– of the spheres
order 58
universe 318
musical 413, 415, 416
– comedy 599
– ear
musician 416
hearing 418
– instruments **417**
– note 413
– voice 580
music-hall 599, 840
musician **416**
musing 451
– on other things 458
musk 400
musket 727
shoulder a – 722
musketeer 726
musketry 727
muslin
semi-transparent 427
musnud
support 215
council 696
scepter 747
muss 59
Mussulman 984
must *necessity* 601
mucor 653
compulsion 744
it – follow 478
I – say 535
mustachio 256
mustard 392, 393
after meat – 135
– gas 663, 727
mustard-seed 193
muster 72, 85
pass – 639
not pass – 651
– courage 861
muster-roll 86
musty 401, 653

nihil – ad rem 10
– tetigit quod non
  ornavit 850
nihilism 989
nihilist 165
nihility 2, 4
nil 2, 4
– admirari
  insensible 823
  no wonder 871
  disapproval 932
– conscire sibi
  nullâ pallescere
  culpâ 946
– desperandum
  858
nill *unwilling* 604
  refuse 764
nim 791
nimble 274, 682
nimble-witted 498,
  842
nimbus
  cloud 353
  halo 420
  glory 873
nimiety 641
nimis, ne quid –
  817
nimium ne crede
  colori 485
n'importe 643
Nimrod 361, 622
nincompoop 501
nine 98
  tuneful –
  music 416
  poetry 597
– days' wonder
  transient 111
  unimportant 643
  no wonder 871
– lives 359
– men's morris 840
– points of the
  law 777
ninefold 98
ninepins 840
ninety 98
ninny 501
Niobe 839
nip *cut* 44
  destroy 162
  shorten 201
  dram 298
  freeze 385
  pungent 392
  drink 959
– in the bud
  check 201
  kill 361
  hinder 706
– up 789
nipperkin 191
nippers 781
nipple 250
Nirwana 981
nis 980
nisi prius 741, 969
Nisus and Euryalus
  890
nisus formativus
  161
nitency 420
niter 392
nitor in adversum
  708

nitrous oxide 376
nit-wit 499, 501
niveous *cold* 383
  white 430
nixe *demon* 980
nixie *fairy* 979
nizam 745
nizy 501
N or M 78
no *zero* 101
  dissent 489
  negation 536
  refusal 764
unable to say –
  605
on – account 761
have – business
  there 843
– chicken 128, 131
– choice 601, 609a
– conjuror 501,
  701
– consequence 643
in – degree 32
at – great distance
  197
– doubt 474, 488
have – end 112
– end of *great* 31
  multitude 102
  length 200
– fear 473
– go 304, 732
at – hand 32
matter of – import
  4
with – interval
  199
– one knows who
  876
– less 639
– longer 122
– love lost be-
  tween them 898
– man's land 187,
  778
– matter
  neglect 460
  unimportant 643
and – mistake 474
– more
  inexistent 2
  past 122
  dead 360
– more than 32
have – notion of
  489
– object 643
– one 4, 187
– other 13, 87
to – purpose
  shortcoming 304
  useless 645
  failure 732
give – quarter 361
– scholar 493
make – scruple of
  602
– great shakes
  small 32
  trifling 643
  imperfect 651
– sooner said than
  done 113, 132
– stranger to 490
– such thing
  non-existent 2

unsubstantial 4
  contrary 14
  dissimilar 18
– surrender 606,
  717
– thank you 764
at – time 107
– wonder 871
Noah's ark 41, 72
nob 210
nobilitate 873
nobility 875
noble *great* 31
  important 642
  rank 873
  peer 875
  disinterested 942
  virtuous 944
noblesse 875
nobody
  unsubstantial 4
  zero 101
  absence 187
  low-born 876
– knows
  ignorance 491
– knows where
  distance 196
– present 187
– would think 508
noctambulation 266
noctivagant
  travel 266
  dark 421
noctograph 421
noctuary 421, 551
nocturnal
  night 126
  dark 421
  black 431
nocturne 415
nocuous 649
nod *wag* 314
  assent 488
  signal 550
  sleep 683
  command 741
  bow 894
– of approbation
  931
– of assent 488
nodding to its fall
  162, 306
noddle 210, 450
noddy 501
node 250
nodosity 250, 256
nods and becks and
  wreathed smiles
  894
nodule 250
nodular 256
nodus, dignus vin-
  dice – 704
Noel 998
noggin 191
noise 402, 404
– abroad 531
make a – in the
  world 873
noiseless 403
noisome
  fetid 401
  bad 649
  unhealthy 657
nolens volens 601
noli me tangere

defiance 715
  excitable 825
  fastidious 868
nolition 603
nolle prosequi 624
nolumus leges
  Angliae mutari
  permanence 141
  continuance 143
  preservation 670
nom de: – guerre
  565
– plume 565
nomad 268
nomadic 266
Nomancy 511
nomenclature **564**
nominal
  unsubstantial 4
  word 562
  name 564
– price 815
nomination 564,
  755
nominee 758
nominis umbra 4
Nomology 963
non:
– compos mentis
  503
– constat 477
– deficit alter 100
– est in ventus 187
– haec in foedera
  536, 610
– nobis Domine
  990
– obstante 707
– placet 489
– possumus
  impossible 471
  obstinate 606
  refusal 764
– nostrum tantas
  componere lites
  471, 713
lex – scripta 963
– semper erit
  aestas 111
– sequitur 477
– sum qualis eram
  140, 160
non-addition 38
non-admission 55
nonage 127
nonagenarian 98
non-appearance
  447
non-assemblage **73**
non-attendance 187
nonce 118
  for the – 118, 134
nonchalance
  neglect 460
  insensibility 823
  indifference 866
non-coincidence 14
non-cohesive 47
non-com. 726
non-commissioned
  officer 745
non-committal 528,
  864
non-completion **730**
non-compliance
  742, 764
nonconformity

difference 15
  exception 83
  dissent 489
  sectarianism 984
non-content 489
non-cooperation
  489, 927
nondescript 83
none 101
– else 87
– to spare 640
– such
  superior 33
  exceptional 83
  very good 648
– in the world 4
– the worse 660
non-endurance 825
nonentity
  inexistence 2
  unsubstantial 4
  unimportant 643
non esse 2
non-essential 6,
  643
non-existence 2
non-expectance 508
non-extension 180a
non-fulfilment 730,
  732
– of one's hopes
  509
non-imitation **20**
non-interference
  inaction 681
  freedom 748
nonius 466
non-juror 489, 984
non-naturals 657
nonny 501
non-observance
  inattention 458
  desuetude 614
  infraction **773**
  dereliction 927
nonpareil 648
  type 591
non-payment **808**
non-performance
  non-completion
  730
  dereliction 927
non-plus
  uncertain 475
  difficulty 704
  conquer 731
non-preparation
  674
non-prevalence 614
non-residence 187
non-resistance 725,
  743
non-resonance
  408a
nonsense
  absurdity 497
  unmeaning 517
  trash 643
talk – *folly* 499
non-subsistence 2
non-success 732
nonsuch [*see* none]
nonsuit *defeat* 731
  fail 732
  condemn 971
nonum prematur in
  annum 133

casion 118
– trial 463
– the whole 50
on dit 532, 588
once *past* 119, 122
  seldom 137
at – 113, 132
– for all *final* 67
  infrequency 137
  tell one - 527
  determine - 604
  choose 609
– in a blue moon
  137
– more 90, 104
– over 457
– upon a time
  time 106
  different time 119
  formerly 122
– in a way 137
Ondine 979
one *identical* 13
  whole 50
  unity 87
  somebody 372
  married 903
  all – to 823
  at – with *agree* 23
  concur 178
  concord 714
  make – of 186
  neither – nor the
    other 610
  of – accord 488
  – and all
    whole 50
    general 78
    unanimous 488
  from – to another
    transfer 783
  – thing with
    another 476
  – of the best 948
  – bone and one
    flesh 903
  – consent 178, 488
  – of these days 121
  – fell swoop 113,
    173
  – fine morning 106
  – and a half 87
  – horse 643
  – idea 481
  – jump 113
  – leg in the grave
    160
  as – man 488, 709
  – mind 178, 488
  – by one
    separately 44
    respectively 79
    unity 87
  both the – and
    the other 89
  the – or the other
    609
  – over the eight
    959
  – and the same 13
  on – side 217, 236
  – step 840
  – in ten thousand
    648, 948
  – at a time 87
  – or two 100
  with – voice 488

– in a way 83
– way or another
  627
at – with
  agree 23
  concur 178
  concord 174
one-eyed 443
oneirocritic 524
oneiromancy 511
oneness 13
onerous *bad* 649
  difficult 704
  burdensome 706
  troublesome 830
oneself 13
  have all to – 777
  kill – 361
  take merit to –
    884
  take upon –
    will 600
    undertake 676
  talk to – 589
  true to – 604*a*
  be – again 660
one-sided
  misjudging 481
  wrong 923
  dishonorable 940
onion 393
onlooker 444
only *small* 32
  simple 42
  single 87
  imperfect 651
  if – 865
  – think 870
  – yesterday 123
only-begotten 87
onomancy 511
onomatopoeia 560,
  564
onset *beginning* 66
  attack 716
onslaught 716
ontology 1
onus *burden* 706
  duty 926
  – probandi
    uncertainty 475
    doubt 485
onward 282
onychomancy 511
onyx 847
oof 800
ooze *emerge* 295
  flow 348
  semiliquid 352
  – out
    disclosure 529
opacity 426
opal 847
opalescent 427, 440
opaque 426
open *begin* 66
  expand 194
  unclose 260
  manifest 525
  reveal 529
  frank 543
  artless 703
  break – 173
  lay – 226
  lay oneself – to
    177
  leave the matter –
    705

pry – 173
throw – 296
– and above board
  703, 939
– air 220, 338
– arms *willing* 602
  friendship 888
  social 892
  courtesy 894
– the ball 62, 66
– a case 476
– country 344
in – court 525, 531
– a discussion 476
– to discussion 475
– the door to
  cause 153
  facilitate 705
  permit 760
with – doors 531
– enemy 891
– eyes *see* 441
  attention 457
  discovery 480*a*
  expectation 507
  inform 527
  undeceive 529
  teach 537
  predetermination
    611
  wonder 870
– fire 716
– house 892
– into
  conversion 144
  river 348
– the lips 529
– the lock 480*a*
– market 799
– one's mind 529
– order 194
– one's purse-
  strings 809
– question 461,
  475
– rupture 713
– sesame 631, 993
– the sluices 297
– space 180
– to suspicion 485
– to *liable* 177
  facile 705
– the trenches 716
– up *begin* 66
  disclose 529
– to the view 446
– war 722, 889
– warfare 722
– the wound 824
opening
  beginning 66
  opportunity 134
  space 180
  gap 198
  aperture 260
open-handed 809,
  816
open-hearted
  veracious 543
  artless 703
  liberal 816
  honorable 939
open-mouthed
  cry 411
  expectation 507
  speak 582
  loquacious 584

desire 865
wonder 870
opera *music* 415
  poetry 597
  drama 599
– glass 445
– hat 225
– house 599
opéra bouffe 599
operculum 261
operae pretium est
  646
operandi, modus
  627, 692
operate *cause* 153
  produce 161
  act 170
  work 680
– upon *motive* 615
operation
  [*see* operate]
  arithmetical – 85
  in – 680
  put in – 677
  surgical – 662
operative
  acting 170
  workman 690
operator
  surgeon 662
  doer 690
operculated 261
operculum 223
operetta 415
operose 686, 704
ophicleide 417
ophiology 368
ophiomancy 511
ophthalmia 443
ophthalmic 441
opiate 174
opine 484
opiniative 481
opiniator 606
opinion 484
  give an – 480
  have too high an –
    of oneself 880
  popular – 488
  system of –s 484
  wedded to an –
    606
opinionate 481, 606
opinionated 474
  self– 880
opiniâtre 481
opinionist 474, 606
opitulation 707
opium *soothe* 174
  deaden sense 376
  bane 663
opium-eater 683
oppidan 188
oppilation 706
opponent 710, 891
opportune
  well-timed 134
  expedient 646
opportunism 605,
  646
opportunity 134
  lose an – 135
oppose *contrary* 14
  counteract 179
  evidence 468
  clash 708
opposite 14

– scale 30
– side 237
opposition
  [*see* oppose] 708
  the – 710
oppositionist 710
oppress *molest* 649
  severe 739
  malevolence 907
oppressed with
  melancholy 837
oppressive *hot* 382
  painful 830
oppressor 739, 913
opprobrium 874
oppugnation 708,
  719
optative 865
optical 441
– instruments 445
– lantern 448
optician 445
optics *light* 420, 445
optics *sight* 441
optimacy 875
optimates 875
optime† 931
optimism 482, 858
optimist 858
  flatterer 935
option 609
optional 600
optometer 443
optometry 445
opulence 803
opuscule 593
or *yellow* 436
  orange 439
  alternative 609
oracle 500, 513
Oracle, Sir –
  positive 474
  vanity 880
  blusterer 887
oracular
  answering 462
  ambiguous 475
  wise 498
  prediction 511
oral *information*
  527
  voice 580
  speech 582
– communication
  588
– evidence 467
orange *round* 249
  colour 439
orangery 371
orarium 999
oration 582
  funeral – 363
orator 582
oratoric 415
oratory
  speaking 582
  place of prayer
    1000
orb *region* 181
  circle 247
  luminary 423
  eye 441
  sphere of action
    625
– of day *sun* 318
  luminary 423
– of night 318

passim	**pastorale** 415	*veteran* 130	**pawky** 702	*inexcitable* 826
dispersed 73	**pastry** *food* 298	*ancestors* 166	**pawl** 45	**peace-maker** 714
place 182	*sweets* 396	*priest* 996	**pawn** 771	*mediator* 724
situation 183	**pasturage**	**patriarchal**	**pawnbroker** 787	*contented* 831
passing *very* 31	*meadow* 344	*ancient* 124	**pax** *hush!* 403	**peace-offering**
transient 111	*herbage* 367	*ancestral* 166	– in bellow 723	*pacification* 723
– bell 363	**pasture** *food* 298	**patriarchate** 737	– vobiscum 894	*mediation* 724
– strange 870	**pasty** *tart* 298	**patrician** 875	**pay** *paint* 223	*gift* 784
– word 527	*like paste* 352	**patrilineal** 11, 166	*profitable* 775	*atonement* 952
pass-key 631	**pat** *pertinent* 23	**patrimony** 780	*defray* 807	**peach** 529
passion	*strike* 276	**patriot** 910	*expend* 809	**peach-colored** 434
emotion 820, 821	*(expedient* 646)	**patrol** *walk* 266	*income* 810	**peacock**
excitability 825	– on the back	*safeguard* 664	*punish* 972	*variegation* 440
pain 828	*induce* 615	*(warning* 668)	*remunerate* 973	*beauty* 845
desire 865	*comfort* 834	**patrolman** 664	in one's –	*proud* 878
love 897	*encourage* 861	**patron**	*servant* 746	*vain* 880
anger 900	*approve* 931	*auxiliary* 711	*hired* 795	*gaudy* 882
ruling – 606	– on the cheek 902	*customer* 795	– in advance 809	**jackdaw** in –'s
Passion-week 998	– on the head	*friend* 890	– attention to 457	*feathers* 701
passionate	*endearment* 902	*benefactor* 912	– back 718	**pea-green** 435
warm 825	**Patagonian** 206	**patronage**	– down 807	**pea-jacket** 225
irascible 901	**patch** *small* 32	*influence* 175	– dues 924	**peak** *height* 206
passionless 823	*change* 140	*aid* 707	– in full 807	*summit* 210
passive *inert* 172	*region* 181	*authority* 737	– homage	*sharp* 253
inaction 681	*blemish* 848	**patronize** 693, 707	*submission* 725	*sicken* 655
obedient 743	– up *restore* 660	**patronymic** 564	*worship* 990	**peaked** 253
inexcitable 826	*compromise* 774	**patten** 225, 998	– the debt of	**peaky** 203
– resister 489	**patchwork**	**patter** *strike* 276	nature 360	**peal** *loud* 404
passivity 172, 989	*mixture* 41	*sound* 407	– no attention &c.	*roll* 407
Passover 998	*discontinuous* 70	*meaningless* 417	to 458, 460	*music* 415
passport	*variegation* 440	*talk* 584	– through the	– of bells 407, 417
indication 550	**pate** *summit* 210	*stage* 599	nose 814	– of laughter 838
instrumentality	*brain* 450	**patterer** 582	– off 718	**pearl** *type* 591
631	**patefaction** 260	**pattern** *model* 22	– off old scores 919	*goodness* 648
order 741	**patella** 191	*perfection* 650	– old debts 807	*ornament* 847
permission 760	**paten** 191	*ornament* 847	out 200, 972	*glory* 873
pass-word	**patent** *open* 260	– after 20	– in one's own	**mother-of–** 440
answer 462	*manifest* 525	**patte de**	coin 718	cast –s before
sign 550	*licence* 760	– mouche 590	– the penalty 952	swine 638
military 722	*property.* 780	– velours 544, 545	– the piper 707	**pearly**
past 122	– medicine 662	**patulous** 194	– regard to 484	*semitransparent*
danger – 664	**pater** 166	**patty** 298	– one's respects	427
insensibility to	– *patriæ* 912	**pauciloquy** 585	894	*colo r* 428
the – 506	**patera** *cup* 191	**paucity** *small* 32	– too much 814	*white* 430
obliteration of	*sacramental* 998	*few* 103	– a visit 892, 894	*grey* 432
the – 506	**paterfamilias** 166	*scanty* 640	– one's way	*variegated* 440
thing of the – 124	**paternal**	**paughty** 878	*defray* 807	**pear-shape** 249
– bearing 830	*father* 166	**Paul Jones** 792	*economy* 817	**peasant** 876
– comprehension	*benevolent* 906	**Paul Pry**	**paymaster** 801	**peat** 388
519	– domicile 189	*curious* 455	**payment** 807	**pebble** *little* 193
– cure 859	**paternity** 166	*prattle* 588	*remuneration* 973	*hard* 323
– dispute 474	**paternoster** 990	**paulo post futurum**	**paynim** 984	– dash 223
– praying for 945	**path** *direction* 278	121	**pays, mal du** –	**peccability** 945
– one's prime 128	*way* 627	**paunch** 191, 250	*regret* 833	**peccable** 947
– recollection 506	cross the – 706	**pauper** 804	*sociality* 892	**peccadillo** 947
– work	*secret* – 530	**pause**	**pea** 249	**peccant** *bad* 649
useless 645	**pathetic** 830	*discontinue* 70	**peace**	*unclean* 653
impaired 659	**pathless**	*cease* 142	*silence* 403	*diseased* 655
paste *attach* 43	*spacious* 180	*quiescence* 265	*concord* 714	– humor 653, 655
cement 45	*closed* 261	*doubt* 485	*amity* **721**	**peccavi** 950
to cement 46	*difficult* 704	*irresolution* 605	at – 714	**peck** *much* 31
pulp 354	**pathognomonic** 550	*repose* 687	*commission of*	*multitude* 102
sham 545	**pathology** 655, 662	**pauvre diable** 804	the – 965	*eat* 298
tinsel 847	**pathos** 821	**pavanne** 840	*justice of the* –	– at *censure* 932
scissors and – 609	**pathoscopic** 820	**pave** 223	967	– of troubles
pastel 556	**pathway** 627	– the way 705	keep the –	*difficulty* 704
pasteurize 652	**patience**	**pavé, on the** – 961	*moderation* 174	*adversity* 735
pasticcio 21, 41	*perseverance* 604a	**pavement** *base* 211	*concord* 714	*pain* 828
pastil 400	*endurance* 826	*covering* 223	make – 723	**peckish** 865
pastime 840	*cards* 840	*path* 627	make – with 831	**Pecksniff** 548
pastor 996	**patient** *sick* 655	**paver** 673	Prince of – 976	**pectinated** 253
pastoral	**patisserie** 298	**pavilion** 189	speak – 831	**peculate** 791
bucolic 370	**patois** 563	**paving** 211	**peaceable**	**peculator** 792
music 415	**patriae: amor** – 910	**pavor** 859	*moderate* 174	**peculiar** 79, 83
poem 597	*pater* – 912	**paw** *touch* 379	**peaceably, get on** –	**peculiarly** 31, 33
religious 995	**patriarch**	*retention* 781	736	**pecuniary** 800
sermon 998	*family* 11	– the ivories 416	**peaceful**	**pecunious** 803

pedagogic 537
pedagogue
  scholar 492
  teacher 540
  pedantic 855
pedagogy 537
pedal 633
  – note 408
  – point 416
pedant *scholar* 492
pedantic
  half-learned 491
  - *style* 577
  affected 855
pedantry 481
peddle *meddle* 683
  hawk 796
peddler 796, 797
peddling
  trifling 643
  miserly 819
pederero 727
pedestal 215
  place on a – 307,
  931
pedestrian 268
pedicel 215
pedicle 215
pedigree 69, 166
pediment 210, 215
pedlar 797
  –'s French 563
pedometer 200
peduncle 215
peek 441
peel *layer* 204
  skin 223
  uncover 226
  – off *separate* 44
peeler 664
peel-house 717
peep 441
  – behind the cur-
  tain 461
  – of day 125
  – into the future
  510
  – out 446, 529
peep-hole 260
peep-show 448, 840
peer *equal* 27
  pry 441
  inquire 461
  lord 875
  – out 446
peerless *supreme* 33
  first rate 648
  glorious 873
  virtuous 944
peeved 900
peevish 895, 901
peg *grade* 71
  hang 214
  project 250
  drink 298, 959
  come down a –
  306
  let down a – 308
  not stir a – 265,
  681
  – away 682
  – to hang on 617
  – on *journey* 266
  – out *die* 360
Pegasus 271
pegomancy 511
pegs *legs* 266

peignoir 225
peindre, fait à –
  845
peine forte et dure
  974
pejorative 483
pelagic 341
pelerine 225
pelf *gain* 775
  property 780
  money 803
pelisse 225
Pelion, Ossa on –
  72, 319
pellet 249, 727
  paper – 643
pellicle 204, 223
pell-mell 59
pellucid 425
pelote 249
pelt *skin* 223
  dress 225
  throw 276
  attack 716
  punish 972
peltry 223
pemmican 298
pen *inclosure* 232
  write 590
  writer 593
  restrain 751
  imprison 752
  ready – 569
  slip of – 495, 568
  stroke of the –
  write 590
  authority 737
  command 741
  – in hand 590
  – and ink 590
  – name 565
  draw the –
  through 552
penal 972
  – *servitude* 972
  – *settlement* 752
penalty 974
  extreme – 972
penance 952, 974
  do – 998
penates, lares et –
  189, 991
penchant
  willing 602
  desire 865
  love 897
pencil *bundle* 72
  - *of light* 420
  write 590
pencil-drawing 556
pencraft 590
pendant *match* 17
  flag 550
  ornament 847
pendency *time* 106
  hanging 214
pendente lite 106
  uncertain 475
  lawsuit 969
pendule 114
pendulous 214, 314
pendulum 114, 214
  motion of a – 314
Penelope, work of –
  645, 730
penetralia 221
  – *mentis* 450, 820

penetrate
  ingress 294
  passage 302
  sagacity 498
  – the soul 824
penetrated with
  484, 821
penetrating
  sagacious 498
  feeling 821
  – *glance* 441
penfold 232
peninsula 342
penitence 950
penitentiary 752,
  996
pen-knife 253
penman 590
  inspired – 985
penmanship 590
pennant 550
pennate 267
penniless 804
pennon 550
penny 800
  not have a – 804
  cost a pretty – 814
  turn a – 775
  no – no paternos-
  ter 812
  in for a – in for a
  pound 768
  – dreadful 594
  – trumpet 410
  – whistle 410
penny-a-liner 534,
  593
penny-a-lining 573
pennyweight 319
penny-wise 819
  – and pound fool-
  ish *caprice* 608
  waste 638
  prodigal 818
pennyworth 812
penology 972
penscript 590
pensée, arrière –
  528
penseroso 837
pensile 214
pension *income* 810
pensioner
  student 541
  servant 746
  receiver 785
pensive 451, 837
penstock 350
pent up 751
  – in one's mem-
  ory 505
pentagon 98, 244
pentahedron 244
pentameter 98, 597
Pentateuch 98, 985
Pentecost 998
Penthesilean 861
penthouse 189, 191
pentile 223
penultimate 67
penumbra 421
penurious 819
penury 804
peon 726
people
  kinsfolk 11
  multitude 102

inhabit 186
  mankind 372
  commonalty 876
  laity 997
pep 171
  – up 171
pepastic 662
pepper *pungent* 392
  condiment 393
  attack 716
  – and salt 432,
  440
peppercorn 643
  – rent 815
peppery
  irascible 901
peptic 662
per 631
  – *contra*
  contrariety 14
  counter-evidence
  468
  opposition 708
  – *procuratio* 755
  – *saltum* 70, 113
  – *se* 87
peradventure 470
peragrate 266
perambulate 266
perambulator
  measure of length
  200
  vehicle 272
perceivable 446
perceive
  be sensible of 375
  see 441
  know 490
percentage 84, 813
perceptible 446
perception 453, 490
perceptive 375
perch *location* 184
  abide 186
  habitation 189
  length 200
  height 206
  support 215
  – up 307
perchance 156, 470
percipience 450
percolate 295, 348
percolator 191
percursory 458
percussion 276
  center of – 222
percussive 277
perdition
  destruction 162
  ruin 732
  loss 776
perdre son Latin
  704
perdrix, toujours –
  841
perdu 528
  enfant – 859, 863
perdurable 110
perdy 535
peregrination 266
peregrinator 268
peremptory
  assertion 535
  firm 604
  authoritative 737
  rigorous 739
  compulsory 744

duty 926
  – denial 536
  – refusal 764
perennial
  continuous 69
  diuturnal 110
  - *plants* 367
perennius, aere –
  873
pererration 266
perfect
  great 31
  entire 52
  excellent 650
  complete 729
perfection 650
  bring to – 729
perfervidum in-
  genium 682
perfidy 874, 940
perflate 349
perforate 260
perforator 262
perforce 601, 744
perform
  produce 161
  do 170
  - *music* 416
  action 680
  achieve 729
  fulfil 772
  – a circuit 629
  – a duty 926
  – the duties of 625
  – a function 644
  – an obligation
  772
  – a part 599, 680
  – a service 998
performable 470
performance
  [*see* perform]
  effect 154
performer
  musician 416
  stage-player 599
  agent 690
  affectation 855
perfume 400
perfunctory 53, 460
pergola 191
perhaps 470, 514
peri 845, 979
periapt 993
pericranium 450
periculous 665
peridot 847
perihelion 197
peril 665
  at your – 909
  take heed at
  one's – 668
perilepsis 476
perimeter 230
period *end* 67
  point 71
  - *of time* 106, 108
  recurrence 138
  at fixed –s 138
  well rounded –s
  577, 578
periodical
  recurring 138
  book 593
periodicity **138**
peripatetic 266, 268
periphery 230

punctilio 939
at the – of 197
come to the –
　special 79
　attention 457
　reasoning 476
　plain language
　576
culminating – 210
disputed – 713
from all –s 180
full of – 574
give –s to 27
go straight to
　the – 278
in – relative 9
　agreeing 23
　conformable 82
knotty – 704
make a – of
　resolution 604
　contention 720
　compulsion 744
　conditions 770
　due 924
　honor 939
nice – 697
on the – of 111,
　121
to the – 572, 642
– an antithesis 578
– at direction 278
　direct attention
　457
　intend 620
　discourtesy 895
　disrespect 929
　censure 932
– of attack 716
at the – of the
　bayonet 173
– of the compass
　278
– of convergence
　74
– of death 360
– in dispute 461
– of etiquette 852
in – of fact 1
– the finger of
　scorn 930
– of honor 939
– of land 250
– a moral 537
– out 155, 457,
　527
– to – race 720
at the – of the
　sword
　violence 173
　severity 739
　compulsion 744
– to attribute 155
　direction 278
　probable 472
　predict 511
　mean 516
– of view 441, 448
point d'appui 215
point-blank
　direct 278
　plain language
　576
　refusal 764
point-champain 874
pointed
　great 31

sharp 253
affirmation 535
markèd 550
concise 572
language 574
pointedly
　intention 620
pointer dog 366
　indicator 550
pointless 843
poise 27, 319, 852
　mental – 498
poison 659, 663
　– gas 722, 727
poisoned 655
commend the –
　chalice 544
poisonous 657, 665
poke
　pocket 191
pig in a –
　uncertain 475
　chance 621
　dawdle 683
　rash 863
– at 276, 716
– the fire 384
– fun at 856
– one's nose in
　682
– out project 250
poker 386
　cards 840
polacca 273
polacre 273
polar 210
　cold 383
– co-ordinates 466
polarization 420
polariscope 445
polarity
　duality 89
　counteraction 179
　contraposition
　237
pole measure of
　length 200
　tall 206
　summit 210
　axis 222
　punt 267
　rotation 312
greasy – 840
opposite –s 237
from – to pole 180
pole-axe 727
polecat 401
pole-star 550, 693
polemic
　discussion 476
　discord 713
　contention 720
　combatant 726
polemoscope 445
police 965
– court 966
– magistrate 967
policeman 664, 965
policy 626, 692
polish smooth 255
　rub 331
　furbish 658
　beauty 845
　ornament 847
　taste 850
　politeness 894
– off finish 729

Polish bank 840
polished
– language 578
　fashionable 852
　polite 894
polisson 949
polite 894
offensive to ears –
　579
– literature 560
– society 852
politic wise 498
　cunning 702
　cautious 864
body –
　mankind 372
　government 737
political economy
　692
politician
　director 694
　proficient 700
politics 702
polity conduct 692
　authority 737
　duty 926
polka 840
poll 85, 609
– tax 812
pollard 193, 201
　tree 367
Poll-parrot 584
pollute soil 653
　corrupt 659
　disgrace 874
pollution
　disease 655
　vice 945
Pollyanna 858
polo 840
polonaise 840
poltroon 862
polyandry 903
polychord 417
polychromatic 428,
　440
polychrome 440,
　556
polygamy 903
polygastric 191
polyglot 522, 560
polygon
　buildings 189
　figure 244
polygraphy 590
polylogy 573
polymorphic 81
polyphonism 580
polypus 250
polyscope 445
polysyllable 561
polytheism 984
pomade 356
pomatum 356
pommel
　support 215
　round 249
　beat 972
Pomona 369
pomp 882
pom-pom 727
pomposity 882
pompous
　language 577
poncho 225
pond 343, 636
　fish – 370

ponder 451
ponderable 316,
　319
ponderation 319,
　480
ponderous 319
– style 574, 579
　dull 843
pondus fumo, dare
　– 481
poniard 727
pons asinorum 519,
　704
pontifical 995
pontificals 999
pontificate 995
pontiff 996
pontoon
　vehicle 272
　boat 273
　way 627
pony 271
poodle 366
pooh, pooh!
　unimportance 643
　contempt 930
pool lake 343
　combination 709
　prize 775
　billiards 840
poop 235
poor weak 160
– reasoning 477
– style 575
　insufficient 640
　trifling 643
　indigent 804
　unhappy 828
cut a – figure 874
– hand 701
– head 499
– house 189
– man 804
– in spirit 881
– stick 501
– thing 914
poorly 160, 655
– off 804
poor-spirited 862
pop noise 406
　unexpected 508
– at 716
– in ingress 294
　insertion 300
– off die 360
– a question 461
– the question
　request 765
　endearment 902
– upon arrive 292
　discover 480a
Pope
　infallibility 474
　priest 996
Popedom 995
Pope Joan 840
Popery 984
pop-gun trifle 643
popinjay 854
poplar tall 206
poppy sedative 174
populace 876
popular
　in demand 865
　celebrated 873
　favorite 897
　approved 931

– opinion 488
popularis, aura –
　873
popularize
　render intelligible
　518
　facilitate 705
　make pleasant
　829
populate 184
population 188, 372
populi, vox –
　publication 531
　election 609
　authority 737
populous
　crowded 72
　multitude 102
　presence 186
porcelain
　baked 384
　sculpture 557
porch entrance 66
　lobby 191
　mouth 231
　opening 260
　church 1000
porcupine 253, 901
pore opening 260
　egress 295
　conduit 350
– over look 441
　apply the mind
　457
　learn 539
porism 461, 480
pornographic 961
porous 260
porpoise 192
porridge 298
porringer 191
port abode 189
　sinistral 239
　gait 264
　arrival 292
　carriage 448
　harbor 666
in – 664
make – 666
– admiral 745
– fire 388
– wine 959
portable small 193
　transferable 270
　light 320
portage 270
portal entrance 66
　mouth 231
　opening 260
portative 193, 270
portcullis 706, 717
let down the – 666
porte-monnaie 802
portend 511
portent 512
portentous
　prophetic 511
　fearful 860
porter janitor 263
　carrier 271, 690
porterage 270
portfolio case 191
　book 593
　magazine 636
　direction 603
　insignia 747
porthole 260

rational
- *quantity* 84
intellectual 450
judicious 498
sane 502
rationale *cause* 153
attribution 155
answer 462
interpretation 322
rationalism 476,
989
rationalization 60
rats in the upper
story 503
rattan 975
ratten 158
rattle *noise* 407
music 417
prattle 584
death – 360
watchman's – 669
- on 584
rattle-snake 913
rattle-traps 780
rattling 836
- pace 274
raucity 405, 410
raucous *hoarse* 581
ravage 162, 659
ravages of time 659
rave *madness* 503
excitement 824,
825
- against 932
ravel *untwist* 60
derange 61
entangle 219
difficulty 704
ravelin 717
ravelled 59
raven *black* 431
hoarse 581
gorge 957
- for 865
ravening 173, 865
ravenous 789, 865
raver 504
ravine *interval* 198
narrow 203
dike 259
channel 350
raving *mad* 503
feeling 821
excitement 824,
825
ravish *seize* 789
please 829
ravished
pleased 827
ravishment 824
raw *immature* 123
sensitive 378
cold 383
color 428
unprepared 674
unskilled 699
- head and bloody
bones 860
- levies 726
- material 635
raw-boned 203
ray 420
- of comfort 831
rayah 745
rayless 421
raze 162
- to the ground

308
razor 253
cut a whetstone
with a – 638
misuse 679
unskilful 699
keen as a – 821
razzia
destruction 162
attack 716
plunder 791
re, in – 9
reabsorb 296
reach *degree* 26
equal 27
distance 196
fetch 270
arrive at 292
river 348
deceive 545
grasp 737
take 789
within – *near* 197
possible 470
- the ear
hearing 418
information 527
- of thought 498
- to *distance* 196
length 200
reach-me-down
673
reaction
compensation 30
reversion 145
counteraction 179
recoil 277
restoration 660
reactionary 145,
607
reactionist 710
read 522, 539
well – 490
- a lecture 537
readable 578
reader *teacher* 540
printer 591
clergyman 996
readership 542
readily 705
reading
speciality 79
knowledge 490
interpretation 522
learning 539
- glass 445
- in 995
reading-desk 1000
readjust 23, 27
readmit 296
ready
expecting 507
willing 602
useful 644
prepare 673
active 682
skilful 698
cash 800
get – 673
make – 673
- to burst forth
825
- made 673
- memory 505
- money 800
- pen 569
- to sink 824

- wit 842
reaffirm 535
reagent 463
real *existing* 1
substantial 3
- *number* 84
true 494
- estate 780
- property 780
- security 771
realism 494
realistic 17
realize
speciality 79
intellect 450
think 451
discover 480a
believe 484
conceive 490
imagine 515
accomplish 729
acquire 775
sell 796
really *wonder* 870
realm *region* 181
people 372
government 737
property 780
realness 1
realty 780
ream 593
reamer 262
reanimate
reproduce 163
life 359
resuscitate 660
reap *shorten* 201
agriculture 371
take 789
- the benefit of
be better for 658
- and carry 775
- the fruits
succeed 731
acquire 775
reward 973
- where one has
not sown 923
- the whirlwind
product 154
failure 732
reappear
repetition 104
reproduce 163
visible 446
restore 660
rear *sequel* 65
end 67
bring up 161
erect 212
back 235
elevate 307
teach 537
in the – 281
- its head
manifest 525
- one's head
pride 878
rear-admiral 745
reason *cause* 153
intellect 450
thought 451
argue 476
wisdom 498
motive 615
by – of 615
feast of – 588

in – *moderate* 174
right 922
listen to – 498
stand to –
certain 474
proof 478
manifest 525
what's the – ? 461
without rhyme
or – 615a
- in a circle 477
- why 153, 615
reasonable
moderate 174
probable 472
judicious 498
sane 502
cheap 815
right 922
- prospect 472
reasoner 476
reasoning 476
reasonless 499
reasons 476
reassemble 72
reassert 535
reassure 858, 861
reasty 401, 653
reave 789
rebate
subtract 38
decrement 40a
moderate 174
discount 813
rebeck 417
rebel 742
rebellion 715
rebellow 412
rebirth 660
reboation 412
rebound 277, 283
rebours, à –
reversion 145
regression 283
difficult 704
rebuff *recoil* 277
resist 719
repulse 732
refuse 764
discourtesy 895
censure 932
rebuild 660
rebuke 932
rebus 533
rebut *answer* 462
counter evidence
468
confute 479
deny 536
rebutter 462, 969
recalcitrant 719,
742
recalcitrate 277,
719
recalescence 382
recall
recollect 505
recant 607
cancel 756
- to life 660
recant *deny* 536
retract 607
resign 756
recapitulate
enumerate 85
repeat 104
describe 594

summarize 596
recast
revolution 146
scheme 626
recede 283, 287
- into the shade
874
receipt
scheme 626
prescription 662
precept 697
security 771
payment 807
- *of money* 810
- in full 807
receive *include* 76
admit 296
belief 484
assent 488
acquire 775
take in 785
take 789
- *money* 810
welcome 892, 894
- Christ 987
received *known* 490
habitual 613
- *maxim* 496
receiver
vessel 191
treasurer 801
official – 967
- of stolen goods
792
receiving 785
recension 85
recent 122, 123
receptacle 191
reception
comprehension 54
inclusion 76
arrival 292
ingestion 296
interview 588
receiving 785
welcome 892, 894
warm – 892
reception-room 191
recess
receptacle 191
corner 244
regression 283
ambush 530
vacation 687
retirement 893
recesses
interior 221
secret – of one's
heart 820
recession
motion from 287
Rechabite 958
réchauffé *copy* 21
repetition 104
food 298
made hot 384
restored 660
recherché 648, 852
recidivation
regression 283
relapse 607, 661
recipe *remedy* 662
precept 697
recipient 191, 785
reciprocal 12, 84
reciprocate
correlation 12

beat a – 623
retreating
  concave 252
retrench subduct 38
  shorten 201
  lose 789
  economize 817
retribution
  retaliation 718
  payment 807
  punishment 972
  reward 973
retrieve restore 660
  acquire 775
retriever dog 366
retroaction
  counteraction 179
  recoil 277
  regression 283
retroactive
  past 122
retrocession
  regression 283
  recession 287
retrograde
  moving back 283
  deteriorated 659
  relapsing 661
retrogression /
  regression 283
  deterioration 659
  relapse 661
retrospection
  past 122
  thought 451
  memory 505
retroussé 245
retroversion 218
retrude 289
return list 86
  repeat 104
  periodic 138
  reverse 145
  recoil 277
  regression 283
  arrival 292
  answer 462
  report 551
  relapse 661
  appoint 755
  profit 775
  restore 790
  proceeds 810
  reward 973
  in –
  compensation 30
  – the compliment
  interchange 148
  retaliate 718
  – to the original
    state 660
  –ed prodigal 950
  – thanks 916, 990
return game 104
return match 104
reunion junction 43
réunion
  assemblage 72
  concord 714
  lieu de – 74
  point de – 74
  social – 892
revamp 140
revanche, en – 718
reveal 529
  – itself 446
reveille 550

réveiller le chat qui
  dort, ne pas –
  668, 864
revel 840, 954
  – in enjoy 377
revelation
  disclosure 480a,
    529
  theological 985
Revelations 985
reveller 840
  drunkard 959
revelling 59, 838
revendicate
  claim 741
  acquisition 775
  due 924
revenge 919
  breathe – 900
revenons à nos -
  moutons 283,
    660
revenue 632, 810
reverberate 277,
  408
reverberatory 386
revere love 897
  respect 928
  piety 987
reverence title 877
  respect 928
  piety 987
  clergy 996
reverenced 500
reverend 877, 996
reverent 987, 990
reverential 928
reverie
  train of thought
    451
  inattention 458
  imagination 515
reversal 218, 607
reverse contrary 14
  inversion 218
  - of a medal 235
  anteposition 237
  adversity 735
  abrogate 756
  cards 840
  – of the shield 468
reverseless 150
reversible 605
reversion
  [see reverse]
  posterity 117
  return 145
  possession 777
  property 780
  succession 783
  remitter 790
reversioner 779
revert repeat 104
  return 145
  turn back 283
revest 790
  - to 457
revest 790
revet 223
reviction 660
review consider 457
  inquiry 461
  judge 480
  recall 505
  periodical 531
  dissertation 595
  compendium 596

entertainment 599
revise 658
  parade 882
reviewer 480, 595
revile 932, 988
reviler 936
revise copy 21
  consider 457
  printing 591
  plan 626
  improve 658
revising barrister
  967
revision, under –
  673
revisit 186
revival
  reproduction 163
  restoration 660
  worship 990
revivalist 996
revive
  reproduce 163
  improve 658
  resuscitate 660
  excite 824
revivify
  reproduce 163
  life 359
  improve 658
  resuscitate 660
revocable 605
revoir, au – 293
revoke 607, 756
revolt resist 719
  disobey 742
  shock 830
  disapproval 932
  – against hate 898
  – at the idea
  dissent 489
revolting
  painful 830
revolution
  periodicity 138
  change 146
  rotation 312
  disobedience 742
revolutionize 140,
  146
revolve
  [see revolution]
  – in the mind 451
revolver 727
revue 599
  intimate – 599
revulsion
  reversion 145
  revolution 146
  inversion 218
  recoil 277
reward 973
reword 104
Reynard
  animal 366
  cunning 702
rez-de-chaussée
  191, 207
rhabdology 85
rhabdomancy 511
Rhadamanthus
  967, 982
rhapsodical
  irregular 139
  imaginary 515
rhapsodist
  fanatic 504

rhapsody
  discontinuity 70
  music 415
  nonsense 497
  fancy 515
  poetry 597
rhetoric speech 582
  flowers of – 577
rheum
  excretion 299
  fluidity 333
  water 337
rhino 800
rhinoceros hide
  376, 823
rhomb 244
rhumb 278
rhyme
  similarity 17
  verse 597
  without – or
    reason
  absurd 497
  caprice 608
  motiveless 615a
rhymeless 598
rhymester 597
rhythm
  periodicity 138
  melody 413
  elegance 578
  verse 597
rhythmical
  - style 578
rialto 799
rib support 215
  ridge 250
  wife 903
ribald vulgar 851
  disreputable 874
  impure 961
riband
  [see ribbon]
ribbed 259
ribbon tie 45
  filament 205
  record 550
  decoration 877
  –s reins 152
  handle the – 693
ribroast 972
rich savory 394
  color 428
  language 577
  abundant 639
  wealthy 803
  beautiful 845
  ornament 847
  – man 803
riches 803
richesses, embarras
  de – 641, 803
richly much 31
  – deserve 924
rick 72, 846
rickety weak 160
  ugly 846
  imperfect 651
rickshaw 272
ricochet 277
ricordo, non mi –
  506
rid deliver 672
  get – of eject 297
  liberation 750
  loose 776
  relinquish 782

riddance 672, 776,
  782
  good – 776
riddle arrange 60
  sieve 260
  secret 533
  clean 652
ride get above 206
  move 266
  break in 370
  – at anchor 265
  – full tilt at 622,
    716
  – hard 274
  – one's hobby 622
  – rough shod
  violence 173
  severity 739
  insolence 885
  illegality 964
  – out the storm
    664
  – and tie
  periodicity 138
  journey 266
  – the whirlwind
    604, 737
rideau, lever de –
  599
ridentem dicere
  verum 836, 842
rider appendix 39
  equestrian 268
rideret Heraclitus
  853
ridge narrow 203
  height 206
  prominence 250
ridicule 856, 929
ridiculous
  absurd 497
  foolish 499
  trifling 643
  grotesque 853
ridiculousness 853
riding district 181
  journey 266
ridotto 840, 892
rifacimento 104,
  660
rife existence 1
  general 78
  influence 175
riff-raff dirt 653
  commonalty 876
  bad folk 949
rifle musket 727
  plunder 791
  – shot 406
rifled cannon 727
rifleman 726
rifler 792
rifles 726
rifle-shooting 840
rift 44, 198
  – within the lute
    651, 713
rig dress 225
  prepare 673
  frolic 840
  strumpet 962
  – the market 794
  run the – upon 929
rigadoon 840
rigging ropes 45
  gear 225
  instrument 633

SHU–SIN

smooth *uniform* 16
calm 174
flattery 213, 251
not rough 255
easy 705
— the bed of death
707, 906
— down 174
— over 174
— the ruffled brow
of care 834
— sailing 705
— water *easy* 705
— the way 705
smooth-bore 727
smoothly, go on —
prosperous 734
smoothness 255
smooth-tongued
544, 933
smother
repress 174
kill 361
stifle sound 581
restrain 751
smoulder *inert* 172
burn 382
latent 526
smous 796, 797
smudge 431, 653,
848
smug *affected* 855
smuggle
introduce 228
steal 791
illegal 964
smuggler 792
smut
dirt 653
impurity 961
smutch 431
snack
small quantity 32
food 298
snacks, go — 778
snaffle 752
snag *projection* 250
sharp 253
danger 667
hindrance 706
snail *slow* 275
snake *undulation*
248
serpent 366
hissing 406
miscreant 913
scotch the — 640
— in the grass
hidden 528
deceiver 548
bad 649
source of danger
667
evil-doer 913
knave 941
snake-like
convoluted 248
snap *break* 44
eat 298
brittle 328
noise 406
rude 895
— at *seize* 789
bite 830
censure 932
— of the fingers
trifle 643

— one's fingers at
defy 715
insolence 885
despise 930
— the thread 70
— up *seize* 789
— one up
censure 932
—shot 554
snap-dragon 840
snappish 901
snare *deception* 545
snarl *growl* 412
rude 895
angry 900
threaten 909
snatch
small quantity 32
seize 789
— at *pursue* 622
seize 789
— a grace beyond
the reach of art
845
— from one's grasp
789
— from the jaws of
death 662, 672
— from under
one's nose 702
— a verdict 545,
702
snatches, by — 70
sneak *hide* 528
coward 862
servile 886
base 940
knave 941
bad man 949
— off, — out of 623
sneer *disparage* 929
contempt 930
blame 932
sneeze *blow* 349
snuffle 409
— at *despise* 930
sneezed at, not to
be — 642
snick 32, 51
snicker 838
sniff *blow* 349
odor 398
discovery 480a
sniffle 349
snigger *laugh* 838
ridicule 856
disrespect 929
sniggle 545
snip
small quantity 32
cut 44
short 201
tailor 225
sniping 716
snippet 32
snip-snap 713
snip-snap-snorem
840
snivel *weep* 839
sniveling
servile 886
snob *vulgar* 851
plebeian 876
servile 886
snobbishness
flattery 933
snood

headdress 225
circle 247
snooker 840
Snooks, Mr. — 876
snooze 683
snozzle 250
snore 411, 683
snort 411, 412
snout 250
snow *ship* 273
ice 383
white 430
snow-ball 72
snow-blindness 443
snow-drift 72
snow-shoe 272
snow-storm 383
snub *short* 201
hinder 706
cast a slur 874
humiliate 879
bluster 885
censure 932
snub-nosed 243
snuff *blow* 349
pungent 392
odor 398
up to — 698, 702
go out like the —
of a candle 360
— out 162, 421
— up 296, 398
snuff-color 433
snuffing, want —
pert 885
snuffle *blow* 349
hiss 409
stammer 583
hypocrisy 988
snuffy 653
snug *closed* 261
comfortable 377
safe 664
prepared 673
content 831
secluded 893
keep — 528, 893
make all — 673
snuggery 189
snugness 827
so *similar* 17
very 31
therefore 476
method 627
— be it 488, 762
— far so good 618
— let it be 681
— much the better
831, 838
— much the worse
832, 835
— to speak 17, 521
soak *immerse* 300
water 337
moist 339
drunkenness 959
— up 340
So-and-so, Mr. —
neology 563
soap *lubricate* 332
oil 356
cleanser 652
soapy *unctuous* 355
servile 886
flattery 933
soar *great* 31
height 206

fly 267
rise 305
sob 839
sober *moderate* 174
wise 498
sane 502
style 576
grave 837
temperate 953
abstinent 958
— down 174, 502
humility 879
in — sadness
affirmation 535
— senses 502
— truth *fact* 494
sober-minded 502
calm 826
humble 879
sobriety 958
sobriquet 565
sob sister 534
so-called 545, 565
soc *jurisdiction* 965
socage 777
soccer 840
sociable
carriage 272
sociality 892
social *mankind* 372
sociable 892
— circle 892
— evil 961
— gathering 892
— science 910
socialism
government 737
participation 778
philanthropy 910
socialist 712
sociality 892
society
mankind 372
party 712
fashion 852
sociality 892
position in — 873
Socinianism 984
sociology 712
sock *hosiery* 225
drama 599
socket 191, 252
socle 215
Socratic method
461
sod 344
beneath the — 363
sodality 712, 888
sodden 339, 384
sofa 215
Sofi 984, 996
soft *stop!* 142
weak 160
moderate 174
smooth 255
not hard 324
moist 339
marsh 345
silence! 403
— *sound* 405
dulcet 413
credulous 486
silly 499
lenient 740
tender 822
timid 862
own to the — im-

peachment 529
— *music* 415
— *pedal* 405
— *sawder* 617, 933
— *soap* 356, 933
— tongue, — words
894
soften [*see* soft]
moderate 174
relieve 834
pity 914
palliate 937
softening of the
brain 158
softer sex 374
soft-hearted 914
softling 160
softness 324
persuasibility 615
soft-spoken 894
soggy 339
soho
attention 457
parley 586
hunting 622
soi-disant
asserting 535
pretender 548
misnomer 565
vain 880
boastful 884
soil *region* 18
land 342
dirt 653
deface 846
till the — 371, 673
soirée 892
sojourn 186, 189
sojourner 188
soke 181
solace *relief* 834
recreation 840
— oneself with
pleasure 827
solar 318
— *system* 318
— *time* 114
solatium 973
sold to the devil 949
soldan [*see* sultan]
solder *join* 43
cement 45
cohere 46
soldier 726
soldier-like 722,
861
sole *alone* 87
base 211
support 215
feme — 904
solecism 568
soleil, coup de —
hot 384
mad 503
solemn
affirmation 535
important 642
grave 837
glorious 873
ostentatious 882
religious 987
worship 990
— *mockery* 882
— *silence* 403
solemnity *rite* 998
solemnization 883
sol-fa 416

retract one's – 283
take – *plan* 626
  prepare 673
  conduct 692
tread in the – of
  281
stercoraceous 653
stereography 591
stereometry 466
stereopticon 445
stereoscope 445
stereoscopic 446
stereotype *copy* 21
  mark 550
  engraving 558
  printing 591
stereotyped
  uniform 16
  stable 150
  habit 613
sterile 169, 645, 732
sterilize 652
sterling *true* 494,
  944
  – coin 800
stern *rear* 235
  severe 739
  discourteous 895
  – necessity 601,
  603
  – truth 494
sternmost 235
sternutation
  sneeze 349
  sound 409
sternway 267
stertorous 402, 580
stet 150
  – pro ratione vo-
    luntas 600
stethoscope 418
stevedore 271, 613,
  690
stew *food* 298
  heat 382
  cook 384
  difficulty 704
  emotion 821
  excitement 825
  annoyance 828
  bagnio 961
  in a – *angry* 900
steward 637
  director 694
  agent 758
  treasurer 801
stewardship 692,
  693
stewpan 386
stichomancy 511
stick *adhere* 46
  cease 142
  staff 215
  stab 260
  remain *quiet* 265
  fool 501
  bungler 701
  weapon 727
  scourge 975
  dirty end of the –
  699
  give the – to 972
  – at *doubt* 485
  averse 603
  – fast *firm* 150
  difficulty 704
  – in one's gizzard

830, 900
  – in 300
  – law 972
  – in the mud
    304, 732
  – at nothing
  resolve 604
  active 682
  rash 863
  – out 250
  – to 143, 604*a*
  – in the throat
  hoarse 581
  not say 585
  dislike 867
  – up 212, 307, 791
  – up for *aid* 707
  applaud 931
  vindicate 937
stickle 603, 616
  – for 720, 794
stickler 606
  severity 739
sticky
  cohering 46
  viscid 352
stiff *rigid* 323
  style 579
  severe 739
  coactive 751
  ugly 846
  affected 855
  haughty 878
  pompous 882
  – breeze 349
stiffen 323
stiff-necked 606
stiffness
  stability 150
stifle *kill* 361
  silence 403
  conceal 528
stifled
  faint sound 405
stifling *hot* 382
stigmatize 874
  censure 932
  accuse 938
stile *way* 627
  hindrance 706
  help a lame dog
    over a – 707
stiletto 262, 727
still
  on the other hand
    30
  moderate 174
  not moving 265
  vaporization 336
  furnace 386
  silent 403
  – less 467
  – life *matter* 316
  painting 556
  – more
  superior 33
  evidence 467
  – small voice 405
  in – water 714
still-born 360, 732
stillroom 636
stillicidium 348
stilted
  elevated 307
  - *style* 577
  ridiculous 853
  affected 855

boasting 884
stilts *support* 215
  on – *high* 206
  elevated 307
  hyperbolical 549
  proud 878
  boasting 884
stimulant 662
stimulate
  energy 171
  violence 173
  incite 615
  excite 824
stimulating
  suggestive 514
stimulus 615
sting *pain* 378
  tingle 380
  poison 663
  excite 824
  mental suffering
    830
  anger 900
stinging
  pungent 392
stingo 298
stingy 819
stink 401
  – in the nostrils
  unpleasant 830
  dislike 867
  hate 898
stink-bomb 727
stink-pot 401
stint *degree* 26
  limit 233
  scanty 640
  begrudge 819
stintless 639
stipend *salary* 973
stipendiary
  subject 749
  receiving 785
  magistrate 967
stipple
  variegate 440
  painting 556
  engraving 558
stipulate 769, 770
  – for 720
stipule 51
stir *energy* 171
  move 264
  agitation 315
  excite 375
  activity 682
  jail 752
  emotion 824
  make a – 642, 682
  – about 682
  – the blood 824,
    900
  – up dissension
    713
  – the embers 163,
    824
  – the feelings 824
  – the fire 384
  – a question 461,
    476
  – one's stumps
    266, 682
  – up *mix* 41
  violent 173
  excite 824
stirps *kin* 11
  source 153

paternity 166
stirring *events* 151
  important 642
  active 682
  – news 532
stirrup
  support 215
  with a foot in the
    – 293
stirrup-cup 293, 959
stitch *junction* 43
  pain 378
  work 680
  – in time 132
  – of work 686
stive 384
stiver 800
stoat 401
stoccado 717
stock *kinship* 11
  quantity 25
  origin 153
  paternity 166
  collar 225
  soup 298
  fool 501
  habitual 613
  materials 635
  store 636
  property 780
  merchandise 798
  money 800
  in – 777
  laughing – 857
  lay in a – 637
  take – *inspect* 457
  accounts 811
  – exchange 799
  – still 265
  – in trade
  means 632
  store 636
  property 780
  merchandise 798
  – with 637
stockade 717
stocked, well – 639
stock exchange 621
stock-farm 370
stocking 225
  hoard 800
stock-jobbing 794
stock operator 621
stocks *prison* 752
  funds 802
  punishment 975
  on the –
  business 625
  preparation 673
  incomplete 730
  – and stones 316,
    823
stocky 201
stodge 957
stoicism
  insensibility 823
  inexcitability 826
  disinterested 942
  temperance 953
stoke 388
stoker 268
stole 999
stolen: – away 671
  – goods 793
stolid 499, 843
stomach *pouch* 191
  taste 390

brook 826
  desire 865
not have the – to
  603
turn the – 830
  – of an ostrich 957
stomacher 225
stone *heavy* 319
  dense 321
  hard 323
  kill 361
  lithography 558
  material 635
  attack 716
  weapon 727
  punish 972
  corner – 642
  go down like a –
    310
  cast the first – at
    938
  heart of – 823, 907
  key– 642
  musical –s 417
  no – unturned
    461, 686
  philosopher's –
    662
  precious – 648
  stepping – 627
  throw a – at
  attack 716
  censure 932
  accuse 938
  throw –s at 907
  tomb– 363
  mark with a
    white – 642
  throw a – in one's
    own garden 699
  – dead 360
  – of Sisyphus 645
stone-blind 442
stone-colored 432
stone-deaf 419
stone's throw 197
stoneware 384
stony 323
stony-hearted 907,
  919
stooge 711, 746, 886
stook 72
stool 215
  between two –s
    704
  – of repentance
    950
  – pigeon 527, 548
stoop *slope* 217
  lower 308
  humble 879
  servile 886
  dishonorable 940
  – to conquer 702
stop *end* 67
  cease 142
  close 261
  rest 265
  silent 403
  danger 665
  inaction 681
  hinder 706
  prohibit 761
  put a – to 142
  – the breath 361
  – the ears 419
  – a flow 348

servant 746
enthral 749
- of dispute 713
- to examination 461
- of inquiry 461
- of thought 454
- to 469, 475
subjection 749
subjective
　intrinsic 5
　immaterial 317
　intellectual 450
subjoin 37
subjugate 731, 749
subjugation 732, 824
subjunctive 37
sublapsarian 984
sublation 38
sublevation 307
sub-lieutenant 745
sublimate
　elevate 307
　lighten 320
　vaporize 336
sublime high 206
　language 574
　beauty 845
　glory 873
　magnanimous 942
　from the - to the ridiculous 853
subliminal 317
sublineation 550
sublunary 318
submarine
　deep 208
　ship 272
　warship 726
　- chaser 726
　- warfare 722
submediant 413
submerge
　destroy 162
　immerse 300
　plunge 310
　steep 337
submersible 273, 726
submersion 208
subministration 707
submission 725
　obedience 743
submissive
　tractable 705
　enduring 826
　humble 879
submit to arbitration 774
submonish 695
submultiple 84
subordinate
　inferior 34
　unimportant 643
　subject 749
subordination 58
suborn 615, 795
subpoena 741, 969
subreption
　falsehood 544
　acquisition 775
subrogation 147
subscribe
　assent 488

aid 707
agree to 769
give 784
subscript 39, 65
subscription
　gift 784
subsequent
　- in order 63
　- in time 117
subserviency
　servility 886
subservient
　instrumental 631
　aid 707
　subject 749
subside 36, 306
subsidiary aid 707
　servant 746
subsidy
　assistance 707
　gift 784
　pay 809
subsist exist 1
　continue 141
　live 359
subsistence 298
subsoil 221, 342
substance
　existence 1
　thing 3
　quantity 25
　inside 221
　matter 316
　texture 329
　important part 642
　wealth 803
　in - 596
　man of - 803
substantial
　existing 1
　hypostatic 3
　material 316
　dense 321
　true 494
　- meaning 516
substantiality 3
substantially
　intrinsically 5
　- true 494
substantiate 467, 924
substantive 1, 3
substitute
　inferior 34
　change 147
　means 634
　deputy 759
substitution 147
substratum
　substance 3
　layer 204
　base 211
　support 215
　interior 221
　materiality 316
substructure 211
subsultory 315
subsume 54
subtend 237
subterfuge 617
　sophistry 477
　lie 546
　cunning 702
subterranean 208
subtile light 320
　rare 322

- texture 329
subtilize rarefy 322
　sophistry 477
subtle slight 32
　light 320
　cunning 702
　- point 704
　- reasoning 476
subtlety 477, 498
subtraction
　subduction 38
　arithmetic 85
　taking 789
subtrahend 38, 84
suburb town 189
　near 197
　environs 227
subvention
　support 215
　aid 707
　gift 784
subversion 146
subvert destroy 162
　invert 218
　depress 308
subway 627
　- train 272
succedaneum 147
succeed follow 63
　posterior 117
　success 731
　transfer 783
　- to acquire 775
succès d'estime 873
success 731
succession
　sequence 63
　continuity 69
　repetition 104
　posteriority 117
　transfer 783
　in quick - 136
　in regular - 138
　- of ideas 451
　- of time 109
successless 732
successor 65, 117
succinct 572
succor 707
succubus 980
succulent
　nutritive 298
　juicy 333
　semiliquid 352
succumb
　fatigue 688
　yield 725
　fail 732
succussion 315
such: - as 17
　- being the case 8
　- like 17
　- a one 372
suchwise 8
suck
　draw off 297
　drink 298
　take 789
　- in 296
　- the blood of 789
sucker 260, 547
suckle 707
suckling infant 129
suction force 157
　reception 296
sudary 652
sudation 299

sudatory 386
sudden
　transient 111
　instantaneous 113
　soon 132
　unexpected 508
　- burst 508
　- death 360
　- and quick in quarrel 901
　- thought 612
sudorific 382
suds froth 353
　in the - 704, 837
sue demand 765
　go to law 969
suet 356
suffer physical pain 378
　disease 655
　allow 760
　feel 821
　endure 826
　moral pain 828
　- for 972
　- punishment 972
sufferance, tenant on - 779
suffice 639
sufficiency 639
suffix adjunct 39
　sequence 63
sequel 65
　letter 561
suffiation 349
suffocate kill 361
　excess 641
suffocating 382, 401
suffocation 361
suffragan 996
suffrage 609
suffragette 742
suffusion
　mixture 41
　feeling 821
　blush 879
sugar 396
sugar-loaf 253
suggest suppose 514
　inform 527
　influence 615
　- itself 451, 515
　- a question 461
suggestio falsi 546
suggestion 626, 695
suggestive
　reminder 505
　significant 516
　descriptive 594
　bawdy 961
sui generis 83
suicidal 162
suicide killing 361
suisse beadle 996
Suisse, point d'argent point de - 812
suit accord 23
　series 69
　class 75
　clothes 225
　expedient 646
　petition 765
　courtship 902
　follow - 19
　law- 969

love- 897
　- the action to the word 550
　- the occasion 646
　do - and service 743
suit case 191
suitable 23, 646
　- season 134
suite sequel 65
　series 69
　escort 88
　retinue 746
　- of rooms 189, 191
suitor
　petitioner 767
　lover 897
　lawsuit 969
sulcated 259
sulky carriage 272
　obstinate 606
　discontented 832
　dejected 837
　sullen 901a
sullen
　obstinate 606
　gloomy 837
　discourteous 895
　sulky 901a
sullenness 901a
sully 653, 874
sulphur 388
　- colored 436
sultan 745
sultry 382
sum number 84
　money 800
　- and substance meaning 516
　synopsis 596
　important part 642
　- total 800
　- up reckon 85
　description 594
　compendium 596
sumless 105
summation 37, 85
summary
　transient 111
　early 132
　short 201
　concise 572
　compendious 596
　illegal 964
　- of facts 594
summer season 125
　support 215
　heat 382
　Indian - 125
　St. Luke's - 125
　St. Martin's - 125
　- lightning 423
　- time 114
summer-house 191
summerset 218
summit top 210
summon 741, 969
　- up 505, 824
　- up courage 861
summum:
　- bonum 618, 827
　- jus 922
sump base 211
　pool 343
　slough 345
　store 636

insolent 885
threat 909
- glibly 584
- nonsense 497
- of signify 516
publish 531
intend 620
- to oneself 589
- oneself out of
  breath 584
- over
confer 588
persuade 615
- to in private 586
- at random
illogical 477
loquacity 584
- together 588
- against time
time 106
protract 110
inaction 681
- of the town
gossip 588
fame 873
talkative 582, 584
talked of 873
talkies 599, 840
talking, fine -
over-estimation
482
tall 206
- hat 225
- talk 884
tallage 812
tallies 85
tallow 356
- candle 423
tallow-faced 429
tally agree 23
list 85, 86
sign 550
credit 805
- with conform 82
tally-ho 622
tally-man 797
talma 225
Talmud 985
talons
authority 737
claws 781
talus 217
tam-o'-shanter 225
tambourine 417
tame inert 172
moderate 174
domesticate 370
teach 537
feeble 575
subjugate 749
insensible 823
calm 826
tameless
violent 173
malevolent 907
Tammany 940
tamp 261, 276
tamper with
alter 140
seduce 615
injure 659
meddle 682
tan color 433
tandem
at length 200
vehicle 272
tang taste 390

bane 663
tangent 199
angle 217
fly off at a -
deviate 279
diverge 291
excitable 825
tangere ulcus 505
tangible
material 316
touch 379
exact 494
sufficient 639
useful 644
tangle 61, 219
tangled 59, 704
weave a - web 704
tango 840
tank pool 343
reservoir 636
armored vehicle
726
tankard 191
tanker 273
tant: - mieux 838
- s'en faut 489
- soit peu 32
tantaene animis
coelestibus irae
900
tantalize balk 509
induce 615
desire 865
tantalizing
exciting 824
Tantalus: torment
of - 507, 865
tantamount 27, 516
tantara 407
tantas componere
lites 723
tanti 642
tantivy speed 274
tantrums 900
tap open 260
plug 263
hit 276
let out 295, 297
sound 406
turn on the - 297
tap-dance 840
tape string 205
measure 466
- machine 553
taper contract 195
narrow 203
candle 423
- to a point 253
tapestry 556, 847
tapinois, en - 528
tapis: on the -
event 151
topic 454
intention 620
plan 626
tap-root 153
taps 550
tapster 746
tar cover 223
sailor 269
pitch 356a
- and feather 929,
972
taradiddle 546
tarantass 272
tarantella 840
tarboosh 225

tardiloquence 583
tardy 133, 275
tare 40a
- and tret 813
tares 645
targe 717
target 620
shield 717
tariff 812
tarmac 635
tarn 343
tarnish
discoloration 429
soil 653
deface 848
disgrace 874
tarpaulin 223
tarry remain 110,
265
later 133
continue 141
- for expect 507
tart pastry 298, 396
acid 397
rude 895
irascible 901
harlot 962
tartan 440
tartane 273
Tartar choleric 901
catch a - dupe 547
unskilful 699
retaliation 718
tartar dirt 653
- emetic 663
Tartarus 982
Tartufe
hypocrisy 544
deceiver 548
impiety 988
task lesson 537
business 625
put to use 677
fatigue 688
command 741
hard - 704
set a - 741
take to - 932
- the memory 505
taskmaster 694
tass 191
tassel 847
taste sapidity 390
experience 821
good taste 850
man of - 850
to one's - savory
394
pleasant 829
love 897
tasteful 850
tasteless insipid
391
tasty 394, 850
tâtonner 463
tatter
small quantity 32
tatterdemalion 876
Tattersalls 799
tatters garments
225
tear to - 162
tatting 847
tattle 588
tattler 532, 588
tattoo
drumming 407

mottled 440
summons 741
taught [see teach]
fastened 43
taunt 929, 938
tauromachy 720
taut 43
tautology 104, 573
tavern 189
tawdry 851
tawny 433, 436
tax inquire 461
employ 677
fatigue 688
command 741
compel 744
request 765
accounts 811
impost 812
discount 813
accuse 938
- one's energies
686
- the memory 505
taxi 266
taxi-cab 272
taxi-driver 268
taxidermy 368
taxis 60
taxonomy 60
tazza 191
Te Deum 990
te fabula narratur,
de - retaliate 718
condemn 971
tea 298
teach 537
- one's grand-
mother 641, 885
- one his place 879
teachable 539
teacher 540, 673
teaching 537
false - 538
teacup, storm in a -
overrate 482, 549
exaggerate 549
teagown 225
team assemblage
69, 72
teamster 694
tea-party 892
tea-pot 191
tear separate 44
violence 173
move rapidly 274
excite 825
weeping 839
- away from 789
- oneself away
623
- asunder one's
bonds 750
- one's hair 839
- out 301
- to pieces
separate 44
destroy 162
- up destroy 162
tear-gas 663, 727
tearful 839
tearing passion 839
tears: draw - 830
shed - 839
- in one's eyes
excited 824
sad 837

tease annoy 830
spite 907
teaser difficult 704
teasing 830
teat 250
tea-table talk 588
technic 698
technica, memoria
- 505
technical
conformable 82
workmanlike 698
- college 542
- education 537
- knowledge 698
- school 542
- term 564
technicality
special 79
cant term 563
formulary 697
technique 556, 698
technocracy 698
technology 698
techy 901
tedious 841
while away the -
hours 681
tedium 841
teem
produce 161
productive 168
abound 639
- with multitude
102
teemful 168
teeming crowd 72
teemless 169
'teens 98
in one's - 127, 129
teeter 314
teeth 330, 781
armed to the -
673, 717, 722
between the - 405
cast in one's - 938
chattering of - 383
have cut one's eye
- 698
in the - of 704, 708
grind one's - 900
the run of one's -
815
set one's - 604
show one's - 900
in spite of one's -
708, 744
make one's - chat-
ter 385, 860
set the - on edge
scrape 331
saw 397
stridor 410
pain the feelings
830
tee 66
teetotalism 953,
958
teetotum 312, 840
teg 366
tegument 223
teind 99
teinoscope 445
tekel upharsin 668
telautograph 553
telegram 532
telegraph

trousers 225
trousseau 225
trouvaille 775
trouvère 597
trover 775, 964
trow *think* 451
  believe 484
  know 490
trowel 191
troy-weight 319
truant *absent* 187
  runaway 623
  idle 682
  apostate 941
truce *cessation* 142
  deliverance 672
  peace 721
  pacification 723
  flag of – 724
trucidation 361
truck *summit* 210
  vehicle 272
  barter 794
truck driver 268
truck farm 371
truckle to
  submit 725
  servile 886
  flatter 933
truckle-bed 215
truck-load 31
truckman 268
truculent 907
trudge 266, 275
truditur dies die
  109
true *real* 1
  straight 246
  assent 488
  accurate 494
  veracious 543
  faithful 772
  honorable 939
  orthodox 983a
  – bill
  vindicate 937
  accuse 938
  lawsuit 969
  see in its –
  colors 480a
  – meaning 516
  – to nature 17
  – to oneself 604a
  – saying 496
  – to scale 494
true-hearted 543,
  939
true-love 897
true-lover's knot
  897, 902
true-penny 939
truism *axiom* 496
  unmeaning 517
trull 962
truly *very* 31
  assent 488
  really 494
  indeed 535
trump *perfect* 650
  honorable 939
  good man 948
  turn up –s 731
  – card *device* 626
  success 731
  – up *falsehood* 544
  accuse 938
trumped up 468,

545, 546
trumpery 517, 643
trumpet *music* 417
  war cry 722
  boast 884
  flourish of –s
  ostentation 882
  celebration 883
  boasting 884
  ear– 418
  penny –
  skill 410
  sound of –
  alarm 669
  speaking – 418
  – blast 404
  – call 550, 741
  – forth 531
trumpeter
  musician 416
  messenger 534
  boaster 884
trumpet-toned 410.
trumpet-tongued
  404, 531
truncate 201, 241
truncated 53
truncheon
  weapon 727
  staff of office 747
  *instrument of
  punishment* 975
trundle 284, 312
trunk *whole* 50
  origin 153
  paternity 166
  box 191
trunk-hose 225
trunnion
  support 215
  projection 250
truss *tie* 43
  pack, packet 72
  support 215
trust
  belief 484
  combination 709
  property 780
  credit 805
  hope 858
  – to a broken reed
  699
  – to the chapter of
  accidents 621
trustee
  consignee 758
  possessor 779
  treasurer 801
trustful 484
trustless 940
trustworthy
  certain 474
  belief 484
  – *memory* 505
  veracious 543
  honorable 939
truth
  exactness 494
  veracity 543
  probity 939
  arrive at the –
  480a
  in – *certainly* 474
  love of – 543
  of a – 535, 543
  prove the – of 937
  religious – 983a

speak the – 529,
  543
in very – 543
Truth, Spirit of –
  976
truthless 544
trutination 319
try *experiment* 463
  adjudge 480
  endeavor 675
  use 677
  lawsuit 969
  – a case 967
  – a cause 480
  – conclusions
  discuss 476
  quarrel 713
  contend 720
  – one's hand 675
  – one's luck 621
  – one 704
  – out 463
  – the patience 830
  – a prisoner 967
  – one's temper 824
  – one's utmost 686
trying 688, 704
tryst 892
trysting-place 74
tsar [*see* czar]
tu quoque 718
  – *argument*
  counter-evidence
  468
  confutation 479
  accuse 938
tub 191
  – *thumper* 582
  – to a whale 545,
  617
tuba 417
tubam trepidat,
  ante – 860, 862
tubby 202
tube 260
  test – 144
tubercle 250
tuberculous 655
tuberosity 250
tubman 968
tubular 260
tubulated 260
tubule 260
tuck *fold* 258
  dagger 727
  – in *locate* 184
  eat 298
  insert 300
tucker 225
tuft *collection* 72
  rough 256
tufted 256
tuft-hunter 836,
  943
tuft-hunting 886,
  933
tug *ship* 273
  pull 285
  effort 686
  – of war 720, 722
  athletic sport 840
tuition 537
tulip *variegated* 440
  gaudy 882
tumble *derange* 61
  destruction 162
  fall 306

agitate 315
  fail 732
  rough and – 59
  – down 665
tumbler *athlete* 159
  glass 191
  actor 599
  buffoon 844
tumbrel 272
tumefaction 194
tumid
  expanded 194
  – *style* 577
tumor
  expansion 194
  prominence 250
tumult *disorder* 59
  agitation 315
  revolt 742
  emotion 825
tumultuous 59, 173
tumulus 363
tun *receptacle* 191
  large 192
  drunkard 959
tunable 413
tund 972
tundra 344
tune 402, 415
  in – 413
  out of –
  unmusical 414
  imperfect 651
  deteriorated 659
  put in –
  prepare 673
  concord 714
  to the – of
  quantity 25
  payment 807
  price 812
  – up 416
tuneful *music* 413
  poetry 597
  – nine 416, 597
tuneless 414
tunic 225
tunicle 999
tuning-fork 417
tunnage 192
tunnel *concave* 252
  opening 260
  passage 627
tup 366, 373
turbe,ɔ 225
turbary 267
turbid 426, 653
turbinated 248, 312
turbine 153
turbulence
  violence 173
  agitation 315
  excitation 825
turbulent 59
Turcism 984
tureen 191
turf *lawn* 344
  grass 367
  fuel 388
  gambling 621
  races 720
  race-course 728
  amusement 840
turgid
  expanded 194
  – *style* 577
  redundant 641

ostentatious 882
Turk
  polygamist 903
  grand – 745
  'bear like the – no
  rival near the
  throne' 878
turkey-trot 840
Turkish bath 386,
  652
turlupinade 842
turmoil
  confusion 59
  violence 173
  agitation 315
turn *state* 7
  crisis 134
  period of time 138
  change 140
  tendency 176
  form 240
  curve 245
  blunt 254
  stroll 266
  deviate 279
  circuition 311
  rotate 312
  aptitude 698
  affections 820
  emotion 821
  dance 840
  nausea 867
  by –s 138, 148
  come in its – 138
  each in its – 148
  meet one at
  every – 641
  take a favorable
  – 658
  give one a –
  aid 707
  excite 824
  do a good – 648,
  906
  ill – 907
  in – 58, 138
  one's luck –s 735
  serve one's – 644
  to a – 494
  take a wrong – 732
  – about 148
  – to account 677,
  775
  – adrift 73, 297
  – aside *change* 140
  deviate 279
  hinder 706
  – one's attention
  from 458
  – away. *eject* 297
  not look 442
  avoid 623
  dismiss 756
  relinquish 782
  – back 145, 283
  – one's back upon
  oppose 708
  refuse 764
  disrespect 929
  contempt 930
  – the brain 503
  – of the cards 156
  – color 821
  – a corner
  go round 311
  succeed 731
  – the corner 140,
  658

unemployed 678, 681
unencumbered 705, 927a
unendeared 898
unending 112
unendowed 158
– with reason 450a
unendurable 830
unenjoyed 841
unenlightened 491, 499
unenslaved 748
unenterprising 864
unentertaining 843
unenthralled 748
unentitled 925
unenvied 929, 930
unequal 28, 139
inequitable 923
– to 640
unequalled 33
unequipped 674
unequitable 923
unequivocal
great 31
sure 474
clear 518
unerring
certain 474
tone 494
innocent 946
unessayed 678
unessential 643
unestablished 185
uneven *diverse* 16a
unequal 28
irregular 139
rough 256
uneventful 643
unexact 495
unexaggerated 494
unexamined 460
unexampled 83
unexceptionable
good 648
legitimate 924
innocent 946
unexcitable 826
unexcited 823, 826
unexciting 174
unexecuted 730
unexempt 177
unexercised 674, 678
unexerted 172
unexhausted 159, 639
unexpanded 195, 203
unexpected
exceptional 83
inexpectation 508
unexpensive 815
unexplained
not known 491
unintelligible 519
latent 626
unexplored
neglected 460
ignorant 491
unseen 526
unexposed 526
unexpressed 536
unexpressive 517
unextended 317

unextinguished 173, 382
unfaded 428
unfading 112
unfailing 141
unfair *false* 544
unjust 923
dishonorable 940
unfaithful 940
unfaltering 604a
unfamiliar 83
unfashionable 83, 851
unfashioned 241, 674
unfasten 44
unfathomable
infinite 105
deep 208
mysterious 519
unfavorable
out of season 135
· *hindrance* 706
obstructive 708
– *chance* 473
unfeared 861
unfeasible 471
unfed 640, 956
unfeeling 376, 823
unfeigned 543
unfelt 823
unfeminine
manly 373
vulgar 851
unfertile 169
unfetter 750
unfettered 748
unfinished 53, 730
unfit
inappropriate 24
impotence 158
inexpedient 647
unskilful 699
wrong 923
undue 925
unfitted
not prepared 674
unfix 44
unfixed 149
unflagging 604a
unflammable 385
unflattering 494, 703
unfledged
young 127, 129
unprepared 674
unflinching
firm 604
persevering 604a
brave 861
unfold
straighten 246
evolve 313
interpret 522
manifest 525
disclose 529
– *a tale* 594
unforbidden 760
unforced 602, 748
unforeseen 508
unforfeited 781
unforgettable 505
unforgiving 919
unforgotten 505
unformed 241, 674
unfortified
pure 42

powerless 158
unfortunate
ill-timed 135
failure 732
adversity 735
unhappy 828
– *woman* 962
unfounded 546
unfrequent 137
unfrequented 893
unfriended
powerless 158
secluded 893
unfriendly
opposed 708
hostile 889
malevolent 907
unfrock 756, 972
unfrozen 382
unfruitful 169
unfulfilled 713, 925
unfurl
unfold 313
– *a flag* 525, 550
unfurnished 640, 674
ungainly 846, 895
ungallant 895
ungarnished 849
ungathered 678
ungenerous 819, 943
ungenial 657
ungenteel 851, 895
ungentle 173, 895
ungentlemanly
vulgar 851
rude 895
dishonorable 940
ungifted 499
unglorified 874
unglue 47
ungodly 989
ungovernable
violent 173
disobedient 742
passionate 825
ungoverned 748
ungraceful
– *language* 579
ugly 846
vulgar 851
ungracious 895, 907
ungrammatical 568
ungranted 764
ungrateful 917
ungratified 832
ungrounded
unsubstantial 4
erroneous 495
ungrudging 816
unguarded
neglected 460
spontaneous 612
unprepared 674
in an – *moment*
unexpectedly 508
unguem, ad – 494, 650
unguent 356
unguibus et rostro 686
unguided
ignorant 491
impulsive 612
unskilled 699
unguilty 946

unhabitable 187
unhabituated 614
unhackneyed 614
unhallowed 988, 989
unhand 750
unhandseled 123
unhandsome 940
unhandy 699
unhappy
adversity 735
pain 828
dejected 837
make – 830
unharbored 185
unhardened
tender 914
innocent 946
penitent 950
unharmonious 24, 414
unharness 750
unhatched 674
unhazarded 664
unhealthy 655, 657
unheard of
exceptional 83
improbable 473
ignorant 491
wonderful 870
unheated 383
unheed, -ed 460
unheeding 458
unhesitating
belief 484
resolved 604
unhewn 241, 674
unhindered 748
unhinge 61, 158
unhinged
impotent '158
insane 503
failure 732
unhitch 44
unholy 989
unhonored 874
unhook (44)
unhoped 508
unhorsed 732
unhostile 888
unhouse 297
unhoused 185
unhurt 670
unicorn
monster 83
carriage 272
unideal *existing* 1
no thought 452
true 494
unification 48, 87
uniform
homogeneous 16
simple 42
orderly 58
regular 80
dress 225
symmetry 242
livery 550
uniformity 16
unilluminated 421
unimaginable 471, 473
wonderful 870
unimaginative 576, 843, 868
unimagined 1, 494
unimitated 20

unimpaired 670
unimpassioned 826
unimpeachable
certain 474
true 494
due 924
approved 931
innocent 946
unimpeached 931, 946
unimpeded 705, 748
unimportance 643
unimpressed 838
unimpressible 823
unimproved 659
unincreased 36
unincumbered
easy 705
exempt 927a
uninduced 616
uninfected 652
uninfectious 656
uninflammable 385
uninfluenced
obstinate 606
unactuated 616
free 768
uninfluential 172, 175a
uninformed 491
uningenuous 544
uninhabit, -able, -ed 187, 893
uninitiated 491, 699
uninjured
perfect 650
healthy 654
preserved 670
uninjurious 656
uninquisitive 456
uninspired 823
uninstructed 491
unintellectual 452, 499
unintelligent 499
unintelligibility 519
unintelligible 519
– *style* 571
render – 538
unintentional
necessary 601
undesigned 621
uninterested 456, 841, 843
unintermitting
unbroken 69
durable 110
continuing 143
persevering 604a
uninterrupted
continuous 69
perpetual 112
unremitting 893
unintroduced 893
uninured 614
uninvented 614
uninvestigated 491
uninvited 893
uninviting 830
union
agreement 23
junction 43
combination 48
concurrence 178
workhouse 189
party 712
concord 714

unpurposed 621
unpursued 624
unqualified
incomplete 52
impotent 158
certain 474
unprepared 674
inexpert 699
unentitled 925
– *truth* 494
unquelled 173
unquenchable
strong 159
desire 865
unquenched
violence 173
heat 382
unquestionable 474
unquestionably 488
unquestioned 474, 488
unquiet
motion 264
agitation 315
excitable 825
unravel *untie* 44
arrange 60
straighten 246
evolve 313
discover 480a
interpret 522
disembarrass 705
unreached 304
unread 491
unready 674
unreal
not existing 2
erroneous 495
imaginary 515
unreasonable
impossible 471
illogical 477
misjudging 481
foolish 499
exorbitant 814
unjust 923
unreclaimed 951
unrecognizable 146
unreconciled 713
unrecorded 552
unrecounted 55
unreduced 31
unrefined 851
unreflecting 458
unreformed 951
unrefreshed 688
unrefuted 478, 494
unregarded
neglected 460
unrespected 929
unregenerate 988
unregistered 552
unreined 748
unrelated 10
unrelenting 914a, 919
unreliable
uncertain 475
irresolute 605
dangerous 665
unrelieved 835
unremarked 460
unremembered 506
unremitting
continuous 69
continuing 110
unvarying 143

persevering 604a
unremoved 184
unremunerated 808
unrenewed 141
unrepealed 141
unrepeated 87, 103
unrepentant 951
unrepining 831
unreplenished 640
unrepressed 173
unreproached 946
unreproved 946
unrequited 806, 917
unresented 918
unresenting 826
unreserved
manifest 525
veracious 543
artless 703
unresisted 743
unresisting 725
unresolved 605
unrespected 929
unrest 149, 264
unrestored 688
unrestrained
capricious 608
unencumbered 705
free 748
unrestricted
undiminished 31
free 748
unretracted 535
unrevenged 918
unreversed 143
unrevoked 143
unrewarded 806, 917
unrhymed 598
unriddle 480a, 529
unrig 645
unrighteous 945
unrip 260
unripe
young 127
sour 397
immature 674
unrivalled 33
unroll *evolve* 313
display 525
unromantic 494
unroot 301
unruffled
calm 174
quiet 265
unaffected 823
placid 826
unruly *violent* 173
obstinate 606
disobedient 742
unsaddle 756
unsafe 665
unsaid 526
unsaleable
useless 645
selling 796
cheap 815
unsaluted 929
unsanctified 988, 939
unsanctioned 925
unsated 865
unsatisfactory
inexpedient 647
bad 649
displeasing 830

discontent 832
unsatisfied 832, 865
unsavouriness 395
unsay *recant* 607
unscanned 460
unscathed 654
unschooled 491
unscientific 477
unscoured 653
unscriptural 984
unscrupulous 940
unseal 529
unsearched 460
unseasonable 24, 135
unseasoned 614, 674
unseat 756
unseemly
inexpedient 647
ugly 846
vulgar 851
undue 925
vicious 945
unseen
invisible 447
neglected 460
latent 526
unseldom 136
unselfish 942
unseparated 46
unserviceable 645
unsettle *derange* 61
unsettled
mutable 149
displaced 185
uncertain 475
– *in one's mind* 503
unsevered 50
unsex 146
unshaded 525
unshaken 159
– *belief* 484
unshapely 846
unshapen 241
unshared 777
unsheathe
– *the sword* 722
unsheltered 665
unshielded 665
unshifting 143
unship 185, 297
unshocked 823
unshorn 50
unshortened 200
unshrinking 604, 861
unsifted 460
unsightly 846
unsinged 670
unskilfulness 699
unslaked 865
unsleeping 604a, 682
unsmooth 256
unsociable 893
unsocial 893
unsoiled 652
unsold 777
unsoldierlike 862
unsolicitous 866
unsolved 526
unsophisticated
simple 42
genuine 494
artless 703

unsorted 59
unsought
avoided 623
unrequested 766
unsound
illogical 477
erroneous 495
deceptive 545
imperfect 651
– *mind* 503
unsown 674
unsparing
abundant 639
severe 739
liberal 816
with an – hand 818
unspeakable 31, 870
unspecified 78
unspent 678
unspied 526
unspiritual 316, 989
unspoiled 648
unspotted
clean 652
beautiful 845
innocent 946
unstable 218
changeable 149
uncertain 475
irresolute 605
precarious 665
– *equilibrium* 149
unstaid 149
unstained
clean 652
honorable 939
unstatesmanlike 699
unsteadfast 605
unsteady
mutable 149
irresolute 605
in danger 665
unstinted 639
unstinting 816
unstirred 823, 826
unstopped
continuing 143
open 260
unstored 640
unstrained
turbid 653
relaxed 687
– *meaning* 516
unstrengthened 160
unstruck 823
unstrung 160
unstudied 460
unsubject 748
unsubmissive 742
unsubservient
useless 645
inexpedient 647
unsubstantial 4
weak 160
rare 322
erroneous 495
imaginary 515
unsubstantiality 4
unsuccessful 732
unsuccessive 70
unsuitable
incongruous 24
(*inexpedient* 647)
– *time* 135

unsullied *clean* 652
honorable 939
(*guiltless* 946)
unsung 526
unsupplied 640
unsupported
weak 160
(*unassisted* 706)
– by evidence 468
unsuppressed 141
unsurmountable 471
unsurpassed 33
unsusceptible 823
unsuspected
belief 484
latent 526
unsuspecting
hopeful 858
unsuspicious
belief 484
artless 703
hope 858
unsustainable 495
unsweet 395
unswept 653
unswerving
straight 246
direct 278
persevering 604a
unsymmetric 83
unsymmetrical 59, 243
unsystematic 59
untainted *pure* 652
healthy 654
honorable 939
untalked of 526
untamed 851, 907
untarnished 939
untasted 391
untaught 491, 674
untaxed 815
unteach 538
unteachable 499, 699
untenable
powerless 158
illogical 477
undefended 725
untenanted 187, 893
unthanked 917
unthankful 917
unthawed 321, 383
unthinkable 471
unthinking
unconsidered 452
involuntary 601
unthought of 452, 460
unthreatened 664
unthrifty
unprepared 674
prodigal 818
unthrone 756
untidy 59, 653
untie 44, 750
– the knot 705
until 106
– now 118
untilled 674
untimely 135
– end 360
untinged 42
untired 689
untiring 604a

remedy 662
Venetian blinds
  351
vengeance 919
  cry to heaven
    for – 923
  with a – 31, 173
vengeful 919
veni vidi vici 731
venial 937
veniam petimusque
    damusque vicis-
    sim 918
venienti occurrere
    morbo 673
venison 394
venom 663, 907
venomous *bad* 649
  poisonous 657
  rude 895
  maleficent 907
vent *opening* 260
  egress 295
  air-pipe 351
  disclose 529
  escape 671
  sale 796
  find – *egress* 295
  passage 302
  publish 531
  escape 671
  give – to 297, 529
  – one's rage 900
  – one's spleen 900
venter 191
veptiduct 351
ventilate
  begin 66
  air 338
  wind 349
  discuss 595
  – a question 461,
    476
ventilator 349, 351
ventosity 349
vent-peg
  stopper 263
  safety 666
  escape 671
ventre
  – à terre 274
  danse du – 840
ventricle 191
ventriloquism 580
venture
  chance 621
  danger 665
  try 675
  courage 861
  I'll – to say 535
venturesome
  undertaking 677
  brave 861
  rash 863
venue 74, 183
Venus *woman* 374
  planet 423
  beauty 845
  love 897
  goddess 919
veracity 543
verandah 191
verbal 562
  – *intercourse* 582,
    588
  – *quibble* 497, 842
verbatim

imitation 19
exact 494
words 562
verbiage
  unmeaning 517
  words 562
  diffuse 573
verbis:
  totidem – 494
  – *ad verbera* 720
verborum, copia –
  diffuse 573
  eloquence 582
  loquacious 584
verbosity
  words 562
  diffuse 573
  loquacity 584
verboten 761
verbum sapienti
  527
verdant 367, 435
verd-antique 435
verdict
  opinion 480
  lawsuit 969
  snatch a – 545,
    702
verdigris 435
verditer 435
verdure 367, 435
verecundiam, argu-
    mentum ad –
  874, 939
verecundity 879,
  881
veredical 543
Verein 712
verge
  tendency 176
  near 197
  edge 231
  limit 233
  direction 278
verger 996
veriest 31
verification 463,
  771
verify 463
  evidence 467
  demonstrate 478
  find out 480a
verily *truly* 494
verisimilitude 472
veritable 494
veritas, nuda – 494
vérité, palais de –
  703
verity 494
verjuice 397
vermicular
  convoluted 248
  worm 366
vermiform 248
vermilion 434
vermin
  animal 366
  unclean 653
  base 876
vernacular
  native 188
  internal 221
  language 560
  habitual 613
vernal 123, 125
vernier
  minuteness 193

– *scale* 466
vero, vitam impen-
    dere – 535, 939
verrons, nous – 507
versatile 149
verse *division* 51
  poetry 597
versed in 490
versicolor 440
versify 597
version *change* 140
  special 79
  interpretation 522
versus 278, 708
vert 435
vertebral 222
vertebrate 366
vertex 210
verticality 212
verticity 312
vertigo
  rotation 312
  delirium 503
verve
  imagination 515
  vigorous language
    574
  energy 682
  feeling 821
very 31
  – best 648
  – image 554
  – many 102
  – minute 113
  – much 31
  – picture 17
  – small 32
  – thing
  identity 13
  agreement 23
  exact 494
  – truc 488
  – well 831
Véry light 423
vesicle *cell* 191
  covering 223
  globe 249
vesicular 191, 260
vespers 126, 990
vespertine 126
vessel
  receptacle 191
  tube 260
  ship 273
vest *place* 184
  dress 225
  – in *belong to* 777
  give 784
Vesta 979
vesta *match* 388
vestal 960
vested *fixed* 150
  legal 963
  – in *located* 184
  – *interest*
  given 780
  due 924
vestibule 66, 191
vestige 551
vestigia:
  veteris – *flammæ*
    505, 613
  – *nulla retrorsum*
    282, 604a
vestment 225, 999
vestry *council* 696
  churchdom 995

church 1000
vesture 225
vesuvian
  match 388
veteran *old* **130**
  adept 700
  warrior 726
veterinary art 370
veteris vestigia
  flammae 505,
    613
veto 761
vetturino 694
vex 830, 898
vexata quaestio 704,
  713
vexation 828, 830
  – of spirit 828
  discontent 832
  resentment 900
vexatious 830
vexed question
  704, 713
vi et armis
  violence 173
  exertion 686
  compulsion 744
viâ 278, 627
viable 359
via lactea 318
viaduct 627
vial 191
vials:
  – of hate 898
  – of wrath 900
viands 298
viaticum
  provision 637
  rite 998
vibrate 314
  – between two
    extremes 149
vibrato 415
vibratory 149
vibroscope 314
vicar *deputy* 759
  clergyman 996
  – of Bray 607, 886
vicarage 1000
vicariate 995
vicarious 147
vicarship 995
vice *deputy* 759
  holder 781
  wickedness **945**
vice versâ
  reciprocal 12
  contrary 14
  interchange 148
vice-admiral 745
Vice-Chancellor
  967
  –'s Court 966
vicegerency 755
vicegerent 758, 759
vice-president 694
vice-regal 759
viceroy
  governor 745
  deputy 759
vicesimal 98
vicinage 197
vicinism 145
vicinity 197, 227
vicious 173, 945
  render – 659
  – *reasoning* 477

vicissitude 149
Vickers gun 727
victim *dupe* 547
  defeated 732
  sufferer 828
victimize *kill* 361
  deceive 545
  injure 649
  baffle 731
victis, væ – 722, 909
victor 731
victoria
  carriage 272
Victoria Cross 733
victory 731
victual *provide* 637
victuals 298
videlicet 79, 522
viduage 905
viduity 905
vie *good* 648
  – with 720
vielle 417
view
  sight 441
  appearance 448
  attend to 457
  opinion 484
  landscape paint-
    ing 556
  intention 620
  bring into – 525
  come into – 446
  commanding – 441
  in – *visible* 446
  intended 420
  expected 507
  keep in – 457
  on – 448
  present to the –
    448
  with a – to 620
  – as 484
  – in a new light
    658
viewer 444
viewless 447
view-point 441
vigesimal 98
vigil *care* 459
vigilance *care* 459
  wisdom 498
  activity 682
  caution 864
vigils *worship* 990
vignette 558, 594,
  847
vigor *strength* 159
  energy 171
  style **574**
  resolution 604
  health 654
  activity 682
viking 792
vile *valueless* 643
  bad 649
  painful 830
  disgraceful 874
  plebeian 876
  dishonorable 940
  vicious 945
vilify *shame* 874
  malediction 908
  censure 932
  detract 934
vilipend
  disrespect 929